Base Ten Grid

(Copy for use in Exercise Problems 3.3 #5, #6, #16; Exercise Problems 3.4 #7, #8; E

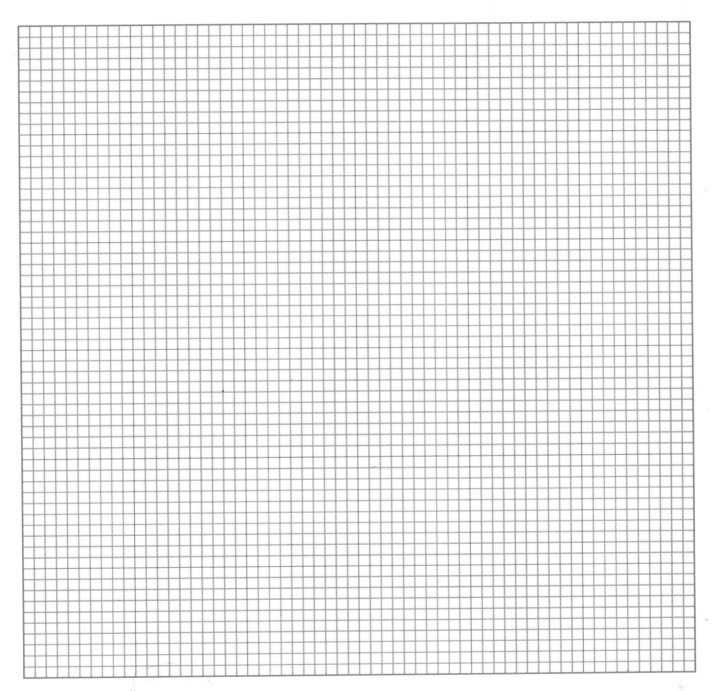

MATHEMATICS
FOR ELEMENTARY TEACHERS
A CONCEPTUAL APPROACH

THIRD EDITION

MATHEMATICS
FOR ELEMENTARY TEACHERS
A CONCEPTUAL APPROACH

Albert B. Bennett, Jr.
University of New Hampshire

L. Ted Nelson
Portland State University

Wm. C. Brown Publishers

Book Team

Editor *Earl McPeek*
Developmental Editor *Theresa Grutz*
Production Editor *Michelle M. Campbell*
Designer *K. Wayne Harms*
Visuals/Design Consultant *Barbara J. Hodgson*
Photo Editor *Robin Storm*
Visuals Processor *Amy L. Saffran*

Wm. C. Brown Publishers

President *G. Franklin Lewis*
Vice President, Publisher *George Wm. Bergquist*
Vice President, Operations and Production *Beverly Kolz*
National Sales Manager *Virginia S. Moffat*
Group Sales Manager *Vincent R. Di Blasi*
Vice President, Editor in Chief *Edward G. Jaffe*
Marketing Manager *Elizabeth Robbins*
Advertising Manager *Amy Schmitz*
Managing Editor, Production *Colleen A. Yonda*
Manager of Visuals and Design *Faye M. Schilling*
Production Editorial Manager *Julie A. Kennedy*
Production Editorial Manager *Ann Fuerste*
Publishing Services Manager *Karen J. Slaght*

WCB Group

President and Chief Executive Officer *Mark C. Falb*
Chairman of the Board *Wm. C. Brown*

Cover photo © Michael Stuckey/Comstock Inc.

Interior and cover design by Karen Mason

Illustrations rendered by Scientific Illustrator's

Copyediting by Lifland et al., Bookmakers

The credits section for this book begins on page 683, and is considered an extension of the copyright page.

Printed in the United States of America by Wm. C. Brown Publishers, 2460 Kerper Boulevard, Dubuque, IA 52001

10 9 8 7 6 5 4 3

Contents

1

Problem Solving

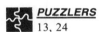
1.1 INTRODUCTION TO PROBLEM SOLVING   2

1.2 PATTERNS AND PROBLEM SOLVING   13

2

Sets and Logic

2.1 SETS AND COUNTING   30

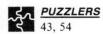

3

Whole Numbers

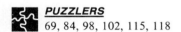

4

Number Theory

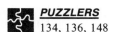

5
Integers and Fractions

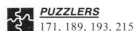
5.1   INTEGERS   152

PROBLEM OPENER   152

Positive and Negative Integers; Uses of Integers; Models for Integers; Addition; Subtraction; Multiplication; Division; Inequality; Properties of Integers; Mental Calculations; Estimation; Problem-Solving Application

COMPUTER INVESTIGATION: Consecutive Differences   171

5.2   INTRODUCTION TO FRACTIONS   172

PROBLEM OPENER   172

Fraction Terminology; Models for Fractions; Equality of Fractions; Common Denominators; Inequality; Density of Fractions; Mixed Numbers and Improper Fractions; Mental Calculations; Estimation; Problem-Solving Application

LABORATORY INVESTIGATION: Paper Folding   193

5.3   OPERATIONS WITH FRACTIONS   194

PROBLEM OPENER   194

Addition; Subtraction; Multiplication; Division; Number Properties; Mental Calculations; Estimation; Problem-Solving Application

LABORATORY INVESTIGATION: Fraction Patterns   215

6

Decimals: Rational and Irrational Numbers

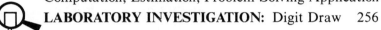

7

Geometric Figures

7.1   PLANE FIGURES   298

PROBLEM OPENER   298

Mathematical Systems; Points, Lines and Planes; Half-Planes, Segments, Rays, and Angles; Problem-Solving Application; Angle Measurements; Perpendicular and Parallel Lines; Problem-Solving Application; Curves and Convex Sets; Polygons; Problem-Solving Application

 LABORATORY INVESTIGATION: Geoboard Polygons   317

7.2   POLYGONS AND TESSELLATIONS   317

PROBLEM OPENER   317

Angles in Polygons; Congruence; Regular Polygons; Constructing Regular Polygons; Tessellations with Polygons; Problem-Solving Application

 LABORATORY INVESTIGATION: Mirror Reflections   329

7.3   SPACE FIGURES   330

PROBLEM OPENER   330

Planes; Polyhedra; Regular Polyhedra; Pyramids and Prisms; Cones and Cylinders; Spheres and Maps*; Problem-Solving Application

 LABORATORY INVESTIGATION: Pyramid Patterns   345

7.4   SYMMETRIC FIGURES   346

PROBLEM OPENER   346

Reflection Symmetry for Plane Figures; Rotation Symmetry for Plane Figures; Reflection Symmetry for Space Figures; Rotation Symmetry for Space Figures; Problem-Solving Application

 LABORATORY INVESTIGATION: Mirror Cards   358

7.5   INTRODUCTION TO LOGO*   359

PROBLEM OPENER   359

Logo Commands; Creating Commands; Recursion; Drawing Polygons; Symmetric Figures; Problem-Solving Application

 COMPUTER INVESTIGATION: Star Polygons   370

*Optional sections and subsections

8
Measurement

8.1 SYSTEMS OF MEASUREMENT 376

PROBLEM OPENER 376
Nonstandard Units of Length; English Units; Metric Units; Precision and Small Measurements; International System of Units; Problem-Solving Application

 CALCULATOR INVESTIGATION: Palindromic Numbers 395

8.2 AREA AND PERIMETER 396

PROBLEM OPENER 396
Nonstandard Units of Area; Standard Units of Area; Perimeter; Areas of Polygons; Circumference and Areas of Circles; Problem-Solving Application

 CALCULATOR INVESTIGATION: Areas of Circles 415

8.3 VOLUME AND SURFACE AREA 416

PROBLEM OPENER 416
Nonstandard Units of Volume; Standard Units of Volume; Surface Area; Volumes of Space Figures; Irregular Shapes; Creating Surface Area*; Problem-Solving Application

LABORATORY INVESTIGATION: Volumes of Cylinders 435

*Optional sections and subsections

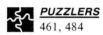
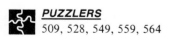
*Optional sections and subsections

11
Statistics

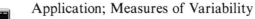

*Optional sections and subsections

12
Probability

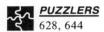
12.1 SINGLE-STAGE EXPERIMENTS 614

12.2 MULTISTAGE EXPERIMENTS 629

Preface

Effective teachers are those who can stimulate students to learn mathematics. Educational research offers compelling evidence that students learn mathematics well only when they construct their own mathematical thinking.*

The revision of this text has been guided by professional reports that have appeared over the past few years. For example, this edition closely parallels courses I and II outlined in the *Recommendations on the Mathematical Preparation of Teachers,* by the Committee of the Undergraduate Program in Mathematics (CUPM), and contains most of the topics covered in courses III and IV of that report. The recommendations in both CUPM's report and the *Curriculum and Evaluation Standards for School Mathematics,* by the National Council of Teachers of Mathematics (NCTM), have influenced us to increase our attention to pedagogical issues, including use of models and visuals and techniques for mental calculation and estimation. This text, together with the activities in *Mathematics for Elementary Teachers: An Activity Approach,* will engage students in a study of mathematics that proceeds from models and manipulatives to diagrams and visual images to ideas represented by abstract symbols. Such a developmental sequence not only furnishes the prospective teacher with a conceptual foundation for mathematics but also provides ideas and methods for teaching mathematics to children.

The primary objective of *Mathematics for Elementary Teachers: A Conceptual Approach* is to present mathematics in a format that prepares teachers to teach elementary school mathematics. Teachers need a firm foundation in the theory of mathematics as it pertains to the elementary school curriculum. They also need ideas and methods for teaching mathematics to elementary school children in a way that will provide an understanding of concepts and generate interest and enthusiasm. The greatest challenge in writing a text for these purposes is to create a proper balance between pedagogical concerns and those of a theoretical and abstract nature. Although this text focuses primarily on teaching content, the extensive use of models and visuals accomplishes two objectives: (1) it assists college students in understanding mathematics concepts, and (2) it provides ideas for teaching mathematics to elementary school children.

CHANGES IN THE THIRD EDITION

The style of this edition is significantly different from that of the first two editions. Although we have retained the numerous photographs and applications of mathematics, the text has been reorganized with a new format. Defined words are in boldface for easy location, key definitions and properties are boxed for quick reference, and historical highlights are displayed apart from the text. New concepts are first introduced with examples and visual diagrams; technical notation is presented after a concept has been developed. Numerous worked examples provide opportunities for students to check their understanding of the concepts being presented.

*Mathematical Sciences Educational Board, *Everybody Counts* (Washington, DC: National Academy Press, 1989), 58.

REVISED AND EXPANDED SEQUENCE OF TOPICS

- Chapter 1 begins with an introduction to problem solving and discusses several problem-solving strategies, as well as Polya's four-step plan. Applications of problem solving occur in each section of the book, and new problem-solving strategies are introduced as needed.
- Chapter 2 provides background for relations and operations on sets and a revised section on logic and the use of conditional statements, Venn diagrams, and valid reasoning.
- The number systems, whole numbers, integers, rational numbers, and real numbers are presented in this order in Chapters 3, 5, and 6 before the topics of geometry and measurement. Most of the historical algorithms for computing that were included in the first two editions have been removed from these chapters, and more attention is given to number properties and techniques for mental calculation and estimation.
- Numeration systems are now discussed in the chapter on whole numbers (Chapter 3), and number theory is covered in a separate chapter (Chapter 4).
- Chapter 6 (decimals) contains an expanded treatment of percents, including mental calculations with percents.
- Instruction on programming in BASIC has been removed from the text, and an introduction to the computer language LOGO is presented in Chapter 7 after the sections on geometric figures and symmetry. The section on LOGO is optional.
- The three sections on measurement in Chapter 8 are now introduced with examples of nonstandard units for length, area, and volume.
- The number system properties are used in Chapter 9, together with properties of equality and inequality, to justify the algebraic steps for solving equations and inequalities. The section on functions and coordinate geometry in Chapter 9 now concentrates mainly on linear functions; an introduction to exponential functions is optional.
- Chapter 10 (geometric mappings) begins with a new section on geometric constructions, and these techniques are then used to construct mappings in the sections on congruence and similarity.
- Statistics (Chapter 11) now precedes the chapter on probability and has been divided into descriptive statistics and inferential statistics. The chapter contains an expanded treatment of graphs, including stem and leaf plots and box and whisker plots.
- Probability (Chapter 12) has been reorganized into the categories of single-stage and multistage experiments. It now covers probability trees and includes more examples of simulations.

SPECIAL FEATURES

PROBLEM-SOLVING APPLICATIONS Seven problem-solving strategies and Polya's four-step plan are introduced in Chapter 1 and used throughout the text. Several additional problem-solving strategies are introduced in the remaining chapters. Each section of the text contains one or more problem-solving applications, which are analyzed with Polya's four-step plan and solved with one or more problem-solving strategies. These problems provide opportunities for instructors to introduce new problem-solving strategies and apply the subject matter of the section. In addition, a segment entitled Featured Strategies in each set of Exercises and Problems presents a problem that is outlined by Polya's four-step plan. The problem-solving strategies used in each chapter are listed in the Table of Contents with page references.

PROBLEM OPENERS Each section of the text begins with a Problem Opener related to the content of that section. These problems are intended to be used as class warm-ups and to promote class discussion. They can be used to open a lesson before the content of the section is introduced to motivate the topics and increase student interest. The solution to each Problem Opener and the problem-solving strategies required are contained in the *Instructor's Resource Manual*. This *Manual* also includes one or more extensions for each Problem Opener, which can be used for class discussions, assignments, or tests.

INVESTIGATIONS The National Council of Supervisors of Mathematics has stated:

> Students need to explore mathematics using manipulatives, measuring devices, models, calculators, and computers. . . . Calculators should be used by students throughout the mathematics program, beginning in the primary grades. As adults, students will use calculators or computers to do difficult computations. They will need facility with single-digit facts, estimation skills, and mental arithmetic, and they must be able to determine if the results obtained from calculators and computers are reasonable.*

Accordingly, following each set of Exercises and Problems, this edition of *Mathematics for Elementary Teachers: A Conceptual Approach* has a Computer Investigation, a Calculator Investigation, or a Laboratory Investigation. These investigations pose open-ended questions that require collecting data, looking for patterns, and forming and verifying conjectures. Such investigations can be used for student papers, class reports, or work in small groups. Each type of investigation is marked with an icon in both the Table of Contents and the text.

MENTAL CALCULATION AND ESTIMATION Mental calculating encourages the development of number sense and the use of number properties, and estimation employs mental calculating techniques. During the past several years increasing numbers of experts have been recommending that schools teach mental calculation and estimation. NCTM's *Curriculum and Evaluation Standards for School Mathematics* states:

> Instruction should emphasize the development of an estimation mind-set. Children should come to know what is meant by an estimate, when it is appropriate to estimate, and how close an estimate is required in a given situation. If children are encouraged to estimate, they will accept estimation as a legitimate part of mathematics.**

Many mathematics educators agree that children will not acquire mental calculating and estimating skills until specific techniques become a regular part of the curriculum. The most common mental calculating and estimating techniques have been included in the chapters on whole numbers, integers, rational numbers, and real numbers. Special exercises designed for practice with these techniques are marked with icons in the Exercises and Problems.

PUZZLERS The text contains over forty mathematics puzzlers, which are listed in the Table of Contents. Most occur at the ends of the Exercises and Problems and are marked by an icon. Answers for the puzzlers are at the beginning of the Answer Section.

---

*National Council of Supervisors of Mathematics, ''Essential Mathematics for the 21st Century'' (Minneapolis, MN: NCSM Essential Mathematics Task Force, 1988), 3–4.

**National Council of Teachers of Mathematics, *Curriculum and Evaluation Standards for School Mathematics* (Reston, VA: 1989), 36.

HISTORICAL HIGHLIGHTS Highlights in mathematical history appear throughout the text to suggest the origins of important ideas and provide background on the lives of some of the world's greatest mathematicians.

WORKED EXAMPLES Numerous examples are posed as questions and followed by solutions.

VISUAL MODELS Mathematical concepts usually are illustrated by diagrams and geometric figures before mathematical terminology and abstractions are introduced.

BOXED FEATURES Key definitions, rules, and properties are displayed in boxes.

KEY TERMS Words and terms that are defined or explained appear in boldface type in the text as well as in the margins.

CHAPTER REVIEWS New words are listed and key ideas are summarized at the end of each chapter.

CHAPTER TESTS Each chapter concludes with a test for evaluating knowledge and understanding of the concepts in that chapter.

BIBLIOGRAPHY A bibliography of additional references is included at the end of each chapter.

ANSWER SECTION Answers for the puzzlers, the odd-numbered Exercises and Problems, and the Chapter Tests appear at the end of the book.

SUGGESTED TEACHING FORMATS AND SEQUENCES

Students must talk with one another as well as in response to the teacher. When the teacher talks most, the flow of ideas and knowledge is primarily from teacher to student. When students make public conjectures and reason with others about mathematics, ideas and knowledge are developed collaboratively, revealing mathematics as constructed by human beings within an intellectual community. They learn to use, in a meaningful context, the tools of mathematical discourse—special terms, diagrams, graphs, sketches, and physical models, as well as symbols. The teacher's role is to initiate and orchestrate this kind of discourse and to use it skillfully to foster student learning.*

The recommendations of recent national reports contain two strong messages:

1. The prevalent mode of mathematics instruction, lecturing while students listen, may be the least effective mode for teaching and learning mathematics.
2. Teachers teach the way they are taught.

We recommend, therefore, that *Mathematics for Elementary Teachers: A Conceptual Approach* be used with the companion activity book *Mathematics for Elementary Teachers: An Activity Approach*. The texts can be used in a combination lecture and lab course, in which lectures on material in the text either precede or follow student work on the related material from the activity book. Alternatively, the course can be

*National Council of Teachers of Mathematics, *Professional Standards for Teaching Mathematics* (Working Draft) (Reston, VA: NCTM, 1989), 32.

a lab course based on the activity sets in the activity book supplemented by the Exercises and Problems from the text. A third possibility is a lecture course based on the text and supplemented by activities from the activity book.

We recommend using one of the following sequences of chapters and sections for a one-semester course; each contains 15 sections.

- **Option 1** 1, 3, 5, 6.1, 6.2, 7.1, 7.2, 8.1, and 8.2
- **Option 2** 1.1, 3, 5, 6.1, 6.2, 7.1, 7.2, 8.1, 11.1, and 12.1
- **Option 3** 1.1, 2, 3, 4.1, 5, and 7

SUPPLEMENTS

INSTRUCTOR'S RESOURCE MANUAL The *Instructor's Resource Manual* for *Mathematics for Elementary Teachers: A Conceptual Approach* contains **solutions for Problem Openers** (including extensions); **solutions for even-numbered Exercises and Problems; answers for Investigations** (Computer, Calculator, and Laboratory); **Chapter Tests with Answers** (two tests for each chapter); and **transparency masters** (various grids and dot paper).

CLASSROOM MANAGEMENT SOFTWARE Wm. C. Brown Publishers provides the following services to users of *Mathematics for Elementary Teachers: A Conceptual Approach.*

- **TestPak 3.0** A free, computerized testing service offers two convenient options. You may use your own Apple® IIe, IIc, or IIGS, Macintosh, or IBM PC to produce tests. A menu-driven test-design program with on-line help screens will guide you through the test-making process. You may select items from the bank, edit existing items, add new items of your own, or have the system randomly select items by chapter, section, or objective.
- **Test Item File** A printed version of all the questions in the TestPak is available. It can serve as a ready reference if you use your own computer to generate tests or use the Call-In Testing Service.
- **Call-In Testing Service** Instructors may obtain a customized student test master and answer key based on their selections from the Test Item File. The master and answer key will be mailed out within two working days of receipt of a request.
- **Computerized Gradebook Software** A record-keeping program is available for computing and graphing individual student and total class records.

COMPUTER PROBLEM-SOLVING DISK A free, copyable *Computer Problem-Solving Disk* containing twenty-one computer programs is available for use with the text. Students may use this disk for gathering data and running simulations for the Computer Investigations in the text. Instructors may use the disk to demonstrate computer simulations and the process of making and verifying conjectures. The disk also contains programs that produce specific sequences of numbers and their sums; factors and prime factors of numbers less than 1 million; rational numbers up to 200 decimal places; and GCF, LCM, means, standard deviations, and compound interest. The disk is programmed for the Apple® II family of computers, the Macintosh computer, and the IBM PC.

Computer Problem-Solving Disk Menu

Triangular Numbers	Palindromic Sums
Palindromic Differences	Number Chains
Frequency of Primes	Standard Deviations
Dice Toss Simulation	Spinner Simulations
Cryptology	Random Digits
Arithmetic Sequence	Geometric Sequence
Factorizations	GCF and LCM
Compound Interest	Repeating Decimals
Dice Sum Distribution	Consecutive Differences
Fibonacci-Type Sequences	Coin Simulations
Finite Differences	

ACTIVITY BOOK *Mathematics for Elementary Teachers: An Activity Approach,* third edition, contains thirty-five activity sets, one corresponding to each section of the text. Each activity set is a sequence of inductive activities and experiments that enables the student to build an understanding of mathematical ideas through the use of models and the discovery of patterns. The activity sets extend the ideas presented in the corresponding sections of the text. For example, attribute pieces are used to illustrate properties of sets; operations in various bases are carried out with multibase pieces; area formulas are developed from geoboard activities; properties of polyhedra are illustrated by models; operations with integers, fractions, and decimals are carried out with various models; distances are approximated with devices for indirect measurement; and empirical probabilities are obtained from probability experiments and simulations. Forty-eight Material Cards, some with colored manipulatives are packaged with *Mathematics for Elementary Teachers: An Activity Approach.* A section on *Ideas for the Elementary Classroom* at the end of each chapter includes a suggested classroom activity and a list of selected sources. There are puzzlers throughout the book and the activity sets are followed by *Just for Fun* enrichment activities.

ACKNOWLEDGMENTS

We thank the many students and instructors who have used the first two editions of this book and contributed comments and thoughtful ideas. We especially acknowledge Mildred Bennett, Sandy Kralovec, Kathy Phaendler, Janette Palmiter, and their students at Portland State University for field testing the third edition of the manuscript and offering helpful suggestions. Special thanks go to Sue Stringer for her careful typing of the manuscript; to Lizabeth Yost for typing the *Instructor's Resource Manual;* to Mildred Bennett, Jeannine Vigerust, and Richard Francis for developing the TestPak; to Ingrid Grabotin and Lizabeth Yost for typing the Test Item File; to Renee Schnider for typing the index; to Albert Bennett III, for programming the Computer Problem-Solving Disk; to Carol Carney, Eleanor Rigdon, and Greg Bennett for proofreading the manuscript; and to Jane Bennett for devoting many hours to reading galleys. We also wish to offer thanks to Quica Ostrander and Sally Lifland of Lifland et al., Bookmakers for their careful and thorough editing of the manuscript.

Special tribute is due to the production team at Wm. C. Brown for their painstaking care and masterful preparation of this edition of the text. We are especially grateful to executive editor Earl McPeek for suggestions on new formatting; to developmental editor Theresa Grutz for her expert advice and guidance; and to Michelle Campbell for capably directing the text production. We also acknowledge typesetter Jane Jaeger and proofreader Dorothy McCarron for flawlessly deciphering the edited manuscript.

Finally, we thank the following reviewers of both the initial outlines and the final manuscript for comments and suggestions that resulted in many significant changes:

Janet J. Brougher, University of Oregon
Verne Byers, University of Maine at Farmington
Richard L. Francis, Southeast Missouri State University
Virginia Ellen Hanks, Western Kentucky University
Dr. Angela Hernandez, University of Montevallo
Virginia L. Keen, Western Michigan State University
Leland W. Knauf, Youngstown State University
Jeannine Vigerust, New Mexico State University

To the Student

This book has been written to help you *understand* the basic concepts of mathematics so that you can help others learn concepts. You will be encouraged to become actively involved by solving worked examples, visualizing mathematical concepts, performing mental calculations, using appropriate technology (calculators and computers), and performing laboratory investigations. You will discover that most mathematical concepts can be developed using manipulatives and visual images and that mathematics is an interesting part of your life and the world around you.

The content of this book reflects the curriculum standards set by the National Council of Teachers of Mathematics for grades K–8, which establish the direction of school mathematics for the 1990s. In the past, elementary school mathematics programs stressed computational rules and speed and accuracy in computing. The focus is now changing, and today's children need to develop conceptual understanding, the ability to reason and communicate through mathematics, and the ability to solve problems. When estimations and approximations are not sufficient, computations can be done with calculators and computers. Children who are able to see mathematics conceptually have a better chance of solving problems and acquiring confidence in their ability to reason.

It is important for you as a future teacher to realize that mathematics is a way of thinking rather than a collection of rules and that it is the conceptual grasp that will help both you and your students learn and apply mathematics. The shaping of mathematical thinking and a mind-set for solving problems needs to begin early in the school curriculum, and the responsibility for this lies with elementary school teachers.

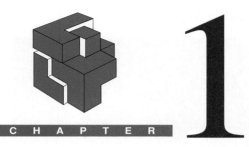

Problem Solving

SPOTLIGHT ON TEACHING

Excerpts from NCTM's Standard 1 for Teaching Mathematics in Grades K–4*

Problem solving should be the central focus of the mathematics curriculum. As such, it is a primary goal of all mathematics instruction and an integral part of all mathematical activity. Problem solving is not a distinct topic but a process that should permeate the entire program and provide the context in which concepts and skills can be learned.

Classrooms with a problem-solving orientation are permeated by thought-provoking questions, speculations, investigations, and explorations; in this environment, the teacher's primary goal is to promote a problem-solving approach to the learning of all mathematics content.

A lesson designed to develop the characteristics of parallelograms can be approached from a problem-solving perspective. The teacher, who has a collection of quadrilaterals like the ones shown, has the children discover the teacher's rule for sorting the shapes. One rule is to have all parallelograms in one loop and all nonparallelograms in the other.

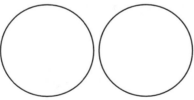
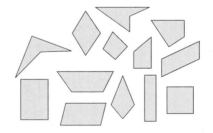

Tile explorations

*Reprinted by permission of the National Council of Teachers of Mathematics.

SECTION 1.1   INTRODUCTION TO PROBLEM SOLVING

☑ *PROBLEM OPENER*

Alice counted 7 cycle riders and 19 cycle wheels going past her house. How many tricycles were there?

There is no more significant privilege than to release the creative power of a child's mind.
Franz F. Hohn

Courtesy of International Business Machines Corporation

"Learning to solve problems is the principal reason for studying mathematics."* This statement by the National Council of Supervisors of Mathematics represents a widespread opinion that problem solving should be the central focus of the mathematics curriculum.

problem
problem solving

A **problem** occurs when a situation you want to resolve arises but no solution is readily apparent. **Problem solving** is the process by which the unfamiliar situation is resolved. A situation that is a problem to one person may not be a problem to another. For example, determining the number of people in 3 cars when each car contains 5 people may be a problem to some elementary school students. They might solve this problem by placing chips in boxes or by making a drawing to represent each car and each person (Figure 1.1) and then counting to determine the total number of people.

Figure 1.1

You may be surprised to know that there are problems in mathematics that are unsolved and have resisted the efforts of some of the best mathematicians to solve them. One such problem was discovered by Arthur Hamann, a seventh-grade student. He noticed that every even number he selected could be written as the difference of two primes.** For example,

$$2 = 5 - 3 \qquad 4 = 11 - 7 \qquad 6 = 11 - 5 \qquad 8 = 13 - 5 \qquad 10 = 13 - 3$$

After showing that this was true for all even numbers less than 250, he predicted that every even number could be written as the difference of two primes. No one has been able to prove or disprove this statement. When a statement is thought to be true but

conjecture

remains unproven, it is called a **conjecture.**

*National Council of Supervisors of Mathematics, "Essential Mathematics for the 21st Century" (Minneapolis, MN: Essential Mathematics Task Force, 1988).

**M. R. Frame, "Hamann's Conjecture," *Arithmetic Teacher* 23 no. 1 (January 1976): 34–35.

Problem solving is the subject of a major portion of research and publishing in mathematics education. Much of this research involves George Polya's heuristics for solving problems. In his book *How To Solve It,* he outlines a four-step process for solving problems:

1. Understanding the problem
2. Devising a plan
3. Carrying out the plan
4. Looking back

His problem-solving steps will be used in this section and in the problem-solving applications throughout the text.

The purpose of this section is to help you become familiar with Polya's four-step
common strategies   process and to acquaint you with some **common strategies** for solving problems: making a drawing, guessing and checking, making a table, using a model, and working backward. Additional strategies will be introduced throughout the text.

MAKING A DRAWING

One of the most helpful strategies for understanding a problem and obtaining ideas for a solution is to *draw pictures and diagrams.* Most likely you have heard the phrase "a picture is worth a thousand words." In the following problem, the drawings will help you to think through the solution.

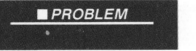

For his wife's birthday, Mr. Jones is planning a dinner party in a large recreation room. There will be 22 people, and in order to seat them all he needs to borrow card tables, the size that seats 1 person on each side. He wants to arrange the tables in a rectangular shape so that they will look like 1 large table. What is the smallest number of tables that Mr. Jones needs to borrow?

Question 1   **Understanding the Problem**   The tables must be placed next to each other, edge to edge, so that they form 1 large rectangular table. If 2 tables are placed end to end, how many people can be seated?

One large table

Question 2   **Devising a Plan**   Drawing pictures of the different possible arrangements of card tables is a natural approach to solving this problem. There are only a few possibilities. The tables can be placed in 1 long row; they can be placed side by side with 2 abreast; etc. How many people can be seated at 5 tables if they are placed end to end in a single row?

Carrying Out the Plan   The following drawings show 2 of the 5 possible arrangements that will seat 22 people. The Xs show that 22 people can be seated in each arrangement. The remaining arrangements, 3 by 8, 4 by 7, and 5 by 6, require 24, 28, and 30 card tables.

Question 3   What is the smallest number of card tables needed?

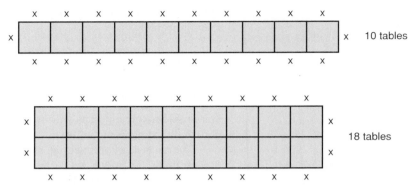

10 tables

18 tables

Looking Back   The drawings show that a single row of tables requires the fewest tables because each end table has places for 3 people and each of the remaining tables has places for 2 people. In all the other arrangements, the corner tables seat only 2 people and the remaining tables seat only 1 person. Therefore, regardless of the number of people, a single row is the arrangement that uses the smallest number of card tables, provided the room is long enough. What is the smallest number of card tables required to seat 38 people?

Question 4

Answers to Questions 1–4
1. 6   **2.** 12   **3.** 10
4. There will be 3 people at each end table and 32 people in between. Therefore, 2 end tables and 16 tables in between will be needed to seat 38 people.

GUESSING AND CHECKING

Sometimes it doesn't pay to guess, as illustrated by the cartoon. On the other hand, many problems can be better understood and even solved by trial-and-error procedures. As Polya said, "Mathematics in the making consists of guesses." If your first guess is off, it may lead to a better guess. Even if guessing doesn't produce the correct answer, you may increase your understanding of the problem and strike upon an idea for solving it. The *guess-and-check* approach is especially appropriate for elementary school children because it puts many problems within their reach.

■ PROBLEM

How far is it from town A to town B in this cartoon?

© 1968 United Features Syndicate, Inc.

Understanding the Problem   There are several bits of information in this problem. Let's see how Peppermint Patty could have obtained a better understanding of the problem with a diagram. First, the towns A, B, C, and D are one after the other, so they can be represented by 4 points on a line, as shown in figure (a). Next, it is 10 miles farther from A to B than from B to C, so we can move point B closer to point C, as in figure (b). It is also 10 miles farther from B to C than from C to D, so point C can be moved closer to point D.

Question 1   Finally, the distance from A to D is given as 390 miles. The problem requires finding what distance?

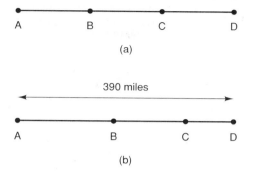

(a)

(b)

Devising a Plan   One method of solving this problem is to guess and then use the result to make a better guess. If the 4 towns were equally spaced, as in figure (a), the distance between each town would be 130 miles ($390 \div 3$). However, the distance from town A to **Question 2**   town B is the greatest. So let's begin with a guess of 150 miles for the distance from A to B. In this case, what is the distance from B to C and C to D?

Carrying Out the Plan   Using a guess of 150 for the distance from A to B produces a total distance from A to D that is greater than 390. If the distance from A to B is 145, then the B to C distance is 135 and the C to D distance is 125. The sum of these distances is **Question 3**   405, which is still too great. What happens if we use a guess of 140 for the distance from A to B?

Looking Back   One of the reasons for *looking back* at a problem is to consider different solutions or approaches. For example, you might have noticed that the first guess, which **Question 4**   produced a distance of 420 miles, was 30 miles too great. How can this observation be used to lead quickly to a correct solution of the original problem?

Answers to Questions 1–4
1. The problem requires finding the distance from A to B.
2. The B to C distance is 140, and the C to D distance is 130.
3. If the A to B distance is 140, then the B to C distance is 130 and the C to D distance is 120. Since the total of these distances is 390, the correct distance from A to B is 140 miles.
4. If the distance between each of the 3 towns is decreased by 10 miles, the incorrect distance of 420 will be decreased to the correct distance of 390. Therefore, the distance between town A and town B is 140 miles.

MAKING A TABLE

A problem can sometimes be solved by listing some or all of the possibilities. A *table* is often convenient for organizing such a list.

■ PROBLEM   Sue and Ann earned the same amount of money, although one worked 6 more days than the other. If Sue earned $36 a day and Ann earned $60 a day, how many days did each work?

Understanding the Problem   Answer a few simple questions to get a feeling for the **Question 1**   problem. How much did Sue earn in 3 days? Did Sue earn as much in 3 days as Ann did in 2 days?

Devising a Plan   One method of solving this problem is to list each day and each **Question 2**   person's total earnings through that day. What is the first amount of total pay that is the same for Sue and Ann, and how many days did it take each of them to earn this amount?

Question 3   **Carrying Out the Plan**   The complete table is shown below. There are 3 amounts in Sue's column that equal amounts in Ann's column. It took Sue 15 days to earn $540. How many days did it take Ann to earn $540, and what is the difference between the numbers of days they each required?

Number of days	Sue's pay	Ann's pay
1	36	60
2	72	120
3	108	(180)
4	144	240
5	(180)	300
6	216	(360)
7	252	420
8	288	480
9	324	(540)
10	(360)	600
11	396	660
12	432	720
13	468	780
14	504	840
15	(540)	900

Question 4   **Looking Back**   You may have noticed that every 5 days Sue earns $180 and every 3 days Ann earns $180. How does this observation suggest a different way to answer the original question?

Answers to Questions 1–4
1. Sue earned $108 in 3 days. Sue did not earn as much in 3 days as Ann did in 2 days.
2. $180. It took Sue 5 days to earn $180, and it took Ann 3 days to earn $180.
3. It took Ann 9 days to earn $540, and the difference between the numbers of days Sue and Ann worked is 6.
4. When Sue has worked 10 days and Ann has worked 6 days (a difference of 4 days), they have each earned $360; when they have worked 15 days and 9 days (a difference of 6 days), respectively, they have each earned $540.

USING A MODEL

Models are important aids for visualizing a problem and suggesting a solution. The recommendations by the Committee on the Undergraduate Program in Mathematics (CUPM) contain frequent references to the use of models for illustrating number relationships and geometric properties.*

whole numbers   The next problem uses **whole numbers,** 0, 1, 2, 3, . . . , and is solved by *using a model*. It involves a well-known story about the German mathematician Karl Gauss. When Gauss was 10 years old, his schoolmaster gave him the problem of computing the sum of whole numbers from 1 to 100. Within a few moments the young Gauss wrote the answer on his slate and passed it to the teacher. Before reading the solution to the following problem, try finding a quick method for computing the sum of whole numbers from 1 to 100.

*Committee on the Undergraduate Program in Mathematics, *Recommendations on the Mathematical Preparation of Teachers* (Berkeley, CA: Mathematical Association of America, 1983).

■ **PROBLEM**

Find an easy method for computing the sum of consecutive whole numbers from 1 to any given number n, $1 + 2 + 3 + \cdots + n$.

Question 1

Understanding the Problem   If the last number in the sum is 8, then the sum is $1 + 2 + 3 + 4 + 5 + 6 + 7 + 8$. If the last number in the sum is 100, then the sum is $1 + 2 + 3 + \cdots + 100$. What is the sum of whole numbers from 1 to 8?

Question 2

Devising a Plan   One method of solving this problem is to cut staircases out of graph paper. The one shown in figure (a) is a 1-through-8 staircase: there is 1 square in the first step, 2 squares in the second step, and so forth, to the last step, which has a column of 8 squares. The total number of squares is the sum $1 + 2 + 3 + 4 + 5 + 6 + 7 + 8$. By using 2 copies of a staircase and placing them together as in figure (b), we can obtain a rectangle whose total number of squares can easily be found by multiplying length by width. What are the dimensions of the rectangle in figure (b) and how many small squares does it contain?

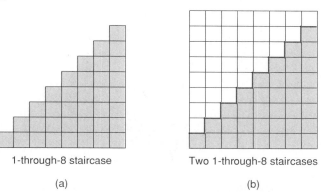

1-through-8 staircase   Two 1-through-8 staircases

(a)   (b)

Question 3

Carrying Out the Plan   Cut out 2 copies of the 1-through-8 staircase and place them together to form a rectangle. Since the total number of squares is 8×9, the number of squares in one of these staircases is $(8 \times 9)/2 = 36$. So, the sum of whole numbers from 1 to 8 is 36. By placing 2 staircases together to form a rectangle, we see that the number of squares in 1 staircase is just half the number of squares in the rectangle. This geometric approach to the problem suggests that the sum of consecutive whole numbers from 1 to any specific number is the product of the last number and the next number, divided by 2. If n represents an arbitrary whole number, what is the sum of whole numbers from 1 to n?

Question 4

Looking Back   To solve the problem Gauss was given, we might think of combining two 1-through-100 staircases to obtain a rectangle with 100×101 squares. Then, dividing by 2 produces the answer: $(100 \times 101)/2 = 5050$.

A numerical approach similar to the staircase model can be used to find the sum $1 + 2 + 3 + \cdots + 100$. If each number is used twice to obtain a sum, 101 will occur 100 times.

$$
\begin{array}{ccccccccc}
1 + & 2 + & 3 + & 4 + \cdots + & 97 + & 98 + & 99 + & 100 \\
100 + & 99 + & 98 + & 97 + \cdots + & 4 + & 3 + & 2 + & 1 \\
\hline
101 + & 101 + & 101 + & 101 + \cdots + & 101 + & 101 + & 101 + & 101
\end{array}
$$

How can these sums be used to obtain the sum of whole numbers from 1 to 100?

Answers to Questions 1–4

1. 36

2. The dimensions are 8 by 9, and there are $8 \times 9 = 72$ small squares.

3. The sum of whole numbers from 1 to n is $n(n + 1)/2$.

4. There are one hundred 101s in this sum, so its total is 100×101. Since each number from 1 to 100 has been used twice, 100×101 must be divided by 2 to obtain the sum of numbers from 1 to 100.

■ HISTORICAL HIGHLIGHT

Carl Friedrich Gauss

Archimedes, Newton, and the German mathematician Carl Friedrich Gauss (1777–1855) are considered to be the three greatest mathematicians of all time. Gauss exhibited a cleverness with numbers at an early age. The story is told that at the age of 3, as he watched his father making out the weekly payroll for laborers of a small brick-laying business, Gauss pointed out an error in the computation. Gauss enjoyed telling the story later in life and used to joke that he could figure before he could talk. Gauss kept a mathematical diary, which contained records of many of his discoveries. Some of the results are entered cryptically. For example,

$$\text{num} = \Delta + \Delta + \Delta$$

is an abbreviated statement that every whole number greater than zero is the sum of 3 or fewer triangular numbers.* (Triangular numbers are introduced later in this chapter.)

WORKING BACKWARD

When you lose or misplace something of value, it is natural to backtrack your steps in hope of discovering where the loss might have occurred. This strategy is similar to a common strategy for solving problems in mathematics. The solution to the following problem illustrates the strategy of *working backward*.

■ PROBLEM

A certain gambler took his week's paycheck to a casino. Aside from a $2 daily entrance fee and a $1 tip to the hatcheck person upon leaving, there were no other expenses. Bad luck plagued the gambler. The first day he lost half the money he had after paying the entrance fee, and the same thing happened on the second day. At the end of the second day, he had $82 remaining. How much was his weekly paycheck?

Question 1

Understanding the Problem   Let's begin by guessing the amount of the paycheck, say $400, to obtain a better feeling for the problem. If the gambler enters the casino with $400, how much money will he have at the end of the first day after he leaves the casino?

Question 2

Devising a Plan   Guessing the amount of the paycheck is one possible strategy, but it requires too many computations. Since we know the gambler has $82 at the end of the second day, a more appropriate strategy for solving the problem is to retrace his steps back through the casino (see the following diagram). First he receives $1 back for the hatcheck. Continue to work back through the second day in the casino. How much money did the gambler have at the beginning of the second day?

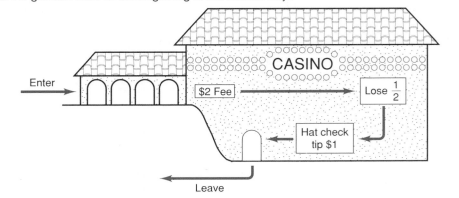

*H. W. Eves, *In Mathematical Circles* (Boston: Prindle, Weber, and Schmidt, 1969), 111–115.

Question 3

Carrying Out the Plan   The gambler had $168 at the beginning of the second day. Continue to work backward through the first day to determine how much money the gambler had at the beginning of that day. How much was the gambler's weekly paycheck?

Question 4

Looking Back   You should now check the solution by beginning with $340, the amount of the paycheck, and going through the expenditures for the 2 days to see if $82 is the remaining amount. This problem can be varied by replacing the $82 at the end of the second day by any amount and working backward to the beginning of the first day. For example, if the gambler had $120 at the end of the second day, what was the amount of the paycheck?

Answers to Questions 1–4
1. $198
2. The following diagram shows that the gambler had $168 at the beginning of the second day.

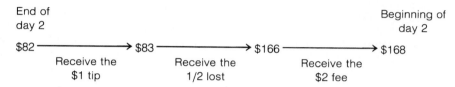

Second day

End of day 2 → $82 → Receive the $1 tip → $83 → Receive the 1/2 lost → $166 → Receive the $2 fee → $168 → Beginning of day 2

3. This diagram shows that the gambler had $340 at the beginning of the first day, so this is the amount of his paycheck.

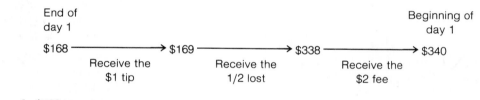

First day

End of day 1 → $168 → Receive the $1 tip → $169 → Receive the 1/2 lost → $338 → Receive the $2 fee → $340 → Beginning of day 1

4. $492

RELATED ACTIVITIES IN
Mathematics for Elementary Teachers: An Activity Approach, 3e

Activity Set 1.1

Tower of Brahma: Experiments to determine the number of moves needed to transfer discs from one needle to another. Strategies: Using a model, forming a table, and solving a simpler problem

Just for Fun

Peg-Jumping Puzzle: Experiments to find ways of interchanging two sets of pegs from one side of a board to another

Sometimes the main difficulty in solving a problem is knowing what question is to be answered.

EXERCISES AND PROBLEMS 1.1

Problems 1 through 4 suggest strategies presented in this section and are analyzed by Polya's four-step process. Other strategies may occur to you. Try to solve each of these problems on your own before answering the questions in parts a, b, c, and d.

1. **Making a Drawing** A well is 20 feet deep. A snail at the bottom climbs up 4 feet each day and slips back 2 feet each night. How many days will it take the snail to reach the top of the well?

   a. *Understanding the Problem* What is the greatest height the snail reaches during the first 24 hours? How far up the well will the snail be at the end of the first 24 hours?

   b. *Devising a Plan* One plan that is commonly chosen is to compute 20/2, since it appears that the snail gains 2 feet each day. However, 10 days is not the correct answer. A second plan is to make a drawing and plot out the snail's daily progress. What is the snail's greatest height during the second day?

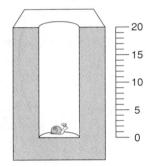

   c. *Carrying Out the Plan* Trace out the snail's daily progress and mark its position at the end of each day. On which day does the snail get out of the well?

   d. *Looking Back* There is a "surprise ending" at the top of the well because the snail does not slip back on the ninth day. Make up a new snail problem, changing the numbers so that there will be a similar surprise ending at the top of the well.

2. **Making a Table** A bank that has been charging a monthly service fee of $2 for checking accounts plus 15 cents for each check written announces that it will change its monthly fee to $3 and each check will cost 8 cents. The bank claims the new plan will save the customer money. How many checks must a customer write per month before the new plan is cheaper than the old plan?

   a. *Understanding the Problem* Try some numbers to get a feeling for the problem. Compute the cost of 10 checks under the old plan and the new plan. Which plan is cheaper for a customer who writes 10 checks a month?

   b. *Devising a Plan* One method of solving this problem is to make a table showing the cost of 1 check, 2 checks, etc., as shown in the next column. How much more does the new plan cost than the old plan for 6 checks?

   c. *Carrying Out the Plan* Extend the table until you reach a point at which the new plan is cheaper than the old plan. How many checks must be written per month for the new plan to be cheaper?

Checks	Cost for old plan	Cost for new plan
1	$2.15	$3.08
2	$2.30	$3.16
3	$2.45	$3.24
4	$2.60	$3.32
5	$2.75	$3.40
6		
7		
8		

   d. *Looking Back* For customers who write 1 check per month, the difference in cost between the old plan and the new plan is 93 cents. What happens to the difference as the number of checks increases? How many checks must a customer write per month before the new plan is 33 cents cheaper?

3. **Guessing and Checking** There are 2 two-digit numbers that satisfy the following conditions: (1) each number has the same digits; (2) the sum of the digits in each number is 10; and (3) the difference between the two numbers is 54. What are the two numbers?

   a. *Understanding the Problem* The numbers 58 and 85 are two-digit numbers that have the same digits. However, the sum of the digits in each number is 13. Find 2 two-digit numbers such that the sum of the digits is 10 and both numbers have the same digits.

   b. *Devising a Plan* Since there are only 9 two-digit numbers whose digits have a sum of 10, the problem can be easily solved by guessing. What is the difference between your 2 two-digit numbers from part a? If this difference is not 54, it can provide information about your next guess.

   c. *Carrying Out the Plan* Continue to guess and check. Which pair of numbers has a difference of 54?

   d. *Looking Back* This problem can be extended by changing the requirement that the sum of the 2 digits equal 10. Solve the problem for the case in which the digits have a sum of 12.

4. *Working Backward* Three girls play 3 rounds of a game. On each round there are 2 winners and 1 loser. The girl who loses on a round has to double the number of chips that each of the other girls has by giving up some of her own chips. Each girl loses 1 round. At the end of 3 rounds, each girl has 40 chips. How many chips did each girl have at the beginning of the game?

a. *Understanding the Problem* Let's select some numbers to get a feeling for this game. Suppose girl A, girl B, and girl C have 70, 30, and 20 chips, respectively, and girl A loses the first round. Girl B and girl C will receive chips from girl A, and thus their supply of chips will double. How many chips will each girl have after this round?

b. *Devising a Plan* Since we know the end result (each girl finished with 40 chips), a natural strategy is to work backward through the 3 rounds to the beginning. Assume that girl C loses the third round. How many chips did each girl have at the end of the second round?

	A	B	C
Beginning			
End of first round			
End of second round			
End of third round	40	40	40

c. *Carrying Out the Plan* Assume that girl B loses the second round and girl A loses the first round. Continue working back through the 3 rounds to determine the number of chips the girls had at the beginning of the game.

d. *Looking Back* Check your answer by working forward from the beginning. The girl with the most chips at the beginning of this game lost the first round. Could the girl with the least chips at the beginning of the game have lost the first round? Try it.

There are often several ways to solve a problem. Strategies are suggested for problems 5 through 11, but you may prefer to use other approaches.

5. Linda picked a basket of apples. She gave half the apples to a neighbor, then 8 apples to her mother, then half the remaining apples to her best friend; she kept the 3 remaining apples for herself. How many apples did she start with in the basket? (Suggested strategy: Working Backward)

6. At left in the following figure is a domino donut with 11 dots on each side. Arrange the 4 single dominoes on the right into a domino donut so that all 4 sides have 12 dots. (Suggested strategies: Using a Model (trace and cut out dominoes) and Guessing and Checking)

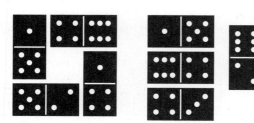

Domino donut

7. In driving from town A to town D, you pass first through town B and then through town C. It is 10 times farther from town A to town B than from B to C, and 10 times farther from B to C than from C to D. If it is 1332 miles from A to D, how far is it from A to B? (Suggested strategies: Making a Drawing and Guessing and Checking)

8. How can you scoop up exactly 6 quarts of water from a river when you have only 2 containers to measure with, a 4-quart bucket and a 9-quart bucket? Assume that there are no markings of partial amounts on the buckets. (Suggested strategies: Guessing and Checking and Making a Table)

9. Harold wrote to 15 people, and the cost of postage was $3.45. If it cost 19 cents to mail a postcard and 29 cents to mail a letter, how many postcards did he write? (Suggested strategy: Making a Table or Guessing and Checking)

10. Sue Ellen and Angela both have $510 in their savings accounts now. They opened their accounts on the same day, at which time Sue Ellen started with twice as much money as Angela. From then on Sue Ellen added $10 to her account each week, and Angela put in $20 each week. How much money did Sue Ellen open her account with? (Suggested strategy: Working Backward)

11. The following patterns can be used to form a cube. A cube has 6 faces: the top and bottom faces, the left and right faces, and the front and back faces. Two faces have been labeled on each of the following patterns. Label the remaining 4 faces on each pattern so that when the cube is assembled with the labels on the outside, each face will be in the right place. (Suggested strategy: Using a Model)

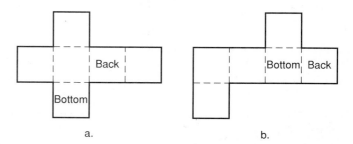

a.   b.

Problems 12 through 19 can be solved by the strategies presented in this section. Once you have solved each problem, write the strategy you used. Then use Polya's idea of looking back to extend the problem or write a related problem.

12. There were ships with 3 masts and ships with 4 masts at the Tall Ships Exhibition. Millie counted a total of 30 masts on the 8 ships she saw. How many of these ships had 4 masts?

13. How can 350 be written as the sum of 4 consecutive whole numbers?

14. When a teacher counted her students in groups of 4, she had 2 left over. When she counted them in groups of 5, she had 1 left over. If 15 of her students were girls and she had more girls than boys, how many students did she have?

15. Three circular cardboard discs have numbers written on the front and back sides. The front sides have the numbers shown below.

By tossing these discs and adding the numbers that show on their faces, we can obtain these totals: 15, 16, 17, 18, 19, 20, 21, and 22. What numbers are written on the back sides of these discs?

16. The curator of an art exhibit wants to place security guards along the 4 walls of a large auditorium so that each wall has the same number of guards. Any guard who is placed in a corner can watch the 2 adjacent walls, but all other guards can watch only 1 wall.
    a. Draw a sketch to show how this can be done with 6 security guards.
    b. Show how this can be done with each of the following numbers of security guards: 7, 8, 9, 10, 11, and 12.
    c. List all numbers less than 100 that are solutions to this problem.

17. How can a chef use an 11-minute hourglass and a 7-minute hourglass to time vegetables that must steam for 15 minutes?

18. By moving adjacent discs 2 at a time, you can change the arrangement of large and small discs shown below to an arrangement in which 3 big discs are side by side, followed by the 3 little discs. Describe the steps.

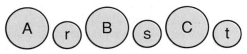

19. Trick questions like the following can help improve problem-solving ability because they require that a person listen and think carefully about the information and the question.
    a. Take 2 apples from 3 apples and what do you have?
    b. A farmer had 17 sheep and all but 9 died. How many sheep did he have left?
    c. I have 2 U.S. coins that total 30 cents. One is not a nickel. What are the 2 coins?
    d. A bottle of cider costs 86 cents. The cider costs 60 cents more than the bottle. How much does the bottle cost?
    e. How much dirt is in a hole 3 feet long, 2 feet wide, and 2 feet deep?
    f. A hen weighs 3 pounds plus half its weight. How much does it weigh?
    g. The score at the end of a baseball game was 7 to 2, and not a man crossed the plate. How could this happen?
    h. Which of the following phrases is correct: (1) "the whites of the egg are yellow" or (2) "the whites of the egg is yellow"?

CALCULATOR INVESTIGATION

Choose any four-digit number, reverse its digits, add the two numbers, and try dividing by 11. For example,

$$7582 + 2857 = 10{,}439,$$

which is divisible by 11 (that is, there is no remainder when it is divided by 11). Try this for some other four-digit numbers. Note: Zero is divisible by 11. Based on your investigation, write T or F under the 4 in the table. Try this for two-digit numbers, three-digit numbers, etc., and write T or F in the table for each number of digits.

Make a conjecture based on the results of this investigation.

Number of digits	2	3	4	5	6	7	8
Divisible by 11 (T or F)							

PUZZLER   Given 4 pieces of chain of 3 links each, explain how all 12 links can be joined into a single circular chain by cutting and rejoining only 3 links.

SECTION 1.2   PATTERNS AND PROBLEM SOLVING

■ PROBLEM OPENER

This matchstick track has 4 squares. If the pattern of squares is continued, how many matches will be needed to build a track with 60 squares?

The great spiral galaxy Andromeda

Patterns play a major role in the solution of problems in all walks of life. Psychologists analyze patterns of human behavior; meteorologists study weather patterns; astronomers seek patterns in the movements of stars and galaxies; and detectives look for patterns among clues. Finding a pattern is such a useful problem-solving strategy in mathematics that some have called it the "art of mathematics."

To find patterns we need to compare and contrast. We must compare to find features that remain constant and contrast to find those that are changing. Patterns appear in many forms. There are number patterns, geometric patterns, word patterns, and letter patterns, to name a few. Try finding a pattern in each of the following sequences and write or sketch the next term.

EXAMPLE A

1,   2,   4,

One Solution   Each term is twice the previous term. The next term is 8.

EXAMPLE B

One Solution   In each block of 4 squares, 1 square is shaded. The upper left, upper right, lower left, and lower right corners are shaded in order. The next term in this sequence has the shaded block in the lower right corner.

EXAMPLE C

Al, Bev, Carl, Donna

One Solution   The first letters of the names are consecutive letters of the alphabet. The next name begins with E.

Finding a pattern requires making educated guesses. You are guessing the pattern based on some observation, and a different observation may lead to another pattern. In Example A the difference between the first and second terms is 1, and the difference between the second and third terms is 2. So, using differences between consecutive terms as the basis of the pattern, we would have a difference of 3 between the third and fourth terms and the fourth term would be 7 rather than 8. In Example C we might use the pattern of alternating masculine and feminine names or of increasing numbers of letters in the names.

PATTERNS IN NATURE

The spiral is a common pattern in nature. It is found in spider webs, seashells, plants, animals, weather patterns, and the shapes of galaxies. The frequent occurrence of spirals in living things can be explained by different growth rates. Living forms curl because the faster-growing (longer) surface lies outside and the slower growing (shorter) surface lies inside. An example of a living spiral is the shell of the mollusk chambered nautilus (Figure 1.2). As it grows, the creature lives in successively larger compartments.

Figure 1.2
Courtesy of the American Museum of National History

Chambered nautilus

A variety of patterns occur in plants and trees. Many of these patterns are related to a famous sequence of numbers called **Fibonacci numbers.** After the first two numbers of this sequence, which are 1 and 1, each successive number may be obtained by adding the two previous numbers.

Fibonacci numbers

1   1   2   3   5   8   13   21   34   55   . . .

The seeds in the center of a daisy are arranged in two intersecting sets of spirals, one turning clockwise and one turning counterclockwise. The number of spirals in each set is a Fibonacci number. Also, the number of petals will often be a Fibonacci number. The daisy in Figure 1.3 has 21 petals.

Figure 1.3

■ HISTORICAL HIGHLIGHT

Month
1st
2nd
3rd
4th
5th

Fibonacci numbers were discovered by the Italian mathematician Leonardo Fibonnaci (ca. 1175–1250) while studying the birthrates of rabbits. Suppose that a pair of baby rabbits is too young to produce more rabbits the first month, but produces a pair of baby rabbits every month thereafter. Each new pair of rabbits will follow the same rule. The pairs of rabbits for the first five months are shown here. The realization that Fibonacci numbers could be applied to the science of plants and trees occurred several hundred years after the discovery of this number sequence.

NUMBER PATTERNS

Number patterns have fascinated people since the beginning of recorded history. One of the earliest patterns to be recognized led to the distinction between **even numbers,**

even numbers

$$0, 2, 4, 6, 8, 10, 12, 14, \ldots$$

odd numbers

and **odd numbers,**

$$1, 3, 5, 7, 9, 11, 13, 15, \ldots$$

The game of "Even and Odd" has been played for generations. To play this game, one person picks up some stones and the other person guesses whether the number of stones is odd or even. If the guess is correct, that person wins.

✓ **PASCAL'S TRIANGLE**   The triangular pattern of numbers shown in Figure 1.4 is Pascal's triangle. It has been of interest to mathematicians for hundreds of years, appearing in China as early as 1303. This triangle is named after the French mathematician Blaise Pascal (1623–1662), who wrote a book on some of its uses.

Figure 1.4

Row zero					1				
Row one				1		1			
Row two			1		2		1		
Row three		1		3		3		1	
Row four	1		4		6		4		1

EXAMPLE D

In the fourth row, each of the numbers 4, 6, and 4 can be obtained by adding the two adjacent numbers from the row above it. What numbers are in the fifth row of Pascal's triangle?

Solution   1   5   10   10   5   1

ARITHMETIC SEQUENCE   Sequences of numbers are often generated by patterns. In the sequences in Example E, each number is obtained from the previous number in the sequence by adding the same number throughout. This number is called the **common difference.** Such a sequence is called an **arithmetic sequence.**

common difference
arithmetic sequence

EXAMPLE E

7,   11,   15,   19,   23, . . .
10,   20,   30,   40,   50, . . .

The first arithmetic sequence has a common difference of 4. What is the common difference for the second sequence? Write the next three terms in each sequence.

Solution   The next three terms in the first sequence in Example E are 27, 31, and 35. The common difference for the second sequence is 10, and the next three terms are 60, 70, and 80.

GEOMETRIC SEQUENCE   In a geometric sequence, each number is obtained by multiplying the previous number by some common number. This number is called the **common ratio,** and the resulting sequence is called a **geometric sequence.***

common ratio
geometric sequence

EXAMPLE F

3,   6,   12,   24,   48, . . .
1,   5,   25,   125,   625, . . .

The common ratio in the first sequence is 2. What is the common ratio in the second sequence? Write the next two terms in each sequence.

Solution   The next two terms in the first sequence in Example F are 96 and 192. The common difference for the second sequence is 5, and the next two terms are 3125 and 15,625.

*The computer programs ARITHMETIC SEQUENCE and GEOMETRIC SEQUENCE on the *Computer Problem-Solving Disc* may be used to obtain any number of a sequence or the sum of the first *n* terms.

triangular numbers

TRIANGULAR NUMBERS   The sequence of numbers illustrated in Figure 1.5 is nei-ther arithmetic nor geometric. These numbers are called **triangular numbers** because of the arrangement of dots that is associated with each number. Since each triangular number is the sum of whole numbers beginning with 1, the formula for the sum of consecutive whole numbers can be used to obtain triangular numbers.

Figure 1.5

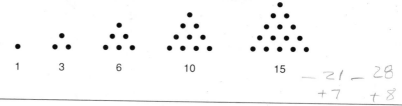

1	3	6	10	15	_ 21 _ 28
					+7 +8

EXAMPLE G

The first triangular number is 1, and the fifth triangular number is 15. What is the sixth triangular number?

Solution   The sixth triangular number is 21.

figurate numbers

There are other types of numbers that receive their names from the numbers of dots in geometric figures (see #12 in Exercises and Problems 1.2). Such numbers are called **figurate numbers** and represent one kind of link between geometry and arith-metic.

finite differences

FINITE DIFFERENCES   Often sequences of numbers don't appear to have a pattern. However, sometimes number patterns can be found by looking at the differences be-tween consecutive terms. This approach is called the method of **finite differences.**

EXAMPLE H

Consider the sequence 0, 3, 8, 15, 24, ... Find a pattern and determine the next term.

Solution   Using the method of finite differences, we can obtain a second sequence of numbers by computing the differences between numbers from the original sequence, as shown below. Then a third sequence is obtained by computing the differences from the second sequence. The process stops when all the numbers in the sequence of differences are equal. In this example, when the sequence becomes all 2s, we stop and work our way back from the bottom row to the original sequence. Assuming the pattern of 2s continues, the next number after 9 is 11, so the next number after 24 is 35.

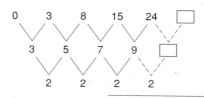

EXAMPLE I

Use the method of finite differences to determine the next term in each sequence.*

1. 3,   6,   13,   24,   39
2. 1,   5,   14,   30,   55,   91

Solution   1. The next number in the sequence is 58.

2. The next number in the sequence is 140.

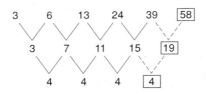

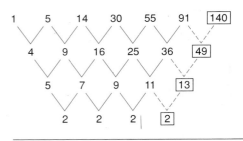

✓ INDUCTIVE REASONING

The process of forming conclusions on the basis of patterns, observations, examples, or experiments is called **inductive reasoning.**

inductive reasoning

EXAMPLE J

Each of the following sums of three consecutive whole numbers is divisible by 3.

$$4 + 5 + 6 = 15 \qquad 2 + 3 + 4 = 9 \qquad 7 + 8 + 9 = 24$$

If we conclude, on the basis of these sums, that "the sum of any three consecutive whole numbers is divisible by 3," we are using inductive reasoning.

Inductive reasoning may be thought of as making an "informed guess." Although this type of reasoning is important in mathematics, it sometimes leads to incorrect results.

EXAMPLE K

Consider the number of regions that can be obtained in a circle by connecting points on the circumference of the circle. Connecting 2 points gives 2 regions; connecting 3 points gives 4 regions; and so on. Each time a new point on the circle is used, the number of regions appears to double.

2 points   3 points   4 points   5 points   6 points

2 regions   4 regions   8 regions   16 regions

The numbers of regions in the circles above are the beginning of the geometric sequence 2, 4, 8, 16, . . . , and it is tempting to conclude that 6 points will produce 32 regions. However, no matter how the 6 points are located on the circle, there will not be more than 31 regions.

*The computer programs ARITHMETIC SEQUENCE and GEOMETRIC SEQUENCE on the *Computer Problem-Solving Disc* may be used to obtain any number of a sequence or the sum of the first *n* terms.

counterexample

COUNTEREXAMPLE   An example that shows that a statement is false is called a **counterexample.** If you have a general statement, test it to see if it is true for a few special cases. You may be able to find a counterexample to show that the statement is not true.

EXAMPLE L

Find two whole numbers for which the following statement is false: The sum of any two whole numbers is divisible by 2.

Solution   It is not true for 7 and 4, since 7 + 4 = 11, and 11 is not divisible by 2. There are pairs of whole numbers for which the statement is true. For example, 3 + 7 = 10, and 10 is divisible by 2. However, the counterexample of the sum of 7 and 4 shows that the statement is not true for all pairs of whole numbers.

Counterexamples can help us to restate a conjecture. The statement in Example L is false, but if it is changed to read, "The sum of two odd numbers is divisible by 2," it becomes a true statement.

EXAMPLE M

For which of the following statements is there a counterexample? If a statement is false, change a condition to produce a true statement.

1. The sum of any four whole numbers is divisible by 2.
2. The sum of any two even numbers is divisible by 2.
3. The sum of any three consecutive whole numbers is divisible by 2.

Solution
1. The following counterexample shows that statement (1) is false: 4 + 12 + 6 + 3 = 25, which is not divisible by 2. If the condition "four whole numbers" is replaced by "four even numbers," the statement becomes true.
2. Statement (2) is true.
3. The following counterexample shows that statement (3) is false: 8 + 9 + 10 = 27, which is not divisible by 2. If the condition "three consecutive whole numbers" is replaced by "three consecutive whole numbers beginning with an odd number," the statement becomes true.

■ *HISTORICAL HIGHLIGHT*

Aristotle (384–322 B.C.), Greek scientist and philosopher, believed that heavy objects fall faster than lighter ones, and this principle was accepted as true for hundreds of years. Then in the sixteenth century, Galileo produced a counterexample by dropping two pieces of metal from the Leaning Tower of Pisa. In spite of the fact that one was twice as heavy as the other, both hit the ground at the same time.

Leaning Tower of Pisa, Pisa, Italy

PROBLEM-SOLVING APPLICATION

solving a simpler problem
finding a pattern

The strategies of **solving a simpler problem** and **finding a pattern** are introduced in the following problem. Simplifying a problem or solving a related but easier problem can help in understanding the given information and devising a plan for the solution. Sometimes the numbers in a problem are large or inconvenient, and finding a solution for smaller numbers can lead to a plan or reveal a pattern for solving the original problem. Read this problem and try solving it. Then read the following four-step solution and compare it to your solution.

■ PROBLEM

There are 15 people in a room, and each person shakes hands exactly once with everyone else. How many handshakes take place?

Understanding the Problem   For each pair of people, there will be 1 handshake. For example, if Paul and Sue shake hands, this is counted as 1 handshake. Thus, the problem is to determine the total number of different ways that 15 people can be paired. How many handshakes will occur when 3 people shake hands?

Question 1

Sue   Paul

Devising a Plan   Fifteen people are a lot of people to work with at one time. Let's simplify the problem and count the number of handshakes for small groups of people. Solving these special cases may give us an idea for solving the original problem. What is the number of handshakes in a group of 4 people?

Question 2

Carrying Out the Plan   We have already noted that there is 1 handshake for 2 people, 3 handshakes for 3 people, and 6 handshakes for 4 people. The following figure illustrates how 6 handshakes will occur among 4 people. Suppose a fifth person joins the group. This person will shake hands with the first 4 people, accounting for 4 more handshakes.

Fifth
person

Similarly, if we bring in a sixth person, this person will shake hands with the first 5 people, and so there will be 5 new handshakes. Suddenly, we can see a pattern developing: the fifth person adds 4 new handshakes; the sixth person adds 5 new handshakes; the seventh person adds 6 new handshakes; and so on until the 15th person adds 14 new handshakes. How many handshakes will there be for 15 people?

Question 3

Question 4

Looking Back   By looking at special cases with numbers smaller than 15, we obtained a better understanding of the problem and an insight for solving it. The pattern we found suggests a method for determining the number of handshakes for any number of people: add the whole numbers from 1 to the number that is 1 less than the number of people. You may recall from Section 1.1 that staircases were used to develop a formula for computing such a sum. How can this formula be used to determine the number of handshakes for 15 people?

Answers to Questions 1–4
1. 3   **2.** 6
3. 1 + 2 + 3 + 4 + 5 + 6 + 7 + 8 + 9 + 10 + 11 + 12 + 13 + 14 = 105
4. The sum of whole numbers from 1 to 14 is (14 × 15)/2 = 105.

RELATED ACTIVITIES IN
Mathematics for Elementary Teachers: An Activity Approach, 3e

Activity Set 1.2   **Geometric Number Patterns:** Geometric patterns for representing number patterns and providing visual support for extending number sequences. (Strategies: Finding a Pattern and Solving a Simpler Problem)

Just for Fun   **Fibonacci Numbers in Nature:** Activities for finding Fibonacci numbers in daisies, cones, and pineapples

---

√ EXERCISES AND PROBLEMS 1.2

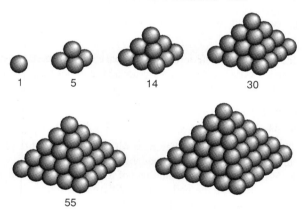

1. One method of stacking cannon balls is to form a pyramid with a square base. The first six such pyramids are shown above.
   a. How many cannon balls are in the sixth pyramid?
   b. Can the method of finite differences be used to find the number of cannon balls in the sixth pyramid?
   c. Describe the tenth pyramid of cannon balls.
   d. Write an expression for the number of cannon balls in the 20th pyramid. (Note: It is not necessary to compute the number.)
   e. For any whole number *n*, write an expression for the number of cannon balls in the *n*th pyramid.

2. The numbers of cubes in the following figures form the beginning of what type of sequence?

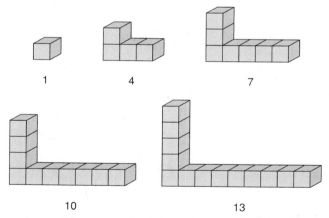

How many blocks will there be in each of the following?
   a. The sixth figure
   b. The 20th figure
   c. The 100th figure
   d. The *n*th figure, for any whole number *n*

3. There are many patterns and number relationships that can be easily discovered on a calendar. Here are a few.
   a. The sum of the three circled dates on the following calendar is 45. For any sum of three consecutive numbers (from the rows), there is a quick method for determining the numbers. Explain how this can be done. Try your method to find three consecutive numbers whose sum is 54.

b. If you are told the sum of any three adjacent dates from a column, it is possible to determine the three numbers. Explain how this can be done and use your method to find the numbers whose sum is 48.

c. The sum of the 3 by 3 array of numbers outlined on the calendar is 99. There is a shortcut method for using this sum to find the 3 by 3 array of numbers. Explain how this can be done. Try your method to find the 3 by 3 array whose sum is 198.

NOVEMBER
1991

Sun	Mon	Tue	Wed	Thu	Fri	Sat
					1	2
3	4	5	6	7	8	9
10	11	12	13	⑭	⑮	⑯
17	18	19	20	21	22	23
24	25	26	27	28	29	30

4. The first few Fibonacci numbers are 1, 1, 2, 3, 5, 8, 13, 21, 34, and 55. Compute the sums shown below and compare the answers with the Fibonacci numbers. Find a pattern and explain how this pattern can be used to find the sums of consecutive Fibonacci numbers, beginning with the first Fibonacci number.

$$1 + 1 + 2 =$$
$$1 + 1 + 2 + 3 =$$
$$1 + 1 + 2 + 3 + 5 =$$
$$1 + 1 + 2 + 3 + 5 + 8 =$$
$$1 + 1 + 2 + 3 + 5 + 8 + 13 =$$
$$1 + 1 + 2 + 3 + 5 + 8 + 13 + 21 =$$

5. Consider the following sequence of numbers:

1 2 3 4 5 6 7 8 9 10 11 12 13 14 15

If we insert "punctuation" according to the following pattern, we obtain equations.

$$1 + 2 = 3 \qquad 4 + 5 + 6 = 7 + 8$$
$$9 + 10 + 11 + 12 = 13 + 14 + 15$$

a. Extend this pattern by writing the next two equations.
b. Does the pattern continue to hold?

6. The products of 1089 and each of the first few digits produce some interesting number patterns. Describe one of these patterns. Will this pattern continue if 1089 is multiplied by 5, 6, 7, 8, and 9?

$$1 \times 1089 = 1089$$
$$2 \times 1089 = 2178$$
$$3 \times 1089 = 3267$$
$$4 \times 1089 = 4356$$
$$5 \times 1089 =$$

7. There are many patterns in Pascal's triangle. Add the first few numbers in the first diagonal, starting from the top. This sum will be another number from the triangle. Will this be true for the sums of the first few numbers in the other diagonals?

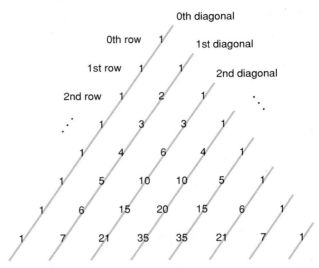

8. Compute the sums of the numbers in the first few rows of Pascal's triangle.
a. What kind of sequence (arithmetic or geometric) do these sums form?
b. What will be the sum of the numbers in row 12 of this triangle?

9. Identify each of the following sequences as arithmetic or geometric. State a rule for obtaining each number from the preceding number. Write the next three numbers in each sequence.

a. 4, 9, 14, 19, . . .   **b.** 15, 30, 60, 120, . . .
c. 24, 20, 16, 12, . . .   **d.** 4, 12, 36, 108, . . .

10. The method of finite differences will sometimes enable you to find the next number in a sequence, but not always.
a. Write the first eight numbers of a geometric sequence and try using the method of finite differences to find the ninth number. Will this method work?
b. Do the same for an arithmetic sequence.

11. Use the method of finite differences to find the next number in each of the following sequences.

a. 1, 2, 7, 22, 53, 106, . . .   **b.** 1, 3, 11, 25, 45, 71, . . .

12. As early as 500 B.C., the Greeks were deeply interested in numbers associated with patterns of dots in the shape of geometric figures. Write the next three figurate numbers and the 100th figurate number in each sequence in parts a, b, and c.
a. Triangular numbers

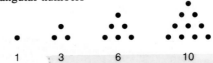

b. Square numbers

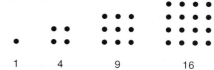

1   4   9   16

c. Pentagonal numbers

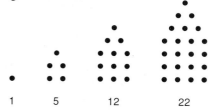

1   5   12   22

13. The Greeks called the numbers represented by the following arrays of dots **oblong numbers.**

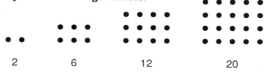

2   6   12   20

a. What is the next oblong number?
b. What is the 20th oblong number?

14. Use the method of finite differences to create a new sequence of numbers from the following sequence of square numbers:

$$1, 4, 9, 16, 25, 36, 49, 64, 81$$

a. What kind of a sequence do you obtain?
b. How can a square array of dots (see exercise 12b) be used to show that the difference of two consecutive square numbers will be an odd number?

15. What kind of reasoning is used to arrive at the conclusion in the following article?

Vitamin C student finds a little is best

By Nancy Hicks
New York Times News Service

NEW YORK – A Canadian researcher has reported finding therapeutic value in using Vitamin C to treat symtoms of the common cold in much lower doses than had been previously recommended.

Dr. Terence W. Anderson, an epidemiologist at the University of Toronto, reported a 30 per cent reduction in the severity of cold symptoms in persons who took only a small amount of Vitamin C – less than 250 milligrams a day regularly, and one gram a day when symptoms of a cold began.

Anderson's conclusion was based on a study of 600 volunteers.

---

16. Continue the pattern of even numbers illustrated below.

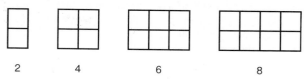

2   4   6   8

a. The fourth even number is 8. Sketch the figure for the ninth even number and determine this number.
b. What is the 45th even number?

17. Continue the pattern of odd numbers illustrated below.

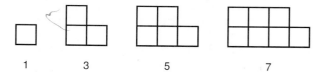

1   3   5   7

a. The fourth odd number is 7. Sketch the figure for the 12th odd number.
b. What is the 35th odd number?

18. If we begin with the number 6, then double it to get 12, and then place the 12 and 6 side by side, the result is 126. This number is divisible by 7. Try this procedure for some other numbers. Find a counterexample that shows that the result is not always divisible by 7.

19. Find a counterexample for each of the following statements.
a. The product of any two whole numbers is evenly divisible by 2.
b. Every whole number greater than 5 is the sum of either two or three consecutive whole numbers. For example, $11 = 5 + 6$ and $18 = 5 + 6 + 7$.

20. Determine which of the following statements are false and give a counterexample for each false statement. If a statement is false, change one of the conditions to obtain a true statement.
a. The product of any three consecutive whole numbers is divisible by 2.
b. The sum of any two consecutive whole numbers is divisible by 2.
c. The sum of any four consecutive whole numbers is divisible by 4.
d. Every whole number greater than zero and less than 15 is either a triangular number or the sum of two or three triangular numbers.

21. In the familiar song "The Twelve Days of Christmas," the total number of gifts received each day is a triangular number. On the first day there was 1 gift, on the second day 3 gifts, on the third day 6 gifts, etc., until the 12th day of Christmas.
a. How many gifts were received on the 12th day?
b. What is the total number of gifts received during all 12 days?

22. For several years Charlie has had a tree farm where he grows blue spruce. The trees are planted in a square array (square arrays are shown in exercise 12b). This year Charlie planted 87 new trees along two adjacent edges of the square to form a larger square. How many trees are in the new square? (Suggested strategy: Making a Drawing)

23. Kay started a computer club and for a while she was the only member. She planned to have each member find 2 new members each month. By the end of the first month she had found two more members. If her plan is carried out, how many members will the club have at the end of

a. 6 months? **b.** 1 year?

(Suggested strategies: Solving a Simpler Problem and Finding a Pattern.)

Featured Strategy: Solving a Simpler Problem

24. You are given 8 coins and a balance scale. The coins are alike in appearance, but one of them is counterfeit and lighter than the others. Find the counterfeit coin using just 2 weighings on the balance scale.

  a. *Understanding the Problem* If there were only 2 coins and 1 was counterfeit and lighter, the bad coin could be determined in just 1 weighing. The balance scale below shows this situation. Is the counterfeit coin on the left or right side of the balance beam?

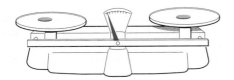

  b. *Devising a Plan* One method of solving this problem is to guess and check. It is natural to begin with 4 coins on each side of the balance beam. Explain why this approach will not produce the counterfeit coin in just 2 weighings. Another method is to simplify the problem and try solving it for fewer coins.

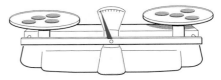

  c. *Carrying Out the Plan* Explain how the counterfeit coin can be found with 1 weighing if there are only 3 coins and 2 weighings if there are 6 coins. By now you may have an idea for solving the original problem. How can the counterfeit coin be found in 2 weighings?

  d. *Looking Back* Explain how the counterfeit coin can be found in 2 weighings when there are 9 coins.

COMPUTER INVESTIGATION

The computer program TRIANGULAR NUMBERS on the *Computer Problem-Solving Disc* prints all the triangular numbers between any two given numbers.

One student was looking at the first few triangular numbers (1, 3, 6, 10, 15, 21) and noticed that the sequence of units digits in those numbers (1, 3, 6, 0, 5, 1) started with 1 and ended with 1.

Questions for Investigation

1. If the triangular numbers are continued beyond 21, will the same units digits be repeated? What patterns can you find?

2. The sequence of units digits eventually contains two consecutive zeros. Are there other pairs of zeros if the sequence is extended?

3. Will the sequence of units digits ever contain three or more consecutive zeros?

4. Use your pattern to develop a method for determining the units digit in any given triangular number—for example, the 5147th triangular number.

PUZZLER

The background in this photo produces an illusion called the Fraser spiral. Can you explain what is wrong with this "spiral"?

CHAPTER REVIEW

1. Problem Solving
   a. **Problem solving** is the process by which an unfamiliar situation is resolved.
   b. **Polya's Four-Step Process**
   Understanding the problem
   Devising a plan
   Carrying out the plan
   Looking back
   c. **Problem-Solving Strategies**
   Making a drawing
   Guessing and checking
   Making a table
   Using a model
   Working backward
   Finding a pattern
   Solving a simpler problem

2. **Unsolved Problems**
   a. There are many unsolved problems in mathematics.
   b. A **conjecture** is a statement that has not been proved, yet is thought to be true.

3. **Patterns**
   a. There are many kinds of patterns. They are found by comparing and contrasting information.

   b. The numbers in the sequence 1, 1, 2, 3, 5, 8, 13, 21, . . . are called **Fibonacci numbers.** The growth patterns of plants and trees frequently can be described by Fibonacci numbers.
   c. **Pascal's triangle** is a triangle of numbers with many patterns. One pattern enables each row to be obtained from the previous row.
   d. An **arithmetic sequence** is a sequence in which each term is obtained by adding a **common difference** to the previous term.
   e. A **geometric sequence** is a sequence in which each term is obtained by multiplying the previous term by a **common ratio.**
   f. The numbers in the sequence 1, 3, 6, 10, 15, 21, . . . are called **triangular numbers.**
   g. **Finite differences** is a method of finding patterns by computing differences of consecutive terms.

4. **Inductive Reasoning**
   a. **Inductive reasoning** is the process of forming conclusions on the basis of observations, patterns, or experiments.
   b. A **counterexample** is an example that shows that a statement is false.

CHAPTER TEST

1. List Polya's four steps in problem solving.

2. List the seven problem-solving strategies that were introduced in this chapter.

3. The numbers in the following sums were obtained by using every other Fibonacci number (circled).

   ①　1　②　3　⑤　8　⑬　21　㉞

   $$1 + 2 =$$
   $$1 + 2 + 5 =$$
   $$1 + 2 + 5 + 13 =$$
   $$1 + 2 + 5 + 13 + 34 =$$

   Compute these sums. What is the relationship between these sums and the Fibonacci numbers?

4. What is the sum of numbers in row nine of Pascal's triangle?

5. Find a pattern in the following sequences and write the next term.

   a. 1, 3, 9, 27, 81,　　b. 3, 6, 9, 12, 15,　　c. 0, 6, 12, 18, 24,
   d. 1, 4, 9, 16, 25,　　e. 3, 5, 11, 21, 35,

6. Classify each sequence in problem 5 as arithmetic, geometric, or neither.

7. Use the method of finite differences to find the next three terms in each sequence.

   a. 1, 5, 14, 30, 55　　　　b. 2, 9, 20, 35,

8. What is the fifth number in each of the following sequences of numbers?

   a. Triangular numbers　　b. Square numbers
   c. Pentagonal numbers

9. What kind of reasoning is used to arrive at the conclusion in the following article?

Operating room work may have health hazards

WASHINGTON (UPI) – There is an increase in cancer and other disease rates among hospital operating room personnel and a report Monday said regular exposure to anesthetic gases appears to be the most likely cause.

A survey of 49,585 operating room personnel indicated that female anesthetists and nurses are the most vulnerable, particularly if they are pregnant.

"The results of the survey strongly suggest that working in the operating room and, presumably, exposure to trace concentrations of anesthetic agents entails a variety of health hazards for operating personnel and their offspring."

10. Find a counterexample for this statement: The sum of any seven consecutive whole numbers is evenly divisible by 4.

Identify the strategy or strategies you use to solve each of the following problems.

11. A 2000-foot-long straight fence has posts that are set 10 feet apart. If the fence begins with a post and ends with a post, determine the number of posts in the entire fence.

12. In a game of chips, Pauli lost half her chips in the first round, then won 50 chips, then lost half her total, and finally won 80 chips. She finished with 170 chips. How many chips did she have at the beginning of the game?

13. The following tower has 5 tiles along its base and 5 rows of tiles. How many tiles will be required to build a tower like this with 25 tiles along its base and 25 rows of tiles?

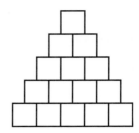

14. Shown below are the first three squares in a pattern. Each square has one more dot on each side than the previous square.

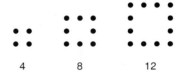

   4   8   12

a. How many dots are there in the fourth square?
b. How many dots are there in the 50th square?

15. There are 78 people around a table. Each person shakes hands with the people to his or her immediate right and left. How many handshakes take place?

16. Two men and 2 boys want to cross a river using a small canoe. The canoe can carry 2 boys or 1 man. How many times must the canoe cross the river to get everyone to the other side?

BIBLIOGRAPHY

Adkins, B. E. "A New Look at an Old Weight Problem." *Arithmetic Teacher* 28 (November 1980): 48–49.

Anderson, D. "The Sum of $1 + 2 + \cdots + 99 + 100$." *Arithmetic Teacher* 31 (November 1983): 50–51.

Balka, D. S. "Digit Delight: Problem-Solving Activities Using 0 through 9." *Arithmetic Teacher* 36 (November 1988): 42–45.

Bartalo, D. B. "Calculators and Problem-Solving Instruction: They Were Made for Each Other." *Arithmetic Teacher* 30 (January 1983): 18–21.

Brown, S. I., and M. Walter. "What If Not?" *Mathematics Teaching* 46 (1969): 38–45.

Bruni, J. V. "Problem Solving for the Primary Grades." *Arithmetic Teacher* 29 (February 1982): 10–15.

Burns, M. "How to Teach Problem Solving." *Arithmetic Teacher* 29 (February 1982): 46–49.

Bush, W. S., and A. Fiala. "Problem Stories: A New Twist on Problem Posing." *Arithmetic Teacher* 34 (December 1986): 6–9.

Campbell, P. F., and H. J. Bamberger. "The Vision of Problem Solving in the Standards." *Arithmetic Teacher* 37 (May 1990): 14–17.

Charles, R. I. "The Role of Problem Solving." *Arithmetic Teacher* 32 (February 1985): 48–50.

Cobb, P., E. Yackel, T. Wood, G. Wheatley, and G. Merkel. "Research into Practice: Creating a Problem-Solving Atmosphere." *Arithmetic Teacher* 36 (September 1988): 46–47.

Day, R. P. "A Problem-Solving Component for Junior High School Mathematics." *Arithmetic Teacher* 34 (October 1986): 14–17.

Dougherty, B. J., and T. Crites. "Applying Number Sense to Problem Solving." *Arithmetic Teacher* 36 (February 1989): 22–25.

Duea, J., and E. Ockenga. "Classroom Problem Solving with Calculators." *Arithmetic Teacher* 29 (February 1982): 50–51.

Easterday, K. E., and C. A. Clothiaux. "Problem-Solving Opportunities." *Arithmetic Teacher* 32 (January 1985): 18–20.

Frank, M. L. "Problem Solving and Mathematical Beliefs." *Arithmetic Teacher* 35 (January 1988): 32–34.

Gathany, T. "Involving Students in Problem Solving." *Mathematics Teacher* 72 (November 1979): 617–621.

Greenes, C. E., and L. Schulman. "Developing Problem-Solving Ability with Multiple-Condition Problems." *Arithmetic Teacher* 30 (October 1982): 18–21.

Jensen, R. J. "Stuck? Don't Give Up! Sub-goal–Generation Strategies in Problem Solving." *Mathematics Teacher* 80 (November 1987): 614–621, 634.

Jones, B. M. "Put Your Students in the Picture for Better Problem Solving." *Arithmetic Teacher* 30 (April 1983): 30–33.

Kenney, M., and S. Bezuszka. "A Square Share: Problem Solving with Squares." *Mathematics Teacher* 77 (September 1984): 414–420.

Krulik, S., and R. Reys, eds. *Problem Solving in School Mathematics,* 1980 Yearbook. Reston, VA: National Council of Teachers of Mathematics, 1980.

Krulik, S., and J. Rudnick. *Problem Solving: A Handbook for Teachers.* Boston: Allyn and Bacon, 1980.

Krulik, S., and J. Rudnick. "Suggestions for Teaching Problem Solving–A Baker's Dozen." *School Science and Mathematics* 81 (January 1981): 37–42.

Krulik, S., and J. Rudnick. "Strategy Gaming and Problem Solving–An Instructional Pair Whose Time Has Come." *Arithmetic Teacher* 31 (December 1983): 26–29.

Lampert, M. "Research into Practice: Arithmetic as Problem Solving." *Arithmetic Teacher* 36 (March 1989): 34–36.

Lee, K. S. "Guiding Young Children in Successful Problem Solving." *Arithmetic Teacher* 29 (January 1982): 15–17.

Liedtke, W. "The Young Child as a Problem Solver." *Arithmetic Teacher* 25 (April 1977): 333–338.

Polya, G. *How To Solve It.* Princeton, NJ: Princeton University Press, 1957.

Rosenbaum, L., K. J. Behounek, L. Brown, and J. V. Burcalow. "Step into Problem Solving with Cooperative Learning." *Arithmetic Teacher* 36 (March 1989): 7–11.

Schaaf, O. F. "Teaching Problem-Solving Skills." *Mathematics Teacher* 77 (December 1984): 694–699.

Slesnick, T. "Problem Solving: Some Thoughts and Activities." *Arithmetic Teacher* 31 (March 1984): 41–43.

Spencer, J., and F. Lester. "Second Graders Can Be Problem Solvers." *Arithmetic Teacher* 29 (September 1981): 15–17.

Suydam, M. N. "Untangling Clues from Research on Problem Solving." *Problem Solving in School Mathematics,* 1980 Yearbook. Reston, VA: National Council of Teachers of Mathematics, 1980.

Suydam, M. N. "Update on Research on Problem Solving: Implications for Classroom Teaching." *Arithmetic Teacher* 29 (February 1982): 56–60.

Szetela, W. "The Problem of Evaluation in Problem Solving: Can We Find Solutions?" *Arithmetic Teacher* 35 (November 1987): 36–41.

Talton, C. F. "Let's Solve the Problem Before We Find the Answer." *Arithmetic Teacher* 36 (September 1988): 40–45.

Thompson, A. "On Patterns, Conjectures, and Proof: Developing Students' Mathematical Thinking." *Arithmetic Teacher* 33 (September 1985): 20–23.

Trotter, T., Jr., and M. D. Myers. "Number Bracelets: A Study in Patterns." *Arithmetic Teacher* 27 (May 1980): 14–17.

Van de Walle, J. A., and H. Holbrook. "Patterns, Thinking, and Problem Solving." *Arithmetic Teacher* 34 (April 1987): 6–12.

Walter, M. "Frame Geometry: An Example in Posing and Solving Problems." *Arithmetic Teacher* 28 (October 1980): 16–18.

Wheatley, C. L., and G. H. Wheatley. "Problem Solving in the Primary Grades." *Arithmetic Teacher* 31 (April 1984): 22–25.

Whitin, D. J. "More Patterns with Square Numbers." *Arithmetic Teacher* 33 (January 1986): 40–42.

Worth, J. "Problem Solving in the Intermediate Grades: Helping Your Students Learn to Solve Problems." *Arithmetic Teacher* 29 (February 1982): 16–19.

Yancey, A. V., C. S. Thompson, and J. S. Yancey. "Children Must Learn to Draw Diagrams." *Arithmetic Teacher* 36 (March 1989): 15–19.

Zur, M., and F. Silverman. "Problem Solving for Teachers." *Arithmetic Teacher* 28 (October 1980): 48–50.

Zweng, M. "The Problem of Solving Story Problems." *Arithmetic Teacher* 27 (September 1979): 2–3.

Sets and Logic

C H A P T E R

SPOTLIGHT ON TEACHING

Excerpts from NCTM's Standards 2 and 3 for Teaching Mathematics in Grades 5–8*

Reasoning is fundamental to the knowing and doing of mathematics. . . . To give more students access to mathematics as a powerful way of making sense of the world, it is essential that an emphasis on reasoning pervade all mathematical activity. Students need a great deal of time and many experiences to develop their ability to construct valid arguments in problem settings and evaluate the arguments of others.

. . . As students' mathematical language develops, so does their ability to reason about and solve problems. Moreover, problem-solving situations provide a setting for the development and extension of communication skills and reasoning ability. The following problem illustrates how students might share their approaches in solving problems:

The class is divided into small groups. Each group is given square pieces of grid paper and asked to make boxes by cutting out pieces from the corners. Each group is given 20 × 20 grid paper. See figure [below]. Students cut and fold the paper to make boxes sized 18 × 18 × 1, 16 × 16 × 2, . . . , 2 × 2 × 9. They are challenged to find a box that holds the maximum volume and to convince someone else that they have found the maximum. . . .

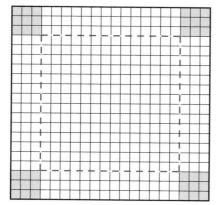
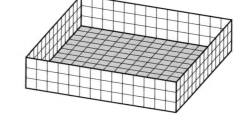

Building a grid-paper box.

*Reprinted by permission of the National Council of Teachers of Mathematics.

SECTION 2.1 SETS AND COUNTING

What is the sum of the
tenth row of this triangle?

$$0$$
$$1 + 2$$
$$3 + 4 + 5$$
$$6 + 7 + 8 + 9$$
$$10 + 11 + 12 + 13 + 14$$

*Two views of the Ishango bone,
found on the shores of Lake
Edward in the Congo*

Long before numbers were invented, numerical records were kept by means of tallies. Archaeologists have unearthed thousands of animal bones marked with groups of notches, which date from prehistoric times. Some anthropologists conjecture that many of these ancient bones are records of days, months, and seasons. One example is the 8000-year-old Ishango bone, which was discovered in East Africa. The marks on this bone occur in several groups that are arranged in columns (see exercise 2 in Exercises and Problems 2.1).

Keeping a tally involves matching sets of objects and marks and is the beginning of the idea of counting. The importance of counting to sets was first recognized by the nineteenth-century mathematician Georg Cantor. He created a new field of mathematics called **set theory.** Cantor used sets to define numbers and, in particular, to develop the theory of infinite sets. Today, sets are one of the major unifying ideas in mathematics, and set terminology is commonly found in elementary school texts.

set theory

■ Historical highlight

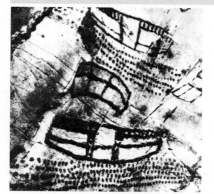

Art symbols dating from 12,000 B.C., found in the El Castillo caves in Spain

During the Old Stone Age (10,000–15,000 B.C.), figures of people and animals and abstract symbols were painted in caves in Spain and France. The symbols were composed of many geometric forms: straight lines, spirals, circles, ovals, and dots. The rows of dots and rectangular figures in this photo were discovered on the walls of the El Castillo caves, Spain, and date from 12,000 B.C. It is conjectured by some scholars that these symbols made up a system for recording the days of the year. It seems likely that numbers were in existence by this time. At first it may only have been necessary to distinguish among one, two, and many objects. The first words for numbers were probably associated with specific things. This influence can be seen in the expressions we have for *two,* such as a *couple* of people, a *brace* of hens, and a *pair* of shoes. Eventually the concepts of twoness, threeness, etc., were separated from physical objects, and the abstract notion of *number* developed.

✓ SETS AND THEIR ELEMENTS

set, elements
describing the elements

There are many words for sets: a *flock* of birds, a *herd* of cattle, a *collection* of paintings, a *bunch* of grapes, a *group* of people, and a *pride* of lions, to name a few. Intuitively, we understand a **set** to be a collection of objects called **elements.**

There are two common methods of specifying a set. One is **describing the elements** of the set with words.

EXAMPLE A

1. "The capitals of the six New England states"
2. "The multiples of 10 from 10 to 500"

listing the elements

The other method of specifying a set is **listing the elements** of the set. When this is done, the elements of the set are written between braces.

EXAMPLE B

1. {Augusta, Concord, Boston, Hartford, Providence, Montpelier}
2. {10, 20, 30, 40, 50, 60, 70, . . . , 490, 500}

If the set of elements is large, as in the case of the set of numbers in Example B, we sometimes begin the list and then use three dots to show that the pattern continues.

empty set
null set

It is possible to have a set with no elements. This set is called the **empty set** or **null set** and is denoted by the set braces with no elements between them, { }, or by the Greek letter phi, Φ.

EXAMPLE C

The set of all whole numbers between 16 and 28 that can be divided evenly by 15 has no elements, so it can be denoted by { } or Φ.

element of
not an element of

It is customary to denote sets by uppercase letters and the elements of sets by lowercase letters. If k is an **element of** set S, we write $k \in S$, and if it is **not an element of** S, we write $k \notin S$. As an example, if we use T to denote the set of numbers in Example B, $60 \in T$ and $55 \notin T$.

VENN DIAGRAMS   Sets are often pictured by using rectangles, circles, or other convenient figures. For example, in Figure 2.1, all whole numbers less than 100 are represented by the region inside the rectangle. All even whole numbers less than 100 are represented by the region inside one circle, and all whole numbers less than 100 that are multiples of 5 represented by the region inside the other circle. Notice there is an overlap of the two circles that could be described as the set of all even whole numbers less than 100 that are multiples of 10. That is, the numbers 0, 10, 20, 30, . . . , 90 are common to both sets. Such figures for representing sets were first used by the Englishman John Venn (1834–1923) and are called **Venn diagrams.**

Venn diagrams

Figure 2.1

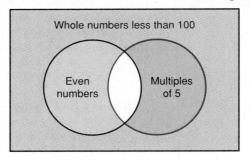
Whole numbers less than 100
Even numbers   Multiples of 5

ATTRIBUTE PIECES   Attribute pieces are geometric models of various shapes, sizes, and colors that are commonly used in elementary schools for illustrating sets. The attribute pieces in Figure 2.2 have 3 attributes: size, shape, and color. There are 3 different shapes: triangular (t), rectangular (r), and hexagonal (h). There are 2 sizes: large (l) and small (s). There are 2 colors: black (b) and white (w).

Figure 2.2

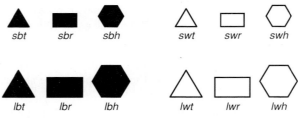

sbt   sbr   sbh   swt   swr   swh

lbt   lbr   lbh   lwt   lwr   lwh

These objects can be classified into sets in many different ways. Here are a few possibilities:

EXAMPLE D

S is the set of small attribute pieces.

L is the set of large attribute pieces.

T is the set of triangles.

H is the set of hexagons.

W is the set of white attribute pieces.

BT is the set of black triangles.

The attribute pieces will be used in the following paragraphs to illustrate set relationships and operations. You may find it helpful to copy and cut out the 12 pieces from the inside cover for use with the examples.

RELATIONSHIPS BETWEEN SETS

There are several ways in which sets may be related to each other. For example, two sets may have no elements in common (disjoint) or all elements in common (equal), or one set may be contained in another (subset). Let's look at some examples.

disjoint

Figure 2.3

DISJOINT SETS   The two sets of attribute pieces in Figure 2.3 have no elements in common. We describe this situation by saying the two sets are **disjoint.**

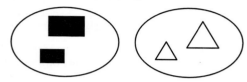

EXAMPLE *E*

Which of the following pairs of sets of attribute pieces are disjoint?

1. *L* (large pieces), *S* (small pieces)
2. *S* (small pieces), *W* (white pieces)
3. *SH* (small hexagons), *BT* (black triangles)

Solution

1. *L* and *S* are disjoint.
2. *S* and *W* have small white pieces in common; they are not disjoint.
3. *SH* and *BT* are disjoint.

---

subset

Figure 2.4

SUBSETS   Figure 2.4 shows that every attribute piece in set *BT* (black triangles) is also in set *T* (triangles). In this case we say that *BT* is a **subset** of *T*.

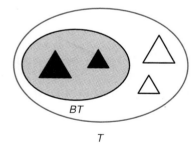

SUBSETS

> If every element of set *A* is also an element of set *B*, then set *A* is a **subset** of *B*. This relationship is written $A \subset B$. If *A* is not a subset of *B*, we write $A \not\subset B$.

EXAMPLE *F*

In which of the following pairs of sets of attribute pieces is the first set a subset of the second?

1. *LR* (large rectangles), *R* (rectangles)
2. *T* (triangles), *S* (small pieces)

Solution

1. *LR* is a subset of *R*. $LR \subset R$
2. *T* is not a subset of *S* because *T* has both large and small triangles. $T \not\subset S$

According to the definition of subset, every set is a subset of itself. For example, $BT \subset BT$, $T \subset T$, and $H \subset H$, because every element in the first set is also in the second set. If we know that $A \subset B$ and that one or more elements of *B* are not in *A*,

proper subset

then *A* is sometimes called a **proper subset** of *B*. As examples, *BT* is a proper subset of *T,* but *H* is not a proper subset of itself.

equal sets

EQUAL SETS   Sets that contain the same elements are called **equal sets.** Sometimes two sets may look different or have different descriptions but be equal. Consider the set *E* of even whole numbers and the set *D* of whole numbers that are divisible by 2. Since every even whole number is divisible by 2, the numbers in set *E* are contained in set *D*. Conversely, since every whole number that is divisible by 2 is an even number, the numbers in set *D* are contained in set *E*. Thus, the two sets have the same numbers and are equal.

EQUAL SETS

> If *A* is a subset of *B* and *B* is a subset of *A*, then both sets have exactly the same elements and they are **equal.** This relationship is written $A = B$. In this case *A* and *B* are just different letters naming the same set.

ONE-TO-ONE CORRESPONDENCE   It is possible to match the elements in the set *SB* (small black) with those in the set *LW* (large white) so that for each element in *SB* there is exactly one element in *LW* and, conversely, for each element in *LW* there is exactly one element in *SB* (Figure 2.5). We refer to this fact by saying that the two sets can be put into **one-to-one correspondence,** or that they are **equivalent sets.**

one-to-one correspondence
equivalent sets

Figure 2.5

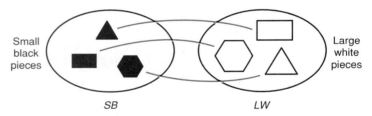

The concepts of number and counting are extensions of the idea of one-to-one correspondence. If two sets can be put into one-to-one correspondence, we say they have the **same number** of elements. To **count** the elements of a set, we match these elements with the whole numbers 1, 2, 3, 4, ... Adults will often point to the objects being counted, and children will sometimes touch each object as they match the objects and whole numbers.

same number
count

The number of elements in the set of small black pieces in Figure 2.5 is 3, because this set can be put into one-to-one correspondence with {1, 2, 3}. It is not possible to put a set of three elements into one-to-one correspondence with any of its proper subsets. For example, set *SB* in Figure 2.5 cannot be put into one-to-one correspondence with any of its proper subsets. Such a set is said to be **finite.**

finite

FINITE SETS

> A set is called **finite** if it *cannot* be put into one-to-one correspondence with any of its proper subsets.

OPERATIONS ON SETS

There are operations that replace two sets by a third set, just as there are operations on numbers that replace two numbers by a third number. *Addition* and *multiplication* are examples of operations on whole numbers; *intersection* and *union* are operations on sets.

INTERSECTION OF SETS   Figure 2.6 shows that the set of small attribute pieces and the set of black attribute pieces have three elements in common. If we form a third set containing these common elements, it is called the **intersection** of the two sets.

intersection

Figure 2.6

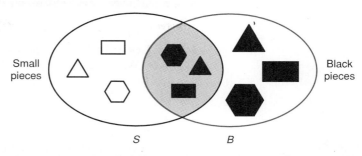

Small pieces — Black pieces

S   B

INTERSECTION OF SETS

> The **intersection** of two sets A and B is the set of all elements that are in both A and B. This operation is written $A \cap B$.

The intersection of the two sets in Figure 2.6 is the set of attribute pieces that are small and black. This new set is indicated by shading the common region inside the curve. The intersection of these sets is written as $S \cap B$.

EXAMPLE G

Find the intersection of these sets of attribute pieces.

1. L (large pieces), H (hexagons)
2. ST (small triangles), BH (black hexagons)
3. SR (small rectangles), S (small pieces)

Solution

1. $L \cap H = \{lbh, lwh\}$
2. $ST \cap BH = \Phi$, because these sets are disjoint.
3. $SR \cap S = SR$, because SR is a subset of S.

The key word in the definition of intersection is "and." In everyday use, as well as in mathematics, the word **and** means that two conditions must be satisfied. For example, if you are required to take the Graduate Record Examination (GRE) *and* the Miller Analogies Test (MAT), you must take both tests.

and

UNION OF SETS   The set of small attribute pieces and the set of black attribute pieces have three pieces in common (Figure 2.7). A new set containing these three pieces and all other pieces within either set is called the **union** of the two sets.

union

Figure 2.7

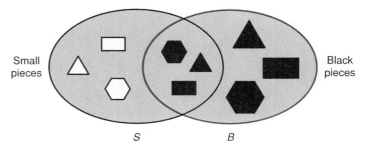

Small pieces — Black pieces

S   B

UNION OF SETS

> The **union** of two sets A and B is the set of all elements that are either in A or in B or in both A and B. This operation is written $A \cup B$.

The union of the two sets in Figure 2.7 is the set of all attribute pieces that are either small or black or both. This new set is indicated by shading the total region inside the two curves. We write the union of these two sets as

$$S \cup B = \{swr, swh, swt, sbt, sbr, sbh, lbt, lbr, lbh\}$$

Example H

Find the union of these sets of attribute pieces.

1. L (large pieces), H (hexagons)
2. ST (small triangles), BH (black hexagons)

Solution

1. $\{lbt, lwt, lbr, lwr, lbh, lwh, sbh, swh\}$
2. $\{sbt, swt, lbh, sbh\}$

Notice that the solution for Example H(1) contains *lbh* and *lwh* only once, even though these two attribute pieces are contained in both sets.

The key word in the definition of union is "or." This word has two different meanings. In everyday use, "or" usually means that it is necessary to satisfy one condition or the other, but not both. For example, "You must take the course *or* pass the qual-
exclusive or   ifying exam." This is called the **exclusive or.** In mathematics the word "or" often means that one condition or the other condition, or both, may be satisfied. This is called the
inclusive or   **inclusive or.** The inclusive or is used in defining the union of sets because an element in the union of two sets may be in the first set or in the second set or in both sets.

Sometimes we wish to consider more than two sets at a time. The Venn diagram in Figure 2.8 shows three sets of attribute pieces: W (white pieces), S (small pieces), and H (hexagonal pieces). This diagram can be used to determine the combinations of operations in the next example.

Example I

List the elements in each set. (First determine the set in parentheses. You may find it helpful to shade the regions of the diagram in Figure 2.8.)

1. $(W \cup S) \cup H$
2. $(W \cap S) \cap H$
3. $(W \cup S) \cap H$
4. $W \cup (S \cap H)$

Solution

1. $\{lwt, lwr, lwh, lbh, swt, swr, swh, sbt, sbr, sbh\}$
2. $\{swh\}$
3. $\{lwh, swh, sbh\}$
4. $\{swh, sbh, swt, swr, lwh, lwt, lwr\}$

Figure 2.8

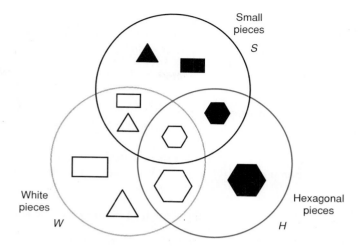

Small
pieces
S

White
pieces
W

Hexagonal
pieces
H

COMPLEMENT OF A SET   Frequently we wish to identify 2 subsets of a set whose union is the whole set. Consider the set of small black attribute pieces and the set of remaining pieces in Figure 2.9. The small black pieces are inside the circle and the others are outside. These 2 subsets are called **complements** of each other because their union is the whole set.

complements

Figure 2.9

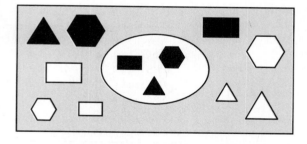

COMPLEMENTARY SETS

> For any given set *U*, if two subsets *A* and *B* are disjoint and their union is *U*, then *A* and *B* are **complements** of each other. This is written $A = B'$ or $B = A'$.

EXAMPLE J

SB is the set of small black attribute pieces. The set of pieces that are not (small and black) is the complement of *SB* (Figure 2.9). This set is denoted by *SB'*.

$$SB = \{sbr,\ sbt,\ sbh\}$$
$$SB' = \{lbt,\ lbh,\ lbr,\ lwt,\ lwh,\ lwr,\ swt,\ swr,\ swh\}$$

universal set

The "given set" referred to in the previous definition is sometimes called the **universal set.** We have been using a universal set of 12 attribute pieces. In problems with whole numbers, the universal set is often the set of whole numbers.

EXAMPLE K

Use the set of whole numbers as the universal set to determine the following complements.

1. What is the complement of the set of even whole numbers?
2. What is the complement of the set of whole numbers that are less than 10?

Solution

1. The set of odd whole numbers
2. The set of whole numbers greater than or equal to 10

complement

The universal set can be any set, but once it is established, each subset has a unique (one and only one) complement. In other words, **complement** is an operation that assigns each set to another set.

PROBLEM-SOLVING APPLICATION

drawing Venn diagrams

Drawing Venn diagrams is a problem-solving strategy for sorting and classifying information. Try solving the following problem by using the information given in the table and drawing 3 overlapping circles, one for each of the 3 networks.

■ PROBLEM

A survey of 120 people was conducted to determine the numbers that watched 3 different television networks. The results are shown in the following table. How many of the 120 people did not watch any of the 3 networks?

Networks	Numbers of people
ABC	55
NBC	30
CBS	40
ABC and CBS	10
ABC and NBC	12
NBC and CBS	8
NBC and CBS and ABC	5

Question 1

Understanding the Problem   The Venn diagram in the following figure shows 3 circles, one to represent each of the 3 networks. Each of the 7 regions inside the circles represents a different category of viewers. For example, people in region *y* watched NBC and CBS but not ABC. What region represents the people who did not watch any of the 3 networks? We need to find the number of people in this region.

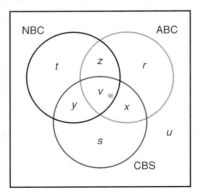

Devising a Plan   We can find the number of people who did not watch any of the 3 networks by first finding the numbers for the 7 regions inside the circles and then subtracting this total from 120. For example, *v* is the intersection of all 3 circles, and the table shows that *v* = 5. Using this number and the fact that there are 8 people in the intersection of NBC and CBS, we can determine the value of *y*. What is the value of *y*?

Question 2

Carrying Out the Plan   Continuing the process described in the previous paragraph, we can determine that $z = 7$ and $x = 5$. Now since there are 40 people represented inside the CBS circle and $v + y + x = 13$, we know that $s = 40 - 13 = 27$. In a similar manner we can determine that $r = 38$ and $t = 15$. So the total number of people represented by the 7 regions is

$$\overset{v}{5} + \overset{y}{3} + \overset{z}{7} + \overset{x}{5} + \overset{s}{27} + \overset{r}{38} + \overset{t}{15} = 100$$

Question 3   How many people did not watch any of the 3 networks?

Looking Back   We solved this problem by finding the number of people in the union of 3 sets and then finding the number of people in the complement. In addition to solving the original problem, the Venn diagram provides much more information. For example, since **Question 4** $s = 27$, we know 27 people watched only CBS. How many people watched both NBC and ABC but not CBS?

Answers to Questions 1–4
1. The region labeled u, which is inside the rectangle but outside the union of the 3 circles
2. $y = 3$ ($y + v = 8$, so $y + 5 = 8$)
3. 20 ($120 - 100 = 20$)
4. 7 ($12 - 5 = 7$)

INFINITE SETS

Are time and space infinite quantities? What do we mean by "infinitely large" and "infinitely small"? First of all we must realize that "very big" and "infinite" are entirely different concepts. There are about 100 billion stars in our galaxy, the Milky Way, and a similar number in the galaxy in Figure 2.10. There are about 1 billion galaxies, and the total number of stars in all of them is a 1 followed by 20 zeros. Although the number of stars is very large, it is not infinite.

Figure 2.10
Galaxy Messier 81, 10 million light-years away

We have an intuitive notion that "infinite" means "without end" or "without bound." These vague terms, however, were not precise enough for mathematicians, and in 1874 Cantor developed the following definition of infinite sets.

INFINITE SETS

> A set is **infinite** if it has a proper subset with which it can be put into one-to-one correspondence.

For example, the set of whole numbers is an infinite set. The set of even numbers is a proper subset of the set of whole numbers because every even number is a whole number and the set of whole numbers contains numbers that are not even (namely, the odd numbers). By matching each whole number with the even number that is twice as big, we can place the numbers of both sets into one-to-one correspondence, as shown below.

$$0 \quad 1 \quad 2 \quad 3 \quad 4 \quad 5 \quad 6 \quad 7 \quad \cdot \quad \cdot \quad \cdot \quad n \quad \cdot \quad \cdot \quad \cdot$$
$$\updownarrow \quad \updownarrow \quad \updownarrow \quad \updownarrow \quad \updownarrow \quad \updownarrow \quad \updownarrow \quad \updownarrow \quad \updownarrow \quad \updownarrow \quad \updownarrow \quad \updownarrow \quad \cdot \quad \cdot \quad \cdot$$
$$0 \quad 2 \quad 4 \quad 6 \quad 8 \quad 10 \quad 12 \quad 14 \quad \cdot \quad \cdot \quad \cdot \quad 2n \quad \cdot \quad \cdot \quad \cdot$$

For every set that is infinite it is possible to find a proper subset with which it can be put into one-to-one correspondence. Notice the distinction between finite and infinite sets. Try as we may, there is no way to form a one-to-one correspondence between the finite set $\{1, 2, 3, 4\}$ and any of its proper subsets.

We have shown that the set of whole numbers is infinite because it can be put into one-to-one correspondence with the set of even numbers. Remember that earlier we defined two sets as having the *same number of elements* if they can be put into one-to-one correspondence. This means that the set of whole numbers and the set of even numbers have the *same number of elements*. In other words, they are *equivalent sets*.

There are many different types of infinite sets. In fact, there is a hierarchy of infinite sets, in which each successive type of set is so much bigger than the previous type of set that they cannot be put into one-to-one correspondence. The first or smallest of the infinite sets is the type that can be put into one-to-one correspondence with the **countably infinite** whole numbers. Sets of this type are said to be **countably infinite.**

RELATED ACTIVITIES IN
Mathematics for Elementary Teachers: An Activity Approach, 3e

Activity Set 2.1   **Sorting and Classifying:** Activities and games with attribute pieces for sorting and classifying, reasoning logically, and formulating and verifying conjectures

Just for Fun   **Attribute Identity Game:** Clues for making and verifying conjectures about the identity of sets of attribute pieces

---

EXERCISES AND PROBLEMS 2.1

1. The notches in the 30,000-year-old Czechoslovakian wolf bone are arranged in two groups. There are 25 notches in one group and 30 in the other. Within each series the notches are in groups of 5. Could this recording system have been devised without number names? without number symbols?

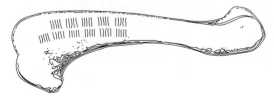

2. Both sides of the 8000-year-old Ishango bone are sketched below. There is 1 row of marks on one side of the bone and 2 rows of marks on the other side. Anthropologists have questioned the significance of the numbers of these marks. Could they be records of game killed or of belongings? Maybe they are intended to show a relationship between numbers? Write the number of marks in each group of marks in these rows.

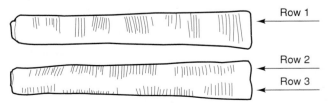

Row 1

Row 2

Row 3

a. Which of these rows suggests a knowledge of multiplication by 2?

b. Can you find other number relationships?

c. In his book *The Roots of Civilization,* Alexander Marshack correlates these marks with phases of the moon and days of a lunar calendar. Using 28 for the number of days in a lunar month, determine how many months are represented by the total number of marks on this bone.*

Use the universal set of 12 attribute pieces and the following sets to answer questions 3 through 6: *W:* white attribute pieces; *H:* hexagonal attribute pieces; *SW:* small white pieces; *SB:* small black pieces; and *L:* large pieces. You may wish to copy and cut out the attribute pieces from the inside cover.

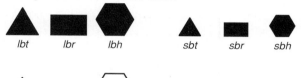

lbt   lbr   lbh   sbt   sbr   sbh

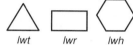 

lwt   lwr   lwh   swt   swr   swh

3. a. Which pairs of sets, if any, can be put into one-to-one correspondence?

b. Which pairs of sets, if any, are equal?

4. a. Which pairs of sets, if any, are disjoint?

b. Which set is a proper subset of another?

5. a. Which attribute pieces are in $W \cap L$?

b. Which attribute pieces are in $W \cup L$?

6. Which of the statements below are true?

a. $swh \in W \cap H$

b. $lwt \in L'$

c. $lbr \in SB \cup W$

7. Use the 12 attribute pieces shown above to list the pieces described below. (Use the inclusive or.)

a. hexagonal and small

b. white and triangular

c. small or white

d. triangular or large

e. not(hexagonal and small)

f. not(small or white)

Given the universal set $U = \{0, 1, 2, 3, 4, 5, 6, 7, 8\}$ and sets $A = \{0, 2, 4, 6, 8\}$, $B = \{1, 3, 5, 7\}$, and $C = \{3, 4, 5, 6\}$, list the elements in the sets described in questions 8 and 9.

8. a. $A \cap C$ b. $C' \cup B$

9. a. $C' \cap A$ b. $(A \cap C) \cup B$

10. For each of the following, draw a Venn diagram so that sets A, B, and C satisfy all of the given conditions.

a. $A \subset B, B \subset C$

b. $C \cap B = \Phi, A \subset C$

c. $(B \cup C) \subset A, B \cap C = \Phi$

d. $A \cap B \neq \Phi, B \cap C \neq \Phi, A \cap C = \Phi$

11. Sketch a three-circle Venn diagram like the one shown here for each of the sets below, and shade the region represented by the set.

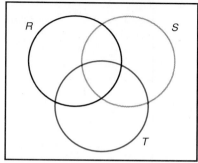

a. $R \cap S$ b. $T \cup R$

c. $(R \cup S) \cap T$ d. $(T \cap S) \cup R$

e. $(R \cup T)'$ f. $(R \cap T) \cap S'$

12. Given that set A has 5 elements and set B has 3 elements, answer the following questions. Draw a sketch of each set.

a. What is the maximum number of elements in $A \cup B$? $A \cap B$?

b. What is the minimum number of elements in $A \cup B$? $A \cap B$?

13. Illustrate the set listed under each figure by shading the figure.

(a)

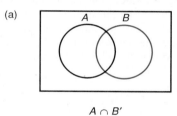

$A \cap B'$

(b)

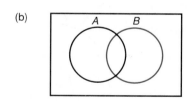

$A' \cup B$

(c)

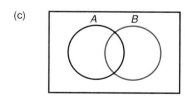

$A' \cup B'$

*For a discussion of these marks, see A. Marshack, *The Roots of Civilization* (New York: McGraw-Hill, 1972), 21–26.

14. Use set notation to identify the shaded region in each of the following sketches.

(a)

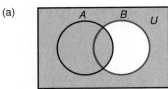

(b)

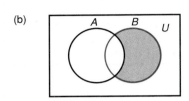

(c)

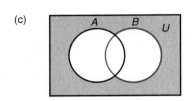

15. The following diagram of human populations was used in investigations correlating the presence or absence of B26+ (a human antigen), RF+ (an antibody protein), spondylitis (an inflammation of the vertebrae), and arthritis (an inflammation of the joints) with the incidence of various rheumatic diseases.

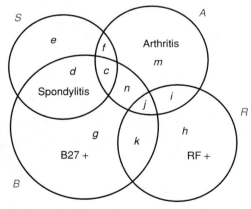

Find the letter(s) of the region(s) corresponding to each of the following sets.

a. $S \cap B$
b. $A \cap R$
c. $(S \cap B) \cap A$
d. $(R \cup A) \cap B$

16. Show that the following sets are infinite.

a. {10, 11, 12, 13, 14, . . .}   **b.** {10, 20, 30, 40, 50, . . .}

17. In a music club with 15 members, 7 people played piano, 6 people played guitar, and 4 people didn't play either of these two instruments. How many people played both piano and guitar?

18. There were 55 people at a high school class reunion. If 16 people had college degrees, 12 people had college degrees and were married, and 14 people were single and did not have college degrees, how many people were married and did not have college degrees?

19. In a survey of 6500 people, 5100 had a car, 2280 had a pet, 5420 had a television set, 4800 had a TV and a car, 1500 had a TV and a pet, 1250 had a car and a pet, and 1100 had a TV, a car, and a pet.

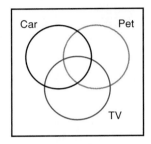

a. Write the number of people in each of the 7 regions inside the circles.
b. How many people had a TV and a pet, but did not have a car?
c. How many people had neither a pet, a TV, nor a car?

20. A class survey found that 25 students watched television on Monday, 20 on Tuesday, and 16 on Wednesday. Of those who watched TV on only 1 of these days, 11 chose Monday, 7 chose Tuesday, and 6 chose Wednesday. If every student watched TV on at least 1 of these days and 7 students watched on all 3 days, find the number of students in the class.*

21. There are 8 blood types, as shown by the Venn diagram. Each circle represents one of three antigens: A, B, or Rh. If A and B are both absent, the blood is type O. If Rh is present, the blood is positive; otherwise it is negative. The table on the following page represents the blood types of 150 people. How many people had the following blood types?

a. B+   **b.** A+   **c.** O+   **d.** O−

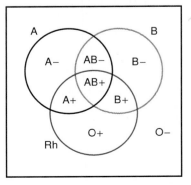

Blood types	Numbers of people
A	60
B	27
Rh	123
A and B	12
B and Rh	17
A and Rh	46
A and B and Rh	9

LABORATORY INVESTIGATION

There are many relationships involving operations on sets. Some of the most interesting involve unions and intersections, together with complements (shown at the right).

To investigate some of these relationships, trace and cut out the 12 attribute pieces from the inside cover. Then list and compare the elements in the following sets to determine which pairs are equal.

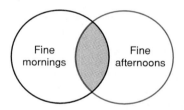

not (hexagonal and black)	$(H \cap B)'$
not hexagonal and not black	$H' \cap B'$
not(hexagonal or black)	$(H \cup B)'$
not hexagonal or not black	$H' \cup B'$

PUZZLER

During a vacation it rained on 13 days, but when it rained in the morning the afternoon was fine, and every rainy afternoon was preceded by a fine morning. There were 11 fine mornings and 12 fine afternoons. How long was the vacation?

SECTION 2.2 LOGIC AND DEDUCTIVE REASONING

■ PROBLEM OPENER

Mike won't take part in the school play if Sue is in it. Tim says that in order for him to participate in the play, Sue must be in it. If Mike is in the play, then Rhonda refuses to be part of it. The director insists that only 1 of the 2 girls and only 1 of the 2 boys be in the play. Who will be chosen?

"When do you want it?"

Lewis Carroll, well-known author of *Alice's Adventures in Wonderland,* also wrote books on logic. At the beginning of his *Symbolic Logic,** he states that logic will give you

> . . . the power to detect fallacies, and to tear to pieces flimsy illogical arguments which you will so continually encounter in books, in newspapers, in speeches, and even in sermons, and which so easily delude those who have never taken the trouble to master this fascinating Art. Try it. That is all I ask of you!

As Lewis Carroll noted, examples of illogical reasoning are common. Consider the following statement.

> If the world ends tomorrow, then you will not have to pay for the printing.

Suppose the world does not end tomorrow. Does this mean there will be a charge for the printing? We will see in this section that this conclusion *does not* follow from the given statements.

DEDUCTIVE REASONING

deductive reasoning
premises

There are two main types of reasoning: *inductive* and *deductive.* In Section 1.2 on problem solving, we obtained conclusions by *inductive reasoning.* With this type of reasoning, conclusions are based on observations. A conclusion from inductive reasoning might be called an "informed guess." **Deductive reasoning,** on the other hand, is the process of obtaining a conclusion from one or more given statements, called **premises.** Here is an example of deductive reasoning in which the conclusion is obtained from two premises.

EXAMPLE A

Premises
1. All whales are mammals.
2. All dolphins are whales.

Conclusion

All dolphins are mammals.

Venn diagrams were used in the early development of logic and are a common means of visualizing information and drawing conclusions. Figure 2.11 uses Venn diagrams to illustrate Example A. Part (a) illustrates the information in the first premise, and part (b) illustrates the information in the second premise. Part (c) is obtained by using the information from (a) and (b). Part (c) shows that all dolphins are contained in the set of mammals, which is the conclusion in Example A.

Figure 2.11

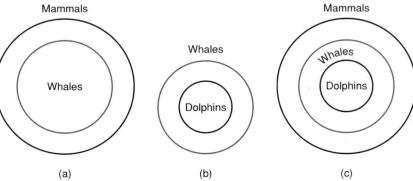

(a)   (b)   (c)

*Lewis Carroll, *Symbolic Logic and the Game of Logic* (New York: Dover Publications, Inc., 1958).

VALID REASONING

valid

The main concern in deductive reasoning is whether or not a conclusion follows logically from the given statements (premises). When a conclusion follows from the given information, it is called **valid.** The conclusion in Example A is valid. Let's consider another example with a valid conclusion.

EXAMPLE B

Premises

1. All salamanders are amphibians.
2. Animals that develop an amnion are not amphibians.

Conclusion

Salamanders do not develop an amnion.

Statement 1 in Example B is illustrated in Figure 2.12 by representing all salamanders, by a circle, which is positioned inside the circle for all amphibians. The region outside the amphibian circle represents all animals that are not amphibians. Statement 2 is illustrated by representing all animals with an amnion by a circle, which is positioned outside the circle for the amphibians. Since the salamanders and the animals with an amnion have separate (non-overlapping) circles, these sets are disjoint, and the conclusion in Example B is valid.

Figure 2.12

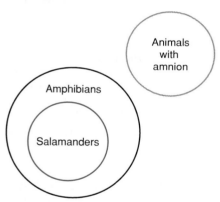

VALID REASONING

When a conclusion follows from the given information, it is called **valid,** and the process of deriving the conclusion is called **valid reasoning.**

---

some

The next example contains the word **some,** which in mathematics means *at least one*. The word "some" could refer to more than one or possibly all the elements of a set.

EXAMPLE C

Premises

1. All customs officials are government employees.
2. Some college graduates are customs officials.

Conclusion

Some college graduates are government employees.

The diagrams in Figure 2.13 illustrate the statements given in Example C. Part (a) represents statement 1, and part (b) represents statement 2. A dot is placed in the intersection of the set of customs officials and the set of college graduates to indicate that there is at least 1 person in both of these sets. Part (c) is a combination of parts (a) and (b). Since the dot in part (c) is inside the circle for the government employees, this diagram shows that the conclusion is valid. Notice that the oval for the college graduates may have people in the regions marked X, but we can't be sure. We can only be sure that there is at least 1 college graduate in the set of customs officials.

Figure 2.13

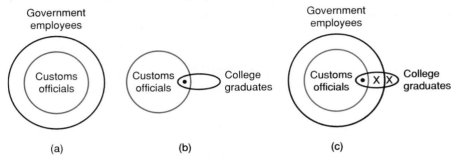

(a)   (b)   (c)

INVALID REASONING

Sometimes a conclusion will not follow from the given information, as in the next example. In this case the conclusion is **invalid.**

invalid

EXAMPLE D

Premises
1. Some members of the Appropriations Committee are Republicans.
2. Some Republicans are on the Welfare Committee.

Conclusion

Some members of the Appropriations Committee are members of the Welfare Committee. (Invalid)

Figure 2.14 shows Venn diagrams representing the information given in statements 1 and 2 of Example D. The overlapping ovals show that some members of the Appropriations Committee are Republicans and some Republicans are members of the Welfare Committee. Notice the use of a dot to indicate that there is at least 1 person in the intersection of each pair of these sets. Since it is possible to represent the information in the premises as shown in the diagram, we are not forced to conclude that the Appropriations Committee and the Welfare Committee have any people in common. Therefore, the conclusion in Example D is invalid.

Figure 2.14

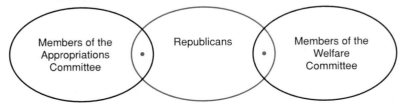

invalid reasoning

When a conclusion does not necessarily follow from the given information, the process of obtaining the conclusion is called **invalid reasoning.**

CONDITIONAL STATEMENTS

Statements of the form "if _____ , then _____ " occur frequently in everyday reasoning and in mathematics.

"if" part   "then" part

If a number is less than 3, then it is less than 8.

conditional statement   A statement in this form is called a **conditional statement.** It has two parts: the "if" part (hypothesis) and the "then" part (conclusion).

A variety of statements can be rewritten in if-then form.

EXAMPLE E

Write the following statements in if-then form.

1. All courses with a grade of C will not count for graduate credit.
2. Every apple contains vitamin C.
3. You will stay in good condition by jogging every day.
4. No students will be admitted after 5 P.M.

Solution

1. If a course has a grade of C, then it will not count for graduate credit.
2. If an object is an apple, then it contains vitamin C.
3. If you jog every day, then you will stay in good condition.
4. If you are a student, then you will not be admitted after 5 P.M.

Example E shows that there are statements without the words "if" and "then" that can be rewritten in if-then form.

Conditional statements can be illustrated by Venn diagrams. Figure 2.15 shows diagrams of the 4 conditional statements in Example E.

Figure 2.15

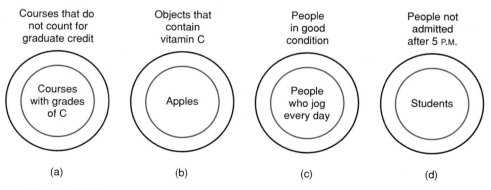

(a)   (b)   (c)   (d)

Every conditional statement "if p, then q" has 3 related conditional statements that can be obtained by negating and/or interchanging the "if" part and the "then" part. The new statements each have special names that show their relationship to the original statement.

Statement	If p, then q.
Converse	If q, then p.
Inverse	If not p, then not q.
Contrapositive	If not q, then not p.

EXAMPLE F

Write the converse, inverse, and contrapositive of the following conditional statement.

Statement: If a person lives in Maine, then the person lives in New England.

Solution

Converse: If a person lives in New England, then the person lives in Maine.

Inverse: If a person does not live in Maine, then the person does not live in New England.

Contrapositive: If a person does not live in New England, then the person does not live in Maine.

The statements from Example F and the corresponding diagram in Figure 2.16 illustrate two important facts. First, a conditional statement and its contrapositive are

logically equivalent

logically equivalent. If one is true, so is the other. If one is false, the other is also false. The two circles in Figure 2.16 represent the information given in the original statement and show that all people who live in Maine are contained in the set of people who live in New England. The people who do not live in New England are outside the large circle. Therefore, if a person does not live in New England, then the person can't live in Maine (the contrapositive).

The second important fact is that if a conditional statement is true, its inverse and converse are *not necessarily true.* They may be true sometimes, but you can't count on it. Figure 2.16 shows that the converse and inverse in Example F are false, because it is possible to have points inside the large circle but outside the small circle.

Figure 2.16

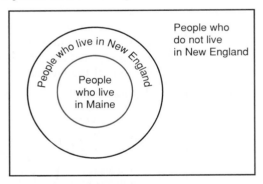

The diagram in Figure 2.17 was done by an elementary school student to show that a statement and its contrapositive have the same meaning.* The region outside the large circle represents the times when the dog does not wear a lead.

Figure 2.17

Karen Brown
If I take my dog for a walk he wears a lead.
When he does not wear a lead he doesn't go for a walk.

*Nuffield Mathematics Project, *Logic* (New York: John Wiley & Sons, 1972).

Example F illustrated that a conditional statement and its converse are not logically equivalent. That is, a conditional statement may be true and its converse may be false. However, when it does happen that a conditional statement and its converse are both true, the two statements are often combined into a single statement by using the words "if and only if." When this is done, the new statement is called a **biconditional** statement.

biconditional

EXAMPLE G

The following statement and its converse are both true. Combine them into one statement by using the words "if and only if."

Statement: If one of two numbers is zero, then the product of the two numbers is zero.

Converse: If the product of two numbers is zero, then one of the two numbers is zero.

Solution

Biconditional: The product of two numbers is zero *if and only if* one of the numbers is zero.

REASONING WITH CONDITIONAL STATEMENTS

In deductive reasoning, the given information (premises) often contains a conditional statement. Here are some examples.

EXAMPLE H

Premises
1. If a person challenges a creditor's report, then the credit bureau will conduct an investigation for that person.
2. Ronald C. Whitney challenged a creditor's report.

Conclusion

The credit bureau will conduct an investigation for Ronald C. Whitney. (Valid)

The diagram in Figure 2.18 shows why the reasoning in Example H is valid. The two circles represent the information in statement 1. Since statement 2 says that Ronald C. Whitney challenged a creditor's report, he is represented by a point inside the small circle, which means that he is also inside the large circle. So the credit bureau will conduct an investigation for Ronald C. Whitney.

Figure 2.18

Law of Detachment

Example H illustrates a characteristic of conditional statements: when a conditional statement is given (premise 1) and the "if" part is satisfied (premise 2), the "then" part will always logically follow. This principle is known as the **Law of Detachment.**

The next two examples illustrate a common source of error in reasoning with conditional statements: assuming that a statement is logically equivalent to its converse or its inverse.

EXAMPLE *I*

Premises
1. If a company fails to have an annual inspection, then its license will be terminated.
2. The Samson Company's license was terminated.

Conclusion

The Samson Company failed to have an annual inspection. (Invalid)

We can see that the conclusion in Example I is invalid by looking at Figure 2.19. This diagram illustrates the information given in the premises and shows that it is possible for the Samson Company to be inside the large circle (satisfying statement 2) but outside the small circle. Since we are not forced to accept the conclusion, it is invalid.

Figure 2.19

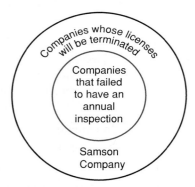

Example I contains two premises. If we could assume the converse of statement 1 to be true, we could replace statement 1 by statement 1′ (its converse).

1. If a company fails to have an annual inspection, then its license will be terminated.
1′. If its license is terminated, then the company failed to have an annual inspection.

Using statement 1′ and statement 2 from Example I, we could then use the Law of Detachment to conclude that the Samson Company failed to have an annual inspection. However, just because a conditional statement is true, we cannot assume its converse is true. That is, we *cannot* use statement 1′. So the conclusion in Example I is invalid. Invalid reasoning that results from assuming the converse of a statement to be true is called **reasoning from the converse.**

reasoning from the converse

Next let's consider the example given at the beginning of this section.

EXAMPLE J

Premises

1. If the world ends tomorrow, then you will not have to pay for the printing.
2. The world does not end tomorrow.

Conclusion

You have to pay for the printing. (Invalid)

The two circles in Figure 2.20 represent the information given in statement 1. That is, a day when the world ends tomorrow is contained in the set of days when there is no charge for the printing. The days when you have to pay for the printing are all outside the large circle. The days when the world does not end tomorrow are outside the small circle, but these days may be inside or outside the large circle. These two possibilities are shown by Xs in Figure 2.20. Therefore, *on the basis of the given information alone,* we are not forced to conclude that you will have to pay for the printing.

Figure 2.20

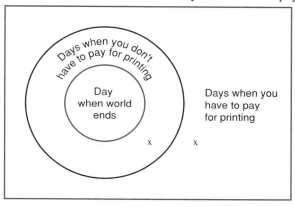

Notice that if we could assume the inverse of premise 1 in Example J to be true, we would know that if the world does not end tomorrow, you will have to pay for the printing. However, a conditional statement and its inverse are not logically equivalent, so the conclusion is invalid. Invalid reasoning that results from assuming the inverse of a conditional statement to be true is called **reasoning from the inverse.**

reasoning for the inverse

PROBLEM-SOLVING APPLICATION

What Is the Name of This Book, by Raymond M. Smullyan, has many original and challenging problems in recreational logic.* The following problem from his book is solved using the problem-solving strategies of *drawing Venn diagrams* and *guessing and checking.*

■ PROBLEM

An enormous amount of loot has been stolen from a store. The criminal (or criminals) took the loot away in a car. Three well-known criminals, A, B, and C, were brought to Scotland Yard for questioning. The following facts were ascertained.

1. No one other than A, B, or C was involved in the robbery.
2. C never pulls a job without using A (and possibly others) as an accomplice.
3. B does not know how to drive.
   Is A innocent or guilty?

Understanding the Problem   Statement 1 says that no one other than A, B, or C was involved in the robbery, but it does not say that all three were involved.

Devising a Plan   One approach is to draw a Venn diagram of the given information to see what conclusions can be reached.

*Raymond M. Smullyan, *What Is the Name of This Book* (Englewood Cliffs, N.J.: Prentice-Hall, 1978), 67.

Carrying Out the Plan Statement 2 can be diagrammed by placing the jobs done by C inside the circle representing jobs done by A (see the following figure) to show that any time C pulls a job, A is also involved. The jobs not done by A are represented by points outside the large circle. Since we are trying to determine whether A is guilty, let's guess and check the results from the diagram. If we guess that A is not guilty and select a point outside the large circle, then we know that C was not involved. What does this line of reasoning show?

Question 1

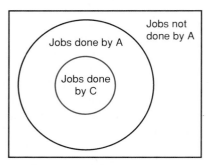

Looking Back Sometimes it is helpful to write a given statement in if-then form and then write its contrapositive. Statement 2 can be written as "If C pulls a job, then A pulls a job." What is the contrapositive of this statement, and how does it help to solve the problem?

Question 2

Answers to Questions 1–2
1. If A and C are not involved, this leaves only B, but B does not drive and could not have done the job alone. Therefore, A must be guilty.
2. If A does not pull the job, then C does not pull the job. The contrapositive tells us that if A is not involved in the job, then C is not involved, which leaves only B. But B cannot do the job alone. Therefore, A must be guilty.

RELATED ACTIVITIES IN
Mathematics for Elementary Teachers: An Activity Approach, 3e

Activity Set 2.2 **Logic Problems for Cooperative Learning Groups:** Logic problems used in a group cooperative learning process for forming and testing hypotheses

Just for Fun **Pica Centro:** A two-person (two-team) game involving opportunities for inductive and deductive reasoning

---

EXERCISES AND PROBLEMS 2.2

1. The diagram and statements above were made by an elementary school student.*
   a. If the first statement is true, is the second statement necessarily true?
   b. Do these two statements have the same meaning?

2. Rewrite each of the following statements in if-then form.
   a. Taking a hard line with a bill collector may lead to a lawsuit.
   b. All employees in Tripak Company must retire by age 65.
   c. A person who files a written application within 31 days of a termination notification will be issued a new policy.
   d. Every pilot must have a physical examination every 6 months.
   e. People under 16 years of age cannot get a driver's license.

*Nuffield Mathematics Project, *Logic* (New York: John Wiley & Sons, 1972).

3. Draw a Venn diagram to illustrate each statement.
   a. All truck drivers are strong people.
   b. Some vegetables are green.
   c. If an animal is a duck, then it has two legs.
   d. If a person was born before 1980, then the person is over 10 years old.

4. Write the converse, inverse, and contrapositive of each statement.
   a. If you take a deduction for your home office, then you must itemize your deductions.
   b. If the Democrats take California, they will win the election.

5. Write the converse, inverse, and contrapositive of each statement.
   a. If switch B is pressed, the camera focus is on manual.
   b. If the weather is fair, the opera will be sold out.

6. Consider the statement "If a number is less than 15, then it is less than 20." Which of the following statements is logically equivalent to this statement?
   a. If a number is not less than 15, then it is not less than 20.
   b. If a number is not less than 20, then it is not less than 15.
   c. If a number is less than 20, then it is less than 15.

7. Write the contrapositive of each of the following statements.
   a. If you subtract $750 for each dependent, then the computer will reject your income tax return.
   b. The cards should be dealt again if there is no opening bid.
   c. If not delighted, return the books at the end of the week's free sing-along.

8. Combine each statement and its converse into a biconditional statement.
   a. If you pay the Durham poll tax, then you are 18 or older. If you are 18 or older, then you pay the Durham poll tax.
   b. If Smith is guilty, then Jones is innocent. If Jones is innocent, then Smith is guilty.

9. Write each biconditional statement as two separate statements: a conditional statement and its converse.
   a. Robinson will be hired if and only if she meets the conditions set by the board.
   b. There will be negotiations if and only if the damaged equipment is repaired.

In exercises 10 through 13, sketch Venn diagrams to determine whether each conclusion follows logically from the premises. Explain your reasoning.

10. *Premises:* All flowers are beautiful. All roses are flowers.
    Conclusion: All roses are beautiful.

11. *Premises:* All teachers are smart. All nice people are smart.
    Conclusion: Some nice people are teachers.

12. *Premises:* Some truck drivers are rich. All musicians are rich.
    Conclusion: Some musicians are truck drivers.

13. *Premises:* All good students are good readers. Some math students are good students.
    Conclusion: Some math students are good readers.

Form a valid conclusion from each set of premises in exercises 14 through 16. Draw a Venn diagram to support your conclusion.

14. *Premises:* If anemia occurs, then something has interfered with the production of red blood cells. The production of red blood cells in this patient is normal.
    Conclusion:

15. *Premises:* If poison is present in the bone marrow, then production of red blood cells will be slowed down. This patient has poison in her bone marrow.
    Conclusion:

16. *Premises:* If there is insufficient vitamin K in the body, there will be a prothrombin deficiency. Mr. Keene does not have a prothrombin deficiency.
    Conclusion:

Advertisements are often misleading and tempt people to draw conclusions that are favorable to a certain product. Determine which of the ads in exercises 17 through 19 present valid conclusions based on the first statements.

17. Great tennis players use Hexrackets. Therefore, if you use a Hexracket, you are a great tennis player.

18. People who use our aluminum siding are satisfied. Therefore, if you don't use our aluminum siding, you won't be satisfied.

19. If you take Sleepwell, you will have extra energy. Therefore, if you don't have extra energy, you are not taking Sleepwell.

Featured Strategy: Making a Table

20. Janet Davis, Sally Adams, Collette Eaton, and Jeff Clark have the occupations of architect, carpenter, diver, and engineer, but not necessarily in that order. Determine each person's occupation.
    (1) The first letters of a person's last name and occupation are different.
    (2) Jeff and the engineer go sailing together.
    (3) Janet lives in the same neighborhood as the carpenter and the engineer.
    a. Understanding the Problem Each person has a different occupation. Davis can't be the diver. Why can't Adams be the architect?
    b. Devising a Plan One approach to this type of problem is to make a table with the names along one edge and the occupations along the other. Then "yes" or "no" can be written in the boxes of the table to record the given information. Explain why "no" can be written four times, as shown in the following table.

	Architect	Carpenter	Diver	Engineer
Davis			No	
Adams	No			
Eaton				No
Clark		No		

c. **Carrying Out the Plan** Each row and column of the table should have exactly one "yes." Continue filling out the table to solve this problem.

d. **Looking Back** One advantage of using such a table is that once "yes" is written in a box, "no" can be written in several other boxes. Each "yes" provides a maximum of how many "no" boxes?

21. Dow, Eliot, Finley, Grant, and Hanley have the following occupations: appraiser, broker, cook, painter, and singer. If three of these people are men, determine each person's sex and occupation.

(1) The broker and the appraiser attended a father-and-son banquet.

(2) The singer, the appraiser, and Grant all belong to the same club.

(3) Dow and Hanley are married to two waiters.

(4) The singer told Finley that he liked science fiction.

(5) The cook owes Hanley $25.

COMPUTER INVESTIGATION

The computer program PALINDROMIC SUMS on the *Computer Problem Solving Disc* computes the sums of numbers and their reverses for any number chosen.

A number is called a palindromic number if it reads the same both forward and backward. For example, 31,413 is a palindromic number. In the example at the right, a number (87) is added to its reverse (78), then the sum (165) is added to its reverse (561), and so forth. Repeating this process four times yields a palindromic number. Will this process always result in a palindromic number?

$$\begin{array}{r} 87 \\ +78 \\ \hline 165 \\ +561 \\ \hline 726 \\ +627 \\ \hline 1353 \\ +3531 \\ \hline 4884 \end{array}$$

Questions for Investigation

1. If you begin with any two-digit number, will the process always result in a palindromic number?

2. Find 1 or more two-digit numbers for which this process requires 2 steps, 3 steps, 4 steps, 6 steps.

3. There are 2 two-digit numbers for which this process of producing a palindromic number requires 24 steps. What are these numbers?

4. Try some numbers with 3 or more digits. There are only 13 three-digit numbers that do not lead to a palindromic number in 23 or fewer steps. Find one of these.

PUZZLER

Lewis Carroll popularized logic by writing comically worded statements and conclusions. The following examples are from his book *Symbolic Logic.* Determine whether the conclusions below are valid or invalid.

No professors are ignorant. All ignorant people are vain.

Conclusion: No professors are vain.

Babies are illogical. Nobody is despised who can manage a crocodile. Illogical persons are despised.

Conclusion: Babies cannot manage crocodiles.

CHAPTER REVIEW

1. **Sets and Venn Diagrams**
   a. A **set** is described as a collection of objects called **elements.**
   b. The elements of a set may be described with **words** or they may be **listed.**
   c. An **empty set,** or **null set,** is a set with no elements.
   d. To show that k is an **element of** set S, we write $k \in S$.
   e. **Venn diagrams** use circles, rectangles, or other shapes to illustrate sets.

2. **Set Relations**
   a. Two sets are **disjoint** if they have no elements in common.
   b. If every element of A is an element of B, then A is called a **subset** of B, written $A \subset B$.
   c. If A is a subset of B and B has elements not contained in A, then A is called a **proper subset** of B.
   d. Two sets are **equal** if they are subsets of each other.
   e. Two sets can be put into **one-to-one correspondence** if it is possible to match each element in one set to exactly one element in the other, and conversely.

   f. Two sets have the **same number** of elements if they can be put into one-to-one correspondence.
   g. A set is said to be **finite** if it cannot be put into one-to-one correspondence with any one of its proper subsets.

3. **Set Operations**
   a. The **intersection** of sets A and B is the set of elements that are in both A and B, written $A \cap B$.
   b. The **union** of sets A and B is the set of elements that are in A or in B or in both A and B, written $A \cup B$.
   c. If A and B are disjoint subsets of a given set U, where $A \cup B = U$, then A and B are **complements** of each other, written $A' = B$ and $B' = A$.
   d. A **universal set** is the set that contains all the elements being considered in a given situation.
   e. **Venn diagrams** are used to illustrate set relations and operations.

4. **Infinite Sets**
   a. A set is **infinite** if it has a proper subset with which it can be put into one-to-one correspondence.
   b. If a set can be put into one-to-one correspondence with the set of whole numbers, it is said to be **countably infinite.**

5. **Deductive Reasoning**
   a. **Deductive reasoning** is the process of obtaining conclusions from one or more given statements called **premises.**
   b. When a conclusion follows from the given information, it is said to be **valid,** and the process of deriving the conclusion is called **valid reasoning.**
   c. When a conclusion does not follow from the given information, the conclusion and the reasoning process are said to be **invalid.**

6. **Conditional Statements**
   a. A statement in if-then form is called a **conditional statement.**

b. Every conditional statement "if p, then q" has three related statements:
   Converse: If q, then p.
   Inverse: If not p, then not q.
   Contrapositive: If not q, then not p.
   c. Two statements are said to be **logically equivalent** if when the first statement is true, the second statement is true and when the first statement is false, the second statement is false.
   d. When a conditional statement is given (premise 1) and the "if" part is satisfied (premise 2), the "then" part will always follow. This principle is known as the **Law of Detachment.**
   e. **Reasoning from the converse** is a type of invalid reasoning that occurs when a conditional statement is true and we assume its converse is true.
   f. When a conditional statement and its converse are combined into one statement by using "if and only if," the new statement is called a **biconditional statement.**

CHAPTER TEST

1. Use the attribute pieces shown below to determine the sets satisfying the given conditions.

   sbt   *sbr*   *sbh*   *swt*   *swr*   *swh*

   a. hexagonal and white
   b. triangular or black
   c. not(white or rectangular)

2. Given the universal set $U = \{0, 1, 2, 3, 4, 5, 6\}$ and the sets $A = \{2, 4, 6\}$ and $B = \{1, 2, 3, 4\}$, determine the following sets.

   a. $A \cap B$ b. $A \cup B$
   c. $A' \cap B$ d. $A \cup B'$

3. Sketch a Venn diagram to illustrate each of the following conditions.
   a. $E \cap F \neq \Phi$
   b. $E \subset G$
   c. $F \cap G = \Phi$ and $E \subset F$
   d. $E \cap G \neq \Phi$ and $(E \cup G) \cap F = \Phi$
   e. $E \subset G$ and $F \subset E$
   f. $E \subset F, G \subset F$, and $E \cap G = \Phi$

4. Use set notation to name the shaded regions below.

   (a)
   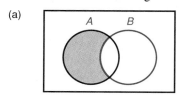

   (b)
   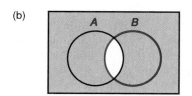

5. Answer each question and draw a diagram to support your conclusion.
   a. If $k \in R \cup S$, is $k \in R \cap S$?
   b. If $x \in T \cap W$, is $x \in T \cup W$?
   c. If $y \in R \cap S$, is $y \in S'$?

6. Show that the following sets are infinite.
   a. $\{100, 101, 102, 103, \ldots\}$
   b. $\{10, 12, 14, 16, 18, \ldots\}$

7. Of 75 cars that were inspected, 12 needed brake repair and 18 needed exhaust-system repair. If the brakes or exhaust systems on 50 of the cars did not need repair, how many cars needed both brake and exhaust-system repairs?

8. In a certain town there live 150 men: 85 are married, 70 have a telephone, 75 own a car, 55 are married and have a telephone, 35 have a telephone and a car, 40 are married and have a car, and 30 are married, have a car, and have a telephone. How many men are single and do not have either a car or a telephone?

9. Rewrite each statement in if-then form.
   a. People who are denied credit have a right to protest to the credit bureau.
   b. All the children who were absent yesterday were absent again today.
   c. Everybody at the party received a gift.

10. Write the converse, inverse, and contrapositive of each of the following statements.
   a. If Mary goes fishing, then her husband goes with her.
   b. If you join the book club, you will receive 5 free books.

11. "If the temperature drops below 10 degrees, the culture dies." This statement is logically equivalent to which of the following statements?
    (1) If the culture dies, the temperature drops below 10 degrees.
    (2) If the temperature does not drop below 10 degrees, the culture does not die.
    (3) If the culture does not die, the temperature does not drop below 10 degrees.

12. Combine the following statement and its converse into a biconditional statement: If there are peace talks, then the prisoners will be set free. If the prisoners are set free, then there will be peace talks.

13. Determine whether each conclusion below is valid or invalid.
    a. *Premises:* All mallards are aggressive birds. Some black ducks are aggressive birds.
       Conclusion: Some black ducks are mallards.
    b. *Premises:* All geometry classes are interesting. Some math classes are geometry classes.
       Conclusion: Some math classes are interesting.
    c. *Premises:* If people are happy, then they have enough to eat. All rich people have enough to eat.
       Conclusion: Some rich people are happy.

14. Use each set of premises to form a valid conclusion.
    a. *Premises:* If a person is healthy, then the person has about 10 times as much lung tissue as necessary. The people in ward *B* have less lung tissue than necessary.
       Conclusion:
    b. If an illegal move is made, the game pieces should be set up as they were before the move. An illegal move was made.
       Conclusion:

15. Determine whether each conclusion below is valid or invalid.
    a. *Premises:* You may keep the books if you like everything about them. John kept the books.
       Conclusion: John liked everything about the books.
    b. *Premises:* If this year's tests are successful, the United States will be using laser communications by 1996. This year's tests were successful.
       Conclusion: The United States will be using laser communications by 1996.

BIBLIOGRAPHY

Adams, V. M. "A Variation on the Algorithm for GCD and LCM?" *Arithmetic Teacher* 30 (November 1982): 46.

Bezuszka, S. J. "A Test for Divisibility by Primes." *Arithmetic Teacher* 33 (October 1985): 36–38.

Bright, G. W. "Teaching Mathematics with Technology: Logical Reasoning." *Arithmetic Teacher* 36 (October 1988): 54–55.

Brown, G. W. "Searching for Patterns of Divisors." *Arithmetic Teacher* 32 (December 1984): 32–34.

Bruni, J., and H. Silverman. "Using Classification to Interpret Consumer Information." *Arithmetic Teacher* 24 (January 1977): 4–12.

Charles, R. I. "The Role of Problem Solving." *Arithmetic Teacher* 32 (February 1985): 48–50.

Cruikshank, D. "Sorting, Classifying and Logic." *Arithmetic Teacher* 21 (November 1974): 588–598.

Dunham, W. "Euclid and the Infinitude of Primes." *Mathematics Teacher* 80 (January 1987): 16–17.

Garofalo, J., and D. K. Mtetwa. "Implementing the Standards: Mathematics as Reasoning." *Arithmetic Teacher* 37 (January 1990): 16–18.

Horak, V., and W. Horak. "Let's Do It: 'Button Bag' Mathematics." *Arithmetic Teacher* 30 (March 1983): 10–16.

O'Regan, P. J. "Intuition and Logic." *Mathematics Teacher* 81 (November 1988): 664–668.

Scott, T. "A Different Attribute Game." *Arithmetic Teacher* 28 (March 1981): 47–48.

Silverman, H. "Teacher Made Materials for Teaching Numbers and Counting." *Arithmetic Teacher* 19 (October 1972): 431–433.

Thompson, A. G. "On Patterns, Conjectures, and Proof: Developing Students' Mathematical Thinking." *Arithmetic Teacher* 33 (September 1985): 20–23.

Vance, J. "The Large-Blue-Triangle: A Matter of Logic." *Arithmetic Teacher* 22 (March 1975): 237–240.

Van de Walle, J., and C. S. Thompson. "Let's Do It: Promoting Mathematical Thinking." *Arithmetic Teacher* 32 (February 1985): 7–13.

Warman, M. "Fun with Logical Reasoning." *Arithmetic Teacher* 29 (May 1982): 26–30.

Whitin, D. J. "Bring On the Buttons." *Arithmetic Teacher* 36 (January 1989): 4–6.

C H A P T E R

3 *Whole Numbers*

SPOTLIGHT ON TEACHING

Excerpts from NCTM's Standards 5 and 6 for Teaching Mathematics in Grades K–4*

Intuition about number relationships helps children make judgments about the reasonableness of computational results and of proposed solutions to numerical problems. Such intuition requires good number sense. . . .

Estimation presents students with another dimension of mathematics; terms such as *about, near, closer to, between,* and *a little less than* illustrate that mathematics involves more than exactness. Estimation interacts with number sense and spatial sense to help children develop insights into concepts and procedures, flexibility in working with numbers and measurements, and an awareness of reasonable results. Estimation skills and understanding enhance the abilities of children to deal with everyday quantitative situations.

If children are to develop good number concepts, considerable instructional time must be devoted to number and numeration. Children's experiences with numbers are most beneficial when the numbers have meaning for them. A variety of place-value tasks that assess children's thinking can be used to identify those numbers that have meaning to individual students. . . .

For children to use both single-digit and multidigit number ideas fluently, written symbols should be linked to physical models and oral names. See figure [below].

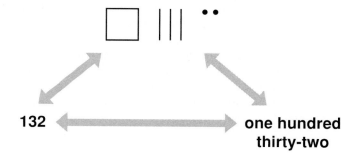

*Reprinted by permission of the National Council of Teachers of Mathematics.

Section 3.1 NUMERATION SYSTEMS

A 7 is written at the right end of a two-digit number, thereby increasing the value of the number by 700. Find the original two-digit number.

Egyptian stone giving an account of the expedition of Amenhotep III in 1450 B.C.

numerals

There are no historical records of the first uses of numbers, their names and their symbols. Written symbols for numbers are called **numerals** and probably were developed before number words, since it is easier to cut notches in a stick than to establish phrases to identify a number.

numeration system

A logically organized collection of numerals is called a **numeration system.** Early numeration systems appear to have grown from tallying. In many of these systems, 1, 2, and 3 were represented by I, I I, and I I I. By 3400 B.C. the Egyptians had an advanced system of numeration for numbers up to and exceeding 1 million. Their first few number symbols show the influence of the simple tally strokes (Figure 3.1).

Figure 3.1

Their symbol for 3 can be seen in the third row from the bottom of the stone inscriptions shown above. What other symbols for single-digit numerals can you see on this stone?

GROUPING AND NUMBER BASES

As soon as it became necessary to count large numbers of objects, the counting process was extended by grouping. Since the fingers furnished a convenient counting device, grouping by 5s was used in some of the oldest methods of counting. The left hand was generally used to keep a record of the number of objects being counted, while the right index finger pointed to the objects. When all 5 fingers had been used, the same hand would be used again to continue counting. In certain parts of South America and Africa, it is still customary to "count by hands": 1, 2, 3, 4, hand, hand and 1, hand and 2, hand and 3, etc.

EXAMPLE A

Use the "count by hands" system to determine the names of the numbers for each of the following sets of dots.

1.

2.

3.

Solution
1. 2 hands and 2
2. 3 hands and 4
3. 4 hands and 3

base   The number of objects used in the grouping process is called the **base.** In Example A the base is 5. By using the numerals 1, 2, 3, and 4 for the first 4 whole numbers and "hand" for the name of the base, it is possible to name numbers up to and including 24 (4 hands and 4).

BASE TEN   As soon as people grew accustomed to counting by the fingers on one hand, it became natural to use the fingers on both hands to group by 10s. In most numeration systems today, grouping is done by 10s. The names of our numbers reflect this grouping process. "Eleven" derives from the medieval German phrase *ein lifon,* meaning *one left over,* and "twelve" is from *twe lif,* meaning *two over ten.* The number names from 13 to 19 have similar derivations. "Twenty" is from *twe-tig,* meaning *two tens,* and "hundred" means *ten times ten.** When grouping is done by 10s, the system

base ten numeration system   is called a **base ten numeration system.**

"You're probably all wondering why I called you here today."

■ *H*ISTORICAL *HIGHLIGHT*

There are many traces of base twenty from different cultures. The Mayas of Yucatan and Aztecs of Mexico had elaborate number systems based on 20. Greenlanders used the expressions "one man" for 20, "two men" for 40, and so on. A similar system was used in New Guinea.

Evidence of grouping by 20 among the ancient Celtics can be seen in the French use of *quatre-vingt* (four-twenty) for 80. In our language the use of "score" suggests past tendencies to count by 20s. Lincoln's familiar Gettysburg Address begins, "Four score and seven years ago." Another example occurs in a childhood nursery rhyme: "Four and twenty blackbirds baked in a pie."

ANCIENT NUMERATION SYSTEMS

EGYPTIAN NUMERATION   The ancient Egyptian numeration system had a base of

hieroglyphics   10. The Egyptians used picture symbols called **hieroglyphics** (figure 3.2).

Figure 3.2

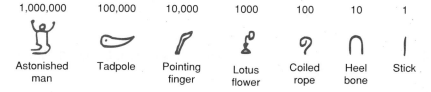

1,000,000	100,000	10,000	1000	100	10	1
Astonished man	Tadpole	Pointing finger	Lotus flower	Coiled rope	Heel bone	Stick

These symbols were repeated the required number of times to represent a number.

*H. W. Eves, *An Introduction to the History of Mathematics,* 3rd ed. (New York: Holt, Rinehart and Winston, 1969), 8–9.

EXAMPLE B

Write the following numbers using Egyptian numerals.

1. 2342
2. 14026

Solution

1.

2.

additive numeration system

The Egyptian numeration system is called an **additive numeration system** because each symbol is repeated as many times as needed. It was the Egyptian custom to write 1s, 10s, and 100s from left to right, rather than from right to left, as we do today. Some Egyptian numerals can be seen in the stone inscriptions on the first page of this section.

EXAMPLE C

Notice the numeral for 743 in the third row from the bottom of the Egyptian stone. The symbols for 3 ones, 4 tens, and 7 hundreds are written from left to right. What other Egyptian numerals can you find on this stone?

Solution

It appears that the third row up contains 45 and the fourth row up has 150. Parts of many other numerals can be seen.

ROMAN NUMERATION   Roman numerals can be found on clock faces, buildings, gravestones, and the preface pages of books. Like the Egyptians, the Romans used base ten and had an additive numeration system. In addition to the symbols for 1, 10, 100, and 1000, there are symbols for 5, 50, and 500. The 7 common symbols are

I	V	X	L	C	D	M
1	5	10	50	100	500	1000

Historical evidence indicates that C is from *centum,* meaning *hundred,* and M is from *milli,* meaning *thousand.* The origin of the other symbols is uncertain. The Romans wrote their numerals so that the numbers they represented were in decreasing order from left to right.

EXAMPLE D

Write the following numbers using Roman numerals.

1. 2342
2. 1996

Solution

1. MMCCCXXXXII
2. MDCCCCLXXXXVI

When a Roman numeral is placed to the left of a numeral for a larger number, as in IX for 9, its position indicates subtraction. The subtractive principle was recognized by the Romans, but they did not make much use of it.* (In fact the subtractive principle has only been in common use for about the past 200 years.) Compare the preceding Roman numeral for 1996 with the following numeral written using the subtractive principle:

MCMXCVI

The Romans had relatively little need for large numbers, so they developed no general system for writing them. In the inscription on a monument commemorating the victory over the Carthaginians in 260 B.C., the symbol ⌂ for 100,000 is repeated 23 times to represent 2,300,000.

MAYAN NUMERATION   The Mayas used base twenty and had a symbol for zero. The Mayan numerals for zero through 19 are shown in Figure 3.3. Notice that there is grouping by 5s within the first 20 numbers.

Figure 3.3

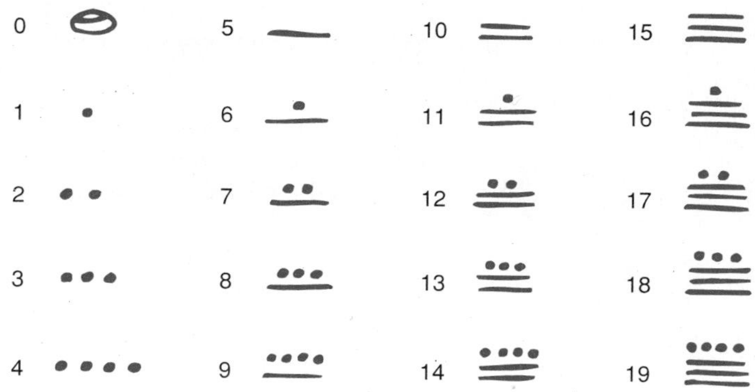

The Mayas wrote their numerals vertically with one numeral below another.

EXAMPLE E

The top numeral in this example, represents 12 times 20, and the lower numeral, represents 16. The complete numeral is 12 × 20 + 16, or 256.

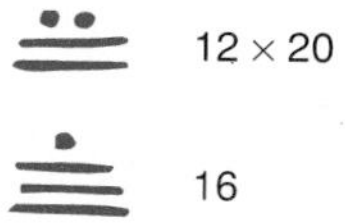

Whenever the Mayas wrote one numeral over the other, as in Example E, the top numeral indicated the number of 20s and the bottom numeral the number of 1s. This is an example of a **positional numeration system** because the position of a numeral indicates its value.**

positional numeration system

---

*D. E. Smith, *History of Mathematics*, 2nd ed. (Lexington, MA: Ginn, 1925), 60.

**The Mayas used a modified base twenty system when they wrote numbers with more than two numerals. For further details on Mayan numeration, see James K. Bidwell, "Mayan Arithmetic," *Mathematics Teacher* 60, no. 7 (November 1967): 762–768.

EXAMPLE F

Write the following numbers using Mayan numerals.

1. 60   2. 106   3. 158

Solution   (1) ● ● ● (3 twenties)   (2) ——— (5 twenties)   (3) ● ● (7 twenties)

⊝ (0)   · ——— (6)   ● ● ● (18)
———
———

Notice the necessity in the Mayan system for a symbol that has the same purpose as our numeral zero. In part (1) of Example F, their symbol for zero occupies the lower place and tells us that the 3 dots have a value of 3 × 20 and there are no 1s.

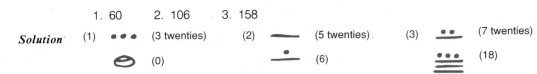

HISTORICAL HIGHLIGHT

There is archaeological evidence that the Mayas were in Central America before 1000 B.C. During the Classical Period (A.D. 300–900), they had a highly developed knowledge of astronomy and a 365-day calendar with a cycle going back to 3114 B.C.

"No, no, no! *Thirty* days hath September!"

HINDU-ARABIC NUMERATION   Much of the world now uses the Hindu-Arabic numeration system. This positional numeration system was named for the Hindus, who invented it, and the Arabs, who transmitted it to Europe. Since it is a base ten numeration system, the only number symbols that are needed are the **digits** 0, 1, 2, 3, 4, 5, 6, 7, 8, and 9. Each digit in a numeral has a name that indicates its position.

digits

EXAMPLE G

Here are the names and values of the digits in 75,063.

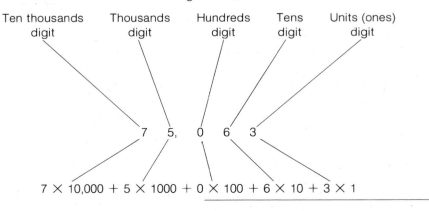

Ten thousands digit   Thousands digit   Hundreds digit   Tens digit   Units (ones) digit

7   5,   0   6   3

$7 \times 10{,}000 + 5 \times 1000 + 0 \times 100 + 6 \times 10 + 3 \times 1$

<table>
<tr><td>**expanded form**
powers of 10</td><td>When we write a number as the sum of the numbers represented by each digit in its numeral (see Example G), we are writing the number in **expanded form.** Another common method of writing a number in expanded form is to use exponents and **powers of 10:** 10^2 for 10×10, 10^3 for $10 \times 10 \times 10$, and so on.</td></tr>
</table>

When we write a number as the sum of the numbers represented by each digit in its numeral (see Example G), we are writing the number in **expanded form.** Another common method of writing a number in expanded form is to use exponents and **powers of 10:** 10^2 for 10×10, 10^3 for $10 \times 10 \times 10$, and so on.

EXAMPLE H

Solution

Write 75,063 in expanded form using powers of 10.

$$75{,}063 = 7 \times 10^4 + 5 \times 10^3 + 0 \times 10^2 + 6 \times 10 + 3$$

place value   Each digit in a numeral has a value that depends on its position. The power of 10 associated with each digit is called the **place value** of the digit.

EXAMPLE I

Solution

Determine the value of each underlined digit and its place value.

1. 7<u>0</u>24   2. 3<u>70</u>,189   3. 49,<u>2</u>38

1. The value is zero and the place value is hundreds.
2. The value is 70,000 and the place value is ten thousands.
3. The value is 200 and the place value is hundreds.

■ HISTORICAL HIGHLIGHT

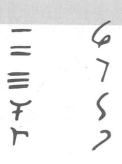

There are various theories about the origin of our digits. It is widely accepted, however, that they originated in India. Notice the resemblance of the Brahmi numerals for 6, 7, 8, and 9 to our numerals. The Brahmi numerals for 1, 2, 4, 6, 7, and 9 were found on stone columns in a cave in Bombay dating from the second or third century B.C.* The oldest dated European manuscript that contains our numerals was written in Spain in A.D. 976. In 1299, merchants in Florence were forbidden to use these numerals. Gradually, over a period of centuries, the Hindu-Arabic numeration system replaced the more cumbersome Roman numeration system.

READING AND WRITING NUMBERS

In English the number names for the whole numbers from 1 to 20 are all single words. The names for the numbers from 21 to 99, with the exceptions of 30, 40, 50, etc., are compound number names that are hyphenated. These names are hyphenated even when they occur as parts of other names. For example, we write "three hundred forty-seven" for 347.

period   Numbers with more than three digits are read by naming the **period** for each group of three digits. Within each period, the digits are read as we would read any number from 1 to 999, and then the name of the period is recited. The names for the first few periods are shown in the following example.

*J. R. Newman, *The World of Mathematics* (New York: Simon and Schuster, 1956), 452–454.

EXAMPLE J

Read the following number.

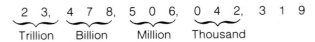

2 3,   4 7 8,   5 0 6,   0 4 2,   3 1 9
Trillion   Billion   Million   Thousand

Solution   This number is read as "twenty-three trillion, four hundred seventy-eight billion, five hundred six million, forty-two thousand, three hundred nineteen."

ROUNDING NUMBERS

If you were to ask a question such as "How many people voted in the 1988 presidential election?" you might be told that in "round numbers" it was about 89 million. Approximations are often as helpful as the exact number, which in this example is 88,930,371.

rounding   One method of **rounding** a number to the nearest million is to write the nearest million greater than the number and the nearest million less than the number and then choose the closer number. Of the following numbers, 88,930,371 is closer to 89,000,000.

89,000,000
88,930,371 rounds to 89,000,000
88,000,000

The more familiar approach to rounding a number uses place value and is stated in the following rule.

RULE FOR ROUNDING NUMBERS

1. Locate the digit with the place value to which the number is to be rounded, and check the digit to its right.
2. If the digit to the right is 5 or greater, then each digit to the right is replaced by zero and the digit with the given place value is increased by 1.
3. If the digit to the right is 4 or less, each digit to the right of the digit with the given place value is replaced by zero.

EXAMPLE K

Round 88,930,371 to the following place values.
1. Ten thousands   2. Thousands   3. Hundreds

Solution   1. Ten thousands place
↓
88,930,371 ─────────────→ rounds to ─────────────→ 88,930,000
2. Thousands place
↓
88,930,371 ─────────────→ rounds to ─────────────→ 88,930,000
3. Hundreds place
↓
88,930,371 ─────────────→ rounds to ─────────────→ 88,930,400

MODELS FOR NUMERATION

There are many models for illustrating positional numeration and place value. The bundles-of-sticks model and base ten number pieces will be introduced in examples L, M, and N and then used to model operations on whole numbers in the remainder of this chapter.

BUNDLES-OF-STICKS (OR STRAWS) MODEL   In this model, units and tens are represented by single sticks and bundles of 10 sticks, respectively. One hundred is represented by a bundle of 10 bundles.

✓ **EXAMPLE L**

The following figure shows the bundle-of-sticks model for representing 148.

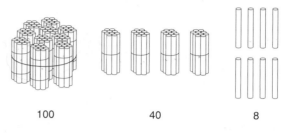

100   40   8

BASE TEN PIECES   In this model, the powers of 10 are represented by objects called **units, longs,** and **flats**: 10 units form a long, and 10 longs form a flat (Figure 3.4). Higher powers of the base can be represented by sets of flats. For example, 10 flats placed in a row represent 1000.

units, longs, flats

Figure 3.4

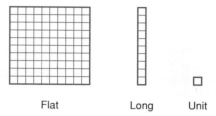

Flat   Long   Unit

EXAMPLE M

Sketch base ten pieces to represent 536.

Solution

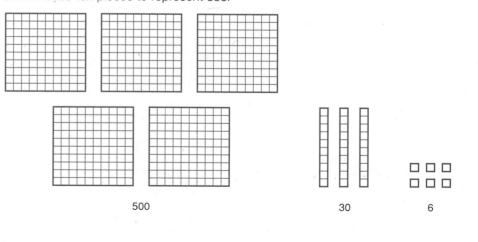

500   30   6

regrouping

Bundles of sticks and base ten pieces can be used to illustrate the concept of **regrouping:** changing one collection to another that represents the same number.

EXAMPLE N

Sketch the minimum number of base ten pieces needed to replace the following collection. Then determine the base ten number represented by the collection.

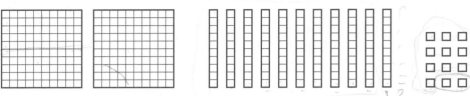

Solution   The new collection will have 3 flats, 2 longs, and 2 units. This collection of base ten pieces represents 322.

PROBLEM-SOLVING APPLICATION

reasoning by analogy

The next problem introduces the strategy of **reasoning by analogy,** which involves forming conclusions based on similar situations. For example, we know that when we add two numbers, *the greater the numbers, the greater the sum.* Reasoning by analogy, we might conclude that *the greater the numbers, the greater the product.* In this case the conclusion is true. This type of reasoning, however, is not always reliable; the conclusion *the greater the numbers, the greater the difference* would be false. The problem-solving strategies of *reasoning by analogy* and *using a model* are used below to solve a problem involving base five positional numeration.

■ PROBLEM

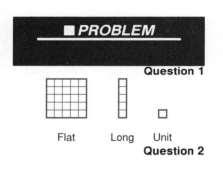

Flat   Long   Unit

Long flat   Flat   Long   Unit

What digits are necessary to represent all numbers in base five positional numeration?

Question 1

Understanding the Problem   The "count by hands" method of counting, which was introduced in the opening pages of this section, is a base five system. In that system, what digits are needed to name any number from 1 to 24?

Devising a Plan   Consider a similar problem: Why are 0, 1, 2, 3, . . . , 9 the only digits needed in base ten? Referring to the base ten pieces, we know that if there are more than 9 of one type of base ten piece, we can replace each group of 10 pieces by a piece representing the next higher power of 10. This suggests using similar pieces for base five. The first 3 base five pieces are shown at the left. How can this model be extended?

Question 2

Carrying Out the Plan   To count using the base five pieces, we can say 1, 2, 3, 4, 1 long, 1 long and 1, 1 long and 2, etc., up to 4 longs and 4—a method similar to that used in the "count by hands" system. We can avoid saying 5 longs because 5 longs can be replaced by 1 flat. In base five positional numeration, 3 flats, 0 longs, and 4 units is written as 304_{five}; the subscript "five" reminds us that we are in base five. Why does any base five numeral require only the digits 0, 1, 2, 3, and 4?

Question 3

Question 4

Looking Back   These models suggest ways to visualize other number bases, such as base two, base seven, or base sixteen. What digits are needed in base two, and what would the base two pieces look like?

Answers to Questions 1–4

1. 0, 1, 2, 3, and 4. For example, 2 hands and 1, 3 hands and 4, etc.
2. The next base five piece has a row of 5 flats.
3. Whenever there are 5 of any base five piece, they can be replaced by the next larger base five piece. If there are no pieces of a given type, the 0 is needed in the numeral to indicate this.
4. The only digits needed in base two are 0 and 1. The first 4 base two pieces are shown at left.

RELATED ACTIVITIES IN
Mathematics for Elementary Teachers: An Activity Approach, 3e

Activity Set 3.1 **Models for Numeration:** Base five and base ten pieces provide models for positional numeration, place value, and regrouping.

Just for Fun **Mind Reading Cards and Game of Nim:** Cards for determining a person's age and a game that provides opportunities for deductive reasoning and looking for patterns. The card design and the game strategy involve binary numbers.

■ *H*ISTORICAL *HIGHLIGHT*

In the fifteenth and sixteenth centuries there were two opposing opinions on the best numeration system and methods of computing. The "abacists" used Roman numerals and computed on the abacus, and the "algorists" used the Hindu-Arabic numerals and place value. The sixteenth-century print at the left shows an abacist competing against an algorist. The abacist is seated at a reckoning table with 4 horizontal lines and a vertical line down the middle. Counters, or chips, placed on lines represented powers of 10. The thousands line was marked with a cross to aid the eye in reading numbers. If more lines were needed, every third line was marked with a cross. This practice gave rise to our modern custom of separating groups of three digits in a numeral by a comma.*

An algorist computing with numerals and an abacist computing with counters

EXERCISES AND PROBLEMS 3.1

1. The chips on the lines of this reckoning table each represent one of the indicated powers of 10.

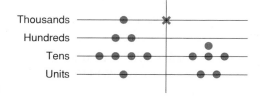

   a. What number is represented on the left side of the reckoning table?
   b. Each chip in a space between the horizontal lines represents half as much as it would on the line above. What number is represented on the right side of this reckoning table?

2. Here is the complete counting system of a twentieth-century Australian tribe that uses only 4 numbers:

Neecha	Boolla	Boolla Neecha	Boolla Boolla
1	2	3	4

   a. If this system were continued, what would be the names for 5 and 6?
   b. How would even numbers differ from odd numbers in a continuation of this system?

3. In the base five system of counting by fingers and grouping by hands, the name for 7 is "1 hand and 2."
   a. What is the name for 22 in this system?
   b. If 25 is called a "hand of hands," what is the name for 37 in this system?

4. The following number names are literal translations of number words taken from primitive languages in various parts of the world.** Follow this pattern, and write in the missing names.
   5: whole hand
   6: 1 on the other hand
   8:
   10:
   11: 1 on the foot
   15:
   16:
   20: man
   21: 1 on the hands of the next man
   25:
   30:
   40:

*D. E. Smith, *History of Mathematics,* 2nd ed. (Lexington, MA: Ginn, 1925), 183–185.

**D. Smeltzer, *Man and Number* (London: A. and C. Black, 1970), 14–15.

5. The following numeration systems were used at different times in different geographical locations. Compare these sets of numerals for the numbers 1 through 10. What similarities can you find? What evidence is there of grouping by 5s?

Babylonian numerals

I	II	III	IIII	V	VI	VII	VIII	VIIII	X

Roman numerals

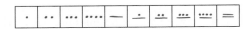

Mayan numerals

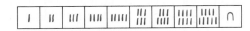

Egyptian numerals

In problems 6 through 8, write each number in the given system.

6. Egyptian numeration:

    a. 3275   b. 40,208   c. 600,000

7. Roman numeration (both without the subtractive principle and with it, if the two forms differ):

    a. 486   b. 1776   c. 2095

8. Mayan numeration:

    a. 15   b. 48   c. 172

9. Perhaps the greatest achievement in the development of numeration systems was the invention of a symbol for zero. The following ancient numeration systems had no zero symbol. How is 603 written in each of these systems?

    a. Egyptian   b. Roman

10. The Greek numerals shown below date from about 1200 B.C. Use these symbols and the additive numeration system to write 2483.

1	10	100	1000
|	—	O	□

11. The Attic-Greek numerals were developed sometime prior to the third century B.C. and came from the first letters of the Greek names for numbers. Use the clues in the following table to find the missing numerals. What base is used in this system?

1	4	8		26
		ΓIII	ΔΓI	

32	52	57	206	
ΔΔΔII		ΓΓII	HHΓI	ΓΔI

12. Write each number in two different ways using expanded form.

    a. 256,049   b. 7088

13. Determine the value of each underlined digit and its place value.

    a. 1478   b. 700,000   c. 2,947,831

14. Write the names of the following numbers.

    a. 5,438,146   b. 31,409

    c. 816,447,210,361   d. 62,340,782,000,000

15. Round 43,668,926 to the nearest

    a. hundred thousand.   b. ten thousand.

    c. thousand.   d. hundred.

16. Make a sketch of each number, using the given model.
    a. 136, using base ten pieces
    b. 47, using the bundle-of-sticks model
    c. 108, using the bundle-of-sticks model
    d. 570, using base ten pieces

17. Sketch the first three base pieces in the following bases:

    a. Base seven   b. Base three

18. In parts a through c, enter the number in the top display into your calculator. What keys must you press to change the display to the one under it without changing the digits that are the same in both displays?

    a. | 1034692. | b. | 938647. | c. | 40000. |
       | 1834692. | | 908047. | | 400000. |

19. Continue the pattern of numbers on the left sides of the equations below. Does the pattern continue to hold on the right sides of the equations?

$$1 \times 9 + 2 = 11$$
$$12 \times 9 + 3 = 111$$
$$123 \times 9 + 4 = 1111$$

Featured Strategies: Making a Drawing, Making a Table, and Finding a Pattern

20. A single-elimination basketball tournament has 247 teams competing for the championship. If the tournament sponsors must pay $20 to have each game refereed, what is the total cost of referees for the tournament?

a. *Understanding the Problem* For every 2 teams that play each other, there is a winner and a loser. The loser is eliminated from the tournament, and the winner plays another team. The following brackets for a four-team tournament show that 3 games are needed to determine a champion.

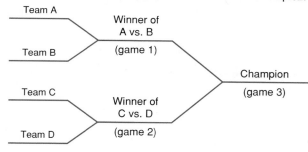

If the number of teams entered in the tournament is not a power of 2, byes are necessary. That is, some teams will be unopposed in the first round so that the number of teams for the second round will be a power of 2. Draw a set of brackets for a seven-team tournament. How many teams will be unopposed in the first round?

b. *Devising a Plan* One approach to solving this problem is to use small numbers and look for a pattern. Complete the following table.

No. of teams	2	3	4	5	6	7	8
Total no. of games	1		3				

c. *Carrying Out the Plan* To solve this problem, use the approach suggested in part b and inductive reasoning, or use your own plan. What is the total cost of referees for the tournament?

d. *Looking Back* The brackets in part a directed our attention to the winning teams. The total number of games played can be more easily determined by thinking about the losing teams. Each game that is played determines one loser. How many losing teams will there be in the tournament?

21. Powers of 2 are used in base two numeration systems. These powers are called **binary numbers.** Here are the first few.

1	2	4	8	16	32	64
2^0	2^1	2^2	2^3	2^4	2^5	2^6

Every positive whole number either is a binary number or can be written as a sum of binary numbers so that each binary number is used only once or not at all. For example, $25 = 16 + 8 + 1$. Write each of the following numbers as a sum of binary numbers, using no binary number more than once.

a. 35   **b.** 42   **c.** 66

CALCULATOR INVESTIGATION

There is something very special about the number 6174. Select any four-digit number whose digits are not all equal and arrange the digits to form the largest possible number—that is, put the digits in decreasing order from left to right. Then form the reverse of this number and subtract it from the larger number. Continue this process by forming the largest possible number from the difference and subtracting its reverse. The example in this table shows the process ending with 6174 after five steps.

Step	Maximum number	Reverse	Difference
1	8421	1248	7173
2	7731	1377	6354
3	6543	3456	3087
4	8730	0378	8352
5	8532	2358	6174

Questions for Investigation

1. If you begin with any four-digit number whose digits are not all equal, will the above process always produce 6174?
2. What happens when this process is applied to three-digit numbers whose digits are not all equal? Is there a special number in this case?
3. What happens when this process is applied to five-digit numbers? Is there a special number in this case?

PUZZLER

It is possible with just 6 different metal weights to weigh on a balance scale any object with a whole-number weight of from 1 to 63 grams. These metal weights are placed on just one side of the scale. What are the 6 weights?

SECTION 3.2   ADDITION AND SUBTRACTION

Use each of the digits 0 through 9 exactly once to obtain the smallest whole number difference.

☐ ☐ ☐ ☐ ☐
− ☐ ☐ ☐ ☐
_____

ALL RIGHT, − I TAKE 2 CLAMS FROM YOU, THEN YOU GIVE ME 3 MORE.

I NOW HAVE 5 CLAMS. 2 + 3 = 5. REMEMBER THAT!

THESE ARITHMETIC LESSONS ARE BREAKING ME.

sum

Children learn addition at an early age using objects. If 2 clams are *put together* with 3 clams, the total number of clams is the **sum** 2 + 3. The idea of *putting sets together,* or *taking their union,* is often used to define addition.

ADDITION OF WHOLE NUMBERS

> If set R has r elements and set S has s elements, and R and S are disjoint, then the **sum** of r plus s, written $r + s$, is the number of elements in the union of R and S. The numbers r and s are called **addends**.

In the definition of addition R and S must be disjoint sets. Otherwise, you could not determine the total number of elements in two sets by adding the number of elements in one set to the number of elements in the other.

√ **EXAMPLE A**

There are 8 people in a group who play the guitar and 6 who play the piano. These are the only people in the group.

1. What is the minimum number of people in this group?
2. What is the maximum number of people in this group?
3. What is the total number of people, if 2 people play both the guitar and the piano?

Solution

1. 8, if the 6 piano players also play the guitar
2. 14, if the sets of piano players and guitar players are disjoint
3. 12, as illustrated below

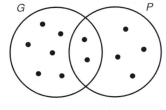

Guitar players   Piano players

MODELS FOR ADDITION ALGORITHMS

✓ **algorithm**

An **algorithm** is a step-by-step procedure for computing. Algorithms for addition involve two separate procedures: (1) adding digits and (2) regrouping, or "carrying" (when necessary), so that the sum is written in positional numeration. The term "carrying" probably originated back when a counter, or chip, was actually carried to the next column on a counting board. Traditionally, a substantial portion of the school mathematics curriculum has involved practice with pencil-and-paper algorithms. As calculators become more readily available, there will be less emphasis on written algorithms. It will always be important, however, to understand algorithms and their use in mental mathematics and estimation.

Many models provide an understanding of addition algorithms. Example B shows how to illustrate the sum of two numbers using the bundle-of-sticks model. The sticks representing these numbers can be placed below each other, just as the numerals are in the addition algorithm. The sum is the total number of sticks in the bundles plus the total number of individual sticks.

EXAMPLE B

The numbers 26 and 38 are represented in the following figure. To compute 26 + 38, we must determine the total number of sticks. There are a total of 5 bundles of sticks (5 tens) and 14 sticks (14 ones). Since there are more than 9 single sticks, they can be regrouped into 1 bundle of 10 sticks and 4 more. Thus there are a total of 6 bundles and 4 sticks. In the addition algorithm, a 4 is recorded in the units column and the extra 10 is recorded by writing a 1 in the tens column.

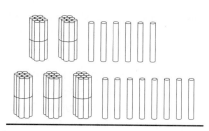
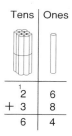

	Tens	Ones
	¹2	6
+	3	8
	6	4

ADDITION ALGORITHMS

There are several ways of providing intermediate steps between the use of physical models for computing sums and the use of algorithms and calculators. One of these is **partial sums**

computing **partial sums.** In this method, the digits for each place value are added and the partial sums are recorded before there is any regrouping.

Two methods of writing partial sums are shown in Example C. In (1) there is seldom a need for regrouping, because if there is more than 1 digit in the partial sum, the digits are placed in different columns. In (2) the regrouping can be done beginning with any partial sum with more than 1 digit.

EXAMPLE C

1.
```
      345
    + 278
      13
      11
      5
    -----
      623
```

2.
$$
\begin{aligned}
345 &= 3 \text{ hundreds} + 4 \text{ tens} + 5 \\
+\,278 &= 2 \text{ hundreds} + 7 \text{ tens} + 8 \\
&= 5 \text{ hundreds} + 11 \text{ tens} + 13
\end{aligned}
$$
Regrouping $\{$ 6 hundreds + 2 tens + 3
= 623

LEFT-TO-RIGHT ADDITION Sometimes it is instructive to examine algorithms from the past. Although it is now customary to add from right to left, beginning with the units digits, this was not always the case. The early Hindus and later the Europeans added from left to right. Since children learn to read from left to right, some may find it natural to add in this direction. It will surprise students to learn that addition does not have to begin with the units digits.

√ **EXAMPLE D**

scratch method

To compute 897 + 537 from left to right, we first add 8 and 5 in the hundreds column (see below). In the second step, the 9 and 3 are added in the tens column and, because carrying is necessary, the 3 in the hundreds column is scratched out and replaced by a 4. In the third step, we add the units digits. Again carrying is necessary, so the 2 in the tens column is scratched out and replaced by a 3. The Europeans called this approach the **scratch method.**

First step	Second step	Third step
897	897	897
+537	+537	+537
13	1̸3̸2	1̸3̸2̸4
	4	43

NUMBER PROPERTIES

A few fundamental properties for operations on whole numbers are so important they are given special names. Four properties for addition are introduced here, and the corresponding properties for multiplication are given in Section 3.3.

CLOSURE PROPERTY FOR ADDITION If you were to select any two whole numbers, their sum would be another unique whole number. This fact is expressed by saying that the whole numbers are **closed for addition.** The word "unique" means *one and only one* and is an important condition because it guarantees that there is only one sum for any two whole numbers. The word "closed" indicates that when an operation is performed on two numbers from a given set, the result is also *in the set,* rather than outside the set. The idea of closure for addition can best be illustrated by considering a set on which addition is not closed. If we select any two numbers from the set of odd numbers {1, 3, 5, 7, . . .}, their sum is not another odd number. So the set of odd numbers is not closed for addition.

closed for addition

CLOSURE PROPERTY FOR ADDITION

> For any two whole numbers *a* and *b*,
>
> *a* + *b* is a unique whole number.

In general, the idea of closure involves a *set* and an *operation.* If we perform the operation with any two or more elements in the set and the result is another element in the set, the operation is closed on that set of elements; if we end up with a result that is not an element of the set, the operation is not closed on that set.

EXAMPLE E

Determine whether the operation is closed for the given set.

1. Subtraction on the set of whole numbers
2. Multiplication on the set of odd numbers
3. Division on the set of whole numbers

Solution   1. Not closed   2. Closed   3. Not closed

identity for addition

IDENTITY PROPERTY FOR ADDITION   Included among the whole numbers is a very special number, zero. Zero is called the **identity for addition,** because when it is added to another number there is *no change*. That is, adding zero to any number leaves the identity of the number unchanged. For example:

$$0 + 5 = 5 \qquad 17 + 0 = 17 \qquad 0 + 0 = 0$$

Zero is unique in that it is the only number that is an identity for addition.

IDENTITY PROPERTY FOR ADDITION

For any whole number b,

$$0 + b = b + 0 = b$$

and zero is a unique identity for addition.

associative property for addition

ASSOCIATIVE PROPERTY FOR ADDITION   In any sum of three numbers, the middle number may be added to (associated with) either of the two end numbers. This property is called the **associative property for addition.**

EXAMPLE F

$$147 + (20 + 6) = (147 + 20) + 6$$

Associative property
for addition

ASSOCIATIVE PROPERTY FOR ADDITION

For any whole numbers a, b, and c,

$$a + (b + c) = (a + b) + c$$

When elementary school students compute by breaking a number into a convenient sum, as in the next example, the *associative property of addition* plays a roll. Arranging numbers to produce sums of 10 is called "making 10s."

EXAMPLE G

$$8 + 7 = 8 + (2 + 5) = (8 + 2) + 5 = 10 + 5 = 15$$

Associative property
for addition

commutative property for addition

COMMUTATIVE PROPERTY FOR ADDITION   When two numbers are added, the numbers may be interchanged (commuted) without affecting the sum. This property is called the **commutative property for addition.**

EXAMPLE H

$$257 + 498 = 498 + 257$$

COMMUTATIVE PROPERTY FOR ADDITION

For any whole numbers *a* and *b*,

$$a + b = b + a$$

As the addition table in Figure 3.5 shows, the commutative property for addition roughly cuts in half the number of basic addition facts that must be memorized. Each sum in the shaded part of the table has a corresponding equal sum in the unshaded part of the table.

Figure 3.5

+	0	1	2	3	4	5	6	7	8	9
0	0	1	2	3	4	5	6	7	8	9
1	1	2	3	4	5	6	7	8	9	10
2	2	3	4	5	6	7	8	9	10	11
3	3	4	5	6	7	8	9	10	11	12
4	4	5	6	7	8	9	10	11	12	13
5	5	6	7	8	9	10	11	12	13	14
6	6	7	8	9	10	11	12	13	14	15
7	7	8	9	10	11	12	13	14	15	16
8	8	9	10	11	12	13	14	15	16	17
9	9	10	11	12	13	14	15	16	17	18

EXAMPLE I

If we know that $3 + 8 = 11$, then, by the commutative property for addition, $8 + 3 = 11$. What do you notice about the locations of these sums in the addition table?

Solution

$3 + 8$ and $8 + 3$ are in opposite parts of the table. If the shaded part of the table is folded onto the unshaded part of the table, these sums will coincide. That is, the table is symmetric about the diagonal from upper left to lower right.

The commutative property also allows us to select convenient combinations of numbers when we are adding.

EXAMPLE J

The numbers 26, 37, and 4 are arranged more conveniently on the right side of the following equation than on the left, because $26 + 4 = 30$ and it is easy to compute $30 + 37$.

$$26 + \underbrace{37 + 4}_{} = 26 + \underbrace{4 + 37}_{} = (26 + 4) + 37 = 30 + 37$$

Commutative property
for addition

INEQUALITY OF WHOLE NUMBERS

number line

unit segment

The inequality of whole numbers can be understood intuitively in terms of the locations of numbers as they occur in the counting process. For example, 3 is less than 5 because it is named before 5 in the counting sequence. This ordering of numbers can be illustrated with a number line. A **number line** is formed by beginning with any line and marking off two points, one labeled zero and the other labeled 1, as shown in Figure 3.6. This **unit segment** is then used to mark off equally spaced points for consecutive whole numbers. For any two numbers, the one that occurs on the left is less than the one that occurs on the right.

One method of marking off unit lengths to form a number line is to use the edges of base ten pieces—the unit for marking off 1 linear unit or the long for marking off 10 units (see Figure 3.6). This use of base ten pieces provides a link between the region model and the linear model for illustrating numbers.

Figure 3.6

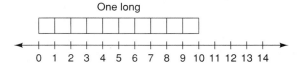

One long

$$0 \quad 1 \quad 2 \quad 3 \quad 4 \quad 5 \quad 6 \quad 7 \quad 8 \quad 9 \quad 10 \quad 11 \quad 12 \quad 13 \quad 14$$

The inequality of whole numbers is defined in terms of addition.

INEQUALITY OF WHOLE NUMBERS

> For any two whole numbers **m** and **n**, **m** is less than **n** (written **m < n**) if and only if there is a nonzero whole number **k** such that **m + k = n**.

less than   greater than

less than or equal to
greater than or equal to

An inequality can be written with the inequality symbol opening to the right or to the left. For example, 4 < 9 means that 4 is **less than** 9; 9 > 4 means that 9 is **greater than** 4. Sometimes the inequality symbol is combined with the equality symbol: ≤ means **less than or equal to,** and ≥ means **greater than or equal to.**

■ *HISTORICAL HIGHLIGHT*

The symbols < and > were first used by the English surveyor Thomas Harriot in 1631. There is no record of why Harriot chose these symbols, but the following conjecture is logical and will help you to remember their meanings. The distances between the ends of the bars in the equality symbol are equal, and in an equation (e.g., 3 = 1 + 2) the number on the left of the sign equals the number on the right. Similarly, 3 < 4 would indicate that 3 is less than 4, because the distance between the bars on the left is less than the distance between the bars on the right. The reasoning is the same whether we write 3 < 4 or 4 > 3. These symbols could easily have evolved into our present notation, < and >, in which the bars completely converge to prevent any misjudgment of the distances.*

SUBTRACTION

Subtraction is usually explained as the *taking away* of a subset of objects from a given set. The word "subtract" literally means *to draw away from under.*

The process of taking away, or subtraction, may be thought of as the opposite of

*This is one of two conjectures on the origin of the inequality symbols, described by H. W. Eves in *Mathematical Circles* (Boston: Prindle, Weber and Schmidt, 1969), 111–113.

inverse operations

the process of putting together, or addition. Because of this dual relationship, subtraction and addition are called **inverse operations.** This relationship is used to define subtraction in terms of addition.

> For any whole numbers r and s, with $r \geq s$, the **difference** of r minus s, written $r - s$, is the whole number c such that $r = s + c$. The number c is called the **missing addend.**

SUBTRACTION OF WHOLE NUMBERS

missing addend

The definition of subtraction says that we can compute the difference $17 - 5$ by determining the **missing addend**—that is, the number that must be added to 5 to give 17. We use this approach when making change. Rather than subtract 83 cents from $1.00 to determine the difference, we pay back the change by counting up from 83 to 100.

In the definition of subtraction there is no need to require r to be greater than or equal to s. In the early school grades, however, before negative numbers are introduced, most examples involve subtracting a smaller number from a larger one.

take-away concept
comparison concept

Two concepts of subtraction occur in problems: the **take-away concept** and the **comparison concept.**

TAKE-AWAY CONCEPT Suppose you have 12 stamps and give away 7. How many stamps will you have left? Figure 3.7 illustrates $12 - 7$ by showing 7 objects being taken away from 12 objects.

Figure 3.7

Take-away concept showing 12 – 7 = 5

COMPARISON CONCEPT Suppose you have 12 stamps and someone else has 7 stamps. How many more stamps do you have than the other person? In this case we compare one collection to another to determine the difference. Figure 3.8 shows that there are 5 more stamps in one collection than in the other.

Figure 3.8

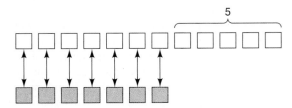

Comparison concept showing 12 – 7 = 5

MODELS FOR SUBTRACTION ALGORITHMS

There are two types of examples to consider in explaining the steps in finding the difference between two multidigit numbers: examples in which borrowing or regrouping is not needed and those in which borrowing or regrouping is needed.

The bundle-of-sticks model and the take-away concept of subtraction are used in Example K to illustrate the subtraction algorithm with regrouping.

EXAMPLE K

To illustrate 53 − 29, we begin with 5 bundles of sticks (5 tens) and 3 sticks (3 ones), as shown. In order to take away 9 sticks, we must regroup one bundle to form 13 single sticks. Once this has been done, we can take away 2 bundles of sticks and 9 sticks, leaving 2 bundles of sticks and 4 single sticks. In the algorithm, the regrouping is recorded by crossing out the 5 and writing a 4 above it.

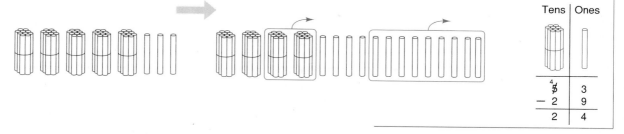

MENTAL CALCULATIONS

Mental calculations are important because they often prove the quickest and most convenient method for obtaining an answer. Performing mental computations requires us to combine a variety of skills: the abilities to use various algorithms, to understand place value and base ten numeration, and to use number properties. Mental calculations are useful in obtaining exact answers, and they are a prerequisite to estimating. Let's consider a few techniques for performing mental calculations.

COMPATIBLE NUMBERS   One mental calculating technique is looking for pairs of numbers whose sum or difference is easy to compute. For example, it is convenient to combine 17 and 43 in the following computation.

$$17 - 12 + 43 = 17 + 43 - 12 = 60 - 12$$

compatible numbers

Using pairs of numbers that are especially easy to compute with is the calculating technique called **compatible numbers.**

EXAMPLE L

Do the following computations in your head.

1. 17 + 12 + 23 + 45
2. 12 − 15 + 82 − 61 + 55

Solution

1. One possibility is to notice that 17 + 23 = 40; then 40 + 45 = 85, and adding 12 produces 97. Another possibility is to notice that 12 + 23 = 35. Then 35 + 45 = 80, and adding 17 produces 97.
2. Here is one possibility: 55 − 15 = 40 and 82 − 61 = 21. Then 40 + 21 = 61, and adding 12 produces 73.

substitutions

SUBSTITUTIONS   Another method of mental calculation is the method of **substitutions,** in which a number is broken down into a convenient sum or difference of numbers. You can easily compute the sum 127 + 38 in your head in many ways. Here are three possibilities:

$$127 + (3 + 35) = (127 + 3) + 35 = 130 + 35 = 165$$
$$127 + (30 + 8) = (127 + 30) + 8 = 157 + 8 = 165$$
$$(125 + 2) + 38 = 125 + (2 + 38) = 125 + 40 = 165$$

EXAMPLE M

Do each computation mentally by substituting a convenient sum or difference for one of the given numbers.

1. 57 + 24
2. 163 − 46

Solution

Below is one possibility for each solution.

1. 57 + 20 + 4 = 77 + 4 = 81
2. 163 − 40 − 6 = 123 − 6 = 117

equal differences

EQUAL DIFFERENCES Another type of substitution that works for subtraction is the method of **equal differences,** which uses the fact that the difference between two numbers is unchanged when both numbers are increased or decreased by the same amount. Figure 3.9 illustrates why this is true when both numbers are increased. No matter how many squares are adjoined to the two rows in this figure, the difference between the numbers of squares in the two rows is 4.

Figure 3.9

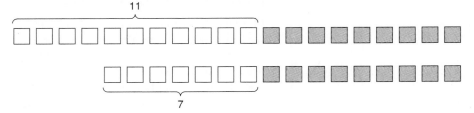

Replacing a difference by an equal but more convenient difference can be very useful.

EXAMPLE N

To compute 47 − 18, first find a more convenient difference by increasing or decreasing both numbers by the same amount.

Solution

Here are several differences that are more convenient.

49 − 20   (Increase both by 2)
50 − 21   (Increase both by 3)
30 − 1   (Decrease both by 17)
40 − 11   (Decrease both by 7)

The difference, 29, is easy to compute in any of these forms.

add up

ADD-UP METHOD A convenient mental method for subtracting is to **add up** from the smaller to the larger number.

EXAMPLE O

Compute each difference by adding up from the smaller to the larger number.

1. 53 − 17
2. 135 − 86

Solution

1. From 17 to 20 is 3, and from 20 to 53 is 33. So the difference is 3 + 33 = 36.
2. From 86 to 100 is 14, and from 100 to 135 is 35. So the difference is 14 + 35 = 49.

ESTIMATION OF SUMS OR DIFFERENCES

In recent years the teaching of estimation has become a top priority in school mathematics programs. Often in everyday applications we need to make a quick calculation that does not have to be exact in order to serve the purpose at hand. Estimation is especially important for developing "number sense" and predicting the reasonableness of answers. With the increased use of calculators, estimation helps students to determine if the correct keys have been pressed.

There are some difficulties in teaching estimation. First, the best estimating technique to use often depends on the numbers involved and the context of the problem. Second, there is no correct answer. An estimate is a "ballpark" figure, and for a given problem there will often be several different estimates.

There are many techniques for estimating. Three common ones, *rounding, using compatible numbers,* and *front-end estimation,* are explained below. After obtaining an estimation, we sometimes need to know if it is less than or greater than the actual answer. This can often be determined from the method of estimation being used.

ROUNDING If an approximate sum or difference is all that is needed, we can round the numbers before computing. The type of problem will often determine what place value the numbers will be rounded to. The following estimates are obtained by rounding to the nearest hundreds and thousands. The symbol $\approx$ means **approximately equal to.**

approximately equal to

EXAMPLE P

Obtain an estimation by rounding each number to the place value of the leading digit.

1. $624 - 289 - 132$
2. $4723 + 419 + 1040$
3. $812 - 245$

Solution

1. $\approx 600 - 300 - 100 = 200$
2. $\approx 5000 + 400 + 1000 = 6400$
3. $\approx 800 - 200 = 600$

Some people prefer rounding each number to the same place value. If each number in problem (2) of Example P were rounded to the nearest thousand, 419 would be rounded to zero and the approximate sum would become $5000 + 0 + 1000 = 6000$. Even when numbers have the same number of digits, they do not have to be rounded to the same place value. A different approximation could be obtained in problem (3) of Example P by rounding 245 to 250 (the nearest tens). We could then use the add-up method to obtain a difference of 550.

$$812 - 245 \approx 800 - 250 = 550$$

COMPATIBLE NUMBERS Sometimes a computation can be simplified by replacing one or more numbers by approximations in order to obtain compatible numbers. For example, to approximate $342 + 250$, we might replace 342 by 350.

$$342 + 250 \approx 350 + 250 = 600$$

Using compatible numbers is a common estimating technique.

EXAMPLE Q   Use compatible numbers to obtain each estimate. Without computing the actual answer, predict whether your estimate is too small or too big.

1. 88 + 37 + 66 + 24
2. 142 − 119
3. 127 + 416 − 288

Solution   Here are some estimations. Others may occur to you.

1. 90 + 40 + 70 + 24 = 224, which is greater than the actual answer.
2. 140 − 120 = 20, which is less than the actual answer.
3. 130 + 400 − 300 = 230, which is less than the actual answer.

front-end estimation   **FRONT-END ESTIMATION**   The method of **front-end estimation** is similar to left-to-right addition, but usually involves only one or two leading digits.

EXAMPLE R   Suppose you have written checks for $417, $683, and $228 and need to determine your approximate balance before writing another check. Without computing an exact sum, how can you determine approximately how much have you spent?

Solution 1   One approach is to use front-end estimation to add the leading digits: 4 + 6 + 2 = 12 (hundreds). You spent approximately $1200.

Solution 2   An obvious improvement is to round each number to the nearest hundred as you add: 4 + 7 + 2 = 13 (hundreds). The approximate amount spent is $1300.

Solution 3   Sometimes front-end estimation involves adding the two leading digits, which in this example are the hundreds and tens digits: 4 + 6 + 2 = 12 (hundreds), and 1 + 8 + 2 = 11 (tens). The estimate is $1200 + $110 = $1310.

Solution 4   To ensure that you maintain a positive balance in your checking account, you may want an estimation that is greater than the actual sum. This estimation can be obtained by computing the sum of the hundreds digits and the sum of the rounded-up tens digits: 4 + 6 + 2 = 12 (hundreds), and 2 + 9 + 3 = 14 (tens). The estimate is $1200 + $140 = $1340.

PROBLEM-SOLVING APPLICATION

making an organized list   The following problem introduces the strategy of **making an organized list.** This problem-solving strategy is closely associated with another strategy called *eliminating possibilities.* Next to guessing and checking, one of the most common approaches to solving problems is systematically searching for or eliminating possibilities.

■ PROBLEM

Karen and Angela are playing darts on the board shown below. Each player throws 3 darts on her turn and adds the numbers on the regions that are hit. The darts always hit the dart

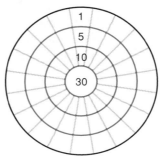

board, and when a dart lands on a line the score is the larger of the two numbers. After 4 turns Karen and Angela notice that their sums for each turn are all different. How many different sums are possible?

Question 1   **Understanding the Problem**   What are the largest and smallest possible sums?

Question 2   **Devising a Plan**   Here are two approaches to finding all the sums. Since the lowest sum is 3 and the highest sum is 90, we can list the numbers from 3 through 90 and determine which can be obtained. Or we can *make an organized list* showing the different regions the 3 darts can strike. For example, if the first 2 darts land in regions 1 and 5, what are the possible scores after the third dart is thrown?

Question 3   **Carrying Out the Plan**   Use one of the above approaches or one of your own to find the different sums and how each can be obtained from the dart board. How many different sums are possible?

Question 4   **Looking Back**   Instead of 4 regions, suppose the dart board had 3 regions. How many different sums would be possible on a dart board with 3 regions numbered 1, 5, and 10?

Answers to Questions 1–4
1. The largest sum is 90 and the smallest is 3.
2. The possible sums are 7, 11, 16, and 36.
3. 20 different sums
4. 10 different sums

RELATED ACTIVITIES IN
Mathematics for Elementary Teachers: An Activity Approach, 3e

Activity Set 3.2   **Adding and Subtracting with Multibase Pieces:** Base five and base ten pieces provide models for addition, subtraction, and regrouping.

Just for Fun   **Force Out:** A two-person game involving addition (or subtraction), with patterns for discovering the winning strategy

---

■ HISTORICAL HIGHLIGHT

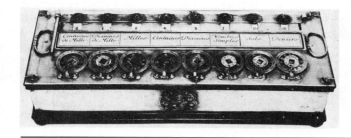

This adding machine was developed by Blaise Pascal in 1642 for computing sums. The machine is operated by dialing a series of wheels with digits from 0 to 9. To carry a number to the next column when a sum is greater than 9, Pascal devised a ratchet mechanism that would advance a wheel 1 digit when the wheel to its right made a complete revolution. The wheels from right to left represent units, tens, hundreds, etc.

EXERCISES AND PROBLEMS 3.2

1. To compute 854 + 629 using the adding machine described above, we would first turn the hundreds, tens, and units wheels 8, 5, and 4 turns, respectively. We would then dial these same wheels 6, 2, and 9 more turns. The sum would appear on indicators at the top of the machine.
   a. Which of these wheels would make more than 1 revolution for this sum?
   b. Which two wheels would be advanced 1 digit because of carrying?

   c. Could this sum be computed by left-to-right addition—that is, by turning the hundreds wheel for both hundreds digits, 8 and 6; then turning the tens wheel for 5 and 2; and then turning the units wheel for 4 and 9?

2. For each of the following, find a whole number, if possible, to make the equation true.

   a. $\square + 11 < 12$ **b.** $9 - \square \geq 5$
   c. $\square - 6 > 10$ **d.** $8 + \square \leq 8$

3. Rewrite each subtraction exercise as an addition exercise.
   a. $247 - \square = 108$ b. $\square - 76 = 231$

4. Sketch base ten pieces to illustrate each computation. Show regrouping.
   a. $46 + 27$
   b. $52 - 36$, using the take-away concept of subtraction
   c. $35 - 18$, using the comparison concept of subtraction

5. Addition is illustrated on a number line by a series of arrows, as shown here.

   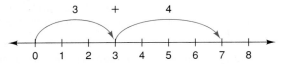

   a. Illustrate $2 + 5$ and $5 + 2$ on a number line.
   b. Use a number line to show that $(2 + 4) + 1 = 1 + (2 + 4)$.
   c. Use a number line to show that $(3 + 4) + 1$ and $(4 + 1) + 3$ are equal.

6. Subtraction is illustrated on a number line by arrows that represent numbers. The number being subtracted is represented by an arrow from right to left, as shown here.

   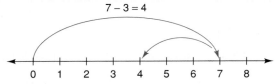

   a. Illustrate $(6 - 3) - 2$ on a number line.
   b. Use a number line to illustrate $6 - 6$.

7. Compute the sums below using the given method. Describe an advantage of each method.
   a. Left-to-right addition:

   $$\begin{array}{r} 726 \\ + 508 \\ \hline \end{array}$$

   b. Partial sums:

   $$\begin{array}{r} 974 \\ + 382 \\ \hline \end{array}$$

8. Which number property shows that the two sides of the equation are equal?
   a. $(38 + 13) + 17 = 38 + (13 + 17)$
   b. $(47 + 62) + 12 = (62 + 47) + 12$
   c. $2 \times (341 + 19) = 2 \times (19 + 341)$
   d. $13 + (107 + 42) = (13 + 107) + 42$

9. Try some numbers in parts a and b to determine whether the properties hold.
   a. Is subtraction commutative?

   $$\square - \triangle \overset{?}{=} \triangle - \square$$

   b. Is subtraction associative?

   $$(\square - \triangle) - \varolessthan \overset{?}{=} \square - (\triangle - \varolessthan)$$

   c. Is addition closed on the set of even numbers?
   d. Is subtraction closed on the set of odd numbers?

10. *Error Analysis* Some types of student errors and misuses of addition are very common. Describe the type of error illustrated in each of the following examples.

    a.
    $$\begin{array}{r} 47 \\ + \ 86 \\ \hline 123 \end{array}$$
    b.
    $$\begin{array}{r} 16 \\ +48 \\ \hline 91 \end{array}$$
    c.
    $$\begin{array}{r} 56 \\ + \ 78 \\ \hline 1214 \end{array}$$
    d.
    $$\begin{array}{r} 35 \\ + \ 46 \\ \hline 171 \end{array}$$

11. *Error Analysis* One common source of elementary school students' errors in subtraction is adding rather than subtracting. When addition is taught first, the students' responses become so automatic that later on they write 8 for the difference $5 - 3$. Try to detect the reason for the error in each of the following computations.

    a.
    $$\begin{array}{r} 84 \\ -36 \\ \hline 52 \end{array}$$
    b.
    $$\begin{array}{r} 52 \\ -38 \\ \hline 24 \end{array}$$
    c.
    $$\begin{array}{r} 46 \\ -27 \\ \hline 73 \end{array}$$
    d.
    $$\begin{array}{r} 94 \\ -37 \\ \hline 12 \end{array}$$

12. Compute exact answers mentally by using compatible numbers or substitutions. Show your method.
    a. $23 + 25 + 28$ b. $128 - 15 + 27 - 50$
    c. $83 + 50 - 13 + 24$ d. $130 + 25 + 70 + 10$
    e. $208 + 554$

13. Use the equal differences method to find a difference that is more convenient for mental computation. Then calculate the exact difference.
    a. $435 - 198$ b. $622 - 115$ c. $245 - 85$

14. Use the add-up method to compute exact differences. Record the numbers you use in the add-up process.
    a. $400 - 185$ b. $535 - 250$ c. $135 - 47$

15. In the table below, round each number to the place value of its leading digit and then compute the sum of each row of numbers.

	83 (think 80)	47 (think 50)	112 (think 100)	Approximate sum
				230
a.	102	38	21	
b.	26	43	59	
c.	25	212	81	
d.	27	68	18	

16. Estimate each sum or difference by replacing one or both numbers by compatible numbers. Show your replacements.

  a. $359 - 192 \approx$ **b.** $712 + 293 \approx$

  c. $882 + 245 \approx$ **d.** $1522 - 486 \approx$

17. Use front-end estimation on the leading digit to estimate each sum below.

  a. $472 + 821 + 306 + 512$

  b. $4721 + 2015 + 3681$

  c. $62 + 85 + 31 + 24 + 88$

18. A homeowner has the following bills to pay for the month of March.

Electricity $86
Heat $128
Water and sewage $94
Property taxes $163
Life insurance $230
Car insurance $65
House insurance $58
Food $541
Doctor's bills $477
Gas and oil $73
Car payments $148
Home mortgage $570
Dentist's bills $109
Recreation $14

  a. Obtain an estimation of how much she owes by rounding each bill to the nearest hundred.

  b. Can the homeowner pay these bills with a monthly salary of $1800?

19. A dealer has 30 cars with air conditioning and 22 cars with standard transmissions. These are the only cars on the lot.

  a. What is the minimum number of cars the dealer has on the lot?

  b. What is the maximum number of cars?

  c. What is the total number of cars, if there are 17 cars with both air conditioning and standard transmissions?

  d. In which case above can the answer be found by adding the number of cars with air conditioning to the number of cars with standard transmissions?

20. A class survey found that 26 students watched the Olympics on television on Saturday and 21 watched on Sunday. Of those who watched the Olympics on only one of these days, 11 chose Saturday and 6 chose Sunday. If every student watched at least one of these days, how many students are in the class?

21. This circle contains the whole numbers from 1 to 7. By adding two or more *neighbor numbers* (numbers that are next to each other), we can get every number from 8 to 28.

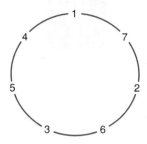

  a. Show how the sums from 8 to 28 can be obtained from this circle.

  b. Arrange the numbers 1, 2, 3, 4, 5, and 6 in a circle so that all sums from 7 to 21 can be obtained. (*Hint:* Study the circle above. The arrangement follows a pattern.) Show how each sum can be obtained.

22. Place the whole numbers from 1 to 19 into the 19 circles of the pattern below so that any three numbers on the same line through the center will give the same sum.

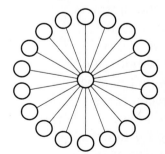

COMPUTER INVESTIGATION

The computer program PALINDROMIC DIFFERENCES on the *Computer Problem-Solving Disc* will compute the differences and print the steps for any number you enter.

In the example at the right, we begin with 723, reverse its digits, and subtract the smaller of the two numbers from the larger. This process of reversing digits and subtracting is continued in steps 2, 3, and 4 until a palindromic number is obtained.

Step 1	Step 2
723	693
−327	−396
396	297

Step 3	Step 4
792	594
−297	−495
495	99

In some cases this process requires many steps, and it is convenient to use a computer program.

Questions for Investigation
1. If you begin with any two-digit or three-digit number, will this process produce a palindromic number?
2. If you begin with a four-digit or five-digit number, will this process result in a palindromic number? If not, are there any patterns that occur?
3. Try this process for some larger numbers to see what happens.

PUZZLER

One night three men registered at the hotel in Hillsville. They were charged $30 for their room. The desk clerk later realized that she had overcharged them by $5 and sent the refund up with the bellboy. The bellboy knew that it would be difficult to split the $5 three ways. Therefore, he kept a $2 "tip" and gave the men only $3. Each man had originally paid $10 and was given back $1. Thus the room cost each man $9. This means that the three men spent $27 for the room plus the $2 tip. What happened to the other dollar?

SECTION 3.3 MULTIPLICATION

■ PROBLEM OPENER

Lee has written a two-digit number in which the units digit is her favorite digit. When she subtracts the tens digit from the units digit, she gets 3. When she multiplies the original two-digit number by 21, she gets a three-digit number whose hundreds digit is her favorite digit and whose tens and units digits are the same as those in her original two-digit number. What is her favorite digit?

State office buildings at the Empire State Plaza, Albany, New York

The skyscraper in the center of the photo in the Problem Opener is called the Tower Building. There is an innovative window-washing machine mounted on top of this building. The machine lowers a cage on a vertical track so that each column of 40 windows can be washed. After 1 column of windows has been washed, the machine moves to the next column. The rectangular face visible in the photo has 36 columns of windows. The total number of windows is $40 + 40 + 40 + \cdots + 40$, a sum in which 40 occurs 36 times. This sum equals the product 36×40, or 1440. We are led to different expressions for the sum and product by considering the rows of windows across the floors. There are 36 windows in each floor on this face of the building and 40 floors. Therefore, the number of windows is $36 + 36 + 36 + \cdots + 36$, a sum in which 36 occurs 40 times. This sum is equal to 40×36, which is also 1440. For sums such as these in which one number is repeated, multiplication is a convenient method for doing addition.

multiplication
repeated addition

Historically, multiplication was developed to replace certain special cases of addition—namely, the cases of *several equal addends*. For this reason we usually see **multiplication** of whole numbers explained and defined as **repeated addition.**

**MULTIPLICATION OF
WHOLE NUMBERS**

> For any whole numbers r and s, the **product** of r **times** s is the sum with s occurring r times. This is written as
>
> $$r \times s = \underbrace{s + s + s + \cdots + s}_{r \text{ times}}$$
>
> The numbers r and s are called **factors.**

rectangular array

One way of representing multiplication of whole numbers is with a **rectangular array** of objects, such as the rows and columns of windows at the beginning of this section. Figure 3.10 shows the close relationship between the use of *repeated addition* and *rectangular arrays* for illustrating products. Part (a) of the figure shows squares in 4 groups of 7 to illustrate $7 + 7 + 7 + 7$, and part (b) of the figure shows the squares pushed together to form a 4 by 7 rectangle.

Figure 3.10

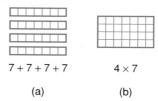

$7 + 7 + 7 + 7$ 4×7

(a)   (b)

In general, $r \times s$ is the number of objects in an r by s rectangular array.

tree diagram

Another way of viewing multiplication is with a figure called a **tree diagram.** Constructing a tree diagram is a counting technique that is useful for certain types of multiplication problems.

EXAMPLE A

A catalog shows jeans available in cotton, brush denim, or stretch denim and in stonewash (*s*), acid wash (*a*), bleached (*b*), or regular color (*r*). How many types of jeans are available?

Solution

A tree diagram for this problem is shown below. The tree begins with 3 branches, each labeled with one of the types of material. Each of these branches leads to 4 more branches, which correspond to the colors. The tree has $3 \times 4 = 12$ end points, one for each of the 12 different types of jeans.

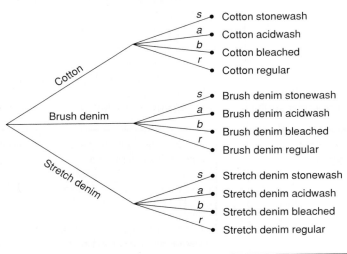

MODELS FOR MULTIPLICATION ALGORITHMS

Physical models for multiplication can generate an understanding of multiplication and suggest or motivate procedures and rules for computing. There are many suitable models for illustrating multiplication. Base ten pieces are used in the following examples.

Figure 3.11 illustrates 3×145 using base ten pieces. First 145 is represented as shown in part (a). Then the base ten pieces for 145 are tripled. The result is 3 flats, 12 longs, and 15 units, as shown in part (b). Finally, the pieces are regrouped: 10 units are replaced by 1 long, leaving 5 units; and 10 longs are replaced by 1 flat, leaving 3 longs. The result is 4 flats, 3 longs, and 5 units, as shown in part (c).

Figure 3.11

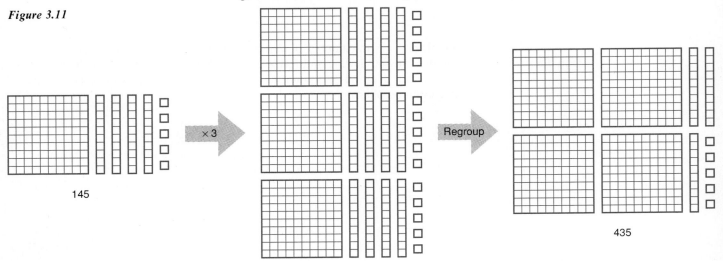

(a)   (b)   (c)

Base ten pieces can be used to illustrate the pencil-and-paper algorithm for computing. Consider the product 3 × 145 shown in Figure 3.11. First a 5, indicating the remaining 5 units in part (c), is recorded in the units column, and the 10 units that have been regrouped are recorded by writing a 1 in the tens column (see below). Then 3 is written in the tens column for the remaining 3 longs, and 1 is recorded in the hundreds column for the 10 longs that have been regrouped. _

Flats	Longs	Units
1	1	
1	4	5
	×	3
4	3	5

The next example illustrates how multiplication by 10 can be carried out with base ten pieces. Multiplying by 10 is especially convenient because 10 units can be placed together to form 1 long, 10 longs to form 1 flat, and 10 flats to form 1 row of flats.

To multiply 34 by 10, we replace each base ten piece for 34 by the base ten piece for the next higher power of ten (Figure 3.12). We begin with 3 longs and 4 units and end with 3 flats, 4 longs, and no units. This illustrates the familiar fact that the product of any whole number and 10 can be computed by placing a zero at the right end of the numeral.

Figure 3.12

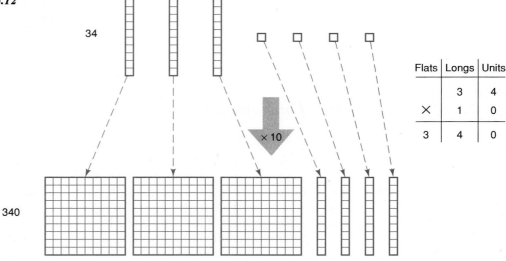

Flats	Longs	Units
	3	4
×	1	0
3	4	0

Computing the product of two numbers by repeated addition of base ten pieces becomes impractical as the size of the numbers increases. For example, computing 18 × 23 would require representing 23 with base ten pieces 18 times. For products involving two-digit numbers, rectangular arrays are more convenient.

To compute 18 × 23, we can draw a rectangle with dimensions 18 by 23 on grid paper (Figure 3.13). The product is the number of small squares in the rectangular array. This number can be easily determined by counting groups of 100 and strips of 10. The total number of small squares is 414. Notice how the array in Figure 3.13 can be viewed as 18 rows of 23, once again showing the connection between the repeated addition and rectangular array views of multiplication.

Figure 3.13

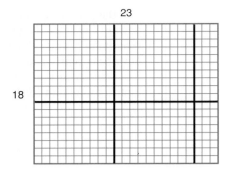

The pencil-and-paper algorithm for multiplication requires computing **partial products.** When a two-digit number is multiplied times a two-digit number, there are 4 partial products.

partial products

The product 13 × 17 is illustrated in Figure 3.14. The 4 regions of the grid represent the 4 partial products. Sometimes it is instructive to draw arrows from each partial product to the corresponding region on the grid.

Figure 3.14

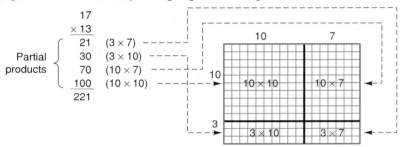

■ *H*ISTORICAL *HIGHLIGHT*

→ 1 × 52 =   52
→ 2 × 52 = 104
  4 × 52 = 208
→ 8 × 52 = 416

      52
     104
   +416
     572

One of the earliest methods of multiplication is found in the Rhind Papyrus. This ancient scroll (ca. 1650 B.C.), more than 5 meters in length, was written to instruct Egyptian scribes in computing with whole numbers and fractions. Beginning with the words "Complete and thorough study of all things, insights into all that exists, knowledge of all secrets . . . ," it indicates the Egyptians' awe of mathematics. Although most of its 85 problems have a practical origin, there are some of a theoretical nature. The Egyptians' algorithm for multiplication was a succession of doubling operations, followed by addition. To compute 11 × 52, they would repeatedly double 52, then add *one* 52, *two* 52s, and *eight* 52s to get *eleven* 52s.

NUMBER PROPERTIES

Four properties for addition of whole numbers were stated in Section 3.2. Four corresponding properties for multiplication of whole numbers are stated below, along with one additional property that relates the operations of addition and multiplication.

CLOSURE PROPERTY
FOR MULTIPLICATION   This property states that the product of any two whole numbers is also a whole number.

CLOSURE PROPERTY FOR MULTIPLICATION

> For any two whole numbers *a* and *b*,
>
> $a \times b$ **is a unique whole number.**

identity for multiplication

IDENTITY PROPERTY FOR MULTIPLICATION   The number 1 is called an **identity for multiplication,** because when multiplied by another number it leaves the identity of the number unchanged. For example:

$$1 \times 14 = 14 \qquad 34 \times 1 = 34 \qquad 1 \times 0 = 0$$

The number 1 is unique in that it is the only number that is an identity for multiplication.

IDENTITY PROPERTY FOR MULTIPLICATION

> For any whole number *b*,
>
> $1 \times b = b \times 1 = b$
>
> and 1 is a unique identity for multiplication.

commutative property for multiplication

COMMUTATIVE PROPERTY FOR MULTIPLICATION   This number property says that in any product of two numbers, the numbers may be interchanged (commuted) without affecting the product. This property is called the **commutative property for multiplication.** For example:

$$347 \times 26 = 26 \times 347$$

COMMUTATIVE PROPERTY FOR MULTIPLICATION

> For any whole numbers *a* and *b*,
>
> $a \times b = b \times a$

The commutative property is illustrated in Figure 3.15, which shows two different views of the same rectangular array. Part (a) of the figure represents 7×5, and part (b) represents 5×7. Since part (b) is obtained by rotating part (a), both figures have the same number of small squares, so 7×5 is equal to 5×7.

Figure 3.15

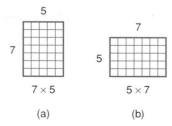

(a)   (b)

As the multiplication table in Figure 3.16 shows, the commutative property for multiplication approximately cuts in half the number of basic multiplication facts that must be memorized. Each product in the shaded part of the table corresponds to an equal product in the unshaded part of the table.

EXAMPLE B

Since $3 \times 7 = 21$, we know by the commutative property for multiplication that $7 \times 3 = 21$. What do you notice about the location of each product in the shaded part of the table relative to the location of the corresponding equal product in the unshaded part of the table?

Solution   If the shaded part of the table is folded onto the unshaded part, each product in the shaded part will coincide with an equal product in the unshaded part. In other words, the table is symmetric about the diagonal from upper left to lower right.

Figure 3.16

×	1	2	3	4	5	6	7	8	9
1	1	2	3	4	5	6	7	8	9
2	2	4	6	8	10	12	14	16	18
3	3	6	9	12	15	18	21	24	27
4	4	8	12	16	20	24	28	32	36
5	5	10	15	20	25	30	35	40	45
6	6	12	18	24	30	36	42	48	54
7	7	14	21	28	35	42	49	56	63
8	8	16	24	32	40	48	56	64	72
9	9	18	27	36	45	54	63	72	81

ASSOCIATIVE PROPERTY FOR MULTIPLICATION   In any product of three numbers, the middle number may be associated with and multiplied by either of the two end numbers. This property is called the **associative property for multiplication.** For example:

associative property for multiplication

$$6 \times (7 \times 4) = (6 \times 7) \times 4$$

Associative property
for multiplication

ASSOCIATIVE PROPERTY FOR MULTIPLICATION

> For any whole numbers *a, b,* and *c,*
>
> $$a \times (b \times c) = (a \times b) \times c$$

Figure 3.17 illustrates the associative property for multiplication. Part (a) of the figure represents 3×4, and part (b) shows 5 of the 3 by 4 rectangles. The number of

Figure 3.17

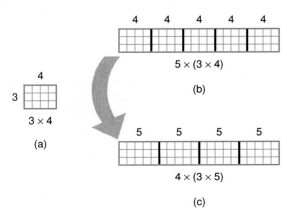

4   4   4   4   4

$5 \times (3 \times 4)$

(b)

4

3   3×4

(a)

5   5   5   5

$4 \times (3 \times 5)$

(c)

small squares in part (b) is 5 × (3 × 4). Part (c) is obtained by subdividing the rectangle in part (b) into 4 copies of a 3 by 5 rectangle. The number of small squares in part (c) is 4 × (3 × 5), which, by the commutative property for multiplication, equals (5 × 3) × 4. Since the numbers of small squares in parts (b) and (c) are equal, 5 × (3 × 4) = (5 × 3) × 4.

The commutative and associative properties are often used to obtain convenient combinations of numbers for mental calculations.

EXAMPLE C

Solution

Try computing 25 × 46 × 4 in your head before reading further.

The easy way to do this is by rearranging the numbers so that 25 × 4 is computed first and then 46 × 100. The following equations show how the commutative and associative properties permit this rearrangement.

Associative property
for multiplication

(25 × 46) × 4 = (46 × 25) × 4 = 46 × (25 × 4)

Commutative property
for multiplication

DISTRIBUTIVE PROPERTY   When multiplying a sum of two numbers by a third number, we can add the two numbers and then multiply by the third number, or we can multiply each number of the sum by the third number and then add the two products.

distributive property for multiplication over addition

To compute 35 × (10 + 2), we can compute 35 × 12, or we can add 35 × 10 to 35 × 2. This property is called the **distributive property for multiplication over addition.**

$$35 \times 12 = 35 \times (10 + 2) = (35 \times 10) + (35 \times 2)$$

Distributive property

DISTRIBUTIVE PROPERTY OF MULTIPLICATION OVER ADDITION

For any whole numbers *a*, *b*, and *c*,

$$a \times (b + c) = (a \times b) + (a \times c)$$

One use of the distributive property is in learning the basic multiplication facts. Elementary school children are often taught the "doubles" (2 + 2 = 4, 3 + 3 = 6, 4 + 4 = 8, etc.) because these number facts together with the distributive property can be used to obtain other multiplication facts.

EXAMPLE D

Solution

How can 7 × 7 = 49 and the distributive property be used to compute 7 × 8?

$$7 \times 8 = 7 \times (7 + 1) = 49 + 7 = 56$$

Distributive property

The distributive property can be illustrated by using rectangular arrays, as in Figure 3.18. The dimensions of the array in part (a) of the figure are 6 by (3 + 4), and the array contains 42 small squares. Part (b) shows the same squares separated into two rectangular arrays with dimensions 6 by 3 and 6 by 4. Since the number of squares in both figures is the same, $6 \times (3 + 4) = (6 \times 3) + (6 \times 4)$.

Figure 3.18

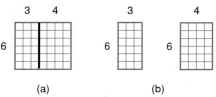

(a)   (b)

The distributive property also holds for multiplication over subtraction.

EXAMPLE E

Show that the two sides of the following equation are equal.

$$6 \times (20 - 8) = (6 \times 20) - (6 \times 8)$$

Solution $6 \times (20 - 8) = 6 \times 12 = 72$ and $(6 \times 20) - (6 \times 8) = 120 - 48 = 72$

MENTAL CALCULATIONS

In the following paragraphs three methods are discussed for performing mental calculations of products. These methods parallel those used for performing mental calculations of sums and differences.

COMPATIBLE NUMBERS   We saw in Example C that the commutative and associative properties permit the rearrangement of numbers in products. Such rearrangements can often generate compatible numbers.

EXAMPLE F

Find a more convenient arrangement that will yield compatible numbers, and compute the following products mentally.

1. $5 \times 346 \times 2$
2. $2 \times 25 \times 79 \times 2$

Solution   1. $5 \times 2 \times 346 = 10 \times 346 = 3460$
2. $2 \times 2 \times 25 \times 79 = 100 \times 79 = 7900$

SUBSTITUTIONS   In certain situations the distributive property is useful for facilitating mental calculations. For example, to compute 21×103, first replace 103 by $100 + 3$ and then compute 21×100 and 21×3 in your head. Try it.

$$21 \times 103 = \underbrace{21 \times (100 + 3)}_{} = \underbrace{2100 + 63}_{} = 2163$$
Distributive property

Occasionally it is convenient to replace a number by the difference of two numbers and use the fact that multiplication distributes over subtraction. Rather than compute 45×98, we can compute 45×100 and subtract 45×2.

$$45 \times 98 = \underbrace{45 \times (100 - 2)}_{} = \underbrace{4500 - 90}_{} = 4410$$
Distributive property

EXAMPLE G   Find a convenient substitution, and compute the following products mentally.

1. 25 × 99
2. 42 × 11
3. 34 × 102

Solution
1. 25 × (100 − 1) = 2500 − 25 = 2475
2. 42 × (10 + 1) = 420 + 42 = 462
3. 34 × (100 + 2) = 3400 + 68 = 3468

EQUAL PRODUCTS   This method of performing mental calculations is similar to the equal differences method used for subtraction. It is based on the fact that the product of two numbers is unchanged when one of the numbers is divided by a given number and the other number is multiplied by the same number. For example, the product 12 × 52 can be replaced by 6 × 104 by dividing 12 by 2 and multiplying 52 by 2. At this point we can mentally calculate 6 × 104 to be 624. Or we can continue the process of dividing and multiplying by 2, replacing 6 × 104 by 3 × 208, which can also be mentally calculated.

Figure 3.19 illustrates why one number in a product can be halved and the other doubled without changing the product. The rectangular array in part (a) of the figure represents 22 × 16. If this rectangle is cut in half by line *h*, the two pieces can be used to form an 11 × 32 rectangle, as in part (b). Notice that 11 is half of 22 and 32 is twice 16. Since the rearrangement has not changed the number of small squares in the two rectangles, the products 22 × 16 and 11 × 32 are equal.

Figure 3.19

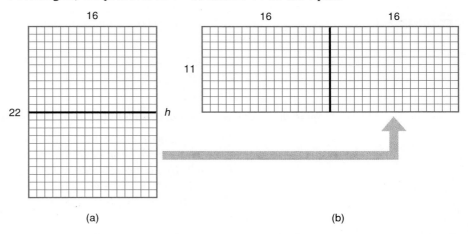

(a)   (b)

The equal products method can also be justified by using number properties. The following equations show that 22 × 16 = 11 × 32. Notice that multiplying by 1/2 and 2 is the same as multiplying by 1. This is a special case of the inverse property for multiplication, which is discussed in Section 5.3.

$$22 \times 16 = 22 \times 1 \times 16 \qquad \text{(Identity property for multiplication)}$$

$$= 22 \times \left(\frac{1}{2} \times 2\right) \times 16 \qquad \text{(Inverse property for multiplication)}$$

$$= \left(22 \times \frac{1}{2}\right) \times (2 \times 16) \qquad \text{(Associative property for multiplication)}$$

$$= 11 \times 32$$

EXAMPLE H

Use the method of equal products to perform the following calculations mentally.

1. 14×4
2. 28×25
3. 15×35

Solution

1. $14 \times 4 = 7 \times 8 = 56$
2. $28 \times 25 = 14 \times 50 = 7 \times 100 = 700$
3. $15 \times 35 = 5 \times 105 = 525$

ESTIMATION OF PRODUCTS

The techniques of *rounding,* using *compatible numbers,* and *front-end estimation* are used in the following examples.

ROUNDING   Products can be estimated by rounding one or both numbers. Computing products by rounding is somewhat more risky than computing sums by rounding, because any error due to rounding becomes multiplied. For example, if we compute 47 $\times$ 28 by rounding 47 to 50 and 28 to 30, the estimated product, $50 \times 30 = 1500$, is greater than the actual product. This may be acceptable if we want an estimate greater than the actual product. For a closer estimate, we can round 47 to 45 and 28 to 30. In this case the estimate is $45 \times 30 = 1350$.

EXAMPLE I

Use rounding to estimate these products. Make any adjustments you feel might be needed.

1. 27×63
2. 81×57
3. 194×26

Solution

Below is one estimate for each product. You may find others.

1. $27 \times 63 \approx 30 \times 60 = 1800$. Notice that since 63 is greater than 27, increasing 27 by 3 has more of an effect on the estimate than decreasing 63 to 60 (see Figure 3.20). So the estimate of 1800 is greater than the actual answer.
2. $81 \times 57 \approx 80 \times 60 = 4800$
3. $194 \times 26 \approx 200 \times 25 = 5000$

Figure 3.20 shows the effect of estimating 27×63 by rounding to 30×60. Rectangular arrays for both products are outlined on the grid. The gray region shows the increase from rounding 27 to 30, and the color region shows the decrease from rounding 63 to 60. Since the gray region is larger than the color region, the estimate is greater than the actual product.

Figure 3.20

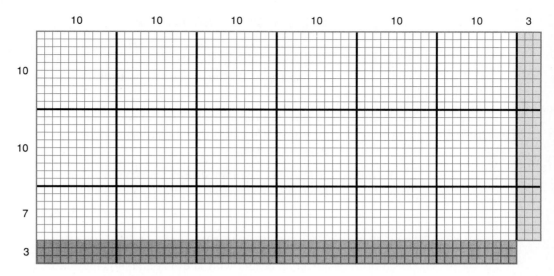

COMPATIBLE NUMBERS Using compatible numbers becomes a powerful tool for estimating products when it is combined with techniques for performing mental calculations. For example, to compute 4 × 237 × 26, we might replace 26 by 25 and use a different combination of numbers.

$$4 \times 237 \times 26 \approx 4 \times 25 \times 237 = 100 \times 237 = 23{,}700$$

EXAMPLE J

Use compatible numbers and mental calculations to compute these products.

1. 2 × 117 × 49   2. 34 × 46 × 3

Solution

1. 2 × 117 × 49 ≈ 2 × 117 × 50 = 100 × 117 = 11,700
2. 34 × 46 × 3 = (3 × 34) × 46 ≈ 100 × 46 = 4600

FRONT-END ESTIMATION This technique is similar to that used for computing sums: the leading digits are used to obtain partial products. One way to estimate 43 × 72 is to multiply the tens digits; 4 × 7 = 28 (hundreds), producing an estimate of 2800. This is one of the 4 partial products. A closer approximation can be obtained by using 2 more partial products—those involving combinations of tens and units digits. Here are 3 of the 4 partial products:

72   72   72
   28 (hundreds)   8 (tens)   21 (tens)
×43   ×43   ×43

(a)   (b)   (c)

The partial sums from (b) and (c) produce 29 (tens), or approximately 30 (tens) = 300, so the estimate can be adjusted upward to 2800 + 300 = 3100.

EXAMPLE K

Use front-end estimation to calculate these products mentally.

1. 64 × 23   2. 58 × 17

Solution

1. 64 × 23 ≈ 1200, using the tens digits. With a combination of tens and units digits, the estimate becomes 1200 + 18 (tens) + 8 (tens) = 1460.
2. 58 × 17 ≈ 500, using the tens digits. This estimate is far too low and can be improved by using the products of tens and units digits: 500 + 35 (tens) + 8 (tens) = 500 + 43 (tens) = 930.

ORDER OF OPERATIONS

Special care must be taken on some calculators when multiplication is combined with addition or subtraction. The numbers and operations will not always produce the correct answer if they are entered into the calculator in the order in which they appear.

EXAMPLE L

Compute 3 + 4 × 5 by entering the numbers into your calculator as they appear from left to right.

Solution   Some calculators will display 35, and others will display 23. The correct answer is 23 because multiplication should be performed before addition:

$$3 + 4 \times 5 = 3 + 20 = 23$$

To avoid confusion, mathematicians have developed the convention that when multiplication occurs with addition and/or subtraction, the multiplication should be performed first. This rule is called **order of operations.**

order of operations

Some calculators are programmed to follow the order of operations. On this type of calculator, any combination of products with sums and differences can be computed by entering the numbers and operations in the order in which they occur from left to right and then pressing the equals key. If a calculator does not follow the order of operations, the products can be computed separately and recorded by hand or saved in the calculator memory.

EXAMPLE M

Use your calculator to evaluate 34 × 19 + 82 × 43. Then check the reasonableness of your answer by rounding and mental calculations.

Solution   The exact answer is 4172. An estimate can be obtained as follows:

$$34 \times 19 + 82 \times 43 \approx 30 \times 20 + 80 \times 40 = 600 + 3200 = 3800$$

Notice that the estimation in Example M is 372 less than the actual product. However, it is useful in judging the reasonableness of the product computed by the calculator: it indicates that the calculator answer is most likely correct. If the numbers are entered into a calculator as they appear from left to right and the calculator is not programmed to follow the order of operations, then the following incorrect result will be obtained:

$$34 \times 19 + 82 \times 43 = 646 + 82 \times 43 = 728 \times 43 = 31,304$$

which is too large by approximately 27,000.

PROBLEM-SOLVING APPLICATION

There is an easy method for mentally computing products of certain two-digit numbers. A few of these products are shown here.

25 × 25 = 625	24 × 26 = 624	71 × 79 = 5609
37 × 33 = 1221	35 × 35 = 1225	75 × 75 = 5625

The following problem reveals the method of computing and uses *rectangular grids* to show why the method works.

■PROBLEM

What is the method of mental calculation for computing the products of the two-digit numbers shown on the previous page, and why does this method work?

Understanding the Problem   There are patterns in the digits in these products. One pattern is that the two numbers in each pair have the same first digit. Find another pattern. What types of two-digit numbers are being used?

Question 1

Devising a Plan   Looking for patterns may help you to find the types of numbers and the method of computing. Another approach is to represent some of these products on a grid. The following grid illustrates 24 × 26; the product is the number of small squares in the rectangle. To determine this number, we can begin by counting large groups of squares. There are 6 hundreds. Explain why this grid is especially convenient for counting the number of hundreds.

Question 2

10   10   6

10

10

4

Carrying Out the Plan   Sketch grids for one or more of the products being considered in this problem. For each grid it is easy to determine the number of hundreds. This is the key to solving the problem. What is the solution to the original problem?

Question 3

Looking Back   Consider the following products of three-digit numbers:

103 × 107 = 11,021   124 × 126 = 15,624

Question 4

Is there a similar method for mentally calculating the products of certain three-digit numbers?

Answers to Questions 1–4
1. In each pair of two-digit numbers, the tens digits are equal and the sum of the units digits is 10.
2. The 2 blocks of 40 squares can be paired with the 2 blocks of 60 squares to form 2 more blocks of 100, as shown below. Then the large 20 by 30 grid represents 6 hundreds. The 4 by 6 grid in the lower right corner represents 4 × 6.

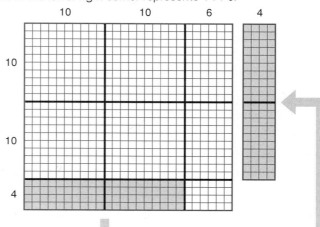

3. The first two digits of the product are formed by multiplying the tens digit times the tens digit plus 1. The remaining digits are obtained by multiplying the two units digits.

4. Yes. For 124 × 126: 12 × 13 = 156 and 4 × 6 = 24, so 124 × 126 = 15,624.

■ **H**ISTORICAL HIGHLIGHT

As late as the seventeenth century, multiplication of large numbers was a difficult task for all but professional clerks. In order to help people "do away with the difficulty and tediousness of calculations," the Scottish mathematician John Napier (1550–1617) invented a method of using rods for performing multiplication. Napier's rods—or "bones," as they are sometimes called—contain multiplication facts for each digit. For example, the rod for the 4s has 4, 8, 12, 16, 20, 24, 28, 32, and 36. This photo of a wooden set shows the fourth, seventh, and ninth rods placed together for computing products that have a factor of 479.

RELATED ACTIVITIES IN
Mathematics for Elementary Teachers: An Activity Approach, 3e

Activity Set 3.3   **Multiplying with Multibase Pieces:** Base five pieces and base ten pieces visually illustrate multiplication, place value, and regrouping.

Just for Fun   **Cross Numbers for Calculators:** Calculator exercises with clues and word problems for completing a cross-number puzzle

---

PUZZLER

Supply the missing digits in this faded document puzzle.

$$
\begin{array}{r}
4\ \square\ \square \\
\times\ \square\ \square\ 7 \\
\hline
\square\ \square\ 8\ 2 \\
1\ 2\ \square\ \square \\
\hline
\square\ \square\ \square\ \square\ \square\ \square
\end{array}
$$

EXERCISES AND PROBLEMS 3.3

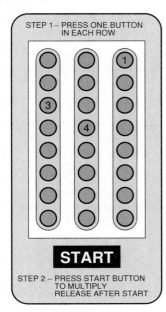

STEP 1 – PRESS ONE BUTTON
IN EACH ROW

START

STEP 2 – PRESS START BUTTON
TO MULTIPLY
RELEASE AFTER START

An exhibit illustrating multiplication at
the California Museum of Science and
Industry

1. The children in the picture above are computing products of 3
numbers from 1 through 8. Each time 3 buttons are pressed on
the switch box, the product is illustrated by lighted bulbs in the
8 by 8 by 8 cube of bulbs. Buttons 3, 4, and 1 are for the product
$3 \times 4 \times 1$. The 12 bulbs in the upper left corner of the cube
will be lighted for this product, as shown in the following figure.
Whenever the third number of the product is 1, the first 2 numbers determine the rectangular array of lighted bulbs on the
front face of the cube (facing children).

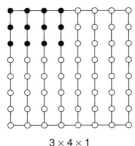

$3 \times 4 \times 1$

Describe the bulbs that will be lighted for the products in parts
a and b.

a. $7 \times 3 \times 1$ **b.** $2 \times 8 \times 1$

The third number in the product determines the number of
times the array on the front face is repeated in the cube. The
24 bulbs in the upper left corner of the next figure will be
lighted for the product $3 \times 4 \times 2$.

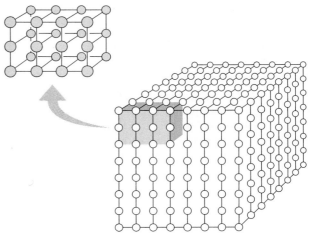

Describe the bulbs that will be lighted for the products in
parts c and d.

c. $6 \times 4 \times 3$ **d.** $1 \times 8 \times 8$

2. Sketch a new set of base ten pieces for each product below, and
show regrouping.
   a. Multiply 247 by 2.

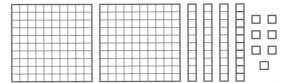

b. Multiply 38 by 5.

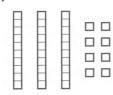

3. Multiplication of whole numbers can be illustrated on a number line by a series of arrows. This number line shows 4 × 2.

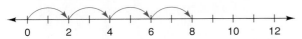

Draw arrow diagrams for the products in parts a and b.

a. 3 × 4   **b.** 2 × 5

c. Use the number line to show that 3 × 4 = 4 × 3.

4. *Error analysis.* Students who know their basic multiplication facts may still have trouble with the steps in the pencil-and-paper multiplication algorithm. Try to detect the type of error in each of the following computations.

a.
$$\begin{array}{r} {\scriptstyle 2} \\ 27 \\ \times\ 4 \\ \hline 48 \end{array}$$

b.
$$\begin{array}{r} {\scriptstyle 2} \\ 18 \\ \times\ 3 \\ \hline 34 \end{array}$$

c.
$$\begin{array}{r} {\scriptstyle 4} \\ 54 \\ \times\ 6 \\ \hline 342 \end{array}$$

d.
$$\begin{array}{r} {\scriptstyle 1} \\ 34 \\ \times 24 \\ \hline 76 \end{array}$$

In problems 5 and 6, use rectangular grids to illustrate the partial products that occur when these products are computed with pencil and paper. Draw arrows from each partial product to its corresponding region on the grid. (You may want to copy the base ten grid from the inside cover to use in the problems.)

5. a.
$$\begin{array}{r} 24 \\ \times\ 7 \\ \hline \end{array}$$
b.
$$\begin{array}{r} 56 \\ \times 73 \\ \hline \end{array}$$

6. a.
$$\begin{array}{r} 84 \\ \times 26 \\ \hline \end{array}$$
b.
$$\begin{array}{r} 39 \\ \times 47 \\ \hline \end{array}$$

7. Which number property is being used in each of the following equalities?
   a. 3 × (2 × 7 + 1) = 3 × (7 × 2 + 1)
   b. 18 + (43 × 7) × 9 = 18 + 43 × (7 × 9)
   c. (12 + 17) × (16 + 5)
      = (12 + 17) × 16 + (12 + 17) × 5
   d. (13 + 22) × (7 + 5) = (13 + 22) × (5 + 7)
   e. (15 × 2 + 9) + 3 = 15 × 2 + (9 + 3)

8. Determine whether the operation is closed for the given set.
   a. Multiplication on the set of even numbers
   b. Multiplication on the set of whole numbers less than 1000
   c. Multiplication on the set of whole numbers greater than 1000

9. Compute the exact products mentally using compatible numbers. Explain your method.
   a. 2 × 83 × 50   **b.** 5 × 3 × 2 × 7
   c. 4 × 2 × 25 × 5   **d.** 5 × 17 × 20

10. Compute the exact products mentally using the fact that multiplication distributes over addition. Show your use of the distributive property.
    a. 18 × 11   **b.** 25 × 12   **c.** 14 × 102

11. Compute the exact products mentally using the fact that multiplication distributes over subtraction. Show your use of the distributive property.
    a. 35 × 19   **b.** 51 × 9   **c.** 30 × 99

12. Use the method of equal products to find numbers that are more convenient for making exact mental calculations. Show the new products that replace the original products.
    a. 24 × 25   **b.** 35 × 60
    c. 16 × 6   **d.** 36 × 5

13. Round the numbers below and mentally estimate the products. Show the rounded numbers and predict whether the estimated products are greater than or less than the actual products. Explain any adjustments you make to improve the estimates.
    a. 22 × 17   **b.** 83 × 31
    c. 71 × 56   **d.** 205 × 29

14. Use compatible numbers and mental calculations to estimate the products. Show your compatible number replacements and predict whether the estimated products are greater than or less than the actual products.
    a. 4 × 76 × 24   **b.** 3 × 34 × 162
    c. 5 × 19 × 74   **d.** 2 × 63 × 2 × 26

15. Estimate the products using front-end estimation and mental calculations. Show two estimates for each product: one using only the tens digits and one using combinations of the tens and units digits.
    a. 36 × 58   **b.** 42 × 27
    c. 62 × 83   **d.** 14 × 62

16. Round the given numbers and estimate each product. Then sketch a rectangular array for the actual product, and on the same figure sketch the rectangular array for the product of the rounded numbers. Shade the regions that show increases and/or decreases due to rounding. (You may want to copy the base ten grid from the inside cover to use on these problems.)
    a. 18 × 62   **b.** 43 × 29
    c. 17 × 28   **d.** 53 × 31

17. Circle the operations in each expression that should be performed first. Estimate each expression mentally and show your method of estimating. Use a calculator to obtain an exact answer and compare this answer to your estimate.
    a. 62 × 45 + 14 × 29   **b.** 36 − 18 × 40 + 15
    c. 114 × 238 − 19 × 605   **d.** 73 − 50 + 17 × 62

18. Estimate the second factor so that the product will fall within the given range. Check your answer with a calculator. Count the number of tries it takes you to land in the range.

	Product	Range
Example	22 × ———	(900, 1000)
	22 × 40 = 880	Too small
	22 × 43 = 946	In the range in two tries

	Product	Range
a.	32 × ———	(800, 850)
b.	95 × ———	(1650, 1750)
c.	103 × ———	(2800, 2900)
d.	76 × ———	(3500, 3600)

19. Consider Figure 3.16 (page 90). There are many patterns in the multiplication table that can be useful in memorizing the basic multiplication facts.
  a. What patterns can you see?
  b. There are several patterns for products involving a factor of 9. Find two of these patterns.

20. A student opened her math book and computed the product of the numbers of the two facing pages. If the product was 68,906, what were the two page numbers?

21. Harry can buy a secondhand car for $2500 cash or pay $500 down and $155 a month for 2 years. How much more will the car cost if he pays for it over a two-year period?

22. Kathy has read 288 pages of her 603-page book. If she reads 35 pages each day, how long will it be before she finishes the book?

23. A store carries 5 styles of backpacks in 4 different sizes. How many backpacks would a person have to look at if he wanted to try all the possibilities?

Featured Strategy: Making an Organized List

24. The 5 tags shown below are placed in a box and mixed. Three tags are then selected at a time. If a player's score is the product of the numbers, how many different scores are possible?

  a. **Understanding the Problem** The problem asks for the number of different scores, so each score can be counted only once. The tags 6, 5, and 1 produce a score of 30. Find three other tags that produce a score of 30.
  b. **Devising a Plan** One method of solving the problem is to form an organized list. If we begin the list with the number 3, there are 6 different possibilities for sets of 3 tags. List these 6 possibilities.

  c. **Carrying Out the Plan** Continue listing the different sets of 3 tags and computing the products. How many different scores are there?
  d. **Looking Back** A different type of organized list can be formed by considering the scores between 6 (the smallest score) and 90 (the greatest score). For example, 7, 8, and 9 can be quickly thrown out. Why?

25. There is a system of finger positions for computing the products of numbers from 6 to 10. Here are the positions for the digits from 6 to 10.

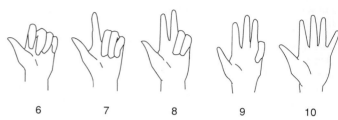

The two numbers that are to be multiplied are each represented on a different hand. The sum of the raised fingers is the number of 10s, and the product of the closed fingers is the number of 1s.
  a. Explain how the position illustrated below shows that 7 × 8 = 56.

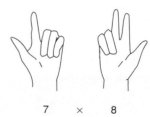

  b. Describe the positions of the fingers for 7 × 6. Does the method work for this product?

26. One of the popular schemes used for multiplying in the fifteenth century is called the **lattice method.** The two numbers to be multiplied, 4826 and 57 in this example, are written above and to the right of the lattice. The partial products are written in the cells. The sums of numbers along the diagonal cells, beginning at the lower right, form the product 275,082.

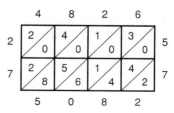

Use the lattice method to compute these products.

a. 34 × 78   **b.** 306 × 923

*COMPUTER
INVESTIGATION*

The computer program NUMBER
CHAINS on the *Computer Problem-
Solving Disc* prints a number chain by
multiplying the units digit by any
number you choose and then adding
the tens digit.

The following task was given to an
elementary school class for practice in
multiplication. Start with a whole number
and then double its units digit and add its
tens digit to obtain a new number. Repeat
this process with each new number. The

$$2 \times 5 + 1$$
$$\downarrow$$
$$15 \rightarrow 11 \rightarrow 3 \rightarrow 6 \rightarrow 12 \rightarrow 5 \rightarrow 10 \rightarrow 1 \rightarrow 2$$
$$\downarrow$$
$$15 \leftarrow 17 \leftarrow 18 \leftarrow 9 \leftarrow 14 \leftarrow 7 \leftarrow 13 \leftarrow 16 \leftarrow 8 \leftarrow 4$$

number chain shown here starts and ends
with 15. A number chain is complete
when any previous number of the chain is
repeated.

Questions for Investigation
1. This number chain has all the whole
   numbers from 1 to 18. What happens
   if we begin the number chain with 19?
   with a number greater than 19?

2. Suppose that instead of doubling the
   units digit we multiply it by 3 (or any
   greater number) and then add the tens
   digit. Will a number chain be
   produced?

3. What patterns exist and what
   conjectures can be made about number
   chains?

PUZZLER

A cryptarithm is a puzzle in which letters
are substituted for digits (0, 1, 2, 3, 4, 5,
6, 7, 8, 9). What are the digits in these
multiplication cryptarithms?

```
      ST              CDE
   ×  RT           ×   ED
      ST            CCEED
     PQR
    PTTT
```

SECTION 3.4   DIVISION AND EXPONENTS

■ PROBLEM OPENER

Using exactly 4 fours and
only addition, subtraction,
multiplication, and
division, write an
expression that equals
each of the numbers from
1 to 10. You do not have
to use all the operations,
and numbers such as 44
are permitted.*

General Motors Terex Titan and
Chevrolet Luv pickup.

One common use of division is to compare two quantities. In the photo above, consider
the relative sizes of the Terex Titan dump truck and the Luv pickup, which is on the
Titan's dump body. The Terex Titan can carry 317,250 kilograms; the Luv pickup has

*Similar equations exist for 5 fives, 6 sixes, etc. See R. Crouse and J. Shuttleworth, ''Playing with Numerals,''
Arithmetic Teacher 21, no. 5 (May 1974): 417–419.

a limit of 450 kilograms. We can determine how many times greater the Titan's capacity is than the Luv's by dividing 317,250 by 450. The answer is 705, which means the Luv pickup will have to haul 705 loads to fill the Titan just once! Sitting in the back of the Luv pickup is a child holding a toy truck. If the toy truck holds 3 kilograms of sand, how many of its loads will be required to fill the Titan?

The division operations used in comparing the sizes of the Terex Titan and the Luv pickup can be checked by multiplication. The load weight of the smaller truck times 705 should equal the load weight of the larger truck. The close relationship between division and multiplication can be used to define division in terms of multiplication.

DIVISION OF WHOLE NUMBERS

> For any whole numbers r and s, with $s \neq 0$, the quotient of r divided by s, written $r \div s$, is the whole number k, if it exists, such that $r = s \times k$.

EXAMPLE A

Mentally calculate each quotient.

   1. $18 \div 3$ 2. $24 \div 6$ 3. $35 \div 5$

Solution

   1. $18 \div 3 = 6$ since $18 = 3 \times 6$
   2. $24 \div 6 = 4$ since $24 = 6 \times 4$
   3. $35 \div 5 = 7$ since $35 = 5 \times 7$

The definition of division, along with Example A, shows why multiplication and division are called inverse operations. We arrive at basic division facts by knowing basic multiplication facts.

dividend
divisor
quotient

There are three basic terms used in describing the division process: dividend, divisor, and quotient. In problem (1) of Example A, 18 is the **dividend,** 3 is the **divisor,** and 6 is the **quotient.** Over the centuries, division has acquired two meanings or uses. David Eugene Smith, in *History of Mathematics,* speaks of the twofold nature of division and refers to the sixteenth-century authors who first clarified the differences between its two meanings.* These two meanings of division, known as partitive (sharing) and measurement (subtractive), are illustrated in the following examples.

EXAMPLE B

Suppose you had 24 tennis balls, which you wanted to divide equally among 3 people. How many tennis balls would each person receive?

Solution

The answer can be determined by separating (partitioning) the tennis balls into 3 equivalent sets. The following figure shows 24 balls divided into 3 groups and illustrates $24 \div 3$. The divisor, 3, indicates the number of groups. This problem

partitive (sharing) concept

illustrates the **partitive (sharing) concept** of division.

---

*D. E. Smith, *History of Mathematics*, 2nd ed. (Lexington, MA: Ginn, 1925), 130.

EXAMPLE C

Suppose you had 24 tennis balls and wanted to give 3 tennis balls to as many people as possible. How many people would receive tennis balls?

Solution   The answer can be determined by subtracting away, or measuring off, as many sets of 3 as possible. The next figure shows the result of this measuring process and illustrates 24 ÷ 3. The divisor, 3, is the number of balls in each group, and the quotient, 8, is the number of groups. This problem illustrates the **measurement (subtractive) concept** of division.

measurement (subtractive) concept

MODELS FOR DIVISION ALGORITHMS

long division   Of the four basic pencil-and-paper algorithms, the algorithm for division, called **long division,** is the most difficult and has traditionally required the most classroom time to master. As the use of calculators in schools increases, long division, especially for three- and four-digit numbers, will be de-emphasized. However, an understanding of division and of algorithms for determining quotients will remain important for mental calculations, estimation, and problem solving.

There are several physical models for illustrating division. Base ten pieces are used in the following examples.

EXAMPLE D

Compute 48 ÷ 4 by sketching base ten pieces.

Solution   1. One possibility is to use the partitive (sharing) concept of division, placing 1 long in each of 4 groups and then 2 units in each group, as shown in the following figure. The *size* of each group, 12, is the quotient of 48 ÷ 4.

2. Another approach is to use the measurement (subtractive) concept of division to form as many groups of 4 units as possible. In this case there are 12 groups of 4 units each, as shown in the next figure. The *number* of groups, 12, is the quotient of 48 ÷ 4.

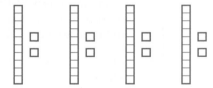

3. A third possibility is to use 4 longs and 8 units to form a rectangular array with one dimension of 4, as shown next. The other dimension is 12, the quotient of 48 ÷ 4.

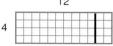

Notice in solution (3) of Example D that by viewing the rectangular array as 4 rows of 12 units each, we are making use of the partitive concept of division, and by viewing the array as 12 columns of 4 units each, we are making use of the measurement concept of division.

Let's see how base ten pieces can be used to illustrate the steps in the long division algorithm.

EXAMPLE E

This example illustrates 378 ÷ 3 using the partitive concept of division. Four steps are described. In each step, as the base ten pieces are divided into groups, the groups are matched to the quotient of the long division algorithm.

Step 1. Begin with 3 flats, 7 longs, and 8 units to represent 378.

Step 2. Partition the flats by placing 1 flat in each of 3 groups. This leaves 7 longs and 8 units.

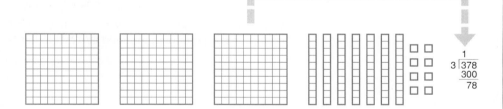

Step 3. Partition the longs by placing 2 longs in each of the 3 groups, leaving 1 long and 8 units.

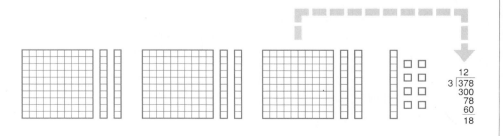

Step 4. Partition the units by placing 6 units in each of the 3 groups. To accomplish this, regroup the remaining long into 10 units.

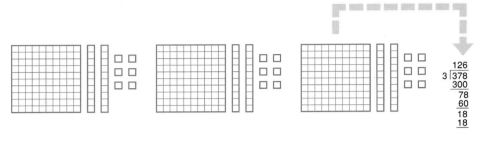

```
       126
  3 ⟌ 378
       300
        78
        60
        18
        18
```

Notice that each of the final groups of base ten pieces represents the quotient, 126.

For small divisors as in Example E, the sharing concept of division is practical because the number of groups is small. For larger divisors, rectangular arrays are convenient. In recent years, the rectangular array approach to illustrating division has become more common.

EXAMPLE F

This example illustrates 336 ÷ 12 using a rectangular array. Three steps are described, and each step is related to the quotient of the long division algorithm.

Step 1. Begin with 3 flats, 3 longs, and 6 units to represent 336.

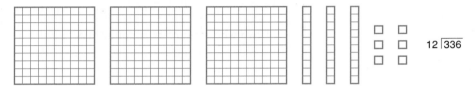

```
  12 ⟌ 336
```

Step 2. Start building a rectangle with one dimension of 12. This can be done by beginning with 1 flat and 2 longs. Then a second flat and 2 more longs can be added on by regrouping the third flat into 10 longs. This leaves 9 longs and 6 units.

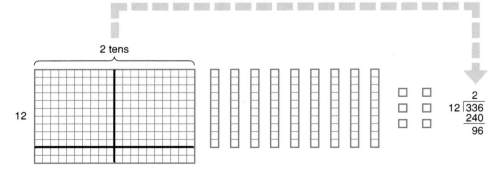

```
         2
  12 ⟌ 336
       240
        96
```

Step 3. Continue building the rectangle by extending it with the remaining 9 longs and 6 units. To accomplish this, regroup one of the longs into 10 units.

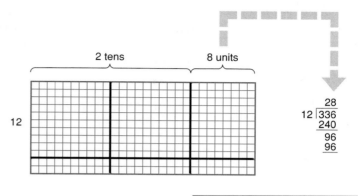

2 tens   8 units

12

$$
\begin{array}{r}
28 \\
12\overline{)336} \\
240 \\
\hline
96 \\
96 \\
\hline
\end{array}
$$

The final dimension of the rectangle in Example F is 28, the quotient of $336 \div 12$. Notice that the rectangular array illustration of division is a visual reminder of the close relationship between division and multiplication: the product of the two dimensions, 12×28, is 336, the number represented by the original set of base ten pieces.

DIVISION ALGORITHM

We have seen that the sum or product of two whole numbers is always another whole number and that this fact is called the closure property. Subtraction and division of whole numbers, on the other hand, are not closed. That is, the difference or quotient of two whole numbers is not always another whole number.

EXAMPLE G

1. $12 - 15$ is not a whole number because there is no whole number c such that $12 = 15 + c$.
2. $38 \div 7$ is not a whole number because there is no whole number k such that $38 = 7 \times k$.

There are times when we want to solve problems involving division of whole numbers even though the quotient is not a whole number. In the case of $38 \div 7$, we can determine the greatest whole number quotient (q) and the remainder (r).

$$
38 = 7 \times \overset{q}{5} + \overset{r}{3}
$$

Notice that the remainder 3 is less than the divisor 7. The fact that such numbers q and r always exist is guaranteed by the following theorem.

DIVISION ALGORITHM

For any whole numbers a and b, with $b \neq 0$, there are whole numbers q and r such that

$$
a = bq + r
$$

and $0 \leq r < b$.

remainder   This theorem says that the **remainder** r is always less than the divisor b. If $r = 0$, then we have the case in which the quotient $a \div b$ is the whole number q.

EXAMPLE H

Compute each quotient, if possible. Otherwise, find the greatest whole number quotient and the remainder.

1. $50 \div 4$ 2. $90 \div 15$ 3. $27{,}094 \div 7$

Solution

1. $50 \div 4$ is not a whole number. The greatest whole number quotient is 12, and the remainder is 2.
2. $90 \div 15 = 6$
3. $27{,}094 \div 7$ is not a whole number. The greatest whole number quotient is 3870, and the remainder is 4.

If $27{,}094 \div 7$ is computed on a calculator, the display will show 3870.5714, which has the whole number quotient 3870 and a decimal. The remainder can be found by computing $27{,}094 - 7 \times 3870$. Some calculators that are especially designed for school children will compute the quotient of two whole numbers and display the remainder as a whole number.*

MENTAL CALCULATIONS

A major strategy in performing mental calculations is replacing a problem by one that can be solved more easily. This approach was used in sections 3.2 and 3.3 for mentally calculating sums, differences, and products; it is described here for division.

equal quotients

EQUAL QUOTIENTS   In calculating a quotient mentally, sometimes it is helpful to use the method of **equal quotients,** in which we divide both the divisor and the dividend by the same number.

EXAMPLE I

The quotient $144 \div 18$ can be replaced by $72 \div 9$ by dividing both 144 and 18 by 2. We know from our basic multiplication facts that $9 \times 8 = 72$, so

$$144 \div 18 = 72 \div 9 = 8$$

Figure 3.21 visually illustrates why both numbers in a quotient can be divided by 2 without changing the quotient. The rectangular array in part (a) of the figure represents $144 \div 18$, and the quotient is the dimension 8. Cutting the rectangle into 2 equal parts at line h divides both the total number of units (144) and one dimension (18) in half, producing the smaller rectangle in part (b) of the figure, with 72 units and a dimension of 9. Notice that the second dimension of the small rectangle (8) is also the second dimension of the original rectangle, and this number is the quotient of both $144 \div 18$ and $72 \div 9$.

---

*Texas Instruments' calculator, the Math Explorer, is described in *It's About T.I.M.E.*, Vol. 1, no. 1 (Lubbock, TX: Texas Instruments, 1989).

Figure 3.21

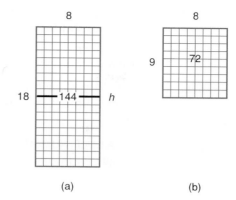

(a)   (b)

The halving process can be carried out several times to replace the numbers in a quotient by smaller numbers. It is also permissible to divide the divisor and dividend by 3, 4, or any other number that divides into both numbers a whole number of times.

EXAMPLE J

Replace each quotient by equal quotients until you can calculate the answer mentally.

1. $180 \div 12$
2. $900 \div 36$
3. $336 \div 48$

Solution   Here are three solutions. Others are possible.

1. $180 \div 12 = 60 \div 4 = 15$ (Divide by 3)
2. $900 \div 36 = 300 \div 12 = 100 \div 4 = 25$ (Divide by 3 twice)
3. $336 \div 48 = 112 \div 16 = 56 \div 8 = 7$ (Divide by 3, then by 2)

ESTIMATION OF QUOTIENTS

ROUNDING   Often we wish to obtain a rough comparison of two quantities in order to determine how many times bigger (or smaller) one is than the other. This may require finding an estimation for a quotient. Rounding numbers is one method of estimating a quotient.

EXAMPLE K

Estimate each quotient by rounding one or both numbers.

1. $472 \div 46$
2. $145 \div 23$
3. $8145 \div 195$

Solution   Here are some possibilities.

1. $472 \div 46 \approx 460 \div 46 = 10$ or $472 \div 46 \approx 500 \div 50 = 10$
2. $145 \div 23 \approx 150 \div 25 = 6$
3. $8145 \div 195 \approx 8000 \div 200 = 40$

Rounding to obtain an approximate quotient can be combined with the process of finding equal quotients (dividing both the divisor and the dividend by the same number).

EXAMPLE L

Find approximations by using rounding and equal quotients.

1. $427 \div 72$
2. $139 \div 18$

Solution

1. $427 \div 72 \approx 430 \div 70 = 43 \div 7 \approx 6$
2. $139 \div 18 \approx 140 \div 18 = 70 \div 9 \approx 8$

COMPATIBLE NUMBERS   Replacing numbers with compatible numbers is a **useful** technique for mentally calculating quotients.

EXAMPLE M

Find one or two compatible numbers to replace the given numbers **and mentally** calculate the quotient.

1. $92 \div 9$
2. $59 \div 16$
3. $485 \div 24$

Solution

Here is one possibility for each quotient.

1. $92 \div 9 \approx 90 \div 9 = 10$
2. $59 \div 16 \approx 60 \div 15 = 4$
3. $485 \div 24 \approx 500 \div 25 = 20$

FRONT-END ESTIMATION   In this technique the leading digits are used to obtain an estimation.

EXAMPLE N

Obtain an approximate quotient by using the leading digits in the divisor and the dividend.

1. $828 \div 210$
2. $7218 \div 2036$
3. $4128 \div 216$

Solution

1. $828 \div 210 \approx 8 \div 2 = 4$
2. $7218 \div 2036 \approx 7 \div 2 = 3\frac{1}{2}$
3. $4128 \div 216 \approx 41 \div 2 = 20\frac{1}{2}$

Notice that in Example N we used two leading digits in 4128 but only one leading digit in 216. By disregarding the ones and tens digits in both 4128 and 216, we kept the leading digits comparable. That is, we divided 41 tens by 2 tens to obtain an estimate of $20\frac{1}{2}$.

EXPONENTS

The large numbers used today were rarely needed a few centuries ago. The word "billion," which is now commonplace, was not adopted until the seventeenth century. Even now, a billion means different things to different people. In the United States it represents 1,000,000,000 (a thousand million), and in England it is 1,000,000,000,000 (a million million).

Our numbers are named according to powers of 10. The first, second, and third powers of 10 are the familiar ten, hundred, and thousand. After this, only every third power of 10 has a new or special name: million, billion, trillion, etc.

10^0	$= 1$	one
10^1	$= 10$	ten
10^2	$= 100$	one hundred
10^3	$= 1000$	**one thousand**
10^4	$= 10,000$	ten thousand
10^5	$= 100,000$	one hundred thousand
10^6	$= 1,000,000$	**one million**
10^7	$= 10,000,000$	ten million
10^8	$= 100,000,000$	one hundred million
10^9	$= 1,000,000,000$	**one billion**
10^{10}	$= 10,000,000,000$	ten billion
10^{11}	$= 100,000,000,000$	one hundred billion
10^{12}	$= 1,000,000,000,000$	**one trillion**

exponentiation

The operation of raising numbers to a power is called **exponentiation.**

EXPONENTIATION

For any number *b* and any whole number *n,* with *b* and *n* not both zero,

$$b^n = b \times b \times b \times b \times \cdots \times b$$

b occurs *n* times

where *b* is called the **base** and *n* is called the **exponent.** In case $n = 0$ or $n = 1$, $b^0 = 1$ and $b^1 = b.$

EXAMPLE O

Evaluate each expression.

1. 3^4 2. 2^5
3. 5^0 4. 3^1

Solution   1. 81   2. 32
3. 1   4. 3

exponential form
*n*th power

A number written in the form b^n is said to be in **exponential form.** In general, the number b^n is called the ***n*th power** of *b;* b^2 and b^3 are usually called *b* squared and *b* cubed. This terminology was inherited from the ancient Greeks, who pictured numbers as geometric arrays of dots. Figure 3.22 illustrates 2^2, a 2 by 2 array of dots in the form of a square, and 2^3, a 2 by 2 by 2 array of dots in the form of a cube.

Figure 3.22

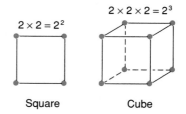

perfect squares

Numbers that can be written as nonzero whole numbers squared are called **perfect squares** (1, 4, 9, 16, 25, . . .), and numbers that can be written as nonzero whole num-

perfect cubes

bers cubed are called **perfect cubes** (1, 8, 27, 64, 125, . . .).

LAWS OF EXPONENTS   Multiplication and division can be performed easily with numbers that are written as powers of the same base. To multiply, we add the exponents, and to divide, we subtract the exponents.

EXAMPLE P

Evaluate each product or quotient. Write the answer in both exponential form and positional numeration.

1. $2^4 \times 2^3$ 2. $2^8 \div 2^3$

Solution

1. $2^4 \times 2^3 = (2 \times 2 \times 2 \times 2) \times (2 \times 2 \times 2) = 2^7 = 128$

2. $2^8 \div 2^3 = \dfrac{2 \times 2 \times 2 \times 2 \times 2 \times 2 \times 2 \times 2}{2 \times 2 \times 2} = 2^5 = 32$

The equations in Example P are special cases of the following rules for computing with exponents.

LAWS OF EXPONENTS

For any number a and all whole numbers m and n, except for the case where the base and exponents are both zero,

$$a^n \times a^m = a^{n+m}$$

$$a^n \div a^m = a^{n-m}, \quad \text{for } a \neq 0.$$

The primary advantage of exponents is their compactness, which makes them convenient for computing with very large numbers and (as we shall see in Chapter 6) very small numbers.

EXAMPLE Q

1. In our galaxy there are 10^{11} (100 billion) stars, and in the observable universe there are 10^9 (1 billion) galaxies. If every galaxy had as many stars as ours, there would be $10^9 \times 10^{11}$ stars. Write this product in exponential form.
2. If 1 out of every 1000 stars had a planetary system, there would be $10^{20} \div 10^3$ stars with planetary systems. Write this quotient in exponential form.
3. If 1 out of every 1000 stars with a planetary system had a planet with conditions suitable for life, there would be $10^{17} \div 10^3$ such stars. Write this quotient in exponential form.

Solution   1. 10^{20} 2. 10^{17} 3. 10^{14}

CALCULATORS   Numbers raised to a power can be computed on a calculator, provided the calculator displays numbers in scientific notation or the numbers do not exceed the capacity of the calculator's display. On most calculators the steps shown in Figure 3.23 will produce the number represented by 4^{10}, if the process is carried out to step 10.

Figure 3.23

Steps	Display
1. Enter 4	4.
2. ☒ 4 =	16.
3. ☒ 4 =	64.
4. ☒ 4 =	256.

The number of steps in the process can be decreased by applying the rule for adding exponents: $a^n \times a^m = a^{n+m}$. To compute 4^{10}, first compute 4^5 on the calculator and then multiply the result, 1024, by itself.

$$4^{10} = 4^5 \times 4^5 = 1024 \times 1024 = 1,048,576$$

Some calculators have exponential buttons for evaluating numbers raised to a power. To compute a number y to some exponential power x, enter the base y into the calculator first, then press the exponential button y^x, and then enter the exponent x. The steps in evaluating 4^{10} are shown in Figure 3.24.

Figure 3.24

Steps	Display
1. Enter 4 (base)	4.
2. $\boxed{y^x}$	4.
3. Enter 10 (exponent)	10.
4. $\boxed{=}$	1048576.

Numbers that are raised to powers will frequently be too long for the calculator display. If you try to compute 4^{15} on a calculator with only 8 places in its display, there will not be room for the answer in positional numeration. Some calculators will automatically convert to scientific notation when numbers in positional numeration are too large for the display (see Section 6.3).

ORDER OF OPERATIONS

The concept of order of operations, discussed in Section 3.3, can now be extended to include division and raising numbers to powers. The order of operations requires that numbers raised to a power be evaluated first; then products and quotients are computed in the order in which they occur from left to right; finally, sums and differences are calculated in the order in which they occur from left to right. An exception to the rule occurs when numbers are written in parentheses. In this case, computations within parentheses should be carried out first.

EXAMPLE R

Evaluate the following expressions.

1. $4 \times 6 + 16 \div 2^3$
2. $4 \times (6 + 16) \div 2^3$
3. $220 - 12 \times 7 + 15 \div 3$
4. $24 \div 4 \times 2 + 15$

Solution

1. 26 (First replace 2^3 by 8; then compute the product and quotient; then add.)
2. 11 (First replace $6 + 16$ by 22; then replace 2^3 by 8; then compute the product and quotient.)
3. 141 (First replace 12×7 by 84 and $15 \div 3$ by 5; then compute the difference and sum.)
4. 27 (First compute $24 \div 4$; then multiply by 2; then add 15.)

Calculators that are programmed to follow the order of operations are very convenient for computing expressions involving several different operations. You may wish to try problem (3) in Example R on your calculator, entering in the numbers and operations as they appear from left to right and then pressing the equality key, to see if you obtain 141.

PROBLEM-SOLVING APPLICATION

The following problem involves numbers in exponential form and is solved using the strategies of *making a table* and *finding a pattern*.

■ PROBLEM

There is a legend that chess was invented for the Indian king Shirham by the grand vizier Sissa Ben Dahir. As a reward, Sissa asked to be given 1 grain of wheat for the first square of the chess board, 2 grains for the second square, 4 grains for the third square, then 8 grains, 16 grains, etc., until each square of the board had been accounted for. The king was surprised at such a meager request until Sissa informed him that this was more wheat than existed in the entire kingdom. What would be the sum of all the grains of wheat for the 64 squares of the chess board?

Understanding the Problem The numbers of grains for the first few squares are shown in the following figure.

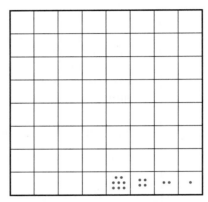

The numbers 1, 2, 4, 8, 16, 32, . . . form a geometric sequence whose common ratio is 2. Sometimes it is convenient to express these numbers as powers of 2.

$$1 \quad 2 \quad 2^2 \quad 2^3 \quad 2^4 \quad 2^5 \quad . . .$$

Question 1 How would the number of grains for the 64th square be written as a power of 2?

Devising a Plan Computing the sum of all 64 binary numbers would be a difficult task. Let's form a table for the first few sums and look for a pattern. Compute the next 3 totals in the following table. How is each total related to a power of 2?

Question 2

Square	No. of grains	Total
1	1	1
2	$1 + 2$	3
3	$1 + 2 + 2^2$	7
4	$1 + 2 + 2^2 + 2^3$	
5	$1 + 2 + 2^2 + 2^3 + 2^4$	
6	$1 + 2 + 2^2 + 2^3 + 2^4 + 2^5$	

Carrying Out the Plan Find a pattern in the preceding table and use it to express the sum of the grains for all 64 squares. What is this sum, written as a power of 2?

Question 3

Looking Back King Shirham was surprised at the total amount of grain because the number of grains for the first few squares is so small. There is more grain for each additional square than for all the preceding squares combined. Why is the number of grains for the 64th square greater than the total number of grains for the first 63 squares?

Question 4

Answers to Questions 1–4

1. 2^{63}

2. The total in each row is 1 less than a power of 2.

3. The total number of grains is $2^{64} - 1$.

4. The total number of grains for the first 63 squares is $2^{63} - 1$, but there are 2^{63} grains for the 64th square.

PUZZLER

Supply the missing digits in this faded document puzzle.

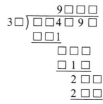

RELATED ACTIVITIES IN

Mathematics for Elementary Teachers: An Activity Approach, 3e

Activity Set 3.4   **Dividing with Base Ten Pieces:** Rectangular arrays illustrate division and the long division algorithm.

Just for Fun   **Calculator Game and Number Tricks:** A calculator keyboard game and number tricks designed for calculators

---

EXERCISES AND PROBLEMS 3.4

1. Circle groups of chips to illustrate $28 \div 7$ using each concept of division.

a. Partitive (sharing) concept

b. Measurement (subtractive) concept

2. Write each division exercise as a multiplication exercise.

a. $68 \div 17 = 4$ **b.** $414 \div 23 = 18$

c. $288 \div 8 = 36$ **d.** $a \div b = c$

3. Write each multiplication exercise as a division exercise.

a. $14 \times 24 = 336$ **b.** $9 \times 8 = 72$

c. $360 \times 10 = 3600$ **d.** $r \times s = t$

4. Find a whole number, if possible, that makes each equation true.

a. $85 \div 17 = \square$ **b.** $\square \div 13 = 14$

c. $216 \div \square = 9$ **d.** $230 \div \square = 15$

5. Illustrate each quotient using the partitive concept of division and circling groups of base ten pieces. Sketch any new pieces that are necessary to show regrouping.

a. $396 \div 3$

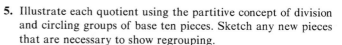

b. $76 \div 4$

6. Use base ten pieces to illustrate the long division algorithm for each quotient below. In separate steps show which base ten pieces correspond to each digit in the quotient.

a. $4\overline{)96}$ (quotient 24)   **b.** $3\overline{)426}$ (quotient 142)

7. Use a rectangular array of base ten pieces to illustrate each quotient below. (Copy the base ten grid from the inside cover.)

a. $72 \div 12$ **b.** $286 \div 26$

8. Show a rectangle that uses all of the base ten pieces listed and has the given dimension. Regrouping may be needed. Label both dimensions of the rectangle. Write a multiplication fact and a division fact illustrated by each rectangle. (Copy the base ten grid from the inside cover.)
   a. 1 flat, 1 long, and 7 units, with one dimension of 13
   b. 3 flats, 3 longs, and zero units, with one dimension of 15
   c. 5 flats, 1 long, and 8 units, with one dimension of 14

9. Below are three problems involving division and zero. The definition of division permits computation of only one of these quotients. The others are not defined. Which quotient can be computed, and what does it equal? Try these quotients on a calculator.
   a. $0 \div 4$ b. $4 \div 0$ c. $0 \div 0$

10. a. What division fact is illustrated by the arrows on this number line?

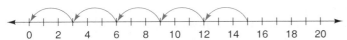

   b. Draw an arrow diagram for $16 \div 8$.

11. *Error Analysis* These examples of long division illustrate four different types of errors. Locate each error.

   a.
   ```
       56 R4
   8)4052
     40
     ──
     52
     48
     ──
      4
   ```

   b.
   ```
      68
   3)258
     24
     ──
     18
     18
     ──
   ```

   c.
   ```
     370
   7)2149
     21
     ──
     49
     49
     ──
   ```

   d.
   ```
     29 R20
   4)136
     8
     ──
     56
     36
     ──
     20
   ```

12. Compute each side of the following equation. Does the right side equal the left side? Try some other numbers in the square, rhombus, and triangle. Can you find a case in which division is not distributive over addition?

$$\left(\boxed{6} + \underline{\triangle}_{15}\right) \div \boxed{3} = \left(\boxed{6} \div \boxed{3}\right) + \left(\underline{\triangle}_{15} \div \boxed{3}\right)$$

13. Is division commutative or associative? Try some numbers in the following equations. It takes only one counterexample to show that a property does not hold.

$$\square \div \triangle \overset{?}{=} \triangle \div \square$$

$$\square \div (\triangle \div \square) \overset{?}{=} (\square \div \triangle) \div \square$$

14. Determine whether each operation below is closed or not closed on the given set.
   a. Addition on the set of odd whole numbers
   b. Division on the set of whole numbers
   c. Multiplication on the set of odd whole numbers
   d. Subtraction on the set of even whole numbers
   e. Addition on $\{0, 1\}$
   f. Multiplication on $\{0, 1\}$

15. Find the greatest whole number quotient and the remainder.
   a. $47{,}208 \div 674$ b. $2018 \div 17$
   c. $13{,}738 \div 24$ d. $107{,}253 \div 86$

16. Use the method of equal quotients to replace the divisor and the dividend in each problem below with smaller numbers. Show the new quotient that replaces the original quotient. Repeat this process, if necessary, until you can mentally calculate the exact quotient.
   a. $90 \div 18$ b. $84 \div 14$
   c. $400 \div 16$ d. $144 \div 16$

17. Round or use compatible numbers to mentally estimate the quotient. Show the new quotient and predict whether it is greater than or less than the exact quotient.
   a. $250 \div 46$ b. $82 \div 19$
   c. $486 \div 53$ d. $8145 \div 195$
   e. $203 \div 50$ f. $241 \div 31$

18. Use front-end estimation with the leading digits to mentally estimate the quotient.
   a. $623 \div 209$ b. $7218 \div 1035$
   c. $938 \div 31$ d. $5634 \div 713$

19. Which of these numbers can be displayed on your calculator in positional numeration? Before trying these on your calculator, round each base and mentally compute its square to obtain an estimation of the number of places in the number.
   a. 589^2 b. 3119^2 c. $89{,}163^2$

20. Compute these products and quotients. Leave your answers in exponential form.
   a. $5^{14} \times 5^{20}$ b. $10^{12} \times 10^{10}$
   c. $10^{32} \div 10^{15}$ d. $3^{22} \div 3^8$

21. Evaluate the following expressions.
   a. $6 + (4 \times 8) - 3$ b. $5 \times 10 - 2 \times 6$
   c. $5 \times (10 - 2) \times 6$ d. $45 \div 3 \times 5 - 2$
   e. $8 - 5 + 2 + 9$

22. The chart below shows the approximate frequencies of some common types of waves. Visible light waves, for example, have a frequency of between 10^{14} and 10^{15} waves or cycles per second.

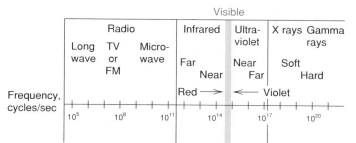

a. The frequency of television waves is 10^8 cycles per second. If a type of x ray has a frequency that is 10^{11} times greater, what is the x-ray frequency?

b. If the frequency of infrared light is 10^{13} cycles per second and it is 1000 times greater than the frequency of microwaves, what is the microwave frequency?

c. If a radio frequency is 10^8 cycles per second and gamma rays have a frequency of 10^{21} cycles per second, how many times greater is the gamma-ray frequency than the radio frequency?

23. Beneath each of the following equations is a sequence of calculator steps. Which sequences produce the correct answers?

a. $8 \times (12 \div 3) = 32$
(1) Enter 8
(2) $\boxed{\times}$
(3) Enter 12
(4) $\boxed{\div}$
(5) Enter 3
(6) $\boxed{=}$

b. $3 \times 4 + 7 = 19$
(1) Enter 3
(2) $\boxed{\times}$
(3) Enter 4
(4) $\boxed{+}$
(5) Enter 7
(6) $\boxed{=}$

c. $17 - 3 \times 5 = 2$
(1) Enter 17
(2) $\boxed{-}$
(3) Enter 3
(4) $\boxed{\times}$
(5) Enter 5
(6) $\boxed{=}$

24. Find a pattern in each of the following sets of equations, and use inductive reasoning to predict the next equation. Evaluate both sides of your new equation.

a. $1^2 + 2^2 + 2^2 = 3^2$
$2^2 + 3^2 + 6^2 = 7^2$
$3^2 + 4^2 + 12^2 = 13^2$

b. $1^3 + 2^3 = 3^2$
$1^3 + 2^3 + 3^3 = 6^2$
$1^3 + 2^3 + 3^3 + 4^3 = 10^2$

25. Suppose you had a chance to work for 22 weeks and could choose one of two methods of payment. You could choose to be paid $1 the first week, $2 the second week, $4 the third week, $8 the fourth week, etc., with the amount doubling each week, or you could choose to receive 2 million dollars in one lump sum.
a. Which method would result in the greater payment?
b. What is the difference in the amounts between these two types of payments?

Featured Strategy: Find a Pattern

26. The chart below illustrates a repeating pattern. If this pattern continues, what symbol will be in the 538th square?

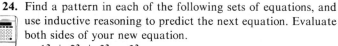

a. **Understanding the Problem** To become more familiar with the problem, extend the pattern a few more squares. What symbol will be in the 19th square?

b. **Devising a Plan** Because the pattern repeats itself after 6 squares, it is suggestive of a clock with 6 symbols. What symbol occurs in squares 6, 12, 18 etc.? Alternatively, you could think of the pattern as pieces of tile 6 squares long. To make the length 32 squares, how many tiles and squares would you need?

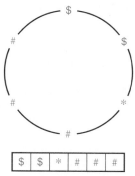

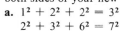

c. **Carrying Out the Plan** Choose a method for finding the symbol on the 538th square. Explain your method.

d. **Looking Back** The lengths and symbols of repeating patterns vary. What will be the 345th digit in the following number, if the pattern continues: 142,857,142,857 . . . ?

27. Look for some patterns in the following triangle of numbers.

$$
\begin{array}{rcl}
1 & = & 1 \\
3 + 5 & = & 8 \\
7 + 9 + 11 & = & 27 \\
13 + 15 + 17 + 19 & = & 64 \\
21 + 23 + 25 + 27 + 29 & = & 125
\end{array}
$$

a. What is the sixth row of this triangle and what is its sum?
b. What is the tenth row of this triangle and what is its sum?

CALCULATOR
INVESTIGATION

One student noticed that 12 divides $10^2 - 2^2$. Further investigation revealed that 23 divides $20^2 - 3^2$ and that 57 divides $50^2 - 7^2$.

Questions for Investigation
1. Will this pattern hold for other two-digit numbers?
2. Will the pattern hold if, instead of taking the difference of the squares, we take their sum? (For example, does 12 divide $10^2 + 2^2$?) Are there other two-digit numbers for which we can use the sum of the squares?
3. Will this pattern hold for three-digit numbers? (For example, does 134 divide $100^2 - 34^2$?)
4. To gain further insight into this investigation, use the distributive property to expand $(10 + 3) \times (10 - 3)$. What does this suggest?

PUZZLER

Krypto is a commercially produced game containing cards numbered from 1 through 25. The object is to combine the numbers on 5 cards that are randomly selected so as to obtain the number on a sixth card, the target number. Any of the four basic operations may be used, but each of the 5 cards must be used once and only once. How can each of the following sets of cards be used with all four operations to obtain the target number?

$$\boxed{22}\ \boxed{19}\ \boxed{2}\ \boxed{14}\ \boxed{10} \rightarrow 7$$
$$\boxed{21}\ \boxed{2}\ \boxed{3}\ \boxed{12}\ \boxed{7} \rightarrow 20$$

CHAPTER REVIEW

1. **Numeration Systems**
   a. A logically organized collection of numerals is called a **numeration system.**
   b. The number of objects used in the grouping process is called the **base.**
   c. In an **additive numeration system,** each symbol is repeated as many times as needed.
   d. The **Egyptian** and **Roman numeration systems** were additive numeration systems.
   e. In a **positional numeration system,** the position of each digit indicates a power of the base.
   f. In a base ten positional numeration system, the power of 10 associated with each digit is called its **place value.**
   g. The **Mayan** and **Hindu-Arabic numeration systems** are positional numeration systems.

2. **Reading and Rounding Numbers**
   a. Numbers with more than three digits are read by naming **periods.** Each period has three digits.
   b. The next three periods after the ones, tens, and hundreds digits are called **thousands, millions,** and **billions.**
   c. To **round** a number to the nearest million means to choose the nearest million.

3. **Models for Numeration**
   a. The **bundle-of-sticks model** and **base ten pieces** are two models for numeration systems.
   b. **Regrouping** is replacing one collection of pieces in a model by another collection that represents the same number.

4. **Whole-Number Operations**
   a. **Addition** is defined in terms of sets.
   b. **Subtraction** is defined as the inverse operation of addition.
   c. **Multiplication** is defined as repeated addition.
   d. **Division** is defined as the inverse operation of multiplication.

   e. There are two concepts of subtraction: the **take-away concept** and the **comparison concept.**
   f. There are two concepts of division: the **partitive concept** and the **measurement concept.**
   g. The operation of raising numbers to a power is called **exponentiation.**
   h. A number written in the form b^n is said to be in **exponential form;** b^n is called the *n*th **power** of b.
   i. For any whole numbers a, n, and m, not allowing 0^0 $a^n \times a^m = a^{n+m}$ and $a^n \div a^m = a^{n-m}$, for $a \neq 0$.

5. **Algorithms for Operations**
   a. An **algorithm** is a step-by-step procedure for computing.
   b. The algorithms for addition and multiplication involve computing **partial sums** and **partial products.**
   c. **Left-to-right addition** is an algorithm that begins with the digits on the left (digits of greatest place value).

6. **Models for Operations**
   a. The **bundle-of-sticks model** and **base ten pieces** are two models for the four basic operations on whole numbers.
   b. A **rectangular array** is a visual method of illustrating the product of two whole numbers.
   c. Constructing a **tree diagram** is a counting technique that involves products of whole numbers.

7. **Number Properties**
   a. **Closure Property for Addition:** For any whole numbers a and b, $a + b$ is a unique whole number.
   b. **Closure Property for Multiplication:** For any whole numbers a and b, $a \times b$ is a unique whole number.
   c. **Identity Property for Addition:** For any whole number b, $0 + b = b + 0 = b$, and 0 is a unique identity for addition.
   d. **Identity Property for Multiplication:** For any whole number b, $1 \times b = b \times 1 = b$, and 1 is a unique identity for multiplication.

e. **Commutative Property for Addition:** For any whole numbers a and b, $a + b = b + a$.

f. **Commutative Property for Multiplication:** For any whole numbers a and b, $a \times b = b \times a$.

g. **Associative Property for Addition:** For any whole numbers a, b, and c, $a + (b + c) = (a + b) + c$.

h. **Associative Property for Multiplication:** For any whole numbers a, b, and c, $a \times (b \times c) = (a \times b) \times c$.

i. **Distributive Property for Multiplication over Addition:** For any whole numbers a, b, and c, $a \times (b + c) = a \times b + a \times c$.

8. **Inequality of Whole Numbers**
   a. For any whole numbers m and n, m is **less than** n if and only if there is a nonzero whole number k such that $m + k = n$. This property is written as $m < n$ or $n > m$.
   b. The inequality symbol and the equality symbol can be combined as $\geq$, which means **greater than or equal to,** or as $\leq$, which means **less than or equal to.**

9. **Mental Calculations**
   a. **Compatible numbers** is the technique of using pairs of numbers that are especially convenient for mental calculations.
   b. **Substitution** is the technique of breaking a number into a convenient sum, difference, or product.
   c. **Equal differences** is the technique of increasing or decreasing both numbers in a difference by the same amount. With such a change, the difference between the two numbers stays the same.

d. **Add up** is the technique of finding a difference by adding up from the smaller number to the larger number.

e. **Equal products** is a type of substitution that uses the fact that the product of two numbers remains the same when one of the numbers is divided by a given number and the other number is multiplied by the given number.

f. **Equal quotients** is a type of substitution that uses the fact that the quotient of two numbers remains the same when both numbers are divided by the same number.

10. **Estimation**
   a. **Rounding** is the technique of replacing one or both numbers in a sum, difference, product, or quotient by an approximate number to obtain an estimation.
   b. **Compatible numbers** is the technique of computing estimations by replacing one or more numbers with convenient approximate numbers.
   c. **Front-end estimation** usually involves computing with only one or two leading digits and is used for obtaining estimations of sums, differences, products, and quotients.

11. **Order of Operations**
   a. The **order of operations** rule requires that when combinations of operations occur in an expression, numbers raised to a power are evaluated first, then products and quotients in the order in which they occur from left to right, then sums and differences in the order in which they occur from left to right.
   b. When **parentheses** are used in an expression, computations within the parentheses should be performed first.

CHAPTER TEST

1. How would 226 be written in each of the following numeration systems?
   a. Egyptian
   b. Roman
   c. Mayan
   d. Base five positional numeration

2. Determine the value of each underlined digit and its place value.
   a. 1<u>4</u>,702,301
   b. 36,0<u>0</u>7,285

3. Round 6,281,497 to the nearest
   a. hundred thousand.
   b. hundred.
   c. thousand.

4. Represent 123 using the given model.
   a. Bundle-of-sticks model
   b. Base ten pieces

5. Sketch base ten pieces to illustrate each computation.
   a. 245 + 182
   b. 362 − 148

6. Compute the sum using the given method.
   a. Left-to-right addition
   483
   +274
   b. Partial sums
   864
   +759

7. Use equal differences to find a replacement for each number that is more convenient for mental calculation. Show the new numbers and determine the answer.
   a. 65 − 19
   b. 843 − 97

8. Use front-end estimation with the leading digits to estimate the value of each computation.
   a. 321 + 435 + 106
   b. 7410 − 2563 + 4602
   c. 32 × 56
   d. 3528 ÷ 713

9. Use equal products to find a replacement for each number that is more convenient for mental computation. Show the new numbers and determine the answer.
   a. 18 × 5
   b. 25 × 28

10. Compute 43 × 28 by showing the partial products. Sketch a rectangular grid to illustrate the product, and draw arrows from each partial product to its corresponding region on the grid.

11. Evaluate the following expressions.
   a. 6 × 4 × 5 − 3
   b. 48 ÷ 4 + 2 × 10
   c. (8 + 3) × 5 − 2

12. Compute the product or quotient. Leave your answer in exponential form.
   a. $3^{12} \div 3^4$
   b. $7^4 \times 7^6$

13. Show how to compute $452 \div 4$ by sketching base ten pieces and using the partitive (sharing) concept of division.

14. Round or use compatible numbers to mentally compute an estimation. Show your number replacements.

    a. $473 + 192$ **b.** $534 - 203$

    c. 993×42 **d.** $350 \div 49$

15. Determine whether each statement is true or false for operations on the set of whole numbers.
    a. If the differences involved are whole numbers, multiplication is distributive over subtraction.
    b. Addition is commutative.
    c. If the differences involved are whole numbers, subtraction is associative.
    d. For nonzero whole numbers, division is commutative.
    e. Subtraction is closed on the set of whole numbers.

16. Find a pattern in the equations below, and use inductive reasoning to predict the right side of the third equation. Then predict the fourth equation. Evaluate both sides of the fourth equation. Does the pattern hold?

$$3^2 + 4^2 = 5^2$$
$$10^2 + 11^2 + 12^2 = 13^2 + 14^2$$
$$21^2 + 22^2 + 23^2 + 24^2 =$$

17. There were 61 athletes at the annual sports banquet who played on either the football team or the baseball team. If 49 were on the football team and 18 were on the baseball team, how many players were on both teams?

18. If pizza is sold in 4 different sizes and can be ordered plain or with any one of 5 different toppings, how many different types of pizza are there?

BIBLIOGRAPHY

Abel, J., G. D. Allinger, and L. Andersen. "Popsicle Sticks, Computers, and Calculators: Important Considerations." *Arithmetic Teacher* 34 (May 1987): 8–12.

Balin, F. "Finger Multiplication." *Arithmetic Teacher* 26 (March 1979): 34–37.

Baroody, A. J. "Children's Difficulties in Subtraction: Some Causes and Cures." *Arithmetic Teacher* 32 (November 1984): 14–19.

Bates, T., and L. Rousseau. "Will the Real Division Algorithm Please Stand Up?" *Arithmetic Teacher* 33 (March 1986): 42–46.

Beard, E., and R. Polis. "Subtraction Facts with Pattern Explorations." *Arithmetic Teacher* 29 (December 1981): 6–9.

Beattie, I. D. "Modeling Operations and Algorithms." *Arithmetic Teacher* 33 (February 1986): 23–28.

Broadbent, F. W. "Lattice Multiplication and Division." *Arithmetic Teacher* 34 (January 1987): 28–31.

Dockweiler, C. J. "Palindromes and the 'Law of 11'." *Arithmetic Teacher* 32 (January 1985): 46–47.

Engelhardt, J. "Using Computational Errors in Diagnostic Teaching." *Arithmetic Teacher* 29 (April 1982): 16–19.

Ewbank, W. A., and J. L. Ginther. "Subtraction Drill with a Difference." *Arithmetic Teacher* 31 (January 1984): 49–51.

Folsom, M. "Operations on Whole Numbers." *Mathematics Learning in Early Childhood.* 1975 Yearbook. Reston, VA: National Council of Teachers of Mathematics, 1975.

Fowler, M. A. "Diagnostic Teaching for Elementary School Mathematics." *Arithmetic Teacher* 27 (March 1980): 34–37.

Grossman, A. S. "A Subtraction Algorithm for the Upper Grades." *Arithmetic Teacher* 32 (January 1985): 44–45.

Hall, W. D. "Division with Base-Ten Blocks." *Arithmetic Teacher* 31 (November 1983): 21–23.

Hall, W. D. "Using Arrays for Teaching Multiplication." *Arithmetic Teacher* 29 (November 1981): 20–21.

Harrison, M., and B. Harrison. "Developing Numeration Concepts and Skills." *Arithmetic Teacher* 33 (February 1986): 18–21, 60.

Hendrickson, A. D. "Verbal Multiplication and Division Problems: Some Difficulties and Some Solutions." *Arithmetic Teacher* 33 (April 1986): 26–33.

Hope, J. "Promoting Number Sense in School." *Arithmetic Teacher* 36 (February 1989): 12–16.

Howden, H. "Teaching Number Sense." *Arithmetic Teacher* 36 (February 1989): 6–11.

Kamii, C., and L. Joseph. "Teaching Place Value and Double-Column Addition." *Arithmetic Teacher* 35 (February 1988): 48–52.

Katterns, B., and K. Carr. "Talking with Young Children about Multiplication." *Arithmetic Teacher* 33 (April 1986): 18–21.

Kline, M. *Why Johnny Can't Add.* New York: St. Martin's, 1973.

Kouba, V. L., et al. "Results of the Fourth NAEP Assessment of Mathematics: Number, Operations, and Word Problems." *Arithmetic Teacher* 35 (April 1988): 14–19.

Krulik, S. "Painless Drilling—Not Your Dentist, but the History of Mathematics." *Arithmetic Teacher* 27 (April 1980): 40–42.

Lappan, G., E. Phillips, and M. J. Winter. "Powers and Patterns: Problem Solving with Calculators." *Arithmetic Teacher* 30 (October 1982): 42–44.

Leutzinger, L. P., and G. Nelson. "Let's Do It: With Powers of Ten." *Arithmetic Teacher* 27 (February 1980): 8–13.

McKillip, W. "Computational Skill in Division: Results and Implications from National Assessment." *Arithmetic Teacher* 28 (March 1981): 34–35.

Moser, J. M., and T. P. Carpenter. "Young Children Are Good Problem Solvers." *Arithmetic Teacher* 30 (November 1982): 24–26.

Musser, G. L. "Let's Teach Mental Algorithms for Addition and Subtraction." *Arithmetic Teacher* 29 (April 1982): 40–42.

O'Neil, D., and R. Jenson. "Some Aids for Teaching Place Value." *Arithmetic Teacher* 29 (December 1981): 6–9.

Payne, J. N. "Research into Practice: Place Value for Tens and Ones." *Arithmetic Teacher* 35 (February 1988): 64–66.

Pearson, E. S. "Summing It All Up: Pre-1900 Algorithms." *Arithmetic Teacher* 33 (March 1986): 38–41.

Quintero, A. H. "Children's Conceptual Understanding of Situations Involving Multiplication." *Arithmetic Teacher* 33 (January 1986): 34–37.

Rathmell, E. "Using Thinking Strategies to Teach the Basic Facts." *Developing Computational Skills.* 1978 Yearbook. Reston, VA: National Council of Teachers of Mathematics, 1978.

Reys, B. J. "Mental Computation." *Arithmetic Teacher* 32 (February 1985): 43–46.

Reys, R. E. "Estimation." *Arithmetic Teacher* 32 (February 1985): 37–41.

Robold, A. "Grid Arrays for Multiplication." *Arithmetic Teacher* 30 (January 1983): 14–17.

Ross, S. H. "Parts, Wholes, and Place Value: A Developmental View." *Arithmetic Teacher* 36 (February 1989): 47–51.

Shaw, R. A., and P. A. Pelosi. "In Search of Computational Errors." *Arithmetic Teacher* 30 (March 1983): 50–51.

Sherrill, J. M. "Magic Squares and Magic Triangles." *Arithmetic Teacher* 35 (October 1987): 44–47.

Sowder, J. T. "Mental Computation and Number Sense." *Arithmetic Teacher* 37 (March 1990): 18–20.

Stanic, G. M. A., and W. D. McKillip. "Developmental Algorithms Have a Place in Elementary School Mathematics Instruction." *Arithmetic Teacher* 36 (January 1989): 14–16.

Stone, J. S. "Place Value and Probability (with Promptings from Pascal)." *Arithmetic Teacher* 27 (March 1980): 47–49.

Suydam, M. "Improving Multiplication Skills." *Arithmetic Teacher* 32 (March 1985): 52.

Thompson, C., and J. Babcock. "A Successful Strategy for Teaching Missing Addends." *Arithmetic Teacher* 26 (December 1978): 38–41.

Thompson, C. S., and A. D. Hendrickson. "Verbal Addition and Subtraction Problems: Some Difficulties and Some Solutions." *Arithmetic Teacher* 33 (March 1986): 21–25.

Thompson, C. S., and J. Van de Walle. "Let's Do It: Transition Boards: Moving from Materials to Symbols in Addition." *Arithmetic Teacher* 28 (December 1980): 4–8.

Thornton, C. A., and P. J. Smith. "Action Research: Strategies for Learning Subtraction Facts." *Arithmetic Teacher* 35 (April 1988): 8–12.

Trafton, P. "Estimation and Mental Arithmetic: Important Components of Computation." *Developing Computational Skills.* 1978 Yearbook. Reston, VA: National Council of Teachers of Mathematics, 1978.

Tucker, B. F. "Seeing Addition: A Diagnosis-Remediation Case Study." *Arithmetic Teacher* 36 (January 1989): 10–11.

Tucker, B. F. "Give and Take: Getting Ready to Regroup." *Arithmetic Teacher* 28 (April 1981): 24–26.

Van de Walle, J., and C. S. Thompson. "Let's Do It: Partitioning Sets for Number Concepts, Place Value, and Long Division." *Arithmetic Teacher* 32 (January 1985): 6–11.

Weiland, L. "Matching Instruction to Children's Thinking about Division." *Arithmetic Teacher* 33 (December 1985): 34–35.

Wheatley, G. H. "Calculators in the Classroom: A Proposal for Curricular Change." *Arithmetic Teacher* 28 (December 1980): 37–39.

Whitin, D. J. "Number Sense and the Importance of Asking 'Why?'" *Arithmetic Teacher* 36 (February 1989): 26–29.

4 *Number Theory*

SPOTLIGHT ON TEACHING

Excerpts from NCTM's Standard 6 for Grades 5–8*

Number theory offers many rich opportunities for explorations that are interesting, enjoyable, and useful. These explorations have payoffs in problem solving, in understanding and developing other mathematical concepts, in illustrating the beauty of mathematics, and in understanding the human aspects of the historical development of number.

Challenging but accessible problems from number theory can be easily formulated and explored by students. For example, building rectangular arrays with a set of tiles can stimulate questions about divisibility and prime, composite, square, even, and odd numbers. [See the figure below.]

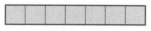

Only 1 rectangle can be
made with 7 tiles, so 7 is prime.

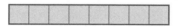

More than 1 rectangle can be made
with 8 tiles, so 8 is composite.

Tile explorations

This activity and others can be extended to investigate other interesting topics, such as abundant, deficient, or perfect numbers; triangular and square numbers; cubes; palindromes; factorials; and Fibonacci numbers. The development of various procedures for finding the greatest common factor of two numbers can foreshadow important topics in the 9–12 curriculum, as students compare the advantages, disadvantages, and efficiency of various algorithms. String art and explorations with star polygons can relate number theory to geometry.

*Reprinted by permission of the National Council of Teachers of Mathematics.

SECTION 4.1 FACTORS AND MULTIPLES

Fifty pennies are placed side by side. Each second penny is replaced by a nickel, each third coin is replaced by a dime, each fourth coin is replaced by a quarter, and each fifth coin is replaced by a half-dollar. What is the value of the fifty coins?

number theory

Number theory is the study of nonzero whole numbers and their relationships. Historically, certain numbers have had special attraction. Perhaps you have a favorite number. Seven is a common favorite number; 3 is also a popular choice. There may be historical reasons for the preference for 3. For example, in the French phrase *très bien,* which means very good, *très* is derived from the word for 3. One of the oldest superstitions is that odd numbers (1, 3, 5, 7, 9, 11, . . .) are lucky. One exception is the common

triskaidekaphobia

fear of 13, called **triskaidekaphobia.** Often hotels will not have a floor numbered 13 and motels will not have a room 13. Is this true in the area where you live? Some people have a particular fear of Friday the 13th. Do you know someone with triskaidekaphobia?

■ *HISTORICAL HIGHLIGHT*

The Pythagoreans (ca. 500 B.C.), a brotherhood of mathematicians and philosophers, believed that numbers had special meanings that could account for all aspects of life. For example, the number 1 represented reason, 2 stood for opinion, 4 was symbolic of justice, and 5 represented marriage. Even numbers were considered weak and earthy, and odd numbers were viewed as strong and heavenly. The numbers 1, 2, 3, and 4 also represented fire, water, air, and earth, and the fact that 1 + 2 + 3 + 4 equals 10 had many meanings. When only 9 heavenly bodies could be found, including the earth, sun, moon, and the sphere of stars, the Pythagoreans imagined a tenth to "balance the earth."*

MODELS FOR FACTORS AND MULTIPLES

factor
multiple

One important type of relationship in number theory is that between a factor and a multiple. If one number is a **factor** of a second (as 3 is a factor of 12), then the second number is a **multiple** of the first (as 12 is a multiple of 3).

*M. Kline, *Mathematics in Western Culture* (New York: Oxford University Press, 1953), 77.

linear model

Let's look at two models for illustrating this relationship: the *linear model* and the *rectangular model*. Rods such as those shown in Figure 4.1 are one type of **linear model.** To determine whether one number is a factor of another, we mark off the rod for one number using a rod representing the other.

In Figure 4.1, the rod for 4 units can be marked off 8 times on the rod that represents 32 units. This shows that $8 \times 4 = 32$. So 8 and 4 are factors of 32, and 32 is a multiple of both 8 and 4.

Figure 4.1

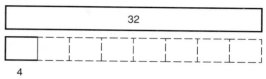

8 and 4 are factors of 32   32 is a multiple of 8 and 4

rectangular model

Figure 4.2 illustrates the **rectangular model.** In this model one number is represented by a rectangular array of squares or tiles and the two dimensions of the rectangle are factors of the number. One way to determine whether a whole number k is a factor of a whole number b is to try building a rectangular array of b tiles such that one dimension of the array is k.

In Figure 4.2, the rectangular array of 84 tiles has 12 rows of tiles. That is, the 84 tiles are divided evenly into 12 rows, so 12 is a factor of 84. Since the 84 tiles are also divided evenly into 7 columns of tiles, 7 is also a factor of 84. Thus the two dimensions of the rectangle, 7 and 12, are factors of 84, and 84 is a multiple of both 12 and 7.

Figure 4.2

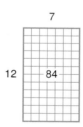

12 and 7 are factors of 84   84 is a multiple of 12 and 7

divides

Another way of stating that 12 is a factor of 84 is to say that 12 **divides** 84. This fact is sometimes written as $12|84$, where the vertical line means *divides.*

> If a and b are whole numbers such that $a \neq 0$ and a is a factor of b, we say that
>
> $$a \text{ divides } b$$
>
> and we write
>
> $$a|b.$$
>
> If a does not divide b, we write $a \nmid b$.

EXAMPLE A

To become more familiar with the *divides* relationship, classify the following statements as true or false.

1. $15|60$
2. $8|30$

3. $3 \not| 19$
4. $18 | 18$
5. $2 | 0$

Solution   1. True   2. False   3. True   4. True   5. True

Notice that *divides* signifies a *relationship* between two numbers; it indicates that one number is divisible by another. It does not indicate the operation of division—that is, dividing one number by another. For example, $3 | 15$ tells us that 3 divides 15, and should not be confused with 3/15, which is equal to the fraction 1/3 and indicates that 1 is to be divided by 3.

PROBLEM-SOLVING APPLICATION

The following problem is solved by using factors and multiples and features the strategies of *guessing and checking* and *making an organized list*.

■ **PROBLEM**

A factory uses machines to sort cards into piles. On one occasion a machine operator obtained the following curious result. When a box of cards was sorted into 7 equal groups, there were 6 cards left over; when the box of cards was sorted into 5 equal groups, there were 4 left over; and when it was sorted into 3 equal groups, there were 2 left. If the machine cannot sort more than 200 cards at a time, how many cards were in the box?

Understanding the Problem   Sorting the cards into groups of 7 is like dividing by 7. Since there were 6 cards left, we know 7 is not a factor of the original number of cards.

Question 1   How can we be sure that 5 and 3 are not factors of the number of cards in the box?

Devising a Plan   One approach is to *guess and check* a few numbers to become more familiar with the problem. Even as you start to guess, you can throw out certain numbers. For example, there could not have been 100 cards, because 5 divides 100. Another approach is to find numbers satisfying one of the conditions. For example, since dividing by 7 leaves a remainder of 6, we can *make an organized list* of numbers satisfying this condition:

13, 20, 27, 34, 41, 48, 55, 62, 69, 76, 83, 90, 97, 104, 111, 118, . . .

Question 2   Then we can find the numbers in this list that leave a remainder of 4 when divided by 5 and a remainder of 2 when divided by 3. What is the smallest number in this list that leaves a remainder of 4 when divided by 5?

Question 3   **Carrying Out the Plan**   The numbers 34, 69, and 104 leave a remainder of 4 when divided by 5. Which of these numbers leaves a remainder of 2 when divided by 3? The answer to this question is the solution to the original problem.

Question 4   **Looking Back**   Another approach is to change the original problem by noticing that if there had been 1 more card in the box, then 7, 5, and 3 would have been factors of the number of cards. Once this number has been found, the number 1 can be subtracted to obtain the original number of cards. What is the smallest nonzero whole number that is divisible by 7, 5, and 3?

Answers to Questions 1–4
1. When the total number of cards is divided by 5, there is a remainder of 4, and when it is divided by 3, there is a remainder of 2; if these numbers were factors, there would be no remainders.
2. 34   **3.** 104   **4.** 105

DIVISIBILITY TESTS

During the gasoline shortage of 1974, the state of Oregon adopted an "odd and even" system of gas rationing. Drivers with odd-numbered license plates could get gasoline on the odd-numbered days of the month, and those with even-numbered plates could get gasoline on the even-numbered days. Some people whose license plate numbers ended in zero were confused as to whether their numbers were odd or even. The solution to this problem lies in the definition of odd and even numbers.

ODD AND EVEN NUMBERS

Any whole number that has 2 as a factor is called an **even number,** and any whole number that does not have 2 as a factor is called an **odd number.**

EXAMPLE B

Would a person with the following license plate have purchased gasoline on the odd-numbered or even-numbered days?

Solution   On even-numbered days, because 1080 has 2 as a factor (2 × 540 = 1080)

In the following paragraphs we will examine a few simple tests for determining whether or not a number is divisible by 2, 3, 4, 5, 6, or 9 without carrying out the division. Before looking at these tests, we present three divisibility theorems.

DIVISIBILITY THEOREMS

1. If a number divides each of two other numbers, then it divides their sum. If $a|b$ and $a|c$, then $a|(b + c)$.
2. If a number divides one of two numbers but not the other, then it will not divide their sum. If $a|b$ and $a \nmid c$, then $a \nmid (b + c)$.
3. If one number divides another number, then it will divide the product of that number and any other whole number. If $a|b$, then $a|kb$.

Figures 4.3 through 4.5 illustrate the three divisibility theorems. To illustrate $a|b$, we draw a rectangle, with a as one dimension. To illustrate $a \nmid c$, we indicate that a rectangle cannot be formed with c tiles which has a as one of its dimensions.

Figure 4.3

If **a divides b** and **a divides c**, then **a divides (b + c)**.

Figure 4.4

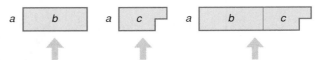

If **a divides b** and **a does not divide c**, then **a does not divide (b + c)**.

Figure 4.5

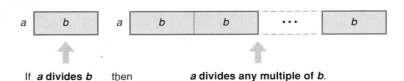

If **a divides b**   then   **a divides any multiple of b**.

EXAMPLE C

Here are examples of the three divisibility theorems.

1. Since $6|54$ and $6|48$, we can conclude that $6|(54 + 48)$. That is, $6|102$.
2. Since $7|42$ but $7 \nmid 50$, we can conclude that $7 \nmid (42 + 50)$. That is, $7 \nmid 92$.
3. Since $13|26$, we can conclude that 13 divides any multiple of 26. For example, $13|(9 \times 26)$, or $13|234$.

TEST FOR DIVISIBILITY BY 2 or 5   A number is divisible by 2 or 5 if the number represented by the units digit is divisible by 2 or 5. This means that a number is divisible by 2 if its units digit is 0, 2, 4, 6, or 8, and it is divisible by 5 if its units digit is 0 or 5.

EXAMPLE D

Classify each statement as true or false and explain why.

1. $2|13,776$ 2. $5|3135$ 3. $2|2461$

Solution

1. True. Since $2|6$, we know that $2|13,776$.
2. True. Since $5|5$, we know that $5|3135$.
3. False. Since $2 \nmid 1$, we know that $2 \nmid 2461$.

To understand why these tests work, let's look at an example. The expanded form of 5273 is

$$5273 = 5 \times 10^3 + 2 \times 10^2 + 7 \times 10 + 3$$

Since 2 divides 10^3, by Divisibility Theorem (3) it also divides any multiple of 10^3 and, in particular, 5×10^3. Similarly, since 2 divides 10^2 and 10, it also divides 2×10^2 and 7×10. Then, by Divisibility Theorem (1), 2 divides the sum of these numbers, which is the portion of the above equation indicated by the brace. Therefore, by Divisibility Theorem (1), 2 will divide the right side of the equation if 2 divides 3; by Divisibility Theorem (2), if 2 does not divide 3, it will not divide the right side of the equation. Since 2 does not divide 3, it does not divide 5273. Similarly, since 5 divides 10^3, 10^2, and 10, it divides the portion of the equation indicated by the brace. However, since 5 does not divide 3, it does not divide 5273. A general proof of the divisibility tests for 2 or 5 for any arbitrary whole number follows the same reasoning.

TEST FOR DIVISIBILITY BY 3 OR 9   A number is divisible by 3 if the sum of its digits is divisible by 3. Similarly, a number is divisible by 9 if the sum of its digits is divisible by 9.

EXAMPLE E

Classify each statement as true or false, and explain why.

1. $3 \mid 2847$ 2. $9 \mid 147{,}389$ 3. $3 \mid 270{,}415$

Solution

1. True, because 3 divides $2 + 8 + 4 + 7 = 21$
2. False, because 9 does not divide $1 + 4 + 7 + 3 + 8 + 9 = 32$
3. False, because 3 does not divide $2 + 7 + 0 + 4 + 1 + 5 = 19$

Let's examine these tests by looking at the expanded form of 2847. Notice the use of the distributive property to obtain the third equation from the second equation. The commutative and associative properties for addition are also needed to obtain the arrangement of numbers in the third equation.

$$
\begin{aligned}
2847 &= 2 \times 10^3 + 8 \times 10^2 + 4 \times 10 + 7 \\
&= 2 \times (999 + 1) + 8 \times (99 + 1) + 4 \times (9 + 1) + 7 \\
&= 2 \times 999 + 8 \times 99 + 4 \times 9 + (2 + 8 + 4 + 7)
\end{aligned}
$$

Since 3 divides 9, 99, 999, etc., by Divisibility Theorems (3) and (1) it also divides the portion of the equation indicated by the brace. Therefore, because of Divisibility Theorems (1) and (2), to determine if 2847 is divisible by 3, it is necessary only to determine if the remaining portion of the equation containing the sum $2 + 8 + 4 + 7$ is divisible by 3. Since 3 does divide this sum, we know that 3 divides 2847.

The expanded form of 2847 in the preceding equation also shows why a similar test works for divisibility by 9. Since 9 divides the portion of the equation indicated by the brace, it will divide 2847 if and only if it divides $2 + 8 + 4 + 7$. In this case 9 does not divide this sum, so it does not divide 2847. A general proof of the divisibility tests for 3 or 9 for any arbitrary whole number follows essentially the same reasoning.

TEST FOR DIVISIBILITY BY 6   If a number is divisible by both 2 and 3, then it is divisible by 6. If it is not divisible by both 2 and 3, then it is not divisible by 6.

EXAMPLE F

Apply the preceding test to determine which of the following numbers are divisible by 6.

1. 561,781   2. 2,100,000,472   3. 123,090,534

Solution

1. 561,781 is not divisible by 2 (because it is odd), so it is not divisible by 6.
2. 2,100,000,472 is not divisible by 3 (because the sum of its digits is 16), so it is not divisible by 6.
3. 123,090,534 is even and divisible by 3, so it is divisible by 6.

TEST FOR DIVISIBILITY BY 4   If the number represented by the last two digits of a number is divisible by 4, then the original number will be divisible by 4.

EXAMPLE G

Use the above test to determine which of the following numbers are divisible by 4.

1. 65,932   2. 476,025,314   3. 113,775,920

Solution

1. 4 | 65,932 because 4 | 32
2. 4 ∤ 476,025,314 because 4 ∤ 14
3. 4 | 113,775,920 because 4 | 20

The expanded form shows why the test for divisibility by 4 works for 65,932.

$$65,932 = 6 \times 10^4 + 5 \times 10^3 + 9 \times 10^2 + 3 \times 10 + 2$$

Since 4 is a factor of 10^4, 10^3, and 10^2, by Divisibility Theorems (3) and (1) it will divide the portion of the expanded form indicated by the brace. Thus whether or not 4 divides 65,932 depends only on whether or not it divides 32. Similar reasoning can be used to prove the test for divisibility by 4 for any arbitrary whole number.

PRIME AND COMPOSITE NUMBERS

One way to classify whole numbers is to consider the number of factors for each number. In the following examples, the rectangular model is used to provide a basis for forming conjectures about numbers of factors.

Figure 4.6 shows three different rectangular arrays for 12, which illustrate that 2, 6, 3, 4, 1, and 12 are factors of 12. Notice that these factors occur in pairs, two factors for each rectangle.

Figure 4.6

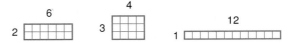

Figure 4.7 shows the arrays for 11 and 10. There is only one array for 11, and its factors are 1 and 11. There are two arrays for 10, and its factors are 2, 5, 1, and 10.

Figure 4.7

Other arrays can be sketched for the numbers from 1 to 9. The following table lists the factors for the numbers from 1 to 12. Notice that the numbers 2, 3, 5, 7, and 11 have exactly two factors. These numbers are called **prime numbers.** Numbers with more than two factors are called **composite numbers.** Since 1 has only one factor, it is classified as *neither prime nor composite.*

prime numbers
composite numbers

Figure 4.8

No.	Factors	No. of factors
1	1	1
2	1, 2	2
3	1, 3	2
4	1, 2, 4	3
5	1, 5	2
6	1, 2, 3, 6	4
7	1, 7	2
8	1, 2, 4, 8	4
9	1, 3, 9	3
10	1, 2, 5, 10	4
11	1, 11	2
12	1, 2, 3, 4, 6, 12	6

EXAMPLE *H*

The table in Figure 4.8 suggests some questions.

1. Will there be numbers other than 1 with only one factor?
2. What kinds of numbers have an odd number of factors?
3. Are there numbers with more than 6 factors?

Solution

1. No
2. Square numbers. For a square number, there will be a square array, which contributes only one factor. So for a square number, the total number of factors will always be odd.
3. Yes. Any number of factors are possible.

EXAMPLE *I*

List the numbers from 13 to 20 and determine whether they are prime or composite.

Solution

The numbers 13, 17, and 19 are prime (each can be represented by only 1 rectangular array), and 14, 15, 16, 18, and 20 are composite (each has 2 or more rectangular arrays).

There is no largest prime because there are an infinite number of prime numbers. Some very large primes have been discovered. From 1876 to 1951, this 39-digit number was the largest known prime:

$$170,141,183,460,469,231,731,687,303,715,884,105,727$$

Now computers make it possible to find a larger prime every few years. In 1983, for example, at the Cray Research Labs in Mendota Heights, Minnesota, David Slowinski found the largest known prime at that time, a number with 39,751 digits. Then in 1985, Slowinski found a prime with 65,050 digits. The search took more than 3 hours on a computer that does 400 million calculations per second.

Prime numbers are difficult to locate because they do not occur in predictable patterns. In fact, there are large stretches of consecutive whole numbers that include no primes. For example, between the numbers 396,733 and 396,833 there are 99 composite numbers.

■ **H**ISTORICAL *HIGHLIGHT*

Knowing the factors of numbers has long been valuable in research involving prime numbers. In 1659 J. H. Rahn published a table listing the factors for all numbers up to 24,000, and in 1668 John Pell of England extended this table to 100,000. The greatest achievement of this sort is the table by J. P. Kulik (1773–1863) from the University of Prague. His table covers all numbers up to 100,000,000.* Finding the factors of numbers is currently of major interest to cryptographers and intelligence agencies, whose code solutions are often based on the prime factors of very large whole numbers.

PRIME NUMBER TEST

One method of determining if a number is prime is checking to see if it has any factors other than itself and 1. This is where the divisibility tests can be useful.

EXAMPLE J

Which of the following numbers are prime?

1. 43,101   2. 24,638   3. 53

Solution

1. Since $3|(4 + 3 + 1 + 0 + 1)$, we know that $3|43,101$, so this number is not prime.
2. Since $2|8$, we know that $2|24,638$, so this number is not prime.
3. 53 is prime.

To determine if a number has factors other than itself and 1, we need only try dividing by prime numbers (2, 3, 5, 7, . . .). There is no need to divide by composite numbers (4, 6, 8, 9, . . .). For example, if 4 divides a number, then 2 divides the number. In other words, if 2 does not divide a number, then 4 will not divide the number.

Let's consider how we might determine that 53 is a prime number. The divisibility tests show that 53 is not divisible by 2, 3, or 5. Checking the primes in order, we next note that 7 is not a factor of 53. So if 53 has any prime factors, they are 11, 13, 17, etc. However, the smallest product of these primes is 11×11, which is greater than 53. This means that 53 cannot be the product of prime factors because their product would be greater than 53. This example suggests the following theorem.

PRIME NUMBER TEST

> Suppose n is a whole number and p is a prime such that $p^2 > n$. If there is no smaller prime that divides n, then n is a prime number.

This theorem tells us which primes we should try as divisors to determine if a number is prime or composite.

EXAMPLE K

Is 421 prime or composite?

Solution

Since $23 \times 23 > 421$, we need only consider 2, 3, 5, 7, 11, 13, 17, and 19 as possible factors of 421. Since none of these primes are factors, 421 is a prime number.

*H. W. Eves, *An Introduction to the History of Mathematics*, 3rd ed. (New York: Holt, Rinehart and Winston, 1969), 149.

SIEVE OF ERATOSTHENES

sieve of Eratosthenes

One way of finding all the primes that are less than a given number is to eliminate those numbers that are not prime. This method was first used by the Greek mathematician Eratosthenes (ca. 230 B.C.) and is called the **sieve of Eratosthenes.** Figure 4.9 illustrates the use of this method to find the primes that are less than 120.

We begin the process by crossing out 1, which is not a prime, and then circling 2 and crossing out all the remaining multiples of 2 (4, 6, 8, 10, . . .). Then 3 is circled and all the remaining multiples of 3 are crossed out (3, 6, 9, 12, . . .). This process is continued by circling 5 and 7 and crossing out their multiples. Since every composite number less than 120 must have at least one prime factor less than 11 (11 × 11 = 121), it is unnecessary to cross out the multiples of primes greater than 7. The numbers in the table that are not crossed out are prime.

Figure 4.9

EXAMPLE L

Examine the locations of the primes in Figure 4.9.

1. What patterns can you see?
2. What is the longest sequence of consecutive numbers that are not prime?

Solution

twin primes

1. Several primes occur in pairs, with one composite number between them: 3 and 5, 5 and 7, and 11 and 13 are the first few such pairs, and 107 and 109 are the largest such pair in this table. Such primes are called **twin primes.** You might also notice that except for 2 and 5, all the primes occur in columns 1, 3, 7, and 9.
2. There are two sequences of 7 numbers that are not prime; the first sequence is the numbers from 90 to 96, and the second sequence is the numbers from 114 to 120.

RELATED ACTIVITIES IN

Mathematics for Elementary Teachers: An Activity Approach, 3e

Activity Set 4.1

Models for Even Numbers, Odd Numbers, Factors, and Primes: Visual illustrations clarify number relationships.

Just for Fun

Spirolaterals: Creative artistic applications involving the concept of least common multiple

PUZZLER

HIT AND RUN

DID YOU GET HIS LICENSE NUMBER?

YES! HIS LICENSE WAS IN TWO PARTS ... A TWO DIGIT NUMBER AND A THREE DIGIT NUMBER. THE TWO DIGIT NUMBER WAS PRIME AND THE SUM OF THE TWO DIGITS WAS A TWO-DIGIT PRIME. THE TENS DIGIT WAS LARGER THAN THE UNITS DIGIT ... IN THE THREE DIGIT PART, THE DIGITS WERE ALL ODD AND DIFFERENT. THE SUM OF THE THREE DIGITS WAS PALINDROMIC. THE SUM OF THE FIRST AND THIRD DIGIT WAS ONE-HALF THE SUM OF THE FIRST AND SECOND.

THAT'S ALL I REMEMBER!

EXERCISES AND PROBLEMS 4.1

1. Some skyscrapers have double-deck elevators to minimize the number of elevator shafts required. People entering the building use the bottom deck of the elevator to arrive at odd-numbered floors, or they take a moving stairway to and from a mezzanine for the top deck of the elevator, which stops at even-numbered floors.

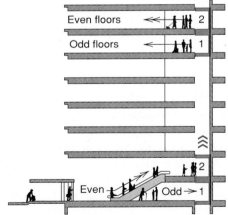

Even floors ← 2
Odd floors ← 1

Even ← | Odd → 1
2

a. Suppose you had to deliver packages to floors 11, 26, 35, and 48. How could you do so with the least amount of elevator riding and walking only one flight of stairs?

b. Describe an efficient scheme for delivering to any number of odd- and even-numbered floors.

2. Classify each of the following statements as true or false.

a. 3|4163   **b.** 2|1670   **c.** 14|84

d. 5∤49   **e.** 1|17   **f.** 13∤13

3. There are several ways of expressing in words the relationship between two numbers when one divides the other. Rewrite each statement in the form *a|b*, using the divides relationship.

a. 7 is a factor of 63.   **b.** 40 is a multiple of 8.

c. 13 is a divisor of 39.   **d.** 36 is divisible by 12.

4. Illustrate statements a and b below with a linear model and statements c and d with a rectangular model.

a. 6|54   **b.** 12|60

c. 7|42   **d.** 43|516

5. Colored rods such as the Cuisenaire Rods® shown below are often found in elementary schools. They may be used as linear models to illustrate the concepts of factors and multiples.*

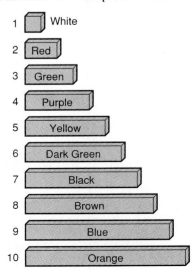

1 White
2 Red
3 Green
4 Purple
5 Yellow
6 Dark Green
7 Black
8 Brown
9 Blue
10 Orange

*Cuisenaire Rods® is a registered trademark of Cuisenaire Company of America, Inc.

A row in which all the rods are the same is called a **one-color train**. Here is a red one-color train representing 12.

| Red | Red | Red | Red | Red | Red |

a. What other Cuisenaire rods can be used to form a one-color train for 12?

b. What one-color trains can be used to represent 15?

c. How many different one-color trains of 2 or more rods will there be for each prime number?

d. If an all-brown train is equal in length to an all-orange train, what can be said about the number of brown rods?

e. If a number can be represented by an all-red train, an all-green train, and an all-black train, it has at least 8 factors. Name these factors.

6. The table in Figure 4.8 (page 131) has no numbers with exactly 5 factors. Find such a number.

7. Each rectangular array of squares gives information about the number of factors of a number. Two rectangles can be formed for the number 6, showing that 6 has factors 2, 3, 1, and 6.

Copy the rectangular grid from the inside cover and use it to sketch as many different rectangular (including square) arrays as possible for each of the following numbers: 15, 16, 30, 25, 17.

a. What kinds of numbers have only 1 rectangular array?

b. Which 3 of the given numbers have an even number of factors? Use your sketches to explain why.

c. Two of the given numbers have square arrays. Make a conjecture about the number of factors for square numbers. Explain how your sketches support your conjecture.

8. Which of the following numbers are divisible by 3? Can the test for divisibility by 3 be used to determine the remainder when a number is divided by 3?

a. 465,076,800 **b.** 100,101,000 **c.** 907,116,341

9. Which number in exercise 8 is divisible by 9?

a. If a number is divisible by 3, is it divisible by 9?

b. If a number is divisible by 9, is it divisible by 3?

10. Which of these numbers are divisible by 4?

a. 47,382 **b.** 512,112

c. 14,710 **d.** 4,328,104,292

e. Explain how divisibility by 4 can be determined without dividing the number by 4.

11. Write each statement in words and classify it as true or false. If the statement is false, show a counterexample.

a. If $a|b$ and $a|c$, then $a|(b + c)$.

b. If $a{\nmid}b$ and $a{\nmid}c$, then $a{\nmid}(b + c)$.

c. If $a|b$ and $b|c$, then $a|c$.

d. If $a|c$ and $b|c$, then $(a + b)|c$.

e. If $a|b$ and $a{\nmid}c$, then $a{\nmid}bc$.

12. The first 10 prime numbers are 2, 3, 5, 7, 11, 13, 17, 19, 23, and 29.

a. Which of these primes would you have to consider as possible factors of 367 in order to determine whether 367 is a prime or composite number?

b. Is 367 prime or composite?

13. The numbers 2, 3, 5, 7, 11, and 13 are not factors of 173. Explain why it is possible to conclude that 173 is prime without checking for more prime factors.

14. Which of the following numbers are prime?

a. 231 **b.** 227

c. 187 **d.** 431

15. Suppose Figure 4.9 were extended to include all the whole numbers up to 300. Explain how the sieve of Eratosthenes could be used to determine all the prime numbers less than 300.

16. The numbers in the following sequence increase by 2, then by 4, then by 6, etc. Continue this sequence until you reach the first number that is not a prime.

17   19   23   29   37

17. To test any number for divisibility by 11, alternately add and subtract the digits from right to left, beginning with the units digit—that is, units digit minus tens digit plus hundreds digit, etc. If the result is divisible by 11, then the original number will be divisible by 11. Use this test on the following numbers. (Note: Zero is divisible by 11.)

a. 63,011,454 **b.** 19,321,488 **c.** 4,209,909,682

d. Will the test for divisibility by 11 work if the digits are alternately added and subtracted from left to right?

18. It is likely that no one will ever find a formula that will give all the primes that are less than an arbitrary number. The following formulas produce primes for a while, but eventually they produce composite numbers.

a. For which of the whole numbers $n = 2$ to 7 is $2^n - 1$ a prime?

b. The formula $n^2 - n + 41$ will give primes, for $n = 1, 2, 3, \ldots, 40$ but not for $n = 41$. Which of the primes less than 100 are given by this formula?

19. There are many conjectures involving primes.

a. The mathematician Christian Goldbach (1690–1764) conjectured that every odd number greater than 5 is the sum of three primes. Verify this conjecture for the following numbers: 21, 27, 31.

b. In 1845 the French mathematician Bertrand conjectured that between any whole number greater than 1 and its double there exists at least one prime. After 50 years this conjecture was proven true by the Russian mathematician Tchebyshev. For the numbers greater than 5 and less than 15, is it true or false that there are at least two primes between every number and its double?

20. If a collection of pencils are placed in rows of 4, there are 2 pencils left. If the pencils are placed in rows of 5, there are 3 left. And if the pencils are placed in rows of 7, there are 5 left. What is the smallest possible number of pencils in the collection?

21. From the numbers 3, 5, 6, 7, 10, 11, 12, and 13, select 5 numbers that produce 15,015 when multiplied together.

22. Joan's age was a factor of her grandfather's age for 6 consecutive years. What were her grandfather's ages during this time?

23. There are long sequences of consecutive whole numbers that include no primes. For example, the following 5 consecutive numbers are not prime. Explain why without computing the products.

$$2 \times 3 \times 4 \times 5 \times 6 + 2$$
$$2 \times 3 \times 4 \times 5 \times 6 + 3$$
$$2 \times 3 \times 4 \times 5 \times 6 + 4$$
$$2 \times 3 \times 4 \times 5 \times 6 + 5$$
$$2 \times 3 \times 4 \times 5 \times 6 + 6$$

a. Construct a sequence of 10 consecutive whole numbers with no primes.

b. Explain how to construct a sequence of 100 consecutive whole numbers with no primes.

Featured Strategies: Using a Model, Making a Table, and Solving a Simpler Problem

24. In a new school built for 1000 students, there were 1000 lockers that were all closed. As the students entered the school, they decided on the following plan. The first student who entered the building opened all 1000 lockers. The second student closed all lockers with even numbers. The third student changed all lockers that were numbered with multiples of 3 (that is, opened those that were closed and closed those that were open). The fourth student changed all lockers numbered with multiples of 4, the fifth changed all lockers numbered with multiples of 5, etc. After 1000 students had entered the building and changed the lockers according to this pattern, which lockers were left open?

a. **Understanding the Problem** To better understand this problem, think about what will happen as each of the first few students enters. For example, after the first three students, will locker #6 be open or closed?

b. **Devising a Plan** Simplifying a problem will sometimes help you to strike on an idea for the solution. Suppose there were only 10 lockers and 10 students. We could number 10 markers to represent the lockers and turn them upside down for open and right side up for closed.

1 2 3 4 5 6 7 8 9 10

Or we could form a table showing the state (open or closed) of each locker after each student passes through.

	Lockers									
	1	2	3	4	5	6	7	8	9	10
Student 1	O	O	O	O	O	O	O	O	O	O
Student 2		C		C		C		C		C
Student 3										

Which of the 10 lockers would be left open after 10 students passed through?

c. **Carrying Out the Plan** Solving the problem for small numbers of students and lockers will help you to see a relationship between the number of each locker and whether it is left open or closed. What types of numbers will be on the lockers that are left open?

d. **Looking Back** How many times will a locker be changed if it is numbered with a prime number?

COMPUTER INVESTIGATION

The computer program FREQUENCY OF PRIMES on the *Computer Problem-Solving Disc* determines the number of primes for given intervals.

There are 15 primes that are less than 50 and 10 primes that are greater than 50 and less than 100.

Questions for Investigation

1. Beginning with 100, are there any other intervals of 50 (100 to 150, 150 to 200, etc.) with 15 or more primes?

2. Does the number of primes in intervals of 50 continue to decrease?

3. What are the frequencies of primes in other intervals, such as intervals of 10? intervals of 100?

4. If there are zero primes in an interval, then all the numbers in that interval are composite. What is the longest interval of consecutive composite numbers you can find? (Hint: Look at printouts of primes.)

PUZZLER

A store manager has an invoice for a shipment of turkey breasts that cost 72 cents a pound. The first and last digits on the receipt are illegible; the manager can read only the middle three digits: $□67.9□. Assuming that 72 is a factor of the whole number □679□, what is the total cost of the turkey breasts?

SECTION 4.2 GREATEST COMMON DIVISOR AND LEAST COMMON MULTIPLE

One thousand lottery tickets for a school function are numbered with whole numbers from 1 to 1000. The winning numbers satisfy the following conditions: the number is even; there is one 7 in the numeral; the sum of the tens and units digits is divisible by 5; and the hundreds digit is greater than the units digit, which is greater than the tens digit. What are the winning numbers?

Census Clock, United States Department of Commerce Building, Washington, D.C.

The census clock pictured above was once located in the lobby of the U.S. Department of Commerce Building and regulated by the Bureau of Census. It showed the estimated population of the United States at any given moment. Four illustrated clock faces displayed the components of population change: births, deaths, immigration, and emigration. Plus and minus signs above the clock faces lit up to indicate when one of these components changed. The clock showed a birth every 10 seconds, a death every 16 seconds, the arrival of an immigrant every 81 seconds, and the departure of an emigrant every 15 minutes.

The times when these lights flashed together can be determined by using multiples of the different time periods of the various clocks.

EXAMPLE A

The plus sign above the birth clock lit at intervals of 10 seconds, and the minus sign for the death clock lit every 16 seconds. If these two indicators both flashed at the same time, when would they flash together again?

Solution

Using a *linear model* for multiples, we can draw a time line showing the flashing periods for each clock. The following line shows that 80 is a common multiple of 10 and 16 and that the clocks would flash together again after 80 seconds.

Birth clock intervals of 10

Death clock intervals of 16

The purpose of this section is to develop the mathematical theory to solve problems involving the *common factors* and *common multiples* of numbers. Prime factorization is one approach used to solve such problems.

■ **HISTORICAL HIGHLIGHT**

Pierre Fermat (1601–1665) has been called the greatest mathematician of the seventeenth century. His greatest achievement was establishing the foundations of number theory. At one time he wrote, "I have found a great number of exceedingly beautiful theorems." His famous Last Theorem, as it is called, states that there are no positive integers x, y, and z such that

$$x^n + y^n = z^n$$

for $n > 2$. For 350 years mathematicians have been searching for a proof of this theorem. Fermat wrote a brief note in the margin of a book saying that he had discovered a truly wonderful proof of this theorem, but the margin was too small to contain it. If Fermat did have such a proof, it has remained lost to this day.*

Pierre Fermat

PRIME FACTORIZATIONS

prime factorization

Composite numbers can always be written as a product of primes. Such a product is called the **prime factorization** of a number. For this reason, prime numbers are often referred to as the *building blocks of the whole numbers.*

EXAMPLE B

Find the prime factorization of each number.

    1. 30   2. 142   3. 429

Solution   1. $2 \times 3 \times 5$ 2. 2×71 3. $3 \times 11 \times 13$

The primes in the prime factorization of a composite number are unique except for their order. For example, any prime factorization of 30 will contain the factors 2, 3, and 5, although possibly not in that order. The uniqueness of prime factors for composite numbers is stated in the following important theorem.

FUNDAMENTAL THEOREM OF ARITHMETIC

> Every composite whole number has one and only one prime factorization (if the order of the factors is disregarded).

This theorem enables us to find the prime factorization of a number by first finding two smaller factors and then continuing, if necessary, to find the factors of these numbers. Once we have only prime factors, the Fundamental Theorem of Arithmetic assures us that this is the only prime factorization.

EXAMPLE C

Find the prime factorization of 300.

Solution   One approach is to note that 300 is even and then divide by 2: $300 = 2 \times 150$. Then, since 150 is even, divide by 2 again: $300 = 2 \times 2 \times 75$. When it is no longer

*E. T. Bell, *Men of Mathematics* (New York: Simon and Schuster, 1965), 56–72.

possible to divide by 2, try dividing by larger primes in order: 3, 5, 7, etc. In this case 3 divides 75, so $300 = 2 \times 2 \times 3 \times 25$, and from this we can see that the prime factorization is $2 \times 2 \times 3 \times 5 \times 5$.

Another approach is to replace 300 by the product of any two of its factors, not necessarily prime factors. For example, $300 = 10 \times 30$. Then each of these factors can be replaced by its factors, and so on. Since $10 = 2 \times 5$ and $30 = 3 \times 10$, we know $300 = 2 \times 5 \times 3 \times 10$. Finally, 10 can be replaced by 2×5, so

$$300 = 2 \times 5 \times 3 \times 2 \times 5 = 2^2 \times 3 \times 5^2$$

Notice that both approaches to the solution of Example C yielded the same prime factors.

Finding the prime factors of a number by first obtaining any two factors and then **factor tree** obtaining their factors is illustrated in Figure 4.10 with a diagram called a **factor tree.** Through a series of steps, a number is broken down into smaller and smaller factors until all the final factors are prime numbers. Three factor trees are shown, with their primes circled at the ends of the "branches."

Figure 4.10

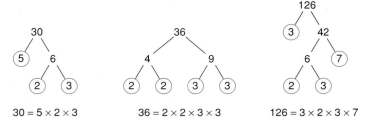

$$30 = 5 \times 2 \times 3 \qquad 36 = 2 \times 2 \times 3 \times 3 \qquad 126 = 3 \times 2 \times 3 \times 7$$

EXAMPLE D

Sketch a factor tree to find the prime factors of 84.

Solution

The Fundamental Theorem of Arithmetic guarantees that the prime factorization is unique, so a factor tree can be started with any two factors of a number. In the factor tree on the left, the first two factors are 7 and 12. In the factor tree on the right, the first two factors are 2 and 42.

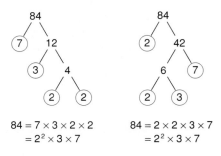

$$84 = 7 \times 3 \times 2 \times 2 \qquad 84 = 2 \times 2 \times 3 \times 7$$
$$= 2^2 \times 3 \times 7 \qquad\qquad = 2^2 \times 3 \times 7$$

FACTORS OF NUMBERS

In Section 4.1 we classified numbers as *prime* or *composite* depending on their number of factors: prime numbers have only two factors, whereas composite numbers have three or more factors. We also saw that the factors of a number can be visualized by sketching rectangular arrays. The rectangles representing the factors of 24 are shown in Figure 4.11. Notice that since 24 is not a square number, each rectangle produces a pair of factors. There are 4 pairs and a total of 8 factors.

Figure 4.11

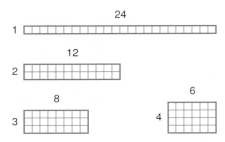

A list of *all* the factors of a number can be obtained by starting with 1 and then considering each whole number, 2, 3, 4, etc., in turn, as a possible factor. For small numbers this can easily be done with mental calculations.

EXAMPLE E

List all the factors of each number.

    1. 20   2. 34

Solution   1. 1, 2, 4, 5, 10, 20   2. 1, 2, 17, 34

Notice that the solutions for Example E list *all* the factors of each number, not just the prime factors.

Another approach to finding the factors of a number is to first find its prime factorization and then use combinations of primes to find all the factors other than 1.

EXAMPLE F

The prime factorization of 273 is 3 × 7 × 13. List all its factors.

Solution   Since 1 is always a factor and each prime is a factor, we can begin the list with 1, 3, 7, and 13. Then we find the products of all pairs of primes: 3 × 7 = 21, 3 × 13 = 39, and 7 × 13 = 91. Finally, the product of all three primes, 3 × 7 × 13 = 273, is also a factor. So the factors of 273 are 1, 3, 7, 13, 21, 39, 91, and 273.

The fact that prime numbers can be used to obtain all the factors of a number is another reason why the prime numbers are called the building blocks of the whole numbers.*

The following problem can be solved by the strategy of *guessing and checking* or by finding the *prime factorization* of a number. Try solving this problem before reading the solution.

PROBLEM-SOLVING APPLICATION

■ PROBLEM

The product of the ages of a group of teenagers is 10,584,000. Find the number of teenagers in the group and their ages.**

Question 1   **Understanding the Problem**   As a first step, it is helpful to list all the possible ages. What are these ages?

---

*The computer program FACTORIZATIONS on the *Computer Problem-Solving Disc* tests any whole number less than 1 million to determine if it is prime or composite. If the number is composite, the computer prints the prime factorization and lists all its factors.

**"Problems of the Month," *The Mathematics Teacher* 82, no. 3 (March 1989): 189.

Question 2

Devising a Plan One approach is to *guess and check*. We might try dividing 10,584,000 by 13, then 14, etc. Another approach is to find the prime factorization of 10,584,000, since the prime factors can be used to build other factors. What is the prime factorization of this number?

Carrying Out the Plan Expressed as a product of prime factors,

$$10,584,000 = 2 \times 2 \times 2 \times 2 \times 2 \times 2 \times 3 \times 3 \times 3 \times 5 \times 5 \times 5 \times 7 \times 7$$

Question 3

The ages of the teenagers can now be obtained by using combinations of these factors. Each 7 must be multiplied by 2, which means that there are two 14-year-olds, and each 5 must be multiplied by 3, which results in three 15-year-olds. Using the remaining 2s, what is the age of the sixth teenager?

Question 4

Looking Back The original problem can be varied by changing the number of teenagers to obtain a new product of ages. The prime factors suggest ways of obtaining new products. For example, we can cross out one 7 and one 2 or two 5s and two 3s. Explain why we cannot change the problem by crossing out only one 3 (or one 2).

Answers to Questions 1–4
1. 13, 14, 15, 16, 17, 18, 19
2. The prime factorization is
$2 \times 2 \times 2 \times 2 \times 2 \times 2 \times 3 \times 3 \times 3 \times 5 \times 5 \times 5 \times 7 \times 7$
3. 16
4. Crossing out only one 3 would leave a factor of 5 with which no number could be paired: 5×2 and 5×7 are not in the teens. Similarly, crossing out one 2 would leave a factor of 7 with which no number could be paired.

GREATEST COMMON FACTOR

common factor

For any two numbers, there is always a number that is a factor of both. The numbers 24 and 36 both have 6 as a factor. When a number is a factor of two numbers, it is called a **common factor.**

EXAMPLE G

1. List all the factors of 24.
2. List all the factors of 36.
3. What are the common factors of 24 and 36?

Solution

1. The factors of 24 are 1, 2, 3, 4, 6, 8, 12, and 24.
2. The factors of 36 are 1, 2, 3, 4, 6, 9, 12, 18, and 36.
3. The common factors of 24 and 36 are 1, 2, 3, 4, 6, and 12.

greatest common factor

Among the common factors of two numbers there will always be a largest number, which is called the **greatest common factor.** The greatest common factor of 24 and 36 is 12. This is sometimes written GCF(24, 36) = 12.

GREATEST COMMON FACTOR

> For any two nonzero whole numbers a and b, the greatest common factor, written GCF(a, b), is the greatest factor (divisor) of both a and b.

The concept of common factor can be illustrated by using separate rods to represent two numbers and then cutting both rods into pieces of common length. The GCF of the two numbers is the length of the pieces of greatest common length. Figure 4.12 shows three possible ways of cutting rods that have lengths of 20 and 30 units. The rods of common length have lengths of 2, 5, and 10. Since there is no greater common length, 10 is the greatest common factor of 20 and 30.

Figure 4.12

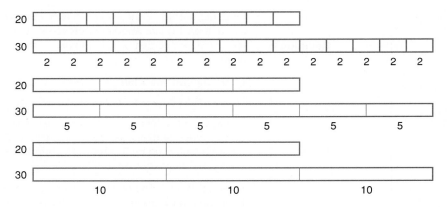

One method of finding the greatest common factor of two numbers is by listing all the factors of both numbers and selecting the greatest one. A more convenient approach, especially for larger numbers, is to use prime factorizations. The GCF of two numbers can be built by using each prime factor the minimum number of times it occurs in both of the numbers.

EXAMPLE H

The following factor trees for 60 and 72 show the prime factors for both numbers.

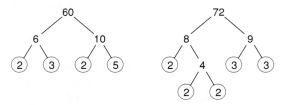

Use these prime factors to obtain GCF(60, 72).

Solution We can see that 2 occurs as a prime factor at least twice and 3 occurs at least once in both 60 and 72. Therefore, we can use these factors to build the GCF, which is $2 \times 2 \times 3 = 12$.

Notice in Example H that 2 occurs as a factor three times in 72 but only twice in 60. So the greatest common factor of 60 and 72 can have 2 as a factor only twice. If 2 occurs three times as a factor of a number, this number will not divide 60.

EXAMPLE I

Find the greatest common factors.

1. GCF(180, 220)   2. GCF(92, 136)   3. GCF(14, 34, 60)

Solution
1. $180 = 2 \times 2 \times 3 \times 3 \times 5$ and $220 = 2 \times 2 \times 5 \times 11$. So GCF(180, 220) = $2 \times 2 \times 5 = 20$, since 2 occurs as a factor twice in both 180 and 220 and 5 occurs as a factor once in both numbers.
2. $92 = 2 \times 2 \times 23$ and $136 = 2 \times 2 \times 2 \times 17$. So GCF(92, 136) = $2 \times 2 = 4$.
3. $14 = 2 \times 7$, $34 = 2 \times 17$, and $60 = 2 \times 2 \times 3 \times 5$. So GCF(14, 34, 60) = 2, since 2 is the only factor common to all three numbers.

relatively prime

Sometimes 1 is the only factor that two numbers have in common. In such cases 1 is the greatest common factor and the two numbers are said to be **relatively prime.**

EXAMPLE J

Determine which pairs of numbers are relatively prime.
1. 8, 9   2. 7, 42   3. 30, 77

Solution

1. 8 and 9 are relatively prime: GCF(8, 9) = 1.
2. 7 and 42 are not relatively prime: GCF(7, 42) = 7.
3. 30 and 77 are relatively prime: GCF(30, 77) = 1.

LEAST COMMON MULTIPLE

Every number has an infinite number of multiples. Here are the first few multiples of 5.

5   10   15   20   25   30   35   40   45   50   55   60   65   70   75

EXAMPLE K

Write the first few multiples of 7.

Solution

7   14   21   28   35   42   49   56   63   70   77   84   91   98   105

common multiple

A number is called a **common multiple** of two numbers if it is a multiple of both. Notice that 35 and 70 occur in both of the preceding lists, so they are common multiples of 5 and 7. The first few multiples of 5 and 7 are shown on the number line in Figure 4.13. Beginning at zero, intervals of 5 units and intervals of 7 units do not coincide again until point 35 on the number line.

Figure 4.13

The next few common multiples of 5 and 7 are 70, 105, 140, 175, and 210. Every pair of nonzero whole numbers has an infinite number of common multiples. Among these common multiples will always be a smallest number, which is called the **least common multiple.** The least common multiple of 5 and 7 is 35. This is sometimes written LCM(5, 7) = 35.

least common multiple

LEAST COMMON MULTIPLE

> For any two nonzero whole numbers *a* and *b,* the least common multiple, written LCM(*a, b*), is the smallest multiple of both *a* and *b.*

Figure 4.14 uses rods to illustrate the concept of least common multiple. Notice that 5 rods of length 4 are required to equal 4 rods of length 5, and that 20 is the smallest length that can be formed by rods of both sizes. The fact that the vertical lines indicating the end of each rod line up only at the left end and the right end of Figure 4.14 shows that the least common multiple of 4 and 5 is 4 × 5 = 20.

Figure 4.14

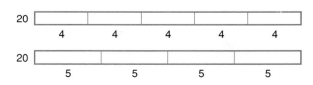

E<small>XAMPLE</small> L

Sketch rods for the following pairs of numbers to illustrate their least common multiple.

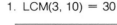

Solution

1. LCM(3, 10) = 30

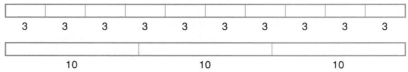

2. LCM(4, 14) = 28

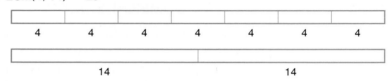

3. LCM(6, 18) = 18

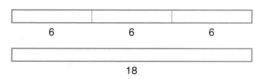

The least common multiple for small numbers can be found by listing the multiples of both numbers. We found the least common multiple of 5 and 7 by listing the first few multiples of 5 and the first few multiples of 7. Another approach, which is more convenient for larger numbers, is to use prime factorizations. The LCM of two numbers can be built from their prime factors by using each prime factor the maximum number of times it occurs in either of the numbers.

E<small>XAMPLE</small> M

Factor trees for 40 and 66 are shown below. Use the prime factors to find LCM(40, 66).

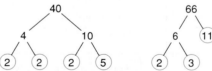

Solution

The factor trees show that 2 occurs three times as a factor of 40 and only once as a factor of 66, so 2 will have to occur three times as a factor in the LCM. Similarly, 5 is a factor of 40, and 3 and 11 are factors of 66, so these numbers will need to be included in the prime factors of the LCM. Therefore, the LCM of 40 and 66 is

$$2 \times 2 \times 2 \times 3 \times 5 \times 11 = 2^3 \times 3 \times 5 \times 11 = 1320$$

Notice in Example M that 2 occurs three times as a factor in 40 and only once as a factor in 66, but it is necessary to have 2 occur three times as a factor in the LCM of 40 and 66.

EXAMPLE N

Find the least common multiples.

   1. LCM(28, 44)   2. LCM(21, 40)   3. LCM(15, 36, 55)

Solution

   1. $28 = 2 \times 2 \times 7$ and $44 = 2 \times 2 \times 11$, so LCM(28, 44) $= 2 \times 2 \times 7 \times 11$
      $= 308$
   2. $21 = 3 \times 7$ and $40 = 2 \times 2 \times 2 \times 5$, so LCM(21, 40) $= 2 \times 2 \times 2 \times 3 \times 5$
      $\times 7 = 840$
   3. $15 = 3 \times 5$, $36 = 2 \times 2 \times 3 \times 3$, and $55 = 5 \times 11$, so LCM(15, 36, 55) $=$
      $2 \times 2 \times 3 \times 3 \times 5 \times 11 = 1980$

You may have noticed some special relationships in Example N. In part (1) of the example, the LCM of 28 and 44 could have been obtained by using all the factors in 28 and 44 and then dividing by the common factors of both numbers. That is,

$$\text{LCM}(28, 44) = \frac{(2 \times 2 \times 7) \times (2 \times 2 \times 11)}{2 \times 2} = \frac{28 \times 44}{\text{GCF}(28, 44)}$$

Similarly, you may have noticed in part (2) of the example that 21 and 40 have no common prime factors—that is, they are relatively prime—so their LCM is the product of the prime factors from both numbers.

$$\text{LCM}(21, 40) = (3 \times 7) \times (2 \times 2 \times 2 \times 5) = 21 \times 40$$

These relationships are stated in the following theorem.

> For positive integers *a* and *b*,
>
> $$\text{LCM}(a, b) = \frac{a \times b}{\text{GCF}(a, b)} \text{ and, when GCF}(a, b) = 1, \text{LCM}(a, b) = a \times b$$

EXAMPLE O

Determine the least common multiples.

   1. LCM(17, 20)   2. LCM(20, 33)   3. LCM(138, 84)

Solution

   1. GCF(17, 20) $= 1$, so LCM(17, 20) $= 17 \times 20 = 340$
   2. GCF(20, 33) $= 1$, so LCM(20, 33) $= 20 \times 33 = 660$
   3. GCF(138, 84) $= 6$, so LCM(138, 84) $= (138 \times 84)/6 = 1932$

Once you have found the prime factors of two numbers, you may find the following schemes helpful for determining their greatest common factor and least common multiple. Notice that the common factors of 198 and 210 are placed under each other in both schemes.*

$$198 = 2 \times 3 \times 3 \qquad\qquad \times 11$$
$$210 = 2 \times 3 \qquad \times 5 \times 7 \qquad\qquad\quad$$
$$\text{GCF} = 2 \times 3 \qquad\qquad\qquad\qquad\qquad\quad$$

$$198 = 2 \times 3 \times 3 \qquad\qquad \times 11$$
$$210 = 2 \times 3 \qquad \times 5 \times 7 \qquad\qquad\quad$$
$$\text{LCM} = 2 \times 3 \times 3 \times 5 \times 7 \times 11$$

*The computer program GCF AND LCM on the *Computer Problem-Solving Disc* prints the GCF and LCM of two or more numbers that are each less than 1 million.

PROBLEM-SOLVING APPLICATION

■ **PROBLEM**

The U.S. Census Clock described at the beginning of this section used flashing lights to indicate birth, death, immigration, and emigration rates. If all 4 lights flashed at the same moment, how long before they would all flash together again?

Understanding the Problem   The birth, death, immigration, and emigration lights flashed every 10, 16, 81, and 900 seconds, respectively. It will take at least 900 seconds (15 minutes) for all 4 lights to flash together again, because the emigrant light flashed only every 900 seconds. Which of the other lights flashed every 900 seconds?

Question 1

Devising a Plan   To obtain an idea for a plan, we can look at a *simpler problem*. At the beginning of this section, a sketch was used to show multiples of 10 and 16 on a number line and to determine that the birth and death lights flashed together every 80 seconds. This suggests visualizing a number line with multiples of 10, 16, 81, and 900.

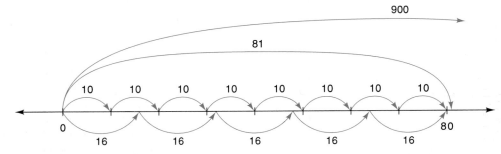

To find the first point beyond zero at which multiples of 10, 16, 81, and 900 coincide, we need to obtain the LCM of these numbers. This requires finding their prime factorizations. What are the prime factorizations of 10, 16, 81, and 900?

Question 2

Carrying Out the Plan   The LCM of 10, 16, 81, and 900 can be built from the prime factors of these numbers.

$$10 = 2 \times 5, 16 = 2 \times 2 \times 2 \times 2, 81 = 3 \times 3 \times 3 \times 3,$$
$$900 = 2 \times 2 \times 3 \times 3 \times 5 \times 5$$

The LCM must contain 2 as a factor four times, 3 as a factor four times, and 5 as a factor twice. So the LCM of 10, 16, 81, and 900 is

$$2 \times 2 \times 2 \times 2 \times 3 \times 3 \times 3 \times 3 \times 5 \times 5 = 32,400$$

Question 3

Thus every 32,400 seconds all 4 lights would flash together. How long is this in hours?

Looking Back   The number of people born in 32,400 seconds would be $32,400 \div 10 = 3240$. Similarly, in 32,400 seconds the number of people who die would be $32,400 \div 16 = 2025$, the number immigrating would be $32,400 \div 81 = 400$, and the number emigrating would be $32,400 \div 900 = 36$. What would be the total gain in population for each 32,400 seconds (9 hours)?

Question 4

Answers to Questions 1–4
1. The birth light, since 10 is a factor of 900
2. The prime factorizations are

$$10 = 2 \times 5$$
$$16 = 2 \times 2 \times 2 \times 2$$
$$81 = 3 \times 3 \times 3 \times 3$$
$$900 = 2 \times 2 \times 3 \times 3 \times 5 \times 5$$

3. 32,400 seconds is equal to 9 hours. ($32400 \div 60 = 540$ minutes, and $540 \div 60 = 9$ hours.)
4. $3240 - 2025 + 400 - 36 = 1579$ people

RELATED ACTIVITIES IN
Mathematics for Elementary Teachers: An Activity Approach, 3e

Activity Set 4.2   **Models for GCF and LCM:** A linear model illustrates concepts and methods of computing greatest common factors and least common multiples.

Just for Fun   **Star Polygons:** An art activity that generates questions that can be answered using the concepts of GCF and LCM

EXERCISES AND PROBLEMS 4.2

1. Find the prime factorization of each number.

   a. 126   **b.** 308

   c. 245   **d.** 442

2. Sketch a factor tree to find the prime factors of each number.

   a. 112   **b.** 385

   c. 390   **d.** 400

3. It has been estimated that life began on earth 1,000,000,000 (1 billion) years ago. How can the Fundamental Theorem of Arithmetic be used to show that 7 is not a factor of this number?

4. List all the factors of each number.

   a. 60   **b.** 182

   c. 180   **d.** 500

5. List all the common factors for each pair of numbers.

   a. 30, 40   **b.** 15, 22

   c. 14, 56   **d.** 23, 64

6. Find each greatest common factor.

   a. GCF(65, 60)   **b.** GCF(8, 30)

   c. GCF(198, 165)   **d.** GCF(280, 168)

   e. GCF(12, 15, 125)   **f.** GCF(118, 7, 24)

7. List 5 common multiples for each pair of numbers.

   a. 4, 14   **b.** 6, 8

   c. 12, 17   **d.** 50, 35

8. Find each least common multiple.

   a. LCM(10, 40)   **b.** LCM(14, 15)

   c. LCM(30, 42)   **d.** LCM(22, 56)

   e. LCM(6, 38, 16)   **f.** LCM(14, 5, 26)

9. The following two rods are marked off in common lengths of 6 units.

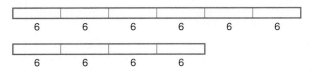

   a. Do these rods provide any information about common factors? or common multiples?

   b. What information is illustrated by these rods?

10. Cuisenaire rods (see exercise 5, page 134) are used below to form an all-green train, which is the same length as an all-yellow train.

   a. Do these rods provide information about common factors or common multiples? What information do they provide?

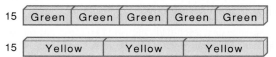

   b. If the purple rods (4 units) and the black rods (7 units) are used to form the shortest possible one-color trains of the same length, how many purple rods and how many black rods will be required?

   c. If an all-brown train (brown rods represent 8 units) equals in length an all-orange train (orange rods represent 10 units), what can be said about the number of brown rods?

   d. If the two trains in part c are the shortest possible, how many brown rods will be required?

11. For a U.S. Census Clock based on the 1990 census, the birth light would flash every 7 seconds; the death light every 15 seconds, the immigration light every 81 seconds, and the emigration light every 900 seconds, to indicate gains and losses in population.

   a. If the birth and death lights flashed at the same time, how many seconds would pass before they flashed together again?

   b. During the time period calculated in part a, what is the gain in population due to births and deaths?

   c. If the birth, death, and immigration lights flashed at the same time, how many seconds would pass before they flashed together again? Is this less than or greater than 1 hour?

   d. For the time period in part c, what is the gain in population due to births, deaths, and immigration?

   e. If all 4 lights flashed at the same time, what is the shortest time before they would all flash together again?

12. Shane has 72 inches of copper wire and 42 inches of steel wire.

   a. What are the largest pieces he can cut these wires into so that each piece is the same length?

   b. How many pieces of wire will he have?

13. A bakery has 300 chocolate chip cookies and 264 peanut butter cookies. The bakers wish to divide the chocolate chip cookies into piles and the peanut butter cookies into piles so that each pile has only one type of cookie, there is the same number of cookies in each pile, and each pile has the largest possible number of cookies.
    a. How many cookies will there be in each pile?
    b. How many piles of chocolate chip cookies will there be?
    c. How many piles of peanut butter cookies will there be?

14. Janice and Bob both work night shifts. When they have the same night off, they go dancing together. If Janice has every fourth night off and Bob has every seventh night off, how often does Janice go dancing with Bob?

15. A clock shop has 3 cuckoo clocks on display. The cuckoos appear at different time intervals. One comes out every 10 minutes, one comes out every 15 minutes, and one comes out every 25 minutes. If they all appear at 5 o'clock, what is the next time they will all come out together?

16. For science day, a school is showing two films: one on volcanoes, which is 24 minutes long, and one on tornadoes, which is 40 minutes long. If they both begin at 8 A.M. and run continuously until 3 P.M., at which times during the day will they both start at the same time?

17. How many zeros are at the right end of the numeral for the product, $1 \times 2 \times 3 \times \cdots \times 98 \times 99 \times 100$?

18. The **proper factors** of a number are all of its factors except the number itself. The Pythagoreans classified a number according to the sum of its proper factors.
    a. A number is **deficient** if the sum of its proper factors is less than the number. Which of these numbers is deficient: 20, 22, 24?
    b. A number is **abundant** if the sum of its proper factors is greater than the number. Which of these numbers is abundant: 23, 30, 35?
    c. A number is **perfect** if the sum of its proper factors is equal to the number. Which of these numbers is perfect: 10, 28, 46?

19. Two sisters, Cindy and Nicole, just bought a special 180-day family health club membership. Cindy will use the club on every second day, and Nicole will use the club on every third day. They go together on the first day. On how many of the 180 days will neither sister use the club?

Featured Strategy: Drawing Venn Diagrams

20. How many whole numbers from 1 to 300 are not multiples of 3 or 5?
    a. **Understanding the Problem** The number of multiples of 3 from 1 to 9 is $9 \div 3 = 3$.

    1 2 ③ 4 5 ⑥ 7 8 ⑨

    How many multiples of 3 are there from 1 to 300? How many multiples of 5 are there?
    b. **Devising a Plan** Since some of the multiples of 3 are also multiples of 5, we need to consider the intersection of the set of multiples of 3 and the set of multiples of 5. How many numbers less than or equal to 300 are multiples of both 3 and 5?
    c. **Carrying Out the Plan** The following Venn diagram helps us to visualize the information. Record the numbers of multiples in the appropriate regions of the diagram, and then determine how many numbers are not multiples of 3 or 5.

    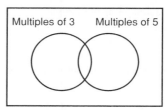

    d. **Looking Back** The Venn diagram helps to answer other questions. How many numbers less than or equal to 300 are multiples of 3 but not multiples of 5?

CALCULATOR INVESTIGATION

Any number less than 900 is prime if none of the following primes are among its factors:

2 3 5 7 11 13 17 19 23 29

Divisibility by the first few primes (2, 3, 5) can be quickly checked by using the divisibility tests.

Questions for Investigation

1. What is the largest three-digit prime number such that each of its digits is prime?
2. What is the smallest three-digit prime number such that each of its digits is prime?
3. What are the 4 largest three-digit numbers that are each the product of two different primes?

PUZZLER

This faded document puzzle uses only the prime digits 2, 3, 5, and 7. How can these numbers be placed in the boxes to create a valid product?

```
    □ □ □
  × □ □
  □ □ □ □
□ □ □ □
□ □ □ □ □
```

CHAPTER REVIEW

1. Number Theory Relationships
  a. **Number theory** is the study of whole numbers and their relationships.
  b. If one number is a **factor** of a second, then the second number is a **multiple** of the first.
  c. If a and b are whole numbers such that a is a factor of b, then a **divides** b, and we write $a|b$. If a does not divide b, we write $a \nmid b$.

2. Models for Factors and Multiples
  a. The **linear model** uses number lines or rods to represent factors and multiples.
  b. In the **rectangular array** model, a number is represented by the number of squares or tiles in an array, and the dimensions of the array are the factors of the number.

3. Divisibility Theorems
  a. For whole numbers a, b, and c, if $a|b$ and $a|c$, then $a|(b + c)$.
  b. For whole numbers a, b, and c, if $a|b$ and $a \nmid c$, then $a \nmid (b + c)$.
  c. For whole numbers a, b, and k, if $a|b$, then $a|bk$.

4. Divisibility Tests
  a. A number is **divisible by 2** if and only if its units digit is divisible by 2.
  b. A number is **divisible by 3** if and only if the sum of its digits is divisible by 3.
  c. A number is **divisible by 4** if and only if the number represented by its tens and units digits is divisible by 4.
  d. A number is **divisible by 5** if and only if its units digit is divisible by 5.
  e. A number is **divisible by 6** if and only if it is divisible by 2 and 3.
  f. A number is **divisible by 9** if and only if the sum of its digits is divisible by 9.
  g. A number is **divisible by 11** if and only if the number obtained by alternately adding and subtracting its digits is divisible by 11.

5. Prime and Composite Numbers
  a. A number with exactly two factors is a **prime number.**
  b. A number with more than two factors is a **composite number.**
  c. The number 1 has only one factor and is neither prime nor composite.
  d. The **prime number test** guarantees that for any whole number n and prime p such that $p^2 > n$, if there is no smaller prime that divides n, then n is a prime number.
  e. The **sieve of Eratosthenes** is a systematic method of eliminating all the numbers less than a given number that are not prime.
  f. The product that expresses a number in terms of primes is called its **prime factorization.**
  g. The **Fundamental Theorem of Arithmetic** states that every composite whole number has one and only one prime factorization (if the order of the factors is disregarded).
  h. A **factor tree** is a diagram for finding the prime factors of a number.
  i. A list of all the factors of a number can be obtained by beginning with 1, listing the prime factors, and then multiplying combinations of the prime factors.

6. GCF and LCM
  a. The **greatest common factor** of two nonzero whole numbers a and b, written GCF(a, b), is the greatest factor the two numbers have in common.
  b. The **least common multiple** of two nonzero whole numbers a and b, written LCM(a, b), is the smallest multiple the two numbers have in common.
  c. If the GCF of two nonzero whole numbers is 1, the numbers are **relatively prime.**
  d. If two numbers are relatively prime, then their LCM is the product of the two numbers.
  e. Number lines and rods are common **linear models** for illustrating the concepts of GCF and LCM.

CHAPTER TEST

1. Determine whether the following statements are true or false.
  a. $3|48{,}025$ **b.** $2|3776$
  c. $6 \nmid 7966$ **d.** $9|4576$

2. Rewrite each statement below in the form $a|b$.
  a. 45 is divisible by 3.
  b. 12 is a factor of 60.
  c. 20 divides 140.
  d. 102 is a multiple of 17.

3. Illustrate the fact that 78 is a multiple of 6 using
  a. a linear model.
  b. a rectangular array model.

4. Rectangular arrays whose dimensions are whole numbers can be used to illustrate the factors of a number. What can be said about the number of rectangular arrays for each of the following types of numbers?
  a. Prime number
  b. Composite number
  c. Square number

5. Determine whether the following statements are true or false.
  a. If 3 divides the units digit of a number, then 3 divides the number.
  b. If a number is divisible by 8, then it is divisible by 4.
  c. If 2 divides the sum of the digits of a number, then 2 divides the number.
  d. If a number is not divisible by 6, then it is not divisible by 3.

6. Which one of the following numbers is prime?
  a. 331   **b.** 351   **c.** 371

7. Write the prime factorization of 1836.

8. List all the factors of 273.

9. Determine whether the following statements are true or false. If a statement is false, show a counterexample.
   a. If $a|b$, then $a|(13 \times b)$.
   b. If $a|(b + c)$, then $a|b$ or $a|c$.
   c. If $a|b$ and $a\nmid c$, then $a\nmid(b + c)$.
   d. If $a|bc$, then $a|b$.

10. List the following.
    a. Four common factors of 30 and 40
    b. Four common multiples 15 and 20
    c. Four common factors of 195 and 255
    d. Five common multiples of 13 and 20

11. Find each GCF or LCM.

    a. GCF(17, 30)   b. LCM(14, 22)

    c. LCM(12, 210)   d. GCF(280, 165)
    e. GCF(18, 28, 36)   f. LCM(6, 15, 65)

12. Sketch linear models to illustrate
    a. the least common multiple of 3 and 8.
    b. the greatest common factor of 15 and 24.

13. One lighthouse light flashes every 10 seconds, and a second lighthouse light flashes every 12 seconds. If they both flash at the same moment, how long before they will both flash together again?

14. How many whole numbers between 1 and 1000 are multiples of either 3 or 7?

15. Mike has 20 strips of wood molding that are each 70 inches long and 6 pieces that are each 28 inches long. He wants to cut all these strips so that each piece has the same length and no wood is left. What is the longest possible length that can be cut?

BIBLIOGRAPHY

Avital, S. "The Plight and Might of Number Seven." *Arithmetic Teacher* 25 (February 1978): 22–24.

Beattie, I. D. "Building Understanding with Blocks." *Arithmetic Teacher* 34 (October 1986): 5–11.

Bezuszka, S. "A Test for Divisibility by Primes." *Arithmetic Teacher* 33 (October 1985): 36–38.

Boyd, B. V. "Learning about Odd and Even Numbers." *Arithmetic Teacher* 35 (November 1987): 18–21.

Brown, G. "Searching for Patterns of Divisors." *Arithmetic Teacher* 32 (December 1984): 32–34.

Burton, G., and J. Knifong. "Definitions for Prime Numbers." *Arithmetic Teacher* 27 (February 1980): 44–47.

Henry, L. "Another Look at Least Common Multiple and Greatest Common Factor." *Arithmetic Teacher* 25 (March 1978): 52–53.

Hohfold, J. "An Inductive Approach to Prime Factors." *Arithmetic Teacher* 29 (December 1981): 28–29.

Hopkins, M. H. "Number Facts—or Fantasy?" *Arithmetic Teacher* 34 (March 1987): 38–42.

Johnson, P. "Understanding the Check of Nines." *Arithmetic Teacher* 26 (November 1978): 54–55.

Kennedy, R. "Divisibility for Integers Ending in 1, 3, 7, or 9." *Mathematics Teacher* 64 (February 1971): 137–138.

Lamb, C., and L. Hutcherson. "Greatest Common Factor and Least Common Multiple." *Arithmetic Teacher* 31 (April 1984): 43–44.

Lappan, G., and M. Winter. "Prime Factorizations." *Arithmetic Teacher* 27 (March 1980): 24–27.

Newman, C. M., and S. B. Turkel. "Integrating Arithmetic and Geometry with Numbered Points on a Circle." *Arithmetic Teacher* 36 (January 1989): 28–31.

Robold, A. "Patterns in Multiples." *Arithmetic Teacher* 29 (April 1982): 21–23.

Roy, S. "LCM and GCF in the Hundred Chart." *Arithmetic Teacher* 26 (December 1978): 53.

Schaefer, M. G. "Motivational Activities in Elementary Mathematics." *Arithmetic Teacher* 28 (May 1981): 17–18.

Scheuer, D., Jr. "All-Star GCF." *Arithmetic Teacher* 26 (November 1978): 34–35.

Sherzer, L. "A Simplified Presentation for Finding the LCM and the GCF." *Arithmetic Teacher* 21 (May 1974): 415–416.

Stern, P. "GCF and LCM, Korean Style!" *Arithmetic Teacher* 32 (December 1984): 3.

5 *Integers and Fractions*

Excerpts from NCTM's Standard 12 for Teaching Mathematics in Grades K–4*

The K–4 instruction should help students understand fractions and decimals, explore their relationship, and build initial concepts about order and equivalence. Because evidence suggests that children construct these ideas slowly, it is crucial that teachers use physical materials, diagrams, and real-world situations in conjunction with ongoing efforts to relate their learning experiences to oral language and symbols. This K–4 emphasis on basic ideas will reduce the amount of time currently spent in the upper grades in correcting students' misconceptions and procedural difficulties.

Fraction symbols, such as ¼ and ¾, should be introduced only after children have developed the concepts and oral language necessary for symbols to be meaningful and should be carefully connected to both the models and oral language.

Children need to use physical materials to explore equivalent fractions and compare fractions. For example, with folded paper strips, children can easily see that ½ is the same amount as ³⁄₆ and that ⅔ is smaller than ¾.

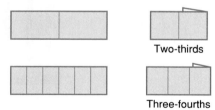

Two-thirds

Three-fourths

*Reprinted by permission of the National Council of Teachers of Mathematics.

SECTION 5.1   INTEGERS

Keeping the single-digit numbers from 1 to 9 in order,

1 2 3 4 5 6 7 8 9

and inserting plus and/or minus signs, we can obtain a sum of 100 in several ways. For example,

$$1 + 2 + 3 - 4 + 5 + 6 + 78 + 9 = 100$$

Find another way.

negative whole numbers

The need for **negative whole numbers** ($^-1$, $^-2$, $^-3$, . . .) originated over 2000 years ago. As trading became more common, whole numbers were needed for two distinctly different uses: to indicate *credits* or *gains* and to indicate *debts* or *losses*. Conventions were developed to permit the use of whole numbers in both cases. About 200 B.C. the Chinese were computing credits with red rods and debts with black rods (Figure 5.1). Similarly, in their writing they used red numerals and black numerals.*

In the United States today it is customary to reverse the color scheme used by the Chinese. Banks often use red numerals to represent amounts below zero ("in the red" is negative). Black numerals are used to represent accounts above zero ("in the black" is positive).

Figure 5.1

Rods for computing
credits and debits

POSITIVE AND NEGATIVE INTEGERS

integers

The negative whole numbers together with the positive whole numbers are called **integers.** A number line with a fixed reference point labeled 0 is a common model for visualizing the integers. The integers are assigned points on the number line that have been marked off in unit lengths to the right and left of zero. For each integer to the right of zero, there is a corresponding integer to the left of zero. These pairs of integers, 2 and $^-2$, 5 and $^-5$, 7 and $^-7$, etc., are called **opposites** or **negatives** of each other (Figure 5.2).

opposites

negatives

Sometimes the integers to the right of zero are labeled $^+1$, $^+2$, $^+3$, etc., in order to emphasize that they are **positive integers** as opposed to **negative integers** ($^-1$, $^-2$, $^-3$,

positive integers

negative integers

*D. E. Smith, *History of Mathematics,* 2nd ed. (Lexington, MA: Ginn, 1925), 257–258.

Figure 5.2

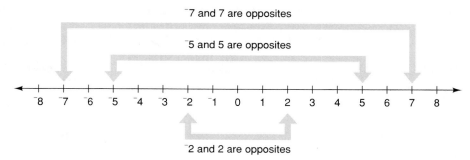

etc). Since minus signs are also used to represent *subtraction,* raising the signs to indicate negative numbers helps to avoid confusion between the two uses of these symbols.

EXAMPLE A

Determine the opposite for each integer.

1. 14   2. 0   3. 1   4. ⁻8

Solution   1. ⁻14   2. 0   3. ⁻1   4. 8

Many calculators have a change-of-sign key that can be used to obtain the opposite of the number in the display. For example, if 35 is in the display, pressing the change-of-sign key changes the display to ⁻35, and pressing the key again produces 35. Such a key is marked in one of three ways: ⎡CS⎤, ⎡CHS⎤, or ⎡+/−⎤.

■ HISTORICAL HIGHLIGHT

Traditionally, it has taken hundreds of years for a new type of number to prove itself necessary and earn a place beside the commonly accepted older numbers. This is especially true of negative numbers. By the seventh century, Hindu mathematicians were using these numbers on a limited basis. They had symbols for negative numbers, such as ⑤ and $\overset{o}{5}$ for ⁻5, and rules for computing with them. However, it was another 1000 years before the Italian mathematician Jerome Cardan (1501–1576) gave the first significant treatment of negative numbers. Cardan called these new numbers "false" and represented each number by writing "m:" in front of the numeral. For example, he wrote "m:3" for negative three. Other writers of this period called negative numbers "absurd numbers." The resistance to negative numbers can be seen as late as 1796, when William Frend, in his text *Principles of Algebra,* argued against their use.

USES OF INTEGERS

positive and negative numbers

The concept of number opposites in the form of positive and negative integers, also referred to as **positive and negative numbers,** is useful whenever we wish to count on both sides of a fixed point of reference. The positive integers indicate one direction, and the negative integers indicate the opposite direction.

CREDITS AND DEBTS   One common example of opposites is *credits*, which are represented by positive numbers, and *debts*, which are represented by negative numbers. The graph in Figure 5.3 shows the U.S. trade balance, which is the difference between exports and imports.

Figure 5.3

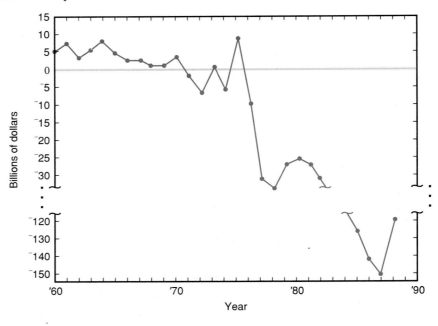

EXAMPLE B

Determine whether the U.S. trade balance was positive or negative for the following periods.

1. 1960 to 1970   2. 1976 to 1988

Solution   1. Positive   2. Negative

TEMPERATURE   Measuring temperature is another familiar use for positive and negative numbers. The fixed reference point on the Celsius thermometer is zero, the temperature at which water freezes. On the Fahrenheit scale, water freezes at 32°. On both scales, temperatures *above* zero are *positive* and those *below* zero are *negative*.

EXAMPLE C

Write the integer for each of the following temperatures.

1. 10° below zero on the Celsius thermometer
2. 20° below 32° on the Fahrenheit thermometer
3. 20° below zero on the Fahrenheit thermometer

Solution   1. ⁻10° Celsius   2. 12° Fahrenheit   3. ⁻20° Fahrenheit

SPORTS   In several sports there are special reference points from which it is convenient to measure with positive and negative numbers. In golf this reference point is *par*, and a score of ⁻4 represents 4 strokes *below par*. In football the yardline at which plays begin is the reference point, and a *loss of yardage* is referred to as *negative yardage*.

TIME   Scientists often find it convenient to designate a given time as "zero time" and then refer to the *time before* and *time after* as being negative and positive, respectively. This practice is followed in the launching of rockets. If the time with respect to blast-off is ⁻15 minutes, then it is 15 minutes before the launch.

ALTITUDE   Sea level is the common reference point for measuring altitudes. Charts and maps that label altitudes below and above sea level use negative and positive numbers. The chart in Figure 5.4 uses negative numbers to show altitudes above the floor of the Atlantic Ocean between South America and Africa.

Figure 5.4

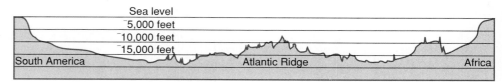

EXAMPLE D

Determine each altitude as an integer.

1. 8500 feet below sea level
2. 300 feet above sea level
3. Sea level

Solution   1. ⁻8500 feet   2. 300 feet   3. 0 feet

MODELS FOR INTEGERS

There are many models for illustrating integers and operations on integers. The *number line model* and the *black and red chips model* will be used on the following pages.

BLACK AND RED CHIPS MODEL   The red and black rods used by the Chinese for positive and negative integers suggest a physical model for the integers. In place of rods we will use chips, and the color scheme will be reversed; that is, black chips will represent positive integers, and red chips negative integers. By establishing that each black chip cancels a red chip (think of each black chip as a $1 credit and each red chip as a $1 debt), we can represent every integer in an infinite number of ways. Three different sets that illustrate the number 3 are shown in Figure 5.5. In part (b) the red chip is canceled by 1 black chip; in part (c) 2 red chips are canceled by 2 black chips.

Figure 5.5

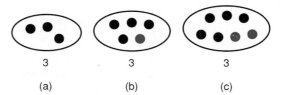

EXAMPLE E

Describe four different sets of chips to represent ⁻4.

Solution   Here are four possibilities: 4 red chips, 5 red chips and 1 black chip, 6 red chips and 2 black chips, 7 red chips and 3 black chips.

ADDITION

Addition of integers can be illustrated by putting together (taking the union of) sets of black and red chips. Figure 5.6 shows sets for ⁻5 and 2 and their union, which contains 5 red chips and 2 black chips. The 2 black chips cancel 2 of the red chips, leaving 3 red chips. This shows that ⁻5 + 2 = ⁻3.

Figure 5.6

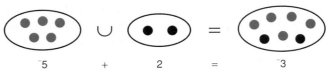

⁻5   +   2   =   ⁻3

Combining a debt of $5 with a credit of $2 reduces the debt to $3.

EXAMPLE F

Sketch sets of chips to illustrate and compute ⁻4 + ⁻3.

Solution

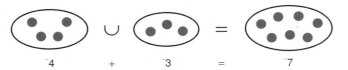

⁻4   +   ⁻3   =   ⁻7

Combining a debt of $4 with a debt of $3 produces a debt of $7.

The usual rules for addition can be discovered by using black and red chips to compute sums of positive and negative integers. For example, when a positive and a negative integer are added, the sum will be positive or negative depending on whether there are more black or red chips. The rule of signs for addition is shown below. In each of the three cases, *a* and *b* represent positive integers. Notice that sums involving negative integers can be obtained by computing sums or differences of positive integers.

**RULE OF SIGNS
FOR ADDITION**

1. Negative plus negative equals negative

$$^-a + {}^-b = {}^-(a + b)$$
$$^-3 + {}^-7 = {}^-(3 + 7) = {}^-10$$

2. Positive plus negative equals positive, if $a > b$

$$a + {}^-b = a - b$$
$$13 + {}^-5 = 13 - 5 = 8$$

3. Positive plus negative equals negative, if $a < b$

$$a + {}^-b = {}^-(b - a)$$
$$6 + {}^-11 = {}^-(11 - 6) = {}^-5$$

The number line is a more abstract model for illustrating addition of positive and negative numbers. To add two numbers, we begin by drawing an arrow from zero to the point that corresponds to the first number. Then, if the second integer is positive, we move from that point to the right on the number line, and if it is negative, we move to the left. Two examples are shown in Figure 5.7.

Figure 5.7

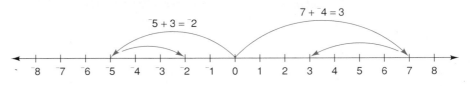

Most calculators are designed to compute with negative as well as positive numbers through use of a change-of-sign key ($\boxed{CS}$ or $\boxed{CHS}$ or $\boxed{+/-}$). For example, to add ⁻715 + ⁻643, you would follow these steps:

	Steps		*Displays*
(1)	715 $\boxed{+/-}$		$\boxed{-715.}$
(2)	$\boxed{+}$		$\boxed{-715.}$
(3)	643 $\boxed{+/-}$		$\boxed{-643.}$
(4)	$\boxed{=}$		$\boxed{-1358.}$

If this special key is not available on your calculator, you can use the rule of signs for addition to first compute the sum or difference of positive integers and then choose the correct sign.

SUBTRACTION

The *take-away model* may be used for subtraction of integers. Figure 5.8 illustrates ⁻6 take away ⁻2. We begin by representing ⁻6 by 6 red chips and then take away 2 red chips.

Figure 5.8

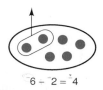

$$^-6 - {}^-2 = {}^-4$$

Taking away a debt of $2 from a debt of $6 leaves a debt of $4.

Traditionally, the take-away model for subtraction is used only when one whole number is subtracted from a larger one. However, it is still possible to use this model in cases such as 3 − 5, where the number being subtracted is the larger one. This can be accomplished by using a suitable representation for 3. For example, instead of representing 3 by 3 black chips, as in set *A* of Figure 5.9, we can represent 3 by 5 black chips and 2 red chips, as in set *B*. Then 5 black chips can be taken away, leaving 2 red chips: 3 − 5 = ⁻2.

Figure 5.9

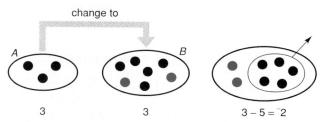

Having a credit of $3 and taking away a credit of $5 leaves a debt of $2.

ADDING OPPOSITES One common method of subtracting an integer is by adding its opposite. If, instead of removing 5 black chips from set *B* in Figure 5.9, we put in 5 red chips, as in Figure 5.10, the final set will still represent ⁻2. In other words, *putting in 5 red chips* has the same effect as *taking away 5 black chips*. This suggests that subtracting 5 is the same as adding its opposite, ⁻5.

Figure 5.10

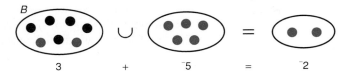

3   +   ⁻5   =   ⁻2

Having a credit of $5 taken away is like incurring a debt of $5.

adding opposites

This approach to subtraction is called **adding opposites.** It enables us to compute the difference of any two integers by computing a sum, as stated in the following definition.

SUBTRACTION OF INTEGERS

For any two integers a and b, $a - b$ is the sum of a plus the opposite of b,

$$a - b = a + {}^-b$$

EXAMPLE G

Compute the following differences.

1. $15 - 7$ 2. $^-14 - 3$ 3. $22 - {}^-5$

Solution

1. $15 - 7 = 15 + {}^-7 = 8$ (The opposite of 7 is $^-7$)
2. $^-14 - 3 = {}^-14 + {}^-3 = {}^-17$ (The opposite of 3 is $^-3$)
3. $22 - {}^-5 = 22 + 5 = 27$ (The opposite of $^-5$ is 5)

The change-of-sign key on a calculator is handy if you wish to subtract negative integers. Here are the keys to press to compute $^-243 - {}^-109$:

	Steps	*Displays*
(1)	243 $\boxed{+/-}$	$\boxed{^-243.}$
(2)	$\boxed{-}$	$\boxed{^-243.}$
(3)	109 $\boxed{+/-}$	$\boxed{^-109.}$
(4)	$\boxed{=}$	$\boxed{^-134.}$

Notice that $^-243 - {}^-109 = {}^-243 + 109$, which can be computed on a calculator by using the change-of-sign key to enter $^-243$ or by commuting the numbers and computing $109 - 243$.

Figure 5.11

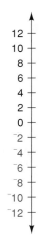

MULTIPLICATION

The familiar rules for multiplying with negative numbers, such as "a negative times a negative is a positive," are easy enough to remember but difficult to illustrate. There are many different approaches that attempt to justify the rules for multiplying with negative numbers in an intuitive manner. Two of these methods are explained in the following paragraphs.

NUMBER LINE MODEL   Products of positive and negative integers can be illustrated on a number line. One number line model uses temperatures. Figure 5.11 shows a thermometer scale, a portion of a vertical number line. To illustrate products we will use the following common conventions:

1. Temperature increases are represented by positive integers and temperature decreases by negative integers.
2. Time in the future is represented by positive integers and time in the past by negative integers.

EXAMPLE H

Compute each product by determining the new or old temperature. You may find it helpful to sketch a vertical number line.

1. If the temperature is now 0°, what will it be 4 hours from now if it increases 3° each hour?

| 4 | × | 3 | = □ |
| 4 hours from now (time in the future) | | 3° increase | Temperature will be ____ |

2. If the temperature is now 0°, what will it be 5 hours from now if it decreases 2° each hour?

| 5 | × | ⁻2 | = □ |
| 5 hours from now (time in the future) | | 2° decrease | Temperature will be ____ |

3. If the temperature is now 0°, what was it 3 hours ago if it has been increasing 5° each hour?

| ⁻3 | × | 5 | = □ |
| 3 hours ago (time in the past) | | 5° increase | Temperature was ___ |

4. If the temperature is now 0°, what was it 4 hours ago if it has been decreasing 2° each hour?

| ⁻4 | × | ⁻2 | = □ |
| 4 hours ago (time in the past) | | 2° decrease | Temperature was ____ . |

Solution

1. The temperature will be 12°:
4 × 3 = 12

2. The temperature will be ⁻10°:
5 × ⁻2 = ⁻10

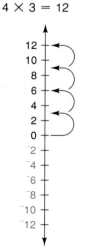
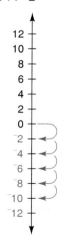

3. The temperature was ⁻15°:
    ⁻3 × 5 = ⁻15

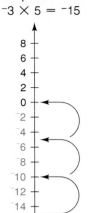

4. The temperature was 8°:
    ⁻4 × ⁻2 = 8

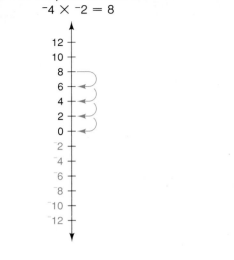

BLACK AND RED CHIPS MODEL   Multiplication by a positive integer can be illustrated by putting in groups of chips. Suppose that on 4 occasions you incur debts of $2. This is represented in Figure 5.12 by 4 groups of 2 red chips; the figure illustrates 4 × ⁻2. Since there are 8 red chips, 4 × ⁻2 = ⁻8.

Figure 5.12

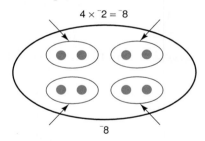

$4 \times {}^-2 = {}^-8$

⁻8

Receiving 4 debts of $2 each is like receiving a debt of $8.

Multiplication by a negative integer can be illustrated by removing groups of chips. For example, suppose you incur 2 debts, each for $3. These are represented in Figure 5.13 by 2 groups of 3 red chips. Paying off both of these debts—that is, removing the 2 groups of 3 red chips—illustrates the product ⁻2 × ⁻3. Notice that removing 6 red chips produces the same result as putting in 6 black chips to cancel the 6 red chips. This suggests that ⁻2 × ⁻3 = 6.

Figure 5.13

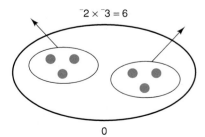

$^-2 \times {}^-3 = 6$

0

Removing 2 debts of $3 each is like removing a debt of $6 or receiving a credit for $6.

EXAMPLE 1

Sketch sets of chips to illustrate each computation. Describe the product in terms of debts and credits.

1. $2 \times 4 = 8$ 2. $4 \times {}^-3 = {}^-12$ 3. ${}^-2 \times {}^-3 = 6$

Solution   1. $2 \times 4 = 8$ (Put in 4 black chips 2 times)

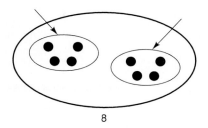

8

Receiving 2 credits of $4 each is like receiving a credit for $8.

2. $4 \times {}^-3 = {}^-12$ (Put in 3 red chips 4 times)

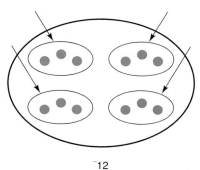

${}^-12$

Receiving 4 debts of $3 each is like receiving a debt of $12.

3. ${}^-2 \times {}^-3 = 6$ (Remove 3 red chips 2 times)

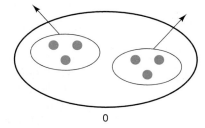

0

Removing 2 debts of $3 each is like removing a debt of $6 or receiving a credit for $6.

The black and red chips model and the number line model illustrate the reasonableness of the rules for multiplying with negative integers. In the following rule of signs for multiplication, *a* and *b* represent positive integers. Notice that products involving negative integers can be obtained by computing products of positive integers.

RULE OF SIGNS FOR MULTIPLICATION

1. Positive times negative equals negative

$$a \times {}^-b = {}^-(a \times b)$$
$$5 \times {}^-2 = {}^-(5 \times 2) = {}^-10$$

2. Negative times positive equals negative

$${}^-a \times b = {}^-(a \times b)$$
$${}^-7 \times 3 = {}^-(7 \times 3) = {}^-21$$

3. Negative times negative equals positive

$${}^-a \times {}^-b = a \times b$$
$${}^-4 \times {}^-5 = 4 \times 5 = 20$$

Products involving negative integers can be computed on a calculator by using the change-of-sign key. Here are the keys to press to compute $^-44 \times {}^-16$:

	Steps	Displays
(1)	44 $\boxed{+/-}$	$\boxed{{}^-44.}$
(2)	$\boxed{\times}$	$\boxed{{}^-44.}$
(3)	16 $\boxed{+/-}$	$\boxed{{}^-16.}$
(4)	$\boxed{=}$	$\boxed{704.}$

However, it is much more convenient, even with a calculator, to use the rule of signs for multiplication to first compute the product of positive integers and then choose the correct sign.

EXAMPLE J

Compute each product.

1. $^-426 \times 83$ 2. $47 \times {}^-2876$ 3. $^-106 \times {}^-17$

Solution

1. Since $426 \times 83 = 35{,}358$ and a negative times a positive equals a negative, $^-426 \times 83 = {}^-35{,}358$.
2. Since $47 \times 2876 = 135{,}172$ and a positive times a negative equals a negative, $47 \times {}^-2876 = {}^-135{,}172$.
3. Since $106 \times 17 = 1802$ and a negative times a negative equals a positive, $^-106 \times {}^-17 = 1802$.

DIVISION

Both the partitive and measurement concepts of division will be used in the following illustrations of division with the black and red chips model.

To show $^-8 \div {}^-2$, we begin with 8 red chips and then measure off, or subtract, as many groups of 2 red chips as possible (see Figure 5.14). Since there are 4 such groups, $^-8 \div {}^-2 = 4$. This illustrates the use of the *measurement concept* of division.

Figure 5.14

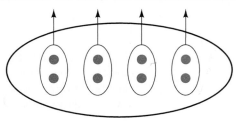

$^-8 \div {}^-2 = 4$

A debt of $2 can be measured off (subtracted from) a debt of $8 a total of 4 times.

To show ⁻6 ÷ 3, we divide 6 red chips into 3 equal groups (see Figure 5.15). Since there are 2 red chips in each group, ⁻6 ÷ 3 = ⁻2. In this illustration the divisor, 3, indicates the number of equal parts into which the set is divided. This illustrates the use of the *partitive concept* of division.

Figure 5.15

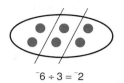

⁻6 ÷ 3 = ⁻2

Sharing a debt of $6 among 3 people gives each person a debt of $2.

In the preceding examples we showed how two different concepts of division are meaningful for negative integers as well as positive integers. In the following definition of division with integers, division is defined in terms of multiplication, just as it was for whole numbers.

DIVISION OF INTEGERS

For any integers a and b, with $b \neq 0$,

$$a \div b = k \text{ if and only if } a = b \times k$$

for some integer k.

EXAMPLE K

Calculate each quotient mentally using the definition of division of integers.

1. ⁻24 ÷ ⁻4   2. 18 ÷ ⁻3   3. ⁻30 ÷ 6

Solution

1. ⁻24 ÷ ⁻4 = 6, since ⁻24 = ⁻4 × 6
2. 18 ÷ ⁻3 = ⁻6, since 18 = ⁻3 × ⁻6
3. ⁻30 ÷ 6 = ⁻5, since ⁻30 = 6 × ⁻5

The inverse relationship between division and multiplication, stated in the preceding definition of division, accounts for the similarity between the rules of signs for division and multiplication with negative integers. In the following rule of signs for division of integers, a and b represent positive integers. Notice in the examples that quotients involving negative integers can be obtained by computing quotients of positive integers.

RULE OF SIGNS FOR DIVISION

1. Positive divided by negative equals negative

$$a \div {}^{-}b = {}^{-}(a \div b)$$
$$24 \div {}^{-}6 = {}^{-}(24 \div 6) = {}^{-}4$$

2. Negative divided by positive equals negative

$$^{-}a \div b = {}^{-}(a \div b)$$
$$^{-}14 \div 2 = {}^{-}(14 \div 2) = {}^{-}7$$

3. Negative divided by negative equals positive

$$^{-}a \div {}^{-}b = a \div b$$
$$^{-}30 \div {}^{-}6 = 30 \div 6 = 5$$

INEQUALITY

less than
greater than

For any two integers on a number line, the number on the left is **less than** the number on the right, and the number on the right is **greater than** the number on the left. For example, in Figure 5.16, $^-8 < ^-3$, $^-7 < ^-4$, and $^-5 < 0$.

Figure 5.16

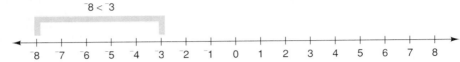

$^-8 < ^-3$

This property is stated more precisely in the following definition of inequality of integers. Although this definition is stated for *less than*, a corresponding statement holds for *greater than*.

INEQUALITY OF INTEGERS

> For any two integers m and n, m is less than n, written $m < n$, if there is a positive integer k such that $m + k = n$.

In thinking about inequalities of negative numbers, you may find it helpful to recall the applications at the beginning of this section. Temperatures of $^-15°$ C and $^-6°$ C are both cold, but $^-15°$ C is colder than $^-6°$ C: $^-15 < ^-6$ because there is a positive integer that can be added to $^-15$ to yield $^-6$ ($^-15 + 9 = ^-6$). Similarly, an altitude of $^-8000$ feet is farther below sea level than an altitude of $^-5000$ feet: $^-8000 < ^-5000$ because there is a positive integer that can be added to $^-8000$ to yield $^-5000$ ($^-8000 + 3000 = ^-5000$).

EXAMPLE **L**

Write the appropriate inequality ($<$ or $>$) for each pair of numbers.

1. $^-37$, $^-55$ 2. $^-110$, 420 3. $^-76$, $^-125$

Solution   1. $^-37 > ^-55$ 2. $^-110 < 420$ 3. $^-76 > ^-125$

PROPERTIES OF INTEGERS

opposite inverse
inverse for addition

INVERSES FOR ADDITION   Addition of integers has one property that addition of whole numbers does not have. For any integer, there is a unique integer, called its **opposite** or **inverse,** such that the integer plus its opposite is equal to zero. We refer to this property by saying that each integer has an **inverse for addition.**

EXAMPLE **M**

Find the integer that satisfies each equation.

1. $174 + \square = 0$ 2. $^-351 + \square = 0$ 3. $0 + \square = 0$

Solution   1. $^-174$ 2. 351 3. 0 (zero is its own inverse)

CLOSURE PROPERTIES   The sum of any two integers is a unique integer, and the product of any two integers is also a unique integer. That is, *addition and multiplication are closed* on the set of integers.

IDENTITY PROPERTIES   Any integer added to zero equals the given integer, and any integer multiplied by 1 equals the given integer. That is, zero is the *identity for addition* and 1 is the *identity for multiplication,* and these are the only identity elements (they are unique) for addition and multiplication of integers.

COMMUTATIVE PROPERTIES   The operations of *addition and multiplication are commutative* for the integers. In particular, these properties hold for negative integers. For example,

$$^-37 + {}^-52 = {}^-52 + {}^-37 \quad \text{and} \quad {}^-37 \times {}^-52 = {}^-52 \times {}^-37$$

ASSOCIATIVE PROPERTIES   The operations of *addition and multiplication are associative* for the integers. These properties hold for any combination of three integers. For the integers $^-7$, $^-2$, and $^-6$,

$$(^-7 + {}^-2) + {}^-6 = {}^-7 + ({}^-2 + {}^-6) \quad \text{and} \quad (^-7 \times {}^-2) \times {}^-6 = {}^-7 \times ({}^-2 \times {}^-6)$$

DISTRIBUTIVE PROPERTY   The *distributive property of multiplication over addition* holds in the set of integers.

EXAMPLE N

Show that the distributive property holds for the following equation by computing both sides of this equation:

$$^-2 \times (3 + {}^-7) = {}^-2 \times 3 + {}^-2 \times {}^-7$$

Solution   Left side of equation: $^-2 \times (3 + {}^-7) = {}^-2 \times {}^-4 = 8$

Right side of equation: $^-2 \times 3 + {}^-2 \times {}^-7 = {}^-6 + 14 = 8$

MENTAL CALCULATIONS

Acquiring number sense is an important objective for elementary school students. Learning to do mental calculations can help them reach this objective. *Mental math techniques* encourage students to use number properties and discover computational shortcuts rather than perform rote calculations.

COMPATIBLE NUMBERS   Finding combinations of compatible numbers is a technique for mental calculation that works with integers as well as with whole numbers.

EXAMPLE O

Do these computations in your head.

1. $50 + {}^-23 + {}^-60$
2. $15 + {}^-26 + 10 + {}^-5$
3. $^-5 \times 18 \times {}^-2$

Solution   One approach to each problem is shown below; your selections of compatible numbers may differ from these.

1. $50 + {}^-60 = {}^-10$, and $^-10 + {}^-23 = {}^-33$
2. $15 + {}^-5 = 10$, $10 + 10 = 20$, and $20 + {}^-26 = {}^-6$
3. $^-5 \times {}^-2 = 10$ and $10 \times 18 = 180$

SUBSTITUTIONS   Using the technique of substitution involves replacing a number by a sum, difference, product, or quotient that is more convenient to use in the computation.

EXAMPLE P

Do each computation mentally using a convenient substitution.

1. $180 + {}^-37$
2. ${}^-6 \times 19$
3. ${}^-150 \div 6$
4. $12 \times {}^-54$

Solution   Different substitutions may occur to you.

1. $180 + {}^-37 = 180 + ({}^-30 + {}^-7)$, and by the associative property for addition this equals $150 + {}^-7 = 143$.
2. ${}^-6 \times 19 = {}^-6 \times (20 + {}^-1)$, and by the distributive property this equals ${}^-120 + 6 = {}^-114$.
3. Using the equal quotients technique described in Section 3.4, we can divide both 150 and 6 by 2. So ${}^-150 \div 6 = {}^-75 \div 3 = {}^-25$. Or both ${}^-150$ and 6 can be divided by 3: ${}^-150 \div 6 = {}^-50 \div 2 = {}^-25$.
4. Using the equal products technique described in Section 3.3, we can divide 12 by 2 and multiply ${}^-54$ by 2: $12 \times {}^-54 = 6 \times {}^-108 = {}^-648$.

ESTIMATION

Computing estimations is one of the most powerful means of acquiring number sense. Estimation requires a knowledge of mental mathematics because one must choose approximate numbers that are convenient for mental calculations.

ROUNDING AND COMPATIBLE NUMBERS   The mental calculating techniques of rounding and compatible numbers are often combined to obtain an estimation.

EXAMPLE Q

Obtain an estimation by rounding and compatible numbers. (Note: In problem (4), division should be performed before addition.)

1. $81 + {}^-32 + 21 + {}^-47$
2. ${}^-53 \times 142 \times {}^-2$
3. $12 \times 67 \times {}^-5$
4. ${}^-250 + 90 \div 32$

Solution   You may find other estimations.

1. $81 + {}^-32 + 21 + {}^-47 \approx (80 + 20) + ({}^-30 + {}^-50) = 100 + {}^-80 = 20$
2. ${}^-53 \times 142 \times {}^-2 \approx {}^-50 \times {}^-2 \times 142 = 100 \times 142 = 14{,}200$
3. $12 \times 67 \times {}^-5 = 12 \times {}^-5 \times 67 = {}^-60 \times 67 \approx {}^-60 \times 70 = {}^-4200$
4. ${}^-250 + 90 \div 32 \approx {}^-250 + 90 \div 30 = {}^-250 + 3 = {}^-247$

Note: The number of negative integers in a product of numbers determines whether the product is positive or negative. Since there are two negative integers in problem (2), the product of the three numbers is positive. Similarly, in problem (3) there is one negative integer, so the answer is negative.

PROBLEM-SOLVING APPLICATION

The following problem involves sums of positive and negative integers. Try solving this problem before reading the solution. You may find it helpful to use the strategies of *solving a simpler problem* and *making an organized list.*

■ PROBLEM

Consider the positive integers from 1 to 25 and their opposites.

$$\pm 1 \ \pm 2 \ \pm 3 \ \pm 4 \ \pm 5 \cdots \pm 21 \ \pm 22 \ \pm 23 \ \pm 24 \ \pm 25$$

Describe all the different numbers that can be obtained by using each integer or its opposite exactly once to form sums of 25 integers.

Understanding the Problem   Each sum must have 25 integers. One possibility is to use the opposites of 1, 2, and 3 and the positive integers from 4 to 25.

$$^-1 + \ ^-2 + \ ^-3 + 4 + 5 + 6 + \cdots + 22 + 23 + 24 + 25 = 313$$

Question 1   The greatest possible sum is 325. What is the least possible sum?

Devising a Plan   Let's solve a simpler problem by using the integers 1, 2, 3, 4, and 5 and their opposites. It is natural to *make an organized list* to consider all the possibilities. This can be done by writing the sum $1 + 2 + 3 + 4 + 5$ and systematically replacing positive integers by their opposites.

$$1 + 2 + 3 + 4 + 5 = 15$$
$$^-1 + 2 + 3 + 4 + 5 = 13$$
$$1 + \ ^-2 + 3 + 4 + 5 = 11$$
$$^-1 + \ ^-2 + 3 + 4 + 5 = 9$$

Question 2   Why can't a sum of zero be obtained from such integers?

Carrying Out the Plan   The list of sums, continued below, reveals a pattern.

$$^-1 + 2 + \ ^-3 + 4 + 5 = 7$$
$$^-1 + 2 + 3 + \ ^-4 + 5 = 5$$
$$^-1 + 2 + 3 + 4 + \ ^-5 = 3$$
$$1 + \ ^-2 + 3 + 4 + \ ^-5 = 1$$
$$1 + 2 + \ ^-3 + 4 + \ ^-5 = \ ^-1$$
$$1 + 2 + 3 + \ ^-4 + \ ^-5 = \ ^-3$$
$$^-1 + 2 + 3 + \ ^-4 + \ ^-5 = \ ^-5$$
$$1 + \ ^-2 + 3 + \ ^-4 + \ ^-5 = \ ^-7$$
$$1 + 2 + \ ^-3 + \ ^-4 + \ ^-5 = \ ^-9$$
$$^-1 + 2 + \ ^-3 + \ ^-4 + \ ^-5 = \ ^-11$$
$$1 + \ ^-2 + \ ^-3 + \ ^-4 + \ ^-5 = \ ^-13$$
$$^-1 + \ ^-2 + \ ^-3 + \ ^-4 + \ ^-5 = \ ^-15$$

We obtain all the odd numbers from 15 to ⁻15. Perhaps you noticed a reason for this. Each time a positive integer is replaced by its opposite, the new sum differs by an even number. For example, if 1 is replaced by ⁻1, the new sum is decreased by 2. Similarly, replacing 2 by ⁻2 decreases the sum by 4; replacing 3 by ⁻3 decreases the sum by 6; etc. Thus we **Question 3**   obtain all the odd numbers from ⁻15 to 15. What does this suggest about the solution to the original problem?

Looking Back   The original problem and the simplified problem considered the positive integers from 1 to 25 and their opposites. Suppose the original problem were changed to **Question 4**   consider the integers from 1 to 24 and their opposites. What sums would be obtained?

Answers to Questions 1–4
1. ⁻325
2. The sum of integers from 1 to 5 is 15, an odd number. Since replacing any one of the numbers from 1 to 5 by its opposite changes the sum by 2 times the number, which is an

even number, such replacements will change the sum of 15 by an even number. Thus the sum of all such integers is an odd number and therefore cannot be zero.

3. The solution will include all odd numbers from 325 to ⁻325.

4. All even numbers from 300 to ⁻300 would be obtained.

RELATED ACTIVITIES IN
Mathematics for Elementary Teachers: An Activity Approach, 3e

Activity Set 5.1   **Models for Operations with Integers:** Activities with black and red chips illustrate the four basic operations with integers.

Just for Fun   **Games for Negative Integers:** Three games involving addition, subtraction, multiplication, and inequality of integers

---

EXERCISES AND PROBLEMS 5.1

Antarctica, the only polar continent, is centered near the South Pole and is covered by a huge ice dome reaching a height of between 2 and 3 miles. One of the hazards of exploration is the hidden crevasses in the ice. This photo shows a crevasse detector operating in Antarctica.

1. a. Following are 5 daytime Fahrenheit temperatures recorded during an Antarctic summer: ⁻18°, ⁻17°, ⁻24°, ⁻34°, and ⁻28°. What is the highest (warmest) of these temperatures?

 b. Winter temperatures in Antarctica are usually below ⁻100° Fahrenheit. What is the lowest (coldest) of the following temperatures: ⁻119°, ⁻98°, ⁻110°, ⁻114°, and ⁻108°?

2. Locate the integers ⁻7, 5, 0, 2, and ⁻4 on a number line, and draw an arrow from each integer to its opposite.

3. Find a positive integer that makes the left side of each equation below equal to the right side. Then write an inequality using < or > for each pair of numbers below the equations.

 a. ⁻3 + □ = ⁻2   **b.** ⁻14 + □ = 3   **c.** ⁻7 + □ = 1
    ⁻3, ⁻2   3, ⁻14   ⁻7, 1

4. Answer each of the following questions with an integer.

 a. A submarine has an altitude of ⁻5500 feet, and it dives down 1500 feet. What is its new altitude in feet?

 b. At ⁻40 minutes in the countdown for a space shuttle launch, technicians began a seven-minute check of the shuttle's compression system. What was the time at the end of this check?

 c. The temperature at 6 A.M. was ⁻15° Fahrenheit, and by noon it had warmed up 8°. What was the noontime temperature?

 d. The nation's trade balance for the first quarter of a year was ⁻23 billion dollars, and for the second quarter it was 9 billion dollars lower. What was the second quarter trade balance in billions of dollars?

5. Use the black and red chips model to sketch three different sets illustrating each integer.

 a. ⁻7   **b.** 0   **c.** 3

6. Use the sets to illustrate the given operations (put in, take away, partition, etc.), and then complete the equations.

a.

3   +   ⁻7   =   ⁻4

b.   **c.**

⁻8 − ⁻3 = ⁻5   ⁻3 × 2 = ⁻6

d.

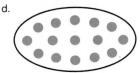

⁻15 ÷ 5 = ⁻3

7. Show a replacement for each set of chips so that the difference can be determined by using the concept of take away. Then complete the equation.

a.

$2 - 5 = {}^-3$

b.

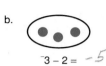

$^-3 - 2 = {}^-5$

8. Answer each question and then write a multiplication fact that the problem illustrates.
   a. If the temperature is now 0°, what was it 5 hours ago if it has been increasing 3° each hour?
   b. If the temperature is now 10°, what will it be 3 hours from now if it decreases 2° each hour?
   c. If the temperature is now 30°, what was it 2 hours ago if it has been decreasing 6° each hour?

9. Draw a number line to illustrate each sum.
   a. $6 + {}^-5 = 1$ **b.** $^-4 + 9$
   c. $^-3 + {}^-4$ **d.** $^-5 + 5$

10. Compute each product or quotient.
   a. $^-6 \times 2 = {}^-12$ **b.** $^-8 \times {}^-3 = 24$
   c. $24 \div {}^-6 = {}^-4$ **d.** $^-20 \div 4 = {}^-5$

11. Find the missing number for each equation.
   a. $4 + \square = {}^-10$ **b.** $6 - \square = 10$
   c. $^-6 \times \square = {}^-12$ **d.** $^-3 + \square = 0$
   e. $^-15 \div \square = {}^-3$ **f.** $^-4 - \square = 7$
   g. $^-1 \times \square = 1$ **h.** $24 \div \square = {}^-8$

12. Which number property of the integers is being used in each of the following equalities?
   a. $^-4 \times \dfrac{16 + {}^-9}{{}^-6 + 13} = {}^-4 \times \dfrac{16 + {}^-9}{13 + {}^-6}$
   b. $^-4 \times ({}^-3 + 3) + {}^-17 = ({}^-4 \times {}^-3) + ({}^-4 \times 3) + {}^-17$
   c. $({}^-8 + 7) + 2 \times ({}^-6 \times {}^-5)$
       $= ({}^-8 + 7) + (2 \times {}^-6) \times {}^-5$
   d. $^-3 \times \dfrac{16 \times {}^-5}{{}^-14 + 2} = {}^-3 \times \dfrac{{}^-5 \times 16}{{}^-14 + 2}$

13. Determine whether the operation is closed for the given set.
   a. Subtraction on the set of integers
   b. Division on the set of integers
   c. Multiplication on the set of negative integers
   d. Addition on the set of negative integers

14. Use compatible numbers or substitution to calculate each sum or difference mentally. Explain your method.
   a. $70 + 43 + {}^-60$
   b. $260 + {}^-49$
   c. $^-125 + 17 + {}^-25 + 13$

15. Use equal products or equal quotients to do each computation mentally.
   a. $24 \times {}^-25$ **b.** $^-90 \div 18$
   c. $^-28 \times 5$ **d.** $400 \div {}^-16$

16. Round each integer to its leading digit, and mentally approximate the sum of the numbers in each row.

	118 Think 100	$^-235$ Think $^-200$	$^-190$ Think $^-200$	485 Think 500	200 Approximate sum
a.	$^-123$	207	$^-315$	186	
b.	$^-238$	175	$^-103$	$^-214$	
c.	78	$^-41$	19	$^-38$	
d.	$^-23$	51	$^-48$	$^-82$	

17. Replace numbers by compatible numbers to obtain estimations. Show how you obtain your estimations.
   a. $^-241 \div 60$ **b.** $64 \times {}^-11 =$
   c. $26 + 59 \div {}^-3$ **d.** $^-31 \times 19$

18. For each problem below, do not compute the answer, just determine whether it is positive or negative. Explain your reasoning.
   a. $^-34 \times 46 \times 381 \times {}^-13$ **b.** $^-22 \times 17 \times 12 + 50$
   c. $41 \times {}^-65 + 500$ **d.** $625 \div {}^-25 + {}^-250$

19. Extend the pattern in each column of equations by writing the next three equations. What multiplication rule for negative numbers is suggested by the last few equations that you write in each column?

   a. $5 \times 3 = 15$ **b.** $3 \times 6 = 18$ **c.** $^-3 \times 3 = {}^-9$
   $5 \times 2 = 10$ $2 \times 6 = 12$ $^-3 \times 2 = {}^-6$
   $5 \times 1 = 5$ $1 \times 6 = 6$ $^-3 \times 1 = {}^-3$
   $5 \times 0 = 0$ $0 \times 6 = 0$ $^-3 \times 0 = 0$

20. The following computations involve the change-of-sign key $\boxed{+/-}$ on a calculator. Determine what computation is being performed and find the answer for each.
   a. $16 \boxed{+/-} + 7 \boxed{+/-}$ **b.** $25 \boxed{+/-} - 30 \boxed{+/-}$
   c. $54 \times 35 \boxed{+/-}$ 1890 **d.** $408 \div 17 \boxed{+/-}$ 24

21. Suppose you have a calculator that does not have a change-of-sign key. Explain how the theorems for operations with integers can be used to compute the following expressions. Find each answer.
   a. $^-487 + {}^-653$ **b.** $360 - {}^-241$
   c. $32 \times {}^-14$ **d.** $336 \div {}^-16$

22. The table below shows yearly percentage increases (positive numbers) and decreases (negative numbers) in energy consumption for petroleum products, natural gas, and coal from 1970 to 1981.*

Year	Annual % increase or decrease energy consumption			
	Total[2]	Refined petroleum products	Natural gas	Coal
1970..........	4.8	4.9	6.7	1.3
1971..........	2.2	3.5	3.1	⁻5.1
1972..........	4.9	7.8	1.0	3.7
1973..........	4.2	5.7	⁻.8	6.8
1974..........	⁻2.5	⁻4.0	⁻3.5	⁻3.2
1975..........	⁻2.8	⁻2.2	⁻8.2	⁻.5
1976..........	5.4	7.5	2.0	7.1
1977..........	2.4	5.5	⁻2.1	1.7
1978..........	2.4	2.3	.4	⁻.8
1979..........	.9	⁻2.2	3.4	9.1
1980..........	⁻3.9	⁻7.9	⁻1.4	2.3
1981..........	⁻2.8	⁻6.4	⁻3.7	3.7

a. Find three consecutive years in which the consumption of petroleum products decreased. What was happening to the consumption of coal during these years?

b. Over the twelve-year period covered by this table, there was one year in which the use of petroleum decreased and the use of natural gas increased. What year was this? *1993*

23. NASA's *Voyager 1* achieved its closest approach to Jupiter (about 280,000 km) on March 5, 1979. In December, 1978, ⁻80 days before its closest approach, the spacecraft swiveled its narrow-angle television camera to begin its observatory phase. The inner squares in the sketch below represent the camera's field of view at four different approach times.

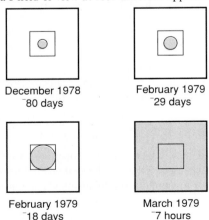

December 1978
⁻80 days

February 1979
⁻29 days

February 1979
⁻18 days

March 1979
⁻7 hours

a. How much time elapsed between the ⁻80 day view and the ⁻29 day view?

b. How much time elapsed between the ⁻18 day view and the ⁻7 hour view?

*U.S. Energy Information Administration.

c. As *Voyager 1* moved away from Jupiter, it examined its moons: Io at ⁺3 hours, Europa at ⁺5 hours, and Ganymede at ⁺14 hours. Thirty-six hours after the ⁻7 hour view, Voyager 1 examined Callisto. How many hours was this after its closest approach to Jupiter?

Featured Strategies: Solving a Simpler Problem and Guessing and Checking

24. How can the integers from ⁻4 to 4 be placed around a circle so that each integer from ⁻10 to 10 can be obtained by adding two or more neighboring numbers (numbers next to each other)?

a. Understanding the Problem The problem requires that the 9 integers from ⁻4 to 4 be used and that the sums involve two or more adjacent integers. The following placement of integers will yield some of the numbers from ⁻10 to 10, but not all of them. For example, $0 = ⁻3 + 0 + 3$, and $1 = 0 + 3 + ⁻4 + 2$. Find some integers from ⁻10 to 10 that cannot be obtained by adding two or more adjacent integers from this circle.

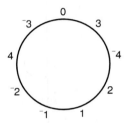

b. Devising a Plan This type of problem can be solved by *guessing and checking* the results. It may also help to *solve a simpler problem*. Consider placing the numbers ⁻2, ⁻1, 0, 1, and 2 around a circle to obtain all the sums from 3 to ⁻3. Show why it doesn't work to place each integer next to its opposite. How should these numbers be placed?

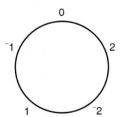

c. Carrying Out the Plan The solution to part b may suggest a solution to the original problem. The requirement that we be able to obtain a sum of 10 and a sum of ⁻10 completely determines the solution. Explain why. How can the integers from ⁻4 to 4 be placed to solve the problem?

d. Looking Back Another observation concerning the original problem is that each of the integers from ⁻4 to 4 can be routinely obtained by adding all the numbers on the circle except the given negative number. Explain why this works.

COMPUTER INVESTIGATION

The computer program CONSECUTIVE DIFFERENCES on the *Computer Problem-Solving Disc* computes the consecutive differences of any *k* integers at the vertices of a *k*-sided polygon, repeating the process as many times as desired.

Select any four integers, and place them at the corners of a square. Then between each pair of numbers write the difference of the larger minus the smaller, and form an inner square whose corners have these differences. Continue this process of taking differences and forming inner squares. (Observations in the 1930s concerning this investigation are attributed to the Italian mathematician E. Ducci.)

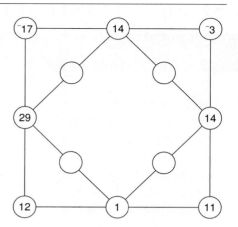

Questions for Investigation
1. If we begin with the square shown here, how many inner squares must we form before we end up with a square whose four numbers are equal?
2. Try some other integers at the four corners. Find four integers for which 5 or more inner squares are needed to obtain all equal numbers.
3. Are there four integers that do not eventually lead to an inner square with all four numbers equal?
4. Any number of integers *k* may be selected and placed at the vertices of a *k*-sided polygon. For what values of *k* will equal numbers be produced?

PUZZLER

A square array of numbers in which the sum of numbers in any horizontal row, vertical column, or diagonal is always the same is called a magic square. Enter the numbers below into the given grid to produce a magic square.

$$^-10, \ ^-8, \ ^-6, \ ^-4, \ 0, \ 2, \ 4, \ 6$$

SECTION 5.2   INTRODUCTION TO FRACTIONS

■ PROBLEM OPENER

Three tired and hungry people had a bag of apples. While the other two were asleep, one of the three awoke, ate 1/3 of the apples, and went back to sleep. Later a second person awoke, ate 1/3 of the remaining apples, and went back to sleep. Finally, the third person awoke and ate 1/3 of the remaining apples, leaving 8 apples in the bag. How many apples were in the bag originally?

Trading floor of the New York Stock Exchange

The sale of stocks and bonds on the New York Stock Exchange is carried out on the three-story trading floor shown in the photo. The prices of stocks are stated in dollars, as well as in halves, fourths, eighths, and sixteenths of a dollar. Historically, whenever a smaller unit of measure was needed, half of the original measure was used. For a still smaller amount, half of a half produced a fourth. Similarly, eighths, sixteenths, and thirty-seconds resulted from repeatedly halving the original unit. The inch, with its halves, fourths, eighths, sixteenths, etc., is a familiar example of this halving process. Another example is shutter speeds on a camera, which are calibrated in fractions of a second: 1/2, 1/4, 1/8, 1/15, 1/30, 1/60, etc. (see #20 in Exercises and Problems 5.2).

■ *HISTORICAL HIGHLIGHT*

unit fractions

The Egyptians were using fractions before 2500 B.C. With the exception of 2/3, all Egyptian fractions were **unit fractions**—that is, fractions with a numerator of 1 (1/3, 1/4, etc.).

In hieratic (sacred) writings like this scroll, the Egyptians placed a dot above a numeral to represent a unit fraction. For example, ∧ represents the number 30, and ∧̇ represents the fraction 1/30. It is interesting to note that as late as the

Egyptian leather scroll describing simple
relations between fractions (ca. 1700 B.C.)

eighteenth century, over 3000 years after the
ancient Egyptians used such symbols, the
symbols $\frac{\cdot}{2}$ and $\frac{\cdot}{4}$ were used in English books
for the fractions 1/2 and 1/4.

Whereas the Egyptians used fractions
with fixed numerators, the Babylonians
(ca. 2000 B.C.) used only fractions with
denominators of 60 and 60^2. The fraction
1/60 was referred to as "the first little part"
and $1/60^2$ as "the second little part." Our use
of minutes, 1/60 of an hour, and seconds,
$1/60^2$ of an hour, was handed down to us
from the Babylonians.

FRACTION TERMINOLOGY

The word "fraction" comes from the Latin word *fractio,* a form of the Latin word
frangere, meaning *to break.* The words "broken number" and "fragment" frequently
were used in the past as synonyms for "fraction." Historically, fractions were first used
for amounts that were less than a whole unit. This is how children first encounter fractions: half of a candy bar, one-third of a pizza, etc. Today fractions include numbers
that are greater than or equal to 1.

fraction   The term **fraction** is used to refer both to a number written in the form *a/b* and
to the numeral *a/b.* You need not be concerned about the distinction between *a/b* as a
number and *a/b* as a numeral; the meaning will be clear from the context. For example,
numerator   when we say the top number of a fraction is called the **numerator** and the bottom number
denominator   is called the **denominator,** we are thinking of the fraction as a symbol or numeral with
two parts. On the other hand, when we say "add the fractions 1/2 and 1/3," we are
thinking of fractions as numbers.

Children in the early grades use fractions whose numerators and denominators are
whole numbers, and those in the later grades use fractions whose numerators and denominators are integers. The numerator and denominator can be any numbers as long
as the denominator is not zero. (See Sections 6.3 and 6.4 for discussions of fractions
involving decimals and irrational numbers.)

MODELS FOR FRACTIONS

Three concepts of fractions will be illustrated by models in the following paragraphs:
the *part-to-whole concept,* the *division concept,* and the *ratio concept.*

part-to-whole concept   **PART-TO-WHOLE CONCEPT**   The most common use of fractions involves the **part-
to-whole concept**—that is, the use of a fraction to denote part of a whole. In the fraction
a/b, the bottom number, *b,* indicates the number of equal parts in a whole, and the top
number, *a,* indicates the number of parts being considered.

EXAMPLE A

Write the fraction for the shaded or lettered part of each figure.

(1)  (2) (3) (4)

Solution   1. $\dfrac{3}{8}$ 2. $\dfrac{7}{16}$ 3. $\dfrac{1}{6}$ 4. $\dfrac{5}{9}$

The Fraction Bars® model is a part-to-whole model for fractions in which the denominator of a fraction is represented by the number of equal parts in a bar and the numerator is the number of shaded parts.*

EXAMPLE B

Write the fraction represented by the shaded portion of each bar.

(1)  (2) (3)

Solution   1. $\dfrac{1}{2}$ 2. $\dfrac{2}{3}$ 3. $\dfrac{3}{4}$

The part-to-whole concept of a fraction also is used in describing part of a set of individual objects.

EXAMPLE C

1. Write the fraction that shows what part of the set is circles.
2. Write the fraction that shows what part of the set is squares.

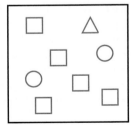

Solution   1. $\dfrac{2}{8}$ of the objects are circles.

2. $\dfrac{5}{8}$ of the objects are squares.

Fractions can be located on a number line using the part-to-whole concept. First select a unit, and then divide this interval into equal parts. To locate the fraction *r/s,* subdivide the unit interval into *s* equal parts, and beginning at zero, count off *r* of these parts. Figure 5.17 shows the sixths and tenths between ⁻1 and 1.

*Fraction Bars® is a registered trademark of Scott Resources, Inc.

Figure 5.17

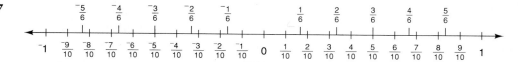

Applications of fractions that involve the part-to-whole concept are numerous. Two examples are shown below.

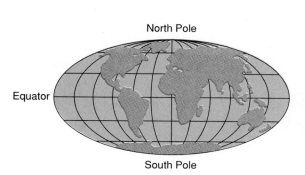

North Pole

Equator

South Pole

Two-thirds of the earth's surface area is covered by water.

Eight-ninths of the volume of an iceberg is under water.

DIVISION CONCEPT   Charlie Brown's little sister Sally has a problem. She is trying to divide 25 by 50. Charlie Brown's comment shows that he thinks of division only in terms of the *measurement concept*—that is, "how many 50s in 25?" However, there is another approach to division. Remember that Section 3.4 discussed two concepts of division: measurement and partitive. With the *partitive concept,* dividing by 50 means there will be 50 parts. If we divide 25 objects of equal size, such as sticks of gum, into 50 equal parts, each part will be one-half of a stick: $25 \div 50 = 1/2$.

© 1967 United Feature Syndicate, Inc.

Here is another illustration of the division concept that involves fractions. Figure 5.18 shows 3 whole bars placed end to end. To compute $3 \div 4$, we use the partitive concept of division and divide the 3 bars into 4 equal parts. This can be done by dividing the 3-bar in half and then dividing each half in half, as shown by the dashed lines. Comparing one of these four parts to a 3/4-bar shows that $3 \div 4 = 3/4$.

Figure 5.18

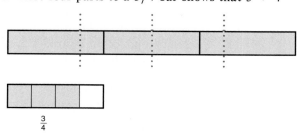

$\frac{3}{4}$

This relationship between fractions and division of numbers is sometimes used to define a fraction as a quotient of two numbers.

> For any numbers *a* and *b*, with *b* ≠ 0,
>
> $$\frac{a}{b} = a \div b$$

One of the major influences in the early development of fractions was the need to solve problems involving division of whole numbers. A problem found in Egyptian writings from 1650 B.C. requires that 4 loaves of bread be divided equally among 10 people. According to the previous definition, 4 ÷ 10 = 4/10, and each person would receive 4/10 of a loaf of bread. Figure 5.19 shows 4 loaves of bread divided into 10 equal parts.

Figure 5.19

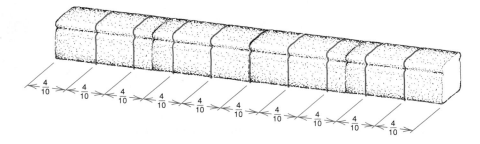

EXAMPLE D

Answer each question with a fraction.

1. Two gallons of cider are poured into 7 containers in equal amounts. How much cider is there in each container?
2. Four acres of land are divided equally into 15 parts. How much land is in each part?

Solution   1. $\frac{2}{7}$ gallon   2. $\frac{4}{15}$ acre

RATIO CONCEPT   Another use of fractions involves the *ratio concept*. In this case fractions are used to compare one amount to another. For example, we might say that a boy's height is 1/3 of his mother's height.

Fractions can be illustrated with Cuisenaire rods by comparing the lengths of two rods (see Figure 5.20). It takes 3 red rods to equal the length of 1 dark green rod in part (a), so the length of the red rod is 1/3 the length of the dark green rod. If the length of the dark green rod is chosen as the unit, then the red rod represents 1/3. If a different unit is selected, the red rod will represent a different fraction. For example, if the yellow rod in part (b) is the unit length, then the red rod represents 2/5, because the length of the red rod is 2/5 the length of the yellow rod. Several different rods can represent the same fraction, depending on the choice of unit. In part (a), 1/3 is represented by a red rod, but if the unit is the length of the blue rod, as in part (c), then the green rod represents 1/3.

Figure 5.21 provides an example of the ratio concept of a fraction. The length of the San Andreas Fault is compared to the length of California's coastal region. Ratios are discussed in more detail in Section 6.3.

Figure 5.20

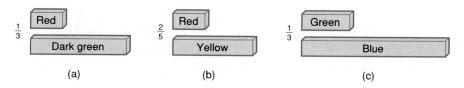

(a)   (b)   (c)

Figure 5.21
The San Andreas Fault runs ¾ of the
length of California's coastal region

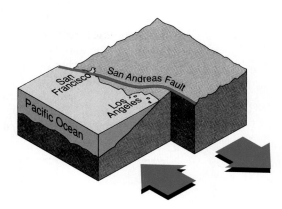

EXAMPLE E

It takes 4 red rods to equal the length of 1 brown rod and 5 white rods to equal the length of 1 yellow rod.

1. If the brown rod is the unit, what is the length of 1 red rod?
2. If the brown rod is the unit, what is the length of 3 red rods?
3. If the yellow rod is the unit, what is the length of 3 white rods?

Solution   1. $\dfrac{1}{4}$ 2. $\dfrac{3}{4}$ 3. $\dfrac{3}{5}$

EQUALITY OF FRACTIONS

Equality of fractions can be illustrated by comparing parts of figures. The charts in Figure 5.22 show that $1/3 = 2/6$, $1/3 = 4/12$, $1/2 = 2/4$, etc.

Figure 5.22

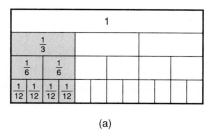   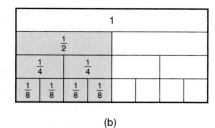

(a)   (b)

EXAMPLE F

Write three more equalities that are illustrated by each of the charts in Figure 5.22.

Solution   Here are some possibilities:

Part (a): $\dfrac{2}{3} = \dfrac{4}{6}$, $\dfrac{2}{3} = \dfrac{8}{12}$, $\dfrac{3}{6} = \dfrac{6}{12}$, $1 = \dfrac{3}{3}$, $1 = \dfrac{6}{6}$

Part (b): $\dfrac{1}{2} = \dfrac{4}{8}$, $\dfrac{1}{4} = \dfrac{2}{8}$, $\dfrac{3}{4} = \dfrac{6}{8}$, $1 = \dfrac{4}{4}$, $1 = \dfrac{8}{8}$

Figure 5.23

Equality of fractions can also be illustrated with sets of objects. For example, 3 out of 12, or 3/12, of the points shown in Figure 5.23 are circled. Viewed in another way, 1/4 of the points are circled, because there are 4 rows, each containing the same number of points, and 1 row is circled. So 3/12 and 1/4 are equivalent fractions representing the same amount.

For every fraction there are an infinite number of other fractions that represent the same number. The Fraction Bars in Figure 5.24 show one method of obtaining fractions equal to 3/4. In part (b), each part of the 3/4-bar has been split into 2 equal parts to show that 3/4 = 6/8. We see that doubling the number of parts in a bar also doubles the number of shaded parts. This is equivalent to multiplying the numerator and denominator of 3/4 by 2. Similarly, part (c) shows that splitting each part of a 3/4-bar into 3 equal parts triples the number of parts in the bar and triples the number of shaded parts. This has the effect of multiplying the numerator and denominator of 3/4 by 3 and shows that 3/4 is equal to 9/12.

Figure 5.24

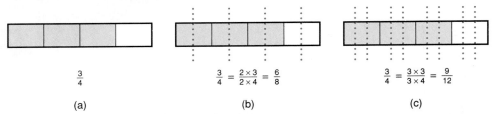

$$\frac{3}{4}$$

(a)

$$\frac{3}{4} = \frac{2 \times 3}{2 \times 4} = \frac{6}{8}$$

(b)

$$\frac{3}{4} = \frac{3 \times 3}{3 \times 4} = \frac{9}{12}$$

(c)

The examples in Figure 5.24 illustrate the *fundamental rule for equality of fractions:* for any fraction, an **equal fraction** will be obtained by multiplying the numerator and denominator by a nonzero number.

equal fraction

FUNDAMENTAL RULE FOR EQUALITY OF FRACTIONS

For any fraction a/b and any number $k \neq 0$,

$$\frac{a}{b} = \frac{ka}{kb}$$

simplifying fractions

SIMPLIFYING FRACTIONS   The definition of equality of fractions justifies a process called **simplifying fractions**. For example, since 6 and 15 have a common factor of 3, 6/15 may be written as a fraction with a smaller numerator and denominator:

$$\frac{6}{15} = \frac{6 \div 3}{15 \div 3} = \frac{2}{5}$$

Figure 5.25 provides an illustration of this equality. Since the number of shaded parts in the bar is 6 and the total number of parts in the bar is 15, both can be divided by 3. By doing so we group the parts of the bar (see the dashed lines) to create 5 equal parts, 2 of which are shaded. This shows that 6/15 is equal to 2/5.

Figure 5.25

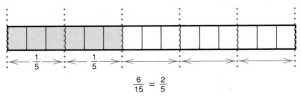

$$\frac{6}{15} = \frac{2}{5}$$

simplified form

Whenever the numerator and denominator of a fraction have a common factor greater than 1, they can be divided by this factor to obtain a fraction in **simplified form.**

EXAMPLE G

Write each fraction in simplified form.

1. $\dfrac{8}{12}$ 2. $\dfrac{24}{28}$ 3. $\dfrac{8}{16}$

Solution

1. $\dfrac{4}{6}$ or $\dfrac{2}{3}$ 2. $\dfrac{12}{14}$ or $\dfrac{6}{7}$ 3. $\dfrac{4}{8}$, $\dfrac{2}{4}$, or $\dfrac{1}{2}$

simplest form
lowest terms

If the numerator and denominator of a fraction are divided by their greatest common factor (GCF), the resulting fraction is called the **simplest form,** and the fraction is said to be in **lowest terms** (Figure 5.26). (Note: There are calculators designed for school children that display fractions. Such calculators indicate when a fraction is not in simplified form, and there is a key for obtaining the fraction in lowest terms.)

Figure 5.26

EXAMPLE H

Determine which fractions are in lowest terms. If a fraction is not in lowest terms, write the fraction in simplest form.

1. $\dfrac{4}{15}$ 2. $\dfrac{^-8}{24}$ 3. $\dfrac{18}{30}$ 4. $\dfrac{10}{21}$ 5. $\dfrac{10}{^-15}$

Solution

1. $\dfrac{4}{15}$ is in lowest terms.

2. GCF($^-8$, 24) = 8, so $\dfrac{^-8}{24} = \dfrac{^-1}{3}$

3. GCF(18, 30) = 6, so $\dfrac{18}{30} = \dfrac{3}{5}$

4. $\dfrac{10}{21}$ is in lowest terms.

5. GCF(10, $^-15$) = 5, so $\dfrac{10}{^-15} = \dfrac{2}{^-3}$

COMMON DENOMINATORS

One of the more important skills in the use of fractions is replacing two fractions with different denominators by two fractions with equal denominators. The fractions 1/6 and 1/4 have different denominators, and the Fraction Bars representing these fractions have different numbers of parts (see Figure 5.27). If each part of the 1/6-bar is split into 2 equal parts and each part of the 1/4-bar is split into 3 equal parts, both bars will have 12 equal parts. The fractions for these new bars, 2/12 and 3/12, have a **common denominator** of 12.

common denominator

Figure 5.27

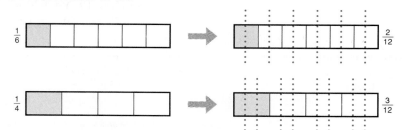

Obtaining the same number of equal parts for two bars is a visual way of finding a common denominator. Another method for finding common denominators of two fractions is to list the multiples of their denominators. The arrows in Figure 5.28 point to the common multiples of 6 and 4. The least common multiple (LCM) of 6 and 4 is 12. This is also the smallest common denominator of 1/6 and 1/4. In general, the **smallest common denominator** of two fractions is the least common multiple of their denominators.

smallest common denominator

Figure 5.28

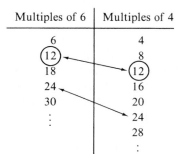

Once a common denominator has been found, two fractions can be replaced by fractions having the same denominator.

$$\frac{1}{6} = \frac{2 \times 1}{2 \times 6} = \frac{2}{12} \qquad \frac{1}{4} = \frac{3 \times 1}{3 \times 4} = \frac{3}{12}$$

EXAMPLE 1

Replace the fractions in each pair by equal fractions having the smallest common denominator.

1. $\dfrac{3}{4}, \dfrac{2}{5}$ 2. $\dfrac{7}{12}, \dfrac{^-3}{8}$ 3. $\dfrac{1}{6}, \dfrac{5}{18}$

Solution

1. LCM(4, 5) = 20; $\dfrac{3}{4} = \dfrac{15}{20}$ and $\dfrac{2}{5} = \dfrac{8}{20}$

2. LCM(12, 8) = 24; $\dfrac{7}{12} = \dfrac{14}{24}$ and $\dfrac{^-3}{8} = \dfrac{^-9}{24}$

3. LCM(6, 18) = 18; $\dfrac{1}{6} = \dfrac{3}{18}$; $\dfrac{5}{18}$ does not need to be replaced.

We can determine whether two fractions are equal by obtaining their common denominators. Consider the fractions 19/62 and 8/27. Using the fundamental rule for equality of fractions, we can multiply the numerator and denominator of 19/62 by 27 and the numerator and denominator of 8/27 by 62.

$$\frac{19}{62} = \frac{27 \times 19}{27 \times 62} \quad \text{and} \quad \frac{8}{27} = \frac{62 \times 8}{62 \times 27}$$

These fractions now have a common denominator, and they are equal if and only if their numerators, 27 × 19 and 8 × 62, are equal. Are the fractions equal? This approach to determining equality suggests the following test for equality of fractions.

TEST FOR EQUALITY OF FRACTIONS

For any fractions *a/b* and *c/d*,

$$\frac{a}{b} = \frac{c}{d} \text{ if and only if } ad = bc$$

EXAMPLE J

Use the test for equality of fractions to determine which pairs of fractions are equal.

1. $\dfrac{42}{105}, \dfrac{14}{35}$ 2. $\dfrac{^-2}{3}, \dfrac{2}{^-3}$ 3. $\dfrac{8}{71}, \dfrac{5}{43}$ 4. $\dfrac{3}{^-9}, \dfrac{4}{^-12}$

Solution

1. $42 \times 35 = 105 \times 14 = 1470$, so $\dfrac{42}{105} = \dfrac{14}{35}$

2. $(^-2)(^-3) = (3)(2) = 6$, so $\dfrac{^-2}{3} = \dfrac{2}{^-3}$

3. $8 \times 43 = 344 \neq 71 \times 5 = 355$, so $\dfrac{8}{71} \neq \dfrac{5}{43}$

4. $3 \times {}^-12 = {}^-9 \times 4 = {}^-36$, so $\dfrac{3}{^-9} = \dfrac{4}{^-12}$

INEQUALITY

Charts such as the one in Figure 5.29 show many different inequalities of fractions.

Figure 5.29

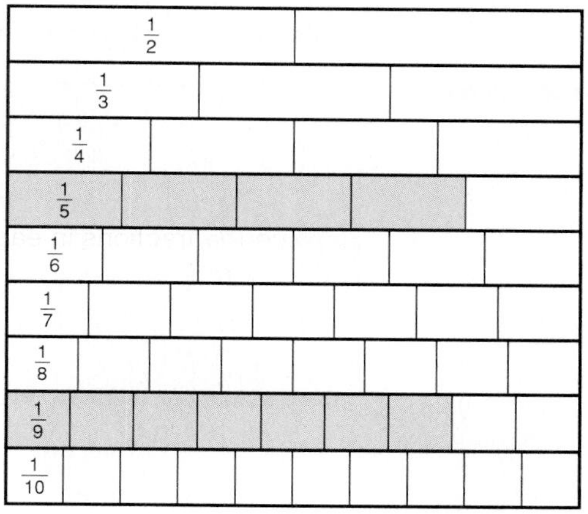

EXAMPLE K

Place the edge of a piece of paper on this chart to determine an inequality for each of the following pairs of fractions.

1. $\dfrac{4}{5}, \dfrac{7}{9}$ 2. $\dfrac{5}{8}, \dfrac{2}{3}$ 3. $\dfrac{2}{7}, \dfrac{3}{10}$ 4. $\dfrac{3}{4}, \dfrac{5}{7}$

Solution

1. $\dfrac{4}{5} > \dfrac{7}{9}$ 2. $\dfrac{5}{8} < \dfrac{2}{3}$ 3. $\dfrac{2}{7} < \dfrac{3}{10}$ 4. $\dfrac{3}{4} > \dfrac{5}{7}$

EXAMPLE L

List a few other inequalities of fractions that are illustrated in Figure 5.29. What patterns of inequalities are there?

Solution

Here are a few of the many inequalities:

$$\frac{1}{4} < \frac{1}{3}, \frac{2}{3} < \frac{3}{4}, \frac{1}{2} < \frac{2}{3}, \frac{5}{8} < \frac{6}{9}, \frac{1}{6} > \frac{1}{7}, \frac{4}{5} > \frac{3}{4}$$

The left edge of Figure 5.29 shows a pattern of decreasing inequalities,

$$\frac{1}{2} > \frac{1}{3} > \frac{1}{4} > \frac{1}{5} > \frac{1}{6} > \frac{1}{7} > \frac{1}{8} > \frac{1}{9} > \frac{1}{10}$$

and the right edge shows an increasing pattern,

$$\frac{1}{2} < \frac{2}{3} < \frac{3}{4} < \frac{4}{5} < \frac{5}{6} < \frac{6}{7} < \frac{7}{8} < \frac{8}{9} < \frac{9}{10}$$

One of the reasons for finding a common denominator for two fractions is to be able to determine the greater fraction. It is difficult to determine whether 5/8 or 3/5 is greater without first replacing them by fractions having a common denominator. The least common multiple of 8 and 5 is 40. Replacing both 5/8 and 3/5 by fractions having a denominator of 40, we see that 5/8 is the greater fraction.

$$\frac{5}{8} = \frac{5 \times 5}{5 \times 8} = \frac{25}{40} \qquad \frac{3}{5} = \frac{8 \times 3}{8 \times 5} = \frac{24}{40}$$

In general, an inequality for two fractions a/b and c/d with positive denominators can be determined by replacing them with fractions having a common denominator,

$$\frac{ad}{bd} \quad \text{and} \quad \frac{bc}{bd}$$

and comparing their numerators, ad and bc.

TEST FOR INEQUALITY OF FRACTIONS

For any fractions a/b and c/d, with b and d positive integers,

$$\frac{a}{b} < \frac{c}{d} \text{ if and only if } ad < bc$$

and

$$\frac{a}{b} > \frac{c}{d} \text{ if and only if } ad > bc$$

EXAMPLE M

Determine an inequality for each pair of fractions.

1. $\dfrac{3}{7}, \dfrac{4}{10}$ 2. $\dfrac{3}{4}, \dfrac{7}{9}$ 3. $\dfrac{^-3}{7}, \dfrac{^-2}{5}$ 4. $\dfrac{1}{2}, \dfrac{1}{^-3}$

Solution

1. $3 \times 10 > 7 \times 4$, so $\dfrac{3}{7} > \dfrac{4}{10}$

2. $3 \times 9 < 4 \times 7$, so $\dfrac{3}{4} < \dfrac{7}{9}$

3. $^-3 \times 5 < 7 \times {}^-2$, so $\dfrac{^-3}{7} < \dfrac{^-2}{5}$

4. $\dfrac{1}{2} > \dfrac{1}{^-3}$ because $\dfrac{1}{2}$ is positive and $\dfrac{1}{^-3}$ is negative.

DENSITY OF FRACTIONS

The integers are evenly spaced on the number line, and for any integer there is a "next" integer, both to its right and to its left. For fractions, however, this is not true.

EXAMPLE N

There is no single fraction that is the *next one* greater than 1/2; instead, there are many such fractions. Use the following number line to find a fraction that is between 1/2 and 6/10.

Solution

One method of finding fractions between two given fractions is to express both fractions with a larger common denominator. The following figure shows several sections of a number line with fractions that are equal to 1/2 and 6/10. By increasing the denominators, we can easily find fractions between 1/2 and 6/10. For example, the third number line shows that the 9 fractions from 51/100 to 59/100 are between 1/2 and 6/10, and the fourth number line shows that the 99 fractions from 501/1000 to 599/1000 are between 1/2 and 6/10.

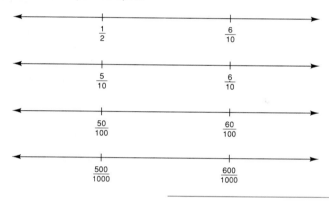

Similarly, there is no fraction next to zero. To state this another way, there is no smallest fraction greater than zero. The following sequence of fractions gets closer and closer to zero, but no matter how far we go in this sequence, these fractions will always be greater than zero.

$$\frac{1}{2}, \frac{1}{4}, \frac{1}{8}, \frac{1}{16}, \frac{1}{32}, \frac{1}{64}, \frac{1}{128}, \cdots$$

These examples are special cases of the more general fact that between any two fractions there is always another fraction. We refer to this property by saying that the fractions are **dense.** Because of this property of denseness, there are an infinite number of fractions between any two fractions.

dense

MIXED NUMBERS AND IMPROPER FRACTIONS

Historically, a fraction stood for part of a whole and represented a number less than 1. The idea that there could be fractions such as 4/4 or 5/4 with numerators greater than or equal to the denominator was uncommon even as late as the sixteenth century. Such fractions are called **improper fractions,** and as their name indicates, at one time they were not thought of as authentic fractions.

improper fractions

When improper fractions are written as a combination of whole numbers and fractions, they are called **mixed numbers.** The numbers below are examples of mixed numbers:

mixed numbers

$$1\frac{1}{5}, 2\frac{3}{4}, 4\frac{2}{3}, 15\frac{1}{8}$$

Placing a whole number and a fraction side by side, as in mixed numbers, indicates the sum of the two numbers. For example, $1\frac{1}{5}$ means $1 + 1/5$. This fact is used in converting a mixed number to an improper fraction. For example,

$$1\frac{1}{5} = 1 + \frac{1}{5} = \frac{5}{5} + \frac{1}{5} = \frac{6}{5} \quad \text{and} \quad 2\frac{3}{4} = 2 + \frac{3}{4} = \frac{8}{4} + \frac{3}{4} = \frac{11}{4}$$

EXAMPLE O

Write a mixed number and an improper fraction to express the shaded amount of each figure. In part (1), each disc represents 1, and in part (2), each bar represents 1.

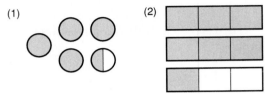

(1)   (2)

Solution

1. $4\frac{1}{2}$ or $\frac{9}{2}$ (Since each whole disc has 2 halves, a total of 9 halves are shaded.)

$$4\frac{1}{2} = 4 + \frac{1}{2} = \frac{8}{2} + \frac{1}{2} = \frac{9}{2}$$

2. $2\frac{1}{3}$ or $\frac{7}{3}$ (Since each whole bar has 3 thirds, a total of 7 thirds are shaded.)

$$2\frac{1}{3} = 2 + \frac{1}{3} = \frac{6}{3} + \frac{1}{3} = \frac{7}{3}$$

EXAMPLE P

Write the missing mixed number above each improper fraction on the following number line, and write the missing improper fraction below each mixed number on the number line.

Solution

$$\frac{-9}{5} = -1\frac{4}{5}, \; -1\frac{3}{5} = \frac{-8}{5}, \; -1\frac{1}{5} = \frac{-6}{5}, \; 1\frac{2}{5} = \frac{7}{5}, \; \frac{8}{5} = 1\frac{3}{5}, \; 1\frac{4}{5} = \frac{9}{5}$$

Notice that in a negative mixed number the negative sign is on only the whole-number part and the fraction is understood to be negative. For example, $^-1\frac{1}{5}$ is equal to $^-1 + {}^-1/5$.

The number line in Example P indicates that the improper fractions 5/5, 10/5, 3/3, and 6/3 are equal to whole numbers. One method of illustrating such equalities is to use the partitive concept of division ($a/b = a \div b$), introduced earlier. For example, 5/5 is 5 divided into 5 equal parts, as shown in Figure 5.30, and 10/5 is 10 divided into 5 equal parts.

300 Students

each box = 3 students

$Ex = 1$ $300 \div 100 = 3$

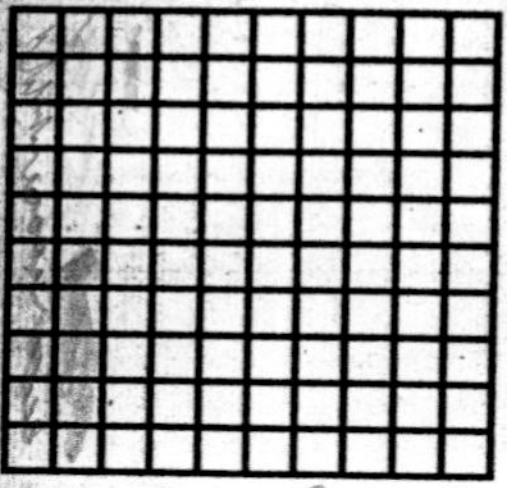

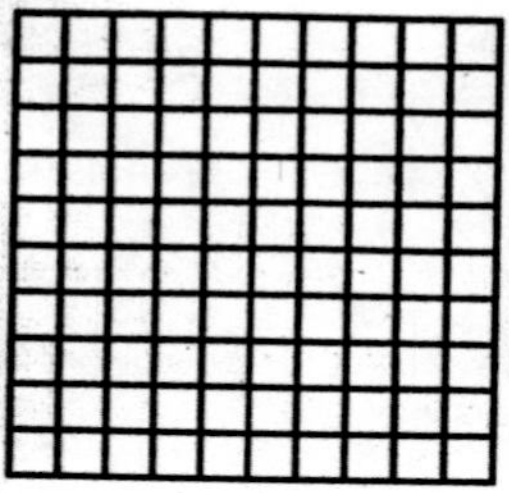

$15 \times 3 = 45$

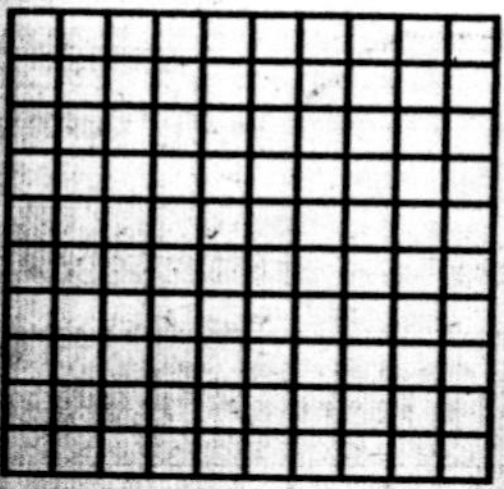

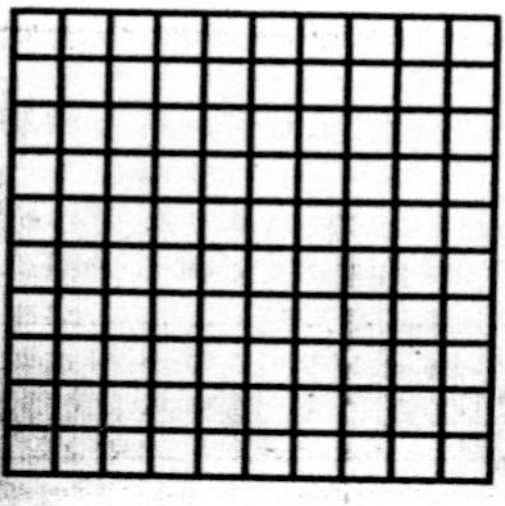

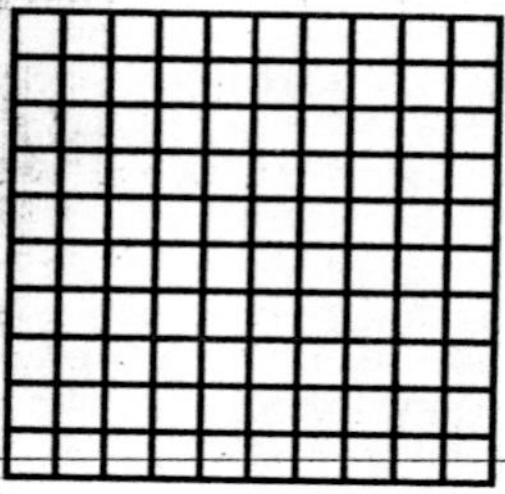

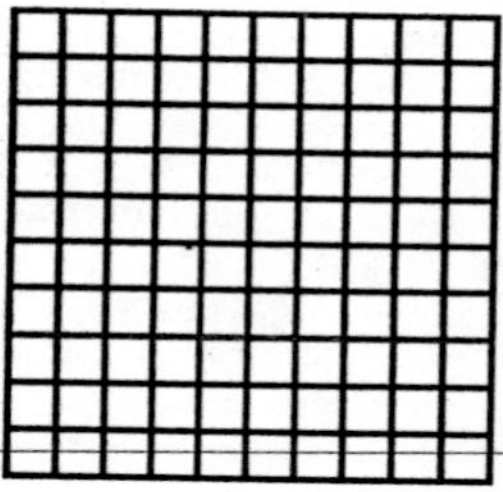

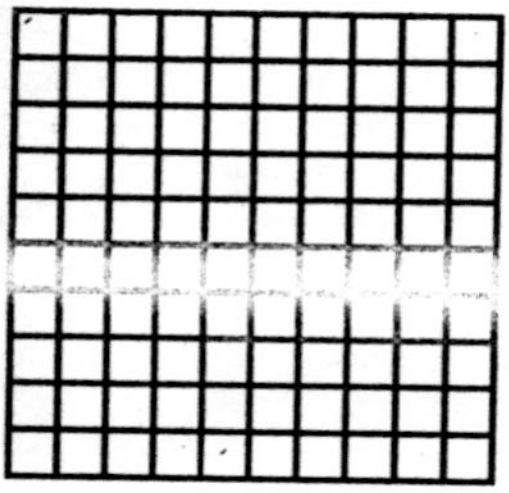

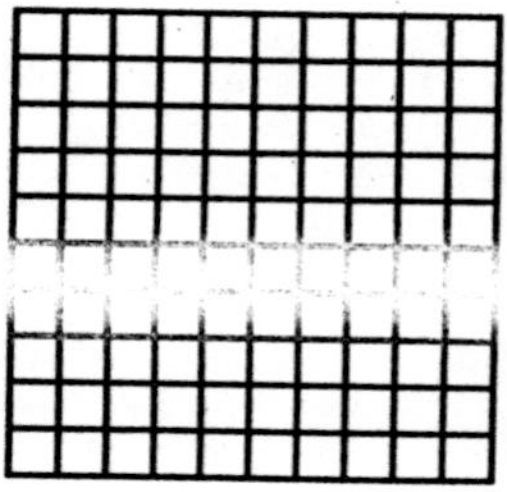

Figure 5.30

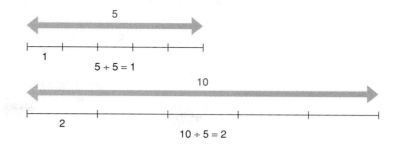

$5 \div 5 = 1$

$10 \div 5 = 2$

MENTAL CALCULATIONS

The *Curriculum and Evaluation Standards for School Mathematics* states that "Fraction symbols, such as 1/4 and 2/3, should be introduced only after children have developed the concepts and oral language necessary for symbols to be meaningful and should be carefully connected to both the models and oral language."* One reason for the use of models is to build number sense for mental calculations. Inequalities of fractions can often be determined by appealing to visual models. For example, the chart in Figure 5.31 shows why it is easy to determine an inequality for two unit fractions: *the more parts in a bar, the smaller the parts.*

Figure 5.31

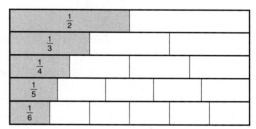

EXAMPLE Q

Use the observation in the paragraph above to mentally determine an inequality for each of the following pairs of fractions.

1. $\dfrac{1}{12}, \dfrac{1}{5}$ 2. $\dfrac{1}{9}, \dfrac{1}{20}$ 3. $\dfrac{1}{11}, \dfrac{1}{3}$

Solution

1. $\dfrac{1}{12} < \dfrac{1}{5}$ because a bar with 12 equal parts has smaller parts than a bar with 5 equal parts.

2. $\dfrac{1}{9} > \dfrac{1}{20}$ because a bar with 9 equal parts has larger parts than a bar with 20 equal parts.

3. $\dfrac{1}{11} < \dfrac{1}{3}$ because a bar with 11 equal parts has smaller parts than a bar with 3 equal parts.

It is also easy to compare two fractions mentally when the numerator of each fraction is 1 less than the denominator of the fraction. For example, to compare 4/5 and 2/3 (see Figure 5.32), we note that a 4/5-bar is within 1/5 of being a whole bar and a 2/3-bar is within 1/3 of being a whole bar. Since $1/5 < 1/3$, a 4/5-bar is closer to a whole bar than a 2/3-bar is. So $4/5 > 2/3$.

*Curriculum and Evaluation Standards for School Mathematics (Reston, VA: National Council of Teachers of Mathematics, 1989), 58.

Figure 5.32

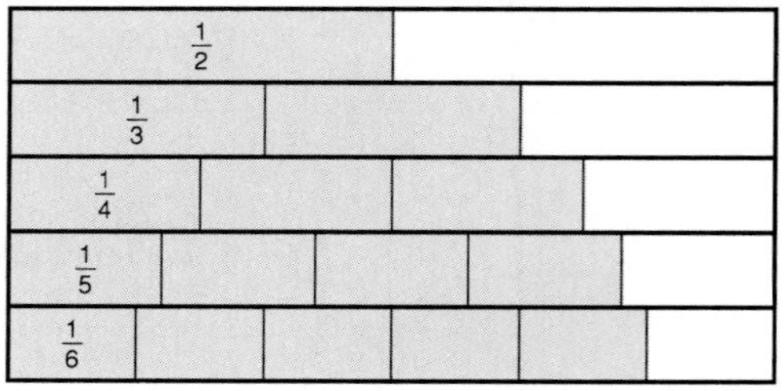

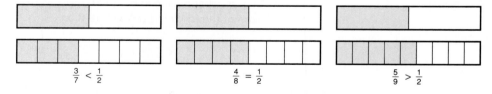

EXAMPLE R

Mentally determine an inequality for each of the following pairs of fractions.

1. $\dfrac{9}{10}, \dfrac{2}{3}$ 2. $\dfrac{3}{4}, \dfrac{14}{15}$ 3. $\dfrac{19}{20}, \dfrac{5}{6}$

Solution

1. $\dfrac{9}{10} > \dfrac{2}{3}$ because $\dfrac{1}{10} < \dfrac{1}{3}$

2. $\dfrac{3}{4} < \dfrac{14}{15}$ because $\dfrac{1}{4} > \dfrac{1}{15}$

3. $\dfrac{19}{20} > \dfrac{5}{6}$ because $\dfrac{1}{20} < \dfrac{1}{6}$

Comparing fractions to 1/2 is also a convenient method of determining inequalities for some pairs of fractions. Consider the fractions 3/7 and 5/9. Figure 5.33 shows that if the numerator is less than half the denominator, the bar for the fraction is less than half shaded and the fraction is less than 1/2. If the numerator is equal to half the denominator, the bar for the fraction is half shaded and the fraction is equal to 1/2. If the numerator is greater than half the denominator, more than half of the bar for the fraction is shaded and the fraction is greater than 1/2. Since $3/7 < 1/2$ and $5/9 > 1/2$, we know that $3/7 < 5/9$.

Figure 5.33

$$\frac{3}{7} < \frac{1}{2} \qquad\qquad \frac{4}{8} = \frac{1}{2} \qquad\qquad \frac{5}{9} > \frac{1}{2}$$

EXAMPLE S

Mentally determine an inequality for each pair of fractions by comparing each fraction to 1/2.

1. $\dfrac{5}{8}, \dfrac{4}{11}$ 2. $\dfrac{7}{15}, \dfrac{5}{9}$ 3. $\dfrac{9}{20}, \dfrac{3}{5}$

Solution

1. $\dfrac{5}{8} > \dfrac{1}{2}$ and $\dfrac{4}{11} < \dfrac{1}{2}$, so $\dfrac{5}{8} > \dfrac{4}{11}$

2. $\dfrac{7}{15} < \dfrac{1}{2}$ and $\dfrac{5}{9} > \dfrac{1}{2}$, so $\dfrac{7}{15} < \dfrac{5}{9}$

3. $\dfrac{9}{20} < \dfrac{1}{2}$ and $\dfrac{3}{5} > \dfrac{1}{2}$, so $\dfrac{9}{20} < \dfrac{3}{5}$

ESTIMATION

Estimations involving fractions are often obtained by rounding. Rounding fractions and mixed numbers to the nearest whole number involves comparing fractions to 1/2. If the fraction is less than 1/2, it is rounded to zero, and if it is greater than 1/2, it is rounded to 1. If the fraction is equal to 1/2, it may be rounded up or down. In this text we will round such fractions up. Similarly, a mixed number is rounded down or up depending on whether the fraction rounds to zero or to 1.

Rounding can be thought of by considering which whole number on a number line a given number is closest to. For example, $2\frac{5}{8}$ is closer to 3 than to 2, so it rounds to 3; and 3/8 is closer to zero than to 1, so it rounds to zero.

Figure 5.34

◁ EXAMPLE T

Round each fraction or mixed number to the nearest whole number.

    1. $\dfrac{2}{5}$ 2. $4\dfrac{3}{7}$ 3. $\dfrac{8}{3}$ 4. $7\dfrac{3}{6}$

Solution   1. 0   2. 4   3. 3   4. 8

Another method of estimating fractions is to replace a fraction by a close approximation that is in simpler form. For example,

$$\frac{7}{22} \approx \frac{7}{21} = \frac{1}{3} \quad \text{and} \quad 1\frac{4}{9} \approx 1\frac{3}{9} = 1\frac{1}{3}$$

EXAMPLE U

Replace each fraction or mixed number by a close approximation that is in simpler form.

    1. $4\dfrac{17}{30}$ 2. $12\dfrac{5}{26}$ 3. $\dfrac{4}{13}$ 4. $\dfrac{19}{80}$

Solution   Here are some possible replacements. Others may occur to you.

    1. $4\dfrac{17}{30} \approx 4\dfrac{15}{30} = 4\dfrac{1}{2}$ 2. $12\dfrac{5}{26} \approx 12\dfrac{5}{25} = 12\dfrac{1}{5}$

    3. $\dfrac{4}{13} \approx \dfrac{4}{12} = \dfrac{1}{3}$ 4. $\dfrac{19}{80} \approx \dfrac{20}{80} = \dfrac{1}{4}$

PROBLEM-SOLVING APPLICATION

The following problem can be solved by *guessing and checking* or by *making a drawing*. Try solving this problem before reading the solution. If you need assistance, read the paragraph entitled Understanding the Problem and then try finding the solution.

PROBLEM

In a certain community 2/3 of the women are married and 1/2 of the men are married. No one in the community is married to a person outside the community. What fraction of the adults are unmarried?

Understanding the Problem   Let's *guess* at some numbers to obtain a better understanding of the problem. For the number of women, we want to select a number that is divisible by 3 (12, 15, 18, 24, 30, 60, etc.) so that we can find 2/3 of it. Suppose we choose a total of 24 women. In this case 16 women (2/3 of 24) are married. Since for each married woman there is a married man, there are 16 married men and thus 32 men in the

Question 1   community. For this example, what fraction of the adults are married and what fraction are unmarried?

Devising a Plan   Another approach is to *make a drawing* to see if it leads to a solution. The married women can be represented by shading 2/3 of a figure and the married men by shading 1/2 of a figure, as shown below. These two figures represent the total population.

Question 2   Why are the shaded regions equal?

Married women

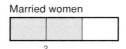

$\frac{2}{3}$

Married men

$\frac{1}{2}$

Carrying Out the Plan   Let's continue the visual approach. If we divide the shaded and unshaded parts of the figure representing the men in half, each new part is the same size

Question 3   as each part of the figure representing the women. How does this show that 4/7 of the people are married and 3/7 are not married?

$\frac{1}{3}$ $\frac{1}{3}$

Women

Men

Looking Back   The visual approach suggests that it is not necessary to know the number of women and men in the community; we will obtain the same answer regardless of the number of women used in the numerical approach. Suppose we select 30 as the number of women. Then there will be 20 married women (2/3 of 30 is 20) and 20 married men. Since

Question 4   1/2 of 40 is 20, there will be 40 men in the community and a total of 70 people. In this case, how many people are not married and what fraction of the people are not married?

Answers to Questions 1–4

1. 32/56 = 4/7 are married and 24/56 = 3/7 are unmarried.

2. There is the same number of married men as married women in the community.

3. There are a total of 7 equal parts: the 4 shaded parts represent the married people, so 4/7 are married; the 3 unshaded parts represent the unmarried people, so 3/7 are not married.

4. 30 people are not married, so 30/70 = 3/7 are not married.

RELATED ACTIVITIES IN

Mathematics for Elementary Teachers: An Activity Approach, 3e

Activity Set 5.2   **Models for Equality and Inequality:** Fraction Bars are used to provide a visual model for the part-to-whole and division concepts of fractions and to illustrate equality, inequality, rounding, and estimation with fractions.

Just for Fun   **Fraction Games:** Two games, one involving inequality of fractions and one involving equality of fractions

PUZZLER

After a cake has been cut into 3 equal pieces, as shown here, a hostess discovers that 4 people each want an equal share of the cake. How can she make one more straight cut so that each of the 4 people gets the same amount of cake?

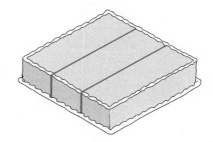

EXERCISES AND PROBLEMS 5.2

1. Only a few different denominators occur in the fractions that appear frequently in newspapers, magazines, sales ads, etc.
   a. Name the different denominators in the fractions in the collage above.
   b. There are many mixed numbers in the collage. Name 10 of them.
   c. Write the mixed numbers in part b as improper fractions.

2. For each figure write two fractions, one for the shaded part and one for the unshaded part.

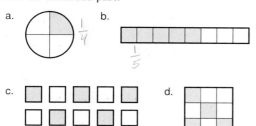

3. Using the given figure and the partitive concept of division, illustrate the quotient. Complete the equation and describe how the answer is obtained from the figure.

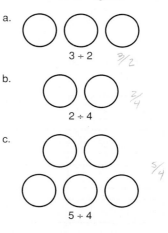

a.

$3 \div 2$ $\frac{3}{2}$

b.

$2 \div 4$ $\frac{2}{4}$

c.

$5 \div 4$ $\frac{5}{4}$

4. Cuisenaire rods can represent various fractions, depending on the choice of the unit rod. If the unit rod is brown, then the purple rod represents 1/2.
   a. What is the unit rod if the purple rod represents 2/3?
   b. If the unit rod is the orange rod, what fraction is represented by the black rod?
   c. If the dark green rod represents 3/4, what is the unit rod?

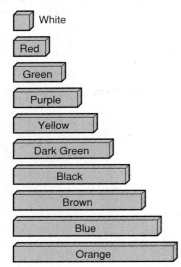

5. Use the array of 12 dots shown here to illustrate each of the following equalities.

   a. $\dfrac{1}{3} = \dfrac{4}{12}$ b. $\dfrac{6}{12} = \dfrac{1}{2}$

   c. $\dfrac{2}{3} = \dfrac{8}{12}$ d. $\dfrac{9}{12} = \dfrac{3}{4}$

6. Write the missing numbers for these fractions.

   a. $\dfrac{7}{8} = \dfrac{28}{32}$ b. $\dfrac{5}{3} = \dfrac{40}{24}$

   c. $\dfrac{2}{3} = \dfrac{12}{18}$ d. $\dfrac{5}{6} = \dfrac{20}{24}$

7. Write each fraction in lowest terms.

   a. $\dfrac{4}{18}$ $\dfrac{2}{9}$ b. $\dfrac{12}{27}$ $\dfrac{4}{9}$

   c. $\dfrac{4}{12}$ $\dfrac{1}{3}$ d. $\dfrac{-16}{24}$ $-\dfrac{2}{3}$

8. Split the parts of these fraction bars to illustrate the given equalities.

   a. $\dfrac{7}{10} = \dfrac{14}{20}$

   b. $\dfrac{6}{7} = \dfrac{18}{21}$

   c. $\dfrac{1}{9} = \dfrac{3}{27}$

   d. $\dfrac{1}{4} = \dfrac{2}{8}$

9. Group the parts of each bar to show why the fraction on the left side of the equation equals the fraction on the right side.

   a.  $\dfrac{9}{12} = \dfrac{3}{4}$

   b. $\dfrac{4}{6} = \dfrac{2}{3}$

   c. $\dfrac{4}{8} = \dfrac{1}{2}$

   d. $\dfrac{8}{10} = \dfrac{4}{5}$

10. Complete the equations so that the fractions in each pair have the smallest common denominator.

    a. $\dfrac{2}{3} =$ b. $\dfrac{1}{6} =$

    $\dfrac{4}{5} =$ $\dfrac{-7}{12} =$

    c. $\dfrac{3}{15} =$ d. $\dfrac{5}{8} =$

    $\dfrac{5}{6} =$ $\dfrac{3}{-10} =$

11. Determine an inequality ($<$ or $>$) for each pair of fractions.

    a. $\dfrac{3}{7} < \dfrac{5}{9}$ b. $\dfrac{1}{4} > \dfrac{1}{6}$ c. $\dfrac{-5}{6} < \dfrac{-7}{8}$

    d. $\dfrac{1}{4} > \dfrac{2}{9}$ e. $\dfrac{3}{8} > \dfrac{1}{3}$ f. $\dfrac{4}{7} > \dfrac{-5}{9}$

12. Between any two fractions there are an infinite number of fractions. Find a fraction that is between the fractions in each pair below.

    a. $\dfrac{1}{20}, \dfrac{1}{10}$ b. $\dfrac{1}{2}, \dfrac{5}{8}$

    c. $\dfrac{1}{3}, \dfrac{1}{4}$ d. $\dfrac{8}{9}, \dfrac{9}{10}$

13. Write each of these fractions as a mixed number or a whole number.

    a. $\dfrac{5}{3}$ $1\dfrac{2}{3}$ b. $\dfrac{8}{8}$ 1 c. $\dfrac{25}{6}$ $4\dfrac{1}{6}$

    d. $\dfrac{-21}{7}$ -3 e. $\dfrac{17}{5}$ $3\dfrac{2}{5}$ f. $\dfrac{18}{2}$ 9

14. Write each of these mixed numbers as a fraction.

    a. $1\dfrac{3}{4}$ $\dfrac{7}{4}$ b. $-2\dfrac{1}{5}$ $-\dfrac{11}{5}$ c. $4\dfrac{2}{3}$ $\dfrac{14}{3}$

    d. $2\dfrac{5}{6}$ $\dfrac{17}{6}$ e. $1\dfrac{3}{7}$ $\dfrac{10}{7}$ f. $3\dfrac{1}{2}$ $\dfrac{7}{2}$

15. For each point indicated on the number lines, write the fraction or improper fraction that identifies it below the line. Then write the mixed number for each improper fraction above the line.

a.

b.

16. Mentally determine an inequality for each pair of fractions and explain your reasoning using a drawing.

   a. $\dfrac{1}{12} > \dfrac{1}{20}$ b. $\dfrac{7}{8} < \dfrac{9}{10}$ c. $\dfrac{5}{12} < \dfrac{6}{11}$

   d. $\dfrac{-1}{50} < \dfrac{-1}{30}$ e. $\dfrac{5}{9} > \dfrac{3}{7}$ f. $\dfrac{11}{12} < \dfrac{19}{20}$

17. Round each fraction or mixed number to the nearest whole number.

   a. $\dfrac{4}{10}$ b. $1\dfrac{1}{3}$ c. $3\dfrac{1}{2}$

   d. $\dfrac{4}{7}$ e. $-2\dfrac{3}{4}$ f. $\dfrac{2}{5}$

18. a. A buyer's guide for single lens reflex cameras gives the following shutter speeds in seconds. Write these numbers in increasing order from smallest to largest.

$$\frac{1}{90},\ \frac{1}{250},\ \frac{1}{60},\ \frac{1}{1000},\ \frac{1}{100}$$

   b. Suppose you need to drill a 3/8-inch hole but the set of drill bits is measured in sixteenths of an inch. What size drill bit should you use?

   c. In order to pass inspection in a certain state, a car's tire treads must have a depth of at least 1/16th of an inch. If the tires on a car have tread depths in inches of 1/2, 1/8, 1/32, and 1/4, which tire will not pass inspection?

19. a. One-fiftieth of the earth's crust is magnesium, and 1/20 of the earth's crust is iron. Is there more iron or more magnesium in the earth's crust?

   b. Pure gold is quite soft. To make it more useful for such items as rings and jewelry, jewelers mix it with other metals such as copper and zinc. Pure gold is marked 24k (24 karat). What fraction of a ring is pure gold if it is marked 14k? Write your answer in lowest terms.

   c. Some health authorities say that we should have 1 gram of protein a day for each kilogram of our weight. There are about 40 grams of protein in a liter of milk. A liter of fat-free milk weighs about 1040 grams. What fraction of milk's weight is protein? Write your answer in lowest terms.

20. The photo at the right shows a shutter-speed knob on top of a 35-mm camera. The numerals on this knob determine the amount of time the camera's shutter stays open. The settings of 4 and 2 following the letter B cause the shutter to remain open for 4 and 2 seconds, respectively. The remaining numerals, 1, 2, 4, 8, etc., represent 1 second and 1/2, 1/4, 1/8, etc., of a second. The fastest opening on this camera is 1/1000th of a second.

Shutter-speed knob on a 35-mm camera

   a. The less light that is available, the longer the shutter must stay open for the film to be properly exposed. Will a shutter setting of 15 allow more or less light than a setting of 60?

   b. If a shutter setting of 250 doesn't allow quite enough light, what number should the dial be set on?

21. The following news clipping shows share prices, in dollars and fractions of a dollar, for a given day for the 5 most active stocks and the 20 top stocks. The first column of numbers contains the daily closing prices. The second column shows whether those prices were up (u), down (d), or unchanged (unc.) from the previous day's price. The third column shows the fraction of a dollar by which each price changed.

   a. Find the closing price in dollars and cents for each of the following stocks: Dow Ch, Gen Elec, and Gulf Oil.

   b. Find the daily price change in cents for these stocks: RCA, Xerox, and Tyco Lb.

5 MOST ACTIVE			
Occid. Pt	17 3/8	d	1/8
Dow Ch	44 3/8	d	1/4
Gn Mot	67 1/4	u	5/8
Aetna Lf	31 1/2	unc.	
Brist My	74	u	3/8

20 TOP STOCKS			
Am T&T	59	u	1/4
RCA	27 1/8	u	1/8
Data Genl	47 5/8	u	3/8
Nat Gyp	14 3/8	unc.	
P Sv Eg	20 3/4	u	1/8
Con Foods	25 1/4	d	1/8
Reyn Ind	60	u	1/4
Pub S.N.H.	20 1/2	unc.	
Xerox	63 3/8	u	3/16
U.S. Steel	47 3/4	d	1/2
Exxon	51 7/8	u	1/2
Whel Fry	22 1/8	d	1/4
Gen Elec	52 3/4	u	1/4
Golf Oil	25 7/8	d	1/4
Polaroid	37 7/8	u	1/4
Unit Tech	33 1/4	u	1/16
Con Edis	18 7/8	d	1/8
Tyco Lb	12 5/8	d	1/4
Ca Pw Pf	27 7/8	unc.	
IBM	271 3/4	u	1/2

Featured Strategies: Guessing and Checking, Solving a Simpler Problem, and Finding a Pattern

22. Five jars, numbered 1 through 5, contain a total of 92 candy bars. If each jar contains 2 more candy bars than the previous jar, how much candy is in each jar?

1   2   3   4   5

a. **Understanding the Problem** Sometimes a problem such as this one can be solved by *guessing* and then adjusting the next guess. Even if no solution is found, you may obtain a better understanding of the problem. Try a few numbers and describe what you learn by guessing.

b. **Devising a Plan** Your guesses in part **a** should suggest that the answers are not whole numbers. Let's simplify the problem by changing the number of candy bars. How many bars will there be in each jar if there are a total of 100 bars?

c. **Carrying Out the Plan** Continue by determining the number of bars in each jar in each of the following cases, assuming there are 100 candy bars.
(1) Each jar has 3 more than the previous jar
(2) Each jar has 4 more than the previous jar
(3) Each jar has 5 more than the previous jar
Look for a pattern in your answers. What general approach to solving this type of problem is suggested? What is the solution to the original problem with 92 candy bars?

d. **Looking Back** Solve this problem for 7 jars containing 92 candy bars, assuming each jar has 2 more bars than the previous jar.

23. Below is a daily report on prices of 5 stocks, showing the lowest and highest price per share for the day.
a. Which of these 5 stocks had the lowest price for the day?
b. Which stock had the highest price for the day?
c. Alaska Airlines finished the day at $8\frac{3}{16}$ dollars. Is this greater than or less than the day's high price for this stock?

Company	Low price	High price
Alaska Airlines	$7\frac{5}{8}$	$8\frac{3}{4}$
Canadian Homestead	$7\frac{15}{16}$	$8\frac{1}{4}$
Mobile Home Indiana	$23\frac{5}{8}$	$24\frac{1}{2}$
Ranger O Can	$19\frac{1}{2}$	$20\frac{3}{8}$
Vintage Enterprise	$28\frac{3}{8}$	$29\frac{3}{4}$

24. The Fibonacci numbers, 1, 1, 2, 3, 5, 8, 13, . . . , occur as the numerators and denominators of fractions associated with patterns of leaf arrangements on trees and plants. The picture shows leaf arrangements on a pear tree branch.

Pear tree stem

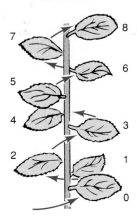

a. If you begin with any leaf on a pear tree branch and count the number of leaves until you reach a leaf that grows from a point just above the first, the number of leaves, not counting the first (zero leaf), will be the Fibonacci number 8. Furthermore, in passing around the branch from a leaf to the leaf directly above, you will make 3 complete turns. This means that each leaf is 3/8 of a turn from its adjacent leaves. The pattern described by this fraction is called phyllotaxis (or leaf divergence). For any given species of tree, the appropriate fraction can be found by counting the leaves (or branches) and the turns around the stem. Fill in the missing numbers in the fractions for phyllotaxis in the following table. (Hint: Look for a relationship between the numerator and denominator in each of the first three fractions.)

Tree	Phyllotaxis
Apple	$\frac{2}{5}$
Pear	$\frac{3}{8}$
Beech	$\frac{1}{3}$
Almond	$\frac{5}{\square}$
Elm	$\frac{\square}{2}$
Willow	$\frac{3}{\square}$

b. The seeds of sunflowers and daisies, the scales of pinecones and pineapples, and the leaves on certain vegetables are arranged in two spirals. In these cases the numerator and denominator of the fraction for phyllotaxis give the number of clockwise and counterclockwise spirals, respectively. Look for a relationship between the numerator and denominator of each fraction in the table at the right and fill in the missing numbers in the fractions for phyllotaxis.

Plant	Phyllotaxis
White pine cone	$\frac{5}{8}$
Pineapple	$\frac{8}{13}$
Daisy	$\frac{21}{34}$
Cauliflower	$\frac{\square}{3}$
Celery	$\frac{1}{\square}$
Medium sunflower	$\frac{55}{\square}$
Large sunflower	$\frac{\square}{144}$

LABORATORY INVESTIGATION

A student had a standard $8\frac{1}{2}$ by 11-inch piece of paper but no ruler. She found that by folding the paper twice she could obtain a length of 6 inches. One of her folds is shown here. She continued to experiment with the sheet of paper and found she could obtain many other lengths.

Questions for Investigation

1. How can a length of 6 inches be obtained from two folds?
2. How can a length of 3 inches be obtained?
3. How can the 3-inch length be used to obtain an 8-inch length?
4. Once you have an 8-inch length, what other lengths can be obtained?
5. A 7-inch length can be obtained by folds that produce two mixed-number lengths. How can this be done?
6. How many other lengths of less than 11 inches can be obtained by folding a standard sheet of paper?

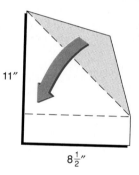

11″

$8\frac{1}{2}″$

PUZZLER

Four books, which are numbered 1 through 4 from left to right, have been placed on a shelf. Each book has 600 pages. The thickness of the 600 pages is 1 inch, and the thickness of each cover is 1/4 of an inch. If a worm begins at page 1 of book 1 and eats to page 600 of book 4, what distance will it have traveled?

Section 5.3 OPERATIONS WITH FRACTIONS

Your father gives half the money in his pocket to your mother, a fourth of what is left to your brother, and a third of what is left to your sister. He then splits the remainder with you. If you get $2, how much did your father start with?

United States space shuttle, Enterprise

Fractions are often used to indicate how much smaller a diagram or model is than the life-size object. For example, the dimensions of the model of the space shuttle in Figure 5.35 are 1/50 of the dimensions of the space shuttle *Enterprise*. This means that each length on the model can be obtained by multiplying the corresponding length on the *Enterprise* by 1/50. In this section we will examine the four basic operations with fractions.

Figure 5.35

■ *HISTORICAL HIGHLIGHT*

Italy's Maria Gaetana Agnesi (1718–1799), a brilliant linguist, philosopher, and mathematician, was the first of twenty-one children of a professor of mathematics at the University of Bologna. By her thirteenth birthday she was fluent in Latin, Greek, Hebrew, French, Spanish and German, as well as her native Italian. In 1748 she published *Instituzioni Analitiche,* two huge volumes containing a complete and unified treatment of algebra, analysis, and recent advances in calculus. This is the first surviving mathematical work written by a woman. Widely acclaimed as a model of clarity and exposition, it was translated into French (1775) and English (1801). In recognition of her exceptional accomplishments, Pope Benedict XIV appointed Agnesi to the chair of mathematics and natural philosophy at the University of Bologna in 1750. Maria Agnesi is said to have been the first woman professor of mathematics on a university faculty.

ADDITION

The concept of addition is the same for fractions as for whole numbers. The addition of whole numbers is illustrated by putting together, or combining, two sets of objects. Similarly, the addition of fractions can be illustrated by combining two amounts.

EXAMPLE A

Suppose that parts of two school days are used for a national testing program: 1/3 of a day is required for test A, and 1/5 of a day is required for test B. Approximately what part of a whole day is used for testing?

Solution One approach to solving this problem is to sketch a figure to represent each amount. The following figures represent 1/3 and 1/5, and we can see that when the shaded amounts are combined the total is approximately 1/2.

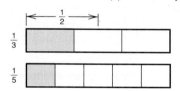

Finding the sum of two fractions is easy when they have the same denominator. Figure 5.36 shows Fraction Bars for 4/6 and 3/6. If the shaded parts of each bar are placed end to end, the total shaded amount is 1 whole bar and 1/6 of a bar. So $4/6 + 3/6 = 7/6$, or $1\frac{1}{6}$.

Figure 5.36

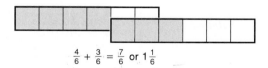

$$\frac{4}{6} + \frac{3}{6} = \frac{7}{6} \text{ or } 1\frac{1}{6}$$

Addition of fractions can also be illustrated on a number line (Figure 5.37) by placing arrows for the fractions end to end.

Figure 5.37

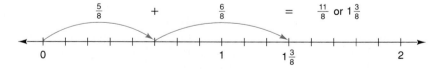

$$\frac{5}{8} \quad + \quad \frac{6}{8} \quad = \quad \frac{11}{8} \text{ or } 1\frac{3}{8}$$

EXAMPLE B

Write each sum as a fraction or a mixed number.

1. $\dfrac{4}{5} + \dfrac{3}{5}$ 2. $\dfrac{2}{9} + \dfrac{6}{9}$ 3. $\dfrac{5}{3} + \dfrac{2}{3}$

Solution   1. $\dfrac{7}{5} = 1\dfrac{2}{5}$ 2. $\dfrac{8}{9}$ 3. $\dfrac{7}{3} = 2\dfrac{1}{3}$

UNLIKE DENOMINATORS The difficulty in adding fractions occurs when the denominators are unequal. The 2/5 bar and the 1/3 bar in part (a) of Figure 5.38 show that 2/5 + 1/3 is greater than 3/5 but less than 4/5. To determine this sum exactly, we must replace the two fractions by fractions having the same denominator. Since the smallest common denominator of 2/5 and 1/3 is 15, these fractions can be replaced by 6/15 and 5/15, as shown in part (b) of Figure 5.38. The sum of these two fractions is 11/15, so 2/5 + 1/3 = 11/15.

Figure 5.38

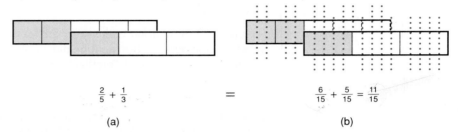

$$\frac{2}{5} + \frac{1}{3}$$

(a)

$$= \qquad \frac{6}{15} + \frac{5}{15} = \frac{11}{15}$$

(b)

Multiplying the denominators of two fractions by each other will always yield a common denominator (but not necessarily the smallest one). Once two fractions have a common denominator, their sum is computed by adding the numerators and retaining the denominator. This is stated in the following rule for adding fractions.

ADDITION OF FRACTIONS

For any fractions a/b and c/d,

$$\frac{a}{b} + \frac{c}{d} = \frac{ad}{bd} + \frac{bc}{bd} = \frac{ad + bc}{bd}$$

EXAMPLE C

Find each sum.

1. $\dfrac{1}{4} + \dfrac{3}{7}$ 2. $\dfrac{5}{6} + \dfrac{^{-}1}{8}$ 3. $\dfrac{7}{10} + \dfrac{9}{20}$

Solution

1. $\dfrac{1}{4} + \dfrac{3}{7} = \dfrac{7}{28} + \dfrac{12}{28} = \dfrac{19}{28}$

2. $\dfrac{5}{6} + \dfrac{^{-}1}{8} = \dfrac{20}{24} + \dfrac{^{-}3}{24} = \dfrac{17}{24}$

3. $\dfrac{7}{10} + \dfrac{9}{20} = \dfrac{14}{20} + \dfrac{9}{20} = \dfrac{23}{20} = 1\dfrac{3}{20}$

MIXED NUMBERS Mixed numbers are combinations of whole numbers and fractions. The sum of two such numbers can be found by adding the whole numbers and fractions separately. If the denominators of the fractions are unequal, as in problem (2) in Example D, a common denominator must be found before the fractions can be added.

EXAMPLE D

Compute each sum.

1. $6\dfrac{2}{5}$
   $+3\dfrac{4}{5}$

2. $3\dfrac{1}{2}$
   $+5\dfrac{2}{3}$

Solution   1. $6\dfrac{2}{5}$

   $+3\dfrac{4}{5}$

   $9\dfrac{6}{5} = 10\dfrac{1}{5}$

2. $3\dfrac{1}{2} = \quad 3\dfrac{3}{6}$

   $+5\dfrac{2}{3} = +5\dfrac{4}{6}$

   $8\dfrac{7}{6} = 9\dfrac{1}{6}$

SUBTRACTION

The concept of subtraction is the same for fractions as for whole numbers. That is, both the take-away concept and the missing addends concept apply to subtraction of fractions. The bars in part (a) of Figure 5.39 show that 1/2 take away 1/6 is 2/6, or that 2/6 must be added to 1/6 to obtain 1/2. Part (b) of the figure illustrates subtraction on a number line and shows that 11/12 take away 7/12 equals 4/12, or that 4/12 must be added to 7/12 to obtain 11/12.

Figure 5.39

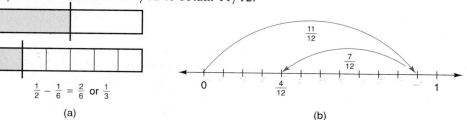

UNLIKE DENOMINATORS   The bars in part (a) of Figure 5.40 show that the difference between 5/6 and 1/4 is greater than 3/6 and less than 4/6. To compute this difference, we can replace these fractions by fractions having a common denominator. The smallest common denominator of 5/6 and 1/4 is 12, so these fractions can be replaced by 10/12 and 3/12, as shown in part (b) of the figure. The difference between these two fractions is 7/12, so 5/6 − 1/4 = 7/12.

Figure 5.40

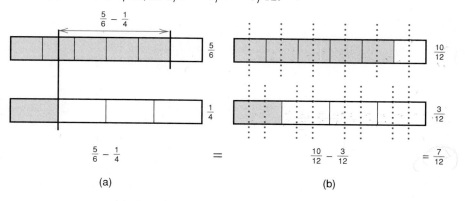

The general rule for subtracting fractions is usually stated using a common denominator that is the product of the two denominators, even though this may not be the smallest common denominator. Once two fractions have a common denominator, their difference is computed by subtracting the numerators and retaining the denominator.

SUBTRACTION OF FRACTIONS

For any fractions a/b and c/d,

$$\frac{a}{b} - \frac{c}{d} = \frac{ad}{bd} - \frac{bc}{bd} = \frac{ad - bc}{bd}$$

EXAMPLE E

Find each difference.

1. $\dfrac{7}{8} - \dfrac{1}{3}$ 2. $\dfrac{1}{2} - \dfrac{4}{5}$ 3. $\dfrac{2}{3} - \dfrac{^{-}1}{4}$

Solution

1. $\dfrac{7}{8} - \dfrac{1}{3} = \dfrac{21}{24} - \dfrac{8}{24} = \dfrac{13}{24}$

2. $\dfrac{1}{2} - \dfrac{4}{5} = \dfrac{5}{10} - \dfrac{8}{10} = \dfrac{^{-}3}{10}$

3. $\dfrac{2}{3} - \dfrac{^{-}1}{4} = \dfrac{8}{12} - \dfrac{^{-}3}{12} = \dfrac{8}{12} + \dfrac{3}{12} = \dfrac{11}{12}$

MIXED NUMBERS   The difference between two mixed numbers can be found by subtracting the whole-number parts and the fractions separately. Sometimes borrowing or regrouping is necessary before this can be done, as in problem (1) in Example F. If the denominators of the fractions in the mixed numbers are unequal, the fractions must be replaced by fractions having a common denominator. In some cases, both borrowing and changing denominators will be necessary before mixed numbers can be subtracted, as in problem (2) in Example F.

EXAMPLE F

Compute each difference.

1. $4\dfrac{1}{5}$ 2. $5\dfrac{1}{6}$

   $-1\dfrac{2}{5}$ $-2\dfrac{3}{4}$

Solution

1. $4\dfrac{1}{5} = 3\dfrac{6}{5}$

   $-1\dfrac{2}{5} = -1\dfrac{2}{5}$

   $\phantom{-1\dfrac{2}{5} = } 2\dfrac{4}{5}$

2. $5\dfrac{1}{6} = 5\dfrac{2}{12} = 4\dfrac{14}{12}$

   $-2\dfrac{3}{4} = -2\dfrac{9}{12} = -2\dfrac{9}{12}$

   $\phantom{-2\dfrac{3}{4} = -2\dfrac{9}{12} = } 2\dfrac{5}{12}$

Figure 5.41

$\frac{1}{3} \times 6 = 2$

MULTIPLICATION

Given a product of two whole numbers $m \times n$, we can think of the first number m as indicating "how many" of the second number. For example, 2×3 means 2 of the 3s. Multiplication of fractions may be viewed in a similar manner. In the product $1/3 \times 6$, the first number tells us "how much" of the second; that is, $1/3 \times 6$ means $1/3$ of 6 (Figure 5.41).

There is a major difference between the outcome of multiplying by a whole number and the outcome of multiplying by a fraction. When we multiply by a whole number greater than 1, the product is greater than the second number being multiplied. However, when we multiply by a fraction less than 1, the product is less than the second number being multiplied. This is often a problem for school children who have been accustomed to multiplying by whole numbers before encountering products with fractions.*

WHOLE NUMBER TIMES A FRACTION   In this case we can interpret multiplication to mean "repeated addition," just as we did with multiplication of whole numbers in Chapter 3. The whole number indicates the number of times the fraction is to be added to itself. Figure 5.42 illustrates $3 \times 2/5$ and shows that this product equals $1\frac{1}{5}$.

Figure 5.42

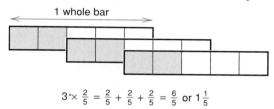

$$3 \cdot \times \frac{2}{5} = \frac{2}{5} + \frac{2}{5} + \frac{2}{5} = \frac{6}{5} \text{ or } 1\frac{1}{5}$$

FRACTION TIMES A WHOLE NUMBER   The product $1/3 \times 4$ means $1/3$ of 4. This product can be illustrated by using 4 bars and dividing each into 3 equal parts (Figure 5.43). The vertical lines partition these bars into equal parts, A, B, and C. Part A, which is one-third of the 4 bars, consists of 4 one-thirds, or 4 thirds.

Figure 5.43

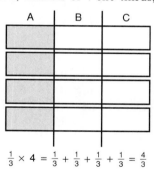

$$\frac{1}{3} \times 4 = \frac{1}{3} + \frac{1}{3} + \frac{1}{3} + \frac{1}{3} = \frac{4}{3}$$

The product $1/3 \times 4$ can also be illustrated by beginning with a 4-bar, as shown in Figure 5.44, and dividing it into 3 equal parts. Each part is $1\frac{1}{3}$ whole bars, so $1/3 \times 4 = 1\frac{1}{3}$.

Figure 5.44

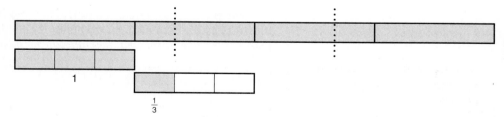

These examples suggest the following definition for products involving a whole number and a fraction.

*According to D. E. Smith, in his *History of Mathematics,* 2nd ed. (Lexington, MA: Ginn, 1925), 225, as early as the fifteenth and sixteenth centuries, writers on the subject of fractions expressed concern over this problem.

WHOLE NUMBER TIMES A FRACTION

For any whole number k and fraction a/b,

$$k \times \frac{a}{b} = \frac{ka}{b}$$

EXAMPLE G

Compute the following products.

1. $3 \times \dfrac{2}{7}$ 2. $\dfrac{2}{5} \times {}^{-}24$ 3. $6 \times \dfrac{3}{8}$

Solution   1. $\dfrac{6}{7}$ 2. $\dfrac{{}^{-}48}{5} = {}^{-}9\dfrac{3}{5}$ 3. $\dfrac{18}{8} = 2\dfrac{2}{8}$

FRACTION TIMES A FRACTION   The product $1/3 \times 1/5$ means $1/3$ of $1/5$. This can be illustrated by using a $1/5$-bar and taking $1/3$ of its shaded amount. In order to do this, the bar in Figure 5.45 has been split into 3 equal parts, A, B, and C. The darker part of the bar is $1/3$ of $1/5$. Each of the new small parts is $1/15$ of a whole bar, so $1/3 \times 1/5 = 1/15$.

Figure 5.45

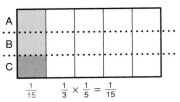

To illustrate $2/3 \times 4/5$, we will use a $4/5$-bar and take $2/3$ of each shaded region. In order to do this, the $4/5$-bar in Figure 5.46 has been split into 3 equal parts, A, B, and C. Each of the new small parts is $1/15$ of a whole bar. The 8 darker parts of the bar represent $8/15$, so $2/3 \times 4/5 = 8/15$.

Figure 5.46

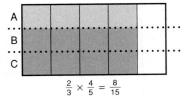

The rule for computing the product of two fractions is suggested in the preceding illustrations. In each of these examples the product can be found by *multiplying numerator by numerator and denominator by denominator.*

MULTIPLICATION OF FRACTIONS

For any fractions a/b and c/d,

$$\frac{a}{b} \times \frac{c}{d} = \frac{ac}{bd}$$

Notice that since the whole number k is equal to the fraction $k/1$, products involving whole numbers and fractions are special cases of the definition of multiplication of fractions.

EXAMPLE H

Compute each product.

1. $\dfrac{1}{2} \times \dfrac{8}{9}$ 2. $\dfrac{4}{7} \times \dfrac{^-2}{5}$ 3. $6 \times \dfrac{4}{5}$

Solution   1. $\dfrac{8}{18}$ or $\dfrac{4}{9}$ 2. $\dfrac{^-8}{35}$ 3. $\dfrac{24}{5}$ or $4\dfrac{4}{5}$

Products involving a mixed number can be computed by replacing the mixed number by an improper fraction.

EXAMPLE I

Compute each product.

1. $\dfrac{3}{4} \times 6\dfrac{1}{5}$ 2. $3\dfrac{1}{8} \times {}^-2\dfrac{1}{3}$

Solution   1. $\dfrac{3}{4} \times 6\dfrac{1}{5} = \dfrac{3}{4} \times \dfrac{31}{5} = \dfrac{93}{20} = 4\dfrac{13}{20}$

2. $3\dfrac{1}{8} \times {}^-2\dfrac{1}{3} = \dfrac{25}{8} \times \dfrac{^-7}{3} = \dfrac{^-175}{24} = {}^-7\dfrac{7}{24}$

DIVISION

Division of fractions can be viewed in much the same way as division of whole numbers. One of the meanings of division of whole numbers is represented by the measurement (subtractive) concept. For example, to explain $15 \div 3$, we often say, "How many times can we subtract 3 from 15?" Similarly, for $3/5 \div 1/10$ we can ask, "How many times can we subtract 1/10 from 3/5?" Figure 5.47 shows that the shaded amount of a 1/10-bar can be subtracted from the shaded amount of a 3/5-bar 6 times. Or, viewed in terms of multiplication, the shaded amount of the 3/5-bar is 6 times greater than the shaded amount of the 1/10-bar.

Figure 5.47

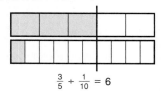

$$\tfrac{3}{5} \div \tfrac{1}{10} = 6$$

This interpretation of division of fractions continues to hold even when the quotient is not a whole number. Figure 5.48 shows that the shaded amount of the 1/3-bar can be subtracted from the shaded amount of the 5/6-bar 2 times, and there is a remainder. Just as in whole-number division, the remainder is then compared to the divisor using a fraction. In this example, the remainder is 1/2 as big as the divisor, so the quotient is $2\frac{1}{2}$.

Figure 5.48

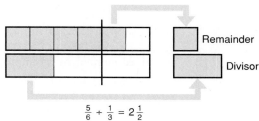

$$\tfrac{5}{6} \div \tfrac{1}{3} = 2\tfrac{1}{2}$$

One of the early methods of dividing one fraction by another was to replace both fractions by fractions having a common denominator. When this is done, the quotient can be obtained by disregarding the denominators and dividing the two numerators. For example,

$$\frac{3}{4} \div \frac{2}{5} = \frac{15}{20} \div \frac{8}{20} = 15 \div 8 = 1\frac{7}{8}$$

It may have been this approach of getting a common denominator that eventually led to the present *invert and multiply* method. In this method of division, which came into general use in the seventeenth century, we invert the divisor and then multiply the two fractions. This method is used below to compute 3/4 divided by 2/5.

$$\frac{3}{4} \div \frac{2}{5} = \frac{3}{4} \times \frac{5}{2} = \frac{15}{8} = 1\frac{7}{8}$$

The following equations show why the invert and multiply method works. Notice in the third expression that since $5/2 \div 5/2 = 1$, we are multiplying $(3/4)/(2/5)$ by 1 (the identity for multiplication). Also, in moving from the third to the fourth expression we use the fact that a number times its reciprocal ($2/5 \times 5/2$) is equal to 1 (the inverse property for multiplication).

$$\frac{3}{4} \div \frac{2}{5} = \frac{\frac{3}{4}}{\frac{2}{5}} = \frac{\frac{3}{4} \times \frac{5}{2}}{\frac{2}{5} \times \frac{5}{2}} = \frac{\frac{3}{4} \times \frac{5}{2}}{1} = \frac{3}{4} \times \frac{5}{2}$$

In a similar manner it can be shown that the invert and multiply method can be used for division of any two fractions.

DIVISION OF FRACTIONS

For any fractions a/b and c/d, with $c/d \neq 0$,

$$\frac{a}{b} \div \frac{c}{d} = \frac{a}{b} \times \frac{d}{c} = \frac{ad}{bc}$$

EXAMPLE **J**

Compute each quotient.

1. $\dfrac{1}{2} \div \dfrac{1}{3}$ 2. $\dfrac{7}{8} \div \dfrac{2}{5}$ 3. $\dfrac{2}{3} \div \dfrac{^-1}{4}$

Solution

1. $\dfrac{1}{2} \div \dfrac{1}{3} = \dfrac{1}{2} \times \dfrac{3}{1} = \dfrac{3}{2} = 1\dfrac{1}{2}$

2. $\dfrac{7}{8} \div \dfrac{2}{5} = \dfrac{7}{8} \times \dfrac{5}{2} = \dfrac{35}{16} = 2\dfrac{3}{16}$

3. $\dfrac{2}{3} \div \dfrac{^-1}{4} = \dfrac{2}{3} \times \dfrac{^-4}{1} = \dfrac{^-8}{3} = ^-2\dfrac{2}{3}$

One method of computing the quotient of two mixed numbers is to replace each mixed number by an improper fraction and use the definition of division of fractions.

EXAMPLE K

Compute each quotient.

1. $5\frac{1}{3} \div 1\frac{1}{8}$ 2. $8\frac{3}{4} \div 2\frac{1}{2}$

Solution

1. $5\frac{1}{3} \div 1\frac{1}{8} = \frac{16}{3} \div \frac{9}{8} = \frac{16}{3} \times \frac{8}{9} = \frac{128}{27} = 4\frac{20}{27}$

2. $8\frac{3}{4} \div 2\frac{1}{2} = \frac{35}{4} \div \frac{5}{2} = \frac{35}{4} \times \frac{2}{5} = \frac{70}{20} = \frac{7}{2} = 3\frac{1}{2}$

(Note: Some calculators are designed to enter and display fractions and perform the four basic operations.)

NUMBER PROPERTIES

The inverse property for addition and the closure, identity, commutative, associative, and distributive properties, which hold for addition and multiplication of integers, also hold for addition and multiplication of fractions. Furthermore, multiplication of fractions has an additional property: *inverses for multiplication*. The rules for adding and multiplying fractions will be used to illustrate each of these properties in the following examples.

ADDITION IS CLOSED   The sum of any two fractions is another unique fraction. This property results from the closure and uniqueness properties for addition and multiplication of integers. Notice how multiplication and addition of integers are needed to compute the following sum of fractions.

$$\frac{^-2}{3} + \frac{4}{5} = \frac{^-2 \times 5}{3 \times 5} + \frac{4 \times 3}{5 \times 3} = \frac{^-10}{15} + \frac{12}{15} = \frac{2}{15}$$

MULTIPLICATION IS CLOSED   The product of any two fractions is another unique fraction. This property is a direct result of the closure and uniqueness properties for multiplication of integers. The equations below show where multiplication of integers is needed.

$$\frac{^-2}{3} \times \frac{4}{5} = \frac{^-2 \times 4}{3 \times 5} = \frac{^-8}{15}$$

IDENTITY FOR ADDITION   The sum of any fraction and zero is the given fraction. This property follows from the fact that zero plus any integer is the given integer.

$$\frac{5}{6} + 0 = \frac{5}{6} + \frac{0}{6} = \frac{5 + 0}{6} = \frac{5}{6}$$

IDENTITY FOR MULTIPLICATION   The product of any fraction and 1 is the given fraction. This property is a result of the corresponding property for integers, which states that 1 times any integer is the given integer.

$$1 \times \frac{^-4}{5} = \frac{1 \times ^-4}{5} = \frac{^-4}{5}$$

ADDITION IS COMMUTATIVE   Two fractions that are being added can be interchanged (commuted) without changing the sum.

$$\frac{7}{8} + \frac{3}{5} = \frac{35}{40} + \frac{24}{40} = \frac{59}{40} = 1\frac{19}{40}$$

$$\frac{3}{5} + \frac{7}{8} = \frac{24}{40} + \frac{35}{40} = \frac{59}{40} = 1\frac{19}{40}$$

This property is illustrated on the number lines in Figure 5.49.

Figure 5.49

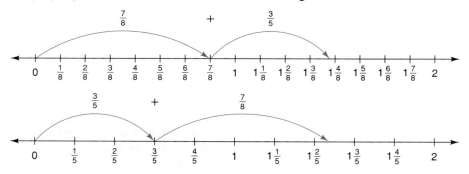

ADDITION IS ASSOCIATIVE   In a sum of three fractions, the middle number may be grouped (associated) with either of the other two numbers.

EXAMPLE **L**

Compute the sum on each side of the equation. (The sums inside the parentheses should be computed first.)

$$\left(\frac{1}{3} + \frac{1}{4}\right) + \frac{1}{6} = \frac{1}{3} + \left(\frac{1}{4} + \frac{1}{6}\right)$$

Solution   Left side: $\left(\dfrac{1}{3} + \dfrac{1}{4}\right) + \dfrac{1}{6} = \dfrac{7}{12} + \dfrac{1}{6} = \dfrac{9}{12}$

Right side: $\dfrac{1}{3} + \left(\dfrac{1}{4} + \dfrac{1}{6}\right) = \dfrac{1}{3} + \dfrac{5}{12} = \dfrac{9}{12}$

MULTIPLICATION IS COMMUTATIVE   Two fractions that are being multiplied can be interchanged (commuted) without changing the product:

$$\frac{1}{2} \times \frac{1}{3} = \frac{1}{6} \text{ and } \frac{1}{3} \times \frac{1}{2} = \frac{1}{6}$$

An illustration of this property is interesting because the processes of taking 1/2 of something and taking 1/3 of something are quite different. To take 1/2 of 1/3, we begin with a 1/3-bar, as shown in part (a) of Figure 5.50, and to take 1/3 of 1/2, we use a 1/2-bar, as shown in part (b) of Figure 5.50. In each figure the darker part of the bar is 1/6 of a whole bar.

Figure 5.50

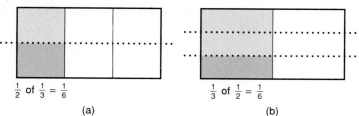

$\frac{1}{2}$ of $\frac{1}{3} = \frac{1}{6}$ $\frac{1}{3}$ of $\frac{1}{2} = \frac{1}{6}$

(a)   (b)

MULTIPLICATION IS ASSOCIATIVE   In a product of three fractions, the middle number may be grouped with either of the other two numbers.

EXAMPLE M

Compute the product on each side of the equation.

$$\left(\frac{1}{2} \times \frac{3}{4}\right) \times \frac{1}{5} = \frac{1}{2} \times \left(\frac{3}{4} \times \frac{1}{5}\right)$$

Solution   Left side: $\left(\dfrac{1}{2} \times \dfrac{3}{4}\right) \times \dfrac{1}{5} = \dfrac{3}{8} \times \dfrac{1}{5} = \dfrac{3}{40}$

Right side: $\dfrac{1}{2} \times \left(\dfrac{3}{4} \times \dfrac{1}{5}\right) = \dfrac{1}{2} \times \dfrac{3}{20} = \dfrac{3}{40}$

MULTIPLICATION IS DISTRIBUTIVE OVER ADDITION   When a sum (or difference) of two fractions is multiplied by a third number, we can add (or subtract) the two fractions and then multiply, or we can multiply both fractions by the third number and then add (or subtract).

EXAMPLE N

Perform the calculations on each side of the equation.

$$\frac{1}{2} \times \left(\frac{3}{4} + \frac{7}{10}\right) = \left(\frac{1}{2} \times \frac{3}{4}\right) + \left(\frac{1}{2} \times \frac{7}{10}\right)$$

Solution   Left side: $\dfrac{1}{2} \times \left(\dfrac{3}{4} + \dfrac{7}{10}\right) = \dfrac{1}{2} \times \left(\dfrac{15}{20} + \dfrac{14}{20}\right) = \dfrac{1}{2} \times \dfrac{29}{20} = \dfrac{29}{40}$

Right side: $\left(\dfrac{1}{2} \times \dfrac{3}{4}\right) + \left(\dfrac{1}{2} \times \dfrac{7}{10}\right) = \dfrac{3}{8} + \dfrac{7}{20} = \dfrac{15}{40} + \dfrac{14}{40} = \dfrac{29}{40}$

---

opposite, or inverse for addition

INVERSES FOR ADDITION   For every fraction there is another fraction, called its **opposite** or **inverse for addition,** such that the sum of the two fractions is zero. The fractions 3/4 and ⁻3/4 are inverses for addition.

$$\frac{3}{4} + \frac{^-3}{4} = \frac{3 + {}^-3}{4} = \frac{0}{4} = 0$$

reciprocal, or inverse for multiplication

INVERSES FOR MULTIPLICATION   For every fraction not equal to zero, there is a nonzero fraction, called its **reciprocal** or **inverse for multiplication,** such that the product of the two numbers is 1. The reciprocal of the fraction 3/8 is 8/3.

$$\frac{3}{8} \times \frac{8}{3} = \frac{3 \times 8}{8 \times 3} = \frac{24}{24} = 1$$

MENTAL CALCULATIONS

The mental calculating techniques we used for computing with whole numbers—*compatible numbers, substitutions,* and *equal differences*—are also appropriate for fractions. We will look at examples of these techniques and point out some of the number properties that make them possible.

COMPATIBLE NUMBERS   Compatible fractions are numbers that can be conveniently combined in a given computation.

EXAMPLE O

Perform each calculation mentally by finding compatible fractions.

1. $2\frac{1}{5} + \frac{2}{3} + 1\frac{4}{5}$

2. $5\frac{5}{6} - \frac{3}{4} + 2\frac{1}{6} + 4$

3. $\frac{1}{3} \times 14 \times 9 \times \frac{1}{2}$

Solution

1. $2\frac{1}{5} + \frac{2}{3} + 1\frac{4}{5} = 2\frac{1}{5} + 1\frac{4}{5} + \frac{2}{3} = 4 + \frac{2}{3} = 4\frac{2}{3}$

2. $5\frac{5}{6} - \frac{3}{4} + 2\frac{1}{6} + 4 = 5\frac{5}{6} + 2\frac{1}{6} + 4 - \frac{3}{4} = 8 + 4 - \frac{3}{4} = 11\frac{1}{4}$

3. $\frac{1}{3} \times 14 \times 9 \times \frac{1}{2} = \frac{1}{3} \times 9 \times 14 \times \frac{1}{2} = 3 \times 7 = 21$

Note: The rearrangements of numbers in these examples require the use of the commutative and associative properties of addition and multiplication of fractions.

Products involving fractions and whole numbers in which the denominator of the fraction divides the whole number can be calculated mentally by dividing the whole number by the denominator. To compute $2/3 \times 24$, we can divide 24 by 3 and multiply the result by 2, as shown in the following equations. We use the fact that $2/3 = 2 \times 1/3$ in the first equation and the associative property for multiplication in the second equation.

$$\frac{2}{3} \times 24 = \left(2 \times \frac{1}{3}\right) \times 24 = 2 \times \left(\frac{1}{3} \times 24\right) = 2 \times 8 = 16$$

canceling

The steps in the preceding equations can be shortened considerably by **canceling** (dividing the denominator of the fraction and the whole number by a common factor).

$$\frac{2}{3} \times 24 = \frac{2}{\cancel{3}} \times \overset{8}{\cancel{24}} = 16$$

EXAMPLE P

Calculate each of the following products mentally using compatible fractions.

1. $\frac{5}{8} \times 32$ 2. $^-54 \times \frac{5}{9}$ 3. $\frac{4}{3} \times 18$

Solution

1. $\frac{5}{8} \times 32 = 5 \times \left(\frac{1}{8} \times 32\right) = 5 \times 4 = 20 \left(\text{or } \frac{5}{\cancel{8}} \times \overset{4}{\cancel{32}} = 20\right)$

2. $^-54 \times \frac{5}{9} = \left(^-54 \times \frac{1}{9}\right) \times 5 = ^-6 \times 5 = ^-30 \left(\text{or } \overset{^-6}{\cancel{^-54}} \times \frac{5}{\cancel{9}} = ^-30\right)$

3. $\frac{4}{3} \times 18 = 4 \times \left(\frac{1}{3} \times 18\right) = 4 \times 6 = 24 \left(\text{or } \frac{4}{\cancel{3}} \times \overset{6}{\cancel{18}} = 24\right)$

SUBSTITUTIONS   Sometimes it is possible to substitute a number for another to obtain compatible fractions. For example,

$$4 \times 2\frac{6}{7} = 4 \times \left(3 - \frac{1}{7}\right) = 12 - \frac{4}{7} = 11\frac{3}{7}$$

EXAMPLE Q

Find a convenient substitution in order to perform each calculation mentally.

1. $2\frac{7}{8} + \frac{1}{4}$ 2. $4\frac{5}{6} - \frac{1}{2}$ 3. $7 \times 2\frac{9}{10}$

Solution

1. $2\frac{7}{8} + \frac{1}{4} = 2\frac{7}{8} + \frac{1}{8} + \frac{1}{8} = 3 + \frac{1}{8} = 3\frac{1}{8}$

2. $4\frac{5}{6} - \frac{1}{2} = 4\frac{2}{6} + \frac{3}{6} - \frac{1}{2} = 4\frac{2}{6}$

3. $7 \times 2\frac{9}{10} = 7 \times \left(3 - \frac{1}{10}\right) = 21 - \frac{7}{10} = 20\frac{3}{10}$

Notice the use of the distributive property to multiply 7 times (3 − 1/10) in problem (3).

EQUAL DIFFERENCES AND ADD UP   Changing two numbers by adding the same amount to both results in the same difference between the two numbers. This technique is very useful in subtracting fractions because in some cases it avoids the need for regrouping (borrowing). For example, to mentally compute $5 - 2\frac{4}{5}$, we can increase both numbers by 1/5 to obtain the difference easily.

$$5 - 2\frac{4}{5} = 5\frac{1}{5} - 3 = 2\frac{1}{5}$$

The reason we can add 1/5 to both numbers is because we are really adding zero (using the identity property for addition), as shown in the first of the next few equations.

$$5 - 2\frac{4}{5} = (5 + 0) - 2\frac{4}{5} = 5 + \left(\frac{1}{5} - \frac{1}{5}\right) - 2\frac{4}{5}$$

$$= \left(5 + \frac{1}{5}\right) - \left(2\frac{4}{5} + \frac{1}{5}\right) = 5\frac{1}{5} - 3 = 2\frac{1}{5}$$

Or the difference can be obtained by adding up from the smaller number to the larger:

$$2\frac{4}{5} + \frac{1}{5} = 3 \text{ and } 3 + 2 = 5, \text{ so } 5 - 2\frac{4}{5} = 2\frac{1}{5}$$

EXAMPLE R

Calculate each difference mentally using the equal differences technique.

1. $3\frac{2}{8} - 1\frac{7}{8}$ 2. $5\frac{3}{10} - 3\frac{9}{10}$ 3. $6\frac{1}{5} - 2\frac{3}{5}$

Solution

1. $3\frac{2}{8} - 1\frac{7}{8} = 3\frac{3}{8} - 2 = 1\frac{3}{8} \left(\text{Increase both by } \frac{1}{8}\right)$

2. $5\dfrac{3}{10} - 3\dfrac{9}{10} = 5\dfrac{4}{10} - 4 = 1\dfrac{4}{10}$ $\left(\text{Increase both by } \dfrac{1}{10}\right)$

3. $6\dfrac{1}{5} - 2\dfrac{3}{5} = 6\dfrac{3}{5} - 3 = 3\dfrac{3}{5}$ $\left(\text{Increase both by } \dfrac{2}{5}\right)$

Note: The add-up method is also convenient for computing each of these differences.

ESTIMATION

Skill at estimating with fractions is especially important, since whole-number approximations are often all that is needed. One of the most common estimating techniques is *rounding*.

ROUNDING   The sum or difference of mixed numbers and fractions can be estimated by rounding each number to the nearest whole number.

$$6\dfrac{1}{3} + 2\dfrac{3}{4} + 1\dfrac{1}{5} \approx 6 + 3 + 1 = 10$$

$$8\dfrac{1}{3} - 2\dfrac{3}{5} \approx 8 - 3 = 5$$

Computing a product by rounding two mixed numbers to the nearest whole number may produce a good estimation, as in the following example.

$$6\dfrac{3}{4} \times 8\dfrac{1}{3} \approx 7 \times 8 = 56 \left(\text{The actual product is } 56\dfrac{1}{4}\right)$$

Or it may give a rough estimation, as in the next example.

$$6\dfrac{1}{2} \times 8\dfrac{1}{2} \approx 7 \times 9 = 63 \left(\text{The actual product is } 55\dfrac{1}{4}\right)$$

A more reliable estimation for $6\frac{1}{2} \times 8\frac{1}{2}$ can be obtained by multiplying the two whole numbers, 6×8, and then adding the products of each fraction times the opposite whole number: $1/2 \times 8$ and $1/2 \times 6$.

$$6\dfrac{1}{2} \times 8\dfrac{1}{2} \approx (6 \times 8) + \left(\dfrac{1}{2} \times 8\right) + \left(6 \times \dfrac{1}{2}\right)$$
$$= 48 + 4 + 3$$
$$= 55$$

Figure 5.51 shows why this method produces a good approximation. The actual product is represented by the region whose dimensions are $6\frac{1}{2}$ by $8\frac{1}{2}$. The approximation is represented by the 6 by 8 colored region and the 1/2 by 6 and 1/2 by 8 colored strips. The 1/2 by 1/2 gray region in the lower right corner represents the difference between the actual product and the approximation, which we obtained in the preceding example. This shows that the difference between the product and the approximation is small.

The distributive property shows how to obtain the four partial products that correspond to the four regions in Figure 5.51. It is used once in going from step 1 to step 2 and twice in going from step 2 to step 3.

Figure 5.51

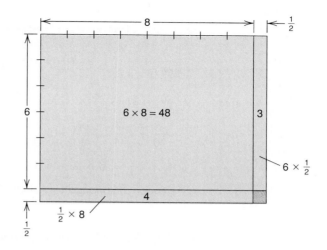

Step 1 $\qquad 6\frac{1}{2} \times 8\frac{1}{2} = \left(6 + \frac{1}{2}\right) \times \left(8 + \frac{1}{2}\right)$

Step 2 $\qquad = \left(6 + \frac{1}{2}\right)8 + \left(6 + \frac{1}{2}\right)\frac{1}{2}$

Step 3 $\qquad = (6 \times 8) + \left(\frac{1}{2} \times 8\right) + \left(6 \times \frac{1}{2}\right) + \left(\frac{1}{2} \times \frac{1}{2}\right)$

Step 4 $\qquad = 48 + 4 + 3 + \frac{1}{4}$

Step 5 $\qquad = 55\frac{1}{4}$

EXAMPLE S

Approximate $10\frac{1}{2} \times 6\frac{1}{5}$ by multiplying the two whole numbers and then adding the products of each fraction times the opposite whole number.

Solution

$$10\frac{1}{2} \times 6\frac{1}{5} \approx (10 \times 6) + \left(\frac{1}{2} \times 6\right) + \left(10 \times \frac{1}{5}\right) = 60 + 3 + 2 = 65$$

COMPATIBLE NUMBERS Replacing a fraction by a reasonably close and compatible fraction can be very useful in obtaining estimations. In a product involving a whole number and a fraction, we can often obtain an approximation by replacing the whole number so that the denominator of the fraction divides the whole number.

$$\frac{2}{7} \times 20 \approx \frac{2}{7} \times 21 = \frac{2}{\cancel{7}} \times \overset{3}{\cancel{21}} = 6$$

Or in a sum or difference, we can replace a fraction by a compatible fraction.

$$3\frac{5}{8} + 9\frac{1}{7} \approx 3\frac{5}{8} + 9\frac{1}{8} = 12\frac{6}{8}, \text{ or } 12\frac{3}{4}$$

EXAMPLE T

Use compatible numbers to estimate each computation mentally.

$$1. \frac{3}{4} \times 31 \qquad 2. 4\frac{7}{10} + 2\frac{2}{11} \qquad 3. 6 \times 2\frac{1}{7}$$

Solution

$$1. \frac{3}{4} \times 31 \approx \frac{3}{4} \times 32 = \frac{3}{\cancel{4}} \times \overset{8}{\cancel{32}} = 24$$

$$2. 4\frac{7}{10} + 2\frac{2}{11} \approx 4\frac{7}{10} + 2\frac{2}{10} = 6\frac{9}{10}$$

3. $6 \times 2\frac{1}{7} \approx 6 \times 2\frac{1}{6} = 12 + 1 = 13$ (Notice in this solution that the distributive property is needed to multiply 6 times $2\frac{1}{6}$, since $2\frac{1}{6} = 2 + \frac{1}{6}$.)

PROBLEM-SOLVING APPLICATION

When two people or machines can accomplish a task at different rates, we sometimes need to determine how much time will be required for them to do the job together. The solutions to such problems often require fractions, and the information can be illustrated by diagrams.

■ PROBLEM

Mary and Bill have the responsibility of mowing their school's soccer field. Mary can mow it in 4 hours with her lawn mower, and Bill can mow it in 6 hours with his lawn mower. How long will it take them if they work together?

Question 1

Understanding the Problem   We know it will require less than 4 hours because Mary can do the job alone in 4 hours. It will require more than 1 hour because Mary can mow 1/4 of the field in 1 hour and Bill can mow 1/6 of the field in 1 hour. What fraction of the field can they mow in 1 hour working together?

Question 2

Devising a Plan   One approach is to *make a drawing*. Since Mary and Bill can mow 1/4 + 1/6 = 5/12 of the field in 1 hour, let's consider a figure to illustrate this part of the total field. The following figure has 12 equal parts, and the 5 shaded parts represent the amount they can mow in 1 hour. According to this diagram, approximately how long (to the nearest hour) will it take them, working together, to mow the field?

1st hour

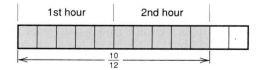

$\frac{5}{12}$

Question 3

Carrying Out the Plan   The next figure shows that in 2 hours they can mow 10/12 of the field and that 2 of the 12 parts remain to be mowed. How long will it take them, working together, to mow the entire field?

| 1st hour | 2nd hour | |

$\frac{10}{12}$

Question 4

Looking Back   Mary and Bill can mow the entire field in $2\frac{2}{5}$ hours (2 hours and 24 minutes). If Bill gets his mower sharpened and can then mow the field in 5 hours, can Mary and Bill working together mow the field in less than 2 hours?

Answers to Questions 1–4

1. $\frac{5}{12}$ 2. 2 hours   3. $2\frac{2}{5}$ hours, or 2 hours and 24 minutes

4. No. Since Mary can mow 1/4 of the field in 1 hour and Bill can mow 1/5 in 1 hour, together they can mow 1/4 + 1/5 = 9/20 in 1 hour. Thus, in 2 hours they can only mow 9/20 + 9/20 = 18/20 of the field.

RELATED ACTIVITIES IN
Mathematics for Elementary Teachers: An Activity Approach, 3e

Activity Set 5.3   **Computing with Fraction Bars:** Fraction Bars are used to illustrate the basic operations of addition, subtraction, multiplication, and division in a visual and intuitive manner.

Just for Fun   **Fraction Games for Operations:** Games with fraction bars for addition, subtraction, and division of fractions

EXERCISES AND PROBLEMS 5.3

$\frac{1}{32}$

$\frac{1}{12}$

$\frac{1}{15}$

1. The fraction by each of the animals shown above tells what fraction of the life-size object the picture is.
  a. The length of the dog in the picture is 1 inch. How long is the corresponding life-size dog?
  b. The height of the trumpeter is $1\frac{1}{2}$ inches. What is the height of the life-size trumpeter?
  c. The claw span of the turkey buzzard is 1/3 of an inch. What is the claw span of the life-size turkey buzzard?

2. Sketch fraction bars to illustrate each computation.

  a. $\frac{3}{10} + \frac{2}{5} = \frac{7}{10}$ **b.** $\frac{5}{6} - \frac{1}{3} = \frac{3}{6}$

  c. $\frac{2}{3} \div \frac{1}{6} = 4$ **d.** $\frac{1}{4} \times 3 = \frac{3}{4}$

  e. $\frac{1}{3} \times \frac{1}{4} = \frac{1}{12}$ **f.** $\frac{1}{3} \times \frac{1}{6} = \frac{1}{18}$

3. a. The figure below can be used to show that $1/3 \times 15 = 5$. Explain how.

Sketch sets of dots to illustrate and determine the following products.

  b. $\frac{3}{8} \times 24$ **c.** $\frac{2}{5} \times 30$

4. a. Place the edge of a piece of paper on the eighths line below and mark off the length $1\frac{1}{8}$. Then place the beginning of this marked-off length at the $1\frac{1}{5}$ point on the fifths line and approximate the sum $1\frac{1}{5} + 1\frac{1}{8}$. What number on the fifths line is this sum closest to?

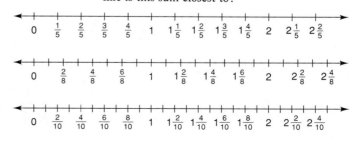

b. Use the number lines to approximate the following sums. On the given line, write the number that the sum is closest to.

$$\frac{4}{5} + 1\frac{3}{8} \text{ (Fifths line)}$$

$$\frac{5}{8} + \frac{7}{10} \text{ (Eighths line)}$$

$$\frac{3}{10} + 1\frac{4}{5} \text{ (Tenths line)}$$

c. Compute these sums and compare them to your approximations.

$$\begin{array}{ccc} \frac{4}{5} & \frac{5}{8} & \frac{3}{10} \\ +1\frac{3}{8} & +\frac{7}{10} & +1\frac{4}{5} \\ \hline \end{array}$$

5. a. Place the edge of a piece of paper on the fifths line in exercise 4 and mark off the length 3/5. Then place the end of this marked-off length at the point $1\frac{7}{8}$ on the eighths line and approximate the difference $1\frac{7}{8} - 3/5$. This number is closest to what number on the eighths line?

b. Use the number lines to approximate each difference. On the given line, write the number that is closest to the difference.

$$1\frac{4}{5} - \frac{5}{8} \text{ (Fifths line)}$$

$$1\frac{1}{8} - \frac{7}{10} \text{ (Eighths line)}$$

$$\frac{9}{10} - \frac{3}{5} \text{ (Tenths line)}$$

c. Compute these differences and compare them to your approximations.

$$\begin{array}{ccc} 1\frac{4}{5} & 1\frac{1}{8} & \frac{9}{10} \\ -\frac{5}{8} & -\frac{7}{10} & -\frac{3}{5} \\ \hline \end{array}$$

6. Perform the operations below. Replace all improper fractions in your answers with whole numbers or mixed numbers and write all fractions in lowest terms.

a. $\frac{2}{3} + \frac{3}{4}$ **b.** $\frac{1}{6} + \frac{3}{8}$ **c.** $\frac{2}{3} \times 6$

d. $\frac{^-3}{4} \times \frac{2}{5}$ **e.** $2\frac{1}{4} + 1\frac{1}{3}$ **f.** $^-1\frac{5}{6} + 3\frac{1}{2}$

g. $2\frac{1}{4} \times 3\frac{1}{2}$ **h.** $14\frac{1}{2} \div 2\frac{1}{4}$ **i.** $\frac{7}{8} - \frac{1}{3}$

j. $\frac{3}{4} - \frac{2}{5}$ **k.** $\frac{3}{4} \div \frac{1}{10}$ **l.** $\frac{2}{3} \div \frac{1}{5}$

m. $3\frac{1}{4} - 1\frac{1}{8}$ **n.** $5\frac{1}{3} - 2\frac{1}{2}$ **o.** $^-3 \div \frac{1}{5}$

p. $4 \times 5\frac{1}{8}$

7. Write the negative (inverse for addition) and the reciprocal (inverse for multiplication) of each number in the table below.

Number	$\frac{7}{8}$	$^-4$	$\frac{^-1}{2}$	10
Negative				
Reciprocal				

8. *Error analysis* In computing with fractions several types of errors frequently occur. In the following example, $3\frac{2}{5}$ should have been replaced by $2\frac{7}{5}$. Instead, the 1 that was borrowed from the 3 was placed in the numerator to form $2\frac{12}{5}$.

$$\begin{array}{ccc} 3\frac{2}{5} & = & 2\frac{12}{5} \\ -\frac{4}{5} & = & -\frac{4}{5} \\ \hline & & 2\frac{8}{5} = 3\frac{3}{5} \end{array}$$

Find plausible reasons for the errors in the computations below.

a. $\frac{1}{4} + \frac{5}{6} = \frac{6}{10}$ **b.** $\frac{7}{8} - \frac{2}{3} = \frac{5}{5}$

c. $\frac{1}{2} \times \frac{3}{8} = \frac{6}{8}$ **d.** $\frac{3}{4} \div \frac{1}{5} = \frac{4}{15}$

e. $\frac{1}{3} + \frac{2}{5} = \frac{6}{8} + \frac{5}{8} = \frac{11}{8}$

9. State the number property that is being used in each of these equalities.

a. $\frac{3}{7} + \left(\frac{2}{9} + \frac{1}{3}\right) = \frac{3}{7} + \left(\frac{1}{3} + \frac{2}{9}\right)$

b. $\frac{3}{7} + \left(\frac{2}{9} \times \frac{9}{2}\right) = \frac{3}{7} + 1$

c. $\frac{2}{9} + \left(\frac{3}{7} + \frac{1}{3}\right) = \left(\frac{2}{9} + \frac{3}{7}\right) + \frac{1}{3}$

d. $\frac{5}{6} \times \left(\frac{3}{4} + \frac{1}{2}\right) = \left(\frac{3}{4} + \frac{1}{2}\right) \times \frac{5}{6}$

e. $\frac{3}{4} \times \frac{5}{6} + \frac{1}{2} \times \frac{5}{6} = \left(\frac{3}{4} + \frac{1}{2}\right) \times \frac{5}{6}$

f. $\frac{7}{8} + \left(\frac{^-2}{3} + \frac{2}{3}\right) = \frac{7}{8} + 0$

10. Determine whether the operation is closed for the given set.
a. Addition for the set of positive fractions
b. Multiplication for the set of negative fractions
c. Division for the set of positive fractions

11. The following problems contain compatible fractions. Use mental calculations and explain your method.

a. $^-2\frac{2}{3} + 5\frac{1}{2} + 6\frac{1}{3} + 1\frac{1}{2}$ **b.** $5\frac{5}{8} + 2\frac{1}{2} - 1\frac{1}{8}$

c. $\frac{^-1}{3} \times \frac{2}{5} \times 12 \times 20$ **d.** $\frac{7}{4} \times 24 + 8$

12. Find a convenient substitution and perform each calculation mentally. Show your substitution.

   a. $3 \times 3\frac{4}{5}$ **b.** $6\frac{7}{10} - 1\frac{1}{2}$ **c.** $12\frac{5}{6} + \frac{1}{3}$

13. Compute each difference by using either the equal differences or add-up technique. Show your method.

   a. $8 - 3\frac{6}{7}$ **b.** $15\frac{3}{10} - 10\frac{9}{10}$ **c.** $7\frac{1}{8} - 3\frac{3}{4}$

14. Round each mixed number to the nearest whole number and compute the sum of numbers in each row.

$7\frac{2}{3}$	$2\frac{3}{4}$	$4\frac{1}{8}$	$5\frac{9}{10}$	21
Think 8	Think 3	Think 4	Think 6	Approximate sum

a.	$1\frac{2}{3}$	$3\frac{1}{4}$	$1\frac{1}{2}$	$2\frac{1}{10}$
b.	$3\frac{4}{5}$	$2\frac{1}{6}$	$3\frac{2}{5}$	$4\frac{1}{2}$
c.	$10\frac{1}{3}$	$5\frac{1}{2}$	$2\frac{7}{8}$	$5\frac{1}{6}$
d.	$6\frac{1}{2}$	$2\frac{3}{4}$	$1\frac{1}{4}$	$2\frac{5}{6}$

15. Approximate the product of each pair of mixed numbers by multiplying the whole numbers and adding the products of the fractions times the opposite whole numbers. Show each step in obtaining the answer.

   a. $4\frac{1}{3} \times 6\frac{1}{2}$ **b.** $5\frac{1}{4} \times 8\frac{2}{5}$

   c. $3\frac{1}{4} \times 4\frac{2}{3}$ **d.** $10\frac{1}{3} \times 6\frac{1}{2}$

16. Estimate each computation mentally using compatible numbers. Show your compatible number replacement.

   a. $\frac{6}{7} \times 34$ **b.** $9\frac{4}{5} + 5\frac{1}{6}$

   c. $8 \times 4\frac{1}{7}$ **d.** $\frac{3}{4} \times 81$

17. Draw a diagram to illustrate the given information and the solution.

   a. What is the fractional amount of the earth's surface covered by oceans or glaciers, if 2/3 is covered by water and 1/10 by glaciers? (Note: Glaciers occur only over land.)

   b. An experiment calls for $8\frac{1}{2}$ ounces of sulfate, but the classroom chemistry kit has only $3\frac{1}{5}$ ounces. How much more sulfate is needed?

   c. In 1897, 48 million pounds of blue shad were caught in the ocean between Maine and Florida. The yearly catch is now 1/6 of the 1897 catch. How many pounds of blue shad are now caught yearly?

18. Draw a diagram to illustrate the given information and the solution.

   a. A school's enrollment decreased by 1/4 because of a reorganization of districts. The new enrollment is 270. What was the school's enrollment before the change?

   b. On Wednesday it rained $1\frac{1}{2}$ inches, and on Thursday it rained only 1/3 as much as it had on Wednesday. What fraction of an inch did it rain on Thursday?

   c. Sound travels 1/5 of a mile in 1 second. How many seconds will it take a sound wave to travel 2 miles?

19. Which of the following sequences of calculator steps will not produce the correct answer? Explain why.

   a. $80 \times 3/5$
   1. 80
   2. $\boxed{\times}$
   3. 3 $\boxed{\div}$ 5
   4. $\boxed{=}$

   b. $80 \div 3/5$
   1. 80
   2. $\boxed{\div}$
   3. 3 $\boxed{\div}$ 5
   4. $\boxed{=}$

20. A taxpayer computes her federal income tax using the following method. Some of the amounts are shown below. Compute the missing amounts.

   (1) 1/3 of base income of $22,000   _____
   (2) 1/5 of averageable income of $12,000   _____
   (3) Line 1 plus line 2   _____
   (4) Tax on line 3 $2,318
   (5) Tax on line 1 $1,630
   (6) Line 4 minus line 5   _____
   (7) Line 6 multiplied by 4   _____
   (8) Line 4 plus line 7 (total tax)   _____

"You'll be happy to know that nobody in the government is out to get you, nobody's reported you for the finder's fee, nor have we received any anonymous tips. You're here only because we think you've been cheating on your return."

21. The following table shows high and low prices for the stocks of 6 companies during one day.

	High price	Low price
Canadian Homestead	$8\frac{1}{4}$	$7\frac{15}{16}$
Drew National	$11\frac{1}{8}$	$9\frac{7}{8}$
General Plywood	$3\frac{3}{4}$	
MEM Company	$26\frac{1}{4}$	$25\frac{5}{8}$
Old Town	$7\frac{3}{4}$	$6\frac{3}{8}$
Sea Container		$16\frac{1}{2}$

   a. General Plywood's low price was 1/8 of a dollar less than its high price for the day. What was its low price?
   b. The day's high price for Sea Container was 3/16 of a dollar above its low price. What was the high price?
   c. What is the difference between the high price and low price of each of these stocks: Drew National, MEM Company, and Old Town?
   d. How much money would a person have saved if he or she had purchased 1000 shares of MEM Company stock at the low price for the day rather than the high price?

Featured Strategies: Guessing and Checking and Drawing Venn Diagrams

22. Mr. Hash bought some plates at a yard sale. After arriving home he found that 2/3 of the plates were chipped, 1/2 were cracked, and 1/4 were chipped and cracked. Only 2 plates were without chips or cracks. How many plates did he buy in all?
   a. **Understanding the Problem** Let's *guess* a number to become more familiar with the problem. If Mr. Hash bought 48 plates, how many were cracked and how many were chipped?
   b. **Devising a Plan** We could continue guessing and checking. Another approach is to *draw a Venn diagram*. The following figure uses circles to represent the chipped plates and the cracked plates. Two plates were neither chipped nor cracked. Since 2/3 were chipped and 1/4 were chipped and cracked, 2/3 − 1/4 = 5/12 were chipped but not cracked. What fraction of the plates were cracked but not chipped?

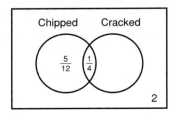

   c. **Carrying Out the Plan** After determining the fraction of the cracked plates that were not chipped, we can add the three fractions to find the fraction of the plates that were chipped and/or cracked. How can this information lead to the solution? How many plates did Mr. Hash buy?
   d. **Looking Back** Suppose that instead of 2 plates there were 3 plates that were neither chipped nor cracked. In this case what would be the total number of plates purchased?

23. Musical notes produced from two strings of equal diameter and tension will vary according to the lengths of the strings. Different fractions of the length of the unit string (the lowest string in the illustration) can be used to produce the notes C, D, E, F, G, A, B, and C (do, re, mi, fa, so, la, ti, do). In particular, if a string is half as long as another, its tone or note will be an octave higher than the longer string.*

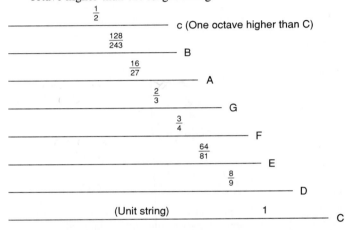

   a. With the exception of two strings, each string from the unit string to the top string is 8/9 of the length of the previous string. For example, the G string is 8/9 of the length of the F string, since 8/9 × 3/4 = 2/3. Which other strings are 8/9 of the length of the preceding strings?
   b. The white piano keys pictured below are the notes of the scale from c to C. All but two of these keys are separated by black keys. How is this observation related to the answer to part a?

24. One painter can paint a room in 2 hours; another painter requires 4 hours to paint the same size room. How long will it take for them to paint the room together?

25. Two-thirds of Mrs. Hoffman's fifth grade students are boys. To make the numbers of boys and girls equal, 4 boys go to the other fifth grade and 4 girls come from that class into Mrs. Hoffman's class. Now one-half of her students are boys. How many students are in Mrs. Hoffman's class?

*See C. F. Linn, *The Golden Mean* (New York: Doubleday, 1974), 9–13, for an elementary explanation of the origin of these fractions.

LABORATORY INVESTIGATION

This tower of bars represents fractions with denominators 2 through 12. Each geometric pattern corresponds to a pattern of fractions. The edge of a piece of paper can be used to line up equalities and inequalities.*

Questions for Investigation

1. Investigate the tower for patterns—there are many. For each geometric pattern, write the corresponding number pattern.

2. One student noticed that the difference between the 1/2-bar and the 1/3-bar is half of 1/3 (see dark line). That is, $1/2 - 1/3 = 1/2 \times 1/3$. Does $1/3 - 1/4 = 1/3 \times 1/4$? Does $1/4 - 1/5 = 1/4 \times 1/5$?

3. If the line at the end of the 1/2-bar (top of tower) is continued down, it divides one of the thirds in half. This shows that $1/2 = 1/3 + 1/2 \times 1/3$. Do the bars show that $2/4 = 2/5 + 1/2 \times 1/5$ or that $3/6 = 3/7 + 1/2 \times 1/7$?

$\frac{1}{2}$		
$\frac{1}{3}$		
$\frac{1}{4}$		
$\frac{1}{5}$		
$\frac{1}{6}$		
$\frac{1}{7}$		
$\frac{1}{8}$		
$\frac{1}{9}$		
$\frac{1}{10}$		
$\frac{1}{11}$		
$\frac{1}{12}$		

PUZZLER

In his will Farmer Smith bequeathed his 17 horses to his 3 sons in the following manner: 1/2 of his horses to the oldest son, Al; 1/3 of his horses to the middle son, Garry; and 1/9 of his horses to the youngest son, Greg. Being fairly capable with fractions, the boys computed their shares to be $8\frac{1}{2}$ horses, $5\frac{2}{3}$ horses, and $1\frac{8}{9}$ horses. However, each boy was disappointed at the prospect of getting parts of a horse, and they fell to quarreling about their predicament. At that point Farmer Smith rode up and, after being informed of their dilemma, proposed the following solution. First he donated his horse, to make a total of 18 horses. Then he gave 1/2 of the horses to Al, 1/3 of the 18 to Garry, and 1/9 of the 18 to Greg. How many horses did each boy receive? What was the total number of these horses? Seeing their satisfaction with his solution, Farmer Smith jumped on his horse and rode away. Why was his solution possible?

CHAPTER REVIEW

1. **Integers**
   a. The negative whole numbers togather with the whole numbers are called **integers.**
   b. For each integer, there is another integer, called its **opposite,** such that their sum is zero.
   c. For any two integers m and n, m is **less than** n, written $m < n$, if there is a positive integer k such that $m + k = n$.
   d. The integers less than zero are called **negative integers** ($^-1, ^-2, ^-3, \ldots$). Often they are denoted by a raised minus sign to avoid confusion with the operation of subtraction.
   e. The integers greater than zero are called **positive integers.** They are sometimes denoted by a raised plus sign to emphasize that they are positive.

2. **Operations on Integers**
   a. **Addition** Positive plus positive equals positive. Negative plus negative equals negative. Negative plus positive may be positive ($^-5 + 8 = 3$), negative ($^-5 + 2 = ^-3$), or zero ($^-5 + 5 = 0$).
   b. **Subtraction** For any two integers n and s, $n - s$ is the sum of n plus the opposite of s.

   c. **Multiplication** Positive times positive equals positive. Positive times negative equals negative. Negative times positive equals negative. Negative times negative equals positive.
   d. **Division** For any integers n and s, with $s \neq 0$, $n \div s = k$ if and only if $n = s \times k$ for some integer k.

3. **Fractions**
   a. A **fraction** is a number in the form a/b, where a and b are any numbers except $b \neq 0$. In this chapter a and b are integers.
   b. In the fraction a/b, a is called the **numerator** and b is called the **denominator.**
   c. There are three concepts of fractions: the **part-to-whole concept,** the **division concept,** and the **ratio concept.**
   d. For any fraction a/b and any number $k \neq 0$, a/b is equal to ka/kb.
   e. To **simplify a fraction** a/b, divide a and b by GCF(a, b).
   f. If GCF(a, b) = 1, then a/b is said to be in **lowest terms** or **simplified.**
   g. The **smallest common denominator** of a/b and c/d is LCM(b, d).

*The computer program GEOMETRIC SEQUENCE on the *Computer Problem-Solving Disc* prints up to 200 terms for this type of sequence and computes their sum. What can be said about the sum of the first 200 terms in the geometric sequence 1/2, 1/4, 1/8, 1/16, . . . ?

h. Between any two fractions there is always another fraction. This property is referred to by saying the fractions are **dense.**

i. If the numerator of a fraction is greater than or equal to the denominator, the fraction is called an **improper fraction.**

j. A number that is written as a whole number and a fraction is called a **mixed number.**

4. Fraction Operations

a. Addition For fractions a/b and c/d,

$$\frac{a}{b} + \frac{c}{d} = \frac{ad + bc}{bd}$$

b. Subtraction For fractions a/b and c/d,

$$\frac{a}{b} - \frac{c}{d} = \frac{ad - bc}{bd}$$

c. Multiplication For fractions a/b and c/d,

$$\frac{a}{b} \times \frac{c}{d} = \frac{ac}{bd}$$

d. Division For fractions a/b and c/d, with $c/d \neq 0$,

$$\frac{a}{b} \div \frac{c}{d} = \frac{a}{b} \times \frac{d}{c} = \frac{ad}{bc}$$

5. Models

a. Black and red chips are used to illustrate integers, with black chips representing positive integers (credits) and red chips representing negative integers (debts).

b. Number lines illustrate integers, with negative integers below zero and positive integers above zero.

c. Fraction Bars and **sets of dots** illustrate the part-to-whole concept of fractions.

d. Cuisenaire rods illustrate the ratio concept of fractions.

e. The part-to-whole concept of fractions can be illustrated with **number lines** by dividing unit intervals into equal numbers of parts.

6. Number Properties

Properties a–j below are true for addition and multiplication of integers and fractions. Property k holds for multiplication of fractions.

a. Addition is closed.

b. Multiplication is closed.

c. Identity for addition.

d. Identity for multiplication.

e. Addition is commutative.

f. Multiplication is commutative.

g. Addition is associative.

h. Multiplication is associative.

i. Multiplication distributes over addition and subtraction.

j. Every number has a unique **inverse for addition** such that the sum of the two numbers is zero.

k. Every fraction not equal to zero has a unique **inverse for multiplication** such that the product of the two fractions is 1.

7. Mental Calculations

a. Compatible numbers is the technique of using pairs of numbers that are especially convenient for mental calculation.

b. Substitutions is the technique of breaking a number into a convenient sum, difference, product, or quotient.

c. Equal differences is the technique of increasing or decreasing both numbers in a difference by the same amount.

d. Add up is the technique of finding a difference by adding up from the smaller number to the larger.

8. Estimation

a. Rounding is the technique of replacing one or more numbers in a sum, difference, product, or quotient by an approximate number to obtain an estimation. Often fractions are rounded to the nearest whole number.

b. Compatible numbers is the technique of computing estimations by replacing one or more numbers with convenient approximate numbers.

CHAPTER TEST

1. Sketch sets of black and red chips to illustrate each operation and determine each answer.

a. $8 + {}^-5$ **b.** ${}^-7 - {}^-3$ **c.** $3 \times {}^-4$

d. ${}^-20 \div {}^-4$ **e.** $6 - 2$ **f.** ${}^-15 \div 3$

2. Sketch a number line to illustrate each sum.

a. ${}^-8 + 3$ **b.** ${}^-8 + {}^-6$

3. Compute each product or quotient.

a. ${}^-7 \times {}^-6$ **b.** $30 \div {}^-5$

c. $8 \times {}^-10$ **d.** ${}^-40 \div {}^-8$

4. Use equal products or equal quotients to calculate each answer mentally. Explain your method.

a. ${}^-16 \times 25$ **b.** $800 \div {}^-16$

5. Use compatible numbers to obtain an estimation. Show your replacement.

a. ${}^-271 \div 30$ **b.** $\frac{1}{8} \times 55$

c. $4 \times 6\frac{1}{5}$ **d.** $11 \times {}^-34$

6. Use each figure to illustrate the operation or equality. Determine the answer for each operation.

a. $6 \div 4$ **b.** $\frac{1}{3} \times 15$

c. $\dfrac{2}{3} \times \dfrac{1}{5}$

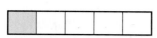

d. $\dfrac{3}{4} = \dfrac{6}{8}$

7. Complete each equation so that the pairs of fractions have the smallest common denominator.

a. $\dfrac{3}{14} =$

$\dfrac{5}{16} =$

b. $\dfrac{1}{24} =$

$\dfrac{^-7}{8} =$

8. Determine an inequality for each pair of fractions.

a. $\dfrac{6}{11}, \dfrac{5}{9}$ **b.** $\dfrac{3}{5}, \dfrac{6}{11}$ **c.** $\dfrac{^-4}{9}, \dfrac{^-3}{7}$

9. Mentally determine an inequality for each pair of fractions and explain your reasoning.

a. $\dfrac{1}{8} > \dfrac{1}{10}$ **b.** $\dfrac{4}{7} > \dfrac{5}{12}$ 48 > 35

c. $\dfrac{1}{2} < \dfrac{7}{12}$ 12 < 14   **d.** $\dfrac{5}{6} < \dfrac{7}{8}$

10. Compute these sums and differences.

a. $\begin{array}{r} 2\frac{1}{6} \\ +4\frac{1}{3} \\ \hline \end{array}$ **b.** $\begin{array}{r} 5\frac{2}{3} \\ -1\frac{1}{5} \\ \hline \end{array}$

c. $\begin{array}{r} 6\frac{5}{8} \\ +1\frac{2}{3} \\ \hline \end{array}$ **d.** $\begin{array}{r} 10\frac{1}{5} \\ -4\frac{5}{6} \\ \hline \end{array}$

11. Compute these products and quotients.

a. $2\dfrac{1}{4} \times 6\dfrac{1}{3}$ **b.** $8\dfrac{4}{5} \div 2\dfrac{1}{8}$

c. $\dfrac{2}{3} \times {}^-14$ **d.** $6 \div 1\dfrac{1}{2}$

12. State the number property that is being used in each of these equations.

a. $6 + \left(\dfrac{3}{5} \times \dfrac{5}{3} \right) = 6 + 1$

b. $\dfrac{3}{4} \times \left(7 + \dfrac{^-1}{2} \right) = \dfrac{3}{4} \times 7 + \dfrac{3}{4} \times \dfrac{^-1}{2}$

c. $\dfrac{2}{3} \times \left(\dfrac{1}{5} + \dfrac{1}{2} \right) = \left(\dfrac{1}{5} + \dfrac{1}{2} \right) \times \dfrac{2}{3}$

d. $8 + \left(\dfrac{4}{5} + \dfrac{^-4}{5} \right) = 8 + 0$

13. True or false:
   a. Subtraction of integers is commutative.
   b. Multiplication is closed for the set of positive integers.
   c. Multiplication is closed for the set of positive fractions.
   d. Division is closed for the set of integers.
   e. Subtraction of fractions is associative.

14. This picture of a blue shark has a length of $1\frac{3}{4}$ inches. The scale factor from an actual blue shark to this picture is $1/120$.

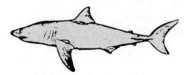

   a. How many feet long is the actual blue shark?
   b. A right whale has a length of approximately 40 feet. If the scale factor from a life-size whale to a picture of the whale is $1/300$, how many inches long is the whale in the picture?

15. A school's new pump can fill the swimming pool in 5 hours; the old pump takes 10 hours. How long will it take to fill the pool if both pumps are used together?

BIBLIOGRAPHY

Battista, M. T. "A Complete Model for Operations on Integers." *Arithmetic Teacher* 30 (May 1983): 26–31.

Bennett, A., Jr., and P. Davidson. *Fraction Bars.* Fort Collins, CO: Scott Resources, 1981.

Bennett, A. B., Jr., and G. L. Musser. "A Concrete Approach to Integer Addition and Subtraction." *Arithmetic Teacher* 23 (May 1976): 332–336.

Bezuk, N. S. "Fractions in the Early Childhood Mathematics Curriculum." *Arithmetic Teacher* 35 (February 1988): 56–60.

Brown, C. "Fractions on Grid Paper." *Arithmetic Teacher* 27 (January 1979): 8–10.

Chang, L. "Multiple Methods of Teaching the Addition and Subtraction of Integers." *Arithmetic Teacher* 33 (December 1985): 14–19.

Chiosi, L. "Fractions Revisited." *Arithmetic Teacher* 31 (April 1984): 46–47.

Coxford, A., and L. Ellerbruch. "Fractional Numbers." *Mathematics Learning in Early Childhood,* 37th Yearbook. Reston, VA: National Council of Teachers of Mathematics, 1975.

Crowley, M., and K. Dunn. "On Multiplying Negative Numbers." *Mathematics Teacher* 78 (April 1985): 252–256.

Curcio, F. R., F. Sicklick, and S. B. Turkel. "Divide and Conquer: Unit Strips to the Rescue." *Arithmetic Teacher* 35 (December 1987): 6–12.

DiDomenico, A. "Discovery of a Property of Consecutive Integers." *Mathematics Teacher* 72 (April 1979): 285–286.

Dirks, M. K. "The Integer Abacus." *Arithmetic Teacher* 31 (March 1984): 50–54.

Edge, D. "Fractions and Panes." *Arithmetic Teacher* 34 (April 1987): 13–17.

Ettline, J. "A Uniform Approach to Fractions." *Arithmetic Teacher* 32 (March 1985): 42–43.

Ewbank, W. A. "LCM—Let's Put It in Its Place." *Arithmetic Teacher* 35 (November 1987): 45–47.

Greenes, C. "Identifying the Gifted Student in Mathematics." *Arithmetic Teacher* 28 (February 1981): 14–17.

Heikkila, F. L. "Maybe We Should Be in the Model Business." *Arithmetic Teacher* 30 (December 1982): 41.

Hollis, L. Y. "Teaching Rational Numbers—Primary Grades." *Arithmetic Teacher* 31 (February 1984): 36–39.

Jacobson, M. "Teaching Rational Numbers—Intermediate Grades." *Arithmetic Teacher* 31 (February 1984): 40–42.

Johnson, J. "Working with Integers." *Mathematics Teacher* 71 (January 1978): 31.

Kiernen, T. "One Point of View: Helping Children Understand Rational Numbers." *Arithmetic Teacher* 31 (February 1984): 3.

Kindle, G. "Droopy, The Number Line, and Multiplication of Integers." *Arithmetic Teacher* 23 (December 1976): 647–650.

Kroll, D. L., and T. Yabe. "A Japanese Educator's Perspective on Teaching Mathematics in the Elementary School." *Arithmetic Teacher* 35 (October 1987): 36–43.

Leutzinger, L., and G. Nelson. "Let's Do It—Fractions with Models." *Arithmetic Teacher* 27 (May 1980): 6–11.

National Council of Teachers of Mathematics. *More Topics in Mathematics for Elementary School Teachers,* 30th Yearbook. Reston, VA.: NCTM, 1968.

Ott, J. M. "A Unified Approach to Multiplying Fractions." *Arithmetic Teacher* 37 (March 1990): 47–49.

Payne, J. N. "Curricular Issues: Teaching Rational Numbers." *Arithmetic Teacher* 31 (February 1984): 14–17.

Payne, J. N. "One Point of View: Sense and Nonsense about Fractions and Decimals." *Arithmetic Teacher* 27 (January 1980): 4–7.

Payne, J. N., and A. E. Towsley. "Implications of NCTM's Standards for Teaching Fractions and Decimals." *Arithmetic Teacher* 37 (April 1990): 23–26.

Peck, D. M., and S. M. Jencks. "Share and Cover." *Arithmetic Teacher* 28 (March 1981): 38–41.

Peterson, J. "Fourteen Different Strategies for Multiplication of Integers, or Why (⁻1)(⁻1) = ⁺1." *Arithmetic Teacher* 19 (May 1972): 396–403.

Post, T. "Fractions: Results and Implications from National Assessment." *Arithmetic Teacher* 28 (May 1981): 26–31.

Prevost, F. "Teaching Rational Numbers—Junior High School." *Arithmetic Teacher* 31 (February 1984): 43–46.

Rees, J. M. "Two-Sided Pies: Help for Improper Fractions and Mixed Numbers." *Arithmetic Teacher* 35 (December 1987): 28–32.

Scott, W. R. "Fractions Taught by Folding Paper Strips." *Arithmetic Teacher* 28 (January 1981): 18–21.

Shookoohi, G. H. "Readiness of Eight-Year-Old Children to Understand the Division of Fractions." *Arithmetic Teacher* 27 (March 1980): 40–43.

Silvia, E. M. "A Look at Division with Fractions." *Arithmetic Teacher* 30 (January 1983): 38–41.

Steiner, E. E. "Division of Fractions: Developing Conceptual Sense with Dollars and Cents." *Arithmetic Teacher* 34 (May 1987): 36–42.

Sweetland, R. "Understanding Multiplication of Fractions." *Arithmetic Teacher* 32 (September 1984): 48–52.

Thiessen, D. "David's Algorithm for the L.C.D." *Arithmetic Teacher* 28 (March 1981): 18.

Van de Walle, J., and C. Thompson. "Let's Do It: Fractions with Fraction Strips." *Arithmetic Teacher* 32 (December 1984): 4–9.

Wiebe, J. H. "Discovering Fractions on a 'Fraction Table'." *Arithmetic Teacher* 33 (December 1985): 49–51.

 **Decimals: Rational and Irrational Numbers**

SPOTLIGHT ON TEACHING

Excerpts from NCTM's Standard 12 for Teaching Mathematics in Grades K–4*

The approach to decimals should be similar to work with fractions, namely, placing a strong and continued emphasis on models and oral language and then connecting this work with symbols. This is necessary if students are to make sense of decimals and use them insightfully. Exploring ideas of tenths and hundredths with models [see figure] can include preliminary work with equivalent decimals, counting sequences, the comparing and ordering of decimals, and addition and subtraction.

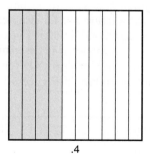
.4

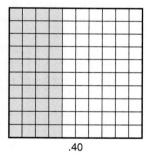
.40

Decimal instruction should include informal experiences that relate fractions to decimals so that students begin to establish connections between the two systems. For example, if students recognize that ½ is the same amount as 0.5, they can use this relationship to determine that 0.4 and 0.45 are a little less than ½ and that 0.6 and 0.57 are a little more than ½. Such activities help children develop number sense for decimals.

*Reprinted by permission of the National Council of Teachers of Mathematics.

SECTION 6.1 DECIMALS AND RATIONAL NUMBERS

A carpenter agrees to work under the condition that he be paid $5.50 every day he works and that he pay $6.60 every day he does not work. At the end of 30 days, he finds he has earned $7.70. How many days did he work?*

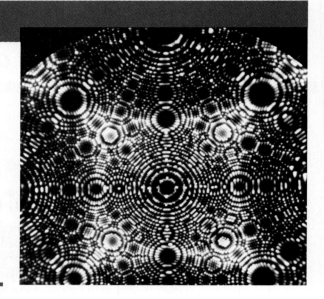

Circular patterns of atoms in an iridium crystal, magnified more than a million times by a field ion microscope

Each dot in the remarkable picture above is an atom in an iridium crystal. The circular patterns show the order and symmetry governing atomic structures. The diameters of atoms, and even the diameters of electrons contained in atoms, can be measured by decimals. Each atom in this picture has a diameter of .000000027 centimeter, and the diameter of an electron is .00000000000056354 centimeter.

The use of decimals is not restricted to describing small objects. The gross national product (GNP) and the national income (NI) for 5 five-year periods are expressed to the nearest tenth of a billion dollars in Figure 6.1.**

Figure 6.1

	1965	1970	1975	1980	1985
GNP (billions)	$691.1	$992.7	$1549.2	$2631.7	$4010.0
NI (billions)	$572.4	$810.7	$1239.4	$2116.6	$3229.9

In our daily lives we encounter decimals in representations of dollar amounts: $17.35, $12.09, $24.00, etc. In the elementary school, pennies, dimes, and dollars are commonly used for teaching decimals.

■ *HISTORICAL HIGHLIGHT*

The person most responsible for our use of decimals is Simon Stevin, a Dutchman. In 1585 Stevin wrote *La Disme,* the first book on the use of decimals. He not only stated the rules for computing with decimals but also pointed out their practical applications. Stevin showed that business calculations with decimals can be performed as easily as those involving only whole numbers. He recommended that the government adopt the decimal system and enforce its use.

*"Problems of the Month," *Mathematics Teacher* 80, no. 7 (October 1987): 555.
***Statistical Abstract of the United States* (Washington, DC: U.S. Government Printing Office, 1988), 407, 411.

As decimals gained acceptance in the sixteenth and seventeenth centuries, a variety of notations were used. Many writers used a vertical bar in place of a decimal point. Here are some examples of how 27.847 was written during this period.

27 | 847   27(847)   27 |847   27 847

27847 . . . ③   27,8ⁱ4ⁱⁱ7ⁱⁱⁱ   27847   27 ⓪ 8 ① 4 ② 7 ③

DECIMAL TERMINOLOGY AND NOTATION

decimal

decimal points

The word "decimal" comes from the Latin *decem,* meaning *ten.* Technically, any number written in base ten positional numeration can be called a decimal. However, **decimal** is most often used to refer only to numbers such as 17.38 and .45, which are expressed with **decimal points.**

There are currently many variations in decimal notation. The English place their decimal point higher above the line than we do in the United States. In other European countries a comma is used in place of a decimal point. A comma and a raised numeral denote a decimal in Scandinavian countries.

United States	*England*	*Europe*	*Scandinavian countries*
82.17	82·17	82,17	82,¹⁷

number of decimal places

place values

The number of digits to the right of the decimal point is called the **number of decimal places.** There are 2 decimal places in 7.08 and 1 decimal place in 104.5. The positions of the digits to the left of the decimal point represent **place values** that are increasing powers of 10 (1, 10, 10^2, 10^3, . . .). The positions to the right of the decimal point represent place values that are decreasing powers of 10 (10^{-1}, 10^{-2}, 10^{-3}, . . .), or reciprocals of powers of 10 (1/10, $1/10^2$, $1/10^3$, . . .). In the decimal 5473.286 (Figure 6.2), the 2 represents 2/10, the 8 represents 8/100, and the 6 represents 6/1000.

Figure 6.2

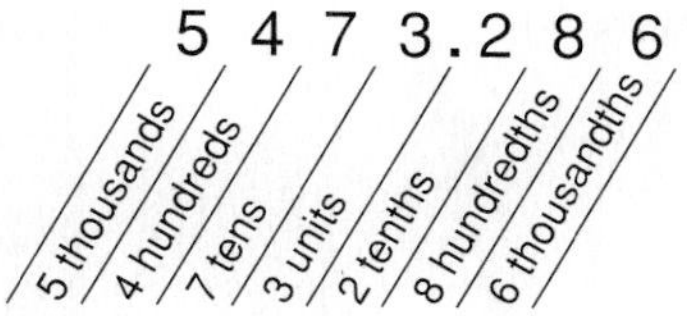

5 4 7 3 . 2 8 6

5 thousands / 4 hundreds / 7 tens / 3 units / 2 tenths / 8 hundredths / 6 thousandths

EXAMPLE A

Express the value of the digit marked by the arrow as a fraction whose denominator is a power of 10.

    ↓   ↓   ↓

1. 47.35   2. 6.089   3. 14.07

Solution   1. $\dfrac{5}{100}$ 2. $\dfrac{9}{1000}$ 3. $\dfrac{0}{10}$

Like whole numbers, decimals can be written in expanded form to show the powers of 10 (Figure 6.3).

Figure 6.3

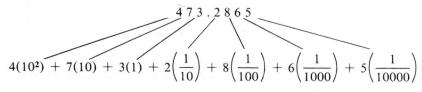

4 7 3 . 2 8 6 5

$$4(10^2) + 7(10) + 3(1) + 2\left(\frac{1}{10}\right) + 8\left(\frac{1}{100}\right) + 6\left(\frac{1}{1000}\right) + 5\left(\frac{1}{10000}\right)$$

READING AND WRITING DECIMALS   The digits to the left of the decimal point are read as a whole number, and the decimal point is read as "and." The digits to the right of the point are also read as a whole number, after which we say the name of the place value of the last digit. For example, 1208.0925 is read "one thousand two hundred eight and nine hundred twenty-five ten-thousandths."

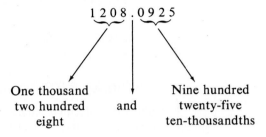

One thousand two hundred eight   and   Nine hundred twenty-five ten-thousandths

---

EXAMPLE B

Write the name of each decimal.

1. 3.472   2. 16.14   3. .3775

Solution

1. Three and four hundred seventy-two thousandths
2. Sixteen and fourteen hundredths
3. Three thousand seven hundred seventy-five ten-thousandths

One place you may see the names of numbers is on bank checks. When writing an amount of money, some people write the decimal part of a dollar in words. Notice that on the bank check in Figure 6.4 it is unnecessary to write "dollars" or "cents." The amount is in terms of dollars, and this unit is printed at the end of the line on which the amount of money is written. Some people write the decimal part of a dollar as a fraction. For example, the amount on this check might have been written as "one hundred seventy-seven and 24/100."

Figure 6.4

MODELS FOR DECIMALS

Models are important for providing conceptual understanding and insight into the use of decimals.

> It is important that decimals be thought of as numbers and the ability to relate them to models should assist in this. We should be spending more time having children become familiar with decimals, their meanings and uses, before rushing directly to decimal computation. Think of the time we spend with counting objects and modeling whole numbers before formal operations with whole numbers are introduced.*

---

*T. P. Carpenter, H. Kepner, M. K. Corbitt, M. M. Lindquist, and R. E. Reys, "Decimals: Results and Implications from National Assessment," *Arithmetic Teacher* 8 (April 1981): 34–37.

DECIMAL SQUARES   The Decimal Squares® model illustrates the part-to-whole concept of decimals. Unit squares are divided into 10, 100, and 1000 equal parts (Figure 6.5), and the decimal tells what part of the square is shaded.*

Figure 6.5

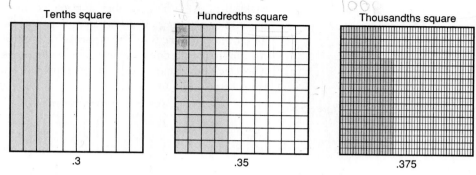

Tenths square

Hundredths square

Thousandths square

.3

.35

.375

Each decimal in Figure 6.5 can be obtained by beginning with the fraction for the shaded amount of the square and obtaining the expanded form of the decimal. For example, the fraction for the square representing 375 parts out of 1000 is 375/1000.

$$\frac{375}{1000} = \frac{300}{1000} + \frac{70}{1000} + \frac{5}{1000} = \frac{3}{10} + \frac{7}{100} + \frac{5}{1000} = .375$$

Similarly, the decimal for 3/10 is .3, and the decimal for 35/100 is .35.

EXAMPLE C

Describe the square that would represent each fraction, and write the decimal for each fraction.

1. $\dfrac{4728}{10,000}$ 2. $\dfrac{6}{100}$

Solution

1. A square with 4728 parts shaded out of 10,000

$$\frac{4728}{10,000} = \frac{4000}{10,000} + \frac{700}{10,000} + \frac{20}{10,000} + \frac{8}{10,000}$$

$$= \frac{4}{10} + \frac{7}{100} + \frac{2}{1000} + \frac{8}{10,000}$$

$$= .4728$$

2. A square with 6 parts shaded out of 100

$$\frac{6}{100} = \frac{0}{10} + \frac{6}{100} = .06$$

The preceding example shows that it is easy to obtain the decimal for a fraction whose denominator is a power of 10; it is just a matter of locating the decimal point. Try the example on your calculator by dividing 4728 by 10,000 and 6 by 100. It is also instructive to enter 4728 into a calculator and then repeatedly divide by 10. Each time the decimal point moves 1 digit to the left.

$$4728 \div 10 = \boxed{472.8}$$
$$\div 10 = \boxed{47.28}$$
$$\div 10 = \boxed{4.728}$$
$$\div 10 = \boxed{.4728}$$

*Decimal Squares® is a registered trademark of Scott Resources, Inc.

In general, to divide an integer by a power of 10, *begin with the units digit and, for each factor of 10, count off a digit to the left to locate the decimal point.*

NUMBER LINE   The number line is a common model for illustrating decimals. One method of marking off a unit from zero to 1 is to use the edge of a Decimal Square, as shown in Figure 6.6. This approach shows the relationship between a *region model* for a unit (the decimal square) and a *linear model* for a unit (the edge of a square). The Decimal Square can be used repeatedly to mark off tenths on the number line from zero to 1, 1 to 2, etc.

Figure 6.6

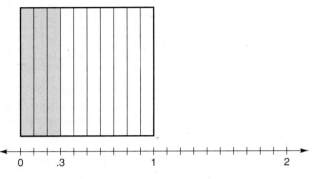

Consider locating the point for .372 on a number line. One approach is to use the expanded form of the decimal,

$$.372 = \frac{3}{10} + \frac{7}{100} + \frac{2}{1000}$$

and locate the point in several steps, as shown in Figure 6.7. First, the point for 3/10 (.3) is located at the end of the third interval, as in Figure 6.6. Second, the expanded form shows that we must add 7/100, so the interval from .3 to .4 is divided into 10 equal parts, which are hundredths. To add 7/100 (.07), we begin at .3 and go to the end of the seventh interval. This is the point for .37. Finally, the interval from .37 to .38 is divided into 10 equal parts, which are thousandths. To add 2/1000, we begin at .37 and go to the end of the second interval. This is the point for .372.

Figure 6.7

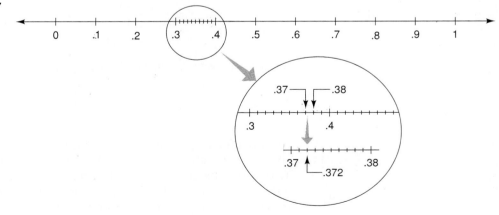

EXAMPLE D

Sketch a number line and mark the approximate location of each decimal.

1. .46   2. 1.75   3. 2.271

Solution

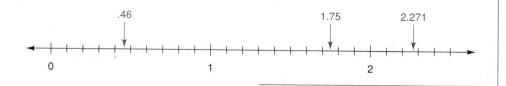

Decimals are used for negative as well as positive numbers. The graph in Figure 6.8 represents increasing and decreasing changes from month to month in the producer price index for finished goods, in tenths of a percent, for 1987.* The producer price index increased from January through September and decreased from October through December.

Figure 6.8

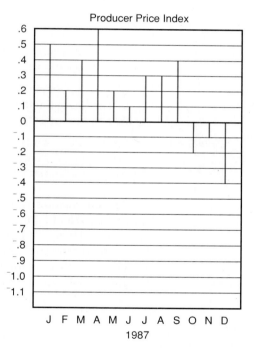

Producer Price Index

J F M A M J J A S O N D
1987

The decimals .2 and ⁻.2 for the months of February and October are opposites. For every decimal, whether positive or negative, there is a corresponding decimal called **opposite, inverse for addition** its **opposite** (or **inverse for addition**) such that the sum of the two decimals is zero. Several decimals and their opposites are shown on the number line in Figure 6.9.

Figure 6.9

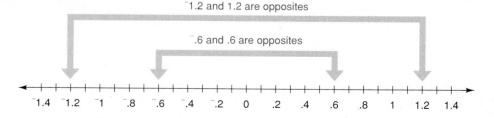

⁻1.2 and 1.2 are opposites

⁻.6 and .6 are opposites

⁻1.4   ⁻1.2   ⁻1   ⁻.8   ⁻.6   ⁻.4   ⁻.2   0   .2   .4   .6   .8   1   1.2   1.4

Producer Price Index News Release (Washington, DC: U.S. Department of Labor, Bureau of Labor Statistics, January, 1988).

EQUALITY OF DECIMALS

Equality of decimals can be illustrated visually by comparing the shaded amounts in their Decimal Squares. Figure 6.10 shows that 4 parts out of 10, 40 parts out of 100, and 400 parts out of 1000 are all represented by the same amount of shading—in each Decimal Square, 4 columns are shaded. This shows that

$$.4 = .40 = .400$$

Figure 6.10

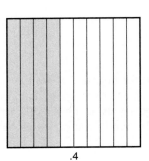
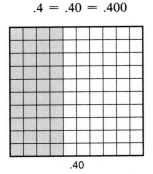
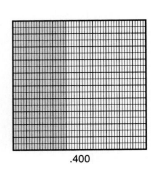

.4   .40   .400

EXAMPLE E

Complete each equation by writing the indicated decimal, and describe the square representing each decimal in the equation.

1. .35 = _____ (thousandths)
2. .670 = _____ (hundredths)
3. .600 = _____ (tenths)

Solution

1. .35 = .350 (35 parts out of 100 and 350 parts out of 1000 are shaded)
2. .670 = .67 (670 parts out of 1000 and 67 parts out of 100 are shaded)
3. .600 = .6 (600 parts out of 1000 and 6 parts out of 10 are shaded)

Decimal Squares also give us a visual model for place value. Consider the Decimal Square for .475 in Figure 6.11. The 4 full columns that are shaded (400 thousandths) represent 4/10 or .4 (400/1000 = 4/10); the 7 small squares that are shaded (70 thousandths) represent 7/100 or .07 (70/1000 = 7/100); and the 5 small parts that are shaded (5 thousandths) represent 5/1000 or .005. Thus the decimal .475 can be thought of as 4 tenths, 7 hundredths, and 5 thousandths.

$$.475 = .4 + .07 + .005$$

Figure 6.11

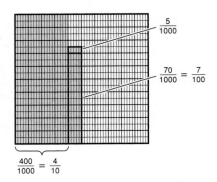

$\frac{5}{1000}$

$\frac{70}{1000} = \frac{7}{100}$

$\frac{400}{1000} = \frac{4}{10}$

INEQUALITY OF DECIMALS

Research indicates that students from elementary school through college often have difficulty determining inequalities for decimals. One source of confusion is thinking of the digits in the decimal as representing whole numbers (see Example F).

Pag 236   chapter 6.1
(25)

Figure 6.12 shows that .47 < .6. Even though 47 is greater than 6, a smaller amount of the square is shaded for .47 than for .6.

Figure 6.12

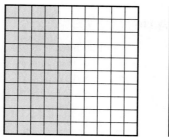
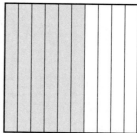

We can also see that .47 < .6 by noting that in the Decimal Square for .47, 4 full columns and part of another are shaded, whereas in the Decimal Square for .6, 6 full columns are shaded. In other words, the digit in the tenths place for .47 is less than the digit in the tenths place for .6. In general, the following *place value test* determines inequalities for decimals.

**PLACE VALUE TEST FOR
INEQUALITY OF DECIMALS**

> The greater of two positive decimals that are both less than 1 will be the decimal with the greater digit in the tenths place. If these digits are equal, this test is applied to the hundredths digits, and so on.

The question in the next example is from a test given as part of a nationwide testing program in schools every 4 years.* Over half of the 13-year-olds who took the test in 1980 selected an incorrect answer.

EXAMPLE F

Which number is the greatest?

1. .19   2. .036   3. .195   4. .2

Solution

One approach is to use the place value test for inequality of decimals. Since 2 is the greatest of the digits in the tenths place of these 4 decimals, .2 is the greatest number. Another approach is to change each decimal to thousandths. This will show that 200 thousandths is the greatest number of thousandths among these 4 decimals.

.190   .036   .195   .200

A visual approach with Decimal Squares shows that 2 full columns of shading (or 2 parts shaded out of 10) is more than 19 parts shaded out of 100 or 195 parts shaded out of 1000.

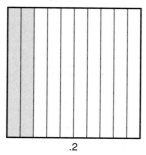
.2

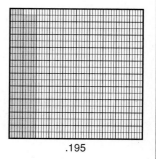
.19   .195

*T. P. Carpenter et al., *Results from the Second Mathematics Assessment of the National Assessment of Educational Progress* (Reston, VA: National Council of Teachers of Mathematics, 1981.)

Note: 47% of the 13-year-olds tested in 1980 selected .195 for the answer to Example F. This error may be due to the fact that 195 is greater than 19, 36, or 2.

RATIONAL NUMBERS

Up to this point, numbers written in the form a/b, where a and b are integers, have been called *fractions*. This is the terminology commonly used in elementary schools. However, the word "fraction" has a more general meaning and includes the quotient of any two numbers, integers or not, as long as the denominator is not zero. Numbers that are quotients of two integers are called **rational numbers.**

rational numbers

RATIONAL NUMBERS

> Any number that can be written in the form a/b, where $b \neq 0$ and a and b are integers, is called a **rational number.**

For example, $1/9$, $^-3/7$, $1/5$, $7/10$, and $^-1/3$ are rational numbers. When the denominator of a rational number equals 1, the rational number equals an integer: $6/1 = 6$, $^-4/1 = ^-4$, $12/1 = 12$, etc. Therefore, integers are also rational numbers.

Rational numbers can be expressed by many different number symbols or numerals. For example, $3/10$ is a rational number and $3/10 = .3$, so $.3$ is also a rational number. In the following paragraphs we will show that all rational numbers a/b can be written as decimals.

We have seen that it is easy to convert a fraction to a decimal if the denominator is a power of 10:

$$\frac{64}{100} = .64 \qquad \frac{7283}{1000} = 7.283 \qquad \frac{54}{10,000} = .0054$$

Sometimes when the denominator is not a power of 10, the fraction can be replaced by an equal number whose denominator is a power of 10. For example, $1/4$ can be replaced by $25/100$ because 100 is a multiple of 4:

$$\frac{1}{4} = \frac{25 \times 1}{25 \times 4} = \frac{25}{100} = .25$$

Since $10 = 2 \times 5$, any power of 10 will have factors of only 2 and 5.

$$10 = 2 \times 5, \ 100 = 10^2 = 2^2 \times 5^2, \ 1000 = 10^3 = 2^3 \times 5^3, \ \ldots$$

Consider replacing $3/8$ by a fraction whose denominator is a power of 10. Since $8 = 2^3$, we need to multiply the numerator and denominator of $3/8$ by 5^3.

$$\frac{3}{8} = \frac{3}{2^3} = \frac{3 \times 5^3}{2^3 \times 5^3} = \frac{375}{10^3} = .375$$

EXAMPLE G

Convert each fraction to a decimal by first writing a fraction whose denominator is a power of 10.

1. $\dfrac{7}{20}$ 2. $\dfrac{3}{25}$ 3. $\dfrac{11}{16}$ 4. $\dfrac{3}{40}$

Solution

1. $\dfrac{7}{20} = \dfrac{35}{100} = .35$ 2. $\dfrac{3}{25} = \dfrac{12}{100} = .12$

3. $\dfrac{11}{16} = \dfrac{11}{2^4} = \dfrac{11 \times 5^4}{2^4 \times 5^4} = \dfrac{6875}{10^4} = .6875$

4. $\dfrac{3}{40} = \dfrac{3}{2^3 \times 5} = \dfrac{3 \times 5^2}{2^3 \times 5^3} = \dfrac{75}{10^3} = .075$

terminating or finite decimals

In the preceding example all of the decimals had a finite number of digits. Such decimals are called **terminating** (or **finite**) **decimals.** However, there are decimals that are not terminating. There is no power of 10 that has 3 as a factor, so 1/3 cannot be written as a fraction whose denominator is a power of 10. In general, we have the following rule.

> If a rational number a/b is in simplest form, it can be written as a terminating decimal if and only if b has only 2s and 5s in its prime factorization.

EXAMPLE H

Which of these rational numbers can be written as terminating decimals?

1. $\dfrac{5}{6}$ 2. $\dfrac{1}{80}$ 3. $\dfrac{9}{15}$ 4. $\dfrac{3}{14}$

Solution

1. 6 has a factor of 3, so 5/6 cannot be written as a terminating decimal.
2. 80 has only factors of 2 and 5, so 1/80 can be written as a terminating decimal.
3. 9/15 = 3/5, and since the denominator of the fraction in simplest form has only 5 as a factor, 9/15 can be written as a terminating decimal.
4. 14 has a factor of 7, so 3/14 cannot be written as a terminating decimal.

Let's consider finding a decimal for 1/3. We know from Section 5.2 that 1/3 = 1 ÷ 3. Figure 6.13 illustrates the first few steps in dividing 1 by 3. Part (a) shows a unit square with 10 tenths shaded and illustrates that 1 ÷ 3 is .3 with .1 remaining. In part (b), the remaining .1 is replaced by 10 hundredths, and dividing by 3 produces .03 with .01 remaining. In part (c), the 1 hundredth is replaced by 10 thousandths, and dividing by 3 produces .003 with .001 remaining. The three steps of the division process in Figure 6.13 produce .3, .03, and .003, which gives a total shaded amount of .333 with .001 remaining.

Figure 6.13

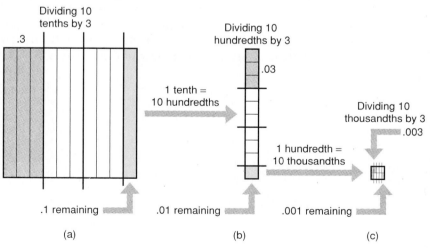

(a)   (b)   (c)

Continuing this process of dividing by 3 shows that the decimal for 1/3 has a repeating pattern of 3s. When a decimal does not terminate and contains a repeating pattern of digits, it is called a **repeating decimal.***

repeating decimal

*The computer program REPEATING DECIMALS on the *Computer Problem-Solving Disc* prints up to 200 decimal places for any fraction that is entered. What can be said about repeating patterns of decimals for 1/p, where p is a prime?

The step-by-step visual illustration in Figure 6.13 has a corresponding numerical division algorithm. The first step is to divide 10 tenths by 3. The result is .3 with .1 remaining. The second step is to divide 10 hundredths by 3. The result of the first two steps is .33 with .01 remaining. In the third step the 10 thousandths are divided by 3. The result of the first three steps is .333 with .001 remaining. This process can be continued to obtain any number of 3s in the decimal approximation for 1/3.

Step 1	Step 2	Step 3
$\begin{array}{r} .3 \\ 3\overline{)1.0} \\ \underline{9} \\ 1 \end{array}$	$\begin{array}{r} .33 \\ 3\overline{)1.00} \\ \underline{9} \\ 10 \\ \underline{9} \\ 1 \end{array}$	$\begin{array}{r} .333 \\ 3\overline{)1.000} \\ \underline{9} \\ 10 \\ \underline{9} \\ 10 \\ \underline{9} \\ 1 \end{array}$

The division algorithm can be used to obtain a terminating or repeating decimal for any rational number. For example, when the numerator of 3/8 is divided by its denominator, the division algorithm shows that the decimal terminates after 3 digits.

$$\begin{array}{r} .375 \\ 8\overline{)3.000} \\ \underline{24} \\ 60 \\ \underline{56} \\ 40 \\ \underline{40} \end{array}$$

On the other hand, when the numerator of 4/7 is divided by its denominator, the quotient does not terminate but repeats the same arrangement of 6 digits (571428) over and over. In this case the decimal is repeating. The reason for this can be seen by looking at the remainders 5, 1, 3, 2, 6 and 4, which are circled below. These 6 numbers, plus zero, are all the possible remainders when a number is divided by 7. So after 6 steps in the process of dividing 4 by 7, the numbers in the decimal quotient repeat. Notice the use of the bar above the 6 digits in the quotient to indicate the repeating **repetend** pattern. The block of digits that is repeated over and over is called the **repetend.**

$$\begin{array}{r} .\overline{571428}5 \\ 7\overline{)4.0000000} \\ \underline{35} \\ (5)0 \\ \underline{49} \\ (1)0 \\ \underline{7} \\ (3)0 \\ \underline{28} \\ (2)0 \\ \underline{14} \\ (6)0 \\ \underline{56} \\ (4)0 \\ \underline{35} \end{array}$$

The preceding example illustrates why every rational number r/s can be represented by either a repeating decimal or a terminating decimal. When r is divided by s, the remainders are always less than s (see the division algorithm, page 107). If a remainder of zero occurs in the division process, as it does when we divide 3 by 8, then the decimal terminates. If there is no zero remainder, then eventually a remainder will be repeated, in which case the digits in the quotient will also start repeating.

Calculators are convenient for finding the decimal representations of fractions. For fractions represented by repeating decimals, such as 7/12 = .5833333333. . . , the number in the calculator display is an approximation because it shows only a few of the digits. For most applications this is sufficient accuracy, and we will not need to be concerned over the fact that the decimal is not exactly equal to the fraction.

EXAMPLE I

Write the decimal for each rational number. Use a bar to show the repetend (repeating digits).

1. $\dfrac{3}{11}$ 2. $\dfrac{5}{6}$ 3. $\dfrac{5}{12}$

Solution   1. $.\overline{27}$ 2. $.8\overline{3}$ 3. $.41\overline{6}$

Notice in the solutions to Example I that the repeating pattern in .83 does not begin until the hundredths digit and the repeating pattern in .416 does not begin until the thousandths digit.

We have seen that every rational number that is the quotient of two integers can be written as a terminating or repeating decimal. Conversely, every terminating or repeating decimal can be written as the quotient of two integers. An example of a terminating decimal written as a quotient is shown below. A method for writing repeating decimals as the quotient of two integers will be shown in Section 6.2.

Terminating decimals can be written as fractions whose denominators are powers of 10. The following equations show why .378 equals 378/1000. In the first equation .378 is written in expanded form. The least common denominator for the fractions is 1000, and their sum is 378/1000.

$$.378 = \frac{3}{10} + \frac{7}{100} + \frac{8}{1000}$$

$$= \frac{300}{1000} + \frac{70}{1000} + \frac{8}{1000}$$

$$= \frac{378}{1000}$$

DENSITY OF RATIONAL NUMBERS

In Chapter 5 we saw examples of the fact that the rational numbers, when written as fractions, are *dense*. That is, between any two such numbers there is always another. To show this we looked at a method for finding a fraction between two given fractions. In the following example we will consider ways of finding a decimal between two given decimals.

EXAMPLE J

Sketch a number line and mark the location of each pair of decimals. Then find another decimal between them.

1. .124 and .125   2. .47 and .621   3. 1.1 and 1.2

Solution   1. .124 = .1240 and .125 = .1250, so the 9 decimals .1241, .1242, .1243, . . . , .1249 are between .124 and .125.

2. Since .47 = .470, any of the thousandths between .470 and .621 may be selected: .471, .472, .473, etc.
3. 1.1 = 1.10 and 1.2 = 1.20, so the 9 decimals 1.11, 1.12, 1.13, . . . , 1.19 are between 1.1 and 1.2.

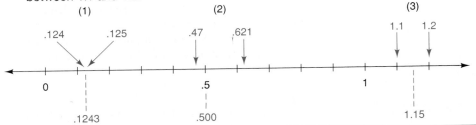

ESTIMATION

Often a calculator display will be filled with the digits of a decimal, when some approximate value is all that is necessary. Rounding to a given place value is the most common method of obtaining decimal estimations.

ROUNDING   Decimals may be rounded to the nearest whole number, nearest tenth, nearest hundredth, etc. Before looking at a rule for rounding decimals, let's consider some visual illustrations.

Squares for three decimals are shown in Figure 6.14. Consider rounding these decimals to the nearest tenth. The decimal .648 rounds to .6 because 6 full columns and *less than half* of the next column are shaded; .863 rounds to .9 because 8 full columns and *more than half* of the next column are shaded; .35 can be either *rounded up* to .4 or *rounded down* to .3, because 3 full columns and *half* of the next column are shaded. In this text we will adopt the policy of *rounding up*.

Figure 6.14

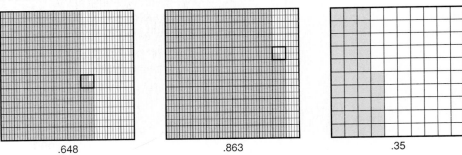

Next consider rounding the decimals in Figure 6.14 to the nearest hundredth. The square for .648 shows that 64 hundredths are shaded (6 full columns and 4 hundredths in the next column); the remaining 8 thousandths are more than half of the next hundredth, so .648 rounds to .65. The Decimal Square for .863 shows that 86 hundredths are shaded (8 full columns and 6 hundredths in the next column); the remaining 3 thousandths are less than half of the next hundredth, so .863 rounds to .86.

EXAMPLE K

Round each decimal to the nearest tenth and hundredth.

1. .283   2. .068   3. 14.649

Solution

1. .283 rounded to the nearest tenth is .3 and to the nearest hundredth is .28.
2. .068 rounded to the nearest tenth is .1 and to the nearest hundredth is .07.
3. 14.649 rounded to the nearest tenth is 14.6 and to the nearest hundredth is 14.65.

Notice in Example K that 14.649 rounded to the nearest tenth is not 14.7. You can confirm this by visualizing a Decimal Square for .649: 6 full columns are shaded and less than half of the next column—49 thousandths—is shaded.

The preceding examples are special cases of the following general rule for rounding decimals. Notice that this is similar to the rule that was stated for rounding whole numbers in Chapter 3.

RULE FOR ROUNDING NUMBERS

1. Locate the place value to which the number is to be rounded and check the digit to its right.
2. If the digit to the right is 5 or greater, then all digits to the right are dropped and the digit with the given place value is increased by 1.
3. If the digit to the right is 4 or less, then all digits to the right of the digit with the given place value are dropped.

EXAMPLE L

Round 1.6825 to the given number of decimal places.

1. 2 decimal places (round to hundredths)
2. 1 decimal place (round to tenths)
3. 3 decimal places (round to thousandths)

Solution

1. $\underset{Hundredths}{1.6825} \longrightarrow 1.68$

2. $\underset{Tenths}{1.6825} \longrightarrow 1.7$

3. $\underset{Thousandths}{1.6825} \longrightarrow 1.683$

Some calculators automatically round decimals that exceed the full display of the calculator. On such calculators, if 2 is divided by 3, the decimal 0.66 . . . 667 will show in the display. Almost all calculators that round off at a digit that is followed by 5 will increase this digit, as described in the preceding rule for rounding numbers. For example, 55/99 is equal to the repeating decimal .5555. . . . If 55 is divided by 99 on a calculator that rounds off, 0.55 . . . 556 will usually show in the display. Try this on your calculator.

PROBLEM-SOLVING APPLICATION

■ PROBLEM

The price of a single pen is 39 cents. This price is reduced if pens are purchased in quantity. The price per pen is always a whole number of cents and never less than 2 cents. If we know that a person bought all the pens in a box for $22.91, we can determine the number of pens. What is this number?

Question 1

Understanding the Problem If the cost per pen is less than 39 cents and it must be a whole number of cents, what are the possibilities for the reduced price?

Devising a Plan Since there are a reasonably small number of possible prices, one approach, if a calculator is available, is to *guess and check*. This can be done by replacing the $22.91 by 2291 and dividing by the whole numbers 38, 37, 36, etc., until a whole number quotient is obtained; or we can divide $22.91 by the decimals .38, .37, .36, etc. Considering this problem as involving whole numbers (whole numbers of pennies) and

Question 2   divisibility suggests another approach: finding the factorization of 2291. How does the fact that there is only one solution tell us that the reduced price in cents is a prime number?

Carrying Out the Plan   A quick use of the divisibility tests for 2, 3, and 5 shows that these numbers are not factors of 2291. Since the prime is less than 39, we need only check the primes 7, 11, 13, 17, 19, 23, 29, 31, and 37. Which prime divides 2291, and what is the number of pens in the box?

Question 3

Looking Back   Suppose we kept the conditions of the problem the same but changed the reduced price for the entire box to $15.17. How many pens would be in the box?

Question 4

Answers to Questions 1–4
1. Whole numbers of cents from 5 to 38
2. If a composite number less than 39 divides 2291, then the factors of the composite number will divide 2291 and there will be more than one possibility for the cost of each pen.
3. 29 is a factor of 2291, so the cost of each pen is 29 cents and there are 79 pens in the box.
4. The first prime less than 39 that divides 1517 is 37. Since 37 × 41 = 1517, the number of pens in the box would be 41.

RELATED ACTIVITIES IN
Mathematics for Elementary Teachers: An Activity Approach, 3e

Activity Set 6.1   **Models for Decimals:** Decimal Squares provide a visual model for the part-to-whole concept of decimals and the concepts of equality, inequality, place value, and estimation.

Just for Fun   **Decimal Games:** A game for equality of decimals, which uses Decimal Squares, and a game for decimal place value

---

EXERCISES AND PROBLEMS 6.1

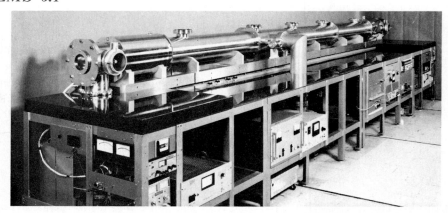

Intervals of time can be measured by this cesium-beam atomic clock to an accuracy of .0000000000001 of a second. This is equivalent to an accuracy of within 1 second every 300,000 years. This strange clock, which is over 19 feet long, is located in Boulder, Colorado and is operated by the National Bureau of Standards.

1. The clock shown above can be adjusted for time intervals as short as one billionth of a second. What is the decimal for
  a. 1 thousandth of a second?
  b. 1 millionth of a second?
  c. 1 billionth of a second?

2. The first book about decimals was written by Simon Stevin in 1585. He used small circled numerals between digits to indicate decimals. Among his examples he wrote 27 + 847/1000 as 27 ⓪ 8 ① 4 ② 7 ③.
  a. Explain how the decimal point could have evolved from this notation.

b. In England this decimal is written as 27 · 847 and in the United States as 27.847. What advantage is there in the English location of the decimal point?

3. For the indicated digit, write a fraction whose denominator is a power of 10.

  a. 23.178   **b.** 7.2016

  c. .0033   **d.** .9999

4. Find the decimal for each fraction and write the name of the decimal.

    a. $\dfrac{42}{100}$ **b.** $\dfrac{64{,}193}{10{,}000}$

    c. $\dfrac{9}{1000}$ **d.** $\dfrac{436}{10}$

5. Write the name of each dollar amount.

    a. $347.96   **b.** $23.50   **c.** $1144.03

6. Draw an arrow from each number to its corresponding point on the number line. Write the number that corresponds to each point labeled with a letter.

7. Write an equal decimal with the given number of decimal places. Briefly describe the Decimal Squares for both decimals in the equation.

    a. .4 = _____ (hundredths)

    b. .47 = _____ (thousandths)

    c. .300 = _____ (tenths)

    d. .270 = _____ (hundredths)

8. Describe Decimal Squares to explain why each of the following is true.

    a. .7 = .70   **b.** .43 = .430   **c.** .45 < .6

    d. .3 > .295   **e.** .085 < .13   **f.** .07 > .035

9. Determine what number is represented by the following figure, if
    a. each small square represents 1 unit.
    b. each large square represents 1 unit.
    c. each 1 × 10 strip represents 1 unit.

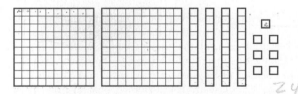

10. Sketch Decimal Squares and describe how to find the decimal for each fraction.

    a. $\dfrac{1}{4}$ **b.** $\dfrac{1}{5}$

    c. $\dfrac{1}{8}$ **d.** $\dfrac{1}{6}$ (to 3 decimal places)

11. Write each fraction as a decimal.

    a. $\dfrac{3}{8}$ **b.** $\dfrac{7}{80}$

    c. $\dfrac{19}{20}$ **d.** $\dfrac{5}{4}$

12. Match each rational number in the first column with an equal rational number in the second column.

$\dfrac{1}{3}$	$.8\overline{3}$
$.25$	$\overline{.34}$
$\dfrac{5}{6}$	$\dfrac{7}{8}$
$.41\overline{6}$	$.\overline{3}$
$.875$	$\dfrac{1}{15}$
$.0\overline{6}$	$\dfrac{1}{4}$
$\dfrac{3}{10}$	$\dfrac{5}{12}$
$\dfrac{34}{99}$	$.3$

13. Which of the following fractions have terminating decimals, and which have repeating decimals?

    a. $\dfrac{7}{17}$ **b.** $\dfrac{2}{9}$ **c.** $\dfrac{6}{15}$

    d. $\dfrac{1}{50}$ **e.** $\dfrac{3}{18}$ **f.** $\dfrac{5}{13}$

14. The following fractions have been approximated by writing their decimals to 3 decimal places. For each fraction, sketch a decimal square with 100 equal parts and explain how the 3 digits can be represented by shading. (Hint: $1/6 = 1 \div 6$.)

    a. $\dfrac{1}{6} \approx .166$ **b.** $\dfrac{1}{7} \approx .142$ **c.** $\dfrac{1}{12} \approx .083$

15. Write the decimal for each fraction. If the decimal is repeating, use a bar to show the repeating digits.

    a. $\dfrac{5}{9}$ **b.** $\dfrac{7}{4}$ **c.** $\dfrac{5}{8}$

16. Replace each decimal in parts a through d with an approximation that is obtained from the leading nonzero digit.

    a. .062   **b.** .0027

    c. .165   **d.** .228

    e. Which approximations above will change if we round to the leading nonzero digit? What are the new approximations?

17. One method of comparing two fractions for inequalities is to find their decimal representations. Use this method to rearrange these fractions in increasing order from left to right:

$$\dfrac{16}{20}, \dfrac{19}{34}, \dfrac{38}{52}, \dfrac{21}{25}, \dfrac{11}{17}$$

18. Round each decimal to the given place value.

    a. .3728 (hundredths)   **b.** .084 (tenths)

    c. 14.3716 (thousandths)   **d.** .349 (tenths)

19. Which of the following decimals is the smallest? Describe decimal squares to support your answer.

    a. .07   **b.** 1.003   **c.** .08

    d. .075   **e.** .3

    f. The preceding question was part of a test on decimals that was given in 1979 to over 7000 students entering college.* Approximately 2/5 of these students chose the incorrect answer of .075. What confusion about decimals might have caused this choice?

20. Money amounts are often rounded to values that can be paid in standard currency. Use the following values for questions a through c: $45.789, $45.443, $45.375, $45.4650, and $45.6749.

    a. Round each amount to the nearest hundredth of a dollar (nearest cent).

    b. Some mortgage lenders round any fraction of a cent up. Using this method, round these amounts up to the nearest hundredth of a dollar.

    c. Some lenders even round up to the nearest dime. Using this method, what are these amounts rounded to the nearest tenth of a dollar?

21. **a.** A catalog lists the following camera weights in ounces: 17.31, 16.25, 15.90, 28.06, and 22.55. What is each weight rounded to the nearest tenth of an ounce?

    b. In one year .20 of the injuries to players in the National Football League were to the knees and .025 were to the arms. Were there more injuries to the knees or to the arms?

    c. A pointer on a water meter is half way between .8 and .9. What is the decimal position of the pointer?

22. **a.** A sewing machine has attachments called throat plates for making eyelets. If the holes on a certain throat plate are .218, .14, .2, and .196 inch in diameter, which is the largest hole?

    b. Physicists have calculated that a cubic foot of air weighs 1.29152 ounces. What is this weight rounded to the nearest tenth of an ounce?

    c. A kilometer is 1000 meters. The length of a soccer field for international matches is 110 meters. What decimal part of a kilometer equals 110 meters?

23. Find the decimal for each of the following fractions and round it to the nearest ten-thousandth (4 decimal places).

    a. $\dfrac{1}{16}$ **b.** $\dfrac{3}{32}$

    c. $\dfrac{7}{64}$ **d.** $\dfrac{35}{64}$

24. Each wrench in a set of socket wrenches is printed with one of the following sizes, in parts of an inch. Arrange the numbers from smallest to largest:

$$\frac{5}{32}, \frac{1}{8}, \frac{3}{16}, \frac{1}{4}, \frac{1}{16}, \frac{3}{32}$$

25. The *Guinness Book of World Records* documents the evolution of sports records in the twentieth century. Three records for the high jump are shown below. Convert the feet and inches into feet, rounding to 2 decimal places.

    a. M. Sweeney: 6′ 5⅝″, U.S., 1895

    b. Zhu Jianhua: 7′ 9¼″, China, 1983

    c. Lester Steers: 6′ 11″, U.S., 1941

Featured Strategies: Solving a Simpler Problem and Making a Table

26. A piece of paper is cut in half, and 1 piece is placed on top of the other. Then the 2 pieces are cut in half, and 1 half is placed on top of the other, forming a stack with 4 pieces. If this process is carried out a total of 25 times and the original piece of paper is .003 inch thick, what is the height of the stack to the nearest foot?

    a. **Understanding the Problem** Simplifying the problem may suggest what needs to be done to obtain a solution. Suppose each piece of paper were 1/2 inch thick. How thick would the stack be after 3 cuts?

    b. **Devising a Plan** Forming a table will help you see a pattern between the number of cuts and the number of pieces of paper. What numbers should appear in the blank lines of the table? What is the number of pieces of paper after 25 cuts, expressed as a power of 2?

Number of cuts	Number of pieces
1	2
2	4
3	8
4	—
5	—
⋮	⋮
25	—

    c. **Carrying Out the Plan** Our simplification in part a suggests that we must multiply the thickness of the paper (.003 or 3/1000 inch) by the total number of pieces of paper. What is the final height of the stack to the nearest foot?

    d. **Looking Back** Another way to think of the height of the final stack is to divide the number of feet by 5280, the number of feet in a mile. How high is the stack to the nearest tenth of a mile?

*A. S. Grossman, "Decimal Notation: An Important Research Finding," *Arithmetic Teacher* 30 (May 1983): 32–33.

CALCULATOR INVESTIGATION

A calculator is a convenient device for discovering patterns and relationships between fractions and repeating decimals. The equations below form the beginning of an interesting pattern.

$$\frac{1}{9} = .111111 \ldots$$

$$\frac{2}{9} = .222222 \ldots$$

$$\frac{3}{9} = .333333 \ldots$$

Questions for Investigation

1. Will the pattern shown at the left continue to hold?
2. What are the decimals for 1/99, 2/99, 3/99, . . . , and is there a pattern? How about 1/999, 2/999, etc.?
3. What patterns can you find in the following equations? Can the patterns be extended?

$$\frac{1}{11} = .090909 \ldots$$

$$\frac{2}{11} = .181818 \ldots$$

$$\frac{3}{11} = .272727 \ldots$$

4. Are there similar patterns for 1/111, 2/111, 3/111, etc.?

PUZZLER

A truck driver noticed that the mileage on the truck odometer was 72,927, a palindromic number. Four hours later the driver was surprised to find that the odometer showed another palindromic number. What was the truck's average speed during this four-hour period?

SECTION 6.2 OPERATIONS WITH DECIMALS

■ PROBLEM OPENER

Helen Chen wants to seed her front lawn. Grass seed can be bought in three-pound boxes that cost $4.50 or in five-pound boxes that cost $6.58. She needs exactly 17 pounds of seed. How many boxes of each size should she purchase to get the best buy?*

A phototimer finish of a 1-mile race between Marty Liquori and Jim Ryun

Electronic timers for athletic competition present decimals to hundredths and thousandths of a second. The above picture shows a phototimer finish of a one-mile race in which Marty Liquori of Villanova beat Jim Ryun of the Oregon Track Club at the 1971 International Freedom Games at Philadelphia's Franklin Field. Both runners were

*C. R. Hirsch, ed., *Activities for Implementing Curricular Themes from the Agenda for Action* (Reston, VA: National Council of Teachers of Mathematics, 1986), 17.

clocked at 3 minutes and 54.6 seconds by officials using hand-operated stopwatches. However, the phototimer clocked Liquori at 3 minutes and 54.54 seconds and Ryun at 3 minutes and 54.75 seconds, a difference of .21 second. What you see is not a simultaneous photograph of the two runners (in which it would appear that they were crossing the finish line together) but a continuous photograph of the finish line showing the runners as they crossed it in the span of .21 second, which is represented in the photo by the space of approximately 2 inches between the men.

ADDITION

The concept of addition of decimals is the same as the concept of addition of whole numbers and fractions: it involves putting together, or combining, two amounts. Figure 6.15 shows a Decimal Square with 47 parts shaded out of 100, representing .47, and a Decimal Square with 36 parts shaded out of 100, representing .36. The total number of shaded parts is 47 + 36 = 83, and since each of these parts is 1 hundredth of a whole square, the total shaded amount represents .83.

Figure 6.15

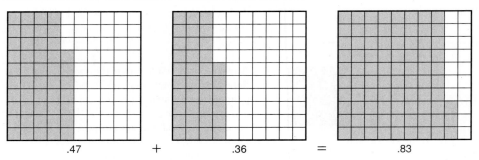

.47   +   .36   =   .83

This example with Decimal Squares indicates why addition of decimals is very similar to addition of whole numbers. We added whole numbers (47 + 36) of parts, and then, taking into account that the small parts were hundredths, we located the decimal point.

The following equations compute this sum using fractions. Notice that in going from the third to the fourth expression we compute the whole number sum 47 + 36.

$$.47 + .36 = \frac{47}{100} + \frac{36}{100} = \frac{47 + 36}{100} = \frac{83}{100} = .83$$

PENCIL-AND-PAPER ALGORITHM   In the pencil-and-paper algorithm, the digits are aligned, tenths under tenths, hundredths under hundredths, etc., as shown in the following example. When the sum of the digits in any column is 10 or greater, regrouping (carrying) is necessary. Since .47 can be thought of as 4 tenths and 7 hundredths and .36 as 3 tenths and 6 hundredths, the sum of the 7 and the 6 in the hundredths column is 13 hundredths.

$$
\begin{array}{r}
\overset{1}{.47} \\
+.36 \\
\hline
.83
\end{array}
$$

Ten of the hundredths can be visualized as 1 tenth; in a decimal square, 10 hundredths fill one column (1/10 of a square). Also, we know that the fraction 10/100 in lowest terms is 1/10. So 1 tenth is regrouped to the tenths column, and 3 is recorded in the hundredths column, as shown above.

EXAMPLE A

Use the pencil-and-paper algorithm to compute each sum, and show the numbers that are regrouped.

1. 62.47 + 114.86   2. 4.039 + 17.18   3. .267 + .5163

Solution

1.   ¹ ¹
      62.47
   +114.86
   ───────
   177.33

2.   ¹ ¹
      4.039
   +17.180
   ───────
   21.219

3.   ¹
      .2670
   +.5163
   ──────
   .7833

Notice in solution (2) of Example A that 17.18 was replaced by 17.180. This can be done because 18 hundredths is equal to 180 thousandths. Similarly, in solution (3), .267 was replaced by .2670.

SUBTRACTION

Subtraction of decimals, like subtraction of whole numbers and fractions, can be illustrated with the take-away concept, as shown in part (a) of Figure 6.16, or with the comparison concept, as shown in part (b). The shaded area in part (a) represents .625, and the arrow shows 238 parts out of 1000 being taken away from 625 parts out of 1000. This leaves 387 parts out of 1000, which represents .387. In part (b), we can compare the shaded amounts of the squares for .75 and .40 to see that the difference is 35 parts out of 100, or .35.

Figure 6.16

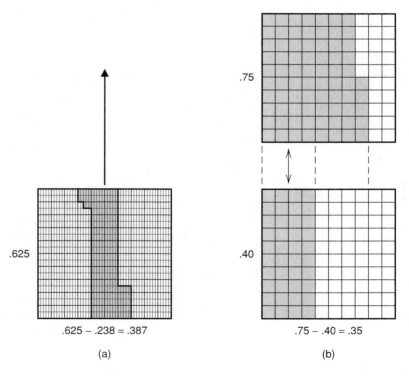

.75

.625

.625 − .238 = .387

(a)

.40

.75 − .40 = .35

(b)

PENCIL-AND-PAPER ALGORITHM   The Decimal Squares provide a visual model for computations of the difference of whole numbers of small parts. This provides a method of viewing subtraction of decimals as subtraction of whole numbers and helps to show the similarity of these operations.

In the pencil-and-paper algorithm for subtraction of decimals, the digits are aligned as they are for addition of decimals. Subtraction then takes place from right to left, with thousandths subtracted from thousandths, hundredths from hundredths, etc. When regrouping (borrowing) is necessary, it is done just as it is in subtracting whole numbers.

In the following example, .625 can be thought of as 6 tenths, 2 hundredths, and 5 thousandths and .238 as 2 tenths, 3 hundredths, and 8 thousandths. In order to subtract 8 thousandths from 5 thousandths, regrouping is needed. Since 1 hundredth equals 10 thousandths ($1/100 = 10/1000$), 1 hundredth can be regrouped from the hundredths column to increase the 5 thousandths to 15 thousandths. Then we can subtract 8 from 15 to obtain 7 in the thousandths column. A slash through the 2 indicates that it has been decreased by 1. Similarly, the 6 in the tenths column is decreased by 1 to obtain 10 more hundredths for the hundredths column ($1/10 = 10/100$). Then 3 is subtracted from 11 to obtain 8 in the hundredths column. Finally, 2 is subtracted from 5 to obtain 3 in the tenths column.

$$
\begin{array}{r}
{}^{5\ 1}\\
.\cancel{6}\cancel{2}5\\
-.238\\
\hline
.387
\end{array}
$$

The following equations show how this difference can be computed using fractions. Notice that we subtract whole numbers in going from the third to the fourth expression.

$$.625 - .238 = \frac{625}{1000} - \frac{238}{1000} = \frac{625 - 238}{1000} = \frac{387}{1000} = .387$$

EXAMPLE B

Use the pencil-and-paper algorithm to compute each difference, and show where regrouping is needed.

1. $46.32 - 18.47$ 2. $.4074 - .356$ 3. $15.06 - 2.743$

Solution

$$
\begin{array}{r}
1.\quad {}^{3\ 5\ \ 2}\\
4\cancel{6}.\cancel{3}2\\
-18.47\\
\hline
27.85
\end{array}
\qquad
\begin{array}{r}
2.\quad {}^{3}\\
.\cancel{4}074\\
-.3560\\
\hline
.0514
\end{array}
\qquad
\begin{array}{r}
3.\quad {}^{4\ \ \ 5}\\
1\cancel{5}.0\cancel{6}0\\
-\ 2.743\\
\hline
12.317
\end{array}
$$

Notice that extra zeros were appended to some of the numbers in solutions (2) and (3) of Example B in order to perform the subtraction.

MULTIPLICATION

The product of a whole number times a decimal can be illustrated by repeated addition. Each of the Decimal Squares in Figure 6.17 has 7 shaded parts. In all there are a total of $2 \times 7 = 14$ shaded parts. This is 4 more shaded parts than would be contained in a whole square, so $2 \times .7 = 1.4$.

Figure 6.17

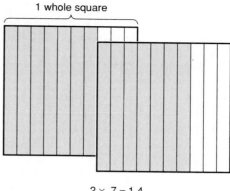

1 whole square

$2 \times .7 = 1.4$

The product of a decimal times a decimal, such as .2 × .3, can be interpreted as .2 of .3. This is illustrated in Figure 6.18 by using a Decimal Square for .3 and taking .2 of its shaded part. To do this we split the shaded part of the Decimal Square for .3 into 10 equal parts. The 6 darker parts of the square represent .2 of .3. Since each of the darker parts is 1 hundredth of a whole square, .2 × .3 = .06.

Figure 6.18

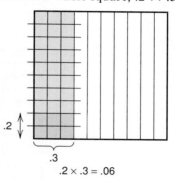

.2

.3

$.2 \times .3 = .06$

PENCIL-AND-PAPER ALGORITHM   The illustrations in Figures 6.17 and 6.18 show that computing products of decimals is closely related to computing products of whole numbers. To compute products involving decimals, we multiply the numbers as though they were whole numbers and then locate the decimal point in the product. The next example shows the product of a one-place decimal and a two-place decimal. The digits do not have to be positioned so that units are above units, tenths above tenths, etc., as they are for addition and subtraction of decimals. The number of decimal places in the answer is the total number of decimal places in the original two numbers.

$$
\begin{array}{r}
27.48 \\
\times \quad 9.2 \\
\hline
5\,4\,9\,6 \\
2\,4\,7\,3\,2 \\
\hline
2\,5\,2.8\,1\,6
\end{array}
$$

The following equations show why 9.2 × 27.48 can be computed by first computing 92 × 2748.

$$9.2 \times 27.48 = \frac{92}{10} \times \frac{2748}{100} = \frac{92 \times 2748}{10 \times 100} = \frac{252{,}816}{1000} = 252.816$$

EXAMPLE C

Use the pencil-and-paper algorithm to compute each product.

1. 3.7 × 2.5
2. 4.6 × .35
3. 1.8 × .473

Solution

1.
```
     2.5
  ×  3.7
   1 7 5
   7 5
   9.2 5
```

2.
```
     .3 5
  ×  4.6
   2 1 0
   1 4 0
   1.6 1 0
```

3.
```
     .4 7 3
  ×  1.8
   3 7 8 4
   4 7 3
   .8 5 1 4
```

The grid (or graph-paper) model that was used for multiplying whole numbers in Chapter 3 can be used to model the products of decimals. The product 2.3 × 1.7 is illustrated in Figure 6.19. The two regions of this rectangle correspond to the two partial products, 2 × 1.7 and .3 × 1.7. The colored region has 3 unit squares and 4 tenths of a unit square; the gray region has 51 hundredths of a unit square.

$$2.3 \times 1.7 = (2 + .3) \times 1.7$$
$$= (2 \times 1.7) + (.3 \times 1.7)$$
$$= 3.4 + .51$$
$$= 3.91$$

Figure 6.19

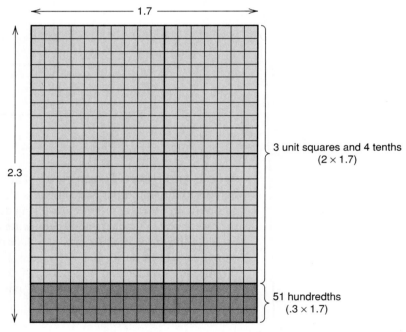

3 unit squares and 4 tenths
(2 × 1.7)

51 hundredths
(.3 × 1.7)

■ *HISTORICAL HIGHLIGHT*

One style of notation used in the sixteenth century called for the number of decimal places to be specified by a circled index to the right of the numeral. For example, 27.487 was represented as 27487 . . . ③, and 9.21 was 921 . . . ②. This notation is especially convenient for computing the product of two decimals. The whole numbers are multiplied, and then the numbers in circles are added to determine the location of the decimal point. Using our present notation, we would place the decimal point between the 3 and the 1 in this product.

$$
\begin{array}{r}
27487 \quad \ldots \ \text{③} \\
\underline{\times 921} \quad \ldots \ \text{②} \\
27487 \\
54974 \\
\underline{247383} \\
25315527 \quad \ldots \ \text{⑤}
\end{array}
$$

MULTIPLYING BY POWERS OF 10   One way to illustrate multiplication of decimals by powers of 10 is to use decimal squares and repeated addition. Figure 6.20 shows squares for .1, .01, and .001 and corresponding squares whose shaded amounts are 10 times greater. Multiplying by higher powers of 10 can be similarly represented—for example, $100 \times .1 = 10$, $100 \times .01 = 1$, etc.

Figure 6.20

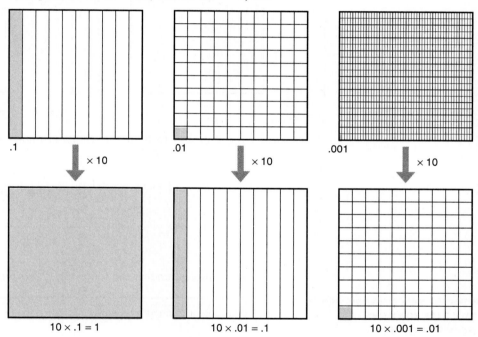

To illustrate $10 \times .165$ with Decimal Squares, we can replace each tenth by 1 whole square, each hundredth by 1 tenth of a square, and each thousandth by 1 hundredth of a square (Figure 6.21).

Figure 6.21

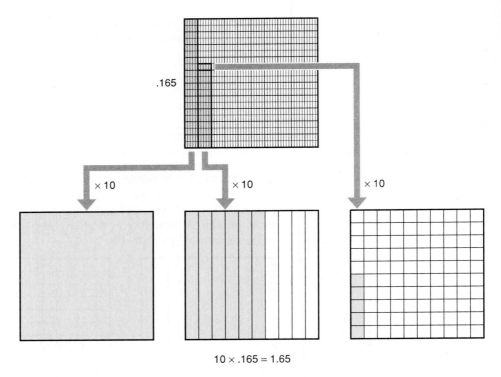

$10 \times .165 = 1.65$

Another way to show the results of multiplying by powers of 10 is to replace the decimal by a sum of fractions.

$$10 \times .165 = 10 \times \left(\frac{1}{10} + \frac{6}{100} + \frac{5}{1000} \right) = \frac{10}{10} + \frac{60}{100} + \frac{50}{1000}$$

$$= 1 + \frac{6}{10} + \frac{5}{100}$$

$$= 1.65$$

These examples suggest the following algorithm.

MULTIPLYING BY POWERS OF 10

To multiply a decimal by a power of 10, move the decimal point 1 place to the right for each power of 10.

EXAMPLE D

Compute each product.

1. $100 \times .45$ 2. 10×14.08 3. $1000 \times .32714$

Solution   1. 45   2. 140.8   3. 327.14

DIVISION

The two concepts of division, the measurement (subtractive) concept and the partitive (sharing) concept, are both useful for illustrating division with decimals. The measurement concept involves repeatedly measuring off or subtracting one amount from another. For example, to compute $.90 \div .15$, determine how many times .15 can be subtracted from .90, or how many times greater .90 is than .15. The Decimal Square in Figure 6.22 has been marked off to show that the quotient is 6.

Figure 6.22

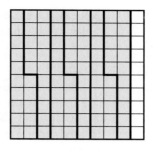

.90 ÷ .15 = 6

Figure 6.23

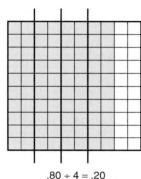

.80 ÷ 4 = .20

To illustrate the division of a decimal by a whole number, we can use the partitive concept. In this case the divisor is the number of equal parts into which a set or region is divided. The shaded part of the Decimal Square in Figure 6.23 has been divided into 4 equal parts to illustrate .80 ÷ 4. Since each part has 20 hundredths, the quotient is .20.

PENCIL-AND-PAPER ALGORITHM   The preceding examples illustrate the close relationship between division of whole numbers and division of decimals. Consider the illustration of dividing .80 by 4 in Figure 6.23. Since the Decimal Square has 80 parts shaded out of 100, we were able to think in terms of whole numbers and divide 80 by 4. Then since the quotient has 20 small squares, each one-hundredth of a whole square, the quotient .80 ÷ 4 is equal to .20. Similar steps are carried out to divide any decimal by a whole number: first divide, using the long division algorithm for whole numbers, and then place the decimal point in the quotient directly above its location in the dividend. These steps are shown here for dividing .80 by 4.

$$\begin{array}{r} .20 \\ 4\overline{)\,.80} \\ \underline{8} \\ 0 \\ \underline{0} \end{array}$$

In the long division algorithm for dividing with decimals, we never actually divide by a decimal. Before we divide, an adjustment is made so that the divisor is always a whole number. For example, the algorithm shown in Figure 6.24 indicates that we are to divide 1.504 by .32. Before dividing, however, we move the decimal points in .32 and 1.504 both 2 places to the right. This has the effect of changing the divisor and the dividend so that we are dividing 150.4 by 32.

Figure 6.24

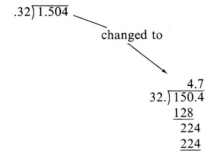

.32$\overline{)\,1.504}$

changed to

$$\begin{array}{r} 4.7 \\ 32.\overline{)\,150.4} \\ \underline{128} \\ 224 \\ \underline{224} \end{array}$$

The rule for dividing by a decimal is to count the number of decimal places in the divisor and then move the decimal points in the divisor and the dividend that many places to the right. In the previous example the decimal points in .32 and 1.504 were moved 2 places to the right because .32 has 2 decimal places. The justification for this process of shifting decimal points is illustrated in the following equations. In the second expression we use the fact that the numerator and denominator of a fraction can be multiplied by the same nonzero number to produce an equal fraction.

$$\frac{1.504}{.32} = \frac{1.504 \times 10^2}{.32 \times 10^2} = \frac{150.4}{32}$$

These equations show that the answer to 1.504 ÷ .32 is the same as that for 150.4 ÷ 32. No further adjustment is needed as long as we shift the decimal points in both the divisor and the dividend by the same amount. Thus division of a decimal by a decimal can always be carried out by dividing a decimal (or whole number) by a whole number.

EXAMPLE E

Use the long division algorithm to compute each quotient.

1. $106.82 \div 7$ 2. $.498 \div .6$ 3. $34.44 \div 1.4$

Solution

```
        15.26              .83               24.6
1.  7) 106.82       2.  .6) .498      3.  1.4) 34.44
       7                   48                 28
       36                  18                 64
       35                  18                 56
       18                                     84
       14                                     84
       42
       42
```

DIVIDING BY POWERS OF 10 In Section 6.1 we saw that a whole number can be divided by a power of 10 by relocating a decimal point. This is also true for dividing decimals by powers of 10, as Figure 6.25 shows for .37 ÷ 10. Since dividing each tenth into 10 equal parts yields 10 hundredths, the 3 tenths (30 hundredths) are replaced by 3 hundredths. Similarly, dividing each hundredth into 10 equal parts gives 10 thousandths, so the 7 hundredths are replaced by 7 thousandths.

Figure 6.25

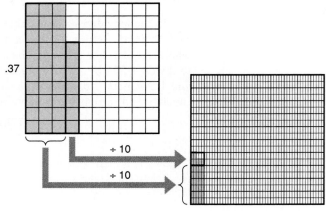

.37 ÷ 10 = .037

The effects of dividing by powers of 10 can be shown by writing the decimals in expanded form. Consider dividing .37 by 10 and 100.

$$.37 \div 10 = \left(\frac{3}{10} + \frac{7}{100}\right) \times \frac{1}{10} = \frac{3}{100} + \frac{7}{1000} = .037$$

$$.37 \div 100 = \left(\frac{3}{10} + \frac{7}{100}\right) \times \frac{1}{100} = \frac{3}{1000} + \frac{7}{10000} = .0037$$

These examples are special cases of the following algorithm.

DIVIDING BY POWERS OF 10

> To divide a decimal by a power of 10, move the decimal point 1 place to the left for each power of 10.

EXAMPLE F

Compute each quotient.

1. .35 ÷ 10   2. 4.6 ÷ 100   3. .8 ÷ 1000

Solution   1. .035   2. .046   3. .0008

ORDER OF OPERATIONS

When addition and subtraction are combined with multiplication and division, care must be taken regarding the order of operations. As in the case of whole numbers, multiplication and division are performed before addition and subtraction. Consider the following example of computing income tax. In 1988, according to Schedule Y in the Internal Revenue Service forms, the tax on earnings greater than $17,850 and less than $43,150 was $2677.50 plus .28 times the amount over $17,850. Therefore, the tax on $24,600 would be

$$\$2677.50 + .28 \times \$6750$$

On calculators that are not designed to follow the order of operations, this tax cannot be computed by entering the numbers and operations into the calculator as they appear from left to right, because .28 will be added to $2677.50. On such calculators this tax can be obtained by computing .28 × 6750 and then adding 2677.50.

EXAMPLE G

Determine the tax on the following amounts according to the 1988 Schedule Y instructions.

1. $32,672   2. $41,320

Solution
1. $2677.50 + .28 × $14,822 = $2677.50 + $4150.16 = $6827.66
2. $2677.50 + .28 × $23,470 = $2677.50 + $6571.60 = $9249.10

REPEATING DECIMALS

In Section 6.1 we saw that terminating decimals can be written as fractions whose denominators are powers of 10.

$$.47 = \frac{47}{100} \qquad 3.802 = \frac{3802}{1000} \qquad 64.3 = \frac{643}{10}$$

Repeating decimals can also be written as quotients of two integers. Consider, for example, .272727. . . . The following steps show how to obtain the fraction for this decimal.

1. Represent the decimal by x.
2. Multiply both sides of the equation by 10^2 in order to move the decimal point past the first repetend (block of 2 repeating digits).

3. Subtract the first equation from the second equation to remove the infinite repeating part of the decimal.
4. Solve for x.

$$x = .272727\ldots$$
$$100x = 27.2727\ldots$$
$$99x = 27$$
$$x = \frac{27}{99} = \frac{3}{11}$$

Similar steps for converting the repeating decimal $.22222\ldots$ are shown below.

1. Represent the decimal by x.
2. Multiply both sides of the equation by 10 to move the decimal point past the first repetend, which in this case has only 1 digit.
3. Subtract the first equation from the second equation.
4. Solve for x.

$$x = .2222\ldots$$
$$10x = 2.222\ldots$$
$$9x = 2$$
$$x = \frac{2}{9}$$

Check the preceding examples by using a calculator to divide the numerators of the fractions by their denominators. Will you obtain the original decimal in each case? (Note: Some calculators are designed for fractions and will convert decimals to fractions.*)

EXAMPLE H

Replace each repeating decimal with a quotient of two integers.

1. $.\overline{17}$ 2. $.\overline{7}$ 3. $.\overline{238}$ 4. $.1\overline{8}$

Solution

1. $\dfrac{17}{99}$ 2. $\dfrac{7}{9}$ 3. $\dfrac{238}{999}$ 4. $\dfrac{2}{11}$

PROPERTIES OF RATIONAL NUMBERS

We have seen that a rational number can always be represented as the quotient of two integers, a/b, or as a decimal. That is, there are two different types of numerals that represent rational numbers. In Section 5.3 we used the definitions of addition and multiplication of fractions to show that these operations satisfy certain number properties. These properties are restated below for the rational numbers.

Closure Properties Addition and multiplication are closed on the set of rational numbers. For any rational numbers a and b, $a + b$ and $a \times b$ are unique rational numbers.

Commutative Properties Addition and multiplication are commutative. For any rational numbers a and b, $a + b = b + a$ and $a \times b = b \times a$.

Associative Properties Addition and multiplication are associative. For any rational numbers a, b, and c, $(a + b) + c = a + (b + c)$ and $(a \times b) \times c = a \times (b \times c)$.

---

*Texas Instruments' calculator the Math Explorer is one such calculator. It is described in *It's About T.I.M.E.*, vol. 1, no. 1 (Lubbock, TX: Texas Instruments, 1989).

Identity Properties The identity for addition is zero, and the identity for multiplication is 1. For any rational number b, there are unique identity elements 0 and 1 such that $0 + b = b$ and $1 \times b = b$.

Inverse Properties For every rational number, there is a unique inverse for addition, and for every nonzero rational number, there is a unique inverse for multiplication. In other words, for any rational number b, there is a unique rational number ^-b such that $b + {}^-b = 0$; and for any rational number $c \neq 0$, there is a unique rational number $1/c$ such that $c \times 1/c = 1$.

Distributive Property Multiplication is distributive over addition. For any rational numbers a, b, and c, $a \times (b + c) = a \times b + a \times c$.

MENTAL COMPUTATION

We have seen that computations with decimals can be carried out by first computing with whole numbers and then placing decimal points. This fact can be used to compute with decimals mentally.

EXAMPLE I

Calculate each answer mentally by first computing with whole numbers and then placing decimal points.

1. .4 × .22	2. .35 + .55	3. 5 × .003
4. .345 − .2	5. .001 × 62	6. .24 ÷ .04

Solution
1. 4 × 22 = 88, and since there are a total of 3 decimal places, .4 × .22 = .088.
2. 35 + 55 = 90, so .35 + .55 = .90.
3. 5 × 3 = 15, and since there are a total of 3 decimal places, 5 × .003 = .015.
4. 345 − 200 = 145, so .345 − .2 = .145.
5. 1 × 62 = 62, and since there are a total of 3 decimal places, .001 × 62 = .062.
6. 24 ÷ 4 = 6, and since both numbers have the same number of decimal places, .24 ÷ .04 = 6.

SUBSTITUTIONS AND ADD UP   The mental calculating techniques for whole numbers can also be used for mental calculations with decimals. For example, to compute .54 − .38, we can use the add-up method:

$$.38 + .02 = .40 \text{ and } .40 + .14 = .54, \text{ so } .38 + .16 = .54$$

Thus .54 − .38 = .16.

EXAMPLE J

Calculate each answer mentally using either the substitutions or the add up techniques.

1. .37 + .28   2. .76 − .29   3. 3 × .98   4. 4.3 × 102

Solution
1. Substitution: .37 + .28 = .37 + (.20 + .08) = .57 + .08 = .65
2. Add up: .29 + .01 = .30 and .30 + .46 = .76, so .29 + .47 = .76, and .76 − .29 = .47
3. Substitution: 3 × .98 = 3 × (1 − .02) = 3 − .06 = 2.94
4. Substitution: 4.3 × 102 = 4.3 × (100 + 2) = 430 + 8.6 = 438.6

COMPATIBLE NUMBERS   Sometimes in computing products mentally it helps to recognize the decimal equivalents of a few simple fractions. Here are some that are useful:

$$.25 = \frac{1}{4}, \ .5 = \frac{1}{2}, \ .75 = \frac{3}{4}, \ .2 = \frac{1}{5}, \ .4 = \frac{2}{5}, \ .6 = \frac{3}{5}, \ .8 = \frac{4}{5}, \ .125 = \frac{1}{8}$$

EXAMPLE K

Compute each product by replacing the decimal by an equivalent fraction.

1. .25 × 800   2. .5 × .6   3. .2 × 30
4. .125 × 24   5. .6 × 45   6. .75 × 12

Solution

1. $\frac{1}{4} \times 800 = 200$ 2. $\frac{1}{2} \times .6 = .3$ 3. $\frac{1}{5} \times 30 = 6$

4. $\frac{1}{8} \times 24 = 3$ 5. $\frac{3}{5} \times \overset{9}{\cancel{45}} = 3 \times 9 = 27$ 6. $\frac{3}{\cancel{4}} \times \overset{3}{\cancel{12}} = 3 \times 3 = 9$

ESTIMATION

There are times when estimations are as helpful as exact computations. The techniques of rounding, front-end estimation, and compatible numbers are illustrated in the following examples.

ROUNDING   Rounding to obtain an estimation mentally will often save time. For example, to make a decision regarding a purchase, all we may need is a rough idea of the cost.

EXAMPLE L

Suppose you are interested in the total cost of a stereo system whose components are priced as follows: tape deck, $219.50; turntable with cartridge, $179; pair of speakers, $284; and receiver, $335.89. Estimate the cost by rounding each amount to the nearest hundred dollars.

Solution   The exact sum and the approximate sum obtained using numbers rounded to the hundreds place are shown below.

Exact sum	Approximate sum
$ 219.50	$ 200
$ 179.00	$ 200
$ 284.00	$ 300
$ 335.89	$ 300
$1018.39	$1000

Notice that the estimation in Example L can be obtained quickly by adding the leading digits if the leading digit in $179 is rounded to 2 and the leading digit in $284 is rounded to 3.

The rectangular grid in Figure 6.26 shows the reasonableness of estimating 1.7 × 3.2 by rounding each number to the nearest whole number. The gray region shows the increase due to rounding 1.7 to 2, and the colored region shows the decrease caused by rounding 3.2 to 3. Notice the 6 unit squares in the grid that illustrate the approximate product. The fact that the gray and colored regions are small compared to the total region shows that the approximate product of $2 \times 3 = 6$ is reasonably close to the actual product. The fact that the gray region is larger than the colored region shows that the approximate product is larger than the actual product.

Figure 6.26

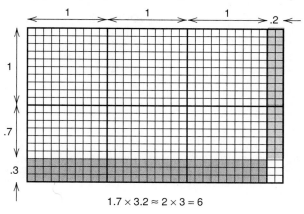

$$1.7 \times 3.2 \approx 2 \times 3 = 6$$

EXAMPLE M

Estimate each product by rounding the decimals to the nearest whole numbers.

1. 4.6×8.21 2. 10.263×5.9

Solution

1. $4.6 \times 8.21 \approx 5 \times 8 = 40$
2. $10.263 \times 5.9 \approx 10 \times 6 = 60$

FRONT-END ESTIMATION   A quick and easy method of obtaining a rough estimation is to use only the leading nonzero digit. For example,

$$762 \times .26 \approx 700 \times .2 = 140$$

EXAMPLE N

Estimate each computation mentally by using the leading nonzero digit in each number.

1. $.328 + .511$ 2. $.361 - .14$ 3. $2.6 \div .53$

Solution

1. $.328 + .511 \approx .3 + .5 = .8$
2. $.361 - .14 \approx .3 - .1 = .2$
3. $2.6 \div .53 \approx 2 \div .5 = 4$

COMPATIBLE NUMBERS   Decimals can be replaced by compatible decimals or compatible fractions—numbers that are more convenient for the given computation. For example, in the sum $3.71 + .24$, it is more convenient to use 3.7 in place of 3.71 and .3 in place of .24.

$$3.71 + .24 \approx 3.7 + .3 = 4$$

EXAMPLE O

Estimate each computation by replacing a decimal by a more compatible decimal or fraction.

1. $6 \div .26$ 2. $1.43 - .5$ 3. $.35 \times 268$
4. $2.87 + 5.15$ 5. $.19 \times 45$ 6. $27.7 - 1.8$

Solution

1. $6 \div .26 \approx 6 \div \dfrac{1}{4} = 24$

2. $1.43 - .5 \approx 1.5 - .5 = 1$

3. $.35 \times 268 \approx \dfrac{1}{3} \times 270 = 90$

4. $2.87 + 5.15 \approx 2.85 + 5.15 = 8$

5. $.19 \times 45 \approx \dfrac{1}{5} \times 45 = 9$

6. $27.7 - 1.8 \approx 27.7 - 1.7 = 26$

Whenever an exact answer is required, an estimation can serve as a guide for detecting large errors. One source of error is misplacing a decimal point when a number is entered into a calculator. Suppose, in computing $.46 \times 34.28$, you mistakenly enter 342.8. Then the calculator will show a product of

$$.46 \times 342.8 = 157.688$$

This error can be discovered by mental estimation: replace .46 by 1/2 and take half of 34.

$$.46 \times 34.28 \approx \dfrac{1}{2} \times 34 = 17$$

Since 17 is much smaller than 157.688, there is an indication of an error in the original computation.

PROBLEM-SOLVING APPLICATION

Occasionally a number is written using both decimal and fraction notation together, as in the next problem. Try solving this problem. If you need help, read as much of the following information as you need.

■ PROBLEM

Unleaded gas sells for 1.18\frac{9}{10}$ a gallon if you use a credit card. The gas pump meter is calibrated for this amount. A discount that lowers the price to 1.14\frac{9}{10}$ per gallon is offered if you choose to pay cash. If you hand the attendant a \$10 bill and ask for \$10 worth of gas, what should the dollar amount on the gas pump read after the attendant has finished?*

Understanding the Problem   These prices use hundredths of a dollar, \$1.18 and \$1.14, plus the fraction 9/10 to indicate 9/10 of a hundredth. 9/10 of a hundredth is $9/10 \times .01$, which is equal to .009. What are the two prices per gallon written as decimals? (Replace the fraction 9/10 by .9.)

Question 1

Devising a Plan   Sometimes *forming a table* with a few calculations will suggest a plan for solving the problem. The following table shows the cost of the first few gallons of gas with cash payment or with credit card payment. For example, 3 gallons of gas will cost $3 \times \$1.149 = \$3.447$ with cash and $3 \times \$1.189 = \$3.567$ with a credit card.

Number of gallons	Cash cost	Credit card cost
1	$1.149	$1.189
2	$2.298	$2.378
3	$3.447	$3.567

*"Problems of the Month," *Mathematics Teacher* 81, no. 9 (December 1988): 738.

Question 2   Since a cash payment of $3.447 will buy 3 gallons of gas (3.447 ÷ 1.149 = 3), how many gallons will a cash payment of $10 buy?

Carrying Out the Plan   Dividing 10 by 1.149 shows that you should receive approximately 8.703 gallons of gas.

$$10 \div 1.149 \approx 8.703$$

Question 3   The cost of purchasing 8.703 gallons of gas with a credit card is 8.703 × $1.189, which is the cost that will show on the gas pump. What is this amount rounded to the nearest hundredth of a dollar?

Question 4   **Looking Back**   Another way to determine the total cost that will show on the gas pump is to determine the extra cost for each gallon when a credit card is used ($1.189 − $1.149 = $.04 or 4 cents) and multiply this difference by the number of gallons, 8.703. What is this extra cost, rounded to the nearest cent? This amount added to $10 will be the dollar amount on the gas pump.

Answers to Questions 1–4
1. $1.189 and $1.149   **2.** Approximately 8.703 gallons   **3.** $10.35   **4.** $.35 (35 cents)

RELATED ACTIVITIES IN
Mathematics for Elementary Teachers: An Activity Approach, 3e

Activity Set 6.2   **Operations with Decimal Squares:** Activities with Decimal Squares illustrate decimal addition, subtraction, multiplication, and division.

Just for Fun   **Decimal Games for Operations:** Three games with Decimal Squares, one for each of the following operations: addition, subtraction, and division

---

PUZZLER   Ken bought some items at the Five and Ten store. All the items were the same price, and the total number of items was the same as the number of cents in the cost of each item. His bill was $6.25. How many items did he buy?

EXERCISES AND PROBLEMS 6.2

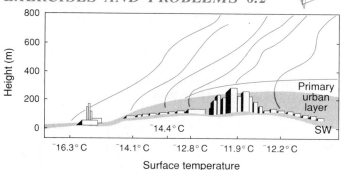

1. The above sketch is from a study showing the influence of surface temperature on air currents. These temperatures are measured on the Celsius scale.
   a. What is the highest surface temperature on this graph?
   b. What is the difference between the highest and lowest surface temperatures?

2. Describe how Decimal Squares can be used to illustrate each of the following computations.
   a. .3 + .45 = .75   **b.** .350 − .2 = .15
   c. 3 × .65 = 1.95   **d.** 10 × .37 = 3.7
   e. .1 × .2 = .02   **f.** .3 × .4 = .12
   g. .75 ÷ .05 = 15   **h.** .60 ÷ 10 = .06

3. In the example shown below, a 1 is regrouped from the hundredths column to the tenths column. This can be explained by adding the fractions for 4 hundredths and 9 hundredths to get 13 hundredths.

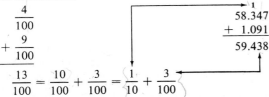

$$\frac{4}{100}$$
$$+ \frac{9}{100}$$
$$\frac{13}{100} = \frac{10}{100} + \frac{3}{100} = \frac{1}{10} + \frac{3}{100}$$

$$58.347$$
$$+ 1.091$$
$$59.438$$

In each of the following exercises, there is one column for which regrouping is needed. Mark this column and use equations to explain how the regrouping takes place.

a.   4.821
     +61.73

b.   .367
      .015
     +.509

c.   66.43
     −41.72

d.   .046
     −.018

4. Use a grid or a sketch to illustrate these products. Label the unit squares in the grid. (Copy the base ten grid from the inside cover of the book.)

a. $2.5 \times 3.7 = 9.25$ b. $1.8 \times 4.6 = 8.28$

5. Use the pencil-and-paper algorithm to compute each product or quotient. Indicate how the location of the decimal point in the product or quotient was found.

a. 3.2×7.8 b. $1.4146 \div .22$
c. $1.44 \div .3$ d. $.012 \times 9.3$

6. Calculate each product or quotient mentally. Explain your method.

a. $100 \times .65$ b. $.01 \times 362$
c. $.7 \div 10$ d. $7.2 \div 100$

7. Write each repeating decimal as a fraction.

a. $.\overline{5}$ b. $.1\overline{4}$ c. $.\overline{217}$

8. Find a decimal that is between each pair of decimals.

a. $.6$ and $.70$ .61.62 - .69   b. $.005$ and $.006$
c. 5.16 and 5.17 d. 13.99 and 14

9. Calculate each answer mentally. Explain your method.

a. $9 \times .6 = 5.4$ b. $.001 \times 5.8$ c. 3.5×99
d. $.337 - .294$ e. $4.3 + .8$ f. 2.6×101

10. Calculate each product mentally by replacing a decimal by an equivalent fraction. Show your replacement.

a. $.25 \times 48$ b. $.5 \times 40.8$ c. $5.5 \times .2$
d. $8 \times .125$ e. $.6 \times 555$ f. $.75 \times 40$

11. Obtain a front-end estimation for each sum or difference. Then obtain a second estimation by rounding to the leading digit.

a. $26.31
      47.66
      21.18
     + 14.92

b. $346.32
      260.40
      118.63
     + 752.01

c. $471.32
     − 113.81

d. $58.14
     − 16.71

12. Estimate each product by rounding the decimals to the nearest whole number. Sketch a rectangular grid that illustrates the actual product. Then sketch and shade the regions that represent the increase due to rounding up and the decrease due to rounding down. Use these regions to predict whether the estimated product is less than or greater than the actual product. (Copy the base ten grid from the inside cover of the book.)

a. 3.4×5.8 b. 6.5×2.1

13. Estimate each computation by replacing a decimal by a compatible decimal or fraction.

a. $8 \div .48$ b. $11.63 + .4$
c. $.34 \times 120$ d. $.23 \times 81.6$

14. The following is a decimal estimation exercise given to 13-year-olds as part of the National Assessment of Educational Progress.* The numbers to the right in the table below show the percentages of students who selected each response on the left.

Estimate the answer to 3.04×5.3.	Percentages
1.6	28%
16	21%
160	18%
1600	23%
I don't know	9%

a. What percent of the students selected the correct response?
b. What kinds of misunderstandings of decimal concepts might have caused students to select each of the incorrect responses?

15. *Error analysis.* Many types of errors can occur in computation, even when a student knows the basic operations with single-digit numbers. Determine which common types of errors were committed in the problems below.

a.   .4
     +.8 = 1.2
      .12

b.   99.40
     −27.86
      71.66

c.   21.8
     × .4 = 8.72
      87.2

d.   9.62
    4)38.6
      36
      26
      24
       2

*M. M. Lindquist, T. P. Carpenter, E. A. Silver, and W. Matthews, "The Third National Mathematics Assessment: Results and Implications for Elementary and Middle Schools," *Arithmetic Teacher* 31 (December 1983): 14–19.

16. Enter 273.5186 into a calculator. What single addition or subtraction can be performed on the calculator to change this number to each number below?

    a. 273.5086 − .01
    b. 273.5196
    c. 273.5786
    d. 273.5193

17. Every decimal except zero has a reciprocal. The product of a decimal times its reciprocal is 1. The reciprocal of 2.318 is 1/2.318, which in decimal form to 7 places is .4314064. Use a calculator to compute the reciprocals of the following decimals. Check your answer by multiplying each number by its reciprocal.

    a. 2.4 . 4
    b. .48
    c. .0046

18. Carry out the following computations for a person whose annual adjusted gross salary is $18,400.
    a. Find the federal tax by multiplying .15 times $18,400.
    b. Find the state tax by multiplying .029 times $18,400.
    c. Find the FICA, or social security tax, by multiplying .0751 times $18,400.
    d. Subtract the sum of the taxes in parts a through c from $18,400 to determine the after-tax amount.

19. Credit card companies have different policies and rates. One company's policies are as follows.
    a. The monthly finance charge on the amount due is determined by the following rule: .0125 times the first $500, .0095 times the next $500, and .0083 times the amount over $1000. What is the finance charge on $1200?
    b. The late charges are .05 times the amount past due. Compute the late charge on $75.25, rounding the answer to the nearest hundredth of a dollar.

20. The basic unit for measuring electricity is the kilowatt-hour (kWh). This is the amount of electrical energy required to operate a 1000-watt appliance for 1 hour. For example, it takes 1 kilowatt-hour of electricity to light 10 one-hundred-watt bulbs for 1 hour. The following table lists the average number of kilowatt-hours required to operate each appliance for 1 month.

Appliance	Kilowatt-hours per month	Cost per month
Microwave oven	15.8	____
Range with oven	97.6	____
Refrigerator	94.7	____
Frost-free refrigerator	152.4	____
Water heater	400.0	____
Radio	7.5	____
Television (black and white)	29.6	____
Television (color)	55.0	____

a. What is the sum of the kilowatt-hours required to operate these 8 appliances for 1 month?

b. At a cost of $.04 for each kilowatt-hour, what is the monthly cost of operating each of these appliances? Round your answers to the nearest penny.

c. Compute the sum of the monthly costs in part b for the 8 appliances.

d. Compute the difference in the monthly costs of electricity for a black and white television and a color television.

e. How much could a person save in 1 year by operating a regular refrigerator rather than a frost-free refrigerator?

21. The greatest record-breaking spree ever occurred in the 1976 Olympic swimming competition, when world records were set in 22 out of 26 events. In one of these events, an East German, Petra Thumer, set a world record in the 400-meter freestyle, winning in 4:09.89 (4 minutes and 9.89 seconds).

    a. Thumer's time was 1.87 seconds faster than the old record. What was the old record?

    b. A world record in the 200-meter freestyle was set by another East German, Kornelia Ender, whose time was 1:59.26. If this rate of speed could be maintained, how long would it take to swim the 400-meter event? Compare this time with Thumer's time for the 400-meter event.

    c. In the 1964 Olympics in Tokyo, Don Schollander, an American, had a winning time of 4:12.2 in the 400-meter freestyle. How many seconds faster was Thumer's time for the 400-meter event?

Featured Strategy: Making a Table

22. In the summer of 1984, Holly and Kathy traveled to Canada. Holly exchanged her U.S. money for Canadian money before leaving. For each 82 cents, she received $1 in Canadian money. Kathy exchanged her money in Canada. For each U.S. dollar, she received $1.20 in Canadian money. Who had the better rate of exchange?

    a. Understanding the Problem Let's answer a few easy questions to become more familiar with the problem. If Holly received $100 in Canadian money, what did it cost her in U.S. money? If Kathy exchanged $50 in U.S. money, how much did she receive in Canadian money?

    b. Devising a Plan It is tempting to conclude that Kathy had the better rate of exchange, because it looks as if she "gained" 20 cents while Holly only "gained" 18 cents. Let's form a table to look at the cost of the first few dollars. Complete the next line of the table.

Holly		Kathy	
U.S.	Canada	U.S.	Canada
$.82	$1	$1	$1.20
$1.64	$2	$2	$2.40

    c. Carrying Out the Plan Extend the table to determine how much it will cost each person in U.S. dollars to buy a gift in Canada for 6 Canadian dollars. Who had the better rate of exchange, Holly or Kathy?

d. Looking Back The results in the table can be used to answer questions involving larger amounts of money. For example, how much less in U.S. money would it cost Holly than Kathy to buy an item for 48 Canadian dollars?

23. Misplacing a decimal point can result in a costly mistake, as described in this newspaper article.

a. This article says that a .05-cent difference was used rather than a half-cent difference. What is the decimal for one-half of a cent?

b. If a bid for 650,000 cartons is .05 of a cent per carton higher than another bid, how many dollars greater is it?

c. If a bid for 650,000 cartons of milk is .5 of a cent per carton higher than another bid, how many dollars greater is it?

d. How much money did the school lose by misplacing the decimal point? (Hint: Use the answers from parts b and c.)

Subtraction error to cost Rochester schools $3,000

By MARK C. BUDRIS
Rochester Bureau Chief

ROCHESTER- An arithmetic error may end up costing the School Department almost $3,000 next year.

School Board Chairman Roland Roberge said Thursday night the subtraction error during a comparison of milk bids led the board to accept a bid it thought was only $298 higher than a second. It was actually $2,986 higher.

"Well, the decimal point was put in the wrong place," Roberge told the board.

He said the error was in turning a half-cent difference in milk prices into a .05-cent difference, which was then multiplied out over the more than 650,000 cartons of milk used in a year by the School Department.

LABORATORY INVESTIGATIO. √

Place 10 cards marked with the digits 0 through 9 in a container, and select them 1 at a time without replacement. As each card is selected, write its digit in one of the boxes shown at the right. As soon as each digit is selected, it must be written in a box, and no changes can be made. This activity can have several goals. One might be forming the largest possible product; another might be forming the smallest product. The activity can be carried out as a game among several people, with each player using each digit as it is selected, or as a solitaire, with one person trying to satisfy a certain goal.

Questions for Investigation

1. What is the largest product that can be formed?

2. What is the product closest to 1?

3. Once 4 digits have been written in the boxes, will the product be changed if the digits in boxes b and d are interchanged?

4. A similar activity might involve sums, differences, or quotients, and the decimals might be to hundredths or thousandths. For example, what is the difference closest to zero that can be formed by placing digits in the following boxes?

PUZZLER

How can the decimals .1, .2, .3, .4, .5, and .6 be placed in the circles so that the sum of the three numbers on each side of the triangle is .9?

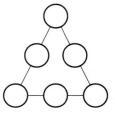

Section 6.3 RATIO, PERCENT, AND SCIENTIFIC NOTATION

■ *PROBLEM OPENER*

A jar with 140 marbles in it weighs 20 ounces, and the same jar with only 100 marbles in it weighs 16 ounces. What is the weight of the jar?

Juxtaposition of photos of planets, each taken by a different spaceship

astronomical unit

One method of measuring large distances in our solar system is to compare each distance to the distance from the earth to the sun. The distance from the earth to the sun is called an **astronomical unit.** The distance from Jupiter to the sun is 5.2 astronomical units, which means that Jupiter is 5.2 times farther from the sun than the earth is. Measuring with astronomical units involves the idea of *ratios,* which is introduced in this section.

■   *HISTORICAL HIGHLIGHT*

Isaac Newton

England's Isaac Newton (1642–1727) was born on Christmas Day of the year in which Galileo died. He was born prematurely and was so small and frail that his mother said he could have fit into a quart pot. Newton once told of how he performed his first scientific experiment as a young man. To determine the strength of the wind, he first broad-jumped with the wind and then broad-jumped against the wind. Comparing these distances with the extent of his broad jump on a calm day, he obtained the strength of the wind, expressed as so many feet strong. Newton is ranked by many as the greatest mathematician the world has produced. His *Principia,* which contains his laws of motion and describes the motions of the planets, is regarded as the greatest scientific work of all time. There are many testimonials to Newton's accomplishments, including the following lines by Alexander Pope:

> Nature and Nature's laws lay hid in night;
> God said, "Let Newton be," and all was light.*

RATIOS

Ratio is one of the most useful ideas in everyday mathematics. A ratio is a pair of positive numbers that is used to compare two sets. The idea of ratio is illustrated in Figure 6.27, which shows that for every 3 chips there are 4 tiles. This ratio is written as 3:4 (read 3 to 4) or as the fraction 3/4.

*H. W. Eves, *In Mathematical Circles* (Boston: Prindle, Weber, and Schmidt, 1969), 7–11.

Figure 6.27

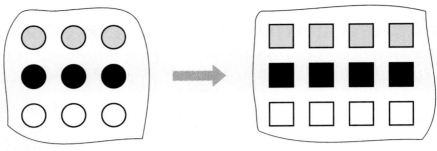

Ratio of 3 to 4

A ratio gives the relative sizes of two sets but not the actual numbers of objects. For example, the fact that the ratio of boys to girls in a certain classroom is 1 to 3 tells us that for every boy there are 3 girls, or that the number of boys is 1/3 the number of girls, but it does not tell us the number of boys or girls.

RATIO

For any two positive numbers *a* and *b*, the **ratio** of *a* to *b* is the fraction *a/b*. This ratio is also written as *a:b*.

EXAMPLE A

In 1987, for every 5 women arrested in the United States, 23 men were arrested.*

1. What is the ratio of the number of men arrested to the number of women arrested?
2. What is the ratio of the number of women arrested to the number of men arrested?

Solution

1. 23:5 or 23/5
2. 5:23 or 5/23

PROPORTIONS

Comparing the relative sizes of large sets through the use of small numbers is a common use of ratios. In Figure 6.28 there are 8 teeth on the small gear and 40 teeth on the large gear. This is a ratio of 8 to 40, and since 8/40 = 1/5 in lowest terms, the ratio of teeth on the small gear to teeth on the large gear is 1 to 5 (1:5).

Figure 6.28

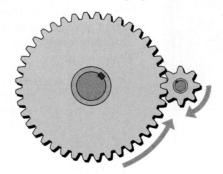

proportion

An equality of ratios is called a **proportion.** Each ratio gives rise to many pairs of equal ratios. For example, in 1986 the ratio of truck accidents to car accidents was 3

Statistical Abstract of the United States, 109th ed. (Washington, DC: U.S. Bureau of the Census, 1989), 173.

to 14. This means that for every 3 truck accidents there were 14 car accidents, for every 6 there were 28, etc., as shown in the following table. These are all equal ratios.*

Truck accidents	Car accidents
3	14
6	28
9	42
12	56
⋮	⋮

PROPORTION

For any two ratios *a/b* and *c/d,*

$$\frac{a}{b} = \frac{c}{d}$$

is called a **proportion.**

Proportions are useful in problem solving. Typically, three of the four numbers in a proportion are given and the fourth is to be found.

EXAMPLE B

If the ratio of teachers to students in a school is 1 to 18 and there are 360 students, how many teachers are there?

Solution   One method for obtaining the solution is to form a table showing equal ratios and continue this list until you reach 360 students.

Number of teachers	Number of students
1	18
2	36
3	54
4	72
⋮	⋮

Another method is to write a proportion as two equal fractions, with □ representing the number of teachers.

$$\frac{1}{18} = \frac{\square}{360}$$

By the fundamental rule for equality of fractions, the numerator and denominator of 1/18 must be multiplied by the same number to obtain an equal fraction. Since the denominator of 1/18 must be multiplied by 20 to get 360 (360 ÷ 18 = 20),

$$\frac{1 \times 20}{18 \times 20} = \frac{20}{360}$$

So the number of teachers is 20.

Statistical Abstract of the United States, 109th ed. (Washington, DC: U.S. Bureau of the Census, 1989), 598.

Historically, the rule of proportions was so valuable to merchants that it was called the *golden rule.* Often we know the price of some quantity and want to determine the price of a different amount.

EXAMPLE C

If 4.8 pounds of flour cost $1.20, how much will 6 pounds cost?

Solution   Use of the ratio of pounds to cost produces the following proportion, with □ representing the cost for 6 pounds.

$$\frac{4.8}{1.20} = \frac{6}{\square}$$

By the rule for equality of fractions, we obtain

$$4.8 \times \square = 1.20 \times 6$$
$$\square = \frac{1.20 \times 6}{4.8}$$
$$\square = 1.5$$

Thus the cost of 6 pounds is $1.50.

PERCENT

percent

The idea of percent is an outgrowth of the use of fractions with denominators of 100. The word **percent** comes from the Latin *per centum,* meaning *out of a hundred.* Percent was first used in the fifteenth century for computing interest, profits, and losses. Currently it has much broader applications, as illustrated by the news clippings in Figure 6.29.

Figure 6.29

Take advantage of the new V.A. financing now available at Greenbrook at only 8% interest

Percents are ways of representing fractions with denominators of 100. For example, if a credit card company charges 15% interest, it means that in addition to paying the amount owed, the card holder must pay 15/100 of the amount owed. Diagrams are one method of gaining an understanding of percents. A 10 by 10 grid with 100 equal parts is a common model in elementary school texts for illustrating decimals (see Figure 6.30). Decimal Squares for tenths, hundredths, and thousandths will be used in this section to describe decimals.

Figure 6.30

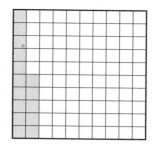

15%

EXAMPLE D

Describe a Decimal Square to represent each percent.

1. 90%   2. 9%   3. 35.5%

Solution

1. 90 parts shaded out of 100 or 9 parts shaded out of 10
2. 9 parts shaded out of 100
3. 35.5 parts shaded out of 100 or 355 parts shaded out of 1000

Notice the similarity between the percent symbol, %, and the numeral 100. This is helpful in remembering how to replace a percent by a fraction or a decimal. First, drop the percent symbol and write the percent as a fraction with a denominator of 100. Then, to obtain a decimal, divide the numerator by the denominator.

EXAMPLE E

Write each percent as a decimal. Then describe a Decimal Square that represents or approximately represents the decimal.

1. 42%   2. 6.8%   3. $21\frac{3}{4}$%   4. 100%

Solution

1. $42\% = \frac{42}{100} = .42$ (42 parts shaded out of 100)

2. $6.8\% = \frac{6.8}{100} = .068$ (between 6 and 7 parts shaded out of 100 or 68 parts shaded out of 1000)

3. $21\frac{3}{4}\% = \frac{21\frac{3}{4}}{100} = \frac{21.75}{100} = .2175$ (between 21 and 22 parts shaded out of 100 or between 217 and 218 parts shaded out of 1000)

4. $100\% = \frac{100}{100} = 1$ (100 parts shaded out of 100)

Example E suggests a shortcut for writing a percent as a decimal: *drop the percent symbol and divide by 100.* Some calculators with percent keys operate in this manner. That is, if the $\boxed{4}$, $\boxed{2}$, and $\boxed{\%}$ keys are pressed, .42 will show in the display. To write a decimal as a percent, reverse the process: write the decimal first as a fraction with a denominator of 100 and then as a percent.

EXAMPLE F

Describe the Decimal Square for each decimal, and then write the decimal as a percent.

1. .07   2. .647   3. 3.25   4. .008

Solution

1. 7 parts shaded out of 100: $.07 = \dfrac{7}{100} = 7\%$

2. 647 parts shaded out of 1000: $.647 = \dfrac{647}{1000} = \dfrac{64.7}{100} = 64.7\%$

3. 3 whole squares and 25 parts shaded out of 100: $3.25 = \dfrac{325}{100} = 325\%$

4. 8 parts shaded out of 1000: $.008 = \dfrac{8}{1000} = \dfrac{.8}{100} = .8\%$

Similarly, to write a fraction as a percent, first write it as a fraction with a denominator of 100. To accomplish this we can use proportions. For example, to write 1/6 as a percent, first find the numerator of a fraction whose denominator is 100.

$$\frac{1}{6} = \frac{\square}{100}$$

To obtain such a fraction, we must multiply the numerator and denominator of 1/6 by the same number. Since $100 \div 6 = 16\frac{2}{3}$, the numerator of 1/6 must be multiplied by $16\frac{2}{3}$. Thus

$$\frac{1}{6} = \frac{16\frac{2}{3}}{100} = 16\frac{2}{3}\%$$

EXAMPLE G

Write each fraction as a percent.

1. $\dfrac{1}{5}$ 2. $\dfrac{1}{8}$ 3. $\dfrac{1}{3}$

Solution

1. $\dfrac{1}{5} = \dfrac{20}{100} = 20\%$

2. $\dfrac{1}{8} = \dfrac{12\frac{1}{2}}{100} = 12\frac{1}{2}\%$

3. $\dfrac{1}{3} = \dfrac{33\frac{1}{3}}{100} = 33\frac{1}{3}\%$

CALCULATIONS WITH PERCENTS

Calculations with percents fall into three categories:

1. Given the *whole* and the *percent*, find the *part*.
2. Given the *whole* and the *part*, find the *percent*.
3. Given the *percent* and the *part*, find the *whole*.

WHOLE AND PERCENT   When the whole and the percent are given, the part can be found by multiplying the percent times the whole. For example, suppose 12% of the 250 teachers in a school have master's degrees. The word *of* is a clue that the percent is acting like a multiplier and that the number of teachers with master's degrees is found by multiplying .12 times 250.

$$12\% \text{ of } 250 = .12 \times 250 = 30$$

Figure 6.31 illustrates the information in the preceding problem. The square is 12% shaded, and the whole square represents 250 teachers. This figure suggests another way to solve the problem. If the whole square represents 250 teachers, then each small hundredths square represents 250/100 = 2.5 teachers. So the number of teachers represented by 12 small squares is 12 × 2.5 = 30.

Figure 6.31

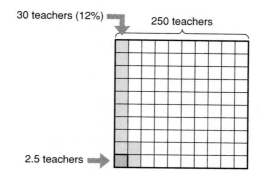

EXAMPLE H

A survey of football players revealed that 20% of 1180 players had knee injuries. How many players had knee injuries?

Solution   20% of 1180 = .20 × 1180 = 236. So 236 players had knee injuries.

PART AND WHOLE   When the part and the whole are given, the percent can be found by writing the fraction for the part of the whole and then writing this fraction as a percent. For example, if 8 of a radio station's top 40 songs for a given week are new songs, then 8/40 of the songs are new. To represent 8/40 as a percent, we can divide 8 by 40 to obtain a decimal and then replace the decimal by a percent.

$$8 \div 40 = .2 \quad \text{and} \quad .2 = \frac{20}{100} = 20\%$$

Figure 6.32 provides a visual approach to solving the preceding problem: 8 is what percent of 40? If we let the total square represent 40, then, since the square has 100 parts, each part represents 40 ÷ 100 = .4. Thus, 2 small squares represent .8, 10 small squares represent 4, and 20 small squares represent 8. Since 20 squares out of 100 is 20%, 8 is 20% of 40.

Figure 6.32

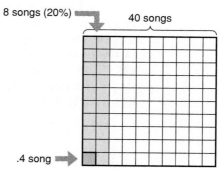

In some cases it is necessary to compare one number to a smaller one. For example, since 90 is 2 times 45, it is 200% of 45.

$$\frac{90}{45} = 2 = \frac{200}{100} = 200\%$$

EXAMPLE I

Determine the following percents.

1. 120 is what percent of 80?
2. 33 is what percent of 11?
3. 60 is what percent of 50?

Solution

1. 120 is 150% of 80: 120/80 = 1.5 = 150/100 = 150%
2. 33 is 300% of 11: 33/11 = 3 = 300/100 = 300%
3. 60 is 120% of 50: 60/50 = 1.2 = 120/100 = 120%

EXAMPLE J

1. If $880 of a $2000 loan has been paid off, what percent has been paid off?
2. If a company's profits were 1.4 billion in 1990 and 1.8 billion in 1991, the 1991 profits were what percent of the 1990 profits?

Solution

1. The fraction of the loan that has been paid off is 880/2000, which equals .44. So 44% of the loan has been paid off.
2. 1.8 is approximately 1.29 times 1.4: 1.8/1.4 ≈ 1.29 = 129/100 = 129%

PERCENT AND PART   When the percent and the part are given, the whole can be found by using a proportion. Suppose a down payment of $14,400 is required for a home loan and this down payment is 18% of the loan. Then the amount of the loan is the missing denominator in the following proportion.

$$\frac{\text{Part}}{\text{Whole}} = \frac{18}{100} = \frac{14,400}{\square}$$

Using the rule for equality of fractions, we can write this equation as

$$18 \times \square = 14,400 \times 100$$
$$\square = \frac{1,440,000}{18}$$
$$\square = 80,000$$

So the amount of the loan is $80,000.

The preceding problem can be illustrated as shown in Figure 6.33. The Decimal Square is 18% shaded, and the shaded amount represents the $14,400 down payment. This figure helps to illustrate the proportion we used to solve the problem. The ratio of the shaded part to the whole is the ratio of 18 to 100, which is equal to the ratio of 14,400 to the total cost. Figure 6.33 also suggests another way to solve the problem. If 18 of the small hundredths squares represent $14,400, then each small square represents $14,400 ÷ 18 = $800. So the total of 100 squares represents 100 × $800 = $80,000.

Figure 6.33

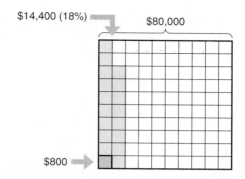

$14,400 (18%) $80,000

$800

EXAMPLE K

Nebraska has 352 one-room schoolhouses. This number is 44% of the total number of one-room schoolhouses in the United States. How many one-room schoolhouses are there in the United States?

Solution The ratio of 44% (44/100) is equal to the ratio of 352 to the total number of one-room schoolhouses.

$$\frac{44}{100} = \frac{352}{\square}$$

Using the rule for equality of fractions, we can rewrite the above equation as

$$44 \times \square = 352 \times 100$$
$$\square = \frac{35,200}{44}$$
$$\square = 800$$

So there are 800 one-room schoolhouses in the United States.

The same procedure can be used for setting up a proportion when the percent is greater than 100. Suppose we know that after a physical exertion test a person's pulse rate is 144 beats per minute, and this is 180% of the person's resting pulse rate. The ratio of 180% (180/100) is equal to the ratio of 144 to the resting pulse rate.

$$\frac{180}{100} = \frac{144}{\square}$$

Using the rule for equality of fractions, we find that

$$180 \times \square = 144 \times 100$$
$$\square = \frac{14,400}{180}$$
$$\square = 80$$

So the person's resting pulse rate is 80 beats per minute.

EXAMPLE L

The school population for the new year in a certain town is 135% of the school population for the previous year. If the new population is 378, how many students did the school have the previous year?

Solution The ratio of 135% (135/100) is equal to the ratio of the new population to the previous year's population.

$$\frac{135}{100} = \frac{378}{\Box}$$

$$135 \times \Box = 378 \times 100$$

$$\Box = \frac{37,800}{135}$$

$$\Box = 280$$

Thus there were 280 students the previous year.

MENTAL CALCULATIONS WITH PERCENTS

The frequent occurrence of percents in everyday life has led people to adopt certain techniques for mental calculations. Two of these, *compatible numbers* and *substitutions,* are introduced here.

COMPATIBLE NUMBERS Certain percents are convenient for calculations. One of these is 10%, because multiplying by .10 is just a matter of moving a decimal point. For example, 10% of 16.50 = .10 × 16.50 = 1.65. Once we know 10% of a number, we can use that amount to determine other percents such as 5%, 15%, 20%, 25%, and 40%. The relationship of these percents to 10% is illustrated in Figure 6.34.

Figure 6.34

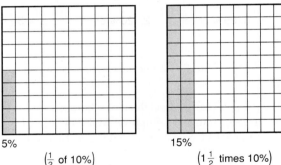

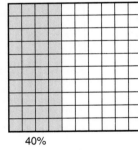

5%
$\left(\frac{1}{2}\text{ of }10\%\right)$

15%
$\left(1\frac{1}{2}\text{ times }10\%\right)$

40%
(4 times 10%)

EXAMPLE M

A store is having a sale and prices are being discounted 15%, 20%, and 25%. Calculate the amount of each discount mentally.

1. 15% of $82   2. 20% of $31.40   3. 25% of $30

Solution

1. Since 10% of $82 = $8.20 and 5% is half as much, 15% of $82 = $8.20 + $4.10 = $12.30.
2. Since 10% of $31.40 = $3.14 and 20% is twice as much, 20% of $31.40 = $6.28.
3. Since 10% of $30 = $3 and 25% = 10% + 10% + 5%, 25% of $30 = $3 + $3 + $1.50 = $7.50.

For some computations it is convenient to replace a percent by a fraction. A few percents and their fractions are shown below; three of these are illustrated in Figure 6.35.

$$10\% = \frac{1}{10} \qquad 12\frac{1}{2}\% = \frac{1}{8} \qquad 20\% = \frac{1}{5} \qquad 25\% = \frac{1}{4} \qquad 33\frac{1}{3}\% = \frac{1}{3}$$

$$50\% = \frac{1}{2} \qquad 66\frac{2}{3}\% = \frac{2}{3} \qquad 75\% = \frac{3}{4} \qquad 80\% = \frac{4}{5}$$

Figure 6.35

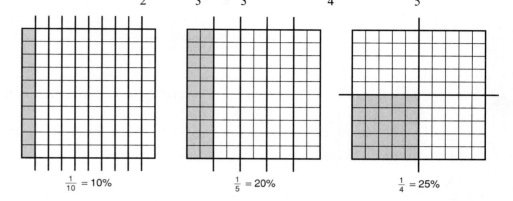

$$\frac{1}{10} = 10\% \qquad\qquad \frac{1}{5} = 20\% \qquad\qquad \frac{1}{4} = 25\%$$

EXAMPLE N

Calculate each percentage mentally by first replacing the percent by a fraction.

1. 25% of 88   2. 20% of 55   3. $33\frac{1}{3}$% of 45   4. 75% of 24

Solution

1. 25% of 88 $= \dfrac{1}{4} \times 88 = 22$

2. 20% of 55 $= \dfrac{1}{5} \times 55 = 11$

3. $33\frac{1}{3}$% of 45 $= \dfrac{1}{3} \times 45 = 15$

4. 75% of 24 $= \dfrac{3}{4} \times 24 = 18$

SUBSTITUTIONS   Some problems allow us to replace a percent by a sum or difference of two percents. For example, to find 90% of 140, we can use the fact that 90% = 100% − 10%.

$$90\% \text{ of } 140 = 100\% \text{ of } 140 - 10\% \text{ of } 140 = 140 - 14 = 126$$

EXAMPLE O

Calculate each percentage mentally by replacing the percent by a sum or difference of two more convenient percents.

1. 95% of 200   2. 110% of 430   3. 45% of 18

Solution

1. 95% of 200 = 100% of 200 − 5% of 200 = 200 − 10 = 190 (Note: 10% of 200 = 20 so 5% of 200 is half of 20.)
2. 110% of 430 = 100% of 430 + 10% of 430 = 430 + 43 = 473
3. 45% of 18 = 50% of 18 − 5% of 18 = 9 − .9 = 8.1 (Note: 10% of 18 = 1.8 so 5% = .9.)

ESTIMATION

COMPATIBLE NUMBERS   Sometimes it is convenient to replace a given percent by an approximation, which may be either another percent or a fraction. For example, percents such as 47%, 52%, and 48%, which are close to 50%, may be replaced by 1/2; percents such as 34%, 35%, and 33%, which are close to $33\frac{1}{3}\%$, are sometimes replaced by 1/3; etc. At times both numbers in a calculation are replaced by approximations to obtain compatible numbers. For example, 24% of $18.75 may be replaced by 1/4 of $20, because 1/4 and $20 are compatible numbers that are approximately equal to the original numbers.

EXAMPLE P

Estimate each percentage mentally by replacing one or both numbers by compatible numbers.

    1. 34% of 62.4   2. 47% of $87.62   3. 8% of 65

Solution   Here are some possible solutions.

    1. $\frac{1}{3} \times 60 = 20$, or $\frac{1}{3} \times 63 = 21$

    2. $\frac{1}{2}$ of $88 = $44, or $\frac{1}{2}$ of $80 = $40 (Note: Since 47% is increased to 1/2, $87.62 is decreased to $80 for the second estimation.)

    3. 10% of 65 = 6.5 or 10% of 60 = 6

When a percent is written as a fraction, replacing the numerator and denominator by compatible numbers often provides a close estimation. For example, when answers to 47 out of 60 questions on a test are correct, 47/60 is the fraction of correct answers. Here are two possibilities for expressing this fraction as a percent:

$$\frac{47}{60} \approx \frac{48}{60} = \frac{8}{10} = 80\%$$

$$\frac{47}{60} \approx \frac{49}{63} = \frac{7}{9} = \frac{77}{99} \approx \frac{77}{100} = 77\%$$

EXAMPLE Q

Determine approximate percents by replacing the numerators and/or denominators by compatible numbers.

    1. $\frac{16}{62}$ 2. $\frac{300}{2490}$ 3. $\frac{42}{87}$

Solution   1. $\frac{16}{62} \approx \frac{15}{60} = \frac{1}{4} = 25\%$ or $\frac{16}{62} \approx \frac{16}{64} = \frac{2}{8} = \frac{1}{4} = 25\%$

    2. $\frac{300}{2490} \approx \frac{300}{2500} = \frac{3}{25} = \frac{12}{100} = 12\%$

    3. $\frac{42}{87} \approx \frac{1}{2} = 50\%$

SCIENTIFIC NOTATION

Large and small numbers are sometimes written using powers of 10. For example, some computers can perform 400,000,000 calculations a second. Using a power of 10, we can write

$$400{,}000{,}000 = 4 \times 100{,}000{,}000 = 4 \times 10^8$$

Decimals that are less than 1 can be written using negative powers of 10. Consider the average human hair, which is approximately .003 of an inch thick.

$$.003 = \frac{3}{1000} = \frac{3}{10^3} = 3 \times 10^{-3}$$

because $1/10^3 = 10^{-3}$. In general, for any numbers x and n, with $x \neq 0$,

$$\frac{1}{x^n} = x^{-n}$$

scientific notation
mantissa
characteristic

Any positive number can be written as the product of a number from 1 to 10 and a power of 10. This method of writing numbers is called **scientific notation.** The number between 1 and 10 is called the **mantissa,** and the exponent of 10 is called the **characteristic.** The product 2.77×10^{12} is a number in scientific notation. The mantissa is 2.77, and the characteristic is 12.

EXAMPLE R

The following table gives five examples of numbers written in scientific notation. Fill in the missing numbers in the last two rows.

	Positional numeration	Scientific notation
Years since age of dinosaurs	150,000,000	1.5×10^8
Seconds of half-life of U-238	142,000,000,000,000,000	1.42×10^{17}
Wave length of gamma ray (m)	.0000000000003048	3.048×10^{-13}
Size of viruses (cm)	.000000914	_____
Orbital velocity of earth (kph)	_____	4.129×10^4

Solution $.000000914 = 9.14 \times 10^{-7}$; $4.129 \times 10^4 = 41{,}290$

Some calculators have a button for displaying numbers in scientific notation. The button may be labeled $\boxed{\text{EE}}$ or $\boxed{\text{EEX}}$ or something similar, where E stands for exponent. If 749,300,000 is entered into such a calculator and the buttons for scientific notation and equality are pressed, the mantissa, 7.493, and the characteristic (or exponent), 8, will appear in the display to denote 7.493×10^8 (Figure 6.36). The base, 10, will not appear in the display.

Figure 6.36

Numbers written in scientific notation are especially convenient for computing. The graph in Figure 6.37 shows increases in the world's population. It wasn't until 1825 that the population reached 1 billion (1×10^9); by 1990 it was 5.1 billion (5.1

$\times$ 10⁹). Since there are about 2.7 $\times$ 10³ square yards of cultivated land per person, the total amount of cultivated land worldwide, in square yards, is

$$(5.1 \times 10^9) \times (2.7 \times 10^3)$$

Rearranging these numbers and using the rule for adding exponents, we can rewrite this product as

$$(5.1 \times 2.7) \times 10^{12}$$

Finally, we compute the product of the mantissas (5.1 $\times$ 2.7) and write the answer in scientific notation:

$$(5.1 \times 2.7) \times 10^{12} = 13.77 \times 10^{12} = 1.377 \times 10^{13}$$

So there are approximately 1.377 $\times$ 10¹³, or 13,770,000,000,000, square yards of cultivated land in the world. Notice in the preceding equation that 13.77 is not between 1 and 10, so we divide by 10 to obtain the mantissa of 1.377 and then increase the characteristic (the power of 10) from 12 to 13. Another advantage of computing in scientific notation is that the products of the mantissas usually can be computed on a calculator without exceeding the capacity of the display.

Figure 6.37

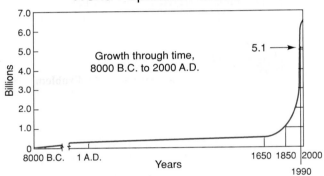

The preceding example illustrates the method of computing products of numbers in scientific notation: (1) multiply the mantissas (numbers from 1 to 10) and (2) add the characteristics (powers of 10).

EXAMPLE S

Compute each product and write the answer in scientific notation.

1. $(6.3 \times 10^4) \times (5.21 \times 10^3)$
2. $(1.55 \times 10^4) \times (8.7 \times 10^{-6})$

Solution

1. $(6.3 \times 5.21) \times (10^4 \times 10^3) = 32.823 \times 10^7$, but since 32.823 is not between 1 and 10, a requirement for scientific notation, we replace it by 3.2823 $\times$ 10.

$$32.823 \times 10^7 = 3.2823 \times 10 \times 10^7 = 3.2823 \times 10^8$$

2. $(1.55 \times 8.7) \times (10^4 \times 10^{-6}) = 13.485 \times 10^{-2}$, but since 13.485 is not between 1 and 10, we replace it by 1.3485 $\times$ 10.

$$13.485 \times 10^{-2} = 1.3485 \times 10 \times 10^{-2} = 1.3485 \times 10^{-1}$$

Calculators that can display numbers in scientific notation will automatically display numbers in this form whenever the numbers are too large or too small for the display. Suppose, for example, you want to compute 473,200 times 639,000, which is 302,374,800,000. If your calculator does not represent numbers in scientific notation, the display will be exceeded and a flashing light or some other type of signal will appear. A calculator with scientific notation will represent this product, which equals 3.023748×10^{11}, as shown in Figure 6.38.

Figure 6.38

Similarly, if a number is too small for the standard display, it will be represented by a mantissa and a negative power of 10. Consider the product .0004 × .000006, which is .0000000024, or 2.4×10^{-9} in scientific notation. If you compute this on a calculator whose display has only 8 places for digits and no scientific notation, it will show a product of 0. On a calculator with scientific notation, a mantissa of 2.4 and a characteristic of $^-9$ will appear in the display, as shown in Figure 6.39.

Figure 6.39

$$\boxed{2.4 \qquad ^-9}$$

PROBLEM-SOLVING APPLICATION

■ PROBLEM

Two elementary school classes have equal numbers of students. The ratio of girls to boys is 3 to 1 in one class and 2 to 1 in the other. If the two classes are combined into one large class, what is the new ratio of girls to boys?

Understanding the Problem   To obtain a better understanding of the ratios, let's select a particular number of students and compute the number of girls and boys. Suppose there are 24 students in each class. The class with the 3 to 1 ratio has 18 girls and 6 boys. How many girls and how many boys are in the class with the 2 to 1 ratio?

Question 1

Devising a Plan   One approach is to *make a drawing* representing the two classes and indicate their ratios. The following figures illustrate the girl-to-boy ratios in the two classes and show that each class is the same size. Why can't we conclude from these figures that the ratio of girls to boys in the combined class is 5 to 2?

Question 2

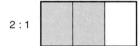   

Carrying Out the Plan   To obtain information from the sketches of the classes, we need to subdivide the parts so that each figure has parts of the same size. The smallest number of such parts is 12, as shown in the following figure. The combined class will have 24 equal parts. What is the ratio of girls to boys in the combined class?

Question 3

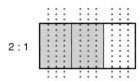   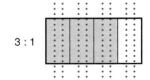

Looking Back   Earlier we chose 24 students per class as a numerical example and from this established girl-to-boy ratios of 18 to 6 and 16 to 8. Do these numbers produce the same ratio for the combined class as that obtained from the sketches?

Question 4

Answers to Questions 1–4

1. 16 girls and 8 boys

2. Because the parts of the sketches are different sizes

3. 17 to 7

4. Yes; the ratio of 34 to 14 is equal to the ratio of 17 to 7.

RELATED ACTIVITIES IN
Mathematics for Elementary Teachers: An Activity Approach, 3e

Activity Set 6.3   **Grid Model for Percent:** A grid model introduces percents as parts out of 100 and is used to illustrate and solve percent problems.

Just for Fun   **Number Search:** Finding equal percents, decimals, and fractions in a newspaper collage

EXERCISES AND PROBLEMS 6.3

In this morning's rush hour, empty seats outnumbered full seats 4 to 1.

In a city the size of Los Angeles, that's 9,000,000 empty seats in cars jammed up on the freeways.
Think about that while you're sitting in traffic.

Share the ride with a friend. It sure beats driving alone.

Presented as a public service by
Eugene Register-Guard
Daily and Sunday

1. The public service ad above points out the need for carpooling to reduce traffic.
   a. According to this ad, what fraction of the car seats are empty during morning rush hour?
   b. In a city the size of Los Angeles, there would be 9,000,000 empty seats during rush hour. How many seats would be filled?

2. a. The ratio of apples to oranges in a gift box is 3 to 2, and there are 18 apples. How many oranges are there?
   b. If the ratio of cars to trucks in a parking lot is 7 to 2 and there are 26 trucks, how many cars are there?
   c. The ratio of U.S. citizens to noncitizens among patent applicants during a given period was 11 to 3. If 407 patent applications were received from U.S. citizens, how many were received from noncitizens?

3. Answer each question, assuming that the rate for the smaller quantity and the rate for the larger quantity are the same. Round each answer to the nearest hundredth of a dollar.
   a. If 1.5 pounds of fish cost $3.12, how much do 3.5 pounds cost?
   b. If 8 ounces of yarn cost $2.66, what is the cost for 20 ounces?
   c. If 10 pounds of nails cost $4.38, what is the cost of 3.2 pounds of the same type of nail?

4. Write each percent as a decimal, and describe a 10 by 10 Decimal Square to illustrate the percent.
   a. 7%   b. 18.2%   c. $34\frac{1}{4}$%

5. Describe a Decimal Square for each decimal, and write the decimal as a percent.
   a. .60   b. .06
   c. .256   d. .003

6. Write each fraction as a percent.
   a. $\frac{7}{25}$ b. $\frac{1}{8}$ c. $\frac{5}{12}$

7. Determine each answer to the nearest tenth.
   a. What is 27% of 160?
   b. 40 is what percent of 200?
   c. If 10% of a number is 4, what is the number?
   d. What is 140% of 65?
   e. 75 is what percent of 50?

8. Determine each answer to the nearest tenth.
   a. What percent of 20 is 14?
   b. What is 12% of 60?
   c. If 12 is 8% of some number, what is the number?
   d. 36.25 is what percent of 14.5?

9. Calculate each percent mentally and explain your method.
   a. 15% of $42   b. 25% of 28
   c. $33\frac{1}{3}$% of 15   d. 5% of $42.60
   e. 10% of $128.50   f. 75% of 32
   g. 90% of $60   h. 110% of 80

10. Estimate each percentage mentally by replacing one or both numbers by compatible numbers. Show your replacements.
    a. 51% of 78.3   b. 23% of 1182
    c. 11% of $19.99   d. 32% of $612.40

11. Calculate approximate percents for the fractions mentally by replacing the numerators or denominators by compatible numbers. Show your replacements.
    a. $\frac{14}{27}$ b. $\frac{9}{38}$ c. $\frac{7}{32}$
    d. $\frac{2}{19}$ e. $\frac{408}{1210}$ f. $\frac{100}{982}$

12. Compute each percent to the nearest tenth of a percent.

a. A down payment of $200 is what percent of the cost of $1460?

b. A 1992 cost of $3.63 is what percent of a 1990 cost of $2.75?

c. A school has collected $744, which is 62% of its goal. What is the total amount of the school's goal?

d. During a flu epidemic, 17% of a school's 283 students were absent on a particular day. How many students were absent?

13. Compute each percent to the nearest tenth of a percent and each dollar amount to the nearest hundredth of a dollar.

a. With a discount of 70%, the cost of a bracelet is $17.99. What is the price before the discount?

b. A cordless intercom system is marked down from $99.99 to 79.99. What percent is the intercom discounted?

c. A teacher's 1991 salary is 107.5% of her 1990 salary. If the 1990 salary is $32,000, what is the 1991 salary?

d. If 6 of the 28 students in a class did not enroll in the school's insurance plan, what percent did enroll in the plan?

14. Write the following numbers in scientific notation.

a. Size of minute insects, in inches = .013

b. Length of a day, in seconds = 86,400

c. Number of years since earth's formation = 3,250,000,000

15. Write the following numbers in positional numeration.

a. Wavelength of X-rays, in inches = 1.2×10^{-9}

b. Approximate length of solar year, in seconds = 3.15569×10^{7}

c. Total number of possible bridge hands = 6.35×10^{11}

16. Write the answers in scientific notation.

a. The velocity of a jet plane is 1.1×10^{3} mph, and the escape velocity of a rocket from earth is 22.7 times faster. Find the rocket's velocity by computing $1.1 \times 10^{3} \times 22.7$.

b. The earth travels 6.21×10^{8} miles around the sun each year in approximately 9×10^{3} hours. Compute $(6.21 \times 10^{8}) \div (9 \times 10^{3})$ to determine the earth's speed in miles per hour.

c. A light-year, the distance that light travels in 1 year, is 5.868×10^{13} miles. The sun is 2.7×10^{4} light-years from the center of our galaxy. Find this distance in miles by computing $5.868 \times 10^{13} \times 2.7 \times 10^{4}$.

d. At one point in *Voyager 1*'s journey to Jupiter, its radio waves traveled 4.62×10^{8} miles to reach the earth. These waves travel at a speed of 3.1×10^{5} miles per second. Compute $(4.62 \times 10^{8}) \div (3.1 \times 10^{5})$ to determine the number of seconds it took these signals to reach the earth.

17. One method of determining which of two packages is the better buy is to determine the price per unit of both packages. For example, each ounce of mix in the large box shown in the following figure costs 3.5 cents ($168¢ \div 48 = 3.5¢$).

a. What is the cost per ounce for the small package?

b. Which is the better buy?

c. If the large box has enough mix for 115 four-inch pancakes, how many four-inch pancakes can be made from the small box?

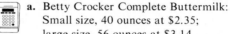

48 ounces	32 ounces
for $1.68	for $1.26

18. Which package in each of the following pairs is the better buy?

a. Betty Crocker Complete Buttermilk:
Small size, 40 ounces at $2.35;
large size, 56 ounces at $3.14

b. Bisquick Variety Baking Mix:
Small size, 20 ounces at $1.17;
large size, 32 ounces at $1.99

c. Plastic tape:
Small roll, 15.2 yards for 69 cents;
large roll, 23.6 yards for $1.60

19. The table below shows the numbers of students and teachers in public elementary schools in several states. The student-teacher ratio for each state is the number of students divided by the number of teachers.

a. Compute these ratios to the nearest tenth.

b. Which state has the best student-teacher ratio?

c. Which has the poorest?

State	Number of teachers	Number of students	Student-teacher ratio
Alabama	17,300	528,000	_____
Florida	38,200	1,042,000	_____
Hawaii	4,700	110,000	_____
Iowa	15,200	351,000	_____
Maine	6,900	153,000	_____
Missouri	24,700	567,000	_____
Oregon	14,900	319,000	_____
Wyoming	3,100	70,000	_____

20. The following figure shows the percentages of injuries to different parts of the body revealed in a study of 1180 injured professional football players. Determine the number of players with each of the following types of injuries, rounded to the nearest whole number.

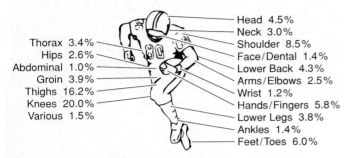

Thorax 3.4%
Hips 2.6%
Abdominal 1.0%
Groin 3.9%
Thighs 16.2%
Knees 20.0%
Various 1.5%

Head 4.5%
Neck 3.0%
Shoulder 8.5%
Face/Dental 1.4%
Lower Back 4.3%
Arms/Elbows 2.5%
Wrist 1.2%
Hands/Fingers 5.8%
Lower Legs 3.8%
Ankles 1.4%
Feet/Toes 6.0%

National Football League 1974 Injuries

a. Head injuries   **b.** Shoulder injuries

c. Injuries to the lower back   **d.** Injuries to feet and toes

21. The cost of a $9.85 item that is being discounted 12% can be determined by subtracting 12% of $9.85 from $9.85. The following equations show that the cost of this item can also be found by taking 88% of $9.85. What number properties are used in the first two of these equations?

$$9.85 - (.12 \times 9.85) = (1 \times 9.85) - (.12 \times 9.85)$$
$$= (1 - .12) \times 9.85$$
$$= .88 \times 9.85$$

Use one of these two methods to compute the discounted cost of each of the following items.
a. Portable typewriter, $209.50 (15% off)
b. Backpacker sleeping bag, $153.95 (20% off)
c. Snowshoes, $86 (28% off)

22. The total cost of a $15.70 item plus a 6% sales tax can be determined by adding 6% of $15.70 to $15.70. The total cost can also be found by multiplying 1.06 times $15.70, as shown by these equations. What number properties are used in the first two equations?

$$15.70 + (.06 \times 15.70) = (1 \times 15.70) + (.06 \times 15.70)$$
$$= (1 + .06) \times 15.70$$
$$= 1.06 \times 15.70$$

Use one of these two methods to compute the cost plus the sales tax for each of the following items. Round each answer to the nearest hundredth of a dollar.
a. Fishing tackle outfit, $48.60 (4% tax)
b. Ten-speed bike, $189 (5% tax)
c. Cassette tape recorder, $69.96 (6% tax)

23. In his will, dated July 17, 1788, Benjamin Franklin stated that he wished "to be useful even after my death if possible," and to this end Franklin left 1000 pounds sterling (about $4570) to be used to make loans to the inhabitants of Boston.*
a. Franklin's will stipulated that not more than 60 pounds, about $274, was to be loaned to apprentices at a 5% annual interest rate. What is the interest on this amount for 1 year?
b. The will also required that at the end of each year the borrower pay off 10% of the total amount owed. Add the interest from part a to $274 to determine the total amount owed at the end of the first year. What is 10% of this amount?
c. Franklin predicted that the 1000 pounds he was leaving would grow to 131,000 pounds in 100 years if loaned at 5% interest compounded yearly. This means that each year the 5% is computed on the total amount in the account, including the past interest. What will 1000 pounds grow to if interest is compounded yearly at 5% for five years?**

24. Population density is a ratio. The ratio for each state is determined by dividing the state's population by its land area in square miles.
a. Calculate the 1988 population densities using the information in the following table. Round each ratio to the nearest tenth.
b. Which of the four states had the greatest increase in population density?

	California	New Jersey	Texas	Arkansas
1988 pop.	28,314,000	7,721,000	16,841,000	2,395,000
Square miles	156,361	7,521	262,134	566,432
1980 density	151.4	979.2	54.3	.7
1988 density	———	———	———	———

25. One astronomical unit is 93,003,000 miles, the earth's average distance from the sun. The distance of the other planets from the sun in astronomical units is their distance divided by 93,003,000. Determine the missing numbers in the following table. Compute each astronomical unit to the nearest tenth.

Planet	Scientific notation	Positional numeration	Astronomical units
Mercury	3.6002×10^7	———	———
Venus	———	67,273,000	———
Earth	9.3003×10^7	———	1
Mars	———	141,709,000	———
Jupiter	4.83881×10^8	———	———
Saturn	———	887,151,000	———
Uranus	1.784838×10^9	———	———
Neptune	———	2,796,693,000	———
Pluto	3.669699×10^9	———	———

*J. Bigelow, *The Life of Benjamin Franklin*, vol. 3 (Philadelphia: J. B. Lippincott, 1893), 470–489. Note: The interest rates given in the exercises are annual interest rates.

**The computer program COMPOUND INTEREST on the *Computer Problem-Solving Disc* computes the amount that results from an investment *P* over *N* years with an interest rate *R*, for different compounding periods (yearly, quarterly, monthly, daily). Was Franklin correct in his hundred-year prediction?

Featured Strategy: Guessing and Checking

26. Suppose an item is on sale at a 20% discount but there is a 5% sales tax. Is the consumer better off if the discount is computed before the tax or if the tax is computed before the discount?

   a. **Understanding the Problem** If the discount is taken first, then the sales tax will be computed on an amount that is less than the original price. If the sales tax is computed first, then the discount will be taken on an amount that is more than the original price. Is one method better for the consumer than the other? Make an intuitive guess.

   b. **Devising a Plan** One approach to this problem is to *guess and check* by trying a few different prices, comparing the results, and using inductive reasoning. What happens when the two methods are used for an item that costs $25?

   c. **Carrying out the Plan** Use the plan suggested in part b, or your own plan, to solve this problem.

   d. **Looking Back** It may have occurred to you to compute the final cost of the item by taking a discount of 15% (20% discount minus 5% tax). Will this method produce the correct result?

   e. **Looking Back Again** The methods described in the original problem result in the payment of different amounts of sales tax to the state. Which method would the owner of the business prefer: discount and then tax, or tax and then discount?

27. After the first term, the top sequence shown below is a geometric sequence. Write the next two numbers in this sequence. Add 4 to each number in the top sequence and divide the results by 10 to complete the lower sequence.

$$0, 3, 6, 12, 24, \underline{\quad}, \underline{\quad}$$
$$.4, .7, \underline{\quad}, \underline{\quad}, \underline{\quad}, \underline{\quad}, \underline{\quad}$$

   a. This famous sequence of numbers is the basis of Bode's Law, which gives an amazingly close approximation of the distances from the first seven planets to the sun in astronomical units. Using this sequence of numbers and inductive reasoning, astronomers predicted that there would be a planet between Mars and Jupiter (see the table at the right). What was the predicted distance in astronomical units of this planet from the sun? (Asteroids were eventually found between Mars and Jupiter; the biggest of these asteroids is Ceres, about 500 miles in diameter.)

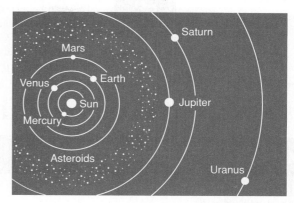

   b. In the 1770s when Bode's Law was discovered, only the first five planets in the table had been discovered. Using Bode's Law, astronomers found Uranus. What would its distance from the sun have been in astronomical units if it had conformed to Bode's Law?

Planet	Distance from sun in astronomical units	Distance predicted by Bode's Law
Mercury	0.4	0.4
Venus	0.7	0.7
Earth	1.0	1.0
Mars	1.52	1.6
Ceres	2.77	—
Jupiter	5.2	5.2
Saturn	9.5	10.0
Uranus	19.2	—
Neptune	30.1	38.8
Pluto	39.5	77.2

COMPUTER INVESTIGATION

The computer program PALINDROMIC SUMS on the *Computer Problem-Solving Disc* computes the sums of decimals and whole numbers and their reverses for any number chosen.

A palindromic decimal is one that reads the same from right to left as from left to right. For example, 37.73 is a palindromic positive decimal, but 5.65 and 988.9 are not. In the example shown here, the process of repeatedly adding a number to its reverse is carried out 3 times before a palindromic decimal is obtained.

$$
\begin{array}{r}
9.7 \\
+ \ 7.9 \\
\hline
17.6 \\
+ \ 6.71 \\
\hline
24.31 \\
+ 13.42 \\
\hline
37.73
\end{array}
$$

Questions for Investigation

1. It takes 24 steps to produce a palindromic number if we begin with 89. How many steps will it take for 8.9?

2. Will every two-digit decimal (4.8, .61, 3.2, .08, etc.) lead to a palindromic number?

3. There are three-digit decimals that will not lead to a palindromic number in fewer than 23 steps. Can you find one?

4. In the examples shown here, it took two steps to produce a palindromic number when we started with 149 but only one step when we started with 1.49. Will the number of steps needed to produce a palindromic number from a decimal always be less than or equal to the number of steps required for the whole number?

$$
\begin{array}{r}
149 \\
+ \ 941 \\
\hline
1090 \\
+ 0901 \\
\hline
1991
\end{array}
\qquad
\begin{array}{r}
1.49 \\
+ 94.1 \\
\hline
95.59
\end{array}
$$

PUZZLER

Two engineering students were discussing the need for engines that conserve energy. One student told of three new devices that could be installed in an engine: one saved 20% on fuel; another saved 30%; and the third saved 50%. "But that's not possible," said the other student, "that's a savings of 100%—the engine wouldn't require any fuel!" What is the total percent of fuel that could be saved if all three devices were used?

SECTION 6.4 IRRATIONAL AND REAL NUMBERS

■ PROBLEM OPENER

If the digits in the decimal .07007000700007 . . . continue this pattern of increasing numbers of zeros followed by 7s (5 zeros and a 7, 6 zeros and a 7, etc.), what will the 100th digit be?

An Egyptian painting, dating from about the fifteenth century B.C., depicting the needs of an advanced society. The upper part shows surveyors with rope.

The number line in Figure 6.40 shows the locations of a few positive rational numbers. Each rational number corresponds to a point on the number line, and between any two such numbers, no matter how close, there is always another rational number. It would seem that there was no room left for any new types of numbers, crowded together as the numbers are.

Figure 6.40

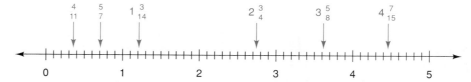

There are, however, points on the number line that correspond to numbers that are not rational. The number $\sqrt{2}$ is an example. This is the number that, when multiplied by itself, equals 2: $\sqrt{2} \times \sqrt{2} = 2$. The following equations show that $\sqrt{2}$ is close to, but greater than, 1.4. Try these products on a calculator. Can you find a number that, when multiplied by itself, is closer to 2?

$$1.4 \times 1.4 = 1.96$$
$$1.41 \times 1.41 = 1.9881$$
$$1.414 \times 1.414 = 1.999396$$
$$1.4142 \times 1.4142 = 1.99996164$$

The beginning of the decimal representation for $\sqrt{2}$ is 1.4142135, but no matter how many decimal places are computed, there will be no repeating pattern as there would be in the case of a rational number.* Such infinite nonrepeating decimal num- **irrational numbers** bers are called **irrational numbers.** It is easy to think of examples of this type of decimal. In the following numeral, each 7 is preceded by one more zero than the previous 7: .07007000700007. . . . Although there is a pattern here, there is no block of digits (repetend) that is repeated over and over, as in the case of a rational number. Therefore this is an irrational number.

EXAMPLE A

Which of the following numbers are irrational?

1. .006006006 . . .   2. .060060006 . . .
3. .731731173111731111 . . .   4. .73737373 . . .

Solution   There is no block of repeating digits in either (2) or (3), so these are irrational numbers.

PYTHAGOREAN THEOREM

Numbers that are not rational were first recognized by the Pythagoreans, followers of the Greek mathematician Pythagoras who lived in the fifth century B.C. It is possible that the discovery of such numbers arose in connection with the Pythagorean theorem. This theorem concerns triangles with a right angle—that is, a 90° angle (see Figure **legs** 6.41). The two shorter sides of such a triangle are called **legs,** and the longest side, **hypotenuse** which is opposite the right angle, is called the **hypotenuse.** The theorem states that for any right triangle, the sum of the areas of the squares on the legs (square A and square B) is equal to the area of the square on the hypotenuse (square C).

Figure 6.41

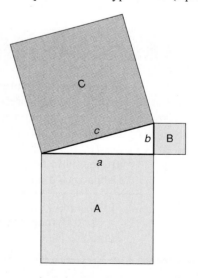

Area A + area B = area C

---

*For a proof that $\sqrt{2}$ is irrational, see R. Courant and H. Robbins, *What Is Mathematics?* (New York: Oxford University Press, 1941), 59–60.

Since the area of a square is the square of the length of the side of the square (see Section 8.2), the area of square A is a^2, the area of square B is b^2, and the area of square C is c^2. So the theorem can be stated as

$$a^2 + b^2 = c^2$$

Figure 6.42 shows a right triangle with legs of lengths 3 and 4 and a hypotenuse of length 5. Notice that the sum of the squares of the lengths of the two legs equals the square of the length of the hypotenuse.

Figure 6.42

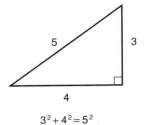

$$3^2 + 4^2 = 5^2$$

Numbers that are not rational may have been discovered by using a right triangle whose legs both have a length of 1, as shown in Figure 6.43. In this case the hypotenuse is the number that, when squared, is $1^2 + 1^2 = 2$. As we have noted, this number is $\sqrt{2}$, which is irrational. Thus the hypotenuse of this triangle has a length that is an irrational number.

Figure 6.43

$$1^2 + 1^2 = (\sqrt{2})^2$$

■ *Historical highlight*

Before the Pythagoreans discovered irrational numbers, they believed that all practical and theoretical affairs of life could be explained by ratios of whole numbers—that is, positive rational numbers. The discovery of line segments whose lengths were not rational numbers caused a logical scandal which threatened to destroy the Pythagorean philosophy. According to one legend, the Pythagoreans attempted to keep the matter secret by taking the discoverer of such numbers, Hippacus, on a sea voyage from which he never returned.

The Pythagorean theorem is one of the most familiar statements in all of mathematics.

PYTHAGOREAN THEOREM

For any right triangle with legs of length a and b and hypotenuse of length c,

$$a^2 + b^2 = c^2$$

EXAMPLE B

Use the Pythagorean theorem to find the missing length in each triangle.

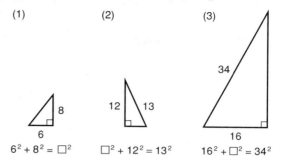

(1) (2) (3)

8

6

$6^2 + 8^2 = \square^2$

12 13

$\square^2 + 12^2 = 13^2$

34

16

$16^2 + \square^2 = 34^2$

Solution

1. $6^2 + 8^2 = 100$. Since $10^2 = 100$, the missing length is 10.
2. $13^2 - 12^2 = 169 - 144 = 25$. Since $5^2 = 25$, the missing length is 5.
3. $34^2 - 16^2 = 1156 - 256 = 900$. Since $30^2 = 900$, the missing length is 30.

There are many proofs of the Pythagorean theorem. *The Pythagorean Proposition* is a book that describes 370 proofs of this theorem.* The proof suggested in Figure 6.44 was known by the Greeks and may have been the one given by Pythagoras. The four triangles in parts (a) and (b) are right triangles, each with the same area. Part (a) has a small square of area a^2, a larger square of area b^2, and four triangles. The total area of the figure in part (a) is $a^2 + b^2 + 4T$, where T is the area of each triangle. Part (b) has a square of area c^2 and four triangles. The total area of the figure in part (b) is $c^2 + 4T$. Since the large square in part (a) and the large square in part (b) both have sides of length $a + b$, they have the same area. Setting these areas equal to each other, we have

$$a^2 + b^2 + 4T = c^2 + 4T$$

and subtracting $4T$ from both sides leaves

$$a^2 + b^2 = c^2$$

Figure 6.44

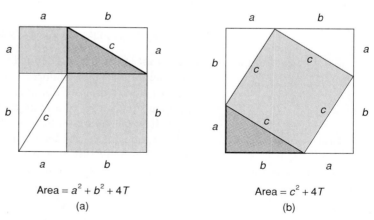

a b

a c a

b c b

a b

Area $= a^2 + b^2 + 4T$

(a)

a b

a

b c c

a c c b

b a

Area $= c^2 + 4T$

(b)

The converse of the Pythagorean theorem also holds. *If the sum of the squares of two sides of a triangle equals the square of the third side, then the triangle is a right triangle.* This means that if you used a rope with 30 knotted intervals of equal length

*E. S. Loomis, *The Pythagorean Proposition* (Washington, DC: National Council of Teachers of Mathematics, 1968).

and formed a triangle of sides 5, 12, and 13, as shown in Figure 6.45, it would be a right triangle. This fact was undoubtedly known by the ancient Egyptians and used by their surveyors to form right triangles (see the photo on page 276).

Figure 6.45

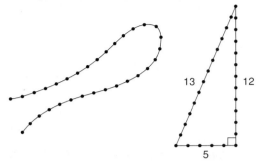

■ *HISTORICAL HIGHLIGHT*

Babylonian stone tablet with approximation of $\sqrt{2}$

The first proof of the Pythagorean theorem is thought to have been given by Pythagoras (ca. 540 B.C.). According to legend, when Pythagoras discovered this theorem he was so overjoyed that he offered a sacrifice of oxen to the gods. The theorem had been used for centuries, however, by the Babylonians and Egyptians. It is illustrated on this 4000-year-old Babylonian tablet, which shows a square and its diagonals. The numbers on this tablet are in base sixty numeration and show that the Babylonians had computed the value of $\sqrt{2}$ to 6 decimal places: 1.414213.

SQUARE ROOTS AND OTHER ROOTS

square root
A **square root** of a number is defined as a number that, when multiplied by itself, yields the original number. For example, 3 is a square root of 9, since $3 \times 3 = 9$. However, $^-3$ is also a square root of 9, because $^-3 \times ^-3 = 9$. Often we are only concerned with the positive square root of a number. For example, suppose the area of the square in Figure 6.46 is 64 square units. Since the area of a square is the product of the length of one side times itself, the length of one side of the square is the positive square root of 64, which is 8. In this example the negative square root, $^-8$, has no meaning. The

principal square root
positive square root of a number is called the **principal square root.**

Figure 6.46

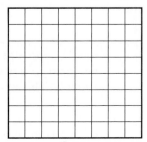

EXAMPLE C

Find the principal square root and the negative square root of each number.

1. 49   2. 20.25   3. .64   4. $\dfrac{1}{4}$

Solution   1. 7, ⁻7   2. 4.5, ⁻4.5   3. .8, ⁻.8   4. $\dfrac{1}{2}$, $\dfrac{-1}{2}$

radical sign   The symbol for the principal square root of a number b is $\sqrt{b}$. The symbol $\sqrt{}$ is called the **radical sign** and was represented first by the letter r, then by $\sqrt{}$, and finally by $\sqrt{}$. The negative square root of b is written as $^-\sqrt{b}$.

> For any positive number **b,**
>
> $$\sqrt{b} \times \sqrt{b} = b$$

EXAMPLE D

Evaluate the following expressions.

1. $\sqrt{14} \times \sqrt{14}$ 2. $(\sqrt{6})^2$ 3. $\sqrt{9} \times \sqrt{9}$

Solution   1. 14   2. 6   3. 9

The square roots of square numbers (1, 4, 9, 16, 25, etc.) are whole numbers. The square roots of all other whole numbers greater than zero ($\sqrt{2}$, $\sqrt{3}$, $\sqrt{5}$, $\sqrt{6}$, $\sqrt{7}$, $\sqrt{8}$, etc.) are irrational. These numbers all have infinite nonrepeating decimals. If a number is entered into a calculator and the square root key $\boxed{\sqrt{x}}$ is pressed, the display will show the principal square root of the number. If the square root of the number is irrational, the decimal that appears in the display will be an approximation.

EXAMPLE E

Classify each number as either rational or irrational. If it is rational, evaluate the square root, and if it is irrational, find an approximation to the nearest tenth.

1. $\sqrt{81}$ 2. $\sqrt{10}$ 3. $\sqrt{30}$

4. $\sqrt{\dfrac{4}{9}}$ 5. $\sqrt{18}$ 6. $\sqrt{.16}$

Solution   1. Rational; 9   2. Irrational; approximately 3.2

3. Irrational; approximately 5.5   4. Rational; $\dfrac{2}{3}$

5. Irrational; approximately 4.2   6. Rational; .4

Even though we cannot write the complete decimals for irrational numbers, these numbers should not be thought of as mysterious or illusive. They are the lengths of line segments, as illustrated by the triangles in Figure 6.47. The legs of the triangle on the left each have a length of 1, so, by the Pythagorean theorem, the hypotenuse is $\sqrt{2}$. The legs of the middle triangle are 1 and $\sqrt{2}$, and the hypotenuse is $\sqrt{3}$. In the triangle on the right, legs of length $\sqrt{2}$ and $\sqrt{3}$ are used to obtain a hypotenuse of $\sqrt{5}$. Line segments of lengths $\sqrt{6}$, $\sqrt{7}$, $\sqrt{8}$, etc., can be constructed in a similar manner.

The lengths of the hypotenuses of the three triangles, $\sqrt{2}$, $\sqrt{3}$, and $\sqrt{5}$, are indicated on the number line below the triangles. Check the locations of these numbers on the number line by using the edge of a piece of paper to mark off the lengths $\sqrt{2}$, $\sqrt{3}$, and $\sqrt{5}$ from the triangles.

Figure 6.47

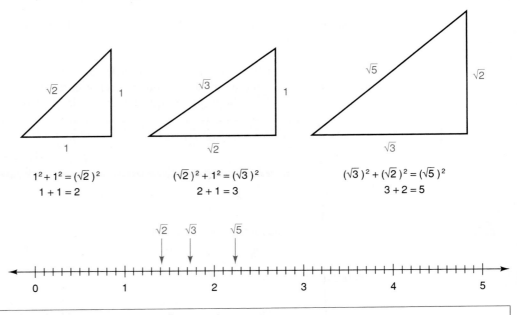

$$1^2 + 1^2 = (\sqrt{2})^2 \qquad (\sqrt{2})^2 + 1^2 = (\sqrt{3})^2 \qquad (\sqrt{3})^2 + (\sqrt{2})^2 = (\sqrt{5})^2$$
$$1 + 1 = 2 \qquad\qquad 2 + 1 = 3 \qquad\qquad\qquad 3 + 2 = 5$$

EXAMPLE F

Find the length of each hypotenuse.

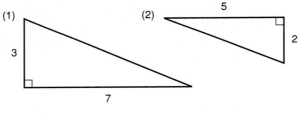

Solution   1. $\sqrt{58}$ 2. $\sqrt{29}$

EXAMPLE G

Mark the approximate location of the length of each hypotenuse from Example F on the following number line.

Solution
1. To the nearest tenth, $\sqrt{58}$ is 7.6, which is 1 tenth beyond 7.5 on the number line.
2. To the nearest tenth, $\sqrt{29}$ is 5.4, which is 1 tenth before 5.5 on the number line.

cube root
perfect cubes

The **cube root** of a number n is written as $\sqrt[3]{n}$. This is the number s such that $s \times s \times s$ equals n. The cube roots of **perfect cubes,** 1, 8, 27, 64, etc., are whole numbers. The cube roots of all other whole numbers are irrational numbers. For example, the cube roots of 4, 10, and 35 are infinite nonrepeating decimals. Their approximate locations are shown on the number line in Figure 6.48. Try cubing these decimals to see how close you get to 4, 10, and 35.

Figure 6.48

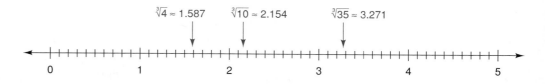

$\sqrt[3]{4} \approx 1.587$ $\sqrt[3]{10} \approx 2.154$ $\sqrt[3]{35} \approx 3.271$

EXAMPLE H

Classify each number as either rational or irrational. If it is rational, find the cube root, and if it is irrational, find an approximation to the nearest tenth.

1. $\sqrt[3]{30}$
2. $\sqrt[3]{125}$
3. $\sqrt[3]{100}$

Solution

1. Irrational; approximately 3.1
2. Rational; 5
3. Irrational; approximately 4.6

*n*th root, index

Fourth roots, fifth roots, etc., can be defined in a similar manner. In general, the **nth root** of a positive number b is written as $\sqrt[n]{b}$, and n is called the **index**. Notice that for square roots ($\sqrt{10}$, $\sqrt{3}$, etc.) the index 2 is not written.

nTH ROOTS

For any positive number b and any positive whole number n,

$$(\sqrt[n]{b})^n = b$$

Some calculators have a button for finding any root (cube root, fourth root, etc.) of a positive number. One common notation for such a button is $\boxed{\sqrt[x]{y}}$. Here are the steps for finding the cube root of 12 using such a calculator. The number in the display in step 4 is only an approximation because $\sqrt[3]{12}$ is an irrational number.

Steps	*Displays*
(1) Enter 12	12.
(2) Press $\boxed{\sqrt[x]{y}}$	12.
(3) Enter 3	3.
(4) $\boxed{=}$	2.289428485

If we use a calculator to cube the decimal in step (4), the display *may or may not* show 12. This will depend on whether the particular calculator we use rounds off. However, it should be noted that the cube of this decimal *is not* equal to 12.

REAL NUMBERS

real numbers

The irrational numbers, together with the rational numbers, form the set of **real numbers**. Figure 6.49 shows the relationships among the familiar sets of numbers. The set of rational numbers and the set of irrational numbers are disjoint, and their union is the set of real numbers, R. The rational numbers, Q, contain the whole numbers, $W = \{0, 1, 2, 3, \ldots\}$, and the integers, $Z = \{0, \pm 1, \pm 2, \pm 3, \ldots\}$. Viewed in another way, the sets W, Z, and Q form an increasing sequence of subsets of R. The set of whole numbers is contained in the set of integers, $W \subset Z$; the set of integers is contained in the set of rational numbers, $Z \subset Q$; and the set of rational numbers is contained in the set of real numbers, $Q \subset R$.

Each whole number is in all of the sets W, Z, Q, and R. Other numbers are in only one, two, or three of these sets. For example, $1/7$ is in the set of rational numbers (Q) and the set of real numbers (R), but not in the set of whole numbers (W) or integers (Z).

Figure 6.49

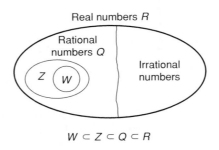

$$W \subset Z \subset Q \subset R$$

EXAMPLE *I*   Use the letters *W, Z, Q,* and *R* to indicate which sets each number is in.

1. ⁻12	2. $\sqrt{15}$	3. .23	4. 130
5. $\dfrac{3}{5}$	6. $.\overline{27}$	7. $\sqrt{10}$	8. $\sqrt{25}$

Solution
1. *Z, Q, R*	2. *R*	3. *Q, R*	4. *W, Z, Q, R*
5. *Q, R*	6. *Q, R*	7. *R*	8. *W, Z, Q, R*

PROPERTIES OF REAL NUMBERS

We have seen that the whole numbers, integers, rational numbers, and real numbers form an increasing sequence, with each set of numbers contained in the next. Although these number systems have several properties in common (the commutative, associative, and distributive properties), each number system was developed because it had number properties that the existing number systems did not have. For example, the whole numbers do not have inverses for addition (negative numbers), so the integers were developed; the integers do not have inverses for multiplication (reciprocals), so the rational numbers were developed. Similarly, the rational numbers lack a number property that the real numbers have.

completeness   The real numbers have the property of *completeness*. Intuitively, we can interpret **completeness** as meaning that all line segments can be measured. If we limit ourselves to the rational numbers, this is not true. For example, we have seen that there is no rational number corresponding to the length of the hypotenuse of a right triangle whose legs have lengths of 1 unit.

real number line   Expressed in a slightly different way, completeness of the real numbers means that there is a one-to-one correspondence between the real numbers and the points on a line. Because of this relationship, a line called the **real number line** is used as a model for the real numbers. Once a zero point has been labeled and a unit has been selected, each real number can be assigned to a point on the line. Each positive real number is assigned a point to the right of zero such that the real number is the distance from this point to the zero point. The negative of this number corresponds to a point that is the same distance to the left of zero. A few examples are shown in Figure 6.50.

Figure 6.50

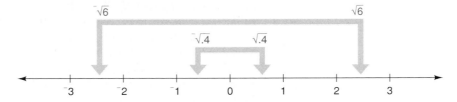

The following are twelve properties of the real number system.

Closure for Addition The sum of any two real numbers is another unique real number. That is, **addition is closed** on the set of real numbers.

Closure for Multiplication The product of any two real numbers is another unique real number. That is, **multiplication is closed** on the set of real numbers.

Addition Is Commutative For any real numbers r and s, $r + s = s + r$.

Multiplication Is Commutative For any real numbers r and s, $r \times s = s \times r$.

Addition Is Associative For any real numbers r, s, and t, $(r + s) + t = r + (s + t)$.

Multiplication Is Associative For any real numbers r, s, and t, $(r \times s) \times t = r \times (s \times t)$.

Identity for Addition For any real number r, $0 + r = r$. Zero is called the **identity for addition,** and it is the only number with this property.

Identity for Multiplication For any real number r, $1 \times r = r$. The number 1 is called the **identity for multiplication,** and it is the only number with this property.

Inverses for Addition For any real number r, there is a unique real number ^{-}r, called its **opposite** or **inverse for addition,** such that $r + {}^{-}r = 0$.

Inverses for Multiplication For any nonzero real number r, there is a unique real number $1/r$, called its **reciprocal** or **inverse for multiplication,** such that $r \times 1/r = 1$.

Multiplication Is Distributive over Addition For any real numbers r, s, and t, $r \times (s + t) = r \times s + r \times t$.

Completeness Property All line segments can be measured with real numbers.

OPERATIONS WITH IRRATIONAL NUMBERS

At first it is difficult to imagine how to perform arithmetical operations with numbers that cannot be expressed exactly in decimal notation. One solution is to replace irrational numbers by rational approximations. The square in Figure 6.51 has sides of length $\sqrt{2}$ units. Since $\sqrt{2} \approx 1.4$, the total length of the four sides is approximately 4×1.4, or 5.6 units. For many purposes this is sufficient accuracy.

Figure 6.51

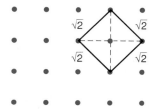

Another solution is to write products and sums without doing the computing. The total length of the sides of the square in Figure 6.51 can be written as $4\sqrt{2}$, which means 4 times $\sqrt{2}$. In this way we indicate the length without approximating it by a decimal.

Is $4\sqrt{2}$ a rational or an irrational number? We know by the property of closure for multiplication of real numbers that $4\sqrt{2}$ is a real number, so it is either rational or irrational. Let's suppose it is a rational number and denote it by r. That is,

$$r = 4\sqrt{2}.$$

Multiplying both sides of this equation by 1/4, we get

$$r \times \frac{1}{4} = \sqrt{2}$$

Now by the property of closure for multiplication of rational numbers, $r \times 1/4$ is a rational number. However, this can't be true because $\sqrt{2}$ is an irrational number and the preceding equation would then have an irrational number equal to a rational number. Since the assumption that $4\sqrt{2}$ is rational leads to a contradiction, $4\sqrt{2}$ must be irrational. A similar argument can be used to prove that *the product of any nonzero rational number and an irrational number is an irrational number.* Thus we can obtain an infinite number of irrational numbers by multiplying each nonzero rational number by $\sqrt{2}$. Let's consider another example of computing with irrational numbers. The total length of the sides of the triangle in Figure 6.52 can be written as $3 + \sqrt{5}$.

Figure 6.52

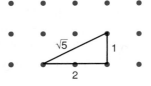

This is also an irrational number, as can be proven by an argument similar to the previous one. For if we assume that $3 + \sqrt{5}$ is a rational number and denote it by s, then

$$s = 3 + \sqrt{5} \quad \text{and} \quad s - 3 = \sqrt{5}$$

But this equation contains a contradiction. Since s and -3 are rational numbers, by the property of closure for addition of rational numbers their sum is also a rational number. But $\sqrt{5}$ is an irrational number. So the assumption that $3 + \sqrt{5}$ is rational is false. In general, the sum of any rational number and irrational number is an irrational number. So once again, an infinite number of irrational numbers can be obtained by adding rational numbers to an irrational number.

EXAMPLE J

Classify each sum or product as rational or irrational, and if it is rational, evaluate the expression.

1. $3\sqrt{24}$ 2. $5\sqrt{36}$ 3. $14 + \sqrt{14}$ 4. $\sqrt{81} + 18$

Solution   1. Irrational   2. Rational; 30   3. Irrational   4. Rational; 27

The total length of the sides of the square in Figure 6.51 and the triangle in Figure 6.52 can be approximated by using rational number approximations for $\sqrt{2}$ and $\sqrt{5}$. However, there are cases in which we can compute with irrational numbers without replacing them by decimal approximations. For example, we know that $\sqrt{2} \times \sqrt{2} = 2$. This can also be seen by looking at the square in Figure 6.51. The area of the square is $\sqrt{2} \times \sqrt{2}$, and we can see that the area is 2 by dividing it into 4 smaller half-squares, or triangles. Thus in this example the product of two irrational numbers is a rational number.

Let's consider another example of a product of two irrational numbers. The rectangle in Figure 6.53 has a length of $\sqrt{18}$ because it is the hypotenuse of a right triangle whose legs each have a length of 3. The width of this rectangle is $\sqrt{2}$. Its area, according to the formula for the area of a rectangle, length times width, is $\sqrt{18} \times \sqrt{2}$. Using a second method, we can show this area to be 6 square units by dividing the rectangle into 2 squares and 8 half-squares, or triangles. These two methods of finding area show that $\sqrt{18} \times \sqrt{2} = 6$. This example illustrates a case in which the product of two different irrational numbers is a rational number.

Figure 6.53

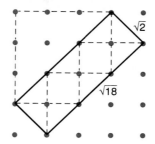

In the preceding example we saw that $\sqrt{18} \times \sqrt{2} = 6$. But since $6 = \sqrt{36} = \sqrt{18 \times 2}$, we see that $\sqrt{18} \times \sqrt{2} = \sqrt{18 \times 2}$. This suggests that *the product of the square roots of two numbers is equal to the square root of the product of the two numbers.* This result is stated in the following theorem.

> For any positive numbers *a* and *b*,
> $$\sqrt{a} \times \sqrt{b} = \sqrt{a \times b}$$

EXAMPLE K

Compute each product and determine if it is rational or irrational.

1. $\sqrt{8} \times \sqrt{6}$ 2. $\sqrt{12} \times \sqrt{3}$ 3. $\sqrt{5} \times \sqrt{20}$ 4. $\sqrt{6} \times \sqrt{10}$

Solution

1. $\sqrt{48}$; irrational   2. $\sqrt{36} = 6$; rational
3. $\sqrt{100} = 10$; rational   4. $\sqrt{60}$; irrational

In addition to allowing us to compute the products of square roots, the preceding theorem is useful for simplifying square roots. For example, $\sqrt{18} = \sqrt{9 \times 2}$ **simplified form** $= \sqrt{9} \times \sqrt{2} = 3\sqrt{2}$. A square root is in **simplified form** if the number under the radical sign has no factor other than 1 that is a square number.

EXAMPLE L

Write each square root in simplified form.

1. $\sqrt{50}$ 2. $\sqrt{54}$ 3. $\sqrt{80}$

Solution

1. $\sqrt{50} = \sqrt{25 \times 2} = \sqrt{25} \times \sqrt{2} = 5\sqrt{2}$
2. $\sqrt{54} = \sqrt{9 \times 6} = \sqrt{9} \times \sqrt{6} = 3\sqrt{6}$
3. $\sqrt{80} = \sqrt{16 \times 5} = \sqrt{16} \times \sqrt{5} = 4\sqrt{5}$

Quotients of real numbers, such as $2 \div \sqrt{3}$, are often written as fractions, such as $2/\sqrt{3}$. When the denominator of a fraction contains a square root, cube root, etc., it is sometimes necessary to find an equal fraction that has a rational number for its denominator. The process of replacing a denominator that is irrational by a denominator that is rational is called **rationalizing the denominator.** The denominator of $2/\sqrt{3}$ can be rationalized by using the fundamental rule for equality of fractions to multiply the numerator and denominator by $\sqrt{3}$.

rationalizing the denominator

$$\frac{2}{\sqrt{3}} = \frac{2 \times \sqrt{3}}{\sqrt{3} \times \sqrt{3}} = \frac{2\sqrt{3}}{3}$$

EXAMPLE M

Rationalize the denominator of each fraction.

1. $\dfrac{1}{\sqrt{2}}$ 2. $\dfrac{-6}{\sqrt{5}}$ 3. $\dfrac{7}{\sqrt{7}}$

Solution

1. $\dfrac{1}{\sqrt{2}} = \dfrac{1 \times \sqrt{2}}{\sqrt{2} \times \sqrt{2}} = \dfrac{\sqrt{2}}{2}$

2. $\dfrac{-6}{\sqrt{5}} = \dfrac{-6 \times \sqrt{5}}{\sqrt{5} \times \sqrt{5}} = \dfrac{-6\sqrt{5}}{5}$

3. $\dfrac{7}{\sqrt{7}} = \dfrac{7 \times \sqrt{7}}{\sqrt{7} \times \sqrt{7}} = \dfrac{7\sqrt{7}}{7} = \sqrt{7}$

PROBLEM-SOLVING APPLICATION

To solve the following problem, we use the Pythagorean theorem and the fact that the length of the sides of a square is the square root of its area. Try solving this problem before reading the solution. You may find the strategies of *making a table* and *finding a pattern* to be useful in obtaining the solution.

■ PROBLEM

The inner square in the sketch below was obtained by connecting the midpoints of the sides of the outer square. If this process of forming smaller inner squares by connecting the midpoints of the sides of the preceding square is continued, what will be the dimensions of the ninth square?

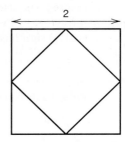

Understanding the Problem The outer square is 2 units by 2 units and has an area of 4. The second square is contained inside the first square and is smaller. What is the length of the sides of the second square, and what is the area of this square?

Question 1

Question 2

Devising a Plan   One approach to solving the problem is to *form a table* listing the lengths of the sides and the areas of the first few squares. The second square has sides of length $\sqrt{2}$ and an area of 2 (see the figure below). What is the length of the sides of the third square, and what is its area?

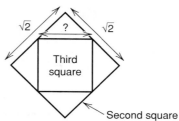

Question 3

Carrying Out the Plan   The following table lists the lengths of the sides and areas of the first 4 squares. Find a pattern and predict the area of the ninth square. What is the length of the sides of the ninth square?

	Square 1	Square 2	Square 3	Square 4	Square 5	Square 6
Length of side	2 by 2	$\sqrt{2}$ by $\sqrt{2}$	1 by 1	$\dfrac{1}{\sqrt{2}}$ by $\dfrac{1}{\sqrt{2}}$		
Area	4	2	1	$\dfrac{1}{2}$		

Question 4

Looking Back   You may have noticed that the area of each square is half the area of the preceding square. Based on this pattern, the area of the ninth square is 1/64. Thus the length of the sides of the ninth square is $\sqrt{1/64} = 1/8$. The fact that the area of each succeeding square decreases by one half is suggested by the following figure. How can the dashed lines be used to show that the inner square has half the area of the outer square?

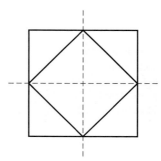

Answers to Questions 1–4

1. The length h of the sides of the second square is the hypotenuse of a triangle whose sides have length 1. The length of the hypotenuse is $\sqrt{2}$, and the area of the second square is $\sqrt{2} \times \sqrt{2} = 2$.

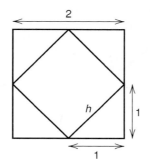

$h^2 = 1^2 + 1^2$

$h^2 = 2$

$h = \sqrt{2}$

2. The length k of the sides of the third square is the hypotenuse of a triangle whose sides have length $\sqrt{2}/2$. The length of the hypotenuse is 1, and the area of the third square is 1.

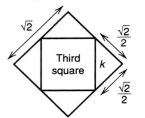

$$k^2 = \left(\frac{\sqrt{2}}{2}\right)^2 + \left(\frac{\sqrt{2}}{2}\right)^2$$

$$k^2 = \frac{2}{4} + \frac{2}{4}$$

$$k = \sqrt{1} = 1$$

3. The area of the ninth square is 1/64, and the length of its sides is $\sqrt{1/64} = 1/8$.

4. The outer square is formed by 8 triangular regions of equal size, and the inner square is formed by 4 of these regions.

RELATED ACTIVITIES IN
Mathematics for Elementary Teachers: An Activity Approach, 3e

Activity Set 6.4   **Irrational Numbers on the Geoboard:** Geoboards are used to form figures whose sides have lengths that are irrational numbers.

Just for Fun   **Golden Rectangles:** A method for constructing golden rectangles and an illustration of how Fibonacci numbers are related to the golden ratio

---

EXERCISES AND PROBLEMS 6.4

There once was a student named Lew,
Who computed the square root of 2.
  When no pattern repeated
  He gave up defeated,
Two million digits is all he would do.

$$\sqrt{2} = 1.41421356241933916628 1975988$$
$$71307959868348906509 6193189$$
$$43242352661427981910 0455546$$
$$61670432543765054609 4505594$$
$$57028253271931476474 1288546$$
$$29784 \ldots$$

"I tend to agree with you—especially since $6 \cdot 10^{-9} \sqrt{t_c}$ is my lucky number."

1. Which of the following numbers are irrational?

a. $\sqrt{49}$ **b.** .131131113 . . .

c. .113113113 . . .   **d.** $\sqrt{14}$

2. Use the Pythagorean theorem to find the missing length for each of the right triangles. Write both the exact answer and the decimal approximation to 1 decimal place.

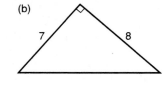

(a)   (b)

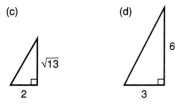

(c)   (d)

3. Find the indicated root of each number.

a. $\sqrt{\dfrac{1}{16}}$ **b.** $\sqrt[3]{64}$ **c.** $\sqrt{9.61}$

d. $\sqrt[3]{8000}$ **e.** $\sqrt{625}$ **f.** $\sqrt[3]{\dfrac{8}{27}}$

4. Classify each number as rational or irrational. If it is rational, find its root, and if it is irrational, find an approximation to the nearest tenth.

a. $\sqrt{18}$ **b.** $\sqrt[3]{216}$ **c.** $\sqrt{\dfrac{1}{9}}$

d. $\sqrt[3]{30}$ **e.** $\sqrt{50}$ **f.** $\sqrt{121}$

5. Write each number as a decimal to the nearest tenth and mark its approximate location on a number line.

a. $\sqrt{7}$ **b.** $\sqrt[3]{30}$ **c.** $\sqrt{3}$

6. Any three whole numbers a, b, and c such that $a^2 + b^2 = c^2$ are called **Pythagorean triples.** We can find such numbers by substituting whole numbers for u and v in the following equations:

$$a = 2uv, \, b = u^2 - v^2, \, c = u^2 + v^2$$

For example, if $u = 5$ and $v = 3$, then a, b, and c have the values shown in the table below. Use the remaining values of u and v in the table to find other values for a, b, and c. Check your answers by showing that $a^2 + b^2 = c^2$.

u	v	a	b	c
2	1			
3	2			
4	3			
4	2			
5	3	30	16	34

7. Form a table like the one shown below and put checks in the appropriate columns to indicate what type of number each number at the left is. For example, ⁻3 is an integer, a rational number, and a real number.

	Whole numbers	Integers	Rational numbers	Real numbers
⁻3		✓	✓	✓
$\dfrac{1}{8}$				
$\sqrt{3}$				
π				
14				
$\dfrac{1.6}{4}$				
.82				

8. Which of the following operations are closed for the given sets? If an operation is not closed, provide an example to show this.
   a. Subtraction on the set of whole numbers
   b. Division by nonzero numbers on the set of rational numbers
   c. Multiplication on the set of irrational numbers
   d. Addition on the set of integers

9. State the property of the real numbers that is being used in each equality.
   a. $\sqrt{3} \times \sqrt{6} = \sqrt{6} \times \sqrt{3}$
   b. $(3 + \sqrt{2}) \times \sqrt{7} = 3\sqrt{7} + \sqrt{2} \times \sqrt{7}$
   c. $(4 + \sqrt{8}) + 2\sqrt{5} = 2\sqrt{5} + (4 + \sqrt{8})$
   d. $^-\sqrt{10} + (\sqrt{10} + 6) = (^-\sqrt{10} + \sqrt{10}) + 6$
   e. $\sqrt{3} \times \left(\dfrac{1}{\sqrt{3}} \times \sqrt{3} \right) = \sqrt{3} \times 1$

10. Classify each sum or product as rational or irrational. If the expression is rational, evaluate it.
   a. $\sqrt{2} \times \sqrt{20}$ **b.** $10 + \sqrt{8}$ **c.** $\sqrt{6} \times \sqrt{24}$
   d. $4\sqrt{15}$ **e.** $\sqrt{25} + 11$ **f.** $\sqrt{7} \times \sqrt{28}$

11. Simplify the following square roots so that the smallest possible whole number is left under the square root symbol.
   a. $\sqrt{45}$ **b.** $\sqrt{48}$ **c.** $\sqrt{60}$

12. We know that $\sqrt{a} \times \sqrt{b} = \sqrt{ab}$ for all positive numbers a and b. Determine whether the following equations are true or false for positive numbers a and b, and if an equation is false, show a counterexample.
   a. $\sqrt{a} + \sqrt{b} = \sqrt{a + b}$ **b.** $\dfrac{\sqrt{a}}{\sqrt{b}} = \sqrt{\dfrac{a}{b}}$

13. Rationalize the denominator of each fraction.
   a. $\dfrac{4}{\sqrt{7}}$ **b.** $\dfrac{3}{2\sqrt{6}}$
   c. $\dfrac{5}{\sqrt{5}}$ **d.** $\dfrac{^-1}{\sqrt{2}}$

14. Use a calculator with a square root key to carry out steps 1 through 4. Write the number that is displayed after step 5.

Steps	Displays
(1) Enter 2	2.
(2) Press $\sqrt{x}$	1.4142135
(3) Press $\sqrt{x}$	1.1892070
(4) Press $\sqrt{x}$	1.0905076
(5) Press $\sqrt{x}$	

   a. If you continue to press the square root key in this example, eventually you will see the same number in every display. What is this number?
   b. What number will eventually show in the display of a calculator if you enter a positive number less than 1 and repeatedly press the square root key?

15. Each day Ed walks past a rectangular athletic field on his way home from school. If the field is being used, Ed walks along two of the sides of the field. If the field is not being used, he cuts across from corner to corner. If he takes 300 steps along one edge of the field and 500 steps along the other edge, approximately how many steps can Ed save by walking from corner to corner?

16. In a game for three students, one opens a book and multiplies the numbers of the facing pages. The other two students race to see who can determine the page numbers. What page numbers yield the following products?

    a. 18,090   **b.** 7482   **c.** 41,820

17. A school's basketball hoop is mounted on a pipe that is cemented into the ground. The hoop is 10 feet above the ground. To stop it from swaying, some students put a brace from behind the hoop to a point on the ground that is 8 feet from the cement base. What is the length of the brace from the hoop to the ground (to the nearest foot)?

18. The infield of a baseball field is a 90 by 90-foot square. The pitching mound is 60.5 feet from home plate. How far is the mound from second base (to the nearest foot)?

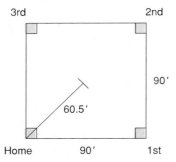

19. A home plate for a baseball field can be formed by making 2 twelve-inch cuts from a square region as shown in the following figure. What are the dimensions of the original square to the nearest tenth of an inch?

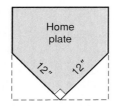

20. A 30-foot ladder is leaning against a house, with the foot of the ladder 8 feet from the house. If the foot of the ladder is pulled 7 more feet from the house, how far down the side of the house will the ladder move (to the nearest foot)?

21. The time it takes a satellite to orbit the earth depends on its apogee and perigee. The *apogee* (A) of a satellite is its greatest distance from the center of the earth, and the *perigee* (P) is its least distance. The formula for the time in hours (T) required for 1 orbit is

$$T = \frac{(A + P)\sqrt{A + P}}{501,186}$$

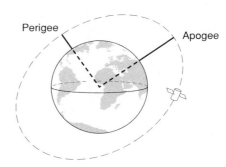

a. Suppose a satellite orbiting the earth has an apogee of 4300 miles and a perigee of 4100 miles. How long does it take to complete 1 orbit (to the nearest tenth of an hour)?

b. Satellites are often placed in circular orbits with apogees and perigees of approximately 26,300 miles. Why is this distance chosen?

Featured Strategy: Making a Drawing

22. Suppose a mile-long metal bridge that was not built to allow for expansion nevertheless expands 2 feet and buckles up at the center. How high will the center be pushed up?

    a. Understanding the Problem The first step in understanding the problem is to *make a drawing*. The distance along the line from A to B represents the bridge, and the curve represents the expanded bridge. Since there are 5280 feet in a mile, what is the distance along the curve from A to B?

    b. Devising a Plan Let's approximate the shape of the buckled bridge by two right triangles, as shown in the next figure. The length from C to B is $5280 \div 2 = 2640$. Explain why the length from D to B is approximately 2641 feet.

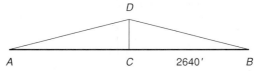

    c. Carrying Out the Plan What is the distance from C to D?

    d. Looking Back If the bridge had been 2 miles long and had expanded 2 feet, how high would the bridge have buckled?

23. For over 2000 years architects and artists have been fond of using a rectangle called the *golden rectangle*. The length of a golden rectangle divided by its width is an irrational number, which when rounded to six decimal places is 1.618033. This irrational number is called the *golden ratio*. Fibonacci numbers are related to the golden ratio. Here are the first 10 Fibonacci numbers.*

1, 1, 2, 3, 5, 8, 13, 21, 34, 55

Golden rectangle

a. Compute the ratios formed by dividing each Fibonacci number by the previous Fibonacci number.
b. Extend the sequence and find 2 consecutive Fibonacci numbers whose ratio to 4 decimal places equals the golden ratio to 4 decimal places.

24. The spiral of right triangles shown here somewhat resembles a cross section of the seashell of the chambered nautilus. It represents the square roots of consecutive whole numbers. The first triangle has two legs of unit length and a hypotenuse of $\sqrt{2}$. This hypotenuse is the leg of the next triangle, which has a hypotenuse of $\sqrt{3}$. Each triangle uses the hypotenuse of the preceding triangle as a leg.

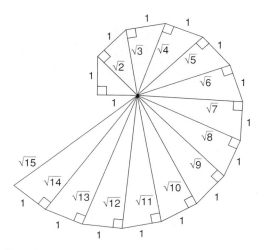

a. Copy the rectangular grid from the inside cover of the book. Identify 2 grid lines to be horizontal and vertical axes, respectively. For each whole number n on the horizontal axis of the grid, plot a point approximately $\sqrt{n}$ units above the axis. The lengths of $\sqrt{n}$ can be measured from the spiral of triangles by using the edge of a piece of paper.
b. Connect the points on the grid. Use the graph to approximate $\sqrt{7.5}$. Could this graph be used to approximate the square root of any number greater than 1 and less than 12?

LABORATORY INVESTIGATION

The Pythagorean theorem can be illustrated visually in several ways. One such illustration is on page 279, and a second is shown by the figure in this investigation.

Square A is divided into 4 regions by 2 dashed lines that pass through its center. One dashed line is parallel to the left edge of square C, and the other dashed line is parallel to the lower edge of square C. If these 4 regions and square B are traced and cut out, they can be arranged to cover square C. Try it.

Questions for Investigation

1. Draw a right triangle with legs of length 1 inch and 2 inches and a square on each of its sides. (Right angles can be drawn by using the corner of a file card.) Subdivide the larger of the squares on the legs into 4 regions as described. Show how these 4 regions and the square on the other leg can be arranged to exactly cover the square on the hypotenuse.
2. Suppose the smaller of the squares on the legs of a right triangle is subdivided into 4 regions, as described. Can these regions and the square on the other leg be arranged to cover the square on the hypotenuse?

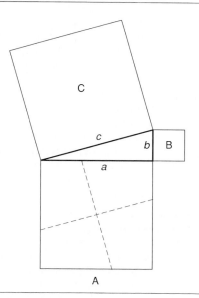

---

*The computer program FIBONACCI-TYPE SEQUENCES on the *Computer Problem-Solving Disc* prints up to 200 terms in a Fibonacci-type sequence beginning with any 2 numbers that are entered and computes the ratio of the last 2 terms. These ratios have something interesting in common.

PUZZLER

A moat filled with crocodiles surrounds an old abandoned castle. The outer and inner edges of the moat form two squares with the same center. The width of the moat is 20 feet. How can a person with no objects other than 2 nineteen-foot planks cross the moat to the castle?

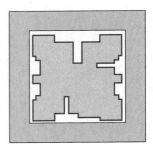

CHAPTER REVIEW

1. Decimals
   a. The word **decimal** comes from the Latin *decem,* meaning *ten.*
   b. The number of digits to the right of the decimal point is called the **number of decimal places.**
   c. The **place values** to the right of the decimal point are decreasing powers of 10.
   d. **Decimal squares** and **number lines** are visual models for decimals.
   e. An **inequality** for decimals less than 1 can be determined by comparing their tenths digits. If these are equal, compare their hundredths digits, etc.

2. Rational Numbers
   a. Any number that can be written in the form a/b, where $b \neq 0$ and a and b are integers, is called a **rational number.**
   b. Every rational number can be represented as either a **terminating** or a **repeating decimal.**
   c. Every terminating or repeating decimal can be written as a rational number in the form a/b.
   d. A rational number a/b in lowest terms can be written as a terminating decimal if and only if b has only 2s or 5s in its prime factorization.
   e. The block of repeating digits in a repeating decimal is called the **repetend.**
   f. The rational numbers are **dense.** That is, between any two such numbers there is always another rational number.
   g. The operations of addition and multiplication on the set of rational numbers satisfy the eleven **number properties** stated in Section 6.2.

3. Operations with Decimals
   a. **Decimal Squares** provide a visual model for decimal operations and can be used to show the similarity between these operations and the operations on whole numbers.
   b. The **pencil-and-paper algorithms** for decimals can be illustrated by computing with fractions.
   c. To compute the product of a decimal and a positive power of 10, move the decimal point 1 place to the right for each factor of 10.
   d. To divide a decimal by a positive power of 10, move the decimal point 1 place to the left for each power of 10.

4. Mental Calculations
   a. Products and quotients of decimals can be calculated mentally by computing with whole numbers and then locating decimal points.
   b. **Compatible numbers** is the technique of using pairs of numbers that are especially convenient for mental calculation. In computing with decimals it is sometimes convenient to use equivalent fractions in place of the decimals.
   c. **Substitution** is the technique of replacing a decimal or a percent by a sum or difference of two decimals or percents.
   d. **Add up** is the technique of obtaining the difference of two decimals by adding up from the smaller to the larger decimal.

5. Estimation
   a. **Compatible numbers** is the technique of computing estimations by replacing one or more numbers with approximate compatible numbers.
   b. **Rounding** is the technique of replacing one or both numbers in a computation with approximate numbers.
   c. **Front-end estimation** is the technique of using the leading nonzero digit to obtain a rough estimation.

6. Ratio and Percent
   a. For any two positive numbers a and b, the **ratio** of a to b ($a{:}b$) is the fraction a/b.
   b. **Proportion** For two equal ratios a/b and c/d, $a/b = c/d$ is called a **proportion.**
   c. The word **percent** is from the Latin *per centum,* meaning *out of a hundred.*
   d. There are three types of computations involving percents: computations using **whole and percent,** computations using **part and whole,** and computations using **percent and part.**

7. Scientific Notation
   a. The method of writing a number as a product of a number from 1 to 10 and a power of 10 is called **scientific notation.**
   b. When a number is written in scientific notation, the part from 1 to 10 is called the **mantissa** and the exponent of 10 is called the **characteristic.**

8. Real Numbers

a. An infinite nonrepeating decimal is called an **irrational number.**

b. The **principal square root** of a positive number b is denoted by $\sqrt{b}$ and is defined to be the positive number that, when multiplied by itself, is b.

c. For any positive number b and any positive whole number n, $\sqrt[n]{b}$ is called the **nth root** of b and defined by $(\sqrt[n]{b})^n = b$.

d. The rational numbers, together with the irrational numbers, form the set of **real numbers.**

e. In addition to the eleven **number properties** stated for the rational numbers, the real numbers have the property of **completeness:** all line segments can be measured with real numbers.

f. The sum or product of a nonzero rational number and an irrational number is an irrational number.

g. For any positive numbers a and b, $\sqrt{a} \times \sqrt{b} = \sqrt{a \times b}$.

h. The process of replacing a denominator that is irrational by a denominator that is rational is called **rationalizing the denominator.**

CHAPTER TEST

1. Describe Decimal Squares to explain each of the following:

a. $.4 > .27$ **b.** $.7 = .70$

c. $.225 < .35$ **d.** $.09 < .1$

2. Write each fraction as a decimal.

a. $\dfrac{3}{4}$ **b.** $\dfrac{7}{100}$ **c.** $\dfrac{2}{3}$

d. $\dfrac{7}{8}$ **e.** $\dfrac{4}{9}$ **f.** $\dfrac{6}{25}$

3. Write each decimal as a fraction.

a. $.278$ **b.** $.\overline{35}$ **c.** $.03$

4. Round each decimal to the given place value.

a. $.878$ (hundredths)   **b.** $.449$ (tenths)

c. $.5096$ (thousandths)   **d.** $.\overline{6}$ (ten thousandths)

5. Perform each operation and describe Decimal Squares to illustrate each answer.

a. $.7 + .6 =$ **b.** $3 \times .4 =$

c. $.62 - .48 =$ **d.** $.80 \div .05 =$

6. Perform the following operations.

a. $.006 + .38 - .2$ **b.** $.62 \times .08$

c. $.14763 \div .21$ **d.** $47 + .8 \times 340$

7. Calculate each answer mentally and explain your method.

a. $100 \times .073$ **b.** $7 \times .6$

c. $4.9 \div 1000$ **d.** $.01 \times 372$

e. 15% of 260 **f.** 25% of 36

8. Estimate each answer by replacing the decimal or percent by a compatible fraction. Show your replacement.

a. $.49 \times 310$ **b.** $.24 \times 416$

c. 33% of 60 **d.** 76% of 40

9. Determine each answer to the nearest tenth.

a. What is 36% of 46?

b. 30 is what percent of 80?

c. 15 is 24% of what number?

d. What is 118% of 125?

e. 322 is what percent of 230?

10. Write each number in scientific notation.

a. 437.8 **b.** $.000106$

11. Classify each number as rational or irrational.

a. $\sqrt{60}$ **b.** $\sqrt[3]{27}$ **c.** $6\sqrt{8}$

d. $\sqrt{10} + 5$ **e.** $\sqrt{\dfrac{1}{4}}$ **f.** $\sqrt[3]{60}$

12. Approximate each number below to 1 decimal place.

a. $\sqrt{34}$ **b.** $\sqrt[3]{18}$

13. Determine whether each operation is closed or not closed and give a reason or show a counterexample.

a. Addition on the set of rational numbers

b. Multiplication on the set of irrational numbers

c. Addition on the set of irrational numbers

14. Simplify each square root.

a. $\sqrt{405}$ **b.** $\sqrt{24}$

15. Find the missing length for each triangle.

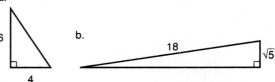

16. Jon paid $187 for a coat that was on sale at 15% off. What was the original price of the coat?

17. A restaurant sells a 20-ounce glass of orange juice for $1.50 and a 16-ounce glass for $1.10. What size glass is the better buy?

18. A rectangular swimming pool has a length of 60 feet and a width of 30 feet. What is the distance from one corner of the pool to the opposite corner, to the nearest tenth of a foot?

19. A fuel company charges monthly finance fees of 1.2% for the first $500 due and .8% for any amount over $500. What is the monthly finance fee for an account with a balance of $650?

20. If the ratio of private school students to public school students in a city is 3 to 16 and there are a total of 18,601 students, how many are in public schools?

BIBLIOGRAPHY

Brumbaugh, F. L. "Big Numbers in a Classroom Model." *Arithmetic Teacher* 29 (November 1981): 18–19.

Carpenter, T., et al. "Decimals: Results and Implications from National Assessment." *Arithmetic Teacher* 28 (April 1981): 34–37.

Carr, M. J. "Get Away from the Table! Make Interest More Interesting." *Mathematics Teacher* 79 (December 1986): 703–705.

Carraher, T. N., and A. D. Schliemann. "Research into Practice: Using Money to Teach about the Decimal System." *Arithmetic Teacher* 36 (December 1988): 42–43.

Cates, W. M. "Ladies and Gentlemen, Start Your Engines." *Arithmetic Teacher* 30 (January 1983): 35–37.

Chow, P., and T. Lin. "Extracting Square Root Made Easy." *Arithmetic Teacher* 29 (November 1981): 48–50.

Cole, B., and H. Weissenfluh. "An Analysis of Teaching Percentages." *Arithmetic Teacher* 21 (March 1974): 226–228.

Comstock, M., and F. Demana. "The Calculator Is a Problem-Solving Concept Developer." *Arithmetic Teacher* 34 (February 1987): 48–51.

Dana, M., and M. Lindquist. "Let's Do It: From Halves to Hundredths." *Arithmetic Teacher* 26 (November 1978): 4–8.

Dewar, J. "Another Look at the Teaching of Percent." *Arithmetic Teacher* 31 (March 1984): 48–49.

Fennell, F. "The Newspaper: A Source for Applications in Mathematics." *Arithmetic Teacher* 30 (October 1982): 22–26.

Firl, D. "Fractions, Decimals and Their Futures." *Arithmetic Teacher* 24 (March 1977): 238–240.

Glatzer, D. "Teaching Percentage: Ideas and Suggestions." *Arithmetic Teacher* 31 (February 1984): 24–26.

Grossman, A. "Decimal Notation: An Important Research Finding." *Arithmetic Teacher* 30 (May 1983): 32–33.

Hannick, F. T. "Using the Memory Functions on Handheld Calculators." *Arithmetic Teacher* 33 (November 1985): 48–49.

Hawkins, V. "The Pythagorean Theorem Revisited: Weighing the Results." *Arithmetic Teacher* 32 (December 1984): 36–37.

Hiebert, J. "Research Report: Decimal Fractions." *Arithmetic Teacher* 34 (March 1987): 22–23.

Hilferty, M. "Some Convenient Fractions for Work with Repeating Decimals." *Mathematics Teacher* 65 (March 1972): 240–241.

Jacobs, J., and E. Herbert. "Making $\sqrt{2}$ Seem 'Real'." *Arithmetic Teacher* 21 (February 1974): 133–136.

Jacobson, M. H. "Teaching Rational Numbers—Intermediate Grades." *Arithmetic Teacher* 31 (February 1984): 40–42.

Kidder, F. "Ditton's Dilemma, or What To Do About Decimals." *Arithmetic Teacher* 28 (October 1980): 44–46.

Markovits, Z., R. Hershkowitz, and M. Bruckheimer. "Estimation, Qualitative Thinking, and Problem Solving." *Mathematics Teacher* 80 (September 1987): 461–464.

Ockenga, E. "Chalk Up Some Calculator Activities for Rational Numbers." *Arithmetic Teacher* 31 (February 1984): 51–53.

Payne, J. "Curricular Issues: Teaching Rational Numbers." *Arithmetic Teacher* 31 (February 1984): 14–17.

Payne, J. "One Point of View: Sense and Nonsense About Fractions and Decimals." *Arithmetic Teacher* 27 (January 1980): 4–7.

Post, T., and K. Cramer. "Research into Practice: Children's Strategies in Ordering Rational Numbers." *Arithmetic Teacher* 35 (October 1987): 33–35.

Prielipp, R. "Decimals." *Arithmetic Teacher* 23 (April 1976): 285–288.

Priester, S. "Sum 9.9: A Game for Decimals." *Arithmetic Teacher* 31 (March 1984): 46–47.

Quintero, A. H. "Helping Children Understand Ratios." *Arithmetic Teacher* 34 (May 1987): 17–21.

Reys, B. J., and R. E. Reys. "Implementing the Standards: Estimation—Direction from the Standards." *Arithmetic Teacher* 37 (March 1990): 22–25.

Schmalz, R. "A Visual Approach to Decimals." *Arithmetic Teacher* 25 (May 1978): 22–25.

Simms, A. J. "Repeating Decimals into Fractions: A Microwave Recipe." *Mathematics Teacher* 80 (January 1987): 61–62.

Skypek, D. "Special Characteristics of Rational Numbers." *Arithmetic Teacher* 31 (February 1984): 10–12.

Strickland, J. F., Jr., and J. Denitto. "The Power of Proportions in Problem Solving." *Mathematics Teacher* 82 (January 1989): 11–13.

Sullivan, K. W. "Money—A Key to Mathematical Success." *Arithmetic Teacher* 29 (November 1981): 34–35.

Swart, W. L. "Fractions vs. Decimals—the Wrong Issue." *Arithmetic Teacher* 29 (October 1981): 17–18.

Teahan, T. "How I Learned to Do Percents." *Arithmetic Teacher* 27 (January 1979): 16–17.

Trafton, P. R., and J. Zawojewski. "Teaching Rational Number Division: A Special Problem." *Arithmetic Teacher* 31 (February 1984): 20–22.

Usiskin, Z., and M. S. Bell. "Ten Often Ignored Applications of Rational-Number Concepts." *Arithmetic Teacher* 31 (February 1984): 48–50.

Wagner, S. "Fun with Repeating Decimals." *Mathematics Teacher* 26 (March 1979): 209–212.

Zawojewski, J. "Initial Decimal Concepts: Are They Really So Easy?" *Arithmetic Teacher* 30 (March 1983): 52–56.

CHAPTER 7   *Geometric Figures*

SPOTLIGHT ON TEACHING

Excerpts from NCTM's Standard 9 for Teaching Mathematics in Grades K–4*

Geometry gives children a different view of mathematics. As they explore patterns and relationships with models, blocks, geoboards, and graph paper, they learn about the properties of shapes and sharpen their intuitions and awareness of spatial concepts. Children's geometric ideas can be developed by having them sort and classify models of plane and solid figures, construct models from straws, make drawings, and create and manipulate shapes on a computer screen. Folding paper cutouts or using mirrors to investigate lines of symmetry are other ways for children to observe figures in a variety of positions, become aware of their important properties, and compare and contrast them. . . .

Spatial sense is an intuitive feel for one's surroundings and the objects in them. To develop spatial sense, children must have many experiences that focus on geometric relationships; the direction, orientation, and perspectives of objects in space; the relative shapes and sizes of figures and objects; and how a change in shape relates to a change in size.

Drawing and sketching shapes is an important part of developing spatial sense. The following spatial-visualization tasks illustrate one productive activity. A figure [such as the segmented circle below] is displayed on an overhead projector for two to three seconds and then children try to draw the figure. The original figure is again briefly displayed, and children make a second attempt at drawing it. Discussion about what the children saw is also important.

Another activity that promotes spatial sense is to have children decide which two-dimensional patterns can be folded to produce a three-dimensional shape. [See the figure below.]

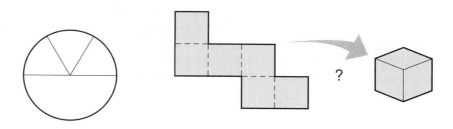

*Reprinted with permission from the *Mathematics Teacher,* © 1987, 1989 by the National Council of Teachers of Mathematics.

SECTION 7.1   PLANE FIGURES

■ *PROBLEM OPENER*

Find a pattern in the 3 figures, and draw the next 2 figures according to the pattern.*

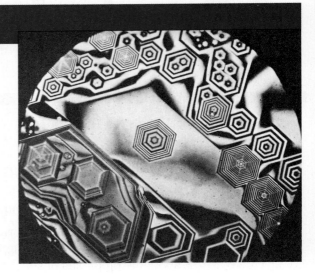

Cross section of cadmium sulfide crystals

We have become so accustomed to hearing about the regularity of patterns in nature that we often take it for granted. Still, it is a source of wonder to see figures with straight edges and uniform angles, such as those in the photo above, occurring in nature.

The study of relationships among lines, angles, surfaces, and solids is a major part of geometry, one of the earliest branches of mathematics. The word **geometry** is from the Latin *geometria,* which means *earth-measure.*

geometry

MATHEMATICAL SYSTEMS

More than 5000 years ago, the Egyptians and Babylonians were using geometry in surveying and architecture. These ancient mathematicians discovered geometric facts and relationships through experimentation and inductive reasoning. Because of their approach, they could never be sure of their conclusions, and in some cases their formulas were incorrect. The ancient Greeks, on the other hand, viewed points, lines, and figures as abstract concepts about which they could reason deductively. They were willing to experiment in order to formulate ideas, but final acceptance of a mathematical statement depended on proof by deductive reasoning. The Greeks' approach was the beginning of mathematical systems.

mathematical system

A **mathematical system** consists of *undefined terms, definitions, axioms,* and *theorems.* There must always be some words that are undefined. "Line" is an example of an undefined term in geometry. We all have an intuitive idea of what a line is, but trying to define it involves more words, such as "straight," "extends indefinitely," "has no thickness," etc. These words would also have to be defined. To avoid this problem of *circularity,* certain basic words such as "point" and "line" are **undefined terms.** These words are then used in **definitions** to define other words. Similarly, there must always be some statements, called **axioms,** that we assume to be true and do not try to prove.

undefined terms
definitions
axioms

theorems

Finally, the axioms, definitions, and undefined terms are used together with deductive reasoning to prove statements called **theorems.**

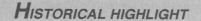

Theorems
↑
Axioms
↑
Undefined terms
and definitions

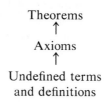

■ **H**ISTORICAL HIGHLIGHT

The crowning achievement of Greek mathematical reasoning was Euclid's *Elements,* a series of 13 books written about 300 B.C. These books contain over 600 theorems, which were obtained by deductive reasoning from 10 basic assumptions called axioms. Although much of the material was drawn from earlier sources, the superbly logical arrangement of the theorems displays the genius of the author. Euclid's *Elements* stood as a model of deductive reasoning for over 2000 years, and few books have been more important to the thought and education of the Western world.*

Euclid

POINTS, LINES, AND PLANES

points

One fundamental notion in geometry is that of a *point.* All geometric figures are sets of points. **Points** are abstract ideas, which we illustrate by dots, corners of boxes, and tips of pointed objects. These concrete illustrations have width and thickness, but points have no dimensions. The following description of a point, from *Mr. Fortune's Maggot,* by Sylvia Townsend Warner, indicates some of the problems associated with teaching elementary school children the concept of a point.**

> Calm, methodical, with a mind prepared for the onset, he guided Lueli down to the beach and with a stick prodded a small hole in it.
> "What is this?"
> "A hole."
> "No, Lueli, it may seem like a hole, but it is a point."
> Perhaps he had prodded a little too emphatically. Lueli's mistake was quite natural. Anyhow, there were bound to be a few misunderstandings at the start.
> He took out his pocket knife and whittled the end of the stick. Then he tried again.
> "What is this?"
> "A smaller hole."
> "Point," said Mr. Fortune suggestively.
> "Yes, I mean a smaller point."
> "No, not quite. It is a point, but it is not smaller. Holes may be of different sizes, but no point is larger or smaller than another point."

---

*D. M. Burton, *The History of Mathematics* (Dubuque, IA: Wm. C. Brown Publishers, 1985), 214–218.
**Quoted in J. R. Newman, *The World of Mathematics,* 4th ed. (New York: Simon and Schuster, 1956), 2254.

line   ✓ A **line** is a set of points that we describe intuitively as being "straight" and extending indefinitely in both directions. The edges of boxes and taut pieces of string or wire are models of lines. The line in Figure 7.1 passes through points *A* and *B* and is denoted by $\overleftrightarrow{AB}$. The arrows indicate that the line continues indefinitely in both directions. If two or more points are on the same line, they are called **collinear.**

collinear

Figure 7.1

A plane is another basic set of points that we do not define precisely. We describe a **plane** as being "flat" like the top of a table, but extending indefinitely. The surfaces of floors and walls are other common models for portions of planes. A plane can be illustrated by a drawing; sometimes arrows are used, as in Figure 7.2, to indicate that it extends and is not bounded.

plane

Figure 7.2

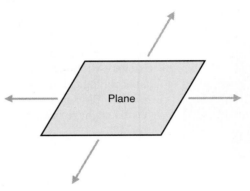

EXAMPLE A

A standard sheet of paper is a model for part of a plane.

1. What part of a sheet of paper might be used as a model for a line?
2. What part of a sheet of paper might be used as a model for a point?
3. How can models of lines and points be obtained by folding a sheet of paper?

Solution

1. Each edge of the paper is a model for part of a line.
2. Each corner of the paper is a model for a point.
3. The crease made by folding a sheet of paper is a model for part of a line. Two folds can produce two lines that intersect in a point.

Points, lines, and planes are undefined terms in geometry that are used to define other terms and geometric figures. The following paragraphs contain some of the more common definitions and examples of figures that occur in planes.

HALF-PLANES, SEGMENTS, RAYS, AND ANGLES

HALF-PLANES   A line in a plane partitions the plane into three disjoint sets: the points on the line and two **half-planes.** Line ℓ in Figure 7.3 partitions the plane into half-planes with point A in one half and point B in the other.

half-planes
opposite half-planes

LINE SEGMENTS   A **line segment** consists of two points on a line and all the points between them (Figure 7.4). The line segment with **endpoints** *A* and *B* is denoted by $\overline{AB}$. To **bisect** a line segment means to divide it into two parts of equal length. The **midpoint** *C* bisects $\overline{AB}$.

line segment
endpoints
bisect
midpoint

Figure 7.3

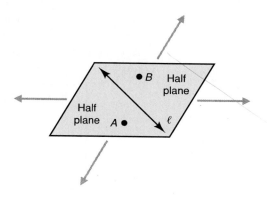

Figure 7.4

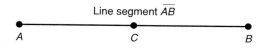

Line segment $\overline{AB}$

HALF-LINES AND RAYS   A point on a line partitions the line into three disjoint sets:

half-lines
ray
endpoint

the point and two **half-lines.** Part (a) of Figure 7.5 shows two half-lines that are de-termined by point *P*. A **ray** consists of a point on a line and all the points in one of the half-lines determined by the point. The ray in part (b), which has *D* as an **endpoint** and contains point *E*, is denoted by $\overrightarrow{DE}$

Figure 7.5

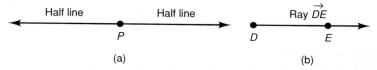

Half line   Half line

P

Ray $\overrightarrow{DE}$

D   *E*

(a)   (b)

angle

vertex, sides of the angle

ANGLES   An **angle** is formed by the union of two rays, as shown in part (a) of Figure 7.6, or by two line segments that have a common endpoint, as in part (b). This endpoint is called the **vertex,** and the rays or line segments are called the **sides of the angle.** The angle with vertex *G*, whose sides contain points *F* and *H*, is denoted by $\angle FGH$. Some-times it is convenient to identify an angle either by its vertex or by a numeral, such as $\angle S$ or $\angle 1$ in part (b).

Figure 7.6

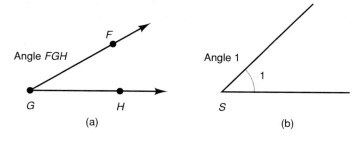

F

Angle *FGH*

G   *H*

(a)

Angle 1

1

S

(b)

EXAMPLE B

Fold a standard sheet of paper to create models of the following terms.

1. Two opposite half-planes
2. A bisected line segment
3. A ray
4. An angle

Solution

1. Any crease creates two half-planes.
2. Fold the paper to obtain a crease and draw a line in the crease, as shown in figure (a). Select two points, *A* and *B* on the line, and fold the line onto itself so that point *A* coincides with point *B*. The point where the new crease intersects segment $\overline{AB}$ is its midpoint and bisects $\overline{AB}$ into two segments.

3. Any crease creates a line, and selecting in a point on the line determines two rays.
4. Any two folds that form creases that intersect in a point create four angles having the point as a vertex. Figure (b) shows angles 1, 2, 3, and 4.

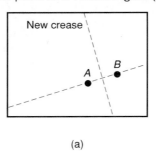

(a)

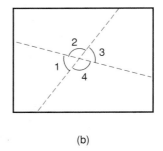

(b)

PROBLEM-SOLVING APPLICATION

The ability to determine the number of line segments between a given number of points has many practical applications. One of these became evident in the early days of the development of the telephone system. The fundamental problem was how to connect two people who wanted to talk. This was done by connecting cords and plugs for each pair of people. In 1884, Ezra T. Gilliland devised a mechanical system that would allow 15 subscribers to reach each other without the aid of an operator.

■ PROBLEM

How many line segments are needed to connect 15 points so that each pair of points forms the ends of a line segment?

Question 1

Understanding the Problem   One line segment connects 2 points, and 3 line segments connect 3 points. How many line segments are needed to connect 4 points?

Question 2

Devising a Plan   Let's examine a few more special cases. Perhaps the strategies of *solving a simpler problem* and *finding a pattern* will lead to a solution. In the following figure, 6 line segments have the points A, B, C, and D as endpoints. How many new line segments are needed to connect E to each of these 4 points, and what is the total number of line segments connecting the 5 points?

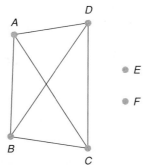

Question 3

Carrying Out the Plan   Placing a sixth point, F, in the diagram, we can see that there will be 5 new line segments from F to the other points and a total of 15 line segments for the 6 points. Find a pattern and complete the following table. How many line segments are required to connect 15 points?

No. of points	2	3	4	5	6	7	8	9	10	15
No. of segments	1	3	6	10	15					

Looking Back   You probably recognize the numbers 1, 3, 6, 10, 15, etc., in the table as triangular numbers (Chapter 1). The nth triangular number is $n(n + 1)/2$. Using this formula, you can determine the number of line segments needed to connect 20 points so that the points in each pair are the endpoints of a line segment. What is this number?

Question 4

Answers to Questions 1–4

1. 6

2. There will be 4 new line segments and a total of 10 line segments for the 5 points.

3. 105

4. The number of line segments needed to connect 20 points is the 19th triangular number: $(19 \times 20)/2 = 190$.

ANGLE MEASUREMENTS

degrees

minutes, seconds

The ancient Babylonians devised a method for measuring angles by dividing a circle into 360 equal parts called **degrees**. One degree ($1°$) is $1/360$ of a complete turn about a circle, as shown in Figure 7.7. Each degree can be divided into 60 equal parts called **minutes,** and each minute can be divided into 60 equal parts called **seconds**. This is the origin of the modern practice of dividing hours into minutes and seconds.

Figure 7.7

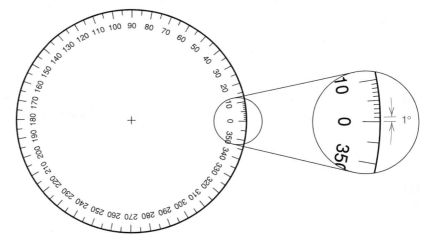

protractor

A **protractor** is a device for measuring angles (Figure 7.8). To measure an angle, place the center of the protractor on the vertex of the angle (B in this example), and line up one side of the angle (BC) with the baseline of the protractor. The protractor in Figure 7.8 shows that $\measuredangle ABC$ has a measure of $60°$.

Figure 7.8

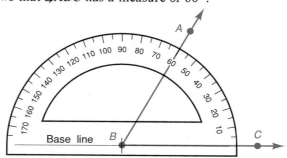

right angle
acute angle
obtuse angle

reflex angle

If an angle has a measure of 90°, as in part (a) of Figure 7.9, it is called a **right angle**; if it is less than 90°, as in part (b), it is called an **acute angle**; if it is greater than 90° and less than 180°, as in part (c), it is called an **obtuse angle**. It is customary to draw ⌐ at the vertex of a right angle. Occasionally we use angles with measures of more than 180°, as shown in part (d) of Figure 7.9. Such an angle is called a **reflex angle**. To indicate an angle with a measure that is greater than 180°, we will draw a circular arc to connect the two sides of the angle.

Figure 7.9

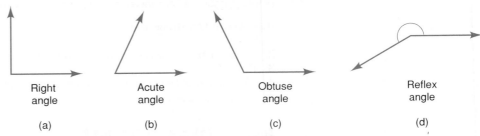

Right angle	Acute angle	Obtuse angle	Reflex angle
(a)	(b)	(c)	(d)

complementary
supplementary

adjacent angles

If the sum of two angles is 90°, the angles are called **complementary**; if their sum is 180°, they are called **supplementary**. Figure 7.10 shows special cases of complementary and supplementary angles in which the pairs of angles share a common side. If two angles have the same vertex, share a common side, and lie on opposite sides of their common side, they are called **adjacent angles**. Angles 1 and 2 are adjacent complementary angles, and angles 3 and 4 are adjacent supplementary angles.

Figure 7.10

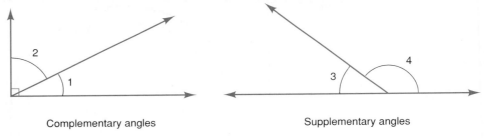

Complementary angles   Supplementary angles

EXAMPLE C

Fold a standard sheet of paper to create models for the following terms.

1. Acute angle   2. Obtuse angle
3. Supplementary angles   4. Complementary angles
5. Adjacent angles

Solution   1, 2, 3, 5 Any crease that intersects an edge of the paper forms supplementary angles with the edges. For example, the crease in figure (a) intersects $\overline{BC}$, forming supplementary angles 1 and 2. The same crease intersects $\overline{AB}$ and forms supplementary angles 3 and 4. Angles 1 and 4 are acute, and angles 2 and 3 are obtuse.

4, 5 Any crease through a corner of the paper forms adjacent complementary angles with the edges. Angles 5 and 6 in figure (b) are complementary adjacent angles.

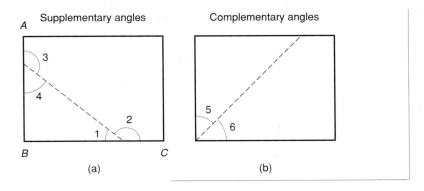

Supplementary angles   Complementary angles

(a)   (b)

Two intersecting lines form several pairs of adjacent supplementary angles. For example, ∠1 and ∠4 in Figure 7.11 are supplementary angles. Nonadjacent angles formed by two intersecting lines, such as ∠2 and ∠4 in Figure 7.11, are called **vertical angles.**

vertical angles

Figure 7.11

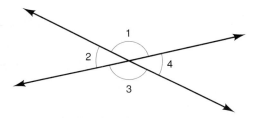

EXAMPLE D

1. Name 4 pairs of supplementary angles in Figure 7.11.
2. Name 2 pairs of vertical angles in Figure 7.11.
3. Fold a sheet of paper to create a model of 2 intersecting lines. Compare the measures of the vertical angles and make a conjecture.

Solution

1. The following pairs of angles are supplementary angles: ∠1 and ∠4; ∠1 and ∠2; ∠2 and ∠3; ∠3 and ∠4.
2. The following pairs of angles are vertical angles: ∠2 and ∠4; ∠1 and ∠3.
3. Two intersecting creases produce vertical angles. Angles 1 and 2 in the figure below are vertical angles. Vertical angles are congruent. This can be illustrated by folding the angles onto each other.

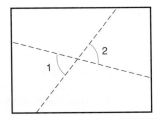

PERPENDICULAR AND PARALLEL LINES

perpendicular

If two lines intersect to form right angles, they are **perpendicular.** Lines m and n in Figure 7.12 are perpendicular; this is indicated by writing $m \perp n$. Two line segments, such as $\overline{AB}$ and $\overline{CD}$, are perpendicular if they lie on perpendicular lines. In this case, we write $\overline{AB} \perp \overline{CD}$ or $\overleftrightarrow{AB} \perp \overleftrightarrow{CD}$.

Figure 7.12

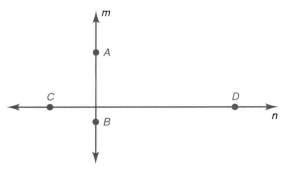

Perpendicular lines

parallel

If two lines are in a plane and they do not intersect, they are **parallel.** Lines *m* and *n* in Figure 7.13 are parallel; this is indicated by writing *m* ‖ *n*. Similarly, two segments are parallel if they lie in parallel lines. Segments $\overline{EF}$ and $\overline{GH}$ are parallel, and we write $\overline{EF}$ ‖ $\overline{GH}$.

Figure 7.13

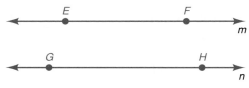

Parallel lines

transversal

alternate interior angles

If two lines *ℓ* and *m* are intersected by a third line *t* (see Figure 7.14), we call line *t* a **transversal.** Two very special angles are created on the alternate sides of the transversal and interior to lines *ℓ* and *m* (angles 1 and 2 in Figure 7.14). These angles are called **alternate interior angles.** If the two lines *ℓ* and *m* are parallel (as in Figure 7.14), *the alternate interior angles have the same measure.* The converse of this statement is also true: *if the alternate interior angles have the same measure,* lines *ℓ* and *m* are parallel. These statements are combined in the following property.

Figure 7.14

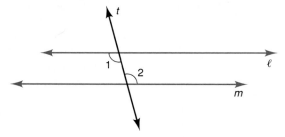

ALTERNATE INTERIOR ANGLES

> If two lines are intersected by a transversal, the lines are parallel if and only if the alternate interior angles created by the transversal have the same measure.

EXAMPLE E

Use a standard sheet of paper to model the following geometric terms: parallel lines, perpendicular lines, lines intersected by a transversal, and alternate interior angles having the same measure. Draw and label these on the paper.

Solution

The opposite edges of the paper are parallel line segments, and any two edges that meet at a corner are perpendicular line segments. Any fold of the paper that intersects the opposite parallel edges of the paper will create alternate interior angles with the same measure.

There are other ways of obtaining parallel and perpendicular lines by folding paper. Two perpendicular lines can be obtained by folding the paper in half along one edge and then folding it in half along the other edge. Two parallel lines can be obtained by folding the paper in half along one edge and then folding it in half again along the same edge.

PROBLEM-SOLVING APPLICATION

■ PROBLEM

What is the maximum number of regions into which a plane can be partitioned by 12 lines?

Understanding the Problem   One line partitions a plane into 2 regions, and 2 intersecting lines partition a plane into 4 regions. What is the maximum number of regions created by 3 lines in a plane?

Question 1

Devising a Plan   It would be difficult to draw 12 lines and count the resulting regions. Let's *make a table* to record the number of regions for the first few lines. This approach may suggest a solution. Three lines divide the plane into 7 regions. What is the maximum number of regions created by 4 lines?

Question 2

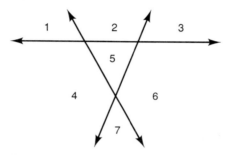

Carrying Out the Plan   The following table lists the maximum number of regions for 1, 2, 3, and 4 lines. Find a pattern and use inductive reasoning to predict the numbers of regions for the next few lines. How many regions will there be for 12 lines?

Question 3

No. of lines	1	2	3	4	5	6	7	8	9	10	11	12
No. of regions	2	4	7	11								

Looking Back   When a fourth line that is not parallel to any of the first 3 lines is drawn on the plane, by definition it will intersect each of the 3 given lines. Also, it will cut across 4 regions, as shown in the figure below. This accounts for 4 new regions. How many lines and how many regions will a fifth nonparallel line intersect?

Question 4

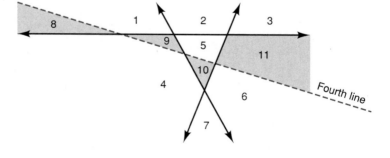

Answers to Questions 1–4

1. 7   **2.** 11

3.

No. of lines	5	6	7	8	9	10	11	12
No. of regions	16	22	29	37	46	56	67	79

4. The fifth line will intersect 4 lines and 5 regions to create 5 new regions.

CURVES AND CONVEX SETS

curve

We can draw a **curve** through a set of points using a single continuous motion (Figure 7.15).

Figure 7.15

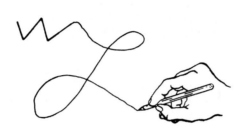

a.

"You don't see many drawings made with one continuous line anymore."

b.

simple curve
simple closed curve
closed curve

Several types of curves are shown in Figure 7.16. Curve A is called a **simple curve** because it starts and stops without intersecting itself. Curve B is a **simple closed curve** because it is a simple curve that starts and stops at the same point. Curve C is a **closed curve,** but since it intersects itself it is not a simple closed curve.

Figure 7.16

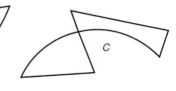

Simple curve   Simple closed curve   Closed curve

EXAMPLE F

Classify each curve as simple, simple closed, or closed.

(1)   (2)   (3)   (4)

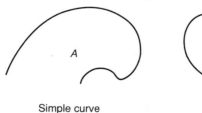

Solution   1. Closed   2. Simple   3. Simple closed   4. Simple closed

Jordan Curve theorem   A well-known theorem in mathematics, called the **Jordan Curve theorem,** states that every simple closed curve partitions a plane into three disjoint sets: the points on the curve, the points in the interior, and the points in the exterior. This means that if K is in the interior and M is in the exterior, then $\overline{KM}$ will intersect the curve (Figure 7.17).

Figure 7.17

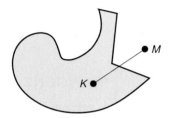

plane region   **CONVEX SETS**   The union of a simple closed curve and its interior is called a **plane region.** Plane regions can be classified as *nonconvex* and *convex.* You may have heard the word "concave" rather than "nonconvex." An object is concave if it is "caved in," like Set F in Figure 7.18, and convex if it is not, like set G. To be more mathematically **convex** precise, we say that a set is **convex** if the line segment joining any two points of the **nonconvex** set lies completely in the set. Set F is **nonconvex** because $\overline{XY}$ is not completely in the set. An intuitive way of thinking about convexity of plane regions is to imagine enclosing the boundary of a figure with a rubber band. If the rubber band touches all points on the boundary (as it will for set G), the set is convex, and if not (as for set F), the set is nonconvex.

Figure 7.18

F   G

Nonconvex   Convex

EXAMPLE G

Classify each region as convex or nonconvex.

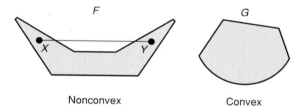

(1)   (2)   (3)

Solution   1. Convex   2. Nonconvex   3. Convex

---

circle   **CIRCLES**   A **circle** is a special case of a simple closed curve whose interior is a convex set (Figure 7.19). Each point on a circle is the same distance from a fixed point called **center, radius** the **center.** A line segment from a point on the circle to its center is a **radius,** and a line **chord** segment whose endpoints are both on the circle is a **chord.** A chord that passes through **diameter** the center is a **diameter.** The words *radius* and *diameter* are also used to refer to the lengths of these line segments. A line that intersects the circle in exactly one point is **tangent, circumference** a **tangent.** The distance around the circle is the **circumference.** The union of a circle **disc** and its interior is called a **disc.**

Figure 7.19

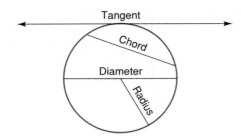

POLYGONS

polygon
polygonal region
sides, vertices

A **polygon** is a simple closed curve that is the union of line segments. The union of a polygon and its interior is called a **polygonal region.** Polygons are classified according to their number of line segments. A few examples are shown in Figure 7.20. The line segments of a polygon are called **sides,** and the endpoints of these segments are **vertices.**

Figure 7.20

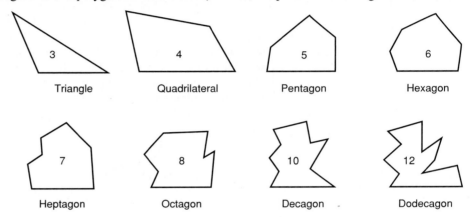

EXAMPLE H

Which of the following figures are polygons?

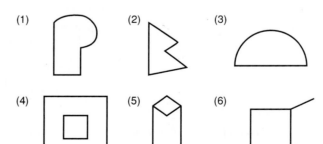

Solution   Figure (2) is the only polygon. Figures (1) and (3) are simple closed curves, but not polygons. Figures (4), (5), and (6) are not simple closed curves.

---

diagonal

Any line segment connecting one vertex of a polygon to a nonadjacent vertex is a **diagonal.** Figure 7.21 shows a pentagon with its 5 diagonals.

Figure 7.21

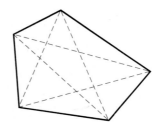

EXAMPLE I

How many diagonals are there in each of the following polygons?

1. Quadrilateral   2. Triangle   3. Hexagon

Solution   1. 2   2. Zero   3. 9

Certain triangles and quadrilaterals occur often enough to be given special names. Several of these are shown in Figure 7.22.

Figure 7.22

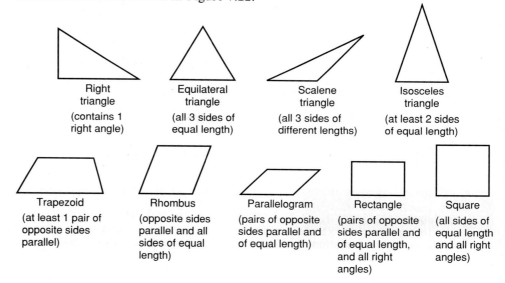

Right triangle
(contains 1 right angle)

Equilateral triangle
(all 3 sides of equal length)

Scalene triangle
(all 3 sides of different lengths)

Isosceles triangle
(at least 2 sides of equal length)

Trapezoid
(at least 1 pair of opposite sides parallel)

Rhombus
(opposite sides parallel and all sides of equal length)

Parallelogram
(pairs of opposite sides parallel and of equal length)

Rectangle
(pairs of opposite sides parallel and of equal length, and all right angles)

Square
(all sides of equal length and all right angles)

EXAMPLE J

Determine whether each statement is true or false, and state a reason.

1. Every square is a rectangle.
2. Every equilateral triangle is an isosceles triangle.
3. Some right triangles are isosceles triangles.
4. Every trapezoid is a parallelogram.
5. Some isosceles triangles are scalene triangles.
6. Every parallelogram is a trapezoid.

Solution

1. True. The opposite sides of a square are parallel and of equal length.
2. True. An equilateral triangle has three sides of equal length, so it has *at least* two sides of equal length.
3. True. A right triangle could have two legs of length 1 and a hypotenuse of length $\sqrt{2}$; the two equal sides would make it an isosceles triangle.
4. False. Some trapezoids have only one pair of opposite parallel sides; a parallelogram must have two pairs of opposite parallel sides.
5. False. All three sides are of different lengths in a scalene triangle.
6. True. A parallelogram has two pairs of opposite parallel sides, so it has *at least* one pair of opposite parallel sides.

EXAMPLE K

Fold a standard sheet of paper to obtain a model of each geometric figure.

1. Isosceles triangle   2. Square   3. Parallelogram

Solution   Here are some possibilities. There are other ways to obtain these figures.

1. Fold the paper in half to obtain point *A*, as shown in figure (a). Then fold to obtain the crease $\overline{AB}$ and fold again to obtain the crease $\overline{AC}$. Line segment $\overline{AB}$ can be folded onto $\overline{AC}$ to show that triangle *ABC* is isosceles.
2. Fold corner *D* [figure (b)] down to point *S* so that $\overline{DF}$ coincides with $\overline{FS}$. With the paper in this folded position, use edge $\overline{DR}$ to draw line $\overline{RS}$. Then figure *DRSF* is a square.
3. Fold the paper in half to obtain points *X* and *Y*, as shown in figure (c). Then fold to obtain the creases $\overline{GX}$ and $\overline{IY}$; *GYIX* is a parallelogram.

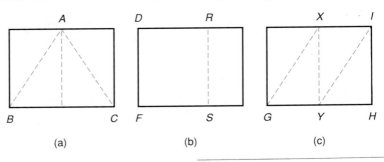

(a)   (b)   (c)

PROBLEM-SOLVING APPLICATION

■ PROBLEM

How many diagonals does a 15-sided polygon have?

Understanding the Problem   A diagonal is a line segment connecting any two nonadjacent vertices of a polygon. Quadrilateral *ABCD*, shown below, has diagonals *AC* and *BD*. Sketch a nonconvex quadrilateral. Does such a quadrilateral have 2 diagonals?

Question 1

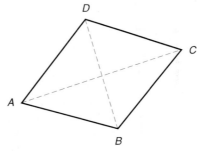

Devising a Plan   One approach is to *simplify the problem* by drawing a few polygons and counting the number of diagonals. By listing these in a table we may be able to find a pattern. How many diagonals are there in each of the following polygons?

Question 2

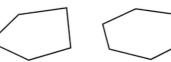

Pentagon   Hexagon   Heptagon

Question 3

Carrying Out the Plan Fill in a few boxes of the table below and *look for a pattern*. Use your pattern and inductive reasoning to complete the table. How many diagonals are there in a 15-sided polygon?

No. of sides	3	4	5	6	7	8	9	10	11	12
No. of diagonals	0	2	5	9						

Question 4

Looking Back Another approach to this problem is to use the result from the Problem-Solving Application on page 302, in which we found the number of line segments connecting 15 points. Since there are 105 line segments connecting 15 points, the number of diagonals in a 15-sided polygon can be found by subtracting 15 (the number of sides in the polygon) from 105. Thus there are 90 diagonals. Use this approach to find the number of diagonals in a 25-sided polygon.

Answers to Questions 1–4
1. Yes
2. Pentagon, 5 diagonals; hexagon, 9 diagonals; heptagon, 14 diagonals
3. 90
4. The number of line segments connecting 25 points is the 24th triangular number: (24 × 25)/2 = 300. Subtracting 25, the number of sides in the polygon, from 300 yields 275 diagonals.

RELATED ACTIVITIES IN
Mathematics for Elementary Teachers: An Activity Approach, 3e

Activity Set 7.1

Figures on Rectangular and Circular Geoboards: Activities involve building convex and nonconvex polygons and various triangles and quadrilaterals on a rectangular geoboard. Central angles and inscribed angles and their relationships are illustrated on a circular geoboard.

Just for Fun

Tangram Puzzles: A paperfolding activity for obtaining the 7 tangram pieces and suggestions for forming geometric figures with these pieces

---

PUZZLER

Cross out 8 line segments and leave 2 squares.

EXERCISES AND PROBLEMS 7.1

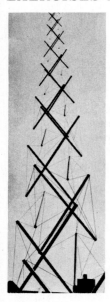

Needle Tower, a sculpture of aluminum and stainless-steel rods and wires

1. The sculpture in the photo has angles formed by steel rods.
   a. What is the approximate measure of these angles? (This can be determined by tracing one angle and measuring it with a protractor.)
   b. Does the measure of the angles decrease, remain the same, or increase as you move from the bottom to the top of the figure? Check your conjecture by tracing.

2. This picture of a cross section of natural sapphire shows angles that each have the same number of degrees.
   a. Are these angles acute or obtuse?
   b. Approximately how many degrees are there in these angles?

Natural sapphire crystal

3. a. List three undefined geometric terms.
   b. List three defined terms whose definitions use one or more of the undefined terms.
   c. Explain why it is necessary to have undefined terms in geometry.

4. Give two examples of physical models that illustrate these terms.

   a. Line segment   b. Triangle
   c. Plane   d. Angle
   e. Point   f. Square

5. Use these polygons to answer the questions that follow.

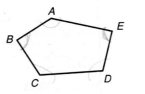 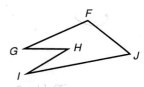

   a. Which angles are acute?
   b. Which angles are obtuse?
   c. Which angles are right angles?
   d. Which angle is a reflex angle (greater than 180°)?

6. Use angles 1 through 10 to identify the following. (Note: Lines ℓ and m are perpendicular.)

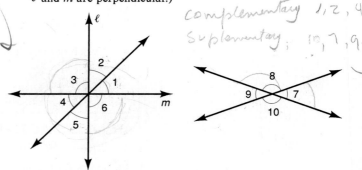

   a. Three pairs of adjacent supplementary angles
   b. Three pairs of vertical angles
   c. Two pairs of adjacent complementary angles

7. Draw a circle that illustrates each of the following geometric situations.
   a. A diameter that is perpendicular to a chord
   b. A line tangent to one end of a radius
   c. Two chords that bisect each other

8. Explain why the angles in each pair in parts *a* through *d* have the same measure. (Note: Lines ℓ and m are parallel.)

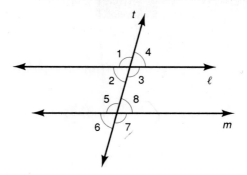

   a. ∡2 and ∡8
   b. ∡2 and ∡4
   c. ∡4 and ∡8 (These angles are called **corresponding angles.**)
   d. ∡1 and ∡7
   e. Explain why ∡3 and ∡8 are supplementary angles.

9. Classify each curve as simple, simple closed, closed, or none of these.

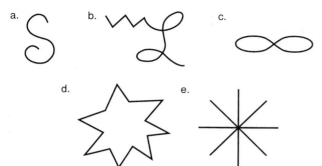

a.   b.   c.

d.   e.

10. Classify each region as convex or nonconvex.

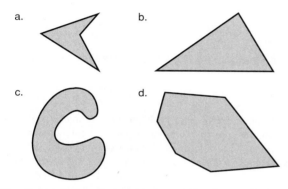

a.   b.

c.   d.

11. The picture below shows three crystals of the mineral staurolite. These crystals are found in all parts of the world. They are especially common in the Shenandoah Valley. The crystal on the far right is known as the "Fairy Stone" of the Appalachian Mountains. This form and the one on the left are often imitated by jewelers.

Crystals of staurolite

a. The ridges on the top of the Fairy Stone form lines that intersect in equal angles. How many degrees are in each of these angles?

b. The ridges on the top of the crystal on the left form 3 lines that intersect in 6 equal angles. How many degrees are in each of these angles?

12. Three lines in a plane may intersect in zero, 1, 2, or 3 points.

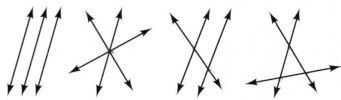

a. How many points of intersection are possible with 4 lines in a plane?

b. How many points of intersection are possible with 5 lines in a plane?

13. Draw some figures to determine whether the following statements are true or false. For each false statement, show a counterexample.

a. The two diagonals of a parallelogram have the same length.

b. Any two angles in a parallelogram that share a common side are supplementary.

c. The two diagonals of a rectangle have the same length.

d. If the two diagonals in a parallelogram have the same length, the parallelogram is a rectangle.

e. If the midpoints of the sides of a rectangle are connected, another rectangle is formed.

f. If the midpoints of the sides of a quadrilateral are connected, a parallelogram is formed.

14. To prepare for their annual volleyball party, the Chase family has laid out a four-sided volleyball court in which two opposite sides have a length of 30 feet and the other two opposite sides have a length of 60 feet.

a. Explain why the court may not be rectangular. What shape might it have?

b. Which statement in #13 can be used to determine if the court is rectangular?

15. In 1891 Almon B. Strowger patented a phone-dialing machine that could connect up to 99 subscribers. How many different two-party calls would such a machine permit?

16. Suppose squares A, B, and C are houses and E, G, and W represent sources of electricity, gas, and water. Try connecting the houses with each utility by drawing lines or curves so that they do not cross each other. It is possible to make only 8 of the 9 connections. Draw these 8 connections.

a. Some of your connections will form a simple closed curve, with the remaining unconnected house and utility on opposite sides of this curve. Find this curve and mark it with dark lines.

b. How does the Jordan Curve Theorem show that 9 connections cannot be completed?

17. The white path in this ornament from the Middle Ages is a curve.

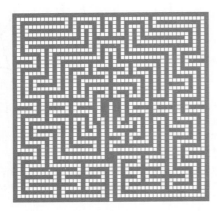

a. Is it a simple curve?
b. Is it a closed curve?

18. The curves shown below are simple closed curves. The Jordan Curve Theorem states that if a point inside a simple closed curve is connected to a point outside the curve, the connecting arc will intersect the curve. Use the fact that points B and D are outside the two curves (i) and (ii) to answer the questions below.

(i)

(ii)

a. Can an arc be drawn from A to B that does not intersect curve (i)? Is A inside or outside the curve?
b. Can an arc be drawn from C to D that does not intersect curve (ii)? Is C inside or outside curve (ii)?
c. Draw line segment $\overline{AB}$. Count the number of times that $\overline{AB}$ intersects curve (i). How can this number be used to tell

when a point is inside or outside a simple closed curve? (Hint: Draw a few simple closed curves.) Check your answer by drawing $\overline{CD}$ for curve (ii).

19. The following simple closed curve is from *Puzzles and Graphs* by John Fujii.* Determine whether the points in each pair below are on the same side of the curve.

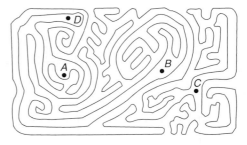

a. A, B **b.** B, C
c. D, C **d.** B, D

Featured Strategies: Solving a Simpler Problem and Making a Table

20. What is the maximum number of points of intersection of 12 lines?
  a. Understanding the Problem The problem asks for the greatest possible number of points of intersection. What is the minimum number of points of intersection of 12 lines?
  b. Devising a Plan The following figure shows that the maximum number of points of intersection of 4 lines is 6. Considering a few other cases for small numbers of lines may reveal a pattern. What is the maximum number of points of intersection of 3 lines?

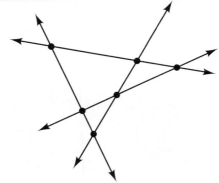

  c. Carrying Out the Plan Look for a pattern and complete the table below. What is the maximum number of points of intersection of 12 lines?

No. of lines	2	3	4	5	6	7	8	9	10	11	12
No. of intersections			6								

  d. Looking Back Use the pattern in part *c* to determine the maximum number of points of intersection of 50 lines.

*John Fujii, *Puzzles and Graphs* (Reston, VA: National Council of Teachers of Mathematics, 1966).

21. An equilateral triangle has three sides of equal length. Fold a sheet of paper to form an equilateral triangle. (Hint: Obtain a center line as in the following figure.)

C   D

LABORATORY INVESTIGATION

The geoboard is a manipulative often used in schools. A square shape is formed by 25 nails in a 5 by 5 array. Line segments, angles, and polygons can be modeled by stretching rubber bands between the nails.

Questions for Investigation

1. The polygon on the geoboard at the right is convex and has 7 sides. What is the convex polygon with the greatest number of sides that can be formed on a geoboard?

2. It is possible to form a nonconvex polygon with over 20 sides on a geoboard. What is the maximum number of sides on such a polygon?

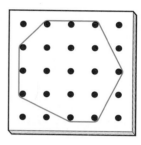

PUZZLER

It is possible to connect *A* to *A'*, *B* to *B'*, and *C* to *C'* so that no curves intersect and the curves are drawn in the interior of the rectangle. How can this be done?

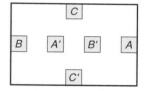

SECTION 7.2 POLYGONS AND TESSELLATIONS

■ *PROBLEM OPENER*

This rectangular region is cut into 8 congruent pieces. In how many ways can a rectangular region be cut into 8 congruent pieces?

8 congruent pieces

Cross section of the gem tourmaline

The triangles in the photo above are another amazing example of geometric figures that occur in nature. In each triangle the sides have the same length and the angles have the same measure. Such special types of polygons are discussed in this section.

ANGLES IN POLYGONS

The vertex angles of a polygon with 4 or more sides can be any size between 0° and 360°. In the hexagon in Figure 7.23, $\angle B$ is less than 20° and $\angle D$ and $\angle A$ are both greater than 180°. In spite of this range of possible sizes, there is a relationship between the sum of all the angles in a polygon and its number of sides.

Figure 7.23

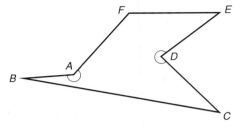

In any triangle, for example, the sum of the 3 angle measures is 180°. This fact was proven by Greek mathematicians in the fourth century B.C. One way of demonstrating this theorem is to draw an arbitrary triangle and cut off its angles, as shown in Figure 7.24. When these angles are placed side by side with their vertices at a point, they form one-half of a revolution (180°) about the point.

Figure 7.24

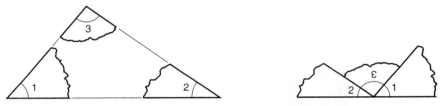

The sum of the angles in a polygon of 4 or more sides can be found by subdividing the polygon into triangles so that the vertices of the triangles are the vertices of the polygon. The quadrilateral in Figure 7.25 is partitioned into 2 triangles whose angles are numbered from 1 through 6. The sum of all 6 angles is 2 × 180°, or 360°. Therefore the sum of the 4 angles of the quadrilateral is 360°, since its angles are made up of these 6 angles.

Figure 7.25

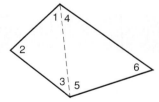

An infinite variety of quadrilaterals can be formed, some convex and others nonconvex. However, since each quadrilateral can be partitioned into 2 triangles such that the vertices of the triangles are also the vertices of the quadrilateral, the sum of the angles of a quadrilateral will always be 360°. A similar approach can be used to find the sum of the angles in any polygon.

EXAMPLE A

Find the sum of all the angles in each polygon.

　　1. Pentagon　　　2. Octagon

Solution

1. A pentagon can be subdivided into 3 triangles, as shown in figure (a). So the total number of degrees in its angles is 3 × 180° = 540°.
2. An octagon can be subdivided into 6 triangles, as shown in figure (b). So the total number of degrees in its angles is 6 × 180° = 1080°.

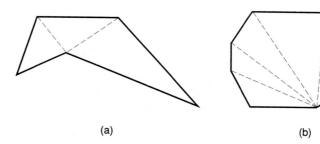

　　　　(a)　　　　　　　　　　　　　　　(b)

CONGRUENCE

congruent

The idea of congruence is quite simple to understand intuitively: two plane figures, such as those in Figure 7.26, are **congruent** if one can be placed on the other so that they coincide. Another way to describe congruent plane figures is to say that they have the same size and shape. (Congruence is presented in more detail in Sections 10.1 and 10.2.)

Figure 7.26

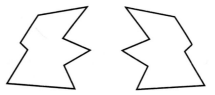

congruent segments
congruent angles

We can be more precise at this point about congruence of line segments and angles. Two **line segments are congruent** if they have the same length, and two **angles are congruent** if they have the same number of degrees (Figure 7.27).

Figure 7.27

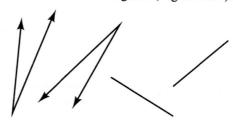

EXAMPLE B

Fold a standard sheet of paper so that it is partitioned into the following figures.

　　1. Four congruent rectangles
　　2. Two congruent right triangles and a rectangle
　　3. Four congruent right triangles
　　4. Sixteen congruent rectangles

Solution   Here are some methods. There are others.

1. Fold the paper twice: once in half perpendicular to one edge and again in half perpendicular to an adjacent edge.
2. Fold a corner of the paper down to obtain a rectangle and the largest possible square. The fold forms the diagonal of the square and bisects it into two right triangles.
3. Fold the paper in half to obtain a rectangle, and then fold along the diagonal of the rectangle.
4. Fold the paper in half perpendicular to the edges a total of 4 times.

REGULAR POLYGONS

regular polygon

Sections 7.1 and 7.2 opened with photos of hexagons and triangles that grow naturally with congruent line segments and congruent angles. The figures in these photos are examples of regular polygons. A polygon is called a **regular polygon** if it satisfies both of the following conditions:

1. all angles are congruent, and
2. all sides are congruent.

A few regular polygons are shown in Figure 7.28.

Figure 7.28

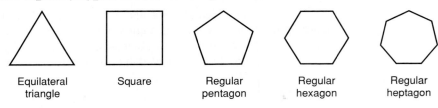

Equilateral   Square   Regular   Regular   Regular
triangle   pentagon   hexagon   heptagon

EXAMPLE **C**

The following figures satisfy only one of the two conditions for regular polygons. For each polygon determine which condition is satisfied and which condition is not satisfied.

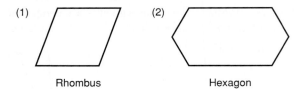

(1)   (2)

Rhombus   Hexagon

Solution   1. The 4 sides are congruent but the 4 angles are not congruent.
2. The 6 angles are congruent but the 6 sides are not congruent.

CONSTRUCTING REGULAR POLYGONS

vertex angle
central angle
exterior angle

There are three special angles in regular polygons (see Figure 7.29). A **vertex angle** is formed by two adjacent sides of the polygon; a **central angle** is formed by connecting the center of the polygon to two adjacent vertices of the polygon; and an **exterior angle** is formed by one side of the polygon and the extension of an adjacent side.

Figure 7.29

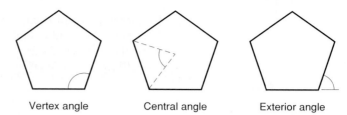

Vertex angle   Central angle   Exterior angle

The sum of the angles in a polygon can be used to compute the number of degrees in each vertex angle of a regular polygon: simply divide the sum of all the angles by the number of angles. For example, part (a) of Figure 7.30 shows a regular pentagon that is subdivided into 3 triangles. Since each vertex of a triangle is a vertex of the pentagon, the sum of the 9 angles in the triangles equals the sum of the 5 angles in the pentagon. So the sum of the angles in the pentagon is 3 × 180°, or 540°. Therefore, each angle in a regular pentagon is 540° ÷ 5, or 108°, as shown in part (b) of Figure 7.30.

Figure 7.30

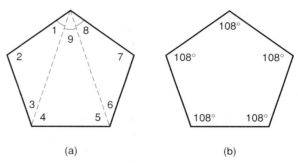

(a)   (b)

Figure 7.31 shows the first four steps in constructing a regular pentagon. The process begins in step (1) as a line segment is drawn and a point for the vertex of the angle is marked. Then in step (2) the baseline of a protractor is placed on the line segment so that the center of the protractor's baseline is at the vertex point, and a 108° angle is drawn. In step (3) two sides of the pentagon are marked off, and in step (4) the protractor is used to draw another 108° angle. This process can be continued to obtain a regular pentagon.

Figure 7.31

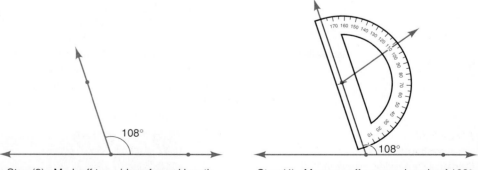

Step (3)   Mark off two sides of equal length.   Step (4)   Measure off a second angle of 108°.

Another approach to constructing regular polygons begins with a circle and uses central angles. The number of degrees in the central angle of a regular polygon is 360 divided by the number of sides in the polygon. A decagon has 10 sides, so each central angle is 360° ÷ 10, or 36° (Figure 7.32).

Figure 7.32

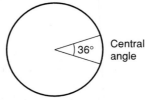

compass

inscribed polygon

Figure 7.33

A four-step sequence for constructing a regular decagon is illustrated in Figure 7.33. The first and third steps use a **compass,** a device for drawing circles and arcs and marking off equal lengths. The decagon that is obtained is said to be *inscribed in the circle.* Any polygon whose vertices are points of a circle is called an **inscribed polygon.**

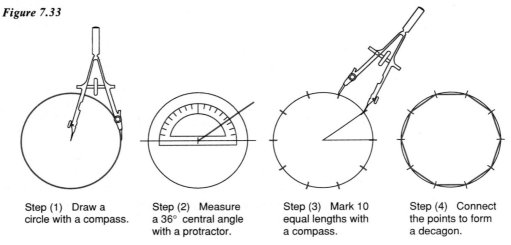

Step (1) Draw a circle with a compass.

Step (2) Measure a 36° central angle with a protractor.

Step (3) Mark 10 equal lengths with a compass.

Step (4) Connect the points to form a decagon.

TESSELLATIONS WITH POLYGONS

tessellation

The hexagonal cells of a honeycomb provide another example of regular polygons in nature (Figure 7.34). The cells in this photo show that regular hexagons can be placed side by side with no uncovered gaps between them. Any arrangement in which non-overlapping figures are placed together to entirely cover a region is called a **tessellation.** Floors and ceilings are often *tessellated,* or *tiled,* with square-shaped material, because squares can be joined together without gaps or overlaps. Equilateral triangles are also commonly used for tessellations. These three types of polygons are the only regular polygons that will tessellate.

Figure 7.34
Honeycomb with eggs
Courtesy of the American Museum of Natural History

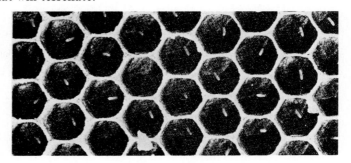

From ancient times tessellations have been used as patterns for rugs, fabrics, pottery, and architecture. The Moors, who settled in Spain in the eighth century A.D., were masters of tessellating walls and floors with colored geometric tiles. Some of their work is shown in Figure 7.35, a photo of a room and bath in the Alhambra, a fortress palace built in the middle of the thirteenth century for Moorish kings.

Figure 7.35
The Sala de Camas, a room in the Alhambra in Granada, Spain

The two tessellations in the center of the photo are made up of nonpolygonal (curved) figures. In the following paragraphs, however, we will concern ourselves only with polygons that tessellate. The triangle is an easy case to consider first. You can see that any triangle will tessellate by simply putting two copies of the triangle together to form a parallelogram (see the shaded region of Figure 7.36). Copies of the parallelogram can then be moved horizontally and vertically. The points at which the vertices of the triangle meet are called the **vertex points** of the tessellation. Since the sum of the angles in a triangle is 180°, the 360° about each vertex point of the tessellation will be covered by using each angle of the triangle twice. In the tessellation shown in Figure 7.36, angles 1, 2, and 3 occur twice about each vertex point.

vertex points

Figure 7.36

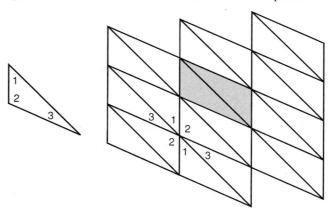

The sizes of the angles in a polygon and the sums of these angles will determine whether the polygon will tessellate. The fact that the sum of the angles in a quadrilateral is 360° suggests that a quadrilateral has the right combination of angles to fit around each vertex point of a tessellation. In the tessellation in Figure 7.37, each angle of the quadrilateral (angles 1, 2, 3, and 4) occurs once about each vertex point of the tessellation.

Figure 7.37

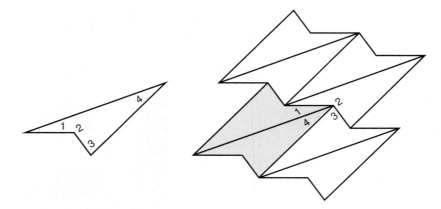

The only regular polygons that will tessellate by themselves are the equilateral triangle, the square, and the regular hexagon. However, if we allow two or more regular polygons in a tessellation, there are other possibilities. Two such tessellations are shown in Figure 7.38. The tessellation in part (a) uses 3 different regular polygons. Notice that each vertex is surrounded by the same arrangement of polygons: hexagon, square, triangle, and square. A tessellation of 2 or more noncongruent regular polygons in which each vertex is surrounded by the same arrangement of polygons is called **semiregular.** Part (b) of Figure 7.38 is a tessellation of regular polygons, but it is *not* semiregular, because some vertices are surrounded by 2 dodecagons and a triangle (see vertex *A*) and others by a dodecagon, 2 triangles, and a square (see vertex *B*).

semiregular

Figure 7.38

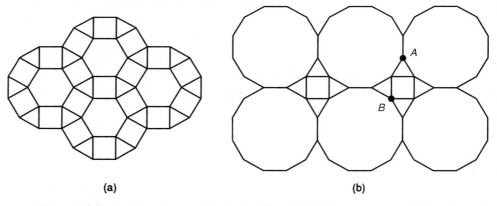

(a)   (b)

The quadrilateral in the tessellation in Figure 7.37 is nonconvex. It is quite surprising that every quadrilateral, convex or nonconvex, will tessellate. This is not true for polygons with more than 4 sides. Although there are some pentagons that will tessellate, there are others that will not tessellate. Similarly, some hexagons will tessellate (for example, a regular hexagon) but not all hexagons.

If we consider only convex polygons, we can prove that *no polygon with more than 6 sides* will tessellate. However, there are countless possibilities for tessellations of nonconvex polygons of more than 6 sides. The tessellation in Figure 7.39 was made using a twelve-sided nonconvex polygon.

Figure 7.39

PROBLEM-SOLVING APPLICATION

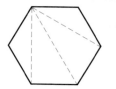

■ PROBLEM

Question 1

Question 2

Question 3

Question 4

What is the measure of each vertex angle in a regular fifty-sided polygon?

Understanding the Problem   Consider a regular polygon with fewer sides. A regular hexagon has 6 congruent vertex angles, and since it can be partitioned into 4 triangles (see figure at left), the sum of all its angles is $4 \times 180° = 720°$. What is the number of degrees in 1 of its vertex angles?

Devising a Plan   The number of degrees in each vertex angle of a regular polygon can be determined once we know the sum of the degrees of all its angles. The total number of degrees in the angles of any polygon can be found by first partitioning the polygon into triangles so that the vertices of the triangles are the same as the vertices of the polygon. Let's make *a table* to determine the number of such triangles for the first few polygons. What is the number of triangles for a hexagon?

No. of sides	3	4	5	6	7	8	9
No. of triangles	1	2	3				
Total no. of degrees	180	2(180)	3(180)				

Carrying Out the Plan   Pentagons, hexagons, and heptagons can be subdivided into 3, 4, and 5 triangles, respectively, as shown below. Notice that connecting 1 vertex of a polygon to each of the other nonadjacent vertices produces exactly 1 triangle for each of the nonadjacent vertices. This suggests that the number of triangles is 2 less than the number of vertices. Using this observation, we can calculate that the sum of the measures of the angles in a fifty-sided polygon is $48 \times 180° = 8640°$. What is the size of each vertex angle in a regular fifty-sided polygon?

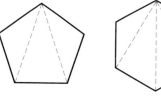

Pentagon   Hexagon   Heptagon

Looking Back   As the number of sides in a regular polygon increases, the shape of the polygon gets closer to a circle, and the size of each vertex angle gets closer to 180°. One of the vertex angles for a fifty-sided regular polygon is shown in the next figure. What is the number of degrees in each vertex angle of a regular one-hundred-sided polygon?

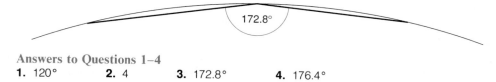

172.8°

Answers to Questions 1–4
1. 120°   **2.** 4   **3.** 172.8°   **4.** 176.4°

RELATED ACTIVITIES IN
Mathematics for Elementary Teachers: An Activity Approach, 3e

Activity Set 7.2

Regular and Semiregular Tessellations: Tessellations with the first few regular polygons are considered, and copies of regular polygons are used to form 8 different semiregular tessellations.

Just for Fun

The Game of Hex: A two-person game involving opportunities for deductive reasoning. There is always a winner in this game, but no winning strategy has yet been found.

PUZZLER

Using only 4 more matchsticks, divide this region into 4 congruent regions. (Hint: Some of the matchsticks may be broken.)

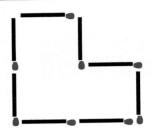

EXERCISES AND PROBLEMS 7.2

Drawing of algae (sea life) by the German biologist Ernst Haeckel (1834–1919)

1. The polygons in the drawing of algae above form the beginning of a tessellation.

  a. There is a regular pentagon at the center. What polygons are adjacent to this pentagon? Are they regular?

  b. There is a second ring of polygons surrounding the inner 6. What kind of polygons are these?

2. Find the sum of all the vertex angles for each polygon.

  a. Hexagon   **b.** Octagon

  c. Decagon   **d.** Fifteen-sided polygon

3. The following figures have been drawn on a square lattice of dot paper. Determine whether each figure is a regular polygon. If it is not, write the condition or conditions that it does not satisfy.

a.

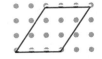

b.

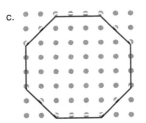

c.

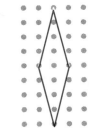

d.

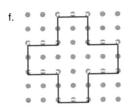

e.

f.

4. The following figure is a regular pentagon, and ∡1 is a central angle. Determine the number of degrees in each of the following angles.

  a. ∡1   **b.** ∡2   **c.** ∡3

5. Write the number of degrees in the central angles of the regular polygons in the following table.

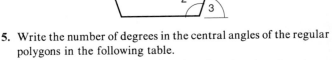

	Triangle	Quadrilateral	Pentagon	Hexagon	Heptagon	Octagon	Nonagon	Decagon		
No. of sides	3	4	5	6	7	8	9	10	20	100
Central angle	120°	90°								

6. This Canadian nickel is a regular dodecagon (12 sides). Assume that you have been asked to design a twelve-sided one-dollar coin that is larger than this nickel. Describe a method for constructing such a polygon.

7. What regular polygons will be formed by the following methods?
   a. Tie a long rectangular strip of paper into a knot and smooth it down (see drawing).

   b. Cut out an equilateral triangle and fold each vertex into the center.
   c. Draw a circle with a compass. Open the compass an amount equal to the radius of the circle, use this distance to mark off points on the circumference, and connect adjacent points.

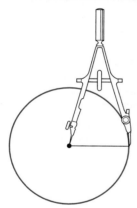

8. The following numbers of degrees are the measures of the central angles of regular polygons. Determine the number of sides in each polygon.
   a. 18°   b. 10°   c. 5°

9. Draw some figures to determine whether the following statements are true or false. For each false statement, show a counterexample.
   a. In any quadrilateral, the sum of the opposite angles is 180°.
   b. A line segment from a vertex of a triangle to the midpoint of the opposite side is called a **median**. The three medians of a triangle meet in a point.
   c. The diagonals of a regular hexagon are congruent.

   d. If the midpoints of the sides of any regular hexagon are connected to form a simple closed curve, this curve is a regular hexagon.
   e. A line segment from a vertex of a triangle that is perpendicular to the opposite side is called an **altitude**. The three altitudes of a triangle meet in a point.
   f. If the midpoints of the sides of any triangle are connected, an equilateral triangle is formed.

10. Which of the following regular polygons will tessellate by themselves? (Copies can be made of regular polygons from the inside cover.)
    a. Equilateral triangle   b. Square
    c. Regular pentagon   d. Regular hexagon
    e. Regular heptagon   f. Regular octagon

11. What condition must be satisfied by the vertex angles of a regular polygon in order for the polygon to tessellate?

12. a. Every quadrilateral will tessellate. Explain why.
    b. Form a tessellation by tracing a few copies of the quadrilateral below. (Copy dot paper from the inside cover.)

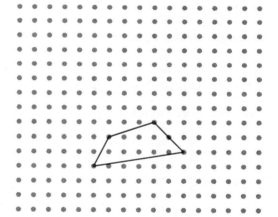

13. Draw a portion of a tessellation that can be made using each of the letters.

    a. 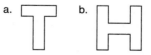   b.   c.

14. A polygon with more than 6 sides will not tessellate if it is convex. The following polygons have more than 6 sides, but they are nonconvex. Sketch a portion of a tessellation for each of these polygons. (Hint: Trace and cut out 1 copy of the figure.)

    a.   b.   c.

15. Which of the following tessellations is semiregular? Explain why.

a.

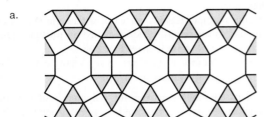

b.

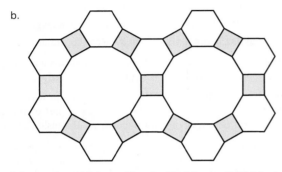

Featured Strategies: Solving a Simpler Problem and Making a Drawing

16. What is the least number of tacks needed to hold up 36 pictures of the same size so that each picture can be seen and each corner is tacked?

a. Understanding the Problem If 2 pictures are tacked up separately, as shown in figure (i), 8 tacks will be required. How many tacks will be needed if the 2 pictures are placed side by side and slightly overlapping, as in figure (ii)?

(i)

(ii)

b. Devising a Plan Simplifying the problem and making a few drawings may provide some ideas. Consider only 4 pictures. How many tacks are needed for each of the following arrangements?

(iv)

c. Carrying Out the Plan The square arrangement of 4 pictures in figure (iv) suggests that we want as many "clusters" like this as possible so that 1 tack can be used for the corners of 4 pictures. Thus we might conjecture that placing the 36 pictures in a square array as shown in figure (v) will minimize the number of tacks. How many tacks does this arrangement require?

(v)

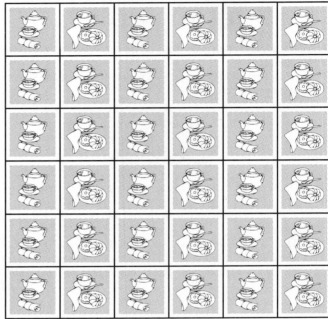

d. Looking Back The grid in figure (v) suggests a method for finding the number of tacks for any square number of pictures. What is the least number of tacks needed for an 8 by 8 array of pictures?

17. Semiregular tessellations can be made using two or more of the following regular polygons. Sketch a portion of a semiregular tessellation that is different from the one shown in part (a) of Figure 7.38. (Hint: Use the given measures of the vertex angles.)

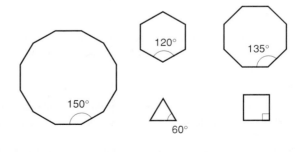

18. The following square figures are made of toothpicks.
   a. How many toothpicks are needed to build the fourth figure?
   b. How many toothpicks are needed to build the 20th figure?

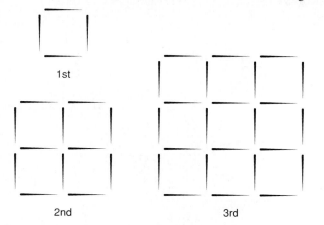

1st

2nd   3rd

19. Gestalt psychology, developed in Germany in the 1930s, is concerned primarily with the laws of perception. What is represented by these polygons and their background?

20. Fold a piece of paper to obtain angles with the following degree measurements.

   a. 90°   **b.** 60°   **c.** 45°

   d. 30°   **e.** 15°   **f.** 150°

   g. 120°

LABORATORY INVESTIGATION

This photo shows two mirrors that are hinged together with tape. The mirrors are placed in front of line ℓ (on a piece of paper) and a toy motorcycle, producing a view of a regular pentagon and 5 motorcycles. Tape two mirrors together and try this experiment, using any small object.

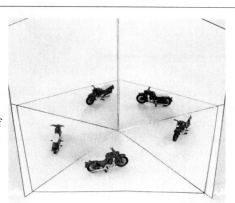

Questions for Investigation

1. What will happen to the pentagon if the angle between the hinged mirrors is increased (the mirrors are opened wider)?

2. What will happen to the figure if the angle between the mirrors is decreased?

3. What is the relationship between the number of objects that can be seen and the angle between the mirrors? (Hint: Trace the positions of the mirrors on the paper and measure the angles. Form a table listing the angle measurements and the corresponding numbers of objects.)

PUZZLER

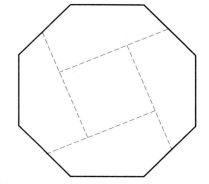

Trace and cut out the pieces of the regular octagon and the regular dodecagon. Show how each set of pieces can be reassembled to form a square.

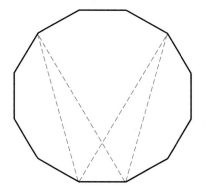

SECTION 7.3 SPACE FIGURES

This is a sketch of a three-dimensional figure that contains 54 small cubes. If the outside of the figure is painted and then the figure is disassembled into 54 individual cubes, how many cubes will have paint on 1 face? 2 faces? 3 faces? zero faces?

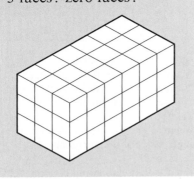

space

Cubic Space Division by M. C. Escher
© 1990 M. C. Escher Heirs/Cordon Art—Baarn—Holland.

In this lithograph by the Dutch artist Maurits C. Escher (1898–1970), the girders intersect at right angles to form the edges of large cubes. The Canadian mathematician H. S. M. Coxeter calls it the cubic honeycomb. By representing space as being filled with cubes of the same size, Escher gives a wonderful sense of infinite space.

The notion of **space** in geometry is an undefined term, just as the ideas of point, line, and plane are undefined. We intuitively think of space as three-dimensional and a plane as only two-dimensional. In his Theory of Relativity, Einstein tied together the three dimensions of space and the fourth dimension of time. He showed that space and time affect each other and give us a four-dimensional universe.

■ *HISTORICAL HIGHLIGHT*

The Russian mathematician Sonya Kovalevsky (1850–1891) is regarded as the greatest woman mathematician to have lived before 1900. Since women were barred by law from institutions of higher learning in Russia, Kovalevsky attended Heidelberg University in Germany. Later she was refused admission to the University of Berlin, which also barred women. Even the famous mathematician Karl Weierstrass, who claimed she had "the gift of intuitive genius," was unable to obtain permission for Kovalevsky to attend his lectures. She obtained her doctorate from the University of Göttingen but was without a teaching position for nine years, until the newly formed University of Stockholm broke tradition and appointed her to an academic position. Kovalevsky's prominence as a mathematician reached its peak in 1888, when she received the famous Prix Bordin from the French Académie des Sciences for her research paper *On the Rotation of a Solid about a Fixed Point*. The selection committee "recognized in this work not only the power of an expansive and profound mind, but also a great spirit of invention."

PLANES

In two dimensions, the figures (lines, angles, polygons, etc.) all occur in a plane. In three dimensions, there are an infinite number of planes. Each plane partitions space into three disjoint sets: the points on the plane and two **half-spaces.** Portions of a few planes are shown in Figure 7.40. Any two planes either are **parallel,** as in part (a), or **intersect** in a line, as in part (b).

half-spaces
parallel planes
intersecting planes

Figure 7.40

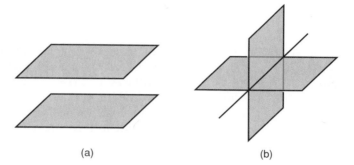

(a)   (b)

dihedral angle

When two planes intersect, we call the angle between the planes a **dihedral angle.** Figure 7.41 shows three dihedral angles and their measures. A dihedral angle is measured by measuring the angle whose sides lie in the planes and are perpendicular to the line of intersection of the two planes. Parts (a), (b), and (c) of Figure 7.41 show examples of obtuse, right, and acute dihedral angles, respectively.

Figure 7.41

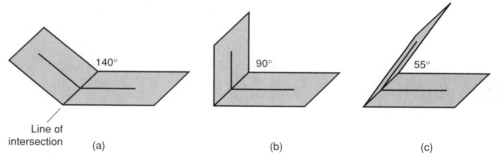

Line of
intersection   (a)   (b)   (c)

When a line m in three-dimensional space does not intersect a plane P, it is parallel to the plane, as in part (a) of Figure 7.42. A line n is perpendicular to a plane Q at a point k if the line is perpendicular to every line in the plane that contains k, as in part (b) of Figure 7.42.

Figure 7.42

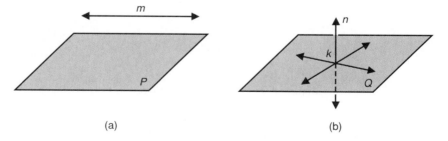

(a)   (b)

POLYHEDRA

The three-dimensional object in Figure 7.43 is a crystal. Its flat pentagonal sides with their straight edges were shaped by nature.

Figure 7.43

polyhedron
faces, edges, vertices
solid

The surface of a figure in space whose sides are polygonal regions, such as the one in Figure 7.43, is called a **polyhedron** (*polyhedra* is the plural). The polygonal regions are called **faces,** and they intersect in the **edges** and **vertices** of the polyhedron. The union of a polyhedron and its interior is called a **solid.** Figure 7.44 shows examples of a polyhedron and two figures that are not polyhedra. The figure in part (a) is a polyhedron because its faces are polygonal regions. The figures in parts (b) and (c) are not polyhedra because one has a curved surface and the other has two faces that are not polygons.

Figure 7.44

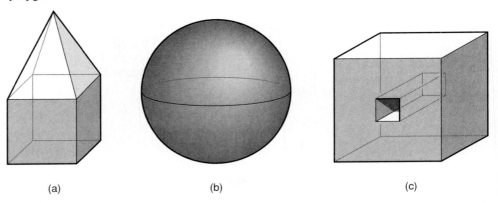

(a)   (b)   (c)

convex   A polyhedron is **convex** if any line segment connecting two of its points is contained inside the polyhedron or on its surface.

EXAMPLE A

Classify the following polyhedra as convex or nonconvex.

(1)   (2)   (3)

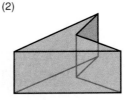
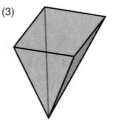

Solution   (1) and (3) are convex; (2) is nonconvex.

REGULAR POLYHEDRA

The best known of all the polyhedra are the *regular polyhedra,* or *Platonic solids.* A
regular polyhedron   **regular polyhedron** is a convex polyhedron whose faces are *congruent regular polygons,* the same number of which meet at each vertex. The ancient Greeks proved that there

are only five regular polyhedra. Models of these polyhedra are shown in Figure 7.45. The **tetrahedron** has 4 triangles for faces; the **cube** has 6 square faces; the **octahedron** has 8 triangular faces; the **dodecahedron** has 12 pentagons for faces; and the **icosahedron** has 20 triangular faces.

tetrahedron
cube, octahedron
dodecahedron
icosahedron

Figure 7.45
From left to right: tetrahedron, cube (hexahedron), octahedron, dodecahedron, icosahedron

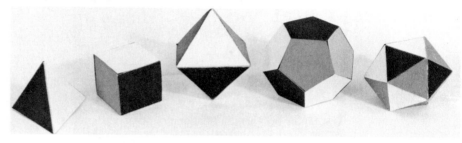

The first three of the regular polyhedra shown in Figure 7.45 are found in nature as crystals. The cube and the octahedron occur in the common mineral pyrite, shown in Figure 7.46. The cube, which is embedded in rock, was found in Vermont, and the octahedron is from Peru. The other regular polyhedra, the dodecahedron and the icosahedron, do not occur as crystals but have been found in the skeletons of microscopic sea animals called radiolarians.

Figure 7.46
Crystals of pyrite

SEMIREGULAR POLYHEDRA   The variety of polyhedra becomes greater when we allow two or more different types of regular polygons for faces. The faces of the boracite crystal in Figure 7.47 are squares and equilateral triangles. This crystal, too, developed its flat, regularly shaped faces naturally, without the help of machines or people. There are only thirteen polyhedra whose faces are two or more regular polygons, the same arrangement of which surround each vertex. They are called **semiregular polyhedra**. The boracite crystal is one of these. Each of its vertices is surrounded by three squares and one equilateral triangle.

semiregular polyhedra

Figure 7.47
Crystals of boracite

Several other semiregular polyhedra are shown in Figure 7.48. You may recognize the combination of hexagons and pentagons in part (a) as the pattern used on the surface of soccer balls.

Figure 7.48

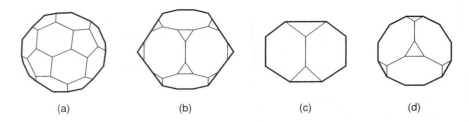

(a)   (b)   (c)   (d)

EXAMPLE B

For each semiregular polyhedron in Figure 7.48, list the polygons in the order in which they occur about any vertex.

Solution   Part (a): hexagon, hexagon, pentagon

Part (b): dodecagon, dodecagon, triangle

Part (c): hexagon, hexagon, triangle

Part (d): octagon, octagon, triangle

PYRAMIDS AND PRISMS

Chances are that when you hear the word "pyramid" you think of the monuments built by the ancient Egyptians. Each of the Egyptian pyramids has a square base and triangular sides rising up to the vertex. This is just one type of pyramid. In general, the **base** of a pyramid can be any polygon, but its sides are always triangular. Pyramids are named according to the shape of their bases. Church spires are familiar examples of pyramids. They are usually square, hexagonal, or octagonal pyramids. The spire in the photo in Figure 7.49 is an octagonal pyramid.

base

Figure 7.49
The Bruton steeple, Williamsburg, Virginia

Several pyramids with different bases are shown in the following example. The vertex that is not contained in the pyramid's base is called the **apex.**

apex

EXAMPLE C

Mark the apex of each pyramid and determine the name of the pyramid.

(1) 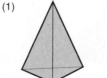   (2)   (3)   (4)

Solution   (1) Triangular pyramid (also called a tetrahedron)

(2) Square pyramid   (3) Pentagonal pyramid   (4) Hexagonal pyramid

PRISMS   Prisms are another common type of polyhedron. You probably remember from your science classes that a prism is used to produce the spectrum of colors ranging from violet to red. Because of the angle between the vertical faces of a prism, light directed into one face will be bent when it passes out through the other face (Figure 7.50).

Figure 7.50

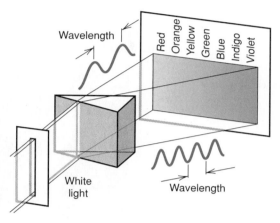

prism, bases

A **prism** has two parallel **bases,** upper and lower, which are congruent polygons. Like pyramids, prisms get their names from the shape of their bases. If the lateral sides of a prism are perpendicular to the bases, as in the case of the triangular, quadrilateral, hexagonal, and rectangular prisms in Figure 7.51, they are rectangles. Such a prism is called a **right prism** or simply a prism. A rectangular prism, the most common type of prism, is sometimes called a **box.** If some of the lateral faces are parallelograms that are not rectangles, as in the pentagonal prism, the prism is called an **oblique prism.** The union of a prism and its interior is called a **solid prism.** A rectangular prism that is a solid is sometimes called a **rectangular solid.**

right prism
box
oblique prism
solid prism
rectangular solid

Figure 7.51

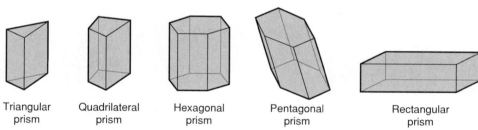

| Triangular prism | Quadrilateral prism | Hexagonal prism | Pentagonal prism | Rectangular prism |

EXAMPLE D

The following figure is a right prism with bases that are regular pentagons.

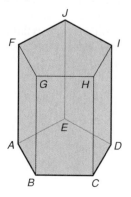

1. What is the measure of the dihedral angle between face *ABGF* and face *BCHG?*
2. What is the measure of the dihedral angle between face *GHIJF* and face *CDIH?*
3. Name two faces that are in parallel planes.

Solution 1. 108° 2. 90° 3. *ABCDE* and *FGHIJ*

The two oblique hexagonal prisms in Figure 7.52 are crystals that grew with these flat, smooth faces and straight edges. Their lateral faces are parallelograms.

Figure 7.52
Prisms of the crystal orthoclase feldspar

CONES AND CYLINDERS

vertex (apex), base
right cone
oblique cone

Figure 7.53

Cones and cylinders are the circular counterparts of pyramids and prisms. Ice-cream cones, paper cups, and party hats are common examples of cones. A cone has a circular region (disc) for a **base** and a lateral surface that slopes to the **vertex (apex).** If the vertex lies directly above the center of the base, the cone is called a **right cone** or usually just a cone; otherwise, it is an **oblique cone** (Figure 7.53).

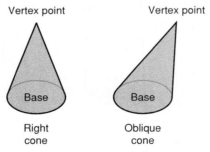

Vertex point   Vertex point

Base   Base

Right cone   Oblique cone

cylinder, bases

right cylinder
oblique cylinder

Figure 7.54

Ordinary cans are models of cylinders. A **cylinder** has two parallel circular **bases** (discs) of the same size and a lateral surface that rises from one base to the other. If the center of the upper base lies directly above the center of the lower base, the cylinder is called a **right cylinder** or simply a cylinder; otherwise, it is an **oblique cylinder** (Figure 7.54). Almost without exception, the cones and cylinders we use are right cones and right cylinders.

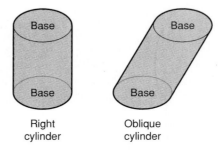

Base   Base

Base   Base

Right cylinder   Oblique cylinder

SPHERES AND MAPS*

The photo in Figure 7.55 is a view of the earth showing its almost perfect spherical shape. It was photographed from the *Apollo 17* spacecraft during its 1972 lunar mission. The dark regions are water. The Red Sea and the Gulf of Aden are near the top center, and the Arabian Sea and Indian Ocean are on the right.

Figure 7.55
Earth, as seen from *Apollo 17* during its 1972 lunar mission

SPHERE

> A **sphere** is the set of points in space that are the same distance from a fixed point called the **center.** The union of a sphere and its interior is called a **solid sphere.**

A line segment joining the center of a sphere to a point on the sphere is called a radius. The length of such a line segment is also called the radius of the sphere. A line segment containing the center of the sphere whose endpoints are on the sphere is called a diameter, and the length of such a line segment is called the diameter of the sphere.

The geometry of the sphere is especially important for navigating on the surface of the earth. You may have noticed that airline maps show curved paths between distant cities. This is because the shortest distance between two points on a sphere is along

great circle

an arc of a **great circle.** In the drawing of the sphere in Figure 7.56, *G* (the colored arc) is the arc of a great circle, because its center is also the center of the sphere, and *B* is not the arc of a great circle. The distance between points *X* and *Y* along an arc *G* is less than the distance between these points along an arc *B*.

Figure 7.56

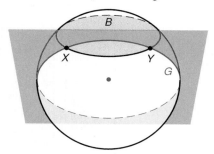

Locations on the earth's surface are often given by naming cities, streets, and buildings. A more general method of describing location uses two systems of circles

parallels of latitude

(Figure 7.57). The circles that are parallel to the equator are called **parallels of latitude** and are shown in part (a). Except for the equator, these circles are not great circles. Each parallel of latitude is specified by an angle from 0° to 90°, both north and south

*This section is optional.

of the equator. For example, New York City is at a northern latitude of 41°, and Sydney, Australia, is at a southern latitude of 34°. The second system of circles is shown in part (b). These circles pass through the North and South Poles and are called **merid-ians of longitude.** These are great circles, and each is perpendicular to the equator. Since there is no natural point at which to begin numbering the meridians of longitude, the meridian that passes through Greenwich, England, was chosen arbitrarily as the zero meridian. Each meridian of longitude is given by an angle from 0° to 180°, both east and west of the zero meridian. The longitude of New York City is 74° West, and that of Sydney, Australia, is 151° East. These two systems of circles provide a grid, or coordinate system, for locating any point on earth and are shown together in part (c).

meridians of longitude

Figure 7.57

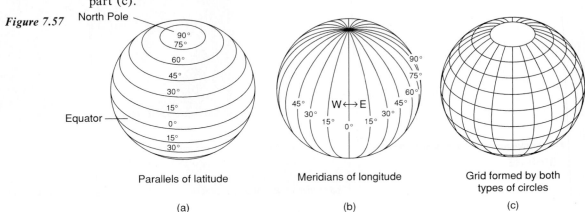

Parallels of latitude

(a)

Meridians of longitude

(b)

Grid formed by both types of circles

(c)

MAP PROJECTIONS   The globe is a spherical map of the earth. Although globes provide the only accurate portrayal of the world, we cannot see the whole globe at one time, nor can distances be measured easily. Maps on a flat surface provide a convenient solution. However, since a sphere cannot be placed flat on a plane without separating or overlapping some of its surface, making maps of the earth is problematic. There are three basic solutions to this problem: copying the earth's surface onto a cylinder, a cone, or a plane (Figure 7.58). These methods of copying are called **map projections.** In each case, some distortions of shapes and distances occur.

map projections

Figure 7.58

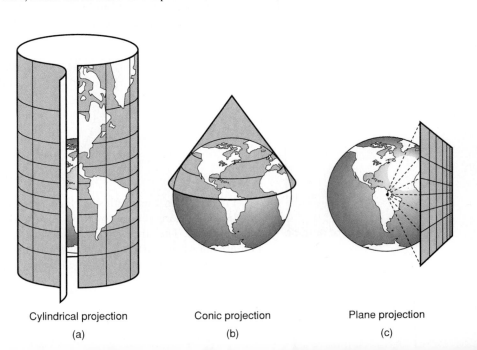

Cylindrical projection

(a)

Conic projection

(b)

Plane projection

(c)

cylindrical projection

A **cylindrical projection** [part (a)] is obtained by placing a cylinder around a sphere and copying the surface of the sphere onto the cylinder. The cylinder is then cut to produce a flat map. Regions close to the equator are reproduced most accurately. The closer we get to the poles, the more the map is distorted.

conic projection

A **conic projection** [part (b)] is produced by copying a portion of the surface of a sphere onto a cone. The cone is then cut and laid flat. This type of map construction is commonly used for countries and other local regions of the earth's surface. The maps of the United States issued by the American Automobile Association are conical projections.

plane projection

A **plane projection** [part (c)] is made by placing a plane next to any point on a sphere and projecting the surface onto the plane. To visualize this process, imagine a light at the center of the sphere and think of the boundary of a country as being pierced with small holes. The light shining through these holes, as shown by the dashed lines in part (c), forms an image of the country on the plane. Less than half of the sphere's surface can be copied onto a plane projection, with the greatest distortion taking place at the outer edges of the plane. A plane projection, unlike cylindrical and conical projections, has the advantage that the distortion is uniform from the center of the map to its edges.

PROBLEM-SOLVING APPLICATION

Euler's formula

There is a remarkable formula that relates the numbers of vertices, edges, and faces of a polyhedron. This formula was first stated by René Descartes about 1635. In 1752 it was discovered again by Leonhard Euler and is now referred to as **Euler's formula.** See if you can discover this formula, either before reading or as you read the parts of the solution presented below.

■ PROBLEM

(a)

What is the relationship among the numbers of faces, vertices, and edges of a polyhedron?

Understanding the Problem   Euler's formula holds for any polyhedron, regular or nonregular. Let's look at a specific example. A cube has 6 faces. How many vertices and edges does it have?

Question 1

Devising a Plan   Let's *make a table,* list the numbers of faces, vertices, and edges for several polyhedra, and look for a relationship. What are the numbers of faces, vertices, and edges for the polyhedra in figures (b), (c), and (d)?

Question 2

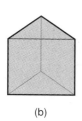   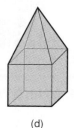

(b)   (c)   (d)

Carrying Out the Plan   The following table contains the numbers of faces, vertices, and edges for the polyhedra in figures (a) through (d). Using F for the number of faces, V for the number of vertices, and E for the number of edges, we can construct Euler's formula from these data. What is Euler's formula?

Question 3

	F	V	E
Figure (a)	6	8	12
Figure (b)	5	6	9
Figure (c)	6	6	10
Figure (d)	9	9	16

Question 4

Looking Back You may remember that an icosahedron has 20 triangular faces, but not remember the number of edges or vertices. Altogether, 20 triangles have a total of 60 edges. Since every 2 edges of a triangle form 1 edge of an icosahedron, this polyhedron has 60 ÷ 2 = 30 edges. Given the numbers of faces and edges for the icosahedron and Euler's formula, $F + V - 2 = E$, we can determine the number of vertices. How many vertices are there?

Answers to Questions 1–4
1. 8 vertices and 12 edges
2. Figure (b): 5 faces, 6 vertices, 9 edges
   Figure (c): 6 faces, 6 vertices, 10 edges
   Figure (d): 9 faces, 9 vertices, 16 edges
3. $F + V - 2 = E$ 4. 12; $20 + V - 2 = 30$

■ **HISTORICAL HIGHLIGHT**

Leonhard Euler

Switzerland's Leonhard Euler (1707–1783) is considered to be the most prolific writer in the history of mathematics. He published over 850 books and papers, and most branches of mathematics contain his theorems. After he became totally blind at the age of 60, he continued his amazing productivity for 17 years by dictating to a secretary and writing formulas in chalk on a large slate. On the 200th anniversary of his birthday in 1907, a Swiss publisher began reissuing Euler's entire collected works; the collection is expected to run to 75 volumes of about 60 pages each.*

RELATED ACTIVITIES IN

Mathematics for Elementary Teachers: An Activity Approach, 3e

Activity Set 7.3 **Models for Regular and Semiregular Polyhedra:** This activity set explores several methods of forming regular polyhedra and uses patterns for forming regular and semiregular polyhedra.

Just for Fun **Instant Insanity:** A popular puzzle with 4 colored cubes, which can be solved by trial and error or deductive reasoning

---

PUZZLER

How can 4 triangles be formed using 6 matchsticks that touch only at their endpoints (do not cross)?

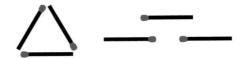

EXERCISES AND PROBLEMS 7.3

Crystals of calcite

1. The crystals crowded together in the photo are growing with flat polygonal faces.
   a. What type of polygon is the top face of these crystals?
   b. What type of polyhedra are formed by these crystals?

*H. W. Eves, *In Mathematical Circles* (Boston: Prindle, Weber, and Schmidt, 1969), 46–49.

2. Which of the following figures are polyhedra?

a.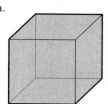

b.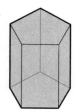

c.

d.

e.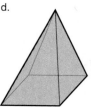

f.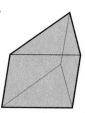

3. Classify these polyhedra as convex or nonconvex.

a.

b.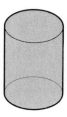

c.

d.

e.

f.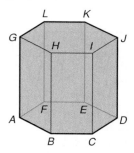

6. Name the following figures and state whether they are right or oblique.

a.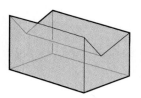

b.

c.

d.

e.

f.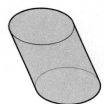

4. The semiregular polyhedra are classified according to the arrangement of regular polygons around each vertex. Proceeding counterclockwise, list the polygons about a vertex of each polyhedron below.

a.

20 hexagons
12 pentagons

b.

32 triangles
6 squares

c.

8 triangles
6 squares

d.

20 hexagons
30 squares
12 decagons

5. Name each of these figures.

a.

b.

c.

7. This figure is a right prism, and its bases are regular hexagons.

a. What face is parallel to face *GHIJKL?*
b. What face is parallel to face *IJDC?*
c. What is the measure of the dihedral angle between face *ABHG* and face *ABCDEF?*
d. What is the measure of the dihedral angle between face *ABHG* and face *BCIH?*

8. Which of the three types of projections would yield the least distorted flat maps of the following regions?
a. Australia
b. North, Central, and South America
c. The entire equatorial region between 30° North latitude and 30° South latitude.

9. Each of the geometric shapes listed below can be seen in the accompanying picture. Try to find the objects.

a. Cone
b. Pyramid
c. Cylinder
d. Sphere
e. Circle
f. 30° angle
g. Rectangle
h. Semicircle
i. Square
j. 45° angle

Thompson Hall, University of New Hampshire

10. Use your knowledge of the spherical coordinate system to match each of the following cities with its approximate longitude and latitude.

Tokyo	38° N and 120° W
San Francisco	56° N and 4° W
Melbourne	35° N and 140° E
Glasgow	35° S and 20° E
Capetown	38° S and 145° E

11. Two points on the earth's surface that are on opposite ends of a line segment through the center of the earth are called **antipodal points.** The coordinates of such points are nicely related. The latitude of one point is as far above the equator as that of the other is below, and the longitudes are supplementary angles (in opposite hemispheres). For example, (30° N, 40° E) is in Saudi Arabia, and its antipodal point (30° S, 140° W) is just off the southern coast of Australia.

a. The globe in the accompanying photo shows that (20° N, 120° W) is a point in the Pacific Ocean just west of Mexico. Its antipodal point is just east of Madagascar. What are its coordinates?

b. The point (30° S, 80° E) is in the Indian Ocean. What are the coordinates of its antipodal point? What country is it in?

Babson College globe: diameter 28 feet, weight 21 tons

12. China is bounded by latitudes of 20° N and 55° N and by longitudes of 75° E and 135° E. It is playfully assumed that if you could dig a hole straight through the center of the earth you would come out in China. For which of the following starting points is this true?

a. Panama (9° N, 80° W)
b. Buenos Aires (35° S, 58° W)
c. New York (41° N, 74° W)

13. The intersection of a plane and a three-dimensional figure is called a **cross section.** The cross section produced by the intersection of a plane and a right cylinder for a plane which is parallel to the base of the cylinder (see figure) is a circle.

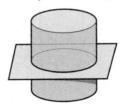

Determine the following cross sections.

a.

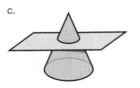

b.

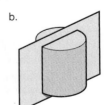

c.

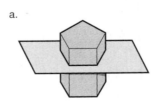

d.

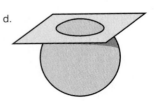

14. *E, F, G, H,* and *C* are the vertices of a square pyramid inside this cube. Name the 5 vertices of 2 more square pyramids that, together with the given pyramid, partition the cube into 3 pyramids.

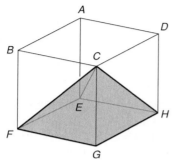

15. A cube can be dissected into triangular pyramids in several ways. Pyramid *FHCA* partitions this cube into 5 triangular pyramids. Name the 4 vertices of each of the other 4 pyramids.

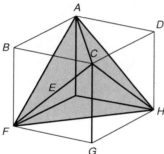

16. The following patterns were formed by joining 6 squares along their edges.
   a. Which two of these patterns will fold into a cube?
   b. Find another pattern of 6 squares that will fold into a cube.

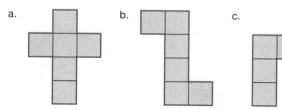

17. One method of describing a three-dimensional figure is to make a drawing of its different views. There are 9 cubes in the following figure (2 are hidden), and the top, right, and front views are shown.

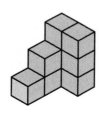

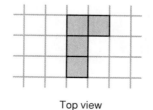

Top view

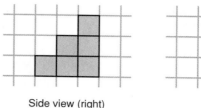

Side view (right) Front view

Sketch three views of each of the following figures. (Note: The only hidden cubes are beneath cubes that can be seen, and the colored faces of the cubes are part of the front views of the figures.)

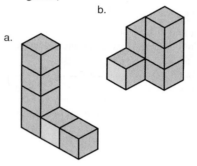

a.   b.   c.

18. Hurricane Ginger was christened on September 10, 1971, and became the longest-lived Atlantic hurricane on record. This tropical storm formed approximately 275 miles south of Bermuda and reached the U.S. mainland 20 days later.

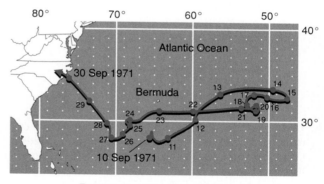

Erratic path of Hurricane Ginger

   a. The storm's coordinates on September 10 were (28° N, 66° W). What were its coordinates on the following dates: September 15, September 23, and September 30?
   b. At this latitude on the earth's surface, each degree of longitude spans a distance of approximately 60 miles. About how many miles did this hurricane travel between September 10 and September 30? (Hint: Use a piece of string.)

19. Sketch or describe how to form a piece of paper into the following figures (without bases).

a.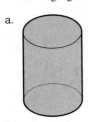
Right circular cylinder

b.
Right circular cone

c.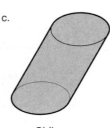
Oblique circular cylinder

Featured Strategies: Making a Drawing and Using a Model

20. The 5 regular polyhedra and the numbers and shapes of their faces are shown in the following table. Determine the missing numbers of vertices and edges.

Polyhedron	Vertices	Faces	Edges
Tetrahedron	—	4 triangles	—
Cube	8	6 squares	12
Octahedron	—	8 triangles	—
Dodecahedron	—	12 pentagons	—
Icosahedron	—	20 triangles	—

a. **Understanding the Problem** The cube is the most familiar of the regular polyhedra. Its 6 faces meet in 12 edges, and its edges meet in 8 vertices. How many vertices and edges does a tetrahedron have?

a.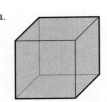

b.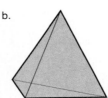

b. **Devising a Plan** One approach is to use a model or a sketch of the polyhedra and count the numbers of vertices and edges. Or once we determine either the number of vertices or the number of edges, the missing number can be obtained by using Euler's formula: $F + V - 2 = E$. Another approach that avoids counting is to use the fact that each pair of faces meets in exactly 1 edge. For example, since a dodecahedron has 12 pentagons for faces and each pair of pentagons shares an edge, the number of edges is $(12 \times 5)/2 = 30$. Using Euler's formula, determine the number of vertices in a dodecahedron.

c. **Carrying Out the Plan** Continue finding the numbers of edges by multiplying the number of faces by the number of sides on a face and dividing by 2. For example, what is the number of edges in an icosahedron? Fill in the rest of the table.

d. **Looking Back** The number of vertices for each regular polyhedron can also be found directly from the number of edges that meet at each vertex. For example, 3 edges meet at each vertex of the dodecahedron, as shown in figure (c)

below. Since there are 12 faces and each face has 5 vertex points, the dodecahedron has $(12 \times 5)/3 = 20$ vertex points. Use this approach to determine the number of vertices for the icosahedron.

c.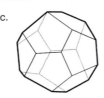
Dodecahedron

d.
Icosahedron

21. The centers of the faces of a cube can be connected to form a regular octahedron. Also, the centers of the faces of an octahedron can be connected to form a cube. Such polyhedra are called **duals.**

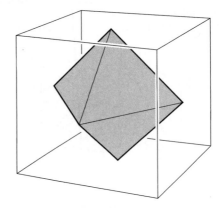

a. How is this dual relationship suggested by the table in #20?
b. Find two other regular polyhedra that are duals of each other.
c. Which regular polyhedron is its own dual?

22. There are six categories of illusions.* One category, called "impossible objects," is produced by drawing three-dimensional figures on two-dimensional surfaces. Find the impossible feature in each of these pictures.

a.

Waterfall by M. C. Escher
© 1990 M. C. Escher Heirs/Cordon Art—
Baarn—Holland.

b.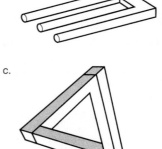

c.

*P. A. Rainey, *Illusions* (Hamden, CT: The Shoe String Press, 1973), 18–43.

23. A second type of illusion involves depth perception. We have accustomed our eyes to see depth when three-dimensional objects are drawn on two-dimensional surfaces. Answer questions a and b by disregarding the depth illusions.

a. Is one of these cylinders larger than the others?

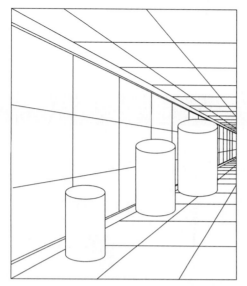

b. Which of the four angles is largest? Which are right angles? (Hint: Use a corner of a piece of paper.)

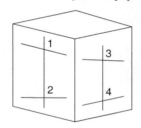

24. The polyhedra shown below illustrate some of the forms crystals may take in nature. The polygons at the tops of the columns are the horizontal cross sections of the polyhedra in the columns.

a. List the numbers of the polyhedra that are pyramids.
b. List the numbers of the polyhedra that are prisms.
c. Which of the polyhedra is most like a dodecahedron?
d. Which of the polyhedra is most like an octahedron?

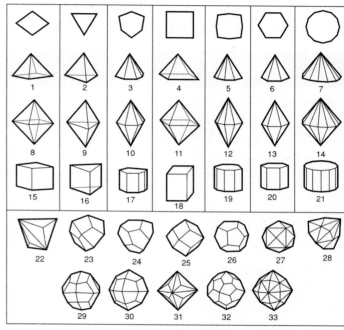

LABORATORY INVESTIGATION

If the pattern at right is traced and cut out, the triangular flaps can be folded up to form a pyramid whose apex is directly above point *P*. (That is, a line containing the apex and point *P* will be perpendicular to the base.) To construct these flaps, we must know the altitude, *h*, of the pyramid.

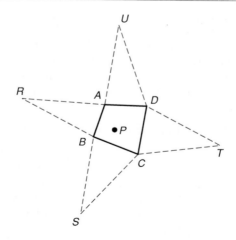

Questions for Investigation

1. How were the vertex points *R*, *S*, *T*, and *U* determined? (Hint: The Pythagorean theorem is needed.)

2. Can triangular flaps be constructed for any polygon and any point *P* in the

same plane [see figures (a) and (b)] so that the flaps fold up to form a pyramid of any given altitude with the apex directly above point *P*?

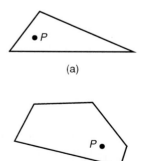

(a)

(b)

PUZZLER

Some wildlife researchers, having pitched camp, set out on an exploratory trip. They walked 15 miles due south, then 15 miles due east, where they saw a bear. Walking 15 miles due north, they returned to their camp. What was the color of the bear?

SECTION 7.4 SYMMETRIC FIGURES

■ PROBLEM OPENER

A vertical line can be drawn through the word MOM so that the left and right sides are mirror images of each other.

$$M \phi M$$

Find a word that can be cut by a horizontal line so that the bottom and top halves are mirror images of each other.

The Taj Mahal, built between 1630 and 1652 on the banks of the Jumna River in Agra, India

The Taj Mahal is considered by many to be the most beautiful building in the world. It is made entirely of white marble and surrounded by a landscaped walled garden on the banks of the Jumna River in Agra, India. It is an octagonal building, and four of its eight faces contain massive arches rising to a height of 33 meters (108 feet). The form and balance of the Taj Mahal can be described by saying it is *symmetrical*. The human race has always found order and harmony in symmetry. Perhaps the most influential factor in our desire for symmetry is the shape of the human body. Even children in their earliest drawings show an awareness of body symmetry.

REFLECTION SYMMETRY FOR PLANE FIGURES

Many years before it became popular to teach geometric ideas in elementary school, cutting out symmetric figures was a common classroom activity. The procedure is to fold a piece of paper and draw a figure that encloses part or all of the crease, as shown in part (a) of Figure 7.59. When the figure is cut out and unfolded, it is symmetrical [see part (b)]. The crease is called a **line of symmetry,** and the figure is said to have **reflection symmetry.**

line of symmetry
reflection symmetry

Figure 7.59

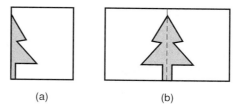

(a)   (b)

Intuitively we understand the idea of reflection symmetry to mean that the two halves of the figure are "the same" or will coincide if one is folded onto the other. The word "reflection" is a natural one to use because of the mirror test for symmetry. If the edge of a mirror is placed along a line of symmetry, the half-figure and its image from the mirror will look like the whole figure. You can test the photo of the building in Figure 7.60 by placing the edge of a mirror along the vertical center line of the photo. With the mirror in this position, half of the building and its reflection will look like the whole building. Since this is the only way the mirror can be placed so that this will happen, the photo of the building has only one line of symmetry.

Figure 7.60

Putnam Hall, University of New Hampshire

The Mira is a convenient device for locating lines of symmetry for plane figures. It is made of Plexiglas so that the user can see through it and at the same time see reflections. If a figure has a line of symmetry, as does the hexagon in Figure 7.61, and the Mira is placed so that the reflection of the figure coincides with the part of the figure behind the Mira, then the edge of the Mira lies on a line of symmetry.

Figure 7.61

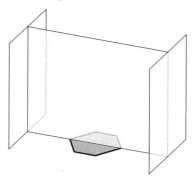

Some figures have more than 1 line of symmetry. To produce a figure with 2 such lines, fold a sheet of paper in half and then in half again, as shown in part (a) of Figure 7.62. Then draw a figure whose endpoints touch the creases, and cut it out. When the paper is opened, the two perpendicular creases will be lines of symmetry for the figure, as shown in part (b) of Figure 7.62.

Figure 7.62

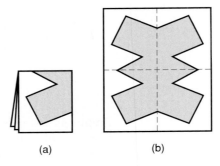

(a)   (b)

EXAMPLE A

Each of the following polygons has 2 or more lines of symmetry. Determine these lines for each figure.

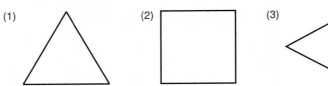

(1)   (2)   (3)

Solution

1. An equilateral triangle has 3 lines of symmetry: 1 line through each vertex, perpendicular to the opposite side.
2. A square has 4 lines of symmetry: 1 horizontal line and 1 vertical line through the midpoints of opposite sides, and 2 lines containing the diagonals.
3. This figure has 2 lines of symmetry: 1 horizontal line through opposite vertices, and 1 vertical line through the midpoints of opposite sides.

line of symmetry

image

The idea of symmetry can be made more precise by adopting the term "image," which is suggested by mirrors. If a line can be drawn through a figure so that each point on one side of the line has a matching point on the other side at the same perpendicular distance from the line, it is a **line of symmetry.** If two points on opposite sides of this line match up, one is called the **image** of the other. A few points and their images have been labeled in Figure 7.63. *A* corresponds to *A′*, *B* to *B′*, *C* to *C′*, and *D* to *D′*. Each line segment connecting a point and its image is perpendicular to the line of symmetry.

Figure 7.63

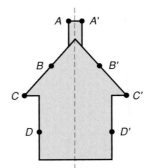

EXAMPLE B

For each of the following figures, show that the dashed line is not a line of symmetry by finding the images of the lettered points.

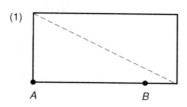

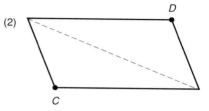

Solution   (1) and (2) The images of points *A, B, C,* and *D* do not lie on the given figures.

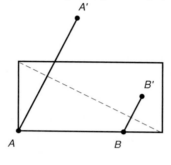

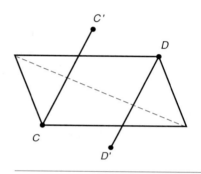

ROTATION SYMMETRY FOR PLANE FIGURES

rotation symmetry

Figure 7.64 may look like a drawing of a plant, but it is a drawing of a type of jellyfish called *Aurelia*. It seems to have the form and balance of a symmetric figure, but it has no lines of reflection. It does, however, have **rotation symmetry,** because it can be turned about its center so that it coincides with itself. For example, if it is rotated 90° clockwise, the top "arm" will move to the 3 o'clock position, the bottom "arm" will move to the 9 o'clock position, etc.

Figure 7.64
Aurelia, the common coastal jellyfish

center of rotation

Let's consider another example of rotation symmetry. Trace Figure 7.65 and mark the center X and the arms *A, B,* and *C.* Cut it out and place it on the page so that both figures coincide. If it is held down by a pencil at point *X,* the top figure can be rotated clockwise so that *A* goes to *B, B* to *C,* and *C* to *A.* This is an example of rotation symmetry, and *X* is called the **center of rotation.** Since the figure is rotated 120° (1/3 of a full turn), it has a *120° rotation symmetry.* From its original position, this figure can also be made to coincide with itself after a 240° clockwise rotation, with *A* going to *C, B* to *A,* and *C* to *B.* This is a *240° rotation symmetry.* Since the figure can be rotated back onto itself after a 360° rotation, the figure also has a *360° rotation symmetry*. Note: Any figure can be rotated 360° using any point as the center of rotation. Thus we will be interested in a 360° rotation symmetry only when a figure has other rotation symmetries.

Figure 7.65

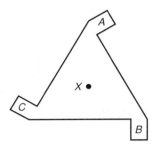

Some figures have both reflection symmetry and rotation symmetry. The regular polygons have both types. The central angles of these polygons determine the angles for the rotation symmetries.

EXAMPLE C

Find all the reflection and rotation symmetries for a regular hexagon.

Solution

Every regular hexagon has 6 reflection symmetries. Figure (1) shows 3 lines of symmetry passing through opposite pairs of parallel sides, and figure (2) shows 3 lines passing through opposite pairs of vertices. Since the central angle in figure (3) is 360° ÷ 6 = 60°, the figure has rotation symmetries of 60°, 120°, 180°, 240°, 300°, and 360°.

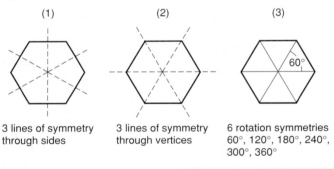

(1)   (2)   (3)

3 lines of symmetry through sides   3 lines of symmetry through vertices   6 rotation symmetries 60°, 120°, 180°, 240°, 300°, 360°

Snowflakes have the reflection and rotation symmetries of the hexagon. Notice the 6 congruent central angles in the snow crystal in Figure 7.66.* Despite the similarity that results from the 6 reflection and 6 rotation symmetries of the hexagon, there is endless variety in the details of snowflakes.

Figure 7.66

*This photo is one of more than 2200 in W. A. Bentley and W. J. Humphreys, *Snow Crystals* (New York: McGraw-Hill, 1931).

REFLECTION SYMMETRY FOR SPACE FIGURES

The idea of reflection symmetry for three-dimensional objects is similar to that for plane figures. With plane figures we found lines such that one half of the figure was the reflection of the other. With figures in space there are *planes of symmetry* such that the two halves look the same. Consider, for example, the antique chair in Figure 7.67. The plane running down the center of the back and across the seat to the front of the chair divides it into left and right halves, which are mirror images of each other. Such a plane is called a **plane of symmetry.** The chair is said to have reflection symmetry.

plane of symmetry

Figure 7.67
Ebonized walnut armchair, dating from between 1865 and 1875

Reflection symmetry for figures in space can be mathematically defined by requiring that for each point on the left side of the chair, there is a corresponding point on the right side such that both points are the same perpendicular distance from the plane of symmetry. For the antique chair, point A corresponds to A' and B corresponds to B'. These points are called images of each other, and the segments $\overline{AA'}$ and $\overline{BB'}$ are perpendicular to the plane of symmetry.

Two-sided symmetry, such as that of the antique chair in Figure 7.67 and the long-horn beetle and zebra butterfly in Figure 7.68, is sometimes called **vertical symmetry** because the plane of symmetry is perpendicular to the ground. Look around and you may be surprised at the number of things that have vertical symmetry.

vertical symmetry

Figure 7.68
Long-horn beetle (*left*) and zebra butterfly (*right*)

EXAMPLE D   Determine the planes of symmetry for each of the following objects.

Solution   The square-top table has 4 vertical planes of symmetry: 1 from front to back, 1 from side to side, and 1 through each diagonal of the top surface. The lamp has 6 vertical planes of symmetry because its shade has 6 congruent sections: 3 planes bisect opposite pairs of sections of the lampshade, and 3 planes pass through opposite pairs of seams of the shade. The wastebasket has 8 vertical planes of symmetry, since its base has the shape of a regular octagon.

ROTATION SYMMETRY FOR SPACE FIGURES

Some three-dimensional objects, such as the table shown in Figure 7.69, have rotation symmetry. If the table is rotated 120°, the legs will change places and the table will be back in the same location or position. That is, leg *A* will go to the position of leg *B*, *B* to *C*, and *C* to *A*. In this example the table can be rotated about line ℓ, which passes **axis of symmetry**   through the center of the table's top and its base. Line ℓ is called the **axis of symmetry**, and the table is said to have rotation symmetry. Since the dihedral angles formed by adjacent legs of this table have measures of 120°, the table has 120°, 240°, and 360° rotation symmetries.

Figure 7.69

The three-legged table in Figure 7.69 also has 3 vertical planes of symmetry, 1 passing through each leg. It is not difficult to find objects with both planes of symmetry and axes of symmetry. The small table, the lamp, and the wastebasket in Example D all have both types of symmetry. Occasionally, however, you will see space figures that have rotation symmetry but no plane of symmetry.

EXAMPLE E

Determine all the rotation symmetries for the paper windmill.

Paper windmill

Solution   The paper windmill has rotation symmetries of 90°, 180°, 270°, and 360° about its axis, which is the line through the center of the windmill and perpendicular to its surface.

PROBLEM-SOLVING APPLICATION

■ PROBLEM

For every plane figure with 2 or more reflection symmetries, there is a relationship between the number of these symmetries and the number of rotation symmetries. What is this relationship?

Question 1   **Understanding the Problem**   There are plane figures with both rotation and reflection symmetries. For example, a rectangle has 2 lines of symmetry. How many rotation symmetries does a rectangle have?

Question 2   **Devising a Plan**   *Making a table* and comparing the numbers of reflection and rotation symmetries may reveal a pattern. A square has 4 reflection symmetries. How many rotation symmetries does a square have?

Question 3   **Carrying Out the Plan**   The numbers of lines of symmetry for several figures are shown below. Determine the numbers of rotation symmetries for these figures and record them in the table. What does this result suggest?

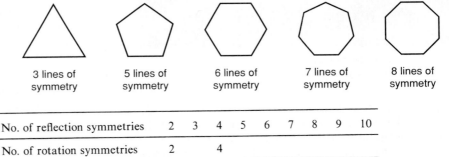

| 3 lines of symmetry | 5 lines of symmetry | 6 lines of symmetry | 7 lines of symmetry | 8 lines of symmetry |

No. of reflection symmetries	2	3	4	5	6	7	8	9	10
No. of rotation symmetries	2		4						

Question 4   **Looking Back**   As the results in the table suggest, if a figure has 2 or more reflection symmetries, it will have the same number of rotation symmetries. The converse, however, is not true. What symmetries does the following figure have?

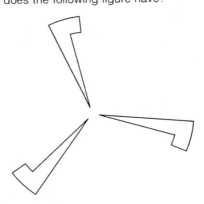

Answers to Question 1–4
1. 2   **2.** 4
3. If a figure has 2 or more reflection symmetries, it will have the same number of rotation symmetries.
4. The figure has rotation symmetries of 120°, 240°, and 360°. It has no reflection symmetries.

RELATED ACTIVITIES IN
Mathematics for Elementary Teachers: An Activity Approach, 3e

Activity Set 7.4   **Creating Symmetric Figures by Paperfolding:** Patterns are included for folding paper into an eight-pointed wind rose, a 16-pointed wind rose, certain star figures, and several types of polygons.

Just for Fun   **Snowflakes:** Steps for creating a variety of hexagonal snowflakes.

EXERCISES AND PROBLEMS 7.4

The Alhambra, built in the thirteenth century for Moorish kings, Granada, Spain

1. The pool, building, and fortress in the section of the Alhambra shown in the photo have a vertical plane of symmetry, about which their left sides are the reflections of their right sides.
   a. List five objects in this picture that have images about the plane of symmetry.
   b. Physical objects can never be perfectly symmetric. In this scene, for example, there are several objects that deviate from perfect symmetry. List three objects that do not have an image for the vertical plane of symmetry.
   c. Several individual items in this photo have vertical lines of symmetry. Name an object in this picture that has a horizontal line of symmetry.

2. In 1850 gold was so plentiful in the United States that dozens of different banks and business firms minted their own coins. Some were square and others had 8 sides, such as this octagonal $50 gold piece.

Panama-Pacific octagonal $50 gold piece

   a. How many rotation symmetries does a regular octagon have?
   b. How many degrees are there in the smallest rotation symmetry?
   c. How many lines of symmetry does a regular octagon have?

3. The following organisms have reflection and rotation symmetries. Determine the number of lines of symmetry and the number of rotation symmetries for each.
   a.

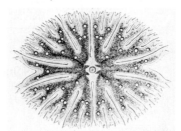

   b.

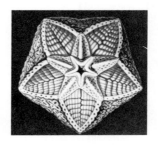

c.

d.

4. Which two of the polygons below have no lines of symmetry? Draw all the lines of symmetry for the remaining polygons. Find the number of rotation symmetries for each figure.

The subject of beauty has been discussed for thousands of years. Aristotle felt that the main elements of beauty are order and symmetry. The American mathematician George Birkhoff (1884–1944) developed a formula for rating the beauty of objects.* Part of his formula involves counting symmetries. If only symmetry is used to rate the beauty of the polygons below, which has the highest rating (counting all lines of reflection and rotation symmetries)? Which is the least beautiful?

a.

b.

c.

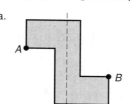 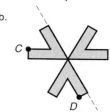

d.

e.

f.

g.

  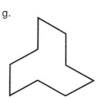

5. Show that the dashed lines in the figures below are not lines of symmetry by finding the images of the lettered points.

a.   b.

6. The mirror test for symmetry is very effective when the reflecting is done with a Mira.** To find a line of symmetry, it is necessary only to move the Mira until the image reflected on the Plexiglas coincides with the portion of the figure behind it. This cannot be done for several of the following figures. Which ones?

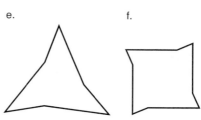

a.   b.

c.

d.

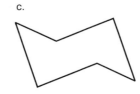

e.   f.

*G. D. Birkhoff, *Aesthetic Measure* (Cambridge, MA: Harvard University Press, 1933), 33–46.

**E. Woodward, "Geometry with a Mira," *Arithmetic Teacher* 25 (November 1977): 117–118.

7. a. Which uppercase letters have two lines of symmetry?
   b. Which letters have two rotation symmetries but no lines of symmetry?

ABCDEFGHIJKLM
NOPQRSTUVWXYZ

8. If you write the letter P on a piece of paper and hold it in front of a mirror, it will look reversed.
   a. Which uppercase letters will not appear reversed when held in front of a mirror?
   b. What type of symmetry do these letters have?
   c. Use the letters from part a to write a word whose reflection in a mirror is also a word.

9. The following figures were formed on circular geoboards. Which of these figures have no lines of symmetry? Determine the number of lines of symmetry for the remaining figures. Find the number of rotation symmetries for each figure that has 2 or more such symmetries, and give the number of degrees for each.

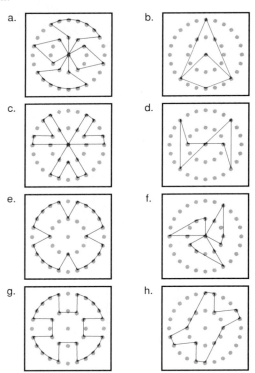

10. Sketch figures with the given symmetries, as they would appear on a circular geoboard.
   a. 1 rotation symmetry and 1 reflection symmetry
   b. 8 rotation symmetries and zero reflection symmetries
   c. 6 rotation symmetries and 6 reflection symmetries

11. Trace the sketches below and complete the figures so that they are symmetric about the dashed line. You might want to first find the image with a mirror or Mira.

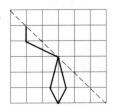 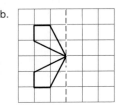

12. Trace the sketches below and complete the figures so that they are symmetric about the 2 perpendicular dashed lines.

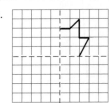 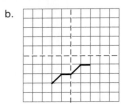

13. How many planes of symmetry does each of the following objects have? (The lampshade has 16 panels.)

   a.

   b.

   c.

14. The figures below are highly symmetric.

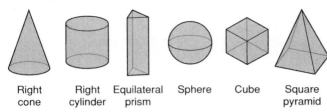

| Right cone | Right cylinder | Equilateral prism | Sphere | Cube | Square pyramid |

a. Which figures have a horizontal plane of symmetry?

b. Does each of these solids have at least 1 vertical plane of symmetry?

c. Give the number of rotation symmetries for each vertical axis of symmetry.

15. List all the symmetries for this figure (a sphere mounted on a pentagonal base).

Sphere with Fish by M. C. Escher

© 1990 M. C. Escher Heirs/Cordon Art— Baarn—Holland.

16. These metalwork designs have many pleasing symmetries. How many rotation symmetries and lines of symmetry does each design have?

a.
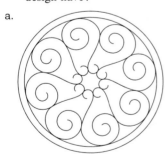

b.

c.
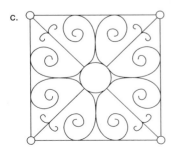

17. How many rotation symmetries does each of the Japanese crests have?

a.   b.

c.   d.

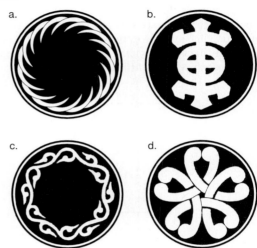

Featured Strategy: Using a Model

18. Crystals are classified into different types according to the number of axes of rotation they have. This photo shows several cubes of a galena crystal. How many axes of symmetry does a cube have?

Intersecting cubes of galena crystals

a. Understanding the Problem One axis of symmetry in the cube below runs through the centers of faces *EFGH* and *ABCD*. What is the total number of axes of symmetry through the faces of the cube? Describe each by listing the pairs of faces.

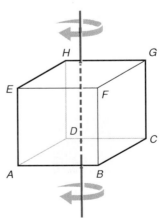

b. Devising a Plan A posterboard or paper model of a cube that can be pierced by a wire is a helpful device for determining rotations that take the cube back onto itself. The following figure suggests some other possibilities for axes of symmetry. One axis passes through the edges $\overline{FG}$ and $\overline{AD}$. How many axes of symmetry pass through the edges of a cube? Describe each by listing pairs of edges.

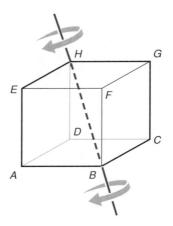

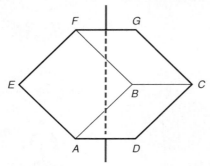

c. Carrying Out the Plan A model will help to show that a cube has 3 types of axes of symmetry: through the faces, through the edges, and through the vertices. The following figure shows the axis through the pair of vertices H and B. How many axes of symmetry are there through pairs of vertices, and what is the total number of axes of symmetry for the cube?

d. Looking Back A cube also has many planes of symmetry. The figure shows a plane that bisects 4 edges of the cube; $\overline{AB}$, $\overline{DC}$, $\overline{HG}$, and $\overline{EF}$. How many planes of symmetry bisect edges of the cube? Describe each by listing the 4 edges.

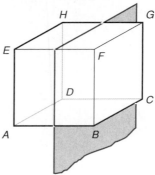

LABORATORY INVESTIGATION

Mirror Cards were developed to teach spatial relationships and symmetry informally in the early grades.* The idea is to use a mirror to match a pattern on one card to that on another.

Questions for Investigation

1. How can the mirror be placed on the card above to obtain the figures shown below? (Note: One cannot be obtained.)

2. What other figures can be obtained from the above card by using a mirror?

  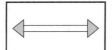

PUZZLER

Subtracting 80 from a certain twentieth-century year (date) with a 180° rotation symmetry yields a nineteenth-century year with both horizontal and vertical lines of symmetry. What are these two years?

---

*M. Walter, "An Example of Informal Geometry: Mirror Cards," *Arithmetic Teacher* 13 (October 1966): 338–352.

SECTION 7.5   INTRODUCTION TO LOGO*

■ *PROBLEM OPENER*

There are 6 different ways in which a 4 by 4 grid can be divided into two congruent parts by cutting along the grid lines. One way is shown here. What are the other 5 ways?

The computer revolution is here. Computers have invaded every aspect of life, from space research to elementary school instruction. The first electronic computer, the ENIAC, was built in 1946 at the University of Pennsylvania. It consisted of 18,000 vacuum tubes, weighed 30 tons, and tended to overheat and break down. Since that time the replacement of tubes by miniaturized circuits has resulted in smaller, more reliable computers. Microcomputers are now widely used in homes and precollege education. The heart of a microcomputer contains miniaturized circuits called **chips,** and each chip contains thousands of electronic circuits. The relative size of a computer chip can be seen in Figure 7.70.

chips

Figure 7.70
Computer chip

Before a computer can perform a task, it must be given step-by-step instructions in words it understands. One of the easiest computer languages, and one that is especially suitable for elementary school children, is **LOGO.** This language was first developed at Massachusetts Institute of Technology (MIT) in the 1970s. Since that time several versions of LOGO have been developed. In this text we will use only those commands in LOGO that are common in most versions of this language.

LOGO

*This section is optional.

LOGO COMMANDS

LOGO was written for children. In experiments at MIT's Artificial Intelligence Laboratory, children drew geometric figures by giving instructions to a mechanical robot called a turtle (see Figure 7.71). As the turtle moved across the floor on large sheets of paper, a pen at its center traced a path. The children could command the turtle to move from one point to another by giving it an angle to turn through and a distance to move.

Figure 7.71
A robot at M.I.T.'s Artificial Intelligence Lab

turtle
heading
start position
home

Now the same thing can be done on a computer screen by moving a small triangular pointer called a **turtle.** The turtle has a position, and at each position on the screen the turtle points in some direction, called its **heading.** The heading is some number of degrees from 0 to 360. The turtle's **start position** is at the center of the screen, heading north. This position is called **home.** Regardless of where the turtle is on the screen, if you type HOME and then press RETURN (or ENTER), the turtle will go to the center of the screen and face north (see Figure 7.72).

Figure 7.72

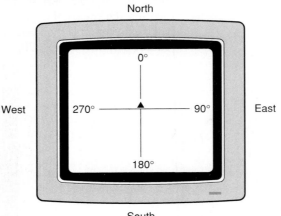

You can move the turtle about by giving it commands. Type FORWARD 30 and press RETURN, and the turtle will move forward 30 turtle steps, tracing its path. Type RIGHT 90 and press RETURN, and the turtle will turn 90° to the right. Type FORWARD 50 and press RETURN, and the turtle will move forward 50 steps, tracing its path. These moves are shown on the screen in Figure 7.73.

Figure 7.73

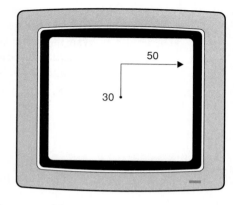

FORWARD 30
RIGHT 90
FORWARD 50

To return the turtle to its home position and clear the screen of all turtle tracks, type HOME CLEARSCREEN and press RETURN.* Sometimes it is helpful to hide the turtle to get a better view of a geometric figure. You can make the turtle invisible by typing HIDETURTLE, and you can make it appear again by typing SHOW-TURTLE. The turtle can be turned right or left any number of degrees, and it can be moved back as well as forward. Here are seven commands and their abbreviations. The RETURN key must be pressed before the computer will carry out any command.**

Command	*Abbreviation*
FORWARD	FD
BACK	BK
RIGHT	RT
LEFT	LT
CLEARSCREEN	CS
HIDETURTLE	HT
SHOWTURTLE	ST

CREATING COMMANDS

A line can be drawn by moving the turtle forward and back. The following commands will produce the line shown in Figure 7.74 and leave the turtle in its start position at the center of the screen.

Figure 7.74

FD 80
BK 160
FD 80

*In Apple LOGO this can be accomplished by typing CLEARSCREEN.

**In the remaining discussion, the RETURN (or ENTER) step will usually not be stated.

procedures

One of the advantages of LOGO is that we can define new commands, called **procedures.** For example, we can give a list of commands a name, and then whenever we type the name the turtle will carry out these commands. We can think of creating a procedure as teaching the turtle a new word. Here is a procedure for drawing the line in Figure 7.74. We named this procedure LINE.

> TO LINE
> FD 80
> BK 160
> FD 80
> END

The TO tells the computer that you are defining a new command. The END tells the computer that you have finished the definition. After you type END and press RETURN, the computer's response, LINE DEFINED, will shown on the screen. Now if you type LINE, the turtle will draw a line in the direction in which it is heading and finish in the position in which it started.

EXAMPLE A

LINE is used three times in the following set of commands. The turtle's initial position is the center of the screen, and its heading is north. Sketch the figure that will be drawn by the turtle in response to these commands.

LINE RT 60 LINE RT 60 LINE RT 60

Solution

The turtle draws a vertical line and makes a right turn of 60°, then repeats this action two more times. The turtle's final heading is 180° (south) because it has turned through three 60° angles.

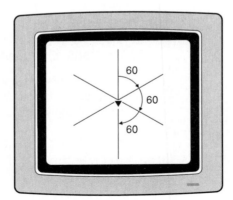

There are times when we want the turtle to move to a new location, but not to draw a path. This can be accomplished by using the command PENUP. When we want the turtle to draw again, we use the command PENDOWN. These commands were used, together with the command LINE, to instruct the turtle to draw the 2 parallel lines shown in Figure 7.75.

Figure 7.75
Two parallel lines

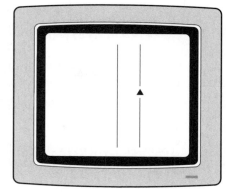

```
LINE
RT 90
PENUP
FD 20
PENDOWN
LT 90
LINE
```

RECURSION

recursion

A powerful feature of computers is their ability to repeat a sequence of commands many times. This type of repetition is called **recursion.** One way of obtaining recursion is through the REPEAT command. For example, instead of using the commands LINE and RT 60 three times to produce three lines at 60° angles, as in Example A, we can use one REPEAT command. This command must include a number, to tell the turtle the number of times the instructions are to be repeated, and a list of instructions, which are typed inside square brackets.

REPEAT 3 [LINE RT 60]

The following commands produce the square in Figure 7.76, whose sides have length 60. Notice that two commands are written on each line. Several commands may be typed on a line before RETURN is pressed.

Figure 7.76

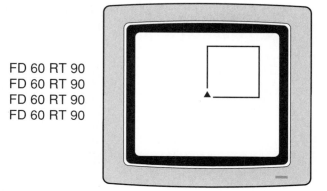

```
FD 60 RT 90
FD 60 RT 90
FD 60 RT 90
FD 60 RT 90
```

Since FD 60 RT 90 is repeated four times, we can accomplish the same result by using the REPEAT command.

REPEAT 4 [FD 60 RT 90]

Now let's use the REPEAT command to define a procedure for drawing a square.

```
TO SQ
  REPEAT 4 [FD 60 RT 90]
END
```

By typing SQ, we instruct the turtle to draw a square whose sides have length 60.

DRAWING POLYGONS

The command HOME is very helpful in drawing polygonal figures because regardless of where the turtle is on the screen, this command will send the turtle back to its start position to complete a closed curve.

EXAMPLE B

Sketch the figure that will be drawn by the following commands.

RT 90 FD 35 LT 90 FD 50 HOME

Solution   These commands instruct the turtle to draw a right triangle. The 2 legs of the triangle are drawn first and then the hypotenuse is formed by sending the turtle home.

Regular polygons are easy to draw using LOGO commands. To draw any regular polygon, the turtle will make a sequence of equal forward moves and equal turns until it has turned a total of 360°. In general, the size of the turn will be 360° divided by the number of sides in the polygon. For example, to draw the regular hexagon in Figure 7.77, the turtle makes 6 forward moves of 50 steps, each followed by a right turn of 60°. These 60° angles are the exterior angles of the hexagon. Each interior angle of the polygon is 120°, the supplement of a 60° turn. Notice that it does not matter where the turtle begins or what direction it is heading; the sequence of 6 moves and turns listed in Figure 7.77 will produce a regular hexagon.

Figure 7.77
Regular hexagon

FD 50 RT 60 FD 50 RT 60 FD 50
RT 60 FD 50 RT 60 FD 50 RT 60
FD 50 RT 60

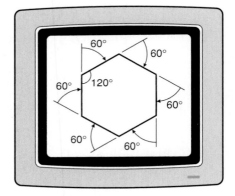

The 12 commands for drawing this hexagon can be condensed into 1 command by using REPEAT, as shown in the following procedure. Once this procedure has been defined, we can obtain the hexagon shown above by typing HEXAGON.

TO HEXAGON
  REPEAT 6 [FD 50 RT 60]
END

EXAMPLE C

What regular polygon will be drawn by the following commands?

REPEAT 10 [FD 15 RT 360/10]

Solution   Since the turtle will take 10 turns, each with 360° ÷ 10 = 36°, a regular decagon with sides of length 15 will be produced.

CIRCLES AND ARCS As the number of sides in a polygon increases, the shape of the polygon becomes closer to a circle. The procedure shown in Figure 7.78 instructs the turtle to draw a regular polygon with 360 sides, which we will call CIRCLE.

Figure 7.78

```
TO CIRCLE
  REPEAT 360 [FD 1 RT 1]
END
```

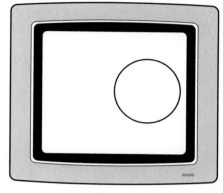

Circle 1

An arc is obtained by drawing part of a circle. The number of 1° turns the turtle makes is the number of degrees in the arc. The following program produces the 90° arc shown in Figure 7.79.

Figure 7.79

```
TO ARC
  REPEAT 90 [FD 1 RT 1]
END
```

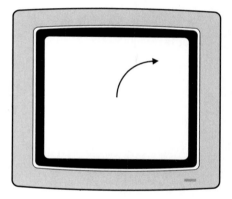

Arc 1

SYMMETRIC FIGURES

Symmetric figures can be obtained by interchanging all RIGHT and LEFT commands in a procedure. When the original figure is combined with the revised figure, the result will be a figure with a vertical line of symmetry. Let's see how this works. The procedure RIGHTVENT produces the vent in Figure 7.80.

Figure 7.80

```
TO RIGHTVENT
  FD 100 RT 90 FD 80 RT 90 FD 50
  RT 90 FD 30 RT 90 FD 20 LT 90
  FD 30 LT 90 FD 70 RT 90 FD 20 RT 90
END
```

Rightvent

Now if we use the commands in the procedure RIGHTVENT, but change each RT to LT and change each LT to RT, the new procedure, called LEFTVENT, will produce a vent that points to the left, as shown in Figure 7.81.

Figure 7.81

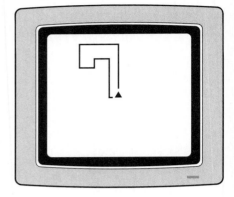

```
TO LEFTVENT
  FD 100 LT 90 FD 80 LT 90 FD 50
  LT 90 FD 30 LT 90 FD 20 RT 90
  FD 30 RT 90 FD 70 LT 90 FD 20 LT 90
END
```

We can now instruct the turtle to draw both of these figures by typing RIGHT-VENT LEFTVENT and pressing RETURN. The resulting figure (Figure 7.82) has 1 line of symmetry, the north-south center line of the screen.

Figure 7.82

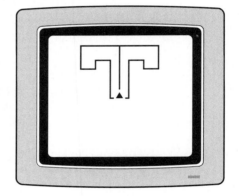

RIGHTVENT LEFTVENT

A figure with rotation symmetry can be created by rotating a given figure. The next set of commands instructs the turtle to draw the flag shown in Figure 7.83.

Figure 7.83

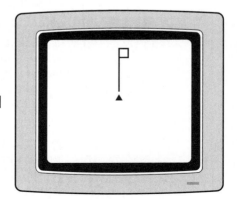

```
TO FLAG
  FD 60
  REPEAT 4 [RT 90 FD 10]
  BK 60
END
```

Flag

Then the procedure FLAG is used with the REPEAT command to create a figure with 5 rotation symmetries (Figure 7.84).

Figure 7.84

REPEAT 5 [FLAG RT 72]

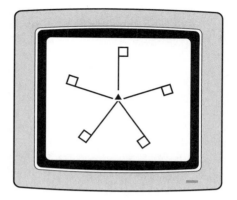

Flag

PROBLEM-SOLVING APPLICATION

Have you ever had to produce a grid by drawing many carefully spaced lines? The steps for using LOGO to draw a grid are developed here.

How can the turtle be instructed to draw an 8 by 8 grid?

Question 1

Understanding the Problem   A *drawing* will help you understand the problem and devise a plan. An 8 by 8 grid is shown in figure (a) below. It requires 9 vertical lines. How many horizontal lines are required?

(a)

Devising a Plan   The need for horizontal and vertical lines suggests using the procedure to draw a line segment and repeating it several times. The following commands, which include the procedure LINE, can be used to draw 9 vertical lines.

REPEAT 9 [LINE PENUP RT 90 FD 20 LT 90 PENDOWN]

Question 2   Figure (b) shows the 9 lines. Where will the turtle be located after drawing the ninth line? If the turtle is repositioned, the same commands can be used again to draw 9 horizontal lines to complete the grid.

(b)

Carrying Out the Plan   After drawing the 9 vertical lines, the turtle will be 20 steps to the right center of the ninth line and headed north. Since half of each line's length is 80 units, the commands

PENUP BK 80 LT 90 FD 100 PENDOWN

Question 3   will put the turtle in position to draw the 9 horizontal lines. What is the turtle's position? The grid can be completed by using the commands used to draw the vertical lines.

Looking Back   The steps for drawing a grid can be defined as a procedure called GRID. **Question 4**   What changes would need to be made in the procedure GRID to decrease the space between the vertical and horizontal lines from 20 units to 15 units?

```
TO GRID
REPEAT 9 [LINE PENUP RT 90 FD 20 LT 90 PENDOWN]
PENUP BK 80 LT 90 FD 100 PENDOWN
REPEAT 9 [LINE PENUP RT 90 FD 20 LT 90 PENDOWN]
```

Answers to Questions 1–4

1. 9   **2.** 20 steps to the right center of the ninth line which is drawn

3. At the bottom of the fifth line, headed west

4. Change FD 20 to FD 15 in two places; change FD 100 to FD 75; change BK 80 to BK 60; and revise the procedure LINE by replacing FD 80 by FD 60 and BK 160 by BK 120.

RELATED ACTIVITIES IN

Mathematics for Elementary Teachers: An Activity Approach, 3e

Activity Set 7.5   **Computer Games in LOGO:** The turtle and a circle are randomly placed on the screen. The objective is to move the turtle inside the circle using the fewest number of moves.

EXERCISES AND PROBLEMS 7.5

1. Sketch the figure the turtle will draw in carrying out the following commands.

```
FD 80 BK 160 FD 80
RT 90 FD 50 LT 90
FD 80 BK 160 FD 80
PENUP RT 90 FD 50 LT 90 PENDOWN
FD 80 BK 160 FD 80
```

2. In Example A the turtle drew 6 spokes of a wheel when given the command LINE and instructed to make right turns of 60°. Use this approach and the REPEAT command to write the commands for drawing 10 spokes.

3. Write the commands for drawing the isosceles triangle in the following figure. The two equal sides have a length of 70 units.

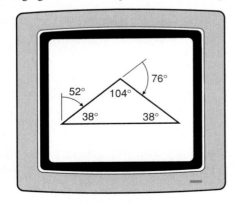

4. Write the commands for drawing a scalene triangle that has an obtuse angle. Sketch the triangle.

5. Write the commands for drawing the following figures.
  a. A nonconvex hexagon
  b. A convex pentagon

6. Define a procedure called PARALLELOGRAM for drawing the parallelogram in the following figure. The sides have lengths of 40 and 70 units.

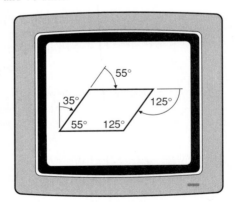

7. Define a procedure for drawing these regular polygons.

  a. Pentagon   **b.** Octagon   **c.** Dodecagon

8. Write a procedure called RTREE for drawing the right side of a tree. Have the turtle return to its start position. Then define a procedure called LTREE by interchanging the RT and LT commands. The two commands RTREE LTREE should produce the complete tree.

9. Use the procedure FLAG from Section 7.5 to write a command for drawing a figure with 10 rotation symmetries.

10. Use the procedure CIRCLE to define a procedure called SLINKY for drawing overlapping circles.

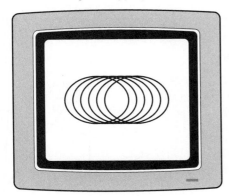

Slinky

11. The procedure ARC from Section 7.5 can be used twice to obtain a petal.
    a. Define a procedure named PETAL.
    b. Use PETAL to define a procedure named FLOWER to draw a flower with 8 petals.

Flower

Featured Strategy: Making a drawing

12. Write a procedure called GRIDSQUARES that instructs the turtle to draw a 3 by 5 array of nonintersecting squares of the same size.

a. **Understanding the Problem** Here is a 2 by 3 array of squares. Draw a 3 by 5 array. Notice that the size of the squares and the distance between them are not given.

b. **Devising a Plan** First you need a procedure to draw a square. Write a procedure to draw a 10 by 10 square. Then, since the same size square is needed 15 times, you can use the REPEAT command.

c. **Carrying Out the Plan** Write the commands to draw the array. (Hint: Do 1 row or 1 column at a time.)

d. **Looking Back** Revise your program to increase the space between the squares.

13. Write the commands for drawing 3 concentric squares, as shown in this figure.

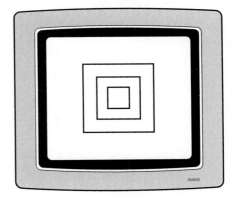

14. A procedure for drawing a figure with many parts, such as a face, can best be created using subprocedures. The following procedure called FACE has 8 subprocedures. In each of these subprocedures except possibly the one for the nose (see hint below), the turtle should start from and return to its home. Design a face, and define the subprocedures for drawing it. (Hint: Once a subprocedure for the left eye, left ear, or left side of the mouth has been defined, the right eye, etc., can be drawn by using the concept of symmetry to obtain a new procedure. The turtle can be used for the nose.)

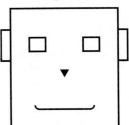

```
TO FACE
BOX  R,EYE  L,EYE  R,EAR  L,EAR
   R,MOUTH  L,MOUTH  NOSE
END
```

COMPUTER INVESTIGATION

Regular polygons can be drawn by using LOGO commands to specify constant forward moves and constant turns, where the number of degrees in the turn is a factor of 360°. For example, the following command produces a regular pentagon with sides of length 80.

REPEAT 5 [FD 80 RT 72]

Some interesting results occur when the number of degrees in the turn is not a factor of 360°.

Questions for Investigation

1. Experiment with the following command by selecting different whole numbers for N and different degrees for □. (Note: Select N large enough so the turtle will complete the figure.)

REPEAT N [FD 80 RT □]

2. What happens when the number of degrees for □ is less than or equal to 120°? between 120° and 180°?

PUZZLER

LOGO commands can be used to instruct the computer to create this five-pointed star. Beginning at H (home), the turtle moves north to I, takes a right turn and moves to C, takes a right turn and moves to D, etc., making 5 equal forward moves and 5 equal turns and ending at H facing north. What is the measure of each right turn, and what is the measure of the angle at I?

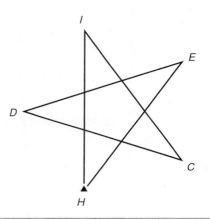

CHAPTER REVIEW

1. Mathematical Systems
   a. A **mathematical system** consists of undefined terms, definitions, axioms, and theorems.
   b. In every mathematical system there must be **undefined words.**
   c. **Definitions** are stated in terms of undefined words or previously defined words.
   d. **Axioms** are statements that are assumed to be true.
   e. **Theorems** are statements that are proved using definitions and axioms together with deductive reasoning.

2. Plane Figures
   a. The terms **point, line,** and **plane** are undefined.
   b. **Half-planes, line segments, rays, angles, parallel lines, perpendicular lines,** and **collinear points** are defined.
   c. Each **angle** is measured in degrees. A **degree** is 1/360 of a complete turn about a circle.
   d. A **protractor** is a device for measuring angles.
   e. Angles are classified as **right, obtuse, acute,** or **reflex.**

   f. Two angles are **complementary** if the sum of their measures is 90° and **supplementary** if the sum of their measures is 180°.
   g. Two intersecting lines form pairs of congruent **vertical angles.**
   h. If two lines are intersected by a third line called a **transversal,** the two lines are parallel if and only if the **alternate interior angles** are congruent.
   i. Curves are classified as **simple, simple closed,** or **closed.**
   j. The union of a simple closed curve and its interior is called a **plane region.**
   k. Plane regions are classified as **convex** or **nonconvex.**
   l. A **circle** is a special type of simple closed curve. **Radius, diameter, circumference, chord, tangent,** and **disc** are defined terms associated with circles.

3. Polygons
   a. A **polygon** is a simple closed curve that is the union of line segments.

b. Polygons are classified according to the number of sides: **triangle, quadrilateral, pentagon,** etc.

c. A polygon is called a **regular polygon** if all of its angles are congruent and all of its sides are congruent.

d. The first three regular polygons are the **equilateral triangle,** the **square,** and the **regular pentagon.**

e. The number of degrees in the **central angle** of a regular polygon is 360 divided by the number of sides in the polygon.

f. An arrangement of nonoverlapping figures that can be placed together to entirely cover a region is called a **tessellation.**

g. The **equilateral triangle, square,** and **regular hexagon** are the only regular polygons that will tessellate.

h. A tessellation with two or more noncongruent regular polygons in which each vertex is surrounded by the same arrangement of polygons is called a **semiregular tessellation.**

4. Space Figures

a. The angle between two intersecting planes is called a **dihedral angle.**

b. The surface of a three-dimensional figure whose sides are polygonal regions is called a **polyhedron.**

c. Polyhedra are classified as **convex** or **nonconvex.**

d. A convex polyhedron whose faces are congruent regular polygons and that has the same arrangement of polygons at each vertex is called a **regular polyhedron** or a **Platonic solid.**

e. A polyhedron whose faces are two or more noncongruent regular polygons and that has the same arrangement of polygons at each vertex is called a **semiregular polyhedron.**

f. **Pyramids, prisms, cones, cylinders,** and **spheres** are common types of figures in space.

g. Points on the earth's surface are located by two systems of circles: **parallels of latitude** and **meridians of longitude.**

h. **Cylindrical, conic,** and **plane projections** are three types of maps of the earth's surface.

5. Symmetry

a. Plane figures can have **reflection symmetries** about lines and **rotation symmetries** about points.

b. A regular polygon with n sides has n reflection symmetries and n rotation symmetries.

c. Every plane figure with reflection symmetries also has rotation symmetries.

d. A plane figure may have rotation symmetries but no reflection symmetries.

e. Space figures have reflection symmetries about planes and rotation symmetries about axes.

6. LOGO

a. LOGO is a computer language that is especially useful for teaching geometry.

b. LOGO commands, such as **FORWARD, BACK, RIGHT,** and **LEFT,** move a triangular pointer called the **turtle.**

c. A sequence of LOGO commands is called a **procedure.**

d. The **REPEAT** command causes **recursion,** whereby the computer repeats a sequence of commands a given number of times.

CHAPTER TEST

1. These figures were obtained by folding rectangular sheets of paper.

(i)  (ii)   (iii)

(iv)  (v)  (vi)

Write the number of the sheet(s) whose shaded region illustrates the polygon.

a. Hexagon **b.** Parallelogram

c. Trapezoid **d.** Equilateral triangle

e. Pentagon **f.** Isosceles triangle

2. Sketch an example of each of the following figures.

a. Nonconvex pentagon

b. Simple closed curve

c. Convex decagon

d. A closed curve that is not simple

3. Identify the following kinds of angles in the figure below.

a. Acute **b.** Reflex

c. Right **d.** Obtuse

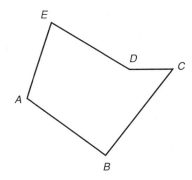

4. Determine whether the statements below are true or false.

a. Every square is a rectangle.

b. Some scalene triangles are right triangles.

c. Every parallelogram is a rectangle.

d. Every rectangle is a parallelogram.

e. Some right triangles are equilateral triangles.

5. Determine the number of degrees in each angle.
   a. The central angle of a regular octagon
   b. A vertex angle of a regular hexagon
   c. An exterior angle of a regular pentagon

6. Determine whether each figure is a regular polygon. If it is not, state the condition it does not satisfy.

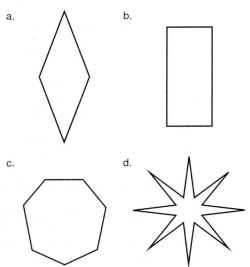

   a.   b.

   c.   d.

7. State whether each of the following polygons will tessellate.

   a. Regular octagon   b. Isosceles triangle

   c. Regular hexagon   d. Nonconvex quadrilateral

   e. Regular pentagon

8. Can an equilateral triangle, a square, and a regular octagon, all of whose sides have the same length, be used together for a semiregular tessellation? Explain your answer.

9. Name each of the following figures, and classify each as right or oblique.

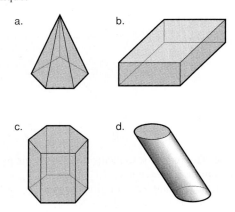

   a.   b.

   c.   d.

e.   f.

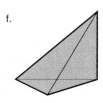

10. Classify each figure as a polyhedron or a nonpolyhedron.

    a. Sphere   b. Prism
    c. Pyramid   d. Cone
    e. Cube   f. Dodecahedron

11. Determine the number of vertices in each of the following polyhedra.
    a. An icosahedron (it has 30 edges)
    b. A semiregular polyhedron with 14 faces and 36 edges

12. Sketch or describe each of the following plane figures.
    a. A figure with 3 lines of symmetry
    b. A figure with 2 rotation symmetries but no lines of symmetry
    c. A figure with 5 rotation symmetries and 5 reflection symmetries

13. Determine the number of planes of symmetry for each figure.
    a. A right prism whose base is a regular octagon
    b. A right cone
    c. A pyramid whose base is a regular pentagon

14. Finish sketching this figure so that it is symmetric about lines m and n.

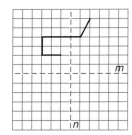

15. Determine the number of lines of symmetry and the number of rotation symmetries for each figure.
    a. A rectangle
    b. A regular heptagon
    c. An equilateral triangle
    d. A parallelogram

16. Write a set of LOGO commands that instruct the turtle to draw a regular octagon.

17. Sketch the figure that the turtle will draw if given the following LOGO commands:

    FD 80 RT 135 FD 100 RT 45 FD 80
    RT 135 FD 100

18. Seven points in a plane can be endpoints for a total of how many line segments?

19. What is the number of degrees in 1 vertex angle of a regular polygon with 40 sides?

20. Suppose the interior of a circle is to be partitioned into the maximum number of regions by line segments. One line will divide it into 2 regions; 2 lines will divide it into 4 regions; and 3 lines will divide it into 7 regions.

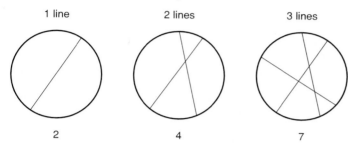

a. What is the maximum number of regions that can be created by 4 lines?

b. Find a pattern and use inductive reasoning to predict the maximum number of regions that can be created by 10 lines.

BIBLIOGRAPHY

Barson, A., and L., Barson. "Ideas (Geometry Activities)." *Arithmetic Teacher* 35 (April 1988): 27–36.

Battista, M. T. "MATHSTUFF Logo Procedures: Bridging the Gap Between Logo and School Geometry." *Arithmetic Teacher* 35 (September 1987): 7–11.

Battista, M. T., and D. H. Clements. "A Case for a Logo-based Elementary School Geometry Curriculum." *Arithmetic Teacher* 36 (November 1988): 11–17.

Billstein, R., S. Libeskind, and J. Lott. *MIT Logo for the Apple.* Menlo Park, CA: Benjamin-Cummings, 1985.

Billstein, R., and J. W. Lott. "The Turtle Deserves a Star." *Arithmetic Teacher* 33 (March 1986): 14–16.

Binswanger, R. "Discovering Division with Logo." *Arithmetic Teacher* 36 (December 1988): 44–49.

Blake, R. N., and C. Verhille. "Semiregular Polyhedra." *Mathematics Teacher* 75 (October 1982): 577–581.

Bledsoe, G. J. "Guessing Geometric Shapes." *Mathematics Teacher* 80 (March 1987): 178–180.

Borenson, H. "Teaching the Process of Mathematical Investigation." *Arithmetic Teacher* 33 (April 1986): 36–38.

Bright, G. W. "Teaching Mathematics with Technology: Logo and Geometry." *Arithmetic Teacher* 36 (January 1989): 32–34.

Bright, G. W., and J. G. Harvey. "Learning and Fun with Geometry Games." *Arithmetic Teacher* 35 (April 1988): 22–26.

Burger, W. F. "Graph Paper Geometry." *Mathematics for the Middle Grades (5–9).* 1982 Yearbook. Reston, VA: National Council of Teachers of Mathematics, 1982.

Burger, W. F. "Geometry." *Arithmetic Teacher* 32 (February 1985): 52–56.

Butzow, J. W. "Y is for Yacht Race: A Game of Angles." *Arithmetic Teacher* 33 (January 1986): 44–48.

Campbell, P. F. "Cardboard, Rubber Bands, and Polyhedron Models." *Arithmetic Teacher* 31 (October 1983): 48–52.

Campbell, P. F. "Microcomputers in the Primary Mathematics Classroom." *Arithmetic Teacher* 35 (February 1988): 22–30.

Charles, R. "Some Guidelines for Teaching Geometry Concepts." *Arithmetic Teacher* 27 (April 1980): 18–20.

Clements, D. C., and M. Battista. "Geometry and Geometric Measurement." *Arithmetic Teacher* 33 (February 1986): 29–32.

Cox, P. "Informal Geometry—More Is Needed." *Mathematics Teacher* 78 (September 1985): 404, 405, 435.

Damarin, S. "What Makes a Triangle." *Arithmetic Teacher* 29 (September 1981): 39–41.

Davis, E. J., et al. "Training Elementary School Teachers to Use Computers—with Emphasis on Logo." *Arithmetic Teacher* 32 (October 1984): 18–25.

Del Grande, G. "Spatial Sense." *Arithmetic Teacher* 37 (February 1990): 14–20.

Edwards, N. T., G. Bitter, and M. M. Hatfield. "Teaching Mathematics with Technology: Measurement in Geometry with Computers." *Arithmetic Teacher* 37 (February 1990): 64–67.

Edwards, R. "Discoveries in Geometry by Folding and Cutting." *Arithmetic Teacher* 24 (March 1977): 196–198.

Giganti, P., Jr., and M. J. Cittadino. "The Art of Tessellation." *Arithmetic Teacher* 37 (March 1990): 6–16.

Heukerott, P. B. "Origami: Paper Folding—the Algorithmic Way." *Arithmetic Teacher* 35 (January 1988): 4–8.

Immerzeel, G. "Geometric Activities for Early Childhood Education." *Arithmetic Teacher* 20 (October 1973): 438–443.

Izard, J. "Developing Spatial Skills with Three-Dimensional Puzzles." *Arithmetic Teacher* 37 (February 1990): 44–47.

Jensen, R., and D. R. O'Neil. "Let's Do It: Informal Geometry Through Geometric Blocks." *Arithmetic Teacher* 29 (May 1982): 4–8.

Juraschek, W. "Get in Touch with Shape." *Arithmetic Teacher* 37 (April 1990): 14–16.

Kaiser, B. "Explorations with Tessellating Polygons." *Arithmetic Teacher* 36 (December 1988): 19–24.

Kerr, D. "The Study of Space Experiences: A Framework for Geometry for Elementary Teachers." *Arithmetic Teacher* 23 (March 1976): 169–174.

Kolnowski, L. W., and J. K. Okey. "Ideas." *Arithmetic Teacher* 34 (April 1987): 26–33.

Kouba, V. L., et al. "Results of the Fourth NAEP Assessment of Mathematics: Measurement, Geometry, Data Interpretation, Attitudes, and Other Topics." *Arithmetic Teacher* 35 (May 1988): 10–16.

Larke, P. J. "Geometric Extravaganza: Spicing Up Geometry." *Arithmetic Teacher* 36 (September 1988): 12–16.

Lott, J., and I. Dayoub. "What Can Be Done with a Mira?" *Mathematics Teacher* 70 (May 1977): 394–399.

Maier, E. "Counting Pizza Pieces and Other Combinatorial Problems." *Mathematics Teacher* 81 (January 1988): 22–26.

McMaster, A. "The Twelve Days of Christmas and the Number of Diagonals in a Polygon." *Mathematics Teacher* 79 (December 1986): 700–702.

Morrell, L. "GE-O-ME-TR-Y." *Arithmetic Teacher* 27 (March 1980): 52.

Moses, B. "Individual Differences in Problem Solving." *Arithmetic Teacher* 30 (December 1982): 10–14.

Newton, J. E. "From Pattern-Block Play to Logo Programming." *Arithmetic Teacher* 35 (May 1988): 6–9.

Onslow, B. "Pentominoes Revisited." *Arithmetic Teacher* 37 (May 1990): 5–9.

Pohl, V. "Producing Curved Surfaces in the Octahedron: Enrichment for Junior High School Students." *Arithmetic Teacher* 34 (November 1986): 30–33.

Reesink, C. J. "Crystals: Through the Looking Glass with Planes, Points, and Rotational Symmetries." *Mathematics Teacher* 80 (May 1987): 377–382.

Sgroi, R. J. "Communicating About Spatial Relationships." *Arithmetic Teacher* 37 (February 1990): 21–23.

Shaw, J. M. "An Easy Dodecahedron." *Mathematics Teacher* 75 (May 1982): 380–382.

Souza, R. "Golfing with a Protractor." *Arithmetic Teacher* 35 (April 1988): 52–56.

Troccolo, J. A. "Polygons Made to Order." *Mathematics Teacher* 80 (January 1987): 44–47.

Usiskin, Z. "Enrichment Activities for Geometry." *Mathematics Teacher* 76 (April 1983): 264–266.

Van de Walle, J., and C. Thompson. "Concepts, Art, and Fun from Simple Tiling Patterns." *Arithmetic Teacher* 31 (November 1980): 4–8.

Van de Walle, J., and C. Thompson. "Cut and Paste for Geometric Thinking." *Arithmetic Teacher* 28 (September 1983): 8–13.

Walter, M. *Boxes, Squares and Other Things.* Reston, VA: National Council of Teachers of Mathematics, 1970.

Wiebe, J. H. "Teaching Mathematics with Technology: Turtle Tips." *Arithmetic Teacher* 37 (May 1990): 28–30.

Willcutt, B. "Triangular Tiles for Your Patio?" *Arithmetic Teacher* 34 (May 1987): 43–45.

Wills, H. "Revisiting the Interior Angles of Polygons." *Mathematics Teacher* 80 (November 1987): 632–634.

Wilson, P. S. "Understanding Angles: Wedges to Degrees." *Mathematics Teacher* 83 (April 1990): 294–300.

Young, J. L. "Improving Spatial Abilities with Geometric Activities." *Arithmetic Teacher* 30 (September 1982): 38–43.

Zurstadt, B. K. "Tessellations and the Art of M. C. Escher." *Arithmetic Teacher* 31 (January 1984): 54–55.

8 *Measurement*

SPOTLIGHT ON TEACHING

Excerpts from NCTM's Standard 10 for Teaching Mathematics in Grades K–4*

Measurement is of central importance to the curriculum because of its power to help children see that mathematics is useful in everyday life and to help them develop many mathematical concepts and skills. . . .

. . . Children need to understand the attribute to be measured as well as what it means to measure. Before they are capable of such understanding, they must first experience a variety of activities that focus on comparing objects directly, covering them with various units, and counting the units. Premature use of instruments or formulas leaves children without the understanding necessary for solving measurement problems.

Many important understandings are associated with a unit of measure. The choice of a unit is arbitrary, but it must have the same attribute as that which is being measured.

The table is about 6 straws long.
The table is about 8 crayons long.

It takes fewer straws than crayons
because the straws are longer.

If children's initial explorations use nonstandard units, they will develop some understandings about units and come to recognize the necessity of standard units in order to communicate.

*Reprinted by permission of the National Council of Teachers of Mathematics.

SECTION 8.1 SYSTEMS OF MEASUREMENT

■ *PROBLEM OPENER*

Train A and train B are on the same track, headed toward each other. Both trains are traveling at 75 miles per hour. When the trains are 300 miles apart, a flea flies from the front of train A to the front of train B, then back to the front of train A, etc., returning back and forth until it is finally crushed by the colliding trains. How long is the flea in flight between the two trains?

Stonehenge, Salisbury Plain, England, believed to have been constructed between 1900 and 1700 B.C.

Figure 8.1
Stonehenge as it might have looked 4000 years ago

The daily rotations of the earth, the monthly changes of the moon, and our planet's yearly orbits about the sun provided some of the first units of measure. The day was divided into parts by sunrise, midday, and sunset; the year was divided into seasons. Some believe that the construction of the prehistoric monument known as Stonehenge, (figure 8.1), in southern England, was an early attempt to measure the length of a year and its seasons. By studying the shadows of the stones, druid priests may have been able to predict the arrival of the summer solstice and the occurrence of eclipses. Eventually, the sundial was invented to measure smaller periods of time, and it remained the principal method of measuring time until the fifteenth century. Modern atomic clocks measure time to within 1 ten-millionth of a second.

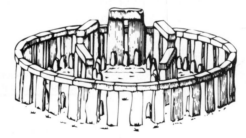

In today's schools, children first learn about concepts of measure with nonstandard units. Later they are often taught both the English and the metric units because both types of units are used in our country. In this section we will look at examples of nonstandard units of measure as well as units of measure in the *English system* and the *metric system*.

NONSTANDARD UNITS OF LENGTH

measuring

The process of **measuring** consists of three steps:

1. Select an object and an attribute to be measured (length, weight, temperature, etc.).

unit of measure

2. Choose a **unit of measure.**

measurement

3. Compare the unit to the object to determine the number of units, called the **measurement.**

hand, span, foot cubit

Many of the first units of measure were parts of the body. The early Babylonian and Egyptian records indicate that the **hand,** the **span,** the **foot,** and the **cubit** were all units of measure. The hand was used as a basic unit of measure by nearly all ancient civilizations and is the basis of the unit that is used today to measure the heights of horses. The height of a horse is measured by the number of hands from the ground to the horse's shoulders, and the hand has been standardized as 4 inches.

Figure 8.2

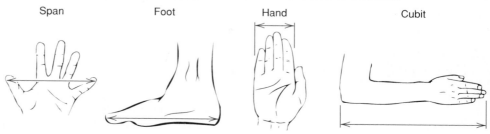

Span   Foot   Hand   Cubit

Elementary school experiences with measuring should provide the chance to relive our early measurement history through measuring activities with body parts.

EXAMPLE A

Choose two units of measure from Figure 8.2 with which to measure one of the following items: the length of a table (or desk), the height of a table, the length or width of a room, or the length of this book. List a few observations from this activity.

Solution   The measurements will vary depending on the units chosen. The smaller the unit, the larger the measure; and the larger the unit, the smaller the measure. The measurement may not be a whole number. Two people may both choose the same unit, such as their hands, and obtain different measurements.

carat

grain stone

Evidence of other early units of measure still exists today. Seeds and stones were common units for measuring weight. The word **carat,** which is the name of a unit of weight for precious stones, was derived from the word for the carob seeds of Mediterranean evergreen trees. *Carat* also expresses the fineness of a gold alloy. "Fourteen carat" means 14 parts of gold to 10 parts of alloy, or that 14 out of 24 parts are pure gold. The **grain,** a unit based on the average weight of grains of wheat, is another unit of weight used by jewelers. Until recently the **stone** was a common unit of weight in England and Canada. A newborn baby would weigh about half a stone.

Such historical examples of units are helpful in understanding the concept of measure and suggest that nonstandard units of measure can be readily invented.

EXAMPLE B

1. Select an object to be used as a nonstandard unit of measure (paper clip, pencil, pen, handspan, etc.) to measure the length or width of a table, desk, chair, or other object near you. First guess, then check your answer.
2. Use the length of the following safety pin to measure the pencil.

Solution   2. The pencil is approximately $5\frac{1}{2}$ safety pin units long.

length   It is possible to find the **length** of an object by counting the number of times a chosen unit can be marked off on the object. Once a unit has been chosen, we assign it a length of 1.

Since it is unlikely that the chosen unit will be marked off a whole number of times, several choices are possible for dealing with the part that is left over: (1) estimate what fraction of the unit is left over, (2) create a smaller unit, or (3) subdivide the unit into an equal number of smaller parts to measure the part that is left over.

EXAMPLE C

Measure the length of the pen below using each of the following units.

1. The length of the large paper clip
2. The length of the small paper clip
3. The length of the plastic twist-tie. The twist-tie has been bent into 4 equal parts.

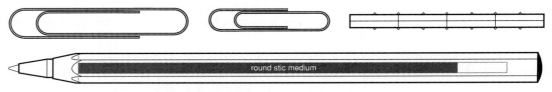

Solution

1. The pen is approximately 3 large paper clip units long.
2. The pen is approximately $4\frac{1}{2}$ small paper clip units long.
3. The pen is approximately $2\frac{3}{4}$ twist-tie units long.

ENGLISH UNITS

LENGTH   As societies evolved, measures became more complex. Since most units of measure had developed independently of each other, it was difficult to change from one unit to another. The English system, for example, arose from a hodgepodge of non-standard units: the **inch** was the length of 3 barleycorns placed end to end, the **foot** was the length of a human foot, and the **yard** was the distance from the nose to the end of an outstretched arm. In the twelfth century, the yard was established by royal decree of King Henry I of England as the distance from his nose to his thumb (Figure 8.3). Gradually, the English system of measurements was standardized. The common units for length are shown in figure 8.4.

inch, foot yard

Figure 8.3

Figure 8.4

English units for length

Inch	in.	$\frac{1}{12}$ foot
Foot	ft	12 inches
Yard	yd	3 feet
Mile	mi	5280 feet

EXAMPLE D

Use the ruler pictured below to answer these questions.

1. What is the length from the tip of your index finger (or thumb) to the first joint?
2. What is the measure of the pencil in Example B?
3. What is the measure of the pen in Example C?
4. Write the number indicated by each arrow above the ruler.

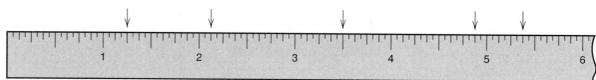

Solution

1. On the average adult hand, this length is approximately 1 in.

2. Approximately $5\frac{7}{8}$ in.

3. Approximately $5\frac{9}{16}$ in.

4. $1\frac{1}{4}$; $2\frac{1}{8}$; $3\frac{1}{2}$; $4\frac{7}{8}$; $5\frac{3}{8}$

cubic inch

Figure 8.5

VOLUME   There are two methods of measuring volume in the English system. One uses cubes whose edges have lengths of 1 inch, 1 foot, or 1 yard. For example, a **cubic inch** is a cube whose edges are each 1 inch long (Figure 8.5).

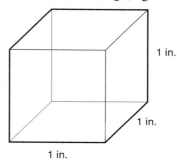

The other method of measuring volume uses measures that evolved from an ancient doubling system. Five of these measures are listed in figure 8.6.

Figure 8.6

English units for volume

Ounce	oz	$\frac{1}{8}$ cup
Cup	c	8 ounces
Pint	pt	2 cups
Quart	qt	2 pints
Gallon	gal	4 quarts

One inconvenience of the English system is that it is difficult to convert from one unit to another.

EXAMPLE E

One gallon is equal to 231 cubic inches. Determine the number of cubic inches (in.^{3}) in each of the following measures.

1. 1 quart   2. 1 cup

Solution

1. Since 4 qt = 1 gal and 231 ÷ 4 = 57.75, there are 57.75 in.^{3} in 1 qt.
2. Since 4 c = 1 qt and 57.75 ÷ 4 = 14.4375, there are 14.4375 in.^{3} in 1 c.

■ **HISTORICAL HIGHLIGHT**

Units of volume

2 mouthfuls	= 1 jigger
2 jiggers	= 1 jack (jackpot)
2 jacks	= 1 jill
2 jills	= 1 cup
2 cups	= 1 pint
2 pints	= 1 quart
2 quarts	= 1 pottle
2 pottles	= 1 gallon
2 gallons	= 1 pail

The *mouthful* is a unit of measure for volume used by the ancient Egyptians. It was also part of an English doubling system: 2 mouthfuls equal 1 jigger; 2 jiggers equal 1 jack; 2 jacks equal 1 jill; etc. The familiar nursery rhyme that begins "Jack and Jill went up the hill" mentions 3 units of volume: the *jack,* the *jill,* and the *pail.* The rhyme was composed as a protest against King Charles I of England for his taxation of the jacks, or jackpots, of liquor sold in taverns. Charles's success at accumulating revenue from the taxes on liquor is the origin of the expression "to hit the jackpot." The phrase "broke his crown" in the nursery rhyme refers to Charles I. Not only did he lose his crown; he lost his head in Britain's civil war not many years after he began taxing jackpots.*

troy unit
avoirdupois unit

WEIGHT   The English system has two systems for measuring weight: one for precious metals, in which there are 12 ounces in a pound (**troy unit**); and one for everyday use, in which there are 16 ounces in a pound (**avoirdupois unit**). The common English units for weight are shown in Figure 8.7.

Figure 8.7

English units for weight

Ounce	oz	$\frac{1}{16}$ pound
Pound	lb	16 ounces
Ton	t	2000 pounds

EXAMPLE F

1. 14.3 pounds equal how many ounces?
2. 3200 pounds equal how many tons?

Solution

1. 228.8 oz (14.3 × 16 = 228.8)
2. 1.6 t (3200 ÷ 2000 = 1.6)

TEMPERATURE   In 1714, Gabriel Fahrenheit, a German instrument maker, invented the first mercury thermometer. The lowest temperature he was able to attain with a mixture of ice and salt he called zero degrees (0°). He used the normal temperature of the human body, which he selected to be 96 degrees (96°), for the upper point of his scale. (With today's more accurate thermometers, we know that human body temperature is about 98.6° on the Fahrenheit scale.) On this scale of temperatures, water freezes at 32° and boils at 212°. This scale is called the **Fahrenheit scale** (Figure 8.8).

Fahrenheit scale

*A. Kline, *The World of Measurement* (New York: Simon and Schuster, 1975), 32–39.

Figure 8.8

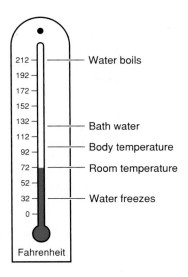

METRIC UNITS

In 1790, in the midst of the French Revolution, the metric system was developed by the French Academy of Sciences. To create a system of "natural standards," the scientists subdivided the length of a meridian from the equator to the North Pole to obtain the basic unit of length, the **meter** (Figure 8.9).

meter

Figure 8.9

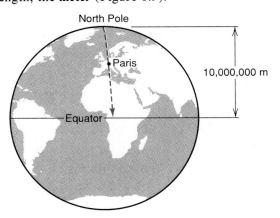

Smaller measures in the metric system are obtained by dividing the basic units into 10, 100, and 1000 parts. Larger measures are 10, 100, and 1000 times greater than the basic units. These measures are named by attaching prefixes to the names of the three basic units (Figure 8.10). The prefixes marked with asterisks are commonly used in everyday nonscientific measurement.

Figure 8.10

Metric prefixes

Greek prefixes	kilo*	1000
	hecto	100
	deca	10
Latin prefixes	deci*	1/10
	centi*	1/100
	milli*	1/1000

mega
micro

There are more prefixes for naming both larger and smaller measures, each new measure being 10 times greater than or 1/10 as great as the previous one. For example, **mega** is the prefix meaning *million,* and **micro** is the prefix meaning *one-millionth.* This relationship between measures is a major advantage of the metric system. Conversion from one measurement to another can be accomplished by multiplying or dividing by powers of 10, which, since we use a base ten numeration system, can be accomplished by moving decimal points.

LENGTH Figure 8.11 shows how the metric system prefixes are used with the meter to obtain other metric units. Notice that as we move from the millimeter to the kilometer, each unit is 10 times greater than the preceding unit. (The common lengths are marked with asterisks.)

Figure 8.11

Metric units for length

Kilometer*	km	1000 m
Hectometer	hm	100 m
Decameter	dkm	10 m
Meter*	m	1 m
Decimeter	dm	1/10 m
Centimeter*	cm	1/100 m
Millimeter*	mm	1/1000 m

To acquire a feeling for the metric units of length, it is helpful to visualize objects having a given length. A meter is roughly the distance from the floor to the waist of an adult or the distance from one shoulder to the fingertips of the opposite outstretched arm, as shown in Figure 8.12. The distance from the floor to a doorknob is usually a little less than a meter. A meter might be used to measure the length of a house, a car, or an athletic field.

Figure 8.12

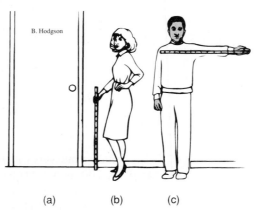

B. Hodgson

(a)   (b)   (c)

centimeter

A **centimeter** is 1/100 of a meter. This is the common unit for such body measurements as height, waist, and hat size. The width of the average fourth grade student's thumbnail is approximately 1 centimeter, as shown in part (a) of Figure 8.13. If the thumb is extended, as shown in part (b), the length from the tip of the index finger to the bottom of the V shape is approximately 1 decimeter (10 centimeters).

Figure 8.13

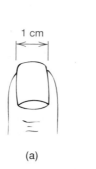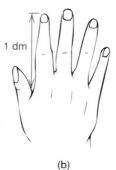

(a)   (b)

millimeter

Occasionally we need a measure smaller than a centimeter. One-tenth of a centimeter is a **millimeter.** The thickness of a pencil lead is approximately 2 millimeters. The ruler shown in Example G has a length between 12 and 13 centimeters, and each centimeter is divided into 10 millimeters.

EXAMPLE G

1. What is your handspan to the nearest centimeter?
2. Which of your finger widths is approximately 1 centimeter?
3. What is the diameter of a penny to the nearest millimeter?

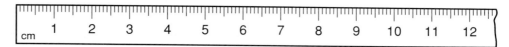

Solution

1. The handspans of adults usually range from 18 cm to 23 cm.
2. The little finger width for an adult is close to 1 cm.
3. The diameter of a penny is 1 cm and 9 mm, or 1.9 cm.

---

kilometer

A **kilometer** is 1000 meters. Distances between cities and countries (and even planets) are measured in kilometers. A kilometer is shorter than a mile, approximately 3/5 as long, as indicated in Figure 8.14.

Figure 8.14

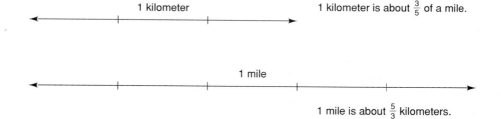

EXAMPLE H

1. If a person walks 3 miles per hour (1 mile every 20 minutes), approximately how many kilometers per hour does the person walk?
2. If a car is traveling 90 kilometers per hour, what is its speed in miles per hour?

Solution

1. Since 1 mile $\approx$ 5/3 km, 3 mi is 3 times greater:

$$3 \times \frac{5}{3} = \frac{15}{3} = 5$$

So the person will walk approximately 5 km per hour (5 kph).

2. Since 1 km ≈ 3/5 mi, 90 km is 90 times greater:

$$90 \times \frac{3}{5} = \frac{270}{5} = 54$$

So the speed of the car is approximately 54 mph.

liter

VOLUME   The basic unit of volume in the metric system is the **liter.** A liter is a little bit bigger than a quart. The capacities of fuel tanks, aquariums, and milk containers are measured in liters. For volumes that are less than a liter, such as those of small bottles or jars, the **milliliter** (1/1000 of a liter) is the common measure. Larger volumes, such as a community's reserve water supply, are measured in **kiloliters** (1000 liters).

milliliter
kiloliter

Figure 8.15 lists the metric system units for volume, which are shown in relationship to the liter. (The common volumes are marked with asterisks.)

Figure 8.15

Metric units for volume

Kiloliter*	kL	1000 L
Hectoliter	hL	100 L
Decaliter	dkL	10 L
Liter*	L	1 L
Deciliter	dL	1/10 L
Centiliter	cL	1/100 L
Milliliter*	mL	1/1000 L

EXAMPLE I

1. 1.3 liters equal how many milliliters?
2. 245 milliliters equal how many liters?
3. 3487 liters equal how many kiloliters?

Solution   1. 1300 mL   2. .245 L   3. 3.487 kL

Notice in Example I how convenient it is to change from one unit to another. Since 1 liter equals 1000 milliliters, the number of milliliters in 1.3 liters is 1.3 × 1000. Similarly, to change from 245 milliliters to liters, we divide by 1000. With metric units, conversions can be done mentally by multiplying and dividing by powers of 10.

A liter is the volume of a cube whose sides each have a length of 10 centimeters [part (a) in Figure 8.16]. Such a cube is called a **cubic decimeter.** The dimensions of the small cube in part (b) are each 1 centimeter. This cube is called a **cubic centimeter.**

cubic decimeter
cubic centimeter

Figure 8.16

1 cubic decimeter (dm³)

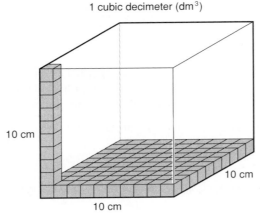

10 cm

10 cm

10 cm

(a) 1 liter equals 1000 cubic centimeters.

1 cubic centimeter (cm³)

(b) 1 cubic centimeter equals 1 milliliter.

Imagine filling the large cube in Figure 8.16 with the smaller cubes. The floor of the large cube is 10 cm by 10 cm and can be covered by 100 cubic centimeters. Since 10 layers of 100 cubes will fill the large cube, a liter has a volume of 1000 cubic centimeters.

Recall that a milliliter is 1/1000 of a liter. Since a cubic centimeter is also 1/1000 of a liter, 1 cubic centimeter equals 1 milliliter.

EXAMPLE J

1. 45 cubic centimeters equal how many milliliters?
2. 1.35 liters equal how many cubic centimeters?
3. 800 cubic centimeters equal how many liters?

Solution

1. 45 mL   2. 1350 cm³   3. .8 L

WEIGHT   In the metric system the word "mass" is often used as a synonym for "weight." Scientists distinguish between *weight* and *mass,* the difference being due to the effect of gravity. We can think of **mass** as the amount of matter that makes up the object. **Weight,** on the other hand, is the force that gravity exerts on the object, and it varies with different locations. An object will weigh more at sea level than on top of a mountain, because the earth's gravity exerts a greater force on it at lower altitudes. The same object in a spaceship would weigh practically nothing. Yet in each of these three locations the amount of material in the object hasn't changed! Because of this situation, it is necessary for scientific purposes to refer to the mass of an object as a measurement that does not change as the object is moved farther from the center of the earth. At sea level the mass and weight of an object are essentially equal. Since the variation in an object's weight between sea level and our highest mountains is very small (.1% difference), we will use the term *weight.*

mass

weight

gram   The basic unit of weight in the metric system is the **gram.** This is a relatively small weight, approximately the weight of a medium-size paper clip or a dollar bill. The weights of many items in grocery stores are measured in grams. Heavier objects are measured in kilograms. A **kilogram** is 1000 grams. To acquire a feeling for this amount, it helps to know the approximate metric weights of a few objects.

kilogram

EXAMPLE K

Use the fact that a kilogram is approximately 2.2 pounds to determine the following weights in kilograms.

1. Your weight
2. The weight of a 10-pound bag of potatoes
3. The weight of a pound of hamburger

Solution

1. A person who weighs 125 lb weighs approximately 57 kg.
2. Approximately 4.5 kg
3. Approximately .5 kg

metric ton   Figure 8.17 shows the metric units for weight and their relationships to the gram. (The common weights are marked with asterisks.) The **metric ton,** not shown in this table, is 1000 kilograms.

Figure 8.17

Metric units for weight

Kilogram*	kg	1000 g
Hectogram	hg	100 g
Decagram	dkg	10 g
Gram*	g	1 g
Decigram	dg	1/10 g
Centigram	cg	1/100 g
Milligram*	mg	1/1000 g

A gram is the weight of 1 cubic centimeter of water. (Since water contracts and expands as its temperature changes, the technical definition calls for water to be at its densest state.) Since 1 cubic centimeter equals 1 milliliter (1/1000 of a liter), 1 milliliter of water also weighs approximately 1 gram. This simple relationship between weight, length, and volume (see Figure 8.18) is another advantage of the metric system over the English system.

Figure 8.18

One cubic centimeter of water equals 1 milliliter of water and weighs approximately 1 gram.

EXAMPLE L

1. 1 liter of water weighs how many kilograms?
2. 48.2 milliliters of water weigh how many grams?
3. 1500 cubic centimeters of water weigh how many kilograms?

Solution   1. 1 kg   2. 48.2 g   3. 1.5 kg

TEMPERATURE   In 1742, about 50 years before the development of the metric system, the Swedish astronomer Anders Celsius devised a temperature scale by selecting zero as the freezing point of water and 100 as the boiling point. He called this system the **centigrade** (100 grades) scale thermometer, but it came to be called the **Celsius scale** in his honor. Some examples of temperatures on the Celsius scale are shown in Figure 8.19.

centigrade, Celsius scale

Figure 8.19

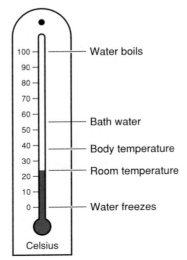

Kelvin scale

Heat is related to the motion of molecules. The faster their motion, the greater the heat. All movement of molecules stops at ⁻273.15° Celsius. The British mathematician and physicist William Thomson, known as Lord Kelvin, called this temperature "absolute zero" and devised the **Kelvin scale,** which increases 1 unit for each increase of 1° Celsius. Thus 273.15 on the Kelvin scale is 0° on the Celsius scale. Both the Celsius and Kelvin scales are part of the metric system. The Celsius scale is used for weather reports, cooking temperatures, and other day-to-day needs; the Kelvin scale is used for scientific purposes.

EXAMPLE M

1. 270.15 on the Kelvin scale equals how many degrees on the Celsius scale?
2. 100° on the Celsius scale equals how many units on the Kelvin scale?

Solution   1. ⁻3°   2. 373.15

■ **H**ISTORICAL HIGHLIGHT

The metric system was a radical change for the French people and met with widespread resistance. Finally in 1837, the French government passed a law forbidding the use of any measures other than those of the new system. Steadily, other nations adopted the metric system. In 1866 the Congress of the United States enacted a law stating that it was lawful to employ the weights and measures of the metric system and that no contract or dealing could be found invalid because of the use of metric units. Today, less than 200 years after its creation, the metric system has been adopted by almost every country except the United States. The U.S. Metric Conversion Act of 1975 set a policy of voluntary conversion with no overall timetable.

PRECISION AND SMALL MEASUREMENTS

The objects in Figure 8.20 are DNA and ribosome molecules in an active chromosome. Each DNA molecule is so small that 100,000 of them lined up side by side will fit into the thickness of this page.

Figure 8.20
DNA and ribosome molecules

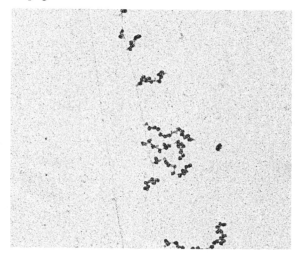

Measurements with this type of precision are possible with the transmission electron microscope. More recently, with the development of the field ion microscope, scientists have been able to view atoms that are 10 times smaller than DNA molecules. The scale in Figure 8.21 shows eight measures in decreasing order from a centimeter down to an **angstrom,** each being 1/10 of the size of the preceding one.

angstrom

Figure 8.21

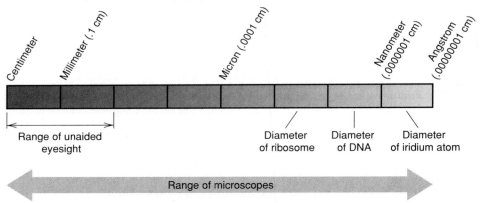

The amount of precision that is possible in taking measurements depends on the smallest unit of the measuring instrument. Using a centimeter ruler, we can determine that the paper clip in part (a) of Figure 8.22 has a length of just over 3 centimeters. If a ruler is marked off in millimeters, as in part (b), the length of the paper clip can be measured as about 32 millimeters, or 3.2 centimeters. With instruments that measure smaller units, we might measure the length of this paper clip to be 3.24, 3.241, or 3.2412 centimeters. It would never be possible, however, to measure its length or the length of any other object exactly.

Figure 8.22

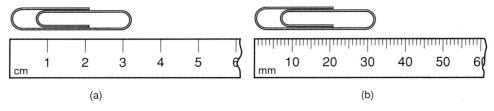

If the smallest unit on the measuring instrument is a millimeter, then the measurement can be approximated to the nearest millimeter. This means that the measurement could be off by one-half of a millimeter, either too much or too little. In general, the **precision** of any measurement is to within one-half of the smallest unit of measure being used.

precision

Conversely, if a measurement is given as 14.5 centimeters, we can assume that it was measured to the nearest tenth of a centimeter and that it is closer to 14.5 centimeters than to 14.4 centimeters or 14.6 centimeters. In other words, it is 14.5 ± .05 centimeters, as shown in Figure 8.23 (.05 is half of one-tenth).

Figure 8.23

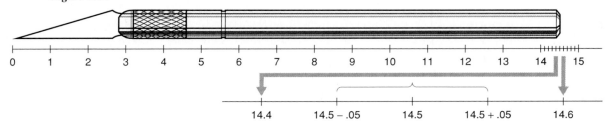

Writing a measurement as 7.62 centimeters indicates that it has been obtained to the nearest one-hundredth of a centimeter and may be off by as much as .005 centimeter (.005 is half of one-hundredth). Sometimes you will see a measurement such as 15.0 centimeters. A zero following the decimal point means that the measurement is accurate to the nearest tenth of a centimeter; 15.0 centimeters implies more precision than does 15 centimeters.

EXAMPLE N

Find the minimum and maximum measurements associated with each of the following measurements.

1. An oven temperature of 246.3° Celsius
2. A baseball bat with a length of 82 centimeters
3. A bag of flour that is labeled 2.27 kilograms

Solution

1. Half of one-tenth is .05, so the temperature is between 246.25° and 246.35° Celsius.
2. Half of 1 is .5, so the length of the bat is between 81.5 and 82.5 cm.
3. Half of .01 is .005, so the weight of the flour is between 2.265 and 2.275 kg.

INTERNATIONAL SYSTEM OF UNITS

International System of Units

second

ampere, candela

mole

The **International System of Units** is a modern version of the metric system that was established by international agreement. Officially abbreviated as SI, this system is built on the metric units discussed previously, but also includes units for time (**second**), electric current (**ampere**), light intensity (**candela**), and the molecular weight of a substance (**mole**). This system provides a logical and interconnected framework for all measurements. To enable the type of precision needed in science today, the meter is now defined in SI units as the distance light travels in 1/299,792,458 of a second, and a second of time is defined as the time required for a wave of the cesium-133 atom to complete 9,192,631,770 cycles.

PROBLEM-SOLVING APPLICATION

■ PROBLEM

This standard set of 11 brass metric weights can be used with a balance scale to weigh any object whose weight is a whole number of grams from 1 to 1600. How can these weights be used to determine that an object weighs 917 grams?

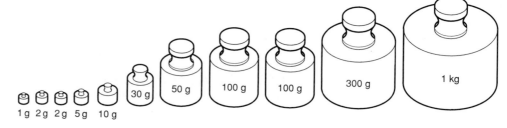

1g 2g 2g 5g 10g   30 g   50 g   100 g   100 g   300 g   1 kg

Question 1

Understanding the Problem   The object to be weighed must be placed on one side of the scale, as shown. The problem is that the 1 kilogram weight is greater than 917 grams and the sum of the remaining 10 weights is less than 917 grams. What is the sum of the remaining 10 brass weights?

Question 2

Devising a Plan One approach is to *guess and check* by experimenting with the weights. If the kilogram weight is placed on the right side of the scale, the scale will tip down on the right. What additional weight will then be needed on the left side of the scale for a balance?

Question 3

Carrying Out the Plan The left side of the scale will need 83 grams, together with the 917 grams, to balance the 1 kilogram. How can 83 grams be obtained from the set of brass weights?

Question 4

Looking Back The key to solving this problem is to place brass weights on both sides of the scale. This is not always necessary. For example, an object that weighs 18 grams can be balanced by placing weights of 10, 5, 2, and 1 gram on one side of the scale. What is the lightest object for which brass weights must be placed on both sides of the scale?

Answers to Questions 1–4
1. 600 g **2.** 83 g **3.** 50 g, 30 g, 2 g, 1g
4. *Forming an organized list,* beginning with the smallest weights, shows that any object weighing between 1 and 20 g can be weighed by placing brass weights on just one side of the scale. The first object that requires the brass weights on both sides of the scale is an object weighing 21 g.

Weights of objects	Sets of weights
1 g	1 g
2 g	2 g
3 g	2 g, 1 g
4 g	2 g, 2 g
⋮	⋮
19 g	10 g, 5 g, 2 g, 2 g
20 g	10 g, 5 g, 2 g, 2 g, 1 g

RELATED ACTIVITIES IN

Mathematics for Elementary Teachers: An Activity Approach, 3e

Activity Set 8.1

Measuring with Metric Units: Activities use the metric measures of millimeter, centimeter, meter, and liter.

Just for Fun

Metric Games: Three games for building familiarity with centimeters and meters

EXERCISES AND PROBLEMS 8.1

"All right—now convert
the whole thing to metric."

1. Although almost all educators agree that we should not teach the metric system by converting back and forth from English units to metric units, it is sometimes helpful to make rough comparisons between the two systems.
   a. What is a 55 mph speed limit approximately equal to in kilometers per hour (kph)?
   b. The distance from Jersey City to New York is 24 mi. Approximately what is this distance in km?
   c. It has been suggested that the speed limit be set at 100 kph. Approximately what would this speed limit be in mph?

2. Measure the length of the scissors shown in the figure using each of the following units.

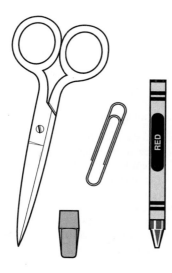

a. The length of the paper clip
b. The length of the eraser
c. The length of the crayon
d. If you had to use one of these units to measure other lengths, which do you think would consistently give you the most "accurate" measurements? Explain.

3. Express the amount of weight the weight lifter is raising in each of the following units.
   a. Grams
   b. Milligrams
   c. Pounds (approximate)

4. Estimate each of the following to the nearest indicated unit. Then use the metric ruler on page 383 to check your estimate.
   a. The thickness of pencil lead (mm)
   b. The width of a pencil (mm)
   c. The diameter of a dime (mm)
   d. The length of a dollar bill (cm)
   e. The width of a standard sheet of typing paper (cm)

5. Estimate each item in the preceding exercise using inches and fractions or decimals for parts of an inch. Then check your estimate by using the inch ruler on page 379.

6. Recipes that use the English system of measurement include teaspoons (tsp) and tablespoons (tbsp or T) as units of measure. If 16 tbsp = 1 c and 3 tsp = 1 tbsp, complete the following.

   a. 1/2 c = _____ tbsp   b. 1/3 c = _____ tsp
   c. 2 qt = _____ c   d. 1 gal = _____ pt
   e. 1 gal = _____ c   f. 1/2 pt = _____ c

7. Complete the following.

   a. 1 mi = _____ yd   b. 4800 lb = _____ tons (t)
   c. 7.5 gal = _____ qt   d. 12.6 ft = _____ yd
   e. 56 ounces (oz) = _____ lb

8. List the following units in order of increasing length: meter, inch, centimeter, kilometer, yard, foot, mile, hectometer.

9. Choose the most realistic measure for each of the following:
   a. Length of a ski: 200 mm, 200 cm, 200 m
   b. Weight of a person: 75 mg, 75 g, 75 kg
   c. Volume of an automobile gas tank: 48 mL, 48L, 48 kL
   d. Weight of a toothpick: 450 mg, 450 g, 450 kg
   e. Height of the Eiffel Tower: 300 cm, 300 m, 300 km
   f. Amount of blood in the human body: 4 mL, 4 L, 4 kL

10. Complete the crossword puzzle by determining the most appropriate metric unit to use for the measurement in each clue.

    Across

    2. Weight of a truck
    5. Length of a building
    7. Volume of a city water supply
    8. Length of a river

    Down

    1. Volume of a gasoline tank
    3. Volume of a perfume bottle
    4. Width of a television screen
    6. Weight of a fifty-cent coin

11. Complete the statement in each clue and write your answers in the cross-number puzzle, placing one digit in each square. (Statements 4 and 9 Across and 6 and 7 Down involve volumes of water.)

    Across

    1. 16.5 cm = _____ mm
    4. 3.15 L weighs approximately _____ g
    5. .12 L = _____ mL
    8. _____ kg = 92,000 g
    9. _____ mL weighs approximately 7.920 kg
    10. _____ m = 5.55 km

    Down

    2. 632,000 L = _____ kL
    3. 4.5 km = _____ m
    6. _____ g is the approximate weight of 432 mL
    7. _____ kg is the approximate weight of 190 L
    8. _____ mg = .9 g
    9. .75 m = _____ cm

12. Each of the grocery story items in the photo is measured either by weight or by volume. Determine which of the following measures goes with each item: 946 mL, 4.536 kg, 567 g, 384 mL, 40 g, and 59 mL.

13. A shopper purchased the following items: tomatoes, 754 g; soup, 772 g; potatoes, 3.45 kg; sugar, 4.62 kg; raisins, 425 g; vegetable shortening, 1.361 kg; and baking powder, 218 g. What was the total weight of this purchase in kilograms?

14. A curtain for a single window can be made from a piece of material that is 1 m wide and 120 cm long. Suppose you need 2 curtains per window and have 6 windows. If the curtain material comes in rolls 1 m wide, how many meters of length will be needed to make curtains for all 6 windows?

15. The following amounts of gasoline have been charged on a credit card: 38.2 L, 26.8 L, 54.3 L, 44.7 L, and 34 L. The price of gasoline is 32 cents per liter.
    a. Use estimation techniques and mental arithmetic to approximate the total cost of the gasoline.
    b. Use a calculator to compute the exact cost.

16. A car owner has her tank filled and notices that the odometer reads 14368.7 (km). After a trip in the country, it takes 34.5 L to fill the tank and the odometer reads 14651.6. How many kilometers per liter is this car getting?

17. A 24 kg bag of birdseed is priced at $16.88. If 75 g of this feed are put in a bird feeder each day, how many days will it be before the bag of seed is empty? Rounded off to the nearest penny, how much does it cost to feed the birds each day?

18. The recipe for a fruit punch calls for these ingredients: 3.5 L of unsweetened pineapple juice; 400 mL of orange juice; 300 mL of lemon juice; 4 L of ginger ale; 2.5 L of soda water; 500 mL of mashed strawberries; and a base of sugar, mint leaves, and water, which has a total volume of 800 mL.
    a. How much punch will the recipe make in liters?
    b. If you serve the punch at a party of 30 people, how many milliliters of punch will there be per person?
    c. This punch was sold at a fair, and each drink of 80 mL cost 25 cents. What was the profit on the sale of this punch if the ingredients cost $12.50?

19. Prescription dosages of the antibiotic garamycin vary from 20 mg for a child to 80 mg for an adult. The garamycin is contained in a vial that has a volume of 2 cm³ (2 mL). The garamycin in each vial weighs 80 mg.

   a. How many cubic centimeters of garamycin are needed for 12 injections of 24 mg each?

   b. How many injections of 60 mg each can be obtained from 24 vials?

20. Measurements can be estimated by comparing the unknown quantity with familiar or known measurements. Obtain the following estimations using the given information.

   a. Estimate the volume of the glass.

1000 ml

   b. Estimate the length and width of the TV screen.

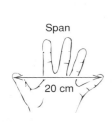

Span

20 cm

   c. Estimate the distance between two towns if a car travels from one town to the other at an average rate of 55 mph and it takes $1\frac{1}{2}$ hours to make the trip.

   d. Estimate the weight of a dozen eggs, including the weight of the carton.

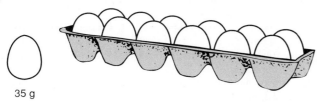

35 g

   e. Estimate the height of the room shown in the photo, assuming that the man is 6 ft tall.

21. The first unit of measure of which there are historical records is the cubit, which is the distance from elbow to fingertips. This unit was used more than 4000 years ago by the Egyptians and Babylonians. The ancient Egyptian cubit shown here measures 52.5 cm and is preserved in the Louvre in Paris.

Ancient Egyptian cubit

   a. How does the Egyptian cubit compare in length with your cubit?

   b. The dimensions of Noah's Ark, as described in the Bible in the sixth chapter of Genesis, are listed in this table. Convert these measures to the nearest meter using the length of the Egyptian cubit. Then convert the measures to the nearest foot (2.54 cm = 1 in.).

	Cubits	Meters	Feet
Length	300	____	____
Breadth	50	____	____
Height	30	____	____

22. The Celsius and Fahrenheit temperature scales are related by the following formulas:

$$C = \frac{5(F - 32)}{9} \text{ and } F = \frac{9C}{5} + 32$$

Four temperatures are described in parts a through d below and indicated on the thermometers. Convert each temperature to Fahrenheit or Celsius (to the nearest tenth of a degree).

   a. Highest recorded temperature, Libya, 1922

   b. At this body temperature, see a doctor.

c. At this temperature, check your car's antifreeze
d. Lowest recorded temperature, Antarctica, 1960

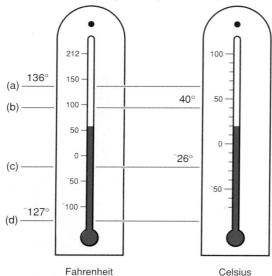

Fahrenheit   Celsius

23. The strand of hair in the following photograph has been magnified 200 times.
   a. Measure the thickness of the magnified strand of hair to the nearest millimeter.
   b. Use the results of part a to determine the thickness of a strand of human hair.
   c. How thick is a strand of human hair in microns (μ)? (1000 μ = 1 mm)
   d. Some of the wires in a microcircuit have a thickness (diameter) of 1 μ. How many times thicker is a human hair than a microcircuit wire?

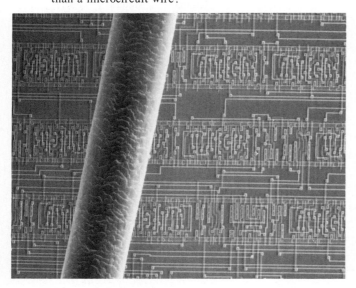

A scanning electron micrograph
magnified 200 times shows a microcircuit
and a human hair

24.

Ready or not – metric system is coming

LOS ANGELES (AP) – The mile run and the 100-yard dash, two of track's glamor races, may soon join the horse-drawn carriage and the five-cent beer as relics of days gone by.

The United States soon will be forced to switch from measuring track meets in yards to measuring them in meters. The Amateur Athletic Union and the National Collegiate Athletic Association have long fought such a switch, but both agree it is becoming mandatory.

Under an international rule which went into effect on June 1, an athlete who runs a race in yards may not qualify for the Olympics, whether he sets a record or not.

As a result of an international rule that went into effect in 1975, track events traditionally measured in yards and miles are now measured in meters, as shown in the next table. Using the fact that 1 yd = 91.5 cm, determine whether the metric event is longer or shorter, and compute the difference in meters and centimeters.

Old race	New race	Difference
a. 100 yd	100 m	_____
b. 220 yd	200 m	_____
c. 440 yd	400 m	_____
d. 880 yd	800 m	_____
e. 1 mi	1500 m	_____

25. A measurement given to a certain unit may be off by as much as plus or minus one-half of that unit. For example, a can of pineapple juice labeled 1.32 L is measured to the nearest hundredth of a liter. Its volume is greater than the minimum of 1.315 L and less than the maximum of 1.325 L. Find the minimum and maximum numbers associated with each of the following measurements.
   a. A two-speed heavy-duty washing machine weighing 112 kg (to the nearest kg)
   b. A patient's temperature of 38.2° C (to the nearest tenth of a degree)
   c. A stereo speaker with a width of 48.3 cm (to the nearest tenth of a cm)
   d. A three-day-old baby weighing 3.46 kg (to the nearest hundredth of a kg)

Featured Strategies: Making a Drawing and Working Backward

26. A special ball, dropped perpendicular to the floor, rebounds to half its previous height on each bounce until the height of its bounce is less than 1 cm. On its fifth bounce, it reaches a height of 6 cm. What is the total distance the ball has traveled when it hits the floor after its fifth bounce? Before reading further, make a drawing and try working backward to solve this problem.

a. **Understanding the Problem** A diagram will help you to visualize the problem. Each bounce can be represented by a vertical line that is half the height of the preceding line. Here is a diagram of the original distance the ball is dropped and the height of its first bounce. Explain why the height of each bounce must be doubled when the total distance the ball travels is computed. Draw the complete diagram for this problem.

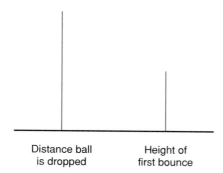

Distance ball
is dropped

Height of
first bounce

b. **Devising a Plan** Working backward is a natural strategy for solving this problem. What is the height of the fourth bounce? What is the total distance traveled during the fourth bounce?

c. **Carrying Out the Plan** Continue working backward to get the height of each bounce and the original distance the ball is dropped. What is the total distance the ball has traveled?

d. **Looking Back** In general, as long as the height of the ball's bounce is not less than 1 cm, the total distance the ball has traveled will be the distance it was dropped plus the sum of 2 times the height of each bounce. Will this general statement be true if the ball does not rebound to half its previous height on each bounce?

27. In 1983, at its General Conference on Weights and Measures, the National Institute of Standards and Technology used the speed of light to define the length of a meter. One meter is the distance light travels in 1/299,792,458 of a second.
   a. How many meters does light travel in 1 second?
   b. What is the speed of light in kilometers per second (km/sec)?

c. In England in 1956, the speed of light was measured as 299,792.4 ± .11 km/sec. Is the speed of light that was used by the General Conference on Weights and Measures within this range?

28. Roof de-icers are designed to prevent ice dams from building up on roofs and gutter pipes. An electric heating cable is clipped to the edge of the roof in a sawtooth pattern. In answering the following questions, assume that this pattern is to run along the edges of a roof and the total length of the edges is 28 meters.

a. How many meters of heating cable will be needed for the edges of the roof, if each meter of roof edge requires 2 meters of cable?

b. In addition, heating cable is placed in gutter pipes and downspouts. Two gutter pipes run along the edges of the roof. Each has a length of 14 m. There are two downspouts, one from each gutter pipe to the ground. Each downspout has a length of 3.2 m. How many meters of cable will be required to go along the gutter pipes and the downspouts if each meter of gutter or downspout requires 1 meter of cable?

c. The heating cable sells for $1.20 per meter. What is the total cost of the cable for the roof, gutter pipes, and downspouts?

29. The distance around the earth's equator is 40,077 km and the population of the United States is approximately 250,000,000 people. If this many people were spaced equally around the equator, what would be the length of the space each person would have, to the nearest centimeter?

CALCULATOR INVESTIGATION

A **palindromic number** such as 17,271 has digits that are the same from left to right as from right to left.

Questions for Investigation
1. The following four-digit palindromic numbers are divisible by 11.

$$1771 \div 11 = 161$$
$$8228 \div 11 = 748$$

Is every four-digit palindromic number divisible by 11?

2. These six-digit palindromic numbers are divisible by 11, and their quotients

are also palindromic numbers. Is this true for every six-digit palindromic number?

$$127,721 \div 11 = 11,611$$
$$258,852 \div 11 = 23,532$$

3. Are eight-digit or ten-digit palindromic numbers divisible by 11?

4. Are there palindromic numbers with an odd number of digits that are divisible by 11?

PUZZLER

A Celsius thermometer and a Fahrenheit thermometer are both placed into a liquid simultaneously. After a period of time, the temperature is the same number on both scales. What is the temperature of the liquid? (Hint: Guess and check by using the formulas in Exercises-Problems 8.1, #22.)

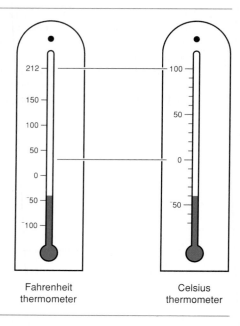

Fahrenheit
thermometer

Celsius
thermometer

SECTION 8.2   AREA AND PERIMETER

■ *PROBLEM OPENER*

Each of the 10 equilateral triangles in the following figure has sides of length 1 unit, and the perimeter of the entire figure is 12 units. What will the perimeter of the figure be if it is extended to include 50 such triangles?

Federal Reserve Bank in Minneapolis

The design of the Federal Reserve Bank in Minneapolis is based on that of a bridge. In fact, this building can be thought of as a bridge that is 10 stories deep. There was no prototype for its structural design. Each floor has an unobstructed area of 60 by 275 feet. No other building had ever included floors that spanned such a length without internal columns.

This bank was designed to fulfill some unusual zoning restrictions. One of these was that the "coverage," or ground area occupied by the building, could be only 2.5% of the area of the city block on which the bank was to be built. In order to satisfy this condition, the bank is supported by two towers and its lower floor is 20 feet above the plaza. A 2.5 acre plaza runs under the building and is entirely public space. The building's coverage is the small amount of area occupied by the two towers.

NONSTANDARD UNITS OF AREA

area

To measure the sizes of plots of land, panes of glass, floors, walls, and other such surfaces, we need a new type of unit, one that can be used to cover a surface. The number of units it takes to cover a surface is called its **area**. Squares have been found to be the most convenient shape for measuring area. If we use the square region in part (a) of Figure 8.24 as the unit square, the area of the colored region in part (b) is 4 square units, because it can be covered by 2 squares and 4 half-squares.

Figure 8.24

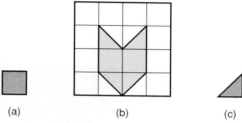

(a)   (b)   (c)

The basic concept involved in calculating area—determining the number of units required to cover a region or surface—is often poorly understood. A Michigan State assessment found that fewer than half of the seventh graders examined could calculate the area of the region in part (b).* Nineteen percent of them thought the area was 6. Can you see why they might have obtained this answer?

Theoretically, the unit for measuring area can have any shape. It can be rectangular, triangular, etc. The only requirement is that the figure must tessellate (cover a region without gaps or overlapping).

EXAMPLE A

What is the area of the colored region in part (b) of Figure 8.24 if the gray triangular region in part (c) is the unit for measuring area?

Solution

Eight triangles are required to cover the colored region, so the area is 8 triangular units.

The earliest units for measuring area were associated with agriculture. The amount of land that could be plowed in a day with the aid of a team of oxen was called an **acre**. In Germany, a scheffel was a volume of seed, and the amount of land that could be sown with this volume of seed became known as a **scheffel of land.**

acre

scheffel of land

Just as nonstandard units for length are helpful in learning about linear measure, nonstandard units for area are important in acquiring an understanding of the concept of area.

*T. G. Coburn, Leah M. Beardsley, and Joseph Payne, *Michigan Educational Assessment Program, Mathematics Interpretive Report, 1973 Grade 4 and 7 Tests.* Guidelines for Quality Mathematics Teaching Monograph Series no. 7. (Birmingham, MI: Michigan Council of Teachers of Mathematics, 1975).

EXAMPLE B

Use each of the following regions as a unit of area to determine the approximate area of the rectangle.

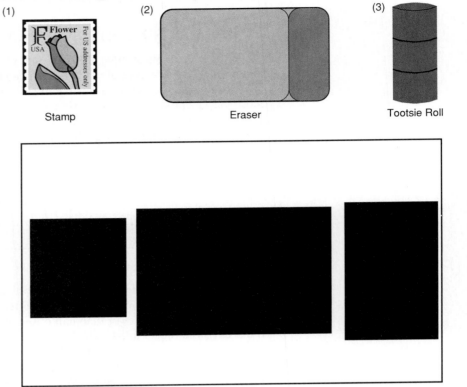

(1) Stamp
(2) Eraser
(3) Tootsie Roll

Solution

1. Approximately 18 to 19 stamp units
2. Approximately 6 to 7 eraser units
3. Approximately 23 to 24 Tootsie Roll units

STANDARD UNITS OF AREA

Eventually more carefully defined units for area were adopted, with the square being the accepted shape of these units.

square inch

ENGLISH UNITS FOR AREA In the English system, area is measured by using squares whose sides have lengths of 1 inch, 1 foot, 1 yard, or 1 mile. Each square unit is named according to the length of its sides. The 1 in. by 1 in. square in Figure 8.25 is a **square inch,** written 1 sq. in. or 1 in.^{2} (think of the exponent 2 as indicating a square).

Figure 8.25

1 in.

1 in.

square foot, square yard square mile

Similarly, we can measure larger areas using a **square foot** (1 ft^2), a **square yard** (1 yd^2), and a **square mile** (1 mi^2).

EXAMPLE C

The different square units are related to each other.

1. How many square inches equal 1 square foot?
2. How many square feet equal 1 square yard?

Solution   1. 144 in.²   2. 9 ft²

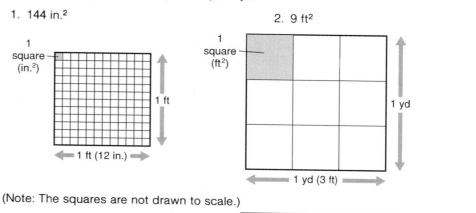

(Note: The squares are not drawn to scale.)

The common units for measuring area in the English system are shown in Figure 8.26.

Figure 8.26

English units for area

Square inch	in.²	$\dfrac{1}{144}$ square foot
Square foot	ft²	144 square inches
Square yard	yd²	9 square feet
Acre	a	43,560 square feet
Square mile	mi²	27,878,400 square feet

square meter

square centimeter
square millimeter

METRIC UNITS FOR AREA   In the metric system there is a square unit for area corresponding to each unit for length. For example, a **square meter** (1 m²) is a square whose sides have a length of 1 meter (shown in Figure 8.27, although not to scale). Square meters are used for measuring the areas of rugs, floors, swimming pools, and other such intermediate-size regions. Smaller areas are measured in square centimeters. A **square centimeter** (1 cm²) is a square whose sides have lengths of 1 centimeter. Even smaller areas are measured with the **square millimeter,** a square whose sides have lengths of 1 millimeter. The actual sizes of the square centimeter and the square millimeter are shown in Figure 8.27.

Figure 8.27

1 square meter (m²)

1 m

1 m

1 square centimeter (cm²)

1 cm

1 cm

1 square millimeter (mm²)

EXAMPLE D

Determine the following relationships between the metric units for area.

1. How many square millimeters equal 1 square centimeter?
2. How many square centimeters equal 1 square meter?

Solution

1. Since each side of a square centimeter has a length of 1 cm and 1 cm = 10 mm, a square centimeter can be covered by 10 × 10 = 100 mm².
2. Since 1 m equals 100 cm, 100 cm² can be placed along each side of a square with dimensions of 1 m by 1 m, and so 10,000 cm² will cover the square meter.

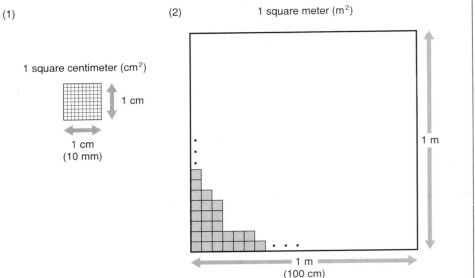

The areas of countries, national forests, oceans, and other such large surfaces are measured with the **square kilometer,** a square whose sides each have a length of 1 kilometer.

Some metric units for area and their relationships are shown in Figure 8.28.

square kilometer

Figure 8.28

Metric units for area

Square millimeter	mm²	$\frac{1}{100}$ square centimeter
Square centimeter	cm²	100 square millimeters
Square meter	m²	10,000 square centimeters
Square kilometer	km²	1,000,000 square meters

PERIMETER

perimeter

Another measure associated with a region is its **perimeter:** the length of its boundary. The perimeter of Figure 8.29 is 23 centimeters, which is greater than the width of this page.

Figure 8.29

Intuitively, it may seem that the area of a region should depend on its perimeter. For example, if one person uses more fence to close in a piece of land than another person, it is tempting to assume the first person has the greater amount of land. However, this is not necessarily true.

EXAMPLE E

Each of the following figures has an area of 4 square centimeters. What is the perimeter of each figure?

(1)   (2)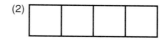

Solution
1. The perimeter is 8 cm.
2. The perimeter is 10 cm.

It is possible for two figures to have the same perimeter but different areas.

EXAMPLE F

Determine the area and perimeter of each figure in square centimeters.

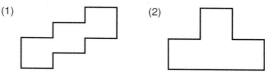

(1)   (2)

Solution
1. The area is 3 cm², and the perimeter is 10 cm.
2. The area is 4 cm², and the perimeter is 10 cm.

AREAS OF POLYGONS

RECTANGLES   Rectangles have right angles and pairs of opposite parallel sides, so unit squares fit onto them quite easily. The rectangle in Figure 8.30 can be covered by 24 whole squares and 6 half-squares. Its area is 27 square units. This area can be obtained from the product 6×4.5, because there are $4\frac{1}{2}$ squares in each of 6 columns. In general, if a rectangle has a length l and a width w, the *area of the rectangle* is the product of its length times its width.

Area of rectangle $= l \times w = lw$

Figure 8.30

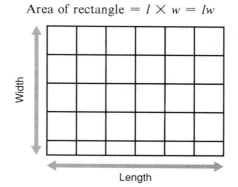

Width

Length

For a given perimeter, the dimensions of a rectangle affects its area. In the photos in Figure 8.31, the same knotted piece of string has been formed into 3 different rectangles. By using the lengths and widths of the rectangles, you can calculate that their perimeters are 36 centimeters. Yet the area decreases from 80 square centimeters (8×10) to 72 square centimeters (6×12) to 32 square centimeters (16×2), as the shape of the rectangle changes. If we continue to decrease the width of the rectangle, we can make its area as small as we please, though the perimeter will remain 36 centimeters.

Figure 8.31
8 cm by 10 cm (*left*); 6 cm by 12 cm (*center*); 16 cm by 2 cm (*right*)

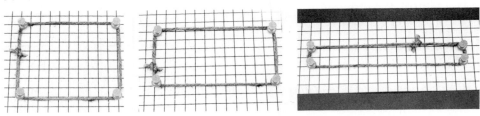

PARALLELOGRAMS Fitting unit squares onto a figure is a good way to acquire an understanding of the concept of area. However, actually placing squares on a region is usually difficult because of the shape of the boundary [see part (a) of Figure 8.32].

One of the basic principles in finding area is that *a region can be cut into parts and reassembled without changing its area.* This principle is useful in developing a formula for the area of a parallelogram. The rectangle in part (b) of Figure 8.32 has been obtained from the figure in part (a) by cutting triangle A from the left side of the parallelogram and moving it to the right side to create a rectangle. The **base** of the rectangle is 5 centimeters and its height is 2 centimeters, so its area is 10 square centimeters. Since the rectangle was obtained by rearranging the parts of the parallelogram, the area of the parallelogram is also 10 square centimeters. Notice that the base of the parallelogram is also 5 centimeters and its **height,** or **altitude** (the perpendicular distance between opposite parallel sides), is 2 centimeters. This suggests that the *area of a parallelogram is the product of its base times its height.*

height, altitude

$$\text{Area of parallelogram} = b \times h = bh$$

Figure 8.32

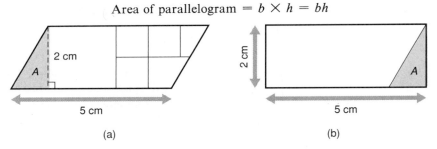

(a)   (b)

For a given perimeter, the area of a parallelogram depends on its shape. The two parallelograms formed by the inside edges of the linkages in the photo in Figure 8.33 both have the same perimeter, but as the parallelogram is skewed more to the right, its height decreases. Since the base of both parallelograms is the same and the area of a parallelogram is the base times the height, the parallelogram with the smaller height has the smaller area. The area of the first parallelogram is approximately 72 square centimeters (9×8), and the area of the second one is approximately 45 square centimeters (9×5). The height of the parallelogram, and consequently its area, can be made arbitrarily small by further skewing the linkages while the perimeter stays constant.

Figure 8.33

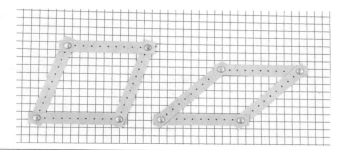

EXAMPLE G

Estimate the area of each parallelogram by visualizing the number of 1 cm by 1 cm squares needed to cover the figure. See if you can come within 1 square centimeter of the correct area. Then compute the area.

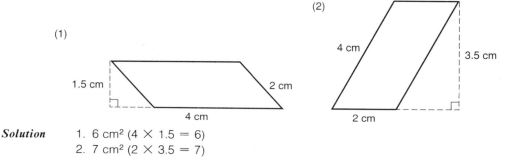

(1)

(2)

1.5 cm

2 cm

4 cm

4 cm

3.5 cm

2 cm

Solution

1. 6 cm² (4 × 1.5 = 6)
2. 7 cm² (2 × 3.5 = 7)

Were your estimates close to these numbers?

TRIANGLES   The triangle in part (a) of Figure 8.34 is covered with 1 cm by 1 cm squares and parts of squares. Can you see why this shows that the area of the triangle is more than 4 square centimeters? Since it is inconvenient to cover the triangle with squares, we will use a different approach to finding its area. Two copies of a triangle can be placed together to form a parallelogram, as shown in part (b). This can be accomplished by rotating the triangle about side $\overline{AB}$. Since the parallelogram has a base of 5 centimeters and a height of 2 centimeters, its area is 10 square centimeters. Thus the area of the triangle is half as much: 5 square centimeters.

Figure 8.34

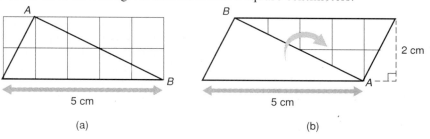

A

B

5 cm

(a)

B

2 cm

A

5 cm

(b)

The preceding example suggests a general approach to finding the area of a triangle: place two copies of the triangle together to form a parallelogram, and then find the area of the parallelogram. If the length of the base of the triangle is b and its height, or altitude (the perpendicular distance to its base from the opposite vertex) is h, the base and altitude of the parallelogram are also b and h (Figure 8.35). So the area of the parallelogram is $b \times h$, and since the parallelogram is formed from two triangles,

$$\text{Area of triangle} = \frac{1}{2} \times b \times h = \frac{1}{2} bh$$

Figure 8.35

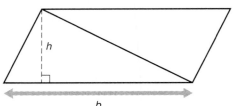

Any side of a triangle may be considered the base, and each base has its corresponding altitude. Regardless of the base and altitude chosen, the triangle will have the same area.

EXAMPLE H

Triangle *ABC* is shown below in two positions, with two different bases and altitudes. One of these altitudes falls outside the triangle. Determine the area of each triangle.

(1)

(2)

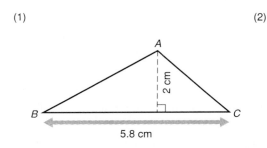

Solution

1. The area is 5.8 cm²: 1/2 × 5.8 × 2 = 5.8.
2. The area is 5.8 cm²: 1/2 × 4 × 2.9 = 5.8.

TRAPEZOIDS   It is inconvenient to cover a trapezoid with square units because of its sloping sides. However, as with a triangle, we can obtain a parallelogram by placing two trapezoids together.

The trapezoid in part (a) of Figure 8.36 has a lower base of length *b* and an upper base of length *u,* and its **height,** or **altitude** (the perpendicular distance between its bases) is *h*. The parallelogram in part (b) was obtained by rotating the trapezoid about side $\overline{AB}$. The parallelogram has a base of $(b + u)$ and a height of *h*, so its area is $(b + u) \times h$. Since the parallelogram is formed from two trapezoids,

$$\text{Area of trapezoid} = \frac{1}{2} \times (b + u) \times h = \frac{1}{2}(b + u)h$$

Figure 8.36

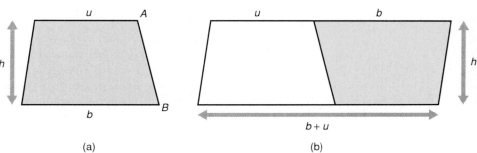

(a)

(b)

EXAMPLE *I*

Estimate the area of the trapezoid in Figure 8.36 by visualizing the number of 1 cm by 1 cm squares needed to cover the figure. See if you can come within 1 square centimeter of obtaining the correct area. Then, using 4 centimeters and 3 centimeters for the lengths of the lower and upper bases and 2.5 centimeters for the height, compute the area of the trapezoid.

Solution

The area of the trapezoid is 8.75 cm²: 1/2 × (4 + 3) × 2.5 = 8.75. Was your estimate close to this number?

CIRCUMFERENCE AND AREAS OF CIRCLES

Circles are part of our natural environment. The sun, the moon, flowers, whirlpools, and cross sections of trees all have circular shapes. The concentric circles in the section of natural pearl in Figure 8.37 were formed by many layers of growth.

Figure 8.37
Concentric circles revealed in a cross section of natural pearl

circumference

CIRCUMFERENCE   The perimeter of, or distance around, a circle is called the **circumference.** There is something deceptive about trying to estimate the circumference of a circle.

EXAMPLE *J*

Estimate the circumference of the pearl in Figure 8.37 in centimeters. Is it less than, approximately equal to, or greater than your handspan?

Solution

The circumference is approximately 14 cm, which is approximately equal to the handspan of many people.

Were you surprised at the solution in Example J? There is a tendency to underestimate the circumferences of circles. Often people estimate the circumference by doubling the diameter. Actually, the circumference is a little greater than 3 times the diameter. This can be illustrated by placing string or a strip of paper around a circular figure, then folding it into three equal parts and comparing one of these parts to the diameter of the circle. The circumference of the pearl, for example, is approximately 14 centimeters, and its diameter is just over 4.5 centimeters.

The exact ratio of the circumference of a circle to its diameter is the irrational number π (pi), which is 3.14159 to the first few decimal places. This ratio is expressed in the following equations, where C is the circumference of a circle, d is the diameter, and r is the radius.

$$\frac{C}{d} = \pi \quad \text{or} \quad C = \pi d \quad \text{or} \quad C = 2\pi r$$

Some calculators have buttons for π. Pressing $\boxed{\pi}$ on a calculator with 10 places for digits will give the number shown in the display in Figure 8.38. However, since π is an irrational number, the number in this display is only a rational number approximation of π. For everyday purposes it is usually sufficient to approximate π by 3.14 or 22/7. We will use 3.14 in this text.

Figure 8.38

EXAMPLE K

The following photo shows a piece of string being stretched around a tennis ball can.

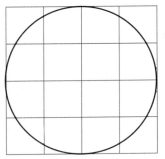

Predict how the length of the string will compare to the height of the can. The can has a diameter of approximately 7 centimeters and a height of approximately 20 centimeters. Compute the length of the string, and compare it to the height of the can.

Solution

It is common for people to predict that the length of the string is less than the height of the can. However, since 3.14 × 7 is approximately 22, the length of the string is approximately 22 cm, which is 2 cm greater than the height of the can.

AREAS OF CIRCLES   The area of a circle can be approximated by counting unit squares and parts of squares which cover the circle.

EXAMPLE L

The following circle has been drawn on a centimeter grid. Approximate its area in square centimeters.

Solution

A first step might be to note that the circle is contained inside a 4 by 4 grid, which indicates that its area is less than 16 cm². Next we can count the squares inside the circle and then combine the parts of the remaining squares, or estimate the parts of the squares outside the circle and subtract their area from 16. A reasonable estimate for the area of the circle is 12 cm².

You might have noticed in Example L that one quarter of the circle is contained in a square and the length of one side of the square is equal to the radius of the circle. This is illustrated in Figure 8.39, which shows that the area of a quarter of the circle with radius r is less than the radius times itself, or r^2. Thus the area of the whole circle is less than $4 \times r^2$.

Figure 8.39

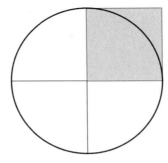

sectors

Let's consider a method for determining the area of a circle. The circle in part (a) of Figure 8.40 has been divided into 16 pie-shaped **sectors**. When these 16 sectors are rearranged and placed together, as shown in part (b), they form a figure whose shape is close to a parallelogram. The length of the base of the parallelogram-like figure is one-half the circumference of the circle, and the height of the figure is approximately the radius of the circle. If the circle is cut into a greater number of sectors, the shape of the resulting parallelogram-like figure will be even closer to a parallelogram. Using the formula for the area of a parallelogram, we can determine the area of the figure in part (b):

$$\text{Area} = b \times h = \frac{1}{2}C \times r = \frac{1}{2}(2\pi r) \times r = \pi r^2$$

which is the formula for the area of a circle.

Figure 8.40

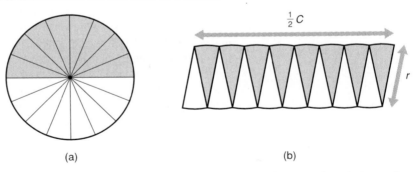

(a)   (b)

Notice that since $\pi \approx 3.14$, the area of a circle is a little more than 3 times the square of the radius of the circle (see Figure 8.39). This fact is sometimes used to estimate the area of a circle.

EXAMPLE M

Approximate the areas of the circles below using a value of 3 for π, and determine how many times greater the area of the large circle is than the area of the small circle.

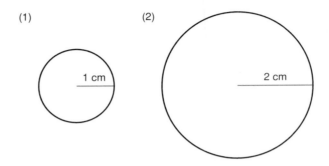

(1)   (2)

1 cm   2 cm

Solution

The area of circle (1) is approximately 3 cm² (3 × 1²), and the area of circle (2) is approximately 12 cm² (3 × 2²). So the circle whose radius is twice as large has an area that is 4 times greater.

■ *HISTORICAL HIGHLIGHT*

Pi has had a long and interesting history. In the ancient Orient, π was frequently taken to be 3. This value also occurs in the King James Bible in nearly identical verses (1 Kings 7:23 and 2 Chronicles 4:2) that describe the circumference of a circular container as being 3 times its diameter.

There have been many attempts to compute π. Archimedes computed π to the equivalent of 2 decimal places, and in 1841 Zacharias Dase computed π to 200 places. In 1873 William Shanks of England computed π to 707 places. In 1946 D. F. Ferguson of England discovered errors starting with the 528th place in Shanks's value for π, and a year later he gave a corrected value of π to 710 places. In recent years electronic computers have calculated π to hundreds of thousands of decimal places. Among the curiosities connected with π are the word devices for remembering the first few decimal places. In the following sentence the number of letters in each word is a digit in π.

3.   1   4   1   5   9   2   6
May I have a large container of coffee?*

PROBLEM-SOLVING APPLICATION

Sometimes it is necessary to find the areas of irregular or nonpolygonal shapes. Some of the water supplied to a leaf by its system of tiny veins is lost through small openings called *stomates*. Botanists collect the water by tying a plastic bag around a branch (Figure 8.41). Then they compute the areas of leaves to determine the amount of water they lose for each square centimeter of surface area.

*This mnemonic and others are given by H. W. Eves, *An Introduction to the History of Mathematics*, 3rd ed. (New York: Holt, Rinehart and Winston, 1969), 94.

Figure 8.41

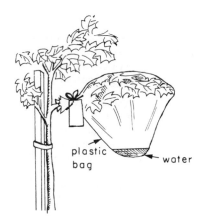

plastic
bag   water

■ **PROBLEM**

If a certain leaf loses 2 milliliters of water in a twenty-four-hour period, how much water does it lose for each square centimeter?

Understanding the Problem   First it is necessary to determine the area of the leaf. If the given leaf has an area of 10 square centimeters, how much water does it lose for each square centimeter?

Question 1

Devising a Plan   One approach to finding the area of a leaf is to trace the leaf on cardboard and cut it out. Comparing the weight of the cutout leaf to the weight and area of the original piece of cardboard by using ratios will give an approximation of the leaf's area. Another approach is to trace the leaf on grid paper and count the number of squares that fall inside the boundary of the leaf. If this approach is used, what can be done with the squares that lie on the boundary?

Question 2

Carrying Out the Plan   The given leaf has been traced on a centimeter grid in the next figure. There are 18 squares, each 1 cm by 1 cm, that fall inside the boundary. So the area of the leaf is at least 18 square centimeters. In order to permit a more accurate estimate for the remainder of the leaf's area, each square on the boundary has been divided into 4 smaller squares. One approach is to count the number of small squares that are half or more than half covered by the leaf. There appear to be 32 such squares. Using the 18 large interior squares and the 32 small boundary squares, we can estimate the area of the leaf.

Question 3   What is the approximate area, and how much water is lost for each square centimeter?

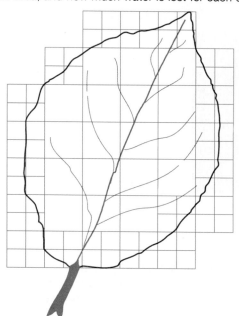

Question 4

Looking Back   The 32 quarter-squares we counted in the preceding step represent 8 square centimeters of leaf area. The process of subdividing boundary squares can be continued to obtain more accurate estimates. For example, if each quarter-square is divided into 4 tiny squares and 136 of these tiny squares are half or more than half covered by the leaf, what is the new estimate of the leaf's area?

Answers to Questions 1–4
1. .2 mL
2. One approach is to combine parts of squares to obtain whole squares. Another is to subdivide the boundary squares.
3. 26 cm²; approximately .08 mL of water is lost per cm² (2 ÷ 26 ≈ .08).
4. Since 16 of the tiny squares have an area of 1 cm², 136 of these tiny squares have an area of 8.5 cm² (136 ÷ 16 = 8.5). So the new estimate of the area of the leaf is 26.5 cm² (18 + 8.5 = 26.5).

RELATED ACTIVITIES IN
Mathematics for Elementary Teachers: An Activity Approach, 3e

Activity Set 8.2   **Areas on Geoboards:** Methods are developed for finding areas of polygons and discovering area formulas and Pick's formula.

Just for Fun   **Pentominoes:** Puzzles and a game with pentominoes are presented. Pentominoes are 12 geometric pieces that each are obtained by joining 5 squares at their edges

---

PUZZLER

The area of the inscribed square is what percent of the area of the circle?

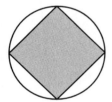

EXERCISES AND PROBLEMS 8.2

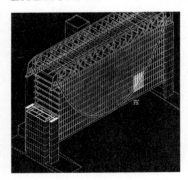

Diagram of the skeletal structure of the Minneapolis Federal Reserve Bank

1. The drawing above shows the skeletal structure of the Minneapolis Federal Reserve Bank. Its 10 floors and the vertical beams partition the front of the bank into congruent rectangles.

The dimensions of these rectangles are approximately 2 m by 4 m.
a. How do the width and height of these rectangles compare to the width of your outstretched arms and the height of the average room?
b. There are 53 rectangles across the front face of the bank. What is the width of the front face of the bank?
c. There are 10 rectangles running from the bottom to the top of the front face of the bank (1 for each floor). What is the height of the front face of the bank?
d. What is the area of the front face?

2. The basic unit for measuring area does not have to be a square. Measure the area of the figure on the grid below using the different units in a, b, and c.

(a)   (b)   (c)

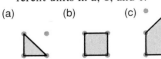

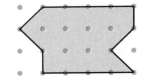

3. Determine the approximate area of the following figure, first using the nonstandard unit in part a and then using the one in part b.

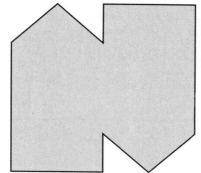

a.

Gum wrapper

b.

Plastic fastener

4. The following question is taken from a mathematics test given to 9-year-olds by the National Assessment of Educational Progress (NAEP).
   a. Which of the following figures has the same area as the 4 by 4 square?

   b. Only 44% of students who took the test chose the 8 by 2 rectangle, and almost as many selected the 3 by 5 rectangle. The selection of the 3 by 5 rectangle may indicate confusion about which two concepts of measurement? Explain why students might have made this choice.

5. a. How many square feet are in 1 square mile?
   b. How many acres are in 1 square mile?
   c. Rhode Island has the least land area of the 50 states. Its area is 1049 square miles. How many acres is this?

6. Each of the following figures has an area of 3 square units. Using the length of the side of a square as the unit of measure, calculate the perimeter of each figure.

a.

b.
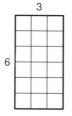

c.

d.
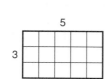

7. a. The **are** (pronounced "air") is a metric unit for measuring the areas of house lots, gardens, and other such medium-size regions. The *are* is equal to the area of a square whose sides measure 10 m each. How many *ares* equal 1 square kilometer?
   b. The **hectare** is the metric unit for measuring larger regions. It is the area of a square whose sides measure 100 m each. How many hectares equal 1 square kilometer?

8. Compute the area of each of these figures in square millimeters. Then determine the area in square centimeters.

a. Rectangle

25 mm
55 mm

b. Parallelogram
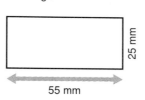
30 mm
60 mm

c. Trapezoid
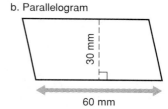
20 mm
30 mm
58 mm

d.
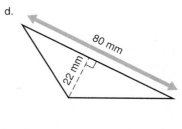
80 mm
22 mm

9. The area of a polygon can be found by subdividing it into smaller regions. Use this principle to find the area of this hexagon.

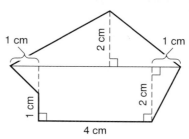

1 cm   2 cm   1 cm
1 cm   2 cm
4 cm

10. A pane of antique stained glass has dimensions of 30 cm by 58 cm. If the glass sells for 25 cents per square centimeter, what is the cost of the pane?

11. A store sells two types of Christmas paper. Type A has four rolls per package and costs $2.99, and each roll is 75 cm by 150 cm. Type B has a single roll that costs $3.19 and is 88 cm by 500 cm. Which type gives you more paper for your money?

12. All-purpose carpeting costs $27.50 per square meter. What is the cost of carpeting a room from wall to wall whose dimensions are 360 cm by 400 cm?

13. Glass for picture frames sells for $20.00 per square meter. What is the total cost of the glass in two picture frames, one of which is 58 cm by 30 cm and the other 40 cm by 60 cm?

14. The length of a kitchen cupboard is 3.5 m. There are three shelves in the cupboard, each 30 cm wide. How many rolls of shelf paper will be needed to cover these shelves, if each roll is 30 cm by 3 m?

15. The instructions on a bag of lawn fertilizer recommend that 35 grams of fertilizer be used for each square meter of lawn. How many square meters of lawn can be fertilized with a 50 kg bag?

16. Some humidity is necessary in homes for comfort, but too much can cause mold and peeling paint. Paint-destroying moisture can come from walls, crawl spaces, and attics.

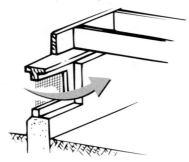

   a. An attic should have 900 cm² of ventilation for each 27 m² of floor area. How many square centimeters of ventilation are needed for an attic with a 4 m by 12 m floor?
   b. A crawl space should have 900 cm² of ventilation for each 27 m² of ceiling area, plus 1800 cm² for each 30 m of perimeter around the crawl space. How many square centimeters of ventilation are needed for a 10 m by 15 m crawl space?

17. The wall shown above at right has a length of 540 cm and a height of 240 cm. A few dimensions are also given around the window and fireplace.
   a. How many square centimeters of wallpaper will it take to paper the wall?
   b. A standard roll of wallpaper is 12.8 m by 53 cm. A store will not sell partial rolls. How many rolls must be purchased to cover this wall?

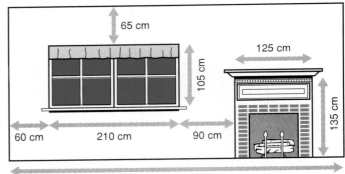

18. Many factors go into assessing the value of a house for tax purposes. Once the proper category has been determined, the assessment rate is per square foot or square meter. Compute the value of the following one-foot dwellings if the assessment rate is $389 per square meter.
   a. Ranch-style: 8 m by 13.75 m
   b. L-shaped consisting of 2 rectangles: 8.7 m by 11 m plus 8 m by 9.5 m
   c. How much tax must be paid on the ranch-style house in part a if the tax rate is $52 on every $1000 of assessed value?

19. The common starfish has five arms. Most species grow as large as 20 to 30 cm in diameter, but some species reach only 1 cm. The starfish shown below, photographed on a centimeter grid, has a diameter of approximately 9.5 cm. What is the approximate area of the underside of this starfish in square centimeters? (Hint: Enclose the starfish in a large square and approximate the area that is not covered.)

20. Below is a brief chronology of some early approximations for π. Compare the decimals for these fractions with the value of π to 15 decimal places:

$$\pi \approx 3.141592653589793$$

Which of these fractions is closest to the value of π? Which of these fractions are equal?

   a. Archimedes (240 B.C.): $\dfrac{223}{71}$

   b. Claudius Ptolemy (A.D. 150): $\dfrac{377}{120}$

c. Tsu Ch'ung-chih (A.D. 480): $\dfrac{355}{113}$

d. Aryabhata (A.D. 530): $\dfrac{62{,}832}{20{,}000}$

e. Bhaskara (A.D. 1150): $\dfrac{3927}{1250}$

21. Of all simple closed curves of equal length, the circle encloses the largest area. Consider the following square and circle.

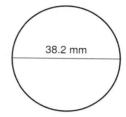

30 mm

a. What is the perimeter of each figure to the nearest millimeter?

b. How much greater (to the nearest square millimeter) is the area of the circle than the area of the square?

22. Rocks are sometimes shaped into discs by the tumbling action of ocean waves. The photo shows four such rocks on a centimeter grid.

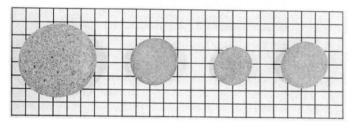

a. Estimate the diameter of the large rock. Use this number to approximate the area of the rock to the nearest square centimeter.

b. What is the difference between the area of the largest rock and the total area of the three smaller rocks?

23. The 1988–1989 Manhattan telephone directory had approximately 1800 pages, each with an 8 inch by 8 inch printed surface.

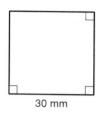

a. If every square inch of printed surface on these pages contained a 50 by 50 array of dots, as shown here, how many dots would there be in this directory?

b. In 1990 the world's population was approximately 5 billion. If each person were represented by 1 dot, about how many of these telephone directories to the nearest tenth would be required to represent everyone in the world?

Featured Strategy: Making a Drawing

24. Draw the largest circle possible on a square piece of paper. Cut the circle out, discarding the trimmings. Inside the circle, draw the largest square possible. Cut the square out, discarding the trimmings. What fraction of the original square piece of paper has been cut off and thrown away?

a. **Understanding the Problem** The shaded portion of this diagram shows the trimmings that will be thrown away in the first step of the paper-cutting process. If the length of a side of the square is 2 cm, what percent of the area of the square is the area of the shaded region?

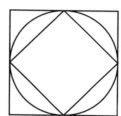

b. **Devising a Plan** One approach to the problem is to compute the total area of the trimmings from the two steps separately. A different approach is suggested by inscribing the second square inside the circle. Shade the total region of the following figure that represents the amount that will be cut off from the original square.

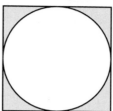

c. **Carrying Out the Plan** Choose a plan from part b or devise one of your own, and use it to determine what fraction of the original square piece of paper is cut off.

d. **Looking Back** Suppose we begin with a circle, inscribe a square, and then inscribe a smaller circle in the square. How does the area of the small circle compare with the area of the large circle? Will the answer be the same as the answer to the original problem?

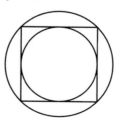

25. A meter trundle wheel is a convenient device for measuring distances along the ground. Every time the wheel makes one complete revolution, it has moved forward 1 meter. If you were to cut this wheel from a square piece of plywood, what would be the dimensions of the smallest square you could use?

26. Physicists study cosmic radiation to learn about properties of our galaxy and levels of sun activity. The proton histogram below contains information on the intensity level of cosmic rays. Region A under the histogram, which is called the **background area,** is compared with the total area of regions A and B.

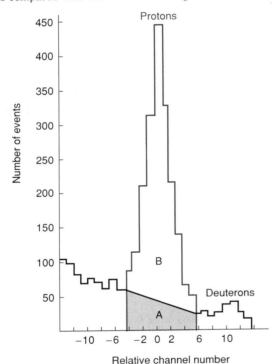

a. What is the approximate area of region A, in square millimeters?

b. What is the approximate area of region B?

c. What is the ratio of the area of region A to the total area of regions A and B to the nearest percent?

27. The seventy-story cylindrical building shown in the photo is the Peachtree Plaza Hotel in Atlanta, Georgia. It contains a seven-story central court with a half-acre lake and over 100 trees. The diameter of this building is 35.36 m (116 ft). According to its architect, John Portman, cylindrical walls were chosen rather than the more common rectangular walls because a circle encloses more area with less perimeter than any other shape.

Peachtree Plaza Hotel in Atlanta, Georgia

a. What is the area of a horizontal cross section of the building (the area of a floor), to the nearest square meter?

b. What is the perimeter, to the nearest meter, of a square that encloses the same area as you found in part a? (Hint: First find the square root of the area in part a.)

c. What is the perimeter of the Peachtree Plaza Hotel to the nearest meter?

d. How many meters longer is the perimeter of the square in part b than the perimeter of the hotel in part c?

e. The Peachtree Plaza Hotel is 230 m (754 ft) tall. This number multiplied by your answer in part d will give the additional wall area that would be needed to enclose the same space if the hotel had a square base rather than a circular one. What is this area?

28. Egyptian scrolls dating from the period between 1850 and 1650 B.C. show many formulas for computing land areas for purposes of taxation. Does the following formula produce the correct area for a quadrilateral with successive sides a, b, c, and d?

$$\text{Area} = \frac{(a + c) \times (b + d)}{4}$$

If not, is the result too large or too small? (Hint: Try this formula on some figures.)

29. The wheel has been called the most important invention of all time. Assume that the diameter of each wheel in this cartoon is 75 cm and that the distance between opposite pairs of wheels is 300 cm. How many revolutions of each wheel will it take to turn this contraption in one complete circle?

"Just because you invented the *wheel*, it doesn't follow logically that you can go on to the *wagon*."

30. The height of a tennis ball can is approximately equal to the circumference of a tennis ball. This can be illustrated by rolling a tennis ball along the edge of a can. The ball will make one complete revolution in rolling from one end of the can to the other. Since a can holds three tennis balls, what does this demonstration imply about the diameter of a ball as compared to its circumference?

CALCULATOR INVESTIGATION

There are many different methods for approximating the area of a circle. The ancient Egyptians used a method described in the Rhind Papyrus (1650 B.C.), which involved finding the area of a square that was approximately equal to the area of the circle.

Questions for Investigation

1. The area of a square whose sides are the same as the diameter of the circle is obviously larger than the area of the circle (see figure). Experiment with some numbers to find what fractional part of the diameter can be used as the side of a square to obtain an approximation for the area of the circle.

2. Another ancient method for finding the area of a circle was to use a piece of rope (or string) whose length was equal to the circumference plus the diameter. A rectangle whose width was

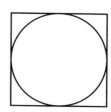

equal to the radius of the circle was then formed from the rope, and the area of the rectangle was used for the area of the circle. Does this method produce an area less than, greater than, or approximately equal to that of the circle?

PUZZLER

Suppose a cable fits tightly around the equator of the earth. If an additional piece is to be spliced in so that the cable can be raised 6 feet above the earth (at all points), approximately how much additional cable will be needed?

SECTION 8.3   VOLUME AND SURFACE AREA

■ PROBLEM OPENER

The number of cubes in these U-shaped figures are the beginning of the sequence

> 5,   28,   81, . . .

If this geometric pattern is continued, how many cubes will there be in the tenth figure?

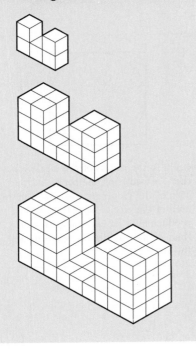

cubic units

Figure 8.42

Liquified natural gas tanker
Aquarius

The huge ship in the photo is the *Aquarius,* one of twelve liquefied natural gas tankers built by the Quincy Shipbuilding Division of General Dynamics. The *Aquarius* is longer than three football fields (285 meters) and carries five spherical aluminum tanks, each with a diameter of 36.58 meters. To appreciate the size of one of these spheres, consider the fact that its diameter is greater than the diameter of one of the floors in the Peachtree Plaza Hotel and greater than the length of a professional basketball court. The space inside these spheres is measured by the number of *unit cubes* that are required to fill it. Each sphere holds the equivalent of 25,000 cubes, each with dimensions of 1 m by 1 m by 1 m.

NONSTANDARD UNITS OF VOLUME

To measure the amount of space in tanks, buildings, refrigerators, cars, and other three-dimensional figures, we need units of measure that are also three-dimensional figures. The number of such units needed to fill a figure is an expression of its **volume.** Cubes are convenient because they pack together without gaps or overlapping. Using the cube in part (a) of Figure 8.42 as the unit cube, we can determine that the volume of the box in part (b) is 24 **cubic units.** The figure shows 12 cubes on the base of the box, and 12 more cubes can be placed above these to fill the box.

(a)

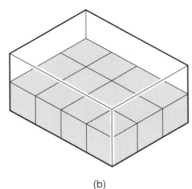

(b)

The first school experiences with measuring volume should involve nonstandard units of measure. Before introducing units of length for the dimensions of a cube, teachers should involve students in activities that require stacking, building, and counting cubes.

EXAMPLE A

Suppose the rectangle below is the base of a box. Determine the approximate number of each of the following units of volume (the die and the cube) that will fit onto this base. (Hint: Trace the front face of each cube.)

(1)   (2)

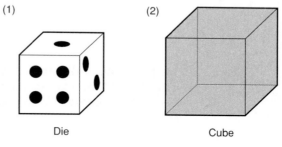

Die   Cube

Solution   1. Approximately 32 dice will cover the base. (If 6 layers of dice fill the box, the volume of the box is 192 dice units.)
              2. Approximately 18 cubes will cover the base. (If 4.5 layers of these cubes fill the box, the volume of the box is approximately 81 cube units.)

The difficulty that children at all grade levels have in understanding the concept of volume is indicated in the next example. Every four years the NAEP (National Assessment of Educational Progress) administers mathematics tests in schools throughout the United States. Example B contains a question on volume from one of these tests.

EXAMPLE B

Students were shown the figure below and asked how many cubes the box contains. What is the correct answer, and what do you think was the incorrect answer most commonly given by the students?

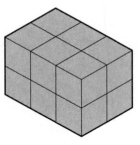

Solution The box contains 12 cubes. Only 6% of the 9-year-olds, 21% of the 13-year-olds, and 43% of the 17-year-olds answered the question correctly.* The most common incorrect answer was 16. Can you see how students might have obtained this answer?

STANDARD UNITS OF VOLUME

For each English unit of length (inches, feet, etc.) and each metric unit of length (centimeter, meter, etc.) there is a corresponding unit of volume, a cube whose three dimensions are the given length.

cubic inch, cubic foot, cubic yard

Figure 8.43

ENGLISH UNITS FOR VOLUME Cubic units are named according to the length of their edges. The most commonly used units for measuring nonliquid volume in the English system are the **cubic inch,** the **cubic foot,** and the **cubic yard.** The cubes for these units are illustrated in Figure 8.43.

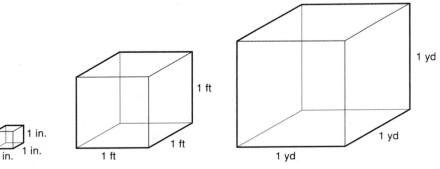

The volume of a microwave oven might be measured in cubic inches. A larger volume, such as that of a room or freezer, might be measured in cubic feet. Even larger volumes, such as the volumes of truckloads of loam or crushed rock, are measured by the cubic yard.

EXAMPLE C

Determine the following English unit relationships.

1. How many cubic inches equal 1 cubic foot?
2. How many cubic feet equal 1 cubic yard?
3. How many cubic inches equal 1.4 cubic feet?

*T. P. Carpenter et al., "Results and Implications of the NAEP Mathematics Assessment: Elementary School," *Arithmetic Teacher* 22 (October 1975): 438–450.

Solution

1. Imagine a box in the shape of a cube whose dimensions are each 1 ft. The base of the box is 12 in. by 12 in., so the floor of the box can be covered by 144 cubes, each of which is 1 in. by 1 in. by 1 in. Since 12 such layers will fill the box, its volume is 1728 in.³ (12 × 144 = 1728).

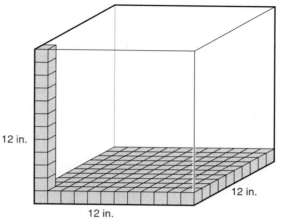

2. Similarly, the floor of a cube-shaped box whose dimensions are each 1 yd can be covered with 9 cubes, each of which is 1 ft by 1 ft by 1 ft. Three such layers will fill the box, so its volume is 27 ft³.

3. Since 1 ft³ = 1728 in.³, 1.4 ft³ = 2419.2 in.³ (1.4 × 1728 = 2419.2).

The English units for volume and their relationships are summarized in Figure 8.44.

Figure 8.44

English units for volume

Cubic inch	in.³	$\dfrac{1}{1728}$ cubic foot
Cubic foot	ft³	1728 cubic inches
Cubic yard	yd³	27 cubic feet

METRIC UNITS FOR VOLUME   The common metric units for measuring nonliquid volume are the **cubic millimeter,** the **cubic centimeter,** and the **cubic meter.** Each unit is named according to the length of the edges of its cube. For example, the edges of the cube for the cubic centimeter each have a length of 1 centimeter. The cubes for the three metric units are shown in Figure 8.45.

**cubic millimeter
cubic centimeter,
cubic, meter**

Figure 8.45

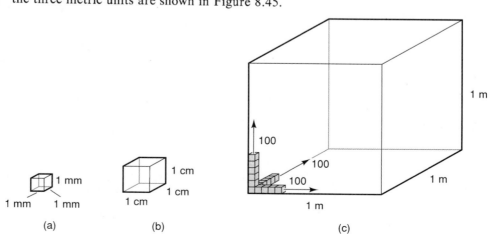

(a)   (b)   (c)

EXAMPLE **D**

Determine the following relationships.

1. How many cubic centimeters equal 1 cubic meter?
2. How many cubic millimeters equal 1 cubic centimeter?
3. How many cubic millimeters equal 3.4 cubic centimeters?

Solution

1. Visualize a cube-shaped box that measures 1 m on each edge [see part (c) of Figure 8.45], and imagine filling it with cubes whose edges measure 1 cm. The floor of the large cube is 100 cm by 100 cm, so it can be covered by 10,000 of the smaller cubes. Since there are 100 such layers, the volume of the box is 1,000,000 cm³ (100 × 10,000).
2. A cube whose edges each have a length of 1 cm has dimensions of 10 mm by 10 mm by 10 mm. So its volume is 1000 mm³ (10 × 10 × 10).
3. Since 1 cm³ = 1000 mm³, 3.4 cm³ = 3400 mm³.

Some of the metric units for volume and their relationships are shown in the following table.

Figure 8.46

Metric units for volume

Cubic millimeter	mm³	$\frac{1}{1000}$ cubic centimeter
Cubic centimeter	cm³	1,000 cubic millimeters
Cubic meter	m³	1,000,000 cubic centimeters

SURFACE AREA

surface area

Another important measure associated with objects in space is their amount of surface. Just as in the case of two-dimensional figures, **surface area** is expressed as the number of unit squares needed to cover the surface.

EXAMPLE **E**

The area of the top of the box in the figure is 9 square centimeters. What is the total surface area, including the base of the box?

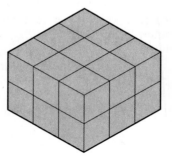

Solution

The top and bottom faces of the box each have an area of 9 cm². The right and left faces each have an area of 6 cm², and the front and back faces each have an area of 6 cm². So the total surface area is 42 cm² (2 × 9 + 2 × 6 + 2 × 6).

The surface area of an object cannot be predicted on the basis of its volume, any more than the perimeter of a figure is determined by the area of the figure.

EXAMPLE F

The box in Example E and the box below each have a volume of 18 cubic centimeters. How do the surface areas of the two boxes compare?

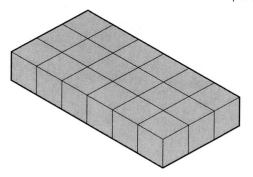

Solution   The top and bottom faces of the box in this figure each have an area of 18 cm²; the right and left sides each have an area of 3 cm²; and the front and back faces each have an area of 6 cm². So the total surface area is 54 cm². This is 12 cm² greater than the surface area of the box in Example E.

Examples E and F show that figures in space can have the same volume but different surface areas. The amount of material you would need to build the box in Example F is about 130% of the amount of material you would need to build the box in Example E (130% of 42 = 1.3 × 42 ≈ 54), although both have a volume of 18 cm³.

VOLUMES OF SPACE FIGURES

PRISMS   In Figure 8.47 the length (20) times the width (10) gives the number of cubes (200) on the floor of the box (or base of the rectangular prism). Since the box can be filled with 6 levels of cubes, it will hold 1200 cubes. This volume of 1200 cubic centimeters can be obtained by multiplying the three dimensions of the box: length × width × height. In general, a rectangular prism with length l, width w, and height h has the following volume:

$$\text{Volume} = \text{length} \times \text{width} \times \text{height } (V = lwh)$$

Figure 8.47

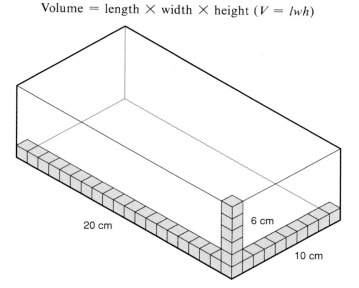

20 cm

6 cm

10 cm

The volume of any prism can be found in a similar way. The base of the prism in Figure 8.48 is a right triangle, which is covered by $4\frac{1}{2}$ cubes. Since 6 levels of $4\frac{1}{2}$ cubes each fill the prism, its volume is 6×4.5, or 27 cubic centimeters.

Figure 8.48

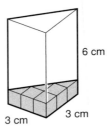

6 cm

3 cm   3 cm

The number of cubes that cover the base of this prism is the same as the area of the base. Therefore, the volume of the prism can be computed by multiplying the area of the base by the height, or altitude, of the prism. In general, the volume of any right prism having a base of area B and a height of h can be computed by the formula,

Volume of prism = area of base × height ($V = Bh$)

The formula for the volume of an oblique prism is suggested by beginning with a stack of cards, as in part (a) of Figure 8.49, and then pushing them sideways to form an oblique prism, as in part (b). If each card in part (a) is 12.5 cm by 7.5 cm and the stack is 5 centimeters high, its volume is $12.5 \times 7.5 \times 5$, or 468.75 cubic centimeters. The base of the oblique prism in part (b) is also 12.5 cm by 7.5 cm, and its height, or altitude (the perpendicular distance between its upper and lower bases), is 5 centimeters. Since both stacks contain the same number of cards, their volumes are both 468.75 cubic centimeters. This means that the volume of the oblique prism can be computed by multiplying the area of its base by its height. In general, *the volume of any prism, right or oblique, is the area of its base times its height.*

Figure 8.49

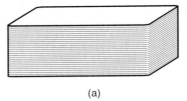   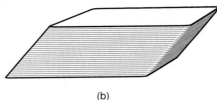

(a)   (b)

EXAMPLE G

Sometimes a prism will have more than one pair of bases, as shown in the following figures. Figure (1) is a right prism whose base is a parallelogram. By turning it so that one of its lateral faces becomes the base, as in figure (2), we can classify the prism as an oblique prism. Determine the volume of each prism, given the following dimensions:

1. Area of base: 280 square centimeters; altitude: 6 centimeters
2. Area of base: 120 square centimeters; altitude: 14 centimeters

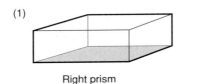

(1)   (2)

Right prism   Oblique prism

Solution   1. 1680 cm³   2. 1680 cm³

The surface area of a prism is the sum of the areas of its bases and faces. In right prisms the faces are rectangles, and in oblique prisms the faces are rectangles and parallelograms.

CYLINDERS   The cylindrical buildings in Figure 8.50 are part of the Renaissance Center in Detroit. Just as with conventional rectangular buildings, architects need to know the volumes and surface areas of these glass-walled cylinders.

Figure 8.50
Renaissance Center in Detroit

To compute the volumes of cylinders, we continue to use unit cubes even though they do not conveniently fit into a cylinder. More than 33 cubes are needed to cover the base of the cylinder in Figure 8.51. Furthermore, since the cylinder has a height of 12 centimeters, it will take *at least* 12 × 33, or 396, cubes to fill the cylinder.

Figure 8.51

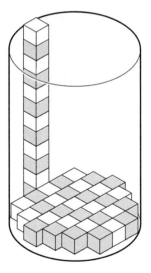

If we were to use smaller cubes in Figure 8.51, they could be packed closer to the boundary of the base and a better approximation would be obtained for the volume of the cylinder. This suggests that the formula for the volume of a cylinder is the same as that for the volume of a prism. For a cylinder with a base of area B and a height of h,

Volume of cylinder = area of base × height ($V = Bh$)

A right cylinder without bases can be formed by joining the opposite edges of a rectangular sheet of paper (Figure 8.52). The circumference of the base of the cylinder is the length of the rectangle, and the height of the cylinder is the height of the rectangle. Therefore, the surface area of the sides of a cylinder is the circumference of the base of the cylinder times its height.

Figure 8.52

h $2\pi r$ r h

For any right cylinder whose base has a radius r and whose height is h, the base has a circumference of $2\pi r$, and the surface area of the side of the cylinder is $2\pi r \times h$. Adding the area of both bases, $2\pi r^2$, to the area of the side of the cylinder produces the total surface area:

$$\text{Surface area of cylinder} = 2\pi rh + 2\pi r^2$$

EXAMPLE H

Compute the volume and surface area of a tennis ball can if the diameter of its base is 7 centimeters and the height of the can is 20 centimeters.

Solution

Surface area: The radius of the base is 3.5 cm, so the top and the base of the can each have an area of 38.465 cm² [3.14 × 3.5²]. The circumference of the can is 21.98 cm, so the lateral surface of the can has an area of 439.6 cm² (20 × 21.98). Thus the total surface area of the can is 516.53 cm², or approximately 517 cm².
Volume: 769.3 cm³ (38.465 × 20)

PYRAMIDS   The Pyramid of Cheops, also known as the Great Pyramid of Egypt, was built about 2600 B.C. and is one of the seven wonders of the ancient world. It has a height of 148 meters. The Transamerica Pyramid in San Francisco (Figure 8.53) has a height of 260 meters and was built in 1972. Even though it is the shorter of these giant pyramids, the Egyptian pyramid has several times more volume. (See #15 in Exercises and Problems 8.3.)

Figure 8.53
Transamerica Pyramid in San Francisco

Pyramid (d) that is inside the cube in part (b) of Figure 8.54 has a square base, *EFGH,* and a height *GC.* This pyramid, together with the 2 pyramids in parts (a) and (c), partition the cube into 3 congruent pyramids. (Can you see how these fit together?) Therefore, the volume of the pyramid in the cube is one-third of the volume of the cube. That is, the volume of the pyramid is one-third of the area of the base of the cube times the height of the cube.

Figure 8.54

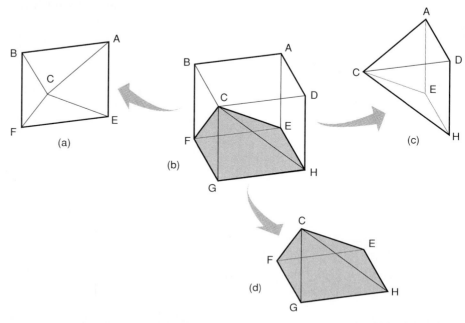

In general, if *B* is the area of the base of a pyramid and *h* is the height, or altitude (perpendicular distance from the apex to the base), of the pyramid,

$$\text{Volume of pyramid} = \frac{1}{3} \times \text{area of base} \times \text{height} \left(V = \frac{1}{3}Bh \right)$$

EXAMPLE I

Determine the volume of the Pyramid of Cheops to the nearest cubic meter. Its square base has sides of length 232.5 meters, and its height is 148 meters.

Solution   The area of the base is 54,056.25 m² (232.5 × 232.5), and

$$\frac{1}{3} \times 54,056.25 \times 148 = 2,666,775$$

So the volume of the pyramid is 2,666,775 m³.

CONES   The pile of crude salt in Figure 8.55 has the shape of a cone with a circular base. The conical shape forms as the salt is poured from above. The salt has been evaporated from ocean water and awaits further purification.

Figure 8.55

The volume of a cone can be approximated by the volume of a pyramid inscribed in the cone. The hexagonal pyramid in Figure 8.56 has a volume of approximately 430 cubic centimeters, which is slightly less than the volume of the cone. As the number of sides in the base of the pyramid increases, its volume becomes closer to the volume of the cone. Since the volume of the pyramid is one-third the area of its base times its height, we can use the same formula to calculate the volume of a cone. In general, for any cone whose base has area B and whose height is h,

$$\text{Volume of cone} = \frac{1}{3} \times \text{area of base} \times \text{height} \left(V = \frac{1}{3}Bh \right)$$

Figure 8.56

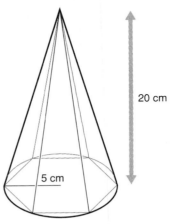

20 cm

5 cm

EXAMPLE J

Determine the volume of the pile of salt in Figure 8.55 to the nearest cubic meter. The height of the cone is 12 meters, and the diameter of its base is 32 meters. Then determine the number of railroad boxcars this salt would fill if each boxcar had a volume of 80 cubic meters.

Solution   The area of the base is 803.84 m². Since

$$\frac{1}{3} \times 803.84 \times 12 = 3215.36$$

the volume of the cone is approximately 3215 m³. This amount of salt would fill about 40 boxcars.

SPHERES   Figure 8.57 shows a view of the earth as seen from the *Apollo 10* spacecraft as it passed over the moon's surface. The earth, the planets, and their moons are all spherical shapes, spinning and orbiting about a spherical sun. There is considerable variation in the volumes of these objects. The earth has about 18 times more volume than the smallest planet, Mercury. The largest planet, Jupiter, is 10,900 times bigger than the earth.

Figure 8.57
View from *Apollo 10* of earth over moon's surface, 1969

The formulas for the volume of a sphere and the surface area of a sphere were known by the ancient Greeks. In fact, Archimedes (ca. 287–212 B.C.) discovered some remarkable relationships between a sphere and the smallest cylinder containing it. *The volume of the sphere is two-thirds the volume of the cylinder,* and *the surface area of the sphere is two-thirds the surface area of the cylinder.*

Figure 8.58 shows a sphere of radius *r*. The smallest cylinder that contains the sphere has a height of 2*r*. The volume of this cylinder is

$$\pi r^2 \times 2r = 2\pi r^3$$

Using the relationship discovered by Archimedes, we know that two-thirds of this volume is the volume of the sphere, or

$$\text{Volume of sphere} = \frac{2}{3} \times 2\pi r^3 = \frac{4}{3}\pi r^3$$

Figure 8.58

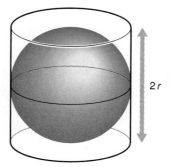

The surface area of the cylinder in Figure 8.58 is the sum of the areas of the two bases and the lateral surface of the cylinder. One base has an area of πr^2, and the two bases together have an area of $2\pi r^2$. Since the circumference of the cylinder is $2\pi r$ and the height of the cylinder is 2*r*, the lateral surface area is $2\pi r \times 2r = 4\pi r^2$. So the total surface area of the cylinder is

$$2\pi r^2 + 4\pi r^2 = 6\pi r^2$$

Using Archimedes discovery once again, we know that two-thirds of this area is the area of the sphere:

$$\text{Surface area of sphere} = \frac{2}{3} \times 6\pi r^2 = 4\pi r^2$$

Thus the surface area of a sphere is *exactly 4 times* the area of a great circle of the sphere.

The area of a circle and the volume of a sphere can be nicely approximated if we think of π as approximately equal to 3. Then the approximate area of the circle is 3 times the square of the circle's radius,

$$\pi r^2 \approx 3r^2$$

and the volume of the sphere is approximately 4 times the cube of the sphere's radius,

$$\frac{4}{3}\pi r^3 \approx \frac{4}{\cancel{3}}\cancel{3}r^3 = 4r^3$$

Figure 8.59

The square on the radius of a circle and the cube on the radius of a sphere are shown in Figure 8.59.

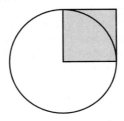

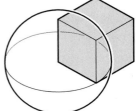

The area of a circle is approximately
3 times the area of the square on its radius.

(a)

The volume of a sphere is approximately
4 times the volume of the cube on its radius.

(b)

EXAMPLE K

Compare the volumes and surface areas of the following two spheres using the estimations suggested in Figure 8.59.

(1)

(2)

1 cm

2 cm

Solution

The volume of sphere (1) is approximately 4 cm³ (4 × 1³), and the volume of sphere (2) is approximately 32 cm³ (4 × 2³). The sphere whose radius is twice as large has a volume that is 8 times greater.

The surface area of sphere (1) is approximately 12 cm² (4 × 3 × 1²), and the surface area of sphere (2) is approximately 48 cm² (4 × 3 × 2²). The sphere whose radius is twice as large has a surface area that is 4 times greater.

■ *HISTORICAL HIGHLIGHT*

Archimedes

Archimedes is considered the greatest creative genius of the ancient world. He earned great renown for his mathematical writings and his mechanical inventions. One familiar legend concerns his launching a large ship using pulleys. Archimedes is reported to have boasted that if he had a fixed fulcrum with which to work, he could move anything: "Give me a place to stand and I will move the earth." Archimedes requested that his tomb be inscribed with a figure of a sphere and a cylinder to commemorate his discovery that the volume of a sphere is two-thirds the volume of the circumscribed cylinder. Many centuries later, the Roman orator Cicero discovered the tomb of Archimedes by identifying the inscription honoring Archimedes's request.*

---

*D. M. Burton, *The History of Mathematics* (Dubuque, IA: Wm. C. Brown Publishers, 1985), 151–155.

IRREGULAR SHAPES

The volume of a figure with an irregular shape can be determined quite easily by submerging it in water and measuring the volume of the water that is displaced. To illustrate this method, we will find the volume in cubic centimeters of the miniature statue in Figure 8.60. Before submerging the statue, we fill the cylinder with water to a height of 700 milliliters. When the statue is placed in the cylinder, the water level rises to the 800-milliliter level. This means that the volume of the statue is equal to the volume of 100 milliliters of water. Since each milliliter of water has a volume of 1 cubic centimeter, the volume of the statue is 100 cubic centimeters.

Figure 8.60

CREATING SURFACE AREA*

A potato can be cooked in a shorter time if it is cut into pieces, ice will melt faster if it is crushed, and coffee beans will provide better coffee if they are ground before they are boiled. The purpose of crushing, grinding, cutting, or, in general, subdividing is to increase the surface area of a substance. You may be aware of this principle and yet be surprised at the rate at which additional surface area is produced.

To illustrate how rapidly surface area can be created, consider a cube that is 2 centimeters on each edge [part (a) of Figure 8.61]. Its volume is 8 cubic centimeters and its surface area is 24 square centimeters. If this cube is cut into 8 smaller cubes, as in part (b), the total volume is still 8 cubic centimeters, but the surface area is doubled, to 48 square centimeters. This can be easily seen by looking at the small cube in the front corner of part (b). Faces a, b, and c contributed 3 square centimeters to

Figure 8.61

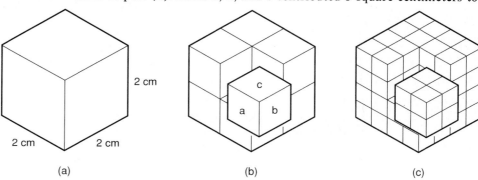

(a)   (b)   (c)

*This section is optional.

the area of the original cube; after the cut, 3 more faces of the small cube are exposed, contributing 3 more square centimeters of area. Since this is true for each of the 8 smaller cubes in part (b), the total increase in surface area is 8×3, or 24 square centimeters.

If we continue the process, cutting each of the centimeter cubes in Figure 8.61 part (b) into 8 smaller cubes, we have 64 cubes whose edges have lengths of 1/2 centimeter [part (c)]. The total volume of these cubes is still 8 cm³, but the second cut has doubled the surface area, increasing it to 96 square centimeters. If the process of halving the dimensions of each small cube is continued, the third set of cuts produces a surface area of $2^3 \times 24$, or 192, square centimeters; after the twelfth set of cuts, the surface area has increased to $2^{12} \times 24$, or 98,304 square centimeters! During this splitting process *the volume has remained the same:* 8 cubic centimeters.

This process of subdividing can also be used to double the surface area of a sphere. If, for example, a sphere of radius 2 centimeters is formed into 8 smaller spheres, each with a radius of 1 centimeter, the total volume will remain the same but the surface area will double. As in the case of the cubes, if we continue this halving process with the smaller spheres, the surface area will double for each set of cuts. Consider the effect when water is sprayed into the air in a fine mist, as from snow-making machines. The surface area of each drop of water is increased many times, allowing the small particles of water to freeze quickly in midair into snowflakes.

PROBLEM-SOLVING APPLICATION

Examples at the beginning of this section showed that, for a given volume, the surface area of a figure can vary. We also saw how surface area can become arbitrarily large while the volume remains constant. These examples suggest the following question: For a given volume, is there a shape that has the least surface area, and if so, what is this shape?

■ PROBLEM

If a rectangular solid has a volume of 24 cubic centimeters, what is the smallest surface area it can have?

Understanding the Problem   Figures made up of 24 cubes can help us consider different shapes. The following rectangular prisms are two possibilities. What is the surface area of each, and which has less surface area?

Question 1

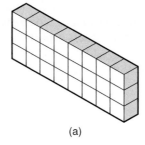
(a)

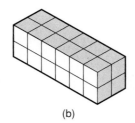
(b)

Question 2

Devising a Plan   One approach is to build (or sketch) figures and compute their surface areas. How many different rectangular prisms can be built using 24 whole cubes, and which has the least surface area?

Question 3

Carrying Out the Plan   A 2 by 3 by 4 prism [figure (c)] has the least amount of surface area of all the figures that can be built from 24 whole cubes. Imagine that the 24 cubes are made of clay that can be molded into one large cube [figure (d)]. What is the length of a side of this cube, and what is the cube's surface area?

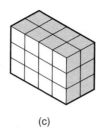

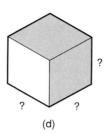

(c)   (d)

Question 4

Looking Back   Each edge of the cube in figure (d) has a length of $\sqrt[3]{24}$ centimeters, or approximately 2.88 centimeters. Thus the area of 1 face is approximately 8.29 square centimeters ($2.88 \times 2.88 \approx 8.29$), and the total surface area of the cube is approximately 50 square centimeters ($6 \times 8.29 \approx 50$). This is 2 square centimeters less than the area of figure (c). Now imagine the 24 cubes of clay being molded into a sphere of volume 24 cubic centimeters. What is the surface area of a sphere that has a volume of 24 cubic centimeters?

Answers to Questions 1–4

1. Prism (a) has a surface area of 70 cm², and prism (b) has a surface area of 56 cm².

2. Six such prisms can be built; the 2 by 3 by 4 prism has the least surface area: 52 cm².

3. The length of a side is $\sqrt[3]{24}$ cm, or approximately 2.88 cm; the cube's surface area is approximately 50 cm².

4. A sphere with a volume of 24 cm³ has a radius of approximately 1.8 cm:

$$\frac{4}{3}\pi(1.8)^3 \approx 24.42 \approx 24$$

A sphere with a radius of 1.8 cm has a surface area of approximately 41 cm²:

$$4\pi(1.8)^2 = 40.6944 \approx 41$$

Notice that the area of the sphere is approximately 9 cm² less than the area of the cube in figure (d). In general, for a given volume, *the sphere is the shape with the least surface area.*

RELATED ACTIVITIES IN
Mathematics for Elementary Teachers: An Activity Approach, 3e

Activity Set 8.3   **Models for Volume and Surface Area:** Volumes and surface areas are computed for models of prisms, pyramids, cylinders, and cones.

Just for Fun   **Soma Cubes:** A seven-piece puzzle made of cubes for constructing various figures.

EXERCISES AND PROBLEMS 8.3

1. a. In the cartoon above, what is the volume of the wheel to the nearest cubic centimeter, if the wheel has a length and height of 1 m, a thickness of 20 cm, and an inner diameter of 46 cm?

b. If this wheel is made of stone that weighs 7 grams per cubic centimeter, what is the weight of the wheel in kilograms?

2. Volume depends on the size of the unit used in measuring. Use each of the following units to find the volume of each figure in parts a through d.

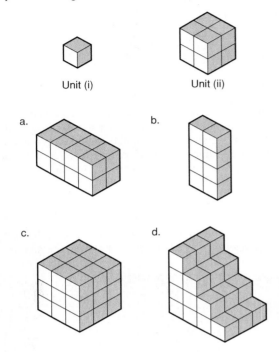

Unit (i)   Unit (ii)

a.   b.

c.   d.

3. **a.** How many cubic inches equal 1 yd³?
   b. How many cubic millimeters equal 1 m³?

4. **a.** How many cubic feet equal 5.2 yd³?
   b. How many cubic centimeters equal .3 m³?

5. Using one of the faces of unit (i) as the unit for area, determine the surface area (including the base) of each figure in parts a through d in #2.

6. The liter is a metric unit approximately equal to 1 quart. A one-quart milk carton has a square base of 7 cm by 7 cm and vertical sides of height 19.3 cm.
   a. What is its volume?
   b. Which has a greater volume, a quart or a liter?

7. Compute the volumes of the figures below to the nearest tenth of a cubic centimeter. Figures c and d have rectangular bases, and figure a has a square base.

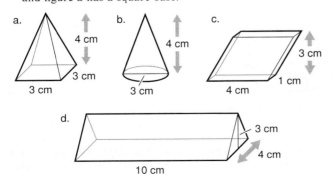

a.   4 cm   3 cm   3 cm
b.   4 cm   3 cm
c.   3 cm   1 cm   4 cm
d.   3 cm   4 cm   10 cm

e.   3 cm
f.   5 cm   10 cm

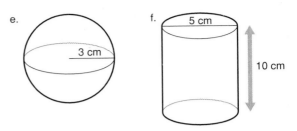

8. Compute the volumes of the following figures in cubic centimeters.

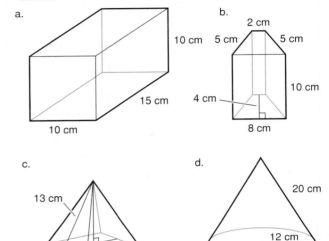

a.   10 cm   15 cm   10 cm
b.   2 cm   5 cm   5 cm   10 cm   4 cm   8 cm
c.   13 cm   10 cm   10 cm
d.   20 cm   12 cm

9. The number of fish that can be put in an aquarium depends on the amount of water the tank holds, the size of the fish, and the capacity of the pump and filter system.

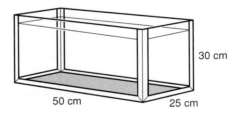

30 cm   50 cm   25 cm

   a. How many liters of water will this tank hold?
   b. The recommended number of tropical fish for this tank is 30. How many cubic centimeters of space would each fish have?
   c. Goldfish need more space and oxygen than tropical fish. Goldfish that are about 5 cm long require 3000 cm³ of water. How many goldfish could live in this tank?

10. The concrete foundation for the office building on the corner of Congress and State streets in Boston required 496 truckloads of concrete and was formed in one continuous pouring carried on over a thirty-hour period.
    a. The concrete was poured to a depth of 1.8 m and covered an area of 2420 m². How many cubic meters of concrete were used?
    b. If each truckload was the same size, what was the volume of each load of concrete to the nearest tenth of a cubic meter?

11. A house with ceilings that are 2.4 m high has 5 rectangular rooms with the following dimensions: 4 m by 5 m; 4 m by 4 m; 6 m by 4 m; 6 m by 6 m; and 6 m by 5.5 m. Which of the following air conditioners will be adequate to cool this house: an 18,000 Btu unit that will cool 280 m³; a 21,000 Btu unit that will cool 340 m³; or a 24,000 Btu unit that will cool 400 m³?

12. A woodshed is 3 m by 2 m by 2 m. If each 1.5 m³ of firewood sells for $25, how much will it cost to completely fill the shed with wood?

13. A catalog describes two types of upright freezers. Type A has a 60 cm by 60 cm by 150 cm storage capacity and costs $339. Type B has a 55 cm by 72 cm by 160 cm storage capacity and costs $379. Which freezer gives you more cubic centimeters for each dollar?

14. A drugstore sells the same brand of talcum powder in two types of cylindrical cans. Can A has a diameter of 5.4 cm, a height of 9 cm, and sells for $1.59. Can B has a diameter of 6.2 cm, a height of 12.4 cm, and sells for $2.99. Which can is the better buy?

15. The Great Pyramid of Egypt has a height of 148 m and a square base with a perimeter of 930 m. The Transamerica Pyramid in San Francisco has a height of 260 m and a square base with a perimeter of 140 m.
    a. How many times greater is the volume of the Great Pyramid than the volume of the Transamerica Pyramid?
    b. The heights (altitudes) of the triangular faces of the Great Pyramid and the Transamerica Pyramid are 188 m and 261 m, respectively. The bases of these triangles are 232.5 m and 35 m, respectively. About how many times greater is the surface area of the four faces of the Great Pyramid than the surface area of the four faces of the Transamerica Pyramid?

16. Swimming pools must be tested daily to determine the pH factor and the chlorine content. Pumps and filters are also necessary, and some pools have heating systems.
    a. What is the depth of a 6 m by 12 m pool to the nearest hundredth of a meter that contains 193 kL of water?
    b. If this pool requires 112 g of chlorine every 2 days, how many kilograms of chlorine should be purchased for a 90-day period?
    c. The Alcoa Solar Heating System for pools has 32 square panels, each 120 cm by 120 cm. Will this heating system fit onto a 5 m by 8 m roof?
    d. Each panel for this system holds 5.68 L of water. What is the total weight of the water in 32 panels to the nearest kilogram?

17. One of the silos pictured here holds corn, and the other holds hay. Chopped corn and hay are blown into the top of the silos through pipes running up from the ground.
    a. The silos have a radius of 3 m and a height of 18 m. What is the volume to the nearest cubic meter of one of these silos? (Use $\pi = 3.14$.)

b. If a blower can load 1 m³ of hay in 3 minutes, how many hours (to the nearest whole number) will it take to fill one of these silos?

18. The spheres shown in the photo were constructed in Charleston, South Carolina, and then towed by tug to Quincy, Massachusetts. Each aluminum sphere for a liquefied natural gas tanker has a diameter of approximately 36.6 m and a weight of 725,750 kg (800 tons).

Spheres for storage of liquified natural gas

a. What is the volume of one sphere?
b. A heavy external coating of insulation on the surface of the sphere enables the sphere to maintain liquefied natural gas at ⁻165° C. How many square meters of insulation are needed for one sphere?

19. This art form is Alex Lieberman's *Argo,* which is at the Walker Art Center in Minneapolis. The entire display weighs about 4535 kg.

a. The cylinder shown in front is 2 m tall and 1 m in diameter. What is its surface area (including the bases) to the nearest hundreth of a square meter?
b. If each square meter of metal in this cylinder weighs 92 kg, what is the weight of the cylinder to the nearest tenth of a kilogram?

Featured Strategies: Making a Drawing and Making a Table

20. An open-top box is to be formed by cutting out squares from the corners of a 50 cm by 30 cm rectangular sheet of material. The height of the box must be a whole number of centimeters. What size squares should be cut out to obtain the box with maximum volume?

  a. Understanding the Problem This diagram shows how the box is to be formed. If 6 cm by 6 cm squares are cut from the corners, the height of the box will be 6 cm. In this case, what will the width and length of the box be?

  b. Devising a Plan One plan for solving this problem is to systematically consider corner squares of increasing size. What is the largest square with whole-number dimensions that can be cut from the corners and still produce a box?

  c. Carrying Out the Plan Complete the following table, and use inductive reasoning to predict the size of the corner squares needed to obtain the box of maximum volume.

Sizes of squares (cm)	Volume of box (cm³)
2 by 2	———
4 by 4	———
6 by 6	———
8 by 8	———
10 by 10	———
12 by 12	———
14 by 14	———

  d. Looking Back The table shows that as the size of the squares at the corners increases, the volume of the box increases for a while and then decreases. Try a few more sizes for the squares, using whole numbers for dimensions, to see if you can obtain a greater volume for the box.

21. Suppose a large cube is built from 1000 small cubes and then painted on all 6 faces. When the large cube is disassembled, how many of the small cubes will be unpainted? Separate the remaining small cubes into groups according to the number of faces painted and compute the number in each group. Generalize this result for an *n* by *n* by *n* cube.

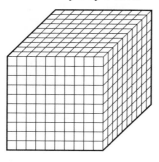

22. A regulation football has a length of approximately 27 cm and a diameter of approximately 16 cm. Describe two different methods of approximating its volume in cubic centimeters.

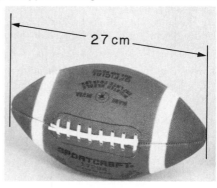
27 cm

23. Assume that a drop of unvaporized gasoline is a sphere with a diameter of 4 mm.

  a. If this drop is divided into 8 smaller drops, each with a diameter of 2 mm, how many times greater is the total surface area of the 8 drops than the surface area of the original drop?

  b. If each drop with a diameter of 2 mm is divided into 8 smaller drops, each with a diameter of 1 mm, how many times greater is the total surface area of the 64 drops than the surface area of the original drop?

  c. If the vaporizing mechanism in a car's engine carries out this splitting process 20 times, how many times is the surface area of the original drop increased?

24. An open-top box is to be formed from a sheet of material 16 in. × 16 in. by cutting out squares with whole-number dimensions from the corners and folding up the edges.

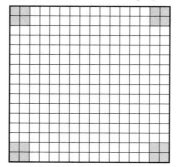

Two such boxes are shown below.

(i) 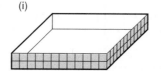   (ii)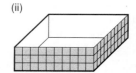

  a. What is the volume of box (i)?
  b. What is the volume of box (ii)?
  c. What are the dimensions and volume of the box having the greatest volume that can be made from the original sheet of material?

25. A cubical block of cement is tossed into a cylindrical tank of water with a diameter of 2 ft, causing the water to rise 1.5 in.
   a. What is the volume of the cube, to the nearest cubic inch?
   b. What is the length of an edge of the cube, to the nearest tenth of an inch?

26. A bank's monthly rental fees for safe deposit boxes with various dimensions are listed below.
   a. Find the volume of each box to the nearest hundredth of a cubic inch. (Suggestion: Change the fractions to decimals.)
   b. What is the cost per cubic inch, to the nearest tenth of a cent, of renting each box?
   c. What happens to the cost per cubic inch as the size of the box increases?

Box size (in.)	Fee
(1) $12\frac{3}{4} \times 4\frac{1}{2} \times 1\frac{1}{2}$	$6.80
(2) $22 \times 4\frac{3}{4} \times 1\frac{1}{2}$	$10.75
(3) $23\frac{3}{4} \times 4\frac{3}{4} \times 2\frac{1}{2}$	$18.40
(4) $21\frac{1}{2} \times 3\frac{5}{8} \times 5$	$23.45
(5) $21\frac{1}{4} \times 5\frac{1}{2} \times 4\frac{3}{4}$	$32.00
(6) $23\frac{3}{4} \times 10 \times 2\frac{3}{4}$	$36.00
(7) $21\frac{1}{4} \times 10\frac{3}{4} \times 3\frac{1}{4}$	$38.60
(8) $21\frac{1}{4} \times 10\frac{1}{2} \times 4\frac{1}{2}$	$50.00

LABORATORY INVESTIGATION

Two students are given rectangular sheets of paper of the same size. The length, l, of the sheet is twice the width, w. By taping together opposite edges of the paper, each forms one of the right cylinders without bases shown at the right.

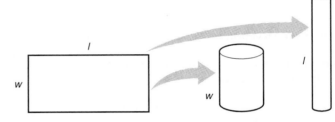

Questions for Investigation
1. Will the two cylinders have the same volume? If not, which will have the greater volume, the cylinder whose height is the width of the sheet or the cylinder whose height is the length of the sheet?
2. Suppose the length of the rectangular sheet is 3 times its width. How will the volumes of the cylinders compare?

PUZZLER

A cylindrical can such as the one shown here is full of water. If you pour the water from the can, how will you know when half the water is gone if you have no measuring device?

CHAPTER REVIEW

   1. Systems of Measurement
   a. Nonstandard units of length, area, and volume provide background for understanding standard units of measure.
   b. The **English system** arose from natural nonstandard units of measure such as the length of a foot. It is used in the United States.
   c. The **metric system** and the **International System of Units** (SI) are based on the meter and are used in almost all countries.
   d. The **precision** of a measurement is to within one-half of the smallest unit of measure used.

e. **Mass** is a measure of a quantity of matter and is not affected by the force of gravity.
f. **Weight** is a measure of the force of gravitational pull on a body.

2. English System
   a. **Units for length: inch** (in.), **foot** (ft), **yard** (yd), and **mile** (mi)
   b. **Units for volume: ounce** (oz), **cup** (c), **pint** (pt), **quart** (qt), and **gallon** (gal)
   c. **Units for weight: ounce** (oz), **pound** (lb), and **ton** (t)
   d. **Temperature** is measured in degrees on the **Fahrenheit scale.**

3. Metric System
   a. The **metric prefixes** are related by powers of 10. (Those with asterisks are the most common.)

kilo*	1000
hecto	100
deca	10
deci	$\frac{1}{10}$
centi*	$\frac{1}{100}$
milli*	$\frac{1}{1000}$

   b. **Units for length: millimeter** (mm), **centimeter** (cm), **meter** (m), and **kilometer** (km)
   c. **Units for volume: milliliter** (mL), **liter** (L), and **kiloliter** (kL).
   d. **Units for weight: milligram** (mg), **gram** (g), and **kilogram** (kg)
   e. **Temperature** is measured in degrees on the **Celsius scale.**

4. Area and Perimeter
   a. The common **English units for area: square inch** (in.²), **square foot** (ft²), **square yard** (yd²), **acre,** and **square mile** (mi²)

   b. The common **metric units for area: square millimeter** (mm²), **square centimeter** (cm²), **square meter** (m²), and **square kilometer** (km²)
   c. **Perimeter** is a measure of the length of the boundary of a region.
   d. **Rectangle:** $A = l \times w$, where l is the length and w is the width of the rectangle.
   e. **Parallelogram:** $A = b \times h$, where b is the length of the base and h is the altitude to the base.
   f. **Triangle:** $A = 1/2 \times bh$, where b is the length of the base and h is the altitude to that base.
   g. **Trapezoid:** $A = 1/2(b + u) \times h$, where b and u are the lengths of the bases and h is the altitude between the bases.
   h. **Circle:** $A = \pi r^2$, where r is the radius of the circle.
   i. The **circumference** C of a circle with diameter d and radius r is $C = \pi d = 2\pi r$.

5. Volume and Surface Area
   a. The common nonliquid **English units for volume: cubic inch** (in.³), **cubic foot** (ft³), and **cubic yard** (yd³)
   b. The common nonliquid **metric units for volume: cubic millimeter** (mm³), **cubic centimeter** (cm³), and **cubic meter** (m³).
   c. **Prism and cylinder:** $V = B \times h$, where B is the area of the base of the prism and h is the altitude.
   d. **Pyramid and cone:** $V = 1/3 \times Bh$, where B is the area of the base and h is the altitude.
   e. **Sphere:** $V = 4/3 \times \pi r^3$, where r is the radius of the sphere.
   f. The **surface area of a prism or pyramid** is the total area of the faces of these polyhedra.
   g. The **surface area of a right cylinder** is $2\pi rh + 2\pi r^2$, where r is the radius of the base and h is the altitude of the cylinder.
   h. The **surface area of a sphere** is $4\pi r^2$, where r is the radius of the sphere.

CHAPTER TEST

(For all questions involving π, approximate π by 3.14.)

1. Indicate the most appropriate metric unit to use in measuring each item.
   a. Weight of a bar of soap
   b. Volume of a bottle of eyedrops
   c. Length of a house
   d. Weight of person
   e. Area of a football field
   f. Volume of a truckload of loam

2. Complete each equality below.
   a. 1 ft = _____ in.   b. 1 yd² = _____ ft²
   c. 3.4 gal = _____ qt   d. 1 qt = _____ oz
   e. 2.5 yd³ = _____ ft³   f. 1 lb = _____ oz

3. Complete each equality below.
   a. 1 g = _____ mg   b. 1 m = _____ cm
   c. 5.2 km = _____ m   d. 2500 mL = _____ L
   e. 1.6 cm² = _____ mm²   f. 1 m³ = _____ cm³

4. Complete each equality below.
   a. 1.6 L of water weighs approximately _____ g
   b. 32° Fahrenheit equals _____ Celsius
   c. 55 cm³ have a volume of _____ mL
   d. 2 dm³ of water weigh _____ kg
   e. 1 km equals approximately _____ mi
   f. 1 kg weighs approximately _____ lb

5. Precision is determined by the smallest unit used for a given measurement. Determine the minimum and maximum measurement for each of the following.
   a. A 5.3 kg bag of dog food
   b. An 85 g tube of toothpaste
   c. A 4.12 oz box of cake mix

6. Find the area of the shaded region below using each of the given units.

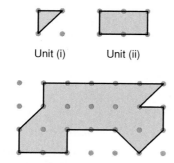

Unit (i)   Unit (ii)

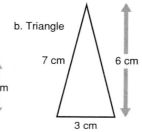

7. Find the area of each figure.

a. Parallelogram

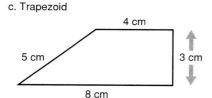

4 cm   3 cm   7 cm

b. Triangle

7 cm   6 cm   3 cm

c. Trapezoid

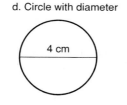

4 cm   5 cm   3 cm   8 cm

d. Circle with diameter

4 cm

8. Edges a and b of a rectangular sheet of paper are taped together to form a cylinder without bases. What is the diameter of the cylinder to the nearest tenth of a centimeter?

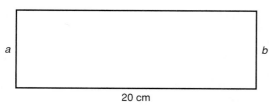

a   b

20 cm

9. Find the area of each shaded region.

a.

15 cm

9 cm

b.

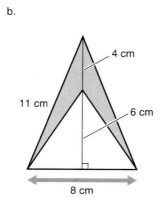

4 cm   11 cm   6 cm   8 cm

10. Find the volume of the figure below using each of the given units.

Unit (i)   Unit (ii)

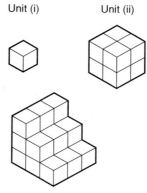

11. Find the volume of each figure if the figures are solid (that is, no missing cubes) and each single cube has a volume of 1 cm³.

a.

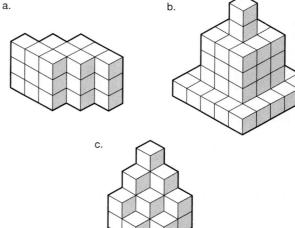

b.

c.

12. Find the volume of each figure.

a. Square pyramid

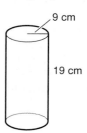

24 cm   14 cm

b. Right cylinder

9 cm   19 cm

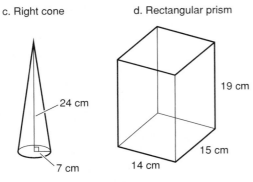

c. Right cone   d. Rectangular prism

24 cm

7 cm

19 cm

15 cm

14 cm

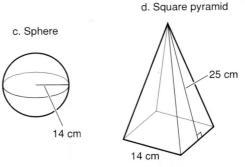

c. Sphere   d. Square pyramid

14 cm

25 cm

14 cm

13. Find the surface area of each figure.

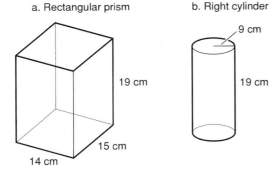

a. Rectangular prism   b. Right cylinder

9 cm

19 cm   19 cm

15 cm

14 cm

14. How many cubic yards of concrete (to the nearest tenth) are needed to make a base for a square patio, if each edge of the square has a length of 11 ft and the cement is poured to a depth of .8 ft?

15. A store sells two types of shelf paper. Type A has dimensions of 5 m by 30 cm and costs $3.70. Type B has dimensions of 4 m by 35 cm and costs $3.50. Which type is the better buy?

16. The cost of a rental car for a two-week, 1600 km trip across northern Spain is $414. The cost does not include gasoline, which is 52 cents per liter. If the car uses 1 L of gasoline per 13 km, what is the total cost for the rental fee plus the gasoline?

BIBLIOGRAPHY

Barson, A., and L. Barson. "Ideas." *Arithmetic Teacher* 35 (May 1988): 20–29.

Battista, M. "Understanding Area and Area Formulas." *Mathematics Teacher* 75 (May 1982): 362–368.

Binswanger, R. "Discovering Perimeter and Area with Logo." *Arithmetic Teacher* 36 (September 1988): 18–24.

Brougher, J. "Discovery Activities with Area and Perimeter." *Arithmetic Teacher* 20 (May 1973): 382–385.

Bruni, J. "Geometry for the Intermediate Grades." *Arithmetic Teacher* 26 (February 1979): 17–19.

Fay, N., and C. Tsairides. "Metric Mall." *Arithmetic Teacher* 37 (September 1989): 6–11.

Harrison, W. B. "How to Make a Million." *Arithmetic Teacher* 33 (September 1985): 46–47.

Harrison, W. R. "What Lies Behind Measurement?" *Arithmetic Teacher* 34 (March 1987): 19–21.

Hart, K. "Which Comes First—Length, Area, or Volume?" *Arithmetic Teacher* 31 (May 1984): 16–18, 26–27.

Hiebert, J. "Units of Measure: Results and Implications from National Assessment." *Arithmetic Teacher* 28 (February 1981): 38–43.

Hiebert, J. "Why Do Some Children Have Trouble Learning Measurement Concepts?" *Arithmetic Teacher* 31 (March 1984): 19–24.

Hildreth, D. J. "The Use of Strategies in Estimating Measurements." *Arithmetic Teacher* 30 (January 1983): 50–54.

Hirstein, J., C. Lamb, and A. Osborne. "Student Misconceptions About Area Measure." *Arithmetic Teacher* 25 (March 1978): 10–16.

Horak, V. M., and W. J. Horak. "Let's Do It: Making Measurement Meaningful." *Arithmetic Teacher* 30 (November 1982): 18–23.

Jamski, W. "So Your Students Know About Area?" *Arithmetic Teacher* 26 (December 1978): 37.

Jensen, R., and D. O'Neil. "Informal Geometry Through Geometric Blocks." *Arithmetic Teacher* 29 (May 1982): 4–8.

Jensen, R., and D. O'Neil. "Meaningful Linear Measurement." *Arithmetic Teacher* 29 (September 1981): 6–12.

Johnson, G. L. "Using a Metric Unit to Help Preservice Teachers Appreciate the Value of Manipulative Materials." *Arithmetic Teacher* 35 (October 1987): 14–20.

Kastner, B. "Number Sense: The Role of Measurement Applications." *Arithmetic Teacher* 36 (February 1989): 40–46.

Kouba, V. L., et al. "Results of the Fourth NAEP Assessment of Mathematics: Measurement, Geometry, Data Interpretation, Attitudes, and Other Topics." *Arithmetic Teacher* 35 (May 1988): 10–16.

Langbort, C. R. "Jar Lids—an Unusual Math Manipulative." *Arithmetic Teacher* 36 (November 1988): 22–25.

Lappan, G., and M. J. Winter. "Sticks and Stones." *Arithmetic Teacher* 29 (March 1982): 38–41.

Leutzinger, L. P., and G. Nelson. "Let's Do It: Meaningful Measurements." *Arithmetic Teacher* 27 (March 1980): 6–11.

Lindquist, M. M. "Implementing the Standards: The Measurement Standard." *Arithmetic Teacher* 37 (October 1989): 22–26.

Malesky, E. M. "Visualization, Estimation, Computation." *Mathematics Teacher* 75 (December 1982): 759–764.

Ott, J. M., D. D. Sommers, and K. Creamer. "But Why Does $C = \pi d$?" *Arithmetic Teacher* 31 (November 1983): 38–40.

Peterson, L. L., and D. R. Camp. "Seven Ways to Find the Area of a Trapezoid." *Mathematics Teacher* 83 (April 1990): 283–286.

Shaw, J. M. "Let's Do It: Student-Made Measuring Tools." *Arithmetic Teacher* 31 (November 1983): 12–15.

Shaw, J. M. "Let's Do It: Exploring Perimeter and Area Using Centimeter Squared Paper." *Arithmetic Teacher* 31 (December 1983): 4–11.

Spitler, G. "The Shear Joy of Area." *Arithmetic Teacher* 29 (April 1982): 36–38.

Szetela, W. "Analogy and Problem Solving: A Tool for Helping Children to Develop a Better Concept of Capacity." *Arithmetic Teacher* 27 (March 1980): 18–22.

Thompson, C., and J. Van de Walle. "Learning About Rulers and Measuring." *Arithmetic Teacher* 32 (April 1985): 8–12.

Vest, F. "Speed of the Earth." *Arithmetic Teacher* 29 (December 1981): 32–33.

Walter, M. "A Common Misconception About Area." *Arithmetic Teacher* 17 (April 1970): 286–289.

Yvon, B. R., J. W. Butzow, and G. W. Marshall. "Training Metric Leaders." *Arithmetic Teacher* 29 (April 1982): 43–47.

Zaslavsky, C. "People Who Live in Round Houses." *Arithmetic Teacher* 37 (September 1989): 18–21.

9 Algebra and Functions

SPOTLIGHT ON TEACHING

Excerpts from NCTM's Standard 9 for Teaching Mathematics in Grades 5–8*

The middle school mathematics curriculum is, in many ways, a bridge between the concrete elementary school curriculum and the more formal mathematics curriculum of the high school. One critical transition is that between arithmetic and algebra. It is thus essential that in grades 5–8, students explore algebraic concepts in an informal way to build a foundation for the subsequent formal study of algebra. Such informal explorations should emphasize physical models, data, graphs, and other mathematical representations rather than facility with formal algebraic manipulation. . . .

The following example illustrates how students can develop a sophisticated understanding of how algebra can be used to model situations and how the algebraic model is related to other models or representations: Working with square tiles, students can explore the question, "Can you add tiles to [the figure below] to make a new figure with a perimeter of 18 units?" (Tiles must touch each other along an entire edge.)

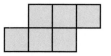

Tile shapes

Students can discover many interesting facts and relationships in exploring this problem. They can discover that adding a tile to fill in a corner where it will touch other tiles along two edges does not change the perimeter at all; that adding a tile that touches another tile along one edge changes the perimeter by exactly two units; and that adding a tile so that it touches three edges actually reduces the perimeter. The students can write algebraic expressions to summarize their discoveries, for example, $p + 2$ or $p - 2$ for adding tiles that touch one or three edges, respectively.

*Reprinted by permission of the National Council of Teachers of Mathematics.

SECTION 9.1 INTRODUCTION TO ALGEBRA

■ PROBLEM OPENER

A whole brick is balanced with 3/4 of a pound and 3/4 of a brick. What is the weight of the whole brick?

"If only he could think in abstract terms."

Algebra is a powerful tool for representing information and solving problems. It originated in Babylonia and Egypt more than 4000 years ago. At first there were no equations, and words were used for variables rather than letters. The Egyptians used words that have been translated as "heap" and "aha" for unknown quantities in their word problems. Here is a problem from the Rhind Papyrus, written by the Egyptian priest Ahmes about 1650 B.C.:

Heap and one-seventh of heap is 19. What is heap?

Today we would use a letter for the unknown quantity and express the given information in an equation.

$$x + \frac{1}{7}x = 19$$

■ HISTORICAL HIGHLIGHT

Germany's Amalie Emmy Noether (1882–1935) is considered to be the greatest woman mathematician of her time. She studied mathematics at the University of Erlangen, where she was one of only two women among nearly a thousand students. In 1907 she received her doctorate in mathematics from the University of Erlangen and eventually was appointed to a lectureship at the University of Göttingen. Noether became the center of an active group of algebraists in Europe, and the mathematics that grew out of her papers and lectures at Göttingen made her one of the pioneers of modern algebra. Her famous papers *The Theory of Ideals in Rings* and *Abstract Construction of Ideal Theory in the Domain of Algebraic Number Fields* are the cornerstones of modern algebra courses now presented to mathematics graduate students.

VARIABLES

variable
placeholder

A letter or symbol that is used to denote an unknown number is called a **variable** or **placeholder.** The letter x in the preceding equation is a variable. One method of introducing variables in elementary schools is with geometric shapes such as $\square$ and $\triangle$. These symbols are less intimidating than letters, and students can replace a variable with a number by writing the numeral inside the geometric shape, like filling in a blank.

To indicate the operations of addition, subtraction, and division with numbers and variables, we use the familiar signs for these operations; for example, $3 + x$, $x - 5$, and $x \div 4$ or $x/4$. A product is indicated by writing a numeral next to a variable. For example, $6x$ represents 6 times x, or 6 times whatever number is used in place of x.

EXAMPLE A

Evaluate the following algebraic expressions for $x = 14$ and $n = 28$.

1. $15 + 3x$ 2. $4n - 6$

3. $\dfrac{n}{7} - 20$ 4. $6x \div 12$

Solution

1. $15 + 3(14) = 15 + 42 = 57$. Notice that when the variable is replaced, parentheses are used; $3(14)$ means 3 times 14.
2. $4(28) - 6 = 112 - 6 = 106$
3. $\dfrac{28}{7} - 20 = 4 - 20 = {}^-16$
4. $6(14) \div 12 = 84 \div 12 = 7$

The concept of variable is often misunderstood, as indicated in the following example, which was taken from a study of 3000 secondary school students in England.*

EXAMPLE B

Students were given the following information and questions. What are the correct answers, and what do you think might have been the most common incorrect answers?

> Cabbages cost 8 pence each and turnips cost 6 pence each. If c stands for the *number* of cabbages bought and t stands for the *number* of turnips bought, what does $8c + 6t$ stand for? What is the total number of vegetables bought?

Solution

The cost of the vegetables is $8c + 6t$, and $c + t$ is the total number of vegetables. 52% of the students thought that $8c + 6t$ meant "8 cabbages and 6 turnips," and 72% wrote 14 for the total number of vegetables.

The number properties are used to simplify algebraic expressions. The *distributive property* is used in the first of the following equations.

$$3x + 5x = (3 + 5)x$$
$$= 8x$$

---

*Dietmar Kuchemann, "Children's Understanding of Numerical Variables," *Mathematics in Schools* 7, no. 4 (September 1978): 23–26.

In the next equations the *identity for multiplication* is first used to replace x by $1x$, and then the *distributive property* is applied to simplify the expression.

$$x + \frac{3}{4}x = 1x + \frac{3}{4}x$$

$$= \left(1 + \frac{3}{4}\right)x$$

$$= 1\frac{3}{4}x$$

EXAMPLE C

Simplify each expression.

1. $13x - 6x$ 2. $9(4x)$ 3. $x + \frac{1}{7}x$

Solution

1. $13x - 6x = (13 - 6)x$ Distributive property
   $= 7x$

2. $9(4x) = [9(4)]x$ Associative property for multiplication
   $= 36x$

3. $x + \frac{1}{7}x = 1x + \frac{1}{7}x$ Identity property for multiplication

   $= \left(1 + \frac{1}{7}\right)x$ Distributive property

   $= 1\frac{1}{7}x$

EQUATIONS

The elementary ideas of algebra can be presented early in school mathematics. Consider the following problem.

EXAMPLE D

Eleanor wins the jackpot in a marble game and doubles her number of marbles. If later she wins 55 more, bringing her total to 127, how many marbles did she have at the beginning?

Solution

One possibility is to work backward from the final total of 127 marbles. Subtracting 55 leaves 72, and so we need to find the number that yields 72 when doubled. This number is 36. A second approach is to work forward to obtain 127 by guessing. A guess of 20 for the original number of marbles will result in $2(20) + 55 = 95$, which is less than 127. Guesses of increasingly larger numbers eventually will lead to a solution of 36 marbles.

Example D says that if some unknown number of marbles is doubled and 55 more are added, the total is 127. This numerical information is stated in the following *equation*.

$$2x + 55 = 127$$

equation An **equation** is a statement of the equality of mathematical expressions; it is a sentence in which the verb is "equals" ($=$). The variable x represents the unknown quantity, which in Example D is the number of marbles.

A *balance scale* is one model for introducing equations in the elementary school. The idea of *balance* is related to the concept of *equality*. A balance scale with its corresponding equation is shown in Figure 9.1. If each chip on the scale has the same weight, the weight on the left side of the scale *equals* (is the same as) the weight on the right side. Similarly, the sum of numbers on the left side of the equation *equals* (is the same as) the number on the right side.

Figure 9.1

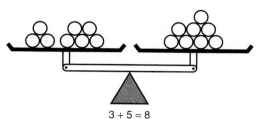

$$3 + 5 = 8$$

The balance scale in Figure 9.2 models the *missing addends* form of addition. The box on the scale may be thought of as *taking the place of*, or *hiding*, the chips needed to balance the scale.

Figure 9.2

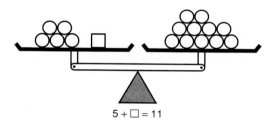

$$5 + \square = 11$$

One approach to determining the number of chips needed to balance the scale is to *guess and check*. Another approach is to notice that by removing 5 chips from both sides of the scale, we obtain the scale shown in Figure 9.3. This scale shows that the box must be replaced by (or is hiding) 6 chips.

Figure 9.3

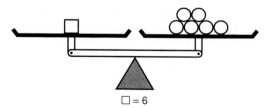

$$\square = 6$$

Similarly, the equation $5 + \square = 11$ can be simplified by subtracting 5 from both sides to obtain $\square = 6$. This simpler equation shows that the variable must be replaced by 6.

SOLVING EQUATIONS

solve an equation
find the solution

To **solve an equation** or **find the solution**(s) means to find all replacements for the variable that make the equation true. The usual approach to solving an equation is to replace it by a simpler equation whose solutions are the same as those of the original equation. Two equations that have exactly the same solution are called **equivalent equations**.

equivalent equations

The *balance scale model* is used in the next two examples to illustrate solving equations. Each step in simplifying the balance scale corresponds to a step in solving the equation.

EXAMPLE E

Solve $3x + 5 = 14$ using the balance scale model and equations. Solving the equations requires the use of several number properties. Step 1 requires the *inverse for addition* and *identity for addition* properties, and step 2 uses the *inverse for multiplication* and *identity for multiplication* properties.

Solution

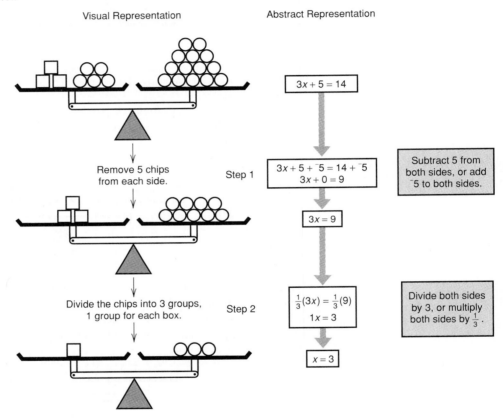

Visual Representation   **Abstract Representation**

$3x + 5 = 14$

Remove 5 chips from each side.   **Step 1**

$3x + 5 + \bar{\,}5 = 14 + \bar{\,}5$
$3x + 0 = 9$

Subtract 5 from both sides, or add $\bar{\,}5$ to both sides.

$3x = 9$

Divide the chips into 3 groups, 1 group for each box.   **Step 2**

$\frac{1}{3}(3x) = \frac{1}{3}(9)$
$1x = 3$

Divide both sides by 3, or multiply both sides by $\frac{1}{3}$.

$x = 3$

Check: If each box on the first balance scale is replaced by 3 chips, the scale will balance with 14 chips on each side. Similarly, if x is replaced by 3 in $3x + 5 = 14$, the equation becomes a true statement.

In the next example the variable occurs on both sides of the equation. The first step is to eliminate the variable from one side of the equation.

EXAMPLE F

Solve $7x + 2 = 3x + 10$ using the balance scale and equations. The *inverse* and *identity number properties for addition and multiplication* are used in steps 1, 2, and 3.

Solution

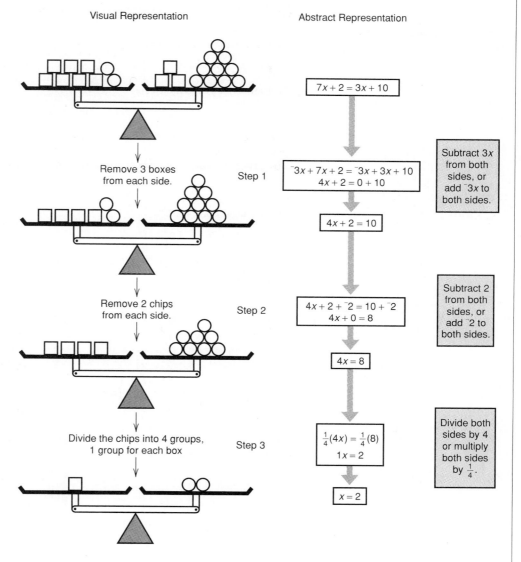

Visual Representation

Abstract Representation

$7x + 2 = 3x + 10$

Remove 3 boxes from each side.   Step 1

$^-3x + 7x + 2 = {}^-3x + 3x + 10$
$4x + 2 = 0 + 10$

Subtract $3x$ from both sides, or add ^-3x to both sides.

$4x + 2 = 10$

Remove 2 chips from each side.   Step 2

$4x + 2 + {}^-2 = 10 + {}^-2$
$4x + 0 = 8$

Subtract 2 from both sides, or add $^-2$ to both sides.

$4x = 8$

Divide the chips into 4 groups, 1 group for each box   Step 3

$\frac{1}{4}(4x) = \frac{1}{4}(8)$
$1x = 2$

Divide both sides by 4 or multiply both sides by $\frac{1}{4}$.

$x = 2$

Check: If each box on the first scale is replaced by 2 chips, the scale will balance with 16 chips on each side. Replacing x by 2 in the equation $7x + 2 = 3x + 10$ makes the equation a true statement and shows that 2 is a solution to this equation.

When the balance scale is used, the same amount must be *put on* or *removed from* each side to maintain a balance. Similarly, with an equation, the *same operation* must be performed on each side to maintain an equality. In other words, *whatever is done to one side of an equation must be done to the other side.* Specifically, several methods can be used to obtain equivalent equations.

1. Add or subtract the same number on both sides.
2. Multiply or divide both sides by the same nonzero number.

3. Replace an expression by an equivalent expression. (The steps in Examples E and F showed how to use several number properties to obtain equivalent expressions.)

The three methods are stated below as the properties of equality.

PROPERTIES OF EQUALITY

Addition (Subtraction) Property

$$a = b \quad \text{if and only if} \quad a + c = b + c$$

Multiplication (Division) Property For $c \neq 0$,

$$a = b \quad \text{if and only if} \quad ac = bc$$

Simplification Any expression can be replaced by an equivalent expression. Doing so usually involves the use of number properties.

EXAMPLE G

Solve these equations.

1. $5x - 9 = 2x + 15$

2. $x + \dfrac{1}{7}x = 19$ (This is the problem posed by the Egyptian priest Ahmes, described on the opening page of this section.)

Solution

1.

$5x - 9 = 2x + 15$	
$^{-}2x + 5x - 9 = {^{-}}2x + 2x + 15$	Addition property of equality
$3x - 9 = 15$	Simplification
$3x - 9 + 9 = 15 + 9$	Addition property of equality
$3x = 24$	Simplification
$\left(\dfrac{1}{3}\right)3x = \left(\dfrac{1}{3}\right)24$	Multiplication property of equality
$x = 8$	Simplification

Check: When x is replaced by 8 in the original equation (or in any of the equivalent equations), the equation is true.

$$5(8) - 9 = 2(8) + 15$$
$$31 = 31$$

2.

$x + \dfrac{1}{7}x = 19$	
$\dfrac{8}{7}x = 19$	Simplification
$\dfrac{7}{8}\left(\dfrac{8}{7}x\right) = \dfrac{7}{8}(19)$	Multiplication property of equality
$x = 16\dfrac{5}{8}$	Simplification

Check: When *x* is replaced by $16\frac{5}{8}$ in the original equation (or any of the equivalent equations), the equation is true.

$$16\frac{5}{8} + \frac{1}{7}\left(16\frac{5}{8}\right) = \frac{133}{8} + \frac{1}{7}\left(\frac{133}{8}\right)$$

$$= \frac{133}{8} + \frac{133}{56}$$

$$= \frac{931}{56} + \frac{133}{56}$$

$$= \frac{1064}{56}$$

$$= 19$$

INEQUALITIES

Not all algebra problems are solved by equations. Consider the following problem.

EXAMPLE H

John has $19 to spend at a carnival. After paying the entrance fee of $3, he finds that each ride costs $2. What are the possibilities for the number of rides he can take?

Solution

This table shows John's total expenses with different numbers of rides. John can take any number of rides from zero to 8 and not spend more than $19.

Number of rides	Expense
0	$3
1	$5
2	$7
3	$9
4	$11
5	$13
6	$15
7	$17
8	$19

Example H says that $3 plus some number of $2 rides must be less than or equal to $19. This numerical information is stated in the following *inequality,* where *x* represents the unknown number of rides:

$$3 + 2x \leq 19$$

inequality

An **inequality** is a statement of the inequality of mathematical expressions; it is a sentence that uses one of the following phrases: "is less than" ($<$), "is less than or equal to" ($\leq$), "is greater than" ($>$), "is greater than or equal to" ($\geq$), or "is not equal to" ($\neq$).

The *balance scale model* is one method of illustrating inequalities. Figure 9.4 illustrates the inequality in Example H. The box can be replaced by any number of chips as long as the beam doesn't tip down on the left side. Some elementary school teachers who use the balance scale model have students tip their arms to imitate the balance scale. Sometimes the teacher places a heavy weight in one of a student's hands and a light weight in the other. This helps students become accustomed to the fact that the amount on the side of the scale that is tipped down is *greater than* the amount on the other side of the scale.

Figure 9.4

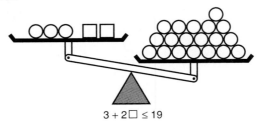

$$3 + 2\square \leq 19$$

One method of finding the number of chips that can be used in place of the box in Figure 9.4 is to think of replacing each box on the scale by the same number of chips, keeping the total number of chips on the left side of the scale less than or equal to 19. Another method is to simplify the scale to determine the possibilities for the number of chips for the box. First, we can remove 3 chips from both sides to obtain the scale setting in Figure 9.5.

Figure 9.5

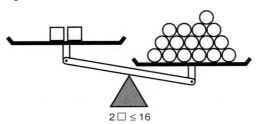

$$2\square \leq 16$$

Next, we can divide the chips on the right side of the scale into two groups, one group for each box on the left side of the scale. The simplified scale in Figure 9.6 shows that replacing the box by 7 or fewer chips will keep the scale tipped down on the right side and that with 8 chips the scale will be balanced.

Figure 9.6

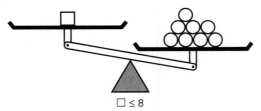

$$\square \leq 8$$

Similarly, the inequality $3 + 2\square \leq 19$ (Figure 9.4) can be simplified by subtracting 3 from both sides and dividing both sides by 2 to obtain $\square \leq 8$. To make this inequality true, we must replace the variable by a number less than or equal to 8.

SOLVING INEQUALITIES

solve an inequality
solutions

equivalent inequalities

To **solve an inequality** means to find all the replacements for the variable that make the inequality true. The replacements that make the inequality true are called **solutions.** Like an equation, an inequality is solved by replacing it by simpler inequalities. Two inequalities that have exactly the same solution are called **equivalent inequalities.** The balance scale model is used in the next example to solve an inequality. Each balance scale has a corresponding inequality.

EXAMPLE 1

Solve $4x + 2 > 14$ using the balance scale model and equivalent inequalities.

Solution

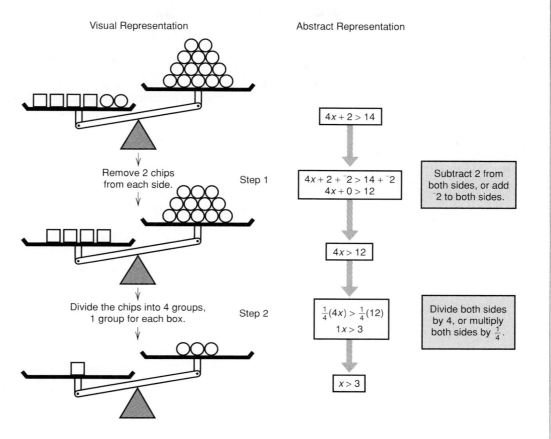

Visual Representation

Abstract Representation

$$4x + 2 > 14$$

Remove 2 chips from each side.   Step 1

$$4x + 2 + {}^-2 > 14 + {}^-2$$
$$4x + 0 > 12$$

Subtract 2 from both sides, or add $^-2$ to both sides.

$$4x > 12$$

Divide the chips into 4 groups, 1 group for each box.   Step 2

$$\tfrac{1}{4}(4x) > \tfrac{1}{4}(12)$$
$$1x > 3$$

Divide both sides by 4, or multiply both sides by $\tfrac{1}{4}$.

$$x > 3$$

Check: If each box on the first balance scale is replaced by more than 3 chips, the scale will stay tipped down on the left. Similarly, if x in the inequality $4x + 2 > 14$ is replaced by any number greater than 3, the inequality is true.

Equivalent inequalities can be obtained using the same steps that were used for obtaining *equivalent equations* (performing the same operation on both sides and replacing an expression by an equivalent expression), with one exception: multiplying or dividing both sides of an inequality by a negative number *reverses the inequality*. For example, $8 > 3$, but if both sides of the inequality are multiplied by $^-1$, we obtain $^-8 < {}^-3$. These inequalities are illustrated in Figure 9.7.

Figure 9.7

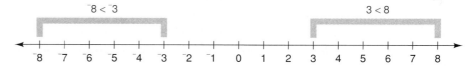

$^-8 < {}^-3$ $3 < 8$

The steps for obtaining equivalent inequalities are listed as properties. (The properties also apply to the inequality *greater than*.)

PROPERTIES OF INEQUALITY

Addition (Subtraction) Property

$$a < b \quad \text{if and only if} \quad a + c < b + c$$

Multiplication (Division) Property

For $c > 0$, $a < b$ if and only if $ac < bc$

For $c < 0$, $a < b$ if and only if $ac > bc$

Simplification Any expression can be replaced by an equivalent expression.

EXAMPLE J

Solve the inequality $4(3x) + 16 < {}^-20$.

Solution

$$4(3x) + 16 < {}^-20$$

$12x + 16 < {}^-20$ Simplification

$(12x + 16) + {}^-16 < {}^-20 + {}^-16$ Addition property for inequality

$12x < {}^-36$ Simplification

$\dfrac{1}{12}(12x) < \dfrac{1}{12}({}^-36)$ Multiplication property for inequality

$x < {}^-3$ Simplification

Check: When there are an infinite number of solutions, as in this example, checking each one is impossible. In this case we can get some indication of whether the inequality was solved correctly by trying a number less than $^-3$ to see if it is a solution. When we replace x in the original inequality by $^-4$, we obtain

$$4[3({}^-4)] + 16 < {}^-20$$
$${}^-48 + 16 < {}^-20$$
$${}^-32 < {}^-20$$

This shows that $^-4$ is a solution. Another common method of checking is to replace x by $^-3$ in the original inequality. Since the properties for obtaining equivalent inequalities are similar to those for obtaining equivalent equations, replacing x by $^-3$ in the original inequality should result in an equality.

$$4[3({}^-3)] + 16 = 4({}^-9) + 16$$
$$= {}^-36 + 16$$
$$= {}^-20$$

These two types of checks together give some assurance that the inequality was solved correctly.

The solutions for an inequality in one variable may be visualized on a number line. The solutions for the inequality in Example J are shown in Figure 9.8. The circle about the point for $^-3$ indicates that this point is not part of the solution. So the solution includes all the points on the half-line extending to the left of the point for $^-3$.

Figure 9.8

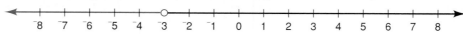

$$^-8 \quad ^-7 \quad ^-6 \quad ^-5 \quad ^-4 \quad ^-3 \quad ^-2 \quad ^-1 \quad 0 \quad 1 \quad 2 \quad 3 \quad 4 \quad 5 \quad 6 \quad 7 \quad 8$$

EXAMPLE K

Solve the inequality $11x - 7 \leq 3x + 23$, and illustrate its solution using a number line.

Solution

$$11x - 7 \leq 3x + 23$$
$$11x - 7 + 7 \leq 3x + 23 + 7 \quad \text{Addition property for inequality}$$
$$11x \leq 3x + 30 \quad \text{Simplification}$$
$$11x - 3x \leq 3x - 3x + 30 \quad \text{Addition property for inequality}$$
$$8x \leq 30 \quad \text{Simplification}$$
$$\frac{1}{8}(8x) \leq \frac{1}{8}(30) \quad \text{Multiplication property for inequality}$$
$$x \leq 3\frac{3}{4} \quad \text{Simplification}$$

Every number less than or equal to $3\frac{3}{4}$ is a solution for the original inequality, and the solution can be shown on a number line as a ray extending to the left whose endpoint is the point for $3\frac{3}{4}$.

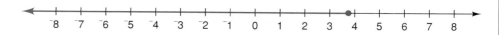

ALGEBRAIC PROOFS

Much of mathematics involves looking for patterns and forming and testing conjectures. This type of mathematics requires *inductive reasoning* (making guesses from observations). Once there appears to be a pattern, or a conjecture is formed, the next step is to use *deductive reasoning* and prove the result. For example, many of the number patterns observed in Section 1.2 can be proven using algebra and the number properties. The following theorem describes a number pattern that we discovered in Chapter 1 using inductive reasoning.

Theorem: The sum of any three consecutive whole numbers is divisible by 3.

Proof: Let x be any whole number. Then $x + 1$ and $x + 2$ are the next two consecutive whole numbers. We must show that $x + (x + 1) + (x + 2)$ is divisible by 3. The commutative and associative properties for addition allow us to rewrite $x + (x + 1) + (x + 2)$ as $3x + 3$. Then, using the distributive property, we can write $3x + 3$ as $3(x + 1)$.

Distributive property

$$x + (x + 1) + (x + 2) = (x + x + x) + (1 + 2) = 3x + 3 = 3(x + 1)$$

Commutative and associative properties for addition

Now $3(x + 1)$ divided by 3 is $x + 1$, and since x is a whole number, $x + 1$ is also a whole number, by the *closure property for addition*. This shows that 3 divides the sum of any three consecutive whole numbers. Furthermore, it shows that the result of dividing such a sum by 3 is the middle number, $x + 1$. For example, $36 + 37 + 38$ divided by 3 is 37.

EXAMPLE L

1. If the sum of three consecutive whole numbers is 261, what are these numbers?
2. If $12,473 + 12,474 + 12,475$ is divided by 3, what is the result?

Solution

1. $261 \div 3 = 87$, so 86, 87, and 88 are the three numbers.
2. By the preceding theorem, the quotient is the middle number, 12,474.

The calendar patterns and relationships that were arrived at by inductive reasoning in #3c of Exercises and Problems 1.2 can now be proven by algebra and deductive reasoning. One of these relationships stated that the sum of any 3 by 3 array from a calendar is 9 times the middle number. For example, the sum of the enclosed numbers on the calendar in Figure 9.9 is $9(11) = 99$.

Figure 9.9

NOVEMBER

1991

Sun	Mon	Tue	Wed	Thu	Fri	Sat
					1	2
3	4	5	6	7	8	9
10	11	12	13	14	15	16
17	18	19	20	21	22	23
24	25	26	27	28	29	30

Theorem: The sum of any 3 by 3 array of dates from a calendar is always 9 times the middle number.

Proof: Figure 9.10 shows an arbitrary 3 by 3 array, with x representing any whole number. The number that is 1 greater than x is $x + 1$, and the number that is 7 greater than x is $x + 7$. (For example, if we let $x = 3$, we obtain the 3 by 3 array of numbers on the calendar in Figure 9.9.)

Figure 9.10

x	$x + 1$	$x + 2$
$x + 7$	$x + 8$	$x + 9$
$x + 14$	$x + 15$	$x + 16$

The commutative and associative properties for addition allow us to write the sum of all the numbers in Figure 9.10 as $9x + 72$, and by the distributive property, $9x + 72$ can be written as $9(x + 8)$:

$$x + (x + 1) + (x + 2) + (x + 7) + (x + 8) + (x + 9) + (x + 14) +$$
$$(x + 15) + (x + 16)$$
$$= 9x + 72$$
$$= 9(x + 8)$$

Since $x + 8$ is the middle number of the 3 by 3 array of numbers in Figure 9.10, the final equation shows that the sum of these numbers is 9 times the middle number of the array.

NUMBER TRICKS   Many simple number tricks and so-called magic formulas can be analyzed by elementary algebra. Select a number and perform the following operations. Add 4 to your number, multiply the result by 6, subtract 9, divide by 3, add 13, divide by 2, and then subtract the number you started with.

If you perform these operations correctly, your final answer will be 9, regardless of the number you started with. This is proven in the following sequence of steps.

Proof: Let N represent an arbitrary real number. The operations described above can be represented algebraically:

Add 4 $\qquad\qquad\qquad N + 4$

Multiply by 6 $\qquad 6(N + 4) = 6N + 24$ Distributive property of multiplication

Subtract 9	$(6N + 24) - 9 = 6N + 15$	Associative property of addition (add $^-9$)
Divide by 3	$\dfrac{6N + 15}{3} = 2N + 5$	Distributive property $\left(\text{multiply by } \dfrac{1}{3}\right)$
Add 13	$(2N + 5) + 13 = 2N + 18$	Associative property of addition
Divide by 2	$\dfrac{2N + 18}{2} = N + 9$	Distributive property $\left(\text{multiply by } \dfrac{1}{2}\right)$
Subtract N	$(N + 9) - N = 9$	Associative and commutative properties of addition

These equations show that it doesn't matter what number N represents. In the final step N is subtracted, and the end result is always 9. Since the number properties we have used hold for all real numbers, N can be a fraction, a decimal, a negative number, or even an irrational number.

PROBLEM-SOLVING APPLICATION

using a variable

Algebra provides a new problem-solving strategy: **using a variable.** Many of the problems in this text that have been solved by *making a drawing, guessing and checking,* and *making an organized list* can now be solved by assigning a variable to the unknown quantity.

■ PROBLEM

Two octogenarians, Eli and Dora, agree to a 12-kilometer race under the following conditions: Eli is to run half the distance and walk half the distance, and Dora is to run half the time and walk the other half of the time. If they both run at 6 kilometers per hour and walk at 3 kilometers per hour, which person will win the race, and what will the winner's time be?

Question 1

Understanding the Problem   First consider Eli, who will run half the distance and walk the other half. The following line segment represents 12 kilometers. Running at a rate of 6 kilometers per hour, Eli will take 1 hour to complete the first half of the race. How long will it take him to walk the second half, and what will his total time be?

1 hour

Start   Finish

Question 2

Devising a Plan   We know the rates at which Dora runs and walks and that the total distance is 12 kilometers. One approach to finding the time she will take to complete the race is to let x represent this time and write an equation. For half of Dora's time, her rate is 6 kilometers per hour. What algebraic expression represents half of Dora's time?

Carrying Out the Plan   Since Dora will run half the time, the number of kilometers she will cover while running is $6(x/2)$, and the number she will cover while walking is $3(x/2)$. The sum of these two distances equals 12 kilometers.

$$6\left(\frac{x}{2}\right) + 3\left(\frac{x}{2}\right) = 12$$

Question 3

The solution to this equation is the time Dora will take to complete the race. Who will win the race, and what will the winning time be?

Question 4

Looking Back   The solution to the preceding equation is $2\frac{2}{3}$. Since Eli requires 3 hours to complete the race, Dora will finish the race 20 minutes ahead of Eli, requiring only $2\frac{2}{3}$ hours. You might have noticed in answering question 1 that Eli spends only 1 of his 3 hours running, which is 1/3 of his time, while Dora spends 1/2 of her time running. Why can't this observation be used to conclude that Dora will win the race?

Answers to Questions 1–4

1. Eli will take 2 hours to walk the last half of the race, for a total of 3 hours to complete the race.

2. $x/2$ represents half of Dora's time.

3.
$$6\left(\frac{x}{2}\right) + 3\left(\frac{x}{2}\right) = 12$$

$$\frac{6x}{2} + \frac{3x}{2} = 12 \qquad \text{Simplification}$$

$$\frac{9x}{2} = 12 \qquad \text{Simplification}$$

$$\frac{2}{9}\left(\frac{9x}{2}\right) = \frac{2}{9}(12) \qquad \text{Multiplication property of equality}$$

$$x = 2\frac{2}{3} \qquad \text{Simplification}$$

So Dora will win the race by finishing in $2\frac{2}{3}$ hours.

4. Since their times are not equal, 1/3 of one time is not necessarily less than 1/2 of another time.

RELATED ACTIVITIES IN

Mathematics for Elementary Teachers: An Activity Approach, 3e

Activity Set 9.1   **Solving Story Problems with Algebra Pieces:** Algebra pieces are used for variables to represent the given information and to find solutions.

Just for Fun   **Algebraic Expression Game:** A game in which two teams match algebraic expressions to word descriptions

---

EXERCISES AND PROBLEMS 9.1

"I tend to agree with you—especially since $6 \cdot 10^{-9}\sqrt{t_c}$ is my lucky number."

1. Given $x = 3$, $y = 1/2$, and $z = {}^{-}7$, evaluate each expression.

   a. $5x - 3y + 15$ **b.** $7(x + z) - 4y$

   c. $\dfrac{x}{y} - 5z + 8$ **d.** $z + 6y - 4x$

2. At the Saturday farmers' market, melons cost \$1.20 each and coconuts cost \$1.45 each. Let m represent the number of melons sold during the day, and let c represent the number of coconuts sold. Write an algebraic expression for each of the following.
   a. The total number of melons and coconuts sold
   b. The cost of all the coconuts sold
   c. The total cost of all the melons and coconuts sold

3. Write the number property that has been used to simplify the expression.

   a. $8(11x) = [(8)(11)]x$ _____

         $= 88x$

   b. $16x - 7x = (16 - 7)x$ _____

         $= 9x$

c. $22x + 3 + {}^-3 = 22x + 0$ _____

$= 22x$ _____

d. $x + \dfrac{1}{5}x = 1x + \dfrac{1}{5}x$ _____

$= \left(1 + \dfrac{1}{5}\right)x$ _____

$= 1\dfrac{1}{5}x$

e. $\dfrac{1}{6}(6x) = \left[\left(\dfrac{1}{6}\right)(6)\right]x$ _____

$= 1x$ _____

$= x$ _____

4. Simplify each expression.

a. $35x + 6x$

b. $\dfrac{{}^-1}{3}\left(\dfrac{x}{5}\right)$

c. $\dfrac{3}{4}x - \dfrac{1}{10}x$

d. $x - \dfrac{1}{3}x$

e. $\dfrac{1}{4}(24x)$

f. $\dfrac{1}{2}\left(\dfrac{x + 6}{2}\right)$

5. In research conducted at the University of Massachusetts, Peter Rosnick found that $37\frac{1}{3}\%$ of a group of 150 engineering students were unable to write the correct equation for the following problem.* Write an equation using variables s and p to represent the following statement: "At this university there are 6 times as many students as professors." Use s for the number of students and p for the number of professors.
a. What is the correct equation?
b. The most common erroneous answer was $6s = p$. Give an explanation for this.

6. The following questions are part of an Algebra I test that was given to 3000 high school students in England to test their knowledge of variables. Perform the operations and answer the questions.
a. Add 4 to $3n$.
b. Multiply $n + 5$ by 4.
c. Which expression represents the largest number: $n + 1$, $n - 3$, $n + 4$, or $n - 7$?
d. (True or false) $2n$ is always greater than $n + 2$.
e. If $e + f = 8$, then $e + f + g =$
f. If $n - 246 = 762$, then $n - 247 =$

7. Determine the number of chips needed to replace each box in order for the scale to balance. Then let x represent the number of chips for each box, and write the corresponding equation that represents each balance scale.

a.

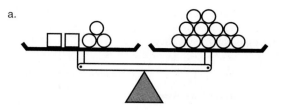

b.

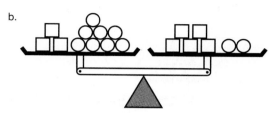

c.

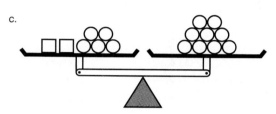

8. Solve each equation.

a. $2x - 18 = 30 + 5x$

b. $\dfrac{3}{4}x - 17 = {}^-2$

c. $3(2x) + 20 = 6(5x - 2)$

d. $8\left(\dfrac{x}{3} - 5\right) = 2x - 6$

9. Each of the following equations has been replaced by a simpler equivalent equation. Write the property of equality that has been used in each step.

a.
$6x - 14 = 2x$
$6x - 14 + 14 = 2x + 14$ Step 1
$6x = 2x + 14$ Step 2

b.
$\dfrac{2}{5}x = 16$

$\dfrac{5}{2}\left(\dfrac{2}{5}x\right) = \dfrac{5}{2}(16)$ Step 1

$x = \dfrac{5}{2}(16)$ Step 2

c.
$6(2x - 5) = 7.3x + 8$
$12x - 30 = 7.3x + 8$ Step 1
$12x - 30 + 30 = 7.3x + 8 + 30$ Step 2
$12x = 7.3x + 38$ Step 3

d.
$11(3x) + 2 = 36$
$33x + 2 = 36$ Step 1
$33x + 2 + {}^-2 = 36 + {}^-2$ Step 2
$33x = 34$ Step 3

---

*Peter Rosnick, "Some Misconceptions Concerning the Concept of a Variable," *Mathematics Teacher* 74, (September 1981): 418–420.

10. Determine the numbers of chips for each box that will keep the scale tipped as shown. Then, using x for a variable, write the corresponding inequality.

a.

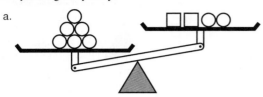

b.

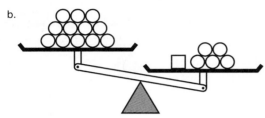

c.

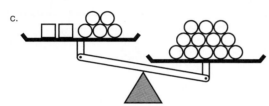

d.

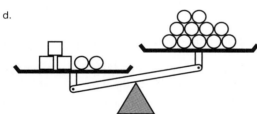

11. Solve each inequality, and illustrate the solution using a number line.

   a. $3x + 5 < x - 4$ b. $3(2x + 7) > 15$

   c. $x + 5 > \dfrac{x}{6}$ d. $3\left(\dfrac{2}{3}x\right) - 6 < 2$

12. Each of the following inequalities has been replaced by a simpler equivalent inequality. Write the property of inequality that has been used in each step.

   a.
   $$3x + 14 < 55$$
   $$3x + 14 + {}^{-}14 < 55 + {}^{-}14 \quad \text{Step 1}$$
   $$3x < 41 \quad \text{Step 2.}$$

   b.
   $$10x < 55$$
   $$\dfrac{1}{10}(10x) < \dfrac{1}{10}(55) \quad \text{Step 1}$$
   $$x < 5\dfrac{1}{2} \quad \text{Step 2}$$

   c.
   $$6x + 11 > 2x - 8$$
   $${}^{-}6x + 6x + 11 > {}^{-}6x + 2x - 8 \quad \text{Step 1}$$
   $$11 > {}^{-}4x - 8 \quad \text{Step 2}$$

   d.
   $${}^{-}3x > x + 15$$
   $$\dfrac{{}^{-}1}{3}({}^{-}3x) < \dfrac{{}^{-}1}{3}(x + 15) \quad \text{Step 1}$$
   $$x < \dfrac{{}^{-}1}{3}(x + 15) \quad \text{Step 2}$$
   $$x < \dfrac{{}^{-}1}{3}x - 5 \quad \text{Step 3}$$

13. It costs Marci 19 cents to mail a postcard and 29 cents to mail a letter. She sent either a postcard or letter to each of 18 people and spent \$4.02. Let x represent the number of postcards she wrote, and write an algebraic expression for each item in parts a through c.
   a. The total cost of the postcards
   b. The number of letters
   c. The total cost of the letters
   d. The sum of the costs in parts a and c is \$4.02. Write and solve an equation to determine the number of postcards Marci mailed.

14. Mr. Dawson purchased some artichokes for 80 cents each and twice as many pineapples for 95 cents each. Altogether he spent \$18.90. Let x represent the number of artichokes, and write an algebraic expression for each item in parts a through c.
   a. The total cost of the artichokes
   b. The number of pineapples
   c. The total cost of the pineapples
   d. The sum of the costs in parts a through c is \$18.90. Write and solve an equation to determine the number of artichokes Mr. Dawson bought.

15. Merle spent \$10.50 for each compact disc and \$8 for each tape. He purchased 3 more tapes than compact discs, and the total amount of money he spent was less than \$120. Let x represent the number of compact discs he purchased, and write an algebraic expression for each item in parts a through c.
   a. The total cost of the compact discs
   b. The number of tapes
   c. The total cost of the tapes
   d. The sum of the costs in parts a through c is less than \$120. Write and solve an inequality to determine the possibilities for the number of compact discs Merle purchased.

16. Sam has 95 cents in change. The coins consist entirely of pennies and nickels, and there are more nickels than pennies. Let x represent the number of nickels, and write an algebraic expression for each item in parts a through c.
   a. The total amount of money in nickels
   b. The total amount of money in pennies
   c. The number of pennies
   d. Write an inequality to indicate that the number of nickels is greater than the number of pennies. Solve the inequality to determine the possibilities for the numbers of nickels.

17. Work each word problem by writing an equation to represent the given information (using x for the unknown) and then solving the equation.

  a. Jeri spends $60 of her paycheck on clothes and then spends half of her remaining money on food. If she has $80 left, what was the amount of her paycheck?

  b. Marcia has 350 ft of fence. After fencing in a square region, she has 110 ft of fence left. What is the length of a side of the square?

18. Work each word problem by writing an equation to represent the given information (using x for the unknown) and then solving the equation.

  a. Rico noticed that if he began with his age, added 24, divided the result by 2, and then subtracted 6, he got his age back. What is his age?

  b. On the day of the field trip, Ms. Sawyer put 1/2 of her students on the bus, 1/5 of her students in the principal's car, and the remaining 9 students in her van. How many students does she have in her class?

19. Work each word problem by writing an inequality (using x for the unknown) and then solving the inequality.

  a. If you add 14 to a certain number, the sum is less than 3 times the number. For what numbers is this true?

  b. Frank and Joni together have a total of 76 seashells, and Joni has more than 3 times as many as Frank. What are the possibilities for the number of seashells Frank has?

20. Work each word problem by writing an inequality (using x for the unknown) and then solving the inequality.

  a. The sum of two consecutive even whole numbers is less than 50. What are the possibilities for this pair of numbers?

  b. The length of the first side of a triangle is a positive integer. The second side is 3 in. longer than the first, and the third side is 3 in. longer than the second. How many such triangles have perimeters of less than 36 in.?

21. Many number tricks can be explained by algebra. Select any number and perform the steps below to see what number you obtain. Add 221 to the number, multiply by 2652, subtract 1326, divide by 663, subtract 870, divide by 4, and subtract the original number. Now let x represent an arbitrary number and use algebra to show that the steps always result in the same number.

22. The distance between oarlocks on a rowboat is called the span of the rowboat. This distance is the basis for computing the proper length of an oar. If the distance between oarlocks is s inches, the length of the oar in feet should be $\dfrac{25(s/2 + 2)}{84}$.

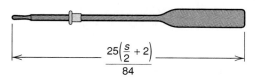

$$\frac{25\left(\dfrac{s}{2} + 2\right)}{84}$$

  a. Determine the proper length of an oar to the nearest tenth of a foot, if the span is 42 inches.

  b. If the length of the oar is 8 ft, determine the proper span of the boat to the nearest inch.

23. Suppose the price of an object is p, the tax is t, and there is a discount d. The discount can be taken first and then the tax computed on the remaining amount, or the tax can be added to the price and then the discount taken.

  a. What is the cost to the customer with each of the preceding methods, if $p = \$24$, $d = 20\%$, and $t = 5\%$?

  b. The cost of using the first method is represented by $(p - dp) + t(p - dp)$. The cost of using the second method is represented by $(p + tp) - d(p + tp)$. Show that these two algebraic expressions are equal.*

Featured Strategy: Using a Variable

24. The teacher asks the class to select a 4 by 4 array of numbers from a 10 by 10 number chart and to use only those numbers for the four-step process described below.

1	2	3	4	5	6	7	8	9	10
11	12	13	14	15	16	17	18	19	20
21	22	23	24	25	26	27	28	29	30
31	32	33	34	35	36	37	38	39	40
41	42	43	44	45	46	47	48	49	50
51	52	53	54	55	56	57	58	59	60
61	62	63	64	65	66	67	68	69	70
71	72	73	74	75	76	77	78	79	80
81	82	83	84	85	86	87	88	89	90
91	92	93	94	95	96	97	98	99	100

1. Circle any number and cross out the remaining numbers in its row and column.

2. Circle another number and cross out the remaining numbers in its row and column.

3. Repeat step 2 until there are 4 circled numbers.

4. Add the 4 circled numbers.

No matter what sum a student comes up with, the teacher will be able to predict the number in the upper left corner of the student's square by subtracting 66 from the sum and dividing the result by 4. Show why this formula works.

  a. **Understanding the Problem** Let's carry out the steps on the 4 by 4 array shown above. The first circled number is 46, and the remaining numbers in its row and column have been crossed out. The next circled number is 38. Continue the four-step process. Does the teacher's formula produce the number in the upper left corner of this 4 by 4 array?

---

*R. M. Knaus and C. G. Knaus, "An Application of an Algebraic Proof," *Mathematics Teacher* 72, (May 1979): 44–45.

b. **Devising a Plan** This problem can be solved by algebra. If we represent the number in the upper left corner by x, the remaining numbers can be represented in terms of x. Complete the next two rows of the 4 by 4 array of algebraic expressions.

$$
\begin{array}{cccc}
x & x+1 & x+2 & x+3 \\
x+10 & x+11 & x+12 & x+13
\end{array}
$$

c. **Carrying out the Plan** Carry out the four-step process on the 4 by 4 array of algebraic expressions you completed in part b. Use the results to show that the teacher's formula works.

d. **Looking Back** One variation on this number trick is to change the size of the array that the student selects. For example, what formula will the teacher use if a 3 by 3 array is selected from the 10 by 10 number chart? (Hint: Use a 3 by 3 algebraic array.) Another variation is to change the number chart. Suppose that a 3 by 3 array is selected from a calendar. What is the formula in this case?

25. Ask a person to write the number of the month of his or her birth and perform the following operations: multiply by 5, add 6, multiply by 4, add 9, multiply by 5, and add the number of the day of birth. When 165 is subtracted from this number, the result is a number that represents the person's month and day of birth. Try it.
Analysis: Let d and m equal the day and month, respectively. The preceding steps are represented by the following algebraic expression. Prove that this expression is equal to $100m + d$.

$$5[4(5m + 6) + 9] + d - 165$$

26. Add the numbers of the day, month, and year you were born; subtract 23 times the day; add 21 times the month; add your age on December 31, 1991. If this result is divisible by 11, you were born on a lucky day.
Analysis: Let d, m, and y equal the day, month, and year of birth, respectively. The preceding steps are represented by the following algebraic expression. Prove that this expression is divisible by 11. In other words, prove that everybody is born on a "lucky day." (Note: $1991 - y$ is your age on December 31, 1991.)

$$(d + m + y) - 23d + 21m + (1991 - y)$$

27. Use the information from the first two balance beams (pictured above on right) to determine the number of nails that are needed to balance 1 cube.*

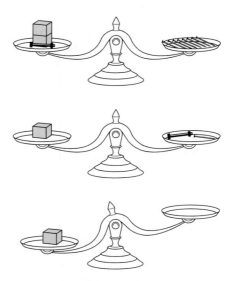

28. Give an algebraic proof of each statement.
   a. The sum of any 3 consecutive dates from a column of a calendar is 3 times the middle number.
   b. The sum of 5 consecutive whole numbers is divisible by 5.

			May			
			1991			
Sun	Mon	Tue	Wed	Thu	Fri	Sat
			1	2	3	4
5	6	7	⑧	9	10	11
12	13	14	⑮	16	17	18
19	20	21	㉒	23	24	25
26	27	28	29	30	31	

29. A class survey found that 25 students watched television on Monday, 20 watched on Tuesday, and 16 watched on Wednesday. Of those who watched TV on only 1 of the days, 11 chose Monday, 7 chose Tuesday, and 6 chose Wednesday. If every student watched on at least 1 of the days and 7 students watched on all 3 days, find the number of students in the class. (Hint: Use the following Venn diagram.)

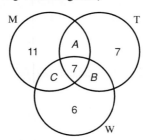

*CALCULATOR
INVESTIGATION*

The digits in the number 2731 have been
written at right 4 times in cyclic order.
That is, in each number the digits are in
the same order if you move from left to
right and then continue again with the
leftmost digit. The sum of the 4 digits in

2731 is 13, and 13 divides 14,443, the
sum of the 4 numbers.

$$
\begin{array}{r}
2731 \\
7312 \\
3127 \\
+\ 1273 \\
\hline
14,443
\end{array}
$$

Questions for Investigation

1. If any four-digit number is written in
cyclic order, will the sum of its digits
divide the sum of the 4 numbers?
2. Investigate this situation for three-digit
and five-digit numbers.
3. If *abcd* represents any four-digit
number, writing each of the 4 numbers
abcd, *bcda*, *cdab*, and *dabc* in
expanded form and computing the sum
will help you to investigate the
situation. What does this show?

PUZZLER

Solve the puzzle at the right, which was
posed by one of America's greatest puzzle
experts, Sam Loyd.*

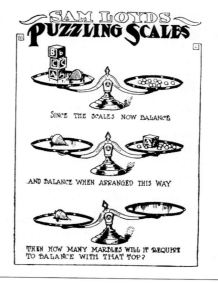

SAM LOYD'S
PUZZLING SCALES

SINCE THE SCALES NOW BALANCE

...AND BALANCE WHEN ARRANGED THIS WAY

THEN HOW MANY MARBLES WILL IT REQUIRE
TO BALANCE WITH THAT TOP?

Mathematical Puzzles of Sam Loyd (New York: Dover Publications, 1959), 101.

SECTION 9.2 FUNCTIONS AND COORDINATE GEOMETRY

■ PROBLEM OPENER

In a guessing game called "What's My Rule," team A makes up a rule, such as "double the number and add 1," and team B tries to guess the rule. To obtain information about the rule, team B selects a number, *x*, and members of team A use their rule on the number to obtain a second number, *y*. Find a rule for the following pairs of numbers.

x	*y*	*x*	*y*	*x*	*y*
1	8	5	26	20	15
2	13	1	2	8	9
8	43	6	37	3	6.5
5	28	12	145	7	8.5
-3	-12	-2	5	12	11

Figure 9.11

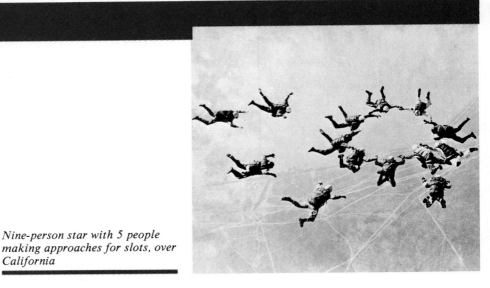

Nine-person star with 5 people making approaches for slots, over California

Two important concepts underlie every branch of mathematics: one is the *set,* and the other, which will be defined in this section, is the *function.*

FUNCTIONS

The distance a skydiver falls is related to the time that elapses during the jump. By the end of the first second, a skydiver has fallen 16 ft, and after 2 seconds, the distance is 62 ft. The distances for the first 30 seconds are shown in the following table.

Distance fallen in free-fall stable-spread position

Seconds	Distance (ft)	Seconds	Distance (ft)
1	16	16	2179
2	62	17	2353
3	138	18	2527
4	242	19	2701
5	366	20	2875
6	504	21	3049
7	652	22	3223
8	808	23	3397
9	971	24	3571
10	1138	25	3745
11	1309	26	3919
12	1483	27	4093
13	1657	28	4267
14	1831	29	4441
15	2005	30	4615

The table in Figure 9.11 matches each time from 1 to 30 seconds with a unique (one and only one) distance. Since the distance fallen depends on time, distance is said to be a *function* of time.

FUNCTION

> A **function** is a rule that relates two sets by assigning each element in the first set to a unique (one and only one) element, called the **image**, in the second set.

domain
range

The two sets for a function have names. The first set is called the **domain**, and the second set is called the **range**. In the skydiving example, the *domain* is the set of whole numbers from 1 to 30, and the *range* is the set of distances. The elements in the domain and range are not always numbers, as shown in the following examples.

EXAMPLE A

Determine the domain and range for each of the following functions.

1. For each triangle there is one and only one area.

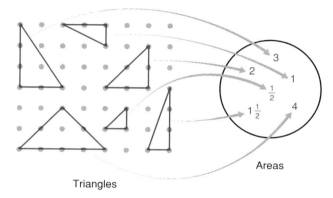

Triangles   Areas

2. For each pair of numbers there is one and only one sum.

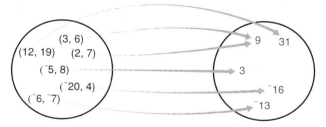

Pairs of numbers   Sums of numbers

3. For each person there is one and only one age.

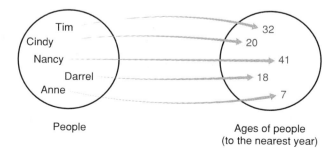

People   Ages of people
                          (to the nearest year)

4. For each polygon there is one and only one perimeter.

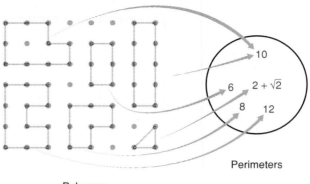

Polygons   Perimeters

5. For every positive integer there is one and only one set of prime factors.

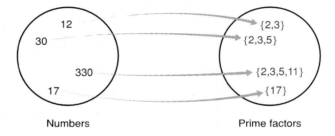

Numbers   Prime factors

Solution

1. Domain: all triangles; range: all positive real numbers
2. Domain: all pairs of real numbers; range: all real numbers
3. Domain: all people; range: whole numbers less than 150
4. Domain: all polygons; range: all positive real numbers
5. Domain: all positive integers; range: all possible sets of prime factors

Not all relationships between sets are functions. Suppose we assign each positive number to its positive and negative square roots (Figure 9.12). Then each number corresponds to two numbers. This violates one of the conditions of the definition of a function, because each number is not assigned to one and only one number.

Figure 9.12

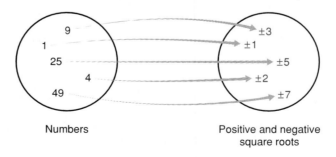

Numbers   Positive and negative
                 square roots

EXAMPLE B

Which of the following are examples of functions?

1. Cats assigned to their heights
2. People assigned to their cars
3. Pencils assigned to their lengths
4. Books assigned to their numbers of pages

Solution

The relationships in 1, 3, and 4 are functions. Each cat has one and only one height, each pencil has one and only one length, and each book has a certain number of pages (that is, one and only one number of pages).
The relationship in 2 is not a function. A person may have more than one car.

A function relating one set of numbers to another can be graphed on a coordinate system. Before considering such graphs, we will discuss the rectangular coordinate system.

RECTANGULAR COORDINATES

There are many types of coordinate systems, each of which is a different method of locating points with respect to some frame of reference. Points on the earth's surface are located by a global coordinate system whose frame of reference is the equator and the zero meridian. Without a frame of reference, the location of a point gives little or no information, as the fellow in Figure 9.13 has just discovered.

Figure 9.13

One frame of reference for points in a plane, such as those on this sheet of paper, is a pair of perpendicular lines called the **x-axis** and the **y-axis.** Every point in the plane, including those on the axes, can be located by an ordered pair of numbers. The first number of the pair (x, y) is called the **x-coordinate** and tells the distance from the *y*-axis. Positive numbers are used for distances to the right of the *y*-axis and negative numbers for distances to the left of the *y*-axis. The second number of the pair (x, y) is called the **y-coordinate** and tells the distance from the *x*-axis. Positive numbers are used above the *x*-axis and negative numbers below. The coordinates of several points are given in Figure 9.14. The intersection of the *x*-axis and the *y*-axis is called the **origin** and has coordinates $(0, 0)$.

x-axis, y-axis

x-coordinate

y-coordinate

origin

Figure 9.14

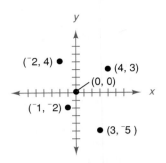

rectangular coordinate system

This method of locating points is called the **rectangular** (or **Cartesian**) **coordinate system.** The name "Cartesian" is in honor of René Descartes, the French mathematician and philosopher who first used this system of coordinates for representing geometric figures.

EXAMPLE C

Graph the line passing through the pair of points whose coordinates are given. Then label one other point on the line and write its coordinates.

1. (3, 5) and (⁻2, 5)
2. (⁻4, 3) and (⁻4, 7)

Solution

1. A line passing through the point (0, 5) and parallel to the x-axis.

2. A line passing through the point (⁻4, 0) and parallel to the y-axis.

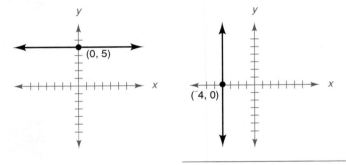

The x-axis and y-axis divide a plane into four regions called quadrants. These are shown in Figure 9.15.

Figure 9.15

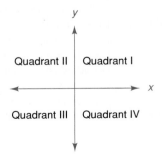

EXAMPLE D

Both the *x*-coordinates and the *y*-coordinates of points in the first quadrant are positive.

1. What can be said about the *x*-coordinates of points in the second and third quadrants?
2. What can be said about the *x*- and *y*-coordinates of points in the third quadrant?

Solution

1. The *x*-coordinates are negative.
2. Both the *x*-coordinates and the *y*-coordinates are negative.

René Descartes

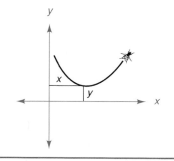

■ **H**ISTORICAL *HIGHLIGHT*

The French mathematician René Descartes (1596–1650) is sometimes referred to as the "father of modern mathematics." Although he made important contributions in the fields of chemistry, physics, physiology, and psychology, he is perhaps best known for his creation of the rectangular coordinate system. Legend has it that the idea of coordinates in geometry came to Descartes while he lay in bed and watched a fly crawling on the ceiling. Noting that each position of the fly could be expressed by two distances from the edges of the ceiling where the walls and ceiling met, Descartes realized that these distances could be related by an equation. That is, each point on a curve has coordinates that are solutions to an equation, and conversely, every two numbers *x* and *y* that are solutions to an equation correspond to a point on a curve. This discovery made it possible to study geometric figures by using equations and algebra. This link between geometry and algebra is one of the greatest mathematical achievements of all times.*

GRAPHS OF FUNCTIONS

In the opening pages of this section we saw several examples of functions: triangles were assigned to their areas, polygons to their perimeters, numbers to prime factors, etc. Consider the function that relates squares and their areas. For each number *x*, which is the length of a side of a square, there corresponds another number x^2, which is the area of the square. In the following ordered pairs of numbers, the first number is from the domain and the second number is from the range.

(1, 1)   (1.5, 2.25)   (2, 4)   (2.5, 6.25)   (3, 9)

The graph of these pairs of numbers is shown in part (a) of Figure 9.16. The length of a side of a square can be any positive real number, so the domain of this function is all positive real numbers. If we choose more numbers from the domain and square these numbers, we find that these ordered pairs lie on the smooth curve shown in part (b). The range of this function is all positive real numbers. For any positive value of *x* from the *x*-axis, the vertical height up to the curve is x^2, as shown in part (c). Since *y* also indicates the vertical distance to points in the coordinate system, $y = x^2$, and this is the equation for the function.

*H. W. Eves, *In Mathematical Circles* (Boston: Prindle, Weber, and Schmidt, 1969), 127–130.

Figure 9.16

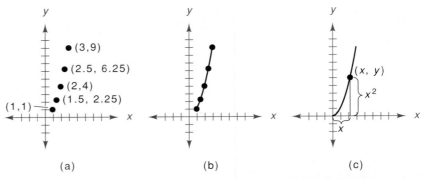

(a)   (b)   (c)

A different function can be obtained by associating the length of each side of a square with its perimeter. That is, each number x, which is the length of a side of a square, corresponds to $4x$, which is the perimeter of the square. The following pairs of numbers from the domain and range of this function have been graphed in Figure 9.17.

(1, 4)   (1.5, 6)   (2, 8)   (2.5, 10)   (3, 12)

Figure 9.17

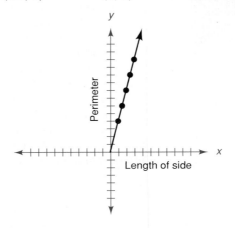

EXAMPLE E

The domain of the function that is graphed in Figure 9.17 is all positive real numbers. That is, any positive real number can be the length of a side of a square. Use this function to answer the following questions.

1. What are the range elements corresponding to the domain elements .5, 1.3, 2.8, and 3.16?
2. What is the range of this function?
3. What is the equation for this function?
4. What is the graph of this function?

Solution

1. (.5, 2), (1.3, 5.2), (2.8, 11.2), (3.16, 12.64)
2. The range is the set of all positive real numbers.
3. $y = 4x$
4. A line

The graph in Figure 9.16 is a curve, and the graph in Figure 9.17 is a line. We will look more closely at functions whose graphs are lines on the following pages. Before doing so, we will discuss the *slopes of lines*.

SLOPES OF LINES

Three lines are shown in Figure 9.18. Each line passes through the origin, and the slope, or steepness, of the lines increases from ℓ to line m to line n.

Figure 9.18

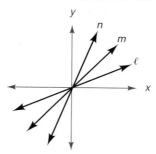

The concept of slope occurs in many applications of mathematics. For example, highway engineers measure the slope, or steepness, of a road by comparing each 100 feet of horizontal distance to the corresponding vertical rise. The Federal Highway Administration recommends a maximum vertical rise of 12 feet for each 100 feet of horizontal distance (see Figure 9.19). Many secondary roads and streets are much steeper. Filbert Street in San Francisco has a vertical rise of approximately 1 foot for each 3 feet of horizontal distance. By comparison, the walls at the ends of the Daytona International Speedway have a vertical rise of 3 feet for each 5 feet of horizontal distance.

Figure 9.19

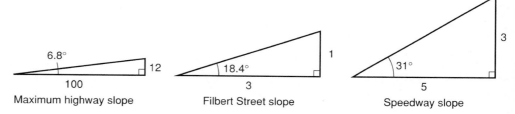

The slope of a line (or line segment) on a rectangular coordinate system is defined in much the same way as the steepness of highways is: two points on the line are selected, and the **slope** of the line containing these points is the difference between the two y-coordinates (the **rise**) divided by the difference between the two x-coordinates (the **run**). Two examples are shown in Figure 9.20. In part (a) the ordered pairs ($^-2$, 2) and (1, 4) are used to compute the slope.

slope

rise

run

$$\text{Rise: } 4 - 2 = 2 \qquad \text{Run: } 1 - {}^-2 = 3 \qquad \text{Slope: } \frac{2}{3}$$

In part (b) the slope is determined from the ordered pairs (2, 9) and (5, 3).

$$\text{Rise: } 3 - 9 = {}^-6 \qquad \text{Run: } 5 - 2 = 3 \qquad \text{Slope: } \frac{{}^-6}{3} = {}^-2$$

Figure 9.20

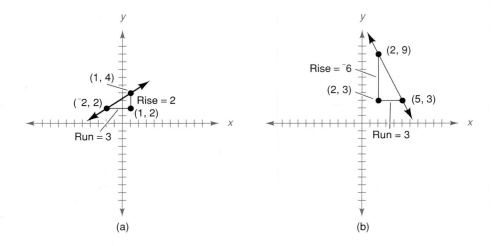

(a)   (b)

EXAMPLE F

Find the run and rise for each pair of points, and determine the slope of the line, if it exists.

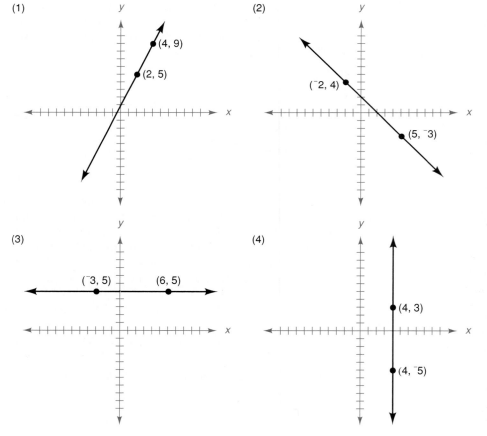

Solution

1. Rise: $9 - 5 = 4$;   run: $4 - 2 = 2$;   slope: $4/2 = 2$
2. Rise: $^-3 - 4 = ^-7$;   run: $5 - ^-2 = 7$;   slope: $^-7/7 = ^-1$
3. Rise: $5 - 5 = 0$;   run: $6 - ^-3 = 9$;   slope: $0/9 = 0$;
4. Rise: $3 - ^-5 = 8$;   run: $4 - 4 = 0$;   slope: undefined

Notice that the line in graph (3) in Example F is parallel to the *x*-axis. All lines that are parallel to the *x*-axis will have a rise of zero and, therefore, a slope of zero. The line in graph (4) in Example F is parallel to the *y*-axis. All lines that are parallel to the *y*-axis will have a run of zero, and since division by zero is undefined, such lines have a slope that is undefined. That is, lines parallel to the *x*-axis *do not have a slope.* Graphs (1) and (2) in Example F show lines with positive and negative slopes. In general, lines that extend from lower left to upper right have a **positive slope,** and lines that extend from upper left to lower right have a **negative slope,** as shown in Figure 9.21.

positive slope
negative slope

Figure 9.21

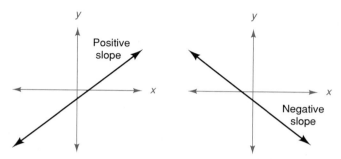

Figure 9.22 shows the rise and run for an arbitrary line $\overleftrightarrow{PQ}$ that is not parallel to the *y*-axis. The slope of such a line is defined below.

Figure 9.22

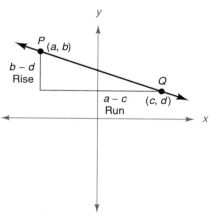

SLOPE OF A LINE

If point P has coordinates (a, b) and point Q has coordinates (c, d) then the slope of the line $\overleftrightarrow{PQ}$ is equal to

$$\frac{b - d}{a - c}, \quad for\ a \neq c$$

LINEAR FUNCTIONS

An observer can estimate the distance to an approaching thunderstorm by counting the seconds between a flash of lightning and the resulting sound of thunder. Every 3 seconds, sound travels approximately 1 kilometer. If you can count up to 6 seconds before hearing the thunder, the storm is approximately 2 kilometers away. In this example, *distance is a function of time.* Here are a few times and their corresponding distances.

$$3 \to 1, \quad 6 \to 2, \quad 9 \to 3, \quad 12 \to 4, \quad 15 \to 5$$

Since each number in the domain is multiplied by 1/3 to obtain the corresponding number for the range, the equation for this function is $y = (1/3)x$, and its graph is the line shown in Figure 9.23.

Figure 9.23

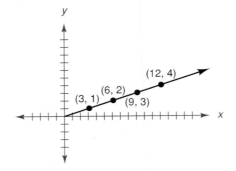

Sound travels faster in water than in air. In water it travels about 1.5 kilometers per second. In 2 seconds it travels 3 kilometers; in 3 seconds it travels 4.5 kilometers; etc. This is another example in which *distance is a function of time*. The graph of this function is a line, and its equation is $y = 1.5x$ (Figure 9.24).

Figure 9.24

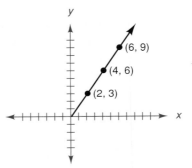

EXAMPLE G

1. Determine the slopes of the lines in Figures 9.23 and 9.24. Which line has the greater slope?
2. Compare the slopes of the lines in Figures 9.23 and 9.24 to the equations of the lines. What do you notice?

Solution

1. The slope of the line in Figure 9.23 is 1/3, and the slope of the line in Figure 9.24 is 3/2, or 1.5. The line in Figure 9.24 has the greater slope.
2. The coefficient of x in each equation is the slope of the graph of the equation.

Both of the preceding equations, $y = (1/3)x$ and $y = 1.5x$, are special cases of the general equation of a line through the origin. For any real number m, the graph of the equation

$$y = mx$$

is a line through the origin with a slope of m.

All lines can be graphed by locating two points on the line. One point on a line whose equation is $y = mx$ is the origin, $(0, 0)$. If we let $x = 1$, a second point is $(1, m)$.

EXAMPLE H

Sketch a rectangular coordinate system and graph the following equations.

1. $y = \dfrac{1}{2}x$ 2. $y = 2x$ 3. $y = 10x$

4. $y = \dfrac{-1}{2}x$ 5. $y = -2x$ 6. $y = -10x$

Solution

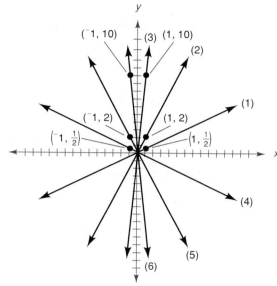

Notice that the greater the positive value of m in the equation $y = mx$, the steeper the slope of the line on the right side of the y-axis, and the smaller the negative value of m, the steeper the slope of the line on the left side of the y-axis.

Next, consider the three lines and their equations in Figure 9.25. Notice that these lines all have a slope of 2 and that this slope can be seen from the equations. Furthermore, the **y-intercept**, the y-coordinate of the point where the line crosses the y-axis, can be seen from the equation. It is zero for the line in part (a), 1 for the line in part (b), and 5 for the line in part (c). The y-intercept also can be easily obtained from these equations by letting $x = 0$.

y-intercept

Figure 9.25

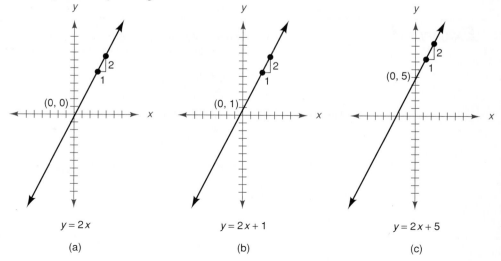

In general, every line (except those parallel to the y-axis) has an equation of the form

$$y = mx + b$$

where m and b are any real numbers; conversely, the graphs of such equations are lines. In this equation m is the slope of the line and b is the y-intercept. When $b = 0$, the equation becomes $y = mx$ and the graph is a line through the origin with a slope of m. If a line is parallel to the y-axis, its equation has the form $x = k$. For example, $x = 6$ is the line passing through $(6, 0)$ and parallel to the y-axis.

EXAMPLE I

Consider the equation $y = 3x + 2$, where x and y are any real numbers. Complete the following table and sketch the graph.

x	0		2		⁻1		⁻3
y		5		11		⁻4	

Solution   (0, 2), (1, 5), (2, 8), (3, 11), (⁻1, ⁻1), (⁻2, ⁻4), (⁻3, ⁻7)

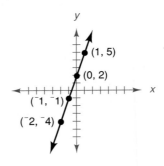

When the equation of a line is written in the form $y = mx + b$, it is said to be in **slope-intercept form**, because the slope, m, of the line and the y-intercept, b, can be read from the equation. When the equation of a line is not in slope-intercept form, it can be rewritten in this form as long as the line is not parallel to the y-axis.

slope-intercept form

EXAMPLE J

Rewrite each equation in slope-intercept form, and determine the slope of the line and the coordinates of the point where the line intersects the x-axis.

1. $y - x = 6$
2. $3x + 4y = 7$

Solution   1. $y - x = 6$
$y - x + x = x + 6$
$y = x + 6$

The slope of the line is 1, and the line intersects the y-axis at (0, 6).

2.
$$3x + 4y = 7$$
$$^-3x + 3x + 4y = ^-3x + 7$$
$$4y = ^-3x + 7$$
$$\frac{1}{4}(4y) = \frac{1}{4}(^-3x + 7)$$
$$y = \frac{^-3}{4}x + \frac{7}{4}$$

The slope of the line is $^-3/4$, and the line intersects the y-axis at $(0, 7/4)$.

linear function

A function is called a **linear function** if and only if its graph is a line that is not parallel to the y-axis. Therefore, all linear functions have equations that can be written in the form $y = mx + b$.

When the slope and the y-intercept of the graph of a linear function are known, the equation can be written immediately. This information is often given in applications. Consider **rates,** such as *miles per hour* or *cost per unit.* These are examples of linear functions. Suppose it costs $8 per hour to rent a lawn mower. It will cost $16 for 2 hours, $24 for 3 hours, etc. If x denotes the number of hours and y the total cost, this information is described by the equation

rates

$$y = 8x$$

Now, if there is an initial fee of $5 in addition to the hourly rate, the equation becomes

$$y = 8x + 5$$

In general, the *rate* is the slope of a line, and the *initial cost* is the y-intercept.

EXAMPLE K

A taxi meter starts at $1.60 and increases at the rate of $1.20 for every minute. Let x represent the number of minutes and y represent the total cost. Write an equation for the total cost as a function of the number of minutes.

Solution

The initial fee is $1.60 and each minute costs $1.20. The total cost in dollars is $y = 1.2x + 1.6$.

EQUATIONS OF LINES   When a function is known to be linear (that is, its graph is a line), we can obtain the equation for the line by using the coordinates of two of its points. Consider the line containing points with coordinates $(^-1, 3)$ and $(2, 9)$. The slope of the line is

$$\frac{9 - 3}{2 - ^-1} = \frac{6}{3} = 2$$

Using an arbitrary point on the line whose coordinates are (x, y), together with the point $(^-1, 3)$, we can express the slope:

$$\frac{y - 3}{x - ^-1}$$

Since the slope of the line is 2,

$$\frac{y - 3}{x - ^-1} = 2$$

Simplifying this equation gives us the equation of the line in slope-intercept form.

$$y - 3 = 2(x - {}^-1)$$
$$y - 3 = 2x + 2$$
$$y = 2x + 5$$

Notice that this equation shows that the slope of the line is 2 and that the y-intercep is 5. The graph of this line is shown in Figure 9.26.

Figure 9.26

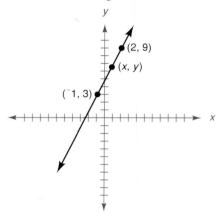

EXAMPLE L

Write the equation of the line containing points whose coordinates are $({}^-4, 7)$ and $(6, {}^-3)$.

Solution   The slope of this line is

$$\frac{{}^-3 - 7}{6 - {}^-4} = \frac{{}^-10}{10} = {}^-1$$

Using an arbitrary point (x, y) and the point $({}^-4, 7)$, we find that the slope is

$$\frac{y - 7}{x - {}^-4} = {}^-1$$

which simplifies to

$$y - 7 = {}^-1(x - {}^-4)$$
$$y - 7 = {}^-x - 4$$
$$y = {}^-x + 3$$

Notice that the equation shows that the slope of this line is $^-1$ and the y-intercept is 3.

EXPONENTIAL FUNCTIONS*

Growth rates of living things are usually graphed as functions of time. If growth can be measured in the early stages of the life of an organ (heart, liver, brain, etc.), organism (plant, animal, insect, etc.), or population (bacteria, animal, insect, etc.), then

lag phase, exponential phase
stationary phase

the growth rate has three phases: the **lag phase,** the **exponential phase,** and the **stationary phase.** These phases are shown on the graph of the growth rate of gourds (Figure 9.27). On this graph the *lag phase* lasts from day 1 to day 4, the *exponential phase*

*This section is optional.

from day 4 to day 12, and the *stationary phase* from day 12 to day 17. Notice that the height of the curve is still increasing in the stationary phase but the growth rate is beginning to slow down.

Figure 9.27

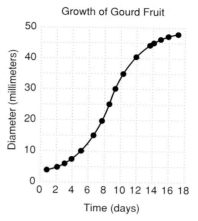

Growth of Gourd Fruit

The production of cells is a function of time. Theoretically, during the exponential phase of growth, 1 cell produces 2 cells, then 4, 8, 16, and so on, in a geometric sequence. The elements of the domain of such a function are *time periods,* and the elements of the range are *numbers of cells.* Here are a few time periods and their corresponding numbers of cells.

$$1 \to 1, \qquad 2 \to 4, \qquad 3 \to 8, \qquad 4 \to 16, \qquad 5 \to 32$$

These pairs of numbers are graphed in Figure 9.28. Since for any positive number x, denoting time, the number of cells is 2^x, the equation for this function is $y = 2^x$.

Figure 9.28

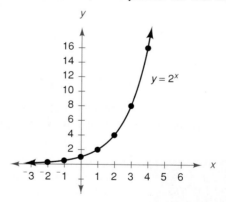

If we let time be negative, as researchers do when they wish to represent time before a fixed time, the graph may be extended to the left of the y-axis (see Figure 9.28). For example, when $x = {}^-3$, $y = 2^{-3} = 1/2^3 = 1/8$. In this case the domain of the function is all real numbers, and the range is all positive real numbers.

EXAMPLE M

Determine the values of y for the equation $y = 2^x$, given the values of x below.

1. $^-1$ 2. $^-2$ 3. $^-4$ 4. 0

Solution

1. $y = 2^{-1} = 1/2^1 = 1/2$
2. $y = 2^{-2} = 1/2^2 = 1/4$
3. $y = 2^{-4} = 1/2^4 = 1/16$
4. $y = 2^0 = 1$

In general, the equation

$$y = k^x$$

exponential function   where k is any positive real number, defines an **exponential function.** The domain of these functions is all real numbers, and the range is all positive real numbers.

EXAMPLE N

Sketch the graph of the function whose equation is $y = 3^x$ by finding the range value that corresponds to each of the following domain values.

$$-2, \quad -1, \quad 0, \quad 1, \quad 2, \quad 3, \quad 4, \quad 5$$

Solution $(-2, 1/9), \ (-1, 1/3), \ (0, 1), \ (1, 3), \ (2, 9), \ (3, 27), \ (4, 81), \ (5, 243)$

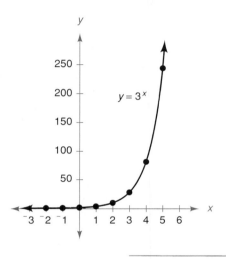

PROBLEM-SOLVING APPLICATION

drawing a graph   The introduction of coordinate geometry and graphing gives us a new problem-solving strategy: **drawing a graph.** This strategy is used in the next problem.

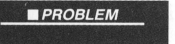

Suppose the average annual cost of heating a home with solar energy is $100, with an initial investment of $8000, and the average annual cost of heating a home with oil is $700, with an initial investment of $2000. Find the number of years before the cost of heating with solar energy will equal the cost of heating with oil.

Question 1   **Understanding the Problem**   Let's look at the total costs for the first few years. In the first year, heating with oil costs $2700 and heating with solar energy costs $8100 (including the initial costs). What is the cost of each system for the first 3 years?

Question 2   **Devising a Plan**   One approach to solving this problem is to write equations for the cost of oil heat and solar heat and graph these equations. The equation for heating with oil is $y = 700x + 2000$, where y is the total cost for the first x years. In terms of the variables x and y, what is the equation for heating with solar energy?

Question 3   **Carrying Out the Plan**   The graphs of the equations for heating with oil and heating with solar energy are shown in the following figure. Use these graphs to determine the number of years before the costs of oil heat and solar heat are equal. What is this cost?

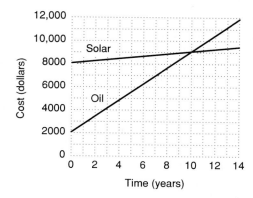

Looking Back   The vertical distances between the cost lines for oil heat and solar heat represent the differences in the costs of these two systems. Use the graph to determine the first year for which the total cost of oil heat will be at least $2000 greater than the total cost of solar heat. What part of the graph represents this difference?

Question 4

Answers to Questions 1–4
1. Solar: $8300; oil: $4100
2. $y = 100x + 8000$
3. In 10 years the total cost of each system is $9000.
4. After the 14th year the cost of oil heat will be at least $2000 greater than the cost of solar heat. This is indicated by the vertical distance between the lines for the two types of heat in year 14.

RELATED ACTIVITIES IN
Mathematics for Elementary Teachers: An Activity Approach, 3e

Activity Set 9.2   **Geometric Patterns and Sequences:** Functions involving whole numbers are obtained by extending geometric patterns of blocks and tile.

Just for Fun   **Coordinate Games:** Two coordinate games on rectangular grids that require the use of rectangular coordinates and areas of plane figures

---

EXERCISES AND PROBLEMS 9.2

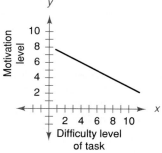

1. Experiments with rats at the University of London tested the conjecture that the motivation level for learning a task is a function of the difficulty of the task.*
   a. What does the graph below show about the level of motivation and the difficulty of the task?
   b. What type of function does this graph represent?

*P. L. Broadhurst, "Emotionality and the Yerkes-Dodson Law," *Journal of Experimental Psychology* 54 (1957): 345–352.

2. Which of the following are examples of functions?
   a. People assigned to their birthdays
   b. Circles assigned to their areas
   c. People assigned to their telephone numbers
   d. Cylinders assigned to their volumes
   e. Hexagons assigned to their perimeters
   f. Pairs of numbers assigned to their products

3. Using the vertices given below, sketch each figure. Find the co-ordinates of the missing vertex. (Note: One of these figures has more than one possible missing vertex.)
   a. Rectangle: $(^-2, 1)$, $(4, 1)$, $(^-2, ^-3)$
   b. Parallelogram: $(^-4, 2)$, $(3, 2)$, $(^-3, 5)$
   c. Square: $(2, ^-1)$, $(4, ^-3)$, $(2, ^-3)$
   d. Rectangle: $(2, 0)$, $(^-4, ^-2)$, $(^-2, ^-4)$

4. List the coordinates for two points on a line that passes through the following quadrants.
   a. Quadrants I, II, and III
   b. Quadrants I and II but not quadrants III or IV
   c. Quadrants I and III but not quadrants II and IV
   d. Quadrants II, III, and IV

5. Consider the function obtained by assigning each radius x of a circle to the area of the circle.
   a. Determine the range value y to the nearest tenth for each of the following domain values, and graph these points. (Copy the coordinate system from the inside cover.)

   $$(1, y), (2, y), (3, y), (4, y), \text{ and } (5, y).$$

   b. Is this function linear?
   c. What is the domain of the function?
   d. What is the range of the function?
   e. What is the equation of the function?

6. Consider the function obtained by assigning the length x of each line segment to half of the length of the line segment.
   a. Determine the range value y for each domain value:

   $$(1, y), (1.5, y), (2, y), (2.5, y), (3, y).$$

   b. Copy the coordinate system from the inside cover and graph the points with the coordinates determined in part a.
   c. What is the equation of this function?
   d. Is this function linear?
   e. What is the domain of the function?
   f. What is the range of the function?

7. Copy the coordinate system from the inside cover and sketch the line containing the points whose coordinates are given. Determine the slope of the line.
   a. $(^-2, ^-6)$ and $(5, 8)$ **b.** $(^-5, ^-2)$ and $(7, ^-2)$
   c. $(^-3, 3)$ and $(8, 8)$ **d.** $(0, 4)$ and $(^-2, 0)$

8. During the past few years Great Britain's pound has been worth between \$1 and \$2 in U.S. currency. Suppose the rate of exchange is \$1.50 for each pound.
   a. What is the cost in dollars of 5 pounds?
   b. What is the cost in pounds of \$25.50?

c. The cost in dollars is a function of the number of pounds. Letting x represent the number of pounds and y the cost in dollars, write the equation for the function and sketch the graph of the function. (Copy the coordinate system from the inside cover.)
   d. Is the function in part c a linear function?

9. Sketch the graph of each equation, where x and y are real numbers. (Copy the coordinate system from the inside cover.)
   a. $y = 3x$ **b.** $y = ^-3x + 8$
   c. $y = 1.2x + 8.4$ **d.** $y = ^-5x$

10. Determine the slope of each line.

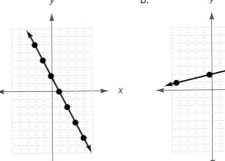

a.   b.

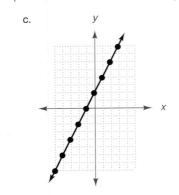

c.

11. The equations of three linear functions and their graphs are shown below.

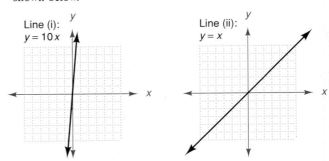

Line (i): $y = 10x$ Line (ii): $y = x$

Line (iii): y

$y = \frac{1}{2}x$

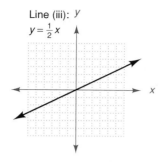

a. What is the slope of each line?
b. On the first coordinate system, can another line be drawn whose slope is greater than that of the given line?
c. Is there any limit to how large the slope of a line can become?
d. On the third coordinate system, can another line be drawn whose slope is less than that of the given line?

12. Determine the slope of the line for each equation below and the coordinates of the point where the line crosses the y-axis.

   a. $y - 3x = 12$ b. $3y - x = 15$
   c. $2x + 3y = 21$ d. $y + 7x - 10 = 0$

13. Write the equation of the line containing the given points.
   a. $(1, 3)$ and $(4, ^-3)$
   b. $(^-1, 12)$ and $(2, 24)$
   c. $(^-8, 2)$ and $(^-8, 6)$

14. Leaky Boat Club charges $1 per hour to rent a canoe. If you are a member of the club, there is no initial fee. Nonmembers who are state residents pay an initial fee of $2, and out-of-state people pay an initial fee of $5. The graphs of these rates are shown below.

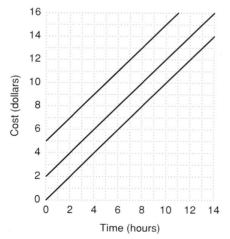

Time (hours)

a. Which line (upper, middle, or lower) represents the cost for state residents who are nonmembers?
b. What is the slope of each line?
c. How much more will it cost an out-of-state resident than a club member to rent a canoe for 8 hours? for 11 hours? Sketch the graphs and indicate the portions of the graph that correspond to these differences. (Copy the coordinate system from the inside cover.)

15. A new push-button phone costs $36 for installation plus $11 each month. Let x be the number of months and y the total cost. Write an equation for the cost of using the phone for x months. What is y when x is 7?

16. A car rental company charges an initial fee of $50 plus 15 cents per mile. Let x be the number of miles and y the total cost. Write an equation for the cost of renting a car to drive x miles. What is y when $x = 860$?

17. A racquetball club charges $15 per month plus $6 for each hour of court time. Let x be the number of hours and y the total cost. Write an equation for the cost per month of playing racquetball for x hours. What is y when $x = 14$?

18. The cost of first-class postage is a function of weight. In 1991 the first ounce cost 29 cents and each additional ounce or fraction thereof cost 23 cents. For example, 1.4 oz cost 52 cents, and 2.7 oz cost 75 cents.
   a. Find the costs for these weights: 3.2 oz, 4.2 oz, and 4.8 oz.
   b. This postal rate applies to letters that weigh less than or equal to 11 oz. Therefore, the domain of this function is all positive numbers less than or equal to 11. There are 11 numbers in the range. List these numbers.
   c. Let x represent weight and y represent cost. Copy the coordinate system from the inside cover and sketch the graph of this function for weights less than or equal to 6 oz.
   d. Is this function linear?

19. Electrical impulses that accompany the beat of the heart are recorded on an electrocardiogram (EKG). The electrocardiograph measures electrical changes in millivolts (1/1000 of a volt). The following graph shows the changes in millivolts (mV) as a function of time for a normal heartbeat.

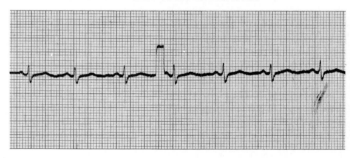

a. How much time is represented on this graph if each small space on the horizontal axis represents .04 second?
b. The tall rectangular part of the graph was caused by a 10 mV signal from the EKG machine. Such a signal is called a calibration pulse. How long did this signal last?
c. This graph shows 7 heartbeats, or pulses. Approximately how much time is there between each pulse (from the end of one pulse to the end of the next pulse)? At this rate how many pulses will there be per minute?

20. Which of the following curves are the graphs of functions? (Hint: Look for values of *x* that may have more than one value of *y*.)

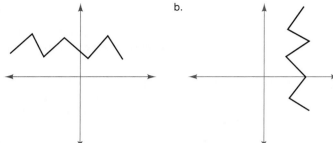

a.   b.

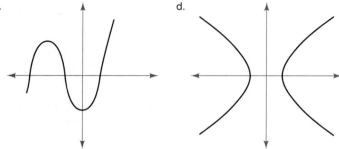

c.   d.

21. Under ideal conditions the size of a colony of *Escherichia coli* bacteria doubles every 20 minutes. A single bacterium will have become a colony of 8 at the end of the first hour. Compute the number of bacteria at the end of hours 2 through 6 and graph the results. Connect these points with a smooth curve. What is the equation of this curve? (Copy coordinate system from inside cover)

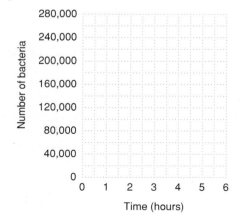

22. Using the coordinate system from the inside cover, graph the following coordinates, where the first number represents time in weeks and the second number represents weight in grams of a corn plant. Connect these points with an S-shaped curve. Mark the approximate locations of the lag, exponential, and stationary phases of this curve. (Copy the coordinate system from the inside cover.)

(1, 10), (2, 30), (3, 50), (4, 90), (5, 140),
(6, 210), (7, 280), (8, 370), (9, 450),
(10, 560), (11, 640), (12, 710), (13, 760),

(14, 800), (15, 840), (16, 860), (17, 880),
(18, 900)

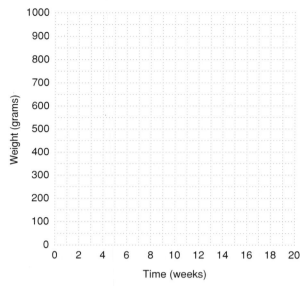

a. For approximately how many weeks was this plant in its exponential growth phase?
b. Approximately how much did its weight increase during the exponential phase?

23. This graph shows population growth in the United States since 1660.

Population Growth in the United States

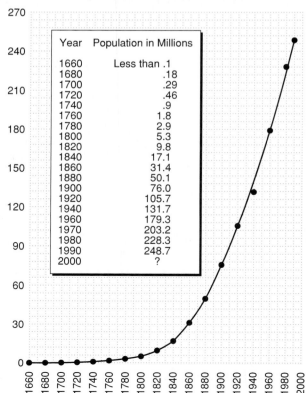

Year	Population in Millions
1660	Less than .1
1680	.18
1700	.29
1720	.46
1740	.9
1760	1.8
1780	2.9
1800	5.3
1820	9.8
1840	17.1
1860	31.4
1880	50.1
1900	76.0
1920	105.7
1940	131.7
1960	179.3
1970	203.2
1980	228.3
1990	248.7
2000	?

a. What was the approximate population in each of the following years: 1930 and 1950?

b. Assuming that the country remains in the exponential phase of the growth curve, predict the approximate population in the year 2000.

Featured Strategy: Drawing a Graph

24. Line segments can be formed on a geoboard by stretching rubber bands between the pegs. Geoboards are usually 5 by 5, but the geoboard shown below is 8 by 8. The line segment on this geoboard has a run of 5 and a rise of 4. Its slope is 4/5. How many line segments with different nonnegative slopes can be formed on this geoboard?

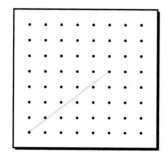

8 by 8 Geoboard

a. Understanding the Problem First notice that it is only necessary to consider the line segments whose left endpoints are at the lower left corner of the geoboard. Why? Explain why we do not want to count line segments that are parallel to the left edge of the geoboard. (Copy the dot grid from the inside cover.)

b. Devising a Plan One approach is to label each point on the geoboard with coordinates. The slope of each line segment can then be determined from the coordinates of its right endpoint. What is the slope of the line on the 4 by 4 geoboard shown below? Explain why it is only necessary to count the points whose coordinates are relatively prime, except for (1, 0).

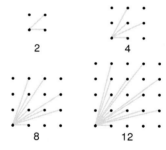

c. Carrying Out the Plan Label the coordinates of each point on the 8 by 8 geoboard, and count the points whose coordinates are relatively prime. The coordinates (1, 0) are not relatively prime. Why? How many line segments with different nonnegative slopes can be formed?

d. Looking Back On any size geoboard, an even number of line segments with different nonnegative slopes can be created. Here are examples of the possible line segments for the first four geoboards. Explain why the number is always even. [Hint: Consider points (a, b) and (b, a).]

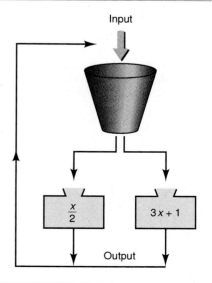

 CALCULATOR INVESTIGATION

The rule for defining a function sometimes involves more than one equation. The function we will investigate has a domain of all positive integers and is defined by the following equations:

$$y = \frac{x}{2} \text{ if } x \text{ is even}$$
$$y = 3x + 1 \text{ if } x \text{ is odd}$$

The diagram of a "function machine" shows how this function is used. First a positive integer, x, is selected as the input and a value, y, is obtained as the output. Each output is then used as the next input, and the process leads to some interesting results.

Questions for Investigation

1. What happens if the input number is a binary number: 1, 2, 4, 8, 16, 32, etc?
2. What happens if the input number is not a binary number?
3. Create your own function to investigate. For example, what results are obtained for the equations $y = x/2$ if x is even and $y = 5x - 1$ if x is odd?

PUZZLER

Diophantus (ca. 250 B.C.) was a great mathematician who brought fame to Alexandria. The brief record we have of his life is related in the following description. His boyhood lasted 1/6 of his life; his beard grew after 1/12 more; he married after 1/7 more; and his son was born 5 years later. The son lived to half his father's age, and the father died 4 years after his son. How many years did Diophantus live?

CHAPTER REVIEW

1. Equations
   a. A letter that is used to denote an unknown number is called a **variable** or **placeholder.**
   b. An equation is a sentence in which the verb is "equals" ($=$). It is a statement of the equality of mathematical expressions. The following are examples of equations: no variables, $17 + 5 = 22$; 1 variable, $15x + 3 = 48$; 2 variables, $y = 6x - 10$.
   c. To **solve an equation** means to find values for the variable that make the equation true.
   d. Two equations that have exactly the same solutions are called **equivalent equations.**
   e. Properties of Equality
      Addition (Subtraction) property:
      $a = b$ if and only if $a + c = b + c$.
      Multiplication (Division) property:
      For $c \neq 0$, $a = b$ if and only if $ac = bc$.
      Simplification: An expression can be replaced by an equivalent expression.

2. Inequalities
   a. An inequality is a sentence that contains $<$, $\leq$, $>$, $\geq$, or $\neq$. It is a statement of the inequality of mathematical expressions. The following are examples of inequalities: no variables, $^-5 < ^-2$; 1 variable, $13x + 5 \geq 28$.
   b. To **solve an inequality** means to find all the values for the variable that make the inequality true.
   c. Two inequalities that have exactly the same solutions are called **equivalent inequalities.**
   d. Properties of Inequality
      Addition (Subtraction) property:
      $a < b$ if and only if $a + c < b + c$.

   Multiplication (Division) property:
   For $c > 0$, $a < b$ if and only if $ac < bc$.
   For $c < 0$, $a < b$ if and only if $ac > bc$.
   Simplification: An expression can be replaced by an equivalent expression

3. Functions
   a. A **function** is a rule that relates each element of a set to a unique element of a second set.
   b. The first set of a function is called the **domain,** and the second set is called the **range.**
   c. A function is a **linear function** if and only if its graph is a line that is not parallel to the y-axis (or, equivalently, if its equation can be written in the form $y = mx + b$, where m and b are real numbers).
   d. A function whose equation is $y = k^x$, where k is any positive real number, is called an **exponential function.**

4. Rectangular Coordinate System
   a. The **rectangular coordinate system** is a method for locating the points on a plane by reference to a pair of perpendicular lines called the x-**axis** and y-**axis.**
   b. The first number in the ordered pair (x, y) is called the x-**coordinate,** and the second number is called the y-**coordinate.**
   c. The **slope** of a line containing points whose coordinates are (a, b) and (c, d) is expressed by $(b - d)/(a - c)$, for $a \neq c$.
   d. Every line that is not parallel to the y-axis has an equation of the form $y = mx + b$. A line that is parallel to the y-axis has an equation of the form $x = k$.
   e. An equation in the form $y = mx + b$ is said to be in **slope-intercept form** because the slope, m, and the y-intercept, b, can be seen from the equation.

CHAPTER TEST

1. Name the number property that has been used to simplify the expression in each step.
   a. $6x + 5x = (6 + 5)x$ Step 1
             $= 11x$
   b. $2\left(\dfrac{1}{2}x\right) = \left[(2)\left(\dfrac{1}{2}\right)\right]x$ Step 1
             $= 1x$ Step 2
             $= x$ Step 3

   c. $7(3x + 5) = 7(3x) + 7(5)$ Step 1
             $= [(7)(3)]x + 7(5)$ Step 2
             $= 21x + 35$
   d. $6x + ^-6x + 15 = 0 + 15$ Step 1
             $= 15$ Step 2

2. Simplify each expression.

   a. $\frac{1}{3}(6x + 30) + 2$

   b. $x - \frac{5}{6}x$

   c. $4\left(\dfrac{14x + 6}{8}\right)$

3. Determine the number of chips needed for each box in order for the scale to stay in the given position.

   a.

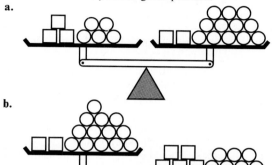

   b.

4. Solve each equation.

   a. $\frac{1}{3}x + 40 = x + 16$

   b. $449 - 34x = \frac{1}{2}(4x + 18)$

5. Solve each inequality.

   a. $7x - 3 < 52 + 2x$ **b.** $6x - 46 > 79 - 4x$

6. Name the property of equality used to obtain the equation in each step from the previous equation.

   a. $\frac{3}{5}x = 2x - 17$

$$\frac{5}{3}\left(\frac{3}{5}x\right) = \frac{5}{3}(2x - 17) \quad \text{Step 1}$$

$$x = \frac{5}{3}(2x - 17) \quad \text{Step 2}$$

   b. $\frac{1}{7}x + 32 = 46x$

$$\frac{1}{7}x + 32 + {}^{-}32 = 46x + {}^{-}32 \quad \text{Step 1}$$

$$\frac{1}{7}x = 46x + {}^{-}32 \quad \text{Step 2}$$

7. Which of the following are examples of functions?

   a. People assigned to their weight

   b. Polygons assigned to their areas

   c. Pets assigned to their owners

   d. Circles assigned to their diameters

8. Consider the function obtained by assigning the diameter x of a circle to its perimeter.

   a. Determine the range values for the following values of x: .1, 1.2, 2.5, and 3. (Use $\pi = 3.14$.)

   b. Graph the coordinates in part a.

   c. What is the equation of this function?

   d. What is the domain of this function?

   e. What is the range of this function?

9. Sketch the graph of each equation.

   a. $y = 6x - 2$ **b.** $3x - 5y = 10$

10. Determine the slope of each line.

   a.

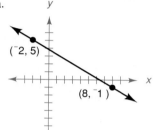

   b.

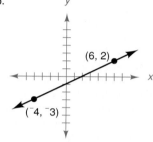

11. Write the equation of the line through the points $(1, {}^{-}7)$ and $(2, 8)$ in slope-intercept form.

12. Determine the slope of the line defined by each equation below and the coordinates of the point where the line crosses the y-axis.

   a. $3y - x = 15$ **b.** $8x + 2y - 22 = 0$

13. A travel company charges \$120 for insurance and \$55 a day to rent a trailer. Let x represent the number of days and y the total cost of renting a trailer.

   a. Write an equation for the cost as a function of time.

   b. What is the slope of the graph of this function?

14. Sketch the graph of $y = 4^x$ for x between $^{-}2$ and 2. What is the name of the function defined by this equation?

15. An electrician normally charges \$15 per hour, but on holidays the charge is \$24 per hour. During a certain period the electrician worked 60 hours and received \$1062. Let x represent the number of holiday hours worked and write an algebraic expression for the items in parts a through c.

   a. The total amount of money received for the holiday hours worked

   b. The number of hours worked on nonholidays

   c. The total amount of money received for working on non-holidays

   d. How many holiday hours did the electrician work?

BIBLIOGRAPHY

Battista, M. T. "Distortions: An Activity for Practice and Exploration." *Arithmetic Teacher* 29 (January 1982): 34–36.

Beard, E. M. L., and A. R. Polis. "Subtraction Facts with Pattern Explorations." *Arithmetic Teacher* 29 (December 1981): 13–14.

Bennett, A. B., Jr. "Visual Thinking and Number Relationships." *Mathematics Teacher* 81 (April 1988): 267–272.

Brieske, T. "Functions, Mappings, and Mapping Diagrams." *Mathematics Teacher* 66 (May 1973): 463–468.

Cetorelli, N. "Teaching Function, Notation." *Mathematics Teacher* 72 (November 1979): 590–591.

Day, R. P. "Helping Students Create Magic Arrays." *Arithmetic Teacher* 36 (November 1988): 46–47.

Graham, K. G., and J. Ferrini-Mundy. "Functions and Their Representations." *Mathematics Teacher* 83 (March 1990): 209–216.

Gustafson, D. A. T. "Skiing the Slopes." *Mathematics Teacher* 80 (December 1987): 733–739.

Hiatt, A. A. "Discovering Mathematics." *Mathematics Teacher* 80 (September 1987): 476–478.

Howden, H. "Implementing the Standards: Patterns, Relationships, and Functions." *Arithmetic Teacher* 37 (November 1989): 18–24.

Johnson, M. L. "Identifying and Teaching Mathematically Gifted Elementary School Children." *Arithmetic Teacher* 30 (January 1983): 25–26, 55–56.

Johnston, A. "Introducing Function and Its Notation." *Mathematics Teacher* 80 (October 1987): 558–564.

Kieren, T. E., and A. T. Olson. "Imagination, Intuition, and Computing in School Algebra." *Mathematics Teacher* 82 (January 1989): 14–17.

Metz, J. R. "Slope as Speed." *Mathematics Teacher* 81 (April 1988): 285–289.

O'Daffer, P. G. "Strategy Spotlight—Write an Equation." *Arithmetic Teacher* 32 (May 1985): 14–15.

Padberg, F. F. "Using Calculators to Discover Simple Theorems—An Example from Number Theory." *Arithmetic Teacher* 28 (April 1981): 21–23.

Papy, F. *Graphs and the Child.* New Rochelle, NY: Cuisenaire Company of America, Inc., 1970.

Papy, F. *Mathematics and the Child.* New Rochelle, NY: Cuisenaire Company of America, Inc., 1971.

Pereira-Mendoza, L. "Graphing and Prediction in the Elementary School." *Arithmetic Teacher* 24 (February 1977): 112–113.

Reys, R. E. "Functioning with a Sticky Model." *Arithmetic Teacher* 29 (September 1981): 18–23.

Robitaille, D. F. "An Investigation of Some Numerical Properties." *Arithmetic Teacher* 29 (May 1982): 13–15.

Smith, L. "Mathematics on the Balance Beam." *School Science and Mathematics* 85 (October 1985): 494–497.

Smith, R. F. "Let's Do It: Coordinate Geometry for Third Graders." *Arithmetic Teacher* 33 (April 1986): 6–11.

Snover, S. L. "Five-Cycle Number Patterns." *Arithmetic Teacher* 29 (March 1982): 22–26.

Terc, M. "Coordinate Geometry—Art and Mathematics." *Arithmetic Teacher* 33 (October 1985): 22–24.

Tredway, D. "Out of Balance." *Arithmetic Teacher* 24 (January 1977): 14–16.

Usiskin, Z. "Why Elementary Algebra Can, Should, and Must Be an Eighth-Grade Course for Average Students." *Mathematics Teacher* 80 (September 1987): 428–438.

Van de Walle, J., and C. S. Thompson. "Let's Do It: A Poster-Board Balance Helps Write Equations." *Arithmetic Teacher* 28 (May 1981): 4–8.

Vissa, J. M. "Coordinate Graphing: Shaping a Sticky Situation." *Arithmetic Teacher* 35 (November 1987): 6–10.

Williams, D. E. "Activities for Algebra." *Arithmetic Teacher* 33 (February 1986): 42–47.

CHAPTER 10 **Geometric Mapping**

SPOTLIGHT ON TEACHING

Excerpts from NCTM's Standard 12 for Teaching Mathematics in Grades 5–8*

Students discover relationships and develop spatial sense by constructing, drawing, measuring, visualizing, comparing, transforming, and classifying geometric figures. Discussing ideas, conjecturing, and testing hypotheses precede the development of more formal summary statements. . . .

Measuring and comparing the sides and angles of similar polygons help students develop and understand the mathematical concept of similar figures. The relationship between the angles and the sides of similar triangles is the foundation of trigonometry. Similarity also can be related to such real-world contexts as photographs, models, projections of pictures, and photocopy machines. Students should explore the relationships among the lengths, areas, and volumes of similar solids. Most students in grades 5–8 incorrectly believe that if the sides of a figure are doubled to produce a similar figure, the area and volume also will be doubled. [See the figure below.]

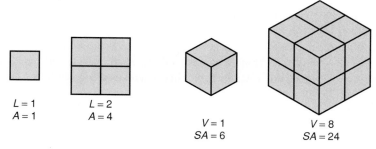

$L = 1$
$A = 1$

$L = 2$
$A = 4$

$V = 1$
$SA = 6$

$V = 8$
$SA = 24$

Area and volume

Investigations of two- and three-dimensional models fosters an understanding of the different growth rates for linear measures, areas, and volumes of similar figures. These ideas are fundamental to measurement and critical to scientific applications.

*Reprinted by permission of the National Council of Teachers of Mathematics.

SECTION 10.1 CONGRUENCE AND CONSTRUCTIONS

■ *PROBLEM OPENER*

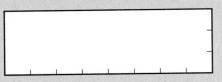

Cut a 3 by 8 rectangle into two congruent parts and form a 2 by 12 rectangle.

"We're here to fix the copier."

congruent

There is an old belief that everyone has a "double"—someone who looks exactly like him or her—somewhere in the world. Two dimensional and three dimensional objects often do look exactly alike. Copy machines are able to make reproductions of two-dimensional figures that have the same *size* and *shape* as the originals. The reproductions are said to be *congruent* to the original figures. Intuitively, we think of two plane figures as **congruent** if one can be moved onto the other so that they coincide. The idea of motion or movement is an important concept in mathematics and will be explored in this chapter.

MAPPINGS

If triangle *ABC* in Figure 10.1 is traced on paper and flipped over, it can be placed on triangle *RST* so that the points of each triangle coincide. The correspondence of point *A* with *R*, *B* with *S*, and *C* with *T* is indicated by

$$A \leftrightarrow R \qquad B \leftrightarrow S \qquad C \leftrightarrow T$$

corresponding vertices

Figure 10.1

We say that *A* corresponds to *R*, *B* corresponds to *S*, and *C* corresponds to *T*. These pairs of vertices are called **corresponding vertices.**

image

mappings

If triangle *ABC* is placed onto triangle *RST*, each point on the first triangle corresponds to exactly one point on the second triangle. This one-to-one correspondence of points is a special type of *function*. In Section 9.2 we discussed functions that assign numbers to numbers. In geometry there are functions that assign points to points, such that to each point in one set there corresponds a unique point, called the **image,** in a second set. Such functions are called **mappings.** In the mapping of △*ABC* to △*RST* in Figure 10.1, the following sides and angles are matched with each other.

Corresponding Sides	Corresponding Angles
$\overline{AB} \leftrightarrow \overline{RS}$	$\angle B \leftrightarrow \angle S$
$\overline{BC} \leftrightarrow \overline{ST}$	$\angle C \leftrightarrow \angle T$
$\overline{AC} \leftrightarrow \overline{RT}$	$\angle A \leftrightarrow \angle R$

corresponding sides
corresponding angles

Such pairs of sides and angles are called **corresponding sides** and **corresponding angles;** these concepts are used in the following definition.

CONGRUENT POLYGONS

> Two polygons are **congruent** if and only if there is a mapping from one to the other such that
>
> 1. corresponding sides are congruent;
> 2. corresponding angles are congruent.

In Figure 10.1, triangle *ABC* and triangle *RST* are congruent because their corresponding sides and angles are congruent. This congruence is indicated by writing $\triangle ABC \cong \triangle RST$.

EXAMPLE A

The following triangles are congruent. Complete the congruence statement $\triangle$ _____ $\cong \triangle$ _____ and list the pairs of corresponding vertices, sides, and angles.

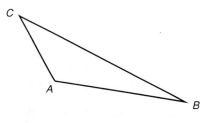
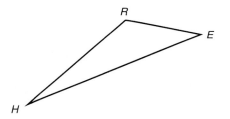

Solution $\triangle ABC \cong \triangle RHE$

Corresponding vertices: $A \leftrightarrow R, B \leftrightarrow H, C \leftrightarrow E$

Corresponding sides: $\overline{AB} \leftrightarrow \overline{RH}, \overline{BC} \leftrightarrow \overline{HE}, \overline{CA} \leftrightarrow \overline{ER}$

Corresponding angles: $\angle A \leftrightarrow \angle R, \angle B \leftrightarrow \angle H, \angle C \leftrightarrow \angle E$

Notice that the order of the letters in the statement of congruence in Example A,

indicates which pairs of vertices, sides, and angles correspond.

To determine if *two* polygons are congruent, we set up a correspondence between their vertices and check to see if their corresponding sides and corresponding angles are congruent. To construct a figure that is congruent to a given figure, we construct corresponding sides and corresponding angles that are congruent to those given. This section introduces techniques for constructing congruent figures.

CONSTRUCTING SEGMENTS AND ANGLES

construction
straightedge

A geometric figure that is produced with a straightedge and compass is called a **construction**. A **straightedge** is used in drawing lines; unlike a ruler, it has no markings. The compass, introduced in Section 7.2, is used in constructing circles and regular polygons. A compass opening of length r can be used to draw a circle of radius r (Figure 10.2).

Figure 10.2

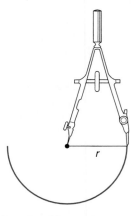

To carry out the constructions in this section you will need a straightedge (or a ruler) and a compass. Try each construction on your own before reading the steps that are given. Attempting each construction will help you to think about the steps that are given, and you may discover a method of your own.

congruent line segments

CONSTRUCTING SEGMENTS   Two **line segments** are **congruent** if they have the same length. For example, if $\overline{AB}$ and $\overline{CD}$ have the same length, then $\overline{AB}$ is congruent to $\overline{CD}$, and we write $\overline{AB} \cong \overline{CD}$. The common method of obtaining a line segment that is congruent to a given segment is to measure the given segment with a ruler and then mark off this length on a line. The following example shows how congruent segments can be constructed using a straightedge and compass.

---

*E*XAMPLE *B*

Construct a line segment that is congruent to segment $\overline{AB}$.

Original segment

Solution   **Step 1** Use a straightedge to draw a line segment that is longer than $\overline{AB}$; label point C.

Step 2 Open the compass to span $\overline{AB}$. Place one end of the compass at point C and mark point D. Then $\overline{AB} \cong \overline{CD}$.

If $\overline{AB}$ in Example B is longer than the opening of the compass, intermediate points can be marked off on $\overline{AB}$. Two such intermediate points are shown in Figure 10.3. The parts of $\overline{AB}$ can then be transferred to the new line using the compass, as in Example B.

Figure 10.3

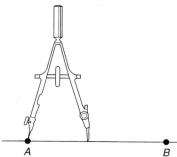

A   B

congruent angles   **CONSTRUCTING ANGLES**   Two **angles** are **congruent** if they have the same measure. For example, if $\angle ABC$ and $\angle DEF$ have the same measure, then $\angle ABC$ is congruent to $\angle DEF$, and we write $\angle ABC \cong \angle DEF$. In Section 7.2 we constructed angles of a given number of degrees by measuring the angles with a protractor. Angles can also be reproduced by using a straightedge and compass.

EXAMPLE C

Construct an angle that is congruent to angle B.

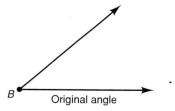

B
Original angle

Solution   **Step 1** Use a straightedge to draw a line segment and label point S.

S

Step 2 Place the end of the compass at point B of the original angle and draw an arc. Label points A and C on the sides of the angle, as shown.

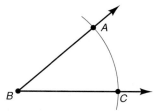

Step 3 Using the same compass opening, place the compass at S on the new line and draw an arc. Label point T as shown.

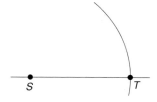

S   T

Step 4 Place the compass at point C of the original angle and adjust the opening to produce an arc through point A.

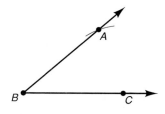

Step 5 Using the same opening, place the compass at point *T* on the new line and draw an arc to locate point *R*.

Step 6 Use a straightedge to connect point *R* to point *S*. Then ∡*ABC* ≅ ∡*RST*.

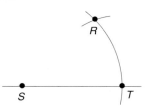

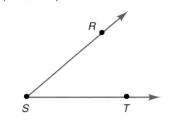

CONSTRUCTING TRIANGLES

Figure 10.4 shows two congruent triangles: △*ABC* ≅ △*DEF*.

Figure 10.4

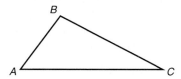
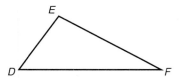

The congruence of the triangles implies a correspondence *A* ↔ *D*, *B* ↔ *E*, and *C* ↔ *F*, such that the corresponding sides and corresponding angles of the triangles are congruent. However, in order to construct a triangle that is congruent to a given triangle, it is not necessary to construct three congruent sides and three congruent angles separately. The following example shows that it is only necessary to construct three congruent sides. The sides of △*ABC* are used in this example.

Example D

Construct a triangle whose sides are congruent to the three line segments given:

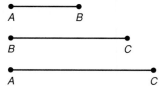

Solution   **Step 1** Use a straightedge and compass to construct *DF*, which is congruent to *AC*.

Step 2 Place the ends of the compass on points *A* and *B* of *AB*. Then place one end of the compass at point *D* and draw an arc. All the points on this arc are a distance of *AB* from point *D*.

Step 3 Place the ends of the compass on points *B* and *C* of $\overline{BC}$. Then place one end of the compass on *F* and draw an arc. The intersection of the two arcs is the third vertex point, *E*.

Step 4 Draw segments $\overline{DE}$ and $\overline{EF}$ to form $\triangle DEF$.

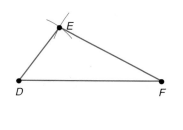

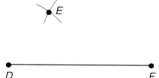

The construction in Example D could have been varied in several ways. For example, we could have begun in step 1 by constructing a segment congruent to either $\overline{AB}$ or $\overline{BC}$. Or in step 2 we could have constructed an arc whose points were a distance of *BC* from point *D*. However, these variations will all result in a triangle that is congruent to $\triangle DEF$. The following *congruence property of triangles* states that constructing a triangle with three sides that are congruent to three sides of another triangle results in two congruent triangles.

SIDE-SIDE-SIDE (SSS)

> If three sides of one triangle are congruent to three sides of another triangle, the two triangles are congruent.

EXAMPLE E

Use the SSS congruence property to show that the following pairs of triangles are congruent. (Note: Small slash marks are used to denote congruent segments on geometric figures. For example, in figure (1) below, $\overline{AD} \cong \overline{BC}$ and $\overline{AB} \cong \overline{DC}$.)

(1)

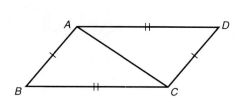

(2)

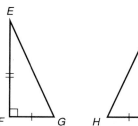

Solution

1. The two triangles are congruent, because the third side of both triangles, $\overline{AC}$, is congruent to itself.
2. Since the legs of the right triangles are congruent ($\overline{EF} \cong \overline{JI}$ and $\overline{FG} \cong \overline{IH}$), the Pythagorean theorem guarantees that hypotenuse $\overline{EG}$ is congruent to hypotenuse $\overline{JH}$.

The fact that three line segments determine the *shape and size* of a triangle is of major importance in the construction of a wide range of objects, from bridges and buildings to playground equipment and furniture. Because of this fact, triangular-shaped supports are more rigid than supports having other polygonal shapes. This can be illustrated by linkages such as those shown in Figure 10.5. The shapes of all these polygons can be changed, except for that of the triangle. For example, the pentagon can be made nonconvex by pushing one of its vertex points into the interior of the polygon, or the hexagon can be reshaped into a convex hexagon. The triangle is the only linkage whose shape cannot be changed.

Figure 10.5

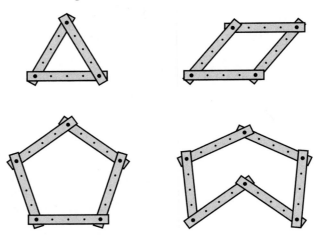

Notice the steel frame made up of triangles that is being lifted into place by the crane in the following photo. What other triangles can you see in this photo?

Figure 10.6
Construction of Lundolm Field House, University of New Hampshire

Example D *should not* lead you to conclude that it is possible to construct a triangle whose sides are congruent to any three given line segments. Consider using the line segments in part (a) of Figure 10.7. First, set the compass opening by placing it on points *C* and *D*, and then draw an arc with center *A*, as shown in part (b). Next, set the compass opening by placing it on points *E* and *F*, and then draw an arc with center *B*. Since the arcs do not intersect, a triangle cannot be constructed from these three segments.

Figure 10.7

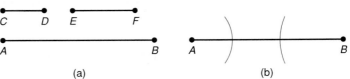

triangle inequality   The preceding demonstration illustrates a property of triangles known as the **triangle inequality.**

TRIANGLE INEQUALITY

The sum of the lengths of any two sides of a triangle is greater than the length of the third side.

EXAMPLE F

Can a triangle be constructed whose sides are congruent to the given segments?

(1)   a
       b
       c

(2)   d
       e
       f

Solution

1. No, because $a + b < c$. Notice that $b + c > a$ and $c + a > b$, but these conditions are not sufficient for a triangle to be constructed.
2. Yes, because the sum of the lengths of any pair of segments is greater than the length of the third segment.

We have seen that if three sides of one triangle are congruent to three sides of another, the triangles are congruent. That is, if three line segments can be used to form a triangle, they determine a unique triangle. Are there other conditions that can be used to determine a unique triangle? The next example focuses on two sides of a tri-angle and the **included angle**—that is, the angle formed by the two sides.

included angle

EXAMPLE G

Construct a triangle such that two of its sides and the included angle are congruent to the two line segments and angle shown below.

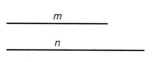

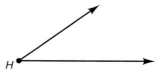

Solution

Step 1 Construct line segment $\overline{AB}$ with length m.

Step 2 Construct an angle congruent to $\angle H$ with A as a vertex.

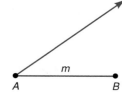

Step 3 Locate point C as shown so that $AC = n$.

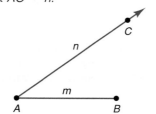

Step 4 Draw segment $\overline{CB}$.

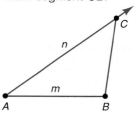

Since the locations of points C and B on the sides of the angle in Example G are determined by the lengths m and n, and since points C and B determine a unique line, it seems reasonable to expect that any triangle constructed by placing $\angle H$ between the two given segments will be congruent to $\triangle ABC$. This result is summarized by the following *congruence property of triangles*.

SIDE-ANGLE-SIDE (SAS)

> If two sides and the included angle of one triangle are congruent to two sides and the included angle of another triangle, the triangles are congruent.

EXAMPLE H

Use the SAS congruence property to determine whether the following pairs of triangles are congruent. (Note: Small slash marks are used to denote congruent angles. For example, $\angle C \cong \angle E$.)

(1)

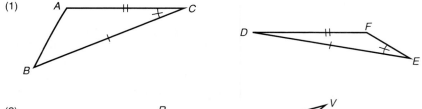

(2)

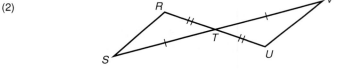

Solution

1. The triangles are not congruent, because $\angle C$ and $\angle D$ which are included between the pairs of congruent sides are not known to be congruent.
2. The triangles are congruent, because $\angle RTS$ and $\angle UTV$ which are included between the pairs of congruent sides are vertical angles, and vertical angles are congruent.

included side

There is one other property of triangles that is useful for showing that two triangles are congruent. This property involves the **included side** of two angles—that is, the side that is common to two angles. For example, $\overline{AB}$ is the included side for $\angle A$ and $\angle B$ in Figure 10.8.

Figure 10.8

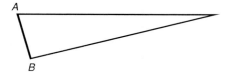

ANGLE-SIDE-ANGLE (ASA)

> If two angles and the included side of one triangle are congruent to two angles and the included side of another triangle, the two triangles are congruent.

EXAMPLE *I*

Use the ASA congruence property to show that the following pairs of triangles are congruent. (Remember, slash marks are used to show congruent segments and congruent angles. So $\overline{AH} \cong \overline{EC}$, $\angle A \cong \angle E$, and $\angle K \cong \angle G$.)

(1)

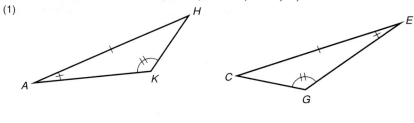

(2)

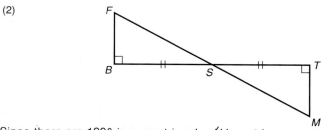

Solution

1. Since there are 180° in every triangle, $\angle H$ must be congruent to $\angle C$. Therefore, $\triangle AKH \cong \triangle EGC$ by the ASA congruence property.
2. Since vertical angles are congruent, $\triangle FSB \cong \triangle MST$ by the ASA congruence property.

CONSTRUCTING BISECTORS

BISECTING SEGMENTS   In the paperfolding examples in Section 7.1, a line segment was bisected by folding the segment onto itself so that the endpoints coincided. In addition to locating the point that bisects the segment, the crease of the paper produces a line perpendicular to the given segment. A line that is perpendicular to a segment

perpendicular bisector   at its midpoint is called the **perpendicular bisector** of the segment.

EXAMPLE *J*

Construct the perpendicular bisector of the line segment below.

A   *B*
Original segment

Solution   **Step 1** Open the compass to span more than half the distance from *A* to *B*. Then, with one end of the compass at *A*, draw an arc in each half-plane determined by $\overleftrightarrow{AB}$.

Step 2 With the same compass opening, place the end of the compass at *B* and draw arcs that intersect the arcs created in step 1. Label the points of intersection of the arcs as *C* and *D*.

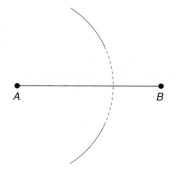

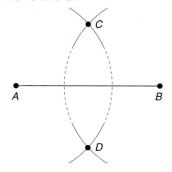

Step 3 Use a straightedge to draw $\overleftrightarrow{CD}$, and label its intersection with $\overline{AB}$ as point M. Then $\overleftrightarrow{CD}$ is the perpendicular bisector of $\overline{AB}$, and M is the midpoint of $\overline{AB}$.

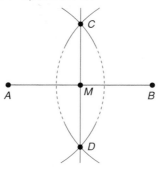

Justification: On the figure in step 3, draw segments $\overline{AC}$, $\overline{BC}$, $\overline{AD}$, and $\overline{BD}$. We know that these segments are all congruent because arcs of the same size were used to locate points C and D; that is, these segments are radii of circles that are the same size. So, by the SSS congruence property, $\triangle ACD \cong \triangle BCD$. Then $\angle ACD \cong \angle BCD$, because these angles are corresponding parts of congruent triangles. Thus $\triangle ACM \cong \triangle BCM$ by the SAS congruence property. Finally, the parts of $\triangle ACM$ and $\triangle BCM$ correspond: $\overline{AM} \cong \overline{BM}$, so M is the midpoint of $\overline{AB}$; $\angle CMA \cong \angle CMB$, and since these angles are supplementary angles, each must be a right angle. So $\overline{CD}$ is the perpendicular bisector of $\overline{AB}$.

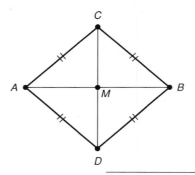

The perpendicular bisector in Example J was constructed by locating two points, C and D, that were equidistant from the endpoints of $\overline{AB}$. Since this distance was chosen arbitrarily, the justification for this construction proves that any point that is equidistant from the endpoints of a segment will be on the perpendicular bisector of the segment. Conversely, an arbitrary point P on the perpendicular bisector of $\overline{AB}$ is equidistant from the endpoints A and B. These facts are summarized in the following theorem.

PERPENDICULAR BISECTOR

> A point is on the perpendicular bisector of a line segment if and only if it is equidistant from the endpoints of the segment.

angle bisector

BISECTING ANGLES   Since $\angle ABD$ in Figure 10.9 is congruent to $\angle DBC$, the ray $\overrightarrow{BD}$ is called the **angle bisector** of $\angle ABC$. If an angle is drawn on paper, the bisector of the angle can be formed by folding one side of the angle onto the other. The crease is the bisector of the angle.

Figure 10.9

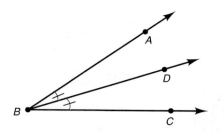

EXAMPLE K

Construct a bisector for the angle below.

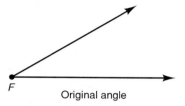

Original angle

Solution

Step 1 Place the end of a compass at point *F* and draw an arc. Label the points where the arc intersects the sides of the angle as *E* and *G*.

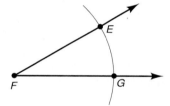

Step 2 Place the end of the compass at point *E* and draw an arc. Repeat this step using point *G* and the same compass opening. Label the intersection of the two arcs as *H*.

Step 3 Draw $\overrightarrow{FH}$, which is the angle bisector of ∡*EFG*.

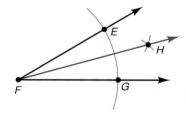

Justification: On the figure in step 3, draw segments $\overline{EH}$ and $\overline{GH}$. Since $\overline{FE} \cong \overline{FG}$ (they were constructed with the same compass opening) and $\overline{EH} \cong \overline{GH}$ (they also were constructed with the same compass opening), $\Delta FEH \cong \Delta FGH$ by the SSS congruence property. Therefore, ∡*EFH* ≅ ∡*GFH*, because these angles are corresponding parts of congruent triangles.

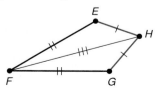

■ **H**ISTORICAL *HIGHLIGHT*

Evariste Galois

For 2000 years, beginning with the ancient Greeks, mathematicians sought to solve the following construction problems using only a straightedge and compass.

1. **Squaring a circle:** Constructing a square whose area equals that of a given circle
2. **Duplicating a cube:** Constructing a cube whose volume is twice that of a given cube
3. **Trisecting an angle:** Constructing rays that trisect a given angle

Algebraic developments by the young French mathematician Evariste Galois (1811–1832) proved that these constructions cannot be done using only a straightedge and compass. Galois died at the age of 20 in a duel, and it wasn't until after his death that his contributions to mathematics were recognized. One important branch of algebra currently bears his name: Galois Theory.*

CONSTRUCTING PERPENDICULAR AND PARALLEL LINES

Construction of a perpendicular bisector, as in Example J, accomplishes two purposes: it locates the midpoint of a segment, and it creates a right angle. Before carrying out the steps in Example L, think about how the steps in constructing the perpendicular bisector can be used to accomplish the construction.

EXAMPLE L

Construct a perpendicular to a line through a point that is not on the line.

Original line and point

Solution

Step 1 Place one end of a compass at point *P* and draw an arc that intersects line *ℓ* in two points. Label these points *A* and *B*.

Step 2 Place the compass at point *A* and draw an arc in the half-plane not containing *P*. With the same compass opening, place the compass at point *B* and draw an arc in the same half-plane. Label the intersection of these arcs as *D*.

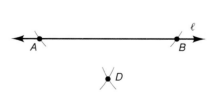

---

*E. T. Bell, *Men of Mathematics* (New York: Simon and Schuster, 1965), 362–377.

Step 3 Use a straightedge to draw $\overleftrightarrow{PD}$. Line $\overleftrightarrow{PD}$ is perpendicular to line ℓ.

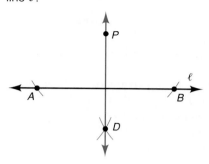

Justification: Since *P* is the same distance from *A* as from *B* (they were constructed with the same compass opening), we know by the perpendicular bisector theorem (page 498) that *P* is on the perpendicular bisector of $\overline{AB}$. Also, *D* is the same distance from *A* and *B*, so it is on the perpendicular bisector of $\overline{AB}$. Since the two points *P* and *D* determine a line, line $\overleftrightarrow{PD}$ is the perpendicular bisector of $\overline{AB}$.

EXAMPLE M

Construct a line parallel to a given line ℓ and through a point *K* that is not on ℓ.

Original line and point

Solution

Step 1 With one end of a compass on point *K*, draw an arc that intersects ℓ at point *A*.

Step 2 With the same compass opening and *A* as center, draw an arc that intersects ℓ at point *B*.

Step 3 With the same compass opening and *B* as center, draw an arc in the same half-plane as *K*.

Step 4 With the same compass opening and *K* as center, draw an arc that intersects the arc drawn in step 3. Label the intersection of the arcs as *C*.

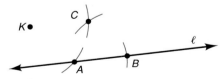

Step 5 Draw line $\overleftrightarrow{KC}$. This line is parallel to ℓ.

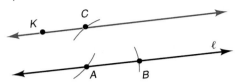

Justification: On the figure in step 5, draw segments $\overline{KA}$, $\overline{CB}$, and $\overline{KB}$. Since $\overline{KA}$, $\overline{AB}$, $\overline{BC}$, and $\overline{KC}$ were constructed as congruent segments, $\triangle KAB \cong \triangle BCK$ by the SSS congruence property. Therefore, $\angle KBA \cong \angle BKC$. Thus since $\angle KBA$ and $\angle BKC$ are congruent alternate interior angles ($\overleftrightarrow{KB}$ is a transversal intersecting $\overleftrightarrow{KC}$ and $\overleftrightarrow{AB}$), line $\overleftrightarrow{KC}$ is parallel to line $\overleftrightarrow{AB}$.

CIRCUMSCRIBING CIRCLES ABOUT TRIANGLES

Section 7.2 illustrated two methods of constructing regular polygons. One method involved marking off equal lengths on a circle to obtain an *inscribed polygon* (a polygon whose vertices are points of the circle). The circle around an inscribed polygon is called **circumscribed circle** a **circumscribed circle.** A circumscribed circle for a pentagon is shown in Figure 10.10. The sides of the pentagon, $\overline{AB}$, $\overline{BC}$, etc., are chords of the circle.

Figure 10.10

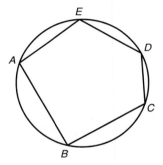

Not all polygons will have a circumscribed circle. However, a circumscribed circle can be constructed for any triangle. Consider the triangle in Figure 10.11.

Figure 10.11

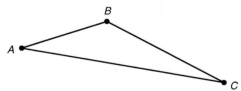

If points A and B are to be on a circle with center O, then OA must equal OB (see Figure 10.12). Thus by the perpendicular bisector theorem, the center of the circumscribed circle must be on the perpendicular bisector of $\overline{AB}$. Similarly, if points B and C are on the circle, then $OB = OC$, and the center of the circle is also on the perpendicular bisector of $\overline{BC}$. So the center of the circle containing A, B, and C can be located by constructing the perpendicular bisectors of $\overline{AB}$ and $\overline{BC}$, as shown in Figure 10.12. The intersection of the perpendicular bisectors is the center of the circumscribed circle about $\triangle ABC$.

Figure 10.12

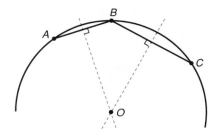

The preceding construction can be checked by using a compass to draw a circle with center *O* and radius *OA*, to see if points *B* and *C* lie on the circle, or by constructing the perpendicular bisector of the third chord, $\overline{AC}$, to determine if it passes through point *O*. Notice that we now have a method for locating the center of any circle if three points of the circle are given: *the center of a circle is the intersection of the perpendicular bisectors of two chords of the circle.*

PROBLEM-SOLVING APPLICATION

■ PROBLEM

A math club is spending the day at a pond (see the figure below) and the question of the length of the pond arises. One of the club members claims the length can be found using congruent triangles. How can this be done?

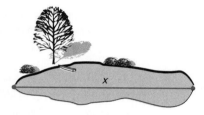

Understanding the Problem   The problem is to determine the distance *x* using congruent triangles.

Devising a Plan   One possibility is to select a point *C* so that points *A*, *B* and *C* form a triangle in which ∡*ACB* and side $\overline{BC}$ can be measured (see the figure below). Then select a point *D* so that $\overline{CD} \cong \overline{CB}$ and ∡*ACD* ≅ ∡*ACB*. Why is △*ACD* ≅ △*ACB*?

Question 1

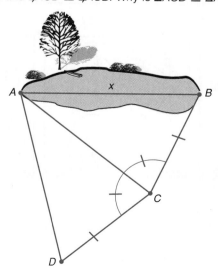

Carrying Out the Plan   Suppose you find that the sides of △*ACD* have the following lengths: *AC* = 2400 feet; *CD* = 1630 feet; and *AD* = 2570 feet. Because of what we know about corresponding parts of congruent triangles, we know that one of these is the length

Question 2   *AB*. Which one?

Question 3   **Looking Back**   The length of the pond can also be found using a right triangle, as shown in the next figure. If the triangle has legs of length 1650 feet and 1970 feet, what is the length of the pond?

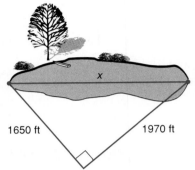

1650 ft   1970 ft

Answers to Questions 1–3
1. Since $\overline{AC}$ is congruent to itself, △*ACB* ≅ △*ACD* by the SAS congruence property.
2. Since $\overline{AD}$ corresponds to $\overline{AB}$, *AB* = 2570 ft.
3. By the Pythagorean theorem,

$$1650^2 + 1970^2 = x^2$$
$$2{,}722{,}500 + 3{,}880{,}900 = x^2$$
$$6{,}603{,}400 = x^2$$
$$2570 \approx x$$

RELATED ACTIVITIES IN

Mathematics for Elementary Teachers: An Activity Approach, 3e

Activity Set 10.1   **Locating Sets of Points in a Plane:** Points in a plane that satisfy given conditions are located and sketched.

Just for Fun   **Line Designs:** Geometric designs formed by connecting sequences of points with line segments

---

EXERCISES AND PROBLEMS 10.1

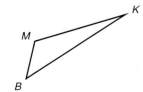 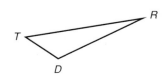

©1979 United Features Syndicate, Inc.

1. The triangles at right are congruent. Determine the corresponding angles and sides in a–f for the congruence and complete the congruence statement in g.

   a. ∡*B* ↔ _____   **b.** ∡*M* ↔ _____

   c. ∡*K* ↔ _____   **d.** $\overline{MB}$ ↔ _____

e. $\overline{BK} \leftrightarrow$ _____   **f.** $\overline{MK} \leftrightarrow$ _____

g. Complete the statement: $\triangle BMK \cong \triangle$ _____

2. If $\triangle ABC \cong \triangle DEF$, list the three pairs of corresponding congruent sides and the three pairs of corresponding congruent angles.

3. The ancient Greeks represented numbers by the lengths of line segments. Addition was represented by the sum of two lengths and subtraction by the difference of two lengths. Use the following segments and a straightedge and compass to construct line segments having the lengths specified in parts a through c. Explain the steps you use.

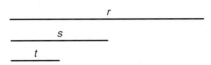

a. $r + s$ **b.** $r - t$ **c.** $r + (s - t)$

4. Show and explain how a straightedge and compass can be used to construct angles that are congruent to the given angles.

(a)

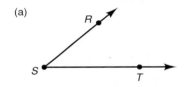

(b)

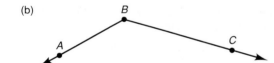

5. Trace each angle and line segment below on a separate sheet of paper. Then show and explain how a straightedge and compass can be used to obtain the construction listed.

a. The perpendicular bisector of $\overline{AB}$

b. The bisector of $\measuredangle DEF$

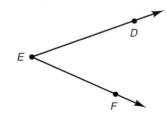

c. A line through K that is perpendicular to line n

d. A line through Q that is parallel to line m

•Q

$\overset{\longleftrightarrow}{} m$

e. A line through S that is perpendicular to $\overline{RS}$

$\underset{R}{\bullet}\rule{4cm}{0.4pt}\underset{S}{\bullet}$

6. The Mira is a Plexiglas device introduced in Section 7.4 for locating lines of symmetry. It can also be used for certain constructions.

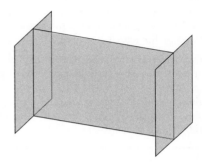

Draw a sketch to show how the Mira can be placed to obtain each construction in #5. Explain your reasoning.

7. Trace the figures below on a piece of paper and construct a circumscribed circle for each figure. Explain the steps in each construction. The figures in parts b, c, and d are regular polygons.

(a)   (b)

(c)   (d)

8. a. Construct a triangle whose sides are congruent to these line segments.

_____

_____

_____

b. Using the line segments in part a, can you construct another triangle that is not congruent to your first triangle? Explain why or why not.

9. The importance of triangles to architecture is due to a basic mathematical fact that is not true of polygons with more than three sides. (Compare the answers to parts a and b with answer to 8b.)

   a. Construct two noncongruent quadrilaterals whose sides are congruent to the line segments shown.

   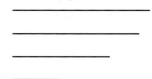

   b. How many noncongruent quadrilaterals can be constructed whose sides are congruent to the four line segments used in part a? (Hint: Imagine changing the shape of a quadrilateral formed by linkages.)

10. If a construction is possible, construct triangles with the following characteristics. (Use a ruler, compass, or protractor as needed.)

    a. Three sides of lengths 5 cm, 6 cm, and 7 cm
    b. Three sides of lengths 5 cm, 6 cm, and 10 cm
    c. Three sides that are congruent to $\overline{AB}$ below

    d. Two sides of length 2 cm and 3 cm and a nonincluded angle with a measure of 60°
    e. Two sides of length 5 cm and an included angle with a measure of 45°
    f. A right triangle with one leg of length 7 cm and one angle with a measure of 35°

11. In parts a and b, construct triangles that have one angle and two sides congruent to the angle and segments shown below.

    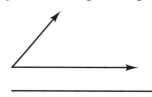

    a. Construct the triangle so that the given angle is included between the two given sides.
    b. Construct the triangle so that the given angle is not included between the two sides.
    c. Compare the triangles in parts a and b. Are they congruent?
    d. What conclusion can you draw from your answer in part c?

12. Construct a triangle in which one side and two angles are congruent to the line segment and angles below. Do two angles and one side determine a unique triangle, or is it possible to construct a second such triangle that is not congruent to the first?

    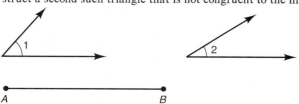

13. In each case below, determine if the given conditions are sufficient to conclude that $\triangle ABC$ is congruent to $\triangle HMS$. Draw diagrams and justify your answers.

    a. $\overline{AB} \cong \overline{HM}$, $\overline{BC} \cong \overline{MS}$, $\overline{AC} \cong \overline{HS}$
    b. $\angle A \cong \angle H$, $\angle B \cong \angle M$, $\angle C \cong \angle S$
    c. $\overline{AB} \cong \overline{HM}$, $\overline{BC} \cong \overline{MS}$, $\angle B \cong \angle M$
    d. $\overline{AB} \cong \overline{HM}$, $\overline{BC} \cong \overline{MS}$, $\angle A \cong \angle H$

14. Construct each of the polygons below using sides congruent to segment $\overline{AB}$. Explain the steps of the construction.

    a. Square
    b. Equilateral triangle
    c. Rhombus

15. There are an infinite number of distances from a line to a point that is not on the line.

    a. Trace line ℓ and point P on a sheet of paper. Use a ruler and compass to locate points on line ℓ that are the following distances from point P: 3 cm, 2 cm, and 1.5 cm.

    b. To the nearest tenth of a centimeter, what is the shortest distance from P to ℓ?
    c. Form a conjecture about the shortest distance from a point that is not on a line, to the line.

16. Use the SSS congruence property to determine which of the following pairs of triangles are congruent. If this property cannot be used, explain why.

    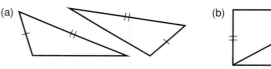

    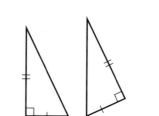

    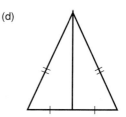

17. Use the SAS congruence property to determine which of the following pairs of triangles are congruent. If this property cannot be used, explain why.

a.

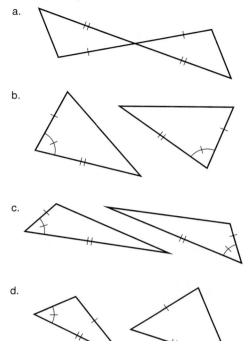

b.

c.

d.

18. Use the ASA congruence property to determine which of the following pairs of triangles are congruent. If this property cannot be used, explain why.

a.

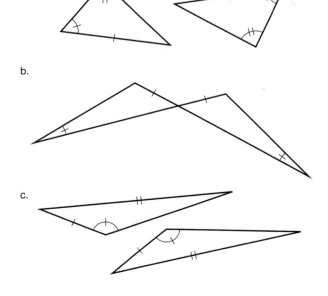

b.

c.

19. Construct an isosceles triangle with two sides congruent to $\overline{AB}$ and one side congruent to $\overline{CD}$.

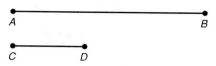

a. Form a conjecture about the angles that are opposite the two congruent sides of an isosceles triangle.

b. In the isosceles triangle below, point K is the midpoint of $\overline{RS}$. What congruence property of triangles can be used to show that $\triangle RKT \cong \triangle SKT$?

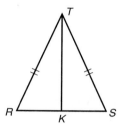

c. How can this congruence be used to show that $\angle R \cong \angle S$?

20. A tangent to a point P on a circle is a line through P that is perpendicular to the radius from the center of the circle to point P. Construct a circle and label a point P on its circumference. Using only a straightedge and compass, construct the tangent to the circle at point P. Show and explain the steps of your construction.

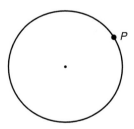

21. It has been proven that it is impossible to trisect every angle using only a straightedge and compass (see Historical Highlight, page 500). However, trisections of certain angles can be constructed. Diagram and list the steps in trisecting a right angle using only a straightedge and compass. (Hint: How can an angle with a measure of 60° be constructed?)

Featured Strategy: Making a Drawing

22. How many different noncongruent triangles can be formed that have two sides and one angle congruent to the line segments and angle below?

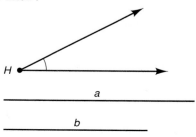

a. **Understanding the Problem** The third side of the triangle can be any length needed to form a triangle with the two given sides and angle. Construct a triangle with two sides and the included angle congruent to the given segments and angle. If another triangle is constructed using the given segments and the given angle as the included angle, will it be congruent to the triangle you constructed?

b. **Devising a Plan** One approach is to *make drawings* that will help you consider different combinations of the given segments and angle systematically. For example, suppose the segment of length b is opposite $\angle H$ in one triangle and the segment of length a is opposite $\angle H$ in the second triangle. Are these two triangles congruent?

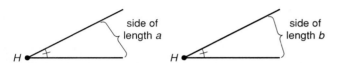

side of length a side of length b

c. **Carrying Out the Plan** Construct triangles using different configurations of the given line segments and angle, and determine if they are congruent. How many noncongruent triangles can be constructed?

d. **Looking Back** Draw a segment of length a, and place the vertex of $\angle H$ at one endpoint, as shown in the following figure. With the point of the compass on the other endpoint of the line segment, draw an arc of length b. This arc intersects two points on one side of $\angle H$ and these points determine two noncongruent triangles, as shown. Suppose a line segment of length b is drawn and $\angle H$ is placed at one endpoint. Will drawing an arc of length a determine two noncongruent triangles?

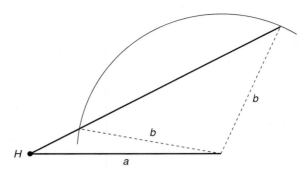

23. In order to measure the width of a river, a ranger stands across the river directly opposite rock R and places a stake at point A on the river's edge. Then she measures off equal distances and places stakes at points B and C so that $AB = BC$. Finally, the ranger moves directly away from the river to a point D, at which stake B and rock R are in a straight line. The diagram illustrates this information.

a. What triangle congruence property (SSS, SAS, ASA) shows that $\triangle ABR \cong \triangle CBD$?

b. How can this congruence be used to measure the width of the river?

Draw a large triangle on a sheet of paper. Conduct the following investigations by folding paper, using a Mira, or using a straightedge and compass to obtain the given constructions.

Questions for Investigation:

1. Construct the perpendicular bisectors of the three sides of a triangle. What

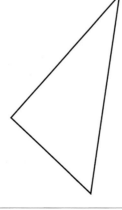

conjecture can you make about these three lines? Will this be true for other triangles?

2. Construct the line passing through each vertex and the midpoint of the opposite side of a triangle. What conjecture can you make about these three lines?

3. Construct the bisectors of the three angles of a triangle. Can you form a conjecture about these three lines?

4. There is a relationship among these three types of construction. What is it?

PUXXLER

The desk calendar at the right consists of two cubes on a stand. How can you number each face on each cube so that the date for each day of any month can be represented above the name of the month? (Note: A single-digit day such as day 3 should be represented by 03.)

SECTION 10.2   CONGRUENCE MAPPINGS

The shaded triangle in the following figure can be mapped onto triangle 3 with 1 reflection. Determine all the triangles onto which the shaded triangle can be mapped with exactly 1 rotation; 1 translation; and 1 reflection.

Day and Night, a woodcut.
© 1990 M. C. Escher Heirs/Cordon Art—Baarn—Holland.

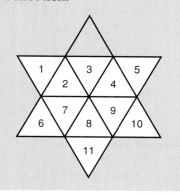

Figure 10.13

In designing the woodcut *Day and Night,* M. C. Escher used geometrical mappings. The particular mappings associated with congruence—translations, reflections, and rotations—will be studied in this section, and examples of how Escher used these mappings to create tessellations will be introduced.

TRANSLATIONS

A **translation** is a special kind of mapping that can be described as a sliding motion. Each point is moved the same distance and in the same direction. The translation in Figure 10.13 maps A to A', B to B', C to C', $\overline{BC}$ to $\overline{B'C'}$, and pentagon K to pentagon K'. This translation is completely determined by point A and its image, A'. That is, given any point X in this figure, we can find its image X' by moving in the *same direction* as from A to A' and the *same distance* as AA'.

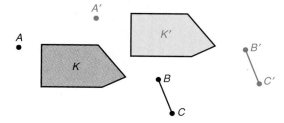

Translations occur with space figures as well as with plane figures. Just as in the case of two-dimensional figures, a translation in three dimensions is described as a sliding motion of points in space in the same direction and for the same distance—for example, a box moving on a conveyor belt or a child going down a slide. The photo in Figure 10.14 shows the results of a sliding motion of the earth's crust, which geologists call a block fault. The arrow points to one side of the fault along which the earth's crust has been displaced.

Figure 10.14
Fault line showing displaced rock

EXAMPLE A

Trace figure (1) and determine the image of the pentagon obtained by a translation that maps *K* to *K'*. Trace figure (2) and determine the image of the three-dimensional figure obtained from a translation that maps *P* to *P'*.

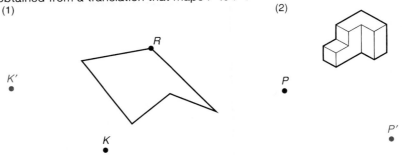

Solution

One method of locating the images of these figures is to use constructions to first find the images of the vertex points. The images of the vertex points can then be connected to obtain the image of the figure. For example, using vertex point *R* on the pentagon, construct a line through *R* that is parallel to $\overline{K'K}$. Then, moving in the direction from *K* to *K'*, locate the image *R'* of *R* so that *RR'* = *KK'*.

Another method of locating the images is to trace the figures. Then slide *K* along $\overline{KK'}$ so that it coincides with *K'* to locate the image of the pentagon, and slide *P* along $\overline{PP'}$ so that it coincides with *P'* to locate the image of the three-dimensional figure.

REFLECTIONS

reflection

line of reflection

fixed points

Figure 10.15

A **reflection** about a line is a mapping that can be described by folding. If this page is folded about line ℓ in Figure 10.15, each point will coincide with its image. E will be mapped to E', F to F', $\overline{EF}$ to $\overline{E'F'}$, and figure M to figure M'. Line ℓ is called a **line of reflection.** Since point S is on ℓ, it does not move for this mapping. S and all other points on ℓ are called **fixed points** for the reflection about ℓ, because each point coincides with (is the same as) its image.

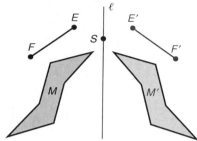

Reflections in space take place about planes. Each point to the left of plane P in Figure 10.16 has a unique image on the right side of P. The sphere is mapped to the sphere, point K to K', and tetrahedron T to tetrahedron T'. Point R and all other points on the plane are fixed points of the mapping. That is, each point on the plane is its own image.

Figure 10.16

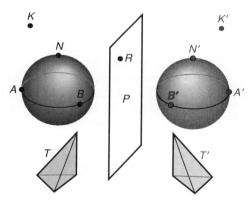

Reflections in space can be illustrated by mirrors. If plane P in Figure 10.16 is replaced by a mirror so that the figures to the left of the mirror are reflected, their images will appear to be in the positions of the figures on the right side of the mirror. Plane P is called the **plane of reflection.**

plane of reflection

Surprisingly clear images can be created by reflections in pools. Pick out some points on the building and their images in the photo in Figure 10.17.

Figure 10.17
Model of the United States Embassy, New Delhi

In the mappings about line ℓ (Figure 10.15) and plane P (Figure 10.16), each point and its image are on lines that are perpendicular to the line or plane of reflection. For example, $\overline{EE'}$ in Figure 10.15 is perpendicular to line ℓ, and $\overline{NN'}$ in Figure 10.16 is perpendicular to plane P. Furthermore, each point is the same distance from the line or plane as is its image. These two conditions hold for all reflections.

EXAMPLE B

Trace figure (1) and determine the image of the quadrilateral obtained from a reflection about line ℓ. Trace figure (2) and determine the image of the three-dimensional figure obtained from a reflection about plane P, which is perpendicular to this page.

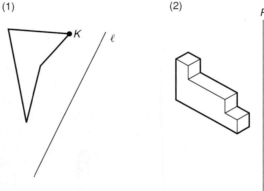

Solution

The image of a polygon can be located by first constructing the images of its vertex points. For example, using vertex point K on the quadrilateral, construct a line through K that is perpendicular to ℓ. Then locate the image K' of K so that K' is on the perpendicular line and the distances from K' to ℓ and from K to ℓ are equal.

Another method is to fold a paper with the traced figures so that line ℓ coincides with itself (or plane P coincides with itself) and trace the image in the opposite half-plane (half-space).

ROTATIONS

rotation

The third type of mapping is a **rotation,** which for plane figures can be described as turning about a point. As an example, consider a 90° rotation about a point O. Place a piece of paper on this page and trace $\overline{FG}$ and quadrilateral $ABCD$ in Figure 10.18. Hold a pencil at point O and rotate the paper 90° in a clockwise direction. (A 90° rotation can be determined by beginning with the edges of the paper parallel to the edges of this page.) Each of the points you trace will coincide with its image after this rotation. Quadrilateral $ABCD$ is mapped to quadrilateral $A'B'C'D'$, and $\overline{FG}$ is mapped

center of rotation

to $\overline{F'G'}$. Point O is called the **center of rotation** and is the only fixed point for this mapping.

Figure 10.18

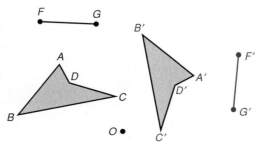

Figures in space are rotated about lines. If the sphere shown in Figure 10.19 is rotated 90° about the vertical axis through N and S, point H will be mapped to H' and point B to B'. Each point will be mapped to a new location except for points N and S, which remain fixed.

Figure 10.19

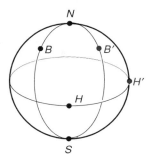

The earth and other spinning objects such as toy tops rotate about axes. The restaurant and observation deck at the top of the sixty-story Space Needle in Seattle, Washington (Figure 10.20) rotate once every 60 minutes about a vertical shaft. Each point on this moving structure traces out a circular path during 1 complete revolution. These moving points are constantly changing their locations and being mapped to each other.

Figure 10.20
Space Needle, Seattle, Washington

EXAMPLE C

Trace the polygon in figure (1) on a piece of paper and determine its image for a 90° clockwise rotation about point O. Line ℓ in figure (2) passes through the opposite faces $ABDC$ and $HFEG$ of the cube. Determine the image of each vertex of the cube for a 90° rotation about line ℓ.

(1)

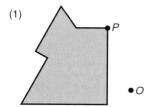

(2)

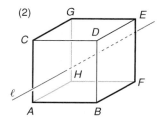

Solution

1. One method of locating the image of the polygon in figure (1) is to use constructions to first find the images of the vertex points. Using vertex point P of the heptagon, construct a right angle having O as the vertex of the angle and $\overrightarrow{OP}$ as one side. Then locate the image P' of P on the other ray of the angle so that $OP = OP'$. A similar construction can be repeated for the other vertex points.

   Another method of finding the image of the polygon is to hold a pencil at point O and rotate the paper 90° clockwise. The figure will be rotated to its new location.

2. The rotation of the cube maps the vertices as follows: $A \rightarrow C$, $C \rightarrow D$, $D \rightarrow B$, $B \rightarrow A$, $H \rightarrow G$, $G \rightarrow E$, $E \rightarrow F$, and $F \rightarrow H$.

COMPOSITION OF MAPPINGS

The wood engraving by M. C. Escher shown in Figure 10.21 combines translations and reflections. The white swan, W, can be mapped onto the black swan, B, by a translation followed by a reflection. This mapping can be carried out by tracing swan W and its center line on a piece of paper and then sliding the paper diagonally to swan B so that the two center lines coincide. The traced swan can now be made to coincide with swan B by a reflection about the center line. A *translation* followed by a *reflection* is called a **glide reflection.**

glide reflection

Figure 10.21
Swans, a wood engraving by M. C. Escher
© 1990 M. C. Escher Heirs/Cordon Art— Baarn—Holland.

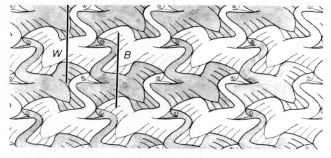

composition of mappings

When one mapping is followed by another, the combination is called a **composition of mappings.** Any combination of translations, reflections, rotations, or glide reflections can be used. In Figure 10.22, a 90° clockwise rotation about point O is followed by a translation of each point 3 spaces to the right. Triangle ABC is mapped to triangle $A'B'C'$ by the rotation, and then the translation maps triangle $A'B'C'$ to triangle $A''B''C''$. The composition of the rotation and translation is the single mapping that takes triangle ABC to triangle $A''B''C''$. In this case, the composition is a 90° rotation about point X. Try it.

Figure 10.22

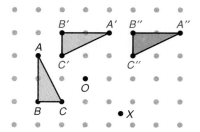

Two-dimensional patterns such as those on wallpaper and tiled floors are created by systematic translations, reflections, and rotations of a basic figure, as illustrated by the next example.

EXAMPLE D

The basic figure in the upper left corner of the following grid has the shape of a mushroom. This figure was repeatedly reflected about the common edge of adjacent squares to obtain the first column of the grid.

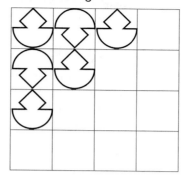

Determine the mapping (translation, reflection, or rotation) that produces each of the following.

1. The top row   2. The second column   3. The second row
4. The diagonal from upper left to lower right

Solution

1. Rotations of 180° about the midpoints of the edges of adjacent squares in the top row
2. Reflections about the common edge of adjacent squares in the second column
3. Rotations of 180° about the midpoints of the edges of adjacent squares in the second row
4. Translations along the diagonal

Composing mappings is similar to performing an operation on numbers. For example, the product of two integers is always another integer (closure property), and the composition of two congruence mappings is always another congruence mapping. The composition of some pairs of mappings is quite easy to determine. A 30° rotation followed by a 45° rotation can be replaced by a 75° rotation, and two translations can always be replaced by one translation.

The situation for reflections is more interesting, as shown in Figure 10.23. For a reflection about line *m*, figure *H* is mapped to *H'*. Then *H'* is mapped to *H''* by a reflection about line *n*. These two reflections can be replaced by a single rotation about point *O* that maps *H* to *H''*.

Figure 10.23

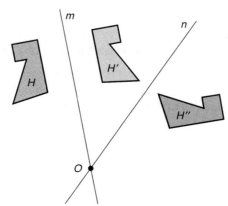

Compositions of different types of mappings, such as a rotation followed by a translation or a reflection followed by a rotation, can also be replaced by a single mapping. It can be proven that the composition of any two of the four mappings (rotation, translation, reflection, or glide reflection) is also a rotation, translation, reflection, or glide reflection. In other words, **composition of congruence mappings is closed.**

composition of congruence mappings is closed

CONGRUENCE

Translations, reflections, rotations, and glide reflections all have something very important in common. If A and B are any two points and A' and B' are their respective images, then the distance between A and B is the same as the distance between A' and B' (Figure 10.24). That is, for these mappings the lengths of the line segments are the same as the lengths of their images. Such mappings are called **distance-preserving mappings.** This property reflects the simple intuitive notion that as figures are rotated, translated, or reflected, their size and shape do not change.

distance-preserving mappings

Figure 10.24

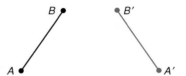

Up to this point we have thought of two figures as being congruent if they have the same size and shape or if one can be made to coincide with the other. The need for a more careful definition of congruence becomes evident when we consider congruence in three dimensions. For example, we need a way of defining congruence for the two kitchen grinders in Figure 10.25, and it does not make sense to say that they coincide.

Figure 10.25

A suitable definition of congruence for both plane and space figures can be given in terms of mappings.

CONGRUENCE

> Two geometric figures are **congruent** if and only if there exists a translation, reflection, rotation, or glide reflection of one figure onto the other.

This definition says that for each of these four mappings, a figure is congruent to its image. Conversely, if two figures are congruent, one can always be mapped to the other by one of these mappings. This definition gives us a way of viewing congruence of both plane and space figures. The plane figures H and H'' in Figure 10.23 are congruent because a rotation maps one to the other. The grinders in Figure 10.25 are congruent because a translation maps one to the other. Each point on the left grinder is mapped to a corresponding point on the right grinder. The distances between any two points on the left grinder, such as points A and B, and between their images, A' and B', are equal. Defining congruence in terms of distance-preserving mappings is the mathematical way of saying that two objects have the same size and shape.

MAPPING FIGURES ONTO THEMSELVES

In their book *Let's Play Math,* Michael Holt and Zoltan Dienes describe the following scheme for coloring pictures of a house.* Cut out a square and color the corners 4 different colors. Both the front and back sides of each corner should be the same color. Place the square on a piece of paper and draw a frame around it (Figure 10.26). At each corner of the frame, write (or draw pictures for) one of the words "wall," "roof," "door," and "window." The entire configuration is called the Rainbow Toy.

Figure 10.26

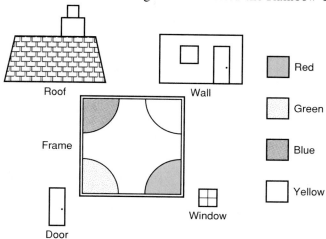

The different positions in which the square can be placed on the frame determine different arrangements of colors for the wall, roof, door, and window of the house. With the square in the position shown in Figure 10.26, we get the colors for house (a) in Figure 10.27. Color schemes for houses (b), (c), and (d) are obtained by rotating the square into 3 different positions; by flipping the square over, we get 4 more positions for the color schemes for houses (e) through (h).

Figure 10.27

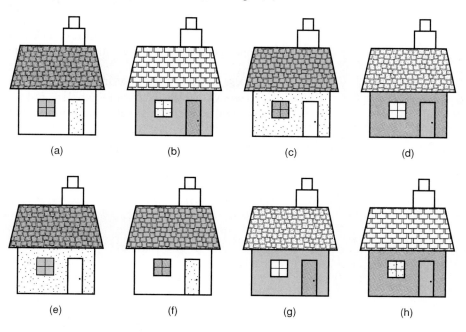

*M. Holt and Z. Dienes, *Let's Play Math* (New York: Walker and Company, 1973), 88–94.

The Rainbow Toy provides an elementary way of illustrating the mappings of a square onto itself. Remember from Section 7.4 that a square has 4 rotational symmetries: 90°, 180°, 270°, and 360°. It also has 4 lines of symmetry (Figure 10.28): 2 diagonal lines d_1 and d_2, a horizontal line h, and a vertical line v. Thus there are 8 mappings of the square onto itself, and these mappings produce the 8 color combinations for the houses in Figure 10.27.

Figure 10.28

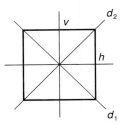

In general, the number of mappings of a plane figure onto itself is the total number of lines of symmetry and rotation symmetries.

EXAMPLE **E**

Determine the number of mappings of each figure onto itself.

1. A rectangle   2. The letter S   3. A regular hexagon

Solution

1. 4, because it has 2 lines of symmetry and 2 rotation symmetries
2. 2, because it has 2 rotation symmetries
3. 12, because it has 6 lines of symmetry and 6 rotation symmetries

---

ESCHER-TYPE TESSELLATIONS*

The Dutch artist M. C. Escher visited the Alhambra in Spain in the 1930s and was inspired by the geometrical tilings of the walls and ceilings to create some very unusual tessellations. He used translations, rotations, and reflections to reshape polygons such as squares, equilateral triangles, and regular hexagons, which are known to tessellate, into nonpolygonal figures that also tessellate. In the following paragraphs we will examine the use of mappings in creating tessellations.

TRANSLATION TESSELLATIONS   One of the simplest ways to create a tessellation is to begin with a square (or a rectangle, a rhombus, or other parallelograms) and change its opposite sides. This technique is illustrated in Figure 10.29.

Figure 10.29

Step 1 Draw a curve from *A* to *B*.

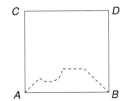

Step 2 Translate the curve to the opposite side of the square so that *A* maps to *C* and *B* maps to *D*.

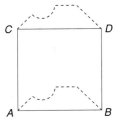

*This section is optional.

Step 3 Draw a curve from *C* to *A*. (Notice that the curve does not have to be within the original figure.)

Step 4 Translate the curve to the opposite side of the square so that *A* maps to *B* and *C* maps to *D*.

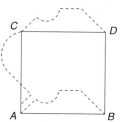 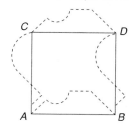

Step 5 Erase the lines of the original square that are not part of the curve to obtain a nonpolygonal figure, and tessellate with this figure.

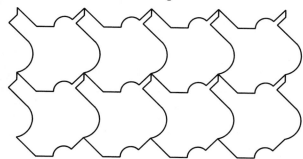

The tessellation in Figure 10.29 can be translated onto itself in many ways: move each figure 1 figure to the right, 2 to the left, etc.

ROTATION TESSELLATIONS   A rotation tessellation is created by beginning with a regular hexagon (Figure 10.30). Rotations are used to alter the sides of the original polygon.

Figure 10.30   **Step 1** Draw a curve from *A* to *B*.

Step 2 Rotate the curve about point *B* so that *A* maps to *C*.

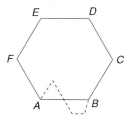 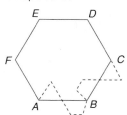

Step 3 Draw a curve from *C* to *D*.

Step 4 Rotate the curve about point *D* so that *C* maps to *E*.

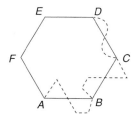 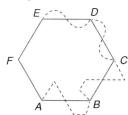

Step 5 Draw a curve from *E* to *F*.

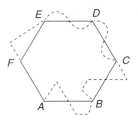

Step 6 Rotate the curve about point *F* so that *E* maps to *A*.

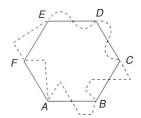

Step 7 Erase the lines of the original hexagon, and form a tessellation with the resulting figure.

The tessellation in Figure 10.30 can be rotated on itself. For example, a rotation of 120° or 240° about point *K* maps the tessellation onto itself.

REFLECTION TESSELLATIONS   The steps for creating a reflection tessellation are shown in Figure 10.31. The basic figure in this case is a rhombus.

Figure 10.31   **Step 1** Draw a curve from *A* to *B*.

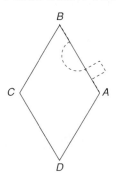

Step 2 Reflect the curve about $\overleftrightarrow{BD}$ so that *A* maps to *C*.

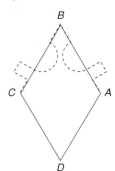

Step 3 Rotate the curve from *B* to *C* about point *C* so that *B* maps to *D*.

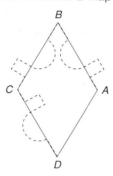

Step 4 Reflect the curve from *C* to *D* about line $\overleftrightarrow{BD}$ so that *C* maps to *A*.

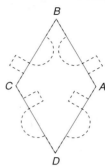

Step 5 Erase the lines of the original rhombus that are not part of the curve, and tessellate with the resulting figure.

The tessellation in Figure 10.31 has many lines about which it can be reflected onto itself.

PROBLEM-SOLVING APPLICATION

■ *PROBLEM*

Given any plane figure and its image for a rotation, how can we determine the center of rotation?

Understanding the Problem The following parallelogram has been rotated a certain number of degrees to its image. The problem is to find the center of rotation.

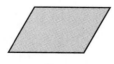

Figure

Image

Devising a Plan One approach is to trace the original figure and then to *guess and check* to locate a point about which the figure can be rotated to coincide with its image. Another approach is to use two chords of a circle. How can chords $\overline{AB}$ and $\overline{CD}$ of the following circle be used to locate the center of the circle?

Question 1

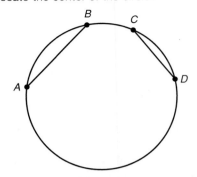

Carrying Out the Plan Each point of the original figure traces an arc as it is rotated to its image point. So the point and its image lie on a circle whose center is the center of rotation. In the following figure, S maps to S', P maps to P', and the perpendicular bisector of $\overline{PP'}$ is ℓ. How can the center of rotation be found?

Question 2

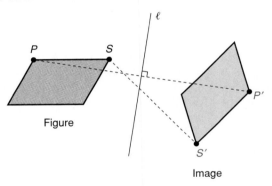

Figure

Image

Question 3 **Looking Back** Check the location of the center of rotation by tracing the original figure and rotating it to its image. How can the measure of the angle of rotation be determined?

Answers to Questions 1–3
1. Draw the perpendicular bisectors of $\overline{AB}$ and $\overline{CD}$. Their intersection is the center of the circle.
2. The intersection of ℓ and the perpendicular bisector of $\overline{SS'}$ is the center of rotation.

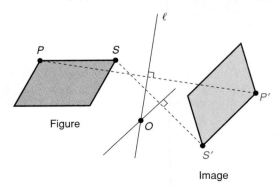

Figure

Image

3. With O as the center of rotation, use a protractor to measure the central angle $\angle POP'$ or $\angle SOS'$.

RELATED ACTIVITIES IN
Mathematics for Elementary Teachers: An Activity Approach, 3e

Activity Set 10.2   **Drawing Escher-Type Tessellations:** Congruence mappings are used to create Escher-type tessellations.

Just for Fun   **Paper Puzzles:** Several puzzles involving sequences of numbers and paperfolding

EXERCISES AND PROBLEMS 10.2

1. The pattern of lines and angles in the above photo was produced by placing 6 photographs of a construction staging side by side.
   a. Are these 6 photographs congruent?
   b. Are the 6 stagings congruent?
   c. What type of mapping is suggested by this picture?

Copy the dot grid from the inside cover of the book to use in sketching the images in #2 through #6.

2. For the translation that takes A to A', sketch the image of the hexagon.

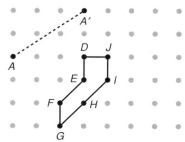

   a. The line through point D and its image is parallel to $\overleftrightarrow{AA'}$. Is this true for every point on the hexagon and its image?

b. If E' and G' are the respective images of E and G, how does the length $E'G'$ compare with the length EG?
c. Compare the area of the hexagon with the area of its image.

3. Sketch the image of the pentagon for a reflection about line ℓ.

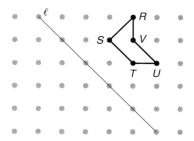

a. If R' is the image of R, what is the measure of the angles formed by the intersection of $\overleftrightarrow{RR'}$ and ℓ?
b. If U' is the image of U, how does the distance from U to ℓ compare with the distance from U' to ℓ?
c. What are the fixed points for this mapping?

4. Sketch the image of the quadrilateral for the 90° rotation about O that takes A to A'. (Trace the figure on a piece of paper and rotate the paper.)

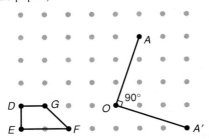

   a. If E' is the image of E, what is the measure of ∡EOE'?
   b. If G' is the image of G, how does the length EG compare with the length E'G'?
   c. Are there any fixed points for this mapping?

5. Map quadrilateral ABCD to quadrilateral A'B'C'D' by a translation that moves point A to A'. Then map quadrilateral A'B'C'D' to quadrilateral A''B''C''D'' by a translation that takes A' to A''.

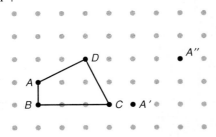

   a. The translation that maps A to A' can be described as "over 4 and down 1." The translation that maps A' to A'' is "over 2 and up 2." Describe the translation that maps A to A''.
   b. What is the image of quadrilateral ABCD for the composition of the following two mappings: the translation that takes A to A' followed by the translation that takes A' to A?

6. Reflect pentagon RSTUV about line m and then reflect its image about line n.

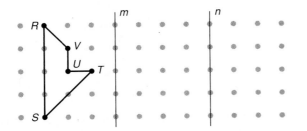

   a. What single mapping (rotation, translation, or reflection) is equal to the composition of these two reflections?
   b. Let R' be the image of R for the reflection about m, and let R'' be the image of R' for the reflection about n. Compare the distance from R to R'' with the distance from line m to line n. What relationship do you find? Will this relationship hold for other points and their images?

7. The hexagons below can be mapped to each other by compositions of reflections about lines m and n.

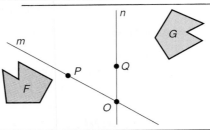

   a. Sketch the image of hexagon F for a reflection about line m. The image from reflecting this image about line n should coincide with hexagon G.
   b. There is a clockwise rotation about point O that will map figure F to figure G. How is the number of degrees in this rotation related to ∡POQ?

8. Trace this figure and points R and S on a piece of paper.

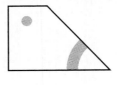

   R •

                                        S •

   a. Locate the image of the figure for the composition of these two mappings: 180° rotation about R followed by a 180° rotation about S.
   b. What single mapping (rotation, translation, reflection, or glide reflection) can be used to replace the two rotations in part a so that the figure is mapped to its image?
   c. Locate the image of the figure for the composition of these two mappings: a 90° clockwise rotation about R followed by a 90° clockwise rotation about S.
   d. What single mapping can be used to replace the two rotations in part c?

9. Complete the pattern in each grid by carrying out the mappings on the basic figure in the small square in the upper left corner of the grid. (Copy the rectangular grid from the inside cover.)
   a. Rows: Rotate 180° about the midpoints of the right sides of the squares.
      Columns: Reflect about the lower side of the squares.

b. Rows: Reflect about the right sides of the squares.
   Columns: Reflect about the lower sides of the squares.

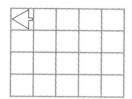

10. Mark off a grid and a square region that can be used as a basic figure to generate this wallpaper pattern. Describe the mappings for obtaining the rows and columns.

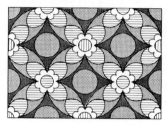

11. The design on the nineteenth-century quilt shown here also occurs in the fourteenth-century Moorish palace the Alhambra. The top row can be generated by a sequence of 180° rotations, beginning with the white figure in the upper left corner.

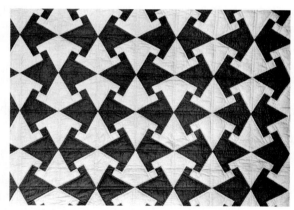

Patchwork quilt with Arabic lattice
pattern, ca. 1850.

Collection of Greenfield Village and the Henry
Ford Museum, Dearborn, Michigan

   a. Locate the centers of rotation for these mappings.
   b. What mapping can be carried out to generate the left column of figures, beginning with the figure in the upper left corner?

12. Isometric grid paper, such as that shown below, is helpful in drawing three-dimensional figures. Sketch the image of each figure for the given mapping. (Copy the isometric grid from the inside cover.)
   a. A translation that maps P to P'

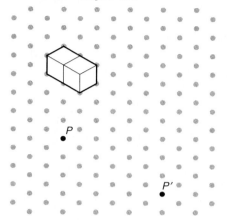

   b. A reflection about plane P, which is perpendicular to this page

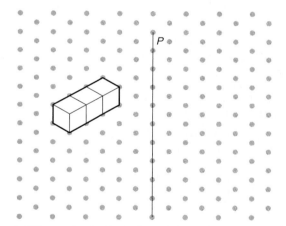

   c. A 90° rotation in the indicated direction about line ℓ.

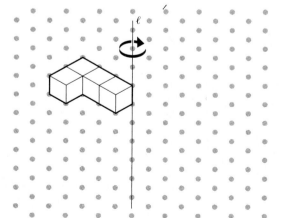

13. Determine the number of congruence mappings of each polygon onto itself and indicate how you determined that number.
    a. Rhombus
    b. Equilateral triangle
    c. Regular octagon
    d. Rectangle
    e. Parallelogram
    f. Regular pentagon

14. Identify the basic figure (rectangle, hexagon, square, or parallelogram) that was used to create the nonpolygonal figure in each tessellation.

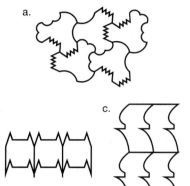

a.

b.   c.

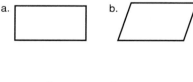

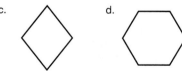

15. Create a nonpolygonal (Escher-type) tessellation of the given type.
    a. A rotation tessellation
    b. A reflection tessellation
    c. A translation tessellation

16. By altering the sides of each polygon, design a nonpolygonal figure that will tessellate.

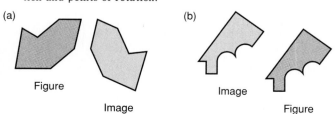

a.   b.

c.   d.

17. Determine the mapping (rotation, translation, or reflection) that maps each figure below to its image. Locate all lines of reflection and points of rotation.

(a)   (b)

Figure

Image

Image

Figure

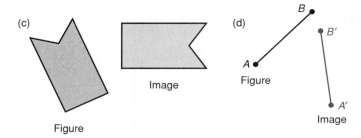

(c)   (d)

Figure

Image

Figure

Image

Featured Strategy: Forming an Organized List

18. How many different ways can 5 consecutive whole numbers be placed in a row so that no 2 consecutive whole numbers are next to each other?
    a. **Understanding the Problem** Here is one solution for the first 5 consecutive whole numbers. If one arrangement can be obtained from another by a reflection, such as the one shown here, then we will consider the two arrangements to be the same. Find another solution.

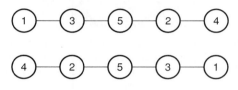

Five in a row

b. **Devising a Plan** This type of problem can be solved by *forming an organized list*. For example, you might begin by listing all the different arrangements with 1 in the first position, then those with 2 in the first position, etc. If you want to eliminate duplication due to reflections, what adjustment must you make in the total number of arrangements?

c. **Carrying Out the Plan** Follow the system suggested above or one of your own to solve this problem.

d. **Looking Back** There are several ways to extend this problem. For example, there are 45 different solutions for 6 consecutive whole numbers; you may want to see if you can find them. Another possibility is using different configurations. How many different solutions are there for the following figure? (Reminder: Two arrangements are the same if they can be obtained from each other by a reflection.)

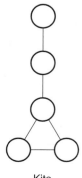

Kite

19. An ornamental design that extends to the right and left (around rooms, buildings, pottery, etc.) is called a **frieze**. The frieze on the following container is mapped onto itself by a translation.

Container with cover, Attica, Greece,
eighth century B.C.

Perkins Collection, Purchase of E. P. Warren
Courtesy, Museum of Fine Arts, Boston.

What transformations (translation, rotation, reflection) will map each of the following frieze patterns onto itself? (Consider these patterns as extending in both directions.)

a.

Chinese ornament painted on porcelain

b.
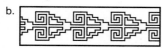

Masonry fret, temple at Mitla, Mexico

c.

French Renaissance ornament from casket

d.

Indian painted lacquer work

20. A translation maps point *P*, with coordinates $(^-2, 1)$, to *P'*, with coordinates $(3, 2)$. Graph these points and draw an arrow from *P* to *P'* to indicate the length and direction of the translation. (Copy the coordinate system from the inside cover.)

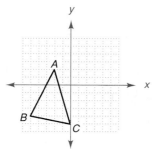

a. Sketch the image of $\triangle ABC$ for this translation.
b. If *A'*, *B'*, and *C'* are the images of *A*, *B*, and *C*, what are their coordinates?

21. Draw the image of quadrilateral *DEFG* for a reflection about the *x*-axis. Label the images of these vertices as *D'*, *E'*, *F'*, and *G'*. (Copy the coordinate system from the inside cover.)

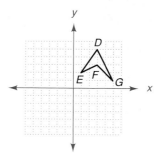

a. What are the coordinates of *D'*, *E'*, *F'*, and *G'*?
b. Reflect quadrilateral *D'E'F'G'* about the *y*-axis and label its vertices *D''*, *E''*, *F''*, and *G''*. What are the coordinates of the vertices of this image?
c. What single rotation will map quadrilateral *DEFG* to quadrilateral *D''E''F''G''*?

22. Mappings are sometimes given by describing what will happen to the coordinates of each point. For example, the mapping $(x, y) \rightarrow (x + 2, y - 3)$ is a translation that maps each point 2 units to the right and 3 units down. To find the image of a particular point, such as $(1, 7)$, substitute these values for *x* and *y* into $(x + 2, y - 3)$. In this case, $(1, 7)$ maps to $(3, 4)$. Find the image of each figure for the given mapping. Label each mapping as a translation, rotation, reflection, or glide reflection. (Copy the coordinate system from the inside cover for the mappings.)

a. $(x, y) \rightarrow (x - 2, y + 1)$ b. $(x, y) \rightarrow (x + 1, ^-y)$

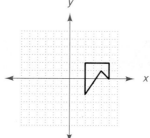
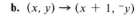

c. $(x, y) \rightarrow (^-x, ^-y)$

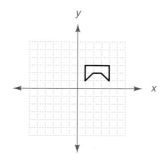

LABORATORY INVESTIGATION

The following steps illustrate a method of altering the sides of an equilateral triangle to obtain a nonpolygonal figure that will tessellate.

Step 1 Draw a curve from A to B.

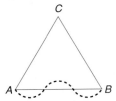

Step 2 Rotate the curve about point B so that A maps to C.

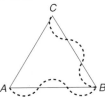

Step 3 Label the midpoint of $\overline{AC}$ as D and draw a curve from D to C. Rotate this curve about D so that C maps to A.

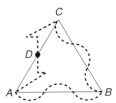

Once the lines of the original triangle have been erased, the figure that remains will tessellate.

Questions for Investigation

1. Which of the transformations (rotation, translation, reflection) will map the tessellation at the left onto itself?

2. Step 3 produces a curve on 1 side of the triangle that is said to have **point symmetry** because it can be rotated onto itself by a 180° rotation. Suppose step 3 is used to produce a curve with point symmetry on all 3 sides of a triangle. Will the resulting figure tessellate?

3. Suppose step 3 is used to create a curve with point symmetry on each of the 6 sides of a regular hexagon. Will the resulting figure tessellate?

PUZZLER

How can the whole numbers from 1 to 8 be placed in the circles of the figure shown here so that any two connected circles do not contain consecutive whole numbers? If we agree that all solutions that can be obtained through rotations and reflections of this diagram are the same, then there is only one solution. Find this unique solution.

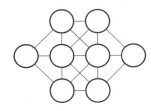

SECTION 10.3   SIMILARITY MAPPINGS

■ PROBLEM OPENER

These two figures are similar. Each dimension of the larger figure is twice the corresponding dimension of the smaller figure. If this doubling of dimensions is continued, how many cubes will there be in the fifth figure?

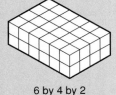

3 by 2 by 1   6 by 4 by 2

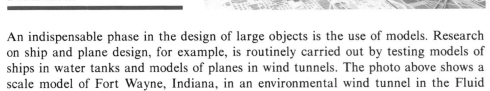

Model of Fort Wayne, Indiana, in a wind tunnel

An indispensable phase in the design of large objects is the use of models. Research on ship and plane design, for example, is routinely carried out by testing models of ships in water tanks and models of planes in wind tunnels. The photo above shows a scale model of Fort Wayne, Indiana, in an environmental wind tunnel in the Fluid

Dynamics and Diffusion Laboratory at Colorado State University. Environmental engineers will study the effects of wind on the scale model of the city in hopes of solving urban smog and pollution problems.

similar   We say that two figures are **similar** if they have the same shape but not necessarily the same size. For example, models of objects are usually similar to the actual objects. All of our familiar optical instruments make use of the principle of similar figures. When you look through a magnifying glass or a microscope, you see an object that is similar to the original figure.

SIMILARITY AND SCALE FACTORS

Similar figures can be created by lights and shadows. Hold a flat object perpendicular to a flashlight's rays, and the light will produce a shadow similar in shape to the original figure (see Figure 10.32). Because the light is from a small bulb and spreads out in the shape of a cone, the shadow is larger than the object.

Figure 10.32

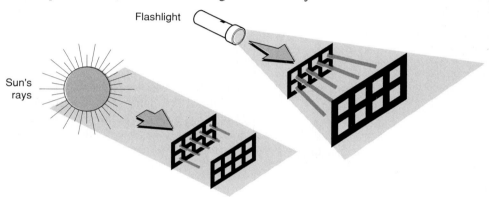

Light rays and shadows are analogous to mappings and their images. For each point on the object there is a corresponding "shadow point," which is its image. The rays of light are like lines projecting from a central source to the object. This type of mapping is illustrated in Figure 10.33. Point *O,* which represents the light source, is

projection point   called the **projection point,** and each point of quadrilateral *ABCD* is mapped to exactly
similarity mapping   one point on quadrilateral *A'B'C'D'*. This type of mapping is called a **similarity mapping.** In this example, *ABCD* is similar to *A'B'C'D'*, and we write *ABCD* ~ *A'B'C'D'*.

Figure 10.33

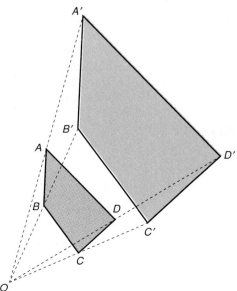

Each point on quadrilateral $A'B'C'D'$ in Figure 10.33 is twice as far from point O as is its corresponding point on quadrilateral $ABCD$. For instance, distance OA' is twice OA, OB' is twice OB, etc. Because of this relationship between points and their images, this mapping is said to have a **scale factor** of 2.

scale factor

If the scale factor for a similarity mapping is greater than 1, the image is an **enlargement** of the original figure. The mapping from figure XZW to figure $X'Z'W'$ in Figure 10.34 has a scale factor of 3. Each image point of figure $X'Z'W'$ is 3 times further from O than is its corresponding point on figure XZW. That is, OX' is 3 times OX, OZ' is 3 times OZ, and OW' is 3 times OW.

enlargement

Figure 10.34

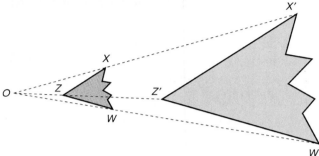

reduction

When the scale factor is less than 1, the image is a **reduction** of the original figure. In the similarity mapping in Figure 10.35, each of the distances from O to points A, B, C, and D has been multiplied by 1/3 to get the image points A', B', C', and D'. That is, the larger figure has been reduced by a scale factor of 1/3.

Figure 10.35

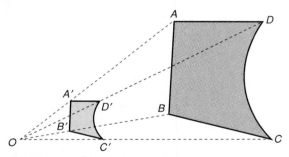

It is even possible for a scale factor to be negative. In that case the original figure and its image are on opposite sides of the projection point, and the image is "upside down" in relation to the original figure. The larger flag shown in Figure 10.36 is projected through point O to the smaller flag using a scale factor of $^-1/2$. In particular, A is mapped to A' and G is mapped to G'. As in the previous examples, the scale factor determines the size of the image. With a scale factor of $^-1/2$, each image point is half as far from the projection point as is its corresponding point on the original figure (and the point and its image are on opposite sides of the projection point). For example, OG' is half of OG, and OA' is half of OA.

Figure 10.36

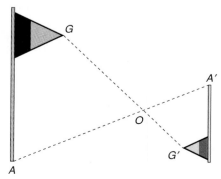

The lenses of our eyes and of cameras create inverted images of scenes, much like the images from a similarity mapping with a negative scale factor (see Figure 10.37). Such lenses are like projection points, producing a scene upside down on the retinas of our eyes or the film of a camera.

Figure 10.37

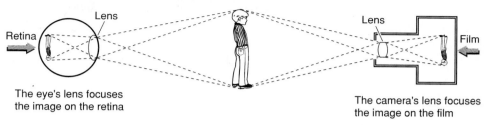

The eye's lens focuses the image on the retina

The camera's lens focuses the image on the film

EXAMPLE A

Determine the scale factor for each mapping.

(1) ... (2) ...

(3) ... (4) ...

Solution

1. Each image point is half as far from *O* as is its corresponding point in the figure: $OA'/OA = 1/2$. So the scale factor is 1/2.
2. Each image point is twice as far from *O* as is its corresponding point on the figure: $OB'/OB = 2$. So the scale factor is 2.
3. $OC'/OC = 1/3$, and since the figure and its image are on opposite sides of the projection point, the scale factor is ⁻1/3.
4. $OD'/OD = 3$, so the scale factor is 3.

We have seen several examples of similarity mappings. For each mapping the original figure and its image are similar. We state this fact as the definition of similar figures.

SIMILAR FIGURES

Two geometric figures are **similar** if and only if there exists a similarity mapping of one figure onto the other.

The definition for similarity also holds for space figures. The two boxes in Figure 10.38 are similar because the smaller one can be mapped onto the larger one by using a projection from point *O* inside the small box. The scale factor for this similarity is

3.6. That is, each vertex of the larger box is 3.6 times farther from point O than is the corresponding vertex of the smaller box. As with plane figures, a scale factor greater than 1 produces an enlargement of a three-dimensional figure, and a scale factor between zero and 1 reduces the original figure.

Figure 10.38

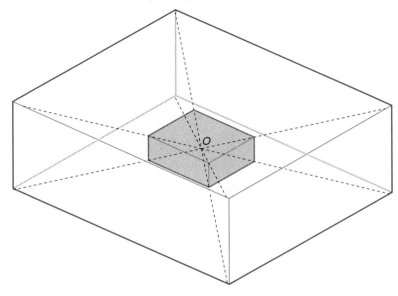

In our study of congruence, the mappings we used (rotations, translations, and reflections) *preserved size and shape.* Similarity mappings, on the other hand, *do not preserve size* but *do preserve shape.*

SIMILAR POLYGONS

Similarity mappings have two important properties. First, the *sizes of angles do not change.* Consider the similarity mapping in Figure 10.39, which maps $\triangle DEF$ to $\triangle D'E'F'$ with a scale factor of 2. In this case,

$$\angle D \cong \angle D', \angle E \cong \angle E', \angle F \cong \angle F'$$

Second, the lengths of line segments all *change by the same multiple,* which is the scale factor. Each side of $\triangle D'E'F'$ is twice as long as its corresponding side in $\triangle DEF$. That is,

$$D'E' = 2(DE), E'F' = 2(EF), D'F' = 2(DF)$$

Another way of stating this condition is to say that the ratios of the lengths of corresponding line segments are equal.

$$\frac{D'E'}{DE} = \frac{E'F'}{EF} = \frac{D'F'}{DF} = \frac{2}{1}$$

Figure 10.39

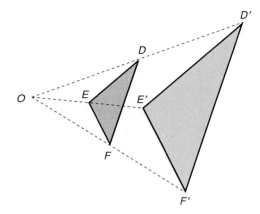

In general, for a scale factor of k, where $k > 0$, each line segment will have an image that is k times as long.

There are many applications of similar figures in which it is inconvenient to set up similarity mappings by using projection points. A solution to this problem is to produce similar figures from measurements of angles and distances. The construction of maps and charts is an example. The polygon on the chart in Figure 10.40 connects 5 points and is approximately similar to the large imaginary polygon over the water that connects the actual landmarks. These positions on the chart were plotted by measuring the 5 vertex angles and 5 distances between these islands. The following theorem verifies that such measurements are all that is necessary to obtain similar polygons.

SIMILAR POLYGONS

Two polygons are similar if and only if there is a mapping from one to the other such that

1. their corresponding angles are congruent;
2. the lengths of their corresponding sides have the same ratio.

Figure 10.40

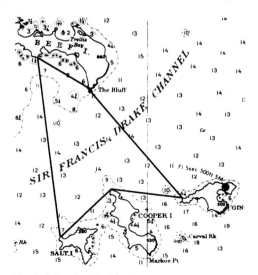

Virgin Islands, West Indies,
scale factor 139,000

EXAMPLE B

If $\triangle ABC$ is similar to $\triangle DEF$ ($\triangle ABC \sim \triangle DEF$), find the lengths of sides $\overline{AB}$ and $\overline{EF}$.

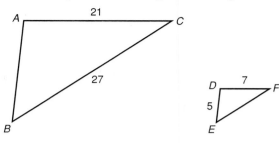

Solution   Since $AC/DF = 21/7 = 3$, the ratio of each pair of corresponding sides is 3. Thus

$$\frac{AB}{DE} = \frac{AB}{5} = 3, \text{ so } AB = 15$$

$$\frac{BC}{EF} = \frac{27}{EF} = 3, \text{ so } EF = 9$$

Notice in Example B that the ratio of any two sides of the first triangle is equal to the ratio of the corresponding two sides of the second triangle. For example,

$$\frac{AC}{AB} = \frac{21}{15} \text{ and } \frac{DF}{DE} = \frac{7}{5}$$

and these two fractions are equal. In general, if two polygons are similar, *the ratio of any two sides of the first polygon is equal to the ratio of the corresponding sides of the second polygon.*

To show that two polygons are similar, it is usually necessary to show that both conditions are satisfied: (1) corresponding angles are congruent, and (2) corresponding sides have the same ratio.

EXAMPLE C

1. Compare the following square and rectangle. Which conditions for similarity do they satisfy? Are they similar?
2. Compare the rectangle and the parallelogram. Which conditions for similarity do they satisfy? Are they similar?

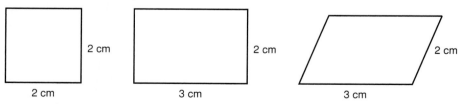

Solution

1. The square and the rectangle have congruent angles (all 90°), but they do not satisfy the second condition for similar polygons because the ratios of the lengths of their sides are not equal: 2/2 ≠ 2/3. So these polygons are not similar.
2. The rectangle and the parallelogram satisfy the second condition for similar polygons because the ratios of the lengths of their sides are equal, but the angles in the rectangle are not congruent to those in the parallelogram. Therefore these polygons are not similar.

SIMILAR TRIANGLES

To determine if two triangles are similar, it is not necessary to check both conditions for similar polygons. Minimum conditions for similarity of triangles are examined in the following examples.

EXAMPLE D

Construct a triangle having two angles congruent to $\angle A$ and $\angle B$.

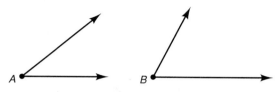

Solution

Draw a line segment of arbitrary length and label its endpoints C and D.

Then construct an angle at C that is congruent to $\angle A$ and an angle at D that is congruent to $\angle B$ (as shown).

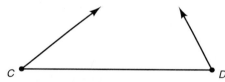

Finally, extend the sides of $\angle C$ and $\angle D$ and label their intersection as E.

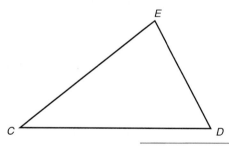

Suppose that instead of beginning with line segment $\overline{CD}$, as in Example D, we begin with $\overline{FG}$, which is half as long. The resulting triangle is shown in Figure 10.41; $\angle F \cong \angle C$ and $\angle G \cong \angle D$.

Figure 10.41

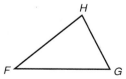

Comparing the lengths of the sides of $\triangle CDE$ and $\triangle FGH$, we see that FH is half of CE, GH is half of DE, and FG is half of CD. So $\triangle CDE \sim \triangle FGH$. This result suggests the following *similarity property of triangles.*

ANGLE-ANGLE (AA)

If two angles of one triangle are congruent to two angles of another triangle, the two triangles are similar.

Notice that for two triangles to be similar, it is only necessary that two angles of one triangle be congruent to two angles of the other triangle, because if that is the case the third angles of the triangles must be equal. Why?

EXAMPLE E

Find a one-to-one correspondence between vertices of each pair of triangles to show that the triangles are similar. Explain why.

(1)

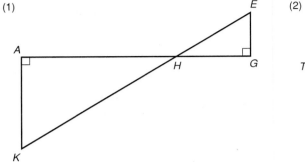

(2)

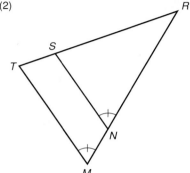

Solution

1. △AKH ~ △GEH by the AA similarity property because ∡A ≅ ∡G and ∡AHK ≅ ∡GHE (they are vertical angles).

2. △RSN ~ △RTM by the AA similarity property because ∡N ≅ ∡M and both triangles contain ∡R.

We have seen that in order to show that two triangles are similar it is only necessary to check the measures of their angles. The following example, on the other hand, considers only the measures of the sides of two triangles.

EXAMPLE F

Two sets of three line segments are shown below. The lengths *r*, *s*, and *t* are three times the corresponding lengths *c*, *d*, and *e*. Construct a triangle from each set of segments and determine if the triangles are similar.

_____ *r* _____	___ *c* ___
_____ *s* _____	__ *d* __
___ *t* ___	_ *e* _

Solution

The following two triangles can be constructed using the construction techniques described in Section 10.1. If the vertices of these triangles are matched so that A ↔ T, B ↔ R, and C ↔ S, the lengths of the corresponding sides have a ratio of 3. Measuring the corresponding angles of the triangles using a protractor—or comparing the angles by tracing on paper—shows that angles A, B, and C are congruent respectively to angles T, R, and S. Thus △ABC ~ △TRS.

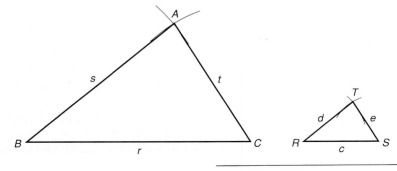

Example F suggests the following *similarity property of triangles.*

SIDE-SIDE-SIDE (SSS)	If the corresponding sides of two triangles are proportional, then the triangles are similar.

EXAMPLE G

Which two of the following three triangles are similar?

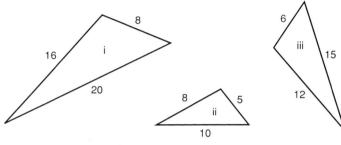

Solution   Triangle i is similar to triangle iii. The ratio of the lengths of their corresponding sides is 4 to 3.

$$\frac{8}{6} = \frac{20}{15} = \frac{16}{12} = \frac{4}{3}$$

PROBLEM-SOLVING APPLICATION

One important application of similar triangles is in making indirect measurements. It is said that the Greek mathematician Thales computed the height of the Great Pyramid of Egypt through indirect measurements. One account describes his use of shadows and similar triangles. The sun is so far away that in a given vicinity the angles formed by its rays and the ground are approximately congruent. If a stick is held perpendicular to the ground, the stick and its shadow form a small right triangle that is similar to the right triangle formed by a pyramid and its shadow. The next problem shows how Thales might have computed the height of the Great Pyramid.

■PROBLEM

Suppose that the distance from the base of the Great Pyramid to the tip of its shadow is 342 feet. Also assume that a 6 foot stick placed perpendicular to the ground casts a 9 foot shadow. If the pyramid has a square base with dimensions of 756 feet by 756 feet, what is the vertical height of the pyramid?

Understanding the Problem   The following drawing shows the stick, the pyramid, and the shadows. Point *A* is the foot of the altitude of the pyramid. The distance from *B* to *C* is 342 ft. What is the distance from *A* to *B*?

Question 1

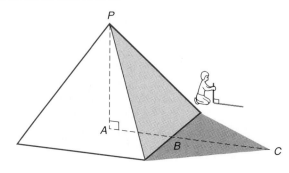

Question 2

Devising a Plan   The stick, the pyramid, and the sun's rays form two similar triangles, as shown in the next figure. Using the ratios of the lengths of corresponding sides, we can find the height of the pyramid. Why is the large triangle similar to the small one?

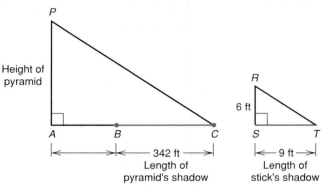

Length of pyramid's shadow

Length of stick's shadow

Question 3

Carrying Out the Plan   In light of the fact that the corresponding sides of similar triangles are proportional, what is the height of the pyramid?

Question 4

Looking Back   Once we have the height of the pyramid, the slant height along the face of the pyramid from B to P can be computed using the Pythagorean theorem. What is this distance?

Answers to Questions 1–4

1. This distance is half the width of the side of the pyramid: $756/2 = 378$.

2. $\angle A$ and $\angle S$ are both right angles. $\angle C$ and $\angle T$ are congruent angles that are formed by the sun's rays and the ground. Therefore, $\triangle PAC \sim \triangle RST$ by the AA similarity property of triangles.

3. $\dfrac{PA}{RS} = \dfrac{AC}{ST}$; $RS = 6$, $AC = 378 + 342 = 720$, and $ST = 9$. So,

$$\frac{PA}{6} = \frac{720}{9}$$

$$PA = \frac{6(720)}{9}$$

$$PA = 480 \text{ ft}$$

4. $\triangle PAB$ is a right triangle with legs $PA = 480$ and $AB = 378$. So by the Pythagorean theorem,

$$480^2 + 378^2 = PB^2$$
$$230{,}400 + 142{,}884 = PB^2$$
$$373{,}284 = PB^2$$
$$611 \approx PB$$

So, the slant height of the face of the pyramid is 611 feet to the nearest foot.

■ *HISTORICAL HIGHLIGHT*

Thales (636–546 B.C.) was one of the earliest of many famous Greek mathematicians and is regarded by historians as the father of geometry. In his early years he traveled widely, learning geometry from the Egyptians and astronomy from the Babylonians. Thales is generally acknowledged as the first to introduce the use of logical proofs based on deductive reasoning, rather than experiments, to support conclusions. Thales was regarded as unusually shrewd in commerce and science, and many anecdotes are told about his cleverness. In one story, one of Thales' mules, loaded with salt for trade, accidentally discovered that if it rolled over in a stream, the contents of its load would dissolve. Thales discouraged this habit by filling the mule's saddlebags with sponges instead of salt. Thales was known as the first of the Seven Sages of Greece, the only mathematician to be so honored. He is supposed to have coined the maxim "Know thyself."

SCALE FACTORS WITH AREA AND VOLUME

The smaller of the two knives in Figure 10.42 is a regular-size Scout knife, whose length is about equal to the width of the palm of your hand. The newspaper clipping says that the bigger knife is "three times larger" than the conventional Scout knife. Does this mean that the length of the larger knife is three times greater or that its surface area or volume is three times greater? Phrases such as "twice as large" and "three times bigger" can be misleading. They often refer to a comparison of linear dimensions, as in the case of these knives (compare their lengths). The "three" in this example refers to the scale factor. It means that the length, width, and height of the big knife are three times greater than the corresponding dimensions of the smaller knife. But what can be said about the relative sizes of the areas or volumes of these knives? In the following paragraphs you will see the effect of scale factors on area and volume.

Figure 10.42
Prepared for anything

Prepared for anything

What could be the world's largest Scout-type knife is ready for the world's largest potato. Wayne Goddard, a professional knife-maker who works at his home at 473 Durham St., Eugene, turned this one out for Dennis and Raymond Ellingsen, Eugene knife collectors. Completely functional, the knife is 24½ inches long when opened. It weighs 4¼ pounds and is three times larger than the conventional Scout knife.

AREA   The two rectangles in Figure 10.43 are similar. The scale factor from the smaller to the larger is 3. That is, the length and width of the larger rectangle are 3 times greater than the length and width of the smaller rectangle. How do their areas compare? The area of the small rectangle is 4×2 square units. Because each of its linear dimensions is increased by a multiple of 3, the area of the larger rectangle is $(3 \times 4) \times (3 \times 2)$ square units. Using the commutative and associative properties for multiplication, we find that

$$(3 \times 4) \times (3 \times 2) = (3 \times 3) \times (4 \times 2)$$
$$= 3^2 \times (4 \times 2)$$

So the area of the large rectangle is 9 (the square of the scale factor 3) times greater than the area of the small rectangle. In general, if one plane figure is similar to another figure by a scale factor of k, where k is any positive real number, then the second figure will have an area k^2 times the area of the first figure.

Figure 10.43

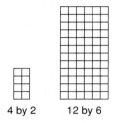

4 by 2   12 by 6

The relationship between scale factor and surface area for three-dimensional figures is the same as that for plane figures. Consider the two boxes shown in Figure 10.44. The scale factor from the small box to the large box is 2. That is, the length, width, and height of the large box are each 2 times greater than the corresponding dimension of the small box. Let's compare the areas of the sides of these boxes. The front side of the small box has an area of 6, and the front side of the large box has an area of 24. The large area is 2^2, or 4, times greater than the small area. A similar comparison between each face of the small box and the corresponding face of the large box shows that the large area is 4 times greater than the small area. In general, the surface areas of two similar figures are related by the *square of their scale factor*. If the scale factor is k, where k is any positive real number, then one figure will have a surface area k^2 times the surface area of the other figure.

Figure 10.44

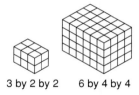

3 by 2 by 2   6 by 4 by 4

EXAMPLE H

1. If the scale factor from a small photo to its enlargement is 3 and the area of the small photo is 15 square inches, what is the area of the large photo?
2. If the surface area of a box is 52 square centimeters and the scale factor from the box to a larger similar box is 2, what is the surface area of the large box?
3. If the scale factor from a figure to its reduction is 1/2 and the figure has a surface area of 76 square feet, what is the surface area of the smaller figure?

Solution

1. $3^2 \times 15 = 135$, so the area of the large photo is 135 in.^{2}.
2. $2^2 \times 52 = 208$, so the surface area of the large box is 208 cm^2.
3. $(1/2)^2 \times 76 = 19$, so the surface area of the smaller figure is 19 ft^2.

VOLUME   There is also a relationship between the volumes of two similar space figures. Consider the volumes of the boxes in Figure 10.44. The volume of the small box is $3 \times 2 \times 2$ cubic units. Because each of its linear dimensions is increased by a scale factor of 2, the volume of the large box is $(2 \times 3) \times (2 \times 2) \times (2 \times 2)$ cubic units. Using the commutative and associative properties for multiplication,

$$(2 \times 3) \times (2 \times 2) \times (2 \times 2) = (2 \times 2 \times 2) \times (3 \times 2 \times 2)$$
$$= 2^3 \times (3 \times 2 \times 2)$$

So the volume of the large box is 8 (the cube of the scale factor 2) times greater than the volume of the small box. In general, if one space figure is similar to another figure by a scale factor of *k,* where *k* is any positive real number, then the second figure will have a volume k^3 times the volume of the first figure.

We are now prepared to examine the relationships between the areas and volumes of the knives shown in Figure 10.42. The scale factor from the small knife to the large knife is 3. Therefore, the large knife has a surface area that is 3^2, or 9, times greater than the surface area of the small knife. The volume of the large knife is 3^3, or 27, times greater than the volume of the small knife.

Let's apply the relationships between scale factor and area and volume to another example.

EXAMPLE 1

The following photo shows a nineteenth-century scale model of a cookstove. This miniature stove was used by a traveling salesperson as a sample and has all the features of a life-size stove. The scale factor from this miniature stove to the life-size stove is 5.

1. If the small stove has a surface area of 300 square centimeters, what is the surface area of the life-size stove?
2. If the oven in the small stove has a volume of 1000 cubic centimeters, what is the volume of the oven in the life-size stove?

Nineteenth-century scale model of a cookstove

Solution

1. $5^2 \times 300 = 7500$, so the large stove has a surface area of 7500 cm².
2. $5^3 \times 1000 = 125{,}000$, so the oven in the large stove has a volume of 125,000 cm³.

SIZES AND SHAPES OF LIVING THINGS*

In the natural world there are some important and interesting relationships between the surface area and volume of similar figures. For every type of animal there is a most convenient size and shape. One factor that governs the size and shape of a living thing is the ratio of its surface area to its volume. All warm-blooded animals at rest lose approximately the same amount of heat for each unit area of skin. Small animals have too much surface area for their volumes; a major reason they spend so much time eating is to keep warm. For example, 5000 mice weigh as much as a person, but their surface area and food consumption are each about 17 times greater! At the other end of the scale, large animals tend to overheat because they have too little surface area for their volumes.

*This section is optional.

Let's take a closer look at the relationship between surface area and volume as the size of an object increases. The table in Figure 10.45 lists the surface areas and volumes of 4 different cubes. As the size of the cube increases, both the surface area and the volume increase, but the volume increases at a faster rate. One way of viewing this change is to form the ratio of surface area to volume. For a 2 by 2 by 2 cube, the ratio is 3, and as the dimensions of the cube increase, the ratio decreases. For a 10 by 10 by 10 cube, the ratio is less than 1.

Figure 10.45

Cube	Surface area	Volume	Area/volume
2 by 2 by 2	24	8	3
3 by 3 by 3	54	27	2
4 by 4 by 4	96	64	1.5
10 by 10 by 10	600	1000	.6

Another way to compare the changes in surface area and volume as the size of a cube increases is with graphs. If the length, width, and height of a cube are x, its area is $6x^2$ and its volume is x^3. The graphs of $y = 6x^2$ and $y = x^3$ in Figure 10.46 show that for $x < 6$, the area is greater than the volume; for $x = 6$, the area equals the volume; and for $x > 6$, the volume is greater than the area.

Figure 10.46

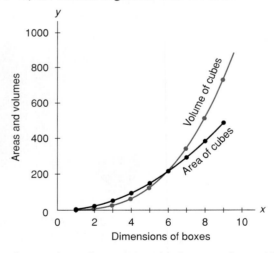

To relate these changes in surface area and volume to the problem of maintaining body temperatures, assume that the cubes shown in Figure 10.47 are animals and that the ideal ratio between surface area and volume is 2. In this case the 2 by 2 by 2 animal has too much surface area (it would tend to be too cold), because its area-to-volume ratio is 3 (24/8); the area-to-volume ratio for the 3 by 3 by 3 animal is 2 (54/27), which is just right; and the 4 by 4 by 4 animal has too little surface area (it would tend to be too hot), because its ratio of area to volume is 1.5 (96/64).

Figure 10.47

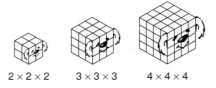

2 × 2 × 2   3 × 3 × 3   4 × 4 × 4

RELATED ACTIVITIES IN
Mathematics for Elementary Teachers: An Activity Approach, 3e

Activity Set 10.3   **Devices for Indirect Measurement:** Several sighting methods are presented for obtaining indirect measurements, including use of the stadiascope, clinometer, hypsometer, and transit.

Just for Fun   **Enlarging Drawings:** Use of grids for producing enlargements of plane figures

EXERCISES AND PROBLEMS 10.3

1. Determine the scale factor for each mapping.

a.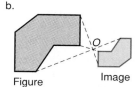

b.

c.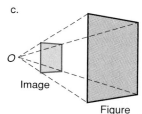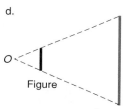

d.

2. For each figure, sketch a similar figure using the given scale factor. (Copy the rectangular grid from the inside cover to use in your sketches.)

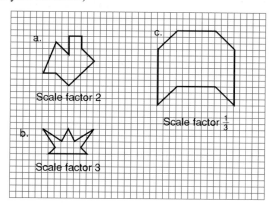

3. Use *O* as a projection point and find the images of triangle T using scale factors of 2, 3, and 1/2. Look for a relationship between the coordinates of the vertices of T and the coordinates of their images. (Copy the rectangular grid from the inside cover.)

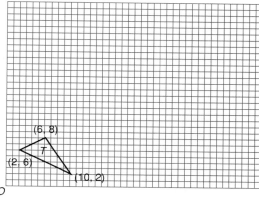

4. The following pairs of polygons are similar. Find each missing length.

a. $\triangle ABC \sim \triangle DEF$

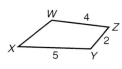

b. $FGHIJ \sim KLMNT$

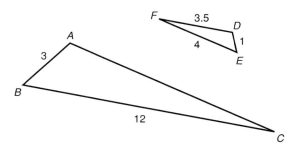

c. $WXYZ \sim RSUV$

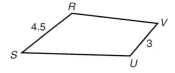

5. Which three of the following triangles are similar to each other? State the reason why.

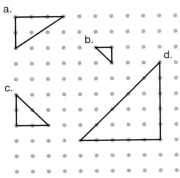

6. Determine whether the triangles in each pair are similar. If so, give a reason and write the similarity correspondence.

a.

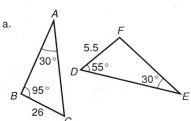

b.

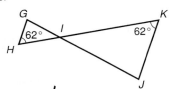

c.

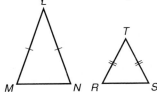

d.

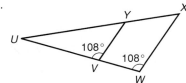

e.

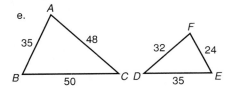

f.

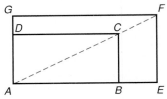

7. Determine whether the following figures are similar, and if so, explain why. If they are not similar, show a counterexample with measurements.
   a. Any 2 squares
   b. Any 2 isosceles triangles
   c. Any 2 rhombuses
   d. Any 2 regular octagons
   e. Any 2 equilateral triangles
   f. Any 2 right triangles
   g. Any 2 congruent polygons

8. Construct the following triangles.
   a. A triangle having sides of length 4 cm and 6 cm and an included angle of 45°
   b. A triangle having sides of length 2 cm and 3 cm and an included angle of 45°
   c. Are the triangles in parts a and b similar?
   d. What conjecture about similar triangles is suggested by these constructions?

9. There is an easy way to test rectangles for similarity. If one rectangle is placed on the other so that their right angles coincide, as shown below, then the rectangles are similar if their diagonals lie on the same line. For example, rectangle *AEFG* is similar to rectangle *ABCD*, but the two rectangles in the right figure are not similar.
   a. Explain why rectangle *ABCD* is similar to rectangle *AEFG*. (Hint: To show that the sides are proportional, use similar triangles.)

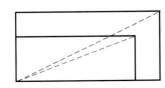

   b. Trace the following rectangles onto another sheet and use the diagonal test to find out which two are similar.

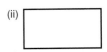

10. Find the distance across the river using the triangles and given measurements. Explain your reasoning.

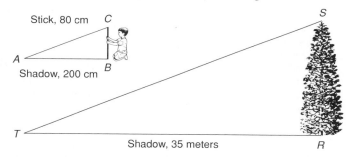

11. The stick and the tree in the following figure form right angles with the ground. Furthermore, ⊿*CAB* and ⊿*STR* are congruent because they are formed by the sun's rays.
   a. Why are the triangles in this figure similar?
   b. Use the given information to find the height of the tree.

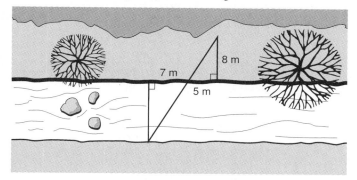

12. During a football game, Beth and her friend were standing next to the goalposts and trying to estimate the height of the posts. Beth noticed that the shadow of the posts was 10 yd, the length of the end zone, and her friend's shadow was 6 ft. Knowing that her friend was 6 ft tall, she quickly computed the height of the goalposts.
   a. Explain with a diagram how this could be done with similar triangles.
   b. What is the height of the posts in feet?
   c. In 1989, a change in football regulations allowed the height of the goalposts to be increased by 10 ft. If the posts Beth saw had been 10 ft higher, what would have been the length of their shadow in yards?

13. Sketch the pentagon and points *K* and *M*. Using the projection points *K* and *M* and a scale factor of 2, draw two images of the pentagon.

   a. Is each image similar to the original pentagon?
   b. Are the two images congruent to each other?
   c. Suppose we continue to use a scale factor of 2 but select another projection point for a mapping. How does the image compare to the first two images?

14. Use the figures in #2 to answer these questions.
   a. How many times greater is the area of its image than the area of the original figure a? the original figure b?
   b. The area of the image of figure c is what fraction of the area of the original figure?

15. Triangle T in #3 has an area of 16 square units. What is the area of the enlargement or reduction for a mapping with the following scale factors?

   a. 2   **b.** 3   **c.** $\frac{1}{2}$

16. A .5 cm by .5 cm square computer chip is shown in this photo. The scale drawing shows the tiny circuits. Assume that the scale factor from the chip to the drawing is 80.

Scale drawing of a computer-on-a-chip; actual chip shown between the fingers in the photograph

   a. What are the dimensions of the drawing?
   b. How many times greater is the surface area of the drawing than the surface area of one face of the chip?

17. These two figures are similar. The scale factor from the small figure to the large figure is 2.

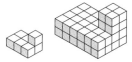

The surface area and volume of the small figure are given in the top row of the following table. Complete the table for figures which are similar to the smaller figure using the given scale factors.

Scale factor	Surface area (sq. units)	Volume (cubic units)
1	26	7
2	—	—
3	—	—
4	—	—
5	—	—

18. This is not an example of trick photography. There are two average-size adults sitting in this chair, and there is room for several more. The scale factor from the small chair to the large chair is 8.

   a. The small chair is 40 cm tall, and its seat is 24 cm wide. What is the height of the large chair, and what is the width of its seat?
   b. How many times more paint will the large chair require than the small chair?
   c. The small chair weighs about 1 kg. Both chairs are made of the same kind of wood. What is the weight of the large chair?

19. Engineers use models of planes to gain information about wing and fuselage (central body) designs. The scale factor from this model of a Boeing B52 to the full-size plane is 100.

Model of a Boeing B52 being adjusted for wind-tunnel test

   a. The lift of an airplane depends on the surface area of its wings. How many times greater is the surface area of the wings of a B52 than the surface area of the wings of its model?
   b. The weight of a plane depends on its volume. How many times greater is the volume of a B52 than the volume of its model?
   c. If the tip of the wing of the model flaps a distance of 3 cm during a wind tunnel test, what is the distance the tip of the wing of a B52 flaps during flight?

20. In *Gulliver's Travels*, by Jonathan Swift, Gulliver went to the kingdom of Lilliput, where he found that he was 12 times taller than the average Lilliputian.

   a. The Lilliputians computed Gulliver's surface area to make him a suit of clothes. About how many times more material would be needed for his suit than for one of theirs?
   b. The Lilliputians computed Gulliver's volume to determine how much he should be fed. About how many times more food would Gulliver require than a Lilliputian?
   c. Tiny people like the Lilliputians can exist only in fairy tales because in real life the ratio of their volume to their surface area would not allow them to maintain the proper body temperature. Would they be too warm or too cold?

21. In parts a, b, and c, similarity mappings are described by relating the coordinates of each point on the given figure to the coordinates of its image. For example, the mapping in part a doubles the coordinates of each point: point $(^-1, 1)$ gets mapped to $(^-2, 2)$. Sketch the images of the given figures. What is the scale factor for each mapping? (Copy the coordinate system from the inside front cover.)
   a. $(x, y) \rightarrow (2x, 2y)$

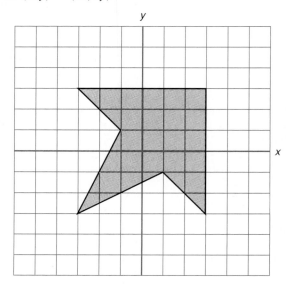

b. $(x, y) \rightarrow \left(\dfrac{x}{2}, \dfrac{y}{2} \right)$

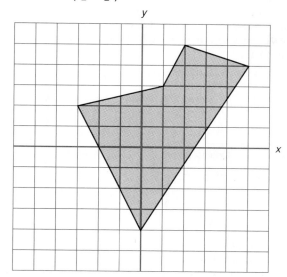

c. $(x, y) \rightarrow (^-3x, ^-3y)$

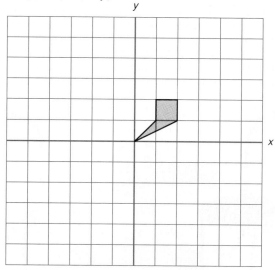

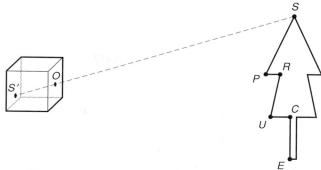

a. Draw lines from the lettered points on this tree through point *O*, and label their images on the back wall (film) of the camera.

b. Sketch the complete image of the tree.

c. *OS* is approximately 66 mm, and *OS'* is approximately 11 mm. What is the scale factor for this projection?

23. Similar figures can be obtained by reproducing a figure from one grid onto another grid of a different size. This procedure is commonly used for enlarging quilting and sewing patterns.

a. What is the scale factor for the enlargement of the patchwork doll?

22. A pinhole camera can easily be made from a box. When the pinhole is uncovered, rays of light reflected from an object strike light-sensitive film. These rays of light travel in straight lines from the object to the pinhole of the camera, like lines through a projection point. Without a lens to gather light rays and increase their intensity, it takes from 60 to 75 seconds for enough light to pass through the pinhole for the image to be recorded.

b. Reproduce the figure from grid A below onto grid B by copying one square at a time. What is the scale factor from grid A to grid B?

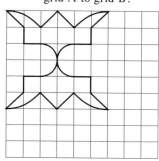

Grid A

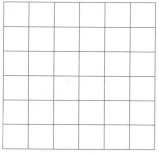

Grid B

c. Reproduce the figure from grid B on page 547 on grid C. What is the scale factor from grid B to grid C?

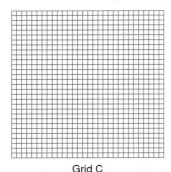

Grid C

d. The scale factor from grid A to grid C is 3/10. How can this scale factor be obtained from the two scale factors in parts b and c?

Featured Strategy: Forming an Organized List

24. The Xerox 7000 copier in Mr. Gary's print shop has 5 switches for determining the size of a reproduction. If switch 1 is used, the reproduction is congruent to the original. Switches 2, 3, 4, and 5 reduce the original size by scale factors of .85, .76, .65, and .58, respectively. Using two switches in sequence, what scale factors can Mr. Gary obtain on this copier?

a. Understanding the Problem These copies of hexagons were obtained from the Xerox 7000. The length of a side of hexagon 2 is .85 times the length of a side of hexagon 1. The smallest hexagon was obtained by using switch 2 to obtain a reproduction of hexagon 1 and then using this reproduction and switch 3. What is the scale factor from hexagon 1 to the smallest hexagon?

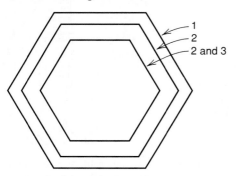

1
2
2 and 3

b. Devising a Plan We could begin by *forming an organized list* of the different ways that switches 2, 3, 4, and 5 can be paired (a switch can be paired with itself). What are they? Why isn't switch 1 included in these pairs?

c. Carrying Out the Plan List the scale factors that can be obtained by using a combination of two switches. Round each scale factor to the nearest hundredth.

d. Looking Back Mr. Gary also has a copier that enlarges the size of a figure by a scale factor of 2. Using this machine once and a setting on the Xerox 7000 once, what additional scale factors can Mr. Gary obtain?

25. The pages of a book come from the printing press as large rectangular sheets of paper. Each sheet is fed through a series of rollers and folded in half several times. A sheet that has been folded once is called a *folio*. Half of a folio is a *quarto*, and half of a quarto is an *octavo*. Each fold is perpendicular to the previous fold.

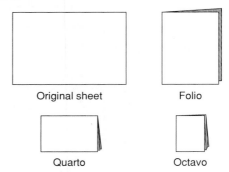

Original sheet   Folio

Quarto   Octavo

a. Which pairs of these rectangles (original, folio, quarto, octavo) are similar? Explain why.

b. If this folding pattern is continued, which of the resulting rectangles will be similar?

26. The setting in the photo below appears to be life-size except for the nickel on the table. These pieces of furniture and dishes were handcrafted in the early 1800s for a dollhouse collection. The miniature cream pitcher holds 2 mL of cream. How much cream would a similar life-size pitcher hold? (*Hint:* Use the nickel on the table to find the scale factor for this photo.)

27. Loop or knot two rubber bands together and hold one end fixed at point *O*. Stretch the rubber bands so that as the knot at point *P* traces one figure, a pencil at point *P'* traces an enlargement. Use this method to enlarge the map of the United States. Assume the distance from *O* to *P'* is 2.3 times the distance from *O* to *P*. How many times greater will the distance from Denver to Kansas City be on the enlarged map than on the small map?

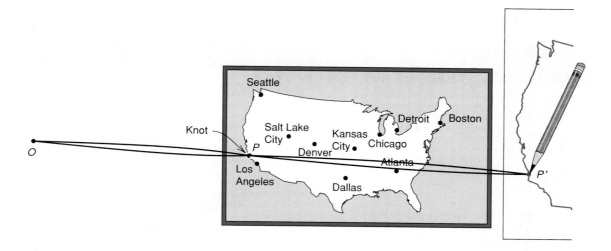

LABORATORY INVESTIGATION

The pantograph is a mechanical device for enlarging and reducing figures by producing a similarity mapping. It can be constructed from four strips of wood, metal, or posterboard that are drilled with equally spaced holes, as shown in this figure. The arms of the pantograph are hinged at points A, B, C, and P so that they move freely. Point O is the projection point and should be held fixed. As point P traces the original figure, a pencil at P' (its image) traces the enlargement. In this figure the arms are set so that point P' is twice as far from the projection point O as is point P, so the scale factor for this mapping is 2. In order to reduce a figure, the pencil is positioned at P, and P' is moved around the boundary of the original figure. With the arms set as shown in the picture, the scale factor for the reduction is 1/2. The pantograph can be changed to obtain different scale factors by adjusting the locations of points B and C. Build a pantograph and experiment with different settings of the arms.

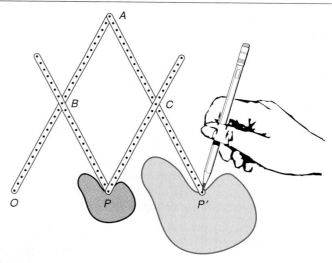

Pantograph, for reproducing similar figures

Questions for Investigation

1. For an enlargement with a scale factor of 2, point B is halfway between O and A, and point C is halfway between A and P'. Where should points B and C be placed for an enlargement with a scale factor of 4? (Hint: To check your answer, use the pantograph to enlarge a unit square. The enlargement should have an area of 16 square units. Why?)

2. What happens to the scale factor for an enlargement as point B is moved toward O and point C is moved toward A?

3. Where should points B and C be placed for an enlargement with a scale factor of 8?

4. What happens to the scale factor for an enlargement as point B is moved toward A and point C is moved toward P'?

PUZZLER

There is a standard rectangular metric size sheet of paper which when cut in half, yields two smaller sheets that are each similar to the original sheet. What is the ratio of the length of the original sheet to the width?*

SECTION 10.4 TOPOLOGICAL MAPPINGS

A monkey made these tracks in the sand by passing from one tree to another. If the monkey did not retrace any tracks, in which tree is it hiding?

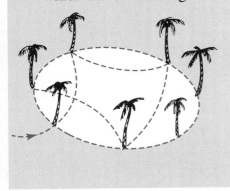

Anamorphic painting of the H. M. S. Victory *by James Steere*

Topology has been called "the mathematics of distortion." It is a special kind of geometry that involves analyzing figures and surfaces that have been twisted, bent, stretched, shrunk, or, in general, distorted from one shape to another. The distortions described above are all examples of topological motions. A figure may be changed so much by a topological motion that it bears little resemblance to the original shape. The above painting of the *H.M.S. Victory* by James Steere is a form of topological distortion called anamorphic art. The reflection of this painting in the cylindrical mirror that has been placed at the center of the picture brings the picture into perspective. It shows the stern of the ship as it appears in the model in Figure 10.48. You may wonder how mathematicians find anything left to study when figures can be so drastically changed. In the following paragraphs we will consider some of the properties of figures that are not changed by topological mappings.

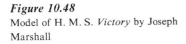

Figure 10.48
Model of H. M. S. *Victory* by Joseph Marshall

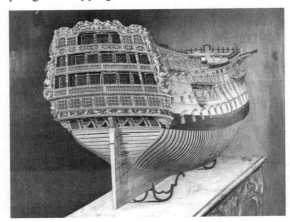

TOPOLOGICAL EQUIVALENCE

Topology is sometimes referred to as "rubber sheet" geometry because when a topological mapping is performed in a plane it is as if the plane were a rubber sheet. As the rubber sheet in Figure 10.49 is stretched, the face is distorted into several shapes. In each picture the original circle has changed shape, but it is still a simple closed curve.

Figure 10.49

topological mapping
topologically equivalent

This stretching of a figure into another shape illustrates a special type of mapping called a **topological mapping.** Any two figures that can be obtained from each other by stretching, bending, or shrinking, without tearing or cutting, are **topologically equivalent.** For example, all simple closed curves are topologically equivalent, and all simple nonclosed curves (including line segments) are topologically equivalent.

EXAMPLE A

Which of these curves are topologically equivalent?

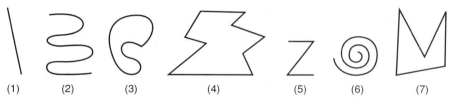

(1)   (2)   (3)   (4)   (5)   (6)   (7)

Solution   Curves (1), (2), (5), and (6) are topologically equivalent. Curves (3), (4), and (7) are topologically equivalent.

---

torus

Similar topological distortions can take place in three dimensions. Think of an object as being made of elastic material. In Figure 10.50 a donut-shaped object, called a **torus,** has been deformed in three steps into the shape of a cup. The cup is topologically equivalent to the torus because, like the torus, it has only one hole, the handle (the inside of the cup is an indentation). Since topologists view the objects in Figure 10.50 as being the same in the sense that they have the same topological properties, a topologist is sometimes playfully described as a person who doesn't know the difference between a donut and a cup of coffee.

Figure 10.50

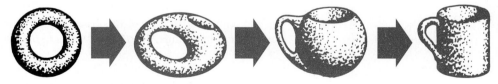

Space figures such as spheres (balls), cubes (boxes), and cylinders (cans) are all topologically equivalent. If we think of them as being made of clay or some other elastic material, any one of them could be deformed into the shape of another without being cut or punctured.

EXAMPLE B

Which of the following objects are topologically equivalent?

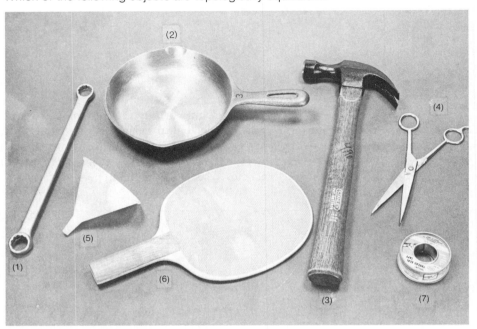

Solution   The following figures are topologically equivalent: (1) and (4); (2), (5), and (7); (3) and (6).

TOPOLOGICAL PROPERTIES

In Section 10.2 we saw that the size and shape of an object remain the same with congruence mappings. To state this another way, these mappings preserve the distance between points and their images. In Section 10.3, we saw that an object changes its size but not its shape with a similarity mapping. In this case, the mapping preserves measures of angles and ratios of the lengths of line segments, but does not preserve distances between points. With topological mappings, both the size and the shape of an object and its image can vary greatly. In other words, topological mappings do not necessarily preserve distances between points, measures of angles, or ratios of the lengths of line segments. In spite of this freedom, some properties of figures are preserved with topological mappings. Two of these are the number of sides and the number of edges of a surface.

NUMBER OF SIDES   The numbers of sides and edges of a surface are preserved with a topological mapping. A sheet of paper has 2 sides and 1 edge; an ant crawling on 1 side must cross over an edge to get to the other side [see part (a) of Figure 10.51]. Deform the sheet by bending or crumpling it in your hands, and it still has 2 sides and 1 edge. The two-sidedness and one-edgedness are properties that are preserved with a topological mapping. A cylindrical band, on the other hand, has 2 sides and 2 edges [part (b) of Figure 10.51]. A surface must be crossed to get from edge to edge, and an edge must be crossed to get from surface to surface.

Figure 10.51

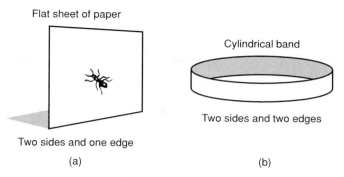

Flat sheet of paper

Two sides and one edge

(a)

Cylindrical band

Two sides and two edges

(b)

In the nineteenth century the German mathematician Ferdinand Moebius (1790–1868) discovered that if he put a half-twist in a strip of paper and fastened the edges, the resulting surface had only 1 edge and 1 side! (See Figure 10.52.) An ant crawling on this surface could reach any other spot on the surface without crawling over an edge. Such a surface is called a **Moebius band** or Moebius strip. Although the Moebius band is only a slight variation of a cylindrical band, these two figures are not topologically equivalent because they have different numbers of sides.

Moebius band

Figure 10.52

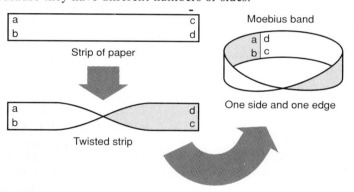

a   c
b   d

Strip of paper

a   d
b   c

Twisted strip

Moebius band

a d
b c

One side and one edge

The Moebius band has fascinated people for years and has appeared in art and literature. It is pictured below in Escher's 1963 woodcut *Moebius Strip II*. In a few cases the Moebius band has been put to practical use. The ribbon in some computer printers is a Moebius band that can be used on both sides. Also, conveyor belts are sometimes Moebius bands so that the entire surface of the band will be used and wear evenly.

Figure 10.53

Moebius Strip II, a woodcut by M. C. Escher

© 1990 M. C. Escher Heirs/Cordon Art—Baarn—Holland.

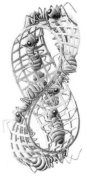

NUMBER OF PUNCTURES   Another property that is preserved by a topological mapping can be described intuitively as the number of punctures or holes.

EXAMPLE C

1. Which of these plane figures are topologically equivalent?

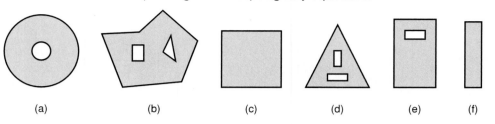

(a)   (b)   (c)   (d)   (e)   (f)

2. Which of these space figures are topologically equivalent?

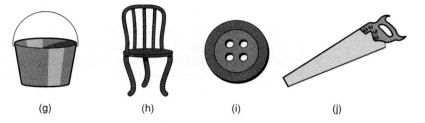

(g)   (h)   (i)   (j)

Solution   1. (a) and (e); (b) and (d); (c) and (f); 2. (g), and (j); (h) and (i).

NETWORKS

In the eighteenth century in the town of Königsberg, Germany (now Kaliningrad, Russia), a favorite pastime was walking along the Pregel River and strolling over the town's 7 bridges (Figure 10.54). During this period a natural question arose: is it possible to take a walk and cross each bridge only once? Before reading further, can you determine the answer? This question was solved by the Swiss mathematician Leonhard Euler. His solution was the beginning of network theory, which is an important branch of topology.

Figure 10.54

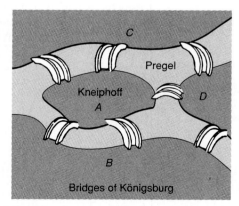

Bridges of Königsburg

Euler represented the 4 land areas of Königsberg (A, B, C, and D in Figure 10.54) as 4 points, and the 7 bridges as 7 lines joining these points. For example, the island of Kniephoff (A) can be reached by 5 bridges, and in the diagram in Figure 10.55 there are 5 lines to point *A*. The 3 lines from point *D* represent 3 bridges, etc. This kind of a diagram is called a *network*. Notice that Euler was concerned not with the size and shape of the bridges and land regions but rather with how the bridges were connected.

Figure 10.55

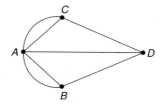

network, vertices
arcs, traversable

A **network** is a collection of points, called **vertices,** and a collection of lines, called **arcs,** connecting these points. A network is **traversable** if you can trace each arc exactly once by beginning at some point and not lifting your pencil from the paper. The problem of crossing each bridge exactly once reduces to one of traversing the network representing these bridges.

odd vertex
even vertex

Euler made the remarkable discovery that whether a network is traversable depends on the number of odd vertices. In the Königsberg network there are an *odd number* of arcs at point *A*, so *A* is called an **odd vertex.** If the number of arcs meeting at a point is *even,* the point is called an **even vertex.** Euler found that the only traversable networks are those that have either *no odd vertices* or *exactly two odd vertices.* Since the Königsberg network has 4 odd vertices, it is not traversable. Therefore, it is not possible to take a walk over the bridges of Königsberg and cross each bridge only once.

EXAMPLE D

Which of the following networks are traversable?

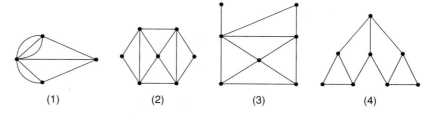

Solution

Network (1) has 2 odd vertices, so it is traversable. Network (2) has no odd vertices, so it is traversable. Networks (3) and (4) have 4 and 6 odd vertices, respectively, so they are not traversable.

We now know how to determine if a network is traversable, but is it possible to predict where you ought to begin in order to trace the network exactly once, and where you will end up? The following example considers this problem.

EXAMPLE E

Each of these networks has 2 odd vertices and is traversable. Show a beginning point and an ending point for each. Form a conjecture about the beginning and ending points of networks with exactly 2 odd vertices.

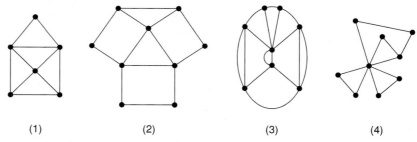

Solution

Conjecture: One odd vertex will be the starting point, and the other odd vertex will be the ending point.

Consider the conjecture in Example E. As a network is traversed, two arcs are used each time we pass through a vertex point: one in arriving at the point and one in leaving. The only way there can be an odd vertex in a traversable network is if that vertex is a beginning point or an ending point.

Next consider a network with no odd vertices.

EXAMPLE F

The following networks have no odd vertices (all vertices are even). Find at least 2 different beginning points for each. Form a conjecture about networks with no odd vertices.

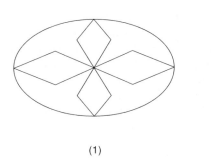 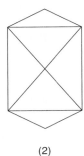 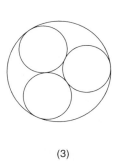

(1)   (2)   (3)

Solution   Conjecture: In a network with all even vertices, the beginning point may be any vertex, and the ending point will be the same vertex.

The conjecture in Example F seems reasonable. Since the arcs occur in pairs at each vertex, beginning at a vertex will always require returning to that vertex.

The facts illustrated in Examples D through F are summarized in the following statements.

TRAVERSABLE NETWORKS

1. A network with exactly two odd vertices is traversable. Either odd vertex may be the beginning point, and the other odd vertex is the ending point.
2. A network with no odd vertices is traversable. Any vertex may be the beginning point, and the same vertex will also be the ending point.
3. A network with more than two odd vertices is not traversable.

FOUR-COLOR PROBLEM   For over 100 years mathematicians believed, but could not prove, that 4 colors were sufficient to color any map in a plane. The only requirement for map coloring is that 2 regions sharing a common boundary have different colors. If 2 regions meet at only one point, they do not share a common boundary. No one had been able to draw a map that required more than 4 colors, but on the other hand, it could not be proven that 4 colors are all that is needed.

EXAMPLE G

Using the conditions stated in the previous paragraph, determine the minimum number of different colors needed to color each map.

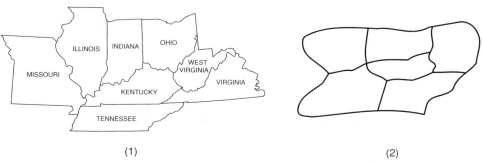

(1)   (2)

Solution   Map (1) requires 4 colors, and map (2) requires 3 colors.

In 1976, two University of Illinois mathematicians, Kenneth Appel and Wolfgang Haken, announced they had proven that 4 colors are all that is necessary to color any map. This result was exciting to mathematicians, and the proof attracted much attention because it was long and made extensive use of computers. The problem was solved by representing map regions as points and boundaries as arcs connecting these points. Using this network approach, Appel and Haken were able to reduce the problem to an examination of 1936 basic map forms. Every map is topologically equivalent to one of these basic forms or else differs in some insignificant way. Appel and Haken fed their map forms into the computer, and after 1200 hours the computer determined that each map can be colored with 4 or fewer colors.

PROBLEM-SOLVING APPLICATION

Network theory has a wide range of applications including determining routes, designing electric circuits, and planning schedules. The solution to the following problem illustrates one use of networks.

■ PROBLEM

A tour guide is planning a tour of a museum. To minimize congestion at doorways, the guide would like to have the tour pass through each door of the museum exactly once. For what type of floor plans is this possible?

Understanding the Problem   The tour may begin at any point inside or outside the museum and end at any point. Show that a tour such as the one described above can be conducted for the floor diagram shown here. Can the tour be started either outside or inside with this floor plan?

Question 1

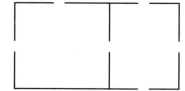

Devising a Plan   One approach is to draw floor diagrams with different numbers of rooms and doors and try planning tours. By counting the numbers of rooms, doors, and doors per room, you may discover a pattern. Another approach is to describe the floor plan by a network and then determine if the network is traversable. Can such a tour be conducted for the following floor plan?

Question 2

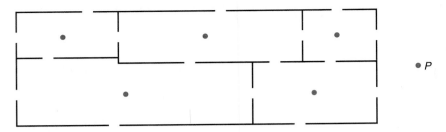

Carrying Out the Plan   The network below illustrates the preceding floor plan. Each room is represented by a vertex point. Notice that a vertex (point *P*) is needed to represent the region outside the floor plan. Is this network traversable? How does the use of networks suggest a general solution to the original problem?

Question 3

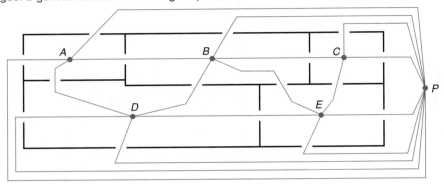

Looking Back   Suppose that in addition to requiring that each door be passed through only once, we also require that the tour begin and end in the same room. For what type of floor plans is this possible?

Question 4

Answers to Questions 1–4

1.

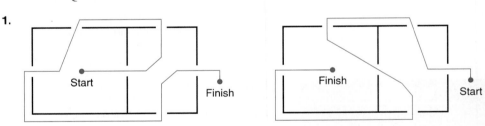

2. No

3. No, because there are 4 odd vertices. In general, a tour that passes through each door exactly once is possible if and only if the network for the floor plan is traversable.

4. This type of tour is possible if the network for the floor plan has no odd vertices.

RELATED ACTIVITIES IN

Mathematics for Elementary Teachers: An Activity Approach, 3e

Activity Set 10.4   **Topological Investigations and Entertainment:** Several activities with Moebius bands are introduced, along with topological tricks and puzzles.

Just for Fun   **Topological Games:** Gale Game (a game on grids) and Sprouts (a network game)

PUZZLER

Make the object shown here using a piece of cardboard, a string, and a ring that is too large to pass through the hole in the panel. The problem is to move the ring from loop A to loop B without cutting or untying the string. How can this be done?

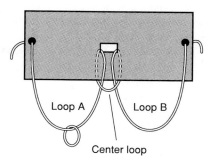

Loop A   Loop B

Center loop

EXERCISES AND PROBLEMS 10.4

1. According to the Swiss psychologist Jean Piaget, children's first discoveries of geometry are topological, and by the age of 3 they can readily distinguish between open and closed figures.* Match up 4 pairs of figures that a child who "thinks topologically" would consider to be the same.

a.

b.

c.

d.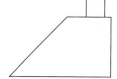

e.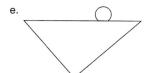

f.

g.

h.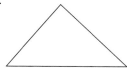

2. Each object in parts a through g is topologically equivalent to either the sphere in figure (i), the torus in figure (ii), or the two-holed object in figure (iii). Match each object to the figure that it is topologically equivalent to.

        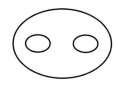

Figure (i)   Figure (ii)   Figure (iii)

a.   b.   c.   d.

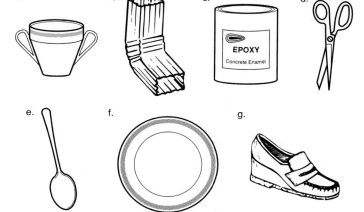

e.   f.   g.

3. Which of these plane figures are topologically equivalent?

a.

b.

c.

d.

e.

f.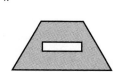

g.

h.

i.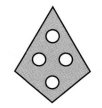

*J. Piaget, "How Children Form Mathematical Concepts," *Scientific American* 189, no. 5 (1953): 74–79.

4. Each of these networks has two odd vertices and is traversable. Show a beginning point and an ending point for each. What is always true about the beginning and ending points of networks with exactly two odd vertices?

a.
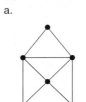

b.
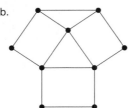

c.
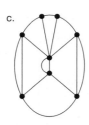

d.

5. Which of the networks below are traversable? Trace each traversable network on a separate piece of paper. Mark a path with arrows, and indicate the beginning and ending points.

a.
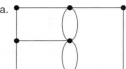

b.
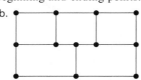

c.
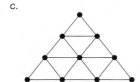

d.
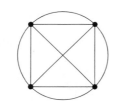

e.
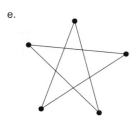

f.
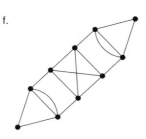

6. The vertices and edges of polyhedra are three-dimensional networks.

Tetrahedron

Cube

Octahedron

Dodecahedron   Icosahedron

a. Which one of the 5 regular polyhedra is traversable?

b. What is the least number of diagonals that need to be drawn on the faces of the cube before the network will be traversable?

7. Many years after Euler proved that it was impossible to take a walk in which each of the 7 bridges of Königsberg is crossed exactly once, an eighth bridge was built. Sketch a network with 4 vertex points for the land areas A, B, C, and D and 8 arcs for the bridges. Is this network traversable?

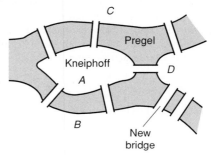

8. Below is a sketch of 2 islands (A, B), 4 land regions (C, D, E, F), and 15 bridges. Is it possible to plan a walk in which each bridge is crossed exactly once? Explain your answer.

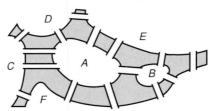

9. Draw a network representing each floor plan below. For which floor plan is it possible to plan a walk in which each door is passed through exactly once?

a.
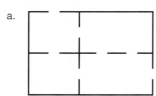

b.
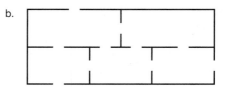

10. For each of the following floor plans, determine if it is possible to plan a walk in which you pass through each door exactly once and begin and end on the outside of the house.

a.

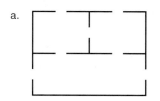

b.

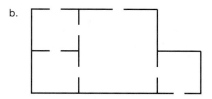

c.

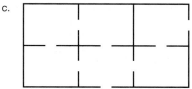

d.

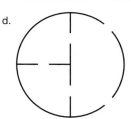

11. Consider networks with 0, 1, 2, 3, and 4 odd vertices. Make a conjecture about the number of odd vertices that are possible in a network.

12. Determine the minimum number of colors required to color each map if regions with a common boundary (other than a single point) must be different colors. (Note: The interiors of the circles in parts (b) and (c) are to be colored.)

a.

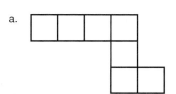

b.

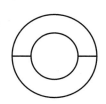

c.

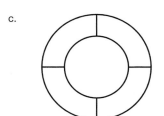

d.

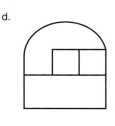

13. When maps are colored, it is desirable to use different colors for regions with a common boundary.
   a. What is the minimum number of colors required to color any map, regardless of the number of regions?
   b. What is the minimum number of colors required to color the map below?

14. Use the maps below to answer questions a and b.
   a. What is the minimum number of colors needed for each map?
   b. What are the numbers of even and odd vertices on each map, not counting the vertices on the outer boundary?

(i)

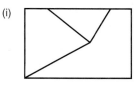

(ii)

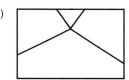

(iii)

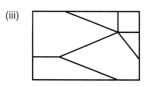

(iv)

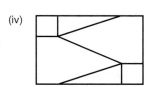

   c. Form a conjecture about the types of vertices on maps that require just two colors. Check your conjecture by drawing more maps.
   d. Form a conjecture about the types of vertices a map must have if it requires 3 or more colors.

15. Some grids are traversable networks and some are not.
   a. Isometric grids (that is, tessellations of equilateral triangles) are traversable. Explain why. Mark beginning and ending points for each grid below.

For parts b through e, copy the rectangular grid from the inside cover.

b. Rectangular grids are not traversable. Explain why.

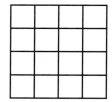

c. A 3 by 3 grid of squares can be made traversable by removing only 3 squares. Mark beginning and ending points for transversing this grid.

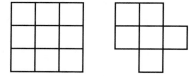

d. Determine the minimum number of squares that must be removed in order for each of the following grids to be traversable.

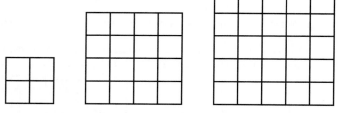

e. Find a pattern in parts c and d and predict the minimum number of squares that must be removed from a 10 by 10 grid of squares in order for the remaining network to be traversable.

f. Write an algebraic expression for the minimum number of squares that must be removed from an n by n grid of squares in order for the remaining network to be traversable.

Featured Strategies: Making a Drawing and Making a Table

16. There is a relationship among the three parts of a network (vertices, arcs, and regions of the plane) that is true for all networks in a plane. What is this relationship?

a. Understanding the Problem Network (i) has 6 vertices, 6 regions (numbered 1 through 6), and 10 arcs. Notice that the outside of the network is counted as 1 region. (The reason for this will be clear later.) How many vertices, regions, and arcs does network (ii) have?

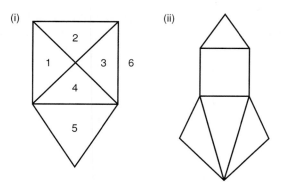

b. Devising a Plan Drawing networks and forming a table showing the numbers of vertices, regions, and arcs may reveal a pattern. Draw a network with 4 vertices and 7 arcs. How many regions does it have? (Don't forget to count the region outside the network.)

c. Carrying Out the Plan The following table lists the numbers of vertices, regions, and arcs for figure (i). Draw some more networks and fill in the table. What relationship is there among the numbers of vertices, regions, and arcs?

Vertices	Regions	Arcs
6	6	10
—	—	—
—	—	—
—	—	—

d. Looking Back If you found the correct relationship in part c, it should hold for any network. Show that the relationship holds for the following special networks.

Counting the outside of the network as 1 region, as required in part a, results in a relationship that is similar to a famous relationship among the vertices, faces, and edges of polyhedra. What is this relationship?

17. Figure A is made up of 4 polygons that are connected by common nonoverlapping sides. Figure B shows that a continuous arc can be drawn that intersects every side of each polygon exactly once.

Figure A   Figure B

a. On which of the following figures can you draw a continuous arc that passes through each side of each polygon? (There is no requirement that the arc begin on the interior of a polygon; however, the arc must not intersect a vertex of the figure.)

(i) 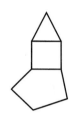   (ii)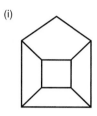

(iii) 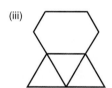   (iv)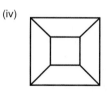

b. Make a conjecture about the conditions under which a continuous arc can be drawn for such polygons.

18. Anamorphic art is a special type of topological mapping.* Finish copying the design in figure 1 onto the corresponding regions of the grid in figure 2. When figure 2 is completed, will it be congruent to figure 1? similar to figure 1?

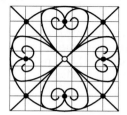

Figure 1

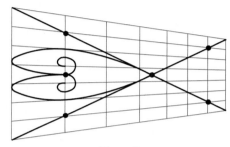

Figure 2

19. The first 3 matchstick figures shown below are the only topologically different figures that can be formed with 3 matches, subject to the condition that the matches meet only at their endpoints with no overlapping. (The figure with 3 matches in a row is topologically equivalent to the Z-shaped pattern.) How many topologically distinct figures can be formed with 4 matches, subject to the above conditions?

*For more details on sketching cylindrical and conical anamorphic pictures, see M. Gardner, "The Curious Magic of Anamorphic Art," *Scientific American* 232, no. 1 (1975).

LABORATORY INVESTIGATION

A Moebius band is formed by taking a strip of paper, twisting it, and taping the edges together (see page 553). Form Moebius bands to use in the following investigations.

Questions for Investigation

1. Cut a Moebius band in half lengthwise, as shown here. What surface results?
2. Beginning one-third of the way in from one edge, cut a Moebius band as shown here, continuing until you return to the beginning point. What is the result?
3. Form two Moebius bands and tape the edge of one perpendicular to the edge of the other. Cut each band lengthwise along its center line as in #1. What happens?
4. Form two cylindrical bands without twists and tape the edge of one band perpendicular to the edge of the other. Predict what will happen if you cut each band lengthwise along its center line, as in #1. Now actually cut the bands. Was your prediction correct?

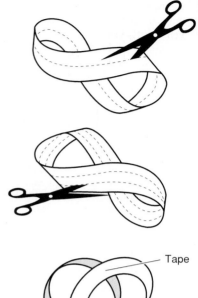

Tape

PUZZLER

Cut two pieces of string. Tie each end of one piece to your wrists and each end of the second piece to a friend's wrists, so that the strings are linked together as shown here. How can the two of you unlink yourselves without untying or cutting the string?

CHAPTER REVIEW

1. Mappings

a. A **mapping** is a function that assigns points to points such that to each point in one set there corresponds a unique point, called the **image,** in the second set.

b. A mapping of $\triangle ABC$ to $\triangle RST$ such that R, S, and T are the images of A, B, and C, respectively, creates the following corresponding parts: **corresponding vertices,** $A \leftrightarrow R$, $B \leftrightarrow S$, $C \leftrightarrow T$; **corresponding sides,** $\overline{AB} \leftrightarrow \overline{RS}$, $\overline{BC} \leftrightarrow \overline{ST}$, $\overline{AC} \leftrightarrow \overline{RT}$; and **corresponding angles,** $\angle A \leftrightarrow \angle R$, $\angle B \leftrightarrow \angle S$, $\angle C \leftrightarrow \angle T$.

c. If figure A is mapped to figure A′ by one mapping and figure A′ is mapped to figure A″ by a second mapping, the single mapping that maps A to A″ is called a **composition of mappings.**

2. Congruence

a. Two polygons are **congruent** if and only if there is a mapping from one to the other such that (1) corresponding sides are congruent and (2) corresponding angles are congruent.

b. An image created by a **translation, reflection, rotation,** or **glide reflection** is congruent to the original figure.

c. **Side-Side-Side** (SSS) If three sides of one triangle are congruent to three sides of another triangle, the triangles are congruent.

d. **Side-Angle-Side** (SAS) If two sides and the included angle of one triangle are congruent to two sides and the included angle of another triangle, the triangles are congruent.

e. **Angle-Side-Angle** (ASA) If two angles and the included side of one triangle are congruent to two angles and the included side of another triangle, the triangles are congruent.

3. **Similarity**

   a. Two polygons are similar if and only if there is a mapping from one to the other such that (1) corresponding angles are congruent and (2) lengths of corresponding sides have the same ratio.

   b. **Angle-Angle** (AA) If two angles of one triangle are congruent to two angles of another triangle, the triangles are similar.

   c. **Side-Side-Side** (SSS) If the corresponding sides of two triangles are proportional, the triangles are similar.

   d. If the **scale factor** for a similarity mapping is greater than 1, the image is an **enlargement.** If the scale factor is less than 1, the image is a **reduction.**

   e. If a plane figure is related to a similar figure by a scale factor of k, where k is any positive real number, then the second figure will have an area k^2 times the area of the first figure.

   f. If a figure in space is related to a similar figure by a scale factor of k, where k is any positive real number, then the second figure will have a volume k^3 times the volume of the first figure.

4. **Topological Equivalence**

   a. Any two figures that can be obtained from each other by stretching, bending, or shrinking, without tearing or cutting, are **topologically equivalent.**

   b. Two three-dimensional figures that are topologically equivalent have the **same number of sides.**

   c. Two three-dimensional figures that are topologically equivalent have the **same number of punctures or holes.**

5. **Geometric Terms**

   a. A line that is perpendicular to a segment at its midpoint is called the **perpendicular bisector** of the segment.

   b. A circle that contains all the vertices of a polygon is called a **circumscribed circle.**

   c. A **network** is a collection of points, called **vertices,** and a collection of lines, called **arcs,** connecting these points.

   d. If the number of arcs meeting at a point is odd, the point is called an **odd vertex.** If the number of arcs is even, the point is called an **even vertex.**

6. **Geometric Properties**

   a. The sum of the lengths of two sides of a triangle is greater than the length of the third side.

   b. A point is on the perpendicular bisector of a line segment if and only if it is equidistant from the endpoints of the segment.

   c. A network is traversable if it has exactly two odd vertices or no odd vertices.

7. **Constructions**

   a. A geometric figure produced with a straightedge and compass is called a **construction.**

   b. Types of constructions:
   Copying a line segment
   Copying an angle
   Bisecting a line segment
   Bisecting an angle
   Constructing a perpendicular to a line through a point not on the line
   Constructing a line parallel to a given line through a point not on the line
   Circumscribing a circle about a triangle

CHAPTER TEST

1. Use a compass and straightedge to carry out each construction. Explain your steps.

   a. The bisector of ∡*A*

   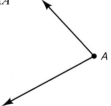

   b. The perpendicular to line *m* through point *Q*

   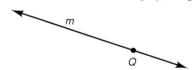

   c. The line through point *P* that is parallel to line ℓ

   d. The perpendicular to line *n* through point *R*

   R •

2. Construct the circumscribed circle about △*ABC*.

   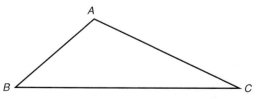

3. Construct a triangle, if possible, whose sides are congruent to the given line segments. If it is not possible, explain why.

   a. ———————————————
   ———————————
   ———————————————

   b. ————————
   ———————————————
   —————————

4. Which of the following pairs of triangles are congruent? For each congruent pair, state the appropriate congruence property of triangles and write the congruence correspondence.

a.

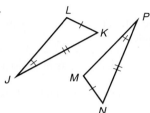

b.

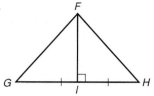

c.

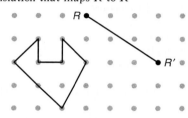

d.

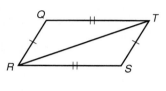

5. Sketch the image for each mapping.
   a. A translation that maps R to R'

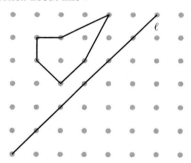

   b. A reflection about line ℓ

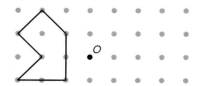

   c. A 90° clockwise rotation about point O

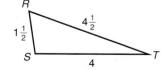

6. Describe the single mapping that is equivalent to the composition of the two given mappings.
   a. A clockwise rotation of 45° followed by a counterclockwise rotation of 70° about the same center of rotation.
   b. A reflection about line ℓ followed by a reflection about line m, when ℓ and m are parallel lines.
   c. A translation from P to P' to the right 12 units and up 8 units, followed by a translation of P' to P'' to the right 5 units and down 10 units

7. Using point O as the projection point, determine the image of each figure for the given scale factor.
   a. Scale factor of 2

   b. Scale factor of $1/3$

   c. Scale factor of $^-1/2$

8. Which of the following pairs of triangles are similar? For each similar pair, state the appropriate similarity property of triangles and write the similarity correspondence.

a.

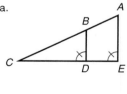

b.

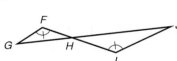

c.

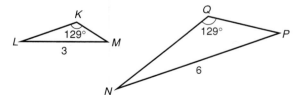

d.

9. If the figures listed below are similar, explain why. If not, sketch a counterexample with measurements.
   a. Two rectangles
   b. Two squares
   c. Two right triangles
   d. Two equilateral triangles
   e. Two congruent quadrilaterals

10. The following figure has a volume of 12 cubic units and a surface area of 32 square units.

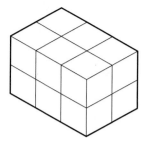

   a. What is the volume of an enlargement with a scale factor of 3?

   b. What is the surface area of an enlargement with a scale factor of 3?

   c. What is the volume of a reduction with a scale factor of 1/2?

   d. What is the surface area of a reduction with a scale factor of 1/2?

11. Match the figures that are topologically equivalent.

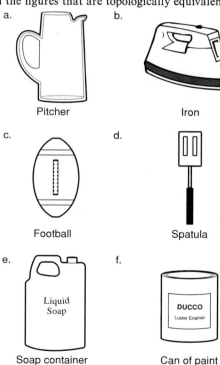

a. Pitcher   b. Iron

c. Football   d. Spatula

e. Liquid Soap — Soap container   f. DUCCO Luster Enamel — Can of paint

12. Determine whether each network is traversable. If so, show a beginning point and an ending point.

   a.   b.

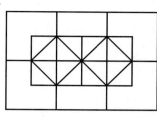

13. A realtor is planning an open house at two locations (see floor plans a and b). Can a tour of each floor plan be conducted so that each door is passed through exactly once, if the tour is to begin outside and end inside? If so, describe a path and the ending point.

   a.

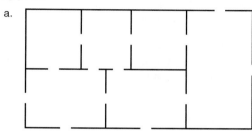

   b.

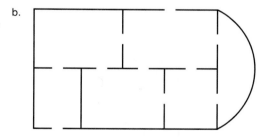

14. The scale factor from a model to a life-size table is 4, and the model and table are both made of the same type of wood.

   a. If the life-size table has a height of 28 in., what is the height of the model?

   b. If the model requires 1/32 qt (1 fl oz) of stain, how many quarts of stain are needed for the life-size table?

   c. If the model weighs 3/4 lb, what is the weight of the life-size table?

15. A person 6 ft tall standing under a streetlight casts a 10 ft shadow on the ground. If the base of the streetlight is 45 ft from the tip of the shadow, what is the height of the streetlight?

BIBLIOGRAPHY

Barr, S. *Experiments in Topology.* New York: Thomas Y. Crowell, 1964.

Bidwell, J. K. "Using Reflections to Find Symmetric and Asymmetric Patterns." *Arithmetic Teacher* 34 (March 1987): 10–15.

Horak, V. M., and W. J. Horak. "Let's Do It: Using Geometry Tiles as a Manipulative for Developing Basic Concepts." *Arithmetic Teacher* 30 (April 1983): 8–15.

Jensen, R. J. "Teaching Mathematics with Technology: Scale Drawings." *Arithmetic Teacher* 35 (May 1988): 36–38.

Johnson, M. "Generating Patterns for Transformations." *Arithmetic Teacher* 24 (March 1977): 191–195.

Kidder, R. "Euclidean Transformations: Elementary School Spaceometry." *Arithmetic Teacher* 24 (March 1977): 201–207.

Lappan, G., and R. Even. "Research into Practice: Similarity in the Middle Grades." *Arithmetic Teacher* 35 (May 1988): 32–35.

Maletsky, E. "Activities: Fun with Flips." *Mathematics Teacher 66* (October 1973): 531–534.

Mathematics Resource Project. *Geometry and Visualization.* Palo Alto, CA: Creative Publications, 1985.

Poggi, J. M. "An Invitation to Topology." *Arithmetic Teacher* 33 (December 1985): 8–11.

Ross, J. "How To Make a Moebius Hat." *Mathematics Teacher* (April 1985): 268–269.

Ryoti, D. E. "Computer Corner [Using the Computer and LOGO to Investigate Symmetry]." *Arithmetic Teacher* 34 (November 1986): 36–37.

Sanok, G. "Living in a World of Transformations." *Arithmetic Teacher* 25 (April 1978): 36–40.

Sawada, D. "Symmetry and Tessellations from Rotational Transformations on Transparencies." *Arithmetic Teacher* 33 (December 1986): 12–13.

Senk, S. L., and D. B. Hirschhorn. "Multiple Approaches to Geometry: Teaching Similarity." *Mathematics Teacher* 83 (April 1990): 274–280.

Sicklick, F., S. B. Turkel, and F. R. Curcio. "The 'Transformation Game'." *Arithmetic Teacher* 36 (October 1988): 37–41.

Woodward, E., and P. G. Buckner. "Reflections and Symmetry—A Second-Grade Miniunit." *Arithmetic Teacher* 35 (October 1987): 8–11.

Zaslavsky, C. "Networks—New York Subways, a Piece of String, and African Traditions." *Arithmetic Teacher* 29 (October 1981): 42–47.

Zurstadt, B. "Tessellations and the Art of M. C. Escher." *Arithmetic Teacher* 31 (January 1984): 54–55.

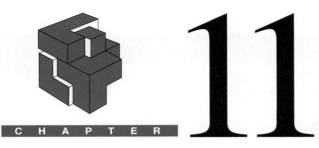

11 *Statistics*

SPOTLIGHT ON TEACHING

Excerpts from NCTM's Standard 10 for Teaching Mathematics in Grades 5–8*

In grades K–4, students begin to explore basic ideas of statistics by gathering data appropriate to their grade level, organizing them in charts or graphs, and reading information from displays of data. These concepts should be expanded in the middle grades. . . . The data to be gathered, organized, and studied should be interesting and relevant; students' interest in themselves and their peers, for example, can motivate them to investigate the "average" student in the class or school. . . .

Random samples, bias in sampling procedures, and limited samples all are important considerations. For instance, would collecting data from the men's and women's basketball teams provide needed information to determine the average height of a college student? Will a larger sample reveal a more accurate picture of the percentage of students with brown hair? The graph [above] illustrates the results of increasing the sample size.

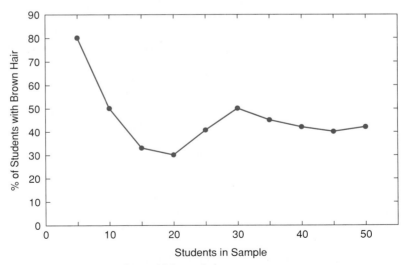

Graph of numbers of students with brown hair

*Reprinted by permission of the National Council of Teachers of Mathematics.

SECTION 11.1 DESCRIPTIVE STATISTICS

A large metropolitan police department made a check of the clothing worn by pedestrians killed in traffic at night. About 4/5 of the victims were wearing dark clothes, and 1/5 were wearing light-colored garments. Explain why this study does not necessarily show that pedestrians are less likely to encounter traffic mishaps at night if they wear something white.

"Hello? Beasts of the Field? This is Lou, over in Birds of the Air. **Anything funny** going on at your end?"

The employees of the Animated Animal Company keep records of the number of toys each machine produces and the number of breakdowns of each machine. Figure 11.1 shows that machine III outproduced machines I and II, and machine II had the most problems. Such numerical information is called **statistics.**

statistics

Figure 11.1

Weekly Record of Birds Produced

	M	T	W	Th	F	Breakdowns
Machine I	165	158	98	125	260	13
Machine II	117	82	46	6	30	24
Machine III	182	243	196	305	261	4

descriptive statistics

inferential statistics

The word "statistics" also means the science of collecting and interpreting data. There are two broad areas of this science: *descriptive statistics* and *inferential statistics*. **Descriptive statistics** is the science of describing data. The number of birds produced each day by machine I is an example of a descriptive statistic. **Inferential statistics** is the science of interpreting data in order to make predictions. Sampling is an important part of inferential statistics. For example, if the manager of Birds of the Air randomly selects 100 birds off the assembly line and finds that 3 are defective, he can estimate that the number of bad birds in a batch of 5000 will be 150. How? This section introduces methods of descriptive statistics.

■ HISTORICAL HIGHLIGHT

Statistics had its beginning in the seventeenth century in the work of the Englishman John Graunt. Graunt used a publication called "Bills of Mortality," which listed births, christenings, and deaths. Here are some of his conclusions: the number of male births exceeds the number of female births; there is a higher death rate in urban areas than in rural areas; and more men than women die violent deaths. Graunt used these statistics in his book *Natural and Political Observations of Mortality*. In his work he summarized great amounts of information to make it understandable (descriptive statistics) and made conjectures about large populations based on small samples (inferential statistics).

CHARTS AND GRAPHS

Graphs provide quick visual summaries of information. Some of the more common graphs are introduced in the following paragraphs.

BAR GRAPHS   The table in Figure 11.2 lists the responses of 40 teachers to a proposal to begin and end the school day one-half hour earlier. Teachers' responses are classified into one of three categories: Favor (F); Oppose (O); or No opinion (N).

Figure 11.2

Teacher	Category	Teacher	Category	Teacher	Category
1	F	14	F	27	N
2	F	15	O	28	O
3	O	16	F	29	F
4	N	17	N	30	O
5	F	18	O	31	F
6	O	19	F	32	F
7	O	20	N	33	N
8	F	21	F	34	F
9	F	22	F	35	O
10	F	23	O	36	F
11	O	24	F	37	N
12	O	25	N	38	F
13	N	26	O	39	O
				40	O

bar graph   The data from the preceding table are summarized by the **bar graph** in Figure 11.3. The intervals on the horizontal axis represent the three categories, and the vertical axis indicates the frequency of responses in each category. Notice that this graph provides a quick summary of the data.

Figure 11.3

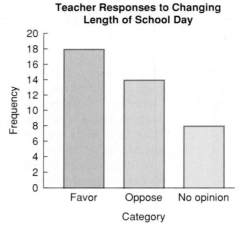

**Teacher Responses to Changing
Length of School Day**

pie chart

PIE CHARTS   A **pie chart** is another way to summarize data visually. A disc (pie) is used to represent the "whole," and its pie-shaped sectors represent the "parts" in proportion to the whole. Consider, for example, the data from Figure 11.2. A total of 40 responses are classified into three categories: 18 in favor, 14 opposed, and 8 with no opinion. These categories represent 18/40, 14/40, and 8/40 of the total responses, respectively. To determine the central angles for the sectors of a pie graph, we multiply these fractions by 360°.

$$\frac{18}{40} \times 360° = 162° \qquad \frac{14}{40} \times 360° = 126° \qquad \frac{8}{40} \times 360° = 72°$$

The pie chart is constructed by first drawing a circle and making three sectors using the central angles in part (a) of Figure 11.4. Then each sector is labeled so that the viewer can easily interpret the results, as in part (b).

Figure 11.4

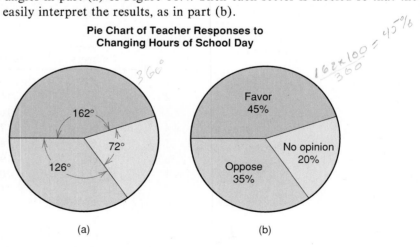

**Pie Chart of Teacher Responses to
Changing Hours of School Day**

(a)   (b)

stem and leaf plot

STEM AND LEAF PLOTS   A **stem and leaf plot** is a quick numerical method of providing a visual summary of data. As the name indicates, this method suggests the stems of plants and their leaves. Consider the following test scores for a class of 26 students:

82, 66, 70, 77, 94, 67, 73, 78, 82, 74, 90, 45, 62,
85, 57, 72, 94, 83, 85, 70, 95, 71, 89, 87, 75, 74

Since the scores in the preceding list range from the 40s to the 90s, the tens digits, 4, 5, 6, 7, 8, and 9, are chosen as the stems, and the unit digits of the numbers will represent the leaves (Figure 11.5). The first step in forming a stem and leaf plot is to list the stem values in increasing order in a column [part (a)]. Next, each leaf value is written in the row corresponding to that number's stem [part (b)]. Here the leaf values have been recorded in the order in which they appear on page 572, but they could be listed in increasing order. The stem and leaf plot shows at a glance the lowest and highest test scores and that the 70s interval has the greatest number of scores.

Figure 11.5

Stem	Leaf		Stem	Leaf
4			4	5
5			5	7
6			6	6 7 2
7			7	0 7 3 8 4 2 0 1 5 4
8			8	2 2 5 3 5 9 7
9			9	4 0 4 5

(a)   (b)

A stem and leaf plot shows where the data are concentrated and the extreme values. You may have noticed that this method of portraying data is like a bar graph turned on its side (rotate this page 90° counterclockwise). Although a stem and leaf plot is not as attractive as a bar graph, it has the advantage of showing all the original data.

A stem and leaf plot that compares two sets of data can be created by forming a central stem and plotting the leaves for the first set of data on one side of the stem and the leaves for the second set on the other side. Suppose the same class of students obtains the following scores on a second test:

85, 89, 70, 76, 49, 66, 71, 71, 75, 82, 73, 77, 68,
79, 55, 91, 52, 63, 64, 84, 81, 68, 73, 67, 66, 72

A stem and leaf plot of scores on both tests is shown in Figure 11.6. In this plot the leaves for both sets of scores have been arranged in order to aid in comparing the test scores. It appears that overall performance was better on the first test. For example, the first test has almost twice as many scores above 80 and half as many scores below 70 as the second test.

Figure 11.6

Second test — Leaf	Stem	First test — Leaf
9	4	5
5 2	5	7
8 8 7 6 6 4 3	6	2 6 7
9 7 6 5 3 3 2 1 1 0	7	0 0 1 2 3 4 4 5 7 8
9 5 4 2 1	8	2 2 3 5 5 7 9
1	9	0 4 4 5

HISTOGRAMS   When data fall naturally into a few categories, they can be illustrated by bar graphs or pie charts. However, data are often spread over a wide range with many different values. In this case it is convenient to group the data in intervals. The data can then be pictured as a bar graph. Such a graph is called a **histogram.** Thus a histogram is just a bar graph for grouped data.

histogram

The following list shows the gestation periods in days for 42 species of animals.

ass 365	deer 201	moose 240
baboon 187	dog 61	mouse 21
badger 60	elk 250	opossum 15
bat 50	fox 52	pig 112

black bear 219	giraffe 425	puma 90
grizzly bear 225	goat (domestic) 151	rabbit 37
polar bear 240	goat (mountain) 184	rhinoceros 498
beaver 122	gorilla 257	sea lion 350
buffalo 278	guinea pig 68	sheep 154
camel 406	horse 330	squirrel 44
cat 63	kangaroo 42	tiger 105
chimpanzee 231	leopard 98	whale 365
chipmunk 31	lion 100	wolf 63
cow 284	monkey 165	zebra 365

Since there are so many different gestation periods, we will group them in intervals. The number of intervals is arbitrary, but usually a number from 5 to 15 is chosen. One method of determining the length of each interval is to first compute the difference between the highest and lowest values, which is $498 - 15 = 483$. Then select the desired number of intervals and determine the interval length. If we select 10 as the number of intervals, then

$$483 \div 10 = 48.3$$

and we may choose 50 (because of its convenience) as the width of each interval. Figure 11.7 lists the number of animals in each interval and is called a **frequency table**.

Figure 11.7   **frequency table**

Frequency table

Interval	0–49	50–99	100–149	150–199	200–249	250–299	300–349	350–399	400–449	450–499
Frequency	6	9	4	5	6	4	1	4	2	1

The histogram for the grouped data in the frequency table is shown in Figure 11.8. We can quickly see from this graph that the greatest number of gestation periods occurs in the interval from 50 to 99 days and that there are only a few animals with gestation periods of over 400 days.

Figure 11.8

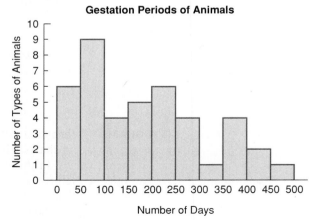

LINE GRAPHS   Another method of presenting data visually is the **line graph**, or **frequency polygon**. This type of graph is often used to show changes over a period of time. For example, the line graph in Figure 11.9 shows the increase in population from 1800 to 1980 at twenty-year intervals. A line graph can be obtained from a bar graph or histogram by connecting the midpoints of the tops of the bars.

line graph
frequency polygon

Figure 11.9

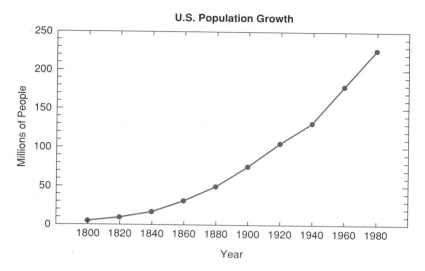

MEASURES OF CENTRAL TENDENCY

measure of central tendency

Another way to summarize data is to represent all values by a single number: a "central" or typical value. A **measure of central tendency** is a number that locates or approximates the "center" of a set of data. There are three measures of central tendency: the *mean*, the *median*, and the *mode*.

MEAN The diagram in part (a) of Figure 11.10 represents the heights of 7 children. One way to represent all the heights by a single number is to "level off" the heights. If 3 centimeters is taken from each of the three tallest heights and distributed among the four shortest, as shown in part (b), the heights level off at 126 centimeters.

Figure 11.10

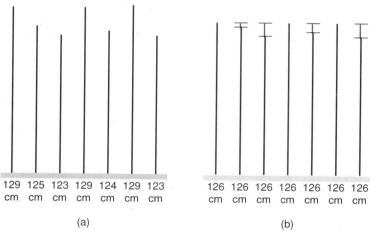

Perhaps you can see by looking at Figure 11.10 why the same result is obtained by adding the 7 numbers,

$$123 + 123 + 124 + 125 + 129 + 129 + 129 = 882$$

and dividing the sum by 7:

$$882 \div 7 = 126$$

mean

This type of "center" number is called the **mean** and is the number we often refer to as the *numerical average* or, simply, the *average*.

MEAN

> The **mean** of a set of data is the sum of all measurements divided by the total number of measurements.
>
> $$\bar{x} = \frac{x_1 + x_2 + x_3 + \cdots + x_n}{n}$$
>
> where x_1, x_2, etc., are n measurements and $\bar{x}$ (read "x bar") denotes the mean.

The table in Figure 11.11 lists the magnitudes of the major earthquakes from 1946 to 1987 and the number of deaths caused by each quake. The death tolls vary from a low of 21 to a high of 800,000. Let's calculate the mean for these data. The sum of the numbers of deaths from the 44 quakes is 1,038,845. The mean is 1,038,845/44, or approximately 23,610 deaths per quake. Notice that this *central number* is higher than all but three of the numbers in this list.

Figure 11.11

Major earthquakes from 1946 to 1987

Date	Place	Deaths	Magnitude
1946 Dec. 21	Japan, Honshu	2000	8.4
1948 June 28	Japan, Fukui	5131	7.3
1949 Aug. 5	Ecuador, Pelileo	6000	6.8
1950 Aug. 15	India, Assam	1530	8.7
1953 Mar. 18	NW Turkey	1200	7.2
1956 June 10–17	N. Afghanistan	2000	7.7
1957 July 2	Northern Iran	2500	7.4
1957 Dec. 13	Western Iran	2000	7.1
1960 Feb. 29	Morocco, Agidir	12,000	5.8
1960 May 21–30	Southern Chile	5000	8.3
1962 Sept. 1	Northwestern Iran	12,230	7.1
1963 July 26	Yugoslavia, Skopje	1100	6.0
1964 Mar. 27	Alaska	114	8.5
1966 Aug. 19	Eastern Turkey	2520	6.9
1968 Aug. 31	Northeastern Iran	12,000	7.4
1970 Mar. 28	Western Turkey	1086	7.4
1970 May 31	Northern Peru	66,794	7.7
1971 Feb. 9	Cal., San Fernando Valley	65	6.5
1972 Apr. 10	Southern Iran	5057	6.9
1972 Dec. 23	Nicaragua	5000	6.2
1974 Dec. 28	Pakistan (9 towns)	5200	6.3
1975 Sept. 6	Turkey (Lice, etc.)	2312	6.8
1976 Feb. 4	Guatemala	22,778	7.5
1976 May 6	Northeast Italy	946	6.5
1976 June 26	New Guinea, Iran, Jaya	443	7.1
1976 July 28	China, Tangshan	800,000	8.2
1976 Aug. 17	Philippines, Mindanao	8000	7.8
1976 Nov. 24	Eastern Turkey	4000	7.9
1977 Mar. 4	Romania, Bucharest, etc.	1541	7.5
1977 Aug. 19	Indonesia	200	8.0
1977 Nov. 23	Northwestern Argentina	100	8.2
1978 June 19	Japan, Sendai	21	7.5
1978 Sept. 16	Northeast Iran	25,000	7.7
1979 Sept. 12	Indonesia	100	8.1
1979 Dec. 12	Colombia, Ecuador	800	7.9
1980 Oct. 10	Northwest Algeria	4500	7.3
1980 Nov. 23	Southern Italy	4800	7.2
1982 Dec. 13	Northern Yemen	2800	6.0
1983 Mar. 31	Southern Columbia	250	5.5
1983 May 26	Japan, Honshu	81	7.7
1983 Oct. 30	Eastern Turkey	1300	7.1
1985 Mar. 3	Chile	146	7.8
1985 Sept. 19–21	Mexico City	4200	8.1
1987 Mar. 5–6	Ecuador	4000	7.3

MEDIAN   We have seen from the earthquake data that the mean is not always a *representative* central number. A second type of central number can be more informative. Consider the heights of the 7 children shown in part (a) of Figure 11.12. In part (b) these heights have been placed in increasing order. There are three heights that are less than and three heights that are greater than the measurement in the fourth position of part (b). Thus it seems reasonable to select this measurement (125 cm) as the representative height. This type of central number is called the **median.** Notice that this number is different from the mean, which is 126 cm.

median

Figure 11.12

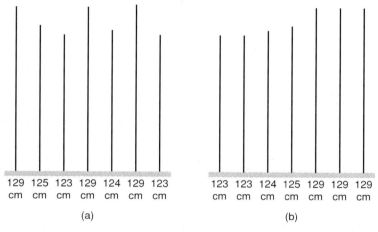

| 129 cm | 125 cm | 123 cm | 129 cm | 124 cm | 129 cm | 123 cm |

(a)

| 123 cm | 123 cm | 124 cm | 125 cm | 129 cm | 129 cm | 129 cm |

(b)

MEDIAN

1. The **median** of a set of data with an odd number of measurements is the middle number when the measurements are listed from smallest to largest (or largest to smallest).
2. The **median** of a set of data with an even number of measurements is the mean of the two middle numbers when the measurements are listed from smallest to largest (or largest to smallest).

The number of earthquake deaths from Figure 11.11 are listed below from smallest to largest. Since the number of measurements is even, we must compute the mean of the two middle numbers. The median for this set of data is 2406, the mean of the two circled numbers. Twenty-two of the numbers are less than 2406, and 22 of the numbers are greater than 2406.

21, 65, 81, 100, 100, 114, 146, 200, 250, 443, 800, 946, 1086, 1100, 1200, 1300, 1530, 1541, 2000, 2000, 2000, 2312, 2500, 2520, 2800, 4000, 4000, 4200, 4500, 4800, 5000, 5000, 5057, 5131, 5200, 6000, 8000, 12,000, 12,000, 12,230, 22,778, 25,000, 66,794, 800,000

MODE   The median seems to be a more representative central number for the earthquake data than the mean, but there are no death tolls that actually equal the median. Let's consider the third type of central measure. Observe that three of the children whose heights are represented in Figure 11.13 are 129 cm tall. This height might be considered the most representative as a central measure because it occurs most frequently. This type of central measure is called the **mode.** Notice that this height is different from the mean (126 cm) and the median (125 cm).

mode

Figure 11.13

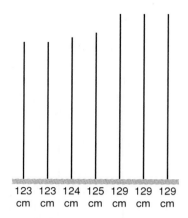

123 123 124 125 129 129 129
cm cm cm cm cm cm cm

MODE

> The **mode** of a set of data is the measurement that occurs most often.

The mode for the earthquake deaths is 2000, a measurement that occurs three times. If a set of data has two different measurements that occur the same number of times, the data have two modes and the set is called **bimodal.**

bimodal

EXAMPLE A

Determine the mean, median, and mode of the earthquake magnitudes in Figure 11.11.

Solution

The mean is approximately 7.3 (322.3/44). To determine the median, we must first list the earthquake magnitudes in increasing order.

5.5, 5.8, 6.0, 6.0, 6.2, 6.3, 6.5, 6.5, 6.8, 6.8, 6.9, 6.9, 7.1, 7.1, 7.1, 7.1, 7.2, 7.2, 7.3, 7.3, 7.3, ⑦.④, ⑦.④, 7.4, 7.5, 7.5, 7.5, 7.7, 7.7, 7.7, 7.7, 7.8, 7.8, 7.9, 7.9, 8.0, 8.1, 8.1, 8.2, 8.2, 8.3, 8.4, 8.5, 8.7

The median is 7.4, the mean of the two circled numbers. There are two modes: 7.1 and 7.7 are measures that each occur four times.

The mean, median, and mode each have their advantages, depending on the type of information desired. In some cases, one measure is clearly more representative of a set of data than another.

EXAMPLE B

Determine the mean, median, and mode for this table of salaries. Which is the best measure of central tendency?

One president	$210,000
One vice-president	120,000
One salesperson	40,000
One supervisor	22,000
One machine operator	20,000
Five mill workers (each earning)	15,000
Six apprentice workers (each earning)	13,000

Solution   The sum of the 16 salaries is

$$\$210,000 + \$120,000 + \$40,000 + \$22,000 + \$20,000 + 5(\$15,000) + 6(\$13,000)$$
$$= \$565,000$$

So the mean is $565,000/16 = $35,312.50. The median is the mean of the eighth and ninth salaries when the salaries are considered in increasing order. Since the eighth and ninth salaries are both 15,000, the median is

$$\frac{\$15,000 + \$15,000}{2} = \$15,000$$

The mode is $13,000, since this salary occurs most frequently. Both the median and the mode are more representative of the majority of salaries than the mean. The mean of $35,312.50 is greater than 13 of the 16 salaries.

PROBLEM-SOLVING APPLICATION

■ PROBLEM

An elementary school principal was interested in computing the mean of the verbal reasoning scores on a differential aptitude test taken by all the students in the school. The mean test score for the 62 students in the Talented and Gifted (TAG) program was 96, and the mean of the scores for the remaining 418 students was 72. What was the mean of the test scores for all the students?

Understanding the Problem   *Drawing a graph* is one way of visualizing the given information. We can think of each of the 418 students as having a score of 72 and each of the 62 TAG students as having a score of 96. The mean for the total group of 480 students can be visualized by "evening off" both columns. Will the mean be closer to 72 or to 96?

Question 1

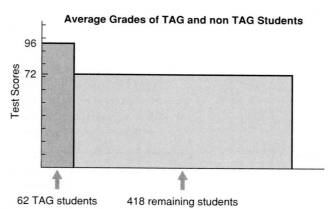

Average Grades of TAG and non TAG Students

62 TAG students   418 remaining students

Devising a Plan   The graph above suggests a plan. The difference between the height of the region representing the TAG students and the height of the region for the remaining students is 96 − 72 = 24. Thus 62 × 24 additional test score points can be "spread" across the top of the graph. To determine the increase in the mean of 72, we can divide the 1488 extra points by the total number of students (480). What is this increase?

Question 2

Carrying Out the Plan   The increase in the mean is 1488 ÷ 480 = 3.1. So if the extra points for the TAG students' scores are evenly spread across the top of the graph, the new mean will be 72 + 3.1 = 75.1. You might have been tempted to obtain the new mean by finding the mean of 96 and 72: (96 + 72)/2 = 84. How does the graph help to show that this is not reasonable for the new mean?

Question 3

Question 4

Looking Back   Another approach to solving the original problem is to find the total of all the scores for the 480 students and then divide by 480. How can the sum of the scores for all 480 students be obtained if we know that the mean for 62 students is 96 and the mean for 418 students is 72?

Answers to Questions 1–4
1. Closer to 72
2. 3.1
3. A horizontal line drawn on the graph at a height of 84 (halfway between 72 and 96) makes it evident that the part of the TAG students' bar above 84 does not have enough area to increase the total graph to a height of 84.
4. The sum of the scores for the total 480 students is

$$62(96) + 418(72) = 36{,}048$$

So the new mean is 36,048/480 = 75.1.

MEASURES OF VARIABILITY

Sometimes we need more than measures of central tendency to describe sets of data. The sets in the following example have the same mean, median, and mode, yet they are very dissimilar.

EXAMPLE C

The numbers in sets A and B have a mean of 23, a median of 20, and a mode of 20. What is the difference between the greatest and smallest values in set A? in set B? Compare these differences.

Set A: 18, 19, 20, 20, 26, 28, 30
Set B: 0, 1, 10, 20, 20, 50, 60

Solution

The difference for set A is 12 (30 − 18), and the difference for set B is 60 (60 − 0), 5 times that of set A.

measure of variability

Example C shows that some sets of data are more varied (spread out) than others. Thus it is necessary to measure the amount of dispersion among data. A **measure of variability** is a number that describes the spread, or variation, in a set of data. We will define two methods of measuring variation: the *range* and the *standard deviation*.

RANGE

The **range** is the difference between the greatest and least values in a set of data.

Even when two sets of data have the same range, there may be differences in the way the data are centered or spread out about the mean. Consider the data and bar graphs in Figure 11.14. The range of the data in both part (a) and part (b) is 4 (the greatest value is 5 and the least value is 1). However, the data represented in part (a) are more centered about the mean and not as spread out as the data represented in part (b).

Figure 11.14

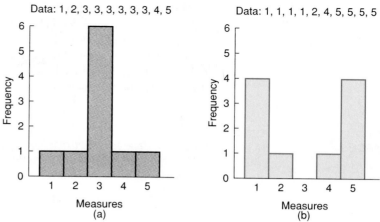

Data: 1, 2, 3, 3, 3, 3, 3, 3, 4, 5

Data: 1, 1, 1, 1, 2, 4, 5, 5, 5, 5

Measures
(a)

Measures
(b)

The data in Figure 11.14 show the need for a measure of variability that is more sensitive than the range.

STANDARD DEVIATION

The **standard deviation** is a measure of variation that is computed using the following steps:

1. Determine the mean.
2. Find the difference between each measure and the mean.
3. Square the differences.
4. Determine the mean of the squared differences.
5. Obtain the square root of this mean. This is the standard deviation, which is denoted by the letter **s**.

$$s = \sqrt{\frac{(x_1 - \bar{x})^2 + (x_2 - \bar{x})^2 + \cdots + (x_n - \bar{x})^2}{n}}$$

where x_1, x_2, etc., are **n** measurements and $\bar{x}$ is the mean.

The tables in Figure 11.15 illustrate the steps for computing the standard deviation for each of the sets of data graphed in Figure 11.14.

Figure 11.15

Set A (mean = 3) 1, 2, 3, 3, 3, 3, 3, 3, 4, 5			Set B (mean = 3) 1, 1, 1, 1, 2, 4, 5, 5, 5, 5		
Measure	Difference from mean	Square of difference	Measure	Difference from mean	Square of difference
x	$x - \bar{x}$	$(x - \bar{x})^2$	x	$x - \bar{x}$	$(x - \bar{x})^2$
1	$1 - 3 = {}^-2$	4	1	$1 - 3 = {}^-2$	4
2	$2 - 3 = {}^-1$	1	1	$1 - 3 = {}^-2$	4
3	$3 - 3 = 0$	0	1	$1 - 3 = {}^-2$	4
3	$3 - 3 = 0$	0	1	$1 - 3 = {}^-2$	4
3	$3 - 3 = 0$	0	2	$2 - 3 = {}^-1$	1
3	$3 - 3 = 0$	0	4	$4 - 3 = 1$	1
3	$3 - 3 = 0$	0	5	$5 - 3 = 2$	4
3	$3 - 3 = 0$	0	5	$5 - 3 = 2$	4
4	$4 - 3 = 1$	1	5	$5 - 3 = 2$	4
5	$5 - 3 = 2$	4	5	$5 - 3 = 2$	4
	Total 10			Total 34	

Mean of squared differences $= \dfrac{10}{10} = 1$

Standard deviation $= \sqrt{1} = 1$

Mean of squared differences $= \dfrac{34}{10} = 3.4$

Standard deviation $= \sqrt{3.4} \approx 1.8$

The standard deviation for set A is 1, and the standard deviation for set B is approximately 1.8 (about twice as large). The larger standard deviation for set B confirms our visual interpretation of the graphs in Figure 11.14: the data graphed in part (b) are more spread out about the mean. In general, the more varied (spread out) the data, the greater the standard deviation, and the less varied the data, the smaller the standard deviation (closer to zero).

EXAMPLE D

Two sets of data and their means are given below. Inspect the sets of data and predict which set has the smaller standard deviation. Compute the standard deviation for both sets of data.

$$\text{Set A: 18, 19, 20, 20, 26, 28, 30} \qquad \text{Mean} = 23$$
$$\text{Set B: 0, 1, 10, 20, 20, 50, 60} \qquad \text{Mean} = 23$$

Solution   The numbers in set A are fairly close together and less spread out than the numbers in set B. So the numbers in set A should have the smaller standard deviation.

Set A ($\bar{x} = 23$)				Set B ($\bar{x} = 23$)		
Measure	Difference from mean	Square of difference		Measure	Difference from mean	Square of difference
x	$x - \bar{x}$	$(x - \bar{x})^2$		x	$x - \bar{x}$	$(x - \bar{x})^2$
30	7	49		60	37	1369
28	5	25		50	27	729
26	3	9		20	-3	9
20	-3	9		20	-3	9
20	-3	9		10	-13	169
19	-4	16		1	-22	484
18	-5	25		0	-23	529
	Total	142			Total	3298

Mean of squared differences

$$= \frac{142}{7} \approx 20.3$$

Standard deviation $\approx \sqrt{20.3} \approx 4.5$

Mean of squared differences

$$= \frac{3298}{7} \approx 471.1$$

Standard deviation $\approx \sqrt{471.1} \approx 21.7$

These standard deviations (4.5 compared to 21.7) show that the measures in set A are less spread out than the measures in set B.

Standard deviations determine intervals about the mean. For set A in Example D, 1 standard deviation above the mean is 23 + 4.5, or 27.5, and 1 standard deviation below the mean is 23 − 4.5, or 18.5 (Figure 11.16). The interval within ±1 standard deviation of the mean is the interval from 18.5 to 27.5. The interval within ±2 standard deviations of the mean is from 14 to 32.

Figure 11.16

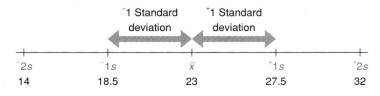

EXAMPLE E

Draw a line, and label the mean and the first two standard deviations ($\pm 1s$ and $\pm 2s$) about the mean for set B in Example D.

Solution

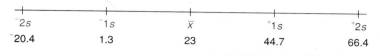

^-2s	^-1s	$\bar{x}$	^+1s	^+2s
$^-20.4$	1.3	23	44.7	66.4

Because the standard deviation measures the spread of data about the mean, it can be used to obtain knowledge about the location of a large percentage of the data.

DISTRIBUTION OF DATA

At least 75% of the measurements in any set of data will lie within 2 standard deviations of the mean (see Figure 11.17).

Figure 11.17

At least 75% of the data are in this interval.

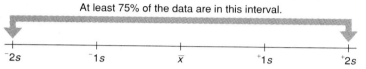

The percent of data within 2 standard deviations of the mean is usually much higher than 75%. In fact, if only 75% of the data in a given set are within 2 standard deviations of the mean, the data have a rather unique distribution (see Computer Investigation, page 590). For sets of data that reflect real-life situations, 90% or more of the data are usually within 2 standard deviations of the mean.

EXAMPLE F

For the set of magnitudes of major earthquakes in Figure 11.11, find the number of measures that are within 2 standard deviations of the mean. The mean is approximately 7.3, and .7 is the standard deviation.

Solution

There are 44 measures, and 42 are within 2 standard deviations of the mean (greater than or equal to 5.9 and less than or equal to 8.7). Since $42/44 \approx .95$, 95% of the magnitudes are within 2 standard deviations of the mean.

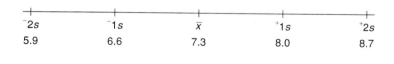

^-2s	^-1s	$\bar{x}$	^+1s	^+2s
5.9	6.6	7.3	8.0	8.7

RELATED ACTIVITIES IN

Mathematics for Elementary Teachers: An Activity Approach, 3e

Activity Set 11.1

Randomness, Sampling, and Simulation in Statistics: Activities illustrate randomness and applications of this concept to sampling and simulations.

Just for Fun

Simulated Racing Game: A two-person simulation game in which the experimental probability of winning a race is determined by sampling

EXERCISES AND PROBLEMS 11.1

"We understand you tore
the little tag off your mattress."

1. The numbers of troops in active service in the 4 major branches of the service (to the nearest hundred thousand) are as follows: Army, 9; Navy, 6; Air Force, 3; and Marine Corps, 2.
   a. Draw a bar graph of the data.
   b. Draw a pie chart of the data.
   c. What is the measure (to the nearest degree) of the central angle in each of the 4 regions of the pie chart?

2. The bar graph below shows the average annual prime rate of interest (to the nearest whole percent) charged by banks for each of the years from 1978 to 1989.*

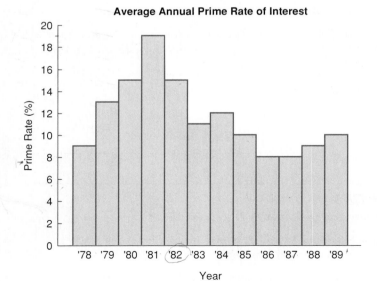

Average Annual Prime Rate of Interest

a. In which year was the prime rate the highest, and what was the rate?
b. In which years was the prime rate the lowest, and what was the rate?
c. In which years did the prime rate decrease, and how much was the decrease?

3. A family's monthly budget is divided as follows: rent, 32%; food, 30%; utilities, 15%; insurance, 4%; medical expenses, 5%; entertainment, 8%; other, 6%.
   a. Draw a pie chart of the data.
   b. What is the measure of the central angle (to the nearest degree) in each of the 7 regions of the chart?

4. The pie chart below represents the percents of federal funds that were spent on programs for the handicapped in public schools in 1987.**
   (For regions A through E the target groups and percents are, respectively, hearing impaired, 1.5%; orthopedically handicapped, 1.3%; other health impaired, 1.2%; visually handicapped, 1.6%; and multi-handicapped, 2.2%.)

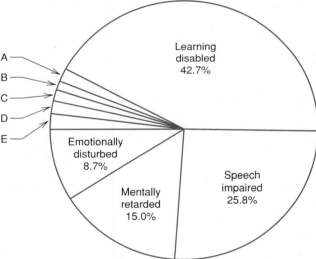

a. What was the total percent spent on programs for learning disabled and speech impaired children?
b. What was the total percent spent on programs for hearing impaired and visually handicapped children?
c. Approximately how many times greater was the amount of money spent on programs for the speech impaired than the amount spent on programs for the emotionally disturbed?

5. The table below shows the percents of elementary schools in the United States in various size categories.*

Size of school (no. of students)	Percent of schools
Under 100	8
100 to 199	12
200 to 299	16
300 to 399	19
400 to 499	16
500 to 599	11
600 to 699	7
700 to 799	4
800 to 899	3
900 to 999	2
1000 or more	2

a. Draw a bar graph of these data.
b. What percent of elementary schools have from 200 to less than 500 students?
c. What percent of elementary schools have 500 or more students?

6. The following scores are from a college mathematics test for elementary school teachers:

92, 75, 78, 90, 73, 67, 85, 80, 58, 87, 62, 74, 74, 76, 89, 95, 72, 86, 80, 57, 89, 97, 65, 77, 91, 83, 71, 75, 67, 68, 57, 86, 62, 65, 72, 75, 81, 72, 76, 69

a. Form a stem and leaf plot of these test scores.
b. How many scores are below 70?
c. What percent of the scores are greater than or equal to 80?

7. The life spans of the 35 U.S. presidents from George Washington to Lyndon Johnson are listed below.

67, 90, 83, 85, 73, 80, 78, 79, 68, 71, 53, 65, 74, 64, 77, 56, 66, 63, 70, 49, 57, 71, 67, 58, 60, 72, 67, 57, 60, 90, 63, 88, 78, 46, 64

a. Form a stem and leaf plot of these data.
b. What percent of the 35 presidents lived to be more than 80 years old?
c. What percent of the 35 presidents did not live to be 60 years old?

8. The following are test scores for two classes that took the same test. (The highest possible score on the test was 60.)

Class 1: 24 scores
34, 44, 53, 57, 19, 50, 41, 56, 38, 27, 56, 49, 39, 24, 41, 50, 45, 47, 35, 51, 40, 44, 48, 43

Class 2: 25 scores
51, 40, 45, 28, 44, 56, 31, 33, 41, 34, 34, 39, 50, 36, 37, 32, 50, 22, 35, 43, 40, 50, 45, 33, 48

a. Form a stem and leaf plot with one stem. Put the leaves for one class on the right side of the stem and the leaves for the other class on the left side. Record the leaves in increasing order.
b. Which class appears to have performed better? Support your answer.

9. The following data represent the weights in kilograms of 53 third-graders.

19.3, 20.2, 22.3, 17.0, 23.8, 24.6, 20.5, 20.3, 21.8, 16.6, 23.4, 25.1, 20.1, 21.6, 22.5, 19.7, 19.0, 18.2, 20.6, 21.5, 27.7, 21.6, 21.0, 20.4, 18.2, 17.2, 20.0, 22.7, 23.1, 24.6, 18.1, 20.8, 24.6, 17.3, 19.9, 20.1, 22.0, 23.2, 18.6, 25.3, 19.7, 20.6, 21.4, 21.2, 23.0, 21.2, 19.8, 22.1, 23.0, 19.1, 25.0, 22.0, 24.2

a. Form a stem and leaf plot of these data, using the tenth digits as the leaves. (Note: It is not necessary to write decimal points.)
b. Which stem value has the most leaves?
c. What are the greatest and least weights?

10. The average annual per capita incomes by states for 1987 are shown in the following table.**

State	Income	State	Income
AL	18,318	MO	19,601
AK	28,008	MT	16,438
AZ	19,610	NE	16,526
AR	16,529	NV	19,521
CA	23,100	NH	19,414
CO	20,736	NJ	23,842
CT	24,322	NM	17,767
DE	20,764	NY	24,634
DC	28,477	NC	17,861
FL	18,674	ND	16,157
GA	19,651	OH	20,568
HI	19,091	OK	18,615
ID	17,062	OR	18,888
IL	22,250	PA	20,408
IN	19,692	RI	18,858
IA	17,292	SC	17,279
KS	18,424	SD	14,963
KY	18,008	TN	18,501
LA	18,707	TX	20,463
ME	17,447	UT	18,303
MD	21,324	VT	17,703
MA	22,486	VA	19,963
MI	23,081	WA	20,110
MN	20,450	WV	18,820
MS	15,938	WI	18,890
		WY	18,817

*Statistical Abstract of the United States, 135.

**Statistical Abstract of the United States, 405.

a. Create a frequency table for these incomes using the intervals shown below.

Interval	Frequency
14,000–14,999	1
15,000–15,999	—
16,000–16,999	—
17,000–17,999	—
18,000–18,999	—
19,000–19,999	—
20,000–20,999	—
21,000–21,999	—
22,000–22,999	—
23,000–23,999	—
24,000–24,999	—
25,000–25,999	—
26,000–26,999	—
27,000–27,999	—
28,000–28,999	—

b. Construct a histogram for the given intervals. (Copy the rectangular grid from the inside cover to use for the histogram.)

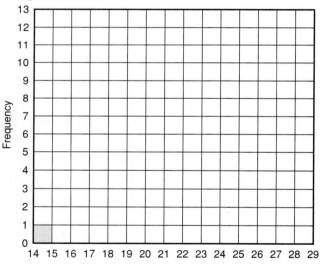

c. Which interval has the greatest frequency of incomes?

d. In how many states was per capita income from $18,000 to less than $20,000?

e. In how many states was per capita income less than $17,000?

---

11. Record snowfalls (to the nearest inch) through 1987 in selected cities are shown in the table below.*

City	Record	City	Record
Juneau	100	Kansas City	20
Hartford	60	Great Falls	58
Wilmington	49	Omaha	31
Washington	21	Reno	24
Chicago	21	Concord	64
Peoria	40	Albany	66
Indianapolis	25	Buffalo	92
Des Moines	23	New York	29
Wichita	34	Bismarck	41
Portland, ME	71	Cincinnati	24
Baltimore	22	Cleveland	54
Boston	42	Columbus	29
Detroit	42	Philadelphia	22
Sault St. Marie	115	Pittsburgh	44
Duluth	77	Sioux Falls	40
Salt Lake City	58	Burlington	78
Spokane	51	Charleston	33
Milwaukee	47	Cheyenne	54
Providence	36	Minneapolis-St. Paul	49

a. Form a frequency table for the snowfall data using the following intervals: 20–29; 30–39; 40–49; 50–59; 60–69; 70–79; 80–89; 90–99; 100–109; 110–119.

b. Draw a histogram for the snowfall data for the intervals in part a.

c. Which interval contains the greatest number of cities?

d. How many cities had record snowfalls of over 50 in.?

12. The line graph below shows the average starting salaries for public school teachers between 1980 and 1987.**

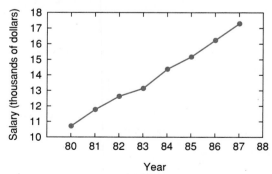

a. Use this graph to predict the average starting salary for public school teachers in 1988.

b. The smallest increase in salaries from one year to the next occurred between which two years?

---

*Statistical Abstract of the United States, 213.

**Statistical Abstract of the United States, 137.

13. The percents of public elementary schools using microcomputers for instruction during the years from 1981 to 1987 are as follows: 1981, 11.1%; 1982, 20.2%; 1983, 68.4%; 1984, 85.1%; 1985, 92.2%; 1986, 95.6%; 1987, 96.4%.*

    a. Draw a line graph of these data, with the years from 1981 to 1987 represented on the horizontal axis.

    b. During which year was the number of schools using microcomputers approximately double what it had been the previous year?

    c. During which year was the number of schools using microcomputers approximately triple what it had been the previous year?

14. Calculate the mean, median, and mode for each set of data.
    a. 4, 7, 6, 2, 4, 5
    b. 0, 1, 5, 0, 2, 0, 3, 1
    c. 4, ⁻3, 2, 8, ⁻2, 0

15. The home run leaders in the National and American Leagues from 1970 to 1989 are listed below.

Home Run Leaders

Year	American League	H.R.
1970	Frank Howard, Washington	44
1971	Bill Melton, Chicago	33
1972	Dick Allen, Chicago	37
1973	Reggie Jackson, Oakland	32
1974	Dick Allen, Chicago	32
1975	George Scott, Milwaukee	
	Reggie Jackson, Oakland	36
1976	Greg Nettles, New York	32
1977	Jim Rice, Boston	39
1978	Jim Rice, Boston	46
1979	Gorman Thomas, Milwaukee	45
1980	Reggie Jackson, New York	
	Ben Oglivie, Milwaukee	41
1981	Bobby Grich, California	
	Tony Ames, Oakland	
	Dwight Evans, Boston	
	Eddie Murry, Baltimore	22
1982	Gorman Thomas, Milwaukee	
	Reggie Jackson, California	39
1983	Jim Rice, Boston	39
1984	Tony Armas, Boston	43
1985	Darrell Evans, Detroit	40
1986	Jesse Barfield, Toronto	40
1987	Mark McGuire, Oakland	49
1988	Jose Canseco, Oakland	42
1989	Fred McGriff, Toronto	36

Year	National League	H.R.
1970	Johnny Bench, Cincinnati	45
1971	Willie Stargell, Pittsburgh	48
1972	Johnny Bench, Cincinnati	40
1973	Willie Stargell, Pittsburgh	44
1974	Mike Schmidt, Philadelphia	36
1975	Mike Schmidt, Philadelphia	38
1976	Mike Schmidt, Philadelphia	38
1977	George Foster, Cincinnati	52
1978	George Foster, Cincinnati	40
1979	Dave Kingman, Chicago	48
1980	Mike Schmidt, Philadelphia	48
1981	Mike Schmidt, Philadelphia	31
1982	Dave Kingman, New York	37
1983	Mike Schmidt, Philadelphia	40
1984	Mike Schmidt, Philadelphia	
	Dale Murphy, Atlanta	36
1985	Dale Murphy, Atlanta	37
1986	Mike Schmidt, Philadelphia	37
1987	Andre Dawson, Chicago	49
1988	Darryl Strawberry, New York	39
1989	Kevin Mitchell, San Francisco	47

a. Compute the mean, median, and mode for numbers of home runs in the National League.

b. Compute the mean, median, and mode for numbers of home runs in the American League.

c. For which league is the mean greater?

d. For which league is the median greater?

e. For which league is the mode greater?

f. In how many different years did the National League's home run leaders hit more home runs than the American League's?

g. Which league's home run leaders have the better record? Support your conclusion.

16. Which measure of central tendency—mean, median, or mode—is best for describing the following instances?

    a. The typical size of hats sold in a store

    b. The typical height of players on a basketball team

    c. The typical age of 7 people in a family, if 6 of them are under 40 and 1 is 96 years old

    d. The typical size of bicycles (by tire size) sold by a bike shop

17. The table below lists the number of nuclear power reactors operating in each of 21 countries in 1987 and their gross capacity in megawatts (1 million watts).*

Country	Number of reactors	Megawatt capacity
United States	108	99,702
Argentina	2	1005
Belgium	7	5718
Brazil	1	657
Canada	18	12,864
China: Taiwan	6	5146
Great Britain	38	12,940
Finland	4	2400
France	53	52,095
India	6	1330
Italy	3	1330
Japan	36	28,046
Netherlands	2	540
Pakistan	1	137
South Africa	2	1930
South Korea	7	5808
Spain	8	5812
Sweden	12	10,095
Switzerland	5	3079
West Germany	19	19,848
Yugoslavia	1	664

a. What is the mean capacity in megawatts (to the nearest tenth) of the reactors in the United States? in France? in Japan? in Great Britain?

b. Which of the four countries in part a has the smallest average megawatt capacity per reactor?

c. What is the mean number of reactors (to the nearest whole number) in these 21 countries? Explain why the mean is a misleading measure of central tendency in this example.

18. The grades of 8 students on a 10-point test were 1, 3, 5, 5, 7, 8, 9, and 10.

a. Compute the mean of these test scores.

b. Compute the standard deviation of these scores.

c. Another class took the same test and had the same mean. What can be said about the two sets of test scores if the second class had a standard deviation of 2?

19. The mean of each of the following sets of data is 6.

Set A: 0, 2, 4, 6, 8, 10, 12
Set B: 3, 4, 5, 6, 7, 8, 9

a. Predict which set of data has the smaller standard deviation.

b. Calculate the standard deviation for both sets of data.

c. Do the standard deviations in part b support your prediction in part a? Explain.

*Statistical Abstract of the United States, 571.

**Statistical Abstract of the United States, 211.

20. The resting pulse rates of 55 people are listed below. The mean of these rates is 72, and the standard deviation is approximately 9.2.

51, 56, 56, 57, 57, 61, 62, 62, 62, 63, 64, 65, 65, 65, 66, 67, 67, 68, 68, 69, 69, 70, 70, 70, 70, 70, 70, 72, 73, 73, 74, 74, 74, 74, 75, 75, 76, 76, 76, 77, 78, 79, 79, 80, 80, 80, 81, 82, 84, 84, 86, 86, 89, 91, 92

a. Circle the pulse rates that are within 1 standard deviation of the mean. What percent of the total do these rates represent?

b. What percent of the rates are within 2 standard deviations of the mean?

c. What percent of the rates are more than 2 standard deviations from the mean?

21. The accompanying bar graphs show the mean monthly amounts of precipitation for Kansas City, Missouri and Portland, Oregon.**

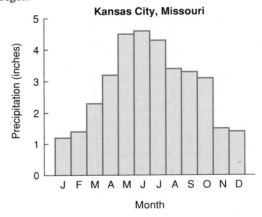

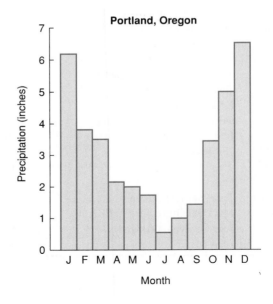

a. In Portland, which two months have the greatest amounts of precipitation (on the average)?

b. In Kansas City, which month has the least amount of precipitation (on the average)?

c. Compare the amounts of precipitation during the summer months (June, July, and August). Which city has the most precipitation during the summer?

d. Both cities have approximately the same annual amounts of precipitation: 35.16 in. for Kansas City and 37.39 in. for Portland. Use these figures to determine a mean monthly amount of precipitation for each city.

Featured Strategy: Drawing a Graph

22. Richard bowled 25 games, and the mean of his scores was 195. His four lowest scores were 126, 130, 134, and 138. If he throws out these four low scores, what is the new mean?

a. Understanding the Problem Throwing out four scores that are below the mean of 195 will result in a higher mean. How many games will be used to determine the new mean?

b. Devising a Plan Sometimes drawing a graph of the given information will suggest a plan. A mean of 195 for 25 games can be pictured as 25 games, each with a score of 195. This is shown in the graph below, in which dashed lines represent the four low scores. What amounts would need to be added to the low scores to bring them up to 195? Devise a plan to determine the new mean when these low scores are thrown out.

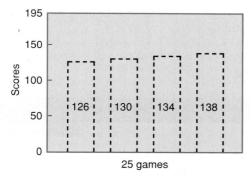

c. Carrying Out the Plan Use your plan to determine the new mean for the 21 games.

d. Looking Back You may have used the approach of determining the total score for the 25 games. What is this total? The four low scores can be subtracted from the total to obtain a new total. Show how to determine the new mean using this approach.

23. The green line in the next figure shows the mean annual mortgage rates for new homes from 1970 to 1987, and the black line shows the mean annual interest rates on treasury bills during the same period.*

a. What was the highest annual mortgage rate (approximate) between 1970 and 1987?

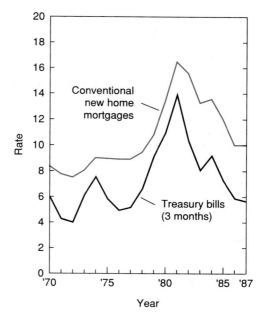

b. What was the lowest annual mortgage rate during these years?

c. What was the annual mortgage rate for 1987?

d. What was the highest annual interest rate for treasury bills?

e. What was the range of the differences between the annual mortgage rate and treasury bill interest rate from 1970 to 1987?

24. People often talk about "the good old days," but how good were they? Here are some surprising facts that were reported by the National Institute of Health Federal Credit Union.

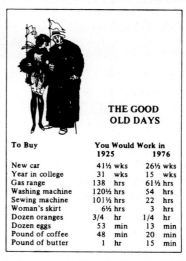

THE GOOD OLD DAYS

To Buy	You Would Work in	
	1925	1976
New car	41½ wks	26½ wks
Year in college	31 wks	15 wks
Gas range	138 hrs	61½ hrs
Washing machine	120½ hrs	54 hrs
Sewing machine	101½ hrs	22 hrs
Woman's skirt	6½ hrs	3 hrs
Dozen oranges	3/4 hr	1/4 hr
Dozen eggs	53 min	13 min
Pound of coffee	48 min	20 min
Pound of butter	1 hr	15 min

a. Divide each amount of work time in 1925 by the corresponding amount of work time in 1976 to find out how many times longer you would have worked for each item in 1925. Compute your answer to two decimal places.

b. Compute the mean of your answers in part a. On the average, how many times longer would you have had to work for these items in 1925?

*Statistical Abstract of the United States, 482.

COMPUTER INVESTIGATION

The computer program STANDARD DEVIATIONS on the *Computer Problem-Solving Disc* computes and prints the mean and standard deviation for any data entered. It also prints the percent of data within ±1, ±2, and ±3 standard deviations of the mean.

Questions for Investigation

1. Suppose a teacher grades a set of tests and computes the mean and standard deviation. Because the grades are low, the teacher decides to add 5 points to each test score:

   Old Scores: 71, 62, 48, 56, 83, 75, 64, 70, 85, 81, 78, 73

New Scores: 76, 67, 53, 61, 88, 80, 69, 75, 90, 86, 83, 78

What happens to the mean and the standard deviation if each measurement is increased by the same amount? Check your conjecture for some other sets of data.

2. What happens to the mean and standard deviation if the same amount is added to each measurement in a strange set of data, such as the one shown in this graph? Experiment with the sets of data given below or create some of your own.

   Set A: 1, 1, 6, 6, 6, 6, 12, 12 (see graph)
   Set B: 1, 2, 3, 4, 5, 100
   Set C: 1, 2, 3, 4, 5, 501, 502, 503, 504, 505

3. In most distributions, over 90% of the data are within 2 standard deviations of the mean. Only very strange distributions have less than 80% (or as little as 75%) of the data in this interval. Try creating a set of data in which less than 80% of the data are within 2 standard deviations of the mean.

PUZZLER

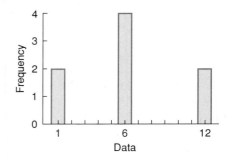

The school ski team drove 120 miles into the mountains at an average speed of 40 miles per hour. The return trip was completed at an average speed of 60 miles per hour. When the coach computed the average speed for the entire trip, he was surprised to find that it was not 50 miles per hour (the average of 40 and 60). What was the average speed for the trip?

SECTION 11.2   INFERENTIAL STATISTICS

■ PROBLEM OPENER

In one survey of trout populations, biologists caught and marked 232 trout from a lake. Three months later the biologists selected a second sample of 329 trout from the lake, and 16 were found to be marked. Assuming that the 232 marked trout intermingled freely with unmarked trout during the three-month period, estimate the number of trout in the lake.

"That's the worst set of opinions I've heard in my entire life."

Making predictions from samples is an important part of *inferential statistics*. Because of the many possibilities for errors, strict procedures must be followed in gathering data. The sample must be large enough, and it must be a representative cross section of the whole.

The need for scientific sampling techniques was dramatically illustrated in the 1936 presidential election. The *Literary Digest,* which had been conducting surveys of elections since 1920, sent questionnaires to 10 million voters (Figure 11.18). Their sample was obtained from telephone directories and lists of automobile owners. By choosing the sample this way, the magazine's editors selected people with above-average incomes (that is, voters who could afford what were relative luxuries at that time: phones and cars) rather than voters from a range of income levels. Based on its sample, the *Digest* predicted that Alfred Landon would win. Instead, the election was a landslide victory for Franklin D. Roosevelt, who had much popular support among middle- and low-income voters.

Figure 11.18

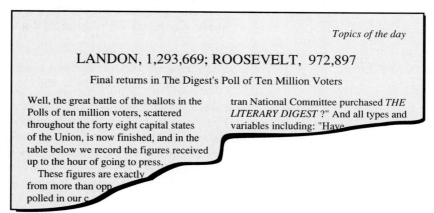

Topics of the day

LANDON, 1,293,669; ROOSEVELT, 972,897

Final returns in The Digest's Poll of Ten Million Voters

Well, the great battle of the ballots in the Polls of ten million voters, scattered throughout the forty eight capital states of the Union, is now finished, and in the table below we record the figures received up to the hour of going to press.

These figures are exactly from more than opp polled in our c

tran National Committee purchased *THE LITERARY DIGEST* ?" And all types and variables including: "Have

SAMPLING

sample
population

A **sample** is a collection of people or objects chosen to represent a larger collection of people or objects called the **population.** For example, when a national poll of 1873 people is used to determine the popularity of a television program, the 1873 people form the sample and all television watchers in the country are the population.

RANDOM SAMPLING   A common method of obtaining a sample from a population is random sampling. If a sample is obtained in such a way that every element in the population has the same chance of being selected, it is called a **random sample** and the process is called **random sampling.**

random sample
random sampling

Randomness is difficult to achieve. Repeatedly tossing a coin may appear to be a random method of making "yes or no" decisions, but imbalances in the coin's weight and tossing it to approximately the same height each time are two factors that could cause a biased result. Similarly, dice and spinners produce fairly random results, but these also have slight biases due to their physical imperfections.

Most random selection processes make use of tables of random digits. Computers can be programmed to generate tables with millions of random digits. The list of random digits in Figure 11.19 is from a computer printout. The digits are printed in pairs and groups of 10 for ease of reading and counting.

Figure 11.19

40 09 18 94 06	62 89 97 10 02	58 63 02 91 44	79 03 55 47 69	14 11 42 33 99
33 19 98 40 42	13 73 63 72 59	26 06 08 92 65	63 08 82 45 85	14 45 81 65 21
69 49 02 58 44	45 45 19 69 33	51 68 97 99 05	77 54 22 70 97	59 06 64 21 68
17 49 43 65 45	04 95 82 76 31	85 53 15 21 70	59 17 27 54 67	07 76 13 95 00
43 13 78 80 55	90 80 88 19 13	13 89 11 00 60	41 86 23 07 60	22 77 93 30 83

To select a random sample from a population, we first assign a number to each element of the population. Then, to ensure randomness, we select an arbitrary starting place in the table.

EXAMPLE A

How can a table of random digits be used to select 10 questions randomly from a list of 50 questions?

Solution   Number the questions from 1 to 50. Then arbitrarily select a pair of numbers from the table in Figure 11.19, say 26, the eleventh pair in the second row. Beginning with this number and moving to the right along the row, list the first 10 different numbers that are less than or equal to 50. These numbers are 26, 6, 8, 45, 14, 21, 49, 2, 44, and 19.

The list of digits in Figure 11.19 may also be used to obtain random single-digit numbers or numbers with 3 or more digits.

EXAMPLE B

How can the list of random digits be used to select a random sample of 65 items from a list of items numbered 1 to 650?

Solution   One way is to start with any digit in the table and list consecutive groups of 3 digits until you have found 65 numbers between 1 and 650. The numerals 001, 002, etc., represent 1, 2, etc., and any triples of numbers from the table that are greater than 650 are discarded. If we use this method with the table of random digits in Figure 11.19 and begin with the first line, 400 is the first number. Then 918, 940, 662, 899, and 710 are discarded because they are greater than 650. The next acceptable number is 025, which represents 25. Continuing this process will produce a random sample.

---

stratified sampling   **STRATIFIED SAMPLING**   In **stratified sampling** a population is divided into groups. The number sampled from each group is then determined by the ratio of the size of the group to the size of the total population.

EXAMPLE C

A city council wants to sample the opinion of the city's adult population of 80,000 people on a plan to build a public swimming pool. The population is divided into three groups—high-income, middle-income, and low-income—and 1500 people are to be sampled. If 16,000 people are low-income, 56,000 middle-income, and 8000 high-income, determine the size of the sample for each income group.

Solution   Since 16,000/80,000 = .2 and .2 × 1500 = 300, 300 people will be sampled from the low-income group. Since 56,000/80,000 = .7 and .7 × 1500 = 1050, 1050 people will be sampled from the middle-income group. Finally, since 8000/80,000 = .1 and .1 × 1500 = 150, 150 people will be sampled from the high-income group.

SKEWED AND SYMMETRIC DISTRIBUTIONS

distribution   The graph of a set of data provides a visual way of illustrating the **distribution** of the data—that is, how the data are clustered together or isolated from each other.

For example, the bar graph in Figure 11.20 shows that about 97 families have no children, about 105 families have 1 child, etc. The most common number of children per family (the mode) is 2. Graphs that show the data piled up at one end of the scale

skewed

skewed to the right

and tapering off toward the other end are called **skewed.** The direction of skewness is determined by the longer "tail" of the distribution. This graph is said to be **skewed to the right** (positively skewed).

Figure 11.20

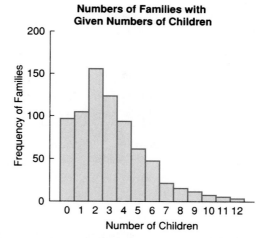

Similarly, a graph may have data piled up at the right with the "tail" extending to the left. This type of graph is said to be **skewed to the left** (negatively skewed). Such a graph is illustrated in Figure 11.21. It shows the numbers of teachers in a school system who drive cars built in the years from 1975 to 1990; the greatest number of teachers have cars that were built in recent years. The mode in this example is the year 1986.

skewed to the left

Figure 11.21

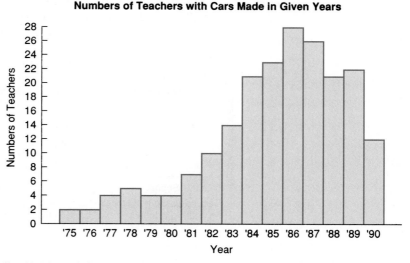

symmetric

A distribution of data in which measurements at equal distances from the center of the distribution occur with the same frequency is said to be **symmetric.** A symmetric distribution and two skewed distributions are shown in Figure 11.22. The graph shows the relative positions of the mean, median, and mode for these distributions. Notice that in a symmetric distribution the mean, median, and mode are all equal.*

---

*The computer program DICE SUM DISTRIBUTION on the *Computer Problem-Solving Disc* simulates the tossing of 1 to 20 dice and graphs the sums for up to 1000 tosses. As the number of tosses increases, what is the shape of the distribution?

Figure 11.22

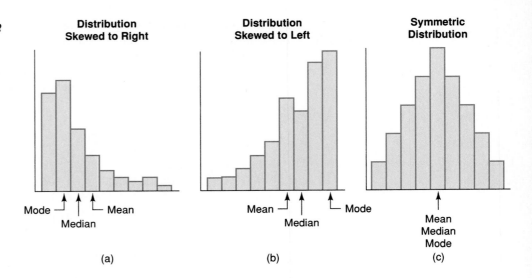

Distribution Skewed to Right

Distribution Skewed to Left

Symmetric Distribution

Mode — Mean
Median
(a)

Mean — Mode
Median
(b)

Mean
Median
Mode
(c)

EXAMPLE D

School test results sometimes produce skewed graphs, especially if the test is too difficult or too easy for the students. Determine the types of distributions of test scores that will occur in each of the following cases.

1. A test designed for fifth graders is given to second graders
2. A test designed for fifth graders is given to fifth graders
3. A test designed for fifth graders is given to eighth graders

Solution

1. The majority of scores will be low, and the distribution will be skewed to the right, as shown in figure (a) below.
2. The distribution of scores will be more or less symmetric, as illustrated in figure (b).
3. The majority of scores will be high, and the distribution will be skewed to the left, as in figure (c).

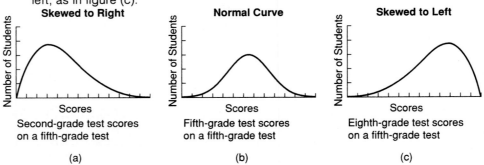

Skewed to Right

Normal Curve

Skewed to Left

Number of Students

Scores

Second-grade test scores on a fifth-grade test

(a)

Number of Students

Scores

Fifth-grade test scores on a fifth-grade test

(b)

Number of Students

Scores

Eighth-grade test scores on a fifth-grade test

(c)

NORMAL DISTRIBUTIONS

As sets of data increase in size and the widths of the bars for their histograms become smaller, the shape of the tops of the histograms approaches a smooth curve. Thus in graphing large sets of data it is customary to approximate the histogram by a smooth curve (Figure 11.23).

Figure 11.23

(a)   (b)

normal curve
normal distribution

A smooth symmetric bell-shaped curve, such as the curve shown in Figure 11.24, is called a **normal curve,** and the distribution of its data is called a **normal distribution.** Normal distributions have certain important properties. About 68% of the values are within 1 standard deviation of the mean; about 95% are within 2 standard deviations of the mean; and about 99.7% fall within 3 standard deviations of the mean. The remaining percent is evenly divided above and below 3 standard deviations. These approximate percents hold for any normal distribution, regardless of the mean or the size of the standard deviation.

Figure 11.24

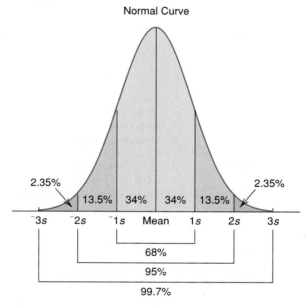

The shapes of normal curves vary, as shown in Figure 11.25. The standard deviation of the data determines the shape of the curve. The smaller the standard deviation, the less spread out the data and the taller and thinner the curve; the larger the standard deviation, the more spread out the data and the lower and flatter the curve. The standard deviations of three sets of data for the normal curves in Figure 11.25 increase from part (a) to part (c).

Figure 11.25

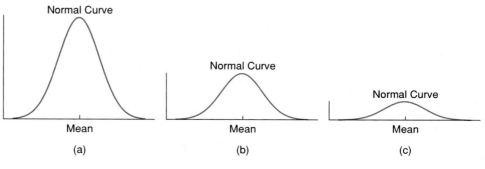

The mean and standard deviation of a normal distribution are used to provide information about the distribution of data, as shown in the next example.

EXAMPLE E

The following graph, showing the distribution of the heights of 8585 men, is an approximation to a nearly normal distribution. The mean is approximately 67 inches (5 feet 7 inches) and the standard deviation is approximately 3 inches.

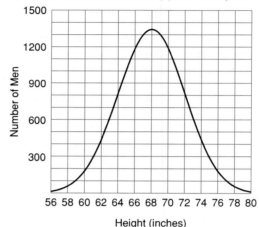

1. How many of these men are between 5 feet 4 inches and 5 feet 10 inches tall?
2. How many men are between 5 feet 1 inch and 6 feet 1 inch tall?
3. How many men are less than 5 feet 1 inch tall?

Solution

1. One standard deviation above and below the mean includes the heights from 5 feet 4 inches to 5 feet 10 inches, and this interval contains 68% of the data. Since .68 × 8585 ≈ 5838, there are approximately 5838 men with heights in this interval.
2. Two standard deviations above and below the mean include the heights from 5 feet 1 inch to 6 feet 1 inch, and this interval contains 95% of the data. Since .95 × 8585 ≈ 8156, there are approximately 8156 men in this interval.
3. More than 2 standard deviations above and below the mean correspond to heights of less than 5 feet 1 inch and more than 6 feet 1 inch; these intervals together contain 5% of the data, so each contains approximately 2.5% of the data. Since .025 × 8585 ≈ 215, there are approximately 215 men who are less than 5 feet 1 inch tall.

■ HISTORICAL HIGHLIGHTS

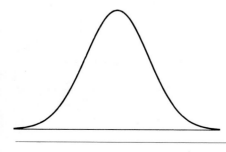

The word "normal" is used to indicate that a normal distribution is very common in nature. About 1833 the Belgian scientist L. A. J. Quetelet collected large amounts of data on human measurements: height, weight, length of limbs, intelligence, etc. He found that all measurements of mental and physical characteristics of human beings tended to be normally distributed. That is, the majority of people have measurements that are close to the mean (average), and measurements further from the mean occur less frequently. Quetelet was convinced that nature aims at creating the perfect person but misses the mark and thus creates deviations on both sides of the ideal.

MEASURES OF RELATIVE STANDING

measure of relative standing

We often wish to determine the relative standing of one measurement in a given set of data—that is, to compare one value with the distribution of all values. This is especially important in analyzing test results. The mean is one common **measure of relative standing.** If the mean of some test scores is 70 and a student has a score of 85, then we know the student has done better than average. However, this information does not tell us how many students scored higher than 70 or whether 85 was the highest score on the test.

PERCENTILES   One popular method of stating a person's relative performance on a test is to give the percent of people who did not score as high. For example, a person who scores higher than 80% of the people taking a test is said to be in the 80th percentile.

_p_TH PERCENTILE

> The **_p_th percentile** of a set of data is a number which is greater than _p_ percent of the data and less than $(100 - p)$ percent of the data.

Percentiles range from a low of 1% to a high of 99%; the 50th percentile is the median. It is customary on standardized tests to establish percentiles for large samples of people. When you take such a test, your score is compared to those of the sample. A percentile score of 65 means that you did better than 65% of the sample group. The table and bar graph in Figure 11.26 show a student's performance on a differential aptitude test. Nine categories are listed in the table at the top of this form: verbal reasoning, numerical ability, VR + NA (verbal reasoning and numerical ability together), abstract reasoning, etc. The raw score in each category represents the number of questions that the student answered correctly. The student's percentile score is obtained by comparing these raw scores with the scores from a sample of thousands of

Figure 11.26

	Verbal Reasoning	Numerical Ability	VR + NA	Abstract Reasoning	Clerical Sp & Acc	Mechanical Reasoning	Space Relations	Language Usage Spelling	Language Usage Grammar
Raw Score	33	31	64	36	41	48	28	56	32
Percentile	90	95	97	80	40	75	70	55	85

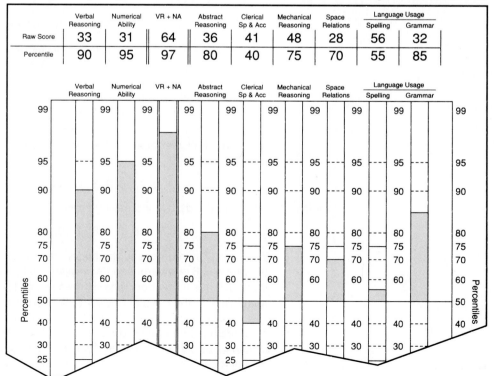

other students. The bar graph is a visual representation of the percentile scores. A horizontal line at the 50th percentile makes it easier to spot scores above and below the median.

EXAMPLE F

1. The verbal reasoning score shown in Figure 11.26 is at the 90th percentile. What does this mean?
2. In which of the nine categories is the student's performance below the median?
3. What percent of the people in the sample group had better spelling scores than this student?

Solution

1. This student's verbal reasoning score is greater than the verbal reasoning scores of 90% of the people in the sample group.
2. In the clerical category
3. 45%

The 50th percentile (median) splits any set of data into two parts: the lower part and the upper part. The median of the lower part is the 25th percentile and is called the **lower quartile**. The median of the upper part is the 75th percentile and is called the **upper quartile**. The 50th percentile (median) is sometimes called the **middle quartile**. The lower quartile, median, and upper quartile are also referred to as the **first, second,** and **third quartiles** and denoted by Q_1, Q_2, and Q_3, respectively. The quartiles split the data into four parts (Figure 11.27).

lower quartile
upper quartile
middle quartile
first, second, third quartiles

Figure 11.27

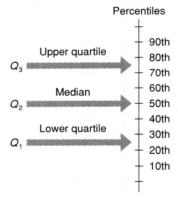

EXAMPLE G

Determine the lower quartile, median, and upper quartile for the following set of data.

$$11, 9, 7, 16, 3, 5, 19, 11, 8, 14, 6, 14, 10, 7, 6, 15, 13$$

Solution

First write the data in increasing order.

$$3, 5, 6, 6, 7, 7, 8, 9, 10, 11, 11, 13, 14, 14, 15, 16, 19$$

There are 17 numbers, and the middle number, or median, is 10. The lower part of the data has 8 numbers, and its median is 6.5, the mean of 6 and 7. Similarly, the upper half has 8 numbers, and its median is 14, the mean of 14 and 14. So the lower quartile is 6.5, the median is 10, and the upper quartile is 14.

Z-SCORES   Percentiles are a method of stating a person's relative standing on a test compared to that of others on the same test. But suppose you wished to compare performances on two different tests. One popular method of determining relative standing is to determine how many standard deviations a test score is from the mean.

EXAMPLE H

John scored 572 on the mathematics part of the Scholastic Aptitude Test (SAT). The mean score for this test was 460, and the standard deviation was 112. Bev scored 28 on the American College Test (ACT), and this test had a mean of 18 and a standard deviation of 5. Who had the better performance?

Solution

John's score of 572 is 1 standard deviation above the mean ($460 + 112 = 572$). Bev's score of 28 is 2 standard deviations above the mean. Even though Bev's score of 28 on the ACT appears much lower than John's score of 572 on the SAT, Bev's performance was better.

The number of standard deviations a measurement is from the mean is called the *z*-score. A *z*-score can be defined for every measure in a set of data.

z-score

Z-SCORE

The *z*-**score** for a measurement x is denoted by

$$z = \frac{x - \bar{x}}{s}$$

where $\bar{x}$ is the mean and s is the standard deviation for the set of data.

Notice that in Example H John has a *z*-score of 1, since

$$z = \frac{572 - 460}{112} = 1$$

and Bev has a *z*-score of 2, since

$$z = \frac{28 - 18}{5} = 2$$

Since most of the data in most sets are usually within 3 standard deviations of the mean, the *z*-score will usually be between ⁻3 and 3. Figure 11.28 shows a few *z*-scores and their relationship to the standard deviation and mean. Notice that if a measurement has a *z*-score of zero, the measurement equals the mean.

Figure 11.28

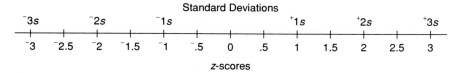

EXAMPLE I

Three students took three different tests with different means and standard deviations. The results are listed below. Which student had the best relative performance and which had the poorest?

Student 1 scored 82 on test 1. The mean on this test was 78.5, and the standard deviation was 2.3.

Student 2 scored 55 on test 2. The mean on this test was 48.2, and the standard deviation was 4.3.

Student 3 scored 392 on test 3. The mean on this test was 460, and the standard deviation was 85.

Solution   Student 1:

$$z = \frac{82 - 78.5}{2.3} \approx 1.52$$

Student 2:

$$z = \frac{55 - 48.2}{4.3} \approx 1.58$$

Student 3:

$$z = \frac{392 - 460}{85} = ^-.8$$

Student 2 had the best relative performance with a z-score of 1.58, and student 3 had the poorest performance. Notice that student 3 scored below the mean on her test, so the z-score is a negative number.

BOX AND WHISKER PLOTS   The z-score is useful for comparing a single measurement from one set of data to a measurement from another set of data, but how can whole sets of data be compared to each other? One method is to use the mean and standard deviation of each set to determine the amount of variability. Another method is to graph the two sets of data to obtain a visual comparison of their distributions. A third method, which is fairly quick and easy to use, involves quartiles and is called a **box and whisker plot.** This method shows the relative sizes of the quartiles as well as the smallest and largest measurements. Consider the following 20 scores on a science test:

box and whisker plot

57, 58, 62, 63, 66, 66, 67, 67, 68, 70, 70, 72, 73, 75, 80, 80, 81, 83, 85, 99

The box and whisker plot for this set of data is shown in Figure 11.29. Notice that the smallest score (57), the greatest score (99), the median, and two quartiles are marked on the line. Above the line there is a rectangular box that extends from the lower quartile (Q_1) to the upper quartile (Q_3) and represents 50% of the scores. The lines running from the ends of the rectangle to the smallest and largest test scores are called the whiskers. The plot shows that 25% of the test scores are in the interval from 66 to 70 (Q_1 to Q_2), and 25% are in the interval from 70 to 80 (Q_2 to Q_3), which is more than twice as long. Also, the length of the whiskers provides information about how close the smallest and greatest measurements are to the quartiles: the smallest test score (57) is much closer to the lower quartile (66) than the greatest score (99) is to the upper quartile (80).

Figure 11.29

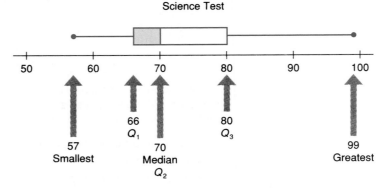

Science Test

EXAMPLE J

Form a box and whisker plot for the following 20 scores on a history test:

55, 59, 64, 64, 68, 70, 73, 75, 76, 79, 81, 81, 82, 84, 85, 85, 87, 92, 95, 98

1. Make a few observations about this plot.
2. Compare the box and whisker plot of scores on the history test to the plot of scores on the science test (Figure 11.29).

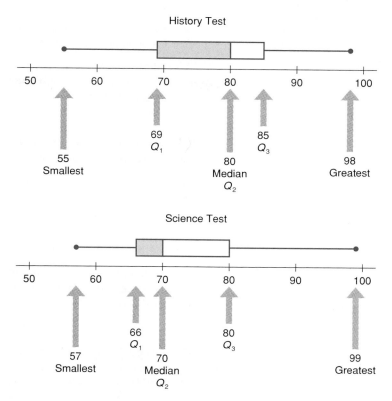

Solution

1. The rectangle in the box and whisker plot for the history test shows that 25% of the scores are in the interval from 69 to 80 (Q_1 to Q_2) and 25% of the scores are in the interval from 80 to 85 (Q_2 to Q_3), which is approximately half as long. Also, 50% of the scores are above 80, and 25% are above 85.

2. A comparison of the box and whisker plots for the history and science tests shows that overall, performance on the history test was better. Although the ranges of both tests are approximately the same ($98 - 55 = 43$ compared to $99 - 57 = 42$), the quartiles for the history test are all higher. For example, the median for the history test (80) equals the upper quartile for the science test. That is, 50% of the scores on the history test are above 80, whereas only 25% of the scores on the science test are above 80. Also, the lower quartile (69) for the history test is approximately equal to the median (70) for the science test, which means that there are approximately twice as many scores below 70 on the science test as on the history test.

SIMULATIONS

There are many statistical problems that are of interest to children but beyond their abilities to solve theoretically. The next example contains a type of problem that might appeal to elementary school children. Such problems are related to sampling and can be solved by conducting experiments.

EXAMPLE K

Each package of a certain brand of cereal contains 1 of 7 cards about superheroes. The students in an elementary school class wanted to know how many boxes of cereal they could expect to buy before getting the entire set.*

*Ann E. Watkins, "Monte Carlo Simulations: Probability the Easy Way," in *Teaching Statistics and Probability*, 1981 Yearbook (Reston, VA: National Council of Teachers of Mathematics, 1981), 203–209.

Solution   The elementary school class solved this problem by writing the names of the 7 superheroes on slips of paper and then performing the following experiment.

1. The 7 slips of paper were put in a bag.
2. A slip was drawn at random from the bag, the superhero's name was tallied, and the slip of paper was returned to the bag.
3. Step 2 was repeated until the name of each superhero had been drawn at least once.
4. The total number of draws was recorded. This total represents the number of boxes needed in this experiment to obtain an entire set of superhero cards.

This experiment was repeated 20 times. Here are the numbers of boxes obtained in the 20 experiments:

20, 14, 27, 18, 17, 15, 19,
19, 19, 20, 16, 11, 15, 21,
15, 22, 20, 28, 12, 26

The average (mean) number of "boxes" for this experiment before getting the entire set of cards is the sum of these numbers divided by 20:

$$\frac{374}{20} = 18.7 \approx 19$$

The students could see that they might have to go through more than 19 boxes to get all 7 cards if they were unlucky or they might collect all 7 cards after buying fewer than 19 boxes if they were lucky.

Monte Carlo method

simulation

Finding an answer to the question in Example K by purchasing boxes of cereal would be expensive. Representing cereal box prizes by writing names on slips of paper and performing an experiment is an example of an approach called the **Monte Carlo method.** In general, this method relies on identifying a model that can be used to *simulate* an event and then performing experiments using the model. **A simulation** is a procedure in which experiments that closely resemble the given situation are conducted repeatedly.

PROBLEM-SOLVING APPLICATION

using a simulation

The Monte Carlo method is a powerful problem-solving technique. This technique will be referred to as **using a simulation.**

■ **PROBLEM**

If people are selected randomly, how many must be selected (on average) to find two who have a birthday in the same month?

Question 1

Understanding the Problem   It might be necessary to select several people to find two with a birthday in the same month. What is the minimum number that must be chosen before this will happen?

Question 2

Devising a Plan   Conducting a simulation will be more convenient than interviewing large numbers of people. One method of simulation involves writing the whole numbers from 1 to 12 on 12 slips of paper and selecting them randomly from a box, returning each slip after it is selected. In this case, each experiment consists of selecting numbers one at a time until the same number is obtained twice. After this experiment has been carried out several times, we can determine the mean of the numbers of selections. Why must each slip of paper be returned to the box after it is selected?

Question 3

Carrying Out the Plan The following numbers were obtained by selecting slips of paper from a box until the same number was chosen twice. Determine the mean (average) size of these groups of numbers. According to this experiment, how many people must be interviewed (on average) to find two with a birthday in the same month?

```
7, 2, 2    1, 9, 10, 3, 5, 6, 9   7, 2, 2    10, 11, 8, 10   11, 9, 2, 3, 7, 9
9, 4, 9    7, 11, 9, 6, 4, 6   5, 9, 9    7, 12, 6, 11, 12   9, 12, 3, 11, 1, 4, 1
12, 2, 8, 6, 6   7, 2, 3, 9, 11, 9   12, 9, 3, 7, 5, 3   7, 2, 11, 4, 10, 5, 12, 9, 7
1, 4, 12, 2, 12   5, 9, 8, 3, 8   11, 11   6, 2, 12, 7, 1, 1   5, 2, 12, 10, 12
```

Question 4

Looking Back Another solution to this problem can be found by using a table of random numbers for the simulation (see below).* One way to use such a table is to select one of the numbers arbitrarily as a beginning point and then, moving from left to right, record pairs of numbers that are greater than zero and less than or equal to 12, with 01, 02, etc., being counted as 1, 2, etc. Solve the original problem by carrying out a simulation using the following list of random digits. What number do you obtain as a solution to the problem using this simulation?

```
89 81 80 69 77 09 86 76 77 71 21 52 23 86 53 95 20 94 29 48 33 37 58 33 93
24 30 87 37 31 80 37 25 47 06 72 78 11 30 08 88 84 78 78 46 51 14 96 58 12
77 02 18 48 54 50 76 36 05 12 33 77 59 58 76 17 68 58 89 84 38 35 42 17 55
58 01 63 92 45 47 24 54 42 80 55 53 09 95 46 98 94 67 27 15 52 56 08 82 56
24 39 68 08 01 15 72 23 88 37 38 00 36 94 14 47 88 90 44 74 28 27 01 71 16
05 61 62 60 18 72 01 75 51 88 52 95 13 39 81 75 76 66 02 76 29 69 77 96 77
62 23 95 43 71 34 38 09 45 82 85 62 72 58 62 74 51 95 87 44 45 01 77 67 26
43 07 96 21 98 68 25 01 17 11 59 32 39 70 13 21 43 81 57 55 86 59 28 45 34
95 78 66 81 10 85 54 62 86 27 44 89 51 18 75 48 62 29 43 54 44 46 13 32 13
55 00 90 00 42 27 01 23 24 10 49 21 46 26 14 82 31 94 54 39 55 07 81 32 57
81 57 86 88 83 81 54 91 42 82 82 14 44 13 30 27 84 31 77 21 88 67 72 04 36
99 94 94 09 62 81 41 09 62 30 95 13 69 92 15 18 76 02 78 22 15 86 90 86 72
```

Answers to Questions 1–4
1. Two
2. There should be an equal chance of any number's being chosen in any selection from the box.
3. The following numbers represent the sizes of the groups: 3, 7, 3, 4, 6, 3, 6, 3, 5, 7, 5, 6, 6, 9, 5, 5, 2, 6, 5. The mean of these numbers is $96/19 \approx 5.05$. Thus on the average approximately 5 people must be chosen before two are found with a birthday in the same month.
4. Starting at the beginning of the list at 89, we obtain the following groups: [09, 06, 11, 08, 12, 02, 05, 12], [01, 09, 08, 08], [01, 01], [05, 01, 02, 09, 01], [07, 01, 11, 10, 01], [10, 07, 04, 09, 09]. The mean size of these groups is approximately 4.8.

RELATED ACTIVITIES IN
Mathematics for Elementary Teachers: An Activity Approach, 3e

Activity Set 11.2   **Statistical Distributions:** These experiments produce data and graphs whose distributions are nearly normal or nearly uniform.

Just for Fun   **Cryptanalysis:** Coding and decoding secret writings

---

*The computer program RANDOM DIGITS on the *Computer Problem-Solving Disc* prints any desired number of random digits in groups of 5.

EXERCISES AND PROBLEMS 11.2

> **Student Flips,
> Finds Penny
> Is Tail Heavy**
>
> by Martin Weil
>
> Washington Post Staff Writer
>
> Edward J. Kelsey, 16, turned his dining room into a penny pitching parlor one day last spring, all in the name of science and statistics.
>
> In ten hours the Northwestern High School senior registered 17,950 coin flips and showed the world that you didn't get as many heads as tails. You get more.
>
> Edward got 464 more, enough to make him study the coins's balance and so discover that the United States Mint produces tail-heavy pennies.

1. As the above article from the *Washington Post* on November 27, 1965 reports, a student recorded 17,950 coin flips and got 464 more heads than tails. He concluded that the U.S. Mint produces tail-heavy coins. For many repeated experiments of 17,950 tosses of a fair coin, we can expect an approximately normal distribution with a mean of 8975 heads and a standard deviation of 67.
   a. The area under a normal curve within ±1 standard deviation of the mean is approximately 68% of the total area under the curve. Therefore, 68% of the time, the number of heads should be between what two numbers?
   b. Numbers above 3 standard deviations from the mean will occur approximately .15% of the time. Therefore, 99.85% of the time the number of heads should be below what number?
   c. Edward Kelsey got 9207 heads. Was he justified in concluding that the coins are tail-heavy?

2. Describe a method for using a table of random digits to obtain each of the following random samples. Then use the table of random digits on page 603 to obtain the sample.
   a. The names of 2 people from a list of 9
   b. Ten test questions from a total of 60
   c. Five people from a group of 30
   d. The health records of 8 children from a class of 25

3. An elementary school has the following numbers of students in grades K–4: grade K, 50; grade 1, 80; grade 2, 90; grade 3, 80; and grade 4, 100. If a stratified sample of 80 children is chosen, how many will be chosen from each grade?

4. There are 18 girls and 12 boys in a class. If stratified sampling is used to select 10 students, how many girls will be selected?

5. Describe the distribution of scores (skewed to the right, symmetric, skewed to the left) for the following tests.
   a. A test designed for third graders and given to first graders
   b. A test designed for sixth graders and given to eighth graders
   c. A test designed for fourth graders and given to second graders
   d. A test designed for second graders and given to second graders

6. Would you expect the distributions of the following sets of data to be skewed to the right, symmetric, or skewed to the left? (Hint: Sketch a graph with some typical values.)
   a. Amounts of time students study in a 24-hour period before an exam
   b. Widths of the handspans of fifth graders
   c. Sneaker sizes of professional basketball players
   d. Heights of college students
   e. Test scores of third graders on a pre-test on fractions at the beginning of the school year
   f. Weights of newborn babies

7. This normal curve shows a distribution of college entrance exam scores that has a mean of 500 and a standard deviation of 100. Use the approximate percents that were given in section 11.2 for a normal curve to answer the following questions.

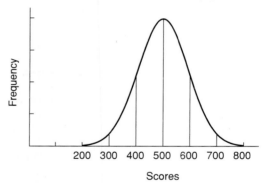

   a. What percent of the students scored between 400 and 600?
   b. What percent of the students scored above 600?
   c. What percent of the students scored below 300?
   d. What percent of the students scored between 300 and 600?

8. One method of grading that uses a normal curve gives students letter grades depending on the standard deviation intervals above or below the mean that contains their score: a grade of F for below ⁻2 standard deviations; D for ⁻2 to ⁻1 standard deviations; C for ⁻1 to 1; B for 1 to 2; and A for above 2 standard deviations. Suppose that on a test given to 50 students the mean score was 78 and the standard deviation was 6.
   a. How many students received a C?
   b. How many students received a grade below C?
   c. How many students received an A?

9. Objects that are manufactured to any set of specifications tend to vary slightly from their specified measurements. In answering the following questions, assume the measurements are normally distributed.

   a. A certain type of bulb has a mean life of 2400 hours with a standard deviation of 200 hours. What percent of these bulbs can be expected to burn longer than 2600 hours?

   b. A brand of crockpots has a mean high temperature of 260° F with a standard deviation of 3° F. If a crockpot's highest temperature is below 254° F or above 266° F, it is considered defective. What percent of these pots can be expected to be defective?

10. A certain university's WATS line can handle as many as 20 calls per minute. The average number of calls per minute during peak periods is 16 with a standard deviation of 4. What percent of the time will the WATS line be overloaded during peak periods? (Assume that the numbers of phone calls are normally distributed during peak period.)

11. This bar graph shows the measures of the diameters (to the nearest inch) of 100 trees of the same species. The mean diameter is 12 in., and the standard deviation is approximately 2 in.

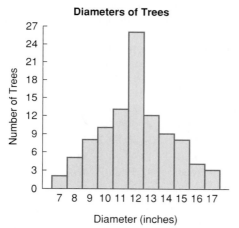

Diameters of Trees

   a. What type of distribution does this graph illustrate?
   b. Make a frequency table showing the numbers of trees of each diameter.
   c. What percent of the diameters are within 1 standard deviation of the mean?
   d. What percent of the trees have diameters within 2 standard deviations of the mean?

12. Trace the graph below on a sheet of paper and mark the approximate locations of the 10th, 25th, 50th, 75th, and 99th percentiles on the horizontal axis.

   a. What percent of the measurements are less than the 30th percentile?
   b. What percent of the measurements are greater than the 90th percentile?
   c. What percent of the measurements are between the 30th and 90th percentiles?
   d. What percent of the measurements are between the median and the 80th percentile?

13. This score form shows one student's scores on a few of the subtests of the Stanford Achievement Test. The top row of numbers listed for each subtest shows the number of questions answered correctly out of the total number of questions on that subtest. The first number in the second row of each column shows the national percentile; the first number in the third row of each column shows the local percentile. For example, this student was in the 90th percentile nationally on the vocabulary test.

Stanford ACHIEVEMENT TEST

	SCORE TYPE	MATH COMP
GR 4 NORMS GR 4.8	RS/NO POSS	29/44
LEVEL INTER 1 FORM E	NAT'L PR-S	54 - 5
STUDENT NO 400000044	LOCAL PR-S	68 - 6
OTHER INFO	GRADE EQUIV	5.5
AGE 9-6 TEST DATE 5/10/91		

READING COMP	VOCAB-ULARY	MATH APPL	SPELLING	LANGUAGE
57/60	32/36	32/40	37/40	40/53
96 - 9	90 -	77 -	86 -	63 -
78 - 7	69 -	62 -	83 -	45 -
PHS	8.4	6.4	8.9	5.4

   a. Nationally, what percent of students scored below this student in mathematics comprehension?
   b. Locally, what percent of students scored below this student in mathematics comprehension?
   c. This student scored higher in reading comprehension than what percent of the national group?
   d. Which of the local percentile scores is not lower than the corresponding national percentile score?
   e. If a local percentile is lower than a national percentile, the local level of achievement is higher than the national level of achievement. Explain why.

14. Rather than being divided into 100 parts, as in the case of percentiles, a distribution is sometimes divided into nine parts called **stanines,** a contraction of the words *standard nine*. Stanines are numbered from a low of 1 to a high of 9, with 5 representing average performance. The stanines that correspond to percentile intervals are shown in the following figure.

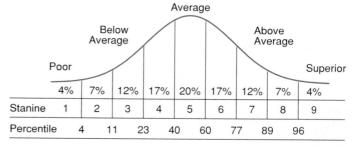

a. Determine the stanine for the 70th percentile.

b. The Stanford Achievement Test chart in exercise 13 records a stanine score beside each percentile. For example, under Math Comp, the 54th percentile corresponds to a stanine score of 5. Determine the 8 stanine scores missing from that chart.

15. Find the lower quartile, median, and upper quartile for each set of data.
   a. 4, 6, 7, 2, 9, 3, 12, 10, 3, 11, 7
   b. 70, 82, 68, 74, 71, 62, 86, 93, 65, 89, 76, 73, 74

16. A student scored 650 on the mathematics part of the Scholastic Aptitude Test (SAT) in a year in which the mean for that subtest was 455 and the standard deviation was 112. When the same student took a university entrance exam for engineers, he scored 140 on a math test that had a mean of 128 and a standard deviation of 9.5.
   a. What was his z-score for each test?
   b. On which of these two tests was his performance stronger, relative to the performance of the other students taking the test?

17. Determine a z-score to the nearest hundredth for each of the following test scores, and rank the scores from poorest to best.
   Test A: Mean, 74.3; standard deviation, 3.6; test score, 81
   Test B: Mean, 3.1; standard deviation, 2.1; test score, 2.8
   Test C: Mean, 6.2; standard deviation, 1.7; test score, 5.3
   Test D: Mean, 720; standard deviation, 146; test score, 840

18. The following is a box and whisker plot for 80 test scores.

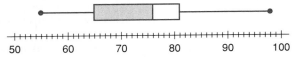

   a. What are the lowest and highest scores?
   b. What is the median score?
   c. What is the upper quartile?
   d. How many of the test scores are below 65?

19. Draw a box and whisker plot for these data:

   52, 61, 67, 75, 79, 81, 82, 83, 90, 93, 96

   a. What is the range of these data?
   b. What observations can you make from the plot regarding the quartiles?

20. The box and whisker plots below illustrate the test scores of 3 classes that took the same test. Which class performed best, and which performed poorest? Support your conclusion.

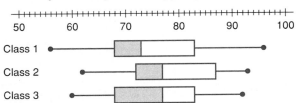

21. This list of the 15 largest states shows the percent (to the nearest tenth) of students completing high school in each state in 1987.*

California	78.9	New Jersey	76.9
Florida	77.1	New York	75.0
Georgia	71.2	N. Carolina	67.8
Illinois	76.4	Ohio	75.6
Indiana	76.0	Pennsylvania	75.5
Massachusetts	80.4	Texas	72.0
Michigan	75.5	Virginia	72.3
Missouri	78.1		

   a. Draw a box and whisker plot of these data.
   b. What is the median percent of students completing high school?
   c. What is true of the median in relationship to the lower quartile and upper quartile?
   d. What is the lower quartile, and what information does it provide about these data?

22. Computer programs generate random numbers for experiments and games. A computer cannot flip coins and roll dice, but it can read numbers and simulate these activities.
   a. Explain how to simulate the flipping of a coin using the following numbers from a random number table. Use your method and record the first 10 "coin tosses."
   b. Devise a way to use these random numbers to simulate the rolling of a die. Use your method and record the first 10 "rolls" of the die.

61 44 34 03 09	05 64 20 54 24
41 17 26 81 06	85 19 76 44 59
73 73 97 24 18	38 25 89 37 20
65 69 66 39 80	13 97 76 63 34
08 60 20 66 68	42 99 28 71 47
72 47 40 14 34	38 57 30 80 89

23. Use a simulation to solve each of the following problems. Describe your method.
   a. A manufacturer puts 1 of 5 different randomly selected colored markers in each box of Crackerjacks. What is the average number of boxes that must be purchased to obtain all 5 markers?
   b. Pepe and Anna are playing a penny-tossing game. The player who can toss 10 heads in the fewest number of tosses wins the game. How many tosses of a fair coin on average are required to obtain 10 heads?
   c. A newly married couple would like to have a child of each sex. Assuming that the chances of a boy or girl are equally likely, what is the average number of children the couple must have in order to have at least 1 boy and 1 girl?

*Statistical Abstract of the United States: 1982–93, 103d ed. (Washington, DC: U.S. Bureau of the Census, 1982), 612.

Featured Strategy: Using a Simulation

24. A cloakroom attendant receives 9 hats from 9 people and gets the hats mixed up. If the hats are returned at random and simultaneously, what is the average number of hats that will go to the correct owners?

    a. Understanding the Problem There are 9 people, and each person has exactly 1 hat. Is it possible that each hat might be returned to its owner?

    b. Devising a Plan One way to approach the problem is to conduct experiments with 9 people and 9 hats, using some random method of returning the hats. Another approach is to design a simulation. How might such a simulation be designed?

    c. Carrying Out the Plan The simulation must be carried out several times to determine the number of "hats" (on average) that will be returned correctly. What is this number?

    d. Looking Back Suppose that instead of 9 hats and 9 people, there are fewer people, each having 1 hat. Will the average number of hats that are returned correctly increase?

25. Graphs of distributions are sometimes intended to be misleading. The scale used on the vertical axis will determine whether the graph of the distribution of sales shown in the table will be skewed. Plot these sales on each of the following bar graphs. (Copy the rectangular grid from the inside cover to reproduce these graphs.) What impressions do these two graphs give to the reader? Which graph better illustrates the true increase in sales. Explain why.

Year	Sales
1986	$191,000,000
1987	191,500,000
1988	193,000,000
1989	195,000,000
1990	198,000,000
1991	200,500,000

(i)

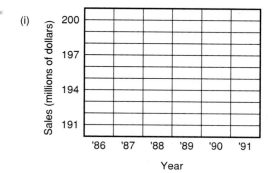

(ii)

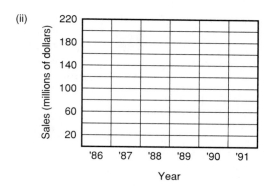

26. The Montagnais and Naskapi, Northern Indian tribes, bake the shoulder blade of a caribou to get guidance on decisions concerning the well-being of their tribe. They determine the direction of the next hunt from the direction of the cracks that appear in the animal's shoulder blade as it is baked. This method of determining direction is a fairly random device that avoids human bias. It suggests that some practices in magic need to be reassessed.*

    a. Explain how a table of random numbers can be used to randomly determine directions of 0° to 360° for hunting.

    b. How can a table of random numbers be used to randomly determine both directions and distances to be traveled for the hunt?

    c. Use your method in part b and the table of random digits on page 603 to determine the direction and distance of your first hunt.

---

*O. K. Moore, "Divination—A New Perspective," *American Anthropologist* 59 (1965): 121–128.

COMPUTER INVESTIGATION

The computer program DICE TOSS SIMULATION on the *Computer Problem-Solving Disc* simulates the toss of 2 or more dice. The computer prints the sum for each toss and the number of tosses needed to obtain a desired sum.

A gambling question that arose in the seventeenth century concerns the number of times 2 dice must be tossed to obtain a double 6 (a sum of 12). Try predicting the average number of tosses needed to obtain a double 6.

Use the computer program to carry out the following investigations.

Questions for Investigation

1. Determine the number of tosses of 2 dice required to obtain a double 6, and repeat this experiment 25 times. What is the mean number of tosses from your experiments?
2. Determine the number of tosses of 2 dice required to obtain a 7 or an 11. Repeat this experiment 25 times and determine the mean number of tosses.

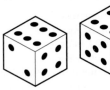

3. Another seventeenth-century gambling question involves tossing 3 dice. Determine the number of tosses of 3 dice required to obtain a sum greater than or equal to 15. Repeat this experiment 25 times. What is the mean number of tosses required to obtain a sum greater than or equal to 15?

PUZZLER

Cryptology is the science of coding and decoding secret messages. Try breaking the following code. It is a statement by the nineteenth-century mathematician Pierre Laplace.*

CA CW GZJHGBHYRZ AOHA H
WVCZQVZ MOCVO YZFHQ MCAO
AOZ VLQWCXZGHACLQ LK
FHJZW LK VOHQVZ WOLERX YZ
ZRZSHAZX AL AOZ GHQB LK AOZ

JLWA CJILGAHQA WEYPZVAW LK
OEJHQ BQLMRZXFZ.

Hint: Make a frequency distribution showing the number of times each letter occurs. The four most often used letters in the English language are e, t, a, and o, in that order. This is also the order in which these letters are used in Laplace's statement above. Substitute these letters for the four most frequently used letters in this code. The letters h, n, i, and s also occur with high frequency in our language. Substitute these letters for the fifth, sixth, seventh, and eighth most frequently used letters in the code.

"I forgot the message!"

CHAPTER REVIEW

1. **Statistics**
   a. **Statistics** can refer to numerical information, called data, or to the science of collecting and interpreting data.
   b. **Descriptive statistics** is the science of describing data.
   c. **Inferential statistics** is the science of interpreting data in order to make predictions.

2. **Charts and Graphs**
   a. **Bar graphs** are used to picture data when there are a small number of distinct categories.
   b. **Pie charts** are used for essentially the same purposes as bar graphs.
   c. **Stem and leaf plots** provide a visual summary of data in numerical form.
   d. **Histograms** are bar graphs of grouped data.
   e. **Line graphs** are often used to show changes over a period of time.
   f. **Box and whisker plots** are used to compare two sets of data.

3. **Measures of Central Tendency**
   a. A **measure of central tendency** is a number that approximates the "center" of a set of data.
   b. There are three measures of central tendency: the **mean** (numerical average), the **mode,** and the **median.**
   c. The **mean** of n numbers is the sum of the numbers divided by n.
   d. The **median** of a set of numbers is the middle number when the numbers are placed in increasing order or, if there is no middle number, the mean of the two middle numbers.
   e. The **mode** of a set of numbers is the number that occurs most often.

4. **Measures of Variability**
   a. A **measure of variability** is a number that describes the spread, or variation, in a set of data.
   b. The **range** is the difference between the greatest and least measures in a set of data.

*The computer program CRYPTOLOGY on the *Computer Problem-Solving Disc* prints the frequency of each letter in any paragraph that is entered.

c. The **standard deviation** is computed by subtracting the mean from each measurement, squaring each difference, finding the mean of the squared differences, and obtaining the square root of this mean.

d. At least 75% of the measurements in any set of data will lie within 2 standard deviations of the mean.

5. Measures of Relative Standing

   a. A **measure of relative standing** is a number that determines the relative position of a measurement in a set of data.

   b. The **pth percentile** of a set of data is a number which is greater than p percent of the data and less than $(100 - p)$ percent of the data.

   c. The 25th percentile of a set of data is known as the **lower quartile,** the 50th percentile is the median, or **middle quartile,** and the 75th percentile is the **upper quartile.**

   d. A z-score can be calculated for any measurement in a set of data. It indicates the number of standard deviations a measurement is from the mean.

6. Sampling

   a. A **sample** refers to a subset taken from a population.

   b. A **random sample** is a sample taken from a population in which every element has the same chance of being selected.

   c. In **stratified sampling** the population is divided into groups and the number sampled from each group is proportional to the size of the group.

7. A **simulation** is a procedure in which experiments that closely resemble the given situation are conducted repeatedly. Identifying a model and carrying out a simulation is called the **Monte Carlo method.**

8. Distributions

   a. The **distribution** of a set of data describes how the data are clustered together or isolated from each other.

   b. If data are concentrated at the right end of a graph with the "tail" extending to the left, the distribution is **skewed to the left.**

   c. If data are concentrated at the left end of a graph with the "tail" extending to the right, the distribution is **skewed to the right.**

   d. A distribution in which measurements at equal distances from the center of the distribution occur with the same frequency is called **symmetric.**

   e. A smooth symmetric bell-shaped curve is called a **normal curve,** and the distribution of its data is called a **normal distribution.**

CHAPTER TEST

The following table shows sources of public school revenues in percents for each state for 1987–1988. Use these data in answering #1 through #5.

PUBLIC SCHOOL REVENUES, BY SOURCE, BY STATE, 1987-88
(in percents)

State	Local and other	Federal	State	Local and other	Federal
Hawaii	91.2	0.1	8.7	Montana	49.3	42.8	7.9
New Mexico	76.3	11.8	11.9	Massachusetts	46.7	47.6	5.7
Washington	73.6	20.6	5.8	Pennsylvania	46.1	49.6	4.3
Alabama	69.9	17.7	12.4	Texas	45.8	47.2	7.0
Kentucky	69.5	20.4	10.1	Kansas	43.8	51.5	4.7
California	69.2	23.4	7.4	New York	43.4	51.6	5.0
Delaware	68.7	23.8	7.5	Rhode Island	43.2	52.5	4.3
Alaska	67.3	25.4	7.3	Iowa	43.2	51.3	5.5
Oklahoma	64.9	29.5	5.6	New Jersey	42.7	53.1	4.2
North Carolina	64.5	29.1	6.4	Wyoming	42.5	52.8	4.7
Arkansas	61.3	29.3	9.4	Connecticut	42.1	53.8	4.1
Idaho	61.2	31.5	7.3	Missouri	40.5	53.7	5.8
West Virginia	61.1	26.8	12.1	Wisconsin	40.2	55.2	4.6
Indiana	60.0	36.0	4.0	Nevada	40.1	55.8	4.1
Utah	57.3	37.0	5.7	Maryland	39.8	54.9	5.3
Minnesota	56.9	38.5	4.6	Colorado	38.8	56.3	4.9
Georgia	58.2	36.3	7.5	Illinois	38.0	54.6	7.4
South Carolina	55.6	36.1	8.3	Vermont	37.0	56.9	6.1
Louisiana	54.8	33.7	11.5	Michigan	35.2	61.2	3.6
Mississippi	54.5	29.8	15.7	Virginia	35.0	60.2	4.8
Maine	54.2	40.2	5.6	South Dakota	27.7	63.3	9.0
Arizona	53.5	43.0	3.5	Oregon	26.7	67.0	6.3
Florida	52.5	40.8	6.7	Nebraska	26.6	68.2	5.2
North Dakota	51.2	41.4	7.4	New Hampshire	7.3	89.6	3.1
Tennessee	50.4	40.0	9.6				
Ohio	49.7	44.6	5.7	United States	50.4	40.0	9.6

Source: NEA *Rankings of the States 1988*

1. a. In which state was the greatest percent of revenue from the state?

   b. In which state was the smallest percent of revenue from the state?

   c. What is the range of percents of revenue supplied by the states?

   d. The states are listed in decreasing order by percents of revenue from state sources. What is the median of these percents?

2. a. Draw a pie chart showing the three sources of revenue for California. Label the size of the central angle for each part of the graph.

   b. Draw a bar graph showing the three sources of revenue for Iowa. Label the axes of the graph.

3. Form a stem and leaf plot of the percents of revenue from the federal government. Use the tens and units digits for the stems and the tenths for the leaves.

4. Form a histogram for the percents of local revenue, using intervals on the horizontal axis of 0% to 9.9%, 10% to 19.9%, 20% to 29.9%, . . . , 80% to 89.9%.

   a. What is the frequency of states in the interval from 20% to 29.9%?

   b. What is the frequency of states in the interval from 80% to 89.9%?

   c. What interval contains the most measurements?

5. a. What is the mean of the percents of local revenue for the 5 states with the greatest percents of local revenue?

   b. What is the mean of the percents of local revenue for the 5 states with the smallest percents of local revenue?

6. a. Which of the following sets of data has the greatest mean?
   b. Which has the greatest range?
   c. Which has the greatest standard deviation?

   Set A: 1, 5, 10, 15, 20
   Set B: 21, 22, 23, 24, 25

7. Draw a box and whisker plot for the following data. Label the three quartiles and the smallest and largest values.

   62, 63, 66, 66, 70, 72, 73, 77, 84, 86, 92, 95, 97

8. Mary obtained a math score of 520 on the SAT; the SAT scores had a mean of 435 and a standard deviation of 105. Her math score on the PSAT (Preliminary Scholastic Aptitude Test) was 56; the PSAT scores had a mean of 44 and a standard deviation of 9.5.
   a. Determine Mary's z-score for the SAT (to the nearest tenth).
   b. Determine Mary's z-score for the PSAT (to the nearest tenth).
   c. On which test was her mathematics performance stronger?

9. A fourth-grade class is given a mathematics pre-test at the beginning of the school year and a post-test at the end of the school year.
   a. Is the distribution of scores on the pre-test most likely to be skewed to the left, skewed to the right, or normal?
   b. Describe the most likely distribution for the post-test.

10. A few of the results from a Stanford Achievement Test taken by a fourth-grader are shown below.

Total Reading	Total Listening	Total Language	Total Math	Basic Bat Tot
107/120	68/76	77/93	81/118	333/407
93 - 8	93 - 8	76 - 6	64 - 6	77 - 7
90 - 8	77 - 7	65 - 6	60 - 6	69 - 6
10.0	9.2	6.5	5.5	8.0

   a. The first row of numbers under each subtest shows the number of questions answered correctly out of the total number of questions on that subtest. What percent to the nearest tenth of the questions on Total Language did this student answer correctly?
   b. The first number in the second row of each column is the student's percentile score relative to the national group. What percent of the national group of students scored below this student in Total Reading?
   c. The first number in the third row of each column is the student's percentile score relative to the local group. This student is at the 60th percentile in Total Math. What does this mean?
   d. The numbers in the fourth row are the grade equivalents indicated by the test results. What do these numbers indicate about this fourth-grader?

11. A district mathematics test for all third-graders had a normal distribution with a mean of 74 and a standard deviation of 11.
   a. What percent of the third-graders tested scored within ±1 standard deviation of the mean?
   b. What percent of the students scored between 52 and 96?

12. Students in two fifth grades were given the same English test. One class of 26 students had a mean of 68, and the second class of 22 students had a mean of 73. What is the mean for the total number of students in both classes (to the nearest tenth)?

13. The mean of three test scores is 74. What must the score on a fourth test be to raise the mean of the four tests to 78?

BIBLIOGRAPHY

Barbella, P. "Realistic Examples in Elementary Statistics." *Mathematics Teacher* 80 (December 1987): 740–743.

Bestgen, B. J. "Making and Interpreting Graphs and Tables: Results and Implications from National Assessment." *Arithmetic Teacher* 28 (December 1980): 26–29.

Burrill, G. "Statistics and Probability." *Mathematics Teacher* 83 (February 1990): 113–118.

Christopher, L. "Graphs Can Jazz Up the Mathematics Curriculum." *Arithmetic Teacher* 30 (September 1982): 28–30.

Davis, G. "Using Data Analysis to Explore Class Enrollment." *Mathematics Teacher* 83 (February 1990): 104–106.

Duncan, D., and B. Litwiller. "Randomness, Normality, and Hypothesis Testing: Experiences for the Statistics Class." *Mathematics Teacher* 74 (May 1981): 368–374.

Goldman, P. H. "Teaching Arithmetic Averaging: An Activity Approach." *Arithmetic Teacher* 37 (March 1990): 38–43.

Hinders, D. C. "Examples of the Use of Statistics in Society." *Mathematics Teacher* 83 (February 1990): 136–141.

Horak, V. M., and W. J Horak. "Let's Do It: Collecting and Displaying the Data Around Us." *Arithmetic Teacher* 30 (September 1982): 16–20.

Hyatt, D. "M and M's Candy: A Statistical Approach." *Arithmetic Teacher* 24 (January 1977): 34.

Jacobson, M. "Graphing in the Primary Grades: Our Pets." *Arithmetic Teacher* 26 (February 1979): 25–26.

Jamski, W. "Introducing Standard Deviation." *Mathematics Teacher* 74 (March 1981): 197–198.

Johnson, E. "Bar Graphs for First Graders." *Arithmetic Teacher* 29 (December 1981): 30–31.

Klitz, R., and J. Hofmeister. "Statistics in the Middle School." *Arithmetic Teacher* 26 (February 1979): 35–36.

Landwehr, J., and A. Watkins. "Stem-and-Leaf Plots." *Mathematics Teacher* 78 (October 1985): 528–532, 537–538.

MacDonald, A. "A Stem-Leaf Plot: An Approach to Statistics." *Mathematics Teacher* 75 (January 1982): 25, 27, 28.

Mullenex, J. L. "Box Plots: Basic and Advanced." *Mathematics Teacher* 83 (February 1990): 108–112.

National Council of Teachers of Mathematics. *Teaching Statistics and Probability.* 1981 Yearbook. Reston, VA: NCTM, 1981.

Olson, A. T. "Exploring Baseball Data." *Mathematics Teacher* 80 (October 1987): 565–569, 584.

Scalzitt, J. "Stand Up and Be Counted." *Arithmetic Teacher* 27 (May 1980): 12–13.

Scheaffer, R. L. "Why Data Analysis." *Mathematics Teacher* 83 (February 1990): 90–93.

Shaw, J. M. "Let's Do It: Dealing with Data." *Arithmetic Teacher* 31 (May 1984): 9–15.

Shaw, J. M. "Let's Do It: Making Graphs." *Arithmetic Teacher* 31 (January 1984): 7–11.

Shulte, A. *Teaching Statistics and Probability.* 1981 Yearbook. Reston, VA: National Council of Teachers of Mathematics, 1981.

Shulte, A. "A Case for Statistics." *Arithmetic Teacher* 26 (February 1979): 24.

Slaughter, J. P. "The Graph Examined." *Arithmetic Teacher* 30 (March 1983): 41–45.

Smith, M. S. "Making Averaging Easier." *Arithmetic Teacher* 29 (December 1981): 40–41.

Smith, R. "Bar Graphs for Five Year Olds." *Arithmetic Teacher* 27 (October 1979): 38–41.

Souviney, R. "Problem Solving Tips for Teachers." *Arithmetic Teacher* 33 (February 1986): 56–57.

Sullivan, D., and M. O'Neil. "THIS IS US! Great Graphs for Kids." *Arithmetic Teacher* 28 (September 1980): 14–18.

Vissa, J. "Sampling Treats from a School of Fish." *Arithmetic Teacher* 34 (March 1987): 36–37.

Zawojewski, J. S. "Research into Practice: Teaching Statistics: Mean, Median, and Mode." *Arithmetic Teacher* 35 (March 1988): 25–26.

12 *Probability*

SPOTLIGHT ON TEACHING

Excerpts from NCTM's Standard 11 for Teaching Mathematics in Grades 5–8*

An understanding of probability and the related area of statistics is essential to being an informed citizen. . . .

The nature of probability encourages a systematic and logical approach to problem solving. Throughout their experimentation and simulation, students should be making hypotheses, testing conjectures, and refining their theories on the basis of new information. . . .

Probability connects many areas of mathematics. For example, fraction concepts play a critical role in the study of probability. Topics such as equivalent fractions, comparison of fractions, addition and multiplication of fractions, as well as whole number operations and the relationships among fractions, decimals, and percents can be reinforced through the study of probability.

Dividing the area of a rectangle into fractional parts to model a probability problem provides an excellent opportunity for students to identify the relationship between concepts in geometry and operations with fractions. (Consider the following example.)

Tom is to pick a path at random [in the maze below]. Use the grid [to the right of the maze] to determine the probability that he will enter room A or room B.

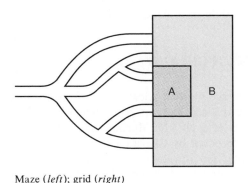

Maze (*left*); grid (*right*)

*Reprinted by permission of the National Council of Teachers of Mathematics.

SECTION 12.1   SINGLE-STAGE EXPERIMENTS

The numbers 3, 4, 5, and 6 are written on four cards. If one number is randomly chosen as the numerator of a fraction and another is randomly chosen as the denominator of the fraction, what is the probability that the fraction is greater than 1 and less than 1½?

"Looks like it might be a nice day tomorrow!"

Probability, a relatively new branch of mathematics, emerged in Italy and France during the sixteenth and seventeenth centuries from studies of strategies for gambling games. From these beginnings probability evolved to have applications in many areas of life. Life insurance companies use probability to estimate how long a person is likely to live; doctors use probability to predict the success of a treatment; and meteorologists use probability to forecast weather conditions.

One of the trends in education in recent years has been to increase emphasis on probability and statistics in the elementary grades. NCTM's *Curriculum and Evaluation Standards for School Mathematics* supports this trend by including statistics and probability as a major strand in the standards for grades K–4. "Collecting, organizing, describing, displaying, and interpreting data, as well as making decisions and predictions on the basis of that information, are skills that are increasingly important in a society based on technology and communication"*

Blaise Pascal

■ *HISTORICAL HIGHLIGHT*

The founders of the mathematical theory of probability were Blaise Pascal (1623–1662) and Pierre Fermat (1601–1665), who developed the principles of this subject in letters to each other during 1654. The initial problem that started their investigation was posed by Chevalier de Mere, a professional gambler. The problem was to determine how the stakes should be divided between two gamblers if they quit before the game was finished. The problem amounts to determining the probability each player has of winning the game at any given stage. The theory that originated in a gambler's dispute is now an essential tool in many disciplines.**

---

*National Council of Teachers of Mathematics, *Curriculum and Evaluation Standards for School Mathematics* (Reston, VA: NCTM, 1989), 54.

**E. T. Bell, *Men of Mathematics* (New York: Simon and Schuster, 1965), 73–89.

PROBABILITIES OF OUTCOMES

Just as probability had its beginning in games of chance, it is often introduced in the early grades through simple games such as those involving spinners. Consider the experiment of spinning the spinner in Figure 12.1. There are 4 possible outcomes: blue, red, green, and yellow. We would expect the color blue to come up about 1/4 of the time if we spin many times. That is, the probability of obtaining blue is 1/4. This probability is indicated by writing.

$$P(\text{Blue}) = \frac{1}{4}$$

Figure 12.1

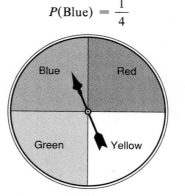

experiment
outcomes
sample space

In general, an activity such as spinning a spinner, tossing a coin, or rolling a die is called an **experiment,** and the different results that can occur are called **outcomes.** The set of all outcomes of an experiment is called the **sample space.**

EXAMPLE A

For each experiment, determine the sample space and the probability of the given outcome.

1. Rolling a regular six-sided die (faces are numbered from 1 to 6) once and obtaining a 2
2. Tossing a coin once and obtaining a head
3. Selecting a green marble on one draw from a box containing 5 green marbles and 7 blue marbles

Solution

1. The sample space contains the numbers from 1 to 6, and $P(2) = 1/6$.
2. The sample space has 2 outcomes, heads (H) and tails (T), and $P(H) = 1/2$.
3. The sample space contains 12 marbles, 5 green (G) and 7 blue (B), and $P(G) = 5/12$.

---

experimental probability

There are two methods of determining probabilities. One is by conducting experiments and observing the results. A probability derived in this fashion is called an **experimental probability.** For example, if a coin is tossed 500 times and 300 heads occur, the experimental probability of obtaining a head is 300/500, or 3/5. The second method of determining probabilities is based on theoretical considerations. Since spinners, dice, coins, and other physical devices for determining random outcomes all have imperfections which lead to biased results, we assign **theoretical probabilities** to the outcomes

theoretical probability

of ideal experiments. Ideally, for example, the spinner shown in Figure 12.1 will be equally likely to stop at any of the 4 colors. So the theoretical probability of obtaining blue is 1/4. From here on the word "probability" will mean *theoretical probability,* unless otherwise stated.

The probability of obtaining one of a group of equally likely outcomes is defined as follows.

**PROBABILITY
OF AN OUTCOME**

> If there are *n* equally likely outcomes, then the **probability** of any given outcome is $1/n$.

Outcomes are not always equally likely, as shown in the next example.

EXAMPLE B

Spinning this spinner will result in 1 of 4 outcomes: blue (B), red (R), green (G), or yellow (Y). Determine the following probabilities.

1. $P(B)$ 2. $P(G)$ 3. $P(Y)$

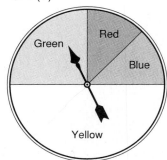

Solution 1. $P(B) = \dfrac{1}{8}$ 2. $P(G) = \dfrac{1}{4}$ 3. $P(Y) = \dfrac{1}{2}$

PROBABILITIES OF EVENTS

Consider the experiment of rolling 2 ordinary dice. The 36 possible outcomes of the sample space are shown in Figure 12.2, and since each outcome is equally likely, the probability of obtaining any given pair of numbers is $1/36$. For example, the probability of obtaining double 6s is $1/36$, because there is only one outcome in which 6 dots show on the top of each die.

Figure 12.2
Thirty-six possible outcomes of rolling 2 dice

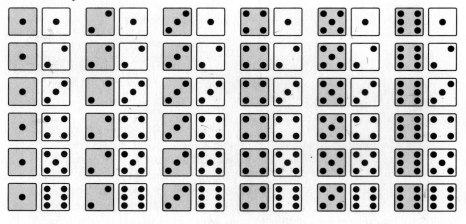

Once we know the complete sample space, as in Figure 12.2, it is possible to answer more difficult questions concerning tosses of 2 dice.

EXAMPLE C

Determine the probabilities of the following outcomes using Figure 12.2.

1. Obtaining a sum less than 4
2. Obtaining a sum of 5
3. Obtaining a sum greater than or equal to 9

Solution

1. There are 3 outcomes whose sum is less than 4, so $P(\text{Sum} < 4) = 3/36 = 1/12$.
2. There are 4 outcomes whose sum is 5, so $P(\text{Sum} = 5) = 4/36 = 1/9$.
3. There are 10 outcomes whose sum is greater than or equal to 9, so $P(\text{Sum} \geq 9) = 10/36 = 5/18$.

Notice that in part (1) of Example C the probability of obtaining a sum less than 4 involves more than one outcome: the pairs (1, 1), (1, 2), and (2, 1) all have a sum less than 4. A subset of outcomes in a sample space is called an **event**. For example, the event with sums of 5 has 4 out of the 36 outcomes, and the event with sums greater than or equal to 9 has 10 out of 36 outcomes.

event

Example C suggests the following rule for obtaining the probability of an event.

PROBABILITY OF AN EVENT

> If all the outcomes of a sample space are equally likely, the **probability of an event** E is
>
> $$P(\text{E}) = \frac{\text{Number of favorable outcomes}}{\text{Total number of outcomes}}$$

Let's use this rule to determine the probability of obtaining a sum of 7 on a toss of 2 dice. Figure 12.2 shows that there are 6 ways this can be done (6 favorable outcomes), so

$$P(\text{Sum} = 7) = \frac{6}{36} = \frac{1}{6}$$

Listing all the outcomes of a sample space (as in Figure 12.2) and counting the favorable outcomes is a common method of determining the probability of an event when there are relatively few outcomes. This approach is used in Examples D and E.

EXAMPLE D

List the sample space for the experiment of tossing 3 coins. Then determine the probabilities of the following events.

1. Obtaining exactly 2 heads
2. Obtaining at least 2 heads

Solution

There are 8 outcomes:

HHH   HHT   HTH   THH   TTT   TTH   THT   HTT

1. There are 3 outcomes with exactly 2 heads (HHT, HTH, and THH), so

$$P(\text{Exactly 2 heads}) = \frac{3}{8}$$

2. There are 4 outcomes with at least 2 heads (HHT, HTH, THH, and HHH), so

$$P(\text{At least 2 heads}) = \frac{4}{8} = \frac{1}{2}$$

✓ **EXAMPLE E**

Five tickets numbered 1, 2, 3, 4, and 5 are placed in a box, and two are selected at random. List the sample space and determine the given probabilities.

1. Obtaining a 1 or a 2 or both
2. Obtaining 2 odd numbers
3. Obtaining the number 6
4. Obtaining a number less than 6

Solution   There are 10 outcomes in the sample space: *without replacement*

$$1, 2 \quad 1, 3 \quad 1, 4 \quad 1, 5 \quad 2, 3 \quad 2, 4 \quad 2, 5 \quad 3, 4 \quad 3, 5 \quad 4, 5$$

1. There are 7 outcomes containing either a 1 or a 2 or both, so

$$P(1 \text{ or } 2 \text{ or both}) = \frac{7}{10}$$

2. There are 3 outcomes in which both numbers are odd, so

$$P(\text{Both odd}) = \frac{3}{10}$$

3. There are no outcomes that include the number 6, so

$$P(6) = 0$$

4. All 10 outcomes include numbers less than 6, so

$$P(\text{Number} < 6) = \frac{10}{10} = 1$$

impossible event

certain event

In part (3) of Example E the event of obtaining the number 6 is the empty set. In this case the event is called an **impossible event,** and it has a probability of zero. At the opposite extreme, the event in part (4) of Example E contains all possible outcomes. Such an event is called a **certain event** and has a probability of 1. Since the number of favorable outcomes is always less than or equal to the total number of outcomes, *the probability of an event is always less than or equal to* 1. These observations are summarized in the following inequality, which holds for any event *E*.

$$0 \leq P(\text{E}) \leq 1$$

We have been computing the probabilities of events by dividing the number of favorable outcomes by the total number of outcomes. Perhaps you have noticed that the probability of an event can also be found by adding the probabilities of the various outcomes in the event. In part (2) of Example E there are 3 outcomes in which both numbers are odd, so the probability of selecting a pair of odd numbers is 3/10. The probability of this event can also be found by adding the probabilities of each outcome:

$$\frac{1}{10} + \frac{1}{10} + \frac{1}{10} = \frac{3}{10}$$

This is a special case of the following property.

PROBABILITY OF EVENTS

The **probability of an event** *E*, which has outcomes $e_1, e_2, \ldots, e_n$, is the sum of the probabilities of the outcomes.

$$P(E) = P(e_1) + P(e_2) + \cdots + P(e_n)$$

This property holds for events with equally likely outcomes as well as for those whose outcomes are not equally likely.

EXAMPLE F

The outcomes of spinning the spinner shown below have these probabilities:

$$P(\text{Purple}) = \frac{1}{12}, \; P(\text{Blue}) = \frac{1}{6}, \; P(\text{Red}) = \frac{1}{6},$$

$$P(\text{Yellow}) = \frac{1}{6}, \; P(\text{Green}) = \frac{1}{12}, \text{ and } P(\text{Orange}) = \frac{1}{3}$$

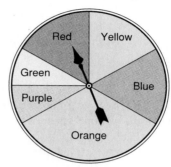

Determine the probabilities of the following events.

1. *E:* Obtaining a primary color (red, blue, or yellow)
2. *T:* Obtaining a color with 6 letters in its name

Solution

1. $P(E) = P(\text{Red}) + P(\text{Blue}) + P(\text{Yellow}) = \frac{1}{6} + \frac{1}{6} + \frac{1}{6} = \frac{3}{6} = \frac{1}{2}$

2. $P(T) = P(\text{Purple}) + P(\text{Orange}) + P(\text{Yellow}) = \frac{1}{12} + \frac{1}{3} + \frac{1}{6} = \frac{7}{12}$

MUTUALLY EXCLUSIVE EVENTS

In Example F, events E and T are not disjoint; that is, they have an outcome (yellow) in common. Thus the probability of E or T cannot be obtained by adding $P(E) + P(T)$. In fact, in this example the sum of these probabilities is greater than 1 (1/2 + 7/12), and we know that probabilities must be less than or equal to 1. However, when two events are *disjoint,* the probability of their union is the sum of their probabilities. Dis-

mutually exclusive events

joint events are called **mutually exclusive events** and have the following property.

MUTUALLY EXCLUSIVE EVENTS

> If events A and B are disjoint, they are called **mutually exclusive events,** and
>
> $$P(A \cup B) = P(A) + P(B)$$

EXAMPLE G

Several events containing the outcomes of spinning the spinner in Example F are defined as follows.

E: Obtaining a primary color (red, blue, or yellow)

T: Obtaining a color with 6 letters in its name

H: Obtaining a color with 5 letters in its name

K: Obtaining a color with 4 letters in its name

N: Obtaining a color with fewer than 6 letters in its name

Use these events to determine the following probabilities.

1. $P(E \cup H)$ 2. $P(T)$ 3. $P(T \cup K)$ 4. $P(N)$

Solution

1. $P(E \cup H) = P(E) + P(H) = \dfrac{1}{2} + \dfrac{1}{12} = \dfrac{7}{12}$

2. $P(T) = \dfrac{7}{12}$

3. $P(T \cup K) = P(T) + P(K) = \dfrac{7}{12} + \dfrac{1}{6} = \dfrac{9}{12} = \dfrac{3}{4}$

4. $P(N) = P(\text{Red}) + P(\text{Blue}) + P(\text{Green}) = \dfrac{1}{6} + \dfrac{1}{6} + \dfrac{1}{12} = \dfrac{5}{12}$

Did you notice that events *T* and *N* in Example G are complementary sets? That is, they have no outcomes in common and their union contains all the outcomes of the sample space. Such events are called **complementary events.** Notice also that $P(T) + P(N) = 7/12 + 5/12 = 1$. In general, if *A* and *B* are complementary events, then we can determine the probability of one by knowing the probability of the other:

complementary event

$$P(A) + P(B) = 1$$

✓ODDS

" BLUE BOY SEEMS TO BE HOLDING BACK A BIT. "

Racetracks state probabilities in terms of odds. Suppose that the odds against Blue Boy's winning are 4 to 1. This means that the racetrack management will match every dollar you bet on Blue Boy with $4. Each time you win, you receive the money you bet plus the money put up by the racetrack. That is, for $1 you receive $5, for $2 you receive $10, etc. The 4 to 1 odds indicate that the racetrack management expects Blue Boy to lose 4 out of every 5 races he runs. Thus the probability of Blue Boy's losing the race is 4/5, and the probability of his winning is 1/5.

This example shows the close relationship between odds and probability: they are different ways of presenting the same information. This relationship is illustrated in Figure 12.3. The bar has 5 equal parts, 4 to represent the unfavorable outcomes (Blue Boy's losing) and 1 to represent a favorable outcome (Blue Boy's winning). The odds of 4 to 1 are shown by the ratio of the 4 unshaded parts to the 1 shaded part. The probability of 4/5 is the ratio of the 4 unshaded parts to the whole (5 parts).

Figure 12.3

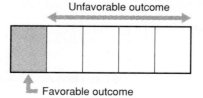

In general, **odds** are ratios. If the **odds in favor** of an event are *n* to *m,* then the probability of the event occurring is $n/(n + m)$ (Figure 12.4). In this case the **odds against** the event are *m* to *n,* and the probability of the event not occurring is $m/(n + m)$.

odds
odds in favor
odds against

Figure 12.4

n favorable outcomes   m unfavorable outcomes

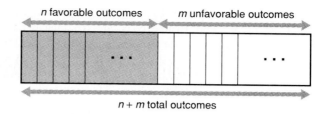

n + m total outcomes

EXAMPLE H

One card is selected at random from an ordinary deck of 52 cards, which contains 4 aces. Determine the following odds and probabilities.

1. Odds of obtaining 1 ace
2. Probability of obtaining 1 ace
3. Odds of not obtaining an ace
4. Probability of not obtaining an ace

Solution

1. Ratio of the number of favorable outcomes to the number of unfavorable outcomes = 4 to 48 = 1 to 12

2. $\dfrac{\text{Number of favorable outcomes}}{\text{Total number of outcomes}} = \dfrac{4}{52} = \dfrac{1}{13}$

3. Ratio of the number of unfavorable outcomes to the number of favorable outcomes = 48 to 4 = 12 to 1

4. $\dfrac{\text{Number of unfavorable outcomes}}{\text{Total number of outcomes}} = \dfrac{48}{52} = \dfrac{12}{13}$

Example H helps us to see that if the odds of an event happening are low, the probability is close to zero, and if the odds are high, the probability is close to 1. The odds of selecting an ace are low, 4 to 48, and the probability is 1/13. Similarly, the odds of selecting a card that is not an ace are high, 48 to 4, and the probability is 12/13.

EXPERIMENTAL PROBABILITY

It is often more difficult to determine a theoretical probability than to determine an experimental probability. Moreover, experimental probabilities involve conducting repeated trials and observing and recording data, activities that are appropriate for school students at all levels.

EXAMPLE I

Consider tossing a bottle cap to determine the experimental probability that it will land with its edge down (see figure). What is this probability for the 50 tosses shown below?

Edge up   Edge down

D U U U D D U D U D
U U U U D U U D U U
U D U U U U U U D U
U U U D U U U D U U
D U U D U D U D U U

Solution

The bottle cap landed with its edge down 15 times out of 50, so the experimental probability for this experiment is 15/50 = 3/10. If many repeated experiments yield approximately the same result, we can conclude that the experimental probability is approximately 3/10.

In many fields the empirical approach is the only means of determining probability. Insurance companies measure the risks against which people are buying insurance in order to set premiums. A person's age and life expectancy are important factors. To compute the probability that a person 20 years old will live to be 65 years old, insurance companies gather birth and death records of large numbers of people and compile mortality tables. One such table appears in Figure 12.5; it shows that out of every 10 million people born in the United States, 6,800,531 will live to age 65. Thus the probability that a newborn baby will live to be 65 is 6,800,531/10,000,000, or about .68 (68%). According to the table, 9,664,994 people will live to age 20. Therefore, the probability of a baby's living to age 20 is about .966, or 96.6%.

Figure 12.5

Age	Number living	Number dying	Age	Number living	Number dying
0	10,000,000	70,800	35	9,373,807	23,528
1	9,929,200	17,475	36	9,350,279	24,685
2	9,911,725	15,066	37	9,325,594	26,112
3	9,896,659	14,449	38	9,299,482	27,991
4	9,882,210	13,835	39	9,271,491	30,132
5	9,868,375	13,322	40	9,241,359	32,622
6	9,855,053	12,812	41	9,208,737	35,362
7	9,842,241	12,401	42	9,173,375	38,253
8	9,829,840	12,091	43	9,135,122	41,382
9	9,817,749	11,879	44	9,093,740	44,741
10	9,805,870	11,865	45	9,048,999	48,412
11	9,794,005	12,047	46	9,000,587	52,473
12	9,781,958	12,325	47	8,948,114	56,910
13	9,769,633	12,896	48	8,891,204	61,794
14	9,756,737	13,562	49	8,829,410	67,104
15	9,743,175	14,225	50	8,762,306	72,902
16	9,728,950	14,983	51	8,689,404	79,160
17	9,713,967	15,737	52	8,610,244	85,758
18	9,698,230	16,390	53	8,524,486	92,832
19	9,681,840	16,846	54	8,431,654	100,337
20	9,664,994	17,300	55	8,331,317	108,307
21	9,647,694	17,655	56	8,223,010	116,849
22	9,630,039	17,912	57	8,106,161	125,970
23	9,612,127	18,167	58	7,980,191	135,663
24	9,593,960	18,324	59	7,844,528	145,830
25	9,575,636	18,481	60	7,698,698	156,592
26	9,557,155	18,732	61	7,542,106	167,736
27	9,538,423	18,981	62	7,374,370	179,271
28	9,519,442	19,324	63	7,195,099	191,174
29	9,500,118	19,760	64	7,003,925	203,394
30	9,480,358	20,193	65	6,800,531	215,917
31	9,460,165	20,718	66	6,584,614	228,749
32	9,439,447	21,239	67	6,355,865	241,777
33	9,418,208	21,850	68	6,114,088	254,835
34	9,396,358	22,551	69	5,859,253	267,241

Example J

Determine the experimental probabilities of the following events using the table in Figure 12.5.

1. That a newborn baby will live to age 60
2. That a person of age 20 will live to be 60 years old
3. That a person of age 50 will live to be 60 years old

Solution
1. Approximately .77
2. Out of 10 million births, there are 9,664,994 people living at age 20 and 7,698,698 living at age 60, so the probability of a person surviving from age 20 to age 60 is 7,698,698/9,664,994 ≈ .797, or approximately 80%.
3. Out of 10 million births, there are 8,762,306 people living at age 50 and 7,698,698 living at age 60, so the probability of a person surviving from age 50 to 60 is 7,698,698/8,762,306 ≈ .879, or approximately 88%.

SIMULATIONS

You may remember from Chapter 11 that a simulation is a procedure in which experiments that closely resemble a real situation are conducted repeatedly. In that chapter simulations provided answers to questions in statistics. Simulations are also used to obtain approximations to theoretical probabilities.

EXAMPLE K

What is the probability that in a group of 5 people chosen at random at least 2 will have a birthday in the same month?

Solution

One approach to this problem is to conduct experiments. Since polling a large number of people to determine their birth months is time consuming, we will use a simulation. The following 20 groups of 5 numbers each were obtained by spinning a spinner labeled with whole numbers from 1 to 12. Since in 12 of the 20 groups the same number occurs 2 or more times, the probability for this simulation is 12/20 = 3/5.*

9 3 9 9 11	7 2 5 4 4	6 9 9 11 12	1 1 10 8 5
1 2 6 12 10	3 9 10 9 1	9 5 9 11 11	7 11 12 2 6
2 7 5 9 2	5 11 4 9 7	11 12 5 8 6	12 3 2 12 8
2 6 3 11 2	7 10 11 7 9	7 2 6 3 12	2 12 5 1 7
7 6 10 9 7	3 8 2 3 12	9 12 4 8 7	6 9 1 4 12

The theoretical basis for approximating probabilities with simulations is called the *Law of Large Numbers*. This law states that the more times a simulation is carried out, the closer the probability,

$$\frac{\text{Number of favorable outcomes}}{\text{Total number of outcomes}}$$

is to the theoretical probability.

Tables of random digits are commonly used for simulations. A portion of such a table is shown in Figure 12.6.

*The computer program SPINNER SIMULATIONS on the *Computer Problem-Solving Disc* simulates the spins of a spinner with whole numbers from 1 to *n* and prints any desired number of results.

Figure 12.6

1000 Random Digits

57455	72455	93949	03017	33463	50612	65976	18630	26080	99135
01177	18110	31846	33144	99175	43471	29341	07096	69643	85566
25107	69058	16098	53085	88020	30108	81469	33487	55936	34594
73312	70522	45206	00165	06447	65724	29908	96532	14636	25790
72526	06721	23176	95705	10722	72474	01434	38573	08089	09806
68868	49240	16140	11046	38620	49148	80338	45266	39020	06304
45101	17710	54682	31812	76734	87045	96291	67557	18680	18886
12672	99918	24766	14132	63739	18576	80955	67381	60403	09892
12201	94684	41296	86044	83170	95446	14032	86602	34998	49065
46062	88535	71445	10422	72088	50200	55509	03741	73748	38899
12483	92564	43692	60562	93982	44567	62843	51987	11525	02695
33791	32729	88363	65524	45698	02573	97181	30352	10505	02352
78160	17311	24688	87381	00257	76315	69875	34128	01483	21765
43595	78341	07757	76471	37801	90306	20915	38132	91714	44436
92750	50923	26074	03327	57400	79251	04823	74914	11445	93818
96564	04624	46940	79735	27074	99264	32920	51271	57583	82685
55645	86878	27211	89358	30594	70161	26045	33370	19425	25961
32582	88628	11166	47654	62462	05080	51664	39828	01770	01607
07866	68988	70054	83887	31538	66864	58710	70349	65126	02265
97092	11334	78242	15410	99001	65756	23979	63446	84808	06072

EXAMPLE L

Try answering the following question by using the table of random digits to carry out a simulation. What is the probability that in a family of 5 children there are 3 boys and 2 girls?

Solution   Let each odd digit from the table in Figure 12.6 represent a boy and each even digit represent a girl. Then examine groups of 5 digits and circle those with 3 odd digits and 2 even digits. Starting at the beginning of the list, we find that the first group with 3 odd and 2 even digits is 72455. There are 30 groups out of the first 100 groups with 3 odd and 2 even digits. These are listed below. Thus the probability based on this simulation is 30/100 = .3. This ratio is an estimation of the theoretical probability of a family's having 3 boys and 2 girls among 5 children.

72455	03017	33463	65976	18110	33144	43471	29341	25107	53085
33487	34594	96532	25790	23176	45101	31812	76734	96291	14132
18576	80955	67381	83170	34998	88535	71445	03741	73748	38899

PROBLEM-SOLVING APPLICATION

Solutions to problems in probability quite often conflict with our intuition. For example, if 2 coins are tossed, the probability of obtaining exactly one head is 50%; however, if 4 coins are tossed, the probability of obtaining exactly 2 heads is not 50%.

■ PROBLEM

To create interest in probability, a teacher asks for a volunteer to play the following game: 4 coins will be tossed and if exactly 2 heads are obtained, the student wins the coins; otherwise, the student loses. What is the probability that the student will win?

Question 1

Understanding the Problem   In order to win, the student must obtain exactly 2 heads. What happens if the student obtains 3 heads or 4 heads?

Devising a Plan   One plan is to toss 4 coins, record the number of heads, and repeat this experiment many times. An experimental probability can then be determined by dividing the number of times exactly 2 heads appear by the total number of tosses. A second plan

Question 2 is to *use a simulation.* In a list of random digits, each even digit can be designated as a head (H) and each odd digit as a tail (T). If the digits from 0 to 9 are used, are there equal numbers of heads and tails?

Carrying Out the Plan Use the list of random digits in Figure 12.6 to carry out a simulation. One way to do this is to consider only the first 4 digits in each group of 5 digits. For example, in the first row of the table, 5 of the 10 groups have exactly 2 "heads" (see **Question 3** the following list). Continue the simulation using the first 10 rows of the table. For this simulation what is the probability of obtaining exactly 2 heads in a toss of 4 coins?

2H   2H   2H   2H   2H

57455 72455 93949 03017 33463 50612 65976 18630 26080 99135

Looking Back The theoretical probability of obtaining exactly 2 heads can be found by listing the 16 different outcomes of tossing 4 coins and counting those with exactly 2 heads **Question 4** (see below). What is this probability? How does it compare to the probability obtained from the simulation?

HTHT   HHHH   HHHT   HHTH   HTHH   THHH   HHTT   HTTH

TTHH   THTH   TTTT   TTTH   TTHT   THTT   HTTT   THHT

Answers to Questions 1–4

1. The student loses.

2. Yes (remember, zero is an even number)

3. Since 42 groups have exactly 2 even digits and 2 odd digits among the first 4 digits, the approximation to the theoretical probability of obtaining exactly 2 heads in tossing 4 coins is 42/100 = .42.

4. Six of the 16 outcomes have exactly 2 heads, so the theoretical probability is 6/16 = .375. This is reasonably close to the probability of .42, which was obtained from the simulation.

RELATED ACTIVITIES IN

Mathematics for Elementary Teachers: An Activity Approach, 3e

Activity Set 12.1   **Probability Experiments:** There are activities for obtaining experimental and theoretical probabilities.

Just for Fun   **Race Track Games:** Two-person racing games to illustrate the probabilities of obtaining different sums from tossing dice

---

EXERCISES AND PROBLEMS 12.1

1. Out of 36 possible outcomes of tossing 2 dice, 6 produce a sum of 7. Complete the following table by computing the probability of rolling each of the other sums. (You may want to use the array of dice shown in Figure 12.2 at the beginning of this section.)

Sum	2	3	4	5	6	7	8	9	10	11	12
Probability						$\frac{6}{36}$					

a. What is the probability of obtaining a sum greater than or equal to 8?

b. What is the probability of obtaining a sum greater than 4 and less than 8?

2. The dice game called craps has the following rules. If the player rolling the dice gets a sum of 7 or 11, he or she wins. If the player rolls a sum of 2, 3, or 12, he or she loses. If the first sum rolled is a 4, 5, 6, 8, 9, or 10, the player continues rolling the dice. After the first roll the player wins if he or she can obtain the first sum rolled before rolling a 7.

a. What is the probability of rolling a 7 or an 11? (See the table in #1.)

b. What is the probability of losing on the first roll?

c. Suppose a player rolls an 8 on the first turn. Which has a greater probability: rolling a 7 on the second turn or rolling another 8?

3. A box contains 7 tickets numbered 1 through 7. One ticket will be selected at random from the box.

a. What is the sample space for this experiment?

b. What is the probability of obtaining an even number?

c. What is the probability of obtaining a number greater than 3?

d. What is the probability of obtaining a prime number?

4. A chip is to be drawn from a box containing the following colored chips: 8 orange, 5 green, 3 purple, and 2 red chips. Describe the sample space and determine the probabilities of selecting the following types of chips.

a. A purple chip

b. A green or purple chip

c. A chip that is not orange

d. A red chip

e. A red or green chip

5. The 5 regular polyhedra, called Platonic solids, are pictured below. These are the only polyhedra that can be used for fair dice. The regular polyhedron with 20 faces (icosahedron) was used as a die by the Egyptians more than 2000 years ago. The faces of these 5 polyhedra are labeled with consecutive whole numbers beginning with 1. For example, the tetrahedron has numbers 1, 2, 3, and 4; the icosahedron has numbers from 1 to 20.

Tetrahedron	Cube	Octahedron	Dodecahedron	Icosahedron
(4 faces)	(6 faces)	(8 faces)	(12 faces)	(20 faces)

Determine the probabilities of rolling the following numbers with each type of die, and record the probabilities in a copy of the following table.

a. A number less than 3

b. An even number

c. The number 2

	Tetra-hedron	Cube	Octa-hedron	Dodeca-hedron	Icosa-hedron
a.					
b.					
c.					

6. For an experiment consisting of spinning the spinner shown here, determine the probabilities below.

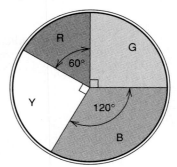

a. $P(B)$ **b.** $P(Y)$

c. $P(R)$ **d.** $P(R \text{ or } B)$

e. $P(R \text{ or } G)$ **f.** $P(R \text{ or } G \text{ or } B)$

7. Four identical chips are lettered A, B, C, and D and placed in a box. An experiment consists of selecting 2 chips at random.

a. List all the outcomes of the sample space.

b. What is the probability that 1 of the 2 chips will be lettered B?

c. What is the probability that 1 chip will be lettered C and the other D?

8. A box contains 3 red marbles and 2 green marbles. An experiment consists of selecting 2 marbles at random from the box.

a. List all the outcomes of the sample space.

b. What is the probability of obtaining 1 red and 1 green marble?

c. What is the probability that both marbles will be red?

9. An experiment consists of tossing a regular die with faces numbered 1 through 6. Use the following events to determine the probabilities below.

E: Obtaining an even number
F: Obtaining a prime number
G: Obtaining an odd number
H: Obtaining a number greater than 4

a. $P(E \cup G)$ and $P(E) + P(G)$

b. $P(F \cup G)$ and $P(F) + P(G)$

c. $P(F \cup H)$ and $P(F) + P(H)$

d. $P(E \cup F)$ and $P(E) + P(F)$

e. Which pairs of probabilities in parts a through d are equal?

10. Consider a regular deck of 52 cards, with 13 cards (including 3 face cards) in each of 4 suits. Use the events below to determine the following probabilities.

   E: Selecting a face card
   F: Selecting an ace
   G: Selecting a spade
   H: Selecting a heart

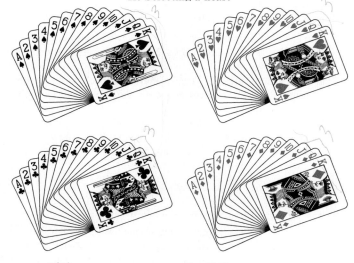

   a. P(E)
   b. P(G)
   c. P(E ∪ F)
   d. P(G ∪ H)

11. The sum of the probability that an event will happen and the probability that the event will not happen is 1. Consider the experiment of selecting 1 card at random from a complete deck of 52 cards. Compute the probabilities of the following events.
   a. Not drawing an ace
   b. Not drawing a face card
   c. Drawing a club, heart, or diamond
   d. Not drawing a black face card

12. Compute the probability and odds of selecting each of the following cards at random from a complete deck of 52 cards.
   a. An ace
   b. A face card
   c. A diamond
   d. A black face card

13. Given the following probabilities, determine the odds in favor of each event.
   a. The probability of living to age 65 is 7/10.
   b. The probability of selecting a person with type O blood is 3/5.
   c. The probability of winning a certain raffle is 1/500.
   d. The probability of rain on Monday is 80%.

14. Gambling syndicates predict the outcomes of sporting events in terms of odds. Convert each of the following odds to a probability.
   a. The odds that the Packers will beat the Rams are 4 to 3.
   b. The odds that the University of Michigan will defeat Ohio State are 7 to 5.
   c. The odds that the Yankees will win the pennant are 10 to 3.
   d. The odds of recovering the missing space capsule are 1 to 4.

15. Determine the experimental probabilities of the following events to the nearest hundredth.
   a. Tossing a paper cup and having it land with its bottom down, if it landed in this position 18 times in 150 tosses
   b. Spinning a spinner and obtaining the color green, if this color was obtained in 46 out of 130 spins
   c. Tossing a tack and having it land with its point up, if it landed in this position on 19 out of 90 tosses

16. The mortality table in Figure 12.5 was computed on the basis of births and deaths among policyholders of several large insurance companies. Use the information in that table to answer the following questions.
   a. What is the experimental probability that a child will live to be 1 year old?
   b. What is the experimental probability that a person will live to age 50?
   c. What is the experimental probability that a person of age 34 will live to age 65?
   d. What is the experimental probability that a 60-year-old person will live to be 65?
   e. If an insurance company has 7000 policyholders of age 28, how many death claims is the company likely to have to pay on behalf of those who do not reach age 29?

17. Use the table of random digits in Figure 12.6 to carry out a simulation that approximates the probability of obtaining at least 5 heads in a toss of 10 fair coins. Describe your simulation.

18. Use the table of random digits in Figure 12.6 to carry out a simulation that approximates the probability of obtaining at least one 6 in 5 rolls of a die. Describe your simulation.

19. Use simulations to approximate the following probabilities. Describe your methods.
   a. What is the probability that in a family of 3 boys and 2 girls the 3 boys were born in succession?
   b. On a certain quiz show people are required to guess which of 3 identical envelopes contains a $1000 bill. What is the probability that exactly 4 out of 8 people will guess the correct envelope?

Featured Strategy: Using a Simulation

20. A machine that sells gumballs for a nickel apiece contains 5 white gumballs and 2 red gumballs. If 2 nickels are put into the machine, what is the probability of obtaining a red gumball, if each gumball has an equal chance of being chosen?

a. Understanding the Problem The problem is to determine the probability of obtaining at least 1 red gumball. If only 1 nickel is put into the machine, what is the probability of obtaining 1 red gumball.

b. Devising a Plan One approach is to use a simulation to approximate the probability. Describe such a simulation.

c. Carrying Out the Plan What probability do you obtain by using your simulation?

d. Looking Back It is also possible to determine the theoretical probability by designating the gumballs as R_1, R_2, W_1, W_2, W_3, W_4, and W_5, listing the outcomes of the sample space, and counting those that contain at least 1 red. What is the theoretical probability obtained with this approach?

21. The Problem-Solving Application on page 624 showed that the probability of obtaining exactly 2 heads in a toss of 4 coins is .375.

a. Use a simulation to approximate the probability of obtaining exactly 3 heads in a toss of 6 fair coins. Describe your simulation.

b. Make a conjecture about the probability of obtaining exactly 10 heads in a toss of 20 fair coins. Will it be less than .5, equal to .5, or greater than .5?

LABORATORY INVESTIGATION

One way of illustrating probability is to assign probabilities to regions in a plane. This square is divided into a 10 by 10 grid, and each cell of the grid is designated by a two-digit number. For example, cell 38 is located by moving horizontally to 3 and vertically to 8. The cells of this grid can be randomly selected using pairs of digits from a table of random digits. For the following investigations, copy the rectangular grid from the inside cover and number the cells.

Questions for Investigation

1. Select a random starting point in the table of random digits in Figure 12.6.

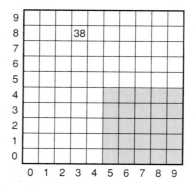

Moving from this starting point to the right along the rows of numbers, tally each of 100 consecutive pairs of numbers by placing a mark in the appropriate cell of your grid. What percent of the 100 marks fall within the shaded region? Will this percent usually be close to 25%? (Note: Some cells will contain more than 1 mark.)

2. What percent of the 100 cells do not contain marks? Try this activity again to see if the percent of cells with no marks remains approximately the same.

3. Suppose that the grid represents a batch of brownies cut into 100 equal pieces and that 100 walnuts were randomly mixed into the batter. Consider the experiment of randomly selecting 1 brownie. Use your marks from one of the preceding activities to determine the probabilities of the following events: obtaining a brownie with no walnuts; obtaining a brownie with 1 walnut; obtaining a brownie with more than 1 walnut.

PUZZLER

How can the faces of two cubes be numbered so that when they are rolled the resulting sum is any whole number from 1 to 12 and each sum has the same probability of occurring?

SECTION 12.2   MULTISTAGE EXPERIMENTS

■ *PROBLEM OPENER*

Make 3 cards of equal size. Label both sides of one card with the letter A, both sides of the second with the letter B, and one side of the third with the letter A and the other side with the letter B. Select a card at random and place it on a table. There will be either an A or a B facing up. What is the probability that the letter facing down on this card is different from the letter facing up?

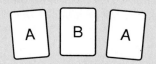

Photo from NASA's Synchronous Meteorological Satellite 1

Meteorologists use computers and probability to analyze weather patterns. In recent years meteorological satellites have improved the accuracy of weather forecasting. NASA's Synchronous Meteorological Satellite 1 sent back this photograph of North and South America on May 28, 1974. Four storms can be seen stretching across the top of the picture from western Canada to the Atlantic Ocean. The structure of cumulus clouds over Florida and the Caribbean Sea allows meteorologists to infer wind speed and direction. Weather forecasts are usually stated in terms of probability, and that probability may be determined from several others. For example, there may be one probability for a cold front and another probability for a change in wind direction. In this section we will see how to use the probabilities of two or more events to determine the probability of a combination of events.

PROBABILITIES OF OUTCOMES

In Section 12.1 we studied single-stage experiments such as spinning a spinner, rolling a die, and tossing a coin. These experiments are over after one step. Now we will study combinations of experiments, called **multistage experiments.**

multistage experiments

Suppose we spin spinner A and then spinner B in Figure 12.7. This is an example of a *two-stage experiment.*

Figure 12.7

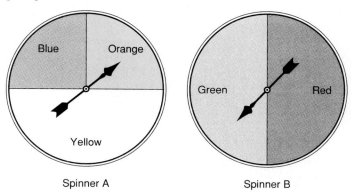

Spinner A   Spinner B

Figure 12.8

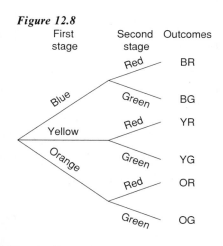

First stage   Second stage   Outcomes

The different outcomes for multistage experiments can be determined by constructing *tree diagrams,* which were used in Chapter 3 as a model for multiplication of whole numbers. Since there are 3 different outcomes from spinner A and 2 different outcomes from spinner B, the experiment of spinning first spinner A and then spinner B has 3 × 2 = 6 outcomes (Figure 12.8).

Figure 12.9 shows the probabilities of obtaining each color and each outcome. Such a diagram is called a **probability tree.** The probability of each of the 6 outcomes can be determined from this probability tree. For example, consider the probability of obtaining BR (blue on spinner A followed by red on spinner B). Since blue occurs 1/4 of the time and red occurs 1/2 of the times that blue occurs, the probability of BR is $1/4 \times 1/2$, or 1/8. This probability is the product of the 2 probabilities along the path that leads to BR. Similarly, the probability of YG (yellow followed by green) is $1/2 \times 1/2 = 1/4$. Notice that the sum of the probabilities for all 6 outcomes is 1.

probability tree

Figure 12.9

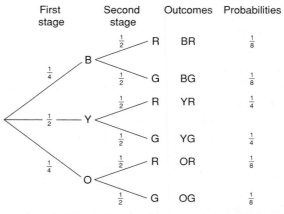

The principle of multiplying along the paths of a probability tree can be generalized as follows. *If the outcomes of an experiment can be represented as the paths of a tree diagram, then the probability of any outcome is the product of the probabilities on its path.*

EXAMPLE A

A die is rolled and a coin is tossed. Sketch the probability tree for this experiment, and determine the probability of rolling a 4 on the die and tossing a tail on the coin.

Solution

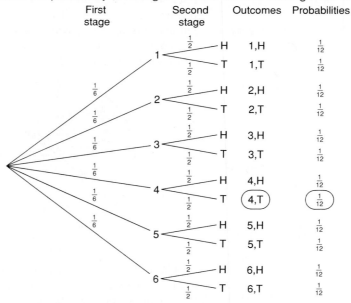

The probability of rolling a 4 and tossing a tail is 1/12. In this two-stage experiment each outcome is equally likely.

An experiment may consist of several stages, as in the next example.

EXAMPLE B

What is the probability that the children in a family of 4 children will be born in the following order: girl, boy, girl, boy?

Solution

It is customary to assume that the probability of a baby's being a girl is 1/2 and the probability of a baby's being a boy is also 1/2.

The probability tree shows that all the outcomes are equally likely and each has a probability of 1/16 (1/2 × 1/2 × 1/2 × 1/2). Since there is only one outcome with the order GBGB, the probability of a family's having a girl, a boy, a girl, and a boy is 1/16.

PROBABILITIES OF EVENTS

Once probabilities have been assigned to the outcomes of a multistage experiment, the probabilities of specific events can be determined. Using the probability tree in Example B, we can determine the probabilities of several events. For example, let E be the event of a family's having 3 girls and 1 boy. Since there are 4 such outcomes,

$$P(E) = \frac{1}{16} + \frac{1}{16} + \frac{1}{16} + \frac{1}{16} = \frac{4}{16} = \frac{1}{4}$$

Or if F is the event of a family's having 2 girls and 2 boys,

$$P(F) = \frac{6}{16} = \frac{3}{8}$$

since there are 6 outcomes with 2 girls and 2 boys.

EXAMPLE C

A box contains 2 red marbles and 1 white marble. A marble is randomly selected and returned to the box, and a second marble is randomly selected. What is the probability of selecting 2 red marbles?

Solution

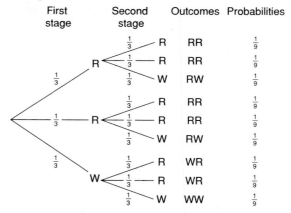

The probability tree shows that there are 9 equally likely outcomes, each with a probability of 1/9. Since there are 4 outcomes with 2 red marbles, the probability of this event is 4/9.

The probability tree in Example C can be simplified by combining branches. Since we are only interested in whether the first marble is red or white, the first stage of the experiment can be represented by 2 branches, one with a probability of 2/3 (selecting a red marble) and one with a probability of 1/3 (selecting a white marble). Similarly, in the second stage we simply wish to distinguish between selecting red and white (Figure 12.10). Notice that the probability of obtaining 2 red marbles is the product of the probabilities along the top branch: $2/3 \times 2/3 = 4/9$.

Figure 12.10

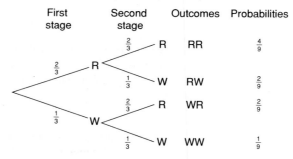

The preceding example suggests the following rule for finding the probabilities of events in multistage experiments.

**MULTIPLICATION RULE
FOR PROBABILITIES**

If event **B** occurs after event **A** has been completed, and $P(A) = a$ and $P(B) = b$ for events **A** and **B**, then the probability of "first **A**, then **B**" is $a \times b$.

EXAMPLE D

What is the probability of rolling a die and obtaining a 4 and then rolling it a second time and obtaining an even number?

Solution

The probability of obtaining a 4 on one roll of a die is 1/6, and the probability of obtaining an even number is 1/2. By the *multiplication rule for probabilities*, the probability of rolling a 4 and then rolling an even number is $1/6 \times 1/2 = 1/12$.

In Example D the result of the first toss of the die has no effect on the result of the second toss. That is, the probability of obtaining an even number on the second roll was not influenced by the outcome of the first roll of the die. These are examples of **independent events.** Similarly, in Example C the event of selecting a red marble on the first draw and the event of selecting a red marble on the second draw are independent events, because the marble from the first draw is replaced. The next example is similar to Example C, but in this case the first marble selected *is not replaced* for the second draw.

independent events

EXAMPLE E

A box contains 2 red marbles and 1 white marble. A marble is selected at random but not returned to the box, and then a second marble is selected. What is the probability of selecting 2 red marbles?

Solution

The probability of selecting a red marble on the first draw is 2/3. So the first stage of the probability tree is the same as that in Figure 12.10. However, because the first marble is not replaced, the probabilities for the second stage are affected. If a red marble is selected on the first draw, then there is 1 red marble and 1 white marble left, so the probability of choosing a red marble on the second draw is 1/2. The top branch of the probability tree shows that the probability of selecting 2 red marbles in this case is $2/3 \times 1/2 = 1/3$.

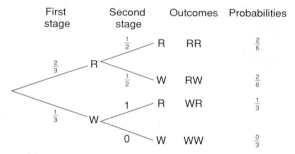

Notice that there is one path leading to RW and one path leading to WR, so the probability of choosing 1 red marble and 1 white marble is $1/3 + 1/3 = 2/3$ when the order in which they are selected is not important. Also, the bottom branch of the tree shows that the probability of selecting 2 white marbles is zero (there is only 1 white marble in the box).

Since in Example E the probability of selecting a red marble on the second draw was affected by the outcome of the first draw, the events in this experiment are called **dependent events.** The probability of dependent events can be computed by using the *multiplication rule for probabilities.* The next two examples involve dependent events.

dependent events

EXAMPLE F

What is the probability of randomly selecting 2 hearts from the 5 cards shown here?

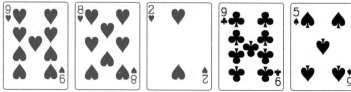

Solution

The probability of obtaining a heart on the first draw is 3/5, and if the first card is a heart, the probability of obtaining a heart on the second draw is 2/4. The probability of obtaining 2 hearts is $3/5 \times 2/4 = 6/20 = 3/10$.

EXAMPLE **G**

Consider the multistage experiment of selecting 1 card from an ordinary deck of 52 cards and then selecting another card without replacing the first. Determine the probabilities of the following events.

1. Selecting 2 clubs
2. Selecting 2 face cards
3. Selecting 2 aces
4. Selecting 2 red cards

Solution

1. There are 13 clubs: $13/52 \times 12/51 = 156/2652 \approx .059$
2. There are 12 face cards: $12/52 \times 11/51 = 132/2652 \approx .050$
3. There are 4 aces: $4/52 \times 3/51 = 12/2652 \approx .005$
4. There are 26 red cards: $26/52 \times 25/51 = 650/2652 \approx .245$

PROBLEM-SOLVING APPLICATION

Many probability problems involve fractions, and partitioning regions into parts is a common model for illustrating fractions. These observations suggest a geometric approach to solving probability problems. The following two-stage probability problem will be solved using a tree diagram and geometric regions.

 **PROBLEM**

The figure shows paths leading to 3 rooms. If you begin at point S and choose a path at random whenever you reach a branch point, what is the probability of entering room A?

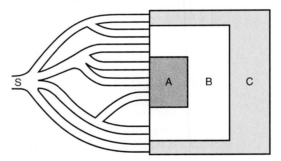

Question 1

Understanding the Problem The probability of taking any 1 of the first 4 paths is 1/4. The probability of taking the top path of the first four paths and then at the next branch point taking the top path (that leads to room C) is $1/4 \times 1/2 = 1/8$. What is the probability of taking the top path of the first four paths and entering room B?

Devising a Plan One approach is to sketch a tree diagram and compute the probability of each outcome.

Question 2

Carrying Out the Plan The following tree diagram shows the probabilities for each branch of the tree. Room B can be entered by 3 paths having probabilities of $1/4 \times 1/2$, $1/4 \times 1/3$, and $1/4 \times 1/2$. The probability of entering room B is the sum of these probabilities. What is the probability of entering room A?

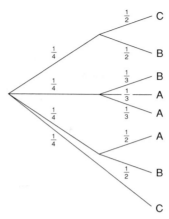

Looking Back   A geometric solution to the problem can be found by subdividing a unit rectangle into parts. Since there are 4 paths at point S and each is equally likely to be chosen, the rectangle is divided into 4 congruent regions, as shown in figure (i). Next, since the upper path leads to 2 equally likely paths, the upper region of the rectangle is partitioned into 2 congruent parts, which are labeled C and B [figure (ii)]. Similarly, the other 3 regions of the rectangle can be partitioned as shown in figure (iii).

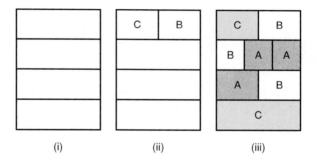

| (i) | (ii) | (iii) |

Question 3

Question 4

Some observations can be made from figure (iii). For example, does room A or room B have the greater probability of being entered? Which of the three rooms has the greatest probability of being entered? To determine the probability of entering each room, we can subdivide the parts of figure (iii) into parts of the same size, as shown in figure (iv). What fractional part of the whole figure are the parts corresponding to room A?

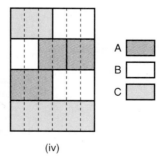

(iv)

Answers to Questions 1–4
1. 1/8
2. 1/4 × 1/3 + 1/4 × 1/3 + 1/4 × 1/2 = 1/12 + 1/12 + 1/8 = 7/24
3. Room B has a greater probability of being entered than room A; room C has the greatest probability of being entered.
4. 7/24

COMPLEMENTARY EVENTS

There are some problems in which the probability of an event can be most easily found by first computing the probability of its complement.

EXAMPLE H

Solution

If a die is tossed 4 times, what is the probability of obtaining *at least* one 6?

Let E be the event of obtaining at least one 6 (this includes the possibility of obtaining one, two, three, or four 6s), and let F be the event of not obtaining any 6s. Then E and F are complementary events, and $P(E) + P(F) = 1$. The probability of not obtaining a 6 on 1 roll of a die is 5/6. So the probability of obtaining no 6s on 4 rolls is

$$P(F) = \frac{5}{6} \times \frac{5}{6} \times \frac{5}{6} \times \frac{5}{6} = \frac{625}{1296} \approx .48$$

and the probability of obtaining at least one 6 is

$$P(E) \approx 1 - .48$$
$$= .52$$

That is, slightly more than half of the time you can expect to obtain at least one 6 in 4 tosses of a die.

Since in Example H obtaining at least one 6 includes several different possibilities (obtaining one 6, two 6s, three 6s, or four 6s), it is easier to consider the probability that this will not happen. The words *at least* are sometimes a clue to the fact that the probability of an event may be more easily found by first computing the probability of its complement.

EXAMPLE I

Solution

Ten teachers have volunteered for a school committee: 7 women and 3 men. If 3 of these people are chosen randomly, what is the probability that *at least* 1 person will be a man?

The probability that a man will not be chosen (that is, that all 3 people will be women) is $7/10 \times 6/9 \times 5/8 \approx .29$. Thus the probability of at least 1 man's being chosen is approximately $1 - .29 = .71$.

There is a well-known problem in probability whose solution often surprises people.

What is the smallest randomly chosen group of people for which there is better than a 50% chance that at least 2 of them will have a birthday on the same day of the year?

Surprisingly, the answer is only 23 people. In fact, there is a 70% probability that among 30 randomly chosen people, 2 will have birthdays on the same day. With 50 randomly chosen people the probability is about 97%. The graph in Figure 12.11 shows that among a group of more than 50 randomly chosen people we can be almost certain of finding 2 with birthdays on the same day.

Figure 12.11

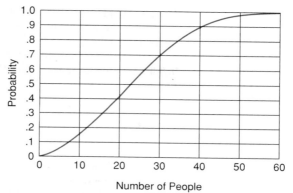

The probability that at least 2 out of 23 people have the same birthday can be found by computing the probability of a complementary event. That is, we can determine the probability that all 23 people have birthdays on different days and then subtract this probability from 1. To begin with, consider the problem for just 2 people. No matter when the first person was born, there is a probability of 364/365 that the second person's birthday will not be on the same day. When a third person joins this group, the probability that his or her birth date will differ from those of the other 2 people is 363/365. Therefore, the probability that 3 people will not share a birth date is 364/365 × 363/365. Similarly, the probability that 23 people will have different birthdays is the following product of 22 numbers:

$$\frac{364}{365} \times \frac{363}{365} \times \frac{362}{365} \times \cdots \times \frac{344}{365} \times \frac{343}{365} \approx .49$$

Therefore, the probability that there will be 2 or more people with birthdays on the same day in a group of 23 people is approximately $1 - .49 = .51$. Make a prediction next time you're in a group of 23 or more people. The odds are in your favor that there will be at least 2 people with birthdays on the same day.

PROBLEM-SOLVING APPLICATION

For cases in which it is difficult to find the probability of a multistage experiment, the probability may be approximated by *carrying out a simulation*. At other times a simulation may be used to check on the reasonableness of a calculation that produces a theoretical probability.

■ PROBLEM

A state lottery has a daily drawing in which 4 ping pong balls are selected at random from among 10 balls numbered 0, 1, 2, . . . , 9. After a ball is selected, it is returned for the next selection. An elementary school student noticed that quite often 2 of the 4 digits drawn are equal. What is the probability that at least 2 out of 4 digits will be equal?

Understanding the Problem   The condition *at least two* includes the possibilities that there may be 2 equal digits, 3 equal digits, or 4 equal digits.

Devising a Plan   One way of determining the probability is to carry out a simulation using the table of random digits in Figure 12.6 (page 624). How can this be done?

Question 1

Carrying Out the Plan   The first 12 groups of 4 digits (using consecutive digits) from the sixth row of the table in Figure 12.6 are shown below. Notice that 6 of these groups have 2 or more equal digits. Continue this simulation through 5 complete rows of the table. What is the probability for this simulation?

Question 2

6886   8492   4016   1401   1046   3862   0491   4880   3384   5266   3902   0063

Looking Back The theoretical probability for this problem can be found by first computing the probability for the complementary event—that is, the probability that all 4 digits are different. After the first digit is drawn, the probability that the second digit will not equal the first digit is 9/10; the probability that the third digit will be different from the first 2 is 8/10; and the probability that the fourth will be different from the first 3 is 7/10. So the probability of selecting 4 different digits is

$$\frac{9}{10} \times \frac{8}{10} \times \frac{7}{10} = \frac{504}{1000} = .504$$

Question 3   What is the theoretical probability that at least 2 of the 4 digits drawn will be equal?

Answers to Questions 1–3
1. Start with any digit in the table and consider groups of 4 digits at a time. The number of groups with 2 or more equal digits divided by the total number of groups is the probability for this simulation.
2. Since 31 out of 62 groups of 4 digits have 2 or more equal digits, the experimental probability for this simulation is 31/62 = .5.
3. The theoretical probability that at least 2 of the 4 digits drawn will be equal is 1 − .504 = .496, or approximately .5.

EXPECTED VALUE

To evaluate the fairness of a game we must consider the prize we can expect to gain as well as the probability of winning. The probability of winning may be fairly small, but if the prize is large enough the game may be a good risk. Consider the following game.

EXAMPLE J

A game involves rolling 2 dice. If the player obtains a sum of 7, he or she is paid $5. Otherwise, the player pays $1. Over a period of time, can the player expect to gain money, lose money, or break even?

Solution   The probability of rolling a sum of 7 is 1/6. Thus for 1 out of every 6 rolls, on the average, the player can expect to receive $5. However, for 5 out of 6 rolls, on the average, the player can expect to pay $1 per roll. Thus over a period of time the player can expect to break even.

The amounts to be won and lost in Example J can be expressed in an equation. Because there is a 1/6 chance of winning $5 and a 5/6 chance of losing $1, the net winnings from the game can be computed as follows:

$$\frac{1}{6}(5) + \frac{5}{6}(^-1) = \frac{5}{6} + \frac{^-5}{6} = 0$$

expected value   This equation expresses the **expected value** of the game; it is generalized in the following definition.

EXPECTED VALUE

If the outcomes of an experiment have values $v_1, v_2, \ldots, v_n$ and the outcomes have probabilities $p_1, p_2, \ldots, p_n$, respectively, then the **expected value** is

$$p_1v_1 + p_2v_2 + \cdots + p_nv_n$$

Sometimes the expected value involves several prizes, and each prize has its own probability of occurring.

EXAMPLE K

The sweepstakes ticket shown has 2 five-digit numbers (1 number is hidden on the left of the ticket, and the digits of the other number are hidden by the 5 dollar signs). The amount you win depends on which digits of the 2 numbers match. If the 2 digits in the ten thousands place are equal, you win $2000; if the two digits in the thousands place are equal, you win $20; etc. (as shown on the lottery ticket). Anyone who wins the $5, $2, or $1-ticket prize is eligible for the $100,000 grand prize. Suppose the probabilities of winning $100,000, $2000, $20, $5, $2, and the $1-ticket prize are 1/1,000,000, 1/20,000, 1/200, 1/25, 1/10, and 1/5, respectively.

1. What is the expected value of this lottery ticket?
2. If each ticket costs $1, will the player who regularly buys them gain or lose money over a period of time?

Solution

1. The expected value is computed by multiplying the amount of each prize by its probability of occurring and adding these products.

$$\frac{1}{1,000,000}(\$100,000) + \frac{1}{20,000}(\$2000) + \frac{1}{200}(\$20) + \frac{1}{25}(\$5) + \frac{1}{10}(\$2) + \frac{1}{5}(\$1)$$
$$= 90 \text{ cents}$$

2. Since the expected value is 90 cents and each ticket costs $1, the player will lose money. On the average, there is a 10 cent loss for each ticket that is purchased.

fair game

A game is called a **fair game** if the net earnings are zero. For example, the game in Example J is a fair game; however, the game in Example K is not a fair game. Most gambling games are not fair games.

EXAMPLE L

A roulette wheel has 38 compartments. Two are numbered 0 and 00 and are colored green. The remaining compartments are numbered 1 through 36; half of these are red, and half are black. With each spin of the wheel, a ball falls into one of the compartments. One way of playing this game is to bet on the red or black color.

1. What is the probability of obtaining a red number on 1 spin?
2. If a player bets $1 on red and wins, the player is paid $1 plus the $1 the player bet. What is the expected value of this game?
3. Is this a fair game?

Solution

1. The probability of obtaining a red number is 18/38 = 9/19.

2. The expected value of this bet is $\frac{18}{38}(\$1) + \frac{20}{38}(\$^{-}1) \approx \$^{-}.05$ (or $^{-}5$ cents).

3. This game is not fair. On the average, a player will lose 5 cents on each spin.

RELATED ACTIVITIES IN
Mathematics for Elementary Teachers: An Activity Approach, 3e

Activity Set 12.2

Multistage Probability Experiments: Experiments with chips, dice, and coins allow students to determine experimental and theoretical probabilities of multistage events.

Just for Fun

Trick Dice: Four special dice with a remarkable property

EXERCISES AND PROBLEMS 12.2

1. For a test of 10 true and false questions, determine the probabilities of the following events, if every question is answered by guessing.
   a. Getting the first 2 questions correct
   b. Getting the first 5 questions correct
   c. Getting all 10 questions correct

2. Consider the two-stage experiment of spinning first the spinner on the left and then the spinner on the right.

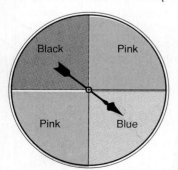

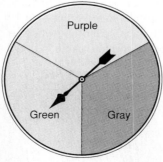

   a. Sketch a probability tree showing all possible outcomes and their probabilities.
   b. What is the probability of obtaining blue followed by green?
   c. What is the probability of obtaining pink followed by purple?

3. Consider the two-stage experiment of randomly selecting a marble from the bowl on the left and then a marble from the bowl on the right.

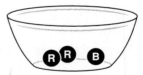

   a. Sketch a probability tree. Show all possible outcomes and their probabilities.
   b. What is the probability of selecting 2 red marbles?
   c. What is the probability of selecting at least 1 red marble?
   d. What is the probability of selecting a yellow marble?

4. A family has 3 children. (Assume that the chances of having a boy or girl are equally likely.)
   a. Draw a probability tree showing all possible combinations of boys and girls.
   b. What is the probability that the family has 2 boys and 1 girl?
   c. What is the probability that the family has at least 1 girl?

5. A fair coin is tossed 4 times.
   a. Draw a probability tree showing all possible outcomes of heads and tails.
   b. What is the probability of obtaining 3 tails and 1 head?
   c. What is the probability of obtaining at least 2 tails?

6. A box contains 7 black and 5 purple marbles. Consider the two-stage experiment of randomly selecting a marble from the box, replacing it, and then selecting a second marble. Determine the probabilities of the following events.
   a. Selecting 2 black marbles
   b. Selecting 1 black and 1 purple marble
   c. Selecting 2 purple marbles

7. Suppose that in exercise #6 the first marble selected is not replaced before the second marble is chosen. Determine the probabilities of the events in #6 a, b, and c.

8. a. If you flipped a fair coin 9 times and got 9 heads, what would be the probability of getting a head on the next toss?
   b. If you rolled a fair die 5 times and got the numbers 1, 2, 3, 4, and 5, what would be the probability of rolling a 6 on the next turn?

9. Classify the following events as dependent or independent and compute their probabilities.
   a. Tossing a coin 3 times and getting 3 heads in a row
   b. Drawing 2 aces from a complete deck of 52 playing cards if the first card selected is not replaced
   c. Rolling 2 dice and getting a sum of 7 twice in succession
   d. Selecting 2 green balls from a bag of 5 green and 3 red balls if the first ball selected is not replaced

10. Alice and Bill make one payment each week, and it is determined by the "debits spinner." Assume each outcome on the spinner is equally likely.

"O.K., Alice, spin the wheel and let's see who gets paid this week."

   a. What is the probability of making a fuel payment 2 weeks in a row?
   b. What is the probability they will not make an electricity payment this week?
   c. If they don't make an electricity payment within the next 3 weeks, their lights will be shut off. What is the probability they will lose their lights?

11. A consumer buys a package of 5 flashbulbs, not knowing that 1 of the bulbs is bad. List the outcomes in the sample space if 2 bulbs are selected randomly and then find the probabilities of the following events.
   a. Both bulbs are good.
   b. One of the bulbs is bad.

12. A college student is considering 6 elective courses taught by 6 different professors. She must select 2 of the courses. The student is unaware that 2 of the 6 courses will be taught by professors who have received distinguished teaching awards. List the elements of the sample space, and then determine the probabilities of the following events, assuming the student chooses her 2 courses randomly.
   a. Not selecting any courses taught by the award-winning professors
   b. Selecting exactly 1 course taught by an award-winning professor
   c. Selecting at least 1 course taught by an award-winning professor

13. A bureau drawer contains 10 black socks and 10 brown socks. Their wearer is a very early riser who selects the socks in the dark. Find the probabilities of the following events.
   a. Selecting 2 socks and having both black
   b. Selecting 2 socks and obtaining 1 black and 1 brown
   c. Selecting 3 socks and obtaining 2 of the same color

14. Determine the probabilities of the following events. (Hint: Use complementary events.)
   a. Getting a sum of 7 at least once on 4 rolls of a pair of dice
   b. Getting at least one 6 on 4 rolls of a die
   c. Getting at least one sum of 7 or 11 on 3 rolls of a pair of dice

15. Mr. and Mrs. Petritz of Butte, Montana have 5 children who were all born on April 15. Answer the following questions, assuming that it is equally likely that a child will be born on any of the 365 days of the year.
   a. After the first Petritz child was born, what was the probability the second child would be born on April 15, if it was not a twin?
   b. If a couple has a child on April 15, what is the probability that their next 4 children will be born on April 15, if there are no multiple births?

16. Assuming that each path in the maze below is equally likely to be chosen, determine the probability of entering room A.

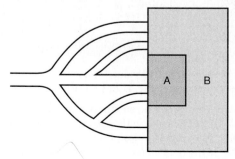

17. Assuming that each path in the maze below is equally likely to be chosen, determine the probability of entering room B.

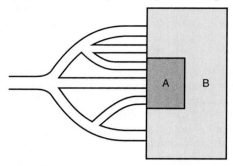

Solve #18 and #19 using (1) a simulation and (2) complementary events. Describe your simulations.

18. A system with 3 components fails if 1 or more components fail. The probability that any given component will fail is 1/10. What is the probability that the system will fail?

19. A manufacturer of bubble gum puts a 5 cent coupon in 1 out of every 5 packages of gum. What is the probability of obtaining at least 1 of these coupons in 4 packages of gum?

20. Suppose there are 3 red, 4 blue, and 5 green chips in a bag and you win by selecting either a red or a green chip. If you get a red chip, you win $3; a green chip pays $2; and a blue chip pays $0.
  a. What is the expected value of this game?
  b. If it costs $1.50 to play this game, is it a fair game?

21. A game consists of rolling a die; the number of dollars you receive is the number that shows on the die. For example, if you roll a 3, you receive $3.
  a. What is the expected value of this game?
  b. What should a person pay in order for this to be a fair game?

22. Five prize amounts are hidden under the 6 rectangles on the lottery ticket shown below. If the same prize amount appears in 3 separate rectangles, the ticket owner wins that prize. The five prizes are $5000, $25, $2, and 1 ticket (worth $1), and the probabilities of winning these prizes on a given ticket are 1/10,000, 1/100, 1/20, and 1/10, respectively.

  a. What is the expected value for one ticket?
  b. If each ticket costs $1, is this a fair game?

23. One way you can bet in roulette is to place a chip on a single number. If the ball lands in the compartment with your number, the house pays you 35 chips plus the chip you bet.
  a. What is the probability that the ball will land on 13?
  b. If each chip is worth $1, what is the expected value of this game?

c. Is the expected value of playing a color (as computed on page 640) greater than, less than, or equal to that of playing a particular number?

Featured Strategy: Solving a Simpler Problem and Using a Simulation

24. Two players have invented a game. A bowl is filled with an equal number of white and red marbles. One player, called the holder, holds the bowl while the other player, called the drawer, is blindfolded and selects 2 marbles. The drawer wins if both marbles are the same color: otherwise, he loses. Which player has the better chance of winning?

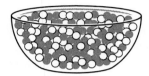

Bowl of marbles

  a. **Understanding the Problem** Either the 2 marbles selected will both be white or both be red or the colors will be different. The drawer feels that he has a 2/3 chance of winning, since there are 3 outcomes and 2 are favorable. Is this true?
  b. **Devising a Plan** One approach is to simplify the problem and try solving it for smaller numbers. What is the probability that the drawer will win if there are 3 red and 3 white marbles in the bowl? Another approach is to use a simulation by placing slips of paper representing marbles in a box and drawing them out 1 at a time.
  c. **Carrying Out the Plan** Who has the better chance of winning this game? What happens to the probability if greater numbers of marbles are used?
  d. **Looking Back** Suppose the game continues with the drawer selecting 2 marbles at a time until there are no marbles left. The drawer wins a point each time the marbles have the same color and otherwise loses a point. Does this game favor the drawer or the holder? (Hint: Try some experiments and determine an empirical probability.)

25. The typical slot machine has 3 wheels that operate independently of one another. Each wheel has 6 different kinds of symbols that occur various numbers of times, as shown in the chart. If any one of the winning combinations appears, the player wins money according to the payoff assigned to each combination. Find the probabilities of the events in parts a through d.

	Wheel I	Wheel II	Wheel III
Cherries	7	7	0
Oranges	3	6	7
Lemons	3	0	4
Plums	5	1	5
Bells	1	3	3
Bars	1	3	1
Totals	20	20	20

a. A bar on wheel I

b. A bar on all 3 wheels

c. Bells on wheels I and II and a bar on wheel III

d. Plums on wheels I and II and a bar on wheel III

26. In an experiment designed to test estimates of probability, people were asked to select one of the two outcomes in parts a and b that would be more likely to occur. Determine which outcome in each case is more likely to occur. Note: Each box has only one winning ticket.

a. 1) Obtaining a winning ticket by drawing once from a box of 10 tickets

2) Obtaining a winning ticket both times by drawing twice with replacement from a box of 5 tickets

b. 1) Obtaining a winning ticket by drawing once from a box of 10 tickets

2) Obtaining a winning ticket at least once by drawing twice with replacement from a box of 20 tickets (Hint: Use complementary events.)

27. In Sweden a motorist was accused of overparking in a restricted time zone. A police officer testified that this particular parked car was seen with the tire valves pointing to 1 o'clock and to 6 o'clock. When the officer returned later (after the allowed parking time had expired), this same car was there with its valves pointing in the same directions—so a ticket was written. The motorist claimed that he had driven the car away from that spot during the elapsed time, and when he returned later the tire valves coincidentally came to rest in the same positions as before. The driver was acquitted, but the judge remarked that if the positions of the tire valves of all 4 wheels had been recorded and found to point in the same direction, the coincidence claim would have been rejected as too improbable.

Assume that because of variations in tire sizes the tires will not turn the same amounts.

a. Using the 12 hour positions, determine the probability that two given tire valves of a car will return to the same position when the car is re-parked.

b. What is the probability that all 4 tire valves will return to the same position?

LABORATORY INVESTIGATION

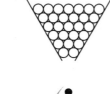

The device in the accompanying photo is called a probability machine and was described by Sir Francis Galton in 1889. There are 10 horizontal rows of pegs in the top half of this device. As a ball falls through the opening at the top center, it strikes the center peg in the top row and has an equal chance of going right or left. At each lower row the ball hits a peg, and in each case it has a 50/50 chance of falling right or left. The balls collect in 11 compartments in the lower half of this device. When a large number of balls are dropped, the distribution of the balls will be approximately normal, with the greatest number in the center compartment and the numbers decreasing as the compartments become further from the center.

Questions for Investigation

1. The probability of a ball's falling into a given compartment can be computed by determining the number of ways a ball can fall into each of the compartments. Consider the following simplified probability machine. The path of 1 ball that has fallen into compartment B is marked with arrows. Determine the number of ways a ball can fall into each of the compartments A, B, C, D, and E, and then determine the probability of a ball's falling into a given compartment. Hint: The total number of ways a ball can enter these 5 compartments is 16.

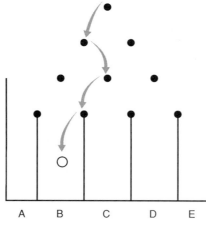

2. Determine the probability of a ball's falling into each compartment of some other simplified probability machines.

3. Look for a pattern. (Hint: The numbers of ways a ball can fall into a compartment is related to Pascal's triangle; see page 16.)

4. Use your pattern to predict the probability of a ball's falling into the center compartment of a probability machine with 11 compartments.

PUZZLER

Suppose you have 3 containers for marbles. Container I holds 1 black marble and 1 white marble; container II holds 1 black and 2 white; and container III holds 1 black and 1 white. If a marble is selected at random from container I and put into container II and a marble is selected at random from container II and put into container III, what is the probability of drawing a black marble from container III?

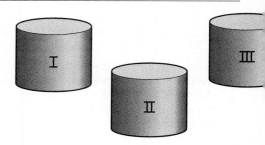

CHAPTER REVIEW

1. **Probability**
   a. Any activity such as spinning a spinner, tossing a coin, or rolling a die is called an **experiment.**
   b. The different results that can occur from an experiment are called **outcomes.**
   c. The set of all outcomes is called the **sample space.**
   d. Probabilities determined from conducting experiments are called **experimental probabilities.**
   e. Probabilities determined from ideal experiments are called **theoretical probabilities.**
   f. If there are n equally likely outcomes, then the **probability of an outcome** is $1/n$.
   g. If the outcomes of an experiment have values $v_1, v_2, \ldots, v_n$ and the outcomes have probabilities $p_1, p_2, \ldots, p_n$, respectively, then the **expected value** of the experiment is
   $$p_1v_1 + p_2v_2 + \cdots + p_nv_n$$
   h. A game is called a **fair game** if the net earnings are zero.

2. **Events**
   a. Any subset of an outcome is called an **event.**
   b. If an event is the empty set, it is called an **impossible event,** and its probability is 0.
   c. If an event contains all possible outcomes, it is called a **certain event,** and its probability is 1.
   d. The **probability of an event** is the sum of the probabilities of its outcomes.

   e. If events A and B are disjoint, they are called **mutually exclusive events.** In this case $P(A \cup B) = P(A) + P(B)$.
   f. If events A and B are complementary sets, they are called **complementary events.** In this case $P(A) + P(B) = 1$.

3. **Odds and Simulations**
   a. The **odds in favor** of an event are the ratio of the number of favorable outcomes (n) to the number of unfavorable outcomes (m). The probability of this event's occurring is $n/(n + m)$.
   b. The **odds against** an event are the ratio of the number of unfavorable outcomes (m) to the number of favorable outcomes (n). The probability of this event's not occurring is $m/(n + m)$.
   c. A **simulation** is a representation of an experiment that uses random numbers or some other device such as spinners or coins.

4. **Multistage Experiments**
   a. A tree diagram showing the outcomes of an experiment and their probabilities is called a **probability tree.**
   b. If A and B are two events and the probability of B is not affected by the occurrence of event A, then these events are called **independent events;** otherwise, they are called **dependent events.**
   c. **Multiplication Rule for Probabilities** If $P(A) = a$ and $P(B) = b$ for independent events A and B, then the probability of "first A, then B" is $a \times b$.

CHAPTER TEST

1. A box contains 6 tickets lettered A, B, C, D, E, and F. Two tickets will be randomly selected from the box (without replacement).
   a. List all the outcomes of the sample space.
   b. What is the probability of selecting tickets A and B?
   c. What is the probability that one of the tickets will be ticket A?

2. A chip is selected at random from a box that contains 3 blue chips, 4 red chips, and 5 yellow chips. Determine the probabilities of selecting each of the following.
   a. A red chip
   b. A red chip or a yellow chip
   c. A chip that is not red

3. A box contains 3 green marbles and 2 orange marbles. An experiment consists of randomly selecting 2 marbles from the box (without replacement).
   a. List all the outcomes of the sample space.
   b. What is the probability of obtaining 2 green marbles?
   c. What is the probability of obtaining 2 orange marbles?
   d. What is the probability of obtaining 1 green and 1 orange marble?

4. The odds of a certain bill's passing through a state's Senate are 7 to 5.
   a. What are the odds of the bill's not passing?
   b. What is the probability that the bill will be passed?

5. A box contains 4 red marbles and 2 yellow marbles. Consider the two-stage experiment of randomly selecting a marble from a box, replacing it, and then selecting a second marble. Determine the probabilities of the following events.
   a. Selecting 2 red marbles
   b. Selecting a red marble on the first draw and a yellow marble on the second
   c. Selecting at least 1 yellow marble

6. Suppose that in exercise #5 the first marble that is selected is not replaced. Determine the probabilities of the events in #5 a, b, and c.

7. A family has 4 children.
   a. Draw a probability tree showing all possible combinations of boys and girls.
   b. What is the probability of the family's having 2 boys and 2 girls?
   c. What is the probability of the family's having at least 2 girls?

8. A contestant on a quiz show will choose 2 out of 7 envelopes (without replacement). If 2 of the 7 envelopes each contain $10,000, what is the probability the contestant will win at least $10,000?

9. The maker of a certain brand of cereal puts a coupon for a free box of cereal in 20% of its boxes. If 3 boxes are purchased, what is the probability of obtaining at least 1 coupon?

10. Players in a die-toss game can win the following amounts: $2 for an even number; $1 for a 1; $3 for a 3; and $5 for a 5.
    a. What is the expected value of the game?
    b. In order for this to be a fair game, what should it cost to play?

11. A certain system fails to operate if any one of 4 relays overloads. The probability of a relay's overloading is .01. What is the probability that the system will fail?

12. An athlete enters three track and field events. She has a .9 probability of winning the 100 meter dash, a .9 probability of winning the low hurdles, and an .8 probability of winning the long jump.
    a. What is the probability that the athlete will win the hurdles and the long jump?
    b. What is the probability that she will win all three events?
    c. What is the probability that she will win at least one of the three events?

BIBLIOGRAPHY

Bruni, J. V., and H. J. Silverman. "Developing Concepts in Probability and Statistics—and Much More." *Arithmetic Teacher* 33 (February 1986): 34–37.

Burns, M. "Put Some Probability in Your Classroom." *Arithmetic Teacher* 30 (March 1983): 21–22.

Choate, S. "Activities in Applying Probability Ideas." *Arithmetic Teacher* 26 (February 1979): 40–42.

Cook, M. "Ideas [Counting Activities]." *Arithmetic Teacher* 36 (September 1988): 31–36.

Enman, V. "Probability in the Intermediate Grades." *Arithmetic Teacher* 26 (February 1979): 38–39.

Fennell, F. "Ya Gotta Play to Win: A Probability and Statistics Unit for the Middle Grades." *Arithmetic Teacher* 31 (March 1984): 26–30.

Halpern, N. "Teaching Probability—Some Legal Applications." *Mathematics Teacher* 80 (February 1987): 150–153.

Hinders, D. "Monte Carlo, Probability, Algebra, and Pi." *Mathematics Teacher* 74 (May 1981): 335–339.

Horak, V. M., and W. J. Horak. "Let's Do It: Take a Chance." *Arithmetic Teacher* 30 (May 1983): 8–15.

Houser, L. L. "Baseball Monte Carlo Style." *Mathematics Teacher* 74 (May 1981): 340–341.

Jones, G. "A Case for Probability." *Arithmetic Teacher* 26 (February 1979): 37–57.

Lappan, G., et al. "Area Models and Expected Value." *Mathematics Teacher* 80 (November 1987): 650–654.

Lappan, G., et al. "Area Models for Probability." *Mathematics Teacher* 80 (March 1987): 217–220.

National Council of Teachers of Mathematics. *Teaching Statistics and Probability.* 1981 Yearbook. Reston, VA: NCTM, 1981.

Nibblelink, W. "Graphing for Any Grade." *Arithmetic Teacher* 30 (November 1982): 28–31.

O'Neil, D. R., and R. Jensen. "Let's Do It: Looking at Facts." *Arithmetic Teacher* 29 (April 1982): 12–15.

Pereira-Mendoza, L. "Using Dice: From Place Value to Probability." *Arithmetic Teacher* 28 (April 1981): 10–12.

Shaw, J. "Roll 'n' Spin." *Arithmetic Teacher* 31 (February 1984): 6–9.

Shulte, A., ed. *The Teaching of Statistics and Probability.* 1981 Yearbook. Reston, VA: National Council of Teachers of Mathematics, 1981.

Shultz, H. S., and B. Leonard. "Probability and Intuition." *Mathematics Teacher* 82 (January 1989): 52–53.

Stone, J. "Place Value and Probability (with Promptings from Pascal)." *Arithmetic Teacher* 27 (March 1980): 47–49.

Travers, K. J. "The Monte Carlo Method: A Fresh Approach to Teaching Probabilistic Concepts." *Mathematics Teacher* 74 (May 1981): 327–334.

Vissa, J. M. "Probability and Combinations for Third Graders." *Arithmetic Teacher* 36 (December 1988): 33–37.

Woodward, E. "A Second-Grade Probability and Graphing Lesson." *Arithmetic Teacher* 30 (March 1983): 23–24.

Answers to Puzzlers

p. 13 Imagine that the links form a circular chain and are numbered from 1 to 12. Four pieces of chain with 3 links each can be obtained by cutting and then joining links #1, #5 and #9. Now, work backward.

p. 24 It is not a spiral but a series of concentric circles. Select a circle and trace it.

p. 43 18 days. There were 5 fine days and 13 days with rain.

p. 54 The first conclusion is invalid.

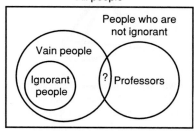

The second conclusion is valid.

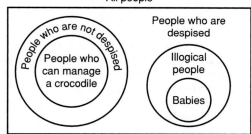

p. 69 The gram weights are the first 6 binary numbers: 1, 2, 4, 8, 16, and 32.

p. 84 There is no missing money. The desk clerk has $25, the bellboy has $2, and each man has $1. The confusion arises when we try to add the $27 (which includes the $2 "tip") to the $2.

p. 98
$$
\begin{array}{r}
426 \\
\times\ 307 \\
\hline
2982 \\
1278 \\
\hline
130{,}782
\end{array}
$$

p. 102
$$
\begin{array}{r}
51 \\
\times\ 61 \\
\hline
51 \\
306 \\
\hline
3111
\end{array}
\qquad
\begin{array}{r}
157 \\
\times\ 75 \\
\hline
11{,}775
\end{array}
$$

p. 115
$$
\begin{array}{r}
9087 \\
39\overline{)354393} \\
351 \\
\hline
339 \\
312 \\
\hline
273 \\
273 \\
\hline
\end{array}
$$

p. 118 $(22 - 19 + 2) \times 14 \div 10 = 7$
$21 \times 2 - 3 - 12 - 7 = 20$

p. 134 The license plate number is 83173.

p. 136 $367.92

p. 148
$$
\begin{array}{r}
775 \\
\times\ 33 \\
\hline
2325 \\
2325 \\
\hline
25{,}575
\end{array}
$$

p. 171

⁻4	⁻6	4
6	⁻2	⁻10
⁻8	2	0

p. 189

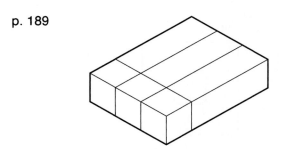

p. 193 $3\frac{1}{2}$ in.

p. 215 The sum of the 3 fractions, $1/2 + 1/3 + 1/9$, is $17/18$, not 1, as we would expect. This means that farmer Brown's will accounted for only $17/18$ of his property. Increasing the total number of horses to 18 allowed the boys to take 17 horses ($17/18$ of the total) and left farmer Smith the horse he had donated to solve the dilemma.

p. 237 The second odometer reading could have been 73,037, 73,137, or 73,237. For these cases the average speeds in miles per hour are 27.5, 52.5, and 77.5, respectively.

p. 253 25 items, each costing 25 cents

p. 256 This is 1 of 4 possible solutions:

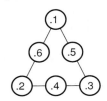

p. 276 72%

p. 294 Place one plank on $\overline{AB}$ so that $AB = 18.8$ ft. Then (by the Pythagorean theorem) $CD = 9.4$ ft. Since $CE \approx 28.3$ ft, $DE \approx 18.9$ ft, so the second plank will reach across the moat along $\overline{DE}$.

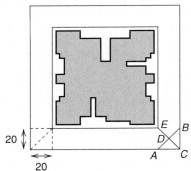

p. 313 One possible solution:

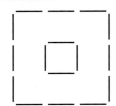

p. 317

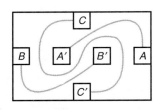

p. 326

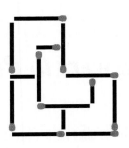

p. 329

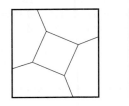

p. 340

p. 346 The bear was white, because the researchers' camp was at the North Pole. The researchers could have been in the vicinity of the South Pole, except that they would not have seen a white bear, or any bear at all—there are no bears at the South Pole. There are, however, an infinite number of locations near the South Pole from which the researchers could start out and make the trip described. Imagine a circle with a circumference of 15 miles around the South Pole. Suppose the researchers' camp was at a point 15 miles north of the circle. Walking 15 miles south from camp would bring them to a point on the circle. Walking 15 miles east would bring them around to the original point on the circle. Walking 15 miles north would bring them back to the point where they started.

p. 358 1961 and 1881

p. 370 Each right turn has a measure of 144°, and the angle at I has a measure of 36°.

p. 396 ⁻40°

p. 410 $2/\pi$, or approximately 63.7%

p. 415 38 ft

p. 435 Watch the surface of the water inside the can as the water is being poured out. Just as the bottom of the can begins to show, the can is half empty.

p. 461 The top weighs 9 marbles.

p. 484 84 years

p. 509 Cube 1: 0, 1, 2, 3, 4, 5
Cube 2: 0, 1, 2, 6, 7, 8
(If its cube is rotated 180°, 6 can be used for 9.)

p. 528

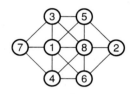

p. 549 $\sqrt{2}$ to 1

p. 559 The ring can be moved from loop A to loop B in five steps.
Step 1: Start the ring on its way by moving it from left to right along Loop A toward the hole of the panel. At this point it cannot continue moving because it will not fit through the hole.
Step 2: Pull the two strings that protrude through the front of the panel until the center loop comes through the hole.
Step 3: Slide the ring along its string and through the center loop. The ring has now almost been moved to loop B.
Step 4: Reach behind the panel and pull the strings and the center loop back through the hole.
Step 5: Move the ring away from the hole and down to Loop B.

p. 564 Slip the string connecting one person's wrists under the string that is around the wrist of the second person and over that person's hands.

p. 590 48 mph

p. 608 "It is remarkable that a science which began with the consideration of games of chance should be elevated to the rank of the most important subjects of human knowledge."

p. 628 Here is one possibility; there are at least three more.
Die 1: 0, 0, 0, 3, 3, 3
Die 2: 1, 2, 3, 7, 8, 9

p. 644 11/24

Answers to Odd-Numbered Exercises and Problems and Chapter Tests

EXERCISES AND PROBLEMS 1.1

1. a. 4 feet; 2 feet   **b.** 6 feet   **c.** On day 9
   d. If the snail climbs 4 feet during the day and slips back 3 feet at night, it will take 17 days for it to climb out of the well.

3. a. 64 and 46   **b.** $64 - 46 = 18$
   c. 82 and 28   **d.** 93 and 39

5. 28 apples

7. 1200 miles from A to B

9. 9 postcards

11.

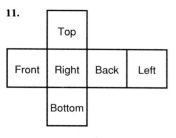

13. $86 + 87 + 88 + 89$

15. 2 is on the back of disc 6; 5 is on the back of disc 7; 9 is on the back of disc 8

17. One way: Start both timers at the same time; put the vegetables in the water when the 7-minute timer finishes; turn the 11-minute timer over when it finishes; vegetables will be steamed in 15 minutes, when the 11-minute timer finishes.

19. a. 2 apples   **b.** 9 sheep
   c. The other coin is a nickel.
   d. The cider costs 73 cents; the bottle costs 13 cents.
   e. No dirt   **f.** 6 pounds
   g. The players were women.
   h. Neither; the whites of the egg are white!

EXERCISES AND PROBLEMS 1.2

1. a. 91   **b.** Yes
   c. Ten layers of cannon balls: the base is 10 by 10, the next layers are 9 by 9, 8 by 8, etc., up to the top level, which has 1 cannon ball.
   d. $1^2 + 2^2 + 3^2 + \cdots + 20^2$ **e.** $1^2 + 2^2 + 3^2 + \cdots + n^2$

3. a., b. 17, 18, 19, and 9, 16, 23: The sum divided by 3 is the middle number.
   c. 14, 15, 16; 21, 22, 23; 28, 29, 30. The sum divided by 9 is the center number of the array.

5. a. $16 + 17 + 18 + 19 + 20 = 21 + 22 + 23 + 24$
     $25 + 26 + 27 + 28 + 29 + 30 = 31 + 32 + 33 + 34 + 35$
   b. Yes

7. Yes

9. a. Arithmetic. Add 5 to each number to get the next number in the series. The next 3 numbers are 24, 29, and 34.
   b. Geometric. Multiply each number by 2. The next 3 numbers are 240, 480, and 960.
   c. Arithmetic. Subtract 4 from each number. The next 3 numbers are 8, 4, and 0.
   d. Geometric. Multiply each number by 3. The next 3 numbers are 324, 972, and 2916.

11. a. 187   **b.** 103

13. a. 30   **b.** $20 \times 21 = 420$

15. Inductive reasoning

17. a.

   b. 69

19. a. $3 \times 5 = 15$, which is not evenly divisible by 2.
   b. 8 cannot be written as the sum of consecutive whole numbers.

21. a. 78   **b.** 364

23. a. 729 (3^6)   **b.** 531,441 (3^{12})

CHAPTER 1 TEST

1. Understanding the problem
Devising a plan
Carrying out the plan
Looking back

2. Making a drawing
Guessing and checking
Making a table
Using a model
Working backward
Finding a pattern
Solving a simpler problem

3. Sums: 3, 8, 21, 55. The sum of the first and third Fibonacci numbers is the fourth Fibonacci number; the sum of the first, third, and fifth Fibonacci numbers is the sixth Fibonacci number; and so forth.

4. 512, or 2^9

5. a. 243   **b.** 18   **c.** 30
   d. 36   **e.** 53

6. a. Geometric   **b.** Arithmetic   **c.** Arithmetic
   d. Neither   **e.** Neither

7. a. 91, 140, 204   **b.** 54, 77, 104

8. a. 15   **b.** 25   **c.** 35

9. Inductive reasoning

10. $2 + 3 + 4 + 5 + 6 + 7 + 8 = 35$, which is not evenly divisible by 4.

11. 201 posts; Making a drawing and/or solving a simpler problem

12. Working backward: $170 - 80 = 90, 90 \times 2 = 180$, $180 - 50 = 130, 130 \times 2 = 260$. She started with 260 chips.
13. 325; Solving a simpler problem and finding a pattern
14. a. 16   **b.** 200; Making a drawing, solving a simpler problem, and finding a pattern
15. 78 handshakes; Making a drawing, solving a simpler problem, and finding a pattern
16. 9 crossings; Making a drawing

EXERCISES AND PROBLEMS 2.1

1. Yes, because the marks may be just tally marks—for example, 1 mark for 1 day. However, the 55 marks in groups of 5 suggest that 5 marks may have been used as a symbol for the number 5.
3. a. SW and SB; W and L **b.** No sets are equal.
5. a. *lwt, lwr, lwh*
  b. *lwt, lwr, lwh, swt, swr, swh, lbt, lbr, lbh*
7. a. *swh, sbh*   **b.** *lwt, swt*
  c. *swt, swr, swh, sbt, sbr, sbh, lwt, lwr, lwh*
  d. *lbt, lbr, lbh, lwt, lwr, lwh, swt, sbt*
  e. *lbt, lbr, lbh, sbt, sbr, lwt, lwr, lwh, swt, swr*
  f. *lbt, lbr, lbh*
9. a. $C' \cap A = \{0, 2, 8\}$
  b. $(A \cap C) \cup B = \{1, 3, 4, 5, 6, 7\}$

11.
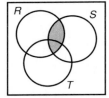
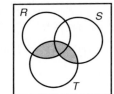
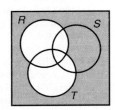

13.
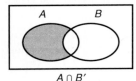

$A \cap B'$ $A' \cup B$

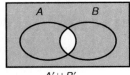

$A' \cup B'$

15. a. *d, c*   **b.** *j, i*   **c.** *c*   **d.** *c, n, j, k*
17. 2 people
19.   **a.**
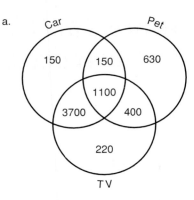

b. 400 people   **c.** 150 people
21. a. 8 people   **b.** 37 people   **c.** 69 people   **d.** 6 people

EXERCISES AND PROBLEMS 2.2

1. a. Yes   **b.** Yes
3. a.
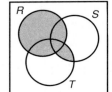
b.
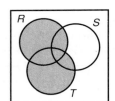

c.
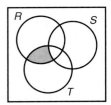
d.
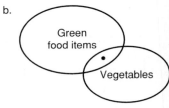

5. a. Converse: If the camera focus is on manual, switch B was pressed.
    Inverse: If switch B is not pressed, the camera focus is not on manual.
    Contrapositive: If the camera focus is not on manual, then switch B was not pressed.
  b. Converse: If the opera is sold out, the weather is fair.
    Inverse: If the weather is not fair, the opera will not be sold out.
    Contrapositive: If the opera is not sold out, the weather is not fair.
7. a. If the computer does not reject your income tax return, then you didn't subtract $750 for each dependent.
  b. If the cards are not dealt again, then there was an opening bid.
  c. If the books are not returned at the end of the week's free sing-a-long, then you are delighted with them.
9. a. If Robinson is hired, then she meets the conditions set by the board.
    If Robinson meets the conditions set by the board, then she will be hired.
  b. If the damaged equipment is repaired, then there will be negotiations.
    If there are negotiations, then the damaged equipment will be repaired.

11. Invalid

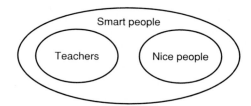

13. Valid

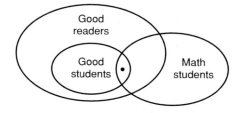

15. This patient's production of red blood cells will be slowed down.
17. Invalid
19. Valid
21.

	Appraiser (man)	Broker (man)	Cook	Painter	Singer (man)	
(woman) Dow	No	No	Yes	No	No	Dow is the cook.
(man) Eliot	No	No	No	No	Yes	Eliot is the singer.
(man) Finley	Yes	No	No	No	No	Finley is the appraiser.
(man) Grant	No	Yes	No	No	No	Grant is the broker.
(woman) Hanley	No	No	No	Yes	No	Hanley is the painter.

CHAPTER 2 TEST

1. a. {swh}   **b.** {sbt, sbr, sbh, swt}   **c.** {sbt, sbh}
2. a. $A \cap B = \{2, 4\}$ **b.** $A \cup B = \{1, 2, 3, 4, 6\}$
   c. $A' \cap B = \{1, 3\}$ **d.** $A \cup B' = \{0, 2, 4, 5, 6\}$
3. a.   E   F   b.   G

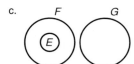

   c.   F   G   d.   E   G   F

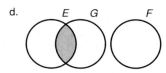

   e.   G   f.   F

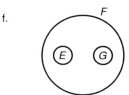

4. a. $A \cap B'$ or $(A' \cup B)'$ **b.** $A' \cup B'$ or $(A \cap B)'$
5. a. Not necessarily

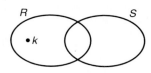

  b. Yes

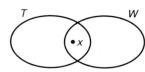

  c. No

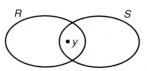

6. Each set can be put into one-to-one correspondence with a proper subset.
  a. {100, 101, 102, 103, . . .}
     ↕   ↕   ↕   ↕
    {110, 111, 112, 113, . . .}

  b. { 10,   12,   14,   16,   18, . . .}
     ↕   ↕   ↕   ↕   ↕
    {100, 120, 140, 160, 180, . . .}

7. 5 cars
8. 20 men
9. a. If you are denied credit, then you have the right to protest to the credit bureau.
  b. If a child was absent yesterday, then the child was absent today.
  c. If you were at the party, then you received a gift.
10. a. Converse: If her husband goes with her, then Mary goes fishing.
    Inverse: If Mary does not go fishing, then her husband does not go with her.
    Contrapositive: If her husband does not go with her, then Mary does not go fishing.
  b. Converse: If you receive 5 free books, then you will join the book club.
    Inverse: If you do not join the book club, then you will not receive 5 free books.
    Contrapositive: If you do not receive 5 free books, then you have not joined the book club.
11. Statement (3)
12. There will be peace talks if and only if the prisoners are set free.
13. a. Invalid   **b.** Valid   **c.** Invalid
14. a. The people in ward B are not healthy.
  b. The game pieces should be set up as they were before the illegal move was made.
15. a. Invalid   **b.** Valid

EXERCISES AND PROBLEMS 3.1

1. a. 1241   **b.** 82
3. a. 4 hands and 2
  b. Hand of hands, 2 hands, and 2

5. In each numeration system, the symbol for 1 is repeated to create the symbols for 2, 3, and 4. In the Babylonian and Egyptian systems, the symbol for 1 is repeated in the symbols for 2 through 9. Grouping by 5s occurs in the Roman and Mayan systems. In these systems, a symbol for 5 is used with the symbols for 1, 2, 3, and 4 to form the symbols for 6, 7, 8, and 9; the symbol for 10 can be formed by combining two symbols for the number 5.

7. **a.** CCCCLXXXVI and CDLXXXVI
   b. MDCCLXXVI
   c. MMLXXXXV and MMXCV

9. **a.** 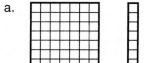 **b.** DCIII

11. Base ten

Hindu-Arabic	1	4	8	16	26
Attic-Greek	Ι	ΙΙΙΙ	ΓΙΙΙ	ΔΓΙ	ΔΔΓΙ

Hindu-Arabic	32	52	57	206	511
Attic-Greek	ΔΔΔΙΙ	ΓΙΙ	ΓΓΙΙ	ΗΗΓΙ	ΓΔΙ

13. **a.** The value is 400; the place value is hundreds.
    b. The value is zero; the place value is thousands.
    c. The value is 2,000,000; the place value is millions.

15. **a.** 43,700,000   **b.** 43,670,000
    c. 43,669,000   **d.** 43,668,900

17.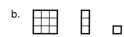
    a.
    b.

19. No, it stops after 9 steps.
21. **a.** 35 = 32 + 2 + 1   **b.** 42 = 32 + 8 + 2
    c. 66 = 64 + 2

EXERCISES AND PROBLEMS 3.2

1. **a.** Units wheel and hundreds wheel
   b. Tens wheel and thousands wheel
   c. Yes
3. **a.** 108 + □ = 247   **b.** 231 + 76 = □
5.
a.
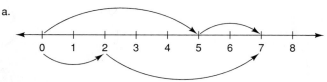

b.
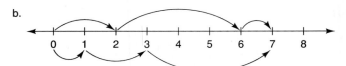
c.
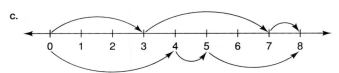

7. **a.** An advantage of this method is that when the digits of highest place value are added first, a subsequent error will affect only the digits of lower place value.

$$\begin{array}{r} 726 \\ + 508 \\ \hline 12\!\!\not7\!\!4 \\ {\scriptstyle 3} \end{array}$$

   b. An advantage of this method is that all digits of column sums are recorded before regrouping. This eliminates the need to add and regroup in the same step.

$$\begin{array}{r} 974 \\ + 382 \\ \hline 6 \\ 15 \\ 12 \\ \hline 1356 \end{array}$$

9. **a.** No. For example, $3 - 5 \neq 5 - 3$
   b. No. For example, $(6 - 4) - 1 \neq 6 - (4 - 1)$
   c. Yes
   d. No. For example, $15 - 7 = 8$, an even number.
11. **a.** The student computed $6 - 4$ (i.e., subtracted the smaller number from the larger).
    b. After a 10 in the tens place was regrouped to units, the 5 was not reduced to 4.
    c. The numbers were added.
    d. The student computed $9 - 7$ and $4 - 3$.
13. **a.** $435 - 198 = 437 - 200 = 237$
    b. $622 - 115 = 627 - 120 = 507$
    c. $245 - 85 = 260 - 100 = 160$
15. **a.** $100 + 40 + 20 = 160$ **b.** $30 + 40 + 60 = 130$
    c. $30 + 200 + 80 = 310$ **d.** $30 + 70 + 20 = 120$
17. **a.** 2000, since $4 + 8 + 3 + 5 = 20$
    b. 9000, since $4 + 2 + 3 = 9$
    c. 270, since $6 + 8 + 3 + 2 + 8 = 27$
19. **a.** 30 cars   **b.** 52 cars   **c.** 35 cars   **d.** Case b
21. **a.** Here are a few selected sums:
    $10 = 5 + 4 + 1$
    $15 = 7 + 2 + 6$
    $19 = 1 + 4 + 5 + 3 + 6$
    $23 = 4 + 1 + 7 + 2 + 6 + 3$

    b.
    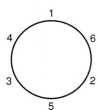

EXERCISES AND PROBLEMS 3.3

1.

a.
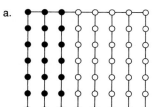

b.
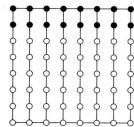

c.
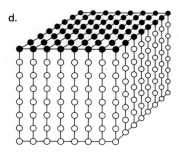
d.

b.
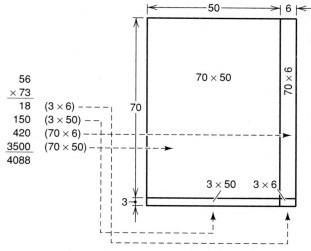

$$\begin{array}{r} 56 \\ \times\,73 \\ \hline 18 \\ 150 \\ 420 \\ 3500 \\ \hline 4088 \end{array}\quad\begin{array}{l} (3\times 6) \\ (3\times 50) \\ (70\times 6) \\ (70\times 50) \end{array}$$

3.
a.

$3 \times 4 = 12$
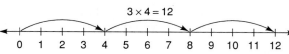

b.

$2 \times 5 = 10$
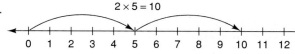

c.

$3 \times 4 = 4 \times 3 = 12$
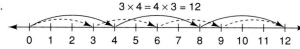

5.

a.
$$\begin{array}{r} 24 \\ \times\,7 \\ \hline 28 \\ 140 \\ \hline 168 \end{array}$$
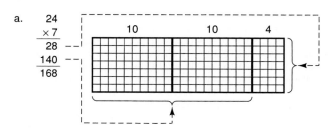

7. a. Commutative property for multiplication
  b. Associative property for multiplication
  c. Distributve property of multiplication over addition
  d. Commutative property for addition
  e. Associative property for addition
9. a. 8300 (Multiply 83 by 100) **b.** 210 (Multiply 21 by 10)
  c. 1000 (Multiply 100 by 10) **d.** 1700 (Multiply 17 by 100)
11. a. $35 \times 19 = 35(20 - 1) = 700 - 35 = 665$
  b. $51 \times 9 = 51(10 - 1) = 510 - 51 = 459$
  c. $30 \times 99 = 30(100 - 1) = 3000 - 30 = 2970$
13. a. $22 \times 17 \approx 20 \times 20 = 400$ (Too big; estimate could be improved by subtracting 20.)
  b. $83 \times 31 \approx 80 \times 30 = 2400$ (Too small; estimate could be improved by adding $2 \times 30 = 60$.)
  c. $71 \times 56 \approx 70 \times 60 = 4200$ (Too big; estimate could be improved by subtracting $3 \times 70 = 210$.)
  d. $205 \times 29 \approx 200 \times 30 = 6000$ (Too big; estimate could be improved by subtracting 50.)
15. a. Front-end estimation:
     $3 \times 5 = 15$, so $36 \times 58 \approx 1500$
     Combinations of tens and hundreds digits:
     $36 \times 58 \approx 30 \times 50 + (6 \times 50) + (8 \times 30) = 2040$
  b. Front-end estimation:
     $4 \times 2 = 8$, so $42 \times 27 \approx 800$
     Combinations of tens and hundreds digits:
     $42 \times 27 \approx 40 \times 20 + (2 \times 20) + (7 \times 40) = 1120$
  c. Front-end estimation:
     $6 \times 8 = 48$, so $62 \times 83 \approx 4800$
     Combinations of tens and hundreds digits:
     $62 \times 83 \approx 60 \times 80 + (2 \times 80) + (3 \times 60) = 5140$
  d. Front-end estimation:
     $1 \times 6 = 6$, so $14 \times 62 \approx 600$
     Combinations of tens and hundreds digits:
     $14 \times 62 \approx 10 \times 60 + (4 \times 60) + (2 \times 10) = 860$
17. a. $62 \otimes 45 + 14 \otimes 29$
     $\approx 60 \times 50 + 10 \times 30$
     $= 3000 + 300$
     $= 3300$
     The exact answer is 3196.
  b. $36 - 18 \otimes 40 + 15$
     $\approx 40 - 20 \times 40 + 15$
     $= 40 - 800 + 15$
     $= {}^{-}745$
     The exact answer is $^{-}669$.
  c. $114 \otimes 238 - 19 \otimes 605$
     $\approx 100 \times 250 - 20 \times 600$
     $= 25{,}000 - 12{,}000$
     $= 13{,}000$
     The exact answer is 15,637.
  d. $73 - 50 + 17 \otimes 62$
     $\approx 70 - 50 + 20 \times 60$
     $= 20 + 1200$
     $= 1220$
     The exact answer is 1077.

19. a. Each row increases by a constant amount (each row is an arithmetic sequence).
Each column increases by a constant amount.
The table is symmetric about the diagonal from upper left to lower right.

b. The sum of the digits in each product is 9. The tens digits in the products (18, 27, 36, . . . , 81) increase from 1 to 8 while the units digits decrease from 8 to 1.

21. $1720

23. 20 backpacks

25. a. The raised fingers represent 5 tens, or 50, and the product of the numbers of closed fingers is $2 \times 3 = 6$.

b. Two raised fingers on one hand and 1 raised finger on the other hand represent 3 tens, or 30, and the product of the numbers of closed fingers is $4 \times 3 = 12$. Since $30 + 12 = 42$, the system works.

EXERCISES AND PROBLEMS 3.4

1. a. Partitive (sharing) concept

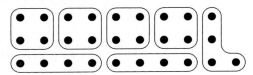

b. Measurement (subtractive) concept

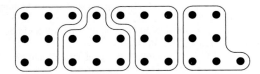

3. a. $336 \div 14 = 24$ **b.** $72 \div 8 = 9$
     c. $3600 \div 10 = 360$ **d.** $s = t \div r$ (or $r = t \div s$)

5.

a.
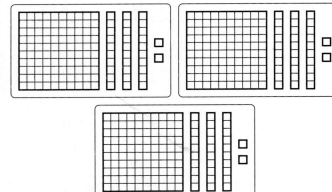
a.

b.
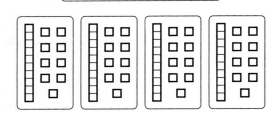

b.

7. a. $72 \div 12 = 6$

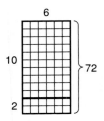

b. $286 \div 26 = 11$

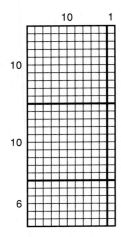

9. a. $0 \div 4 = 0$ **b.** Undefined   **c.** Undefined

11. a. In the second step of the division algorithm, $5 \div 8$ is 0 with a remainder of 5. The zero should have been placed in the quotient.

b. The 6 and 8 in the quotient were placed in the wrong columns.

c. In the second step of the division algorithm, $4 \div 7$ is 0 with a remainder of 4. The zero should have been placed in the quotient above the 4.

d. In the first step of the division algorithm, the remainder, 5, is greater than the divisor, 4. The remainder should be less than the divisor.

13. Division is not commutative: $8 \div 4 \neq 4 \div 8$. Division is not associative: $24 \div (12 \div 2) \neq (24 \div 12) \div 2$, since $4 \neq 1$.

15. a. 70 remainder 28   **b.** 118 remainder 12
     c. 572 remainder 10   **d.** 1247 remainder 11

17. a. $250 \div 46 \approx 250 \div 50 = 5$ (Less than the exact quotient)

b. $82 \div 19 \approx 80 \div 20 = 4$ (Less than the exact quotient)

c. $486 \div 53 \approx 500 \div 50 = 10$ (Greater than the exact quotient)

d. $8145 \div 195 \approx 8200 \div 200 = 41$ (Less than the exact quotient)

e. $203 \div 50 \approx 200 \div 50 = 4$ (Less than the exact quotient)

f. $241 \div 31 \approx 240 \div 30 = 8$ (Greater than the exact quotient)

19. a. 6 places   **b.** 7 places   **c.** 10 places

21. a. 35   **b.** 38   **c.** 240
     d. 73   **e.** 14

23. The sequences in parts a and b produce the correct answers on all calculators. The sequence in part c produces the correct answer if the calculator follows the rules for the order of operations.

25. a. The doubling payment plan
     b. $97,152

27. a. $31 + 33 + 35 + 37 + 39 + 41 = 216$
     b. $91 + 93 + 95 + 97 + 99 + 101 + 103 + 105 + 107 + 109 = 1000$

CHAPTER 3 TEST

1. a.
   b. CCXXVI
   c. (symbol)
   d. 1401_{five}

2. a. The value is 4 million; the place value is millions.
   b. The value is zero; the place value is ten thousands.

3. a. 6,300,000   **b.** 6,281,500
   c. 6,281,000

4.   a.

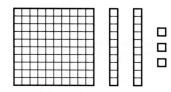

   b.

5. a. $245 + 182 = 427$

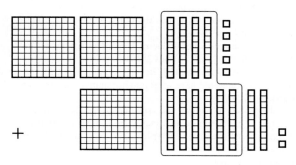

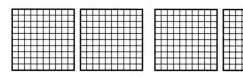

b. $362 - 148 = 214$

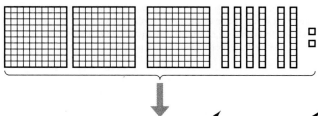

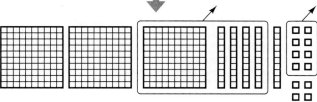

6. a.
$$\begin{array}{r} 483 \\ + 274 \\ \hline 657 \\ 7 \end{array}$$

b.
$$\begin{array}{r} 864 \\ + 759 \\ \hline 13 \\ 11 \\ 15 \\ \hline 1623 \end{array}$$

7. a. $65 - 19 = 66 - 20 = 46$
   b. $843 - 97 = 846 - 100 = 746$

8. a. $321 + 435 + 106 \approx 300 + 400 + 100 = 800$
   b. $7410 - 2563 + 4602 \approx 7000 - 2000 + 4000 = 9000$
   c. $32 \times 56 \approx 30 \times 50 = 1500$
   d. $3528 \div 713 \approx 3000 \div 700 \approx 4$

9. a. $18 \times 5 = 3 \times 30 = 90$
   b. $25 \times 28 = 100 \times 7 = 700$

10.

$$\begin{array}{r} 28 \\ \times 43 \\ \hline 24 \\ 60 \\ 320 \\ 800 \\ \hline 1204 \end{array}$$

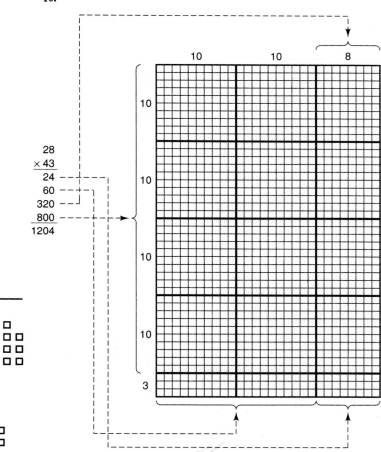

11. a. 117   **b.** 32   **c.** 53
12. a. 3^8 **b.** 7^{10}

13.

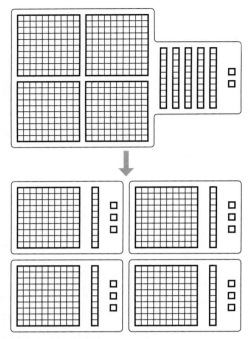

14. Other answers are possible.
   a. $473 + 192 \approx 500 + 200 = 700$
   b. $534 - 203 \approx 500 - 200 = 300$
   c. $993 \times 42 \approx 1000 \times 40 = 40,000$
   d. $350 \div 49 \approx 350 \div 50 = 7$
15. a. True   **b.** True
   c. False   **d.** False   **e.** False
16. $21^2 + 22^2 + 23^2 + 24^2 = 25^2 + 26^2 + 27^2$
   $36^2 + 37^2 + 38^2 + 39^2 + 40^2 = 41^2 + 42^2 + 43^2 + 44^2$
   $7230 = 7230$
17. 6 players
18. 24 types of pizza

EXERCISES AND PROBLEMS 4.1

1. a. Take the escalator to the elevator that serves the even-numbered floors and deliver to the 26th and 48th floors. Then walk down to the 47th floor and use the elevator that serves the odd-numbered floors to deliver to the 35th and 11th floors. Return to the street level on the elevator that serves the odd-numbered floors.
   b. If the highest floor to be delivered to has an odd number, deliver to all the odd-numbered floors first. Then walk down one flight of stairs and use the elevator for the even-numbered floors. A similar plan can be used if the highest floor to be delivered to has an even number.
3. a. 7|63   **b.** 8|40   **c.** 13|39   **d.** 12|36
5. a. White, green, purple, dark green
   b. White, green, yellow
   c. One
   d. For every 5 brown rods there will be 4 orange rods.
   e. 1, 2, 3, 7, 6, 14, 21, 42

7.

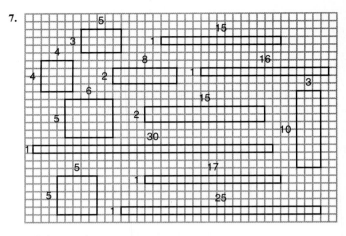

   a. Prime numbers
   b. 15, 30, 17
   c. Square numbers have an odd number of factors.
9. 465,076,800 is divisible by 9.
   a. Not necessarily   **b.** Yes
11. a. If a divides b and a divides c, then a divides the sum $b + c$. True
   b. If a does not divide b and a does not divide c, then a does not divide the sum $b + c$. False: $2 \nmid 5$ and $2 \nmid 7$ but $2 | (5 + 7)$
   c. If a divides b and b divides c, then a divides c. True
   d. If a divides c and b divides c, then the sum $a + b$ divides c. False: $2|6$ and $3|6$ but $(2 + 3) \nmid 6$
   e. If a divides b and a does not divide c, then a does not divide the product bc. False: $2|2$ and $2 \nmid 3$ but $2 | 2 \times 3$
13. No number less than 13 divides 173. But if a number n greater than 13 divided 173, there would have to be another number m less than 13 that divided 173. Why?
15. Carry out the process of circling and crossing out multiples until the prime number 17 has been circled. Since every composite number less than 300 has at least one prime factor less than or equal to 17, the process ends when 17 is circled.
17. There are other solutions
   a. Divisible by 11   **b.** Not divisible by 11
   c. Divisible by 11   **d.** Yes
19. a. There are other sums. $21 = 3 + 7 + 11$; $27 = 3 + 11 + 13$; $31 = 7 + 11 + 13$
   b. True
21. $3 \times 5 \times 7 \times 11 \times 13 = 15,015$
23. Using the fact that if $a|b$ and $a|c$, then $a|(b + c)$, we see that 2 is a factor of $2 \times 3 \times 4 \times 5 \times 6 + 2$ because it is a factor of both $2 \times 3 \times 4 \times 5 \times 6$ and 2. Similarly, 3 is a factor of the next number; 4 is a factor of the next number; etc.
   a. The following 10 numbers have factors of 2, 3, 4, . . . 11, respectively. Other sequences are possible.

   $2 \times 3 \times 4 \times 5 \times 6 \times 7 \times 8 \times 9 \times 10 \times 11 + 2$
   $2 \times 3 \times 4 \times 5 \times 6 \times 7 \times 8 \times 9 \times 10 \times 11 + 3$
   $2 \times 3 \times 4 \times 5 \times 6 \times 7 \times 8 \times 9 \times 10 \times 11 + 4$
   $\vdots$
   $2 \times 3 \times 4 \times 5 \times 6 \times 7 \times 8 \times 9 \times 10 \times 11 + 11$

   b. Let n be the product of the whole numbers from 2 through 101. The numbers $n + 2, n + 3, n + 4, . . . n + 101$ form a sequence of 100 consecutive composite numbers: $n + 2$ is divisible by 2; $n + 3$ is divisible by 3; $n + 4$ is divisible by 4; etc.

EXERCISES AND PROBLEMS 4.2

1. a. $126 = 2 \times 3 \times 3 \times 7 = 2 \times 3^2 \times 7$
 b. $308 = 2 \times 2 \times 7 \times 11 = 2^2 \times 7 \times 11$
 c. $245 = 5 \times 7 \times 7 = 5 \times 7^2$
 d. $442 = 2 \times 13 \times 17$
3. 1,000,000,000 has a unique factorization containing only 2s and 5s. Since there is no other factorization, 7 is not a factor.
5. a. 1, 2, 5, 10   **b.** 1   **c.** 1, 2, 7, 14   **d.** 1
7. a. 28, 56, 84, 112, 140   **b.** 24, 48, 72, 96, 120
 c. 204, 408, 612, 816, 1020   **d.** 350, 700, 1050, 1400, 1750
9. a. Common factors
 b. 6 is a common factor of the length of both rods
11. a. 105 seconds
 b. If you started counting after the lights flashed together, there would be a gain in population of 8 people.
 c. 2835 seconds, which is less than an hour
 d. If you started counting after the lights flashed together, there would be 405 births, 189 deaths and 35 immigrants. This would be a gain in population of 251 people.
 e. 56,700 seconds, or 945 minutes, or 15.75 hours
13. a. 12 cookies   **b.** 25 piles   **c.** 22 piles
15. 150 minutes later, or at 7:30
17. 24 (5 occurs as a factor 24 times and 2 occurs as a factor at least 24 times)
19. If Cindy and Nicole go together on the first day, then there will be 60 days out of 180 on which neither uses the club.

CHAPTER 4 TEST

1. a. False   **b.** True   **c.** True   **d.** False
2. a. 3|45   **b.** 12|60   **c.** 20|140   **d.** 17|102
3.
 a.
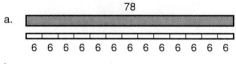
 b.
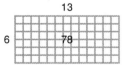
4. a. Exactly one array.
 b. Two or more arrays.
 c. One or more arrays, one of which is a square.
5. a. False   **b.** True   **c.** False   **d.** False
6. a. Prime   **b.** Composite   **c.** Composite
7. $1836 = 2^2 \times 3^3 \times 17$
8. 1, 3, 7, 13, 21, 39, 91, 273
9. a. True   **b.** False: $2|(5 + 7)$ but $2{\not|}5$ and $2{\not|}7$
 c. True   **d.** False: $2|3 \times 6$ but $2{\not|}3$
10. a. 1, 2, 5, 10
 b. The 4 smallest common multiples are 60, 120, 180, and 240.
 c. 1, 3, 5, 15
 d. The 5 smallest common multiples are 260, 520, 780, 1040, and 1300.
11. a. 1   **b.** 154   **c.** 420
 d. 5   **e.** 2   **f.** 390

12.
 a.
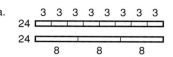
 b.
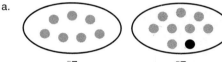
13. 60 seconds
14. 428
15. 14 inches

EXERCISES AND PROBLEMS 5.1

1. a. $^-17°$ **b.** $^-119°$
3. a. $^-3 + \boxed{1} = ^-2$ **b.** $^-14 + \boxed{17} = 3$
 $^-3 < ^-2$ $3 > ^-14$
 c. $^-7 + \boxed{8} = 1$
 $^-7 < 1$

5.
 a.
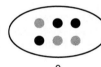
 b.
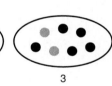
 c.
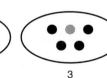

7.
 a.
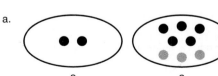
 b.
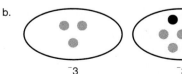

9.

a.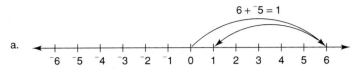

b.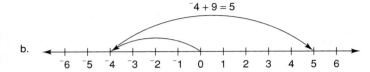

c.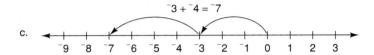

d.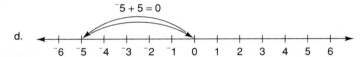

11. a. $^-14$ b. $^-4$ c. 2
    d. 3   e. 5   f. $^-11$
    g. $^-1$ h. $^-3$

13. a. Closed   b. Not closed
    c. Not closed   d. Closed

15. a. Divide 24 by 4 and multiply $^-25$ by 4: $24 \times {}^-25 = 6 \times {}^-100$
    $= {}^-600$
   b. Divide both numbers by 9: $^-90 \div 18 = {}^-10 \div 2 = {}^-5$
   c. Multiply 5 by 2 and divide $^-28$ by 2: $^-28 \times 5 = {}^-14 \times 10$
    $= {}^-140$
   d. Divide both numbers by 4: $400 \div {}^-16 = 100 \div {}^-4 = {}^-25$

17. a. $^-241 \div 60 \approx {}^-240 \div 60 = {}^-4$
   b. $64 \times {}^-11 \approx 64 \times {}^-10 = {}^-640$
   c. $26 + 59 \div {}^-3 \approx 26 + 60 \div {}^-3 = 6$
   d. $^-31 \times 19 \approx {}^-30 \times 20 = {}^-600$

19. a. $5 \times {}^-1 = {}^-5$
    $5 \times {}^-2 = {}^-10$
    $5 \times {}^-3 = {}^-15$
    A positive number times a negative number equals a negative number.
   b. $^-1 \times 6 = {}^-6$
    $^-2 \times 6 = {}^-12$
    $^-3 \times 6 = {}^-18$
    A negative number times a positive number equals a negative number.
   c. $^-3 \times {}^-1 = 3$
    $^-3 \times {}^-2 = 6$
    $^-3 \times {}^-3 = 9$
    A negative number times a negative number equals a positive number.

21. a. Compute $487 + 653$ and negate the answer:
    $^-487 + {}^-653 = {}^-(487 + 653) = {}^-1140$
   b. Compute $360 + 241$: $360 - {}^-241 = 360 + 241 = 601$
   c. Compute 32×14 and negate the answer:
    $32 \times {}^-14 = {}^-(32 \times 14) = {}^-448$
   d. Compute $336 \div 16$ and negate the answer:
    $336 \div {}^-16 = {}^-(336 \div 16) = {}^-21$

23. a. 51 days   b. 17 days and 17 hours   c. 29 hours

EXERCISES AND PROBLEMS 5.2

1. a. 2, 3, 4, and 8
   b.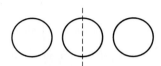
    $7\frac{1}{8}$, $7\frac{5}{8}$, $24\frac{1}{2}$, $27\frac{3}{4}$, $5\frac{1}{8}$, $11\frac{1}{4}$, $32\frac{7}{8}$, $27\frac{1}{4}$, $18\frac{1}{2}$, $21\frac{5}{8}$
   c. $\frac{57}{8}$, $\frac{61}{8}$, $\frac{49}{2}$, $\frac{111}{4}$, $\frac{41}{8}$, $\frac{45}{4}$, $\frac{263}{8}$, $\frac{109}{4}$, $\frac{37}{2}$, $\frac{173}{8}$

3. a. $3 \div 2 = 1\frac{1}{2}$

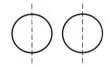

   b. $2 \div 4 = \frac{1}{2}$

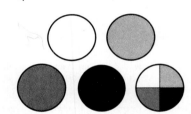

   c. $5 \div 4 = 1\frac{1}{4}$

5. a. $\frac{1}{3} = \frac{4}{12}$ b. $\frac{6}{12} = \frac{1}{2}$

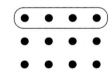

   c. $\frac{2}{3} = \frac{8}{12}$ d. $\frac{9}{12} = \frac{3}{4}$

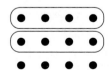

7. a. $\frac{2}{9}$ b. $\frac{4}{9}$ c. $\frac{1}{3}$ d. $\frac{^-2}{3}$

9.

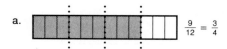

a. $\dfrac{9}{12} = \dfrac{3}{4}$

b. $\dfrac{4}{6} = \dfrac{2}{3}$

c. $\dfrac{4}{8} = \dfrac{1}{2}$

d. $\dfrac{8}{10} = \dfrac{4}{5}$

11. a. $\dfrac{3}{7} < \dfrac{5}{9}$ **b.** $\dfrac{1}{4} > \dfrac{1}{6}$ **c.** $\dfrac{-5}{6} > \dfrac{-7}{8}$

     d. $\dfrac{1}{4} > \dfrac{2}{9}$ **e.** $\dfrac{3}{8} > \dfrac{1}{3}$ **f.** $\dfrac{4}{7} > \dfrac{-5}{9}$

13. a. $1\dfrac{2}{3}$ **b.** 1   **c.** $4\dfrac{1}{6}$

     d. $^-3$ **e.** $3\dfrac{2}{5}$ **f.** 9

15.

a.

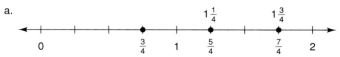

b.

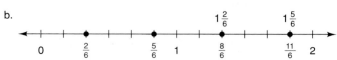

17. a. 0   **b.** 1   **c.** 4
     d. 1   **e.** $^-3$ **f.** 0

19. a. More iron   **b.** $\dfrac{7}{12}$ **c.** $\dfrac{40}{1040} = \dfrac{1}{26}$

21. a. Dow Ch, $44.38   **b.** RCA, up 12.5 cents
     Gen Elec, $52.75   Xerox, up 18.75 cents
     Gulf Oil, $25.88   Tyco Lb, down 25 cents
23. a. Alaska Airlines   **b.** Vintage Enterprise
     c. Less than the day's high

EXERCISES AND PROBLEMS 5.3

1. a. 32 inches   **b.** 18 inches   **c.** 5 inches
3. a. 15 objects are put in 3 groups of 5 objects. So ⅓ of 15 is 5.

     b. $\dfrac{3}{8} \times 24 = 9$

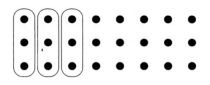

c. $\dfrac{2}{5} \times 30 = 12$

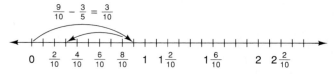

5. a. $1\dfrac{7}{8} - \dfrac{3}{5}$ is closest to $1\dfrac{2}{8}$ on the eighths line.

b.

$$1\dfrac{4}{5} - \dfrac{5}{8} \approx 1\dfrac{1}{5}$$

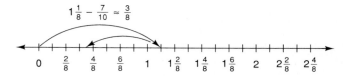

$$1\dfrac{1}{8} - \dfrac{7}{10} \approx \dfrac{3}{8}$$

$$\dfrac{9}{10} - \dfrac{3}{5} = \dfrac{3}{10}$$

c. $1\dfrac{4}{5} = 1\dfrac{32}{40}$ $1\dfrac{1}{8} = 1\dfrac{5}{40} = 1\dfrac{45}{40}$ $\dfrac{9}{10} = \dfrac{9}{10}$

     $-\dfrac{5}{8} = \dfrac{25}{40}$ $-\dfrac{7}{10} = \dfrac{28}{40} = \dfrac{28}{40}$ $-\dfrac{3}{5} = \dfrac{6}{10}$

     $1\dfrac{7}{40}$ $\dfrac{17}{40}$ $\dfrac{3}{10}$

7.

Number	$\dfrac{7}{8}$	$^-4$	$\dfrac{-1}{2}$	10
Negative	$\dfrac{-7}{8}$	4	$\dfrac{1}{2}$	$^-10$
Reciprocal	$\dfrac{8}{7}$	$\dfrac{-1}{4}$	$^-2$	$\dfrac{1}{10}$

9. a. Commutative property for addition
     b. Inverse for multiplication
     c. Associative property for addition
     d. Commutative property for multiplication
     e. Distributive property
     f. Inverse for addition

11. a. $\left(6\dfrac{1}{3} - 2\dfrac{2}{3}\right) + \left(5\dfrac{1}{2} + 1\dfrac{1}{2}\right) = 3\dfrac{2}{3} + 7 = 10\dfrac{2}{3}$

     b. $\left(5\dfrac{5}{8} - 1\dfrac{1}{8}\right) + 2\dfrac{1}{2} = 4\dfrac{4}{8} + 2\dfrac{1}{2} = 7$

     c. $\left(\dfrac{-1}{3} \times 12\right) \times \left(\dfrac{2}{5} \times 20\right) = {}^-4 \times 8 = {}^-32$

     d. $\dfrac{7}{4} \times \overset{6}{24} + 8 = 50$

13. a. Equal differences $\left(\text{Add } \dfrac{1}{7} \text{ to both}\right)$:

$$8 - 3\frac{6}{7} = 8\frac{1}{7} - 4 = 4\frac{1}{7}$$

b. Adding up:

$$\frac{1}{10} \qquad 4\frac{3}{10}$$

$$10\frac{9}{10} \curvearrowright 11 \curvearrowright 15\frac{3}{10}$$

So $15\dfrac{3}{10} - 10\dfrac{9}{10} = 4\dfrac{4}{10}$

c. Equal differences $\left(\text{Add } \dfrac{1}{4} \text{ to both}\right)$:

$$7\frac{1}{8} - 3\frac{3}{4} = 7\frac{3}{8} - 4 = 3\frac{3}{8}$$

15. a. $4\dfrac{1}{3} \times 6\dfrac{1}{2}$

$$\approx 4 \times 6 + \frac{1}{3} \times 6 + \frac{1}{2} \times 4$$
$$= 24 + 2 + 2$$
$$= 28$$

b. $5\dfrac{1}{4} \times 8\dfrac{2}{5}$

$$\approx 5 \times 8 + \frac{1}{4} \times 8 + \frac{2}{5} \times 5$$
$$= 40 + 2 + 2$$
$$= 44$$

c. $3\dfrac{1}{4} \times 4\dfrac{2}{3}$

$$\approx 3 \times 4 + \frac{1}{4} \times 4 + \frac{2}{3} \times 3$$
$$= 12 + 1 + 2$$
$$= 15$$

d. $10\dfrac{1}{3} \times 6\dfrac{1}{2}$

$$\approx 10 \times 6 + \frac{1}{3} \times 6 + \frac{1}{2} \times 10$$
$$= 60 + 2 + 5$$
$$= 67$$

17. a. $\dfrac{23}{30}$

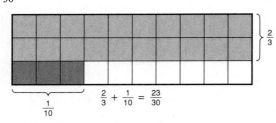

$$\frac{2}{3} + \frac{1}{10} = \frac{23}{30}$$

b. $5\dfrac{3}{10}$ ounces $\left(8\dfrac{1}{2} - 3\dfrac{1}{5} = 5\dfrac{3}{10}\right)$

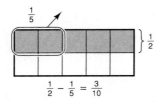

$$\frac{1}{2} - \frac{1}{5} = \frac{3}{10}$$

c. 8 million pounds

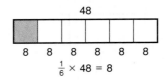

$$\frac{1}{6} \times 48 = 8$$

19. a. This sequence of steps will produce the correct answer because

$$80 \times \frac{3}{5} = (80 \times 3) \div 5$$

b. This sequence of steps will not produce the correct answer because

$$80 \div \frac{3}{5} \neq (80 \div 3) \div 5$$

21. a. $3\dfrac{5}{8}$ **b.** $16\dfrac{11}{16}$

c. Drew National, $1\dfrac{1}{4}$; MEM Company, $\dfrac{5}{8}$; Old Town, $1\dfrac{3}{8}$

d. \$625

23. a. D, E, A, B

b. The pairs of notes that are separated by black keys correspond to the pairs of strings in part a in which one string is 8/9 of the length of the other.

25. 24 students

CHAPTER 5 TEST

1. a.

$$8 \quad + \quad {}^-5 \quad = \quad {}^-3$$

b.

$${}^-7 - {}^-3 = {}^-4$$

c.

$$3 \times {}^-4 = {}^-12$$

d.

$${}^-20 \div {}^-4 = 5$$

e.

$$6 - 2 = 4$$

f.

$${}^-15 \div 3 = {}^-5$$

a.

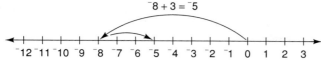

$$^-8 + 3 = ^-5$$

b.

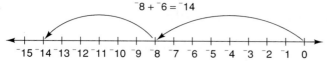

$$^-8 + ^-6 = ^-14$$

3. a. 42   **b.** ⁻6   **c.** ⁻80   **d.** 5

4. a. $^-16 \times 25 = ^-4 \times 4 \times 25 = ^-4 \times 100 = ^-400$
  b. $800 \div ^-16 = 200 \div ^-4 = 100 \div ^-2 = ^-50$

5. a. $^-271 \div 30 \approx ^-270 \div 30 = ^-9$

  b. $\dfrac{1}{8} \times 55 \approx \dfrac{1}{8} \times 56 = 7$

  c. $4 \times 6\dfrac{1}{5} \approx 4 \times \left(6 + \dfrac{1}{4} \right) = 24 + 1 = 25$

  d. $11 \times ^-34 \approx 10 \times ^-35 = ^-350$

6. a. $6 \div 4 = 1\dfrac{1}{2}$

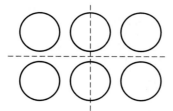

  b. $\dfrac{1}{3} \times 15 = 5$

  c. $\dfrac{2}{3} \times \dfrac{1}{5} = \dfrac{2}{15}$

  d. $\dfrac{3}{4} = \dfrac{6}{8}$

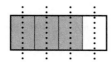

7. a. $\dfrac{3}{14} = \dfrac{24}{112}$ **b.** $\dfrac{1}{24} = \dfrac{1}{24}$

     $\dfrac{5}{16} = \dfrac{35}{112}$ $\dfrac{^-7}{8} = \dfrac{^-21}{24}$

8. a. $\dfrac{6}{11} < \dfrac{5}{9}$ **b.** $\dfrac{3}{5} > \dfrac{6}{11}$ **c.** $\dfrac{^-4}{9} < \dfrac{^-3}{7}$

9. a. ⅛ > ¹⁄₁₀. For two figures of the same size, 1 out of 10 equal parts is less than 1 out of 8 equal parts.
  b. ⁴⁄₇ > ⁵⁄₁₂. ⁴⁄₇ is greater than ½, ⁵⁄₁₂ is less than ½.
  c. ½ < ⁷⁄₁₂. ⁷⁄₁₂ is greater than ⁶⁄₁₂ = ½.
  d. ⁵⁄₆ < ⅞. A whole with ⅛ missing is greater than a whole with ⅙ missing.

10. a. $6\dfrac{1}{2}$ **b.** $4\dfrac{7}{15}$ **c.** $8\dfrac{7}{24}$ **d.** $5\dfrac{11}{30}$

11. a. $14\dfrac{1}{4}$ **b.** $4\dfrac{12}{85}$ **c.** $-9\dfrac{1}{3}$ **d.** 4

12. a. Inverse for multiplication
  b. Distributive property
  c. Commutative property for multiplication
  d. Inverse for addition

13. a. False   **b.** True   **c.** True
  d. False   **e.** False

14. a. 210 inches or 17.5 feet   **b.** $1\dfrac{3}{5}$ inches

15. $3\dfrac{1}{3}$ hours

EXERCISES AND PROBLEMS 6.1

1. a. .001   **b.** .000001   **c.** .000000001
3. a. 7/100   **b.** 6/10,000   **c.** 3/1000   **d.** 9/10
5. a. Three hundred forty-seven and ninety-six hundredths dollars
  b. Twenty-three and fifty hundredths dollars
  c. One thousand one hundred forty-four and 3 hundreths dollars
7. a. .40; a square with 100 equal parts, 40 of which are shaded
  b. .470; a square with 1000 equal parts, 470 of which are shaded
  c. .3; a square with 10 equal parts, 3 of which are shaded
  d. .27; a square with 100 equal parts, 27 of which are shaded
9. a. 247   **b.** 2.47   **c.** 24.7
11. a. .375   **b.** .0875   **c.** .95   **d.** 1.25
13. The fractions in a, b, e, and f have repeating decimals. The fractions in c and d have terminating decimals.
15. a. .5̄   **b.** 1.75   **c.** .625
17. $\dfrac{19}{34}, \dfrac{11}{17}, \dfrac{38}{52}, \dfrac{16}{20}, \dfrac{21}{25}$
19. a–e. .07 is the smallest. Its decimal square has 7 parts shaded out of 100. The decimal square for .08 has 8 parts shaded out of 100; and the decimal square for .075 has 75 parts shaded out of 1000 or $7\frac{1}{2}$ parts shaded out of 100. The decimal square for .3 has 3 parts shaded out of 10 of 30 parts shaded out of 100. 1.003 is represented by 1 whole shaded square and 3 parts shaded out of 1000.
  f. Students may have believed that the more decimal places there are, the smaller the decimal.
21. a. 17.3, 16.3, 15.9, 28.1, 22.6   **b.** Knees   **c.** .85
23. a. .0625   **b.** .0938   **c.** .1094   **d.** .5469
25. a. 6.47 feet   **b.** 7.77 feet   **c.** 6.92 feet

EXERCISES AND PROBLEMS 6.2

1. a. ⁻11.9° C   **b.** 4.4° C (⁻11.9 − ⁻16.3)

3. a.

$$
\begin{array}{r}
\overset{1}{4.821} \\
+\ 61.73 \\
\hline
66.551
\end{array}
\qquad
\frac{8}{10} + \frac{7}{10} = \frac{15}{10} = \frac{10}{10} + \frac{5}{10} = 1 + \frac{5}{10}
$$

b.

$$
\begin{array}{r}
\overset{2}{.367} \\
.015 \\
+\ .509 \\
\hline
.891
\end{array}
\qquad
\frac{7}{1000} + \frac{5}{1000} + \frac{9}{1000} = \frac{21}{1000} = \frac{20}{1000} + \frac{1}{1000}
$$
$$
= \frac{2}{100} + \frac{1}{1000}
$$

c. The 10 tenths are used to increase the 4 in the tenths column to 14 tenths.

$$
\begin{array}{r}
\overset{5}{6\cancel{6}.43} \\
-\ 41.72 \\
\hline
24.71
\end{array}
\qquad
6 = 5 + 1 = 5 + \frac{10}{10}
$$

d. The 10 thousandths are used to increase the 6 in the thousandths column to 16 thousandths.

$$
\begin{array}{r}
\overset{3}{.0\cancel{4}6} \\
-\ .018 \\
\hline
.028
\end{array}
\qquad
\frac{4}{100} = \frac{3}{100} + \frac{1}{100} = \frac{3}{100} + \frac{10}{1000}
$$

5. a. 24.96; multiply 32 times 78 and count off 2 decimal places.
   b. 6.43; divide 141.46 by 22.
   c. 4.8; divide 14.4 by 3.
   d. .1116; multiply 12 times 93 and count off 4 decimal places.

7. a. $\dfrac{5}{9}$ **b.** $\dfrac{14}{99}$ **c.** $\dfrac{217}{999}$

9. a. Compute $9 \times 6 = 54$ and count off 1 decimal place to obtain 5.4.
   b. Move the decimal point in 5.8 a total of 3 places to the left to obtain .0058.
   c. Compute $3.5 \times 100 = 350$ and subtract 3.5 to obtain 346.5.
   d. Add 6 thousandths to both numbers to obtain $.343 - .300$ and then subtract .300 to obtain .043.
   e. Compute $4.2 + .8 = 5.0$ and then add .1 to obtain 5.1.
   f. Compute $2.6 \times 100 = 260$ and add 2.6 to obtain 262.6.

11. a. Front-end estimation: $90, rounding to leading digit: $110
   b. Front-end estimation: $1300, rounding to leading digits: $1500
   c. Front-end estimation: $300, rounding to leading digit: $400
   d. Front-end estimation: $40, rounding to leading digit: $40

13. a. $8 \div .5 = 16$ **b.** $11.60 + .4 = 12$
   c. $\dfrac{1}{3} \times 120 = 40$ **d.** $\dfrac{1}{4} \times 80 = 20$

15. a. The 2 should have been written in the tenths column and the 1 in the ones column.
   b. The 6 in the hundredths column was not subtracted (possibly zero was subtracted from 6). This error caused a subsequent error in the tenths column.
   c. The decimal point in the product was placed under the decimal point in the two given numbers. Perhaps 1 decimal place was counted off rather than 2.
   d. The remainder of 2 was recorded in the quotient.

17. a. $.41\overline{6}$ **b.** $2.08\overline{3}$ **c.** 217.3913
19. a. $12.66   **b.** $3.76

---

21. a. 4 minutes and 11.76 seconds
   b. If this rate could be maintained, it would take 3 minutes and 58.52 seconds to swim 400 meters. This is 11.37 seconds faster than Thumer's time.
   c. 2.31 seconds
23. a. .5 cent   **b.** $325   **c.** $3250   **d.** $2925

EXERCISES AND PROBLEMS 6.3

1. a. $\dfrac{4}{5}$ **b.** 2,250,000

3. a. $7.28   **b.** $6.65   **c.** $1.40
5. a. 60% (60 parts shaded out of 100)
   b. 6% (6 parts shaded out of 100)
   c. 25.6% (25 and 6 tenths parts shaded out of 100 or 256 parts shaded out of 1000)
   d. .3% (3 tenths of a part shaded out of 100 or 3 parts shaded out of 1000)
7. a. 43.2   **b.** 20%   **c.** 40   **d.** 91   **e.** 150%
9. a. 10% of $42 is $4.20, and half of this is $2.10. So 15% of 42 is $4.20 + $2.10 = $6.30.
   b. 25% of 28 is $1/4 \times 28 = 7$.
   c. $33\frac{1}{3}$% of 15 is $1/3 \times 15 = 5$.
   d. 10% of $42.60 is $4.26, so 5% of 42.60 is $2.13.
   e. To determine 10% of $128.50, move the decimal point 1 place to the left to obtain $12.85.
   f. 75% of 32 is $3/4 \times 32 = 24$.
   g. 10% of $60 is $6, so 90% of $60 is $54.
   h. 10% of 80 is 8, so 110% of 80 is 88.

11. a. $\dfrac{14}{27} \approx \dfrac{14}{28} = 50\%$ **b.** $\dfrac{9}{38} \approx \dfrac{9}{36} = 25\%$

   c. $\dfrac{7}{32} \approx \dfrac{8}{32} = 25\%,\ \dfrac{7}{32} \approx \dfrac{7}{35} = 20\%$ **d.** $\dfrac{2}{19} \approx \dfrac{2}{20} = 10\%$

   e. $\dfrac{408}{1210} \approx \dfrac{400}{1200} = 33\dfrac{1}{3}\%$ **f.** $\dfrac{100}{982} \approx \dfrac{100}{1000} = 10\%$

13. a. $59.97   **b.** 20%   **c.** $34,400   **d.** 78.6%
15. a. .0000000012   **b.** 31,556,900   **c.** 635,000,000,000
17. a. Approximately 3.9 cents per ounce
   b. The large box   **c.** Approximately 77 pancakes
19. a. Alabama, 30.5 to 1; Florida, 27.3 to 1; Hawaii, 23.4 to 1; Iowa, 23.1 to 1; Maine, 22.2 to 1; Missouri, 23.0 to 1; Oregon, 21.4 to 1; Wyoming, 22.6 to 1
   b. Oregon has the best student-teacher ratio.
   c. Alabama has the poorest student-teacher ratio.
21. The identity property for multiplication in the first equation and the distributive property for multiplication over addition in the second equation.
   a. $178.08   **b.** $123.16   **c.** $61.92
23. a. $13.70   **b.** $28.77   **c.** 1276.28 pounds
25. Mercury: 36,002,000; .4 unit
   Venus: 6.7273×10^7; .7 unit
   Earth: 93,003,000; 1.0 unit
   Mars: 1.41709×10^8; 1.5 units
   Jupiter: 483,881,000; 5.2 units
   Saturn: 8.87151×10^8; 9.5 units
   Uranus: 1,784,838,000; 19.2 units
   Neptune: 2.796693×10^9; 30.1 units
   Pluto: 3,669,699,000; 39.5 units

27. 0, 3, 6, 12, 24, 48, 96
.4, .7, 1.0, 1.6, 2.8, 5.2, 10.0
a. 2.8 astronomical units
b. 19.6 astronomical units

EXERCISES AND PROBLEMS 6.4

1. The numbers in b and d are irrational.

3. a. $\dfrac{1}{4}$ **b.** 4   **c.** 3.1

d. 20   **e.** 25   **f.** $\dfrac{2}{3}$

5. a. $\sqrt{7} \approx 2.6$ **b.** $\sqrt[3]{30} \approx 3.1$ **c.** $\sqrt{3} \approx 1.7$

7.

	Whole numbers	Integers	Rational numbers	Real numbers
$^-3$		✓	✓	✓
$\dfrac{1}{8}$			✓	✓
$\sqrt{3}$				✓
π				✓
14	✓	✓	✓	✓
$\dfrac{1.6}{4}$			✓	✓
$.\overline{82}$			✓	✓

9. a. Commutative property for multiplication
b. Distributive property
c. Commutative property for addition
d. Associative property for addition
e. Inverse property for multiplication

11. a. $3\sqrt{5}$ **b.** $4\sqrt{3}$ **c.** $2\sqrt{15}$

13. a. $\dfrac{4\sqrt{7}}{7}$ **b.** $\dfrac{\sqrt{6}}{4}$ **c.** $\sqrt{5}$ **d.** $\dfrac{^-\sqrt{2}}{2}$

15. 217 steps
17. 13 feet
19. 17.0 by 17.0 inches
21. a. 1.5 hours
b. In this position the satellite takes approximately 24 hours to make 1 orbit of the earth. Therefore, the satellite stays in the same position relative to the earth.
23. a. Here are the first eight ratios for consecutive pairs of Fibonacci numbers: 1, 2, 1.5, 1.$\overline{6}$, 1.6, 1.625, 1.6153846, 1.6190476, 1.6176471
b. $233 \div 144 \approx 1.6180556$

CHAPTER 6 TEST

1. a. The decimal square for .4 has 4 full columns shaded, but the decimal square for .27 has less than 3 full columns shaded.
b. The decimal square with 7 parts shaded out of 10 has the same amount of shading as the decimal square with 70 parts shaded out of 100.
c. The decimal square for .225 has less than 3 full columns shaded, but the decimal square for .35 has more than 3 full columns shaded.
d. The decimal square for .09 has less than 1 full column shaded, but the square for .1 has 1 full column shaded.
2. a. .75   **b.** .07   **c.** .$\overline{6}$
d. .875   **e.** .$\overline{4}$ **f.** .24
3. a. $\dfrac{278}{1000}$ **b.** $\dfrac{35}{99}$ **c.** $\dfrac{3}{100}$
4. a. .88   **b.** .4   **c.** .510   **d.** .6667
5. a. 1.3: The total amount of shading in 2 squares, one with 6 columns shaded out of 10 and one with 7 columns shaded out of 10, is 13 shaded columns, or 1 completely shaded square and 3 shaded columns.
b. 1.2: The total amount of shading in 3 squares, each with 4 columns shaded out of 10, is 12 shaded columns, or 1 completely shaded square and 2 shaded columns.
c. .14: If a square has 62 parts shaded out of 100, and 48 of the shaded parts are taken away, 14 parts shaded out of 100 remain.
d. 16: If a square has 80 parts shaded out of 100, and 5 of the 80 shaded parts are removed at a time, the process can be done 16 times, or the 80 shaded parts can be divided into 16 groups, each containing 5 shaded parts.
6. a. .186   **b.** .0496   **c.** .703   **d.** 319
7. a. Move the decimal point in .073 a total of 2 places to the right to obtain 7.3.
b. Compute $7 \times 6 = 42$ and count off 1 decimal place to obtain 4.2.
c. Move the decimal point in 4.9 a total of 3 places to the left to obtain .0049.
d. Move the decimal point in 372 a total of 2 places to the left to obtain 3.72.
e. 10% of 260 is 26, and half of this is 13. So 15% of 260 is $26 + 13 = 39$.
f. 25% of 36 is $1/4 \times 36 = 9$.

8. a. $\dfrac{1}{2} \times 310 = 155$ **b.** $\dfrac{1}{4} \times 416 = 104$

c. $\dfrac{1}{3} \times 60 = 20$ **d.** $\dfrac{3}{4} \times 40 = 30$

9. a. 16.6   **b.** 37.5%   **c.** 62.5
d. 147.5   **e.** 140%
10. a. 4.378×10^2 **b.** 1.06×10^{-4}
11. a. Irrational   **b.** Rational   **c.** Irrational
d. Irrational   **e.** Rational   **f.** Irrational
12. a. 5.8   **b.** 2.6
13. a. Closed by the closure property for rational numbers
b. Not closed ($\sqrt{2} \times \sqrt{8} = 4$)
c. Not closed ($^-\sqrt{3} + \sqrt{3} = 0$)
14. a. $9\sqrt{5}$ **b.** $2\sqrt{6}$
15. a. $2\sqrt{13}$ **b.** $\sqrt{319}$
16. $220
17. 16-ounce glass
18. 67.1 feet
19. $7.20
20. 15,664 students

EXERCISES AND PROBLEMS 7.1

1. **a.** 70°   **b.** It remains the same.
3. **a.** Point, line, plane
   b. Collinear, half-plane, segment, ray, angle, half-line
   c. To avoid circularity
5. **a.** Angles *G, I,* and *J*   **b.** Angles *A, C, D,* and *F*
   c. Angles *B* and *E*   **d.** Angle *H*
7. **a.** Diameter $\overline{CD}$ ⊥ chord $\overline{RS}$.
   b. Line ℓ is tangent to radius $\overline{OD}$.
   c. Chords $\overline{AB}$ and $\overline{CD}$ bisect each other.

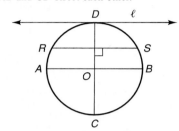

9. **a.** Simple   **b.** None of these
   c. Closed   **d.** Simple closed
   e. None of these
11. **a.** 90°   **b.** 60°
13. **a.** False; a parallelogram that is not a rectangle will have one diagonal longer than the other.
    b. True   **c.** True   **d.** True
    e. False; the resulting figure will be a parallelogram if the rectangle is not a square.
    f. True
15. 4851
17. **a.** Yes   **b.** No
19. **a.** No   **b.** No   **c.** No   **d.** Yes
21. Use $\overline{CD}$ as one side of the triangle and fold point *D* onto the center line to point *E* so that $CD = CE$. Then $\triangle CDE$ is an equilateral triangle.

EXERCISES AND PROBLEMS 7.2

1. **a.** Hexagons; no, they are not regular.
   b. Hexagons and heptagons
3. **a.** Regular polygon
   b. All angles are not congruent and all sides are not congruent.
   c. All sides are not congruent.
   d. All angles are not congruent.
   e. All angles are not congruent and all sides are not congruent.
   f. All angles are not congruent.
5.

No. of sides	3	4	5	6	7	8	9	10	20	100
Central angle	120°	90°	72°	60°	51.4°	45°	40°	36°	18°	3.6°

7. **a.** Pentagon   **b.** Hexagon   **c.** Hexagon
9. **a.** False; a trapezoid with two adjacent 90° angles, one acute angle, and one obtuse angle will have opposite angles whose sum is not 180°.
   b. True
   c. False; if three diagonals are drawn from one vertex of a regular hexagon, one will be longer than the other two.
   d. True

e. True
f. False; beginning with an isosceles triangle whose sides are 20 inches, 20 inches, and 1 inch and connecting the midpoints of the sides will produce a triangle with one side that is shorter than the other two sides.
11. The measure of each vertex angle must be a factor of 360.
13.

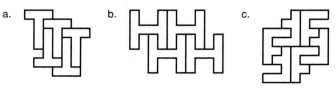

15. **a.** Not semiregular; some vertices are surrounded by 2 squares and 3 triangles, and other vertices are surrounded by 2 squares, 1 triangle, and 1 hexagon.
    b. Semiregular; each vertex has the same arrangement of polygons.
17. There are 6 semiregular tessellations that each use 2 regular polygons. The arrangements of the polygons are octagon, octagon, square; dodecagon, dodecagon, equilateral triangle; square, square, equilateral triangle, equilateral triangle, equilateral triangle; square, equilateral triangle, square, equilateral triangle, equilateral triangle; hexagon and 4 equilateral triangles; and hexagon, equilateral triangle, hexagon, equilateral triangle. In addition to the one in part (a) of Figure 7.38, there is another semiregular tessellation that uses 3 regular polygons. It is shown in part b of #15.
19. The word LOVE

EXERCISES AND PROBLEMS 7.3

1. **a.** Hexagon   **b.** Hexagonal prisms
3. **a.** Nonconvex   **b.** Convex   **c.** Convex
5. **a.** Pentagonal pyramid   **b.** Cone (or right cone)
   c. Hexagonal prism   **d.** Square pyramid
   e. Cylinder (or right cylinder)   **f.** Triangular prism
7. **a.** *ABCDEF*   **b.** *GLFA*   **c.** 90°   **d.** 120°
9. **a.** Three near the top of the tower and two on the front part of the building
   b. Roof of the tower
   c. Two columns up the sides of the tower
   d. Light globe in front of the building
   e. Circumference of the clock
   f. Hands of the clock
   g. Windows
   h. Windows on the right and left sides of the front of the building
   i. Windows below the clock
   j. Edges of the roof of the tower
11. **a.** (20°S, 60°E)   **b.** (30°N, 100°W); the United States
13. **a.** Pentagon   **b.** Rectangle
    c. Circle   **d.** Circle
15. *CFGH, AEFH, ABCF,* and *ACDH*
17.   **a.**

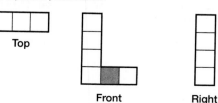

b.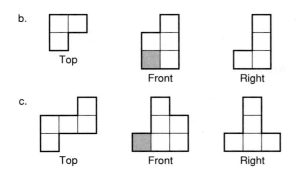
Top   Front   Right

c.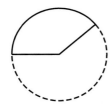
Top   Front   Right

19. a. Roll up a rectangular sheet of paper and tape the opposite edges.
b. Cut out and roll up a sector of a disc and tape the radii.

c. Hold the right cylinder from part a at an angle, dip the ends at the same angle into a liquid, and cut off the moistened part. Cutting along the taped edges produces the following pattern.

21. a. The number of faces in a cube equals the number of vertices in an octahedron, and the number of faces in an octahedron equals the number of vertices in a cube.
b. The dodecahedron and icosahedron are duals.
c. A tetrahedron
23. a. No
b. Angle 1 is largest. Angles 2 and 3 are right angles.

EXERCISES AND PROBLEMS 7.4

1. a. The left hedge and right hedge; the window in the left turret and the window in the right turret; the center arch and itself; the arches on the left and the arches on the right; the surface of the pool and itself. In general, nearly every object to the left of the center of the picture has a corresponding object to the right.
b. The trees and the rectangular window on the right side of the fortress do not have images. There are other windows and openings on the fortress that do not have images for the vertical plane of symmetry.
c. The rectangular window on the right side of the fortress and the surface of the pool have horizontal lines of symmetry.
3. a. 2 lines of reflection and 2 rotation symmetries
b. 5 lines of reflection and 5 rotation symmetries
c. 6 lines of reflection and 6 rotation symmetries
d. 23 lines of reflection and 23 rotation symmetries

5. a. 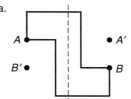   **b.**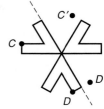

7. a. H, X, O, and I have 2 lines of symmetry.
b. N, S, and Z have 2 rotation symmetries but no lines of symmetry.
9. Figures d, f, and h have no lines of symmetry.
a. 2 lines of symmetry and 2 rotation symmetries, 180° and 360°
b. 1 line of symmetry
c. 3 lines of symmetry and 3 rotation symmetries, 120°, 240°, and 360°.
d. 2 rotation symmetries, 180° and 360°
e. 4 lines of symmetry and 4 rotation symmetries, 90°, 180°, 270°, and 360°
f. 3 rotation symmetries, 120°, 240°, and 360°
g. 4 lines of symmetry and 4 rotation symmetries, 90°, 180°, 270°, and 360°
h. 2 rotation symmetries, 180° and 360°

11. a. 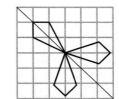   **b.**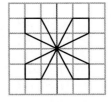

13. a. 16   **b.** 1   **c.** 2
15. 5 planes of symmetry and 5 rotation symmetries
17. a. 16   **b.** 2   **c.** 6   **d.** 5

EXERCISES AND PROBLEMS 7.5

1.

3.   RT 52 FD 70 RT 76 FD 70 HOME

5. Other answers are possible.

a.   FD 40 RT 45 FD 40 RT 80 FD 60
RT 120 FD 30 LT 110 FD 50 HOME

b.   FD 40 RT 45 FD 40 RT 30 FD 70
RT 90 FD 130 HOME

7.
   a. TO PENTAGON
        REPEAT 5 [FD 70 RT 72]
        END

   b. TO OCTAGON
        REPEAT 8 [FD 50 RT 45]
        END

   c. TO DODECAGON
        REPEAT 12 [FD 35 RT 30]
        END

9.
      REPEAT 10 [FLAG RT 36]

11.
   a. TO PETAL
        ARC RT 90 ARC RT 90
        END

   b. TO FLOWER
        REPEAT 8 [PETAL RT 45]
        END

13.
   PENUP BK 10 RT 90 BK 10 LT 90
   PENDOWN REPEAT 4 [FD 20 RT 90]
   PENUP BK 10 RT 90 BK 10 LT 90
   PENDOWN REPEAT 4 [FD 40 RT 90]
   PENUP BK 10 RT 90 BK 10 LT 90
   PENDOWN REPEAT 4 [FD 60 RT 90]

CHAPTER 7 TEST

1. **a.** (iv)   **b.** (iii)   **c.** (ii) and (iii)
   d. (i)   **e.** (vi)   **f.** (i) and (v)

2.   a.   b.

   c.   d.

3. **a.** C and E   **b.** D   **c.** B   **d.** A
4. **a.** True   **b.** True   **c.** False
   d. True   **e.** False
5. **a.** 45°   **b.** 120°   **c.** 72°
6. **a.** All angles are not congruent.   **b.** All sides are not congruent.
   c. All sides are not congruent.   **d.** All angles are not congruent.
7. **a.** No   **b.** Yes   **c.** Yes
   d. Yes   **e.** No

8. No. The measure of a vertex angle of a regular octagon is 135°, and 135 cannot be combined with multiples of 60 and 90 (the degrees in the angles of the triangle and the square) to equal 360.
9. **a.** Right pentagonal pyramid
   b. Right rectangular prism
   c. Right hexagonal prism
   d. Oblique cylinder
   e. Right cone
   f. Oblique triangular pyramid
10. **a.** Nonpolyhedron   **b.** Polyhedron
   c. Polyhedron   **d.** Nonpolyhedron
   e. Polyhedron   **f.** Polyhedron
11. **a.** 12   **b.** 24
12. **a.** An equilateral triangle

   b.

   c. A regular pentagon
13. **a.** 9   **b.** An infinite number   **c.** 5

14.

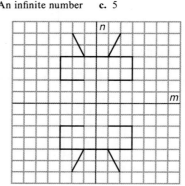

15. **a.** 2 lines of symmetry and 2 rotation symmetries
   b. 7 lines of symmetry and 7 rotation symmetries
   c. 3 lines of symmetry and 3 rotation symmetries
   d. 2 rotation symmetries

16.   REPEAT 8 [FD 55 RT 45]

17.

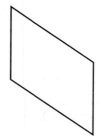

18. 21
19. 171°
20. **a.** 11   **b.** 56

EXERCISES AND PROBLEMS 8.1

1. a. 92 kph   **b.** 40 k   **c.** 60 mph
3. a. 202,500 g   **b.** 202,500,000 mg   **c.** 445 lb
5. a. $\frac{1}{32}$ in.   **b.** $\frac{1}{4}$ in.

   c. $\frac{11}{16}$ in.   **d.** $6\frac{3}{16}$ in.

   e. $8\frac{1}{2}$ in.

7. a. 1760 yd   **b.** 2.4 tons   **c.** 30 qt
   d. 4.2 yd   **e.** 3.5 lb
9. a. 200 cm   **b.** 75 kg   **c.** 48 L
   d. 450 mg   **e.** 300 m   **f.** 4 L
11.

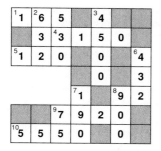

13. 11.6 kg
15. a. Rounding to the nearest multiple of 10 gives 40 + 30 + 50 + 40 + 30 = 190, and 1/3 of this is approximately $63.
   b. $63.36
17. 320 days; 5 cents per day
19. a. 7.2 cm³   **b.** 32 injections
21. a. Most cubits are less than 52.5 cm.
   b. Length: 158 m; breadth: 26 m; height: 16 m. Or length: 517 ft; breadth: 86 ft; height: 52 ft
23. a. 17 mm   **b.** 17/200 mm = .085 mm
   c. 85 μ   **d.** 85 times thicker
25. a. 111.5 kg to 112.5 kg   **b.** 38.15°C to 38.25°C
   c. 48.25 cm to 48.35 cm   **d.** 3.455 kg to 3.465 kg
27. a. 299,792,458 m   **b.** 299,792.458 km/sec   **c.** Yes
29. 16 cm

EXERCISES AND PROBLEMS 8.2

1. a. The width of these rectangles is greater than the width of the outstretched arms of the average adult, and the height of these rectangles is greater than the height of an average room.
   b. 106 m   **c.** 40 m   **d.** 4240 m²
3. a. Approximately 4/3 or $1\frac{1}{3}$ gum wrappers
   b. Approximately 4 plastic fasteners
5. a. 27,878,400 ft²   **b.** 640 acres   **c.** 671,360 acres
7. a. 10,000 ares   **b.** 100 hectares
9. 15.5 cm²
11. Type A
13. $8.28
15. Approximately 1428.6 m²
17. a. 90,675 cm²   **b.** Two rolls
19. 40 cm²
21. a. Square, 120 mm; circle, 120 mm   **b.** 246 mm²

23. a. 2.88×10^8 **b.** 17.4 directories
25. Approximately 31.8 cm by 31.8 cm
27. a. 982 m²   **b.** 125 m   **c.** 111 m
   d. 14 m   **e.** 3220 m²
29. 4 revolutions

EXERCISES AND PROBLEMS 8.3

1. a. 166,779 cm³   **b.** 1167.453 kg
3. a. 46,656 in.³   **b.** 1,000,000,000 mm³
5. a. 40 square units   **b.** 28 square units
   c. 54 square units   **d.** 68 square units
7. a. 12 cm³   **b.** 9.4 cm³   **c.** 12 cm³
   d. 60 cm³   **e.** 113.0 cm³   **f.** 196.3 cm³
9. a. 37.5 L   **b.** 1250 cm³   **c.** 12
11. 21,000 Btu units
13. Type B
15. a. About 25 times greater   **b.** About 5 times greater
17. a. 509 m³   **b.** 25 hr
19. a. 7.85 m²   **b.** 722.2 kg
21. 512 of the small cubes will be unpainted.

10 by 10 by 10 cube

No. of painted faces	3	2	1	0
No. of cubes	8	12 × 8	6 × 8²	8³

Here are the results for an *n* by *n* by *n* cube with $n \geq 2$.

No. of painted faces	3	2	1	0
No. of cubes	8	12(n − 2)	6(n − 2)²	(n − 2)³

23. a. 2 times greater   **b.** 4 times greater
   c. 2^{20} (more than 1 million)
25. a. 678 in.³   **b.** 8.8 in. ($\sqrt[3]{678} \approx 8.8$)

CHAPTER 8 TEST

1. a. Gram   **b.** Milliliter   **c.** Meter
   d. Kilogram   **e.** Square meter   **f.** Cubic meter
2. a. 12   **b.** 9   **c.** 13.6
   d. 32   **e.** 67.5   **f.** 16
3. a. 1000   **b.** 100   **c.** 5200
   d. 2.5   **e.** 160   **f.** 1,000,000
4. a. 1600   **b.** 0°   **c.** 55
   d. 2   **e.** 3/5   **f.** 2.2
5. a. Minimum, 5.25 kg; maximum, 5.35 kg
   b. Minimum, 84.5 g; maximum, 85.5 g
   c. Minimum, 4.115 oz; maximum, 4.125 oz
6. Area using unit (i): 26 square units; area using unit (ii): 6.5 square units
7. a. 21 cm²   **b.** 9 cm²
   c. 18 cm²   **d.** 12.56 cm²
8. 6.4 cm
9. a. 54 cm²   **b.** 16 cm²
10. Volume using unit (i): 18 cubic units; volume using unit (ii): 2.25 cubic units
11. a. 27 cm³   **b.** 54 cm³   **c.** 27 cm³
12. a. 1568 cm³   **b.** 4832.46 cm³
   c. 1230.88 cm³   **d.** 3990 cm³

13. a. 1522 cm²   **b.** 1582.56 cm²
    c. 2461.76 cm²   **d.** 896 cm²
14. 3.6 yd³
15. Type A
16. $478

EXERCISES AND PROBLEMS 9.1

1. a. 28.5   **b.** ⁻30   **c.** 49   **d.** ⁻16
3. a. Associative property for multiplication
   b. Distributive property
   c. Inverse property for addition and identity property for addition
   d. Identity property for multiplication and distributive property
   e. Associative property for multiplication, inverse property for multiplication, and identity property for multiplication
5. a. $6p = s$
   b. One possible reason for writing $6s = p$ is that the statement says, "6 times as many students."
7. a. 4 chips per box; $2x + 3 = 11$
   b. 3 chips per box; $3x + 8 = 5x + 2$
   c. 2 chips per box; $2x + 5 = 9$
9. a. Step 1: Addition property of equality
   Step 2: Simplification
   b. Step 1: Multiplication property of equality
   Step 2: Simplification
   c. Step 1: Simplification (distributive property)
   Step 2: Addition property of equality
   Step 3: Simplification
   d. Step 1: Simplification
   Step 2: Addition property of equality
   Step 3: Simplification
11. a. $x < {}^-4\frac{1}{2}$

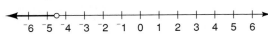

   b. $x > {}^-1$

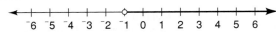

   c. $x > {}^-6$

   d. $x < 4$

13. a. .19x   **b.** $18 - x$ **c.** $.29(18 - x)$
   d. $.19x + .29(18 - x) = \$4.02$
   $x = 12$ Marci mailed 12 postcards.
15. a. 10.5x   **b.** $x + 3$ **c.** $8(x + 3)$
   d. $10.5x + 8(x + 3) < 120$
   $x < 5.189$
   Merle bought either 1, 2, 3, 4, or 5 compact discs.

17. a. Let x equal the amount of the paycheck.

$$60 + \frac{1}{2}(x - 60) + 80 = x$$
$$x = 220$$

The total paycheck is $220.
   b. Let x equal the length of a side of the square.

$$4x + 110 = 350$$
$$x = 60$$

A side of the square is 60 ft long.
19. a. Let x equal the unknown number.

$$14 + x < 3x$$
$$x > 7$$

The statement is true for any number greater than 7.
   b. Let x equal Frank's number of shells. Then Joni's number of shells is $76 - x$, which is greater than 3 times Frank's number.

$$76 - x > 3x$$
$$x < 19$$

Frank can have from 1 to 18 shells.
21. Let x equal an arbitrary number.
   Add 221:
   $x + 221$
   Multiply by 2652:
   $2652(x + 221) = 2652x + 586{,}092$
   Subtract 1326:
   $2652x + 586{,}092 - 1326 = 2652x + 584{,}766$
   Divide by 663:
   $$\frac{2652x + 584{,}766}{663} = 4x + 882$$
   Subtract 870:
   $4x + 882 - 870 = 4x + 12$
   Divide by 4:
   $$\frac{4x + 12}{4} = x + 3$$
   Subtract x:
   $(x + 3) - x = 3$
   Regardless of the original number, the result is always 3.
23. a. Discount and then tax:
   $[24 - .2(24)] + .05[24 - .2(24)] = \$20.16$
   Tax and then discount:
   $(24 + .05 \times 24) - .2(24 + .05 \times 24) = \$20.16$
   With either method the cost to the customer is $20.16.
   b. $(p - dp) + t(p - dp) = (p + tp) - d(p + tp)$
   $p - dp + tp - tdp = p + tp - dp - dtp$
25. $5[4(5m + 6) + 9] + d - 165$

$$= 5[20m + 24 + 9] + d - 165$$
$$= (100m + 165) + d - 165$$
$$= 100m + d$$

27. 3 nails
29. $A = 5$, $B = 1$, and $C = 2$, so there are 39 students in the class.

EXERCISES AND PROBLEMS 9.2

1. a. As the level of difficulty increases, the level of motivation decreases.
   b. Linear

3. a. $(4, {}^-3)$ **b.** $(4, 5)$ or $(2, {}^-1)$ or $({}^-10, 5)$ **d.** $y = {}^-5x$
 c. $(4, {}^-1)$ **d.** $(0, 2)$

5. a. $(1, 3.1), (2, 12.6), (3, 28.3), (4, 50.2), (5, 78.5)$
 b. No
 c. The set of positive real numbers
 d. The set of all positive real numbers
 e. $y = \pi x^2$

7. a. Slope $= 2$ **b.** Slope $= 0$
 c. Slope $= 5/11$ **d.** Slope $= 2$

9. a. $y = 3x$

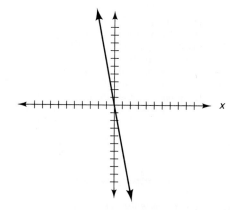

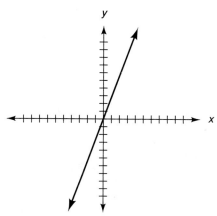

b. $y = {}^-3x + 8$

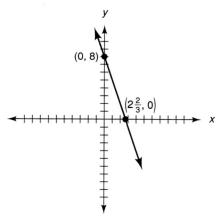

c. $y = 1.2x + 8.4$

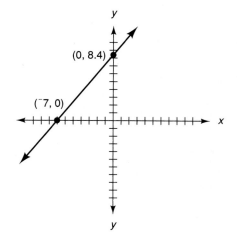

11. a. Slope of line i $= 10$; slope of line ii $= 1$; slope of line iii $= 1/2$
 b. Yes **c.** No **d.** Yes

13. a. $y = {}^-2x + 5$ **b.** $y = 4x + 16$ **c.** $x = {}^-8$

15. $y = 11x + 36$
 $x = 7, y = 113$

17. $y = 6x + 15$
 $x = 14, y = 99$

19. a. 4.68 seconds **b.** .12 second
 c. Approximately .68 second; this is a pulse rate of approximately 88 beats per minute.

21. The equation for this curve is $y = 8^x$, where x is the number of hours and y is the number of bacteria.

Time (hours)	No. of bacteria
1	8
2	64
3	512
4	4096
5	32,768
6	262,144

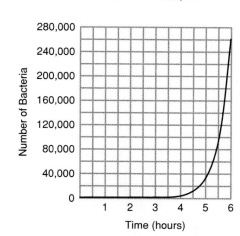

23. a. 1930: 120,000,000; 1950: 162,000,000
 b. 300,000,000

CHAPTER 9 TEST

1. a. Step 1: Distributive property
  b. Step 1: Associative property for multiplication
    Step 2: Inverse property for multiplication
    Step 3: Identity property for multiplication
  c. Step 1: Distributive property
    Step 2: Associative property for multiplication
  d. Step 1: Inverse property for addition
    Step 2: Identity property for addition

2. a. $2x + 12$ **b.** $x/6$ **c.** $7x + 3$

3. a. 7 chips   **b.** More than 2 chips

4. a. $x = 36$ **b.** $x = 12\frac{2}{9}$

5. a. $x < 11$ **b.** $x > 12.5$

6. a. Step 1: Multiplication property for equality
    Step 2: Simplification
  b. Step 1: Addition property for equality
    Step 2: Simplification

7. a. Function   **b.** Function
  c. Not a function   **d.** Function

8. a. (.1, .314), (1.2, 3.768), (2.5, 7.85), (3, 9.42)

b.

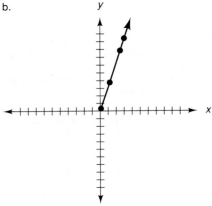

  c. $y = 3.14x$
  d. All positive real numbers
  e. All positive real numbers

9. a. $y = 6x - 2$

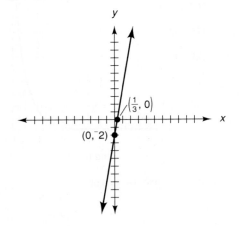

b. $3x - 5y = 10$

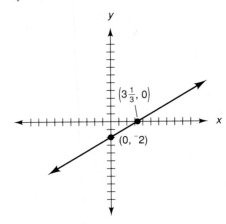

10. a. Slope $= {}^-3/5$ **b.** Slope $= 1/2$

11. $y = 15x - 22$

12. a. Slope is $1/3$; y-intercept is $(0, 5)$
  b. Slope is $^-4$; y-intercept is $(0, 11)$

13. a. $y = 55x + 120$ **b.** Slope $= 55$

14. $y = 4^x$ is an exponential function.

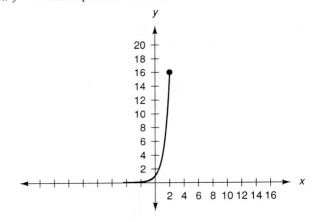

15. a. $24x$ **b.** $60 - x$
  c. $15(60 - x)$ **d.** 18 hours

EXERCISES AND PROBLEMS 10.1

1. a. $\angle T$ **b.** $\angle D$ **c.** $\angle R$
  d. $\overline{DT}$ **e.** $\overline{TR}$ **f.** $\overline{DR}$
  g. $\triangle TDR$

3. **a.**

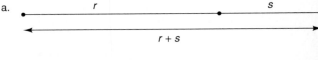

c.

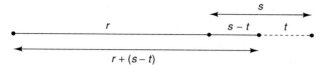

$$r + (s - t)$$

5. a. See steps for bisecting a line segment, page 497.
  b. See steps for bisecting an angle, page 499.
  c. See steps for constructing a perpendicular to a line through a given point, page 500.
  d. See steps for constructing a line parallel to a given line, page 501.
  e. Extend $\overline{RS}$ to point B; use a compass and locate point A so that $AS = SB$; use a compass to draw arcs intersecting at point D so that D is equidistant from A and B; $\overline{DS} \perp \overline{RS}$.

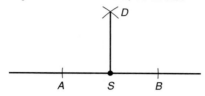

7. For all 4 polygons, construct the perpendicular bisector of any two sides of the polygon. Their intersection is the center of the circumscribed circle whose radius is the distance from the center to any vertex of the polygon.

9.
  a.   b.

  b. An infinite number of quadrilaterals can be constructed.

11.
  a.   b.

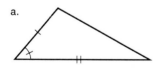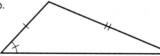

  b. This is one of two possibilities.
  c. No, the triangles are not congruent.
  d. Two sides and one angle of a triangle may be congruent to two sides and one angle of a second triangle and yet the triangles are not necessarily congruent.
13. a. $\triangle ABC \cong \triangle HMS$ by the SSS congruence property.
  b. $\triangle ABC$ is not necessarily congruent to $\triangle HMS$.
  c. $\triangle ABC \cong \triangle HMS$ by the SAS congruence property.
  d. $\triangle ABC$ is not necessarily congruent to $\triangle HMS$.
15. a. One of two possible points on line ℓ for each distance.

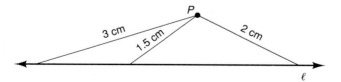

b. 1.1 cm
  c. The shortest distance from a point to a line is the length of the perpendicular line segment from the line to the point.
17. a, b, and **c.** The triangles are congruent by the SAS congruence property.
  d. The triangles are not necessarily congruent because the congruent angles are not the included angles for the pairs of congruent sides.
19. a. They are congruent.
  b. Since $\overline{RT} \cong \overline{ST}$, $\overline{RK} \cong \overline{SK}$, and $\overline{KT}$ is common to both triangles, $\triangle RKT \cong \triangle SKT$ by the SSS congruence property.
  c. Since $\triangle RKT \cong \triangle SKT$, the triangles are congruent, $\angle R \cong \angle S$ by corresponding parts.
21. To trisect right $\angle ABC$, open a compass to span $\overline{BC}$ and draw an arc with B as center. With the same compass opening, draw an arc with C as center and that intersects the first arc at point D. Then $\triangle BDC$ is an equilateral triangle and $\angle DBC$ has a measure of 60°. Bisecting this angle will provide a trisection of $\angle ABC$.

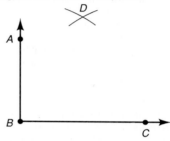

23. a. Since $\overline{AB} \cong \overline{CB}$, $\angle RAB$ and $\angle DCB$ are right angles, and $\angle RBA \cong \angle DBC$ (because they are vertical angles), the triangles are congruent by the ASA congruence property.
  b. CD can be measured, and by corresponding parts, $\overline{CD} \cong \overline{AR}$.

EXERCISES AND PROBLEMS 10.2

1. a. No   **b.** Yes   **c.** Translation mapping
3. a. 90°   **b.** The distances are equal.
  c. All points on ℓ
5. a. Over 6 and up 1   **b.** Quadrilateral $ABCD$
7.   a.

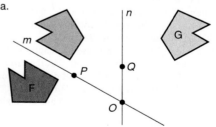

  b. The number of degrees in the angle of rotation is twice the number of degrees in $\angle POQ$.

9. a.   b.

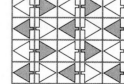

11. a. The centers of rotation are shown in the following figure.

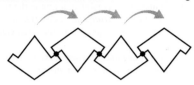

b. Reflections, or 180° rotations about the lower point of the figure.

13. a. Two, because a rhombus has rotation symmetries of 180° and 360°

b. Six: 3 rotation symmetries and 3 reflection symmetries

c. Sixteen: 8 rotation symmetries and 8 reflection symmetries

d. Four: 2 rotation symmetries (180° and 360°) and 2 reflection symmetries

e. Two rotation symmetries

f. Ten: 5 rotation symmetries and 5 reflection symmetries

15. a. See rotation tessellations, page 519.

b. See reflection tessellations, page 520.

c. See translation tessellations, page 518.

17. a. Reflection about line ℓ, which is the perpendicular bisector of any line segment whose endpoints are a point on the figure and its image

b. Translation

c. Rotation about point O, which is the intersection of the perpendicular bisectors of two line segments whose end points are pairs of points on the figure and their images

d. Rotation about point Q, which is the intersection of the perpendicular bisectors of $\overline{AA'}$ and $\overline{BB'}$.

19. a. A translation

b. A translation or horizontal reflection

c. A translation or vertical reflection

d. A translation

21. a. $D'(3,^-5)$, $E'(1,^-2)$, $F'(3,^-3)$, $G'(5,^-1)$

b. $D''(^-3,^-5)$, $E''(^-1,^-2)$, $F''(^-3,^-3)$, $G''(^-5,^-1)$

c. A 180° rotation about the origin

EXERCISES AND PROBLEMS 10.3

1. a. 2   **b.** $^-1/2$ **c.** 1/3   **d.** 4

3. For scale factors of 2, 3, and 1/2, the point (2, 6) is mapped to (4, 12), (6, 18), and (1, 3), respectively. In general, for a scale factor of k, point (a, b) will be mapped to (ka, kb).

5. Triangles b, c, and d are similar because the lengths of their corresponding sides are proportional. Note that the ratio of the lengths of pairs of legs in triangles b, c, and d is 1, whereas the ratio of the lengths of the legs in triangle a is 2/3 (or 3/2).

7. a. Similar (corresponding sides proportional and all angles 90°)

b. Not necessarily similar

c. Not necessarily similar

d. Similar (corresponding sides proportional and all angles 135°)

e. Similar (corresponding sides proportional and all angles 60°)

f. Not necessarily similar

g. Similar (the lengths of corresponding sides have a proportion of 1 and corresponding angles are congruent)

9. a. $\triangle ABC$ is similar to $\triangle AEF$. Therefore, $AB/AE = BC/EF = AC/AF$. Also, $\triangle ACD$ is similar to $\triangle AFG$, so $AD/AG = DC/GF = AC/AF$. All angles in both rectangles equal 90°. Therefore, the corresponding sides of $ABCD$ and $AEFG$ are proportional and their corresponding angles are equal.

b. Rectangle (iii) is similar to rectangle (iv).

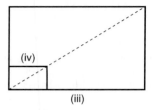

(iii)

11. a. Since there are 180° in every triangle, the third angles of these triangles are also congruent. Thus the triangles are similar by the AAA similarity property.

b. 14 m

13. a. Yes   **b.** Yes   **c.** All three images are congruent.

15. a. 64 square units   **b.** 144 square units   **c.** 4 square units

17.

Scale factor	Surface area (sq. units)	Volume (cubic units)
1	26	7
2	104	56
3	234	189
4	416	448
5	650	875

19. a. 10,000 times greater   **b.** 1,000,000 times greater

c. 3 m

21. a. Scale factor = 2

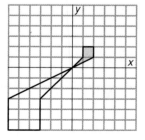

b. Scale factor = 1/2

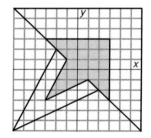

c. Scale factor = $^-3$

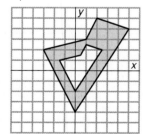

23. a. 3 **b.** 3/2 **c.** 1/5
  d. By multiplying the first 2 scale factors together
25. a. The original sheet is similar to the quarto with a scale factor of
    1/2, because the two adjacent edges of the original sheet were both
    folded in half to obtain the quarto; and the folio is similar to the
    octavo with a scale factor of 1/2 because two adjacent edges of the
    folio were both folded in half.
  b. Every other rectangle will be similar to the original sheet; and
    beginning with the folio, every other rectangle will be similar to the
    folio.
27. 2.3 times greater

EXERCISES AND PROBLEMS 10.4

1. a and g; b and h; c and f; d and e
3. a, e, and h; b and f; c and g; d and i
5. a. Traversable. Either odd vertex can be a beginning point.

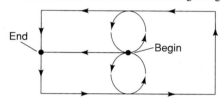

  b, d. Not traversable
  c, e, and **f.** Traversable. Any vertex can be a beginning point.
7. Yes, it is traversable.

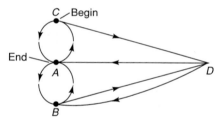

9. Floor plan a
11. Every network has an even number of odd vertices (0, 2, 4, . . .).
13. a. 4 **b.** 4
15. a. Isometric grids are traversable because all vertices are even, and
    any vertex may be a beginning point.
  b. Rectangular grids are not traversable because all vertices on the
    outer boundary are odd except for the corner vertices.
  c. The beginning point can be either of the two odd vertices; the
    ending point will be the other vertex.
  d. Remove 1 square from the 2 × 2 grid; remove 5 squares from the
    4 × 4 grid; remove 7 squares from the 5 × 5 grid.
  e. The number of squares to remove from a 10 × 10 grid is the
    ninth odd number, 17.
  f. The number of squares to remove from an $n \times n$ grid is the
    $(n - 1)$th odd number, $2n - 1$.
17. a. Figures (i), (ii), and (iv)
  b. There must be exactly zero, 1, or 2 regions with an odd number of
    sides.
19. Five

CHAPTER 10 TEST

1. a. Using any compass opening and A as center draw arcs
    intersecting the sides of ∠A in points B and C. With the same
    compass opening and points B and D as centers, draw intersecting
    arcs at point D. Line segment $\overline{DA}$ is the bisector.

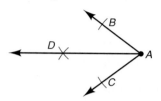

  b. Using the same compass opening and point Q as center, locate
    points A and B on line m so that $AQ = BQ$. With the same
    compass opening and A and B as centers, draw arcs intersecting at
    point D in one half-plane and point C in the other half-plane.
    Then line segment $\overline{DC} \perp m$.

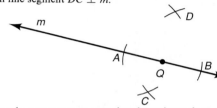

  c. Using the same compass opening throughout, draw arcs so that
    $PA = AB = BC = PC$, as shown in the following figure.
    Line $\overleftrightarrow{PC} \parallel \ell$.

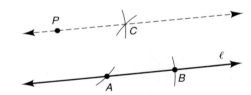

  d. With R as center, draw arcs intersecting line n so that
    $RA = RB$. With the same compass opening and A and B as
    centers, draw arcs intersecting at D so that $AD = BD$. Line
    segment $\overline{RD} \perp n$.

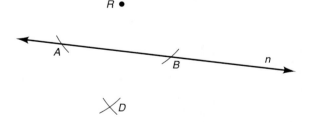

2. Construct the perpendicular bisectors of $\overline{BA}$ and $\overline{AC}$. The intersection
    of these bisectors is the center of the circle whose radius is the
    distance from the center to any vertex of the triangle.

3.   **a.**

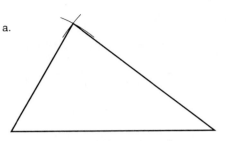

   b. A triangle cannot be constructed with the given segments because the sum of the lengths of the two shorter segments is less than the length of the third segment.

4. **a.** $\triangle ABC \cong \triangle DEC$ by the ASA congruence property
   b. $\triangle FGI \cong \triangle FHI$ by the SAS congruence property
   c. Since the two congruent angles are not included between the pairs of congruent sides, the triangles are not necessarily congruent.
   d. $\triangle RQT \cong \triangle TSR$ by the SSS congruence property

5.   **a.**

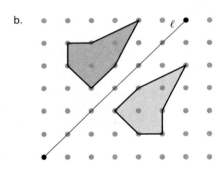

   b.

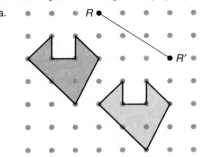

   c.

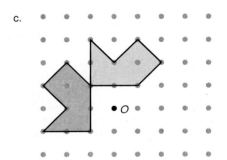

6. **a.** A counterclockwise rotation of 25°
   b. A translation twice the distance between lines ℓ and m
   c. A translation of P to the right 17 units and down 2 units

7. **a.** Scale factor of 2

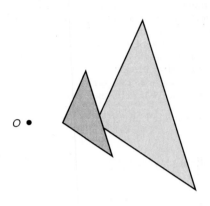

   b. Scale factor of 1/3

   c. Scale factor of ⁻1/2

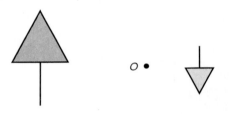

8. **a.** $\triangle BDC \sim \triangle AEC$ by the AAA similarity property
   b. $\triangle FGH \sim \triangle IJH$ by the AAA similarity property
   c. These triangles are not necessarily similar.
   d. $\triangle RST \sim \triangle WUV$ by the SSS similarity property
9. **a.** Not necessarily similar because sides need not be proportional.

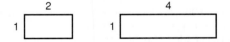

   b. Similar because corresponding sides are proportional and corresponding angles are congruent
   c. Not necessarily similar because sides need not be proportional, and all pairs of corresponding angles need not be congruent.

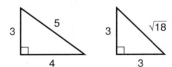

   d. Similar because corresponding sides are proportional and corresponding angles are congruent
   e. Similar because corresponding sides have a proportion of 1 and corresponding angles are congruent
10. **a.** 324 cubic units   **b.** 288 square units
   c. 1.5 cubic units   **d.** 8 square units

11. a and d; b and e; c and f

12. a. Not traversable   **b.** Not traversable

13. a. Yes. Begin outside and end in the room with the 5 doors at the lower left.

b. No

14. a. 7 in.   **b.** 1/2 qt   **c.** 48 lb

15. 27 ft

EXERCISES AND PROBLEMS 11.1

1.   Persons on Active Duty

a.

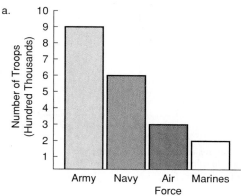

b.

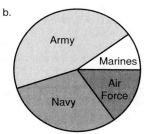

c. Army, 162°; Navy, 108°; Air Force, 54°; Marine Corps, 36°

3.   a.   Family's Monthly Budget

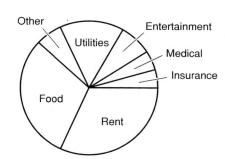

b. Rent, 115°; food, 108°; utilities, 54°; insurance, 14°; medical, 18°; entertainment, 29°; other, 22°

5.

a.   Percent Distribution of Elementary Schools According to Size (Student Enrollment)

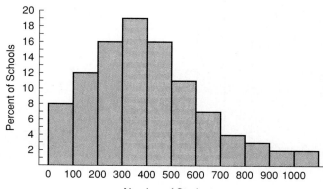

b. 51%   **c.** 29%

7. a.

Stem	Leaf
9	0 0
8	3 5 0 8
7	3 8 9 1 4 7 0 1 2 8
6	7 8 5 4 6 3 7 0 7 0 3 4
5	3 6 7 8 7
4	9 6

b. Approximately 14%   **c.** 20%

9. a.

Stem	Leaf
27	7
26	
25	1 3 0
24	6 6 6 2
23	8 4 1 2 0 0
22	3 5 7 0 1 0
21	8 6 5 6 0 4 2 2
20	2 5 3 1 6 4 0 8 1 6
19	3 7 0 9 7 8 1
18	2 2 1 6
17	0 2 3
16	6

b. The stem for 20   **c.** Greatest weight, 27.7 kg; least weight, 16.6 kg

11. a.

Interval	Frequency
20–29	11
30–39	4
40–49	9
50–59	5
60–69	3
70–79	3
80–89	0
90–99	1
100–109	1
110–119	1

b.

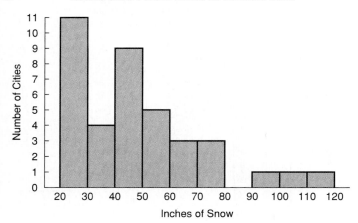

Record Snow Falls in Inches for Selected Cities

c. The interval 20–29   d. 14 cities

13. a.

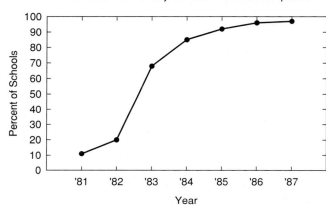

Percents of Elementary Schools with Microcomputers

   b. 1982   c. 1983
15. a. Mean, 41.5; median, 40; modes, 37, 40, and 48
   b. Mean, 38.35; median, 39; modes, 32 and 39
   c. National League
   d. National League
   e. National League
   f. 13 years
   g. The National League; all measures of central tendency are greater for the N.L. than for the A.L., and N.L. hitters hit more home runs in nearly two-thirds of the years listed.
17. a. United States, 923.2; France, 982.9; Japan, 779.1; Great Britain, 340.5
   b. Great Britain
   c. 16 reactors; 15 of these 21 countries have fewer than 16 reactors.
19. a. Set B   b. Set A: 4; set B: 2
   c. Yes. The data in set A are more spread out and have the greater standard deviation.
21. a. December and January
   b. January   c. Kansas City
   d. Kansas City, 2.93 in.; Portland, 3.12 in.
23. a. 16.5%   b. 7.5%   c. 10%   d. 14%
   e. The smallest difference was approximately 1%, and the largest difference was approximately 5%, so the range was 4%.

EXERCISES AND PROBLEMS 11.2

1. a. 8908 and 9042   b. 9176   c. Yes
3. Grade K, 10; grade 1, 16; grade 2, 18; grade 3, 16; grade 4, 20
5. a. Skewed to the right   b. Skewed to the left
   c. Skewed to the right   d. Symmetric
7. a. 68%   b. 16%   c. 2.5%   d. 81.5%
9. a. 16%   b. 5%
11. a. A normal distribution
   b.

Diameter (inches)	No. of trees
7	2
8	5
9	8
10	10
11	13
12	26
13	12
14	9
15	8
16	4
17	3

   c. 70%   d. 95%
13. a. 54%   b. 68%   c. 96%
   d. The score for mathematics comprehension
   e. A lower local percentile means that at the local level fewer students scored below the given student on a given subtest than at the national level.
15. a. Lower quartile, 3; median, 7; upper quartile, 10
   b. Lower quartile, 69; median, 74; upper quartile, 84
17. Test C, ⁻.53; test B, ⁻.14; test D, .82; test A, 1.86
19. a. The range is 44.
   b. The 2 lower quartiles are larger than the 2 upper quartiles; 50% of the values are above 81 and 25% are above 90.

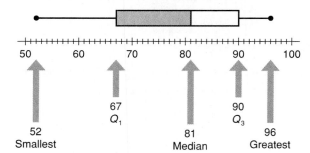

21. a.

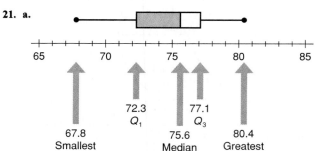

   b. 75.6%
   c. The median is closer to the upper quartile.
   d. The lower quartile of 72.3 means that in one-fourth of these 15 states, less than 72.3% of all students complete high school.

23. a. Approximately 11.4 boxes. Label each of 5 slips of paper with the name of a different color. Place the slips in a container and randomly select 1 at a time (with replacement). Compute the average number of selections needed to obtain all 5 colors.

b. The average number of tosses before 10 heads can be expected is 20. Using a table of random numbers, choose even numbers for heads and odd numbers for tails. Count sequences until 10 heads are obtained and then compute the average number of digits in each sequence.

c. The average number of children a couple must have to be sure of having a child of each sex is 3. Label one slip of paper "boy" and one slip of paper "girl." Place them in a container and randomly select 1 at a time (with replacement). Compute the average number of selections required to select each slip of paper once.

25. The top graph gives the impression of substantial increases in sales from 1986 to 1991, whereas the bottom graph gives the impression of slight increases. The top graph is misleading; it suggests that sales doubled from 1987 to 1988 and from 1988 to 1990. The bottom graph better illustrates the true sales increases.

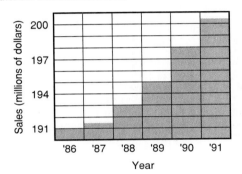

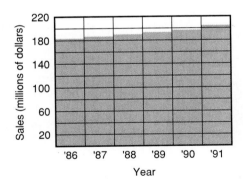

CHAPTER 11 TEST

1. a. Hawaii   **b.** New Hampshire   **c.** 83.9%
d. 50.05 (the mean of 50.4 and 49.7)

2.
a. Sources of Revenue for
California Public Schools

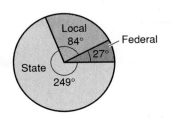

b.
Sources of Revenue for
Iowa Public Schools

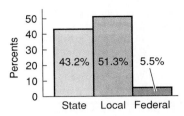

3.

Stem	Leaf
15	7
14	
13	
12	4 1
11	9 5
10	1
9	4 6 0
8	7 3
7	4 5 3 3 5 4 9 0 4
6	4 7 1 3
5	8 6 7 6 7 7 0 5 8 3 2
4	0 6 3 7 3 2 7 1 6 1 9 8
3	5 6 1

4.   Frequency Distribution of States in Categories of Local School Revenue

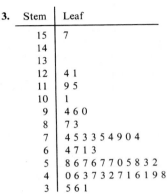

a. 10   **b.** 1   **c.** 50% to 59%
5. a. 69.86%   **b.** 14.12%
6. a. Set B   **b.** Set A   **c.** Set A

7.

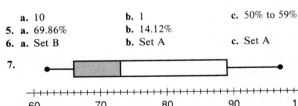

8. a. .8   **b.** 1.3   **c.** On the PSAT
9. a. Skewed to the right   **b.** Normal

10. a. 82.8%   **b.** 93%
   c. On the Total Math subtest, the scores of 60% of local students were lower than this student's score.
   d. This student is performing at grades levels much higher than the fourth grade.
11. a. 68%   **b.** 95%
12. 70.3
13. 90

EXERCISES AND PROBLEMS 12.1

1.

Sum	2	3	4	5	6	7	8	9	10	11	12
Probability	$\frac{1}{36}$	$\frac{2}{36}$	$\frac{3}{36}$	$\frac{4}{36}$	$\frac{5}{36}$	$\frac{6}{36}$	$\frac{5}{36}$	$\frac{4}{36}$	$\frac{3}{36}$	$\frac{2}{36}$	$\frac{1}{36}$

   a. 5/12   **b.** 5/12
3. a. The whole numbers from 1 to 7
   b. 3/7   **c.** 4/7   **d.** 4/7
5.

	Tetrahedron	Cube	Octahedron	Dodeca-hedron	Icosahedron
a. A number less than 3	$\frac{1}{2}$	$\frac{1}{3}$	$\frac{1}{4}$	$\frac{1}{6}$	$\frac{1}{10}$
b. An even number	$\frac{1}{2}$	$\frac{1}{2}$	$\frac{1}{2}$	$\frac{1}{2}$	$\frac{1}{2}$
c. The number 2	$\frac{1}{4}$	$\frac{1}{6}$	$\frac{1}{8}$	$\frac{1}{12}$	$\frac{1}{20}$

7. a. A, B   A, C   A, D   B, C   B, D   C, D
   b. 1/2   **c.** 1/6
9. a. 1 and 1   **b.** 2/3 and 1
   c. 2/3 and 5/6   **d.** 5/6 and 1
   e. Since E and G are the only disjoint sets, only the pair in part a have equal probabilities.
11. a. 12/13   **b.** 10/13   **c.** 3/4   **d.** 23/26
13. a. 7 to 3   **b.** 3 to 2   **c.** 1 to 499   **d.** 4 to 1
15. a. .12   **b.** .35   **c.** .21
17. Let even digits represent heads and odd digits represent tails. Arbitrarily select a sequence of 10 digits from the table and count the number of heads. Carry out this experiment repeatedly, recording the number of heads in each sequence of 10 digits. The probability is approximately .62.
19. a. Label 3 slips of paper B and 2 slips of paper G, and put them in a hat. Randomly select these slips one at a time without replacing them, and record the sequence of Bs and Gs. Carry out this experiment many times, and divide the number of times that 3 Bs occur in succession by the total number of experiments. The theoretical probability of having 3 boys in succession is .3.
   b. Label 3 slips of paper $1000, $0, and $0, and put them in a hat. Randomly select one of the slips, and then replace it. Repeat this process for a total of 8 times. Record the number of $1000 slips. Carry out this experiment of 8 random selections many times, and divide the number of times that exactly four $1000 slips are obtained by the total number of experiments. The theoretical probability that 4 out of 8 people will guess the correct envelope is approximately .17.

21. a. Use a table of random digits, letting even digits represent heads and odd digits represent tails. Check sequences of 6 digits, and compute the experimental probability of having exactly 3 heads. The theoretical probability is .3125.
   b. Less than .5. The theoretical probability of obtaining exactly 10 heads in 20 tosses is approximately .18.

EXERCISES AND PROBLEMS 12.2

1. a. 1/4   **b.** 1/32   **c.** 1/1024
3. a.

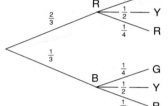

   b. 1/6   **c.** 3/4   **d.** 1/2

5. a.

   b. 1/4   **c.** 11/16
7. a. 7/22   **b.** 35/66   **c.** 5/33
9. a. Independent, 1/8   **b.** Dependent, 1/221
   c. Independent, 1/36   **d.** Dependent, 5/14
11. If G_1, G_2, G_3, and G_4 are the 4 good flashbulbs and B is the bad bulb,
   the sample space is
   $G_1 G_2$ $G_1 G_3$ $G_1 G_4$ G_1 B $G_2 G_3$
   $G_2 G_4$ G_2 B $G_3 G_4$ G_3 B G_4 B
   a. 3/5   **b.** 2/5
13. a. $10/20 \times 9/19 \approx .24$ **b.** $2(10/20 \times 10/19) \approx .53$
   c. 1
15. a. 1/365   **b.** $(1/365)^4 \approx 5.6 \times 10^{-11}$
17. 7/18
19. Approximately .59; that is, $[1 - (4/5)^4]$. A simulated probability
   can be obtained using a random device in which a given number or
   object has a 1/5 probability of occurring. Many experiments in which
   this device is used 4 times will produce a simulated probability.
21. a. $(1/6)(\$1 + \$2 + \$3 + \$4 + \$5 + \$6) = \$3.50$
   b. \$3.50
23. a. 1/38   **b.** $\left(\dfrac{1}{38}\right)(\$35) + \left(\dfrac{37}{38}\right)(\$-1) \approx \$^-.05$ or $^-5¢$

   c. The expected values are equal.
25. a. 1/20
   b. $1/20 \times 3/20 \times 1/20 = .000375$
   c. $1/20 \times 3/20 \times 1/20 = .000375$
   d. $5/20 \times 1/20 \times 1/20 = .000625$
27. a. $1/144 \approx .007$ **b.** $1/20{,}736 \approx .00005$

CHAPTER 12 TEST

1. a. AB, AC, AD, AE, AF, BC, BD
    BE, BF, CD, CE, CF, DE, DF, EF
   b. 1/15   **c.** 1/3
2. a. 1/3   **b.** 3/4   **c.** 2/3
3. a. $G_1 G_2$ $G_1 G_3$ $G_1 O_1$ $G_1 O_2$ $G_2 G_3$
     $G_2 O_1$ $G_2 O_2$ $G_3 O_1$ $G_3 O_2$ $O_1 O_2$
   b. 3/10   **c.** 1/10   **d.** 3/5
4. a. 5 to 7   **b.** 7/12
5. a. 4/9   **b.** 2/9   **c.** 5/9
6. a. 2/5   **b.** 4/15   **c.** 3/5

7. a.

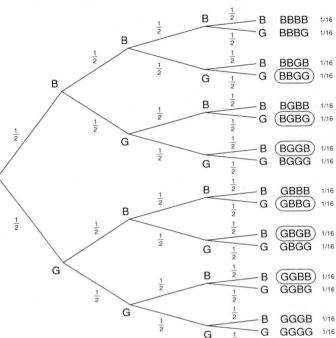

   b. 3/8   **c.** 11/16
8. 11/21
9. .488
10. a. $\$2\left(\dfrac{1}{2}\right) + \$1\left(\dfrac{1}{6}\right) + \$3\left(\dfrac{1}{6}\right) + \$5\left(\dfrac{1}{6}\right) = \$2.50$

   b. \$2.50
11. .039, or approximately 4% $[1 - (.99)^4]$
12. a. .72   **b.** .648   **c.** .998

Credits

Text and Illustrations

Chapter 1

p. 1: Courtesy of International Business Machines Corporation. p. 4: Reproduced from *HOW TO TAKE A CHANCE* by Darell Huff, Illustrated by Irving Geis., by permission of W. W. Norton & Company, Inc. Copyright © 1959 by W. W. Norton & Company, Inc. Copyright renewed by Darrell Huff & Irving Geis. p. 9: B.C. by permission of Johnny Hart and Field Enterprises, Inc. p. 19: Courtesy Italian Government Travel Office. p. 23: © 1975 by The New York Times Company. Reprinted by permission. p. 26: Reprinted by permission of United Press International.

Chapter 2

p. 43: Courtesy of John Demchuck. fig. 2.17: Reproduced from: Nuffield Mathematics Project (1972) *Logic*. Wiley/Chambers/Murray. Reprinted by permission. p. 42: Venn diagram from 1977 *Encyclopedia Britannica Book of the Year* reprinted by courtesy of Encyclopedia Britannica, Inc. p. 52: Reproduced from: Nuffield Mathematics Project (1972) *Logic*. Wiley/Chambers/Murray. Reprinted by permission. p. 42: Reprinted with permission from the Mathematics Teacher, © 1987, 1989 by the National Council of Teachers of Mathematics.

Chapter 3

p. 59: Drawing by Malcolm Hancock; © 1973 New Yorker Magazine, Inc. p. 62: Drawing by Kovarsky; The New Yorker Magazine, Inc. p. 67: Reprinted from the Margarita Philosophia of Gregor Reisch, 1503. p. 70: B.C. by permission of Johnny Hart and Field Enterprises, Inc. 84: Drawing by Dana Fradon; © 1976 The New Yorker Magazine, Inc. p. 102: Krypto, produced by M.P.H. Company, Inc. South Bend, Indiana 46624.

Chapter 4

p. 124: B.C. by permission of Johnny Hart and Field Enterprises, Inc. p. 127: Reprinted by courtesy of Agencia J.B., Rio de Janeiro. p. 134: Reprinted from *Aftermath IV*, Dale Seymour et al. Courtesy of Creative Publications. p. 134: Otis Elevator Illustration reprinted from *Architecturial Record,* March 1970. © 1970 by McGraw Hill, Inc. with all rights reserved. p. 140: Reprinted with permission from the *Mathematics Teacher,* © 1987, 1989 by The National Council of Teachers of Mathematics.

Chapter 5

p. 152: B.C. by permission of Johnny Hart and Field Enterprises Inc. fig. 5.4: Adapted from the *Book of Popular Science,* courtesy of Grolier Inc. p. 170: Redrawn from a photo by courtesy of National Aeronautics and Space Administration. p. 174: Fractions Bars model from the Fraction Bars® Materials by Albert B. Bennett, Jr. and Patricia Davidson © 1981 Permission of Scott Resources, Inc. Fort Collins Colorado. p. 175: From the *Book of Knowledge,* © 1960 by permission of Grolier Inc. p. 211: Illustrations from *Webster's New International Dictionary*, Second Edition © 1959 used by permission of G. & C. Merriam Co., publishers of the Merriam-Webster Dictionaries. p. 213: Drawing by Dana Fradon; © 1973 New Yorker Magazine, Inc. p. 217: Illustration from *Webster's New International Dictionary*, Second Edition © 1959 used by permission of G. & C. Merriam Co., Publishers of the Mirriam-Webster Dictionaries.

Chapter 6

p. 220: Reprinted with permission from the *Mathematics Teacher,* © 1987, 1989 by the National Council of Teachers of Mathematics. p. 237: Reprinted with permission from *Activities for Implementing Curricular Themes from the Agenda for Action,* © 1986 by the National Council of Teachers of Mathematics. p. 252: Reprinted with permission from the *Mathematics Teacher,* © 1987, 1989 by the National Council of Teachers of Mathematics. p. 253: Redrawn from permission by D. Reidel Publishing Company. p. 256: Reprinted by courtesy of Foster's Daily Democrat, Dover, New Hampshire. fig 6.37: Redrawn from data by courtesy of the Population Reference Bureau Inc. p. 272: Courtesy U.S. Department of Transportation and the Advertising Council. p. 273: Reprinted by permission of the Pillsbury Company. p. 274: Courtesy of the Stanford Research Institute, J. Grippo (Project Manager). p. 290: Reprinted with permission from Sidney Harris. fig. 6.5: Decimas Squares model from the Decimal Squares Materials by Albert B. Bennett Jr., © 1981 Permission of Scott Resources, Inc. Fort Collins, Colorado.

Chapter 7

p. 298: Reprinted with permission from the *Mathematics Teacher,* © 1987, 1989 by the National Council of Teachers of Mathematics. fig. 7.15: Reprinted with permission from Sidney Harris. p. 316: Copyright © 1974 by Charles F. Linn. Reprinted by permission of Doubleday & Company, Inc. p. 316: Reprinted by Courtesy of the National Council of Teachers of Mathematics. p. 317: Courtesy of General Motors Research Laboratories. p. 327: Photos from *Collecting Rare Coins For Profit,* by Q. David Bowers. Courtesy of Harper & Row Publishers 1975. fig. 7.57: Drawings reprinted with permission from *Encyclopedia Britannica*, 14th edition, © 1972 by Encyclopedia Britannica, Inc. fig. 7.58: "Reprinted with permission from Collier's Encyclopedia. © 1989 Macmillan Educational Corporation." p. 330: Reprinted with permission from *Collier's Encyclopedia.* © 1976 Macmillan Educational Corporation. p. 343: Courtesy of National Aeronautics and Space Administration. p. 351: B.C. by permission of Johnny Hart and Field Enterprises, Inc. p. 357: Reprinted from *Early American Design Motifs*, by Suzanne E. Chapman (New York: Dover Publications, Inc. 1974). p. 357: Reprinted from *Symbols, Signs and Signets,* by Ernst Lehner (New York: Dover Publications, Inc. 1950).

Chapter 8

p. 376: Courtesy of British Tourist Authority, New York. fig. 8.3: From *The Book of Knowledge.* © 1960 by permission of Grolier Incorporated. fig. 8.20: Courtesy of O. L. Miller and Barbara A. Hamkalo, Oak Ridge National Laboratory. p. 391: Reprinted with permission from Sidney Harris. p. 391: Reprinted from *Popular Science,* with permission. © 1975 Times Mirror Magazines, Inc. p. 393: Trustees of the Science Museum, London. p. 394: Reprinted with permission from The Associated Press. fig. 8.41: Based on drawing from *Mathematics and Living Things,* Student Text. School Mathematics Study Group, 1965. Reprinted by permisssion of Leland Stanford Junior University. p. 414: Courtesy Dr. William Webber University of New Hampshire. p. 415: By John A. Ruge, reprinted from the Saturday Review. p. 431: B.C. by permission of Johnny Hart and Field Enterprises Inc.

Chapter 9

pp. 442 and 456: Reprinted with permission from Sidney Harris. p. 460: Reprinted from the Arithmetic Teacher, (Oct. 1972) © 1972 by the National Council of Teachers of Mathematics, Inc. Used by permission. p. 460: Reprinted by permission of the publisher from *Math Puzzles* by Sam Loyd, editor Martin Gardner (New York: Dover Publications. Inc. 1959). p. 461: Courtesy of U.S. Parachute Association. fig. 9.13: Drawing by Chas Addams; © 1974 The New Yorker Magazine Inc. fig. 9.27: Graph from *Mathematics and Living Things,*

Teachers Commentary, School Mathematics Study Group, © 1965 Reprinted by permission of Leland Stanford Junior University. p. 479: Courtesy of Jim and Lisa Aschbacher. p. 481: Courtesy of Dr. Richard A. Petrie. p. 482: Graph from *Mathematics and Living Things*, Teacher's Commentary, School Mathematics Study Group. © 1965. Reprinted by Permission of Leland Stanford Junior University.

Chapter 10

p. 488: Reprinted by permission Saturday Review, © 1976 & V. Gene Meyers. fig. 10.27: Reproduced from the book, *Let's Play Math*, by Michael Holt and Zoltan Dienes. Copyright © 1973 by Michael Holt and Zoltan Dienes used by permission of Publisher, Walker and Company. p. 523: Courtesy John P. Adams University of New Hampshire. p. 527: Reproduced by permission of the publisher from *Aesthetic Measure* by George D. Birkhoff (Cambridge, MA: Harvard University Press). © 1933 by the President and Fellows of Harvard College; 1961 by Garrett Birkhoff. fig. 10.40: produced by permission of the National Ocean Survey (NOAA). U.S. Department of Commerce. p. 549: Reprinted with permission from the *Mathematics Teacher*, © 1987, 1989 by the National Council of Teachers of Mathematics.

Chapter 11

p. 570: Drawing by Ziegler; © 1974 The New Yorker Magazine, Inc. p. 571: "Bills of Mortality" from DEVILS, DRUGS AND DOCTORS by Howard W. Haggard, M.D. Copyright 1929, © 1957 by Howard W. Haggard. Reprinted by permission on Harper & Row, Publishers, Inc. fig. 11.11: *The Work Almanac & Book of Facts*, 1989 edition, © Newspaper Enterprise Association, Inc.; 1988 New York, NY 10166. p. 584: Copyright © 1975. Reprinted by permission of Saturday Review and Robert D. Ross. p. 587: *The World Almanac & Book of Facts*, 1989 edition, © Newspaper Enterprise Association, Inc., 1988 New York, NY 10166. p. 589: From *The Peoples Almanac*, 1975 Edition by David Wallechinsky and Irving Wallace. Copyright © 1975 by David Wallechinsky and Irving Wallace. Reprinted by permission of Doubleday & Company, Inc. p. 590: Drawing by Webber; © 1975 The New Yorker Magazine, Inc. fig 11.26: Redrawn from the Differential Aptitude Tests. Copyright © 1972, 1973 by The Psychological Corporation. Reproduced by special permission of the publisher. p. 604: Reprinted by courtesy of Washington Post. p. 605: Reproduced by permission from the Stanford Achievement Test, 7th Edition. Copyright © 1982 by Harcourt Brace Jovanovich Inc. All rights reserved. p. 608: Copyright 1965. Reprinted by permission of Saturday Review and Ed Fisher. p. 610: Reproduced by permission from the Stanford Achievement Test, 7th edition copyright © 1982 by Harcourt Brace Jovanovich Inc. All rights reserved.

Chapter 12

p. 614: Courtesy of Leonard Toss. p. 620: Joseph Zeix, Cartoonist. fig. 12.5: Mortality Table for *Principles of Insurance* Eighth Edition, by Robert Mehr and Emmerson Cammack, © 1985. p. 679: Reprinted by Courtesy of R.D. Irwin, Inc. p. 625: B.C. by permission of Johnny Hart and Field Enterprises, Inc. p. 639: Reprinted by permission of the New Hampshire Sweepstakes Commission. p. 641: Reprinted from *Ladies Home Journal*, February 1976, by courtesy of Henry R. Martin, cartoonist. p. 642: Reprinted by permission of the New Hampshire Sweepstakes Commission.

Photo Credits

Chapter 1

Page 2: Courtesy of International Business Machines Corporation; p. 8: Courtesy of British Information Systems; p. 13: Palomar Observatory Photograph; 1.2: Courtesy Department of Library Services, American Museum of Natural History; 1.3: Ron Bergeron; p. 19: Courtesy of the Italian Government Travel Office; p. 24: Reproduced from An Introduction to Color by Ralph M. Evans © 1948 John Wiley and Sons, Inc. Reprinted by Permission.

Chapter 2

Page 30: Courtesy of Dr. Jean de Heinzelin; p. 31: Courtesy of Musee de l'Homme; 2.10: Palomar Observatory Photograph.

Chapter 3

Page 58: Reproduced by Courtesy of the Trustees of the British Museum; p. 81: Reprinted by permission from "More About Computers" © 1974 by International Business Machines, Corp.; p. 84: Courtesy of N.Y. State Office of General Services; p. 98: Courtesy of Deutshces Museum, Munich; p. 99: From the exhibition "Mathematica: A World of Numbers & Beyond," made by the Office of Charles and Ray Eames for IBM Corporation; p. 102: Courtesy of TEREX Division, General Motors.

Chapter 4

Page 137: Courtesy of U.S. Bureau of Census; p. 138: Bettmann Archives.

Chapter 5

Page 168: Official U.S. Navy Photograph; p. 172: New York Stock Exchange, Inc.; p. 173: Courtesy of the Trustees of the British Museum; p. 175: Official U.S. Navy Photograph; p. 191: Courtesy of Minolta Corporation; p. 194: Courtesy of Rockwell International; 5.35: Reprinted by Courtesy of Calspan Corporation.

Chapter 6

Page 220: Courtesy of Professor Erwin W. Mueller, The Pennsylvania State University; p. 234: Courtesy of National Institute of Standards and Technology; p. 237: Courtesy of the Bulova Watch Company, Inc.; p. 257: Courtesy of NASA; p. 257: Bettmann Archives; p. 273: By permission of the Pillsbury Company; p. 276: Courtesy of Lehnert and Landrock, Cairo; p. 280: Yale Babylonia Collection.

Chapter 7

Page 298: Courtesy of General Motors Research Laboratory; p. 299: Bettmann Archives; p. 314: Hirshhorn Museum and Sculpture Garden, Smithsonian Institution; p. 314: Reproduced from "Handbook of Gem Identification," by Richard T. Liddicoat, Jr. Reprinted by permission of the Gemological Institute of America; p. 315: B. M. Shaub; p. 317: B. M. Shaub; p. 317: Courtesy Department of Library Services, American Museum of Natural History; 7.35: MAS, Barcelona, Spain; p. 326: Reproduced from "Art Forms in Nature" by Ernst Haeckel © 1974 Dover Publications, Inc.; p. 329: Talbot Lovering; 7.43: B. M. Shaub; 7.45: Talbot Lovering; 7.46: B.M. Shaub; 7.47: Reproduced from "Minerology," by Ivan Kostov, © 1968 Courtesy of the author; 7.49: Reproduced from "The Public Buildings of Williamsburg," by Marcus Whitten, published by The Colonial Williamsburg Foundation and distributed by Holt, Rinehart and Winston; 7.52: B. M. Shaub; 7.55: Courtesy of NASA; p. 340: Bettmann Archives; p. 340: B. M. Shaub; p. 342: Courtesy of John P. Adams, University of New Hampshire; p. 342: Courtesy of Babson College, Wellesley, Massachusetts; p. 346: Courtesy of Government of India Tourist Office; 7.60: Courtesy of University of New Hampshire Media Services; 7.66: Reproduced from Snow Crystals by W. A. Bentley and W. J. Humphreys. Reprinted by Courtesy of McGraw-Hill Book Company; 7.67: Reprinted by Courtesy of the magazine "Antiques"; 7.68: Courtesy of Entomology Department, University of New Hampshire. Photo by Ron Bergeron; 7.69: Courtesy of Lathrops Ethan Allen, Dover N.H. Photo by Ron Bergeron; p. 352: (Left and right) Courtesy of Lothrops Ethan Allen, Dover, N.H. Photo by Ron Bergeron (Center) Courtesy of Jamaica Lamp Company, Queensville, New York; p. 354: Courtesy of the Spanish National Tourist Office; p. 354: Courtesy of The American Numismatic Society, New York; pp. 354, 355: Reproduced from "Art Forms in Nature," Ernst Haeckel © 1974 Dover Publications, Inc.; p. 355: Ron Bergeron; p. 356: (Left) Courtesy of Erie Glass Company, Parkridge, Illinois; (Center and right) Courtesy of Lothrops Ethan Allen, Dover, New Hampshire. Photo by Ron Bergeron; p. 357: B. M. Shaub; 7.70: Courtesy of Rockwell International Corporation; p. 359: Courtesy of Radio Shack, A Division of Tandy Corporation; 7.71: Courtesy MIT News Office.

Chapter 8

Page 387: British Tourist Authority; 8.20: Courtesy of O. L. Miller and Barbara A. Hamkalo, Oak Ridge National Library; p. 392: Ron Bergeron; p. 394: General Electric Research and Development Center; p. 396: Courtesy of the Federal Reserve Bank of Minneapolis; 8.31: Ron Bergeron; 8.33: Talbot Lovering; 8.37: Courtesy of Gemological Institute of America; p. 406: Ron Bergeron; p. 410: Courtesy of Gunnar Birkerts and Associates, Architects; Photo by Bob Coyle; p. 412: Ron Bergeron; p. 413: Ron Bergeron; p. 414: Reprinted by permission of Peachtree Plaza; p. 415: Talbot Lovering; p. 416: Courtesy of General Dynamics, Quincy Shipbuilding Division; 8.50: Courtesy of Renaissance Center; 8.53: Reprinted by permission of Transamerica Corporation; 8.55: Courtesy of Leslie Salt, Co., Newark, California; 8.57: Courtesy of NASA; p. 428: Historical Pictures Service, Inc.; 8.60: Talbot Lovering; p. 433: Photo by Herb Moyer.

Reprinted by permission from Rodney Sanderson; p. 433: Courtesy of General Dynamics, Quincy Shipbuilding Division; p. 433: Collection: Mrs. Harry Lynde Bradley, André Emmerich Gallery; p. 434: Ron Bergeron.

Chapter 9

Page 462: Courtesy U.S. Parachute Association; p. 467: The Bettmann Archive.

Chapter 10

10.6: Courtesy University of New Hampshire Media Services; p. 500: Reproduced from "A Concise History of Mathematics," Dirk J. Stiruk. © 1984 Dover Publications, Inc.; 10.14: Courtesy of U.S. Geological Survey; 10.17: Courtesy of U.S. Department of State; 10.20: Courtesy of Travel Marketing, Inc. Seattle; 10.25: Courtesy of Rival Manufacturing Company; p. 525: Collection of Greenfield Village and The Henry Ford Museum, Dearborn, Michigan; p. 527: Perkins

Collection, Purchase of E. P. Warren, Courtesy Museum of Fine Arts, Boston; p. 528: Courtesy of J. E. Cermak, Fluid Dynamics and Diffusion Laboratory, Colorado State University; 10.42: Photo by Wayne Goddard. Description of Knife reprinted by permission of the Register Gaurd, Eugene Oregon; p. 541: Courtesy of Sally Ann Foley. Photo by Ron Bergeron; p. 545: Courtesy of Rockwell International Corporation; p. 546: Courtesy of Sydney Rogers Chair Company, Georgetown, Massachusetts; p. 546: Courtesy of Boeing; p. 548: Courtesy of Sally Ann Foley. Photo by Ron Bergeron; p. 550: British Crown Copyright. Science Museum, London; 10.48: Photo Science Museum, London; 10.49: Talbot Lovering; p. 552: Ron Bergeron.

Chapter 12

Page 614: Bettmann Archive; p. 629: Courtesy of NASA; p. 639: Ron Bergeron; p. 643: From the exhibition "Mathematica: A World of Numbers and Beyond" made by the Office of Charles and Ray Eames for IBM Corporation

Index